INSIGHT:
The Experience of
Literature

INSIGHT:

The Experience of Literature
American Literature
English Literature

The Carnegie Curriculum Study Center
under Project English

BEEKMAN W. COTTRELL

LOIS S. JOSEPHS

ROBERT C. SLACK

ERWIN R. STEINBERG

INSIGHT:
The Experience of Literature

EDITED BY

Beekman W. Cottrell

Department of English, Carnegie-Mellon University

UNDER THE GENERAL EDITORSHIP OF

Erwin R. Steinberg

Dean, College of Humanities and Social Sciences,
Carnegie-Mellon University

NOBLE AND NOBLE, PUBLISHERS, INC.

NEW YORK · CHICAGO · DALLAS · LOS ANGELES · TORONTO

BEEKMAN W. COTTRELL received his Ph.D. in English from Columbia University. Since 1953 he has been on the faculty of Carnegie-Mellon University (formerly Carnegie Institute of Technology), where he is currently associate professor of English. In 1960 he took a year's leave of absence to serve as Director of the American Institute of Languages in Baghdad. Dr. Cottrell has published essays on a number of modern writers—Graham Greene, William Faulkner, Robert Penn Warren—and on Shakespeare's *A Winter's Tale*. Collaborating with Dr. Lois Josephs, a fellow member of the Carnegie Curriculum Study Center in English, he has written several articles on English education for the *English Journal*. He has also lectured widely on modern literature, the theater, and the art of film. Dr. Cottrell is film critic for the *Pittsburgh Point*.

ERWIN R. STEINBERG received his Ph.D. from New York University. Since 1946 he has held teaching and administrative posts at Carnegie-Mellon University. From 1963 to 1964 he also served as coordinator of all PROJECT ENGLISH programs for the U.S. Office of Education, and since 1963 has been Chairman of the Committee of Examiners, General Examination in English Composition for Educational Testing Service. Dr. Steinberg is the author of a monograph, *Needed Research in the Teaching of English,* issued by the U.S. Government Printing Office. In addition, he has published essays on the modern novel and the teaching of English for *Modern Fiction Studies,* the *English Journal, College English, PMLA,* and other journals. He is editor of *The Rule of Force* and (with W. M. Schutte) of *Personal Integrity,* collections of readings for college students.

Contents

Preface

G O O D literature speaks for itself. Because the reader should experience it directly, we have deliberately omitted such materials as introductions, background essays, and study questions. At the end of each volume in *Insight: The Experience of Literature*, however, there are brief statements about each of the writers represented in that volume. The reader will also notice that virtually all of the works are reproduced without expurgation, abridgment, or condensation. We feel strongly that, except in unusual instances, works of literature should be read as intended by the writer.

This series is an outgrowth of the work done in the Curriculum Study Center in English at Carnegie-Mellon University, a cooperative venture between Carnegie-Mellon and seven school systems in and around Pittsburgh. We are indebted to the students, instructors, and administrators who experimented with us in demonstrating the validity of the basic concepts of a new program in literature. After careful evaluation of the program, many of the specific works of literature have been changed and the instructor's manual rewritten. We are especially indebted to Mildred B. Wolfe, now on the Carnegie-Mellon faculty, who served as administrative assistant not only in the Center but also in the publishing project.

Carnegie-Mellon University　　　　　　　　　　　　　　　　B.W.C.
Pittsburgh, Pa.　　　　　　　　　　　　　　　　　　　　　L.S.J.
　　　　　　　　　　　　　　　　　　　　　　　　　　　　R.C.S.
　　　　　　　　　　　　　　　　　　　　　　　　　　　　E.R.S.

INTRODUCTION

Old Milon

GUY DE MAUPASSANT

THE broad sunlight threw its burning rays on the fields, and under this shower of flame life burst forth in glowing vegetation from the earth. As far as the eye could see, the soil was green; and the sky was blue to the verge of the horizon.

The Norman farms scattered through the plain seemed at a distance like little woods enclosed each in a circle of thin beech trees. Coming closer, on opening the worm-eaten stile, one fancied that he saw a giant garden, for all the old apple trees, as knotted as the peasants, were in blossom. The weather-beaten black trunks, crooked, twisted, ranged along the enclosure, displayed beneath the sky their glittering domes, rosy and white. The sweet perfume of their blossoms mingled with the heavy odors of the open stables and with the fumes of the steaming dunghill, covered with hens and their chickens.

It was midday. The family sat at dinner in the shadow of the pear tree planted before the door—the father, the mother, the four children, the two maidservants, and the three farm laborers. They scarcely uttered a word. Their fare consisted of soup and of a stew composed of potatoes mashed up in lard.

From time to time one of the maidservants rose and went to the cellar to draw a pitcher of cider.

The husband, a big fellow of about forty, stared at a vine, still bare of leaves, which stood close to the farmhouse, twining like a serpent under the shutters the entire length of the wall.

He said, after a long silence:

"The old man's vine is blossoming early this year. Perhaps it will bear good fruit."

The peasant's wife also turned around, and gazed at the vine without speaking.

This vine was planted exactly in the place where the old man had been shot.

It was during the war of 1870. The Prussians were occupying the entire country. General Faidherbe, with the Army of the North, was at their head.

Now the Prussian staff had taken up its quarters in this farmhouse. The peasant who owned it, Old Milon, received them, and gave them the best treatment he could.

For a whole month the German vanguard remained on the lookout in the village. The French were posted ten leagues away without moving, and yet, each night, some of the Uhlans disappeared.

All the isolated scouts, those who were sent out on patrol, whenever they started in groups of two or three, never came back.

They were picked up dead in the morning in a field, near a farmyard, or in a ditch. Even their horses were found lying on the roads with their throats cut by a saber stroke. These murders seemed to have been accomplished by the same men, who could not be discovered.

The country was terrorized. Peasants were shot on mere information, women imprisoned, attempts were made to obtain revelations from children by fear.

But, one morning, Old Milon was found stretched out in his stable with a gash across his face.

Two disemboweled Uhlans were seen lying three kilometers away from the farmhouse. One of them still grasped in his hand his blood-stained weapon. He had fought and defended himself.

A council of war having been immediately constituted, in the open air, in front of the farmhouse, the old man was brought before it.

He was sixty-eight years old. He was small, thin, a little crooked, with long hands resembling the claws of a crab. His faded hair, scanty and slight, like the down on a young duck, allowed his scalp to be plainly seen. The brown, creased skin of his neck showed the big veins which sank under his jaws and reappeared at his temples. He was regarded in the district as a miser and a hard man in business transactions.

He was made to stand among four soldiers in front of the kitchen table, which had been carried out of the house for the purpose. Five officers and the Colonel sat facing him. The Colonel was the first to speak.

"Father Milon," he said, in French, "since we came here we have had nothing to say of you but praise. You have always been obliging, and even considerate toward us. But today a terrible accusation rests on you, and the matter must be cleared up. How did you get the wound on your face?"

The peasant gave no reply.

The Colonel went on:

"Your silence condemns you, Milon. But I want you to answer me, do you understand? Do you know who has killed the two Uhlans who were found this morning near the crossroads?"

The old man said in a clear voice:

"I did!"

The Colonel, surprised, remained silent for a second, looking steadfastly at the prisoner. Old Milon maintained his impassive demeanor, his air of rustic stupidity, with downcast eyes, as if he were talking to his curé. There was only one thing that could reveal his internal agitation, the way in which he slowly swallowed his saliva with a visible effort, as if he were choking.

The old peasant's family—his son Jean, his daughter-in-law, and two little children—stood ten paces behind, scared and dismayed.

The Colonel continued:

"Do you know also who killed all the scouts of our army whom we have found every morning, for the past month, lying here and there in the fields?"

The old man answered with the same brutal impassiveness:

"It was I!"

"It was you, then, that killed them all?"

"All of them—yes . . . I."

"You alone?"

"I alone."

"Tell me the way you managed to do it?"

This time the peasant appeared to be affected; the necessity of speaking at some length embarrassed him.

"I know myself. I did it the way I found easiest."

The Colonel proceeded:

"I warn you, you must tell me everything. You will do well, therefore, to make up your mind about it at once. How did you begin it?"

The peasant cast an uneasy glance toward his family, who remained in a listening attitude behind him. He hesitated for another second or so, then all of a sudden he made up his mind.

"I came home one night about ten o'clock, and the next day you were here. You and your soldiers seized two hundred francs worth of property from me, including a cow and two sheep. So I said to myself: as many times as they take fifty francs worth of stuff, just that many times will I make them pay for it. But then I had other things in my heart, which I'll tell you about now. I came across one of your cavalrymen smoking his pipe near my ditch just behind my barn. I went and took my scythe off the hook, and I came back with short steps from behind while he lay there without hearing anything. And I cut off his head with one stroke, like a feather, while he only said 'Oof!' You have only to look at the bottom of the pond; you'll find them there in a coal bag with a big stone tied to it.

"I got an idea into my head. I took all he had on him from his boots to his cap, and I hid them in the bakehouse in the Martin wood behind the farmyard."

The old man stopped. The officers, speechless, looked at one another. The examination was resumed, and this is what they were told.

Once he had accomplished this murder, the peasant lived with one thought: "To kill the Prussians!" He hated them with the sly and ferocious hatred of a peasant who was at the same time covetous and patriotic. He had got an idea into his head, as he put it. He waited for a few days.

He was allowed to go and come freely, to go out and return just as he pleased, as long as he was humble, submissive, and obliging toward the conquerors.

Now, every evening he saw the cavalrymen bearing dispatches leaving the farmhouse; and he went out, one night, after discovering the name of the village to which they were going, and after picking up by associating with the soldiers the few words of German he needed.

He made his way through his farmyard, slipped into the wood, reached the bakehouse, walked to the end of the long passage, and having found the clothes of the soldier which he had hidden there, he put them on. Then he went prowling about the fields, creeping along, keeping to the slopes so as to avoid observation, listening to the least sounds, restless as a poacher.

When he believed the time had arrived he took up his position at the roadside, and hid himself in a clump of brushwood. He still waited. Finally, near midnight, he heard the galloping of a horse's hoofs on the hard soil of the road. The old man put his ear to the ground to make sure that only one cavalryman was approaching; then he got ready.

The Uhlan came on at a very quick pace, carrying some dispatches. He rode forward with watchful eyes and strained ears. As soon as he was no more than ten paces away, Old Milon dragged himself across the road, groaning: *"Hilfe! hilfe!"* ("Help! help!").

The cavalryman drew up, recognized a German soldier dismounted, believed that he was wounded, leaped down from his horse, drew near the prostrate man, never suspecting anything, and, as he stooped over the stranger, he received in the middle of the stomach the long, curved blade of the saber. He sank down without any death throes, merely quivering with a few last shudders.

Then the Norman, radiant with the mute joy of an old peasant, rose up, and merely to please himself, cut the dead soldier's throat. After that, he dragged the corpse to the ditch and threw it in.

The horse was quietly waiting for its rider. Milon got into the saddle and started across the plain at a gallop.

At the end of an hour, he perceived two more Uhlans approaching the staffquarters, side by side. He rode straight toward them, crying: *"Hilfe! hilfe!"* The Prussians let him come on, recognizing the uniform without any distrust.

And like a cannonball the old man shot between the two, bringing both of them to the ground with his saber and a revolver. The next thing he did was to cut the throats of the horses—the German horses! Then, softly, he reentered the bakehouse and hid his horse in the dark passage. There he took off the uniform, put on once more his own old clothes, and going to his bed, slept till morning.

For four days he did not stir out, awaiting the close of the open inquiry as to the cause of the soldiers' deaths, but, on the fifth day, he started out again, and by a similar stratagem killed two more soldiers.

Thenceforth, he never stopped. Each night he wandered about, prowled through the country at random, cutting down Prussians, sometimes here, sometimes there, galloping through the deserted fields under the moonlight, a lost Uhlan, a hunter of men. Then, when he had finished his task, leaving behind him corpses lying along the roads, the old horseman went to the bakehouse, where he concealed both the animal and the uniform. About midday he calmly returned to the spot to give the horse oats and water, and he took good care of the animal, for he demanded a lot of work from it.

But, the night before his arrest, one of the soldiers he attacked put himself on his guard, and cut the old peasant's face with a slash of a saber.

He had, however, killed both of them. He had even managed to go back and hide his horse and put on his everyday garb, but, when he reached the stable, he was overcome by weakness and was not able to make his way into the house.

He had been found lying on the straw, his face covered with blood.

When he had finished his story, he suddenly lifted his head and glanced proudly at the Prussian officers.

The Colonel, tugging at his mustache, asked:

"Have you anything more to say?"

"No, nothing more; we are even. I killed sixteen, not one more, not one less."

"You know you have to die?"

"I ask for no mercy!"

"Have you been a soldier?"

"Yes, I served at one time. And it was you Germans that killed my father, who was a soldier of the first Emperor, not to speak of my youngest son François, whom you killed last month near Evreux. I owed this to you, and I've paid you back. We're quits."

The officers stared at one another.

The old man went on:

"Eight for my father, eight for my son—that pays it off! I sought for no quarrel with you. I don't know you! I only know where you came from. You came to my house here and ordered me about as if the house was yours. I have had my revenge, and I'm glad of it!"

And stiffening up his old frame, he folded his arms in the attitude of a humble hero.

The Prussians held a long conference. A captain, who had also lost a son the month before, defended the brave old farmer.

Then the Colonel rose and, advancing toward Old Milon, he said, lowering his voice:

"Listen, old man! There is perhaps one way of saving your life—it is—"

But the old peasant was not listening to him, and, fixing his eyes directly on the German officer, while the wind made the scanty hair move to and fro on his skull, he made a frightful grimace, which shriveled up his pinched face scarred by the saber stroke, and puffing out his chest, he spat, with all his strength, right into the Prussian's face.

The Colonel, stupefied, raised his hand, and for the second time the peasant spat in his face.

All the officers sprang to their feet and yelled out orders at the same time.

In less than a minute, the old man, still as impassive as ever, was stood up against the wall and shot, while he smiled at Jean, his eldest son, first and then at his daughter-in-law and the two children, who were staring with terror at the scene.

The Stranger's Note

LIN YUTANG

IT WAS toward the noon hour. The day was hot and few passengers were on the street. Wang Erh's teahouse was situated two streets back of the covered passages and bazaars in the center of the East City, where the best restaurants were. The morning crowd, which had come to his teahouse for a cup of tea and exchange of gossip and news, had dispersed, and Wang Erh was washing his teapots and stacking them, some two dozen, on a shelf. This done, he took his pipe and prepared to enjoy a rest, when he saw a tall, well-dressed man walk into his shop. The visitor's bushy eyebrows and deep black eyes gave him a striking appearance.

Wang Erh had never seen this man before, but that did not surprise him. All sorts of people came to his shop; that was what made running a teahouse interesting. Businessmen and their families, scholars, salesmen, gamblers, cheats, and passing strangers all came to rest and refresh themselves. The tall stranger selected an inside table, and he gave the impression of being a little secretive, even a little nervous. Wang Erh saw that he was preoccupied, and thought it would be better to leave him alone.

Soon a boy peddler passed by in the street, calling aloud, "Fried partridge *hutu!* Hey-yo, delicious fried partridge!"

The gentleman called him in. The boy, whose head was shaven like a monk's, laid his tray on the table and began to pierce some *hutu* together on a stick, sprinkling some salt on it.

"Please, sir, here's your partridge."

"Leave it there. What's your name?"

"Seng-erh, that is my name, because I look like a little monk," said the boy with an innocent smile.

"Would you like to earn some extra money, little monk?"

"Certainly." The boy's eyes brightened.

"I want to ask you to do something for me."

The tall gentleman pointed to a house, number four from the corner, down an alley which opened on the street at a point just facing the tea-house. "Do you know who lives in that house?" he asked.

"That is the house of Mr. Huangfu, an officer of the palace, in charge of official uniforms."

"Oh, is he? Do you know how many persons are living in the house?"

"Just three. The palace officer, his young wife, and a little foster daughter."

"Good. Do you know the lady?"

"She seldom comes out of her house. But she often buys partridge from me and I know her. Why do you ask?"

The stranger saw that Wang Erh was not looking, so he took out a case and poured some fifty coins on the boy's tray, at which the boy's eyes brightened. "That's for you," he said.

He then showed the boy a package, which contained a pair of gold cable bracelets, two short hair brooches, and a note. "Give these three things to that lady. But remember, if you see the husband, do not give them to him. Is that clear?"

"I am to give these things to the lady. I am not to give them to the palace officer."

"Right. After you give the lady the note, wait for an answer. If she does not come with you, tell me what she says."

The boy went to the house, but when he lifted the screen and peeped in, he saw the palace officer sitting in the front room looking directly at the door. Huangfu was a short man in his forties, with broad shoulders and a wide, flat, rather rectangular face. He had been on duty at the palace for the last three months and had come home only two days ago.

"What are you doing here?" shouted the officer and ran after the boy, who had immediately started to run away. Huangfu grabbed him by the shoulder and shook him violently. "What do you mean by peeping in at my door and running away like that?"

"A gentleman asked me to deliver a package to your wife. He told me not to give it to you."

"What is in it?"

"I will not tell you. The gentleman told me not to give it to you."

The officer gave the boy's head such a loud whack that the boy winced and reeled.

"Hand them to me!" he shouted in his throaty, officer's voice.

The boy could only do as he was told, still protesting, "They are not for you. They are for her."

Huangfu broke open the package and saw the bracelets, the pair of hair brooches, and the note which read as follows:

Dear Mrs. Huangfu: You may think this presumptuous of me, but since I saw you at the restaurant, I have not been able to put you out of my mind. I would love to call on you, but that ass of your husband has returned. May I beg to see you alone? Come with the messenger of this note, or tell me how I can meet you. I am sending these little things as tokens of my great esteem.

Your admirer, (unsigned)

The officer ground his teeth. Raising his eyebrows, he asked coldly, "Who gave you this message?"

Seng-erh pointed to Wang Erh's shop just outside the alley, and said, "A gentleman with bushy eyebrows, great big eyes, a snub nose, and a wide mouth gave them to me."

Huangfu grabbed the boy by the arm and dragged him to the shop. The stranger was gone. In spite of Wang Erh's protests, the officer took the boy back to his house and locked him in. The boy was now thoroughly frightened.

Huangfu was shaking with anger. He called his wife out with a commanding voice. The young wife was a delicate and rather pretty woman of twenty-four, with a small, intelligent face. She saw that her husband was white and panting, and she could not understand what had happened.

"Look at these!" said her husband, grimly staring at her.

Mrs. Huangfu seated herself leisurely in a chair. She took out the articles and stared at them.

"Read the note!"

She read it and slowly shook her head. "Is this letter for me? It must be a mistake. Who sent it?"

"How do I know who sent it? You know! Whom did you have dinner with during the three months when I was on duty?"

"You know me well," replied the young wife gently. "I would not do such a thing. We have been married for seven years. Have I ever done anything a wife should not do?"

"Then where does the note come from?"

"How can I know?"

Unable to explain the letter and clear herself, the wife began weeping. "What kind of a strange disaster has fallen out of a clear, blue sky!" she wailed. Without warning her husband struck her on the face. Mrs. Huangfu cried aloud and ran into the house.

The palace officer called for the thirteen-year-old maid, Ying-erh, his foster daughter. Her short sleeves revealed her plump arms, red from washing. She stood stiffly erect, awaiting an order, trembling a little as she always did before her master. Fearfully she watched his movements. He took down from the wall a piece of bamboo and threw it on the floor. Then he took a rope and tied the maid's hands, swinging the other end of the rope across a beam in the roof. He hauled the girl up and, holding the bamboo in his hand, he asked, "Tell me, whom did the mistress dine with when I was away?"

"There was no one," replied the girl in a terror-stricken voice.

Huangfu began to beat the maid with the bamboo, and his wife, inside, trembled hearing her screams. The flogging and questioning went on for some time. Unable to stand it any longer the maid at last said, "When you were away, Mother slept with a certain person every night."

"That's better," said the master. He let her down and untied her.

"Now tell me, who was the fellow who slept with your mother every night in my absence?"

The girl wiped her eyes and said with hatred in her voice, "I will tell you. She slept every night with me."

"I will get to the bottom of this!" he swore, and went out, locking the door behind him.

The wife and foster daughter looked at one another. Mrs. Huangfu saw the bruises on the young girl's arms and back, and rushed to wash her wounds, crying, "The beast!"

The wife shuddered at the sight of the blood which had reddened the basin of water. As she poured it down the gutter, she muttered again, "The brutal beast."

The girl stood looking at her kind foster mother and said, "If it were not for you, I would have gone back to our village. And you should, too, Mother."

"Hush, you mustn't say that."

Mrs. Huangfu looked dazed, unable to understand what had happened. At last, she turned to the boy, who was cowering in a corner of the room, and asked, "What was the stranger like?"

The boy repeated the description and told her the story. The wife and her foster daughter sat silent, completely puzzled.

Half an hour later, the husband returned with four officers of the law. Dragging the partridge boy forward, he said to the men, "Take down his name." The men did as they were told, having respect for Huangfu's position as a palace officer.

"Don't go away yet. There are more persons inside." He called out to his wife and maid and demanded that all three be arrested.

"How dare we arrest the lady?"

"You have to. A murder is involved."

Frightened by his words, the men took down the names and escorted the prisoners out of the house. A crowd of neighbors had gathered outside. As Mrs. Huangfu stepped out of the door screen, she instinctively shrank back, and said to her husband, *"Koko,* I never thought I would see this day. You should have used your head and taken time to find out who sent the letter. It's such a disgrace!"

The officers had already pushed her outside the door. The neighbors made way for her to pass.

"If you were afraid of disgrace, you shouldn't have done it," answered her husband.

The wife said to him, "Why don't you ask our close neighbors if a man ever stepped inside our door during your absence? The idea of accusing me!"

"I will!" replied her husband angrily.

The neighbors, not knowing what the wife was accused of, were altogether bewildered. They sympathized with the wife and shook their heads in answer to the husband's question.

Huangfu went with the accused to proffer charges before the magistrate, Chien of Kaifeng. Chien had a round, plump face and seemed to be a man of infinite patience, incapable of being excited by anything. The husband submitted the letter and the gifts and made the formal charge. The magistrate ordered the prisoners to be held in detention pending investigation.

Two jail officers, Shan Ting and Shan Chienhsing, were in charge of questioning the prisoners. They began with the wife.

Mrs. Huangfu stated that she was born in a village near the city, that she had lost her mother early, and her father at the age of seventeen, and that she had no close relatives. She had married her husband the following year, and they had been happily married for seven years. No relatives or visitors had come to her house during her husband's absence, and she never dined with anybody at home or in a restaurant, except her husband. She had no idea who could have sent the note.

"Why is it that you never see your relatives? Don't they come and see you?"

"My husband does not like it. Once my cousin, Chang Erh, came to see us to beg my husband for a job. He didn't get the job because it wasn't easy to get. My husband asked me to stop seeing my relatives after that, and I did."

"You do everything your husband tells you to?"

"Yes, I do."

"Do you often go out to the theatre, where you might be seen by people?"

"No."

"Why not?"

"He does not take me."

"And you don't go out alone?"

"No."

"Do you go to restaurants for dinner?"

"Very rarely. I am happy at home. Oh yes, several days ago, the night when he came back from the palace, he did not like my food and took me to a restaurant near by."

"And you two dined alone?"

"Yes."

The woman's neighbors were called in. In general they corroborated the wife's story. They had never seen any visitor at her house, nor had they seen her go out except with her husband. She was a woman who kept very close to the house. The neighbors had a rather good opinion of her and called her *Siaoniangtse,* "Young Mistress," because she was so small, although there was no "old mistress" in the house. A neighboring woman said the husband was short-tempered and mistreated the wife, who was always meek and submissive and never complained. The neighbor said Mrs. Huangfu looked like "a bird feeding from one's hand."

On the third day, Shan Chienhsing was standing in front of the magistrate's office, thinking about the mystery, when he saw the husband pass by. Huangfu came up to him and gave him a greeting.

"How is the case proceeding?" he asked. "Three days have passed. Perhaps you have received a present from the sender of the note and purposely delayed action."

"Nonsense! The case is not so easily concluded. Your wife insists on her innocence and we have learned nothing to prove otherwise. You did not send the note yourself by any chance?"

"Don't talk to me like that. We are happily married." Huangfu was angry.

"What do you propose to do?" asked Shan.

"If the court cannot clear the case, I will demand a divorce."

Shan went into his office and prepared the documents. That afternoon he presented his report to the magistrate. Magistrate Chien ordered the couple and the witnesses to trial the next day.

The magistrate first questioned the little boy. Then he turned to the thirteen-year-old maid as the most important witness. He banged the court gavel, an iron paperweight, by way of frightening her and spoke in a harsh, severe voice:

"You know everything that has been going on in the house, don't you?"

"I do."

"Did you see any visitor or visitors when your master was away?"

The maid answered impatiently, "If there were any visitor, would I not have seen him?"

The magistrate gave another loud bang with his gavel and shouted, "You little liar! You dare to lie in my presence! I will send you to jail for this."

The maid was frightened, but she said firmly, "Your Honor, I have not lied to you. My mistress stayed in the house all the time. You cannot wrong a good woman." She broke down, whimpering and sobbing.

The magistrate was impressed by the maid's testimony.

"Now then," he addressed the husband, "a charge of theft must be proven with the stolen goods in the thief's possession, and a charge of adultery must be proved by producing a corespondent. I cannot condemn your wife without more evidence than a note from an anonymous stranger. You may have some enemy who planted this note." He looked at the woman and continued, "Certainly some one is trying to cause trouble. Don't you think you ought to take her home and try to find out who sent the note?"

The husband was adamant. "Under the circumstances, Your Honor, I am not willing to take her home."

"You may be making a mistake," warned the magistrate.

"I shall be satisfied if you will grant me a divorce," said Huangfu. He could not help looking at his wife out of the corner of his eye.

After more questioning, the magistrate said to the woman, "Your husband insists on a divorce. I hate to break up marriages. What do you think?"

"My conscience is clear. But if he wants a divorce, I shall not protest."

The divorce was granted according to the husband's wish. The boy and the maid were released and ordered to be taken back to their parents.

The wife completely broke down when the court was adjourned. Divorce was a great disgrace to the woman, and she had not expected it because her guilt had not been established.

"I did not know you could be so cruel after seven years of marriage. You know I have no place to go now," said the wife to her husband. "I will rather die than have my name dishonored."

"That is none of my business," replied Huangfu and abruptly turned his back.

Only Ying-erh, the girl, stood by her.

"Ying-erh," said the wife. "Thank you for what you did. It is of no help now. You can go home to your parents. I have nowhere to go and I cannot keep you. Go home like a good girl."

They parted in tears.

The woman, now left all alone, could not completely realize what had happened. Aimlessly, she made her way through the streets and crowds without seeing anything. The day was darkening, and she wandered to the Tienhan Bridge on the Pien River where she stood looking out at the locks and congested water traffic. The masts of the boats stood close together rocking and swaying in the evening wind, giving her a heady sensation, as if she were rocking with them. She watched the golden disc of the sun disappear behind a distant hill, and realized she had come to the end of her road. She would never see the sun again.

Just as she was about to jump into the river, some one pulled her back. She turned around and saw an old woman, well over fifty, dressed in black. Her hair was thin and grayish-white.

"Daughter, what do you take your own life for?"

Mrs. Huangfu stared at her.

"Do you know me? I don't suppose you do," said the old woman.

"No," replied the young woman.

"I am your poor auntie. Since your marriage to the palace officer, I have not dared to come and bother you. It was so long ago when I saw you as a child. The other day I heard from the neighbors that you were involved in a lawsuit with your husband, and I came every day to ask for news. I hear that the magistrate has decreed a divorce. But why jump into the river?"

"My husband does not want me and I have no place to go. Why should I live?"

"Come, come, you can stay with your old auntie," said the old woman. Her voice was strong for her age. "Such a young woman trying to end her own life! What nonsense!"

Mrs. Huangfu was not at all sure whether this old woman really was her aunt, but she allowed the woman to take her along, without a will of her own.

They went first to a wine shop where the old woman ordered her a drink. When the young woman came to the aunt's house she found it was situated in a quiet, out-of-the-way alley. It was fairly decent looking, furnished with green curtains and armchairs and tables.

"Auntie, are you living all alone? How do you support yourself?"

The old woman whose name was Hu, answered with a laugh. "Oh, I make a living somehow. I used to call you 'Missie.' I forget your name."

"My name is Chunmei," answered Mrs. Huangfu, and she did not push her question further.

The old woman, Hu, was very kind to her, and for the first days she made her guest rest. Chunmei lay in bed thinking of the sudden and strange turn of her life.

Several days later, the old woman said to her, "You must be strong. I am not really your auntie, but I wanted to save a young girl's life when I saw you about to take the jump. You are young and pretty. You have your life before you." Her old eyes narrowed into slits. "Do you still love your husband who has so brutally disowned you and left you to die?"

Chunmei looked up from her pillow and answered, "I don't know."

"I don't blame you," said the old woman. "But wake up, my daughter. You are still young and you shouldn't suffer yourself to be pushed around by people. Forget your husband, and get over your misery. Young people sometimes have foolish sentiments, I know. I have crossed more bridges than you have crossed streets. Life is like that. Up and down, up and down it goes, round and round in a circle. I lost my husband at twenty-eight. How old are you?" Chunmei gave her age. "Well, I was a few years older than you are now, but here I am. Look at me." Even though her face was lined, and the skin of her neck was a little loose, she seemed in perfect health. "You take a good rest and in a little time you will get over it. Life is like going on a road. You fall down. What then? Do you sit down and cry and refuse to get up? No, you pick yourself up and go on again. From what you told me, he is a rascal. Why, he has not deserted you. He has thrown you out. So what are you lying here moping about?"

Chunmei listened to her words and felt better. "What can I do? I can't be living with you forever."

"Don't worry. Take a good rest and get strong again. Then when you are well, find a good man and remarry. Pretty eyes and a pretty face like yours never need to go hungry."

"Thank you, Auntie. I already feel better."

Mrs. Huangfu could not help feeling grateful to the old woman for saving her life and helping her recover her spirits during this bitter period of her life.

They had dinner together every night. Old woman Hu always liked a little rice wine with her dinner; wine was the "water of life," according to her. "There's nothing like a little wine for recovering your faith in life," she said. "At my age, it makes me feel good and young once more." Chunmei admired the spirit of this hearty woman.

After dinner, they heard a man's voice calling outside,

"Hu *potse,* Hu *potse!*" The old woman went hastily to open the door.

"Why do you close the door so early?" asked the man. It had been raining that day, and she had locked the door rather early.

The old woman asked him to sit down, but the man said he had to go away immediately, and remained standing. Chunmei saw from the back room that he was tall and had thick eyebrows and big eyes. Her attention was arrested and she looked at him carefully from behind the screen. His mouth could be called broad, and his nose was not pointed, more or less answering the boy's description. Her heart pounded, but she made no sign of her suspicion.

"What is this?" asked the tall man in a tone of impatience. "It is already a month since you sold the three hundred dollars' worth of things. I want the money."

"They were sold, as I told you," replied Auntie Hu. "They are in my client's place, but what can I do if he has not paid up? As soon as he pays, I shall turn over the money to you."

"But this is long enough—longer than usual. Bring the money as soon as you receive it."

The gentleman left and Auntie Hu came inside looking quite upset.

"Who was the visitor?" asked Chunmei.

"I will tell you, Chunmei. The gentleman's name is Hung. He says he was the magistrate of Tsaichow and is now retired. I don't believe him. I know he lies, but he is a great fellow. He often asks me to sell some of his jewels. He says he is an agent for jewelers. Maybe he is, maybe he isn't. But he has good jewels, and the other day he asked me to sell some for him. They were sold but my client hasn't paid. I don't blame him for being impatient."

"Do you know him well?"

"Yes, in a business way—perhaps more. I never saw a fellow quite like him. I can't make him out. He is liberal with his money. When he sees I am in need of money, he gives me some without my asking for it. The next time he comes, I will introduce him to you."

Chunmei's interest was greatly aroused, but she tried not to show it.

Hung came again and again, and Chunmei was introduced to him as a relative of Auntie Hu. She was torn between the desire to find out if he was the stranger who had changed her life, and her liking for his undeniable charm. She could not quite get rid of the suspicion that he might be the very man they had been looking for, and she tried to make his face fit the partridge boy's description of the mysterious stranger. The point which bothered her most was whether his nose could be called snub.

At one of their meetings, she sat staring at him, lost in thought.

"What are you staring at me for?" remarked Hung in his jocular way. "Every physiognomist tells me I have a lucky face and lucky ear lobes." He pulled his heavy lobes, and said, "See? I always brought luck to people."

Hung was alternately amusing, helpful, and attentive. He was flashily dressed and inordinately vain. Because he had traveled a great deal, he could tell entertaining stories, and his swagger was part of his charm. But he was also interested in others. He asked Chunmei to tell her story and listened with sympathy. He took her part, interrupting only to express his disgust with the ex-husband's outrageous cruelty. His sympathy for her seemed sincere, even if he might be courting her.

After their second meeting he had asked Chunmei to sew on a button for him. Chunmei was fascinated. She saw that he really had business transactions to come and see the old woman about, but now he provided excuses for many more visits. He always brought a bottle with him, and sweetmeats and new delicacies which he had promised the women; he would announce that he was coming for supper, complain of hunger, and then have the insolence to teach Chunmei how to prepare a dish of ham and candied ginger in his own way. When a man had the courage to command, it gave a woman pleasure to obey.

"What do you think of that rascal?" Auntie Hu asked Chunmei when he left.

"I think he is an interesting person."

"He asked me the other day to do something for him which I have not yet been able to do."

"What was it?"

"He is living alone. The other day he asked me to find a woman and make a match for him. Why don't you let me make the arrangements and suggest the match to him? I can see that he likes you and will be delighted at the suggestion."

"I see," said Chunmei thoughtfully.

"You see what? He is a charming man. What is holding you back? If you still haven't got over that ass of an ex-husband of yours, you are the greatest fool I know. Isn't he a fine fellow? He has money and will be able to take care of you, and you will be off my hands."

"I must tell you, Auntie," said Chunmei. "I like him, but there is something I should like to clear up."

"What is it?"

"I have an idea he might be the unknown person who sent the note, and broke up our marriage."

Auntie Hu broke into such laughter that Chunmei felt embarrassed.

"He answers the description, more or less, you know."

"What nonsense? How many tall men are there in the world, and how many have heavy eyebrows and big eyes? Is that his fault? Suppose he *was* that stranger, what then? You have been punished for eating a cake which you didn't eat. You've paid the price, and the cake is here. It's yours. If I were you, I would marry the stranger, just to show him off to that brute who was your husband."

Chunmei did not know what to think. If Hung was not the stranger, she would be doing herself a lot of good, and if he was, she would be doing her ex-husband no harm. She began to feel the sweetness of revenge.

The next time Hung came, she was gayer than usual. She had decided to test him.

He had brought his own bottle, and said, "Come on, drink to my luck in meeting such a fair lady as you."

"No, I will drink to your lucky ear lobes," the young woman replied. The drink helped her a lot. She could not contain her curiosity any longer, and in the next breath, she surprised herself by remarking, "The stranger was said to look like you."

"Really? I am honored. Think of a man who had the courage to do such a thing! If I had seen you before, I would have wanted to do the same thing, even if you were married to a duke. Once I did have an affair with a duke's mistress. You don't believe me? I don't suppose you would. However, here's to my lucky ear lobes!" He poured himself another cup and finished it at one gulp.

"See how he lies," remarked Auntie Hu pleasantly.

"Be sensible," said Hung, putting down his cup. "You have never seen the man. How do you know whether he is tall or short? But your husband was a brute to leave a pretty woman like you."

"Yes, he gave me no chance," she said. "It is all over now. What do I care? I am just curious to know who sent the note." In spite of herself, her eyes were a little red.

"Forget about the brute," said Hung. "Come on, drink. Such a pretty face is not made for tears. He did not want you, and you are still thinking of him. Oh, what a world, what a world!"

Chunmei was completely confused. The old woman encouraged her to drink and forget. Almost in revenge, she kept on drinking. Later in the evening, she became very gay. For the first time she realized she was free. She had never quite felt it before. It gave her a wonderful feeling of elation. She kept repeating in a silly way, "Yes, I have no husband . . . Yes, I have no husband."

"Yes, forget," said Hung.

"Yes, forget," said Chunmei. "Say you are not the stranger, are you?"

"Don't talk nonsense. What would you do if I were?"

"I would love you for setting me free from that brute husband of mine. Would it not be funny if my husband saw me drinking with the stranger here tonight?"

"Your former husband, I beg your pardon," corrected Hung. "You know what it would prove? It would prove that you had known the stranger and dined with him before. Thousands of women have done things behind their husbands' backs and are not divorced. You are divorced without having been unfaithful. What a world!"

"You are a devil," said Chunmei, and she began to laugh, and her laughter was gay as it had never been when she was Mrs. Huangfu.

"Am I?" asked Hung, and he put his arms around her.

She smiled up at him and said dreamily, "Hello, stranger," and offered him her lips.

Somehow she felt a sense of victory.

After their marriage Hung took her to live in a house far out in the western suburb. She had not thought it possible that she could be so happy. They talked and laughed and Chunmei seemed to be consciously trying to make up for what she had missed before. He often took her to small restaurants and she went with him gladly. He seemed well-to-do and was liberal with his money. He loved to press money into her palms and never asked her for an account, as Huangfu had. Then, too, he had friends whom he often invited home for dinner. It was as different as possible from her life with her former husband.

Hung had never openly admitted that he was the stranger. He always had a way of turning aside the question, or he would admit it with such a swagger that it seemed impossible to take him seriously. But one afternoon, after a little drink and some cold partridge, which they had bought from a street hawker, he was feeling very happy, and for once he made a slip of the tongue. "You know I sometimes think of that poor partridge boy—" he checked himself immediately and added lamely—"from what you told me about him." And Chunmei knew.

That night in bed after she had put out the light, Chunmei asked him, "Tell me why did you send that note?"

There was a long silence.

"He bullied you, didn't he?" he said at last.

"You knew? You had seen me?"

"Of course I knew. You don't know what a ridiculous couple you two made, like a swan married to a toad."

"Where did you see me?"

"I saw you the first time trailing your feet behind him on Kungchien Street. I stopped to ask you for road directions. He pulled you away roughly with a stern, censorious look I could not forget. That was last spring. You wouldn't remember. I thought of you as a bird in a cage. I was struck by you from the moment I saw you. I will let that bird free, I said to myself. I took a lot of trouble to find out. You had enemies, you know."

"I?" Chunmei gasped.

"You know that relative of yours, Chang Erh, who stayed in your house for some time to beg your husband for a job?"

"*You* know Chang Erh?"

"Yes. Do you know why your clan people never came to see you? Because of your husband's treatment of Chang Erh. He came home and told everybody in the village about it. I was in love with you and it was driving me crazy. I pictured you as a fairy enchained by a monster."

"But how could you do such a thing? I never had dinner with you. And I was happy."

"Yes, as happy as a bird in a cage. Remember two days before I sent you that fatal letter, when your husband had just come home, you dined at the Taiho restaurant in the passage with him? I was there, sitting at the next table. Yes, you were very happy. It didn't take me two minutes to see that you were afraid of him. I detested the fellow. I noticed that he never once consulted you about your food. He ordered what *he* liked, and you ate humbly, sweetly, submissively. I was boiling with rage. I tried to arrange to see you, but that partridge boy bungled it. I was madly in love with you and followed the trial every day through Auntie Hu. I had hoped he would divorce you, but I did not expect it to turn out exactly as I wished."

Next morning, she saw Hung writing a letter. She waited until he had finished, and then quickly snatched it from him and said laughingly, "Do you know what this letter means in my hands, if I hand it over to the court?"

Hung felt a slight shock and immediately recovered himself. "You won't," he said.

"Why won't I?"

"I know you mean the handwriting, but don't forget that you are living with the adulterer now. At the most, you will merely be convicted of adultery, and the judge cannot convict a person twice."

"You devil!"

She bent and kissed him, a long hot kiss.

"You are biting me," Hung protested jokingly.

"That is how much I love you!"

New Year came around. Chunmei used to go with her former husband to Siangkuoshih on that day to pray for a lucky year. She suggested to Hung their doing it, and they went to the temple together.

Huangfu, too, remembered their visit at the Siangkuoshih on every New Year's Day. He had been feeling desolate and unhappy since the settlement at court. The mystery of the stranger had never been solved, and he had gone back to the palace again. Now that he was separated from his wife, he remembered more and more her good qualities, and the more he thought about her, the more he believed in her innocence. Everything pointed to it: her own behavior during the arrest and trial, and the testimony of the maid and the neighbors. His remorse was bitter. He forced himself to put on a good gown, took a box of incense, and went to the temple.

As usual, there was a big crowd at the temple on New Year's Day. As Huangfu came out, he saw his former wife going in with a tall man. They did not see him, so he waited outside for them to come out, chatting idly with a seller of clay dolls. When he saw them come down the temple steps, he hid himself in the crowd, trembling with anger and jealousy.

He followed them till they got outside the gate, and then he called to her from behind. Chunmei turned around and recognized him with a start. He was shabby and thin, and there was a new sad look on his face.

"Oh, you!" she cried with evident annoyance and contempt. Her tone and carriage were so different from his submissive wife that for a moment he thought she must be somebody else.

"Chunmei, what are you doing here? Come home, I need you." He glanced at Hung briefly.

"Who are you?" demanded Hung. "I should ask you to stop bothering this lady." Turning to Chunmei, he asked, "What is this man to you?"

"He is my former husband," she replied.

"Come home, Chunmei. I have forgiven you. I am lonely. I was wrong about you." Huangfu's tone was almost plaintive.

"He is not your husband any more, is he?" Hung asked the woman, accenting his words slowly and fixing his eyes on her.

Chunmei looked at Hung and answered, "No."

"May I speak to you for a moment?" Huangfu asked her again. Chunmei looked at Hung, and he nodded and stood aside.

"What do you want?" asked Chunmei. Her voice was suddenly angry.

"Who is this man you are with?"

"Is it any business of yours what I do now?" Her voice was bitter.

"For old times' sake," he begged. "Come home. I want you."

Chunmei went a step closer. Her eyes shone and she raised her voice. "Let's make this clear," she said. "You did not want me. I told you I was innocent. You would not believe me, and did not care whether I lived or died. You said it was none of your business. Luckily I did not die, and what I do is none of your business now."

Huangfu's face changed. He laid his hands on her tightly, and she struggled to get free, shouting, "Let me alone! Let me alone!"

The former husband was so surprised that his grip relaxed. She broke away and went to Hung.

"Leave her alone, you bully!" shouted Hung.

He took her hand, and they walked off without another word. Huangfu stood alone, stupefied. As they walked down the street, they heard him calling to her from behind them:

"But I have forgiven you, Chunmei! I have forgiven you!"

From The Stream of Days

TĀHĀ HUSSEIN

I

FOR the first two or three weeks of his stay in Cairo he was lost in bewilderment. All he knew was that he had left the country behind him and settled in the capital as a student attending lectures at the Azhar. It was more by imagination than by sense that he distinguished the three phases of his day.

Both the house he lived in and the path that led to it were strange and unfamiliar. When he came back from the Azhar he turned to the right through a gateway which was open during the daytime and shut at night; after evening prayer there was only a narrow opening left in the middle of the door. Once through it, he became aware of a gentle heat playing on his right cheek, and a fine smoke teasing his nostrils; while on the left he heard an odd gurgling sound which at once puzzled and delighted him.

For several days, morning and evening, he listened curiously to this sound, but lacked the courage to inquire what it might be. Then one day he gathered from a chance remark that it came from the bubbling of a *narghile*[1] smoked by tradesmen of the district. It was provided for them by the proprietor of the café from which the gentle heat and the fine smoke cloud issued.

He walked straight on for a few steps before crossing a damp, roofed-in space in which it was impossible to stand firmly because of the slops thrown there by the café proprietor. Then he came out into an open

[1] *narghile:* a water pipe, similar to a hookah.

passageway; but this was narrow and filthy and full of strange, elusive smells, which were only moderately unpleasant early in the day and at nightfall, but as the day advanced and the heat of the sun grew stronger, became utterly intolerable.

He walked straight on through this narrow passage; but rarely did he find it smooth or easy. More often than not his friend would have to push him either this way or that so as to avoid some obstacle or other. Then he would continue in the new direction, feeling his way toward a house either to left or right, until he had passed the obstacle and taken the old direction again. He hurried along nervously at his companion's side, breathing the nauseous smells, and half-deafened by the medley of sounds that came from all sides at once, left and right, above and below, to meet in midair, where they seemed to unite above the boy's head, layer upon layer, into a single fine mist.

There was in fact a remarkable variety of sounds. Voices of women raised in dispute, of men shouting in anger or peaceably talking together; the noise of loads being set down or picked up; the song of the water carrier crying his wares; the curse of a carter to his horse or mule or donkey; the grating sound of cart wheels; and from time to time this confused whirl of sounds was torn by the braying of a donkey or the whinnying of a horse.

As he passed through this babel, his thoughts were far away, and he was scarcely conscious of himself or of what he was doing; but at a certain point on the road he caught the confused sound of conversation through a half-open door on the left; then he knew that a pace or two further on he must turn to the left up a staircase which would bring him to his lodging.

It was an ordinary sort of staircase, neither wide nor narrow, and its steps were of stone; but since it was used very frequently in both directions, and no one troubled to wash or sweep it, the dirt piled up thickly and stuck together in a compact mass on the steps, so that the stone was completely covered up, and whether you were going up or coming down the staircase appeared to be made of mud.

Now whenever the boy went up or down a staircase he was obliged to count the steps. But long as were the years he stayed in this place, and countless the times he negotiated this staircase, it never occurred to him to count the number of its steps. He learned at the second or third time of climbing it that after going up a few steps he had to turn a little to the left before continuing his ascent, leaving on his right an opening through which he never penetrated, though he knew that it led to the first floor of the building in which he lived for so many years.

This floor was not inhabited by students, but by workers and tradesmen.

He left the entrance to it on his right, and went on up to the second floor. There his harassed spirit found rest and relief; lungfuls of fresh air drove away the sense of suffocation with which he had been oppressed on that filthy staircase, and then too there was the parrot, whistling on without a break, as if to testify before all the world to the tyranny of her Persian master, who had imprisoned her in an abominable cage, and would sell her tomorrow or the day after to another man who would treat her in exactly the same way. And when he was rid of her and had laid hands on the cash, he would buy a successor for her who would be cooped up in the same prison pouring forth the same curses on her master, and waiting as her sister had waited to be passed on from hand to hand, and from cage to cage, while everywhere she went that plaintive cry of hers would delight the hearts of men and women.

When our friend reached the top of the staircase he breathed in the fresh air that blew on his face, and listened to the voice of the parrot calling him toward the right. He obeyed, turning through a narrow corridor, past two rooms in which two Persians lived. One of these was still a young man, while the other was already past middle age. The one was as morose and misanthropic as the other was genial and good-natured.

At last the boy was home. He entered a room like a hall, which provided for most of the practical needs of the house. This led on to another room, large but irregular in shape, which served for social and intellectual needs. It was bedroom and dining room, reading room and study, and a room for conversation by day or by night. Here were books and crockery and food; and here the boy had his own particular corner, as in every room he occupied or visited at all frequently.

This place of his was on the left inside the door. After advancing a pace or two he found a mat spread on the ground, and above that an old but quite serviceable carpet. Here he sat in the daytime, and here he slept at night, with a pillow for his head and a rug to cover him. On the opposite side of the room was his elder brother's pitch, a good deal higher than his own. He had a mat spread on the ground, and a decent carpet on top of that, then a felt mattress, and above that a long, wide piece of bedding stuffed with cotton, and finally, crowning all, a coverlet. Here the young sheikh[2] would sit with his close friends. They were not obliged to prop up their backs against the bare wall, as the boy did, having cushions to pile up on the rugs. At night this couch was transformed into a bed on which the young sheikh slept.

---

[2] *sheikh:* The word *sheikh* meant originally "old man" or "elder." In this translation it is used in two senses: (1) as more or less equivalent to *âlim,* "doctor," and so teacher at the Azhar; (2) "scholar" or aspirant to learning, as here.

II

This was all the boy ever learned about his immediate surroundings. The second phase of his life consisted in the tumultuous journey between his home and the Azhar. He went out through the covered passage till he felt the heat of the café on his left cheek, and heard the bubbling of the *narghile* on his right. In front of him was a shop which played an important part in his life; it belonged to El-Hagg Firûz, who supplied the neighborhood with most of the necessities of life. In the morning he sold boiled beans,[3] prepared in the usual variety of ways. But El-Hagg Firûz used to boast the special virtues of his beans—and raise their prices accordingly. He had plain beans, beans in fat, beans in butter, beans in every kind of oil; he added, if required, all sorts of spices. As for the students, they adored these beans, and often made far too large a meal of them. So by mid-morning they were already dull in the head, and at the noon lecture they slept.

When evening came El-Hagg Firûz sold his customers their supper: cheese, olives, milled sesame, or honey. To the more luxurious he supplied boxes of tuna or sardines. And to a few of them perhaps, as night approached, he sold things which have no name, and nothing to do with food, things spoken of in a whisper, yet passionately vied for.

The boy used to overhear these whisperings; sometimes he half understood, but as a rule the whole transaction was a mystery to him. As the days passed by and he grew older, he came to see through these subtle hints and ambiguities. What he learned then obliged him to overhaul his standards of judgment, and to revise his valuation both of people and of things.

El-Hagg Firûz was a tall, jet-black fellow, and anything but talkative. But when he did speak he mumbled his words and lisped out his Arabic in a fashion which made an ineffaceable impression on the boy. He is always reminded of it by the story of Ziad and his pupil in *El-Bayan wal-Tabyîn*.[4] Ziad asked his pupil to say: "We have been given a pony." Instead of which he repeated it so: "We have been given a bony." "Wretch!" said Ziad, annoyed. "If you can't say pony, say horse instead." Whereupon the boy replied: "We have been given an arse." Ziad, shocked, reverted to the "bony" as the lesser evil.

El-Hagg Firûz held a unique position in the neighborhood and among

---

[3] *boiled beans: fool,* the brown bean which is the staple diet of the Egyptian masses.
[4] *El-Bayan wal-Tabyîn: Book of Exposition and Demonstration:* a treatise on rhetoric, constituting a huge anthology of Arab eloquence, by El-Jâhiz, a prolific and original author of the Basra school (ninth century).

the students especially. It was to him that they went when their money ran out toward the end of the month, or when their remittances were overdue. He it was who gave them food on credit, lent them a piaster or two from time to time, and helped them out in all kinds of emergencies. No wonder his name was as often on their lips as those of the most learned sheikhs of the Azhar.

But this was not all. El-Hagg Firûz was essential to the students in yet another way. It was to him that were addressed all the letters bringing them news of their families, or enclosing flimsy notes which they took to the post office with empty pockets, to return with the jingle of silver falling cheerily on their ears and into their very hearts.

Naturally not a single student missed an opportunity of passing the time of day morning and evening at El-Hagg Firûz' shop, or of casting a quick furtive glance at the spot where letters were waiting to be collected. How often one of them would go home grasping a sealed envelope which was spotted with oil and butter stains; yet despite its greasiness that envelope was more precious in his eyes than any composition or textbook on law, grammar or theology.

On leaving the covered passage, then, the boy found himself in front of El-Hagg Firûz' shop; his friend would take him a few paces in that direction to greet El-Hagg Firûz and to inquire if there was a letter for him or not; the reply would bring either smiles or frowns to his face. Then he turned away to the left, and walked straight forwards down the long narrow street crowded with passersby. It was full of students, merchants, tradesmen, laborers; carts drawn by donkeys, horses or mules; carters shouting out warnings or curses at the men, women or children blocking their path. Then on each side of the street were different kinds of shops, in many of which was prepared the meager diet of the poor. The smells that issued from them were abominable, but that did not prevent them from delighting most of the passersby, whether they were students, laborers or porters. Some of them turned aside to these shops and bought a scrap of food to gulp down on the spot, or take home and eat, either alone or with others. And some of them, assailed by this battery of smells, remained unmoved. They were tempted but did not yield. Their eyes saw, their nostrils smelled, their appetite was stirred; but, alas, their pockets were empty. They passed on with yearning in their souls and with bitterness and resentment in their hearts; yet at the same time they were content with their lot and accepted it with resignation.

In some other shops a quiet, unhurried trade was transacted, almost without any words passing at all. If anything was said, it was under the breath, so as scarcely to be heard. In spite of this—or perhaps for this

very reason—the trade in question brought great wealth and prosperity to
those who practiced it. To all appearances the majority of these shops
dealt only in coffee and soap, though some of them also sold sugar and rice.

As he passed through all this a warm interest stirred in the boy. But he
would have understood practically nothing had not his friend from time to
time volunteered an explanation. He continued on his way, sometimes
walking firmly forwards, sometimes swerving aside. When the road was
clear he marched with a sure step, but stumbled and faltered on its edges
when it was crowded or twisty. At last he came to a spot where he had to
turn a little to the left and then plunge into a lane as narrow and crooked
and filthy as could be. Its atmosphere was foul with an abominable medley
of smells, and from time to time weak, hollow voices which reflected
its misery and wrong echoed back cries for charity to the footfalls of
passersby, begging at the sound of steps, as if life had only been percepti-
ble through the ears. They were answered by other voices: the thin, harsh,
strangled cries of those winged creatures which love darkness and desola-
tion and ruins. Often enough these noises were accompanied by the
flutter of wings, which sometimes, to his horror, shaved past his ear or
his face. Instinctively his hand would fly up for protection, and for sometime afterwards his heart would be throbbing with apprehension.

On he walked with his friend along this narrow, dark, twisting alley,
now rising, now descending, now going straight on, now turning to left or
right. And all the time these loathsome sounds assailed him, sometimes
from in front, and sometimes from behind, but never without dismaying
him. After a time he felt his heart lighten and his lungs expand, and knew
that the moment of release had come. He heaved one sigh of relief, loaded
with all the weight of his anxiety and distress.

Now he breathed freely and easily, as if he were taking in great drafts
of life from the fresh air which flowed over him as he left the bat-ridden
alley. On he went along the road, which twisted treacherously under his
feet for a few moments, then became firm again so that he could step
forward easily and with confidence. His heart thrilled with joy at the strange
harmony of sounds which came to his ears as he walked along the pleasant,
peaceful street. On one side of him was the Mosque of Sayyidna-l-
Hussein,[5] and on the other a series of small shops. How often he
would stop at one of these during the days that followed, and what good
things he tasted there! Soaked figs and their juice in summertime, and in

---

[5] *Sayyidna-l-Hussein:* Sayyidna (lit. *Our Master*) Hussein was the grandson of the
Prophet; he and his descendants were considered the true Caliphs by the Shi'ite ("sep-
aratist") sect, as opposed to the Sunnis (traditionalists). The mosque is of the Otto-
man period.

winter *bassbûssa*,[6] which diffused a warm glow of well-being through the body. Sometimes he would stop at a Syrian retailer's to choose from a variety of foods, hot or cold, salt or sweet. Their taste gave him inexpressible pleasure, yet if they were offered him now he would be afraid they might make him ill, or even poison him.

He continued along this street until he came to a place where the voices grew louder and more numerous. He realized that the roads divided here and that he could branch right or left, go straight on, or turn about. "Here are the crossroads," said his companion. "If you go right you reach the Sikka El-Gadida, then the Musky, then 'Ataba El-Khadra. To the left you have Sharia El-Darrâssa. But we must go straight on into Sharia El-Halwagi, the street of learning and hard work. It is so narrow that if you stretched out your arms left and right you could almost touch both walls. Now you are walking between a number of small bookshops. There are books of every kind in them, new and old, good and bad, in print or manuscript."

How many a pleasant and rewarding halt did our friend make in that narrow street, which remained fixed in his memory later on, after his life had changed its course.

But this time he must hurry past. His guide had to be at the Azhar before the lecture began. Here they were, arrived at the Barbers' Gate. He took off his sandals, laid them one on top of the other, then picked them up in his hand as he followed his companion. A little further on he stepped over a shallow threshold into the quiet courtyard of the Azhar, and felt a cool morning breeze blow refreshingly upon his face. And so he entered the third phase of this new life of his.

III

This third phase of his existence was the one he loved best of all. In his own room he endured all the pains of exile. It was like a foreign country to him, and he never became familiar with its contents, except perhaps those nearest to him. He did not live in it in the same sense that he had lived in his country home or in other familiar rooms where nothing was unknown to him. He passed his days there in exile from people and things alike, and in such anguish of heart that the oppressive air he breathed there brought him no rest or refreshment, but only heaviness and pain.

Nor was there any doubt of his preferring these hours in the Azhar to the agitated journey back and forth, whose hazards drove him almost to

[6] *bassbûssa:* nut-cake of Syrian origin.

despair. It was not only his steps that were confused and unsteady; his very heart was overwhelmed by that unnerving perplexity which perverts a man's purposes and drives him blindly onwards, not only along the material road which he needs must follow, but also along the free paths of the mind, feckless and without a plan. Not only was he distracted by the hubbub and tumult that eddied around him. He was distressed at the unsteadiness of his walk and the impossibility of harmonizing his own quiet, faltering steps with the firm and even brutal pace of his companion.

It was only in the third phase of his day that he found rest and security. The fresh breeze that blew across the court of the Azhar at the hour of morning prayer met him with a welcome and inspired him with a sense of security and hope. The touch of this breeze on his forehead, damp with sweat from that feverish journey, resembled nothing so much as the kisses his mother used to give him during his early years, when he chanted verses from the Koran to her, or entertained her with a story he had heard at the village school; or when, as a pale, delicate infant, he abandoned the corner in which he had been reciting the litany from the *sura* Ya-Sin to go and carry out some household task or other.

Those kisses revived his heart and filled him not only with tenderness but with hope and confidence. The breeze which welcomed him in the court of the Azhar, no less, brought rest after weariness, calm after tumult, a smile after gloomy looks. However, he as yet knew nothing of the Azhar, and had not the least idea what he would find there. But it was enough for him to brush with his bare feet the ground of that court, to feel on his face the caress of its morning breeze, and to realize that around him the Azhar was preparing to awake from its drowsiness, that its inertia would soon give place to activity. He began to recover consciousness of himself, as life returned to him. He felt the conviction of being in his own country, among his own people, and lost all sense of isolation, all sadness. His soul blossomed forth, and with every fiber of his being he yearned to discover . . . well, what? Something he was a stranger to, though he loved it and felt irresistibly drawn toward it—knowledge. How many times had he heard this word, and longed to find out its hidden meaning! His impression of it was vague enough, to be sure; but of this he was convinced, that knowledge had no limits and that people might spend their whole lives in acquiring a few drops of it. He too wished to devote his whole life to it and to win as much of it as he could, however little that might be. His father and the learned friends who came to visit him had spoken of knowledge as a boundless ocean, and the child had never taken this expression for a figure of speech or a metaphor, but as the simple truth. He had come to Cairo and to the Azhar with the intention of throw-

ing himself into this ocean and drinking what he could of it, until the day
he drowned. What finer end could there be for a man of spirit than to
drown himself in knowledge? What a splendid plunge into the beyond!

All these thoughts suddenly thronged into his young spirit, filling it and
taking possession of it, blotting out the memory of that desolate room, of
the turbulent, twisty road, and even of the country and its delights. They
convinced him that it was no mistake or exaggeration to be consumed with
love for the Azhar as well as with regret for the country.

The boy paced on with his companion until he had crossed the court and
mounted the shallow step which is the threshold of the Azhar itself. His
heart was all modesty and humility, but his soul was filled with glory and
pride. His feet stepped lightly over the worn-out mats that were laid out
across the floor, leaving a bare patch here and there, as if on purpose
to touch the feet which passed over them with something of the benediction
attached to that holy ground. The boy used to love the Azhar at this moment, when worshipers were finishing their early-morning prayer and going
away, with the marks of drowsiness still in their eyes, to make a circle
round some column or other and wait for the teacher who was to give a
lecture on tradition or exegesis, first principles or theology.[7]

At this moment the Azhar was quiet, and free from the strange intermingled murmurs that filled it from sunrise until evening prayer. You could
only hear the whispered conversations of its inmates or the hushed but
steady voice of some young man reciting the Koran. Or you might come
upon a worshiper who had arrived too late for the common service, or had
gone on to perform extra prayers after completing the statutory number.
Or maybe you would hear a teacher beginning his lecture in the languid
tone of a man who has awakened from sleep and said his prayers but has
not yet eaten anything to give him strength and energy. He starts in a quiet,
husky voice: "In the name of God, the merciful, the compassionate: Praise
be to God, father of the worlds. May His peace and blessing be upon our
lord Muhammad, the most noble of the prophets, upon his family and his
companions. These are the words of the author of the Book, may God rest
his soul and grant us the fruits of his learning. Amen!"

The students listened to the lecture with the same quiet languor in which
it was given. There was a striking contrast between the different tones the
sheikhs used at the early-morning and midday lectures. At dawn their
voices were calm and gentle, with traces of drowsiness in them. At noon
they were strong and harsh, but fraught too with a certain sluggishness in-
duced by the lunch they had just eaten, the baked beans and pickles and

[7] *tradition . . . theology:* These are the four primary subjects of the traditional
Azharite course.

so on which made up the usual fare of an Azharite at this time. At dawn
the voices seemed to beg humbly for favor from the great authorities of
the past, while by noon they were attacking them almost as if they were
adversaries. This contrast always astonished and delighted the boy.

On he went with his friend up the two steps leading into the *liwân*.[8]
There beside one of those sacred pillars, to which a chair was bound by
a great chain, our friend was deposited by his companion, who left him with
these words: "Wait there and you will hear a lecture on tradition; when
mine is over I will return and fetch you." His companion's lecture was on
the first principles of Islamic law, given by Sheikh Rậdy, God rest his soul.
The textbook was the *Tahrîr* of El-Kemal Ibn El-Humam. When the boy
heard this sentence, every word filled him at once with awe and curiosity.
First principles of law? What science was this? Sheikh Rậdy? Who could he
be? *Tahrîr?*[9] What was the meaning of this word? El-Kemal Ibn El-
Humam? Could there be a more wonderful pair of names? How true it
was that knowledge is a boundless ocean, full of unimaginable benefit for any thoughtful being who is ready to plunge into it. The
boy's admiration for this lecture especially grew deeper every day as he listened to his brother and his brother's friends studying their lesson beforehand. What they read sounded very strange, but there was no doubt of its
fascination.

As he listened the boy used to burn with longing to grow six or seven
years older, so that he might be able to understand it, to solve its riddles
and ambiguities, to be master of the whole subject as those distinguished
young men were, and to dispute with the teachers about it as they did.
But for the present he was compelled to listen without understanding.
Time and again he would turn over some sentence or other in his mind on
the chance of finding some sense in it. But he achieved nothing by all this,
except perhaps a greater respect for knowledge and a deeper reverence for
his teachers, together with modesty as to his own powers and a deter-
mination to work harder.

There was one sentence in particular. How many sleepless nights it cost
him! How many days of his life it overcast! Sometimes it tempted him
to miss an elementary lecture—for he had understood his first lessons without difficulty—and so led him on to playing truant from the sheikh's lecture
on tradition, in order to speculate on what he had heard from the lips of
those older students.

The sentence which took possession of him in this way was certainly a

8 *liwân:* colonnade surrounding the central court of the mosque.
9 *Tahrîr:* "Correct Reformulation" (of the first principles of law). The work was
written in the fifteenth century.

remarkable one. It would fall echoing in his ears as he lay on the threshold of sleep, and drag him back to a wakefulness which lasted all night through. This was the sentence: "Right is the negation of negation." What could these words mean? How could negation be negated? What might such negation be? And how could the negation of negation be right?[10] The sentence began to whirl round in his head like the ravings of delirium in a sick man's brain, until one day it was driven out of his mind by one of El-Kafrawy's[11] *Problems*. This problem he understood at once and was able to argue about. Thus he came at last to feel that he had begun to taste the water of the boundless ocean of knowledge.

The boy sat beside the pillar, toying with the chain and listening to the sheikh on tradition. He understood him perfectly, and found nothing to criticize in his lesson except the cascade of names which he poured forth on his listeners in giving the source and authorities for each tradition. It was always "so-and-so tells us" or "according to so-and-so." The boy could not see the point of these endless chains of names, or this tedious tracing of sources. He longed for the sheikh to have done with all this and come down to the tradition itself. As soon as he did so the boy listened with all his heart. He memorized the tradition and understood it, but showed not the slightest interest in the sheikh's analysis, which reminded him too well of the explanations given by the Imam of the mosque in his country village and the sheikh who used to teach him the elements of law.

While the sheikh proceeded with his lesson the Azhar began gradually to wake up, as if stirred out of its torpor by the voices of the teachers holding forth, and by the discussions which arose between them and the students, amounting sometimes almost to quarrels. The students came closer, the voices rose higher, the echoes intermingled and the sheikhs raised their voices again, so that the students might be able to hear them, ever higher and higher, up to the final climax of the words "God is all-wise." For meanwhile other students had come up to wait for a lecture on law by another sheikh, or maybe the same one; so he had no choice but to end the early-morning lecture and begin the next. Then the boy's companion would return, take him by the hand without a word and drag him off all urgently to another place, where he dumped him like a piece of luggage and abandoned him again.

---

[10] *This was . . . right:* As the context is legal, the sentence means: "Property is a counterclaim against a counterclaim," or the assertion of a right against all comers. In a different context the words might well mean: "Truth is the refutation of refutation," or the rebuttal of skepticism.

[11] *El-Kafrawy:* An Azharite grammarian of the eighteenth century.

The boy realized that he had been transferred to the law class. He would listen to this lecture until it came to an end and both sheikhs and students went off. Then he would stay rooted to the spot until his friend came back from Sayyidna-l-Hussein, where he had been attending a lecture on law given by Sheikh Bakhît, God rest his soul.

Now Sheikh Bakhît was prolix in the extreme, and his students used to harass him with objections. So he never finished the lesson until the middle of the morning. Then the boy's companion would return to where he was, take him by the hand without a word and lead him out of the Azhar. And so back he went through the second phase along the road between the Azhar and his lodgings into the third and final phase, where he was left alone in his place in the corner on the old carpet stretched out over a rotten worn-out mat.

The Bet

ANTON CHEKHOV

I T WAS a dark autumn night. The old banker was pacing from corner to corner of his study, recalling to his mind the party he gave in the autumn fifteen years before. There were many clever people at the party and much interesting conversation. They talked among other things of capital punishment. The guests, among them not a few scholars and journalists, for the most part disapproved of capital punishment. They found it obsolete as a means of punishment, unfitted to a Christian State, and immoral. Some of them thought that capital punishment should be replaced universally by life imprisonment.

"I don't agree with you," said the host. "I myself have experienced neither capital punishment nor life imprisonment, but if one may judge *a priori,* then in my opinion capital punishment is more moral and more humane than imprisonment. Execution kills instantly, life imprisonment kills by degrees. Who is the more humane executioner, one who kills you in a few seconds or one who draws the life out of you incessantly, for years?"

"They're both equally immoral," remarked one of the guests, "because their purpose is the same, to take away life. The State is not God. It has no right to take away that which it cannot give back, if it should so desire."

Among the company was a lawyer, a young man of about twenty-five. On being asked his opinion, he said:

"Capital punishment and life imprisonment are equally immoral; but if I were offered the choice between them, I would certainly choose the second. It's better to live somehow than not to live at all."

There ensued a lively discussion. The banker who was then younger and more nervous suddenly lost his temper, banged his fist on the table, and, turning to the young lawyer, cried out:

"It's a lie. I bet you two millions you wouldn't stick in a cell for even five years."

"If you mean it seriously," replied the lawyer, "then I bet I'll stay not five but fifteen."

"Fifteen! Done!" cried the banker. "Gentlemen, I stake two millions."

"Agreed. You stake two millions, I my freedom," said the lawyer.

So this wild, ridiculous bet came to pass. The banker, who at that time had too many millions to count, spoiled and capricious, was beside himself with rapture. During supper he said to the lawyer jokingly.

"Come to your senses, young man, before it's too late. Two millions are nothing to me, but you stand to lose three or four of the best years of your life. I say three or four, because you'll never stick it out any longer. Don't forget either, you unhappy man, that voluntary is much heavier than enforced imprisonment. The idea that you have the right to free yourself at any moment will poison the whole of your life in the cell. I pity you."

And now the banker, pacing from corner to corner, recalled all this and asked himself:

"Why did I make this bet? What's the good? The lawyer loses fifteen years of his life and I throw away two millions. Will it convince people that capital punishment is worse or better than imprisonment for life? No, no! all stuff and rubbish. On my part, it was the caprice of a well-fed man; on the lawyer's, pure greed of gold."

He recollected further what happened after the evening party. It was decided that the lawyer must undergo his imprisonment under the strictest observation, in a garden wing of the banker's house. It was agreed that during the period he would be deprived of the right to cross the threshold, to see living people, to hear human voices, and to receive letters and newspapers. He was permitted to have a musical instrument, to read books, to write letters, to drink wine and smoke tobacco. By the agreement he could communicate, but only in silence, with the outside world through a little window specially constructed for this purpose. Everything necessary, books, music, wine, he could receive in any quantity by sending a note through the window. The agreement provided for all the minutest details, which made the confinement strictly solitary, and it obliged the lawyer to remain exactly fifteen years from twelve o'clock of November 14th, 1870, to twelve o'clock of November 14th, 1885. The least attempt on his part to violate the conditions, to escape if only for two minutes before the time, freed the banker from the obligation to pay him the two millions.

During the first year of imprisonment, the lawyer, as far as it was possible to judge from his short notes, suffered terribly from loneliness and boredom. From his wing day and night came the sound of the piano. He rejected wine and tobacco. "Wine," he wrote, "excites desires, and desires are the chief foes of a prisoner; besides, nothing is more boring than to drink good wine alone," and tobacco spoiled the air in his room. During the first year the lawyer was sent books of a light character; novels with complicated love interest, stories of crime and fantasy, comedies, and so on.

In the second year the piano was heard no longer and the lawyer asked only for classics. In the fifth year, music was heard again, and the prisoner asked for wine. Those who watched him said that during the whole of that year he was only eating, drinking, and lying on his bed. He yawned often and talked angrily to himself. Books he did not read. Sometimes at night he would sit down to write. He would write for a long time and tear it all up in the mornings. More than once he was heard to weep.

In the second half of the sixth year, the prisoner began zealously to study languages, philosophy, and history. He fell on these subjects so hungrily that the banker hardly had time to get books enough for him. In the space of four years about six hundred volumes were bought at his request. It was while that passion lasted that the banker received the following letter from the prisoner: "My dear jailer, I am writing these lines in six languages. Show them to experts. Let them read them. If they do not find one single mistake, I beg you to give orders to have a gun fired off in the garden. By the noise I shall know that my efforts have not been in vain. The geniuses of all ages and countries speak in different languages; but in them all burns the same flame. Oh, if you knew my heavenly happiness now that I can understand them!" The prisoner's desire was fulfilled. Two shots were fired in the garden by the banker's order.

Later on, after the tenth year, the lawyer sat immovable before his table and read only the New Testament. The banker found it strange that a man who in four years had mastered six hundred erudite volumes should have spent nearly a year in reading one book, easy to understand and by no means thick. The New Testament was then replaced by the history of religions and theology.

During the last two years of his confinement the prisoner read an extraordinary amount, quite haphazard. Now he would apply himself to the natural sciences, then he would read Byron or Shakespeare. Notes used to come from him in which he asked to be sent at the same time a book on chemistry, a textbook of medicine, a novel, and some treatise on philosophy or theology. He read as though he were swimming in the sea among broken pieces of wreckage, and in his desire to save his life was eagerly grasping one piece after another.

II

The banker recalled all this, and thought:

"Tomorrow at twelve o'clock he receives his freedom. Under the agreement, I shall have to pay him two millions. If I pay, it's all over with me. I am ruined forever. . . ."

Fifteen years before he had too many millions to count, but now he was afraid to ask himself which he had more of, money or debts. Gambling on the Stock Exchange, risky speculation, and the recklessness of which he could not rid himself even in old age, had gradually brought his business to decay; and the fearless, self-confident, proud man of business had become an ordinary banker, trembling at every rise and fall in the market.

"That cursed bet," murmured the old man clutching his head in despair. . . . "Why didn't the man die? He's only forty years old. He will take away my last farthing, marry, enjoy life, gamble on the Exchange, and I will look on like an envious beggar and hear the same words from him every day: 'I'm obliged to you for the happiness of my life. Let me help you.' No, it's too much! The only escape from bankruptcy and disgrace—is that the man should die."

The clock had just struck three. The banker was listening. In the house everyone was asleep, and one could hear only the frozen trees whining outside the windows. Trying to make no sound, he took out of his safe the key of the door which had not been opened for fifteen years, put on his overcoat, and went out of the house. The garden was dark and cold. It was raining. A damp, penetrating wind howled in the garden and gave the trees no rest. Though he strained his eyes, the banker could see neither the ground, nor the white statues, nor the garden wing, nor the trees. Approaching the garden wing, he called the watchman twice. There was no answer. Evidently the watchman had taken shelter from the bad weather and was now asleep somewhere in the kitchen or the greenhouse.

"If I have the courage to fulfill my intention," thought the old man, "the suspicion will fall on the watchman first of all."

In the darkness he groped for the steps and the door and entered the hall of the garden wing, then poked his way into a narrow passage and struck a match. Not a soul was there. Someone's bed, with no bedclothes on it, stood there, and an iron stove loomed dark in the corner. The seals on the door that led into the prisoner's room were unbroken.

When the match went out, the old man, trembling from agitation, peeped into the little window.

In the prisoner's room a candle was burning dimly. The prisoner himself sat by the table. Only his back, the hair on his head and his hands were visible. Open books were strewn about on the table, the two chairs, and on the carpet near the table.

Five minutes passed and the prisoner never stirred once. Fifteen years' confinement had taught him to sit motionless. The banker tapped on the window with his finger, but the prisoner made no movement in reply. Then the banker cautiously tore the seals from the door and put the key into the lock. The rusty lock gave a hoarse groan and the door creaked. The banker expected instantly to hear a cry of surprise and the sound of steps. Three minutes passed and it was as quiet inside as it had been before. He made up his mind to enter.

Before the table sat a man, unlike an ordinary human being. It was a skeleton, with tight-drawn skin, with long curly hair like a woman's, and a shaggy beard. The color of his face was yellow, of an earthy shade; the cheeks were sunken, the back long and narrow, and the hand upon which he leaned his hairy head was so lean and skinny that it was painful to look upon. His hair was already silvering with gray, and no one who glanced at the senile emaciation of the face would have believed that he was only forty years old. On the table, before his bended head, lay a sheet of paper on which something was written in a tiny hand.

"Poor devil," thought the banker, "he's asleep and probably seeing millions in his dreams. I have only to take and throw this half-dead thing on the bed, smother him a moment with the pillow, and the most careful examination will find no trace of unnatural death. But, first, let us read what he has written here."

The banker took the sheet from the table and read:

> Tomorrow at twelve o'clock midnight, I shall obtain my freedom and the right to mix with people. But before I leave this room and see the sun I think it necessary to say a few words to you. On my own clear conscience and before God who sees me I declare to you that I despise freedom, life, health, and all that your books call the blessings of the world.
>
> For fifteen years I have diligently studied earthly life. True, I saw neither the earth nor the people, but in your books I drank fragrant wine, sang songs, hunted deer and wild boar in the forests, loved women. . . . And beautiful women, like clouds ethereal, created by the magic of your poets' genius, visited me by night, and whispered to me wonderful tales,

which made my head drunken. In your books I climbed the summits of Elbruz and Mont Blanc and saw from there how the sun rose in the morning, and in the evening suffused the sky, the ocean and the mountain ridges with a purple gold. I saw from there how above me lightnings glimmered, cleaving the clouds; I saw green forests, fields, rivers, lakes, cities; I heard sirens singing, and the playing of the pipes of Pan; I touched the wings of beautiful devils who came flying to me to speak of God. . . . In your books I cast myself into bottomless abysses, worked miracles, burned cities to the ground, preached new religions, conquered whole countries. . . .

Your books gave me wisdom. All that unwearying human thought created in the centuries is compressed to a little lump in my skull. I know that I am cleverer than you all.

And I despise your books, despise all worldly blessings and wisdom. Everything is void, frail, visionary and delusive as a mirage. Though you be proud and wise and beautiful, yet will death wipe you from the face of the earth like the mice underground; and your posterity, your history, and the immortality of your men of genius will be as frozen slag, burned down together with the terrestrial globe.

You are mad, and gone the wrong way. You take falsehood for truth and ugliness for beauty. You would marvel if suddenly apple and orange trees should bear frogs and lizards instead of fruit, and if roses should ·begin to breathe the odor of a sweating horse. So do I marvel at you, who bartered heaven for earth. I do not want to understand you.

That I may show you indeed my contempt for that by which you live, I waive the two millions of which I once dreamed as of paradise, and which I now despise. That I may deprive myself of my right to them, I shall come out from here five minutes before the stipulated term, and thus shall violate the agreement.

When he had read, the banker put the sheet on the table, kissed the head of the strange man, and began to weep. He went out of the wing. Never at any other time, not even after his terrible losses on the Exchange, had he felt such contempt for himself as now. Coming home, he lay down on his bed, but agitation and tears kept him a long time from sleeping. . . .

The next morning the poor watchman came running to him and told him that they had seen the man who lived in the wing climb through the window into the garden. He had gone to the gate and disappeared. The banker instantly went with his servant to the wing and established the escape of his prisoner. To avoid unnecessary rumors he took the paper with the renunciation from the table and, on his return, locked it in his safe.

SOCIAL CONCERNS

An Enemy of the People

HENRIK IBSEN

CHARACTERS

DR. THOMAS STOCKMANN, *Medical Officer of the Municipal Baths*

MRS. STOCKMANN, *his wife*

PETRA, *their daughter, a teacher*

EJLIF
MORTEN $\big\}$ *their sons (aged 13 and 10 respectively)*

PETER STOCKMANN, *the Doctor's elder brother; Mayor of the Town and Chief Constable, Chairman of the Baths' Committee, etc., etc.*

MORTEN KIIL, *a tanner (Mrs. Stockmann's adoptive father)*

HOVSTAD, *editor of the "People's Messenger"*

BILLING, *subeditor*

CAPTAIN HORSTER

ASLAKSEN, *a printer*

MEN *of various conditions and occupations, some few women, and a troop of schoolboys—the audience at a public meeting*

The action takes place in a coast town in southern Norway.

45

ACT ONE

SCENE: DR. STOCKMANN'S *sitting room. It is evening. The room is plainly but neatly appointed and furnished. In the right-hand wall are two doors; the farther leads out to the hall, the nearer to the doctor's study. In the left-hand wall, opposite the door leading to the hall, is a door leading to the other rooms occupied by the family. In the middle of the same wall stands the stove, and, further forward, a couch with a looking glass hanging over it and an oval table in front of it. On the table, a lighted lamp, with a lampshade. At the back of the room, an open door leads to the dining room.* BILLING *is seen sitting at the dining table, on which a lamp is burning. He has a napkin tucked under his chin, and* MRS. STOCKMANN *is standing by the table handing him a large plateful of roast beef. The other places at the table are empty, and the table somewhat in disorder, a meal having evidently recently been finished.*

MRS. STOCKMANN: You see, if you come an hour late, Mr. Billing, you have to put up with cold meat.

BILLING (*as he eats*): It is uncommonly good, thank you—remarkably good.

MRS. STOCKMANN: My husband makes such a point of having his meals punctually, you know——

BILLING: That doesn't affect me a bit. Indeed, I almost think I enjoy a meal all the better when I can sit down and eat all by myself and undisturbed.

MRS. STOCKMANN: Oh well, as long as you are enjoying it. (*Turns to the hall door, listening.*) I expect that is Mr. Hovstad coming too.

BILLING: Very likely.

[PETER STOCKMANN *comes in. He wears an overcoat and his official hat, and carries a stick.*]

PETER STOCKMANN: Good evening, Katherine.

MRS. STOCKMANN (*coming forward into the sitting room*): Ah, good evening—is it you? How good of you to come up and see us!

PETER STOCKMANN: I happened to be passing, and so——(*looks into the dining room*)——but you have company with you, I see.

MRS. STOCKMANN (*a little embarrassed*): Oh, no—it was quite by chance he came in. (*Hurriedly.*) Won't you come in and have something, too?

PETER STOCKMANN: I! No, thank you. Good gracious—hot meat at night! Not with my digestion.

MRS. STOCKMANN: Oh, but just once in a way——

PETER STOCKMANN: No, no, my dear lady; I stick to my tea and bread and butter. It is much more wholesome in the long run—and a little more economical, too.

MRS. STOCKMANN (*smiling*): Now you mustn't think that Thomas and I are spendthrifts.

PETER STOCKMANN: Not you, my dear; I would never think that of you. (*Points to the* DOCTOR'S *study.*) Is he not at home?

MRS. STOCKMANN: No, he went out for a little turn after supper—he and the boys.

PETER STOCKMANN: I doubt if that is a wise thing to do. (*Listens.*) I fancy I hear him coming now.

MRS. STOCKMANN: No, I don't think it is he. (*A knock is heard at the door.*) Come in! (HOVSTAD *comes in from the hall.*) Oh, it is you, Mr. Hovstad!

HOVSTAD: Yes, I hope you will forgive me, but I was delayed at the printer's. Good evening, Mr. Mayor.

PETER STOCKMANN (*bowing a little distantly*): Good evening. You have come on business, no doubt.

HOVSTAD: Partly. It's about an article for the paper.

PETER STOCKMANN: So I imagined. I hear my brother has become a prolific contributor to the "People's Messenger."

HOVSTAD: Yes, he is good enough to write in the "People's Messenger" when he has any home truths to tell.

MRS. STOCKMANN (*to* HOVSTAD): But won't you——?

[*Points to the dining room.*]

PETER STOCKMANN: Quite so, quite so. I don't blame him in the least, as a writer, for addressing himself to the quarters where he will find the readiest sympathy. And, besides that, I personally have no reason to bear any ill will to your paper, Mr. Hovstad.

HOVSTAD: I quite agree with you.

PETER STOCKMANN: Taking one thing with another, there is an excellent spirit of toleration in the town—an admirable municipal spirit. And it all springs from the fact of our having a great common interest to unite us—an interest that is in an equally high degree the concern of every right-minded citizen——

HOVSTAD: The Baths, yes.

PETER STOCKMANN: Exactly—our fine, new, handsome Baths. Mark my words, Mr. Hovstad—the Baths will become the focus of our municipal life! Not a doubt of it!

MRS. STOCKMANN: That is just what Thomas says.

PETER STOCKMANN: Think how extraordinarily the place has developed within the last year or two! Money has been flowing in, and there is some life and some business doing in the town. Houses and landed property are rising in value every day.

HOVSTAD: And unemployment is diminishing.

PETER STOCKMANN: Yes, that is another thing. The burden of the poor rates has been lightened, to the great relief of the propertied classes; and that relief will be even greater if only we get a really good summer this year, and lots of visitors—plenty of invalids, who will make the Baths talked about.

HOVSTAD: And there is a good prospect of that, I hear.

PETER STOCKMANN: It looks very promising. Inquiries about apartments and that sort of thing are reaching us every day.

HOVSTAD: Well, the Doctor's article will come in very suitably.

PETER STOCKMANN: Has he been writing something just lately?

HOVSTAD: This is something he wrote in the winter, a recommendation of the Baths—an account of the excellent sanitary conditions here. But I held the article over, temporarily.

PETER STOCKMANN: Ah, some little difficulty about it, I suppose?

HOVSTAD: No, not at all; I thought it would be better to wait till the spring, because it is just at this time that people begin to think seriously about their summer quarters.

PETER STOCKMANN: Quite right; you were perfectly right, Mr. Hovstad.

MRS. STOCKMANN: Yes, Thomas is really indefatigable when it is a question of the Baths.

PETER STOCKMANN: Well—remember, he is the Medical Officer to the Baths.

HOVSTAD: Yes, and what is more, they owe their existence to him.

PETER STOCKMANN: To him? Indeed! It is true I have heard from time to time that some people are of that opinion. At the same time I must say I imagined that I took a modest part in the enterprise.

MRS. STOCKMANN: Yes, that is what Thomas is always saying.

HOVSTAD: But who denies it, Mr. Stockmann? You set the thing going and made a practical concern of it; we all know that. I only meant that the idea of it came first from the Doctor.

PETER STOCKMANN: Oh, ideas—yes! My brother has had plenty of them in his time—unfortunately. But when it is a question of putting an idea into practical shape, you have to apply to a man of different mettle, Mr. Hovstad. And I certainly should have thought that in this house at least——

MRS. STOCKMANN: My dear Peter——

HOVSTAD: How can you think that——?

MRS. STOCKMANN: Won't you go in and have something, Mr. Hovstad? My husband is sure to be back directly.

HOVSTAD: Thank you, perhaps just a morsel.

[*Goes into the dining room.*]

PETER STOCKMANN (*lowering his voice a little*): It is a curious thing that these farmers' sons never seem to lose their want of tact.

MRS. STOCKMANN: Surely it is not worth bothering about! Cannot you and Thomas share the credit as brothers?

PETER STOCKMANN: I should have thought so; but apparently some people are not satisfied with a share.

MRS. STOCKMANN: What nonsense! You and Thomas get on so capitally together. (*Listens.*) There he is at last, I think.

[*Goes out and opens the door leading to the hall.*]

DR. STOCKMANN (*laughing and talking outside*): Look here—here is another guest for you, Katherine. Isn't that jolly? Come in, Captain Horster; hang your coat up on this peg. Ah, you don't wear an overcoat. Just think, Katherine; I met him in the street and could hardly persuade him to come up! (CAPTAIN HORSTER *comes into the room and greets* MRS. STOCKMANN. *He is followed by* DR. STOCKMANN.) Come along in, boys. They are ravenously hungry again, you know. Come along, Captain Horster; you must have a slice of beef.

[*Pushes* HORSTER *into the dining room.* EJLIF *and* MORTEN *go in after them.*]

MRS. STOCKMANN: But, Thomas, don't you see——?

DR. STOCKMANN (*turning in the doorway*): Oh, is it you, Peter? (*Shakes hands with him.*) Now that is very delightful.

PETER STOCKMANN: Unfortunately I must go in a moment——

DR. STOCKMANN: Rubbish! There is some toddy just coming in. You haven't forgotten the toddy, Katherine?

MRS. STOCKMANN: Of course not; the water is boiling now.

[*Goes into the dining room.*]

PETER STOCKMANN: Toddy too!

DR. STOCKMANN: Yes, sit down and we will have it comfortably.

PETER STOCKMANN: Thanks, I never care about an evening's drinking.

DR. STOCKMANN: But this isn't an evening's drinking.

PETER STOCKMANN: It seems to me—— (*looks toward the dining room*) It is extraordinary how they can put away all that food.

DR. STOCKMANN (*rubbing his hands*): Yes, isn't it splendid to see young people eat? They have always got an appetite, you know! That's as it should be. Lots of food—to build up their strength! They are the people who are going to stir up the fermenting forces of the future, Peter.

PETER STOCKMANN: May I ask what they will find here to "stir up," as you put it?

DR. STOCKMANN: Ah, you must ask the young people that—when the time comes. We shan't be able to see it, of course. That stands to reason—two old fogies, like us——

PETER STOCKMANN: Really, really! I must say that is an extremely odd expression to——

DR. STOCKMANN: Oh, you mustn't take me too literally, Peter. I am so heartily happy and contented, you know. I think it is such an extraordinary piece of good fortune to be in the middle of all this growing, germinating life. It is a splendid time to live in! It is as if a whole new world were being created around one.

PETER STOCKMANN: Do you really think so?

DR. STOCKMANN: Ah, naturally you can't appreciate it as keenly as I. You have lived all your life in these surroundings, and your impressions have got blunted. But I, who have been buried all these years in my little corner up north, almost without ever seeing a stranger who might bring new ideas with him—well, in my case it has just the same effect as if I had been transported into the middle of a crowded city.

PETER STOCKMANN: Oh, a city——!

DR. STOCKMANN: I know, I know; it is all cramped enough here, compared with many other places. But there is life here—there is promise—there are innumerable things to work for and fight for; and that is the main thing. (*Calls.*) Katherine, hasn't the postman been here?

MRS. STOCKMANN (*from the dining room*): No.

DR. STOCKMANN: And then to be comfortably off, Peter! That is something one learns to value, when one has been on the brink of starvation, as we have.

PETER STOCKMANN: Oh, surely——

DR. STOCKMANN: Indeed I can assure you we have often been very hard put to it, up there. And now to be able to live like a lord! Today, for instance, we had roast beef for dinner—and, what is more, for supper too. Won't you come and have a little bit? Or let me show it to you, at any rate? Come here——

PETER STOCKMANN: No, no—not for worlds!

DR. STOCKMANN: Well, but just come here then. Do you see, we have got a table cover?

PETER STOCKMANN: Yes, I noticed it.

DR. STOCKMANN: And we have got a lampshade too. Do you see? All out of Katherine's savings! It makes the room so cozy. Don't you think so? Just stand here for a moment—no, no, not there—just here, that's it! Look now, when you get the light on it altogether—I really think it looks very nice, doesn't it?

PETER STOCKMANN: Oh, if you can afford luxuries of this kind——

DR. STOCKMANN: Yes, I can afford it now. Katherine tells me I earn almost as much as we spend.

PETER STOCKMANN: Almost—yes!

DR. STOCKMANN: But a scientific man must live in a little bit of style. I am quite sure an ordinary civil servant spends more in a year than I do.

PETER STOCKMANN: I daresay. A civil servant—a man in a well-paid position——

DR. STOCKMANN: Well, any ordinary merchant, then! A man in that position spends two or three times as much as——

PETER STOCKMANN: It just depends on circumstances.

DR. STOCKMANN: At all events I assure you I don't waste money unprofitably. But I can't find it in my heart to deny myself the pleasure of entertaining my friends. I need that sort of thing, you know. I have lived for so long shut out of it all that it is a necessity of life to me to mix with young, eager, ambitious men, men of liberal and active minds; and that describes every one of those fellows who are enjoying their supper in there. I wish you knew more of Hovstad——

PETER STOCKMANN: By the way, Hovstad was telling me he was going to print another article of yours.

DR. STOCKMANN: An article of mine?

PETER STOCKMANN: Yes, about the Baths. An article you wrote in the winter.

DR. STOCKMANN: Oh, that one! No, I don't intend that to appear just for the present.

PETER STOCKMANN: Why not? It seems to me that this would be the most opportune moment.

DR. STOCKMANN: Yes, very likely—under normal conditions.

[*Crosses the room.*]

PETER STOCKMANN (*following him with his eyes*): Is there anything abnormal about the present conditions?

DR. STOCKMANN (*standing still*): To tell you the truth, Peter, I can't say just at this moment—at all events not tonight. There may be much that is very abnormal about the present conditions—and it is possible there may be nothing abnormal about them at all. It is quite possible it may be merely my imagination.

PETER STOCKMANN: I must say it all sounds most mysterious. Is there something going on that I am to be kept in ignorance of? I should have imagined that I, as Chairman of the governing body of the Baths——

DR. STOCKMANN: And I should have imagined that I—— Oh, come, don't let us fly out at one another, Peter.

PETER STOCKMANN: Heaven forbid! I am not in the habit of flying out at people, as you call it. But I am entitled to request most emphatically that all arrangements shall be made in a business-like manner, through the proper channels, and shall be dealt with by the legally constituted authorities. I can allow no going behind our backs by any roundabout means.

DR. STOCKMANN: Have I ever at any time tried to go behind your backs?

PETER STOCKMANN: You have an ingrained tendency to take your own way, at all events; and that is almost equally inadmissible in a well-ordered community. The individual ought undoubtedly to acquiesce in subordinating himself to the community—or, to speak more accurately, to the authorities who have the care of the community's welfare.

DR. STOCKMANN: Very likely. But what the deuce has all this got to do with me?

PETER STOCKMANN: That is exactly what you never appear to be willing to learn, my dear Thomas. But, mark my words, someday you will have to suffer for it—sooner or later. Now I have told you. Good-bye.

DR. STOCKMANN: Have you taken leave of your senses? You are on the wrong scent altogether.

PETER STOCKMANN: I am not usually that. You must excuse me now if I—— (*calls into the dining room*) Good night, Katherine. Good night, gentlemen.

[*Goes out.*]

MRS. STOCKMANN (*coming from the dining room*): Has he gone?

DR. STOCKMANN: Yes, and in such a bad temper.

MRS. STOCKMANN: But, dear Thomas, what have you been doing to him again?

DR. STOCKMANN: Nothing at all. And, anyhow, he can't oblige me to make my report before the proper time.

MRS. STOCKMANN: What have you got to make a report to him about?

DR. STOCKMANN: Hm! Leave that to me, Katherine.——It is an extraordinary thing that the postman doesn't come.

[HOVSTAD, BILLING, *and* HORSTER *have got up from the table and come into the sitting room.* EJLIF *and* MORTEN *come in after them.*]

BILLING (*stretching himself*): Ah! one feels a new man after a meal like that.

HOVSTAD: The Mayor wasn't in a very sweet temper tonight, then.

DR. STOCKMANN: It is his stomach; he has a wretched digestion.

HOVSTAD: I rather think it was us two of the "People's Messenger" that he couldn't digest.

MRS. STOCKMANN: I thought you came out of it pretty well with him.

HOVSTAD: Oh yes; but it isn't anything more than a sort of truce.

BILLING: That is just what it is! That word sums up the situation.

DR. STOCKMANN: We must remember that Peter is a lonely man, poor chap. He has no home comforts of any kind; nothing but everlasting business. And all that infernal weak tea wash that he pours into himself! Now then, my boys, bring chairs up to the table. Aren't we going to have that toddy, Katherine?

MRS. STOCKMANN (*going into the dining room*): I am just getting it.

DR. STOCKMANN: Sit down here on the couch beside me, Captain Horster. We so seldom see you. Please sit down, my friends.

[*They sit down at the table.* MRS. STOCKMANN *brings a tray, with a spirit lamp, glasses, bottles, etc., upon it.*]

MRS. STOCKMANN: There you are! This is arrack, and this is rum, and this one is the brandy. Now everyone must help himself.

DR. STOCKMANN (*taking a glass*): We will. (*They all mix themselves some toddy.*) And let us have the cigars. Ejlif, you know where the box is. And you, Morten, can fetch my pipe. (*The two boys go into the room on the right.*) I have a suspicion that Ejlif pockets a cigar now and then!—but I take no notice of it. (*Calls out.*) And my smoking cap too, Morten. Katherine, you can tell him where I left it. Ah, he has got it. (*The boys bring the various things.*) Now, my friends. I stick to my pipe, you know. This one has seen plenty of bad weather with me up north. (*Touches glasses with them.*) Your good health! Ah! it is good to be sitting snug and warm here.

MRS. STOCKMANN (*who sits knitting*): Do you sail soon, Captain Horster?

HORSTER: I expect to be ready to sail next week.

MRS. STOCKMANN: I suppose you are going to America?

HORSTER: Yes, that is the plan.

MRS. STOCKMANN: Then you won't be able to take part in the coming election.

HORSTER: Is there going to be an election?

BILLING: Didn't you know?

HORSTER: No, I don't mix myself up with those things.

BILLING: But you do not take an interest in public affairs?

HORSTER: No, I don't know anything about politics.

BILLING: All the same, one ought to vote, at any rate.

HORSTER: Even if one doesn't know anything about what is going on?

BILLING: Doesn't know! What do you mean by that? A community is like a ship; everyone ought to be prepared to take the helm.

HORSTER: Maybe that is all very well on shore, but on board ship it wouldn't work.

HOVSTAD: It is astonishing how little most sailors care about what goes on on shore.

BILLING: Very extraordinary.

DR. STOCKMANN: Sailors are like birds of passage; they feel equally at home in any latitude. And that is only an additional reason for our being all the more keen, Hovstad. Is there to be anything of public interest in tomorrow's "Messenger"?

HOVSTAD: Nothing about municipal affairs. But the day after tomorrow I was thinking of printing your article——

DR. STOCKMANN: Ah, devil take it—my article! Look here, that must wait a bit.

HOVSTAD: Really? We had just got convenient space for it, and I thought it was just the opportune moment——

DR. STOCKMANN: Yes, yes, very likely you are right; but it must wait all the same. I will explain to you later.

[PETRA *comes in from the hall, in hat and cloak and with a bundle of exercise books under her arm.*]

PETRA: Good evening.

DR. STOCKMANN: Good evening, Petra; come along.

[*Mutual greetings;* PETRA *takes off her things and puts them down on a chair by the door.*]

PETRA: And you have all been sitting here enjoying yourselves, while I have been out slaving!

DR. STOCKMANN: Well, come and enjoy yourself too!

BILLING: May I mix a glass for you?

PETRA (*coming to the table*): Thanks, I would rather do it; you always mix it too strong. But I forgot, Father—I have a letter for you.
[*Goes to the chair where she has laid her things.*]

DR. STOCKMANN: A letter? From whom?

PETRA (*looking in her coat pocket*): The postman gave it to me just as I was going out——

DR. STOCKMANN (*getting up and going to her*): And you only give it to me now!

PETRA: I really had not time to run up again. There it is!

DR. STOCKMANN (*seizing the letter*): Let's see, let's see, child! (*Looks at the address.*) Yes, that's all right!

MRS. STOCKMANN: Is it the one you have been expecting so anxiously, Thomas?

DR. STOCKMANN: Yes, it is. I must go to my room now and—— Where shall I get a light, Katherine? Is there no lamp in my room again?

MRS. STOCKMANN: Yes, your lamp is already lit on your desk.

DR. STOCKMANN: Good, good. Excuse me for a moment——
[*Goes into his study.*]

PETRA: What do you suppose it is, Mother?

MRS. STOCKMANN: I don't know; for the last day or two he has always been asking if the postman has not been.

BILLING: Probably some country patient.

PETRA: Poor old dad!—he will overwork himself soon. (*Mixes a glass for herself.*) There, that will taste good!

HOVSTAD: Have you been teaching in the evening school again today?

PETRA (*sipping from her glass*): Two hours.

BILLING: And four hours of school in the morning——

PETRA: Five hours.

MRS. STOCKMANN: And you have still got exercises to correct, I see.

PETRA: A whole heap, yes.

HORSTER: You are pretty full up with work too, it seems to me.

PETRA: Yes—but that is good. One is so delightfully tired after it.

BILLING: Do you like that?

PETRA: Yes, because one sleeps so well then.

MORTEN: You must be dreadfully wicked, Petra.

PETRA: Wicked?

MORTEN: Yes, because you work so much. Mr. Rörlund says work is a punishment for our sins.

EJLIF: Pooh, what a duffer you are, to believe a thing like that!

MRS. STOCKMANN: Come, come, Ejlif!

BILLING (*laughing*): That's capital!

HOVSTAD: Don't you want to work as hard as that, Morten?

MORTEN: No, indeed I don't.

HOVSTAD: What do you want to be, then?

MORTEN: I should like best to be a Viking.

EJLIF: You would have to be a pagan then.

MORTEN: Well, I could become a pagan, couldn't I?

BILLING: I agree with you, Morten! My sentiments, exactly.

MRS. STOCKMANN (*signaling to him*): I am sure that is not true, Mr. Billing.

BILLING: Yes, I swear it is! I am a pagan, and I am proud of it. Believe me, before long we shall all be pagans.

MORTEN: And then shall we be allowed to do anything we like?

BILLING: Well, you see, Morten——

MRS. STOCKMANN: You must go to your room now, boys; I am sure you have some lessons to learn for tomorrow.

EJLIF: I should like so much to stay a little longer——

MRS. STOCKMANN: No, no; away you go, both of you.

[*The boys say good night and go into the room on the left.*]

HOVSTAD: Do you really think it can do the boys any harm to hear such things?

MRS. STOCKMANN: I don't know, but I don't like it.

PETRA: But you know, Mother, I think you really are wrong about it.

MRS. STOCKMANN: Maybe, but I don't like it—not in our own home.

PETRA: There is so much falsehood both at home and at school. At home one must not speak, and at school we have to stand and tell lies to the children.

HORSTER: Tell lies?

PETRA: Yes, don't you suppose we have to teach them all sorts of things that we don't believe?

BILLING: That is perfectly true.

PETRA: If only I had the means I would start a school of my own, and it would be conducted on very different lines.

BILLING: Oh, bother the means!

HORSTER: Well, if you are thinking of that, Miss Stockmann, I shall be delighted to provide you with a schoolroom. The great big old house my father left me is standing almost empty; there is an immense dining room downstairs——

PETRA (*laughing*): Thank you very much; but I am afraid nothing will come of it.

HOVSTAD: No, Miss Petra is much more likely to take to journalism, I expect. By the way, have you had time to do anything with that English story you promised to translate for us?

PETRA: No, not yet; but you shall have it in good time.

[DR. STOCKMANN *comes in from his room with an open letter in his hand.*]

DR. STOCKMANN (*waving the letter*): Well, now the town will have something new to talk about, I can tell you!

BILLING: Something new?

MRS. STOCKMANN: What is this?

DR. STOCKMANN: A great discovery, Katherine.

HOVSTAD: Really?

MRS. STOCKMANN: A discovery of yours?

DR. STOCKMANN: A discovery of mine. (*Walks up and down.*) Just let them come saying, as usual, that it is all fancy and a crazy man's imagination! But they will be careful what they say this time, I can tell you!

PETRA: But, Father, tell us what it is.

DR. STOCKMANN: Yes, yes—only give me time, and you shall know all about it. If only I had Peter here now! It just shows how we men can go about forming our judgments, when in reality we are as blind as any moles——

HOVSTAD: What are you driving at, Doctor?

DR. STOCKMANN (*standing still by the table*): Isn't it the universal opinion that our town is a healthy spot?

HOVSTAD: Certainly.

DR. STOCKMANN: Quite an unusually healthy spot, in fact—a place that deserves to be recommended in the warmest possible manner either for invalids or for people who are well——

MRS. STOCKMANN: Yes, but my dear Thomas——

DR. STOCKMANN: And we have been recommending it and praising it— I have written and written, both in the "Messenger" and in pamphlets——

HOVSTAD: Well, what then?

DR. STOCKMANN: And the Baths—we have called them the "main artery of the town's life blood," the "nerve center of our town," and the devil knows what else——

BILLING: "The town's pulsating heart" was the expression I once used on an important occasion——

DR. STOCKMANN: Quite so. Well, do you know what they really are, these great, splendid, much-praised Baths, that have cost so much money— do you know what they are?

HOVSTAD: No, what are they?

MRS. STOCKMANN: Yes, what are they?

DR. STOCKMANN: The whole place is a pesthouse!

PETRA: The Baths, Father?

MRS. STOCKMANN (*at the same time*): Our Baths!

HOVSTAD: But, Doctor——

BILLING: Absolutely incredible!

DR. STOCKMANN: The whole Bath establishment is a whited, poisoned sepulcher, I tell you—the gravest possible danger to the public health! All the nastiness up at Mölledal, all that stinking filth, is infecting the water in the conduit pipes leading to the reservoir; and the same cursed, filthy poison oozes out on the shore too——

HORSTER: Where the bathing place is?

DR. STOCKMANN: Just there.

HOVSTAD: How do you come to be so certain of all this, Doctor?

DR. STOCKMANN: I have investigated the matter most conscientiously. For a long time past I have suspected something of the kind. Last year we had some very strange cases of illness among the visitors—typhoid cases, and cases of gastric fever——

MRS. STOCKMANN: Yes, that is quite true.

DR. STOCKMANN: At the time, we supposed the visitors had been infected before they came; but later on, in the winter, I began to have a different opinion; and so I set myself to examine the water, as well as I could.

MRS. STOCKMANN: Then that is what you have been so busy with?

DR. STOCKMANN: Indeed I have been busy, Katherine. But here I had none of the necessary scientific apparatus, so I sent samples, both of the drinking water and of the seawater, up to the University, to have an accurate analysis made by a chemist.

HOVSTAD: And have you got that?

DR. STOCKMANN (*showing him the letter*): Here it is! It proves the presence of decomposing organic matter in the water—it is full of infusoria. The water is absolutely dangerous to use, either internally or externally.

MRS. STOCKMANN: What a mercy you discovered it in time.

DR. STOCKMANN: You may well say so.

HOVSTAD: And what do you propose to do now, Doctor?

DR. STOCKMANN: To see the matter put right—naturally.

HOVSTAD: Can that be done?

DR. STOCKMANN: It must be done. Otherwise the Baths will be absolutely useless and wasted. But we need not anticipate that; I have a very clear idea what we shall have to do.

MRS. STOCKMANN: But why have you kept this all so secret, dear?

DR. STOCKMANN: Do you suppose I was going to run about the town gossiping about it, before I had absolute proof? No, thank you. I am not such a fool.

PETRA: Still, you might have told us——

DR. STOCKMANN: Not a living soul. But tomorrow you may run around to the old Badger——

MRS. STOCKMANN: Oh, Thomas! Thomas!

DR. STOCKMANN: Well, to your grandfather, then. The old boy will have something to be astonished at! I know he thinks I am cracked—and there are lots of other people think so too, I have noticed. But now these good folks shall see—they shall just see! (*Walks about, rubbing his hands.*) There will be a nice upset in the town, Katherine; you can't imagine what it will be. All the conduit pipes will have to be relaid.

HOVSTAD (*getting up*): All the conduit pipes?

DR. STOCKMANN: Yes, of course. The intake is too low down; it will have to be lifted to a position much higher up.

PETRA: Then you were right after all.

DR. STOCKMANN: Ah, you remember, Petra—I wrote opposing the plans before the work was begun. But at that time no one would listen to me. Well, I am going to let them have it now! Of course, I have prepared a report for the Baths Committee; I have had it ready for a week, and was only waiting for this to come. (*Shows the letter.*) Now it shall go off at once. (*Goes into his room and comes back with some papers.*) Look at that! Four closely written sheets!——and the letter shall go with them. Give me a bit of paper, Katherine—something to wrap them up in. That will do! Now give it to—to—(*stamps his foot*)—what the deuce is her name?—give it to the maid, and tell her to take it at once to the Mayor.

[MRS. STOCKMANN *takes the packet and goes out through the dining room.*]

PETRA: What do you think Uncle Peter will say, Father?

DR. STOCKMANN: What is there for him to say? I should think he would be very glad that such an important truth has been brought to light.

HOVSTAD: Will you let me print a short note about your discovery in the "Messenger"?

DR. STOCKMANN: I shall be very much obliged if you will.

HOVSTAD: It is very desirable that the public should be informed of it without delay.

DR. STOCKMANN: Certainly.

MRS. STOCKMANN (*coming back*): She has just gone with it.

BILLING: Upon my soul, Doctor, you are going to be the foremost man in the town!

DR. STOCKMANN (*walking about happily*): Nonsense! As a matter of fact, I have done nothing more than my duty. I have only made a lucky find—that's all. Still, all the same——

BILLING: Hovstad, don't you think the town ought to give Dr. Stockmann some sort of testimonial?

HOVSTAD: I will suggest it, anyway.

BILLING: And I will speak to Aslaksen about it.

DR. STOCKMANN: No, my good friends, don't let us have any of that nonsense. I won't hear of anything of the kind. And if the Baths Committee should think of voting me an increase of salary, I will not accept it. Do you hear, Katherine?— I won't accept it.

MRS. STOCKMANN: You are quite right, Thomas.

PETRA (*lifting her glass*): Your health, Father!

HOVSTAD *and* BILLING: Your health, Doctor! Good health!

HORSTER (*touches glasses with* DR. STOCKMANN): I hope it will bring you nothing but good luck.

DR. STOCKMANN: Thank you, thank you, my dear fellows! I feel tremendously happy! It is a splendid thing for a man to be able to feel that he has done a service to his native town and to his fellow citizens. Hurrah, Katherine!

[*He puts his arms round her and whirls her round and round, while she protests with laughing cries. They all laugh, clap their hands, and cheer the* DOCTOR. *The boys put their heads in at the door to see what is going on.*]

CURTAIN

ACT TWO

SCENE: *The same. The door into the dining room is shut. It is morning.* MRS. STOCKMANN, *with a sealed letter in her hand, comes in from the dining room, goes to the door of the* DOCTOR'S *study and peeps in.*

MRS. STOCKMANN: Are you in, Thomas?

DR. STOCKMANN (*from within his room*): Yes, I have just come in. (*Comes into the room.*) What is it?

MRS. STOCKMANN: A letter from your brother.

DR. STOCKMANN: Aha, let us see! (*Opens the letter and reads:*) "I return herewith the manuscript you sent me"—(*reads on in a low murmur*) Hm!——

MRS. STOCKMANN: What does he say?

DR. STOCKMANN (*putting the papers in his pocket*): Oh, he only writes that he will come up here himself about midday.

MRS. STOCKMANN: Well, try and remember to be at home this time.

DR. STOCKMANN: That will be all right; I have got through all my morning visits.

MRS. STOCKMANN: I am extremely curious to know how he takes it.

DR. STOCKMANN: You will see he won't like it's having been I, and not he, that made the discovery.

MRS. STOCKMANN: Aren't you a little nervous about that?

DR. STOCKMANN: Oh, he really will be pleased enough, you know. But, at the same time, Peter is so confoundedly afraid of anyone's doing any service to the town except himself.

MRS. STOCKMANN: I will tell you what, Thomas—you should be good-natured, and share the credit of this with him. Couldn't you make out that it was he who set you on the scent of this discovery?

DR. STOCKMANN: I am quite willing. If only I can get the thing set right. I——

[MORTEN KIIL *puts his head in through the door leading from the hall, looks round in an inquiring manner, and chuckles.*]

MORTEN KIIL (*slyly*): Is it—is it true?

MRS. STOCKMANN (*going to the door*): Father!—is it you?

DR. STOCKMANN: Ah, Mr. Kiil—good morning, good morning!

MRS. STOCKMANN: But come along in.

MORTEN KIIL: If it is true, I will; if not, I am off.

DR. STOCKMANN: If what is true?

MORTEN KIIL: This tale about the water supply. Is it true?

DR. STOCKMANN: Certainly it is true. But how did you come to hear it?

MORTEN KIIL (*coming in*): Petra ran in on her way to the school——

DR. STOCKMANN: Did she?

MORTEN KIIL: Yes; and she declares that—— I thought she was only making a fool of me, but it isn't like Petra to do that.

DR. STOCKMANN: Of course not. How could you imagine such a thing?

MORTEN KIIL: Oh well, it is better never to trust anybody; you may find you have been made a fool of before you know where you are. But it is really true, all the same?

DR. STOCKMANN: You can depend upon it that it is true. Won't you sit down? (*Settles him on the couch.*) Isn't it a real bit of luck for the town——

MORTEN KIIL (*suppressing his laughter*): A bit of luck for the town?

DR. STOCKMANN: Yes, that I made the discovery in good time.

MORTEN KIIL (*as before*): Yes, yes, yes!—But I should never have thought you the sort of man to pull your own brother's leg like this!

DR. STOCKMANN: Pull his leg!

MRS. STOCKMANN: Really, Father dear——

MORTEN KIIL (*resting his hands and his chin on the handle of his stick and winking slyly at the* DOCTOR): Let me see, what was the story? Some kind of beast that had got into the water pipes, wasn't it?

DR. STOCKMANN: Infusoria—yes.

MORTEN KIIL: And a lot of these beasts had got in, according to Petra—a tremendous lot.

DR. STOCKMANN: Certainly; hundreds of thousands of them, probably.

MORTEN KIIL: But no one can see them—isn't that so?

DR. STOCKMANN: Yes; you can't see them.

MORTEN KIIL (*with a quiet chuckle*): Damme—it's the finest story I have ever heard!

DR. STOCKMANN: What do you mean?

MORTEN KIIL: But you will never get the Mayor to believe a thing like that.

DR. STOCKMANN: We shall see.

MORTEN KIIL: Do you think he will be fool enough to——?

DR. STOCKMANN: I hope the whole town will be fools enough.

MORTEN KIIL: The whole town! Well, it wouldn't be a bad thing. It would just serve them right, and teach them a lesson. They think themselves so much cleverer than we old fellows. They hounded me out of the council; they did, I tell you—they hounded me out. Now they shall pay for it. You pull their legs too, Thomas!

DR. STOCKMANN: Really, I——

MORTEN KIIL: You pull their legs! (*Gets up.*) If you can work it so that the Mayor and his friends all swallow the same bait, I will give ten pounds to a charity—like a shot!

DR. STOCKMANN: That is very kind of you.

MORTEN KIIL: Yes, I haven't got much money to throw away, I can tell you; but if you can work this, I will give five pounds to a charity at Christmas.

[HOVSTAD *comes in by the hall door.*]

HOVSTAD: Good morning! (*Stops.*) Oh, I beg your pardon——

DR. STOCKMANN: Not at all; come in.

MORTEN KIIL (*with another chuckle*): Oho!—is he in this too?

HOVSTAD: What do you mean?

DR. STOCKMANN: Certainly he is.

MORTEN KIIL: I might have known it! It must get into the papers. You know how to do it, Thomas! Set your wits to work. Now I must go.

DR. STOCKMANN: Won't you stay a little while?

MORTEN KIIL: No, I must be off now. You keep up this game for all it is worth; you won't repent it, I'm damned if you will!

[*He goes out;* MRS. STOCKMANN *follows him into the hall.*]

DR. STOCKMANN (*laughing*): Just imagine—the old chap doesn't believe a word of all this about the water supply.

HOVSTAD: Oh, that was it, then?

DR. STOCKMANN: Yes, that was what we were talking about. Perhaps it is the same thing that brings you here?

HOVSTAD: Yes, it is. Can you spare me a few minutes, Doctor?

DR. STOCKMANN: As long as you like, my dear fellow.

HOVSTAD: Have you heard from the Mayor yet?

DR. STOCKMANN: Not yet. He is coming here later.

HOVSTAD: I have given the matter a great deal of thought since last night.

DR. STOCKMANN: Well?

HOVSTAD: From your point of view, as a doctor and a man of science, this affair of the water supply is an isolated matter. I mean, you do not realize that it involves a great many other things.

DR. STOCKMANN: How do you mean?——Let us sit down, my dear fellow. No, sit here on the couch. (HOVSTAD *sits down on the couch,* DR. STOCK-MANN *on a chair on the other side of the table.*) Now then. You mean that——?

HOVSTAD: You said yesterday that the pollution of the water was due to impurities in the soil.

DR. STOCKMANN: Yes, unquestionably it is due to that poisonous morass up at Mölledal.

HOVSTAD: Begging your pardon, Doctor, I fancy it is due to quite another morass altogether.

DR. STOCKMANN: What morass?

HOVSTAD: The morass that the whole life of our town is built on and is rotting in.

DR. STOCKMANN: What the deuce are you driving at, Hovstad?

HOVSTAD: The whole of the town's interests have, little by little, got into the hands of a pack of officials.

DR. STOCKMANN: Oh, come!—they are not all officials.

HOVSTAD: No, but those that are not officials are at any rate the officials' friends and adherents; it is the wealthy folk, the old families in the town, that have got us entirely in their hands.

DR. STOCKMANN: Yes, but after all, they are men of ability and knowledge.

HOVSTAD: Did they show any ability or knowledge when they laid the conduit pipes where they are now?

DR. STOCKMANN: No, of course that was a great piece of stupidity on their part. But that is going to be set right, now.

HOVSTAD: Do you think that will be all such plain sailing?

DR. STOCKMANN: Plain sailing or no, it has got to be done, anyway.

HOVSTAD: Yes, provided the press takes up the question.

DR. STOCKMANN: I don't think that will be necessary, my dear fellow; I am certain my brother——

HOVSTAD: Excuse me, Doctor; I feel bound to tell you I am inclined to take the matter up.

DR. STOCKMANN: In the paper?

HOVSTAD: Yes. When I took over the "People's Messenger," my idea was to break up this ring of self-opinionated old fossils who had got hold of all the influence.

DR. STOCKMANN: But you know you told me yourself what the result had been; you nearly ruined your paper.

HOVSTAD: Yes, at the time we were obliged to climb down a peg or two, it is quite true, because there was a danger of the whole project of the Baths coming to nothing if they failed us. But now the scheme has been carried through, and we can dispense with these grand gentlemen.

DR. STOCKMANN: Dispense with them, yes; but we owe them a great debt of gratitude.

HOVSTAD: That shall be recognized ungrudgingly. But a journalist of my democratic tendencies cannot let such an opportunity as this slip. The bubble of official infallibility must be pricked. The superstition must be destroyed, like any other.

DR. STOCKMANN: I am wholeheartedly with you in that, Mr. Hovstad; if it is a superstition, away with it!

HOVSTAD: I should be very reluctant to bring the Mayor into it, because he is your brother. But I am sure you will agree with me that truth should be the first consideration.

DR. STOCKMANN: That goes without saying. (*With sudden emphasis.*) Yes, but—but——

HOVSTAD: You must not misjudge me. I am neither more self-interested nor more ambitious than most men.

DR. STOCKMANN: My dear fellow—who suggests anything of the kind?

HOVSTAD: I am of humble origin, as you know; and that has given me opportunities of knowing what is the most crying need in the humbler ranks of life. It is that they should be allowed some part in the direction of public affairs, Doctor. That is what will develop their faculties and intelligence and self-respect——

DR. STOCKMANN: I quite appreciate that.

HOVSTAD: Yes—and in my opinion a journalist incurs a heavy responsibility if he neglects a favorable opportunity of emancipating the masses—the humble and oppressed. I know well enough that in exalted circles I shall be called an agitator, and all that sort of thing; but they may call what they like. If only my conscience doesn't reproach me, then——

DR. STOCKMANN: Quite right! Quite right, Mr. Hovstad. But all the same—devil take it! (*A knock is heard at the door.*) Come in!

[ASLAKSEN *appears at the door. He is poorly but decently dressed, in black, with a slightly crumpled white neckcloth; he wears gloves and has a felt hat in his hand.*]

ASLAKSEN (*bowing*): Excuse my taking the liberty, Doctor——

DR. STOCKMANN (*getting up*): Ah, it is you, Aslaksen!

ASLAKSEN: Yes, Doctor.

HOVSTAD (*standing up*): Is it me you want, Aslaksen?

ASLAKSEN: No; I didn't know I should find you here. No, it was the Doctor I——

DR. STOCKMANN: I am quite at your service. What is it?

ASLAKSEN: Is what I heard from Mr. Billing true, sir—that you mean to improve our water supply?

DR. STOCKMANN: Yes, for the Baths.

ASLAKSEN: Quite so, I understand. Well, I have come to say that I will back that up by every means in my power.

HOVSTAD (*to the* DOCTOR): You see!

DR. STOCKMANN: I shall be very grateful to you but——

ASLAKSEN: Because it may be no bad thing to have us small tradesmen at your back. We form, as it were, a compact majority in the town—if we choose. And it is always a good thing to have the majority with you, Doctor.

DR. STOCKMANN: That is undeniably true; but I confess I don't see why such unusual precautions should be necessary in this case. It seems to me that such a plain, straightforward thing——

ASLAKSEN: Oh, it may be very desirable, all the same. I know our local authorities so well; officials are not generally very ready to act on proposals that come from other people. That is why I think it would not be at all amiss if we made a little demonstration.

HOVSTAD: That's right.

DR. STOCKMANN: Demonstration, did you say? What on earth are you going to make a demonstration about?

ASLAKSEN: We shall proceed with the greatest moderation, Doctor. Moderation is always my aim; it is the greatest virtue in a citizen—at least, I think so.

DR. STOCKMANN: It is well known to be a characteristic of yours, Mr. Aslaksen.

ASLAKSEN: Yes, I think I may pride myself on that. And this matter of the water supply is of the greatest importance to us small tradesmen. The Baths promise to be a regular gold mine for the town. We shall all make our living out of them, especially those of us who are householders. That is why we will back up the project as strongly as possible. And as I am at present Chairman of the Householders' Association——

DR. STOCKMANN: Yes——?

ASLAKSEN: And, what is more, local secretary of the Temperance Society —you know, sir, I suppose, that I am a worker in the temperance cause?

DR. STOCKMANN: Of course, of course.

ASLAKSEN: Well, you can understand that I come into contact with a great many people. And as I have the reputation of a temperate and law-abiding citizen—like yourself, Doctor—I have a certain influence in the town, a little bit of power, if I may be allowed to say so.

DR. STOCKMANN: I know that quite well, Mr. Aslaksen.

ASLAKSEN: So you see it would be an easy matter for me to set on foot some testimonial, if necessary.

DR. STOCKMANN: A testimonial?

ASLAKSEN: Yes, some kind of address of thanks from the townsmen for your share in a matter of such importance to the community. I need scarcely say that it would have to be drawn up with the greatest regard to moderation, so as not to offend the authorities—who, after all, have the reins in their hands. If we pay strict attention to that, no one can take it amiss, I should think!

HOVSTAD: Well, and even supposing they didn't like it——

ASLAKSEN: No, no, no; there must be no discourtesy to the authorities, Mr. Hovstad. It is no use falling foul of those upon whom our welfare so closely depends. I have done that in my time, and no good ever comes of it. But no one can take exception to a reasonable and frank expression of a citizen's views.

DR. STOCKMANN (*shaking him by the hand*): I can't tell you, dear Mr. Aslaksen, how extremely pleased I am to find such hearty support among my fellow citizens. I am delighted—delighted! Now, you will take a small glass of sherry, eh?

ASLAKSEN: No, thank you; I never drink alcohol of that kind.

DR. STOCKMANN: Well, what do you say to a glass of beer, then?

ASLAKSEN: Nor that either, thank you, Doctor. I never drink anything as early as this. I am going into town now to talk this over with one or two householders, and prepare the ground.

DR. STOCKMANN: It is tremendously kind of you, Mr. Aslaksen; but I really cannot understand the necessity for all these precautions. It seems to me that the thing should go of itself.

ASLAKSEN: The authorities are somewhat slow to move, Doctor. Far be it from me to seem to blame them——

HOVSTAD: We are going to stir them up in the paper tomorrow, Aslaksen.

ASLAKSEN: But not violently, I trust, Mr. Hovstad. Proceed with moderation, or you will do nothing with them. You may take my advice; I have gathered my experience in the school of life. Well, I must say good-bye, Doctor. You know now that we small tradesmen are at your back at all events, like a solid wall. You have the compact majority on your side, Doctor.

DR. STOCKMANN: I am very much obliged, dear Mr. Aslaksen. (*Shakes hands with him.*) Good-bye, good-bye.

ASLAKSEN: Are you going my way, toward the printing office, Mr. Hovstad?

HOVSTAD: I will come later; I have something to settle up first.

ASLAKSEN: Very well.

[*Bows and goes out;* STOCKMANN *follows him into the hall.*]

HOVSTAD (*as* STOCKMANN *comes in again*): Well, what do you think of that, Doctor? Don't you think it is high time we stirred a little life into all this slackness and vacillation and cowardice?

DR. STOCKMANN: Are you referring to Aslaksen?

HOVSTAD: Yes, I am. He is one of those who are floundering in a bog—decent enough fellow though he may be, otherwise. And most of the people here are in just the same case—seesawing and edging first to one side and then to the other, so overcome with caution and scruple that they never dare to take any decided step.

DR. STOCKMANN: Yes, but Aslaksen seemed to me so thoroughly well-intentioned.

HOVSTAD: There is one thing I esteem higher than that; and that is for a man to be self-reliant and sure of himself.

DR. STOCKMANN: I think you are perfectly right there.

HOVSTAD: That is why I want to seize this opportunity, and try if I cannot manage to put a little virility into these well-intentioned people for once. The idol of Authority must be shattered in this town. This gross and inexcusable blunder about the water supply must be brought home to the mind of every municipal voter.

DR. STOCKMANN: Very well; if you are of the opinion that it is for the good of the community, so be it. But not until I have had a talk with my brother.

HOVSTAD: Anyway, I will get a leading article ready; and if the Mayor refuses to take the matter up——

DR. STOCKMANN: How can you suppose such a thing possible?

HOVSTAD: It is conceivable. And in that case——

DR. STOCKMANN: In that case I promise you—— Look here, in that case you may print my report—every word of it.

HOVSTAD: May I? Have I your word for it?

DR. STOCKMANN (*giving him the MS.*): Here it is; take it with you. It can do no harm for you to read it through, and you can give it back to me later on.

HOVSTAD: Good, good! That is what I will do. And now good-bye, Doctor.

DR. STOCKMANN: Good-bye, good-bye. You will see everything will run quite smoothly, Mr. Hovstad—quite smoothly.

HOVSTAD: Hm!—we shall see.

[*Bows and goes out.*]

DR. STOCKMANN (*opens the dining room door and looks in*): Katherine! Oh, you are back, Petra?

PETRA (*coming in*): Yes, I have just come from the school.

MRS. STOCKMANN (*coming in*): Has he not been here yet?

DR. STOCKMANN: Peter? No. But I have had a long talk with Hovstad. He is quite excited about my discovery. I find it has a much wider bearing than I at first imagined. And he has put his paper at my disposal if necessity should arise.

MRS. STOCKMANN: Do you think it will?

DR. STOCKMANN: Not for a moment. But at all events it makes me feel proud to know that I have the liberal-minded, independent press on my side. Yes, and—just imagine—I have had a visit from the Chairman of the Householders' Association!

MRS. STOCKMANN: Oh! What did he want?

DR. STOCKMANN: To offer me his support too. They will support me in a body if it should be necessary. Katherine—do you know what I have got behind me?

MRS. STOCKMANN: Behind you? No, what have you got behind you?

DR. STOCKMANN: The compact majority.

MRS. STOCKMANN: Really? Is that a good thing for you, Thomas?

DR. STOCKMANN: I should think it was a good thing. (*Walks up and down rubbing his hands.*) By Jove, it's a fine thing to feel this bond of brotherhood between oneself and one's fellow citizens!

PETRA: And to be able to do so much that is good and useful, Father!

DR. STOCKMANN: And for one's own native town into the bargain, my child!

MRS. STOCKMANN: That was a ring at the bell.

DR. STOCKMANN: It must be he, then. (*A knock is heard at the door.*) Come in!

PETER STOCKMANN: (*comes in from the hall*): Good morning.

DR. STOCKMANN: Glad to see you, Peter!

MRS. STOCKMANN: Good morning, Peter. How are you?

PETER STOCKMANN: So so, thank you. (*To* DR. STOCKMANN) I received from you yesterday, after office hours, a report dealing with the condition of the water at the Baths.

DR. STOCKMANN: Yes. Have you read it?

PETER STOCKMANN: Yes, I have.

DR. STOCKMANN: And what have you to say to it?

PETER STOCKMANN (*with a sidelong glance*): Hm!——

MRS. STOCKMANN: Come along, Petra.

[*She and* PETRA *go into the room on the left.*]

PETER STOCKMANN (*after a pause*): Was it necessary to make all these investigations behind my back?

DR. STOCKMANN: Yes, because until I was absolutely certain about it——

PETER STOCKMANN: Then you mean that you are absolutely certain now?

DR. STOCKMANN: Surely you are convinced of that.

PETER STOCKMANN: Is it your intention to bring this document before the Baths Committee as a sort of official communication?

DR. STOCKMANN: Certainly. Something must be done in the matter—and that quickly.

PETER STOCKMANN: As usual, you employ violent expressions in your report. You say, among other things, that what we offer visitors in our Baths is a permanent supply of poison.

DR. STOCKMANN: Well, can you describe it any other way, Peter? Just think—water that is poisonous, whether you drink it or bathe in it! And this we offer to the poor sick folk who come to us trustfully and pay us at an exorbitant rate to be made well again!

PETER STOCKMANN: And your reasoning leads you to this conclusion, that we must build a sewer to draw off the alleged impurities from Mölledal and must relay the water conduits.

DR. STOCKMANN: Yes. Do you see any other way out of it? I don't.

PETER STOCKMANN: I made a pretext this morning to go and see the town engineer, and, as if only half seriously, broached the subject of these proposals as a thing we might perhaps have to take under consideration sometime later on.

DR. STOCKMANN: Sometime later on!

PETER STOCKMANN: He smiled at what he considered to be my extravagance, naturally. Have you taken the trouble to consider what your proposed alterations would cost? According to the information I obtained, the expenses would probably mount up to fifteen or twenty thousand pounds.

DR. STOCKMANN: Would it cost so much?

PETER STOCKMANN: Yes; and the worst part of it would be that the work would take at least two years.

DR. STOCKMANN: Two years? Two whole years?

PETER STOCKMANN: At least. And what are we to do with the Baths in the meantime? Close them? Indeed, we should be obliged to. And do you suppose anyone would come near the place after it had got about that the water was dangerous?

DR. STOCKMANN: Yes, but, Peter, that is what it is.

PETER STOCKMANN: And all this at this juncture—just as the Baths are beginning to be known. There are other towns in the neighborhood with qualifications to attract visitors for bathing purposes. Don't you suppose they would immediately strain every nerve to divert the entire stream of strangers to themselves? Unquestionably they would; and then where should we be? We should probably have to abandon the whole thing, which has cost us so much money—and then you would have ruined your native town.

DR. STOCKMANN: I—should have ruined——!

PETER STOCKMANN: It is simply and solely through the Baths that the town has before it any future worth mentioning. You know that just as well as I.

DR. STOCKMANN: But what do you think ought to be done, then?

PETER STOCKMANN: Your report has not convinced me that the condition of the water at the Baths is as bad as you represent it to be.

DR. STOCKMANN: I tell you it is even worse!—or at all events it will be in summer, when the warm weather comes.

PETER STOCKMANN: As I said, I believe you exaggerate the matter considerably. A capable physician ought to know what measures to take —he ought to be capable of preventing injurious influences or of remedying them if they become obviously persistent.

DR. STOCKMANN: Well? What more?

PETER STOCKMANN: The water supply for the Baths is now an established fact, and in consequence must be treated as such. But probably the Committee, at its discretion, will not be disinclined to consider the question of how far it might be possible to introduce certain improvements consistent with a reasonable expenditure.

DR. STOCKMANN: And do you suppose that I will have anything to do with such a piece of trickery as that?

PETER STOCKMANN: Trickery!!

DR. STOCKMANN: Yes, it would be a trick—a fraud, a lie, a downright crime toward the public, toward the whole community!

PETER STOCKMANN: I have not, as I remarked before, been able to convince myself that there is actually any imminent danger.

DR. STOCKMANN: You have not! It is impossible that you should not be convinced. I know I have represented the facts absolutely truthfully and fairly. And you know it very well, Peter, only you won't acknowledge it. It was owing to your action that both the Baths and the water conduits were built where they are; and that is what you won't acknowledge—that damnable blunder of yours. Pooh!—do you suppose I don't see through you?

PETER STOCKMANN: And even if that were true? If I perhaps guard my reputation somewhat anxiously, it is in the interests of the town. Without moral authority I am powerless to direct public affairs as seems, to my judgment, to be best for the common good. And on that account— and for various other reasons, too—it appears to me to be a matter of importance that your report should not be delivered to the Committee. In the interests of the public, you must withhold it. Then, later on, I will raise the question and we will do our best, privately; but nothing of this unfortunate affair—not a single word of it—must come to the ears of the public.

DR. STOCKMANN: I am afraid you will not be able to prevent that now, my dear Peter.

PETER STOCKMANN: It must and shall be prevented.

DR. STOCKMANN: It is no use, I tell you. There are too many people that know about it.

PETER STOCKMANN: That know about it? Who? Surely you don't mean those fellows on the "People's Messenger"?

DR. STOCKMANN: Yes, they know. The liberal-minded, independent press is going to see that you do your duty.

PETER STOCKMANN (*after a short pause*): You are an extraordinarily independent man, Thomas. Have you given no thought to the consequences this may have for yourself?

DR. STOCKMANN: Consequences?—for me?

PETER STOCKMANN: For you and yours, yes.

DR. STOCKMANN: What the deuce do you mean?

PETER STOCKMANN: I believe I have always behaved in a brotherly way to you—have always been ready to oblige or to help you?

DR. STOCKMANN: Yes, you have, and I am grateful to you for it.

PETER STOCKMANN: There is no need. Indeed, to some extent I was forced to do so—for my own sake. I always hoped that, if I helped to improve your financial position, I should be able to keep some check on you.

DR. STOCKMANN: What!! Then it was only for your own sake!

PETER STOCKMANN: Up to a certain point, yes. It is painful for a man in an official position to have his nearest relative compromising himself time after time.

DR. STOCKMANN: And do you consider that I do that?

PETER STOCKMANN: Yes, unfortunately, you do, without even being aware of it. You have a restless, pugnacious, rebellious disposition. And then there is that disastrous propensity of yours to want to write about every sort of possible and impossible thing. The moment an idea comes into your head, you must needs go and write a newspaper article or a whole pamphlet about it.

DR. STOCKMANN: Well, but is it not the duty of a citizen to let the public share in any new ideas he may have?

PETER STOCKMANN: Oh, the public doesn't require any new ideas. The public is best served by the good, old-established ideas it already has.

DR. STOCKMANN: And that is your honest opinion?

PETER STOCKMANN: Yes, and for once I must talk frankly to you. Hitherto I have tried to avoid doing so, because I know how irritable you are; but now I must tell you the truth, Thomas. You have no conception what an amount of harm you do yourself by your impetuosity. You complain of the authorities, you even complain of the government— you are always pulling them to pieces; you insist that you have been neglected and persecuted. But what else can such a cantankerous man as you expect?

DR. STOCKMANN: What next! Cantankerous, am I?

PETER STOCKMANN: Yes, Thomas, you are an extremely cantankerous man to work with—I know that to my cost. You disregard everything that you ought to have consideration for. You seem completely to forget that it is me you have to thank for your appointment here as Medical Officer to the Baths——

DR. STOCKMANN: I was entitled to it as a matter of course!—I and nobody else! I was the first person to see that the town could be made into a flourishing watering place, and I was the only one who saw it at that time. I had to fight single-handed in support of the idea for many years; and I wrote and wrote——

PETER STOCKMANN: Undoubtedly. But things were not ripe for the scheme then—though, of course, you could not judge of that in your out-of-the-way corner up north. But as soon as the opportune moment came I—and the others—took the matter into our hands——

DR. STOCKMANN: Yes, and made this mess of all my beautiful plan. It is pretty obvious now what clever fellows you were!

PETER STOCKMANN: To my mind the whole thing only seems to mean that you are seeking another outlet for your combativeness. You want to pick a quarrel with your superiors—an old habit of yours. You cannot put up with any authority over you. You look askance at anyone who occupies a superior official position; you regard him as a personal enemy, and then any stick is good enough to beat him with. But now I have called your attention to the fact that the town's interests are at stake —and, incidentally, my own too. And therefore I must tell you, Thomas, that you will find me inexorable with regard to what I am about to require you to do.

DR. STOCKMANN: And what is that?

PETER STOCKMANN: As you have been so indiscreet as to speak of this delicate matter to outsiders, despite the fact that you ought to have treated it as entirely official and confidential, it is obviously impossible to hush it up now. All sorts of rumors will get about directly, and everybody who has a grudge against us will take care to embellish these rumors. So it will be necessary for you to refute them publicly.

DR. STOCKMANN: I! How? I don't understand.

PETER STOCKMANN: What we shall expect is that, after making further investigations, you will come to the conclusion that the matter is not by any means as dangerous or as critical as you imagined in the first instance.

DR. STOCKMANN: Oho!—so that is what you expect!

PETER STOCKMANN: And, what is more, we shall expect you to make public profession of your confidence in the Committee and in their readiness to consider fully and conscientiously what steps may be necessary to remedy any possible defects.

DR. STOCKMANN: But you will never be able to do that by patching and tinkering at it—never! Take my word for it, Peter; I mean what I say, as deliberately and emphatically as possible.

PETER STOCKMANN: As an officer under the Committee, you have no right to any individual opinion.

DR. STOCKMANN (*amazed*): No right?

PETER STOCKMANN: In your official capacity, no. As a private person, it is quite another matter. But as a subordinate member of the staff of the Baths, you have no right to express any opinion which runs contrary to that of your superiors.

DR. STOCKMANN: This is too much! I, a doctor, a man of science, have no right to——!

PETER STOCKMANN: The matter in hand is not simply a scientific one. It is a complicated matter, and has its economic as well as its technical side.

DR. STOCKMANN: I don't care what it is! I intend to be free to express my opinion on any subject under the sun.

PETER STOCKMANN: As you please—but not on any subject concerning the Baths. That we forbid.

DR. STOCKMANN (*shouting*): You forbid!——You! A pack of——

PETER STOCKMANN: *I* forbid it—I, your chief; and if I forbid it, you have to obey.

DR. STOCKMANN (*controlling himself*): Peter—if you were not my brother——

PETRA (*throwing open the door*): Father, you shan't stand this!

MRS. STOCKMANN (*coming in after her*): Petra, Petra!

PETER STOCKMANN: Oh, so you have been eavesdropping.

MRS. STOCKMANN: You were talking so loud, we couldn't help——

PETRA: Yes, I was listening.

PETER STOCKMANN: Well, after all, I am very glad——

DR. STOCKMANN (*going up to him*): You were saying something about forbidding and obeying?

PETER STOCKMANN: You obliged me to take that tone with you.

DR. STOCKMANN: And so I am to give myself the lie, publicly?

PETER STOCKMANN: We consider it absolutely necessary that you should make some such public statement as I have asked for.

DR. STOCKMANN: And if I do not—obey?

PETER STOCKMANN: Then we shall publish a statement ourselves to reassure the public.

DR. STOCKMANN: Very well; but in that case I shall use my pen against you. I stick to what I have said; I will show that I am right and that you are wrong. And what will you do then?

PETER STOCKMANN: Then, I shall not be able to prevent your being dismissed.

DR. STOCKMANN: What?

PETRA: Father—dismissed!

MRS. STOCKMANN: Dismissed!

PETER STOCKMANN: Dismissed from the staff of the Baths. I shall be obliged to propose that you shall immediately be given notice, and shall not be allowed any further participation in the Baths' affairs.

DR. STOCKMANN: You would dare to do that!

PETER STOCKMANN: It is you that are playing the daring game.

PETRA: Uncle, that is a shameful way to treat a man like Father!

MRS. STOCKMANN: Do hold your tongue, Petra!

PETER STOCKMANN (*looking at* PETRA): Oh, so we volunteer our opinions already, do we? Of course. (*To* MRS. STOCKMANN) Katherine, I imagine you are the most sensible person in this house. Use any influence you may have over your husband, and make him see what this will entail for his family as well as——

DR. STOCKMANN: My family is my own concern and nobody else's!

PETER STOCKMANN: ——for his own family, as I was saying, as well as for the town he lives in.

DR. STOCKMANN: It is I who have the real good of the town at heart! I want to lay bare the defects that sooner or later must come to the light of day. I will show whether I love my native town.

PETER STOCKMANN: You, who in your blind obstinacy want to cut off the most important source of the town's welfare?

DR. STOCKMANN: The source is poisoned, man! Are you mad? We are making our living by retailing filth and corruption! The whole of our flourishing municipal life derives its sustenance from a lie!

PETER STOCKMANN: All imagination—or something even worse. The man who can throw out such offensive insinuations about his native town must be an enemy of our community.

DR. STOCKMANN (*going up to him*): Do you dare to——!

MRS. STOCKMANN (*throwing herself between them*): Thomas!

PETRA (*catching her father by the arm*): Don't lose your temper, Father!

PETER STOCKMANN: I will not expose myself to violence. Now you have had a warning; so reflect on what you owe to yourself and your family. Good-bye.

[*Goes out.*]

DR. STOCKMANN (*walking up and down*): Am I to put up with such treatment as this? In my own house, Katherine! What do you think of that!

MRS. STOCKMANN: Indeed, it is both shameful and absurd, Thomas——

PETRA: If only I could give Uncle a piece of my mind——

DR. STOCKMANN: It is my own fault. I ought to have flown out at him long ago!—shown my teeth!—bitten! To hear him call me an enemy to our community! Me! I shall not take that lying down, upon my soul!

MRS. STOCKMANN: But, dear Thomas, your brother has power on his side——

DR. STOCKMANN: Yes, but I have right on mine, I tell you.

MRS. STOCKMANN: Oh yes, right—right. What is the use of having right on your side if you have not got might?

PETRA: Oh, Mother!—how can you say such a thing!

DR. STOCKMANN: Do you imagine that in a free country it is no use having right on your side? You are absurd, Katherine. Besides, haven't I got the liberal-minded, independent press to lead the way, and the compact majority behind me? That is might enough, I should think!

MRS. STOCKMANN: But, good heavens, Thomas, you don't mean to——?

DR. STOCKMANN: Don't mean to what?

MRS. STOCKMANN: To set yourself up in opposition to your brother.

DR. STOCKMANN: In God's name, what else do you suppose I should do but take my stand on right and truth?

PETRA: Yes, I was just going to say that.

MRS. STOCKMANN: But it won't do you any earthly good. If they won't do it, they won't.

DR. STOCKMANN: Oho, Katherine! Just give me time, and you will see how I will carry the war into their camp.

MRS. STOCKMANN: Yes, you carry the war into their camp, and you get your dismissal—that is what you will do.

DR. STOCKMANN: In any case I shall have done my duty toward the public —toward the community. I, who am called its enemy!

MRS. STOCKMANN: But toward your family, Thomas? Toward your own home! Do you think that is doing your duty toward those you have to provide for?

PETRA: Ah, don't think always first of us, Mother.

MRS. STOCKMANN: Oh, it is easy for you to talk; you are able to shift for yourself, if need be. But remember the boys, Thomas; and think a little, too, of yourself, and of me——

DR. STOCKMANN: I think you are out of your senses, Katherine! If I were to be such a miserable coward as to go on my knees to Peter and his damned crew, do you suppose I should ever know an hour's peace of mind all my life afterwards?

MRS. STOCKMANN: I don't know anything about that; but God preserve us from the peace of mind we shall have, all the same, if you go on defying him! You will find yourself again without the means of subsistence, with no income to count upon. I should think we had had enough of that in the old days. Remember that, Thomas; think what that means.

DR. STOCKMANN (*collecting himself with a struggle and clenching his fists*):

And this is what this slavery can bring upon a free, honorable man! Isn't it horrible, Katherine?

MRS. STOCKMANN: Yes, it is sinful to treat you so, it is perfectly true. But, good heavens, one has to put up with so much injustice in this world —— There are the boys, Thomas! Look at them! What is to become of them? Oh, no, no, you can never have the heart——

[EJLIF and MORTEN *have come in while she was speaking, with their school books in their hands.*]

DR. STOCKMANN: The boys——! (*Recovers himself suddenly.*) No, even if the whole world goes to pieces, I will never bow my neck to this yoke!

[*Goes toward his room.*]

MRS. STOCKMANN (*following him*): Thomas—what are you going to do!

DR. STOCKMANN (*at his door*): I mean to have the right to look my sons in the face when they are grown men.

[*Goes into his room.*]

MRS. STOCKMANN (*bursting into tears*): God help us all!

PETRA: Father is splendid! He will not give in.

[*The boys look on in amazement;* PETRA *signs to them not to speak.*]

CURTAIN

ACT THREE

SCENE: *The editorial office of the "People's Messenger." The entrance door is on the left-hand side of the back wall; on the right-hand side is another door with glass panels through which the printing room can be seen. Another door in the right-hand wall. In the middle of the room is a large table covered with papers, newspapers, and books. In the foreground on the left a window, before which stand a desk and a high stool. There are a couple of easy chairs by the table, and other chairs standing along the wall. The room is dingy and uncomfortable; the furniture is old, the chairs stained and torn. In the printing room the compositors are seen at work, and a printer is working a hand press.* HOVSTAD *is sitting at the desk, writing.* BILLING *comes in from the right with* DR. STOCKMANN'S *manuscript in his hand.*

BILLING: Well, I must say!

HOVSTAD (*still writing*): Have you read it through?

BILLING (*laying the MS. on the desk*): Yes, indeed I have.

HOVSTAD: Don't you think the Doctor hits them pretty hard?

BILLING: Hard? Bless my soul, he's crushing! Every word falls like—how shall I put it?—like the blow of a sledgehammer.

HOVSTAD: Yes, but they are not the people to throw up the sponge at the first blow.

BILLING: That is true; and for that reason we must strike blow upon blow until the whole of this aristocracy tumbles to pieces. As I sat in there reading this, I almost seemed to see a revolution in being.

HOVSTAD (*turning round*): Hush!—Speak so that Aslaksen cannot hear you.

BILLING (*lowering his voice*): Aslaksen is a chicken-hearted chap, a coward; there is nothing of the man in him. But this time you will insist on your own way, won't you? You will put the Doctor's article in?

HOVSTAD: Yes, and if the Mayor doesn't like it——

BILLING: That will be the devil of a nuisance.

HOVSTAD: Well, fortunately we can turn the situation to good account, whatever happens. If the Mayor will not fall in with the Doctor's project, he will have all the small tradesmen down on him—the whole of the Householders' Association and the rest of them. And if he does fall in with it, he will fall out with the whole crowd of large shareholders in the Baths, who up to now have been his most valuable supporters——

BILLING: Yes, because they will certainly have to fork out a pretty penny——

HOVSTAD: Yes, you may be sure they will. And in this way the ring will be broken up, you see, and then in every issue of the paper we will enlighten the public on the Mayor's incapability on one point and another, and make it clear that all the positions of trust in the town, the whole control of municipal affairs, ought to be put in the hands of the Liberals.

BILLING: That is perfectly true! I see it coming—I see it coming; we are on the threshold of a revolution!

[*A knock is heard at the door.*]

HOVSTAD: Hush! (*Calls out.*) Come in! (DR. STOCKMANN *comes in by the street door.* HOVSTAD *goes to meet him.*) Ah, it is you, Doctor! Well?

DR. STOCKMANN: You may set to work and print it, Mr. Hovstad!

HOVSTAD: Has it come to that, then?

BILLING: Hurrah!

DR. STOCKMANN: Yes, print away. Undoubtedly it has come to that. Now they must take what they get. There is going to be a fight in the town, Mr. Billing!

BILLING: War to the knife, I hope! We will get our knives to their throats, Doctor!

DR. STOCKMANN: This article is only a beginning. I have already got four or five more sketched out in my head. Where is Aslaksen?

BILLING (*calls into the printing room*): Aslaksen, just come here for a minute!

HOVSTAD: Four or five more articles, did you say? On the same subject?

DR. STOCKMANN: No—far from it, my dear fellow. No, they are about quite another matter. But they all spring from the question of the water supply and the drainage. One thing leads to another, you know. It is like beginning to pull down an old house, exactly.

BILLING: Upon my soul, it's true; you find you are not done till you have pulled all the old rubbish down.

ASLAKSEN (*coming in*): Pulled down? You arc not thinking of pulling down the Baths surely, Doctor?

HOVSTAD: Far from it; don't be afraid.

DR. STOCKMANN: No, we meant something quite different. Well, what do you think of my article, Mr. Hovstad?

HOVSTAD: I think it is simply a masterpiece——

DR. STOCKMANN: Do you really think so? Well, I am very pleased, very pleascd.

HOVSTAD: It is so clear and intclligible. One need have no special knowledge to understand the bearing of it. You will have every enlightened man on your side.

ASLAKSEN: And every prudent man, too, I hope?

BILLING: The prudent and the imprudent—almost the whole town.

ASLAKSEN: In that case we may venture to print it.

DR. STOCKMANN: I should think so!

HOVSTAD: We will put it in tomorrow morning.

DR. STOCKMANN: Of course—you must not lose a single day. What I wanted to ask you, Mr. Aslaksen, was if you would supervise the printing of it yourself.

ASLAKSEN: With pleasure.

DR. STOCKMANN: Take care of it as if it were a treasure! No misprints—every word is important. I will look in again a little later; perhaps you will be able to let me see a proof. I can't tell you how eager I am to see it in print, and see it burst upon the public——

BILLING: Burst upon them—yes, like a flash of lightning!

DR. STOCKMANN: ——and to have it submitted to the judgment of my intelligent fellow townsmen. You cannot imagine what I have gone

through today. I have been threatened first with one thing and then
with another; they have tried to rob me of my most elementary rights
as a man——

BILLING: What! Your rights as a man!

DR. STOCKMANN: ——they have tried to degrade me, to make a coward of
me, to force me to put personal interests before my most sacred con-
victions——

BILLING: That is too much—I'm damned if it isn't.

HOVSTAD: Oh, you mustn't be surprised at anything from that quarter.

DR. STOCKMANN: Well, they will get the worst of it with me; they may assure themselves of that. I shall consider the "People's Messenger" my
sheet anchor now, and every single day I will bombard them with one
article after another, like bombshells——

ASLAKSEN: Yes, but——

BILLING: Hurrah!—it is war, it is war!

DR. STOCKMANN: I shall smite them to the ground—I shall crush them—I
shall break down all their defenses, before the eyes of the honest public! That is what I shall do!

ASLAKSEN: Yes, but in moderation, Doctor—proceed with moderation——

BILLING: Not a bit of it, not a bit of it! Don't spare the dynamite!

DR. STOCKMANN: Because it is not merely a question of water supply and
drains now, you know. No—it is the whole of our social life that we
have got to purify and disinfect——

BILLING: Spoken like a deliverer!

DR. STOCKMANN: All the incapables must be turned out, you understand—
and that in every walk of life! Endless vistas have opened themselves
to my mind's eye today. I cannot see it all quite clearly yet, but I shall
in time. Young and vigorous standard-bearers—those are what we need
and must seek, my friends; we must have new men in command at all
our outposts.

BILLING: Hear, hear!

DR. STOCKMANN: We only need to stand by one another, and it will all be
perfectly easy. The revolution will be launched like a ship that runs
smoothly off the stocks. Don't you think so?

HOVSTAD: For my part, I think we have now a prospect of getting the
municipal authority into the hands where it should lie.

ASLAKSEN: And if only we proceed with moderation, I cannot imagine that
there will be any risk.

DR. STOCKMANN: Who the devil cares whether there is any risk or not?
What I am doing, I am doing in the name of truth and for the sake of
my conscience.

HOVSTAD: You are a man who deserves to be supported, Doctor.

ASLAKSEN: Yes, there is no denying that the Doctor is a true friend to the town—a real friend to the community, that he is.

BILLING: Take my word for it, Aslaksen, Dr. Stockmann is a friend of the people.

ASLAKSEN: I fancy the Householders' Association will make use of that expression before long.

DR. STOCKMANN (*affected, grasps their hands*): Thank you, thank you, my dear staunch friends. It is very refreshing to me to hear you say that; my brother called me something quite different. By Jove, he shall have it back, with interest! But now I must be off to see a poor devil. I will come back, as I said. Keep a very careful eye on the manuscript, Aslaksen, and don't for worlds leave out any of my notes of exclamation! Rather put one or two more in! Capital, capital! Well, good-bye for the present—good-bye, good-bye!

[*They show him to the door and bow him out.*]

HOVSTAD: He may prove an invaluably useful man to us.

ASLAKSEN: Yes, so long as he confines himself to this matter of the Baths. But if he goes further afield, I don't think it would be advisable to follow him.

HOVSTAD: Hm!—that all depends——

BILLING: You are so infernally timid, Aslaksen!

ASLAKSEN: Timid? Yes, when it is a question of the local authorities, I am timid, Mr. Billing; it is a lesson I have learned in the school of experience, let me tell you. But try me in higher politics, in matters that concern the government itself, and then see if I am timid.

BILLING: No, you aren't, I admit. But this is simply contradicting yourself.

ASLAKSEN: I am a man with a conscience, and that is the whole matter. If you attack the government, you don't do the community any harm, anyway; those fellows pay no attention to attacks, you see—they go on just as they are, in spite of them. But *local* authorities are different; they *can* be turned out, and then perhaps you may get an ignorant lot into office who may do irreparable harm to the householders and everybody else.

HOVSTAD: But what of the education of citizens by self-government—don't you attach any importance to that?

ASLAKSEN: When a man has interests of his own to protect, he cannot think of everything, Mr. Hovstad.

HOVSTAD: Then I hope I shall never have interests of my own to protect!

BILLING: Hear, hear!

ASLAKSEN (*with a smile*): Hm! (*Points to the desk.*) Mr. Sheriff Stensgaard was your predecessor at that editorial desk.

BILLING (*spitting*): Bah! That turncoat.

HOVSTAD: I am not a weathercock—and never will be.

ASLAKSEN: A politician should never be too certain of anything, Mr. Hovstad. And as for you, Mr. Billing, I should think it is time for you to be taking in a reef or two in your sails, seeing that you are applying for the post of secretary to the Bench.

BILLING: I——!

HOVSTAD: Are you, Billing?

BILLING: Well, yes—but you must clearly understand I am doing it only to annoy the bigwigs.

ASLAKSEN: Anyhow, it is no business of mine. But if I am to be accused of timidity and of inconsistency in my principles, this is what I want to point out: my political past is an open book. I have never changed, except perhaps to become a little more moderate, you see. My heart is still with the people; but I don't deny that my reason has a certain bias toward the authorities—the local ones, I mean.

[*Goes into the printing room.*]

BILLING: Oughtn't we to try and get rid of him, Hovstad?

HOVSTAD: Do you know anyone else who will advance the money for our paper and printing bill?

BILLING: It is an infernal nuisance that we don't possess some capital to trade on.

HOVSTAD (*sitting down at his desk*): Yes, if we only had that, then——

BILLING: Suppose you were to apply to Dr. Stockmann?

HOVSTAD (*turning over some papers*): What is the use? He has got nothing.

BILLING: No, but he has got a warm man in the background, old Morten Kiil—"the Badger," as they call him.

HOVSTAD (*writing*): Are you so sure *he* has got anything?

BILLING: Good Lord, of course he has! And some of it must come to the Stockmanns. Most probably he will do something for the children, at all events.

HOVSTAD (*turning half round*): Are you counting on that?

BILLING: Counting on it? Of course, I am not counting on anything.

HOVSTAD: That is right. And I should not count on the secretaryship to the Bench either, if I were you; for I can assure you—you won't get it.

BILLING: Do you think I am not quite aware of that? My object is precisely *not* to get it. A slight of that kind stimulates a man's fighting power—it is like getting a supply of fresh bile—and I am sure one needs that badly enough in a hole-and-corner place like this, where so seldom anything happens to stir one up.

HOVSTAD (*writing*): Quite so, quite so.

BILLING: Ah, I shall be heard of yet!—Now I shall go and write the appeal to the Householders' Association.

[*Goes into the room on the right.*]

HOVSTAD (*sitting at his desk, biting his penholder, says slowly*): Hm!—that's it, is it? (*A knock is heard.*) Come in! (PETRA *comes in by the outer door.* HOVSTAD *gets up.*) What, you!—here?

PETRA: Yes, you must forgive me——

HOVSTAD (*pulling a chair forward*): Won't you sit down?

PETRA: No, thank you; I must go again in a moment.

HOVSTAD: Have you come with a message from your father, by any chance?

PETRA: No, I have come on my own account. (*Takes a book out of her coat pocket.*) Here is the English story.

HOVSTAD: Why have you brought it back?

PETRA: Because I am not going to translate it.

HOVSTAD: But you promised me faithfully——

PETRA: Yes, but then I had not read it. I don't suppose you have read it, either?

HOVSTAD: No, you know quite well I don't understand English; but——

PETRA: Quite so. That is why I wanted to tell you that you must find something else. (*Lays the book on the table.*) You can't use this for the "People's Messenger."

HOVSTAD: Why not?

PETRA: Because it conflicts with all your opinions.

HOVSTAD: Oh, for that matter——

PETRA: You don't understand me. The burden of this story is that there is a supernatural power that looks after the so-called good people in this world and makes everything happen for the best in their case—while all the so-called bad people are punished.

HOVSTAD: Well, but that is all right. That is just what our readers want.

PETRA: And are you going to be the one to give it to them? For myself, I do not believe a word of it. You know quite well that things do not happen so in reality.

HOVSTAD: You are perfectly right, but an editor cannot always act as he would prefer. He is often obliged to bow to the wishes of the public in unimportant matters. Politics is the most important thing in life—for a newspaper, anyway; and if I want to carry my public with me on the path that leads to liberty and progress, I must not frighten them away. If they find a moral tale of this sort in the serial at the bottom of the page, they will be all the more ready to read what is printed above it; they feel more secure, as it were.

PETRA: For shame! You would never go and set a snare like that for your readers; you are not a spider!

HOVSTAD (*smiling*): Thank you for having such a good opinion of me. No; as a matter of fact, that is Billing's idea and not mine.

PETRA: Billing's!

HOVSTAD: Yes; anyway he propounded that theory here one day. And it is Billing who is so anxious to have that story in the paper; I don't know anything about the book.

PETRA: But how can Billing, with his emancipated views——

HOVSTAD: Oh, Billing is a many-sided man. He is applying for the post of secretary to the Bench, too, I hear.

PETRA: I don't believe it, Mr. Hovstad. How could he possibly bring himself to do such a thing?

HOVSTAD: Ah, you must ask him that.

PETRA: I should never have thought it of him.

HOVSTAD (*looking more closely at her*): No? Does it really surprise you so much?

PETRA: Yes. Or perhaps not altogether. Really, I don't quite know——

HOVSTAD: We journalists are not worth much, Miss Stockmann.

PETRA: Do you really mean that?

HOVSTAD: I think so sometimes.

PETRA: Yes, in the ordinary affairs of everyday life, perhaps; I can understand that. But now, when you have taken a weighty matter in hand——

HOVSTAD: This matter of your father's, you mean?

PETRA: Exactly. It seems to me that now you must feel you are a man worth more than most.

HOVSTAD: Yes, today I do feel something of that sort.

PETRA: Of course you do, don't you? It is a splendid vocation you have chosen—to smooth the way for the march of unappreciated truths and new and courageous lines of thought. If it were nothing more than because you stand fearlessly in the open and take up the cause of an injured man——

HOVSTAD: Especially when that injured man is—ahem!—I don't rightly know how to——

PETRA: When that man is so upright and so honest, you mean?

HOVSTAD (*more gently*): Especially when he is your father, I meant.

PETRA (*suddenly checked*): *That?*

HOVSTAD: Yes, Petra—Miss Petra.

PETRA: Is it *that,* that is first and foremost with you? Not the matter itself? Not the truth?—not my father's big generous heart?

HOVSTAD: Certainly—of course—that too.

PETRA: No, thank you; you have betrayed yourself, Mr. Hovstad, and now I shall never trust you again in anything.

HOVSTAD: Can you really take it so amiss in me that it is mostly for your sake——?

PETRA: I am angry with you for not having been honest with my father. You talked to him as if the truth and the good of the community were what lay nearest to your heart. You have made fools of both my father and me. You are not the man you made yourself out to be. And that I shall never forgive you—never!

HOVSTAD: You ought not to speak so bitterly, Miss Petra—least of all now.

PETRA: Why not now, especially?

HOVSTAD: Because your father cannot do without my help.

PETRA (looking him up and down): Are you that sort of man too? For shame!

HOVSTAD: No, no, I am not. This came upon me so unexpectedly—you must believe that.

PETRA: I know what to believe. Good-bye.

ASLAKSEN (coming from the printing room, hurriedly and with an air of mystery): Damnation, Hovstad!—(Sees PETRA.) Oh, this is awkward——

PETRA: There is the book; you must give it to someone else.

[Goes toward the door.]

HOVSTAD (following her): But, Miss Stockmann——

PETRA: Good-bye.

[Goes out.]

ASLAKSEN: I say—Mr. Hovstad——

HOVSTAD: Well, well!—what is it?

ASLAKSEN: The Mayor is outside in the printing room.

HOVSTAD: The Mayor, did you say?

ASLAKSEN: Yes, he wants to speak to you. He came in by the back door—didn't want to be seen, you understand.

HOVSTAD: What can he want? Wait a bit—I will go myself. (Goes to the door of the printing room, opens it, bows, and invites PETER STOCKMANN in.) Just see, Aslaksen, that no one——

ASLAKSEN: Quite so.

[Goes into the printing room.]

PETER STOCKMANN: You did not expect to see me here, Mr. Hovstad?

HOVSTAD: No, I confess I did not.

PETER STOCKMANN (looking round): You are very snug in here—very nice indeed.

HOVSTAD: Oh——

PETER STOCKMANN: And here I come, without any notice, to take up your time!

HOVSTAD: By all means, Mr. Mayor. I am at your service. But let me relieve you of your——(*Takes* STOCKMANN's *hat and stick and puts them on a chair.*) Won't you sit down?

PETER STOCKMANN (*sitting down by the table*): Thank you. (HOVSTAD *sits down.*) I have had an extremely annoying experience today, Mr. Hovstad.

HOVSTAD: Really? Ah well, I expect with all the various business you have to attend to——

PETER STOCKMANN: The Medical Officer of the Baths is responsible for what happened today.

HOVSTAD: Indeed? The Doctor?

PETER STOCKMANN: He has addressed a kind of report to the Baths Committee on the subject of certain supposed defects in the Baths.

HOVSTAD: Has he indeed?

PETER STOCKMANN: Yes—has he not told you? I thought he said——

HOVSTAD: Ah, yes—it is true he did mention something about——

ASLAKSEN (*coming from the printing room*): I ought to have that copy——

HOVSTAD (*angrily*): Ahem!—there it is on the desk.

ASLAKSEN (*taking it*): Right.

PETER STOCKMANN: But look there—that is the thing I was speaking of!

ASLAKSEN: Yes, that is the Doctor's article, Mr. Mayor.

HOVSTAD: Oh, is *that* what you were speaking about?

PETER STOCKMANN: Yes, that is it. What do you think of it?

HOVSTAD: Oh, I am only a layman—and I have only taken a very cursory glance at it.

PETER STOCKMANN: But you are going to print it?

HOVSTAD: I cannot very well refuse a distinguished man——

ASLAKSEN: I have nothing to do with editing the paper, Mr. Mayor——

PETER STOCKMANN: I understand.

ASLAKSEN: I merely print what is put into my hands.

PETER STOCKMANN: Quite so.

ASLAKSEN: And so I must——

[*Moves off toward the printing room.*]

PETER STOCKMANN: No, but wait a moment, Mr. Aslaksen. You will allow me, Mr. Hovstad?

HOVSTAD: If you please, Mr. Mayor.

PETER STOCKMANN: You are a discreet and thoughtful man, Mr. Aslaksen.

ASLAKSEN: I am delighted to hear you think so, sir.

PETER STOCKMANN: And a man of very considerable influence.

ASLAKSEN: Chiefly among the small tradesmen, sir.

PETER STOCKMANN: The small taxpayers are the majority—here as everywhere else.

ASLAKSEN: That is true.

PETER STOCKMANN: And I have no doubt you know the general trend of opinion among them, don't you?

ASLAKSEN: Yes, I think I may say I do, Mr. Mayor.

PETER STOCKMANN: Yes. Well, since there is such a praiseworthy spirit of self-sacrifice among the less wealthy citizens of our town——

ASLAKSEN: What?

HOVSTAD: Self-sacrifice?

PETER STOCKMANN: It is pleasing evidence of a public-spirited feeling, extremely pleasing evidence. I might almost say I hardly expected it. But you have a closer knowledge of public opinion than I.

ASLAKSEN: But, Mr. Mayor——

PETER STOCKMANN: And indeed it is no small sacrifice that the town is going to make.

HOVSTAD: The town?

ASLAKSEN: But I don't understand. Is it the Baths——?

PETER STOCKMANN: At a provisional estimate, the alterations that the Medical Officer asserts are desirable will cost somewhere about twenty thousand pounds.

ASLAKSEN: That is a lot of money, but——

PETER STOCKMANN: Of course, it will be necessary to raise a municipal loan.

HOVSTAD (*getting up*): Surely you never mean that the town must pay——?

ASLAKSEN: Do you mean that it must come out of the municipal funds?—out of the ill-filled pockets of the small tradesmen?

PETER STOCKMANN: Well, my dear Mr. Aslaksen, where else is the money to come from?

ASLAKSEN: The gentlemen who own the Baths ought to provide that.

PETER STOCKMANN: The proprietors of the Baths are not in a position to incur any further expense.

ASLAKSEN: Is that absolutely certain, Mr. Mayor?

PETER STOCKMANN: I have satisfied myself that it is so. If the town wants these very extensive alterations, it will have to pay for them.

ASLAKSEN: But, damn it all—I beg your pardon—this is quite another matter, Mr. Hovstad!

HOVSTAD: It is, indeed.

PETER STOCKMANN: The most fatal part of it is that we shall be obliged to shut the Baths for a couple of years.

HOVSTAD: Shut them? Shut them altogether?

ASLAKSEN: For two years?

PETER STOCKMANN: Yes, the work will take as long as that—at least.

ASLAKSEN: I'm damned if we will stand that, Mr. Mayor! What are we householders to live upon in the meantime?

PETER STOCKMANN: Unfortunately, that is an extremely difficult question to answer, Mr. Aslaksen. But what would you have us do? Do you suppose we shall have a single visitor in the town, if we go about proclaiming that our water is polluted, that we are living over a plague spot, that the entire town——

ASLAKSEN: And the whole thing is merely imagination?

PETER STOCKMANN: With the best will in the world, I have not been able to come to any other conclusion.

ASLAKSEN: Well then, I must say it is absolutely unjustifiable of Dr. Stockmann—I beg your pardon, Mr. Mayor——

PETER STOCKMANN: What you say is lamentably true, Mr. Aslaksen. My brother has, unfortunately, always been a headstrong man.

ASLAKSEN: After this, do you mean to give him your support, Mr. Hovstad?

HOVSTAD: Can you suppose for a moment that I——?

PETER STOCKMANN: I have drawn up a short résumé of the situation as it appears from a reasonable man's point of view. In it I have indicated how certain possible defects might suitably be remedied without outrunning the resources of the Baths Committee.

HOVSTAD: Have you got it with you, Mr. Mayor?

PETER STOCKMANN (*fumbling in his pocket*): Yes, I brought it with me in case you should——

ASLAKSEN: Good Lord, there he is!

PETER STOCKMANN: Who? My brother?

HOVSTAD: Where? Where?

ASLAKSEN: He has just gone through the printing room.

PETER STOCKMANN: How unlucky! I don't want to meet him here, and I had still several things to speak to you about.

HOVSTAD (*pointing to the door on the right*): Go in there for the present.

PETER STOCKMANN: But——?

HOVSTAD: You will only find Billing in there.

ASLAKSEN: Quick, quick, Mr. Mayor—he is just coming.

PETER STOCKMANN: Yes, very well; but see that you get rid of him quickly.
[*Goes out through the door on the right, which* ASLAKSEN *opens for him and shuts after him*].

HOVSTAD: Pretend to be doing something, Aslaksen.

[*Sits down and writes.* ASLAKSEN *begins foraging among a heap of newspapers that are lying on a chair.*]

DR. STOCKMANN (*coming in from the printing room*): Here I am again.
[*Puts down his hat and stick.*]

HOVSTAD (*writing*): Already, Doctor? Hurry up with what we were speaking about, Aslaksen. We are very pressed for time today.

DR. STOCKMANN (*to* ASLAKSEN): No proof for me to see yet, I hear.

ASLAKSEN (*without turning round*): You couldn't expect it yet, Doctor.

DR. STOCKMANN: No, no; but I am impatient, as you can understand. I shall not know a moment's peace of mind till I see it in print.

HOVSTAD: Hm!—it will take a good while yet, won't it, Aslaksen?

ASLAKSEN: Yes, I am almost afraid it will.

DR. STOCKMANN: All right, my dear friends; I will come back. I do not mind coming back twice if necessary. A matter of such great importance—the welfare of the town at stake—it is no time to shirk trouble. (*Is just going, but stops and comes back.*) Look here—there is one thing more I want to speak to you about.

HOVSTAD: Excuse me, but could it not wait till some other time?

DR. STOCKMANN: I can tell you in half a dozen words. It is only this. When my article is read tomorrow and it is realized that I have been quietly working the whole winter for the welfare of the town——

HOVSTAD: Yes, but, Doctor——

DR. STOCKMANN: I know what you are going to say. You don't see how on earth it was any more than my duty—my obvious duty as a citizen. Of course it wasn't; I know that as well as you. But my fellow citizens, you know——! Good Lord, think of all the good souls who think so highly of me——!

ASLAKSEN: Yes, our townsfolk have had a very high opinion of you so far, Doctor.

DR. STOCKMANN: Yes, and that is just why I am afraid they—— Well, this is the point; when this reaches them, especially the poorer classes, and sounds in their ears like a summons to take the town's affairs into their own hands for the future——

HOVSTAD (*getting up*): Ahem! Doctor, I won't conceal from you the fact——

DR. STOCKMANN: Ah!—I knew there was something in the wind! But I won't hear a word of it. If anything of that sort is being set on foot——

HOVSTAD: Of what sort?

DR. STOCKMANN: Well, whatever it is—whether it is a demonstration in my honor, or a banquet, or a subscription list for some presentation to me—whatever it is, you must promise me solemnly and faithfully to put a stop to it. You too, Mr. Aslaksen; do you understand?

HOVSTAD: You must forgive me, Doctor, but sooner or later we must tell you the plain truth——

[*He is interrupted by the entrance of* MRS. STOCKMANN, *who comes in from the street door.*]

MRS. STOCKMANN (*seeing her husband*): Just as I thought!

HOVSTAD (*going toward her*): You too, Mrs. Stockmann?

DR. STOCKMANN: What on earth do *you* want here, Katherine?

MRS. STOCKMANN: I should think you know very well what I want.

HOVSTAD: Won't you sit down? Or perhaps——

MRS. STOCKMANN: No, thank you; don't trouble. And you must not be offended at my coming to fetch my husband; I am the mother of three children, you know.

DR. STOCKMANN: Nonsense!—we know all about that.

MRS. STOCKMANN: Well, one would not give you credit for much thought for your wife and children today; if you had had that, you would not have gone and dragged us all into misfortune.

DR. STOCKMANN: Are you out of your senses, Katherine? Because a man has a wife and children, is he not to be allowed to proclaim the truth —is he not to be allowed to be an actively useful citizen—is he not to be allowed to do a service to his native town?

MRS. STOCKMANN: Yes, Thomas—in reason.

ASLAKSEN: Just what I say. Moderation is everything.

MRS. STOCKMANN: And that is why you wrong us, Mr. Hovstad, in enticing my husband away from his home and making a dupe of him in all this.

HOVSTAD: I certainly am making a dupe of no one——

DR. STOCKMANN: Making a dupe of me! Do you suppose *I* should allow myself to be duped?

MRS. STOCKMANN: It is just what you do. I know quite well you have more brains than anyone in the town, but you are extremely easily duped, Thomas. (*To* HOVSTAD) Please realize that he loses his post at the Baths if you print what he has written——

ASLAKSEN: What!

HOVSTAD: Look here, Doctor——

DR. STOCKMANN (*laughing*): Ha—ha!—just let them try! No, no—they will take good care not to. I have got the compact majority behind me, let me tell you!

MRS. STOCKMANN: Yes, that is just the worst of it—your having any such horrid thing behind you.

DR. STOCKMANN: Rubbish, Katherine!—Go home and look after your house and leave me to look after the community. How can you be so afraid, when I am so confident and happy? (*Walks up and down, rubbing his hands.*) Truth and the People will win the fight, you may be certain! I see the whole of the broad-minded middle class marching like a victorious army——! (*Stops beside a chair.*) What the deuce is that lying there?

ASLAKSEN: Good Lord!

HOVSTAD: Ahem!

DR. STOCKMANN: Here we have the topmost pinnacle of authority!

[*Takes the* MAYOR'S *official hat carefully between his fingertips and holds it up in the air.*]

MRS. STOCKMANN: The Mayor's hat!

DR. STOCKMANN: And here is the staff of office, too. How in the name of all that's wonderful——?

HOVSTAD: Well, you see——

DR. STOCKMANN: Oh, I understand. He has been here trying to talk you over. Ha—ha!—he made rather a mistake there! And as soon as he caught sight of me in the printing room——(*bursts out laughing*)—— did he run away, Mr. Aslaksen?

ASLAKSEN (*hurriedly*): Yes, he ran away, Doctor.

DR. STOCKMANN: Ran away without his stick or his—— Fiddlesticks! Peter doesn't run away and leave his belongings behind him. But what the deuce have you done with him? Ah!—in there, of course. Now you shall see, Katherine.

MRS. STOCKMANN: Thomas—please don't——!

ASLAKSEN: Don't be rash, Doctor.

[DR. STOCKMANN *has put on the* MAYOR'S *hat and taken his stick in his hand. He goes up to the door, opens it, and stands with his hand to his hat at the salute.* PETER STOCKMANN *comes in, red with anger.* BILLING *follows him.*]

PETER STOCKMANN: What does this tomfoolery mean?

DR. STOCKMANN: Be respectful, my good Peter. I am the chief authority in the town now.

[*Walks up and down.*]

MRS. STOCKMANN (*almost in tears*): Really, Thomas!

PETER STOCKMANN (*following him about*): Give me my hat and stick.

DR. STOCKMANN (*in the same tone as before*): If you are chief constable, let me tell you that I am the Mayor—I am the master of the whole town, please understand!

PETER STOCKMANN: Take off my hat, I tell you. Remember it is part of an official uniform.

DR. STOCKMANN: Pooh! Do you think the newly awakened lion-hearted people are going to be frightened by an official hat? There is going to be a revolution in the town tomorrow, let me tell you. You thought you could turn me out; but now I shall turn you out—turn you out of all

your various offices. Do you think I cannot? Listen to me. I have triumphant social forces behind me. Hovstad and Billing will thunder in
the "People's Messenger," and Aslaksen will take the field at the head of
the whole Householders' Association——

ASLAKSEN: That I won't, Doctor.

DR. STOCKMANN: Of course you will——

PETER STOCKMANN: Ah!—may I ask, then, if Mr. Hovstad intends to
join this agitation?

HOVSTAD: No, Mr. Mayor.

ASLAKSEN: No, Mr. Hovstad is not such a fool as to go and ruin his paper
and himself for the sake of an imaginary grievance.

DR. STOCKMANN (*looking round him*): What does this mean?

HOVSTAD: You have represented your case in a false light, Doctor, and
therefore I am unable to give you my support.

BILLING: And after what the Mayor was so kind as to tell me just now
I——

DR. STOCKMANN: A false light! Leave that part of it to me. Only print my
article; I am quite capable of defending it.

HOVSTAD: I am not going to print it. I cannot and will not and dare not
print it.

DR. STOCKMANN: You dare not? What nonsense!—you are the editor; and
an editor controls his paper, I suppose!

ASLAKSEN: No, it is the subscribers, Doctor.

PETER STOCKMANN: Fortunately, yes.

ASLAKSEN: It is public opinion—the enlightened public—householders and
people of that kind; they control the newspapers.

DR. STOCKMANN (*composedly*): And I have all these influences against
me?

ASLAKSEN: Yes, you have. It would mean the absolute ruin of the community if your article were to appear.

DR. STOCKMANN: Indeed.

PETER STOCKMANN: My hat and stick, if you please. (DR. STOCKMANN
takes off the hat and lays it on the table with the stick. PETER STOCK-
MANN *takes them up.*) Your authority as Mayor has come to an untimely end.

DR. STOCKMANN: We have not got to the end yet. (*To* HOVSTAD) Then it
is quite impossible for you to print my article in the "People's Messenger"?

HOVSTAD: Quite impossible—out of regard for your family as well.

MRS. STOCKMANN: You need not concern yourself about his family, thank
you, Mr. Hovstad.

PETER STOCKMANN (*taking a paper from his pocket*): It will be sufficient, for the guidance of the public, if this appears. It is an official statement. May I trouble you?

HOVSTAD (*taking the paper*): Certainly; I will see that it is printed.

DR. STOCKMANN: But not mine. Do you imagine that you can silence me and stifle the truth? You will not find it so easy as you suppose. Mr. Aslaksen, kindly take my manuscript at once and print it as a pamphlet —at my expense. I will have four hundred copies—no, five—six hundred.

ASLAKSEN: If you offered me its weight in gold, I could not lend my press for any such purpose, Doctor. It would be flying in the face of public opinion. You will not get it printed anywhere in the town.

DR. STOCKMANN: Then give it back to me.

HOVSTAD (*giving him the MS.*): Here it is.

DR. STOCKMANN (*taking his hat and stick*): It shall be made public all the same. I will read it out at a mass meeting of the townspeople. All my fellow citizens shall hear the voice of truth!

PETER STOCKMANN: You will not find any public body in the town that will give you the use of their hall for such a purpose.

ASLAKSEN: Not a single one, I am certain.

BILLING: No, I'm damned if you will find one.

MRS. STOCKMANN: But this is too shameful! Why should everyone turn against you like that?

DR. STOCKMANN (*angrily*): I will tell you why. It is because all the men in this town are old women—like you; they all think of nothing but their families, and never of the community.

MRS. STOCKMANN (*putting her arm into his*): Then I will show them that an—an old woman can be a man for once. I am going to stand by you, Thomas!

DR. STOCKMANN: Bravely said, Katherine! It shall be made public—as I am a living soul! If I can't hire a hall, I shall hire a drum, and parade the town with it and read it at every street corner.

PETER STOCKMANN: You are surely not such an arrant fool as that!

DR. STOCKMANN: Yes, I am.

ASLAKSEN: You won't find a single man in the whole town to go with you.

BILLING: No, I'm damned if you will.

MRS. STOCKMANN: Don't give in, Thomas. I will tell the boys to go with you.

DR. STOCKMANN: That is a splendid idea!

MRS. STOCKMANN: Morten will be delighted; and Ejlif will do whatever he does.

DR. STOCKMANN: Yes, and Petra!—and you too, Katherine!

MRS. STOCKMANN: No, I won't do that; but I will stand at the window and watch you, that's what I will do.

DR. STOCKMANN (*puts his arms round her and kisses her*): Thank you, my dear! Now you and I are going to try a fall, my fine gentlemen! I am going to see whether a pack of cowards can succeed in gagging a patriot who wants to purify society!

[*He and his wife go out by the street door.*]

PETER STOCKMANN (*shaking his head seriously*): Now he has sent *her* out of her senses, too.

CURTAIN

ACT FOUR

SCENE: *A big, old-fashioned room in* CAPTAIN HORSTER'S *house. At the back, folding doors, which are standing open, lead to an anteroom. Three windows in the left-hand wall. In the middle of the opposite wall a platform has been erected. On this is a small table with two candles, a water-bottle and glass, and a bell. The room is lit by lamps placed between the windows. In the foreground on the left there is a table with candles and a chair. To the right is a door and some chairs standing near it. The room is nearly filled with a crowd of townspeople of all sorts, a few women and schoolboys being among them. People are still streaming in from the back, and the room is soon filled.*

FIRST CITIZEN (*meeting another*): Hullo, Lamstad! You here too?

SECOND CITIZEN: I go to every public meeting, I do.

THIRD CITIZEN: Brought your whistle too, I expect!

SECOND CITIZEN: I should think so. Haven't you?

THIRD CITIZEN: Rather! And old Evensen said he was going to bring a cowhorn, he did.

SECOND CITIZEN: Good old Evensen!

[*Laughter among the crowd.*]

FOURTH CITIZEN (*coming up to them*): I say, tell me what is going on here tonight.

SECOND CITIZEN: Dr. Stockmann is going to deliver an address attacking the Mayor.

FOURTH CITIZEN: But the Mayor is his brother.

FIRST CITIZEN: That doesn't matter; Dr. Stockmann's not the chap to be afraid.

THIRD CITIZEN: But he is in the wrong; it said so in the "People's Messenger."

SECOND CITIZEN: Yes, I expect he must be in the wrong this time, because neither the Householders' Association nor the Citizens' Club would lend him their hall for his meeting.

FIRST CITIZEN: He couldn't even get the loan of the hall at the Baths.

SECOND CITIZEN: No, I should think not.

A MAN IN ANOTHER PART OF THE CROWD: I say—who are we to back up in this?

ANOTHER MAN, BESIDE HIM: Watch Aslaksen, and do as he does.

BILLING (*pushing his way through the crowd, with a writing case under his arm*): Excuse me, gentlemen—do you mind letting me through? I am reporting for the "People's Messenger." Thank you very much!

[*He sits down at the table on the left.*]

A WORKMAN: Who was that?

SECOND WORKMAN: Don't you know him? It's Billing, who writes for Aslaksen's paper.

[CAPTAIN HORSTER *brings in* MRS. STOCKMANN *and* PETRA *through the door on the right.* EJLIF *and* MORTEN *follow them in.*]

HORSTER: I thought you might all sit here; you can slip out easily from here, if things get too lively.

MRS. STOCKMANN: Do you think there will be a disturbance?

HORSTER: One can never tell—with such a crowd. But sit down, and don't be uneasy.

MRS. STOCKMANN (*sitting down*): It was extremely kind of you to offer my husband the room.

HORSTER: Well, if nobody else would——

PETRA (*who has sat down beside her mother*): And it was a plucky thing to do, Captain Horster.

HORSTER: Oh, it is not such a great matter as all that.

[HOVSTAD *and* ASLAKSEN *make their way through the crowd.*]

ASLAKSEN (*going up to* HORSTER): Has the Doctor not come yet?

HORSTER: He is waiting in the next room.

[*Movement in the crowd by the door at the back.*]

HOVSTAD: Look—here comes the Mayor!

BILLING: Yes, I'm damned if he hasn't come after all!

[PETER STOCKMANN *makes his way gradually through the crowd, bows courteously, and takes up a position by the wall on the left. Shortly afterwards* DR. STOCKMANN *comes in by the right-hand door.*

He is dressed in a black frockcoat, with a white tie. There is a little feeble applause, which is hushed down. Silence is obtained.]

DR. STOCKMANN (*in an undertone*): How do you feel, Katherine?

MRS. STOCKMANN: All right, thank you. (*Lowering her voice.*) Be sure not to lose your temper, Thomas.

DR. STOCKMANN: Oh, I know how to control myself. (*Looks at his watch, steps onto the platform, and bows.*) It is a quarter past—so I will begin. [*Takes his MS. out of his pocket.*]

ASLAKSEN: I think we ought to elect a chairman first.

DR. STOCKMANN: No, it is quite unnecessary.

SOME OF THE CROWD: Yes—yes!

PETER STOCKMANN: I certainly think, too, that we ought to have a chairman.

DR. STOCKMANN: But I have called this meeting to deliver a lecture, Peter.

PETER STOCKMANN: Dr. Stockmann's lecture may possibly lead to a considerable conflict of opinion.

VOICES IN THE CROWD: A chairman! A chairman!

HOVSTAD: The general wish of the meeting seems to be that a chairman should be elected.

DR. STOCKMANN (*restraining himself*): Very well—let the meeting have its way.

ASLAKSEN: Will the Mayor be good enough to undertake the task?

THREE MEN (*clapping their hands*): Bravo! Bravo!

PETER STOCKMANN: For various reasons, which you will easily understand, I must beg to be excused. But fortunately, we have among us a man who I think will be acceptable to you all. I refer to the President of the Householders' Association, Mr. Aslaksen.

SEVERAL VOICES: Yes—Aslaksen! Bravo, Aslaksen!

[DR. STOCKMANN *takes up his MS. and walks up and down the platform.*]

ASLAKSEN: Since my fellow citizens choose to entrust me with this duty, I cannot refuse.

[*Loud applause.* ASLAKSEN *mounts the platform.*]

BILLING (*writing*): "Mr. Aslaksen was elected with enthusiasm."

ASLAKSEN: And now, as I am in this position, I should like to say a few brief words. I am a quiet and peaceable man, who believes in discreet moderation, and—and—in moderate discretion. All my friends can bear witness to that.

SEVERAL VOICES: That's right! That's right, Aslaksen!

ASLAKSEN: I have learned in the school of life and experience that moderation is the most valuable virtue a citizen can possess——

PETER STOCKMANN: Hear, hear!

ASLAKSEN: ——and moreover that discretion and moderation are what enable a man to be of most service to the community. I would therefore suggest to our esteemed fellow citizen, who has called this meeting, that he should strive to keep strictly within the bounds of moderation.

A MAN BY THE DOOR: Three cheers for the Moderation Society!

A VOICE: Shame!

SEVERAL VOICES: Sh!—Sh!

ASLAKSEN: No interruptions, gentlemen, please! Does anyone wish to make any remarks?

PETER STOCKMANN: Mr. Chairman.

ASLAKSEN: The Mayor will address the meeting.

PETER STOCKMANN: In consideration of the close relationship in which, as you all know, I stand to the present Medical Officer of the Baths, I should have preferred not to speak this evening. But my official position with regard to the Baths and my solicitude for the vital interests of the town compel me to bring forward a motion. I venture to presume that there is not a single one of our citizens present who considers it desirable that unreliable and exaggerated accounts of the sanitary condition of the Baths and the town should be spread abroad.

SEVERAL VOICES: No, no! Certainly not! We protest against it!

PETER STOCKMANN: Therefore, I should like to propose that the meeting should not permit the Medical Officer either to read or to comment on his proposed lecture.

DR. STOCKMANN (*impatiently*): Not permit!—— What the devil!——

MRS. STOCKMANN (*coughing*): Ahem!—ahem!

DR. STOCKMANN (*collecting himself*): Very well. Go ahead!

PETER STOCKMANN: In my communication to the "People's Messenger," I have put the essential facts before the public in such a way that every fair-minded citizen can easily form his own opinion. From it you will see that the main result of the Medical Officer's proposals—apart from their constituting a vote of censure on the leading men of the town—would be to saddle the taxpayers with an unnecessary expenditure of at least some thousands of pounds.

[*Sounds of disapproval among the audience, and some catcalls.*]

ASLAKSEN (*ringing his bell*): Silence, please, gentlemen! I beg to support the Mayor's motion. I quite agree with him that there is something behind this agitation started by the Doctor. He talks about the Baths; but it is a revolution he is aiming at—he wants to get the administration of the town put into new hands. No one doubts the honesty of the Doctor's intentions—no one will suggest that there can be any two opinions as to that. I myself am a believer in self-government for the people, provided it does not fall too heavily on the taxpayers. But that would be the case here; and that is why I will see Dr. Stockmann damned—I beg your pardon—before I go with him in the matter. You can pay too dearly for a thing sometimes; that is my opinion.

[*Loud applause on all sides.*]

HOVSTAD: I, too, feel called upon to explain my position. Dr. Stockmann's agitation appeared to be gaining a certain amount of sympathy at first, so I supported it as impartially as I could. But presently we had reason to suspect that we had allowed ourselves to be misled by misrepresentation of the state of affairs——

DR. STOCKMANN: Misrepresentation!——

HOVSTAD: Well, let us say a not entirely trustworthy representation. The Mayor's statement has proved that. I hope no one here has any doubt as to my liberal principles; the attitude of the "People's Messenger" toward important political questions is well known to everyone. But the advice of experienced and thoughtful men has convinced me that in purely local matters a newspaper ought to proceed with a certain caution.

ASLAKSEN: I entirely agree with the speaker.

HOVSTAD: And, in the matter before us, it is now an undoubted fact that Dr. Stockmann has public opinion against him. Now, what is an editor's first and most obvious duty, gentlemen? Is it not to work in harmony with his readers? Has he not received a sort of tacit mandate to work persistently and assiduously for the welfare of those whose opinions he represents? Or is it possible I am mistaken in that?

VOICES FROM THE CROWD: No, no! You are quite right!

HOVSTAD: It has cost me a severe struggle to break with a man in whose house I have been lately a frequent guest—a man who till today has been able to pride himself on the undivided goodwill of his fellow citizens—a man whose only, or at all events whose essential, failing is that he is swayed by his heart rather than his head.

A FEW SCATTERED VOICES: That is true! Bravo, Stockmann!

HOVSTAD: But my duty to the community obliged me to break with him. And there is another consideration that impels me to oppose him, and, as far as possible, to arrest him on the perilous course he has adopted; that is, consideration for his family——

DR. STOCKMANN: Please stick to the water supply and drainage!

HOVSTAD: ——consideration, I repeat, for his wife and his children for whom he has made no provision.

MORTEN: Is that us, Mother?

MRS. STOCKMANN: Hush!

ASLAKSEN: I will now put the Mayor's proposition to the vote.

DR. STOCKMANN: There is no necessity! Tonight I have no intention of dealing with all that filth down at the Baths. No; I have something quite different to say to you.

PETER STOCKMANN (*aside*): What is coming now?

A DRUNKEN MAN (*by the entrance door*): I am a taxpayer! And therefore I have a right to speak too! And my entire—firm—inconceivable opinion is——

A NUMBER OF VOICES: Be quiet at the back there!

OTHERS: He is drunk! Turn him out!

[*They turn him out.*]

DR. STOCKMANN: Am I allowed to speak?

ASLAKSEN (*ringing his bell*): Dr. Stockmann will address the meeting.

DR. STOCKMANN: I should like to have seen anyone, a few days ago, dare to attempt to silence me as has been done tonight! I would have defended my sacred rights as a man, like a lion! But now it is all one to me; I have something of even weightier importance to say to you.

[*The crowd presses nearer to him,* MORTEN KIIL *conspicuous among them.*]

DR. STOCKMANN (*continuing*): I have thought and pondered a great deal, these last few days—pondered over such a variety of things that in the end my head seemed too full to hold them——

PETER STOCKMANN (*with a cough*): Ahem!

DR. STOCKMANN: ——but I got them clear in my mind at last, and then I saw the whole situation lucidly. And that is why I am standing here tonight. I have a great revelation to make to you, my fellow citizens! I will impart to you a discovery of a far wider scope than the trifling matter that our water supply is poisoned and our medicinal Baths are standing on pestiferous soil.

A NUMBER OF VOICES (*shouting*): Don't talk about the Baths! We won't hear you! None of that!

DR. STOCKMANN: I have already told you that what I want to speak about is the great discovery I have made lately—the discovery that all the sources of our *moral* life are poisoned and that the whole fabric of our civic community is founded on the pestiferous soil of falsehood.

VOICES OF DISCONCERTED CITIZENS: What is that he says?

PETER STOCKMANN: Such an insinuation——!

ASLAKSEN (*with his hand on his bell*): I call upon the speaker to moderate his language.

DR. STOCKMANN: I have always loved my native town as a man only can love the home of his youthful days. I was not old when I went away from here; and exile, longing, and memories cast, as it were, an additional halo over both the town and its inhabitants. (*Some clapping and applause.*) And there I stayed, for many years, in a horrible hole

far away up north. When I came into contact with some of the people
that lived scattered about among the rocks, I often thought it would
have been more service to the poor half-starved creatures if a veterinary
doctor had been sent up there, instead of a man like me.

[*Murmurs among the crowd.*]

BILLING (*laying down his pen*): I'm damned if I have ever heard!——

HOVSTAD: It is an insult to a respectable population!

DR. STOCKMANN: Wait a bit! I do not think anyone will charge me with
having forgotten my native town up there. I was like one of the eider
ducks brooding on its nest, and what I hatched was—the plans for these
Baths. (*Applause and protests.*) And then when fate at last decreed for
me the great happiness of coming home again—I assure you, gentlemen,
I thought I had nothing more in the world to wish for. Or rather, there
was one thing I wished for—eagerly, untiringly, ardently—and that was
to be able to be of service to my native town and the good of the community.

PETER STOCKMANN (*looking at the ceiling*): You chose a strange way of
doing it—ahem!

DR. STOCKMANN: And so, with my eyes blinded to the real facts, I reveled in happiness. But yesterday morning—no, to be precise, it was yesterday afternoon—the eyes of my mind were opened wide, and the
first thing I realized was the colossal stupidity of the authorities——

[*Uproar, shouts, and laughter.* MRS. STOCKMANN *coughs persistently.*]

PETER STOCKMANN: Mr. Chairman!

ASLAKSEN (*ringing his bell*): By virtue of my authority!——

DR. STOCKMANN: It is a petty thing to catch me up on a word, Mr. Aslaksen. What I mean is only that I got scent of the unbelievable piggishness
our leading men had been responsible for down at the Baths. I can't
stand leading men at any price!—I have had enough of such people in
my time. They are like billy goats in a young plantation; they do mischief everywhere. They stand in a free man's way, whichever way he
turns, and what I should like best would be to see them exterminated like
any other vermin——

[*Uproar.*]

PETER STOCKMANN: Mr. Chairman, can we allow such expressions to pass?

ASLAKSEN (*with his hand on his bell*): Doctor!

DR. STOCKMANN: I cannot understand how it is that I have only now acquired a clear conception of what these gentry are, when I had almost
daily before my eyes in this town such an excellent specimen of them—
my brother Peter—slow-witted and hidebound in prejudice——

[*Laughter, uproar, and hisses.* MRS. STOCKMANN *sits coughing assiduously.* ASLAKSEN *rings his bell violently.*]

THE DRUNKEN MAN (*who has got in again*): Is it me he is talking about? My name's Petersen, all right—but devil take me if I——

ANGRY VOICES: Turn out that drunken man! Turn him out.

[*He is turned out again.*]

PETER STOCKMANN: Who was that person?

FIRST CITIZEN: I don't know who he is, Mr. Mayor.

SECOND CITIZEN: He doesn't belong here.

THIRD CITIZEN: I expect he is a lumberman from over at—— (*the rest is inaudible.*)

ASLAKSEN: He had obviously had too much beer—— Proceed, Doctor; but please strive to be moderate in your language.

DR. STOCKMANN: Very well, gentlemen, I will say no more about our leading men. And if anyone imagines, from what I have just said, that my object is to attack these people this evening, he is wrong—absolutely wide of the mark. For I cherish the comforting conviction that these parasites—all these venerable relics of a dying school of thought—are most admirably paving the way for their own extinction; they need no doctor's help to hasten their end. Nor is it folk of that kind who constitute the most pressing danger to the community. It is not they who are most instrumental in poisoning the sources of our moral life and infecting the ground on which we stand. It is not they who are the most dangerous enemies of truth and freedom among us.

SHOUTS FROM ALL SIDES: Who then? Who is it? Name! Name!

DR. STOCKMANN: You may depend upon it I shall name them! That is precisely the great discovery I made yesterday. (*Raises his voice.*) The most dangerous enemy of truth and freedom among us is the compact majority—yes, the damned, compact Liberal majority—that is it! Now you know!

[*Tremendous uproar. Most of the crowd are shouting, stamping, and hissing. Some of the older men among them exchange stolen glances and seem to be enjoying themselves.* MRS. STOCKMANN *gets up, looking anxious.* EJLIF *and* MORTEN *advance threateningly upon some schoolboys who are playing pranks.* ASLAKSEN *rings his bell and begs for silence.* HOVSTAD *and* BILLING *both talk at once, but are inaudible. At last quiet is restored.*]

ASLAKSEN: As Chairman, I call upon the speaker to withdraw the ill-considered expressions he has just used.

DR. STOCKMANN: Never, Mr. Aslaksen! It is the majority in our community that denies me my freedom and seeks to prevent my speaking the truth.

HOVSTAD: The majority always has right on its side.

BILLING: And truth too, by God!

DR. STOCKMANN: The majority *never* has right on its side. Never, I say!

That is one of these social lies against which an independent, intelligent man must wage war. Who constitutes the majority of the population in a country? Is it the clever folk or the stupid? I don't imagine you will dispute the fact that at present the stupid people are in an absolutely overwhelming majority all the world over. But, good Lord!—you can never pretend that it is right that the stupid folk should govern the clever ones! (*Uproar and cries.*) Oh, yes—you can shout me down, I know! but you cannot answer me. The majority has *might* on its side—unfortunately; but *right* it has *not*. I am in the right—I and a few other scattered individuals. The minority is always in the right.

[*Renewed uproar.*]

HOVSTAD: Aha!—so Dr. Stockmann has become an aristocrat since the day before yesterday!

DR. STOCKMANN: I have already said that I don't intend to waste a word on the puny, narrow-chested, short-winded crew whom we are leaving astern. Pulsating life no longer concerns itself with them. I am thinking of the few, the scattered few among us, who have absorbed new and vigorous truths. Such men stand, as it were, at the outposts, so far ahead that the compact majority has not yet been able to come up with them; and there they are fighting for truths that are too newly born into the world of consciousness to have any considerable number of people on their side as yet.

HOVSTAD: So the Doctor is a revolutionary now!

DR. STOCKMANN: Good heavens—of course I am, Mr. Hovstad! I propose to raise a revolution against the lie that the majority has the monopoly of the truth. What sort of truths are they that the majority usually supports? They are truths that are of such advanced age that they are beginning to break up. And if a truth is as old as that, it is also in a fair way to become a lie, gentlemen. (*Laughter and mocking cries.*) Yes, believe me or not, as you like; but truths are by no means as long-lived as Methuselah—as some folk imagine. A normally constituted truth lives, let us say, as a rule seventeen or eighteen, or at most twenty years; seldom longer. But truths as aged as that are always worn frightfully thin, and nevertheless it is only then that the majority recognizes them and recommends them to the community as wholesome moral nourishment. There is no great nutritive value in that sort of fare, I can assure you; and, as a doctor, I ought to know. These "majority truths" are like last year's cured meat—like rancid, tainted ham; and they are the origin of the moral scurvy that is rampant in our communities.

ASLAKSEN: It appears to me that the speaker is wandering a long way from his subject.

PETER STOCKMANN: I quite agree with the Chairman.

DR. STOCKMANN: Have you gone clean out of your senses, Peter? I am sticking as closely to my subject as I can; for my subject is precisely this, that it is the masses, the majority—this infernal compact majority—that poisons the sources of our moral life and infects the ground we stand on.

HOVSTAD: And all this because the great, broad-minded majority of the people is prudent enough to show deference only to well-ascertained and well-approved truths?

DR. STOCKMANN: Ah, my good Mr. Hovstad, don't talk nonsense about well-ascertained truths! The truths of which the masses now approve are the very truths that the fighters at the outposts held to in the days of our grandfathers. We fighters at the outposts nowadays no longer approve of them; and I do not believe there is any other well-ascertained truth except this, that no community can live a healthy life if it is nourished only on such old, marrowless truths.

HOVSTAD: But instead of standing there using vague generalities, it would be interesting if you would tell us what these old, marrowless truths are that we are nourished on.

[*Applause from many quarters.*]

DR. STOCKMANN: Oh, I could give you a whole string of such abominations; but to begin with I will confine myself to one well-approved truth, which at bottom is a foul lie, but upon which, nevertheless, Mr. Hovstad and the "People's Messenger" and all the "Messenger's" supporters are nourished.

HOVSTAD: And that is———?

DR. STOCKMANN: That is, the doctrine you have inherited from your forefathers and proclaim thoughtlessly far and wide—the doctrine that the public, the crowd, the masses are the essential part of the population—that they constitute the People—that the common folk, the ignorant and incomplete element in the community, have the same right to pronounce judgment and to approve, to direct, and to govern as the isolated, intellectually superior personalities in it.

BILLING: Well, damn me if ever I——

HOVSTAD (*at the same time, shouting out*): Fellow citizens, take good note of that!

A NUMBER OF VOICES (*angrily*): Oho!—we are not the People! Only the superior folks are to govern, are they?

A WORKMAN: Turn the fellow out, for talking such rubbish!

ANOTHER: Out with him!

ANOTHER (*calling out*): Blow your horn, Evensen!

[*A horn is blown loudly, amidst hisses and an angry uproar.*]

DR. STOCKMANN (*when the noise has somewhat abated*): Be reasonable!

Can't you stand hearing the voice of truth for once? I don't in the least expect you to agree with me all at once; but I must say I did expect Mr. Hovstad to admit I was right, when he had recovered his composure a little. He claims to be a freethinker——

VOICES (*in murmurs of astonishment*): Freethinker, did he say? Is Hovstad a freethinker?

HOVSTAD (*shouting*): Prove it, Dr. Stockmann! When have I said so in print?

DR. STOCKMANN (*reflecting*): No, confound it, you are right!—you have never had the courage to. Well, I won't put you in a hole, Mr. Hovstad. Let us say it is I that am the freethinker, then. I am going to prove to you, scientifically, that the "People's Messenger" leads you by the nose in a shameful manner when it tells you that you—that the common people, the crowd, the masses are the real essence of the People. That is only a newspaper lie, I tell you! The common people are nothing more than the raw material of which a People is made. (*Groans, laughter, and uproar.*) Well, isn't that the case? Isn't there an enormous difference between a well-bred and an ill-bred strain of animals? Take, for instance, a common barn-door hen. What sort of eating do you get from a shriveled-up old scrag of a fowl like that? Not much, do you? And what sort of eggs does it lay? A fairly good crow or a raven can lay pretty nearly as good an egg. But take a well-bred Spanish or Japanese hen, or a good pheasant or a turkey—then you will see the difference. Or take the case of dogs, with whom we humans are on such intimate terms. Think first of an ordinary common cur—I mean one of the horrible, coarse-haired, low-bred curs that do nothing but run about the streets and befoul the walls of the houses. Compare one of these curs with a poodle whose sires for many generations have been bred in a gentleman's house, where they have had the best of food and had the opportunity of hearing soft voices and music. Do you not think that the poodle's brain is developed to quite a different degree from that of the cur? Of course it is. It is puppies of well-bred poodles like that that showmen train to do incredibly clever tricks—things that a common cur could never learn to do even if it stood on its head.

[*Uproar and mocking cries.*]

A CITIZEN (*calls out*): Are you going to make out we are dogs, now?

ANOTHER CITIZEN: We are not animals, Doctor!

DR. STOCKMANN: Yes, but, bless my soul, we *are,* my friend! It is true we are the finest animals anyone could wish for; but, even among us, exceptionally fine animals are rare. There is a tremendous difference between poodle-men and cur-men. And the amusing part of it is that Mr.

Hovstad quite agrees with me as long as it is a question of four-footed animals——

HOVSTAD: Yes, it is true enough as far as they are concerned.

DR. STOCKMANN: Very well. But as soon as I extend the principle and apply it to two-legged animals, Mr. Hovstad stops short. He no longer dares to think independently, or to pursue his ideas to their logical conclusion; so he turns the whole theory upside down and proclaims in the "People's Messenger" that it is the barn-door hens and street curs that are the finest specimens in the menagerie. But that is always the way, as long as a man retains the traces of common origin and has not worked his way up to intellectual distinction.

HOVSTAD: I lay no claim to any sort of distinction. I am the son of humble countryfolk, and I am proud that the stock I come from is rooted deep among the common people he insults.

VOICES: Bravo, Hovstad! Bravo! Bravo!

DR. STOCKMANN: The kind of common people I mean are not only to be found low down in the social scale; they crawl and swarm all around us —even in the highest social positions. You have only to look at your own fine, distinguished Mayor! My brother Peter is every bit as plebeian as anyone that walks in two shoes——

[*Laughter and hisses.*]

PETER STOCKMANN: I protest against personal allusions of this kind.

DR. STOCKMANN (*imperturbably*): ——and that, not because he is, like myself, descended from some old rascal of a pirate from Pomerania or thereabouts—because that is who we are descended from——

PETER STOCKMANN: An absurd legend. I deny it!

DR. STOCKMANN: ——but because he thinks what his superiors think and holds the same opinions as they. People who do that are, intellectually speaking, common people; and that is why my magnificent brother Peter is in reality so very far from any distinction—and consequently also so far from being liberal-minded.

PETER STOCKMANN: Mr. Chairman——!

HOVSTAD: So it is only the distinguished men that are liberal-minded in this country? We are learning something quite new!

[*Laughter.*]

DR. STOCKMANN: Yes, that is part of my new discovery too. And another part of it is that broad-mindedness is almost precisely the same thing as morality. That is why I maintain that it is absolutely inexcusable in the "People's Messenger" to proclaim, day in and day out, the false doctrine that the masses, the crowd, the compact majority have the monopoly of broad-mindedness and morality—and that vice and corruption and every kind of intellectual depravity are the result of culture, just as all the filth that is draining into our Baths is the result of the tanneries up at Mölledal! (*Uproar and interruptions.* DR. STOCK-MANN *is undisturbed, and goes on, carried away by his ardor, with a smile.*) And yet this same "People's Messenger" can go on preaching that the masses ought to be elevated to higher conditions of life! But, bless my soul, if the "Messenger's" teaching is to be depended upon, this very raising up the masses would mean nothing more, nor less than setting them straightway upon the paths of depravity! Happily, the theory that culture demoralizes is only an old falsehood that our forefathers believed in and we have inherited. No, it is ignorance, poverty, ugly conditions of life that do the devil's work! In a house which does not get aired and swept every day—my wife Katherine maintains that the floor ought to be scrubbed as well, but that is a debatable question —in such a house, let me tell you, people will lose within two or three years the power of thinking or acting in a moral manner. Lack of oxygen weakens the conscience. And there must be a plentiful lack of oxygen in very many houses in this town. I should think, judging from the fact that the whole compact majority can be unconscientious enough to wish to build the town's prosperity on a quagmire of falsehood and deceit.

ASLAKSEN: We cannot allow such a grave accusation to be flung at a citizen community.

A CITIZEN: I move that the Chairman direct the speaker to sit down.

VOICES (*angrily*): Hear, hear! Quite right! Make him sit down!

DR. STOCKMANN (*losing his self-control*): Then I will go and shout the truth at every street corner! I will write it in other towns' newspapers! The whole country shall know what is going on here!

HOVSTAD: It almost seems as if Dr. Stockmann's intention were to ruin the town.

DR. STOCKMANN: Yes, my native town is so dear to me that I would rather ruin it than see it flourishing upon a lie.

ASLAKSEN: This is really serious.

[*Uproar and catcalls.* MRS. STOCKMANN *coughs, but to no purpose; her husband does not listen to her any longer.*]

HOVSTAD (*shouting above the din*): A man must be a public enemy to wish to ruin a whole community!

DR. STOCKMANN (*with growing fervor*): What does the destruction of a community matter, if it lives on lies! It ought to be razed to the ground, I tell you! All who live by lies ought to be exterminated like vermin! You will end by infecting the whole country; you will bring about such a state of things that the whole country will deserve to be ruined.

And if things come to that pass, I shall say from the bottom of my heart: "Let the whole country perish, let all these people be exterminated!"

VOICES FROM THE CROWD: That is talking like an out-and-out enemy of the people!

BILLING: There sounded the voice of the people, by all that's holy!

THE WHOLE CROWD (*shouting*): Yes, yes! He is an enemy of the people! He hates his country! He hates his own people!

ASLAKSEN: Both as a citizen and as an individual, I am profoundly disturbed by what we have had to listen to. Dr. Stockmann has shown himself in a light I should never have dreamed of. I am unhappily obliged to subscribe to the opinion which I have just heard my estimable fellow citizens utter; and I propose that we should give expression to that opinion in a resolution. I propose a resolution as follows: "This meeting declares that it considers Dr. Thomas Stockmann, Medical Officer of the Baths, to be an enemy of the people."

[*A storm of cheers and applause. A number of men surround the* DOCTOR *and hiss him.* MRS. STOCKMANN *and* PETRA *have got up from their seats.* MORTEN *and* EJLIF *are fighting the other schoolboys for hissing; some of their elders separate them.*]

DR. STOCKMANN (*to the men who are hissing him*): Oh, you fools! I tell you that——

ASLAKSEN (*ringing his bell*): We cannot hear you now, Doctor. A formal vote is about to be taken; but, out of regard for personal feelings, it shall be by ballot and not verbal. Have you any clean paper, Mr. Billing?

BILLING: I have both blue and white here.

ASLAKSEN (*going to him*): That will do nicely; we shall get on more quickly that way. Cut it up into small strips—yes, that's it. (*To the meeting*) Blue means no; white means yes. I will come round myself and collect votes.

[PETER STOCKMANN *leaves the hall.* ASLAKSEN *and one or two others go round the room with the slips of paper in their hats.*]

FIRST CITIZEN (*to* HOVSTAD): I say, what has come to the Doctor? What are we to think of it?

HOVSTAD: Oh, you know how headstrong he is.

SECOND CITIZEN (*to* BILLING): Billing, you go to their house—have you ever noticed if the fellow drinks?

BILLING: Well, I'm hanged if I know what to say. There are always spirits on the table when you go.

THIRD CITIZEN: I rather think he goes quite off his head sometimes.

FIRST CITIZEN: I wonder if there is any madness in his family?

BILLING: I shouldn't wonder if there were.

FOURTH CITIZEN: No, it is nothing more than sheer malice; he wants to get even with somebody for something or other.

BILLING: Well certainly he suggested a rise in his salary on one occasion lately, and did not get it.

THE CITIZENS (*together*): Ah!—then it is easy to understand how it is!

THE DRUNKEN MAN (*who has got among the audience again*): I want a blue one, I do! And I want a white one too!

VOICES: It's that drunken chap again! Turn him out!

MORTEN KIIL (*going up to* DR. STOCKMANN): Well, Stockmann, do you see what these monkey tricks of yours lead to?

DR. STOCKMANN: I have done my duty.

MORTEN KIIL: What was that you said about the tanneries at Mölledal?

DR. STOCKMANN: You heard well enough. I said they were the source of all the filth.

MORTEN KIIL: My tannery too?

DR. STOCKMANN: Unfortunately, your tannery is by far the worst.

MORTEN KIIL: Are you going to put that in the papers?

DR. STOCKMANN: I shall conceal nothing.

MORTEN KIIL: That may cost you dear, Stockmann.

[*Goes out.*]

A STOUT MAN (*going up to* CAPTAIN HORSTER, *without taking any notice of the ladies*): Well, Captain, so you lend your house to enemies of the people?

HORSTER: I imagine I can do what I like with my own possessions, Mr. Vik.

THE STOUT MAN: Then you can have no objection to my doing the same with mine.

HORSTER: What do you mean, sir?

THE STOUT MAN: You shall hear from me in the morning.

[*Turns his back on him and moves off.*]

PETRA: Was that not your owner, Captain Horster?

HORSTER: Yes, that was Mr. Vik, the ship owner.

ASLAKSEN (*with the voting papers in his hands, gets up on to the platform and rings his bell*): Gentlemen, allow me to announce the result. By the votes of everyone here except one person——

A YOUNG MAN: That is the drunk chap!

ASLAKSEN: By the votes of everyone here except a tipsy man, this meeting of citizens declares Dr. Thomas Stockmann to be an enemy of the people. (*Shouts and applause.*) Three cheers for our ancient and honorable citizen community! (*Renewed applause.*) Three cheers for our able and energetic Mayor, who has so loyally suppressed the promptings of family feeling! (*Cheers.*) The meeting is dissolved.

[*Gets down.*]

BILLING: Three cheers for the Chairman!

THE WHOLE CROWD: Three cheers for Aslaksen! Hurrah!

DR. STOCKMANN: My hat and coat, Petra! Captain, have you room on your ship for passengers to the New World?

HORSTER: For you and yours we will make room, Doctor .

DR. STOCKMANN (*as* PETRA *helps him into his coat*): Good. Come, Katherine! Come, boys!

MRS. STOCKMANN (*in an undertone*): Thomas, dear, let us go out by the back way.

DR. STOCKMANN: No back ways for me, Katherine. (*Raising his voice.*) You will hear more of this enemy of the people, before he shakes the dust off his shoes upon you! I am not so forgiving as a certain Person; I do not say: "I forgive you, for ye know not what ye do."

ASLAKSEN (*shouting*): That is a blasphemous comparison, Dr. Stockmann!

BILLING: It is, by God! It's dreadful for an earnest man to listen to.

A COARSE VOICE: Threatens us now, does he?

OTHER VOICES (*excitedly*): Let's go and break his windows! Duck him in the fjord!

ANOTHER VOICE: Blow your horn, Evensen! Pip, pip!

[*Hornblowing, hisses, and wild cries.* DR. STOCKMANN *goes out through the hall with his family,* HORSTER *elbowing a way for them.*]

THE WHOLE CROWD (*howling after them as they go*): Enemy of the People! Enemy of the People!

BILLING (*as he puts his papers together*): Well, I'm damned if I go and drink toddy with the Stockmanns tonight!

[*The crowd press toward the exit. The uproar continues outside; shouts of* "Enemy of the People!" *are heard from without.*]

CURTAIN

ACT FIVE

SCENE: DR. STOCKMANN'S *study. Bookcases and cabinets containing specimens line the walls. At the back is a door leading to the hall; in the foreground on the left, a door leading to the sitting room. In the right-hand wall are two windows, of which all the panes are broken. The* DOCTOR'S *desk, littered with books and papers, stands in the middle of the room, which is in disorder. It is morning.* DR. STOCKMANN, *in dressing gown, slippers, and a smoking cap, is bending down and raking with an umbrella under one of the cabinets. After a little while he rakes out a stone.*

DR. STOCKMANN (*calling through the open sitting-room door*): Katherine, I have found another one.

MRS. STOCKMANN (*from the sitting room*): Oh, you will find a lot more yet, I expect.

DR. STOCKMANN (*adding the stone to a heap of others on the table*): I shall treasure these stones as relics. Ejlif and Morten shall look at them every day, and when they are grown up they shall inherit them as heirlooms. (*Rakes about under a bookcase.*) Hasn't—what the deuce is her name?—the girl, you know—hasn't she been to fetch the glazier yet?

MRS. STOCKMANN (*coming in*): Yes, but he said he didn't know if he would be able to come today.

DR. STOCKMANN: You will see he won't dare to come.

MRS. STOCKMANN: Well, that is just what Randine thought—that he didn't dare to, on account of the neighbors. (*Calls into the sitting room.*) What is it you want, Randine? Give it to me. (*Goes in and comes out again directly.*) Here is a letter for you, Thomas.

DR. STOCKMANN: Let me see it. (*Opens and reads it.*) Ah!—of course.

MRS. STOCKMANN: Who is it from?

DR. STOCKMANN: From the landlord. Notice to quit.

MRS. STOCKMANN: Is it possible? Such a nice man——

DR. STOCKMANN (*looking at the letter*): Does not dare do otherwise, he says. Doesn't like doing it, but dare not do otherwise—on account of his fellow citizens—out of regard for public opinion. Is in a dependent position—dare not offend certain influential men——

MRS. STOCKMANN: There, you see, Thomas!

DR. STOCKMANN: Yes, yes, I see well enough; the whole lot of them in the town are cowards; not a man among them dares do anything for fear of the others. (*Throws the letter onto the table.*) But it doesn't matter to us, Katherine. We are going to sail away to the New World, and——

MRS. STOCKMANN: But, Thomas, are you sure we are well advised to take this step?

DR. STOCKMANN: Are you suggesting that I should stay here, where they have pilloried me as an enemy of the people—branded me—broken my windows! And just look here, Katherine—they have torn a great rent in my black trousers, too!

MRS. STOCKMANN: Oh, dear!—and they are the best pair you have got!

DR. STOCKMANN: You should never wear your best trousers when you go out to fight for freedom and truth. It is not that I care so much about the trousers, you know; you can always sew them up again for me. But that the common herd should dare to make this attack on me, as if they were my equals—that is what I cannot, for the life of me, swallow!

MRS. STOCKMANN: There is no doubt they have behaved very ill to you, Thomas; but is that sufficient reason for our leaving our native country for good and all?

DR. STOCKMANN: If we went to another town, do you suppose we should not find the common people just as insolent as they are here? Depend upon it, there is not much to choose between them. Oh, well, let the curs snap—that is not the worst part of it. The worst is that, from one end of this country to the other, every man is the slave of his Party. Although, as far as that goes, I daresay it is not much better in the free West either; the compact majority, and liberal public opinion, and all that infernal old bag of tricks are probably rampant there too. But there things are done on a larger scale, you see. They may kill you, but they won't put you to death by slow torture. They don't squeeze a free man's soul in a vise, as they do here. And, if need be, one can live in solitude. (*Walks up and down.*) If only I knew where there was a virgin forest or a small South Sea island for sale, cheap——

MRS. STOCKMANN: But think of the boys, Thomas.

DR. STOCKMANN (*standing still*): What a strange woman you are, Katherine! Would you prefer to have the boys grow up in a society like this? You saw for yourself last night that half the population are out of their minds; and if the other half have not lost their senses, it is because they are mere brutes, with no sense to lose.

MRS. STOCKMANN: But, Thomas dear, the imprudent things you said had something to do with it, you know.

DR. STOCKMANN: Well, isn't what I said perfectly true? Don't they turn every idea topsy-turvy? Don't they make a regular hotchpotch of right and wrong? Don't they say that the things I know are true are lies? The craziest part of it all is the fact of these "liberals," men of full age, going about in crowds imagining that they are the broad-minded party! Did you ever hear anything like it, Katherine?

MRS. STOCKMANN: Yes, yes, it's mad enough of them, certainly; but——
(PETRA *comes in from the sitting room.*) Back from school already?

PETRA: Yes. I have been given notice of dismissal.

MRS. STOCKMANN: Dismissal?

DR. STOCKMANN: You too?

PETRA: Mrs. Busk gave me my notice; so I thought it was best to go at once.

DR. STOCKMANN: You were perfectly right, too!

MRS. STOCKMANN: Who would have thought Mrs. Busk was a woman like that?

PETRA: Mrs. Busk isn't a bit like that, Mother; I saw quite plainly how it hurt her to do it. But she didn't dare do otherwise, she said; and so I got my notice.

DR. STOCKMANN (*laughing and rubbing his hands*): She didn't dare do otherwise, either! It's delicious!

MRS. STOCKMANN: Well, after the dreadful scenes last night——

PETRA: It was not only that. Just listen to this, Father!

DR. STOCKMANN: Well?

PETRA: Mrs. Busk showed me no less than three letters she received this morning——

DR. STOCKMANN: Anonymous, I suppose?

PETRA: Yes.

DR. STOCKMANN: Yes, because they didn't dare to risk signing their names, Katherine!

PETRA: And two of them were to the effect that a man, who has been our guest here, was declaring last night at the Club that my views on various subjects are extremely emancipated——

DR. STOCKMANN: You did not deny that, I hope?

PETRA: No, you know I wouldn't. Mrs. Busk's own views are tolerably emancipated, when we are alone together; but now that this report about me is being spread, she dare not keep me on any longer.

MRS. STOCKMANN: And someone who had been a guest of ours! That shows you the return you get for your hospitality, Thomas!

DR. STOCKMANN: We won't live in such a disgusting hole any longer. Pack up as quickly as you can, Katherine; the sooner we can get away the better.

MRS. STOCKMANN: Be quiet—I think I hear someone in the hall. See who it is, Petra.

PETRA (*opening the door*): Oh, it's you, Captain Horster! Do come in.

HORSTER (*coming in*): Good morning. I thought I would just come in and see how you were.

DR. STOCKMANN (*shaking his hand*): Thanks—that is really kind of you.

MRS. STOCKMANN: And thank you, too, for helping us through the crowd, Captain Horster.

PETRA: How did you manage to get home again?

HORSTER: Oh, somehow or other. I am fairly strong, and there is more sound than fury about these folk.

DR. STOCKMANN: Yes, isn't their swinish cowardice astonishing? Look here, I will show you something! There are all the stones they have thrown through my windows. Just look at them! I'm hanged if there are more than two decently large bits of hardstone in the whole heap; the rest are nothing but gravel—wretched little things. And yet they stood out there bawling and swearing that they would do me some violence; but as for *doing* anything—you don't see much of that in this town.

HORSTER: Just as well for you this time, Doctor!

DR. STOCKMANN: True enough. But it makes one angry all the same; because if someday it should be a question of a national fight in real earnest, you will see that public opinion will be in favor of taking to one's heels, and the compact majority will turn tail like a flock of sheep, Captain Horster. That is what is so mournful to think of; it gives me so much concern, that—— No, devil take it, it is ridiculous to care about it! They have called me an enemy of the people, so an enemy of the people let me be!

MRS. STOCKMANN: You will never be that, Thomas.

DR. STOCKMANN: Don't swear to that, Katherine. To be called an ugly name may have the same effect as a pin scratch in the lung. And that hateful name—I can't get quit of it. It is sticking here in the pit of my stomach, eating into me like a corrosive acid. And no magnesia will remove it.

PETRA: Bah!—you should only laugh at them, Father.

HORSTER: They will change their minds someday, Doctor.

MRS. STOCKMANN: Yes, Thomas, as sure as you are standing here.

DR. STOCKMANN: Perhaps, when it is too late. Much good may it do them! They may wallow in their filth then and rue the day when they drove a patriot into exile. When do you sail, Captain Horster?

HORSTER: Hm!—that was just what I had come to speak about——

DR. STOCKMANN: Why, has anything gone wrong with the ship?

HORSTER: No; but what has happened is that I am not to sail in it.

PETRA: Do you mean that you have been dismissed from your command?

HORSTER (*smiling*): Yes, that's just it.

PETRA: You too.

MRS. STOCKMANN: There, you see, Thomas!

DR. STOCKMANN: And that for the truth's sake! Oh, if I had thought such a thing possible——

HORSTER: You mustn't take it to heart; I shall be sure to find a job with some ship owner or other, elsewhere.

DR. STOCKMANN: And that is this man Vik—a wealthy man, independent of everyone and everything! Shame on him!

HORSTER: He is quite an excellent fellow otherwise; he told me himself he would willingly have kept me on, if only he had dared——

DR. STOCKMANN: But he didn't dare? No, of course not.

HORSTER: It is not such an easy matter, he said, for a party man——

DR. STOCKMANN: The worthy man spoke the truth. A party is like a sausage machine; it mashes up all sorts of heads together into the same mincemeat—fatheads and blockheads, all in one mash!

MRS. STOCKMANN: Come, come, Thomas dear!

PETRA (*to* HORSTER): If only you had not come home with us, things might not have come to this pass.

HORSTER: I do not regret it.

PETRA (*holding out her hand to him*): Thank you for that!

HORSTER (*to* DR. STOCKMANN): And so what I came to say was that if you are determined to go away, I have thought of another plan——

DR. STOCKMANN: That's splendid!—if only we can get away at once.

MRS. STOCKMANN: Hush!—wasn't that someone knocking?

PETRA: That is Uncle, surely.

DR. STOCKMANN: Aha! (*Calls out.*) Come in!

MRS. STOCKMANN: Dear Thomas, promise me definitely——

[PETER STOCKMANN *comes in from the hall.*]

PETER STOCKMANN: Oh, you are engaged. In that case, I will——

DR. STOCKMANN: No, no, come in.

PETER STOCKMANN: But I wanted to speak to you alone.

MRS. STOCKMANN: We will go into the sitting room in the meanwhile.

HORSTER: And I will look in again later.

DR. STOCKMANN: No, go in there with them, Captain Horster; I want to hear more about——

HORSTER: Very well, I will wait, then.

[*He follows* MRS. STOCKMANN *and* PETRA *into the sitting room.*]

DR. STOCKMANN: I daresay you find it rather drafty here today. Put your hat on.

PETER STOCKMANN: Thank you, if I may. (*Does so.*) I think I caught cold last night; I stood and shivered——

DR. STOCKMANN: Really? I found it warm enough.

PETER STOCKMANN: I regret that it was not in my power to prevent those excesses last night.

DR. STOCKMANN: Have you anything particular to say to me besides that?

PETER STOCKMANN: (*taking a big letter from his pocket*): I have this document for you, from the Baths Committee.

DR. STOCKMANN: My dismissal?

PETER STOCKMANN: Yes, dating from today. (*Lays the letter on the table.*) It gives us pain to do it; but, to speak frankly, we dared not do otherwise on account of public opinion.

DR. STOCKMANN (*smiling*): Dared not? I seem to have heard that word before, today.

PETER STOCKMANN: I must beg you to understand your position clearly. For the future you must not count on any practice whatever in the town.

DR. STOCKMANN: Devil take the practice! But why are you so sure of that?

PETER STOCKMANN: The Householders' Association is circulating a list from house to house. All right-minded citizens are being called upon to give up employing you; and I can assure you that not a single head of a family will risk refusing his signature. They simply dare not.

DR. STOCKMANN: No, no; I don't doubt it. But what then?

PETER STOCKMANN: If I might advise you, it would be best to leave the place for a little while——

DR. STOCKMANN: Yes, the propriety of leaving the place *has* occurred to me.

PETER STOCKMANN: Good. And then, when you have had six months to think things over, if, after mature consideration, you can persuade yourself to write a few words of regret, acknowledging your error——

DR. STOCKMANN: I might have my appointment restored to me, do you mean?

PETER STOCKMANN: Perhaps. It is not at all impossible.

DR. STOCKMANN: But what about public opinion, then? Surely you would not dare to do it on account of public feeling.

PETER STOCKMANN: Public opinion is an extremely mutable thing. And, to be quite candid with you, it is a matter of great importance to us to have some admission of that sort from you in writing.

DR. STOCKMANN: Oh, that's what you are after, is it? I will just trouble you to remember what I said to you lately about foxy tricks of that sort!

PETER STOCKMANN: Your position was quite different then. At that time you had reason to suppose you had the whole town at your back——

DR. STOCKMANN: Yes, and now I feel I have the whole town *on* my back ——(*flaring up*)——I would not do it if I had the devil and his dam on my back——! Never—never, I tell you!

PETER STOCKMANN: A man with a family has no right to behave as you do. You have no right to do it, Thomas.

DR. STOCKMANN: I have no right! There is only one single thing in the world a free man has no right to do. Do you know what that is?

PETER STOCKMANN: No.

DR. STOCKMANN: Of course you don't, but I will tell you. A free man has no right to soil himself with filth; he has no right to behave in a way that would justify his spitting in his own face.

PETER STOCKMANN: This sort of thing sounds extremely plausible, of course; and if there were no other explanation for your obstinacy—— But as it happens there is.

DR. STOCKMANN: What do you mean?

PETER STOCKMANN: You understand very well what I mean. But, as your brother and as a man of discretion, I advise you not to build too much upon expectations and prospects that may so very easily fail you.

DR. STOCKMANN: What in the world is all this about?

PETER STOCKMANN: Do you really ask me to believe that you are ignorant of the terms of Mr. Kiil's will?

DR. STOCKMANN: I know that the small amount he possesses is to go to an institution for indigent old workpeople. How does that concern me?

PETER STOCKMANN: In the first place, it is by no means a small amount that is in question. Mr. Kiil is a fairly wealthy man.

DR. STOCKMANN: I had no notion of that!

PETER STOCKMANN: Hm!—hadn't you really? Then I suppose you had no notion, either, that a considerable portion of his wealth will come to your children, you and your wife having a life income from the capital. Has he never told you so?

DR. STOCKMANN: Never, on my honor! Quite the reverse; he has consistently done nothing but fume at being so unconscionably heavily taxed. But are you perfectly certain of this, Peter?

PETER STOCKMANN: I have it from an absolutely reliable source.

DR. STOCKMANN: Then, thank God, Katherine is provided for—and the children too! I must tell her this at once——(*calls out*)——Katherine, Katherine!

PETER STOCKMANN (*restraining him*): Hush, don't say a word yet!

MRS. STOCKMANN (*opening the door*): What is the matter?

DR. STOCKMANN: Oh, nothing, nothing; you can go back. (*She shuts the door.* DR. STOCKMANN *walks up and down in his excitement.*) Provided for!——Just think of it, we are all provided for! And for life! What a blessed feeling it is to know one is provided for!

PETER STOCKMANN: Yes, but that is just exactly what you are not. Mr. Kiil can alter his will any day he likes.

DR. STOCKMANN: But he won't do that, my dear Peter. The "Badger" is much too delighted at my attack on you and your wise friends.

PETER STOCKMANN (*starts and looks intently at him*): Ah, that throws a light on various things.

DR. STOCKMANN: What things?

PETER STOCKMANN: I see that the whole thing was a combined maneuver on your part and his. These violent, reckless attacks that you have made against the leading men of the town, under the pretense that it was in the name of truth——

DR. STOCKMANN: What about them?

PETER STOCKMANN: I see that they were nothing else than the stipulated price for that vindictive old man's will.

DR. STOCKMANN (*almost speechless*): Peter—you are the most disgusting plebeian I have ever met in all my life.

PETER STOCKMANN: All is over between us. Your dismissal is irrevocable —we have a weapon against you now.

[*Goes out.*]

DR. STOCKMANN: For shame! For shame! (*Calls out.*) Katherine, you must have the floor scrubbed after him! Let—what's her name—devil take it, the girl who has always got soot on her nose——

MRS. STOCKMANN (*in the sitting room*): Hush, Thomas, be quiet!

PETRA (*coming to the door*): Father, grandfather is here, asking if he may speak to you alone.

DR. STOCKMANN: Certainly he may. (*Goes to the door.*) Come in, Mr. Kiil. (MORTEN KIIL *comes in.* DR. STOCKMANN *shuts the door after him.*) What can I do for you? Won't you sit down?

MORTEN KIIL: I won't sit. (*Looks around.*) You look very comfortable here today, Thomas.

DR. STOCKMANN: Yes, don't we?

MORTEN KIIL: Very comfortable—plenty of fresh air. I should think you have got enough today of that oxygen you were talking about yesterday. Your conscience must be in splendid order today, I should think.

DR. STOCKMANN: It is.

MORTEN KIIL: So I should think. (*Taps his chest.*) Do you know what I have got here?

DR. STOCKMANN: A good conscience, too, I hope.

MORTEN KIIL: Bah!—No, it is something better than that.

[*He takes a thick pocketbook from his breast pocket, opens it, and displays a packet of papers.*]

DR. STOCKMANN (*looking at him in astonishment*): Shares in the Baths?

MORTEN KIIL: They were not difficult to get today.

DR. STOCKMANN: And you have been buying——?

MORTEN KIIL: As many as I could pay for.

DR. STOCKMANN: But, my dear Mr. Kiil—consider the state of the Baths' affairs!

MORTEN KIIL: If you behave like a reasonable man, you can soon set the Baths on their feet again.

DR. STOCKMANN: Well, you can see for yourself that I have done all I can, but—— They are all mad in this town!

MORTEN KIIL: You said yesterday that the worst of this pollution came from my tannery. If that is true, then my grandfather and my father before me, and I myself, for many years past, have been poisoning the town like three destroying angels. Do you think I am going to sit quiet under that reproach?

DR. STOCKMANN: Unfortunately, I am afraid you will have to.

MORTEN KIIL: No, thank you. I am jealous of my name and reputation. They call me "the Badger," I am told. A badger is a kind of pig, I believe; but I am not going to give them the right to call me that. I mean to live and die a clean man.

DR. STOCKMANN: And how are you going to set about it?

MORTEN KIIL: You shall cleanse me, Thomas.

DR. STOCKMANN: I!

MORTEN KIIL: Do you know what money I have bought these shares with? No, of course you can't know—but I will tell you. It is the money that Katherine and Petra and the boys will have when I am gone. Because I have been able to save a little bit after all, you know.

DR. STOCKMANN (*flaring up*): And you have gone and taken Katherine's money for *this!*

MORTEN KIIL: Yes, the whole of the money is invested in the Baths now. And now I just want to see whether you are quite stark, staring mad, Thomas! If you still make out that these animals and other nasty things of that sort come from my tannery, it will be exactly as if you were to flay broad strips of skin from Katherine's body, and Petra's, and the boys'; and no decent man would do that—unless he were mad.

DR. STOCKMANN (*walking up and down*): Yes, but I *am* mad; I *am* mad!

MORTEN KIIL: You cannot be so absurdly mad as all that, when it is a question of your wife and children.

DR. STOCKMANN (*standing still in front of him*): Why couldn't you consult me about it, before you went and bought all that trash?

MORTEN KIIL: What is done cannot be undone.

DR. STOCKMANN (*walks about uneasily*): If only I were not so certain about it——! But I am absolutely convinced that I am right.

MORTEN KIIL (*weighing the pocketbook in his hand*): If you stick to your mad idea, this won't be worth much, you know.
[*Puts the pocketbook in his pocket.*]

DR. STOCKMANN: But, hang it all! it might be possible for science to discover some prophylactic, I should think—or some antidote of some kind——

MORTEN KIIL: To kill these animals, do you mean?

DR. STOCKMANN: Yes, or to make them innocuous.

MORTEN KIIL: Couldn't you try some ratsbane?

DR. STOCKMANN: Don't talk nonsense! They all say it is only imagination, you know. Well, let it go at that! Let them have their own way about it! Haven't the ignorant, narrow-minded curs reviled me as an enemy of the people?—and haven't they been ready to tear the clothes off my back, too?

MORTEN KIIL: And broken all your windows to pieces!

DR. STOCKMANN: And then there is my duty to my family. I must talk it over with Katherine; she is great on those things.

MORTEN KIIL: That is right; be guided by a reasonable woman's advice.

DR. STOCKMANN (*advancing toward him*): To think you could do such a preposterous thing! Risking Katherine's money in this way, and putting me in such a horribly painful dilemma! When I look at you, I think I see the devil himself——

MORTEN KIIL: Then I had better go. But I must have an answer from you before two o'clock—yes or no. If it is no, the shares go to a charity, and that this very day.

DR. STOCKMANN: And what does Katherine get?

MORTEN KIIL: Not a halfpenny. (*The door leading to the hall opens, and* HOVSTAD *and* ASLAKSEN *make their appearance.*) Look at those two!

DR. STOCKMANN (*staring at them*): What the devil!—have *you* actually the face to come into my house?

HOVSTAD: Certainly.

ASLAKSEN: We have something to say to you, you see.

MORTEN KIIL (*in a whisper*): Yes or no—before two o'clock.

ASLAKSEN (*glancing at* HOVSTAD): Aha!

[MORTEN KIIL *goes out.*]

DR. STOCKMANN: Well, what do you want with me? Be brief.

HOVSTAD: I can quite understand that you are annoyed with us for our attitude at the meeting yesterday——

DR. STOCKMANN: Attitude, do you call it? Yes, it was a charming attitude! I call it weak, womanish—damnably shameful!

HOVSTAD: Call it what you like; we could not do otherwise.

DR. STOCKMANN: You *dared* not do otherwise—isn't that it?

HOVSTAD: Well, if you like to put it that way.

ASLAKSEN: But why did you not let us have word of it beforehand?— just a hint to Mr. Hovstad or to me?

DR. STOCKMANN: A hint? Of what?

ASLAKSEN: Of what was behind it all.

DR. STOCKMANN: I don't understand you in the least.

ASLAKSEN (*with a confidential nod*): Oh, yes, you do, Dr. Stockmann.

HOVSTAD: It is no good making a mystery of it any longer.

DR. STOCKMANN (*looking first at one of them and then at the other*): What the devil do you both mean?

ASLAKSEN: May I ask if your father-in-law is not going round the town buying up all the shares in the Baths?

DR. STOCKMANN: Yes, he has been buying Baths' shares today; but——

ASLAKSEN: It would have been more prudent to get someone else to do it—someone less nearly related to you.

HOVSTAD: And you should not have let your name appear in the affair. There was no need for anyone to know that the attack on the Baths came from you. You ought to have consulted me, Dr. Stockmann.

DR. STOCKMANN (*looks in front of him; then a light seems to dawn on him and he says in amazement*): Are such things conceivable? Are such things possible?

ASLAKSEN (*with a smile*): Evidently they are. But it is better to use a little finesse, you know.

HOVSTAD: And it is much better to have several persons in a thing of that sort, because the responsibility of each individual is lessened, when there are others with him.

DR. STOCKMANN (*composedly*): Come to the point, gentlemen. What do you want?

ASLAKSEN: Perhaps Mr. Hovstad had better——

HOVSTAD: No, you tell him, Aslaksen.

ASLAKSEN: Well, the fact is that, now we know the bearings of the whole affair, we think we might venture to put the "People's Messenger" at your disposal.

DR. STOCKMANN: Do you dare do that now? What about public opinion? Are you not afraid of a storm breaking upon our heads?

HOVSTAD: We will try to weather it.

ASLAKSEN: And you must be ready to go off quickly on a new tack, Doctor. As soon as your invective has done its work——

DR. STOCKMANN: Do you mean, as soon as my father-in-law and I have got hold of the shares at a low figure?

HOVSTAD: Your reasons for wishing to get the control of the Baths are mainly scientific, I take it.

DR. STOCKMANN: Of course; it was for scientific reasons that I persuaded the old "Badger" to stand in with me in the matter. So we will tinker at the conduit pipes a little, and dig up a little bit of the shore, and it shan't cost the town a sixpence. That will be all right—eh?

HOVSTAD: I think so—if you have the "People's Messenger" behind you.

ASLAKSEN: The Press is a power in a free community, Doctor.

DR. STOCKMANN: Quite so. And so is public opinion. And you, Mr. Aslaksen—I suppose you will be answerable for the Householders' Association?

ASLAKSEN: Yes, and for the Temperance Society. You may rely on that.

DR. STOCKMANN: But, gentlemen—I really am ashamed to ask the question—but, what return do you——?

HOVSTAD: We should prefer to help you without any return whatever, believe me. But the "People's Messenger" is in rather a shaky condition; it doesn't go really well; and I should be very unwilling to suspend the paper now, when there is so much work to do here in the political way.

DR. STOCKMANN: Quite so; that would be a great trial to such a friend of the people as you are. (*Flares up.*) But I am an enemy of the people, remember! (*Walks about the room.*) Where have I put my stick? Where the devil is my stick?

HOVSTAD: What's that?

ASLAKSEN: Surely you never mean——?

DR. STOCKMANN (*standing still*): And suppose I don't give you a single penny of all I get out of it? Money is not very easy to get out of us rich folk, please to remember!

HOVSTAD: And you please to remember that this affair of the shares can be represented in two ways!

DR. STOCKMANN: Yes, and you are just the man to do it. If I don't come to the rescue of the "People's Messenger," you will certainly take an evil view of the affair; you will hunt me down, I can well imagine—pursue me—try to throttle me as a dog does a hare.

HOVSTAD: It is a natural law; every animal must fight for its own livelihood.

ASLAKSEN: And get its food where it can, you know.

DR. STOCKMANN (*walking about the room*): Then you go and look for yours in the gutter, because I am going to show you which is the strongest animal of us three! (*Finds an umbrella and brandishes it above his head.*) Ah, now——!

HOVSTAD: You are surely not going to use violence!

ASLAKSEN: Take care what you are doing with that umbrella.

DR. STOCKMANN: Out of the window with you, Mr. Hovstad!

HOVSTAD (*edging to the door*): Are you quite mad?

DR. STOCKMANN: Out of the window, Mr. Aslaksen! Jump, I tell you! You will have to do it, sooner or later.

ASLAKSEN (*running round the writing table*): Moderation, Doctor—I am a delicate man—I can stand so little——(*calls out*)——Help, help!
   [MRS. STOCKMANN, PETRA, *and* HORSTER *come in from the sitting room.*]

MRS. STOCKMANN: Good gracious, Thomas! What is happening?

DR. STOCKMANN (*brandishing the umbrella*): Jump out, I tell you! Out into the gutter!

HOVSTAD: An assault on an unoffending man! I call you to witness, Captain Horster.

[*Hurries out through the hall.*]

ASLAKSEN (*irresolutely*): If only I knew the way about here——
　　　　　　[*Steals out through the sitting room.*]
MRS. STOCKMANN (*holding her husband back*): Control yourself, Thomas!
DR. STOCKMANN (*throwing down the umbrella*): Upon my soul, they
　　have escaped after all.
MRS. STOCKMANN: What did they want you to do?
DR. STOCKMANN: I will tell you later on; I have something else to think
　　about now. (*Goes to the table and writes something on a calling
　　card.*) Look there, Katherine; what is written there?
MRS. STOCKMANN: Three big No's; what does that mean?
DR. STOCKMANN: I will tell you that too, later on. (*Holds out the card to
　　PETRA.*) There, Petra; tell sooty-face to run over to the "Badger's"
　　with that, as quickly as she can. Hurry up!
　　　　　　[PETRA *takes the card and goes out to the hall.*]
DR. STOCKMANN: Well, I think I have had a visit from every one of the
　　devil's messengers today! But now I am going to sharpen my pen till they
　　can feel its point; I shall dip it in venom and gall; I shall hurl my
　　inkpot at their heads!
MRS. STOCKMANN: Yes, but we are going away, you know, Thomas.
　　　　　　[PETRA *comes back.*]
DR. STOCKMANN: Well?
PETRA: She has gone with it.
DR. STOCKMANN: Good!——Going away, did you say? No, I'll be hanged
　　if we are going away! We are going to stay where we are, Katherine!
PETRA: Stay here?
MRS. STOCKMANN: Here, in the town?
DR. STOCKMANN: Yes, here. This is the field of battle—this is where the
　　fight will be. This is where I shall triumph! As soon as I have had my
　　trousers sewn up I shall go out and look for another house. We must
　　have a roof over our heads for the winter.
HORSTER: That you shall have in my house.
DR. STOCKMANN: Can I?
HORSTER: Yes, quite well. I have plenty of room, and I am almost never
　　at home.
MRS. STOCKMANN: How good of you, Captain Horster!
PETRA: Thank you!
DR. STOCKMANN (*grasping his hand*): Thank you, thank you! That is one
　　trouble over! Now I can set to work in earnest at once. There is an
　　endless amount of things to look through here, Katherine! Luckily I
　　shall have all my time at my disposal, because I have been dismissed
　　from the Baths, you know.
MRS. STOCKMANN (*with a sigh*): Oh, yes, I expected that.

DR. STOCKMANN: And they want to take my practice away from me, too. Let them! I have got the poor people to fall back upon, anyway—those that don't pay anything; and, after all, they need me most, too. But, by Jove, they will have to listen to me; I shall preach to them in season and out of season, as it says somewhere.

MRS. STOCKMANN: But, dear Thomas, I should have thought events had shown you what use it is to preach.

DR. STOCKMANN: You are really ridiculous, Katherine. Do you want me to let myself be beaten off the field by public opinion and the compact majority and all that devilry? No, thank you! And what I want to do is so simple and clear and straightforward. I only want to drum into the heads of these curs the fact that the liberals are the most insidious enemies of freedom—that party programs strangle every young and vigorous truth—that considerations of expediency turn morality and justice upside down—and that they will end by making life here unbearable. Don't you think, Captain Horster, that I ought to be able to make people understand that?

HORSTER: Very likely; I don't know much about such things myself.

DR. STOCKMANN: Well, look here—I will explain! It is the party leaders that must be exterminated. A party leader is like a wolf, you see—like a voracious wolf. He requires a certain number of smaller victims to prey upon every year, if he is to live. Just look at Hovstad and Aslaksen! How many smaller victims have they not put an end to—or at any rate maimed and mangled until they are fit for nothing except to be householders or subscribers to the "People's Messenger"! (*Sits down on the edge of the table.*) Come here, Katherine—look how beautifully the sun shines today! And this lovely spring air I am drinking in!

MRS. STOCKMANN: Yes, if only we could live on sunshine and spring air, Thomas.

DR. STOCKMANN: Oh, you will have to pinch and save a bit—then we shall get along. That gives me very little concern. What is much worse is that I know of no one who is liberal-minded and high-minded enough to venture to take up my work after me.

PETRA: Don't think about that, Father; you have plenty of time before you.——Hullo, here are the boys already!

[EJLIF *and* MORTEN *come in from the sitting room.*]

MRS. STOCKMANN: Have you got a holiday?

MORTEN: No; but we were fighting with the other boys between lessons——

EJLIF: That isn't true; it was the other boys were fighting with us.

MORTEN: Mr. Rörlund said we had better stay at home for a day or two.

DR. STOCKMANN (*snapping his fingers and getting up from the table*): I have it! I have it, by Jove! You shall never set foot in the school again!

THE BOYS: No more school!

MRS. STOCKMANN: But, Thomas——

DR. STOCKMANN: Never, I say. I will educate you myself; that is to say, you shan't learn a blessed thing——

MORTEN: Hooray!

DR. STOCKMANN: ——but I will make liberal-minded and high-minded men of you. You must help me with that, Petra.

PETRA: Yes, Father, you may be sure I will.

DR. STOCKMANN: And my school shall be in the room where they insulted me and called me an enemy of the people. But we are too few as we are; I must have at least twelve boys to begin with.

MRS. STOCKMANN: You will certainly never get them in this town.

DR. STOCKMANN: We shall. (*To the boys*) Don't you know any street urchins—regular ragamuffins?

MORTEN: Yes, Father, I know lots!

DR. STOCKMANN: That's capital! Bring me some specimens of them. I am going to experiment with curs, just for once; there may be some exceptional heads among them.

MORTEN: And what are we going to do, when you have made liberal-minded and high-minded men of us?

DR. STOCKMANN: Then you shall drive all the wolves out of the country, my boys!

[EJLIF *looks rather doubtful about it;* MORTEN *jumps about crying* "Hurrah!"]

MRS. STOCKMANN: Let us hope it won't be the wolves that will drive you out of the country, Thomas.

DR. STOCKMANN: Are you out of your mind, Katherine? Drive me out! Now—when I am the strongest man in the town!

MRS. STOCKMANN: The strongest—now?

DR. STOCKMANN: Yes, and I will go so far as to say that now I am the strongest man in the whole world.

MORTEN: I say!

DR. STOCKMANN (*lowering his voice*): Hush! You mustn't say anything about it yet, but I have made a great discovery.

MRS. STOCKMANN: Another one?

DR. STOCKMANN: Yes. (*Gathers them round him, and says confidentially:*) It is this, let me tell you—that the strongest man in the world is he who stands most alone.

MRS. STOCKMANN (*smiling and shaking her head*): Oh, Thomas, Thomas!

PETRA (*encouragingly, as she grasps her father's hands*): Father!

CURTAIN

Youth, Beautiful Youth

HERMANN HESSE

EVEN my Uncle Matthäus was pleased, after his fashion, to see me again. When a young man who has been in foreign parts for several years comes back home one day and turns out to have done rather well for himself, even the coolest relations will smile and gladly shake his hand.

The small brown suitcase in which I was carrying my worldly goods was still brand-new, with a sound lock and gleaming straps. It contained two clean suits, plenty of underwear, a new pair of boots, a number of books and photographs, two handsome pipes, and a small pistol. In addition I had with me my violin case and a knapsack full of trifles, two hats, a cane and an umbrella, a light coat, and a pair of overshoes. All these things were stout and new, and moreover, sewed into my breast pocket, I had more than two hundred marks in savings and a letter promising me a good position abroad for the coming autumn. It all made quite a respectable outfit. And now, with my journeyman's years behind me, I was returning with all this equipment. I came back a man of the world to my home town, which I had left as a diffident problem child.

With creeping caution the train descended the hill in great winding curves, and with each turn the houses, streets, river, and gardens of the town below came closer and grew more distinct. Soon I could distinguish the roofs and pick out the familiar ones; soon, too, I could count the windows and recognize the stork nests. And while childhood and boyhood and a thousand precious memories of home were wafted toward me out of the valley, my sense of arrogant triumph at the homecoming slowly melted away. My desire to make a big impression upon all those people down there

125

yielded to a feeling of grateful astonishment. Homesickness, which in the course of the years had ceased to trouble me, assailed me powerfully in this last quarter-hour. Every clump of broom near the station platform and every familiar garden fence became strangely precious to me, and I asked each to forgive me for having been able to forget it and get along without it for so long.

When the train passed above our garden, I saw someone standing at the topmost window of the old house and waving a large towel. That must have been my father. And on the veranda my mother and the maid were standing, also waving, and from the top chimney faint blue smoke from the fire for the coffee flowed up into the warm air and out over the little town. All this now belonged to me again; it had all waited for me and was now welcoming me.

At the station the bearded old platform attendant ran about just as excited as he had always been, herding people away from the tracks, and among the people I saw my sister and my younger brother looking for me expectantly. For my baggage, my brother had brought along the little express wagon that had been our pride all through our boyhood. On it we placed my suitcase and knapsack. Fritz pulled and I followed along behind with my sister. She reproved me for wearing my hair so short now, but thought my mustache handsome and my new suitcase very elegant. We laughed and looked into each other's eyes, and from time to time clasped hands again and nodded to Fritz, who went on ahead with the little cart, but kept turning around to look at me. He was as tall as I and had filled out nicely. As he walked ahead of us, I suddenly remembered that when we had been boys I had sometimes hit him in the course of quarrels. I saw again his child's face and his offended or sorrowful eyes, and I felt something of the same painful penitence I had always felt in those days as soon as my anger had ebbed away. Now Fritz strode along, tall and grown up, and already with blond down around his chin.

We went down the avenue of cherry and rowan trees and passed the upper footbridge, a new store, and many old, unchanged houses. Then came the corner by the bridge, and there as always stood my father's house, with open windows, through which I could hear our parrot chortling, and my heart pounded for joy and for all the memories. I went through the cool, dark stone gateway and down the wide stone walk and hurried up the stairs. My father came down them to meet me. He kissed me, smiled, and patted me on the back. Then he led me silently by the hand to the upper door of the vestibule, where my mother was waiting and took me in her arms.

Then the maid, Christine, came running up and shook hands with me, and I went on into the living room, where the coffee stood ready, and greeted Polly, the parrot. He recognized me at once, climbed from the edge of his cage roof onto my finger, and lowered his beautiful gray head for me to stroke. The room was freshly papered, but otherwise everything remained the same—from the portraits of grandparents and the china closet to the tall clock with its old-fashioned decorations of lilacs. The cups stood ready on the set table, and in my cup was a small bunch of mignonette, which I took out and stuck in my lapel.

Opposite me sat my mother, looking at me and putting soft rolls on my plate. She admonished me not to talk so much that I should forget to eat, and then she herself asked me one question after another that I had to answer. Father listened in silence, stroked his beard, which had turned gray, and looked at me through his glasses with an air of kind scrutiny. And as I reported my experiences, acts, and successes—without being excessively modest—I could not help feeling that I must thank these two for the best of all.

This first day I wanted to see nothing but my dear old home; there would be time enough tomorrow and later on for everything else. And so after the coffee we went through all the rooms, through kitchen, corridors, and bedchambers, and almost everything was just as it had been before. The few innovations I discovered already seemed old and obvious to the others, and they disputed over whether these changes had not already been made in my day.

In the small garden that lies on the slope of the hill between ivied walls, the afternoon sun fell upon neat paths and rough limestone edgings, upon the half-filled water barrel and the beautiful, vivid flower beds, so that everything seemed smiling. We sat down on the veranda in comfortable chairs. The sunlight flowed, muted, warm, and pale green, through the large transparent leaves of the syringa. A few bees that had lost their way buzzed about, heavy and intoxicated. In gratitude for my return Father bared his head and said the Lord's Prayer. We stood still with folded hands, and though the unusual solemnity dampened my spirits slightly, I nevertheless heard the old and sacred words with gladness, and I spoke the Amen gratefully.

Then Father went to his study, my brother and sister ran off, and the whole house became quiet. I sat alone at the table with my mother. This was the moment I had long been looking forward to, and also dreading. For though my homecoming was glad and welcome, my life in the past several years had not been entirely pure and innocent.

Now Mother looked at me with her beautiful warm eyes and read my face. Perhaps she was considering what to say and what to ask about. I sat in embarrassed silence, playing with my fingers. I was prepared for an examination that on the whole would not be altogether inglorious, but which in certain of its details was bound to make me feel abashed.

For a while she looked quietly into my eyes. Then she took my hand in her fine, small ones.

"Do you still pray a little sometimes?" she asked softly.

"Not any more of late," I had to say, and she gave me a slightly troubled look.

"You'll learn how again," she said then.

And I said: "Perhaps."

Then she was silent for a while, and at last asked: "But you do want to be an upright man, don't you?"

To that I could say yes. And now, instead of putting awkward questions to me, she stroked my hand and nodded to me in a manner that meant she trusted me, even though I made no confessional. And then she asked me about my clothes and laundry, for in the past two years I had taken care of myself and no longer sent things home to be laundered and repaired.

"Tomorrow we will look through everything together," she said after I made my report, and with that the interrogation was over.

Soon afterward my sister came out to the veranda and asked me to come into the house with her. In the parlor she sat down at the piano and took out the music we'd played long ago, which I had neither sung nor heard for so long, but had not forgotten. We sang songs of Schubert and Schumann, and then we set to singing German and foreign folksongs until it was time for supper. My sister set the table while I talked with the parrot, who was supposed to be a male in spite of his name, Polly. He could say a great many things; he mimicked our voices and our laughter and accorded each of us a special and precisely graduated degree of friendliness. He was most intimate with my father, who could do anything he wanted with him; then came my brother, then Mamma, then myself, and last of all my sister, of whom Polly was a little chary.

Polly was the only pet in our house, and was just like one of the children, having been with us for twenty years. He loved conversation, laughter, and music, but not in his immediate vicinity. When he was alone and heard people talking animatedly in the adjoining room, he listened sharply, joined in the conversation and laughed in his good-natured, ironic fashion. And sometimes when he sat alone and quite unobserved on his climbing bars, when everything was silent and the sun shone warmly into the room, he would begin in deep, contented tones to hail life and praise God. His song sounded like a flute; it was solemn, warm, and heartfelt, like the self-forgetful singing of a child at play.

After supper I spent half an hour watering the garden. When I came in again, wet and dirty, I heard from the walk a half-familiar girl's voice speaking inside the house. Quickly I wiped my hands on my handkerchief and entered. There, in a lavender dress and a big straw hat, sat a tall, beautiful girl. When she stood up, looked at me, and held out her hand, I recognized Helene Kurz, a friend of my sister's, with whom I had once upon a time been in love.

"So you still recognize me?" I said smugly.

"Lotte told me you'd come home," she said pleasantly. But I would have liked it better if she had simply said yes. She had grown tall and very pretty indeed. I could think of nothing else to say and went over to the flowers by the window, while she chatted with Mother and Lotte.

My eyes gazed out on the street and my fingers toyed with the geranium leaves, but my thoughts were elsewhere. I saw a slate-cold winter evening; I was ice-skating on the river between the high alder bushes, sweeping in timorous semicircles as I followed at a distance the figure of a girl who scarcely knew how to skate and was being guided by another girl.

Her voice, grown much fuller and deeper than it had been, now sounded familiar and yet almost unknown to me. She had become a young lady, and I felt not in the least her equal in age and station. Rather, it was as though I were still fifteen years old. When she left, I shook hands with her again, but made a needlessly low and ironic bow and said: "Good night, Miss Kurz."

"So she's back home again?" I asked afterward.

"Where else should she be?" Lotte wondered, and I preferred to drop the subject.

At ten o'clock sharp the house was locked up and my parents went to bed. As he kissed me good-night, my father laid his arm around my shoulders and said softly: "It's good to have you back home again. Are you glad, too?"

Everybody went to bed—the maid, too, had bid us good-night some time before—and after doors had opened and shut a few times, a profound nocturnal silence settled over the entire house.

Beforehand I had got myself a mug of beer and chilled it. I now set it on the table in my room, and as smoking was not permitted in the living rooms of our house, I filled a pipe now and lit it. My two windows looked out over the dark, quiet courtyard, from which stone steps led uphill to the garden. Up above I saw the pines silhouetted black against the sky, and above them the stars twinkling.

I stayed up for more than an hour, watching the moths flitting around my lamp, and slowly blowing my clouds of smoke toward the open windows. Long, silent processions of images passed through my mind, countless memories of home and boyhood days—a vast, silent host rising and glimmering and vanishing again like waves on the surface of a lake.

Next morning I put on my best suit as a token of respect for my native town and my many old acquaintances, and to make it quite clear that I had done well and not come home a poor devil. Above our narrow valley the summer sky was radiantly blue. A haze of dust rose from the white avenues. In front of the near-by post office stood the mail carriages from the forest villages, and in the street small children played with marbles and soft balls.

My first stroll took me over the old stone bridge, the oldest structure in the town. I contemplated the small Gothic chapel on the bridge, which in former days I had raced past hundreds of times. Then I leaned on the parapet and looked up and down the swift green river. The cozy old mill with the white wheel painted on its gable end had vanished, and in its place stood a large new brick building. But otherwise nothing was changed, and, as of old, innumerable geese and ducks swam about on the water and waddled on the banks.

On the other side of the bridge I encountered my first acquaintance, a schoolmate who had gone into the tanning trade. He was wearing a shiny orange-yellow leather apron. He gave me a groping, uncertain look but did not quite recognize me. Pleased, I nodded to him and strolled on, while he looked back after me and kept trying to recall.

At the window of his workshop I greeted the coppersmith with the marvelous white beard. Then I looked in on the turner, who let the belt of his lathe hum and offered me a pinch of snuff. Then came the market square with its big fountain and the quaint town-hall arcade. The bookseller's shop was there. And though the old fellow had long ago given me a bad character because of my ordering Heine's works, I dropped in and bought a pencil and a picture postcard. From here it had never been far to the school buildings, and so I took a look at the old barracks as I passed. At the gates I scented the familiar, nervous smell of schoolrooms, and scurried on with a sigh of relief to the church and the parsonage.

By the time I had drifted around a few more of the narrow streets and had been shaved at the barber's, it was ten o'clock, time to pay my visit to Uncle Matthäus. I went through the handsome courtyard into his fine house, dusted off my trousers in the cool passageway, and knocked on the door of the living quarters. Inside I found my aunt and her two daughters sewing. Uncle was already at his office. Everything in this house breathed a spirit of pure, old-fashioned industry, a bit austere and emphatically utilitarian, but also serene and reliable. It was a house of eternal sweeping, dusting, washing, sewing, knitting, and spinning, and nevertheless the daughters found time to make music, and do it very well. Both played the piano and sang, and if they did not know the more modern composers, they were all the more familiar with Handel, Bach, Haydn, and Mozart.

Aunt jumped up to greet me. Her daughters finished their stitches first and then shook hands with me. To my amazement, I was treated quite like a guest of honor and taken into the visitors' room. Moreover, Aunt Berta could not be dissuaded from offering me a glass of wine and assorted pastries. Then she sat down opposite me in one of the company chairs. The daughters stayed at their work in the other room.

This time I was partly subjected to the examination that my kind mother had spared me yesterday. But here too I was not required to embellish an unsatisfactory state of affairs in the telling. My aunt was passionately interested in the personalities of certain well-known preachers, and she questioned me at length about the churches and ministers in all the towns I had lived in. A few small embarrassments cropped up, but with good will we glossed over these and joined in lamenting the death some ten years before of a famous prelate whose sermons I might have been able to hear in Stuttgart if he had lived.

Then the conversation turned to my fortunes, experiences, and prospects, and we decided that I had had good luck and was well started.

"Who would have thought it six years ago?" she remarked.

"Was I really so badly off then?" I could not help asking.

"No, I wouldn't exactly say that. But still your parents were really worried then."

"So was I," I wanted to say, but on the whole she was right, and I did not want to revive the quarrels of the past.

"I guess that is true," I therefore said, and nodded soberly.

"I gather you have tried quite a number of trades."

"Yes, certainly, Aunt. And I regret none of them. For that matter, I don't intend to keep my present one indefinitely."

"You don't say! Do you mean that? When you've just got yourself such a good position? Almost two hundred marks a month—why, that is splendid for a young man."

"Who knows how long it will last, Aunt?"

"What a way to talk! It will last all right if you stick right to it."

"Well, let us hope so. But now I must go upstairs to see Aunt Lydia, and then drop in on Uncle at the office. So good-bye for now, Aunt Berta."

"Yes, adieu. It has been a great pleasure to me. Be sure to come around again."

"Of course."

I bade good-bye to the two girls in the living room and from the doorway called another farewell to Aunt. Then I climbed the bright, wide stair-case. And if before I had had the feeling that I was breathing an old-fashioned atmosphere, I now entered one positively antique.

In two tiny rooms upstairs lived an octogenarian great-aunt who re-ceived me with the delicacy and gallantry of bygone times. There were watercolor portraits of great-great-uncles, antimacassars, purses with bou-quets of flowers and landscapes embroidered on them in beads, oval picture frames, and a fragrance of sandalwood and delicate old perfume.

Aunt Lydia was wearing a purple dress cut very plain. Except for her nearsightedness and a faint shaking of her head, she was amazingly youth-ful and spry. She drew me down on a narrow settee, and instead of talk-ing about the distant past asked me about my life and my ideas. She was interested in everything, attentive to everything I said. Old as she was, and remote and ancestral though her rooms smelled and looked, she had gone on frequent travels up to only two years before. Though she did not wholly approve of it, she had a clear and by no means entirely unfavorable con-ception of the contemporary world, and she liked to refresh and fill out her view of it. At the same time she possessed a charming and graceful adroit-ness in conversation. When you sat with her, the talk flowed on without pauses and was somehow always interesting and pleasant.

When I left, she kissed me and dismissed me with a gesture of blessing which I have never seen anyone else employ.

I looked up Uncle Matthäus in his office, where he sat bent over news-papers and catalogues. I had made up my mind not to sit down and to leave shortly, and Uncle made it easy for me.

"So you are back in the country again?" he said.

"Yes, back again. It's been a long time."

"And now you are doing well, so I hear?"

"Quite well, thank you."

"You will drop in and say hello to my wife, won't you?"

"I already have been to see her."

"Oh, you have. Good boy. Well then, that's fine."

Whereupon he lowered his gaze to his catalogue again and held out his hand toward me. As he had picked approximately the right direction, I shook his hand quickly and went out with a contented feeling.

Now the official visits were done with, and I went home to dine. In my honor there were rice and roast veal. After dinner my brother, Fritz, took me aside and led me up to his room, where my butterfly collection hung on the wall under glass. My sister wanted to chat with us and stuck her head in at the door, but Fritz importantly waved her away. "No, we have a secret," he said.

Then he scrutinized my face, and when he saw me looking sufficiently curious, he drew a box out from under the bed. The lid of the box was covered with a sheet of tin and weighed down by several good-sized stones.

"Guess what's inside," he said in a low, crafty voice.

I thought about our former hobbies and experiments and guessed: "Lizards?"

"No."

"Ring snakes?"

"Not a bit."

"Caterpillars?"

"No, nothing alive."

"No? Then why is the box shut so tight?"

"There are things more dangerous than caterpillars."

"Dangerous? Aha—powder?"

Instead of replying he removed the lid and I saw inside the box a good-sized arsenal: packages of powder of varying fineness, charcoal, tinder, fuses, lumps of sulfur, boxes of saltpeter, and iron filings.

"Well, what do you say?"

I knew that my father would have been unable to sleep a wink if he had known that a box of such materials was stored in the boys' room. But Fritz was glowing so with joy and the pleasure of having sprung his surprise that I expressed this thought only by a mild remark and instantly accepted his reassurances. For I myself had a certain responsibility for all this, and I was looking forward to a fireworks display as eagerly as an apprentice to quitting time.

"Will you go in with me?" Fritz asked.

"Of course. We can set the stuff off at night, in gardens here and there, eh?"

"Sure we can. Recently I set off a grenade with half a pound of powder in it, out on the meadows outside of town. It boomed like an earthquake. But now I'm out of money, and we still need all sorts of stuff."

"I'll contribute three marks."

"That's the boy! Then we'll have rockets and giant crackers."

"But you'll be careful, eh?"

"Careful! Nothing's ever happened to *me!*"

This was a reference to a bad accident I had had with fireworks at the age of fourteen; it had missed by a hair costing me my eyesight and my life.

Now he showed me the supplies and the various pieces he had started, initiated me into the mysteries of some of his new experiments and inventions, and stirred up my curiosity about others that he intended to show me and was keeping a deep dark secret for the present. This took up the whole of his noon hour, and then he had to go back to work. After he left I had no sooner covered up the sinister box and stowed it away under the bed than Lotte came in and asked me to come for a walk with her and Papa.

"How does Fritz strike you?" Father said. "He's grown up, hasn't he?"

"Oh yes."

"And is a good deal more serious, don't you think? He's beginning to outgrow his childish pranks at last. Yes, now all my children are grown up."

Getting there anyway, I thought, and felt a bit ashamed. But it was a glorious afternoon; the poppies flamed in the grainfields, the red corn cockles smiled. We walked along slowly, talking of nothing but enjoyable matters. Well-known paths and orchards, the familiar margins of woods, greeted me and beckoned to me; times past rose up once more, sweet and radiant, as though everything had been good and perfect in those days.

"Now I must ask you something," Lotte said. "I have been thinking of inviting a friend of mine here for a few weeks."

"Have you? Where from?"

"From Ulm. She's two years older than me. What do you think? Now that we have you here, that's the main thing, and you must tell me right out if her visit would bother you."

"What's she like?"

"She's taken the teacher's examination——"

"Oh Lord!"

"Not 'Oh Lord' at all. She's very nice and certainly no bluestocking—not at all. In fact, she hasn't gone in for teaching."

"Why not?"

"You'll have to ask her that yourself."

"Then she is coming?"

"Stupid! It depends on you. If you think you'd rather have just the family all together, she can come some other time. That's why I'm asking you."

"I'll toss a coin."

"If you feel that way about it, say yes right off."

"All right, yes."

"Good. Then I'll write to her today."

"And send her my regards."

"That will hardly overwhelm her with pleasure."

"Incidentally, what is her name?"

"Anna Amberg."

"Amberg is nice. And Anna is a saint's name, but a dull one, if only because you can't make a nickname out of it."

"Would you like Anastasia better?"

"Yes—that could be shortened to Stasi or Stasel."

Meanwhile we had reached the top of the hill, which from one terrace to the next had seemed almost upon us, but had kept receding. Now from a rock we looked down across the queerly foreshortened, steeply sloping fields through which we had climbed, to the town, far below in the narrow valley. Behind us, on rolling land, the black pine forest ran for mile upon mile, broken here and there by narrow meadows or a strip of grainfield that gleamed in sharp contrast to the dark color of the woods.

"Really, no other place is so beautiful as this," I said pensively.

My father smiled and looked at me. "It is your homeland, son. And it is beautiful; that is true."

"Is your homeland more beautiful, Papa?"

"No, but wherever your childhood was, everything is beautiful and sacred. Haven't you ever been homesick, my boy?"

"Oh yes, now and then I have been."

Near by was a wooded spot where in my boyhood days I had often captured robin redbreasts. And a bit farther on there must be the remains of a stone fort that we children had once built. But Father was tired, and after a short rest we turned back and descended the hill by another road.

I wished I could find out a little more about Helene Kurz, but I dared not bring up her name for fear of exposing myself. In the peacefulness and idleness of being home, and with the happy prospect of several weeks of a lazy holiday before me, my youthful heart was beginning to be stirred by longings and plans for romance. All that was needed was a handy pretext. But that was just what I lacked, and the more I was haunted by the image of that beautiful young lady, the more difficult it became for me to ask without embarrassment about her and her circumstances.

As we walked slowly homeward, we gathered large bunches of flowers from the margins of the fields. This was an art I had not practiced for a long time. In our household Mother had established the custom of keeping not only potted plants, but also fresh flowers on all the tables and chests of drawers. In the course of years a great many simple vases, glasses, and jars had been assembled, and we children scarcely ever returned from a walk without bringing home flowers, ferns, or small branches of trees and shrubs.

It seemed to me that I had not even looked at wildflowers for years. For they look very different when you notice them in passing, with an artistic pleasure, as islands of color in a world of green, and when you kneel or stoop to examine them singly and choose the finest for picking. I discovered tiny hidden plants whose blossoms reminded me of outings in my school-days, and others that my mother particularly liked or had given special private names. These same flowers were all still to be found, and each of them awakened a memory. Out of every blue or yellow calyx my joyous childhood looked up at me, looked with unwonted dearness and nearness into my eyes.

In what we called the salon of our house stood several tall cases of plain pine. Stuffed into these, standing or lying in confused heaps, was a hoard of books dating back several generations. They were not in any kind of order and were rather neglected. As a small boy I had found and read here *Robinson Crusoe* and *Gulliver's Travels,* in yellowed editions with gay woodcuts. Then I had turned to old stories of seafarers and explorers, and later to a good many more literary works, such as *Siegwart, Story of a Monastery, The New Amadis, The Sorrows of Werther,* and Ossian. Later still, I took up the many books by Jean Paul, Stilling, Walter Scott, Platen, Balzac, and Victor Hugo, as well as the small edition of Lavater's *Physiognomy* and numerous sets of pretty little almanacs, pocket-sized booklets, and popular calendars, the older ones illustrated with copper engravings by Chodowiecki, the later ones by Ludwig Richter, and the Swiss ones with woodcuts by Disteli.

Now on evenings when there was no family music-making or when I was not manufacturing firecrackers with Fritz, I could take one or another volume from this treasure store into my room and blow the smoke of my pipe into the yellowed pages over which my grandparents had sighed, raved enthusiastically, and pondered. My brother had gutted and consumed for his fireworks one volume of Jean Paul's *Titan.* When I had read the first two volumes and was hunting for the third, he confessed his crime, but claimed that the volume had been in bad shape anyway.

These evenings were always pleasant and entertaining. We sang; Lotte played the piano and Fritz the fiddle; Mamma told stories of our childhood. Polly fluted away in his cage and refused to go to bed. Father rested at the window or pasted away at a scrapbook for his small nephews.

But I did not at all feel it as a disturbing note when one evening Helene Kurz dropped in again to chat for half an hour. Again and again I looked at her with a sense of amazement at how beautiful and perfect she had become. When she arrived, the candles on the piano were almost burned down, and she joined in the singing of a two-voiced song. But I sang very low, so that I could hear every note of her rich voice. I stood behind her and looked through her brown hair at the candlelight gleaming golden, saw how her shoulders moved slightly as she sang, and thought how delicious it would be to run my hand just a little over her hair.

Without much logic, I had the feeling that we were linked by certain memories of former days because I had been in love with her around the time of my confirmation. Now her casual friendliness was a mild disappointment to me. For it did not occur to me that the relationship had existed only on my side, and that she had known nothing about it.

Afterward, when she took her leave, I picked up my hat and walked to the glass door with her.

"Good-night," she said. But instead of taking her hand, I said: "I'll walk you home."

She laughed.

"Oh, no need of that, thank you. You know it isn't customary here."

"Isn't it?" I said, and let her pass. But then my sister took her blue-ribboned straw hat and called out: "I'll go along too."

And the three of us descended the stairs. I eagerly opened the heavy front gate and we stepped out into the warm dusk and walked slowly through the town, across the bridge and the market square, and up to the steep outlying hill where Helene's parents lived. The two girls chattered away like starlings, and I listened and was glad to be with them and one member of a trio. Sometimes I walked more slowly, pretending I was looking up at the sky for weather signs, and lagged a step behind so that I could see how straight and freely she carried her dark head and how firmly and evenly her slender body stepped forward.

At her house Helene shook hands with us and went in. I saw her hat gleaming for a moment in the dark vestibule before the door clapped shut.

"Yes," Lotte said, "she really is a fine girl, isn't she? And there's something so sweet about her."

"There certainly is. How do things stand with your girl friend? Is she coming soon?"

"I wrote to her yesterday."

"Hm, I see. Well, shall we go home the same way?"

"Oh, we might go by the way of the gardens, at that."

We walked down the narrow lane between the garden fences. It was already dark, and we had to watch where we were going, for there were many sagging plank steps on the path and loose pickets leaning out from the fences.

We had almost reached our garden and could see the living-room lamp burning inside the house. Suddenly a low voice said: "Pst! Pst!" and my sister was frightened. But it was our brother, Fritz, who had hidden in the garden to meet us.

"Stand still and watch!" he called to us. Then he lit a fuse with a sulfur match and came over to us.

"Fireworks again?" Lotte scolded him.

"There won't be much of a bang," Fritz assured her. "Just watch, it's my own invention."

We waited until the fuse had burned down. Then it began to crackle and shoot out small reluctant sparks, like wet gunpowder. Fritz was glowing with pleasure.

"Now it will come, in a second, first white fire, then a small bang and a red flame, then a pretty blue one!"

It did not turn out as he expected. Instead, after some jerking and shooting of sparks the precious invention went up all at once, with a loud boom and blast pressure and a white cloud of smoke.

Lotte laughed, and Fritz was unhappy. As I tried to console him, the dense smoke drifted away with solemn deliberation over the dark gardens.

"We did get just a glimpse of the blue," Fritz began, and I admitted that. Then, almost tearfully, he described in detail the making of his pyrotechnical triumph and how it should have gone off.

"We'll try it again," I said.

"Tomorrow?"

"No, Fritz. Let's make it next week."

I might just as well have said tomorrow. But my mind was full of thoughts of Helene Kurz and was lost in the dream of some wonderful happiness that might dawn for me tomorrow—perhaps that she would visit again in the evening or that she might suddenly take a liking to me. In short, I was now engrossed in things that seemed to me more important and more exciting than all the fireworks in the world.

We crossed the garden to the house and found our parents at the backgammon board in the living room. It was all so simple and natural and could not be any different. And yet everything has turned out so differently that today it all seems infinitely remote to me. For today my old home no longer exists for me. The old house, the garden, and the veranda, the familiar rooms, furniture and pictures, the parrot in his big cage, the dear old town, and the whole valley have become strange to me and no longer belong to me. Mother and Father are dead, and my childhood home is nothing but memories and homesickness. No road leads me back there any longer.

Around eleven o'clock at night, when I was sitting over a fat volume of Jean Paul, my small oil lamp began to grow dim. It sputtered and made tiny, anxious noises; the flame became red and sooty, and when I examined it and turned the wick up and down, I saw that it was out of oil. I felt sorry about the fine novel I was reading, but it would not do to go groping around in the dark house now, looking for oil.

And so I blew out the smoking lamp and went to bed in a bad temper. Outside, a warm wind had sprung up and was blowing gently through the pines and the lilac bushes. In the grassy yard down below, a cricket was chirping. I could not fall asleep and again began thinking of Helene. I could hope for no more from this well-bred, beautiful girl than to go on looking at her with vain longing, and that was as painful as it was pleasurable. I felt hot and wretched when I imagined her face, the sound of her rich voice, and her walk, the firm and energetic rhythm of her footsteps as she had walked down the street and across the market square this evening.

Finally I jumped up out of bed. I was much too warm and restive to sleep. I went to the window and looked out. Among wispy strips of cloud the waning moon floated pallidly. The cricket was still singing in the yard. What I would have liked best was to go out walking for an hour or so. But our front door was always locked at ten o'clock, and if it ever had to be opened and used after that hour, this always signified an event, something unusual, disturbing, and adventurous. I did not even know where the door key hung.

I remembered again bygone years when as an adolescent I had sometimes thought our home life was virtual slavery. And at night, with a guilty conscience and adventurous defiance, I had slipped out of the house to have a mug of beer at a tavern that stayed open late. To get out I had used the back door to the garden, which was fastened only by bolts; then I would clamber over the fence and reach the street by way of the narrow lane between the adjoining gardens.

I put on my trousers—the air was so warm that no more clothing was necessary—took my shoes in my hand, and stole out of the house barefoot. Clambering over the garden fence, I set out on a slow stroll through the sleeping town, walking upstream along the river, which flowed along with muted whispers and played with small quivering reflections of the moonlight.

To be up and about outdoors at night, beneath the silent sky and beside quietly flowing water, is always mysterious and stirs the soul to its very depths. At such times we are closer to our origins; we feel a kinship with animals and plants, feel dim memories of a primeval life before houses and towns were built, when man, the homeless wanderer, could regard the woods, streams, mountains, wolves, and hawks as his equals and could love them as friends or hate them as deadly foes. Night also removes our customary sense of community life; when lights are no longer burning and human voices can no longer be heard, one who is still awake feels solitary and sees himself parted from others and thrown upon his own resources. Then that most terrible of all human feelings, that of being inescapably alone, of having to live alone and to taste and endure alone sorrow, fear, and death, underlies our every thought—to the young and healthy only an intimation and warning, to the feeble a real dread.

I too felt something of this. At least my ill humor faded and gave way to quiet contemplation. It pained me to think that beautiful, desirable

Helene would probably never think of me with emotions like those I felt toward her; but I also knew that the grief of an unrequited love was not going to kill me, and I had a vague premonition that life, mysterious life, held darker abysses and worse vicissitudes than a young man's vacation sorrows.

Nevertheless, my stirred-up blood remained warm and, independently of my will, created out of the sluggish breeze caressing hands and a girl's brown hair, so that this walk late at night made me neither tired nor sleepy. So I walked over the rowen grass of the pale fields on the banks of the river, removed my light clothing, and plunged into the cool water. The swift current instantly forced me to put up a stiff resistance. I swam upstream for a quarter of an hour. Depression and melancholy streamed off me with the refreshing river water. Cooled and somewhat tired, I found my clothes again, slipped into them still wet, and returned home and to bed in a light, tranquil frame of mind.

After the excitement of the first few days I gradually fell in with the quiet normality of life at home. How I had roamed around in the outside world, drifting from city to city, knowing many different sorts of people, sometimes working, sometimes dreaming, sometimes studying, and sometimes spending nights carousing, living for a while on bread and milk and then for a while on books and cigars, a different person every month. And here everything was the same as it had been ten and twenty years before. Here the days and weeks ran on in a serene, even tempo. And I, who had become estranged from all this and accustomed to an unstable life of variegated experiences, fitted into this again as if I had never been away. I took an interest in people and things that I had completely forgotten for years, and missed nothing of all that the outside world had meant to me.

The hours and days ran along for me as easily as summer clouds, without leaving a trace behind; each was a colorful picture and each a floating emotion, rising in a rush of music, sounding forth, and soon fading dreamily away. I watered the garden, sang with Lotte, firecrackered with Fritz, chatted with Mother about foreign places and with Father about the latest events in the world; I read Goethe and Jens Peter Jacobsen, and one thing passed into another and went well with the other, and nothing seriously mattered either way.

At the time what seriously mattered to me was Helene Kurz and my feeling for her. But that too existed like everything else; it moved me for hours at a time, then was submerged again for hours. Constant alone was my pulsating, joyous feeling of being alive, the feeling of a swimmer who moves along in smooth water, unhurried and aimless, without effort and without a care. In the woods the jay shrieked and the bilberries ripened; in the garden, roses bloomed and fiery nasturtiums. I took part in it all, thought the world glorious, and wondered what life would be like when eventually I too would become a real man, old and sensible.

One afternoon a large raft came floating through the town. I jumped aboard it, lay down on a pile of boards, and floated downriver for a few hours, past farms and villages and under bridges, while above me the air quivered and sultry clouds seethed with faint thunder, and under me the cool water of the river slapped and laughed fresh and foamy. I imagined that Helene was along; I had abducted her, and we were sitting hand in hand and showing each other the splendors of the world from here all the way downstream to Holland.

When I left the raft far down in the valley, I jumped short and landed in the water up to my chest. But on the warm walk home my steaming clothes dried on my body. And when I reached the first houses of the town again, dusty and weary after my long tramp, I met Helene Kurz wearing a red blouse. I lifted my hat and she nodded, and I thought again of my daydream, of her traveling down the river with me hand in hand and speaking to me as an intimate, and then for the rest of that evening it all seemed hopeless to me and I thought myself a silly dreamer and stargazer. Nevertheless, before going to sleep I smoked my handsome pipe, with two grazing deer painted on its porcelain bowl, and read *Wilhelm Meister* until after eleven o'clock.

The following evening at about half past eight I went up to the Pinnacle with my brother, Fritz. We had a heavy package with us, which we took turns carrying. It contained a dozen giant crackers, six skyrockets, three large grenades, and a variety of small things.

The air was tepid, blue-tinted, and filled with shreds of cloud in motion, which drifted gently away over the church tower and the peaks of the hills, frequently covering the pallid first stars of evening. At the Pinnacle we first rested for a short while after our climb, and I looked down on our narrow river valley lying below in its pale twilight colors. As I looked at the town and the next village, at the bridges and mill dam and the narrow, shrub-lined river, the twilight mood and the thought of that beautiful girl stole upon me together. I would have preferred to be dreaming there alone and waiting for the moon. But that could not be, for my brother had already unpacked and startled me by exploding two crackers from behind my back; he had linked them with a string, tied them to a pole, and held them out close to my ears.

I was a little annoyed. But Fritz laughed so uproariously and was so pleased with himself that I was quickly infected and joined in. In quick succession we set off three extra-powerful grenades and listened to the tremendous reports booming up and down the valley and dying away in long, rolling echoes. Then came more firecrackers, squibs, and a large catherine-wheel, and to finish it off we slowly sent one after another of our fine sky-rockets mounting into the now black night sky.

"You know, a real good rocket like that is almost like worshiping God," said my brother, who sometimes liked to use figures of speech. "Or like singing a beautiful song, don't you think? It's so solemn."

On the way home we tossed our last firecracker into the shingler's yard, at the nasty yard dog, who howled in terror and went on barking ferociously after us for a quarter of an hour. We came home high-spirited and black-fingered, like two young rascals who have been up to all sorts of tricks. And to our parents we sang the praises of our lovely evening walk, the view of the valley and the star-strewn sky.

One morning while I was at the window cleaning out my pipe, Lotte came running up and called: "Well, my girl friend is arriving today, at eleven."

"Anna Amberg?"

"Yes. You'll come with me to meet her, won't you?"

"All right."

I was not particularly pleased at the prospect of this guest, to whom I had not given a thought. But there was nothing to do about it, and so toward eleven o'clock I went to the railroad station with my sister. We arrived too early and walked up and down in front of the station.

"Perhaps she will be riding second-class," Lotte said.

I stared incredulously at her.

"She might be. Her family are well-to-do, and though she hasn't any airs . . ."

I shuddered. I imagined a fashionable lady with mincing manners and a pile of baggage stepping out of the second-class car and finding my father's comfortable home pitiful and myself not at all good enough for her.

"If she's traveling second-class, she may just as well travel right past here, for all I care."

Lotte was annoyed and was going to answer me sharply, but then the train pulled in and stopped, and Lotte ran quickly toward it. I followed her at a leisurely pace and saw her girl friend getting out of a third-class car, armed with a gray silk umbrella, a traveling-rug, and a modest suitcase.

"Anna, this is my brother."

I said hello, and because in spite of the third class I didn't know what she would think of my taking her suitcase myself, light as it was, I beckoned the porter and handed it to him. Then I walked along into the city beside the two girls, wondering at how much they had to tell each other. But I took a liking to Miss Amberg. Of course, I was a bit disappointed that she was not especially pretty, but to make up for that there was something pleasant about her face and voice that was soothing and awakened confidence.

I can still see the way my mother received the two of them at the glass door. Mother had a knack for reading people's faces, and anyone whom she welcomed with her smile, after a first searching look, could be prepared for a good time in her home. I can still see how she looked into Anna Amberg's eyes and then nodded to her and gave her both hands, taking her into her heart and making her at home without saying a word. My suspicion that the stranger would be an intruder promptly vanished, for she took the proffered hands and friendliness with quiet cordiality, and from the very first hour became part of our household.

With all the acumen of my young years, I decided that first day that this pleasant girl had an innocent, natural serenity. She might not know too much about life, but she was a worthwhile chum. I had a dim suspicion of the existence of a higher and worthier serenity that some can acquire out of trouble and suffering, and some never acquire at all; but this I did not really know from experience. For the time being, I remained unaware that our guest possessed this rare kind of tranquil cheerfulness.

Girls with whom one could chum around and talk about life and literature were not often met with in my sphere of life in those days. Up to now I had regarded my sister's girl friends either as objects to fall in love with or as creatures of no importance at all. To associate with a young lady without constraint, and to be able to chat with her about all sorts of things as if she were one of my own friends, was something new and delightful to me. In spite of being on equal terms with her, I sensed in her voice, language, and way of thinking the feminine tone, and I found this warm and sweet.

Quite incidentally I was rather abashed to notice how quietly and skillfully and with what absence of fuss Anna fitted herself into our life and accustomed herself to our ways. For all of the friends I had ever brought home as vacation guests had always made a bit of a to-do and brought with them an alien atmosphere. Even I myself had been louder and more self-important than was needful in the first days after my homecoming.

At times I was amazed at how little special consideration Anna seemed to require. In conversation I could even be almost rude without seeing any sign that she was offended. How different it was with Helene Kurz, by contrast! Toward her, even in the most animated talk, I would not have dared to use anything but the most careful and respectful phrases.

As it happened, Helene Kurz came to see us quite often during this time, and seemed to be fond of my sister's friend. One day we were all invited to a gathering in the garden at Uncle Matthäus's. Coffee and cake were served, and afterward gooseberry wine; in the intervals we played harmless children's games or strolled decorously along the garden paths, whose neatness and precision of themselves imposed dignified behavior.

It was strange to me to see Helene and Anna together and to talk with both at once. With Helene Kurz, who as always looked wonderful, I could talk only about superficial matters, but I did so in the prissiest tone, while with Anna I could chat about even the most interesting subjects without any agitation or sense of strain. And while I was grateful to her, finding conversation with her relaxing and reassuring, I kept glancing away from her to the other, the far prettier girl whose looks ravished me and yet always left me unsatisfied.

My brother, Fritz, was wretchedly bored. After he had eaten as much cake as he could hold, he suggested several rougher games, some we would not enter into, and others we quickly abandoned. In between he drew me aside and complained that the afternoon was terribly insipid. When I shrugged, he alarmed me by confessing that he had a firecracker in his pocket which he intended to set off later on when the girls would, as usual, take their time about bidding each other good-bye. I had to argue hard to dissuade him. He then took himself off to the remotest corner of the big garden and lay down under the gooseberry bushes. But I betrayed him by laughing with the others over his childish bad temper, though I was sorry for him and understood his feelings very well.

My two cousins, Aunt Berta's daughters, were quite easy to handle. They were altogether unspoiled and drank in with grateful eagerness jokes that had long since lost all sheen of newness. Uncle had withdrawn immediately after the coffee. Aunt Berta stayed with Lotte most of the time; she was quite willing to dismiss me after I had a few words with her on the art of putting up berries, which made her very pleased with me. And so I hung around the two girls and in pauses of the conversation wondered why it is so much more difficult to talk with a girl you are in love with. I should have liked very much to pay some kind of homage to Helene, but I could think of nothing. Finally I cut two of the many roses in the garden and gave one to Helene, the other to Anna Amberg.

That was the last entirely unclouded day of my holiday. The following day I heard from a casual acquaintance that Helene Kurz had recently been a frequent visitor to such and such a family, and that an engagement would soon be announced. He mentioned this incidentally, among many other items of news, and I was careful not to let on that it meant anything to me. But even though it was only a rumor, I had in any case scarcely dared to hope for much from Helene, and was now convinced that she was out of reach entirely. I returned home utterly unhinged and fled to my room.

Under the circumstances and with my youthful resiliency, I could not go on sorrowing for very long. But for several days I refused all amusement. I took long, lonely walks in the woods, hung around the house feeling sad and vacant, and spent evenings behind closed windows improvising on the violin.

"Is something the matter, my boy?" Papa said to me, laying his hand on my shoulder.

"I didn't sleep well," I replied quite truthfully. I could not manage to tell him any more. But he said something then that I have often recalled since.

"A sleepless night," he said, "is always a bad business. But it is endurable if we have good thoughts. When we lie still and do not sleep, we easily become vexed and turn our minds to vexatious things. But we can also use our wills and think good thoughts."

"Can we?" I wondered. For in recent years I had begun to doubt the existence of free will.

"Yes, we can!" Father said emphatically.

I can still remember distinctly the very hour when, after several days of being bitter and gloomy, I came to myself again, forgot my unhappiness, and began living with others and being gay again. We were all sitting in the living room over afternoon coffee; only Fritz was not there. The others were merry and talkative, but I kept quiet and did not participate, though secretly I was already feeling once more a need to chat and be lively. As young people will, I had surrounded my sorrow with a wall of silence and defiant obstinacy. After the considerate custom of our household, the others had let me alone and respected my obvious low spirits, and now I could not get up the courage to tear down my wall. A short while before, my feeling had been genuine and necessary to me; now I was pretending it, boring myself with it. Moreover, I was ashamed because my period of penance had lasted so short a time.

Suddenly the tranquillity of our afternoon coffee was shattered by a jaunty flourish of trumpets, a bold and challenging run of rapid tones that made us all leap to our feet.

"There's a fire!" my sister cried out in alarm.

"That would be a funny fire alarm."

"Then soldiers are going to be quartered on us."

Meanwhile we had all rushed headlong to the windows. On the street, right in front of our house, we saw a swarm of children, and in the midst of them, seated on a huge white horse, was a trumpeter clad in scarlet, his horn and habit resplendent in the sunlight. This remarkable person looked up at all the windows as he trumpeted; he had a tanned face, with a tremendous Hungarian mustachio. He went on frenziedly blowing his horn, mixing his themes with all sorts of random improvisations, until all the windows in the vicinity were crowded with onlookers. Then he put down his instrument, stroked his mustache, placed his left hand on his hip while with his right hand he reined in the restive horse, and delivered a speech. He was passing through, he said, and only for this one single day would his world-famous troupe be stopping in the town. On the earnest pleas of the citizens he would give a "gala performance" that very evening on the meadow near the marsh. There would be "trained horses, elegant balancing acts and a grand pantomime as well." Admission for adults was twenty pfennigs, children ten. Having given his announcement and made sure that all understood, the rider blew one more blast of his shining horn and rode off, followed by the flock of children and a dense white cloud of dust.

The laughter and the joyous anticipation that the circus rider's appearance had stirred up among us was a great help to me. I took advantage of the opportunity to drop my gloomy airs and join in the excitement of the others. Promptly I invited the two girls to the evening performance. After some demurring Papa gave us his permission, and the three of us at once sauntered down to the meadow to take a look at the show. We found two men busy marking off a round arena and fencing it in with rope. Then they began putting up a high scaffolding. Near by, on the steps of a green van, a frightfully fat old woman sat knitting. A pretty white poodle lay at her feet. While we were looking on, the rider returned from town, tied the white horse behind the van, removed his flashy red garments, and in shirt-sleeves helped the others set up the scaffolding.

"Poor fellows!" Anna Amberg said. But I said I couldn't see what there was to pity about them. I took up the defense of the circus performers and praised their free, merry gypsy life to the skies. There was nothing I would like better than to go with them, I said; to walk the tightrope and after the performance take the plate around.

"I'd love to see that," Anna laughed merrily.

Whereupon I took my hat instead of a plate, made the gestures of a man taking up a collection, and humbly asked for a small contribution for the clown. Anna put her hand in her pocket, fumbled for a moment, and then threw a pfennig into my hat. I thanked her and dropped it into my vest pocket.

The gaiety I had been repressing burst out of me with stunning force. I was high-spirited as a child all that day. Perhaps being aware of my own fickleness had something to do with this.

In the evening we took Fritz along and went to the performance. Even before we got there we were akindle with excitement and anticipatory pleasure. At the meadow a crowd was surging aimlessly hither and thither. Children stood about, silent and blissful, their eyes wide with expectancy; young rapscallions teased everybody and knocked one another over in front of people's feet; onlookers settled down in the chestnut trees, and the constable strode around with his helmet on. Around the arena a row of seats had been set up; in the center of the arena stood a four-armed scaffold with cans of oil depending from its arms. These were now lit; the crowd pressed closer; the row of seats slowly filled; and above the arena and the many heads swayed the sooty red flame of the kerosene torches.

We had found places on one of the plank seats. A hand organ sounded out, and the ringmaster appeared in the arena with a small black pony. The clown came in with him and began a conversation, punctuated by many slaps in the face, which evoked loud applause. It began with the clown's asking some insolent question. Answering with a slap in the face, the ringmaster said: "Do you think I'm a camel?"

To which the clown replied: "Now, sir, I know quite well what the difference is between you and a camel."

"Oh, you do, clown? What is the difference?"

"Why, ringmaster, a camel can work for a week without drinking. But you can drink for a week without working."

Another slap, more applause. And so it went on, and even as I marveled at the crudeness of the jokes and the simplicity of the grateful audience, I myself laughed along with everybody else.

The pony made leaps, jumped over a bench, counted to twelve, and played dead. Then came a poodle that jumped through hoops, danced on two legs, and did military drill. In between, the clown constantly reappeared. Then came a goat, a very pretty little animal that balanced itself on a chair.

Finally the clown was asked whether all he could do was stand around and crack jokes. Whereupon he quickly threw off his bulky clown's costume, appeared in red tights, and climbed up the high rope. He was a handsome fellow and did his act well. But even if he had not, it was a fine sight to see the red figure illuminated by the flames of the torches suspended far up under the dark-blue night sky.

Since the performance had taken longer than planned, the pantomime had to be cut out. We too had stayed out beyond our usual hour, and we set off for home at once.

All during the performance we had kept up a lively chatter. I had been sitting next to Anna Amberg, and though we had made nothing but casual remarks to each other, I had been aware all the time of her warm closeness, and now on the way home I missed it a little.

Because I lay in my bed for a long time without falling asleep, I had time to think about that. And as I did so, I became uncomfortably and shamefully conscious of my faithlessness. How had I been able to give up beautiful Helene Kurz so quickly? But with the help of some sophistical reasoning that night and during the next few days, I settled the matter quite neatly and solved all the apparent contradictions to my own satisfaction.

That night, before finally going to sleep, I lit the lamp again, found in my vest pocket the pfennig coin that Anna had given me in jest, and studied it tenderly. It bore the date 1877—in other words, it was just as old as myself. I wrapped it in white paper, labeled it with the initials A. A. and the day's date, and placed it in the innermost slot of my wallet, as a lucky penny.

Half of my holiday—and the first half of a holiday is always longer than the second—had long since passed, and after a week of violent thunderstorms the summer began to grow gradually older and wiser. But I, as though nothing else in the world was of any importance, steered lovelorn, with fluttering pennons, through the almost imperceptibly shortening days; I charged each day with a golden hope and in gay bravado watched each one coming, shining, and going without wishing to stop it and without regretting its passing.

Certainly this bravado sprang from the amazing insouciance of youth, but my mother was also partly to blame for it. For without saying a word about the matter, she let me see that she was well disposed toward my friendship with Anna. Associating with this intelligent and well-mannered girl had certainly done me good; there was no denying that. And it seemed to me that Mamma would also approve a deeper and closer relationship with Anna. So there was no need for worry and concealment, and I behaved toward Anna as I would have toward a dear sister.

Such a situation, however, was far from what I wanted, and after a while this static chumminess between us at times became almost painful to me. For I wished to emerge from the well-fenced garden of friendship into the broad, unbounded fields of love, and had no idea how I could imperceptibly lure my unsuspecting friend out on the open roads. But out of this very conflict there arose, during the last part of my vacation, a deliciously free state of suspension between contentment and desiring more which remains in my memory as a state of great happiness.

So we passed pleasant summer days in our fortunate household. With Mother I had meanwhile returned to the old relationship of a child, so that I could talk to her about my life without constraint, could confess past faults and discuss plans for the future. I still remember one morning how we sat in the arbor winding yarn. I had told Mother what had happened to my belief in God and had finished by asserting that if I were ever to become a believer again, someone would have to come along and convert me.

At this my mother smiled and looked at me. After meditating for a while she said: "Probably no one will ever come along and convert you. But gradually you yourself will learn that it isn't possible to go on through life without faith. For knowledge is good for nothing, you know. Every day you are apt to see someone whom you thought you knew through and through do something that proves how little you really know people or can be certain about anything. And yet people need something they can rely upon; people need certainty. And then it is always better to turn to the Saviour rather than to some professor or Bismarck or anyone else."

"Why?" I asked. "After all, there isn't so much that we know for certain about the Saviour."

"Oh, we know enough. And then too—in the course of ages there have been individuals here and there who were able to die with self-confidence and without fear. It is said that Socrates was one, and there were some others—but not many. In fact, they were very few, and if they were able to die calmly and composedly, it was not because of their wisdom, but because their hearts and consciences were pure. Very well, let us say that these few people were right—each one right for himself. But how many of us are like them? As against these few, you see on the other side thousands upon thousands of poor, ordinary people who have nevertheless been able to die willingly and with composure because they believed in the Saviour. Your grandfather lay suffering terribly for fourteen months before he was granted relief; yet he did not complain and suffered all that pain and death almost cheerfully because the Saviour was his consolation."

And finally Mother said: "I know quite well that I cannot convince you. Faith does not come through reason, any more than love. But you will some day learn that reason does not cover everything, and when you have come to that point, then in your extremity you will snatch at anything that seems to offer support. Perhaps then you will remember some of the things we have said today."

I helped Father in the garden, and often when I went for walks I would bring back a sackful of forest soil for him to use on his potted plants. With Fritz I invented new fireworks and burned my fingers setting them off. With Lotte and Anna Amberg I spent whole mornings or afternoons in the woods, helping to pick berries and look for flowers. I read aloud to them from my favorite books and discovered new places for strolls.

The fine summer days ran into one another. I had become accustomed to being about Anna all the time, and when I thought that this would soon come to an end, dark clouds blackened the bright blue of my vacation sky.

And as all loveliness and sweetness is mortal and has its destined end, day after day of this summer, too, slipped through my fingers—this summer which in memory seems to have brought my youth to a close. The family began to talk of my impending departure. Mother once more went carefully through my stock of clothing, mending a few things, and on the day I packed she presented me with two pairs of substantial gray woolen socks that she had knitted herself; neither of us knew that it was to be her last gift to me.

Long dreaded and yet surprising when it came, the last day finally arrived. It was a fair, blue late summer day, with lacy clouds and a soft southeast breeze that played in the garden among the roses, still blooming in great numbers—a breeze that gathered all the fragrance of the summer until, toward noon, it grew tired and went to sleep. Because I had decided to make the most of the day and not to leave until late evening, we young people decided to spend the afternoon on an outing. That left the morning hours for my parents, and I sat between the two of them on the sofa in Father's study. Father had saved a few farewell presents for me. Now, with a kind of joking tone that concealed his emotion, he gave them to me. There was a small old-fashioned purse with a sum of money in it; a pen to carry in the pocket; and a neatly bound notebook that he had made himself and in which he had written in his austere hand a dozen good maxims. He advised me to be sparing but not stingy with the money; to use the pen to write home frequently; and if I found any more good maxims that my experience had tested, to set them down in the notebook beside those others which in his own life he had found useful and true.

We sat together more than two hours, and my parents told me a good many stories of the past, of our own childhood, of theirs, and of the lives of their parents; stories that were new to me and struck me as important. I have forgotten much of what they said, and as at intervals my thoughts kept wandering away to Anna, I may well have not listened to all of the earnest and weighty things they said. But what has remained with me is a vivid memory of that morning in the study and a feeling of deep gratitude and reverence for both my parents, whom today I see in an aura of purity and holiness which no other human beings have for me.

But at the time the farewell I had to take in the afternoon touched me far more deeply. Soon after lunch I set out with the two girls along the road over the mountain. Our destination was a lovely forest gorge, a steep-walled tributary valley of our river.

At first my solemn mood made the other two silent and thoughtful. But when we reached the peak of the mountain, from where the winding valley and forested hills could be seen through the tall red trunks of the firs, I wrenched myself out of my depression with a loud whoop. The girls laughed and instantly started to sing a hiking song. It was *"O Täler weit, o Höhen,"*[1] an old favorite of Mother's, and as I sang along I recalled many joyous outings in the woods in my childhood and on past vacations. Just as soon as the last notes of the song died away, we began, as though by agreement, to talk about those times and about Mother. We spoke of those times with gratitude and pride, for we had had a glorious youth, and I walked hand in hand with Lotte until Anna, laughing, took my other hand.

---

[1] *"O Täler . . . Höhen":* "Oh wide valleys, oh heights."

Then we strode along the road that ran on the ridge, the three of us swinging our hands in a kind of dance, and it was a joy to be alive.

Then we climbed down a steep, slanting footpath that led to a brook at the bottom of the deep gorge. From a distance we could hear the brook leaping over stones and ledges. Farther upstream along the brook was a favorite inn of ours, where I had invited the two girls to have coffee, cake, and ice cream with me. Descending the hill and along the brook we had to walk in single file, and I remained behind Anna, looking at her and trying to think of some way to speak alone with her before the day ended.

Finally a pretext occurred to me. We were close to our destination and had arrived at a grassy spot covered with wild pinks. I suggested to Lotte that she go on ahead to order the coffee and have a nice garden table set for us, while Anna and I gathered a big bouquet of ferns and flowers, this being such a fine spot to pick them. Lotte thought this a good idea and went ahead. Anna sat down on a moss-covered rock and began plucking fronds of fern.

"So this is my last day," I began.

"Yes, it's too bad. But you will surely be coming home again soon, won't you?"

"Who knows? Not next year, at any rate, and even if I do come again, it won't be the same."

"Why not?"

"Well, it would be if you should happen to be here again!"

"You know that's not altogether out of the question. But, after all, your coming home this time had nothing to do with me."

"Because I didn't know you then."

"Yes, of course. But you aren't even helping me. You might hand me a few of those pinks over there."

I pulled myself together.

"I'll pick them by and by. But at the moment something else is more important to me. You see, now I have a few minutes alone with you, and that is what I have been waiting for all day. Because—since I must leave today, you know—well, I wanted to ask you, Anna——"

She looked at me, her intelligent face grave and somewhat troubled.

"Wait!" she interrupted my stumbling speech. "I think I know what you want to say to me. And now I must ask you sincerely not to say it!"

"Not say it?"

"No, Hermann. I cannot tell you now why that cannot be, but I don't mind your knowing. Ask your sister some other time, later on. She knows all about it. We have so little time now, and it's a sad story; let's not be sad today. Let us make our bouquet now, until Lotte comes back. And for the rest, let us stay good friends and be jolly together for the rest of this day. Will you?"

"I would if I could."

"All right, then listen. My case is the same as yours: there's someone I care for and cannot have. But when that's how it is, there's all the more reason to cling to the friendship, kindness, and fun that come your way from other quarters, don't you think? That is why I say let us stay good friends and for this last day at least have fun together. Shan't we?"

I murmured yes, and we shook hands on it. The brook sported in its bed and sprayed drops of water up at us; our bouquet grew huge and vivid; and before long we heard my sister's voice approaching us, singing and calling out. When she reached us, I pretended I wanted to drink. I knelt by the brook's edge and dipped my forehead and eyes into the cold, flowing water for a short while. Then I took up the bouquet and we walked together the short distance to the inn.

There under a maple tree a table was set for us, with ice cream, coffee, and cookies. The innkeeper's wife welcomed us, and to my own surprise I found I could talk and answer people and eat as though all were well. I became almost gay; I made a little after-dinner speech and laughed unforcedly when the others laughed.

I will never forget with what simplicity and kindness and amiability Anna helped me to get over my humiliation and sadness that afternoon. Without betraying the fact that something had occurred between us, she treated me with a wonderful friendliness that helped me to act normal. I was filled with the greatest respect for her older and deeper sorrow and for the serene manner in which she bore it.

The narrow forest gorge was filling with early evening shadows when we started out again. But on the ridge, which we reached after a quick climb, we caught up with the sinking sun and walked for another hour in its warm light before we lost sight of it again as we descended to the town. I looked back at the sun one last time as it hovered, large and pink among the tops of the black pines, and I thought that tomorrow, far from here, I would see it again in foreign places.

In the evening, after I had taken my leave of all in the household, Lotte and Anna walked with me to the station and waved after me as the train slid away into the darkness.

I stood at the window of the car and looked out on the town, where street lamps were already lit and windows glowed brightly. As the train approached our garden, I caught sight of a powerful blood-red flare. There stood my brother, Fritz, holding a Bengal light in each hand. At the very moment that I waved to him and rode by, he sent a skyrocket shooting straight up into the air. Leaning out, I saw it mount and pause, describe a gentle arc, and vanish in a rain of red sparks.

Biryuk[1]

IVAN TURGENEV

I WAS coming back from hunting one evening alone in a racing droshky.[2] I was six miles from home; my good trotting mare galloped bravely along the dusty road, pricking up her ears with an occasional snort; my weary dog stuck close to the hind wheels, as though he were fastened there. A tempest was coming on. In front, a huge, purplish storm cloud slowly rose from behind the forest; long, gray rain clouds flew over my head and to meet me; the willows stirred and whispered restlessly. The suffocating heat changed suddenly to a damp chilliness; the darkness rapidly thickened. I gave the horse a lash with the reins, descended a steep slope, pushed across a dry watercourse overgrown with brushwood, mounted the hill, and drove into the forest. The road ran before me, bending between thick hazel bushes, now enveloped in darkness; I advanced with difficulty. The droshky jumped up and down over the hard roots of the ancient oaks and limes, which were continually intersected by deep ruts—the tracks of cart wheels; my horse began to stumble. A violent wind suddenly began to roar overhead; the trees blustered; big drops of rain fell with slow tap and splash on the leaves; there came a flash of lightning and a clap of thunder. The rain fell in torrents. I went on a step or so, and soon was forced to stop; my horse foundered; I could not see an inch before me. I managed to take refuge somehow in a spreading bush. Crouching down and covering my face, I waited patiently for the storm to blow over, when suddenly, in a

[1] *Biryuk:* Russian for wolf. In the province of Orel it is used to denote a lone, misanthropic man.
[2] *droshky:* four-wheeled carriage commonly used at that time for country travel.

flash of lightning, I saw a tall figure on the road. I began to stare intently in that direction—the figure seemed to have sprung out of the ground near my droshky.

"Who's that?" inquired a ringing voice.

"Why, who are you?"

"I'm the forester here."

I mentioned my name.

"Oh, I know! Are you on your way home?"

"Yes. But, you see, in such a storm. . . ."

"Yes, there is a storm," replied the voice.

A pale flash of lightning lit up the forester from head to foot; a brief crashing clap of thunder followed at once upon it. The rain lashed with redoubled force.

"It won't be over just directly," the forester went on.

"What's to be done?"

"I'll take you to my hut, if you like," he said abruptly.

"That would be a service."

"Please to take your seat."

He went up to the mare's head, took her by the bit, and pulled her up. We set off. I held on to the cushion of the droshky, which rocked "like a boat on the sea," and called my dog. My poor mare splashed with difficulty through the mud, slipped, and stumbled; the forester hovered before the shafts to right and to left like a ghost. We drove rather a long while; at last my guide stopped. "Here we are home, sir," he observed in a quiet voice. The gate creaked; some puppies barked a welcome. I raised my head, and in a flash of lightning I made out a small hut in the middle of a large yard, fenced in with hurdles.[3] From the one little window there was a dim light. The forester led his horse up to the steps and knocked at the door. "Coming, coming!" we heard in a little shrill voice; there was the patter of bare feet, the bolt creaked, and a girl of twelve, in a little old smock tied round the waist with list,[4] appeared in the doorway with a lantern in her hand.

"Show the gentleman a light," he said to her, "and I will put your droshky in the shed."

The little girl glanced at me, and went into the hut. I followed her.

The forester's hut consisted of one room, smoky, low-pitched, and empty, without curtains or partition. A tattered sheepskin hung on the wall. On the bench lay a single-barreled gun; in the corner lay a heap of rags; two great pots stood near the oven. A pine splinter was burning on the table, flickering up and dying down mournfully. In the very middle of

---

[3] *hurdles:* twigs interwoven to form a fence.

[4] *list:* a piece of cloth.

the hut hung a cradle, suspended from the end of a long horizontal pole. The little girl put out the lantern, sat down on a tiny stool, and with her right hand began swinging the cradle, while with her left she attended to the smoldering pine splinter. I looked round—my heart sank within me; it's not cheering to go into a peasant's hut at night. The baby in the cradle breathed hard and fast.

"Are you all alone here?" I asked the little girl.

"Yes," she uttered, hardly audibly.

"You're the forester's daughter?"

"Yes," she whispered.

The door creaked, and the forester, bending his head, stepped across the threshold. He lifted the lantern from the floor, went up to the table, and lighted a candle.

"I daresay you're not used to the splinter light?" said he, and he shook back his curls.

I looked at him. Rarely has it been my fortune to behold such a comely creature. He was tall, broad-shouldered, and in marvelous proportion. His powerful muscles stood out in strong relief under his wet homespun shirt. A curly black beard hid half of his stern and manly face; small brown eyes looked out boldly from under broad eyebrows which met in the middle. He stood before me, his arms held lightly akimbo.

I thanked him, and asked his name.

"My name's Foma," he answered, "and my nickname's Biryuk."

"Oh, *you're* Biryuk."

I looked with redoubled curiosity at him. From my Yermolaï[5] and others I had often heard stories about the forester Biryuk, whom all the peasants of the surrounding districts feared as they feared fire. According to them there had never been such a master of his business in the world before. "He won't let you carry off a handful of brushwood; he'll drop upon you like a fall of snow, whatever time it may be, even in the middle of the night, and you needn't think of resisting him—he's strong, and as cunning as the devil. . . . And there's no getting at him, anyhow; neither by brandy nor by money; there's no snare he'll walk into. More than once good folks have planned to put him out of the world, but no—it's never come off."

That was how the neighboring peasants spoke of Biryuk.

"So you're Biryuk," I repeated; "I've heard talk of you, brother. They say you show no mercy to anyone."

"I do my duty," he answered grimly; "it's not right to eat the master's bread for nothing."

[5] *Yermolaï:* his servant.

He took an ax from his girdle and began splitting splinters.

"Have you no wife?" I asked him.

"No," he answered, with a vigorous sweep of the ax.

"She's dead, I suppose?"

"No . . . yes . . . she's dead," he added, and turned away. I was silent; he raised his eyes and looked at me.

"She ran away with a traveling peddler," he brought out with a bitter smile. The little girl hung her head; the baby waked up and began crying; the little girl went to the cradle. "There, give it him," said Biryuk, thrusting a dirty feeding bottle into her hand. "Him, too, she abandoned," he went on in an undertone, pointing to the baby. He went up to the door, stopped, and turned round.

"A gentleman like you," he began, "wouldn't care for our bread, I daresay, and except bread, I've——"

"I'm not hungry."

"Well, that's for you to say. I would have heated the samovar,[6] but I've no tea. . . . I'll go and see how your horse is getting on."

He went out and slammed the door. I looked round again. The hut struck me as more melancholy than ever. The bitter smell of stale smoke choked my breathing unpleasantly. The little girl did not stir from her place, and did not raise her eyes; from time to time she jogged the cradle, and timidly pulled her slipping smock up onto her shoulder; her bare legs hung motionless.

"What's your name?" I asked her.

"Ulita," she said, her mournful little face drooping more than ever.

The forester came in and sat down on the bench.

"The storm's passing over," he observed, after a brief silence; "if you wish it, I will guide you out of the forest."

I got up; Biryuk took his gun and examined the fire pan.

"What's that for?" I inquired.

"There's mischief in the forest. . . . They're cutting a tree down on Mares' Ravine," he added, in reply to my look of inquiry.

"Could you hear it from here?"

"I can hear it outside."

We went out together. The rain had ceased. Heavy masses of storm cloud were still huddled in the distance; from time to time there were long flashes of lightning; but here and there overhead the dark blue sky was already visible; stars twinkled through the swiftly flying clouds. The outline

6 *samovar:* Russian tea urn heated by charcoal fire.

of the trees, drenched with rain, and stirred by the wind, began to stand
out in darkness. We listened. The forester took off his cap and bent his
head. . . . "Th— . . . there!" he said suddenly, and he stretched out his
hand: "See what a night he's pitched on." I had heard nothing but the
rustle of the leaves. Biryuk led the mare out of the shed. "But, perhaps,"
he added aloud, "this way I shall miss him."

"I'll go with you . . . if you like?"

"Certainly," he answered, and he backed the horse in again; we'll catch
him in a trice, and then I'll take you. Let's be off."

We started, Biryuk in front, I following him. Heaven only knows how
he found out his way, but he only stopped once or twice, and then merely
to listen to the strokes of the ax.

"There," he muttered, "do you hear? Do you hear?"

"Why, where?"

Biryuk shrugged his shoulders. We went down into the ravine; the wind
was still for an instant; the rhythmical strokes reached my hearing distinctly. Biryuk glanced at me and shook his head. We went farther through
the wet bracken and nettles. A slow muffled crash was heard. . . .

"He's felled it," muttered Biryuk. Meantime the sky had grown clearer
and clearer; there was a faint light in the forest. We clambered at last out
of the ravine.

"Wait here a little," the forester whispered to me. He bent down, and,
raising his gun above his head, vanished among the bushes. I began listening with strained attention. Across the continual roar of the wind faint
sounds from close by reached me; there was a cautious blow of an ax on
the brushwood, the crash of wheels, the snort of a horse. . . .

"Where are you off to? Stop!" the iron voice of Biryuk thundered suddenly. Another voice was heard in a pitiful shriek, like a trapped hare. . . .
A struggle was beginning.

"No, no, you've made a mistake," Biryuk declared, panting; "you're not
going to get off. . . ."

I rushed in the direction of the noise, and ran up to the scene of the
conflict, stumbling at every step. A felled tree lay on the ground, and near
it Biryuk was busily engaged holding the thief down and binding his hands
behind his back with a kerchief. I came closer. Biryuk got up and set him
on his feet. I saw a peasant drenched with rain, in tatters, and with a long,
disheveled beard. A sorry little nag, half covered with a stiff mat, was
standing by, together with a rough cart. The forester did not utter a word;
the peasant too was silent; his head was shaking.

"Let him go," I whispered in Biryuk's ears; "I'll pay for the tree."

Without a word Biryuk took the horse by the mane with his left hand; in his right he held the thief by the belt. "Now turn round, you rat!" he said grimly.

"The bit of an ax there, take it," muttered the peasant.

"No reason to lose it, certainly," said the forester, and he picked up the ax. We started. I walked behind. . . . The rain began sprinkling again, and soon fell in torrents. With difficulty we made our way to the hut. Biryuk pushed the captured horse into the middle of the yard, led the peasant into the room, loosened the knot in the kerchief, and made him sit down in a corner. The little girl, who had fallen asleep near the oven, jumped up and began staring at us in silent terror. I sat down on the locker.

"Ugh, what a downpour!" remarked the forester. "You will have to wait till it's over. Won't you lie down?"

"Thanks."

"I would have shut him in the store loft, on your honor's account," he went on, indicating the peasant; "but you see the bolt—"

"Leave him here; don't touch him," I interrupted.

The peasant stole a glance at me from under his brows. I vowed inwardly to set the poor wretch free, come what might. He sat without stirring on the locker. By the light of the lantern I could make out his worn, wrinkled face, his overhanging yellow eyebrows, his restless eyes, his thin limbs. . . . The little girl lay down on the floor, just at his feet, and again dropped asleep. Biryuk sat at the table, his head in his hands. A cricket chirped in the corner . . . the rain pattered on the roof and streamed down the windows; we were all silent.

"Foma Kuzmich," said the peasant suddenly in a thick, broken voice; "Foma Kuzmich!"

"What is it?"

"Let me go."

Biryuk made no answer.

"Let me go . . . hunger drove me to it; let me go."

"I know you," retorted the forester severely; "your set's all alike—all thieves."

"Let me go," repeated the peasant. "Our manager . . . we're ruined, that's what it is—let me go!"

"Ruined, indeed! . . . Nobody need steal."

"Let me go, Foma Kuzmich. . . . Don't destroy me. Your manager, you know yourself, will have no mercy on me; that's what it is."

Biryuk turned away. The peasant was shivering as though he were in the throes of fever. His head was shaking, and his breathing came in broken gasps.

"Let me go," he repeated with mournful desperation. "Let me go; by God, let me go! I'll pay; see, by God, I will! By God, it was through hunger! . . . The little ones are crying, you know yourself. It's hard for us, see."

"You needn't go stealing, for all that."

"My little horse," the peasant went on, "my poor little horse, at least . . . our only beast . . . let it go."

"I tell you, I can't. I'm not a freeman; I'm made responsible. You oughtn't to be spoiled, either."

"Let me go! It's through want, Foma Kuzmich, want—and nothing else —let me go!"

"I know you!"

"Oh, let me go!"

"Ugh, what's the use of talking to you! Sit quiet, or else you'll catch it. Don't you see the gentleman, hey?"

The poor wretch hung his head. . . . Biryuk yawned and laid his head on the table. The rain still persisted. I was waiting to see what would happen.

Suddenly the peasant stood erect. His eyes were glittering, and his face flushed dark red. "Come, then, here; strike yourself, here," he began, his eyes puckering up and the corners of his mouth dropping; "come, cursed destroyer of men's souls! drink Christian blood, drink."

The forester turned round.

"I'm speaking to you, Asiatic, bloodsucker, you!"

"Are you drunk, or what, to set to being abusive?" began the forester, puzzled. "Are you out of your senses, hey?"

"Drunk! Not at your expense, cursed destroyer of souls—brute, brute, brute!"

"Ah, you—I'll show you!"

"What's that to me? It's all one; I'm done for; what can I do without a home? Kill me—it's the same in the end; whether it's through hunger or like this—it's all one. Ruin us all—wife, children . . . kill us all at once. But, wait a bit, we'll get at you!"

Biryuk got up.

"Kill me, kill me," the peasant went on in savage tone; "kill me; come, come, kill me. . . ." The little girl jumped up hastily from the ground and stared at him. "Kill me, kill me!"

"Silence!" thundered the forester, and he took two steps forward.

"Stop, Foma, stop," I shouted; "let him go. . . . Peace be with him."

"I won't be silent," the luckless wretch went on. "It's all the same— ruin, anyway—you destroyer of souls, you brute; you've not come to ruin yet. . . . But wait a bit; you won't have long to boast of; they'll wring your neck; wait a bit!"

Biryuk clutched him by the shoulder. I rushed to help the peasant. . . .

"Don't touch him, master!" the forester shouted to me.

I should not have feared his threats, and already had my fist in the air; but to my intense amazement, with one pull he tugged the kerchief off the peasant's elbows, took him by the scruff of the neck, thrust his cap over his eyes, opened the door, and shoved him out.

"Go to the devil with your horse!" he shouted after him. "But mind, next time. . . ."

He came back into the hut and began rummaging in the corner.

"Well, Biryuk," I said at last, "you've astonished me; I see you're a splendid fellow."

"Oh, stop that, master," he cut me short with an air of vexation; "please don't speak of it. But I'd better see you on your way now," he added; "I suppose you won't wait for this little rain. . . ."

In the yard there was the rattle of the wheels of the peasant's cart.

"He's off, then!" he muttered; "but next time!"

Half an hour later he parted from me at the edge of the wood.

My Lord, the Baby

RABINDRANATH TAGORE

I

RAICHARAN was twelve years old when he came as a servant to his master's house. He belonged to the same caste as his master and was given his master's little son to nurse. As time went on the boy left Raicharan's arms to go to school. From school he went on to college, and after college he entered the judicial service. Always, until he married, Raicharan was his sole attendant.

But, when a mistress came into the house, Raicharan found two masters instead of one. All his former influence passed to the new mistress. This was compensated for by a fresh arrival. Anukul had a son born to him, and Raicharan by his unsparing attentions soon got a complete hold over the child. He used to toss him up in his arms, call to him in absurd baby language, put his face close to the baby's, and draw it away again with a grin.

Presently the child was able to crawl and cross the doorway. When Raicharan went to catch him, he would scream with mischievous laughter and make for safety. Raicharan was amazed at the profound skill and exact judgment the baby showed when pursued. He would say to his mistress with a look of awe and mystery: "Your son will be a judge someday."

New wonders came in their turn. When the baby began to toddle, that was to Raicharan an epoch in human history. When he called his father Ba-ba and his mother Ma-ma and Raicharan Chan-na, then Raicharan's ecstasy knew no bounds. He went out to tell the news to all the world.

After a while Raicharan was asked to show his ingenuity in other ways. He had, for instance, to play the part of a horse, holding the reins between his teeth and prancing with his feet. He had also to wrestle with his little charge, and if he could not, by a wrestler's trick, fall on his back defeated at the end, a great outcry was certain.

About this time Anukul was transferred to a district on the banks of the Padma. On his way through Calcutta he bought his son a little go-cart. He bought him also a yellow satin waistcoat, a gold-laced cap, and some gold bracelets and anklets. Raicharan was wont to take these out and put them on his little charge with ceremonial pride whenever they went for a walk.

Then came the rainy season, and day after day the rain poured down in torrents. The hungry river, like an enormous serpent, swallowed down terraces, villages, cornfields, and covered with its flood the tall grasses and wild casuarinas on the sandbanks. From time to time there was a deep thud, as the riverbanks crumbled. The unceasing roar of the main current could be heard from far away. Masses of foam, carried swiftly past, proved to the eye the swiftness of the stream.

One afternoon the rain cleared. It was cloudy, but cool and bright. Raicharan's little despot did not want to stay in on such a fine afternoon. His lordship climbed into the go-cart. Raicharan, between the shafts, dragged him slowly along till he reached the rice fields on the banks of the river. There was no one in the fields, and no boat on the stream. Across the water, on the farther side, the clouds were rifted in the west. The silent ceremonial of the setting sun was revealed in all its glowing splendor. In the midst of that stillness the child, all of a sudden, pointed with his finger in front of him and cried: "Chan-na! Pitty fow."

Close by on a mud flat stood a large *Kadamba* tree in full flower. My lord, the baby, looked at it with greedy eyes, and Raicharan knew his meaning. Only a short time before he had made, out of these very flower balls, a small go-cart; and the child had been so entirely happy dragging it about with a string, that for the whole day Raicharan was not made to put on the reins at all. He was promoted from a horse into a groom.

But Raicharan had no wish that evening to go splashing knee-deep through the mud to reach the flowers. So he quickly pointed his finger in the opposite direction, calling out: "Oh, look, baby, look! Look at the bird." And with all sorts of curious noises he pushed the go-cart rapidly away from the tree.

But a child destined to be a judge cannot be put off so easily. And besides, there was at the time nothing to attract his eyes. And you cannot keep up forever the pretense of an imaginary bird.

The little Master's mind was made up, and Raicharan was at his wits' end. "Very well, baby," he said at last, "you sit still in the cart, and I'll go and get you the pretty flower. Only mind you don't go near the water."

As he said this, he made his legs bare to the knee and waded through the oozing mud toward the tree.

The moment Raicharan had gone, his little Master went off at racing speed to the forbidden water. The baby saw the river rushing by, splashing and gurgling as it went. It seemed as though the disobedient wavelets themselves were running away from some greater Raicharan with the laughter of a thousand children. At the sight of their mischief, the heart of the human child grew excited and restless. He got down stealthily from the go-cart and toddled off toward the river. On his way he picked up a small stick and leaned over the bank of the stream pretending to fish. The mischievous fairies of the river with their mysterious voices seemed to be inviting him into their playhouse.

Raicharan had plucked a handful of flowers from the tree and was carrying them back in the end of his cloth, with his face wreathed in smiles. But when he reached the go-cart, there was no one there. He looked on all sides and there was no one there. He looked back at the cart and there was no one there.

In that first terrible moment his blood froze within him. Before his eyes the whole universe swam round like a dark mist. From the depth of his broken heart he gave one piercing cry: "Master, Master, little Master!"

But no voice answered "Chan-na." No child laughed mischievously back; no scream of baby delight welcomed his return. Only the river ran on, with its splashing, gurgling noise as before—as though it knew nothing at all and had no time to attend to such a tiny human event as the death of a child.

As the evening passed by, Raicharan's mistress became very anxious. She sent men out on all sides to search. They went with lanterns in their hands and reached at last the banks of the Padma. There they found Raicharan rushing up and down the fields, like a stormy wind, shouting the cry of despair: "Master, Master, little Master!"

When they got Raicharan home at last, he fell prostrate at his mistress' feet. They shook him, and questioned him, and asked him repeatedly where he had left the child; but all he could say was that he knew nothing.

Though everyone held the opinion that the Padma had swallowed the child, there was a lurking doubt left in the mind. For a band of gypsies had been noticed outside the village that afternoon, and some suspicion rested on them. The mother went so far in her wild grief as to think it possible that Raicharan himself had stolen the child. She called him aside with piteous entreaty and said: "Raicharan, give me back my baby. Oh! give me back my child. Take from me any money you ask, but give me back my child!"

Anukul tried to reason his wife out of this wholly unjust suspicion: "Why on earth," he said, "should he commit such a crime as that?"

The mother only replied: "The baby had gold ornaments on his body. Who knows?"

It was impossible to reason with her after that.

II

Raicharan went back to his own village. Up to this time he had had no son, and there was no hope that any child would now be born to him. But it came about before the end of a year that his wife gave birth to a son and died.

An overwhelming resentment at first grew up in Raicharan's heart at the sight of this new baby. At the back of his mind was resentful suspicion that it had come as a usurper in place of the little Master. He also thought it would be a grave offense to be happy with a son of his own after what had happened to his master's little child. Indeed, if it had not been for a widowed sister, who mothered the new baby, it would not have lived long.

But a change gradually came over Raicharan's mind. A wonderful thing happened. This new baby began to crawl about and cross the doorway with mischief in its face. It also showed an amusing cleverness in making its escape to safety. Its voice, its sounds of laughter and tears, its gestures, were those of the little Master. On some days, when Raicharan listened to its crying, his heart suddenly began thumping wildly against his ribs, and it seemed to him that his former little Master was crying somewhere in the unknown land of death because he had lost his Chan-na.

Phailna (for that was the name Raicharan's sister gave to the new baby) soon began to talk. It learned to say Ba-ba and Ma-ma with a baby accent. When Raicharan heard those familiar sounds the mystery suddenly became clear. The little Master could not cast off the spell of his Chan-na, and therefore he had been reborn in his own house.

The arguments in favor of this were, to Raicharan, altogether beyond dispute:

> (i) The new baby was born soon after his little Master's death.
> (ii) His wife could never have accumulated such merit as to give birth to a son in middle age.
> (iii) The new baby walked with a toddle and called out Ba-ba and Ma-ma. There was no sign lacking which marked out the future judge.

Then suddenly Raicharan remembered that terrible accusation of the mother. "Ah," he said to himself with amazement, "the mother's heart was right. She knew I had stolen her child." When once he had come to this conclusion, he was filled with remorse for his past neglect. He now gave himself over, body and soul, to the new baby, and became its devoted attendant. He began to bring it up as if it were the son of a rich man. He bought a go-cart, a yellow satin waistcoat, and a gold-embroidered cap. He melted down the ornaments of his dead wife and made gold bangles and anklets. He refused to let the little child play with anyone of the neighborhood and became himself its sole companion day and night. As the baby grew up to boyhood, he was so petted and spoiled and clad in such finery that the village children would call him "Your Lordship," and jeer at him; and older people regarded Raicharan as unaccountably crazy about the child.

At last the time came for the boy to go to school. Raicharan sold his small piece of land and went to Calcutta. There he got employment with great difficulty as a servant and sent Phailna to school. He spared no pains to give him the best education, the best clothes, the best food. Meanwhile he lived himself on a mere handful of rice and would say in secret: "Ah! my little Master, my dear little Master, you loved me so much that you came back to my house. You shall never suffer from any neglect of mine."

Twelve years passed away in this manner. The boy was able to read and write well. He was bright and healthy and good-looking. He paid a great deal of attention to his personal appearance and was specially careful in parting his hair. He was inclined to extravagance and finery, and spent money freely. He could never quite look on Raicharan as a father, because, though fatherly in affection, he had the manner of a servant. A further fault was this, that Raicharan kept secret from everyone that he himself was the father of the child.

The students of the hostel, where Phailna was a boarder, were greatly amused by Raicharan's country manners, and I have to confess that behind his father's back Phailna joined in their fun. But, in the bottom of their hearts, all the students loved the innocent and tender-hearted old man, and Phailna was very fond of him also. But, as I have said before, he loved him with a kind of condescension.

Raicharan grew older and older, and his employer was continually finding fault with him for his incompetent work. He had been starving himself for the boy's sake. So he had grown physically weak and was no longer up to his work. He would forget things, and his mind became dull and stupid. But his employer expected a full servant's work out of him and would not brook excuses. The money that Raicharan had brought with him from the sale of his land was exhausted. The boy was continually grumbling about his clothes and asking for more money.

III

Raicharan made up his mind. He gave up the situation where he was working as a servant, and left some money with Phailna and said: "I have some business to do at home in my village and shall be back soon."

He went off at once to Baraset, where Anukul was magistrate. Anukul's wife was still broken down with grief. She had had no other child.

One day Anukul was resting after a long weary day in court. His wife was buying, at an exorbitant price, an herb from a mendicant quack, which was said to ensure the birth of a child. A voice of greeting was heard in the courtyard. Anukul went out to see who was there. It was Raicharan. Anukul's heart was softened when he saw his old servant. He asked him many questions and offered to take him back into service.

Raicharan smiled faintly and said in reply: "I want to make obeisance to my mistress."

Anukul went with Raicharan into the house, where the mistress did not receive him as warmly as his old master. Raicharan took no notice of this, but folded his hands, and said: "It was not the Padma that stole your baby. It was I."

Anukul exclaimed: "Great God! Eh! What! Where is he?"

Raicharan replied: "He is with me. I will bring him the day after tomorrow."

It was Sunday. There was no magistrate's court sitting. Both husband and wife were looking expectantly along the road, waiting from early morning for Raicharan's appearance. At ten o'clock he came, leading Phailna by the hand.

Anukul's wife, without question, took the boy into her lap, and was wild with excitement, sometimes laughing, sometimes weeping, touching him, kissing his hair and his forehead, and gazing into his face with hungry, eager eyes. The boy was very good-looking and dressed like a gentleman's son. The heart of Anukul brimmed over with a sudden rush of affection.

Nevertheless, the magistrate in him asked: "Have you any proofs?"

Raicharan said: "How could there be any proof of such a deed? God alone knows that I stole your boy, and no one else in the world."

When Anukul saw how eagerly his wife was clinging to the boy, he realized the futility of asking for proofs. It would be wiser to believe. And then—where could an old man like Raicharan get such a boy from? And why should his faithful servant deceive him for nothing?

"But," he added severely, "Raicharan, you must not stay here."

"Where shall I go, Master?" said Raicharan, in a choking voice, folding his hands. "I am old. Who will take an old man as a servant?"

The mistress said: "Let him stay. My child will be pleased. I forgive him."

But Anukul's magisterial conscience would not allow him. "No," he said, "he cannot be forgiven for what he has done."

Raicharan bowed to the ground and clasped Anukul's feet. "Master," he cried, "let me stay. It was not I who did it. It was God."

Anukul's conscience was worse stricken than ever, when Raicharan tried to put the blame on God's shoulders.

"No," he said, "I could not allow it. I cannot trust you anymore. You have done an act of treachery."

Raicharan rose to his feet and said: "It was not I who did it."

"Who was it then?" asked Anukul.

Raicharan replied: "It was my fate."

But no educated man could take this for an excuse. Anukul remained obdurate.

When Phailna saw that he was the wealthy magistrate's son, and not Raicharan's, he was angry at first, thinking that he had been cheated all this time of his birthright. But seeing Raicharan in distress, he generously said to his father: "Father, forgive him. Even if you don't let him live with us, let him have a small monthly pension."

After hearing this, Raicharan did not utter another word. He looked for the last time on the face of his son; he made obeisance to his old master and mistress. Then he went out and was mingled with the numberless people of the world.

At the end of the month Anukul sent him some money to his village. But the money came back. There was no one there of the name of Raicharan.

Two Poems

PO CHÜ-I

Golden Bells

When I was almost forty
I had a daughter whose name was Golden Bells.
Now it is just a year since she was born;
She is learning to sit and cannot yet talk.
Ashamed—to find that I have not a sage's heart:
I cannot resist vulgar thoughts and feelings.
Henceforward I am tied to things outside myself:
My only reward—the pleasure I am getting now.
If I am spared the grief of her dying young,
Then I shall have the trouble of getting her married.
My plan for retiring and going back to the hills
Must now be postponed for fifteen years!

Remembering Golden Bells

Ruined and ill—a man of two score;
    Pretty and guileless—a girl of three.
Not a boy—but still better than nothing:
To soothe one's feeling—from time to time a kiss!
There came a day—they suddenly took her from me;
Her soul's shadow wandered I know not where.

And when I remember how just at the time she died
She lisped strange sounds, beginning to learn to talk,
Then I know that the ties of flesh and blood
Only bind us to a load of grief and sorrow.
At last, by thinking of the time before she was born,
By thought and reason I drove the pain away.
Since my heart forgot her, many days have passed
And three times winter has changed to spring.
This morning, for a little, the old grief came back,
Because, in the road, I met her foster-nurse.

Tell Freedom

PETER ABRAHAMS

And judgment is turned away backward, and justice standeth afar off
for truth is fallen in the street, and equity cannot enter.
—ISAIAH

WEDNESDAY was crackling day. On that day the children of the
location made the long trek to Elsburg siding for the squares of pig's
rind that passed for our daily meat. We collected a double lot of cow dung
the day before; a double lot of *moeroga*.[1]

I finished my breakfast and washed up. Aunt Liza was at her washtub in
the yard. A misty, sickly sun was just showing. And on the open veld the
frost lay thick and white on the grass.

"Ready?" Aunt Liza called.

I went out to her. She shook the soapsuds off her swollen hands and
wiped them on her apron. She lifted the apron and put her hand through
the slits of the many thin cotton dresses she wore. The dress nearest the
skin was the one with the pocket. From this she pulled a sixpenny piece.
She tied it in a knot in the corner of a bit of colored cloth.

"Take care of that. . . . Take the smaller piece of bread in the bin but
don't eat it till you start back. You can have a small piece of crackling with
it. Only a small piece, understand?"

"Yes, Aunt Liza."

"All right."

I got the bread and tucked it into the little canvas bag in which I would
carry the crackling.

[1] *moeroga:* wild spinach.

170

" 'Bye, Aunt Liza." I trotted off, one hand in my pocket, feeling the cloth where the money was. I paused at Andries' home.

"Andries!" I danced up and down while I waited. The cold was not so terrible on bare feet if one did not keep still.

Andries came trotting out of their yard. His mother's voice followed; desperate and plaintive:

"I'll skin you if you lose the money!"

"Women!" Andries said bitterly.

I glimpsed the dark, skinny woman at her washtub as we trotted across the veld. Behind, and in front of us, other children trotted in twos and threes.

There was a sharp bite to the morning air I sucked in; it stung my nose so that tears came to my eyes; it went down my throat like an icy draught; my nose ran. I tried breathing through my mouth but this was worse. The cold went through my shirt and shorts; my skin went pimply and chilled; my fingers went numb and began to ache; my feet felt like frozen lumps that did not belong to me, yet jarred and hurt each time I put them down. I began to feel sick and desperate.

"Jesus God in heaven!" Andries cried suddenly.

I looked at him. His eyes were rimmed in red. Tears ran down his cheeks. His face was drawn and purple, a sick look on it.

"Faster," I said.

"Think it'll help?"

I nodded. We went faster. We passed two children, sobbing and moaning as they ran. We were all in the same desperate situation. We were creatures haunted and hounded by the cold. It was a cruel enemy who gave no quarter. And our means of fighting it were pitifully inadequate. In all the mornings and evenings of the winter months, young and old, big and small, were helpless victims of the bitter cold. Only toward noon and the early afternoon, when the sun sat high in the sky, was there a brief respite. For us, the children, the cold, especially the morning cold, assumed an awful and malevolent personality. We talk of "It." "It" was a half-human monster with evil thoughts, evil intentions, bent on destroying us. "It" was happiest when we were most miserable. Andries had told me how "It" had, last winter, caught and killed a boy.

Hunger was an enemy too, but one with whom we could come to terms, who had many virtues and values. Hunger gave our *pap*,[2] *moeroga,* and crackling a feastlike quality. We could, when it was not with us, think and talk kindly about it. Its memory could even give moments of laughter. But

[2] *pap:* a kind of porridge made with crushed corn.

the cold of winter was with us all the time. "It" never really eased up. There were only more bearable degrees of "It" at high noon and on mild days. "It" was the real enemy. And on this Wednesday morning, as we ran across the veld, winter was more bitterly, bitingly, freezingly real than ever.

The sun climbed. The frozen earth thawed, leaving the short grass looking wet and weary. Painfully, our feet and legs came alive. The aching numbness slowly left our fingers. We ran more slowly in the more bearable cold.

In climbing, the sun lost some of its damp look and seemed a real, if cold, sun. When it was right overhead, we struck the sandy road which meant we were nearing the siding. None of the others were in sight. Andries and I were alone on the sandy road on the open veld. We slowed down to a brisk walk. We were sufficiently thawed to want to talk.

"How far?" I said.

"A few minutes," he said.

"I've got a piece of bread," I said.

"Me too," he said. "Let's eat it now."

"On the way back," I said. "With a bit of crackling."

"Good idea. . . . Race to the fork."

"All right."

"Go!" he said.

We shot off together, legs working like pistons. He soon pulled away from me. He reached the fork in the road some fifty yards ahead.

"I win!" he shouted gleefully, though his teeth still chattered.

We pitched stones down the road, each trying to pitch farther than the other. I won and wanted to go on doing it. But Andries soon grew weary with pitching. We raced again. Again he won. He wanted another race, but I refused. I wanted pitching, but he refused. So, sulking with each other, we reached the pig farm.

We followed a fenced-off pathway round sprawling white buildings. Everywhere about us was the grunt of pigs. As we passed an open doorway, a huge dog came bounding out, snarling and barking at us. In our terror, we forgot it was fenced in and streaked away. Surprised, I found myself a good distance ahead of Andries. We looked back and saw a young white woman call the dog to heel.

"Damn Boer dog," Andries said.

"Matter with it?" I asked.

"They teach them to go for us. Never get caught by one. My old man's got a hole in his bottom where a Boer dog got him."

I remembered I had outstripped him.

"I won!" I said.

"Only because you were frightened," he said.

"I still won."

"Scare arse," he jeered.

"Scare arse, yourself!"

"I'll knock you!"

"I'll knock you back!"

A couple of white men came down the path and ended our possible fight. We hurried past them to the distant shed where a queue had already formed. There were grown-ups and children. All the grown-ups, and some of the children, were from places other than our location.

The line moved slowly. The young white man who served us did it in a leisurely fashion, with long pauses for a smoke. Occasionally he turned his back.

At last, after what seemed hours, my turn came. Andries was behind me. I took the sixpenny piece from the square of cloth and offered it to the man.

"Well?" he said.

"Sixpence crackling, please."

Andries nudged me in the back. The man's stare suddenly became cold and hard. Andries whispered into my ear.

"Well?" the man repeated coldly.

"Please, *baas*,"[3] I said.

"What d'you want?"

"Sixpence crackling, please."

"What?"

Andries dug me in the ribs.

"Sixpence crackling, please, *baas*."

"What?"

"Sixpence crackling, please, *baas*."

"You new here?"

"Yes, *baas*." I looked at his feet while he stared at me.

At last he took the sixpenny piece from me. I held my bag open while he filled it with crackling from a huge pile on a large canvas sheet on the ground. Turning away, I stole a fleeting glance at his face. His eyes met mine, and there was amused, challenging mockery in them. I waited for Andries at the back of the queue, out of the reach of the white man's mocking eyes.

The cold day was at its mildest as we walked home along the sandy road. I took out my piece of bread and, with a small piece of greasy crackling, still warm, on it, I munched as we went along. We had not yet made our

[3] *baas:* master.

peace so Andries munched his bread and crackling on the other side of the road.

"Dumb fool!" he mocked at me for not knowing how to address the white man.

"Scare arse!" I shouted back.

Thus, hurling curses at each other, we reached the fork. Andries saw them first and moved over to my side of the road.

"White boys," he said.

There were three of them. Two of about our own size and one slightly bigger. They had school bags and were coming toward us up the road from the siding.

"Better run for it," Andries said.

"Why?"

"No, that'll draw them. Let's just walk along, but quickly."

"Why?" I repeated.

"Shut up," he said.

Some of his anxiety touched me. Our own scrap was forgotten. We marched side by side as fast as we could. The white boys saw us and hurried up the road. We passed the fork. Perhaps they would take the turning away from us. We dared not look back.

"Hear them?" Andries asked.

"No."

I looked over my shoulder.

"They're coming," I said.

"Walk faster," Andries said. "If they come closer, run."

"Hey, *klipkop*!"[4]

"Don't look back," Andries said.

"Hottentot!"

We walked as fast as we could.

"Bloody Kaffir!"

Ahead was a bend in the road. Behind the bend were bushes. Once there, we could run without their knowing it till it was too late.

"Faster," Andries said.

They began pelting us with stones.

"Run when we get to the bushes," Andries said.

The bend and the bushes were near. We would soon be there.

A clear young voice carried to us:

"Your fathers are dirty black bastards of baboons!"

"Run!" Andries called.

---

[4] *klipkop:* stonehead.

A violent, unreasoning anger suddenly possessed me. I stopped and turned.

"You're a liar!" I screamed.

The foremost boy pointed at me:

"An ugly black baboon!"

In a fog of rage I went toward him.

"Liar!" I shouted. "My father was better than your father!"

I neared them. The bigger boy stepped between me and the one I was after.

"My father was better than your father! Liar!"

The big boy struck me a mighty clout on the side of the face. I staggered, righted myself, and leaped at the boy who had insulted my father. I struck him on the face, hard. A heavy blow on the back of my head nearly stunned me. I grabbed at the boy in front of me. We went down together.

"Liar!" I said through clenched teeth, hitting him with all my might.

Blows rained on me, on my head, my neck, the side of my face, my mouth, but my enemy was under me and I pounded him fiercely, all the time repeating:

"Liar! Liar! Liar!"

Suddenly, stars exploded in my head. Then there was darkness.

I emerged from the darkness to find Andries kneeling beside me.

"God, man! I thought they'd killed you."

I sat up. The white boys were nowhere to be seen. Like Andries, they'd probably thought me dead and run off in panic. The inside of my mouth felt sore and swollen. My nose was tender to the touch. The back of my head ached. A trickle of blood dripped from my nose. I stemmed it with the square of colored cloth. The greatest damage was to my shirt. It was ripped in many places. I remembered the crackling. I looked anxiously about. It was safe, a little off the road on the grass. I relaxed. I got up and brushed my clothes. I picked up the crackling.

"God, you're dumb!" Andries said. "You're going to get it! Dumb arse!"

I was too depressed to retort. Besides, I knew he was right. I was dumb. I should have run when he told me to.

"Come on," I said.

One of many small groups of children, each child carrying his little bag of crackling, we trod the long road home in the cold winter afternoon.

There was tension in the house that night. When I got back Aunt Liza had listened to the story in silence. The beating or scolding I expected did not come. But Aunt Liza changed while she listened, became remote and withdrawn. When Uncle Sam came home she told him what had happened. He, too, just looked at me and became more remote and withdrawn than usual. They were waiting for something; their tension reached out to me, and I waited with them, anxious, apprehensive.

The thing we waited for came while we were having our supper.

We heard a trap pull up outside.

"Here it is," Uncle Sam said and got up.

Aunt Liza leaned back from the table and put her hands in her lap, fingers intertwined, a cold, unseeing look in her eyes.

Before Uncle Sam reached it, the door burst open. A tall, broad white man strode in. Behind him came the three boys. The one I had attacked had swollen lips and a puffy left eye.

" 'Evening, *baas*!" Uncle Sam murmured.

"That's him," the bigger boy said, pointing at me.

The white man stared till I lowered my eyes.

"Well?" he said.

"He's sorry, *baas*," Uncle Sam said quickly. "I've given him a hiding he won't forget soon. You know how it is, *baas*. He's new here, the child of a relative in Johannesburg and they don't all know how to behave there. You know how it is in the big towns, *baas*." The plea in Uncle Sam's voice had grown more pronounced as he went on. He turned to me. "Tell the *baas* and young *basies* how sorry you are, Lee."

I looked at Aunt Liza and something in her lifelessness made me stubborn in spite of my fear.

"He insulted my father," I said.

The white man smiled.

"See, Sam, your hiding couldn't have been good."

There was a flicker of life in Aunt Liza's eyes. For a brief moment she saw me, looked at me, warmly, lovingly, then her eyes went dead again.

"He's only a child, *baas*," Uncle Sam murmured.

"You stubborn too, Sam?"

"No, *baas*."

"Good. . . . Then teach him, Sam. If you and he are to live here, you must teach him. Well. . . . ?"

"Yes, *baas*."

Uncle Sam went into the other room and returned with a thick leather thong. He wound it once round his hand and advanced on me. The man and boys leaned against the door, watching. I looked at Aunt Liza's face. Though there was no sign of life or feeling on it, I knew suddenly, instinctively, that she wanted me not to cry.

Bitterly, Uncle Sam said:

"You must never lift your hand to a white person. No matter what happens, you must never lift your hand to a white person. . . ."

He lifted the strap and brought it down on my back. I clenched my teeth and stared at Aunt Liza. I did not cry with the first three strokes. Then, suddenly, Aunt Liza went limp. Tears showed in her eyes. The thong came down on my back, again and again. I screamed and begged for mercy. I groveled at Uncle Sam's feet, begging him to stop, promising never to lift my hand to any white person. . . .

At last, the white man's voice said:

"All right, Sam."

Uncle Sam stopped. I lay whimpering on the floor. Aunt Liza sat like one in a trance.

"Is he still stubborn, Sam?"

"Tell the *baas* and *basies* you are sorry."

"I'm sorry," I said.

"Bet his father is one of those who believe in equality."

"His father is dead," Aunt Liza said.

"Good night, Sam."

"Good night, *baas*. Sorry about this."

"All right, Sam." He opened the door. The boys went out first, then he followed. "Good night, Liza."

Aunt Liza did not answer. The door shut behind the white folk, and soon we heard their trap moving away. Uncle Sam flung the thong viciously against the door, slumped down on the bench, folded his arms on the table, and buried his head on his arms. Aunt Liza moved away from him, came on the floor beside me, and lifted me into her large lap. She sat rocking my body. Uncle Sam began to sob softly. After some time, he raised his head and looked at us.

"Explain to the child, Liza," he said.

"You explain," Aunt Liza said bitterly. "You are the man. You did the beating. You are the head of the family. This is a man's world. You do the explaining."

"Please, Liza. . . ."

"You should be happy. The whites are satisfied. We can go on now."

With me in her arms, Aunt Liza got up. She carried me into the other room. The food on the table remained half eaten. She laid me on the bed on my stomach, smeared fat on my back, then covered me with the blankets. She undressed and got into bed beside me. She cuddled me close, warmed me with her own body. With her big hand on my cheek, she rocked me, first to silence, then to sleep.

For the only time of my stay there, I slept on a bed in Elsburg.

When I woke next morning Uncle Sam had gone. Aunt Liza only once referred to the beating he had given me. It was in the late afternoon, when I returned with the day's cow dung.

"It hurt him," she said. "You'll understand one day."

That night, Uncle Sam brought me an orange, a bag of boiled sweets, and a dirty old picture book. He smiled as he gave them to me, rather anxiously. When I smiled back at him, he seemed to relax. He put his hand on my head, started to say something, then changed his mind and took his seat by the fire.

Aunt Liza looked up from the floor where she dished out the food.

"It's all right, old man," she murmured.

"One day. . . ." Uncle Sam said.

"It's all right," Aunt Liza repeated insistently.

The long winter passed. Slowly, day by day, the world of Elsburg became a warmer place. The cracks in my feet began to heal. The spells of bearable, noonday cold gave way to warmth. The noise of the veld at night became a din. The freezing nights changed, became bearable; changed again, became warm. Warm nights and hot days!

Summer had come, and with its coming the world became a softer, kindlier, more beautiful place. Sunflowers began blooming in people's yards. And people themselves began to relax and laugh. When, one evening, as I came in with some washing from the line, I heard Uncle Sam's voice raised in laughter, and saw him and Aunt Liza playing. I knew summer had really come. Later that same evening he went into the other room and returned with a guitar. Aunt Liza beamed.

"Open the door?"

Uncle Sam nodded. He played. Soon people from the other houses came, in ones and twos, till our little room was crowded. Someone sang with his arms on his wife's shoulders, a love song:

> I'll be your sweetheart,
> If you will be mine. . . .

Summer had come indeed.

In the long summer afternoons, after my day's work, I went down to the river. Sometimes Andries and some of the other children went with me. Often I went alone.

Often, with others, or alone, I climbed the short willows with their long drooping branches. The touch of the willow leaf on the cheek gives a feeling of cool wonder. Often I jumped from stone to stone on the broad bed of the shallow, clear, fast-flowing river. Sometimes I found little pools of idle water, walled off by stones from the flow. I tickled long-tailed tadpoles in these. The sun on the water touched their bodies with myriad colors.

Sometimes I watched the *springhaas*—the wild rabbit of the veld—go leaping across the land, almost faster than my eye could follow. And sometimes I lay on my back, on the green grass; on the bank of the river, and looked up at the distant sky, watching thin, fleecy white clouds form and re-form and trying to associate the shapes with people and things I knew. I loved being alone by the river. It became my special world.

Each day I explored a little more of the river, going farther up or down stream, extending the frontiers of my world. One day, going farther downstream than I had been before, I came upon a boy. He was on the bank on the other side from me. We saw each other at the same time and stared. He was completely naked. He carried two finely carved sticks of equal size and shape, both about his own height. He was not light brown, like the other children of our location, but dark brown, almost black. I moved almost to the edge of the river. He called out in a strange language.

"Hello!" I shouted.

He called out again, and again I could not understand. I searched for a place with stones, then bounded across. I approached him slowly. As I drew near, he gripped his sticks more firmly. I stopped.

He spoke harshly, flung one stick on the ground at my feet, and held the other ready as though to fight.

"Don't want to fight," I said.

I reached down to pick up the stick and return it to him. He took a step forward and raised the one in his hand. I moved back quickly. He stepped back and pointed at the stick on the ground. I shook my head.

"Don't want to fight."

I pushed the stick toward him with my foot, ready to run at the first sign of attack. I showed my new, stubby teeth in a tentative smile. He said something that sounded less aggressive. I nodded, smiling more broadly. He relaxed, picked up the stick, and transferred both to his left hand. He smacked his chest.

"Joseph! Zulu!"

I smacked my own chest.

"Lee. . . ." But I didn't know what I was apart from that.

He held out his hand. We shook. His face lit up in a sunny smile. He said something and pointed downstream. Then he took my arm and led me down.

Far downstream, where the river skirted a hillside, hidden by a cluster of willows, we came on a large clear pool. Joseph flung his sticks on the ground and dived in. He shot through the water like a tadpole. He went down and came up. He shouted and beckoned me to come in. I undressed and went in more tentatively. Laughing, he pulled me under. I came up gasping and spluttering, my belly filled with water. He smacked me on the back and the water shot out of my mouth in a rush. When he realized I could not swim he became more careful. We spent the afternoon with Joseph teaching me to swim. At home, that evening, I stood beside Aunt Liza's washtub.

"Aunt Liza. . . ."

"Yes?"

"What am I?"

"What are you talking about?"

"I met a boy at the river. He said he was Zulu."

She laughed.

"You are Colored. There are three kinds of people: white people, Colored people, and black people. The white people come first, then the Colored people, then the black people."

"Why?"

"Because it is so."

Next day, when I met Joseph, I smacked my chest and said: "Lee Colored!"

He clapped his hands and laughed.

Joseph and I spent most of the long summer afternoons together. He learned some Afrikaans from me; I learned some Zulu from him. Our days were full.

There was the river to explore.

There were my swimming lessons, and others.

I learned to fight with sticks; to weave a green hat of young willow wands and leaves; to catch frogs and tadpoles with my hands; to set a trap for the *springhaas*; to make the sounds of the river birds.

There was the hot sun to comfort us. . . .

There was the green grass to dry our bodies. . . .

There was the soft clay with which to build. . . .

There was the fine sand with which to fight. . . .

There were our giant grasshoppers to race. . . .

There were the locust swarms when the skies turned black and we caught them by the hundreds. . . .

There was the rare taste of crisp, brown-baked, salted locusts. . . .

There was the voice of the wind in the willows. . . .

There was the voice of the heaven in the thunderstorms. . . .

There were the voices of two children in laughter, ours. . . .

There were Joseph's tales of black kings who lived in days before the white man. . . .

At home, I said:

"Aunt Liza. . . ."

"Yes?"

"Did we have Colored kings before the white man?"

"No."

"Then where did we come from? Joseph and his mother come from the black kings who were before the white man."

And laughing, and ruffling my head, she said:

"You talk too much. . . . Go'n wash up."

And to Joseph, next day, I said:

"We didn't have Colored kings before the white man."

And he comforted me and said:

"It is of no moment. You are my brother. Now my kings will be your kings. Come: I have promised the mother to bring you home. She awaits you. I will race you to the hill."

From the top of the hill I looked into a long valley where cattle grazed. To the right, on the sloping land, nestled a cluster of mud huts. Around each hut was a wall built of mud.

"That is my home." Joseph pointed.

We veered right and went down to it. From a distance, we saw a woman at the gate of one of the huts.

"There is the mother!" He walked faster.

She was barefooted. She wore a slight skirt that came above her knees. A child was strapped to her back. The upper part of her body was naked except for the cloth across her chest that supported the child. Round her neck, arms, and legs were strings of white beads. As we drew near, I saw that she was young. And her broad, round face was beautiful. Her black eyes were liquid soft. She called out a greeting and smiled. Joseph pushed me forward.

"This is my brother, Lee of the Coloreds, little mother."

"Greetings, Mother," I said.

"I greet you, my son," she said softly, a twinkle in her eyes.

"As the man of my house has told you, food awaits. Come."

"See!" Joseph puffed out his chest. To his mother he said, "He would not believe when I told him I was the man in our house."

"He is indeed," she said.

Circling the hut was a raised platform. We sat on this while she brought us the food; salted fried locusts and corn on the cob. She sat nearby and watched us eating.

"Show the mother," Joseph said, and took another bite at the *mealies*. "Show the mother you are not circumcised yet."

I showed her.

"This is strange," she said. "Have you no initiation schools?"

"No!" Joseph said.

"Then when do you enter manhood?"

"He does not know."

"Is it true?" She looked at me.

I nodded.

"He's still a child!" Joseph cried. "So big and a child!"

Christmas came and it was a feast of eating and laughter. I spent half my time at home with Aunt Liza and Uncle Sam and the other half with Joseph and the little mother.

My sixth birthday came. Joseph and the little mother and I celebrated it by the river.

Then, early one morning, just as the first cold touches crept into the morning air, Joseph came to our location.

I was washing up when I heard young voices shouting:

"Look at the naked Kaffir! Lee's Kaffir!"

I rushed out. Joseph came gravely to me.

"I come to take leave, my brother. My father has died in the mines so we go back to our land."

He stood straight and stern, not heeding the shouts of the children about. He was a man. This was the burden of his manhood. I had learned so much from him, so I said equally coldly:

"I must take leave of the little mother."

"She is a woman. She weeps."

We ran all the way there. . . .

When the little cart had taken them away, I climbed the hill and went down to the river. I carried Joseph's two sticks with me. These were his parting gift to his brother. "Defend yourself," he had said. "I will make others."

I walked along the river that had been our kingdom. Now it was a desolate place. Joseph had been here with me; now Joseph had gone. Before I realized it, my tears flowed fast. There had been much between us.

So the summer passed. The autumn came. The leaves went brown on the willows by the river. They fluttered to the ground and turned to mold. The long days shortened suddenly. The cold came. Winter had come to torture us again.

Return: Two Poems

ABIOSEH NICOL

Up-Country

Then I came back
Sailing down the Guinea coast,
Loving the sophistication
Of your brave new cities:
Dakar, Accra, Cotonou,
Lagos, Bathurst, and Bissau,
Freetown, Libreville.
Freedom is really in the mind.

Go up-country, they said,
To see the real Africa.
For whomsoever you may be,
That is where you come from.
Go for bush—inside the bush
You will find your hidden heart,
Your mute ancestral spirit.

And so I went,
Dancing on my way.

On An African Beach

Here I stand
On the white-fringed edge of the world:
Its limits are my mind.
Let your white sun
Wash my strong brown body.

I feel the crinkle of your golden sands
Under the yellow soles of my feet.
If I lose this certain grip,
If this blue sea washes all of you away,
I will have been widowed
By the moon's rising tide.

I have taken you for better or for worse,
Yet between the thick and the thin
Of this ebbing flow I cannot form a whole.

But if with love again
I turn my face towards you, Africa,
Turning away from the faithless horizon,
Your green mountains will give me
My fulfillment.

The Prisoner

PO CHÜ-I

Tartars led in chains,
Tartars led in chains!
Their ears pierced, their faces bruised—they are driven into
the land of Ch'in.
The Son of Heaven took pity on them and would not have
them slain.
He sent them away to the south-east, to the lands of Wu
and Yüeh.
A petty officer in a yellow coat took down their names
and surnames.
They were led from the city of Ch'ang-an under escort of
an armed guard.
Their bodies were covered with the wounds of arrows,
their bones stood out from their cheeks.
They had grown so weak they could only march a single
stage a day.
In the morning they must satisfy hunger and thirst with
neither plate nor cup:
At night they must lie in their dirt and rags on beds that
stank with filth.
Suddenly they came to the Yangtze River and remembered
the waters of Chiao.
With lowered hands and levelled voices they sobbed a
muffled song.

Then one Tartar lifted up his voice and spoke to the
      other Tartars,
"*Your* sorrows are none at all compared with *my* sorrows."
Those that were with him in the same band asked to hear
      his tale:
   As he tried to speak the words were choked by anger.
He told them "I was born and bred in the town of
      Liang-yüan..
In the frontier wars of Ta-li[1] I fell into the Tartar's hands.
Since the days the Tartars took me alive forty years have passed:
They put me into a coat of skins tied with a belt of rope.
Only on the first of the first month might I wear my
      Chinese dress.
As I put on my coat and arranged my cap, how fast the
      tears flowed!
I made in my heart a secret vow I would find a way home:
I hid my plan from my Tartar wife and the children she had
      borne me in the land.
I thought to myself, 'It is well for me that my limbs are
      still strong.'
And yet, being old, in my heart I feared I should never live
      to return.
The Tartar chieftains shoot so well that the birds are afraid
      to fly:
From the risk of their arrows I escaped alive and fled
      swiftly home.
Hiding all day and walking all night I crossed the Great Desert.
Where clouds are dark and the moon black and the sands
      eddy in the wind.
Frightened, I sheltered at the Green Grave,[2] where the frozen
      grasses are few:
Stealthily I crossed the Yellow River, at night, on the thin ice,
Suddenly I heard Han[3] drums and the sound of soldiers coming:
I went to meet them at the road-side, bowing to them as
      they came.
But the moving horsemen did not hear that I spoke the
      Han tongue:

[1] *Ta-li:* the period Ta-li, A.D. 766–780.
[2] *Green Grave:* the grave of Chao-chün, a Chinese girl who in 33 B.C. was "bestowed upon the Khan of the Hsiung-nu as a mark of Imperial Regard." Hers was the only grave in this desolate district on which grass would grow.
[3] *Han:* i.e., Chinese.

Their Captain took me for a Tartar born and had me bound
in chains.
They are sending me away to the south-east, to a low and
swampy land:
No one now will take pity on me: resistance is all in vain.
Thinking of this, my voice chokes and I ask of Heaven above,
Was I spared from death only to spend the rest of my years
in sorrow?
My native village of Liang-yüan I shall not see again:
My wife and children in the Tartars' land I have fruitlessly
deserted.
When I fell among Tartars and was taken prisoner, I pined
for the land of Han:
Now that I am back in the land of Han, they have turned
me into a Tartar.
Had I but known what my fate would be, I would not have
started home!
For the two lands, so wide apart, are alike in the sorrow
they bring.
Tartar prisoners in chains!
Of all the sorrows of all the prisoners mine is the hardest
to bear!
Never in the world has so great a wrong befallen the lot
of man—
A Han heart and a Han tongue set in the body of a Turk."

The Dwarf Trees

SEAMI MOTOKIYO

CHARACTERS

THE PRIEST, LORD TOKIYORI *disguised*
TSUNEYO GENZAYEMON, *a former retainer of Tokiyori*
GENZAYEMON'S WIFE
TOKIYORI'S MINISTER, *and* FOLLOWERS
CHORUS

PRIEST: No whence nor whither know I, only onward,
    Onward my way.

I am a holy man of no fixed abode. I have been traveling through the land of Shinano; but the snow lies thick. I had best go up to Kamakura now and wait there. When Spring comes I will set out upon my pilgrimage.

    [*He walks round the stage singing his song of travel.*]

    Land of Shinano, Peak of Asama,
    Thy red smoke rising far and near! Yet cold
    Blows the great wind whose breath
    From Greatwell Hill is fetched.
    On to the Village of Friends—but friendless I,
    Whose self is cast aside, go up the path
    Of Parting Hill, that from the temporal world
    Yet further parts me. Down the river, down
    Runs my swift raft plank-nosed to Plank-nose Inn,
    And to the Ford of Sano I am come.

I have traveled so fast that I am come to the Ford of Sano in the country of Kōzuke. Ara! It is snowing again. I must seek shelter here. (*Goes to the wing and knocks.*) Is there anyone in this house?

TSUNEYO'S WIFE (*raising the curtain that divides the hashigakari[1] from the stage*): Who is there?

PRIEST: I am a pilgrim; pray lodge me here tonight.

WIFE: That is a small thing to ask. But since the master is away, you cannot lodge in this house.

PRIEST: Then I will wait here till he comes back.

WIFE: That must be as you please. I will go to the corner and watch for him. When he comes I will tell him you are here.

[*Enter* TSUNEYO *from the wing, making the gesture of one who shakes snow from his clothes.*]

TSUNEYO: Ah! How the snow falls! Long ago when I was in the World I loved to see it:

"Hither and thither the snow blew like feathers plucked
      from a goose;
Long, long I watched it fall, till it dressed me in a white
      coat."[2]

So I sang; and the snow that falls now is the same that I saw then. But I indeed am frost-white[3] that watch it!

Oh how shall this thin dress of Kefu cloth
Chase from my bones the winter of today,
Oh pitiless day of snow!
      [*He sees his* WIFE *standing waiting.*]

What is this! How comes it that you are waiting here in this great storm of snow?

WIFE: A pilgrim came this way and begged for a night's lodging. And when I told him you were not in the house, he asked if he might wait till you returned. That is why I am here.

TSUNEYO: Where is this pilgrim now?

WIFE: There he stands!

PRIEST: I am he. Though the day is not far spent, how can I find my way in this great storm of snow? Pray give me shelter for the night.

TSUNEYO: That is a small thing to ask; but I have no lodging fit for you; I cannot receive you.

[1] *hashigakari:* the runway in backstage center between the dressing room and the stage.

[2] *"Hither . . . white coat":* Po Chü-i's *Works,* iii. 13.

[3] *frost-white:* alluding partly to the fact that he is snow-covered, partly to his gray hairs.

PRIEST: No, no. I do not care how poor the lodging may be. Pray let me stay here for one night.

TSUNEYO: I would gladly ask you to stay, but there is scarce space for us two, that are husband and wife. How can we give you lodging? At the village of Yamamoto yonder, ten furlongs farther, you will find a good inn. You had best be on your way before the daylight goes.

PRIEST: So you are resolved to turn me away?

TSUNEYO: I am sorry for it, but I cannot give you lodging.

PRIEST (*turning away*): Much good I got by waiting for such a fellow! I will go my way.

[He goes.]

WIFE: Alas, it is because in a former life we neglected the ordinances[4] that we are now come to ruin. And surely it will bring us ill fortune in our next life, if we give no welcome to such a one as this! If it is by any means possible for him to shelter here, please let him stay.

TSUNEYO: If you are of that mind, why did you not speak before? (*Looking after the* PRIEST) No, he cannot have gone far in this great snowstorm. I will go after him and stop him. Hie, traveler, hie! We will give you lodging. Hie! The snow is falling so thick that he cannot hear me. What a sad plight he is in. Old-fallen snow covers the way he came and snow new fallen hides the path where he should go. Look, look! He is standing still. He is shaking the snow from his clothes; shaking, shaking. It is like that old song:

> "At Sano Ferry
> No shelter found we
> To rest our horses,
> Shake our jackets,
> In the snowy twilight."

That song was made at Sano Ferry,
At the headland of Miwa on the Yamato Way.

CHORUS: But now at Sano on the Eastern Way
Would you wander weary in the snow of twilight?
Though mean the lodging,
Rest with us, oh rest till day!

[The PRIEST goes with them into the hut.]

TSUNEYO (*to his* WIFE): Listen. We have given him lodging, but have not laid the least thing before him. Is there nothing we can give?

WIFE: It happens that we have a little boiled millet;[5] we can give him that if he will take it.

---

[4] *ordinances:* Buddhist ordinances, such as hospitality to priests.
[5] *boiled millet:* food of the poorest peasants.

TSUNEYO: I will tell him. (*To the* PRIEST) I have given you lodging, but I have not yet laid anything before you. It happens that we have a little boiled millet. It is coarse food, but pray eat it if you can.

PRIEST: Why, that's a famous dish! Please give it me.

TSUNEYO (*to* WIFE): He says he will take some; make haste and give it to him.

WIFE: I will do so.

TSUNEYO: Long ago when I was in the World I knew nothing of this stuff called millet but what I read of it in poems and songs. But now it is the prop of my life.

> Truly Rosei's dream of fifty years' glory
> That he dreamed at Kántán on lent pillow propped
> Was dreamed while millet cooked, as yonder dish now.
> Oh if I might but sleep as he slept, and see in my dream
> Times that have passed away, then should I have comfort;
> But now through battered walls

CHORUS: Cold wind from the woods
> Blows sleep away and the dreams of recollection.
> [*While the* CHORUS *sings these words an* ATTENDANT *brings on to the stage the three dwarf trees.*]

TSUNEYO: How cold it is! And as the night passes, each hour the frost grows keener. If I had but fuel to light a fire with, that you might sit by it and warm yourself? Ah! I have thought of something. I have some dwarf trees. I will cut them down and make a fire of them.

PRIEST: Have you indeed dwarf trees?

TSUNEYO: Yes, when I was in the World I had a fine show of them; but when my trouble came I had no more heart for tree fancying, and gave them away. But three of them, I kept—plum, cherry and pine.[6] Look, there they are, covered with snow. They are precious to me; yet for this night's entertainment I will gladly set light to them.

PRIEST: No, no, that must not be. I thank you for your kindness, but it is likely that one day you will go back to the World again and need them for your pleasure. Indeed it is not to be thought of.

TSUNEYO: My life is like a tree the earth has covered;
> I shoot no blossoms upward to the world.

WIFE: And should we burn for you
> These shrubs, these profitless toys,

---

[6] *plum, cherry and pine:* these have an almost sacred status in Japanese life, and the cultivation of dwarf trees is a fine art.

TSUNEYO: Think them the faggots of our Master's servitude.[7]
WIFE: For snow falls now upon them, as it fell
TSUNEYO: When he to hermits of the cold
     Himalayan Hills was carrier of wood.
WIFE: So let it be.
CHORUS: "Shall I from one who has cast life aside,
     Dear life itself, withhold these trivial trees?"
           [TSUNEYO *goes and stands by the dwarf trees.*]
     Then he brushed the snow from off them, and when he
       looked,
     "I cannot, cannot," he cried, "O beautiful trees,
     Must I begin?
     You, plum tree, among bare boughs blossoming
     Hard by the window, still on northward face
     Snow-sealed, yet first to scent
     Cold air with flowers, earliest of Spring;
     'You first shall fall.'
     You by whose boughs on mountain hedge entwined
     Dull country folk have paused and caught their breath,[8]
     Hewn down for firewood. Little had I thought
     My hand so pitiless!"
           [*He cuts down the plum tree.*]
     "You, cherry (for each Spring your blossom comes
     Behind the rest), I thought a lonely tree
     And reared you tenderly, but now
     I, I am lonely left, and you, cut down,
     Shall flower but with flame."
TSUNEYO: You now, O pine, whose branches I had thought
     One day when you were old to lop and trim,
     Standing you in the field, a football post,[9]
     Such use shall never know.
     Tree, whom the winds have ever wreathed
     With quaking mists, now shimmering in the flame

---

[7] *our Master's servitude:* referring to Shākyamuni, who went through a period of servitude in his early life. Shākyamuni is a manifestation of the Buddha and the manifestation most likely to be revealed to us in this world. Buddhism officially began in
Japan in A.D. 552, when a bronze image of Shākyamuni was presented to the emperor
by Korea.
[8] *"Dull . . . breath":* using words from a poem by Michizane (A.D. 845–903).
[9] *football-post:* A considerable amount of religious ritual accompanies Japanese sport,
it should be noted, even in our day; this is most apparent to Westerners in exhibi-
tions of *judo* and *sumo* wrestling.

Shall burn and burn.
Now like a beacon, sentinels at night
Kindle by palace gate to guard a king,
Your fire burns brightly.
Come, warm yourself.

PRIEST: Now we have a good fire and can forget the cold.

TSUNEYO: It is because you lodged with us that we too have a fire to sit by.

PRIEST: There is something I must ask you: I would gladly know to what clan my host belongs.

TSUNEYO: I am not of such birth; I have no clan name.

PRIEST: Say what you will, I cannot think you a commoner. The times may change; what harm will you get by telling me your clan?

TSUNEYO: Indeed I have no reason to conceal it. Know then that Tsuneyo Genzayemon, Lord of Sano, is sunk to this!

PRIEST: How came it, sir, that you fell to such misery?

TSUNEYO: Thus it was: kinsmen usurped my lands, and so I became what I am.

PRIEST: Why do you not go up to the Capital and lay your case before the Shikken's court?

TSUNEYO: By further mischance it happens that Lord Saimyōji himself is absent upon pilgrimage. And yet not all is lost; for on the wall a tall spear still hangs, and armor with it; while in the stall a steed is tied. And if at any time there came from the City news of peril to our master——

Then, broken though it be I would gird this armor on,
And rusty though it be I would hold this tall spear,
And lean-ribbed though he be I would mount my horse
    and ride
Neck by neck with the swiftest,
To write my name on the roll.
And when the fight began
Though the foe were many, yet would I be the first
To cleave their ranks, to choose an adversary
To fight with him and die.
    [*He covers his face with his hands; his voice sinks again.*]
But now, another fate, worn out with hunger
To die useless. Oh despair, despair!

PRIEST: Take courage; you shall not end so. If I live, I will come to you again. Now I go.

TSUNEYO *and* WIFE: We cannot let you go. At first we were ashamed that you should see the misery of our dwelling; but now we ask you to stay with us awhile.

PRIEST: Were I to follow my desire, think you I would soon go forth into the snow?

TSUNEYO *and* WIFE: After a day of snow even the clear sky is cold, and tonight——

PRIEST: Where shall I lodge?

WIFE: Stay with us this one day.

PRIEST: Though my longing bides with you——

TSUNEYO *and* WIFE: You leave us?

PRIEST: Farewell, Tsuneyo!

BOTH: Come back to us again.

CHORUS (*speaking for* PRIEST): "And should you one day come up to the City, seek for me there. A humble priest can give you no public furtherance, yet can he find ways to bring you into the presence of Authority. Do not give up your suit." He said no more. He went his way—he sad to leave them and they to lose him from their sight.

[*Interval of six months.*]

TSUNEYO (*standing outside his hut and seeming to watch travelers on the road*): Hie, you travelers! Is it true that the levies are marching to Kamakura? They are marching in great force, you say? So it is true. Barons and knights from the Eight Counties of the East all riding to Kamakura! A fine sight it will be. Tasseled breastplates of beaten silver; swords and daggers fretted with gold. On horses fat with fodder they ride; even the grooms of the relay horses are magnificently appareled. And along with them (*miming the action of leading a horse*) goes Tsuneyo, with horse, armor and sword that scarce seem worthy of such names. They may laugh, yet I am not, I think, a worse man than they; and had I but a steed to match my heart, then valiantly——(*making the gesture of cracking a whip*)——you laggard!

CHORUS: The horse is old, palsied as a willow bough; it cannot hasten. It is lean and twisted. Not whip or spur can move it. It sticks like a coach in a bog. He follows far behind the rest.

PRIEST (*again ruler of Japan,*[10] *seated on a throne*): Are you there?

ATTENDANT: I stand before you.

PRIEST: Have the levies of all the lands arrived?

ATTENDANT: They are all come.

PRIEST: Among them should be a knight in broken armor, carrying a rusty sword, and leading his own lean horse. Find him, and bring him to me.

[10] Hōjō no Tokiyori ruled at Kamakura from 1246 till 1256. He then became a priest and traveled through the country incognito in order to acquaint himself with the needs of his subjects.

ATTENDANT: I tremble and obey. (*Going to* TSUNEYO) I must speak with
  you.
TSUNEYO: What is it?
ATTENDANT: You are to appear immediately before my lord.
TSUNEYO: Is it I whom you are bidding appear before his lordship?
ATTENDANT: Yes, you indeed.
TSUNEYO: How can it be I? You have mistaken me for some other.
ATTENDANT: Oh no, it is you. I was told to fetch the most ill-conditioned
  of all the soldiers; and I am sure you are he. Come at once.
TSUNEYO: The most ill-conditioned of all the soldiers?
ATTENDANT: Yes, truly.
TSUNEYO: Then I am surely he.
      Tell your lord that I obey.
ATTENDANT: I will do so.
TSUNEYO: I understand; too well I understand. Some enemy of mine has
  called me traitor, and it is to execution that I am summoned before the
  Throne. Well, there is no help for it. Bring me into the Presence.
CHORUS: He was led to where on a great daïs
      All the warriors of this levy were assembled
      Like a bright bevy of stars.
      Row on row they were ranged,
      Samurai and soldiers:
      Swift scornful glances, fingers pointed
      And the noise of laughter met his entering.
TSUNEYO: Stuck through his tattered, his old side-sewn sash,
      His rusty sword sags and trails—yet he undaunted,
      "My Lord, I have come."
              [*He bows before the Throne.*]
PRIEST: Ha! He has come, Tsuneyo of Sano!

Have you forgotten the priest whom once you sheltered from the snow-
storm? You have been true to the words that you spoke that night at
Sano:

      "If at any time there came news from the City of peril
            to our master
      Then broken though it be, I would gird this armor on,
      And rusty though it be, I would hold this tall spear,
      And bony though he be, I would mount my horse and ride
      Neck by neck with the swiftest."

These were not vain words; you have come valiantly. But know that this
levy of men was made to this purpose: to test the issue of your words

whether they were spoken false or true; and to hear the suits of all those that have obeyed my summons, that if any among them have suffered injury, his wrongs may be righted. And first in the case of Tsuneyo I make judgment. To him shall be returned his lawful estate, thirty parishes in the land of Sano. But above all else one thing shall never be forgotten, that in the great snowstorm he cut down his trees, his treasure, and burnt them for firewood. And now in gratitude for the three trees of that time—plum, cherry and pine—we grant to him three fiefs, Plumfield in Kaga, Cherrywell in Etchū and Pinebranch in Kōzuke. He shall hold them as a perpetual inheritance for himself and for his heirs; in testimony whereof we give this title deed, by our own hand signed and sealed, together with the safe possession of his former lands.

TSUNEYO: Then Tsuneyo took the deeds.

CHORUS: He took the deeds, thrice bowing his head.

[*Speaking for* TSUNEYO.]

"Look, all you barons!

[TSUNEYO *holds up the documents.*]

Look upon this sight
And scorn to envy turn!"
Then the levies of all the lands
Took leave of their Lord
And went their homeward way.

TSUNEYO: And among them Tsuneyo.

CHORUS: Among them Tsuneyo,
Joy breaking on his brow,
Rides now on splendid steed
To the Boat Bridge of Sano, to his lands once torn
Pitiless from him as the torrent tears
That Bridge of Boats at Sano now his own.

Saturday Night in the Village

GIACOMO LEOPARDI

The day
is ready to close;
the girl takes the downward
path homeward from the vineyard,
and jumps from crevice to crevice
like a goat, as she holds a swath
of violets and roses
to decorate her hair and bodice
tomorrow as usual for the Sabbath.

Her grandmother sits,
facing the sun going out,
and spins and starts to reason
with the neighbors, and renew the day,
when she used to dress herself for the holiday
and dance away
the nights—still quick and healthy,
with the boys, companions of her fairer season.

Once again the landscape is brown,
the sky drains to a pale blue,
shadows drop from mountain and thatch,
the young moon whitens.
As I catch
the clatter of small bells,

sounding in the holiday,
I can almost say
my heart takes comfort in the sound.
Children place their pickets
and sentinels,
and splash round and round
the village fountain.
They jump like crickets,
and make a happy sound.
The field-hand,
who lives on nothing,
marches home whistling,
and gorges on the day of idleness at hand.

Then all's at peace;
the lights are out;
I hear the rasp of shavings,
and the rapping hammer
of the carpenter, working all night
by lanternlight—
hurrying and straining himself
to increase his savings
before the whitening day.

This is the most kind
of the seven days; tomorrow, you will wait
and pray for Sunday's boredom and anguish
to be extinguished
in the workday's grind
you anticipate.

Lively boy,
the only age you are alive
is like this day of joy,
a clear and breathless Saturday
that heralds life's holiday.
Rejoice, my child,
this is the untroubled instant.
Why should I undeceive you?
Let it not grieve you,
if the following day is slow to arrive.

Waiting for the Barbarians

C. P. CAVAFY

What are we waiting for, gathered in the market-place?

The barbarians are to arrive today.

Why so little activity in the Senate?
Why do the Senators sit there without legislating?

Because the barbarians will arrive today.
Why should the Senators bother with laws now?
The barbarians, when they come, will do the law-making.

Why has our emperor risen so early,
and why does he sit at the largest gate of the city
on the throne, in state, wearing the crown?

Because the barbarians will arrive today.
And the emperor is waiting to receive
their leader. He has even prepared
a parchment for him. There
he has given him many titles and names.

Why did our two consuls and our praetors go out
today in the scarlet, the embroidered, togas?
Why did they wear bracelets with so many amethysts,

and rings with brilliant sparkling emeralds?
Why today do they carry precious staves
splendidly inlaid with silver and gold?

> Because the barbarians will arrive today;
> and such things dazzle barbarians.

And why don't the worthy orators come as always
to make their speeches, say what they have to say?

> Because the barbarians will arrive today;
> and they are bored by eloquence and public speaking.

What does this sudden uneasiness mean,
and this confusion? (How grave the faces have become!)
Why are the streets and squares rapidly emptying,
and why is everyone going back home so lost in thought?

> Because it is night and the barbarians have not come.
> And some men have arrived from the frontiers
> and they say that there are no barbarians any longer.

And now, what will become of us without barbarians?
Those people were a kind of solution.

The Athlete and the Philosopher

XENOPHANES OF COLOPHON

Now, supposing a man were to win the prize for the foot race
    at Olympia, there where the precinct of Zeus stands beside
the river, at Pisa: or if he wins the five-contests, or the wrestling,
    or if he endures the pain of boxing and wins, or that new
and terrible game they call the pankration, contest of all holds:
    why, such a man will obtain honor, in the citizens' sight,
and be given a front seat and be on display at all civic occasions,
    and he would be given his meals all at the public expense,
and be given a gift from the city to take and store for safekeeping.
    If he won with the chariot, too, all this would be granted to him,
and yet he would not deserve it, as I do. Better than brute strength
    of men, or horses either, is the wisdom that is mine.
But custom is careless in all these matters, and there is no justice
    in putting strength on a level above wisdom which is sound.
For if among the people there is one who is a good boxer,
    or one who excels in wrestling or in the five-contests,
or else for speed of his feet, and this is prized beyond other
    feats of strength that men display in athletic games,
the city will not, on account of this man, have better government.
    Small is the pleasure the city derives from one of its men
if he happens to come first in the games by the banks of Pisa.
    This does not make rich the treasure house of the state.

All Quiet on the Western Front

ERICH MARIA REMARQUE

This book is to be neither an accusation nor a confession,
and least of all an adventure, for death is not
an adventure to those who stand face to face with it.
It will try simply to tell of a generation
of men who, even though they may have escaped its shells,
were destroyed by the war.

Grateful acknowledgment is made to Mr. Remarque for granting permission to reprint his work IM WESTEN NICHTS NEUES copyright 1928 by Ullstein A.G.; copyright renewed 1956 by Erich Maria Remarque. *All Quiet on the Western Front* copyright 1929, 1930 by Little, Brown and Company; copyright renewed 1957, 1958 by Erich Maria Remarque.

Chapter I

W E are at rest five miles behind the front. Yesterday we were relieved, and now our bellies are full of beef and haricot beans. We are satisfied and at peace. Each man has another messtinful for the evening; and, what is more, there is a double ration of sausage and bread. That puts a man in fine trim. We have not had such luck as this for a long time. The cook with his carroty head is begging us to eat; he beckons with his ladle to everyone that passes and spoons him out a great dollop. He does not see how he can empty his stewpot in time for coffee. Tjaden and Müller have produced two washbasins and had them filled up to the brim as a reserve. In Tjaden this is voracity, in Müller it is foresight. Where Tjaden puts it all is a mystery, for he is and always will be as thin as a rake.

What's more important still is the issue of a double ration of smokes. Ten cigars, twenty cigarettes, and two quids of chew per man; now that is decent. I have exchanged my chewing tobacco with Katczinsky for his cigarettes, which means I have forty altogether. That's enough for a day.

It is true we have no right to this windfall. The Prussian is not so generous. We have only a miscalculation to thank for it.

Fourteen days ago we had to go up and relieve the front line. It was fairly quiet on our sector, so the quartermaster who remained in the rear had requisitioned the usual quantity of rations and provided for the full company of one hundred and fifty men. But on the last day an astonishing number of English field guns opened up on us with high explosive, drumming ceaselessly on our position, so that we suffered heavily and came back only eighty strong.

Last night we moved back and settled down to get a good sleep for once; Katczinsky is right when he says it would not be such a bad war if only one could get a little more sleep. In the line we have had next to none, and fourteen days is a long time at one stretch.

It was noon before the first of us crawled out of our quarters. Half an hour later every man had his messtin and we gathered at the cookhouse, which smelled greasy and nourishing. At the head of the queue of course were the hungriest—little Albert Kropp, the clearest thinker among us and therefore the first to be lance corporal; Müller, who still carries his school textbooks with him, dreams of examinations, and during a bombardment mutters propositions in physics; Leer, who wears a full beard and has a preference for the girls from officers' brothels. And as the fourth, myself, Paul Bäumer. All four are eighteen years of age, and all four joined up from the same class as volunteers for the war.

Close behind us were our friends: Tjaden, a skinny locksmith of our own age, the biggest eater of the company. He sits down to eat as thin as a grasshopper and gets up as big as a bug in the family way; Haie Westhus, of the same age, a peat digger, who can easily hold a ration loaf in his hand and say: Guess what I've got in my fist; then Detering, a peasant, who thinks of nothing but his farmyard and his wife; and finally Stanislaus Katczinsky, the leader of our group, shrewd, cunning, and hardbitten, forty years of age, with a face of the soil, blue eyes, bent shoulders, and a remarkable nose for dirty weather, good food, and soft jobs.

Our gang formed the head of the queue before the cookhouse. We were growing impatient, for the cook paid no attention to us.

Finally Katczinsky called out to him: "Say, Heinrich, open up the soup kitchen. Anyone can see the beans are done."

He shook his head sleepily: "You must all be there first." Tjaden grinned: "We are all here."

The sergeant-cook still took no notice. "That may do for you," he said. "But where are the others?"

"They won't be fed by you today. They're either in the dressing station or pushing up daisies."

The cook was quite disconcerted as the facts dawned on him. He was staggered. "And I have cooked for one hundred and fifty men——"

Kropp poked him in the ribs. "Then for once we'll have enough. Come on, begin!"

Suddenly a vision came over Tjaden. His sharp, mousy features began to shine, his eyes grew small with cunning, his jaws twitched, and he whispered hoarsely: "Man! then you've got bread for one hundred and fifty men too, eh?"

The sergeant-cook nodded, absent-minded and bewildered.

Tjaden seized him by the tunic. "And sausage?"

Ginger nodded again.

Tjaden's chaps quivered. "Tobacco too?"

"Yes, everything."

Tjaden beamed: "What a beanfeast! That's all for us! Each man gets— wait a bit—yes, practically two issues."

Then Ginger stirred himself and said: "That won't do."

Then we got excited and began to crowd around.

"Why won't that do, you old carrot?" demanded Katczinsky.

"Eighty men can't have what is meant for a hundred and fifty."

"We'll soon show you," growled Müller.

"I don't care about the stew, but I can only issue rations for eighty men," persisted Ginger.

Katczinsky got angry. "You might be generous for once. You haven't drawn food for eighty men. You've drawn it for the Second Company. Good. Let's have it then. We are the Second Company."

We began to jostle the fellow. No one felt kindly toward him, for it was his fault that the food twice came up to us in the line too late and cold. Under shellfire he wouldn't bring his kitchen up near enough, so that our soup carriers had to go much farther than those of the other companies. Now Bulcke of the First Company is a much better fellow. He is as fat as a hamster in winter, but he trundles his pots when it comes to that right up to the very front line.

We were in just the right mood, and there would certainly have been a dustup if our company commander had not appeared. He informed himself of the dispute, and only remarked: "Yes, we did have heavy losses yesterday."

He looked in the dixie. "The beans look good."

Ginger nodded. "Cooked with meat and fat."

The lieutenant looked at us. He knew what we were thinking. And he knew many other things too, because he came to the company as a non-com and was promoted from the ranks. He lifted the lid from the dixie again and sniffed. Then passing on he said: "Serve out the whole issue. We can do with it. And bring me a plateful too."

Ginger looked sheepish as Tjaden danced round him.

"It doesn't cost you anything! One would think the quartermaster's store belonged to him! And now get on with it, you old blubbersticker, and don't you miscount either."

"You be hanged!" spat out Ginger. When things get beyond him he throws up the sponge altogether; he just goes to pieces. And as if to show that all things were now the same to him, of his own free will he shared out half a pound of synthetic honey equally among us.

Today is wonderfully good. The mail has come, and almost every man has a couple of letters.

Kropp pulls out one. "Kantorek sends you all his best wishes."

We laugh. Müller throws his cigarette away and says: "I wish he was here."

Kantorek had been our schoolmaster, an active little man in a gray tail-coat, with a face like a shrewmouse. He was about the same size as Corporal Himmelstoss, the "Terror of Klosterberg." It is very queer that the unhappiness of the world is so often brought on by small men. They are so much more energetic and uncompromising than the big fellows. I have always taken good care to keep out of sections with small company commanders. They are mostly confounded little martinets.

During drilltime Kantorek gave us long lectures until the whole of our class went under his shepherding to the District Commandant and volunteered. I can see him now, as he used to glare at us through his spectacles and say in a moving voice: "Won't you join up, Comrades?"

These teachers always carry their feelings ready in their waistcoat pockets and fetch them out at any hour of the day. But we didn't think of that then.

There was, indeed, one of us who hesitated and did not want to fall into line. That was Josef Behm, a plump, homely fellow. But he did allow himself to be persuaded, otherwise he would have been ostracized. And perhaps more of us thought as he did, but no one could very well stand out, because at that time even one's parents were ready with the word "coward"; no one had the vaguest idea what we were in for. The wisest were just the poor and simple people. They knew the war to be a misfortune, whereas people who were better off were beside themselves with joy, though they should have been much better able to judge what the consequences would be.

Katczinsky said that was a result of their upbringing. It made them stupid. And what Kat said, he had thought about.

Strange to say, Behm was one of the first to fall. He got hit in the eye during an attack, and we left him lying for dead. We couldn't bring him with us, because we had to come back helter-skelter. In the afternoon suddenly we heard him call and saw him outside creeping toward us. He had only been knocked unconscious. Because he could not see, and was mad with pain, he failed to keep under cover, and so was shot down before anyone could go and fetch him in.

Naturally we couldn't blame Kantorek for this. Where would the world be if one brought every man to book? There were thousands of Kantoreks, all of whom were convinced that there was only one way of doing well, and that way theirs.

And that is just why they let us down so badly.

For us lads of eighteen they ought to have been mediators and guides to the world of maturity, the world of work, of duty, of culture, of progress— to the future. We often made fun of them and played jokes on them, but in our hearts we trusted them. The idea of authority, which they represented, was associated in our minds with a greater insight and a manlier wisdom. But the first death we saw shattered this belief. We had to recognize that our generation was more to be trusted than theirs. They surpassed us only in phrases and in cleverness. The first bombardment showed us our mistake, and under it the world as they had taught it to us broke in pieces.

While they continued to write and talk, we saw the wounded and dying. While they taught that duty to one's country is the greatest thing, we already knew that death throes are stronger. But for all that we were no mutineers, no deserters, no cowards—they were very free with all these expressions. We loved our country as much as they; we went courageously into every action; but also we distinguished the false from the true, we had suddenly learned to see. And we saw that there was nothing of their world left. We were all at once terribly alone; and alone we must see it through.

Before going over to see Kemmerich we pack up his things: he will need them on the way back.

In the dressing station there is great activity; it reeks as ever of carbolic, ether, and sweat. Most of us are accustomed to this in the billets, but here it makes one feel faint. We ask for Kemmerich. He lies in a large room and receives us with feeble expressions of joy and helpless agitation. While he was unconscious someone had stolen his watch.

Müller shakes his head: "I always told you that nobody should carry as good a watch as that."

Müller is rather crude and tactless, otherwise he would hold his tongue, for anybody can see that Kemmerich will never come out of this place again. Whether he finds his watch or not will make no difference. At the most one will only be able to send it to his people.

"How goes it, Franz?" asks Kropp.

Kemmerich's head sinks.

"Not so bad . . . but I have such a damned pain in my foot."

We look at his bed covering. His leg lies under a wire basket. The bed covering arches over it. I kick Müller on the shin, for he is just about to tell Kemmerich what the orderlies told us outside: that Kemmerich has lost his foot. The leg is amputated. He looks ghastly, yellow, and wan. In his face there are already the strained lines that we know so well, we have seen them now hundreds of times. They are not so much lines as marks. Under the skin the life no longer pulses, it has already pressed out to the boundaries of the body. Death is working through from within. It already has command in the eyes. Here lies our comrade, Kemmerich, who a little while ago was roasting horseflesh with us and squatting in the shell holes. He it is still and yet it is not he any longer. His features have become uncertain and faint, like a photographic plate on which two pictures have been taken. Even his voice sounds like ashes.

I think of the time when we went away. His mother, a good plump matron, brought him to the station. She wept continually, her face was bloated and swollen. Kemmerich felt embarrassed, for she was the least composed of all; she simply dissolved into fat and water. Then she caught sight of me and took hold of my arm again and again, and implored me to look after Franz out there. Indeed he did have a face like a child, and such frail bones that after four weeks' pack carrying he already had flat feet. But how can a man look after anyone in the field!

"Now you will soon be going home," says Kropp. "You would have had to wait at least three or four months for your leave."

Kemmerich nods. I cannot bear to look at his hands, they are like wax. Under the nails is the dirt of the trenches, it shows through blue-black like poison. It strikes me that these nails will continue to grow like long, fantastic cellar plants long after Kemmerich breathes no more. I see the picture before me. They twist themselves into corkscrews and grow and grow, and with them the hair on the decayed skull, just like grass in a good soil, just like grass, how can it be possible——

Müller leans over. "We have brought your things, Franz."

Kemmerich signs with his hand. "Put them under the bed."

Müller does so. Kemmerich starts on again about the watch. How can one calm him without making him suspicious?

Müller reappears with a pair of airman's boots. They are fine English boots of soft, yellow leather which reach to the knee and lace all the way —they are things to be coveted.

Müller is delighted at the sight of them. He matches their soles against his own clumsy boots and says: "Will you be taking them with you, Franz?"

We all three have the same thought; even if he should get better, he would be able to use only one—they are no use to him. But as things are now it is a pity that they should stay here; the orderlies will of course grab them as soon as he is dead.

"Won't you leave them with us?" Müller repeats.

Kemmerich doesn't want to. They are his most prized possessions.

"Well, we could exchange," suggests Müller again. "Out here one can make some use of them." Still Kemmerich is not to be moved.

I tread on Müller's foot; reluctantly he puts the fine boots back again under the bed.

We talk a little more and then take our leave.

"Cheerio, Franz."

I promise him to come back in the morning. Müller talks of doing so too. He is thinking of the lace-up boots and means to be on the spot.

Kemmerich groans. He is feverish. We get hold of an orderly outside and ask him to give Kemmerich a dose of morphine.

He refuses. "If we were to give morphine to everyone we would have to have tubfuls——"

"You only attend to officers properly," says Kropp viciously.

I hastily intervene and give him a cigarette. He takes it.

"Are you usually allowed to give it, then?" I ask him.

He is annoyed. "If you don't think so, then why do you ask?"

I press a couple more cigarettes into his hand. "Do us the favor——"

"Well, all right," he says.

Kropp goes in with him. He doesn't trust him and wants to see. We wait outside.

Müller returns to the subject of the boots. "They would fit me perfectly. In these boots I get blister after blister. Do you think he will last till tomorrow after drill? If he passes out in the night, we know where the boots——

Kropp returns. "Do you think——?" he asks.

"Done for," says Müller emphatically.

We go back to the huts. I think of the letter that I must write tomorrow to Kemmerich's mother. I am freezing. I could do with a tot of rum. Müller pulls up some grass and chews it. Suddenly little Kropp throws his cigarette away, stamps on it savagely, and looking round him with a broken and distracted face, stammers: "Damned swine, the damned swine!"

We walk on for a long time. Kropp has calmed himself; we understand; he sees red, out here every man gets like that sometime.

"What has Kantorek written to you?" Müller asks him.

He laughs. "We are the Iron Youth."

We all three smile bitterly. Kropp rails: he is glad that he can speak.

Yes, that's the way they think, these hundred thousand Kantoreks! Iron Youth. Youth! We are none of us more than twenty years old. But young? Youth? That is long ago. We are old folk.

Chapter II

IT is strange to think that at home in the drawer of my writing table there lies the beginning of a play called "Saul" and a bundle of poems. Many an evening I have worked over them—we all did something of the kind—but that has become so unreal to me that I cannot comprehend it anymore. Our early life is cut off from the moment we came here, and that without our lifting a hand. We often try to look back on it and to find an explanation, but never quite succeed. For us young men of twenty everything is extraordinarily vague, for Kropp, Müller, Leer, and me, for all of us whom Kantorek calls the "Iron Youth." All the older men are linked up with their previous life. They have wives, children, occupations, and interests, they have a background which is so strong that the war cannot obliterate it. We young men of twenty, however, have only our parents, and some, perhaps, a girl—that is not much, for at our age the influence of parents is at its weakest and girls have not yet got a hold over us. Besides this there was little else—some enthusiasm, a few hobbies, and our school. Beyond this our life did not extend. And of this nothing remains.

Kantorek would say that we stood on the threshold of life. And so it would seem. We had as yet taken no root. The war swept us away. For the others, the older men, it is but an interruption. They are able to think beyond it. We, however, have been gripped by it and do not know what the end may be. We know only that in some strange and melancholy way we have become a wasteland. All the same, we are not often sad.

Though Müller would be delighted to have Kemmerich's boots, he is really quite as sympathetic as another who could not bear to think of such a thing for grief. He merely sees things clearly. Were Kemmerich able to make any use of the boots, then Müller would rather go barefoot over barbed wire than scheme how to get hold of them. But as it is the boots are quite inappropriate to Kemmerich's circumstances, whereas Müller can make good use of them. Kemmerich will die; it is immaterial who gets them. Why, then, should Müller not succeed to them? He has more right than a hospital orderly. When Kemmerich is dead it will be too late. Therefore Müller is already on the watch.

We have lost all sense of other considerations, because they are artificial. Only the facts are real and important for us. And good boots are scarce.

Once it was different. When we went to the District Commandant to enlist, we were a class of twenty young men, many of whom proudly shaved for the first time before going to the barracks. We had no definite plans for our future. Our thoughts of a career and occupation were as yet of too unpractical a character to furnish any scheme of life. We were still crammed full of vague ideas which gave to life, and to the war also, an ideal and almost romantic character. We were trained in the army for ten weeks and in this time more profoundly influenced than by ten years at school. We learned that a bright button is weightier than four volumes of Schopenhauer. At first astonished, then embittered, and finally indifferent, we recognized that what matters is not the mind but the boot brush, not intelligence but the system, not freedom but drill. We became soldiers with eagerness and enthusiasm, but they have done everything to knock that out of us. After three weeks it was no longer incomprehensible to us that a braided postman should have more authority over us than had formerly our parents, our teachers, and the whole gamut of culture from Plato to Goethe. With our young, awakened eyes we saw that the classical conception of the Fatherland held by our teachers resolved itself here into a renunciation of personality such as one would not ask of the meanest servant— salutes, springing to attention, parade marches, presenting arms, right wheel, left wheel, clicking the heels, insults, and a thousand pettifogging details. We had fancied our task would be different, only to find we were to be trained for heroism as though we were circus ponies. But we soon accustomed ourselves to it. We learned, in fact, that some part of these things was necessary, but the rest merely show. Soldiers have a fine nose for such distinctions.

By threes and fours our class was scattered over the platoons among Frisian fishermen, peasants, and laborers with whom we soon made friends. Kropp, Müller, Kemmerich, and I went to No. 9 platoon under Corporal Himmelstoss.

He had the reputation of being the strictest disciplinarian in the camp, and was proud of it. He was a small, undersized fellow with a foxy, waxed moustache, who had seen twelve years' service and was in civil life a postman. He had a special dislike for Kropp, Tjaden, Westhus, and me, because he sensed a quiet defiance.

I have remade his bed fourteen times in one morning. Each time he had some fault to find and pulled it to pieces. I have kneaded a pair of prehistoric boots that were as hard as iron for twenty hours—with intervals of course—until they became as soft as butter and not even Himmelstoss could find anything more to do to them; under his orders I have scrubbed out the Corporals' Mess with a toothbrush. Kropp and I were given the job of clearing the barrack square of snow with a handbroom and a dustpan,

and we would have gone on till we were frozen had not a lieutenant acci-
dentally appeared who sent us off and hauled Himmelstoss over the coals.
But the only result of this was to make Himmelstoss hate us more. For six
weeks consecutively I did guard every Sunday and was hut orderly for the
same length of time. With full pack and rifle I have had to practice on a
soft, wet, newly plowed field the "Prepare to advance, advance!" and the
"Lie down!" until I was one lump of mud and finally collapsed. Four hours
later I had to report to Himmelstoss with my clothes scrubbed clean, my
hands chafed and bleeding. Together with Kropp, Westhus, and Tjaden I
have stood at attention in a hard frost without gloves for a quarter of an
hour at a stretch, while Himmelstoss watched for the slightest movement
of our bare fingers on the steel barrel of the rifle. I have run eight times
from the top floor of the barracks down to the courtyard in my shirt at
two o'clock in the morning because my drawers projected three inches
beyond the edge of the stool on which one had to stack all one's things.
Alongside me ran the corporal, Himmelstoss, and trod on my bare toes. At
bayonet practice I had constantly to fight with Himmelstoss, I with a
heavy iron weapon while he had a handy wooden one with which he easily
struck my arms till they were black and blue. Once, indeed, I became so
infuriated that I ran at him blindly and gave him a mighty jab in the stomach and knocked him down. When he reported me the company commander laughed at him and told him he ought to keep his eyes open; he
understood Himmelstoss, and apparently was not displeased at his discom-
fiture. I became a past master on the horizontal bars and strove to surpass
my instructor at physical jerks—we have trembled at the mere sound of
his voice, but this runaway post-horse never got the better of us.

One Sunday as Kropp and I were lugging a latrine bucket on a pole
across the barrack yard, Himmelstoss came by, all polished up and spry for
going out. He planted himself in front of us and asked how we liked the
job. In spite of ourselves we tripped and emptied the bucket over his legs.
He raved, but the limit had been reached.

"That means clink," he yelled.

But Kropp had had enough. "There'll be an inquiry first," he said, "and
then we'll unload."

"Mind how you speak to a noncommissioned officer!" bawled Himmelstoss. "Have you lost your senses? You wait till you're spoken to. What
will you do, anyway?"

"Show you up, Corporal," said Kropp, his thumbs in line with the seams
of his trousers.

Himmelstoss saw what we meant and went off without saying a word.

But before he disappeared he growled: "You'll drink this!"—but it was the end of his authority. He tried it on once more in the plowed field with his "Prepare to advance, advance" and "Lie down." We obeyed each order, since an order's an order and has to be obeyed. But we did it so slowly that Himmelstoss became desperate. Carefully we went down on our knees, then on our hands, and so on; in the meantime, quite infuriated, he had given another command. But before we had even begun to sweat he was hoarse. After that he left us in peace. He did indeed always refer to us as swine, but there was, nevertheless, a certain respect in his tone.

There were many other staff corporals, the majority of whom were more decent. But above all each of them wanted to keep his good job there at home as long as possible, and that he could do only by being strict with the recruits.

Practically every conceivable polishing job in the entire camp fell to us and we often howled with rage. Many of us became ill through it; Wolf actually died of inflammation of the lung. But we would have felt ridiculous had we hauled down our colors. We became hard, suspicious, pitiless, vicious, tough—and that was good; for these attributes had been entirely lacking in us. Had we gone into the trenches without this period of training most of us would certainly have gone mad. Only thus were we prepared for what awaited us. We did not break down, but endured; our twenty years, which made many another thing so grievous, helped us in this. But by far the most important was that it awakened in us a strong, practical sense of *esprit de corps,* which in the field developed into the finest thing that arose out of the war—comradeship.

I sit by Kemmerich's bed. He is sinking steadily. Around us is a great commotion. A hospital train has arrived and the wounded fit to be moved are being selected. The doctor passes by Kemmerich's bed without once looking at him.

"Next time, Franz," I say.

He raises himself on the pillow with his elbows. "They have amputated my leg."

He knows it too, then. I nod and answer: "You must be thankful you've come off with that."

He is silent.

I resume: "It might have been both legs, Franz. Wegeler has lost his right arm. That's much worse. Besides, you will be going home." He looks at me. "Do you think so?"

"Of course."

"Do you think so?" he repeats.

"Sure. Once you've got over the operation."

He beckons me to bend down. I stoop over him and he whispers: "I don't think so."

"Don't talk rubbish, Franz, in a couple of days you'll see for yourself. What is it anyway—an amputated leg? here they patch up far worse things than that."

He lifts one hand. "Look hère though, these fingers."

"That's the result of the operation. Just eat decently and you'll soon be well again. Do they look after you properly?"

He points to a dish that is still half full. I get excited. "Franz, you must eat. Eating is the main thing. That looks good too."

He turns away. After a pause he says slowly: "I wanted to become a head forester once."

"So you may still," I assure him. "There are splendid artificial limbs now, you'd hardly know there was anything missing. They are fixed onto the muscles. You can move the fingers and work and even write with an artificial hand. And besides, they will always be making new improvements."

For a while he lies still. Then he says: "You can take my lace-up boots with you for Müller."

I nod and wonder what to say to encourage him. His lips have fallen away, his mouth has become larger, his teeth stick out and look as though they were made of chalk. The flesh melts, the forehead bulges more prominently, the cheekbones protrude. The skeleton is working itself through. The eyes are already sunken in. In a couple of hours it will be over.

He is not the first I have seen thus; but we grew up together and that always makes it a bit different. I have copied his essays. At school he used to wear a brown coat with a belt and shiny sleeves. He was the only one of us, too, who could do the giant's turn on the parallel bars. His hair flew in his face like silk when he did it. Kantorek was proud of him for it. But he couldn't endure cigarettes. His skin was very white; he had something of the girl about him.

I glance at my boots. They are big and clumsy, the breeches are tucked into them, and standing up one looks well built and powerful in these great drainpipes. But when we go bathing and strip, suddenly we have slender legs again and slight shoulders. We are no longer soldiers but little more than boys; no one would believe that we could carry packs. It is a strange moment when we stand naked; then we become civilians, and almost feel ourselves to be so. When bathing, Franz Kemmerich looked as slight and frail as a child. There he lies now—but why? The whole world ought to pass by this bed and say: "That is Franz Kemmerich, nineteen and a half years old, he doesn't want to die. Let him not die!"

My thoughts become confused. This atmosphere of carbolic and gangrene clogs the lungs, it is a thick gruel, it suffocates.

It grows dark. Kemmerich's face changes color, it lifts from the pillow and is so pale that it gleams. The mouth moves slightly. I draw near to him. He whispers: "If you find my watch, send it home——"

I do not reply. It is no use anymore. No one can console him. I am wretched with helplessness. This forehead with its hollow temples, this mouth that is now merely a slit, this sharp nose! And the fat, weeping woman at home to whom I must write. If only the letter were sent off already!

Hospital orderlies go to and fro with bottles and pails. One of them comes up, casts a glance at Kemmerich, and goes away again. You can see he is waiting, apparently he wants the bed.

I bend over Franz and talk to him as though that could save him: "Perhaps you will go to the convalescent home at Klosterberg, among the villas, Franz. Then you can look out from the window across the fields to the two trees on the horizon. It is the loveliest time of the year now, when the corn ripens; at evening the fields in the sunlight look like mother-of-pearl. And the lane of poplars by the Klosterbach, where we used to catch sticklebacks! You can build an aquarium and keep fish in it, and you can go out without asking anyone—you can even play the piano if you want to."

I lean down over his face, which lies in the shadow. He still breathes, lightly. His face is wet, he is crying. What a fine mess I have made of it with my foolish talk!

"But Franz"—I put my arm round his shoulders and put my face against his. "Will you sleep now?"

He does not answer. The tears run down his cheeks. I would like to wipe them away but my handkerchief is too dirty.

An hour passes. I sit tensely and watch his every movement in case he may perhaps say something. What if he were to open his mouth and cry out! But he only weeps, his head turned aside. He does not speak of his mother or his brothers and sisters. He says nothing; all that lies behind him; he is entirely alone now with his little life of nineteen years, and cries because it leaves him. This is the most disturbing and hardest parting that ever I have seen, although it was pretty bad too with Tiedjen, who called for his mother—a big bear of a fellow who, with wild eyes full of terror, held off the doctor from his bed with a dagger until he collapsed.

Suddenly Kemmerich groans and begins to gurgle.

I jump up, stumble outside, and demand: "Where is the doctor? Where is the doctor?"

As I catch sight of the white apron I seize hold of it: "Come quick, Franz Kemmerich is dying."

He frees himself and asks an orderly standing by: "Which will that be?"

He says: "Bed 26, amputated thigh."

He sniffs: "How should I know anything about it, I've amputated five legs today"; he shoves me away, says to the hospital orderly: "You see to it," and runs off to the operating room.

I tremble with rage as I go along with the orderly. The man looks at me and says: "One operation after another since five o'clock this morning. You know today alone there have been sixteen deaths—yours is the seventeenth. There will probably be twenty altogether——"

I become faint, all at once I cannot do any more. I won't revile anymore, it is senseless, I could drop down and never rise up again.

We are by Kemmerich's bed. He is dead. The face is still wet from the tears. The eyes are half open and yellow like old horn buttons.

The orderly pokes me in the ribs. "Are you taking his things with you?" I nod.

He goes on. "We must take him away at once, we want the bed. Outside they are lying on the floor."

I collect the things, untie Kemmerich's identification disk, and take it away. The orderly asks about the paybook. I say that it is probably in the Orderly Room, and go. Behind me they are already hauling Franz on to a waterproof sheet.

Outside the door I am aware of the darkness and the wind as a deliverance. I breathe as deep as I can, and feel the breeze in my face, warm and soft as never before. Thoughts of girls, of flowery meadows, of white clouds suddenly come into my head. My feet begin to move forward in my boots, I go quicker, I run. Soldiers pass by me, I hear their voices without understanding. The earth is streaming with forces which pour into me through the soles of my feet. The night crackles electrically, the front thunders like a concert of drums. My limbs move supply, I feel my joints strong, I breathe the air deeply. The night lives, I live. I feel a hunger, greater than comes from the belly alone.

Müller stands in front of the hut and waits for me. I give him the boots. We go in and he tries them on. They fit well.

He roots among his supplies and offers me a fine piece of saveloy.[1] With it goes hot tea and rum.

---

[1] *saveloy*: pork sausage.

Chapter III

REINFORCEMENTS have arrived. The vacancies have been filled and the sacks of straw are already laid out in the huts. Some of them are old hands but there are twenty-five men of a later draft from the base. They are about two years younger than us. Kropp nudges me: "Seen the infants?"

I nod. We stick out our chests, shave in the open, shove our hands in our pockets, inspect the recruits, and feel ourselves to be stone-age veterans.

Katczinsky joins us. We stroll past the horse boxes and go over to the reinforcements, who have already been issued with gas masks and coffee.

"Long time since you've had anything decent to eat, eh?" Kat asks one of the youngsters.

He grimaces. "For breakfast, turnip bread—lunch, turnip stew—supper, turnip cutlets and turnip salad." Kat gives a knowing whistle.

"Bread made of turnips? You've been in luck, it's nothing new for it to be made of sawdust. But what do you say to haricot beans? Have some?"

The youngster turns red: "You can't kid me."

Katczinsky merely says: "Fetch your messtin."

We follow curiously. He takes us to a tub beside his straw sack. It is nearly half full of a stew of beef and beans. Katczinsky plants himself in front of it like a general and says:

"Sharp eyes and light fingers! That's what the Prussians say."

We are surprised. "Great guts, Kat, how did you come by that?" I ask him.

"Ginger was glad I took it. I gave him three pieces of parachute silk for it. Cold beans taste fine, too."

Grudgingly he gives the youngster a portion and says:

"Next time you come with your messtin have a cigar or a chew of tobacco in your other hand. Get me?" Then he turns to us. "You get off scot free, of course."

Katczinsky never goes short; he has a sixth sense. There are such people everywhere but one does not appreciate it at first. Every company has one or two. Katczinsky is the smartest I know. By trade he is a cobbler, I believe, but that hasn't anything to do with it; he understands all trades. It's a good thing to be friends with him, as Kropp and I are, and Haie Westhus too, more or less. But Haie is rather the executive arm operating under Kat's orders when things come to blows. For that he has his qualifications.

For example, we land at night in some entirely unknown spot, a sorry hole, that has been eaten out to the very walls. We are quartered in a small dark factory adapted to the purpose. There are beds in it, or rather bunks—a couple of wooden beams over which wire netting is stretched.

Wire netting is hard. And there's nothing to put on it. Our waterproof sheets are too thin. We use our blankets to cover ourselves.

Kat looks at the place and then says to Haie Westhus: "Come with me." They go off to explore. Half an hour later they are back again with arms full of straw. Kat has found a horse box with straw in it. Now we might sleep if we weren't so terribly hungry.

Kropp asks an artilleryman who has been some time in this neighborhood: "Is there a canteen anywhere abouts?"

"Is there a what?" he laughs. "There's nothing to be had here. You won't find so much as a crust of bread here."

"Aren't there any inhabitants here at all, then?"

He spits. "Yes, a couple. But they mostly loaf round the cookhouse and beg."

"That's a bad business!—Then we'll have to pull in our belts and wait till the rations come up in the morning."

But I see Kat has put on his cap.

"Where to, Kat?" I ask.

"Just to explore the place a bit." He strolls off. The artilleryman grins scornfully. "Let him explore! But don't be too hopeful about it."

Disappointed we lie down and consider whether we couldn't have a go at the iron rations. But it's too risky; so we try to get a wink of sleep.

Kropp divides a cigarette and hands me half. Tjaden gives an account of his national dish—broad beans and bacon. He despises it when not flavored with bog myrtle, and, "for God's sake, let it all be cooked together, not the potatoes, the beans, and the bacon separately." Someone growls that he will pound Tjaden into bog myrtle if he doesn't shut up. Then all becomes quiet in the big room—only the candles flickering from the necks of a couple of bottles and the artilleryman spitting every now and then.

We stir a bit as the door opens and Kat appears. I think I must be dreaming; he has two loaves of bread under his arm and a blood-stained sandbag full of horseflesh in his hand.

The artilleryman's pipe drops from his mouth. He feels the bread. "Real bread, by God! and still hot too!"

Kat gives no explanation. He has the bread, the rest doesn't matter. I'm sure that if he were planted down in the middle of the desert, in half an hour he would have gathered together a supper of roast meat, dates, and wine.

"Cut some wood," he says curtly to Haie.

Then he hauls out a frying pan from under his coat, and a handful of salt as well as a lump of fat from his pocket. He has thought of everything. Haie makes a fire on the floor. It lights up the empty room of the factory. We climb out of bed.

The artilleryman hesitates. He wonders whether to praise Kat and so perhaps gain a little for himself. But Katczinsky doesn't even see him, he might as well be thin air. He goes off cursing.

Kat knows the way to roast horseflesh so that it's tender. It shouldn't be put straight into the pan, that makes it tough. It should be boiled first in a little water. With our knives we squat round in a circle and fill our bellies.

That is Kat. If for but one hour in a year something eatable were to be had in some one place only, within that hour, as if moved by a vision, he would put on his cap, go out and walk directly there, as though following a compass, and find it.

He finds everything—if it is cold, a small stove and wood, hay and straw, a table and chairs—but above all food. It is uncanny; one would think he conjured it out of the air. His masterpiece was four boxes of lobsters. Admittedly we would rather have had a good beefsteak.

We have settled ourselves on the sunny side of the hut. There is a smell of tar, of summer, and of sweaty feet. Kat sits beside me. He wants to talk. Today we have been practicing saluting because Tjaden failed to salute a major. Kat can't get it out of his head.

"You see, we are losing the war because we can salute too well," he says.

Kropp stalks up, with his breeches rolled up and his feet bare. He lays out his washed socks to dry on the grass.

The two begin to argue. At the same time they lay a bottle of beer on the result of an air fight that's going on above us. Katczinsky won't budge from the opinion, which as an old front hog, he rhymes:

> Give 'em all the same grub and all the same pay
> And the war would be over and done in a day.

Kropp on the other hand is a thinker. He proposes that a declaration of war should be a kind of popular festival with entrance tickets and bands, like a bullfight. Then in the arena the ministers and generals of the two countries, dressed in bathing drawers and armed with clubs, can have it out among themselves. Whoever survives, his country wins. That would be much simpler and more just than this arrangement, where the wrong people do the fighting.

The subject is dropped. Then the conversation turns to drill.

A picture comes before me. Burning midday in the barrack yard. The heat hangs over the square. The barracks are deserted. Everything sleeps. All one hears is the drummers practicing; they have installed themselves anywhere and practice brokenly, dully, monotonously. What a concord! Midday heat, barrack square, and drummers beating!

The windows of the barracks are empty and dark. From some of them trousers are hanging to dry. The rooms are cool and one looks toward them longingly.

O dark, musty platoon huts, with the iron bedsteads, the bedding, the lockers and the stools! Even you can become the object of desire; out here you have a faint resemblance to home; your rooms, full of the smell of stale food, sleep, smoke, and clothes!

Katczinsky paints it all in lively colors. What would we not give to be able to go back to it! But we must not pursue that line of thought any further.

Those early morning hours of instruction—"What are the parts of the 98 rifle?"—the midday hours of physical training—"Pianist, forward! By the right, quick march. Report to the cookhouse for potato peeling."

We indulge in reminiscences. Kropp laughs suddenly and says: "Change at Löhne!"

That was our corporal's favorite game. Löhne is a railway junction. In order that our fellows going on leave shouldn't get lost there, Himmelstoss used to practice the change in the barrack room. We had to learn that at Löhne, to reach the branch line, we must pass through a subway. The beds represented the subway and each man stood at attention on the left side of his bed. Then came the command: "Change at Löhne!" and like lightning everyone scrambled under the bed to the opposite side. We practiced this for a whole hour——

Meanwhile the German airplane has been shot down. Like a comet it bursts into a streamer of smoke and falls headlong. Kropp has lost the bottle of beer. Disgruntled he counts out the money from his wallet.

"Surely Himmelstoss was a very different fellow as a postman," say I, after Albert's disappointment has subsided. "Then how does it come that he's such a bully as a drill sergeant?"

The question revives Kropp, more particularly as he hears there's no more beer in the canteen. "It's not only Himmelstoss, there are lots of them. As sure as they get a stripe or a star they become different men, just as though they'd swallowed concrete."

"That's the uniform," I suggest.

"Roughly speaking it is," says Kat, and prepares for a long speech; "but the root of the matter lies elsewhere. For instance, if you train a dog to eat potatoes and then afterwards put a piece of meat in front of him, he'll snap at it, it's his nature. And if you give a man a little bit of authority he behaves just the same way, he snaps at it too. The things are precisely the same. In himself man is essentially a beast, only he butters it over like a slice of bread with a little decorum. The army is based on that; one man must always have power over the other. The mischief is merely that each one has much too much power. A noncom can torment a private, a lieutenant a noncom, a captain a lieutenant, until he goes mad. And because they know they can, they all soon acquire the habit more or less. Take a simple case: we are marching back from the parade ground dog-tired. Then comes the order to sing. We are glad enough to be able to trail arms but we sing spiritlessly. At once the company is turned about and has to do another hour's drill as punishment. On the march back the order to sing is given again, and once more we start. Now what's the use of all that? It's simply that the company commander's head has been turned by having so much power. And nobody blames him. On the contrary, he is praised for being strict. That, of course, is only a trifling instance, but it holds also in very different affairs. Now I ask you: Let a man be whatever you like in peacetime, what occupation is there in which he can behave like that without getting a crack on the nose? He can only do that in the army. It goes to the heads of them all, you see. And the more insignificant a man has been in civil life the worse it takes him."

"They say, of course, there must be discipline," ventures Kropp meditatively.

"True," growls Kat, "they always do. And it may be so; still it oughtn't to become an abuse. But you try to explain that to a blacksmith or a laborer or a workman, you try to make that clear to a simple soldier—and that's what most of them are here. All he understands is that he has been properly trained so that when he comes up to the front he thinks he knows exactly what he should do in every circumstance and what not. It's simply amazing, I tell you, that the ordinary soldier survives so long up here in the front line. Simply amazing!"

No one protests. Everyone knows that drill ceases only in the front line and begins again a few miles behind, with all the absurdities of saluting and parade. It is an iron law that the soldier must be employed under every circumstance.

Here Tjaden comes up with a flushed face. He is so excited that he stutters. Beaming with satisfaction he stammers out: "Himmelstoss is on his way. He's coming to the front!"

Tjaden has a special grudge against Himmelstoss, because of the way he educated him in the barracks. Tjaden wets his bed, he does it at night in his sleep. Himmelstoss maintained that it was sheer laziness and invented a method worthy of himself for curing Tjaden.

He hunted up another wet-a-bed, named Kindervater, from a neighboring hut, and quartered him with Tjaden. In the huts there were the usual bunks, one above the other in pairs, with mattresses of wire netting. Himmelstoss put these two so that one occupied the upper and the other the lower bunk. The man underneath was of course disgusted. The next night they were changed over and the lower one put on top so that he could retaliate. That was Himmelstoss's system of self-education.

The idea was low but not ill-conceived. Unfortunately it accomplished nothing, because the first assumption was wrong: it was not laziness in either of them. Anyone who looked at their sallow skin could see that. The matter ended in one of them always sleeping on the floor, where he frequently caught cold.

Meanwhile Haie sits down beside us. He winks at me and rubs his paws thoughtfully. We once spent the finest day of our army life together—the day before we left for the front. We had been allotted to one of the recently formed regiments, but were first to be sent back for equipment to the garrison, not to the reinforcement depot, of course, but to another barracks. We were due to leave next morning early. In the evening we prepared ourselves to square accounts with Himmelstoss.

We had sworn for weeks past to do this. Kropp had even gone so far as to propose entering the postal service in peacetime in order to be Himmelstoss's superior when he became a postman again. He reveled in the thought of how he would grind him. It was this that made it impossible for him to crush us altogether—we always reckoned that later, at the end of the war, we would have our revenge on him.

In the meantime we decided to give him a good hiding. What could he do to us anyhow if he didn't recognize us and we left early the next morning?

We knew which pub he used to visit every evening. Returning to the barracks he had to go along a dark, uninhabited road. There we waited for him behind a pile of stones. I had a bedcover with me. We trembled with suspense, hoping he would be alone. At last we heard his footstep, which we recognized easily, so often had we heard it in the mornings as the door flew open and he bawled: "Get up!"

"Alone?" whispered Kropp.

"Alone."

I slipped around the pile of stones with Tjaden.

Himmelstoss seemed a little elevated; he was singing. His belt buckle gleamed. He came on unsuspectingly.

We seized the bedcover, made a quick leap, threw it over his head from behind, and pulled it round him so that he stood there in a white sack unable to raise his arms. The singing stopped. The next moment Haie Westhus was there, and spreading out his arms he shoved us back in order to be first in. He put himself in position with evident satisfaction, raised his arm like a signal mast and his hand like a coal shovel, and fetched such a blow on the white sack as would have felled an ox.

Himmelstoss was thrown down, he rolled five yards and started to yell. But we were prepared for that and had brought a cushion. Haie squatted down, laid the cushion on his knees, felt where Himmelstoss's head was, and pressed it down on the pillow. Immediately his voice was muffled. Haie let him get a gasp of air every so often, when he would give a mighty yell that was immediatey hushed.

Tjaden unbuttoned Himmelstoss's braces and pulled down his trousers, holding the whip meantime in his teeth. Then he stood up and set to work.

It was a wonderful picture: Himmelstoss on the ground, Haie bending over him with a fiendish grin and his mouth open with bloodlust, Himmelstoss's head on his knees; then the convulsed, striped drawers, the crossed legs, executing at every blow most original movements in the lowered breeches, and towering over them like a woodcutter the indefatigable Tjaden. In the end we had to drag him away to get our turn.

Finally Haie stood Himmelstoss on his feet again and gave one last personal remonstrance. As he stretched out his right arm preparatory to giving him a box on the ear he looked as if he were going to reach down a star.

Himmelstoss staggered. Haie stood him up again, made ready, and fetched him a second, well-aimed beauty with the left hand. Himmelstoss yelled and fell down on all fours cursing. His striped postman's backside gleamed in the moonlight.

We disappeared at full speed.

Haie looked round once again and said wrathfully, satisfied and rather mysteriously:

"Revenge is black pudding."

Himmelstoss ought to have been pleased; his saying that we should each educate one another had borne fruit for himself. We had become successful students of his methods.

He never discovered whom he had to thank for the business. At any rate he scored a bedcover out of it; for when we returned a few hours later to look for it, it was no longer to be found.

That evening's work made us more or less content to leave next morning. And an old buffer was pleased to describe us as "young heroes."

Chapter IV

WE have to go up on wiring fatigue.[2] The motor trucks roll up after dark. We climb in. It is a warm evening and the twilight seems like a canopy under whose shelter we feel drawn together. Even the stingy Tjaden gives me a cigarette and then a light.

We stand jammed in together, shoulder to shoulder, there is no room to sit. But we do not expect that. Müller is in a good mood for once; he is wearing his new boots.

The engines drone, the trucks bump and rattle. The roads are worn and full of holes. We dare not show a light so we lurch along and are often almost pitched out. That does not worry us, however. It can happen if it likes; a broken arm is better than a hole in the guts, and many a man would be thankful enough for such a chance of finding his way home again.

Beside us stream the munition columns in long files. They are making the pace, they overtake us going forward. We joke with them and they answer back.

A wall becomes visible, it belongs to a house which lies on the side of the road. I suddenly prick up my ears. Am I deceived? Again I hear distinctly the cackle of geese. A glance at Katczinsky—a glance from him to me; we understand one another.

"Kat, I hear some aspirants for the frying pan over there."

He nods. "It will be attended to when we come back. I have their number."

Of course Kat has their number. He knows all about every leg of goose within a radius of fifteen miles.

The trucks arrive at the artillery lines. The gun emplacements are camouflaged with bushes against aerial observation, and look like a kind of military Feast of the Tabernacles. These branches might seem gay and cheerful were not cannon embowered there.

The air becomes acrid with the smoke of the guns and the fog. The fumes of powder taste bitter on the tongue. The roar of the guns makes our truck stagger, the reverberation rolls raging away to the rear, everything quakes. Our faces change imperceptibly. We are not, indeed, in the front line, but only in the reserves, yet in every face can be read: This is the Front, now we are within its embrace.

It is not fear. Men who have been up as often as we have become thick-skinned. Only the young recruits are agitated. Kat explains to them:

---

[2] *wiring fatigue*: an army detail, stringing up barbed wire.

"That was a twelve-inch. You hear the explosion first and afterwards comes the sound of the gun."

But the hollow sound of the firing does not reach us. It is swallowed up in the general murmur of the front. Kat listens: "There'll be a bombardment tonight."

We all listen. The front is restless. "The Tommies are firing already," says Kropp.

The shelling can be heard distinctly. It is the English batteries to the right of our section. They are beginning an hour too soon. According to us they start punctually at ten o'clock.

"What's got them?" says Müller. "Their clocks must be fast."

"There'll be a bombardment, I tell you, I can feel it in my bones." Kat shrugs his shoulders.

Three shells land beside us. The burst of flame shoots across the fog, the fragments howl and drone. We shiver and are glad to think that we shall be back in the huts early in the morning.

Our faces are neither paler nor more flushed than usual; they are not more tense nor more flabby—and yet they are changed. We feel that in our blood a contact has shot home. That is no figure of speech; it is fact. It is the front, the consciousness of the front, that makes this contact. The moment that the first shells whistle over and the air is rent with the explosions, there is suddenly in our veins, in our hands, in our eyes, a tense waiting, a watching, a profound growth, a strange sharpening of the senses. The body with one bound is in full readiness.

It often seems to me as though it were the vibrating, shuddering air that with a noiseless leap springs upon us; or as though the front itself emitted an electric current which awakened unknown nerve centers.

Every time it is the same. We start out for the front plain soldiers, either cheerful or gloomy; then come the first gun emplacements and every word of our speech has a new ring.

When Kat stands in front of the hut and says: "There'll be a bombardment," that is merely his own opinion; but if he says it here, then the sentence has the sharpness of a bayonet in the moonlight, it cuts clean through the thought, it thrusts nearer and speaks to this unknown thing that is awakened in us, a dark meaning—"There'll be a bombardment." Perhaps it is our inner and most secret life that shivers and falls on guard.

To me the front is a mysterious whirlpool. Though I am in still water far away from its center, I feel the whirl of the vortex sucking me slowly, irresistibly, inescapably into itself.

From the earth, from the air, sustaining forces pour into us—mostly from the earth. To no man does the earth mean so much as to the soldier. When he presses himself down upon her long and powerfully, when he buries his face and his limbs deep in her from the fear of death by shell-fire, then she is his only friend, his brother, his mother; he stifles his terror and his cries in her silence and her security; she shelters him and gives him a new lease of ten seconds of life, receives him again and often forever.

Earth!—Earth!—Earth!

Earth with thy folds, and hollows and holes, into which a man may fling himself and crouch down! In the spasm of terror, under the hailing of annihilation, in the bellowing death of the explosions, O Earth, thou grantest us the great resisting surge of new-won life. Our being, almost utterly carried away by the fury of the storm, streams back through our hands from thee, and we, thy redeemed ones, bury ourselves in thee, and through the long minutes, in a mute agony of hope, bite into thee with our lips!

At the sound of the first droning of the shells we rush back, in one part of our being, a thousand years. By the animal instinct that is awakened in us we are led and protected. It is not conscious; it is far quicker, much more sure, less fallible, than consciousness. One cannot explain it. A man is walking along without thought or heed—suddenly he throws himself down on the ground and a storm of fragments flies harmlessly over him— yet he cannot remember either to have heard the shell coming or to have thought of flinging himself down. But had he not abandoned himself to the impulse he would now be a heap of mangled flesh. It is this other, this second sight in us, that has thrown us to the ground and saved us, without our knowing how. If it were not so, there would not be one man alive from Flanders to the Vosges.

We march up, moody or good-tempered soldiers—we reach the zone where the front begins and become on the instant human animals.

An indigent-looking wood receives us. We pass by the soup kitchens. Under cover of the wood we climb out. The trucks turn back. They are to collect us again in the morning, before dawn.

Mist and the smoke of guns lie breast-high over the fields. The moon is shining. Along the road troops file. Their helmets gleam softly in the moonlight. The heads and the rifles stand out above the white mist, nodding heads, rocking carriers of guns.

Farther on the mist ends. Here the heads become figures; coats, trousers, and boots appear out of the mist as from a milky pool. They become a column. The column marches on, straight ahead, the figures resolve themselves into a block, individuals are no longer recognizable, the dark wedge presses onward, fantastically topped by the heads and weapons floating off on the milky pool. A column—not men at all.

Guns and munition wagons are moving along a crossroad. The backs of the horses shine in the moonlight, their movements are beautiful, they toss their heads, and their eyes gleam. The guns and the wagons float before the dim background of the moonlit landscape, the riders in their steel helmets resemble knights of a forgotten time; it is strangely beautiful and arresting.

We push on to the pioneer dump. Some of us load our shoulders with pointed and twisted iron stakes; others thrust smooth iron rods through rolls of wire and go off with them. The burdens are awkward and heavy.

The ground becomes more broken. From ahead come warnings: "Look out, deep shell holes on the left"—"Mind, trenches"——

Our eyes peer out, our feet and our sticks feel in front of us before they take the weight of the body. Suddenly the line halts; I bump my face against the roll of wire carried by the man in front and curse.

There are some shell-smashed trucks in the road. Another order: "Cigarettes and pipes out." We are getting near the line.

In the meantime it has become pitch-dark. We skirt a small wood and then have the front line immediately before us.

An uncertain, red glow spreads along the skyline from one end to the other. It is in perpetual movement, punctuated with the bursts of flame from the muzzles of the batteries. Balls of light rise up high above it, silver and red spheres which explode and rain down in showers of red, white, and green stars. French rockets go up, which unfold a silk parachute to the air and drift slowly down. They light up everything as bright as day, their light shines on us and we see our shadows sharply outlined on the ground. They hover for the space of a minute before they burn out. Immediately fresh ones shoot up to the sky, and again green, red, and blue stars.

"Bombardment," says Kat.

The thunder of the guns swells to a single heavy roar and then breaks up again into separate explosions. The dry bursts of the machine guns rattle. Above us the air teems with invisible swift movement, with howls, pipings, and hisses. They are the smaller shells—and among them, booming through the night like an organ, go the great coal boxes and the heavies. They have a hoarse, distant bellow like a rutting stag and make their way high above the howl and whistle of the smaller shells. It reminds me of flocks of wild geese when I hear them. Last autumn the wild geese flew day after day across the path of the shells.

The searchlights begin to sweep the dark sky. They slide along it like gigantic tapering rulers. One of them pauses, and quivers a little. Immediately a second is beside him, a black insect is caught between them and tries to escape—the airman. He hesitates, is blinded and falls.

At regular intervals we ram in the iron stakes. Two men hold a roll and the others spool off the barbed wire. It is that awful stuff with close-set, long spikes. I am not used to unrolling it and tear my hand.

After a few hours it is done. But there is still some time before the trucks come. Most of us lie down and sleep. I try also, but it has turned too chilly. Near to the sea one is constantly waked by the cold.

Once I fall fast asleep. Then waking suddenly with a start I do not know where I am. I see the stars, I see the rockets, and for a moment have the impression that I have fallen asleep at a garden fête. I don't know whether it is morning or evening, I lie in the pale cradle of the twilight and listen for soft words which will come, soft and near—am I crying? I put my hand to my eyes, it is so fantastic; am I a child? Smooth skin—it lasts only a second, then I recognize the silhouette of Katczinsky. The old veteran, he sits quietly and smokes his pipe—a covered pipe of course. When he sees I am awake, he says: "That gave you a fright. It was only a nosecap, it landed in the bushes over there."

I sit up, I feel myself strangely alone. It's good Kat is there. He gazes thoughtfully at the front and says:

"Mighty fine fireworks if they weren't so dangerous."

One lands behind us. Two recruits jump up terrified. A couple of minutes later another comes over, nearer this time. Kat knocks out his pipe. "It makes a glow."

Then it begins in earnest. We crawl away as well as we can in our haste. The next lands fair among us. Two fellows cry out. Green rockets shoot up on the skyline. Barrage. The mud flies high, fragments whizz past. The crack of the guns is heard long after the roar of the explosions.

Beside us lies a fair-headed recruit in utter terror. He has buried his face in his hands, his helmet has fallen off. I fish hold of it and try to put it back on his head. He looks up, pushes the helmet off, and like a child creeps under my arm, his head close to my breast. The little shoulders heave. Shoulders just like Kemmerich's. I let him be. So that the helmet should be of some use I stick it on his behind—not for a jest, but out of consideration, since that is his highest part. And though there is plenty of meat there, a shot in it can be damned painful. Besides, a man has to lie a whole month on his belly in the hospital, and afterwards he would be almost sure to have a limp.

It's got someone pretty badly. Cries are heard between the explosions.

At last it grows quiet. The fire has lifted over us and is now dropping on the reserves. We risk a look. Red rockets shoot up to the sky. Apparently there's an attack coming.

Where we are it is still quiet. I sit up and shake the recruit by the shoulder. "All over, kid! It's all right this time."

He looks round him dazedly. "You'll get used to it soon," I tell him.

He sees his helmet and puts it on. Gradually he comes to. Then suddenly he turns fiery red and looks confused. Cautiously he reaches his hand to his behind and looks at me dismally.

I understand at once: Gun-shy. That wasn't the reason I had stuck his helmet over it. "That's no disgrace," I reassure him: "Many's the man before you has had his pants full after the first bombardment. Go behind that bush there and throw your underpants away. Get along———"

He goes off. Things become quieter, but the cries do not cease. "What's up, Albert?" I ask.

"A couple of columns over there have got it in the neck."

The cries continue. It is not men, they could not cry so terribly.

"Wounded horses," says Kat.

It's unendurable. It is the moaning of the world, it is the martyred creation, wild with anguish, filled with terror, and groaning.

We are pale. Detering stands up. "God! For God's sake! Shoot them!"

He is a farmer and very fond of horses. It gets under his skin. Then, as if deliberately, the fire dies down again. The screaming of the beasts becomes louder. One can no longer distinguish whence in this now quiet, silvery landscape it comes; ghostly, invisible, it is everywhere, between heaven and earth it rolls on immeasurably. Detering raves and yells out: "Shoot them! Shoot them, can't you? damn you again!"

"They must look after the men first," says Kat quietly.

We stand up and try to see where it is. If we could only see the animals we should be able to endure it better. Müller has a pair of glasses. We see a dark group, bearers with stretchers, and larger black clumps moving about. Those are the wounded horses. But not all of them. Some gallop away in the distance, fall down, and then run on farther. The belly of one is ripped open, the guts trail out. He becomes tangled in them and falls, then he stands up again.

Detering raises his gun and aims. Kat hits it up in the air. "Are you mad———?"

Detering trembles and throws his rifle on the ground.

We sit down and hold our ears. But this appalling noise, these groans and screams penetrate, they penetrate everywhere.

We can bear almost anything. But now the sweat breaks out on us. We must get up and run, no matter where, but where these cries can no longer be heard. And it is not men, only horses.

From the dark group stretchers move off again. Then single shots crack out. The black heap is convulsed and becomes thinner. At last! But still it is not the end. The men cannot overtake the wounded beasts which fly in their pain, their wide-open mouths full of anguish. One of the men goes down on his knee, a shot—one horse drops—another. The last one props himself on his forelegs and drags himself round in a circle like a merry-go-round; squatting, it drags round in circles on its stiffened forelegs; apparently its back is broken. The soldier runs up and shoots it. Slowly, humbly, it sinks to the ground.

We take our hands from our ears. The cries are silenced. Only a long-drawn, dying sigh still hangs on the air.

Then again only the rockets, the singing of the shells, and the stars—and they shine out wonderfully.

Detering walks up and down cursing: "Like to know what harm they've done." He returns to it once again. His voice is agitated, it sounds almost dignified as he says: "I tell you it is the vilest baseness to use horses in the war."

We go back. It is time we returned to the trucks. The sky is become a bit brighter. Three o'clock in the morning. The breeze is fresh and cool, the pale hour makes our faces look gray.

We trudge onward in single file through the trenches and shell holes and come again to the zone of mist. Katczinsky is restive, that's a bad sign.

"What's up, Kat?" says Kropp.

"I wish I were back home." Home—he means the huts.

"It won't last much longer, Kat."

He is nervous. "I don't know, I don't know——"

We come to the communication trench and then to the open fields. The little wood reappears; we know every foot of ground here. There's the cemetery with the mounds and the black crosses.

That moment it breaks out behind us, swells, roars, and thunders. We duck down—a cloud of flame shoots up a hundred yards ahead of us.

The next minute under a second explosion part of the wood rises slowly in the air, three or four trees sail up and then crash to pieces. The shells begin to hiss like safety valves—heavy fire——

"Take cover!" yells somebody—"Cover!"

The fields are flat, the wood is too distant and dangerous—the only cover is the graveyard and the mounds. We stumble across in the dark, and as though spirited away, every man lies glued behind a mound.

Not a moment too soon. The dark goes mad. It heaves and raves. Darknesses blacker than the night rush on us with giant strides, over us and away. The flames of the explosions light up the graveyard.

There is no escape anywhere. By the light of the shells I try to get a view of the fields. They are a surging sea, daggers of flame from the explosions leap up like fountains. It is impossible for anyone to break through it.

The wood vanishes, it is pounded, crushed, torn to pieces. We must stay here in the graveyard.

The earth bursts before us. It rains clods. I feel a smack. My sleeve is torn away by a splinter. I shut my fist. No pain. Still that does not reassure me: wounds don't hurt till afterwards. I feel the arm all over. It is grazed but sound. Now a crack on the skull, I begin to lose consciousness. Like lightning the thought comes to me: Don't faint, sink down in the black broth and immediately come up to the top again. A splinter slashes into my helmet, but has traveled so far that it does not go through. I wipe the mud out of my eyes. A hole is torn up in front of me. Shells hardly ever land in the same hole twice, I'll get into it. With one bound I fling myself down and lie on the earth as flat as a fish; there it whistles again, quickly I crouch together, claw for cover, feel something on the left, shove in beside it, it gives way, I groan, the earth leaps, the blast thunders in my ears, I creep under the yielding thing, cover myself with it, draw it over me, it is wood, cloth, cover, cover, miserable cover against the whizzing splinters.

I open my eyes—my fingers grasp a sleeve, an arm. A wounded man? I yell to him—no answer—a dead man. My hand gropes further, splinters of wood—now I remember again that we are lying in the graveyard.

But the shelling is stronger than everything. It wipes out the sensibilities, I merely crawl still deeper into the coffin, it should protect me, and especially as Death himself lies in it too.

Before me gapes the shell hole. I grasp it with my eyes as with fists. With one leap I must be in it. There, I get a smack in the face, a hand clamps onto my shoulder—has the dead man waked up?—the hand shakes me, I turn my head, in the second of light I stare into the face of Katczinsky, he has his mouth wide open and is yelling. I hear nothing, he rattles me, comes nearer, in a momentary lull his voice reaches me: "Gas—Gaas—Gaaas—Pass it on."

I grab for my gas mask. Some distance from me there lies someone. I think of nothing but this: That fellow there must know: Gaaas—Gaaas——

I call, I lean toward him, I swipe at him with the satchel, he doesn't see—once again, again—he merely ducks—it's a recruit—I look at Kat desperately, he has his mask ready—I pull out mine too, my helmet falls to one side, it slips over my face, I reach the man, his satchel is on the side nearest me, I seize the mask, pull it over his head, he understands, I let go and with a jump drop back into the shell hole.

The dull thud of the gas shells mingles with the crashes of the high explosives. A bell sounds between the explosions, gongs, and metal clappers warning everyone—Gas—Gas—Gaas.

Someone plumps down behind me, another. I wipe the goggles of my mask clear of the moist breath. It is Kat, Kropp, and someone else. All four of us lie there in heavy, watchful suspense and breathe as lightly as possible.

These first minutes with the mask decide between life and death: is it tightly woven? I remember the awful sights in the hospital: the gas patients who in day-long suffocation cough their burned lungs up in clots.

Cautiously, the mouth applied to the valve, I breathe. The gas still creeps over the ground and sinks into all hollows. Like a big, soft jellyfish it floats into our shell hole and lolls there obscenely. I nudge Kat, it is better to crawl out and lie on top than to stay here where the gas collects most. But we don't get as far as that; a second bombardment begins. It is no longer as though the shells roared; it is the earth itself raging.

With a crash something black bears down on us. It lands close beside us; a coffin thrown up.

I see Kat move and I crawl across. The coffin has hit the fourth man in our hole on his outstretched arm. He tries to tear off his gas mask with the other hand. Kropp seizes him just in time, twists the hand sharply behind his back, and holds it fast.

Kat and I proceed to free the wounded arm. The coffin lid is loose and bursts open, we are easily able to pull it off, we toss the corpse out, it slides down to the bottom of the shell hole, then we try to loosen the underpart.

Fortunately the man swoons and Kropp is able to help us. We no longer have to be careful, but work away till the coffin gives with a sigh before the spade that we have dug in under it.

It has grown lighter. Kat takes a piece of the lid, places it under the shattered arm, and we wrap all our bandages round it. For the moment we can do no more.

Inside the gas mask my head booms and roars—it is nigh bursting. My lungs are tight, they breathe always the same hot, used-up air, the veins on my temples are swollen, I feel I am suffocating.

A gray light filters through to us. I climb out over the edge of the shell hole. In the dirty twilight lies a leg torn clean off; the boot is quite whole, I take that all in at a glance. Now someone stands up a few yards distant. I polish the windows, in my excitement they are immediately dimmed again, I peer through them, the man there no longer wears his mask.

I wait some seconds—he has not collapsed—he looks around and makes a few paces—rattling in my throat I tear my mask off too and fall down, the air streams into me like cold water, my eyes are bursting, the wave sweeps over me and extinguishes me.

The shelling has ceased. I drag myself to the crater and tell the others. They take off their masks. We lift up the wounded man, one taking his splintered arm. And so we stumble off hastily.

The graveyard is a mass of wreckage. Coffins and corpses lie strewn about. They have been killed once again; but each of them that was flung up saved one of us.

The hedge is destroyed, the rails of the light railway are torn up and rise stiffly in the air in great arches. Someone lies in front of us. We stop; Kropp goes on alone with the wounded man.

The man on the ground is a recruit. His hip is covered with blood; he is so exhausted that I feel for my water bottle where I have rum and tea. Kat restrains my hand and stoops over him.

"Where's it got you, comrade?"

His eyes move. He is too weak to answer.

We cut off his trousers carefully. He groans. "Gently, gently, it is much better——"

If he has been hit in the stomach he oughtn't to drink anything. There's no vomiting, that's a good sign. We lay the hip bare. It is one mass of mincemeat and bone splinters. The joint has been hit. This lad won't walk anymore.

I wet his temples with a moistened finger and give him a swig. His eyes move again. We see now that the right arm is bleeding as well.

Kat spreads out two wads of dressing as wide as possible so that they will cover the wound. I look for something to bind loosely round it. We have nothing more, so I slit up the wounded man's trouser leg still farther in order to use a piece of his underpants as a bandage. But he is wearing none. I now look at him closely. He is the fair-headed boy of a little while ago.

In the meantime Kat has taken a bandage from a dead man's pocket and we carefully bind the wound. I say to the youngster who looks at us fixedly: "We're going for a stretcher now——"

Then he opens his mouth and whispers: "Stay here——"

"We'll be back again soon," says Kat. "We are only going to get a stretcher for you."

We don't know if he understands. He whimpers like a child and plucks at us: "Don't go away——"

Kat looks around and whispers: "Shouldn't we just take a revolver and put an end to it?"

The youngster will hardly survive the carrying, and at the most he will only last a few days. What he has gone through so far is nothing to what he's in for till he dies. Now he is numb and feels nothing. In an hour he will become one screaming bundle of intolerable pain. Every day that he can live will be a howling torture. And to whom does it matter whether he has them or not——

I nod. "Yes, Kat, we ought to put him out of his misery."

He stands still a moment. He has made up his mind. We look around—but we are no longer alone. A little group is gathering, from the shell holes and trenches appear heads.

We get a stretcher.

Kat shakes his head. "Such a kid——" He repeats it: "Young innocents——"

Our losses are less than was to be expected—five killed and eight wounded. It was in fact quite a short bombardment. Two of our dead lie in the upturned graves. We had merely to throw the earth in on them.

We go back. We trot off silently in single file one behind the other. The wounded are taken to the dressing station. The morning is cloudy. The bearers make a fuss about numbers and tickets, the wounded whimper. It begins to rain.

An hour later we reach our trucks and climb in. There is more room now than there was.

The rain becomes heavier. We take out waterproof sheets and spread them over our heads. The rain rattles down and flows off at the sides in streams. The trucks bump through the holes, and we rock to and fro in a half-sleep.

Two men in the front of the truck have long forked poles. They watch for telephone wires which hang crosswise over the road so densely that they might easily pull our heads off. The two fellows take them at the right moment on their poles and lift them over behind us. We hear their call "Mind—wire—," dip the knee in a half-sleep and straighten up again.

Monotonously the trucks sway, monotonously come the calls, monotonously falls the rain. It falls on our heads and on the heads of the dead up in the line, on the body of the little recruit with the wound that is so much too big for his hip; it falls on Kemmerich's grave; it falls in our hearts.

An explosion sounds somewhere. We wince, our eyes become tense, our hands are ready to vault over the side of the truck into the ditch by the road.

It goes no farther—only the monotonus cry: "Mind—wire"—our knees bend—we are again half asleep.

Chapter V

KILLING each separate louse is a tedious business when a man has
hundreds. The little beasts are hard and the everlasting cracking with
one's fingernails very soon becomes wearisome. So Tjaden has rigged up
the lid of a boot-polish tin with a piece of wire over the lighted stump of a
candle. The lice are simply thrown into this little pan. Crack! and they're
done for.

We sit around with our shirts on our knees, our bodies naked to the
warm air and our hands at work. Haie has a particularly fine brand of
louse: they have a red cross on their heads. He suggests that he brought
them back with him from the hospital at Thourhout, where they attended
personally on a surgeon general. He says he means to use the fat that
slowly accumulates in the tin lid for polishing his boots, and roars with
laughter for half an hour at his own joke.

But he hasn't much success today; we are too preoccupied with another
affair.

The rumor has materialized. Himmelstoss has come. He appeared yesterday; we've already heard the well-known voice. He seems to have over-
done it with a couple of young recruits on the plowed field at home, and
unknown to him the son of the local magistrate was watching. That cooked
his goose.

He will meet some surprises here. Tjaden has been meditating for hours
what to say to him. Haie gazes thoughtfully at his great paws and winks at
me. The thrashing was the high-water mark of his life. He tells me he often
dreams of it. Kropp and Müller are amusing themselves. From somewhere or other, probably the pioneer cookhouse, Kropp has bagged for
himself a messtinful of beans. Müller squints hungrily into it but checks
himself and says: "Albert, what would you do if it were suddenly peacetime again?"

"There won't be any civil life," says Albert bluntly.

"Well, but if—" persists Müller, "what would you do?"

"Clear out of this!" growls Kropp.

"Of course. And then what?"

"Get drunk," says Albert.

"Don't talk rot, I mean seriously——"

"So do I," says Kropp, "what else should a man do?"

Kat becomes interested. He levies tribute on Kropp's tin of beans, swal-
lows some, then considers for a while and says: "You might get drunk
first, of course, but then you'd take the next train for home and mother.
Peacetime, man, Albert——"

He fumbles in his oilcloth pocketbook for a photograph and suddenly shows it all round. "My old people!" Then he puts it back and swears: "Damned lousy war——"

"It's all very well for you to talk," I tell him. "You've a wife and children."

"True," he nods, "and I have to see to it that they've something to eat."

We laugh. "They won't lack for that, Kat, you'd scrounge it from somewhere."

Müller is insatiable and gives himself no peace. He wakes Haie Westhus out of his dream. "Haie, what would you do if it was peacetime?"

"Give you a kick in the backside for the way you talk," I say. "How will it come about exactly?"

"How does the cow dung come on the roof?" retorts Müller laconically, and turns to Haie Westhus again.

It is too much for Haie. He shakes his freckled head:

"You mean when the war's over?"

"Exactly. You've said it."

"Well, there'd be women of course, eh?"—Haie licks his lips.

"Sure."

"By Jove yes," says Haie, his face melting, "then I'd grab some good buxom dame, some real kitchen wench with plenty to get hold of, you know, and jump straight into bed. Just you think, boys, a real featherbed with a spring mattress; I wouldn't put trousers on again for a week."

Everyone is silent. The picture is too good. Our flesh creeps. At last Müller pulls himself together and says:

"And then what?"

A pause. Then Haie explains rather awkwardly: "If I were a noncom I'd stay with the Prussians and serve out my time."

"Haie, you've got a screw loose, surely!" I say.

"Have you ever dug peat?" he retorts good-naturedly. "You try it."

Then he pulls a spoon out of the top of his boot and reaches over into Kropp's messtin.

"It can't be worse than digging trenches," I venture.

Haie chews and grins: "It lasts longer though. And there's no getting out of it, either."

"But, man, surely it's better at home."

"Some ways," says he, and with open mouth sinks into a daydream.

You can see what he is thinking. There is the mean little hut on the moors, the hard work on the heath from morning till night in the heat, the miserable pay, the dirty laborer's clothes.

"In the army in peacetime you've nothing to trouble about," he goes on, "your food's found every day, or else you kick up a row; you've a bed, every week clean underwear like a perfect gent, you do your noncom's duty, you have a good suit of clothes; in the evening you're a free man and go off to the pub."

Haie is extraordinarily set on his idea. He's in love with it.

"And when your twelve years are up you get your pension and become a village bobby, and you can walk about the whole day."

He's already sweating on it. "And just you think how you'd be treated. Here a dram, there a pint. Everybody wants to be well in with a bobby."

"You'll never be a noncom though, Haie," interrupts Kat.

Haie looks at him sadly and is silent. His thoughts still linger over the clear evenings in autumn, the Sundays in the heather, the village bells, the afternoons and evenings with the servant girls, the fried bacon and barley, the carefree evening hours in the alehouse——

He can't part with all these dreams so abruptly; he merely growls: "What silly questions you do ask."

He pulls his shirt over his head and buttons up his tunic.

"What would you do, Tjaden?" asks Kropp.

Tjaden thinks only of one thing. "See to it that Himmelstoss doesn't get past me."

Apparently he would like most to have him in a cage and sail into him with a club every morning. To Kropp he says warmly: "If I were in your place I'd see to it that I became a lieutenant. Then you could grind him till the water in his backside boils."

"And you, Detering?" asks Müller like an inquisitor. He's a born schoolmaster with all his questions.

Detering is sparing with his words. But on this subject he speaks. He looks at the sky and says only the one sentence: "I would go straight on with the harvesting."

Then he gets up and walks off.

He is worried. His wife has to look after the farm. They've already taken away two of his horses. Every day he reads the papers that come, to see whether it is raining in his little corner of Oldenburg. They haven't brought the hay in yet.

At this moment Himmelstoss appears. He comes straight up to our group. Tjaden's face turns red. He stretches his length on the grass and shuts his eyes in embarrassment.

Himmelstoss is a little hesitant, his gait becomes slower. Then he marches up to us. No one makes any motion to stand up. Kropp looks up at him with interest.

He continues to stand in front of us and wait. As no one says anything he launches a "Well?"

A couple of seconds go by. Apparently Himmelstoss doesn't quite know what to do. He would like most to set us all on the run again. But he seems to have learned already that the front line isn't a parade ground. He tries it on though, and by addressing himself to one instead of to all of us hopes to get some response. Kropp is nearest, so he favors him.

"Well, you here too?"

But Albert's no friend of his. "A bit longer than you, I fancy," he retorts.

The red moustache twitches: "You don't recognize me anymore, what?"

Tjaden now opens his eyes. "I do though."

Himmelstoss turns to him: "Tjaden, isn't it?"

Tjaden lifts his head. "And do you know what you are?"

Himmelstoss is disconcerted. "Since when have we become so familiar? I don't remember that we ever slept in the gutter together?"

He has no idea what to make of the situation. He didn't expect this open hostility. But he is on his guard: someone has already dinned some rot into him about getting a shot in the back.

The question about the gutter makes Tjaden so mad that he becomes almost witty: "No, you slept there by yourself."

Himmelstoss begins to boil. But Tjaden gets in ahead of him. He must bring off his insult: "Wouldn't you like to know what you are? A dirty hound, that's what you are. I've been wanting to tell you that for a long time."

The satisfaction of months shines in his dull pig's eyes as he spits out: "Dirty hound!"

Himmelstoss lets fly too, now. "What's that, you muckrake, you dirty peat stealer? Stand up there, bring your heels together when your superior officer speaks to you."

Tjaden winks solemnly. "You take a run and jump at yourself, Himmelstoss."

Himmelstoss is a raging book of army regulations. The Kaiser couldn't be more insulted. "Tjaden, I command you, as your superior officer: Stand up!"

"Anything else you would like?" asks Tjaden.

"Will you obey my order or not?"

Tjaden replies, without knowing it, in the well-known classical phrase.

At the same time he ventilates his backside.

"I'll have you court-martialed," storms Himmelstoss.

We watch him disappear in the direction of the Orderly Room. Haie and Tjaden burst into a regular peat digger's bellow. Haie laughs so much that he dislocates his jaw, and suddenly stands there helpless with his mouth wide open. Albert has to put it back again by giving it a blow with his fist.

Kat is troubled: "If he reports you, it'll be pretty serious."

"Do you think he will?" asks Tjaden.

"Sure to," I say.

"The least you'll get will be five days' close arrest," says Kat.

That doesn't worry Tjaden. "Five days' clink are five days' rest."

"And if they send you to the Fortress?" urges the thoroughgoing Müller.

"Well, for the time being the war will be over so far as I am concerned."

Tjaden is a cheerful soul. There aren't any worries for him. He goes off with Haie and Leer so that they won't find him in the first flush of the excitement.

Müller hasn't finished yet. He tackles Kropp again.

"Albert, if you were really at home now, what would you do?"

Kropp is contented now and more accommodating:

"How many of us were there in the class exactly?"

We count up: out of twenty, seven are dead, four wounded, one in a madhouse. That makes twelve privates.

"Three of them are lieutenants," says Müller. "Do you think they would still let Kantorek sit on them?"

We guess not: we wouldn't let ourselves be sat on for that matter.

"What do you mean by the threefold theme in 'William Tell'?" says Kropp reminiscently, and roars with laughter.

"What was the purpose of the Poetic League of Göttingen?" asks Müller suddenly and earnestly.

"How many children had Charles the Bald?" I interrupt gently.

"You'll never make anything of your life, Bäumer," croaks Müller.

"When was the Battle of Zana?" Kropp wants to know.

"You lack the studious mind, Kropp, sit down, three minus——" I wink.

"What offices did Lycurgus consider the most important for the state?" asks Müller, pretending to take off his pince-nez.

"Does it go: 'We Germans fear God and none else in the whole world,' or 'We, the Germans, fear God and——' " I submit.

"How many inhabitants has Melbourne?" asks Müller.

"How do you expect to succeed in life if you don't know that?" I ask Albert hotly.

Which he caps with: "What is meant by Cohesion?"

We remember mighty little of all that rubbish. Anyway, it has never been the slightest use to us. At school nobody ever taught us how to light a cigarette in a storm of rain, nor how a fire could be made with wet wood

—nor that it is best to stick a bayonet in the belly because there it doesn't get jammed, as it does in the ribs.

Müller says thoughtfully: "What's the use. We'll have to go back and sit on the forms again."

I consider that out of the question. "We might take a special exam."

"That needs preparation. If you do get through, what then? A student's life isn't any better. If you have no money, you have to work like the devil."

"It's a bit better. But it's rot all the same, everything they teach you."

Kropp supports me: "How can a man take all that stuff seriously when he's once been out here?"

"Still, you must have an occupation of some sort," insists Müller, as though he were Kantorek himself.

Albert cleans his nails with a knife. We are surprised at this delicacy. But it is merely pensiveness. He puts the knife away and continues: "That's just it. Kat and Detering and Haie will go back to their jobs because they had them already. Himmelstoss too. But we never had any. How will we ever get used to one after this, here?"—he makes a gesture toward the front.

"We'll want a private income, and then we'll be able to live by ourselves in a wood," I say, but at once feel ashamed of this absurd idea.

"But what will really happen when we go back?" wonders Müller, and even he is troubled.

Kropp gives a shrug. "I don't know. Let's get back first, then we'll find out."

We are all utterly at a loss. "What could we do?" I ask.

"I don't want to do anything," replies Kropp wearily. "You'll be dead one day, so what does it matter? I don't think we'll ever go back."

"When I think about it, Albert," I say after a while, rolling over on my back, "when I hear the word 'peacetime,' it goes to my head; and if it really came, I think I would do some unimaginable thing—something, you know, that it's worth having lain here in the muck for. But I can't even imagine anything. All I do know is that this business about professions and studies and salaries and so on—it makes me sick, it is and always was disgusting. I don't see anything—I don't see anything at all, Albert."

All at once everything seems to me confused and hopeless.

Kropp feels it too. "It will go pretty hard with us all. But nobody at home seems to worry much about it. Two years of shells and bombs—a man won't peel that off as easy as a sock."

We agree that it's the same for everyone; not only for us here, but everywhere, for everyone who is of our age; to some more, and to others less. It is the common fate of our generation.

Albert expresses it: "The war has ruined us for everything."

He is right. We are not youth any longer. We don't want to take the world by storm. We are fleeing. We fly from ourselves. From our life. We were eighteen and had begun to love life and the world; and we had to shoot it to pieces. The first bomb, the first explosion, burst in our hearts. We are cut off from activity, from striving, from progress. We believe in such things no longer, we believe in the war.

The Orderly Room shows signs of life. Himmelstoss seems to have stirred them up. At the head of the column trots the fat sergeant major. It is queer that almost all pay sergeant majors are fat.

Himmelstoss follows him, thirsting for vengeance. His boots gleam in the sun.

We get up.

"Where's Tjaden?" the sergeant puffs.

No one knows, of course. Himmelstoss glowers at us wrathfully. "You know very well. You won't say, that's the fact of the matter. Out with it!"

Fatty looks round inquiringly; but Tjaden is not to be seen. He tries another way.

"Tjaden will report at the Orderly Room in ten minutes."

Then he steams off with Himmelstoss in his wake.

"I have a feeling that next time we go up wiring I'll be letting a bundle of wire fall on Himmelstoss's leg," hints Kropp.

"We'll have quite a lot of jokes with him," laughs Müller.

That is our sole ambition: to knock the conceit out of a postman.

I go into the hut and put Tjaden wise. He disappears.

Then we change our possy and lie down again to play cards. We know how to do that: to play cards, to swear, and to fight. Not much for twenty years—and yet too much for twenty years.

Half an hour later Himmelstoss is back again. Nobody pays any attention to him. He asks for Tjaden. We shrug our shoulders.

"Then you'd better find him," he persists. "Haven't you been to look for him?"

Kropp lies back in the grass and says: "Have you ever been out here before?"

"That's none of your business," retorts Himmelstoss. "I expect an answer."

"Very good," says Kropp, getting up. "See up there where those little white clouds are? Those are antiaircraft. We were over there yesterday. Five dead and eight wounded. It was a lot of fun. Next time, when you go up with us, before they die the fellows will come up to you, click their heels, and ask stiffly: 'Please may I go? Please may I hop it? We've been waiting here a long time for someone like you.' "

He sits down again and Himmelstoss disappears like a comet.

"Three days' CB," Kat conjectures.

"Next time I'll let fly," I say to Albert.

But that is the end. The case comes up for trial in the evening. In the Orderly Room sits our Lieutenant, Bertinck, and calls us in one after another.

I have to appear as a witness and explain the reason of Tjaden's insubordination.

The story of the bed-wetting makes an impression. Himmelstoss is recalled and I repeat my statement.

"Is that right?" Bertinck asks Himmelstoss.

He tries to evade the question, but in the end has to confess, for Kropp tells the same story.

"Why didn't someone report the matter, then?" asks Bertinck.

We are silent: he must know himself how much use it is reporting such things in the army. It isn't usual to make complaints in the army. He understands it all right though, and lectures Himmelstoss, making it plain to him that the front isn't a parade ground. Then comes Tjaden's turn, who gets a long sermon and three days' open arrest. He gives Kropp a wink and one day's open arrest. "It can't be helped," he says to him regretfully. He is a decent fellow.

Open arrest is quite pleasant. The clink was once a fowlhouse; there we can visit the prisoners, we know how to manage it. Close arrest would have meant the cellar.

They used to tie us to a tree, but that is forbidden now. In many ways we are treated quite like men.

An hour after Tjaden and Kropp are settled in behind their wire netting we make our way in to them. Tjaden greets us crowing. Then we play skat far into the night. Tjaden wins of course, the lucky wretch.

When we break up Kat says to me: "What do you say to some roast goose?"

"Not bad," I agree.

We climb up on a munition wagon. The ride costs us two cigarettes. Kat has marked the spot exactly. The shed belongs to a regimental headquarters. I agree to get the goose and receive my instructions. The outhouse is behind the wall and the door shuts with just a peg.

Kat hoists me up. I rest my foot in his hands and climb over the wall. Kat keeps watch below.

I wait a few moments to accustom my eyes to the darkness. Then I recognize the shed. Softly I steal across, lift the peg, pull it out, and open the door.

I distinguish two white patches. Two geese, that's bad: if I grab one the other will cackle. Well, both of them—if I'm quick, it can be done.

I make a jump. I catch hold of one and the next instant the second. Like a madman I bash their heads against the wall to stun them. But I haven't quite enough weight. The beasts cackle and strike out with their feet and wings. I fight desperately, but Lord! what a kick a goose has! They struggle and I stagger about. In the dark these white patches are terrifying. My arms have grown wings and I'm almost afraid of going up into the sky, as though I held a couple of captive balloons in my fists.

Then the row begins; one of them gets his breath and goes off like an alarm clock. Before I can do anything, something comes in from outside; I feel a blow, lie outstretched on the floor, and hear awful growls. A dog. I steal a glance to the side, he makes a snap at my throat. I lie still and tuck my chin into my collar.

It's a bulldog. After an eternity he withdraws his head and sits down beside me. But if I make the least movement he growls. I consider. The only thing to do is to get hold of my small revolver, and that too before anyone arrives. Inch by inch I move my hand toward it.

I have the feeling that it lasts an hour. The slightest movement and then an awful growl; I lie still, then try again. When at last I have the revolver my hand starts to tremble. I press it against the ground and then say over to myself: Jerk the revolver up, fire before he has a chance to grab, and then jump up.

Slowly I take a deep breath and become calmer. Then I hold my breath, whip up the revolver, it cracks, the dog leaps howling to one side, I make for the door of the shed and fall head over heels over one of the damned geese.

At full speed I seize it again, and with a swing toss it over the wall and clamber up. No sooner am I on top than the dog is up again as lively as ever and springs at me. Quickly I let myself drop. Ten paces away stands Kat with the goose under his arm. As soon as he sees me we run.

At last we can take a breather. The goose is dead, Kat saw to that in a moment. We intend to roast it, without telling anybody. I fetch a stove and wood from the hut and we crawl into a small deserted lean-to which we use for such purposes. The single window space is heavily curtained. There is a sort of hearth, an iron plate set on some bricks. We kindle a fire.

Kat plucks and cleans the goose. We put the feathers carefully to one side. We intend to make two cushions out of them with the inscription: "Sleep soft under shellfire." The sound of the gunfire from the front penetrates into our refuge. The glow of the fire lights up our faces, shadows dance on the wall. Sometimes a heavy crash and the hut shivers. Airplane bombs. Once we hear a stifled cry. A hut must have been hit.

Airplanes drone; the tack-tack of machine guns breaks out. But no light that could be observed shows from us.

We sit opposite one another, Kat and I, two soldiers in shabby coats, cooking a goose in the middle of the night. We don't talk much, but I believe we have a more complete communion with one another than even lovers have.

We are two men, two minute sparks of life; outside is the night and the circle of death. We sit on the edge of it crouching in danger, the grease drips from our hands, in our hearts we are close to one another, and the hour is like the room: flecked over with the lights and shadows of our feelings cast by a quiet fire. What does he know of me or I of him? Formerly we should not have had a single thought in common—now we sit with a goose between us and feel in unison, and are so intimate that we do not even speak.

It takes a long time to roast a goose, even when it is young and fat. So we take turns. One bastes it while the other lies down and sleeps. A grand smell gradually fills the hut.

The noises without increase in volume, pass into my dream and yet linger in my memory. In a half-sleep I watch Kat dip and raise the ladle. I love him, his shoulders, his angular, stooping figure—and at the same time I see behind him woods and stars, and a clear voice utters words that bring me peace, to me, a soldier in big boots, belt, and knapsack, taking the road that lies before him under the high heaven, quickly forgetting and seldom sorrowful, forever pressing on under the wide night sky.

A little soldier and a clear voice, and if anyone were to caress him he would hardly understand, this soldier with the big boots and shut heart, who marches because he is wearing big boots, and has forgotten all else but marching. Beyond the skyline is a country with flowers, lying so still that he would like to weep. There are sights there that he has not forgotten, because he never possessed them—perplexing, yet lost to him. Are not his twenty summers there?

Is my face wet, and where am I? Kat stands before me, his gigantic, stooping shadow falls upon me like home. He speaks gently, he smiles and goes back to the fire.

Then he says: "It's done."

"Yes, Kat."

I stir myself. In the middle of the room shines the brown goose. We take out our collapsible forks and our pocket knives and each cuts off a leg. With it we have army bread dipped in gravy. We eat slowly and with gusto.

"How does it taste, Kat?"

"Good! And yours?"

"Good, Kat."

We are brothers and press on one another the choicest pieces. Afterwards I smoke a cigarette and Kat a cigar. There is still a lot left.

"How would it be, Kat, if we took a bit to Kropp and Tjaden?"

"Sure," says he.

We carve off a portion and wrap it up carefully in newspaper. The rest we thought of taking over to the hut. Kat laughs, and simply says: "Tjaden."

I agree, we will have to take it all.

So we go off to the fowlhouse to wake them. But first we pack away the feathers.

Kropp and Tjaden take us for magicians. Then they get busy with their teeth. Tjaden holds a wing in his mouth with both hands like a mouth organ, and gnaws. He drinks the gravy from the pot and smacks his lips:

"May I never forget you!"

We go to our hut. Again there is the lofty sky with the stars and the oncoming dawn, and I pass on beneath it, a soldier with big boots and a full belly, a little soldier in the early morning—but by my side, stooping and angular, goes Kat, my comrade.

The outlines of the huts are upon us in the dawn like a dark, deep sleep.

Chapter VI

THERE are rumors of an offensive. We go up to the front two days earlier than usual. On the way we pass a shelled schoolhouse. Stacked up against its longer side is a high double wall of yellow, unpolished, brand-new coffins. They still smell of fir, and pine, and the forest. There are at least a hundred.

"That's a good preparation for the offensive," says Müller astonished.

"They're for us," growls Detering.

"Don't talk rot," says Kat to him angrily.

"You be thankful if you get so much as a coffin," grins Tjaden, "they'll slip you a waterproof sheet for your old Aunt Sally of a carcass."

The others jest too, unpleasant jests, but what else can a man do?—The coffins are really for us. The organization surpasses itself in that kind of thing.

Ahead of us everything is simmering. The first night we try to get our bearings. When it is fairly quiet we can hear the transports behind the enemy lines rolling ceaselessly until dawn. Kat says they do not go back but are bringing up troops—troops, munitions, and shells.

The English artillery has been strengthened, that we can detect at once. There are at least four more batteries of twenty-fives to the right of the farm, and behind the poplars they have put in trench mortars. Besides these they have brought up a number of those little French beasts with instantaneous fuses.

We are in low spirits. After we have been in the dugouts two hours our own shells begin to fall in the trench. This is the third time in four weeks. If it were simply a mistake in aim no one would say anything, but the truth is that the barrels are worn out. The shots are often so uncertain that they land within our own lines. Tonight two of our men were wounded by them.

The front is a cage in which we must await fearfully whatever may happen. We lie under the network of arching shells and live in a suspense of uncertainty. Over us Chance hovers. If a shot comes, we can duck, that is all; we neither know nor can determine where it will fall.

It is this Chance that makes us indifferent. A few months ago I was sitting in a dugout playing skat; after a while I stood up and went to visit some friends in another dugout. On my return nothing more was to be seen of the first one, it had been blown to pieces by a direct hit. I went back to the second and arrived just in time to lend a hand digging it out. In the interval it had been buried.

It is just as much a matter of chance that I am still alive as that I might have been hit. In a bombproof dugout I may be smashed to atoms and in the open may survive ten hours' bombardment unscathed. No soldier outlives a thousand chances. But every soldier believes in Chance and trusts his luck.

We must look out for our bread. The rats have become much more numerous lately because the trenches are no longer in good condition. Detering says it is a sure sign of a coming bombardment.

The rats here are particularly repulsive, they are so fat—the kind we call corpse rats. They have shocking, evil, naked faces, and it is nauseating to see their long, nude tails.

They seem to be mighty hungry. Almost every man has had his bread gnawed. Kropp wrapped his in his waterproof sheet and put it under his head, but he cannot sleep because they run over his face to get at it. Detering meant to outwit them: he fastened a thin wire to the roof and suspended his bread from it. During the night when he switched on his pocket torch he saw the wire swinging to and fro. On the bread was riding a fat rat.

At last we put a stop to it. We cannot afford to throw the bread away, because already we have practically nothing left to eat in the morning, so we carefully cut off the bits of bread that the animals have gnawed.

The slices we cut off are heaped together in the middle of the floor. Each man takes out his spade and lies down prepared to strike. Detering, Kropp, and Kat hold their pocket lamps ready.

After a few minutes we hear the first shuffling and tugging. It grows, now it is the sound of many little feet. Then the torches switch on and every man strikes at the heap, which scatters with a rush. The result is good. We toss the bits of rat over the parapet and again lie in wait.

Several times we repeat the process. At last the beasts get wise to it, or perhaps they have scented the blood. They return no more. Nevertheless, before morning the remainder of the bread on the floor has been carried off.

In the adjoining sector they attacked two large cats and a dog, bit them to death and devoured them.

Next day there is an issue of Edam cheese. Each man gets almost a quarter of a cheese. In one way that is all to the good, for Edam is tasty—but in another way it is vile, because the fat red balls have long been a sign of a bad time coming. Our forebodings increase as rum is served out. We drink it of course; but are not greatly comforted.

For days we loaf about and make war on the rats. Ammunition and hand grenades become more plentiful. We even overhaul the bayonets—that is to say, the ones that have a saw on the blunt edge. If the fellows over there catch a man with one of those he's killed at sight. In the next sector some of our men were found whose noses were cut off and their eyes poked out with their own saw-bayonets. Their mouths and noses were stuffed with sawdust so that they suffocated.

Some of the recruits have bayonets of this kind; we take them away and give them the ordinary kind.

But the bayonet has practically lost its importance. It is usually the fashion now to charge with bombs and spades only. The sharpened spade is a more handy and many-sided weapon; not only can it be used for jabbing a man under the chin, but it is much better for striking with because of its greater weight; and if one hits between the neck and shoulder it easily cleaves as far down as the chest. The bayonet frequently jams on the thrust and then a man has to kick hard on the other fellow's belly to pull it out again; and in the interval he may easily get one himself. And what's more, the blade often gets broken off.

At night they send over gas. We expect the attack to follow and lie with our masks on, ready to tear them off as soon as the first shadow appears.

Dawn approaches without anything happening—only the everlasting, nerve-racking roll behind the enemy lines, trains, trains, trucks, trucks; but what are they concentrating? Our artillery fires on it continually, but still it does not cease.

We have tired faces and avoid each other's eyes. "It will be like the Somme," says Kat gloomily. "There we were shelled steadily for seven days and nights." Kat has lost all his fun since we have been here, which is bad, for Kat is an old front hog, and can smell what is coming. Only Tjaden seems pleased with the good rations and the rum; he thinks we might even go back to rest without anything happening at all.

It almost looks like it. Day after day passes. At night I squat in the listening post. Above me the rockets and parachute lights shoot up and float down again. I am cautious and tense, my heart thumps. My eyes turn again and again to the luminous dial of my watch; the hands will not budge. Sleep hangs on my eyelids, I work my toes in my boots in order to keep awake. Nothing happens till I am relieved—only the everlasting rolling over there. Gradually we grow calmer and play skat and poker continually. Perhaps we will be lucky.

All day the sky is hung with observation balloons. There is a rumor that the enemy is going to put tanks over and use low-flying planes for the attack. But that interests us less than what we hear of the new flamethrowers.

We wake up in the middle of the night. The earth booms. Heavy fire is falling on us. We crouch into corners. We distinguish shells of every caliber.

Each man lays hold of his things and looks again every minute to reassure himself that they are still there. The dugout heaves, the night roars and flashes. We look at each other in the momentary flashes of light, and with pale faces and pressed lips shake our heads.

Every man is aware of the heavy shells tearing down the parapet, rooting up the embankment and demolishing the upper layers of concrete. When a shell lands in the trench we note how the hollow, furious blast is like a blow from the paw of a raging beast of prey. Already by morning a few of the recruits are green and vomiting. They are too inexperienced.

Slowly the gray light trickles into the post and pales the flashes of the shells. Morning is come. The explosion of mines mingles with the gunfire.

That is the most dementing convulsion of all. The whole region where they go up becomes one grave.

The reliefs go out, the observers stagger in, covered with dirt, and trembling. One lies down in silence in the corner and eats, the other, a reservist reinforcement, sobs; twice he has been flung over the parapet by the blast of the explosions without getting any more than shellshock.

The recruits are eyeing him. We must watch them, these things are catching, already some lips begin to quiver. It is good that it is growing daylight; perhaps the attack will come before noon.

The bombardment does not diminish. It is falling in the rear too. As far as one can see it spouts fountains of mud and iron. A wide belt is being raked.

The attack does not come, but the bombardment continues. Slowly we become mute. Hardly a man speaks. We cannot make ourselves understood.

Our trench is almost gone. At many places it is only eighteen inches high, it is broken by holes, and craters, and mountains of earth. A shell lands square in front of our post. At once it is dark. We are buried and must dig ourselves out. After an hour the entrance is clear again, and we are calmer because we have had something to do.

Our company commander scrambles in and reports that two dugouts are gone. The recruits calm themselves when they see him. He says that an attempt will be made to bring up food this evening.

This sounds reassuring. No one had thought of it except Tjaden. Now the outside world seems to draw a little nearer: if food can be brought up, think the recruits, then it can't really be so bad.

We do not disabuse them; we know that food is as important as ammunition and only for that reason must be brought up.

But it miscarries. A second party goes out, and it also turns back. Finally Kat tries, and even he reappears without accomplishing anything. No one gets through, not even a fly is small enough to get through such a barrage.

We pull in our belts tighter and chew every mouthful three times as long. Still the food does not last out; we are damnably hungry. I take out a scrap of bread, eat the white and put the crust back in my knapsack; from time to time I nibble at it.

The night is unbearable. We cannot sleep, but stare ahead of us and doze. Tjaden regrets that we wasted the gnawed pieces of bread on the rats. We would gladly have them again to eat now. We are short of water, too, but not seriously yet.

Towards morning, while it is still dark, there is some excitement.

Through the entrance rushes in a swarm of fleeing rats that try to storm the walls. Torches light up the confusion. Everyone yells and curses and slaughters. The madness and despair of many hours unloads itself in this outburst. Faces are distorted, arms strike out, the beasts scream; we just stop in time to avoid attacking one another.

The onslaught has exhausted us. We lie down to wait again. It is a marvel that our post has had no casualties so far. It is one of the few deep dugouts.

A corporal creeps in; he has a loaf of bread with him. Three people have had the luck to get through during the night and bring some provisions. They say the bombardment extends undiminished as far as the artillery lines. It is a mystery where the enemy gets all his shells.

We wait and wait. By midday what I expected happens. One of the recruits has a fit. I have been watching him for a long time, grinding his teeth and opening and shutting his fists. These hunted, protruding eyes, we know them too well. During the last few hours he has had merely the appearance of calm. He had collapsed like a rotten tree.

Now he stands up, stealthily creeps across the floor, hesitates a moment, and then glides toward the door. I intercept him and say: "Where are you going?"

"I'll be back in a minute," says he, and tries to push past me.

"Wait a bit, the shelling will stop soon."

He listens and for a moment his eye becomes clear. Then again he has the glowering eyes of a mad dog, he is silent, he shoves me aside.

"One minute, lad," I say. Kat notices. Just as the recruit shakes me off Kat jumps in and we hold him.

Then he begins to rave: "Leave me alone, let me go out, I will go out!"

He won't listen to anything and hits out, his mouth is wet and pours out words, half-choked, meaningless words. It is a case of claustrophobia, he feels as though he is suffocating here and wants to get out at any price. If we let him go he would run about everywhere regardless of cover. He is not the first.

Though he raves and his eyes roll, it can't be helped, and we have to give him a hiding to bring him to his senses. We do it quickly and mercilessly, and at last he sits down quietly. The others have turned pale; let's hope it deters them. This bombardment is too much for the poor devils, they have been sent straight from a recruiting depot into a barrage that is enough to turn an old soldier's hair gray.

After this affair the sticky, close atmosphere works more than ever on our nerves. We sit as if in our graves waiting only to be closed in.

Suddenly it howls and flashes terrifically, the dugout cracks in all its joints under a direct hit, fortunately only a light one that the concrete blocks are able to withstand. It rings metallically, the walls reel, rifles, helmets, earth, mud, and dust fly everywhere. Sulfur fumes pour in.

If we were in one of those light dugouts that they have been building lately instead of this deep one, not one of us would now be alive.

But the effect is bad enough even so. The recruit starts to rave again and two others follow suit. One jumps up and rushes out, we have trouble with the other two. I start after the one who escapes and wonder whether to shoot him in the leg—then it shrieks again, I fling myself down and when I stand up the wall of the trench is plastered with smoking splinters, lumps of flesh, and bits of uniform. I scramble back.

The first recruit seems actually to have gone insane. He butts his head against the wall like a goat. We must try tonight to take him to the rear. Meanwhile we bind him, but in such a way that in case of attack he can be released at once.

Kat suggests a game of skat: it is easier when a man has something to do. But it is no use, we listen for every explosion that comes close, miscount the tricks, and fail to follow suit. We have to give it up. We sit as though in a hissing boiler that is being belabored from without on all sides.

Night again. We are deadened by the strain—a deadly tension that scrapes along one's spine like a gapped knife. Our legs refuse to move, our hands tremble, our bodies are a thin skin stretched painfully over repressed madness, over an almost irresistible, bursting roar. We have neither flesh nor muscles any longer, we dare not look at one another for fear of some incalculable thing. So we shut our teeth—it will end—it will end—perhaps we will come through.

Suddenly the nearer explosions cease. The shelling continues but it has lifted and falls behind us, our trench is free. We seize the hand grenades, pitch them out in front of the dugout and jump after them. The bombardment has stopped and a heavy barrage now falls behind us. The attack has come.

No one would believe that in this howling waste there could still be men; but steel helmets now appear on all sides out of the trench, and fifty yards from us a machine gun is already in position and barking.

The wire entanglements are torn to pieces. Yet they offer some obstacle. We see the storm troops coming. Our artillery opens fire. Machine guns rattle, rifles crack. The charge works its way across. Haie and Kropp begin with the hand grenades. They throw as fast as they can, others pass them, the handles with the strings already pulled. Haie throws seventy-five yards, Kropp sixty, it has been measured, the distance is important. The enemy as they run cannot do much before they are within forty yards.

We recognize the distorted faces, the smooth helmets: they are French.

They have already suffered heavily when they reach the remnants of the barbed-wire entanglements. A whole line has gone down before our machine guns; then we have a lot of stoppages and they come nearer.

I see one of them, his face upturned, fall into a wire cradle. His body collapses, his hands remain suspended as though he were praying. Then his body drops clean away and only his hands with the stumps of his arms, shot off, now hang in the wire.

The moment we are about to retreat three faces rise up from the ground in front of us. Under one of the helmets a dark pointed beard and two eyes that are fastened on me. I raise my hand, but I cannot throw into those strange eyes; for one mad moment the whole slaughter whirls like a circus round me, and these two eyes that are alone motionless; then the head rises up, a hand, a movement, and my hand grenade flies through the air and into him.

We make for the rear, pull wire cradles into the trench and leave bombs behind us with the string pulled, which ensure us a fiery retreat. The machine guns are already firing from the next position.

We have become wild beasts. We do not fight, we defend ourselves against annihilation. It is not against men that we fling our bombs, what do we know of men in this moment when Death with hands and helmets is hunting us down—now, for the first time in three days we can see his face, now, for the first time in three days we can oppose him; we feel a mad anger. No longer do we lie helpless, waiting on the scaffold, we can destroy and kill, to save ourselves, to save ourselves and be revenged.

We crouch behind every corner, behind every barrier of barbed wire, and hurl heaps of explosives at the feet of the advancing enemy before we run. The blast of the hand grenades impinges powerfully on our arms and legs; crouching like cats we run on, overwhelmed by this wave that bears us along, that fills us with ferocity, turning us into thugs, into murderers, into God only knows what devils; this wave that multiplies our strength with fear and madness and greed of life, seeking and fighting for nothing but our deliverance. If your own father came over with them you would not hesitate to fling a bomb into him.

The forward trenches have been abandoned. Are they still trenches? They are blown to pieces, annihilated—there are only broken bits of trenches, holes linked by tracks, nests of craters, that is all. But the enemy's casualties increase. They did not count on so much resistance.

It is nearly noon. The sun blazes hotly, the sweat stings in our eyes, we wipe it off on our sleeves, and often blood with it. At last we reach a trench that is in a somewhat better condition. It is manned and ready for the counterattack, it receives us. Our guns open up in full blast and cut off the enemy attack.

The lines behind us stop. They can advance no farther. The attack is crushed by our artillery. We watch. The fire lifts a hundred yards and we break forward. Beside me a lance corporal has his head torn off. He runs a few steps more while the blood spouts from his neck like a fountain.

It does not come quite to hand-to-hand fighting; they are driven back. We arrive once again at our shattered trench and pass on beyond it.

Oh, this turning back again! We reach the shelter of the reserves and yearn to creep in and disappear—but instead we must turn round and plunge again into the horror. If we were not automatons at that moment we would continue lying there, exhausted, and without will. But we are swept forward again, powerless, madly savage and raging; we will kill, for they are still our mortal enemies; their rifles and bombs are aimed against us, and if we don't destroy them, they will destroy us.

The brown earth, the torn, blasted earth, with a greasy shine under the sun's rays; the earth is the background of this restless, gloomy world of automatons, our gasping is the scratching of a quill, our lips are dry, our heads are debauched with stupor—thus we stagger forward, and into our pierced and shattered souls bores the torturing image of the brown earth with the greasy sun and the convulsed and dead soldiers, who lie there—it can't be helped—who cry and clutch at our legs as we spring away over them.

We have lost all feeling for one another. We can hardly control ourselves when our hunted glance lights on the form of some other man. We are insensible, dead men, who through some trick, some dreadful magic, are still able to run and to kill.

A young Frenchman lags behind, he is overtaken, he puts up his hands, in one he still holds his revolver—does he mean to shoot or to give himself up?—a blow from a spade cleaves through his face. A second sees it and tries to run farther; a bayonet jabs into his back. He leaps in the air, his arms thrown wide, his mouth wide open, yelling; he staggers, in his back the bayonet quivers. A third throws away his rifle, cowers down with his hands before his eyes. He is left behind with a few other prisoners to carry off the wounded.

Suddenly in the pursuit we reach the enemy line.

We are so close on the heels of our retreating enemies that we reach it almost at the same time as they. In this way we suffer few casualties. A machine gun barks, but is silenced with a bomb. Nevertheless, the couple of seconds have sufficed to give us five stomach wounds. With the butt of his rifle Kat smashes to pulp the face of one of the unwounded

machine gunners. We bayonet the others before they have time to get
out their bombs. Then thirstily we drink the water they have for cooling
the gun.

Everywhere wire cutters are snapping, planks are thrown across the entanglements, we jump through the narrow entrances into the trenches.
Haie strikes his spade into the neck of a gigantic Frenchman and throws his
first hand grenade; we duck behind a breastwork for a few seconds, then
the whole section of trench before us is empty. The next throw whizzes
obliquely over the corner and clears a passage; as we run past we toss
handfuls down into the dugouts, the earth shudders, it crashes; dully and
stifled, we stumble over slippery lumps of flesh, over yielding bodies; I
fall into an open belly on which lies a clean new officer's cap.

The fight ceases. We lose touch with the enemy. We cannot stay here
long but must retire under cover of our artillery to our own position. No
sooner do we know this than we dive into the nearest dugouts, and with
the utmost haste seize on whatever provisions we can see, especially the
tins of corned beef and butter, before we clear out.

We get back pretty well. There has been no further attack by the enemy.
We lie for an hour panting and resting before anyone speaks. We are so
completely played out that in spite of our great hunger we do not think
of the provisions. Then gradually we become something like men again.

The corned beef over there is famous along the whole front. Occasionally it has been the chief reason for a flying raid on our part, for our
nourishment is generally bad; we have a constant hunger.

We bagged five tins altogether. The fellows over there are well looked
after; it seems a luxury to us with our hunger pangs, our turnip jam, and
meat so scarce that we simply grab at it. Haie has scored a thin loaf
of white French bread, and stuck it in behind his belt like a spade. It is a
bit bloody at one corner, but that can be cut off.

It is a good thing we have something decent to eat at last; we still have
a use for all our strength. Enough to eat is just as valuable as a good
dugout; it can save our lives; that is the reason we are so greedy for it.

Tjaden has captured two water bottles full of cognac. We pass them
round.

The evening benediction begins. Night comes, out of the craters rise the
mists. It looks as though the holes were full of ghostly secrets. The white
vapor creeps painfully round before it ventures to steal away over the
edge. Then long streaks stretch from crater to crater.

It is chilly. I am on sentry and stare into the darkness. My strength is
exhausted as always after an attack, and so it is hard for me to be alone with

my thoughts. They are not properly thoughts; they are memories which in my weakness turn homeward and strangely move me.

The parachute lights shoot upwards—and I see a picture, a summer evening, I am in the cathedral cloister and look at the tall rose trees that bloom in the middle of the little cloister garden where the monks lie buried. Around the walls are the stone carvings of the Stations of the Cross. No one is there. A great quietness rules in this blossoming quadrangle, the sun lies warm on the heavy gray stones, I place my hand upon them and feel the warmth. At the right-hand corner the green cathedral spire ascends into the pale blue sky of the evening. Between the glowing columns of the cloister is the cool darkness that only churches have, and I stand there and wonder whether, when I am twenty, I shall have experienced the bewildering emotions of love.

The image is alarmingly near; it touches me before it dissolves in the light of the next star shell.

I lay hold of my rifle to see that it is in trim. The barrel is wet, I take it in my hand and rub off the moisture with my fingers.

Between the meadows behind our town there stands a line of old poplars by a stream. They were visible from a great distance, and although they grew on one bank only, we called them the poplar avenue. Even as children we had a great love for them, they drew us vaguely thither, we played truant the whole day by them and listened to their rustling. We sat beneath them on the bank of the stream and let our feet hang over in the bright, swift waters. The pure fragrance of the water and the melody of the wind in the poplars held our fancies. We loved them dearly, and the image of those days still makes my heart pause in its beating.

It is strange that all the memories that come have these two qualities. They are always completely calm, that is predominant in them; and even if they are not really calm, they become so. They are soundless apparitions that speak to me, with looks and gestures, silently, without any word—and it is the alarm of their silence that forces me to lay hold of my sleeve and my rifle lest I should abandon myself to the liberation and allurement in which my body would dilate and gently pass away into the still forces that lie behind these things.

They are quiet in this way, because quietness is so unattainable for us now. At the front there is no quietness and the curse of the front reaches so far that we never pass beyond it. Even in the remote depots and rest areas the droning and the muffled noise of shelling is always in our ears. We are never so far off that it is no more to be heard. But these last few days it has been unbearable.

Their stillness is the reason why these memories of former times do not awaken desire so much as sorrow—a strange, incomprehensible melancholy. Once we had such desires—but they return not. They are past, they belong to another world that is gone from us. In the barracks they called forth a rebellious, wild craving for their return; for then they were still bound to us, we belonged to them and they to us, even though we were already absent from them. They appeared in the soldiers' songs which we sang as we marched between the glow of the dawn and the black silhouettes of the forests to drill on the moor, they were a powerful remembrance that was in us and came from us.

But here in the trenches they are completely lost to us. They arise no more; we are dead and they stand remote on the horizon, they are an apparition, a mysterious reflection drawing us home, that we fear and love without hope. They are strong and our desire is strong—but they are unattainable, and we know it.

And even if these scenes of our youth were given back to us we would hardly know what to do. The tender, secret influence that passed from them into us could not arise again. We long to be in them and to move in them; we long to remember and to love them and to be stirred by the sight of them. But it would be like gazing at the photograph of a dead comrade; those are his features, it is his face, and the days we spent together take on a mournful life in the memory; but the man himself it is not.

We could never again, as the same beings, take part in those scenes. It was not any recognition of their beauty and their significance that attracted us, but the communion, the feeling of a comradeship with the things and events of our existence, which cut us off and made the world of our parents a thing incomprehensible to us—for then we surrendered ourselves to events and were lost in them, and the least little thing was enough to carry us down the stream of eternity. Perhaps it was only the privilege of our youth, but as yet we recognized no limits and saw nowhere an end. We had that thrill of expectation in the blood which united us with the course of our days.

Today we would pass through the scenes of our youth like travelers. We are burned up by hard facts; like tradesmen we understand distinctions, and like butchers, necessities. We are no longer untroubled—we are indifferent. We long to be there; but could we live there?

We are forlorn like children, and experienced like old men, we are crude and sorrowful and superficial—I believe we are lost.

My hands grow cold and my flesh creeps; and yet the night is warm. Only the mist is cold, this mysterious mist that trails the dead before us and sucks from them their last, creeping life. By morning they will be pale and green and their blood congealed and black.

Still the parachute rockets shoot up and cast their pitiless light over the stony landscape, which is full of craters and frozen lights like a moon. The blood beneath my skin brings fear and restlessness into my thoughts. They become feeble and tremble, they desire warmth and life. They cannot endure without sympathy and communion, they are disordered before the naked picture of despair.

I hear the rattle of the messtins and immediately feel a strong desire for warm food; it would do me good and comfort me. Painfully I force myself to wait until I am relieved.

Then I go into the dugout and find a mug of barley. It is cooked in fat and tastes good, I eat it slowly. I remain quiet, though the others are in a better mood, for the shelling has died down.

The days go by and the incredible hours follow one another as a matter of course. Attacks alternate with counterattacks and slowly the dead pile up in the field of craters between the trenches. We are able to bring in most of the wounded that do not lie too far off. But many have long to wait and we listen to them dying.

For one of them we search two days in vain. He must be lying on his belly and unable to turn over. Otherwise it is hard to understand why we cannot find him; for it is only when a man has his mouth close to the ground that it is impossible to gauge the direction of his cry.

He must have been badly hit—one of those nasty wounds, neither so severe that they exhaust the body at once and a man dreams on in a half-swoon, nor so light that a man endures the pain in the hope of becoming well again. Kat thinks he has either a broken pelvis or a shot through the spine. His chest cannot have been injured, otherwise he would not have such strength to cry out. And if it were any other kind of wound it would be possible to see him moving.

He grows gradually hoarser. The voice sounds so desperate that it prevails everywhere. The first night some of our fellows go out three times to look for him. But when they think they have located him and crawl across, next time they hear the voice it seems to come from somewhere else altogether.

We search in vain until dawn. We scrutinize the field all day with glasses, but discover nothing. On the second day the calls are fainter; that will be because his lips and mouth have become dry.

Our company commander has promised special leave with three days extra to anyone who finds him. That is a powerful inducement, but we would do all that is possible without that; for his cry is terrible. Kat and Kropp even go out in the afternoon, and Albert gets the lobe of his ear shot off in consequence. It is to no purpose, they come back without him.

It is easy to understand what he cries. At first he called only for help—the second night he must have some delirium, he talks with his wife and his children, we often detect the name Elise. Today he merely weeps. By evening the voice dwindles to a croaking. But it persists still through the whole night. We hear it so distinctly because the wind blows toward our line. In the morning when we suppose he must already have long gone to his rest, there comes across to us one last gurgling rattle.

The days are hot and the dead lie unburied. We cannot fetch them all in, if we did we should not know what to do with them. The shells will bury them. Many have their bellies swollen up like balloons. They hiss, belch, and make movements. The gases in them make noises.

The sky is blue and without clouds. In the evening it grows sultry and the heat rises from the earth. When the wind blows toward us it brings the smell of blood, which is heavy and sweet. This deathly exhalation from the shell holes seems to be a mixture of chloroform and putrefaction, and fills us with nausea and retching.

The nights become quiet and the hunt for copper driving bands and the silken parachutes of the French star shells begins. Why the driving bands are so desirable no one knows exactly. The collectors merely assert that they are valuable. Some have collected so many that they will stoop under the weight of them when we go back.

But Haie at least gives a reason. He intends to give them to his girl to supplement her garters. At this the Frisians explode with mirth. They slap their knees: "By Jove though, he's a wit, Haie is, he's got brains." Tjaden especially can hardly contain himself; he takes the largest of the rings in his hand and every now and then puts his leg through it to show how much slack there is.

"Haie, man, she must have legs like, legs——" his thoughts mount somewhat higher, "and a behind too she must have, like a——like an elephant!"

Haie beams, proud that his girl should receive so much appreciation.

"She's a nice bit," he says with self-satisfaction.

The parachutes are turned to more practical uses. According to the size of the bust three or perhaps four will make a blouse. Kropp and I use them as handkerchiefs. The others send them home. If the women could see at what risk these bits of rag are often obtained, they would be horrified.

Kat surprises Tjaden endeavoring with perfect equanimity to knock the driving band off a dud. If anyone else had tried it the thing would have exploded, but Tjaden always has his luck with him.

One morning two butterflies play in front of our trench. They are brimstone butterflies, with red spots on their yellow wings. What can they be looking for here? There is not a plant nor a flower for miles. They settle on the teeth of a skull. The birds too are just as carefree, they have long since accustomed themselves to the war. Every morning larks ascend from No Man's Land. A year ago we watched them nesting; the young ones grew up too.

We have a spell from the rats in the trench. They are in No Man's Land —we know what for. They grow fat; when we see one we have a crack at it. At night we hear again the rolling behind the enemy lines. All day we have only the normal shelling, so that we are able to repair the trenches. There is always plenty of amusement, the airmen see to that. There are countless fights for us to watch every day.

Battle planes don't trouble us, but the observation planes we hate like the plague; they put the artillery on to us. A couple of minutes after they appear, shrapnel and high explosives begin to drop on us. We lose eleven men in one day that way, and five of them stretcher bearers. Two are so smashed that Tjaden remarks you could scrape them off the wall of the trench with a spoon and bury them in a messtin. Another has the lower part of his body and his legs torn off. Dead, his chest leans against the side of the trench, his face is lemon yellow, in his beard still burns a cigarette. It glows until it dies out on his lips.

We put the dead in a large shell hole. So far there are three layers, one on top of the other.

Suddenly the shelling begins to pound again. Soon we are sitting up once more with the rigid tenseness of blank anticipation.

Attack, counterattack, charge, repulse—these are words, but what things they signify! We have lost a good many men, mostly recruits. Reinforcements have again been sent up to our sector. It is one of the new regiments, composed of young fellows called up during last year. They have had hardly any training, and are sent into the field with only a theoretical knowledge. They do know what a hand grenade is, it is true, but they have very little idea of cover, and what is most important of all, have no eye for it. A fold in the ground has to be quite eighteen inches high before they can see it.

Although we need reinforcement, the recruits give us almost more trouble than they are worth. They are helpless in this grim fighting area, they fall like flies. The present method of fighting from posts demands knowledge and experience; a man must have a feeling for the contours of the ground, an ear for the sound and character of the shells, must be able to decide beforehand where they will drop, how they will burst, and how to shelter from them.

The young recruits of course know none of these things. They get killed simply because they can hardly tell shrapnel from high explosive, they are mown down because they are listening anxiously to the roar of the big coal boxes falling far in the rear, and miss the light, piping whistle of the low-spreading little daisy cutters. They flock together like sheep instead of scattering, and even the wounded are shot down like hares by the airmen.

Their pale turnip faces, their pitiful clenched hands, the miserable courage of these poor devils, the desperate charges and attacks made by these poor brave devils, who are so terrified that they dare not cry out loudly, but with battered chests and torn bellies and arms and legs only whimper softly for their mothers and cease as soon as one looks at them.

Their sharp, downy, dead faces have the awful expressionlessness of dead children.

It brings a lump into the throat to see how they go over, and run and fall. A man would like to spank them, they are so stupid, and to take them by the arm and lead them away from here where they have no business to be. They wear gray coats and trousers and boots, but for most of them the uniform is far too big, it hangs on their limbs, their shoulders are too narrow, their bodies too slight; no uniform was ever made to these childish measurements.

Between five and ten recruits fall to every old hand.

A surprise gas attack carries off a lot of them. They have not yet learned what to do. We found one dugout full of them, with blue heads and black lips. Some of them in a shell hole took their masks off too soon; they did not know that the gas lies longest in the hollows; when they saw others on top without masks they pulled theirs off too and swallowed enough to scorch their lungs. Their condition is hopeless, they choke to death with hemorrhages and suffocation.

In one part of the trench I suddenly run into Himmelstoss. We dive into the same dugout. Breathless we are all lying one beside the other waiting for the charge.

When we run out again, although I am very excited, I suddenly think: "Where's Himmelstoss?" Quickly I jump back into the dugout and find him with a small scratch lying in a corner pretending to be wounded. His face looks sullen. He is in a panic; he is new to it too. But it makes me mad that the young recruits should be out there and he here.

"Get out!" I spit.

He does not stir, his lips quiver, his moustache twitches.

"Out!" I repeat.

He draws up his legs, crouches back against the wall, and shows his teeth like a cur.

I seize him by the arm and try to pull him up. He barks.

That is too much for me. I grab him by the neck and shake him like a sack, his head jerks from side to side.

"You lump, will you get out—you hound, you skunk, sneak out of it, would you?" His eye becomes glassy, I knock his head against the wall—"You cow"—I kick him in the ribs—"You swine"—I push him toward the door and shove him out head first.

Another wave of our attack has just come up. A lieutenant is with them. He sees us and yells: "Forward, forward, join in, follow." And the word of command does what all my banging could not. Himmelstoss hears the order, looks round him as if awakened, and follows on.

I come after and watch him go over. Once more he is the smart Himmelstoss of the parade ground, he has even outstripped the lieutenant and is far ahead.

Bombardment, barrage, curtain fire, mines, gas, tanks, machine guns, hand grenades—words, words, but they hold the horror of the world.

Our faces are encrusted, our thoughts are devastated, we are weary to death; when the attack comes we shall have to strike many of the men with our fists to waken them and make them come with us—our eyes are burned, our hands are torn, our knees bleed, our elbows are raw.

How long has it been? Weeks—months—years? Only days. We see time pass in the colorless faces of the dying, we cram food into us, we run, we throw, we shoot, we kill, we lie about, we are feeble and spent, and nothing supports us but the knowledge that there are still feebler, still more spent, still more helpless ones there who, with staring eyes, look upon us as gods that escape death many times.

In the few hours of rest we teach them. "There, see that waggletop? That's a mortar coming. Keep down, it will go clean over. But if it comes this way, then run for it. You can run from a mortar."

We sharpen their ears to the malicious, hardly audible buzz of the smaller shells that are not so easily distinguished. They must pick them out from the general din by their insect-like hum—we explain to them that these are far more dangerous than the big ones that can be heard long beforehand.

We show them how to take cover from aircraft, how to simulate a dead man when one is overrun in an attack, how to time hand grenades so that they explode half a second before hitting the ground; we teach them to fling themselves into holes as quick as lightning before the shells with instantaneous fuses; we show them how to clean up a trench with a handful of bombs; we explain the difference between the fuse length of the enemy bombs and our own; we put them wise to the sound of gas shells—show them all the tricks that can save them from death.

They listen, they are docile—but when it begins again, in their excitement they do everything wrong.

Haie Westhus drags off with a great wound in his back through which the lung pulses at every breath. I can only press his hand; "It's all up, Paul," he groans and bites his arm because of the pain.

We see men living with their skulls blown open; we see soldiers run with their two feet cut off, they stagger on their splintered stumps into the next shell hole; a lance corporal crawls a mile and a half on his hands dragging his smashed knee after him; another goes to the dressing station and over his clasped hands bulge his intestines; we see men without mouths, without jaws, without faces; we find one man who has held the artery of his arm in his teeth for two hours in order not to bleed to death. The sun goes down, night comes, the shells whine, life is at an end.

Still the little piece of convulsed earth in which we lie is held. We have yielded no more than a few hundred yards of it as a prize to the enemy. But on every yard there lies a dead man.

We have been relieved. The wheels roll beneath us, we stand dully, and when the call "Mind—wire" comes, we bend our knees. It was summer when we came up, the trees were still green, now it is autumn and the night is gray and wet. The trucks stop, we climb out—a confused heap, a remnant of many names. On either side stand people, dark, calling out the numbers of the regiments, the companies. And at each call a little group separates itself off, a small handful of dirty, pallid soldiers, a dreadfully small handful, and a dreadfully small remnant.

Now someone is calling the number of our company, it is, yes, the company commander, he has got one too, his arm is in a sling. We go over to him and I recognize Kat and Albert; we stand together, lean against each other, and look at one another.

And we hear the number of our company called again and again. He will call a long time, they do not hear him in the hospitals and shell holes.

Once again: "Second Company, this way!"

And then more softly: "Nobody else Second Company?"

He is silent, and then huskily he says: "Is that all?" and gives the order: "Number!"

The morning is gray, it was still summer when we came up, and we were one hundred and fifty strong. Now we freeze, it is autumn, the leaves rustle, the voices flutter out wearily: "One—two—three—four——" and cease at thirty-two. And there is a long silence before the voice asks: "Anybody else?"—and waits and then says softly: "In squads——" and then breaks off and is only able to finish: "Second Company——" with difficulty: "Second Company——march easy!"

A line, a short line, trudges off into the morning. Thirty-two men.

Chapter VII

THEY have taken us farther back than usual to a field depot so that we can be reorganized. Our company needs more than a hundred reinforcements.

In the meantime, when we are off duty, we loaf around. After a couple of days Himmelstoss comes up to us. He has had the bounce knocked out of him since he has been in the trenches and wants to get on good terms with us. I am willing enough, because I saw how he brought Haie Westhus in when he was hit in the back. Besides he's decent enough to treat us at the canteen when we are out of funds. Only Tjaden is still reserved and suspicious.

But he is won over, too, when Himmelstoss tells us that he is taking the place of the sergeant cook who has gone on leave. As a proof he produces on the spot two pounds of sugar for us and a half-pound of butter specially for Tjaden. He even sees to it that we are detailed the next two or three days to the cookhouse for potato and turnip peeling. The grub he gives us there is real officers' fare.

Thus for the moment we have the two things a soldier needs for contentment: good food and rest. That's not much when one comes to think of it. A couple of years ago we would have despised ourselves terribly. But now we are quite happy. It is all a matter of habit—even the front line.

Habit is the explanation of why we seem to forget things so quickly. Yesterday we were under fire, today we act the fool and go foraging through the countryside, tomorrow we go up to the trenches again. We forget nothing really. But so long as we have to stay here in the field, the front-line days, when they are past, sink down in us like a stone; they are too serious for us to be able to reflect on them at once. If we did that, we should have been destroyed long ago. I soon found out this much—terror can be endured so long as a man simply ducks; but it kills, if a man thinks about it.

Just as we turn into animals when we go up to the line, because that is the only thing which brings us through safely, so we turn into wags and loafers when we are out resting. We can do nothing else, it is a sheer necessity. We want to live at any price; so we cannot burden ourselves with feelings which, though they might be ornamental enough in peacetime, would be out of place here. Kemmerich is dead, Haie Westhus is dying, they will have a job with Hans Kramer's body at the Judgment Day, piecing it together after a direct hit; Martens has no legs anymore. Meyer is dead, Max is dead, Beyer is dead. Hämmerling is dead, there are a hundred and twenty wounded men lying somewhere or other; it is a damnable business, but what has it to do with us now—we live. If it were possible for us to save them, then it would be seen how much we cared—we would have a shot at it though we went under ourselves; for we can be damned quixotic when we like; fear we do not know much about—terror of death, yes; but that is a different matter, that is physical.

But our comrades are dead, we cannot help them, they have their rest—and who knows what is waiting for us? We will make ourselves comfortable and sleep, and eat as much as we can stuff into our bellies, and drink and smoke so that the hours are not wasted. Life is short.

The terror of the front sinks deep down when we turn our backs upon it; we make grim, coarse jests about it; that keeps us from going mad; as long as we take it that way we maintain our own resistance.

But we do not forget. It's all rot that they put in the war news about the good humor of the troops, how they are arranging dances almost before they are out of the front line. We don't act like that because we are in a good humor: we are in a good humor because otherwise we should go to pieces. If it were not so we could not hold out much longer; our humor becomes more bitter every month.

And this I know: all these things that now, while we are still in the war, sink down in us like a stone, after the war shall waken again, and then shall begin the disentanglement of life and death.

The days, the weeks, the years out here shall come back again, and our dead comrades shall then stand up again and march with us, our heads shall be clear, we shall have a purpose, and so we shall march, our dead comrades beside us, the years at the Front behind us——against whom, against whom?

Some time ago there was an army theater in these parts. Colored posters of the performances are still sticking on a hoarding. With wide eyes Kropp and I stand in front of it. We can hardly credit that such things still exist. A girl in a light summer dress, with a red patent-leather belt about her hips! She is standing with one hand on a railing and with the other she holds a straw hat. She wears white stockings and white shoes, fine buckle shoes with high heels. Behind her smiles a blue lake with white-horses, at the side is a bright bay. She is a lovely girl with a delicate nose, red lips, and slender legs, wonderfully clean and well cared for, she certainly bathes twice a day and never has any dirt under her nails. At most perhaps a bit of sand from the beach.

Beside her stands a man in white trousers, a blue jacket, and sailor's cap; but he interests us much less.

The girl on the poster is a wonder to us. We have quite forgotten that there are such things, and even now we hardly believe our eyes. We have seen nothing like it for years, nothing like it for happiness, beauty, and joy. That is peacetime, that is as it should be; we feel excited.

"Just look at those thin shoes though, she couldn't march many miles in those," I say, and then begin to feel silly, for it is absurd to stand in front of a picture like this and think of nothing but marching.

"How old would she be?" Kropp asks.

"About twenty-two at the most," I hazard.

"Then she would be older than us! She is not more than seventeen, let me tell you!"

It gives us gooseflesh.

"That would be good, Albert, what do you think?"

He nods. "I have white trousers at home too."

"White trousers," says I, "but a girl like that——"

We look askance at one another. There's not much to boast of here—two ragged, stained, and dirty uniforms. It is hopeless to compete.

So we proceed to tear the young man with the white trousers off the hoarding, taking care not to damage the girl. That is something towards it.

"We could go and get deloused, anyway," Kropp then suggests.

I am not very enthusiastic because it doesn't do one's clothes any good and a man is lousy again inside two hours. But when we have considered the picture once more, I declare myself willing. I even go further.

"We might see if we could get a clean shirt as well——"

"Socks might be better," says Albert, not without reason.

"Yes, socks too perhaps. Let's go and explore a bit."

Then Leer and Tjaden stroll up; they look at the poster and immediately the conversation becomes smutty. Leer was the first of our class to have intercourse, and he gave stirring details of it. After his fashion he enjoys himself over the picture, and Tjaden supports him nobly.

It does not distress us exactly. Who isn't smutty is no soldier; it merely does not suit us at the moment, so we edge away and march off to the delousing station with the same feeling as if it were a swell gentlemen's outfitters.

The houses in which we are billeted lie near the canal. On the other side of the canal there are ponds flanked with poplars—on the other side of the canal there are women, too.

The houses on our side have been abandoned. On the other side, though, one occasionally sees inhabitants.

In the evening we go swimming. Three women come strolling along the bank. They walk slowly and don't look away, although we have no bathing suits.

Leer calls out to them. They laugh and stop to watch us. We fling remarks at them in broken French, anything that comes into our heads,
hastily and all jumbled together, anything to detain them. They are not
especially wonderful pieces, but then where are such to be had about here?

There is one slim little brunette. Her teeth gleam when she laughs. She
has quick movements, her dress swings loosely about her legs. Although the
water is cold we are very jovial and do our best to interest them so that they
will stay. We try to make jokes and they answer with things we cannot
understand; we laugh and beckon. Tjaden is more crafty. He runs into the
house, gets a loaf of army bread and holds it up.

That produces a great effect. They nod and beckon us to come over.
But we don't dare to do that. It is forbidden to cross to the opposite bank.
There are sentries on all the bridges. It's impossible without a pass. So we
indicate that they should come over to us; but they shake their heads and
point to the bridge. They are not allowed to pass either. They turn away
and walk slowly down the canal, keeping along the towpath all the way.
We accompany them swimming. After a few hundred yards they turn off
and point to a house that stands a little distance away among the trees and
shrubbery.

Leer asks if they live there.

They laugh—sure, that's their house.

We call out to them that we would like to come, sometime when the
guards cannot see us. At night. Tonight.

They raise their hands, put them together, rest their faces on them, and
shut their eyes. They understand. The slim brunette does a two-step. The
blonde girl twitters: "Bread—good——"

Eagerly we assure them that we will bring some with us. And other tasty
bits too, we roll our eyes and try to explain with our hands. Leer nearly
drowns trying to demonstrate a sausage. If it were necessary we would
promise them a whole quartermaster's store. They go off and frequently
turn and look back. We climb out on the bank on our side of the canal and
watch to see whether they go into the house for they might easily have been
lying. Then we swim back.

No one can cross the bridge without leave, so we will simply have to
swim over at night. We are full of excitement. We cannot last out without a
drink, so we go to the canteen where there is beer and a kind of punch.

We drink punch and tell one another lying tales of our experiences. Each
man gladly believes the other man's story, only waiting impatiently till he
can cap it with a taller one. Our hands are fidgety, we smoke countless
cigarettes, until Kropp says: "We might as well take them a couple of
cigarettes too." So we put some inside our caps to keep them.

The sky turns apple green. There are four of us, but only three can go;

we must shake off Tjaden, so ply him with rum and punch until he rocks. As it turns dark we go to our billets, Tjaden in the center. We are all glowing and full of a lust for adventure. The little brunette is mine, we settled that by cutting for her.

Tjaden drops on his sack of straw and snores. Once he wakes up and grins so craftily that we are alarmed and begin to think he is cheating, and that we have given him the punch to no purpose. Then he drops back again and sleeps on.

We each get hold of a whole army loaf and wrap it up in newspaper. The cigarettes we put in too, as well as three good rations of liver sausage that were issued to us this evening. That makes a decent present.

We stow the things carefully in our boots; we have to take them to protect our feet against treading on wire and broken glass on the other bank. As we must swim for it we can take no other clothes. But it is not far and quite dark.

We make off with our boots in our hands. Swiftly we slip into the water, lie on our backs and swim, holding the boots with their contents up over our heads.

We climb out carefully on the opposite bank, take out the packages and put on our boots. We put the things under our arms. And so, all wet and naked, clothed only in our boots, we break into a trot. We find the house at once. It lies among the trees. Leer trips over a root and skins his elbows.

"No matter," he says gaily.

The windows are shuttered. We slip round the house and try to peer through the cracks. Then we grow impatient. Suddenly Kropp hesitates:

"What if there's a Major in with them?"

"Then we just clear off," grins Leer, "he can try to read our regimental numbers here," and smacks his behind.

The door of the courtyard stands open. Our boots make a great clatter. The house door opens, a chink of light shines through and a woman cries out in a scared voice.

"Ssh, ssh! *camerade—bon ami*——" we say, and show our packages protestingly.

The other two are now on the scene, the door opens wide and the light floods over us. They recognize us and all three burst into laughter at our appearance. They rock and sway in the doorway, they laugh so much. How supple their movements are!

"*Un moment*——" They disappear and throw us bits of clothing which we gladly wrap round ourselves. Then we venture in. A small lamp burns in the room, which is warm and smells a little of perfume. We unwrap our parcels and hand them over to the women. Their eyes shine, it is obvious that they are hungry.

Then we all become rather embarrassed. Leer makes the gestures of eating, and then they come to life again and bring out plates and knives and fall to on the food, and they hold up every slice of liver sausage and admire it before they eat it, and we sit proudly by.

They overwhelm us with their chatter—we understand very little of it, but we listen and the words sound friendly. No doubt we all look very young. The little brunette strokes my hair and says what all the French women say: "*La guerre—grand malheur—pauvres garçons——*"

I hold her arm tightly and press my lips into the palm of her hand. Her fingers close round my face. Close above me are her bewildering eyes, the soft brown of her skin and her red lips. Her mouth speaks words I do not understand. Nor do I fully understand her eyes; they seem to say more than we anticipated when we came here.

There are other rooms adjoining. In passing I see Leer, he has made a great hit with the blonde. And he knows it, too. But I—I am lost in remoteness, in weakness, and in a passion to which I yield myself trustingly. My desires are strangely compounded of yearning and misery. I feel giddy, there is nothing here that a man can hold on to. We have left our boots at the door, they have given us slippers instead, and now nothing remains to recall for me the assurance and self-confidence of the soldier: no rifle, no belt, no tunic, no cap. I let myself drop into the unknown, come what may —yet, in spite of all, I feel somewhat afraid.

The little brunette contracts her brows when she is thinking; but when she talks they are still. And often the sound does not quite become a word but suffocates or floats away over me half finished; an arch, a pathway, a comet. What have I known of it—what do I know of it?—The words of this foreign tongue, that I hardly understand, they caress me to a quietness, in which the room grows dim, and dissolves in the half-light, and only the face above me lives and is clear.

How various is a face; but an hour ago it was strange and now it is touched with a tenderness that comes, not from it, but out of the night, the world and the blood, all these things seem to shine in it together. The objects in the room are touched by it and transformed, they become isolated, and I feel almost awed at the sight of my clear skin when the light of the lamp falls upon it and the cool brown hand passes over it.

How different all this is from the conditions in the soldiers' brothels, to which we are allowed to go, and where we have to wait in long queues. I wish I never thought of them; but desire turns my mind to them involuntarily and I am afraid, for it might be impossible ever to be free of them again.

But then I feel the lips of the little brunette and press myself against them, my eyes close and I let it all fall from me, war and terror and grossness, in order to awaken young and happy; I think of the picture of the girl on the poster and, for a moment, believe that my life depends on winning her. And if I press ever deeper into the arms that embrace me, perhaps a miracle may happen. . . .

So, after a time we find ourselves reassembled again. Leer is in high spirits. We pull on our boots and take our leave warmly. The night air cools our hot bodies. The rustling poplars loom large in the darkness. The moon floats in the heavens and in the waters of the canal. We do not run, we walk beside one another with long strides.

"That was worth a ration loaf," says Leer.

I cannot trust myself to speak, I am not in the least happy.

Then we hear footsteps and dodge behind a shrub.

The steps come nearer, close by us. We see a naked soldier, in boots, just like ourselves; he has a package under his arm, and gallops onward. It is Tjaden in full course. He has disappeared already.

We laugh. In the morning he will curse us.

Unobserved, we arrive again at our sacks of straw.

I am called to the Orderly Room. The company commander gives me a leave pass and a travel pass and wishes me a good journey. I look to see how much leave I have got. Seventeen days—fourteen days' leave and three days for traveling. It is not enough and I ask whether I cannot have five days for traveling. Bertinck points to my pass. There I see that I am not to return to the front immediately. After my leave I have to report for a course of training to a camp on the moors.

The others congratulate me. Kat gives me good advice, and tells me I ought to try to get a base job. "If you are smart, you'll hang on to it."

I would rather not have gone for another eight days; we are to stay here that much longer and it is good here.

Naturally I have to stand the others drinks at the canteen. We are all a little bit drunk. I become gloomy: I will be away for six weeks—that is lucky of course, but what may happen before I get back? Shall I meet all these fellows again? Already Haie has gone—who will the next be?

As we drink, I look at each of them in turn. Albert sits beside me and smokes, he is silent, we have always been together; opposite squats Kat, with his drooping shoulders, his broad thumb, and calm voice—Müller, with the protruding teeth and the booming laugh—Tjaden, with his mousy eyes—Leer who has grown a full beard and looks at least forty.

Over us hangs a dense cloud of smoke. Where would a soldier be without tobacco? The canteen is his refuge, and beer is far more than a drink, it is a token that a man can move his limbs and stretch in safety. We do it ceremonially, we stretch our legs out in front of us and spit deliberately, that is the only way. How it all rises up before a man when he is going away the next morning!

At night we go again to the other side of the canal. I am almost afraid to tell the little brunette that I am going away, and when I return we will certainly be far away from here; we will never see one another again. But she merely nods and takes no special notice. At first I am at a loss to understand, then it suddenly dawns on me. Yes, Leer is right: if I were going up to the front, then she would have again called me "*pauvre garçon*"; but merely going on leave—she does not want to hear about that, that is not nearly so interesting. May she go to the devil with her chattering talk. A man dreams of a miracle and wakes up to loaves of bread.

Next morning, after I have been deloused, I go to the railhead. Albert and Kat come with me. At the halt we learn that it will be a couple of hours yet before the train leaves. The other two have to go back to duty. We take leave of one another.

"Good luck, Kat; good luck, Albert."

They go off and wave once or twice. Their figures dwindle. I know their every step and movement; I would recognize them at any distance. Then they disappear. I sit down on my pack and wait.

Suddenly I become filled with a consuming impatience to be gone.

I lie down on many a station platform; I stand before many a soup kitchen; I squat on many a bench—then at last the landscape becomes gloomy, mysterious, and familiar. It glides past the western windows with its villages, their thatched roofs like caps, pulled over the whitewashed, half-timbered houses, its cornfields, gleaming like mother-of-pearl in the slanting light, its orchards, its barns and old lime trees.

The names of the stations begin to take on meaning and my heart trembles. The train stamps and stamps onward, I stand at the window and hold on to the frame. These names mark the boundaries of my youth.

Smooth meadows, fields, farmyards; a solitary team moves against the skyline along the road that runs parallel to the horizon—a barrier, before which peasants stand waiting, girls waving, children playing on the embankment, roads, leading into the country, smooth roads without artillery.

It is evening, and if the train did not rattle I should cry out. The plain unfolds itself.

In the distance, the soft, blue silhouette of the mountain ranges begins to appear. I recognize the characteristic outline of the Dolbenberg, a jagged comb,[3] springing up precipitously from the limit of the forests. Behind it should lie the town.

---

[3] *comb*: a narrow valley or ravine (sometimes *coomb*).

But now the sun streams through the world, dissolving everything in its golden-red light, the train swings round one curve and then another; far away, in a long line one behind the other, stand the poplars, unsubstantial, swaying and dark, fashioned out of shadow, light, and desire.

The field swings round as the train encircles it, and the intervals between the trees diminish; the trees become a block and for a moment I see one only—then they reappear from behind the foremost tree and stand out a long line against the sky until they are hidden by the first houses.

A street crossing. I stand at the window, I cannot drag myself away. The others put their baggage ready for getting out. I repeat to myself the name of the street that we cross over—Bremerstrasse—Bremerstrasse——

Below there are cyclists, trucks, men; it is a gray street and a gray subway—it embraces me as though it were my mother.

Then the train stops, and there is the station with noise and cries and sentries. I pick up my pack and fasten the straps, I take my rifle in my hand and stumble down the steps.

On the platform I look round; I know no one among the people hurrying to and fro. A Red Cross sister offers me something to drink. I turn away, she smiles at me too foolishly, so obsessed with her own importance: "Just look, I am giving a soldier coffee!"—she calls me "Comrade," but I will have none of it.

Outside in front of the station the stream roars alongside the street, it rushes foaming from the sluices of the mill bridge. There stands the old, square watchtower, in front of it the great mottled lime tree and behind it the evening.

Here we have often sat—how long ago it is—we have passed over this bridge and breathed the cool, acid smell of the stagnant water; we have leaned over the still water on this side of the lock, where the green creepers and weeds hang from the piles of the bridge—and on hot days we rejoiced in the spouting foam on the other side of the lock and told tales about our schoolteachers.

I pass over the bridge, I look right and left; the water is as full of weeds as ever, and it still shoots over in gleaming arches; in the tower building laundresses still stand with bare arms as they used to over the clean linen, and the heat from the ironing pours out through the open windows. Dogs trot along the narrow street, before the doors of the houses people stand and follow me with their gaze as I pass by, dirty and heavy laden.

In this confectioner's we used to eat ices, and there we learned to smoke cigarettes. Walking down the street I know every shop, the colonial warehouses, the pharmacist's, the tobacconist's. Then at last I stand before the brown door with its worn latch and my hand grows heavy. I open the door and a wonderful freshness comes out to meet me, my eyes are dim.

The stairs creak under my boots. Upstairs a door rattles, someone is looking over the railing. It is the kitchen door that was opened, they are cooking potato cakes, the house reeks of it, and today of course is Saturday; that will be my sister leaning over. For a moment I am shy and lower my head, then I take off my helmet and look up. Yes, it is my eldest sister.

"Paul," she cries, "Paul——"

I nod, my pack bumps against the banisters; my rifle is so heavy.

She pulls a door open and calls: "Mother, Mother, Paul is here."

I can go no farther—Mother, Mother, Paul is here.

I lean against the wall and grip my helmet and rifle. I hold them as tight as I can, but I cannot take another step, the staircase fades before my eyes, I support myself with the butt of my rifle against my feet and clench my teeth fiercely, but I cannot speak a word, my sister's call has made me powerless, I can do nothing, I struggle to make myself laugh, to speak, but no word comes, and so I stand on the steps, miserable, helpless, paralyzed, and against my will the tears run down my cheeks.

My sister comes back and says: "Why, what is the matter?"

Then I pull myself together and stagger onto the landing. I lean my rifle in a corner, I set my pack against the wall, place my helmet on it, and fling down my equipment and baggage. Then I say fiercely: "Bring me a handkerchief."

She gives me one from the cupboard and I dry my face. Above me on the wall hangs the glass case with the colored butterflies that once I collected.

Now I hear my mother's voice. It comes from the bedroom.

"Is she in bed?" I ask my sister.

"She is ill——" she replies.

I go in to her, give her my hand, and say as calmly as I can: "Here I am, Mother."

She lies still in the dim light. Then she asks anxiously:

"Are you wounded?" and I feel her searching glance.

"No, I have got leave."

My mother is very pale. I am afraid to make a light.

"Here I lie now," says she, "and cry instead of being glad."

"Are you sick, Mother?" I ask.

"I am going to get up a little today," she says and turns to my sister, who is continually running to the kitchen to watch that the food does not burn; "and put out the jar of preserved whortleberries—you like that, don't you?" she asks me.

"Yes, Mother, I haven't had any for a long time."

"We might almost have known you were coming," laughs my sister, "there is just your favorite dish, potato cakes, and even whortleberries to go with them too."

"And it is Saturday," I add.

"Sit here beside me," says my mother.

She looks at me. Her hands are white and sickly and frail compared with mine. We say very little, and I am thankful that she asks nothing. What ought I to say? Everything I could have wished for has happened. I have come out of it safely and sit here beside her. And in the kitchen stands my sister making the evening bread and singing.

"Dear boy," says my mother softly.

We were never very demonstrative in our family; poor folk who toil and are full of cares are not so. It is not their way to protest what they already know. When my mother says to me "dear boy," it means much more than when another uses it. I know well enough that the jar of whortleberries is the only one they have had for months, and that she has kept it for me; and the somewhat stale cakes that she gives me, too. She has taken a favorable opportunity of getting a few and has put them all by for me.

I sit by her bed, and through the window the chestnut trees in the beer garden opposite glow in brown and gold. I breathe deeply and say over to myself: "You are at home, you are at home." But a sense of strangeness will not leave me, I can find nothing of myself in all these things. There is my mother, there is my sister, there my case of butterflies, and there the mahogany piano—but I am not myself there. There is a distance, a veil between us.

I go and fetch my pack to the bedside and turn out the things I have brought—a whole Edam cheese, that Kat provided me with, two loaves of army bread, three-quarters of a pound of butter, two tins of liver sausage, a pound of dripping, and a little bag of rice.

"I suppose you can make some use of that——"

They nod.

"Is it pretty bad for food here?" I inquire.

"Yes, there's not much. Do you get enough out there?"

I smile and point to the things I have brought. "Not always quite so much as that, of course, but we fare reasonably well."

Erna goes out to bring in the food. Suddenly my mother seizes hold of my hand and asks falteringly: "Was it very bad out there, Paul?"

Mother, what should I answer to that! You would not understand, and never realize it. And you never should realize it. Was it bad, you ask.—— You, Mother——I shake my head and say: "No, Mother, not so very. There are always a lot of us together so it isn't so bad."

"Yes, but Heinrich Bredemeyer was here just lately and he said it was terrible out there now, with the gas and all the rest of it."

It is my mother who says that. She says: "With the gas and all the rest of it." She does not know what she is saying, she is merely anxious for me. Should I tell her how we once found three enemy trenches with their garrison all stiff as though stricken with apoplexy? Against the parapet, in the dugouts, just where they were, the men stood and lay about, with blue faces, dead.

"No, Mother, that's only talk," I answer, "there's not very much in what Bredemeyer says. You see for instance, I'm well and fit——"

Before my mother's tremulous anxiety I recover my composure. Now I can walk about and talk and answer questions without fear of having suddenly to lean against the wall because the world turns soft as rubber and my veins become brimstone.

My mother wants to get up. So I go for a while to my sister in the kitchen. "What is the matter with her?" I ask.

She shrugs her shoulders: "She has been in bed two months now, but we did not want to write and tell you. Several doctors have been to see her. One of them said it is probably cancer again."

I go to the District Commandant to report myself. Slowly I wander through the streets. Occasionally someone speaks to me. I do not delay long for I have little inclination to talk.

On my way back from the barracks a loud voice calls out to me. Still lost in thought I turn around and find myself confronted by a Major. "Can't you salute?" he blusters.

"Sorry, Major," I say in embarrassment, "I didn't notice you."

"Don't you know how to speak properly?" he roars.

I would like to hit him in the face, but control myself, for my leave depends on it. I click my heels and say: "I did not see you, Herr Major."

"Then keep your eyes open," he snorts. "What is your name?" I give it. His fat red face is furious. "What regiment?"

I give him full particulars. Even yet he has not had enough. "Where are they?"

But I had had more than enough and say: "Between Langemark and Bixschoote."

"Eh?" he asks, a bit stupefied.

I explain to him that I arrived on leave only an hour or two since, thinking that he would then trot along. But not at all. He gets even more furious: "You think you can bring your front-line manners here, what? Well, we don't stand that sort of thing. Thank God, we have discipline here!"

"Twenty paces backwards, double march!" he commands.

I am mad with rage. But I cannot say anything to him; he could put me under arrest if he liked. So I double back, and then march up to him. Six paces from him I spring to a stiff salute and maintain it until I am six paces beyond him.

He calls me back again and affably gives me to understand that for once he is pleased to put mercy before justice. I pretend to be duly grateful. "Now, dismiss!" he says. I turn about smartly and march off.

That ruins the evening for me. I go back home and throw my uniform into a corner; I ought to have done that before. Then I take out my civilian clothes from the wardrobe and put them on.

I feel awkward. The suit is rather tight and short, I have grown in the army. Collar and tie give me some trouble. In the end my sister ties the bow for me. But how light the suit is, it feels as though I had nothing on but a shirt and underpants.

I look at myself in the glass. It is a strange sight. A sunburned, overgrown candidate for confirmation gazes at me in astonishment.

My mother is pleased to see me wearing civilian clothes; it makes me less strange to her. But my father would rather I kept my uniform on so that he could take me to visit his acquaintances.

But I refuse.

It is pleasant to sit quietly somewhere, in the beer garden for example, under the chestnuts by the skittle alley.[4] The leaves fall down on the table and on the ground, only a few, the first. A glass of beer stands in front of me, I've learned to drink in the army. The glass is half empty, but there are still a few good swigs ahead of me, and besides, I can always order a second and a third if I wish to. There are no bugles and no bombardments, the children of the house play in the skittle alley, and the dog rests his head against my knee. The sky is blue, between the leaves of the chestnuts rises the green spire of St. Margaret's Church.

This is good, I like it. But I cannot get on with the people. My mother is the only one who asks no questions. Not so my father. He wants me to tell him about the front; he is curious in a way that I find stupid and distressing; I no longer have any real contact with him. There is nothing he likes more than just hearing about it. I realize he does not know that a man cannot talk of such things; I would do it willingly, but it is too dangerous for me to put these things into words. I am afraid they might then become gigantic and I be no longer able to master them. What would become of us if everything that happens out there were quite clear to us?

So I confine myself to telling him a few amusing things. But he wants to know whether I have ever had a hand-to-hand fight. I say "No," and get up and go out.

[4] *skittle alley*: an area where a game similar to bowling is played.

But that does not mend matters. After I have been startled a couple of times in the street by the screaming of the tramcars, which resembles the shriek of a shell coming straight for one, somebody taps me on the shoulder. It is my German master, and he fastens on me with the usual question: "Well, how are things out there? Terrible, terrible, eh? Yes, it is dreadful, but we must carry on. And after all, you do at least get decent food out there, so I hear. You look well, Paul, and fit. Naturally it's worse here. Naturally. The best for our soldiers every time, that goes without saying."

He drags me along to a table with a lot of others. They welcome me, a headmaster shakes hands with me and says: "So you come from the front? What is the spirit like out there? Excellent, eh? Excellent?"

I explain that no one would be sorry to be back home.

He laughs uproariously. "I can well believe it! But first you have to give the Froggies a good hiding. Do you smoke? Here, try one. Waiter, bring a beer as well for our young warrior."

Unfortunately I have accepted the cigar, so I have to remain. And they are all so dripping with goodwill that it is impossible to object. All the same I feel annoyed and smoke like a chimney as hard as I can. In order to make at least some show of appreciation I toss off the beer in one gulp. Immediately a second is ordered; people know how much they are indebted to the soldiers. They argue about what we ought to annex. The headmaster with the steel watch chain wants to have at least the whole of Belgium, the coal areas of France, and a slice of Russia. He produces reasons why we must have them and is quite inflexible until at last the others give in to him. Then he begins to expound just whereabouts in France the breakthrough must come, and turns to me: "Now, shove ahead a bit out there with your everlasting trench warfare—smash through the Johnnies and then there will be peace."

I reply that in our opinion a breakthrough may not be possible. The enemy may have too many reserves. Besides, the war may be rather different from what people think.

He dismisses the idea loftily and informs me I know nothing about it. "The details, yes," says he, "but this relates to the whole. And of that you are not able to judge. You see only your little sector and so cannot have any general survey. You do your duty, you risk your lives, that deserves the highest honor—every man of you ought to have the Iron Cross—but first of all the enemy line must be broken through in Flanders and then rolled up from the top."

He blows his nose and wipes his beard. "Completely rolled up they must be, from the top to the bottom. And then to Paris."

I would like to know just how he pictures it to himself, and pour the third glass of beer into me. Immediately he orders another.

But I break away. He stuffs a few more cigars into my pocket and sends me off with a friendly slap. "All of the best! I hope we will soon hear something worthwhile from you."

I imagined leave would be different from this. Indeed, it was different a year ago. It is I of course that have changed in the interval. There lies a gulf between that time and today. At that time I still knew nothing about the war, we had been only in quiet sectors. But now I see that I have been crushed without knowing it. I find I do not belong here anymore, it is a foreign world. Some of these people ask questions, some ask no questions, but one can see that they are quite confident they know all about it; they often say so with their air of comprehension, so there is no point in discussing it. They make up a picture of it for themselves.

I prefer to be alone, so that no one troubles me. For they all come back to the same thing, how badly it goes and how well it goes; one thinks it is this way, another that; and yet they are always absorbed in the things that go to make up their own existence. Formerly I lived in just the same way myself, but now I feel no contact here any longer.

They talk to me too much. They have worries, aims, desires, that I cannot comprehend. I often sit with one of them in the little beer garden and try to explain to him that this is really the only thing: just to sit quietly, like this. They understand of course, they agree, they may even feel it so too, but only with words, only with words, yes, that is it—they feel it, but always with only half of themselves, the rest of their being is taken up with other things, they are so divided in themselves that none feels it with his whole essence; I cannot even say myself exactly what I mean.

When I see them here, in their rooms, in their offices, about their occupations, I feel an irresistible attraction in it, I would like to be here, too, and forget the war; but also it repels me, it is so narrow, how can that fill a man's life, he ought to smash it to bits; how can they do it, while out at the front the splinters are whining over the shell holes and the star shells go up, the wounded are carried back on waterproof sheets and comrades crouch in the trenches.——They are different men here, men I cannot properly understand, whom I envy and despise. I must think of Kat and Albert and Müller and Tjaden, what will they be doing? No doubt they are sitting in the canteen, or perhaps swimming—soon they will have to go up to the front line again.

In my room behind the table stands a brown leather sofa. I sit down on it.

On the walls are pasted countless pictures that I once used to cut out of the newspapers. In between are drawings and postcards that have come my way. In the corner is a small iron stove. Against the wall opposite stand the bookshelves with my books.

I used to live in this room before I was a soldier. The books I bought gradually with money I earned by coaching. Many of them are second hand, all the classics for example, one volume in blue cloth boards cost one mark twenty pfennig. I bought them complete because I was thorough-going, I did not trust the editors of selections, even though they may have chosen all the best. So I purchased only "collected works." I read most of them with laudable zeal, but few of them really appealed to me. I preferred the other books, the moderns, which were, of course, much dearer. A few I came by not quite honestly, I borrowed and did not return them because I did not want to part with them.

One shelf is filled with schoolbooks. They are not so well cared for, they are badly thumbed, and pages have been torn out for certain purposes. Then below are periodicals, papers, and letters all jammed in together with drawings and rough sketches.

I want to think myself back into that time. It is still in the room, I feel it at once, the walls have preserved it. My hands rest on the arms of the sofa; now I make myself at home and draw up my legs so that I sit comfortably in the corner, in the arms of the sofa. The little window is open, through it I see the familiar picture of the street with the rising spire of the church at the end. There are a couple of flowers on the table. Penholders, a shell as a paperweight, the inkwell—here nothing is changed.

It will be like this too, if I am lucky, when the war is over and I come back here for good. I will sit here just like this and look at my room and wait.

I feel excited; but I do not want to be, for that is not right. I want that quiet rapture again. I want to feel the same powerful, nameless urge that I used to feel when I turned to my books. The breath of desire that then arose from the colored backs of the books shall fill me again, melt the heavy, dead lump of lead that lies somewhere in me, and waken again the impatience of the future, the quick joy in the world of thought—it shall bring back again the lost eagerness of my youth. I sit and wait.

It occurs to me that I must go and see Kemmerich's mother; I might visit Mittelstaedt too, he should be at the barracks. I look out of the window—beyond the sober picture of the street appears a range of hills, distant and light; it changes to a clear day in autumn, and I sit by the fire with Kat and Albert and eat potatoes baked in their skins.

But I do not want to think of that, I sweep it away. The room shall speak, it must catch me up and hold me, I want to feel that I belong here, I want to hearken and know when I go back to the front that the war will sink down, be drowned utterly in the great homecoming tide, know that it will then be past forever, and not gnaw us continually, that it will have none but an outward power over us.

The backs of the books stand in rows. I know them all still, I remember arranging them in order. I implore them with my eyes: Speak to me— take me up—take me, Life of my Youth—you who are carefree, beautiful —receive me again——

I wait, I wait.

Images float through my mind, but they do not grip me, they are mere shadows and memories.

Nothing—nothing——

My disquietude grows.

A terrible feeling of foreignness suddenly rises up in me. I cannot find my way back, I am shut out though I entreat earnestly and put forth all my strength.

Nothing stirs; listless and wretched, like a condemned man, I sit there and the past withdraws itself. And at the same time I fear to importune it too much, because I do not know what might happen then. I am a soldier, I must cling to that.

Wearily I stand up and look out of the window. Then I take one of the books, intending to read, and turn over the leaves. But I put it away and take out another. There are passages in it that have been marked. I look, turn over the pages, take up fresh books. Already they are piled up beside me. Speedily more join the heap—papers, magazines, letters.

I stand there dumb. As before a judge.

Dejected.

Words, Words, Words—they do not reach me.

Slowly I place the books back in the shelves.

Nevermore.

Quietly, I go out of the room.

Still, I do not give up hope. I do not, indeed, go to my room anymore, but comfort myself with the thought that a few days are not enough to judge by. Afterwards—later on—there is plenty of time for that.

So I go over to see Mittelstaedt in the barracks, and we sit in his room; there is an atmosphere about it that I do not like but with which I am quite familiar.

Mittelstaedt has some news ready for me that electrifies me on the spot. He tells me Kantorek has been called up as a territorial.[5]

"Just think of it," says he, and takes out a couple of good cigars, "I come back here from the hospital and bump right into him. He stretches out his

---

[5] *territorial*: a soldier called up for home defense.

paw to me and bleats: 'Hello, Mittelstaedt, how are you?'—I look at him and say: 'Territorial Kantorek, business is business and schnapps is schnapps, you ought to know that well enough yourself. Stand to attention when you speak to a superior officer.' You should have seen his face! A cross between a dud and a pickled cucumber. He tried once again to chum up. So I snubbed him a bit harder. Then he brought up his biggest guns and asked confidentially: 'Would you like me to use my influence so that you can take an emergency exam?' He was trying to remind me of those things, you know. Then I got mad and I reminded him of something instead. 'Territorial Kantorek, two years ago you preached us into enlisting; and among us there was one, Josef Behm, who didn't want to enlist. He was killed three months before he would have been called up in the ordinary way. If it had not been for you he would have lived just that much longer. And now: Dismiss. You will hear from me later.' It was easy to get put in charge of his company. First thing I did was to take him to the stores and fit him out with a suitable equipment. You will see in a minute."

We go out to the parade ground. The company has fallen in. Mittelstaedt stands them at ease and inspects.

Then I see Kantorek and am scarcely able to stifle my laughter. He is wearing a faded blue tunic. On the back and in the sleeves there are big dark patches. The overcoat must have belonged to a giant. The black, worn breeches are just as much too short; they reach barely halfway down his calf. The boots, tough old clodhoppers, with turned-up toes and laces at the side, are much too big for him. But as a compensation the cap is too small, a terribly dirty, mean little pillbox. The whole outfit is just pitiful.

Mittelstaedt stops in front of him: "Territorial Kantorek, do you call those buttons polished? You seem as if you can never learn. Inadequate, Kantorek, quite inadequate——"

It makes me bubble with glee. In school Kantorek used to chasten Mittelstaedt with exactly the same expression—"Inadequate, Mittelstaedt, quite inadequate."

Mittelstaedt continues to upbraid him: "Look at Boettcher now, there's a model for you to learn from."

I can hardly believe my eyes. Boettcher is there too, Boettcher, our school porter. And he is a model! Kantorek shoots a glance at me as if he would like to eat me. But I grin at him innocently, as though I do not recognize him anymore.

Nothing could look more ludicrous then his forage cap and his uniform. And this is the object before whom we used to stand in anguish, as he sat up there enthroned at his desk, spearing at us with his pencil for our mistakes in those irregular French verbs with which afterwards we made so little headway in France. That is barely two years ago—and now here stands Territorial Kantorek, the spell quite broken, with bent knees, arms like pothooks, unpolished buttons and that ludicrous outfit—an impossible soldier. I cannot reconcile this with the menacing figure at the schoolmaster's desk. I wonder what I, the old soldier, would do if this skinful of woe ever dared to say to me again: "Bäumer, give the imperfect of *aller.*' "

Then Mittelstaedt makes them practice skirmishing, and as a favor appoints Kantorek squad leader.

Now in skirmishing, the squad leader has always to keep twenty paces in front of his squad; if the order comes "On the march, about turn," the line of skirmishers simply turns about, but the squad leader, who now finds himself suddenly twenty paces in rear of the line, has to rush up at the double and take his position again twenty paces in front of the squad. That makes altogether forty paces double march. But no sooner has he arrived than the order "On the march, about turn" comes again and he once more has to race at top speed another forty paces to the other side. In this way the squad has made merely the turnabout and a couple of paces while the squad leader dashes backwards and forwards. That is one of Himmelstoss's well-worn recipes.

Kantorek can hardly expect anything else from Mittelstaedt, for he once messed up the latter's chance of promotion, and Mittelstaedt would be a big fool not to make the best of such a good opportunity as this, before he goes back to the front again. A man might well die easier after the army has given him just one such stroke of luck.

In the meantime Kantorek is dashing up and down like a wild boar. After a while Mittelstaedt stops the skirmish and begins the very important exercise of creeping.

On hands and knees, carrying his gun in regulation fashion, Kantorek shoves his absurd figure over the sand immediately in front of us. He is breathing hard, and his panting is music.

Mittelstaedt encourages Kantorek the Territorial with quotations from Kantorek the Schoolmaster. "Territorial Kantorek, we have the good fortune to live in a great age, we must all humble ourselves and for once put aside bitterness."

Kantorek sweats and spits out a dirty piece of wood that has lodged in his teeth.

Mittelstaedt stoops down and says reproachfully: "And in the trifles never lose sight of the great adventure, Territorial Kantorek!"

It amazes me that Kantorek does not explode with a bang, especially when, during physical exercises, Mittelstaedt copies him to perfection, seizing him by the seat of his trousers as he is climbing along the horizontal bar, so that he can just raise his chin above the beam, and then starts to give him good advice. That is exactly what Kantorek used to do to him at school.

The extra fatigues are next detailed off. "Kantorek and Boettcher, bread fatigue! Take the handcart with you."

In a couple of minutes the two set off together pushing the barrow. Kantorek in a fury walks with his head down. But the porter is delighted to have scored light duty.

The bakehouse is away at the other end of the town, and the two must go there and back through the whole length of it.

"They've done that a couple of times already," grins Mittelstaedt. "There are still a few people waiting to see them."

"Excellent," I say, "but hasn't he reported you yet?"

"He did try. Our CO laughed like the deuce when he heard the story. He hasn't any time for schoolmasters. Besides, I'm sweet with his daughter."

"He'll mess up the examination for you."

"I don't care," says Mittelstaedt calmly. "Besides, his complaint came to nothing because I could show that he had had hardly anything but light duty."

"Couldn't you polish him up a bit?" I ask.

"He's too stupid, I couldn't be bothered," answers Mittelstaedt contemptuously.

What is leave?—A pause that only makes everything after it so much worse. Already the sense of parting begins to intrude itself. My mother watches me silently—I know she counts the days—every morning she is sad. It is one day less. She has put away my pack, she does not want to be reminded by it.

The hours pass quickly if a man broods. I pull myself together and go with my sister to the butcher's to get a pound of bones. That is a great luxury and people line up early in the morning and stand waiting. Many of them faint.

We have no luck. After waiting by turns for three hours the queue disperses. The bones have not lasted out.

It is a good thing I get my rations. I bring them to my mother and in that way we all get something decent to eat.

The days grow ever more strained and my mother's eyes more sorrowful. Four days left now. I must go and see Kemmerich's mother.

I cannot write that down. This quaking, sobbing woman who shakes me and cries out on me: "Why are you living then, when he is dead?"—who drowns me in tears and calls out: "What are you there for at all, child, when you——"—who drops into a chair and wails: "Did you see him? Did you see him then? How did he die?"

I tell her he was shot through the heart and died instantaneously. She looks at me, she doubts me: "You lie. I know better. I have felt how terribly he died. I have heard his voice at night, I have felt his anguish—tell the truth, I want to know it, I must know it."

"No," I say, "I was beside him. He died at once."

She pleads with me gently: "Tell me. You must tell me. I know you want to comfort me, but don't you see, you torment me far more than if you told me the truth? I cannot bear the uncertainty. Tell me how it was and even though it will be terrible, it will be far better than what I have to think if you don't."

I will never tell her, she can make mincemeat out of me first. I console her, but she strikes me as rather stupid all the same. Why doesn't she stop worrying? Kemmerich will stay dead whether she knows about it or not. When a man has seen so many dead he cannot understand any longer why there should be so much anguish over a single individual. So I say rather impatiently: "He died immediately. He felt absolutely nothing at all. His face was quite calm."

She is silent. Then she says slowly: "Will you swear it?"

"Yes."

"By everything that is sacred to you?"

Good God, what is there that is sacred to me?—such things change pretty quickly with us.

"Yes, he died at once."

"Are you willing never to come back yourself, if it isn't true?"

"May I never come back if he wasn't killed instantaneously."

I would swear to anything. But she seems to believe me. She moans and weeps steadily. I have to tell how it happened so I invent a story and I almost believe it myself.

As I leave she kisses me and gives me a picture of him. In his recruit's uniform he leans on a round rustic table with legs made of birch branches. Behind him a wood is painted on a curtain, and on the table stands a mug of beer.

It is the last evening at home. Everyone is silent. I go to bed early, I seize the pillow, press it against myself, and bury my head in it. Who knows if I will ever lie in a featherbed again?

Late in the night my mother comes into my room. She thinks I am asleep, and I pretend to be so. To talk, to stay awake with one another, it is too hard.

She sits long into the night although she is in pain and often writhes. At last I can bear it no longer and pretend I have just wakened up.

"Go and sleep, Mother, you will catch cold here."

"I can sleep enough later," she says.

I sit up. "I don't go straight back to the front, Mother. I have to do four weeks at the training camp. I may come over from there one Sunday, perhaps."

She is silent. Then she asks gently: "Are you very much afraid?"

"No, Mother."

"I would like to tell you to be on your guard against the women out in France. They are no good."

Ah! Mother, Mother! You still think I am a child—why can I not put my head in your lap and weep? Why have I always to be strong and self-controlled? I would like to weep and be comforted, too; indeed I am little more than a child; in the wardrobe still hang my short, boy's trousers—it is such a little time ago, why is it over?

"Where we are there aren't any women, Mother," I say as calmly as I can.

"And be very careful at the front, Paul."

Ah, Mother, Mother! Why do I not take you in my arms and die with you? What poor wretches we are!

"Yes, Mother, I will."

"I will pray for you every day, Paul."

Ah! Mother, Mother! Let us rise up and go out, back through the years, where the burden of all this misery lies on us no more, back to you and me alone, Mother!

"Perhaps you can get a job that is not so dangerous."

"Yes, Mother, perhaps I can get into the cookhouse—that can easily be done."

"You do it then, and if the others say anything——"

"That won't worry me, Mother——"

She sighs. Her face is a white gleam in the darkness.

"Now you must go to sleep, Mother."

She does not reply. I get up and wrap my cover round her shoulders.

She supports herself on my arm, she is in pain. And so I take her to her room. I stay with her a little while.

"And you must get well again, Mother, before I come back."

"Yes, yes, my child."

"You ought not to send your things to me, Mother. We have plenty to eat out there. You can make much better use of them here."

How destitute she lies there in her bed, she, that loves me more than all the world. As I am about to leave, she says hastily: "I have two pairs of underpants for you. They are all wool. They will keep you warm. You must not forget to put them in your pack."

Ah! Mother! I know what these underpants have cost you in waiting, and walking, and begging! Ah! Mother, Mother! how can it be that I must part from you? Who else is there that has any claim on me but you? Here I sit and there you are lying, and we have so much to say, that we could never say it.

"Good night, Mother."

"Good night, my child."

The room is dark. I hear my mother's breathing, and the ticking of the clock. Outside the window the wind blows and the chestnut trees rustle.

On the landing I stumble over my pack, which lies there already made up, because I have to leave early in the morning.

I bite into my pillow. I grasp the iron rods of my bed with my fists. I ought never to have come here. Out there I was indifferent and often hopeless—I will never be able to be so again. I was a soldier, and now I am nothing but an agony for myself, for my mother, for everything that is so comfortless and without end.

I ought never to have come on leave.

Chapter VIII

I ALREADY know the camp on the moors. It was here that Himmelstoss gave Tjaden his education. But now I know hardly anyone here; as ever, all is altered. There are only a few people that I have occasionally met before.

I go through the routine mechanically. In the evenings I generally go to the Soldiers' Home, where the newspapers are laid out, but which I do not read; still, there is a piano there that I am glad enough to play on. Two girls are in attendance, one of them is young.

The camp is surrounded with high barbed-wire fences. If we come back late from the Soldiers' Home we have to show passes. But those who are on good terms with the guard can get through, of course.

Between the junipers and the birch trees on the moor we practice company drill each day. It is bearable if one expects nothing better. We advance at a run, fling ourselves down, and our panting breath moves the stalks of the grasses and the flowers of the heather to and fro. Looked at so closely one sees the fine sand is composed of millions of the tiniest pebbles as clear as if they had been made in a laboratory. It is strangely inviting to dig one's hands into it.

But most beautiful are the woods with their line of birch trees. Their color changes with every minute. Now the stems gleam purest white, and between them, airy and silken, hangs the pastel green of the leaves; the next moment all changes to an opalescent blue, as the shivering breezes pass down from the heights and touch the green lightly away; and again in one place it deepens almost to black, as a cloud passes over the sun. And this shadow moves like a ghost through the dim trunks and passes far out over the moor to the sky—then the birches stand out again like gay banners on white poles, with their red and gold patches of autumn-tinted leaves.

I often become so lost in the play of soft light and transparent shadow that I almost fail to hear the commands. It is when one is alone that one begins to observe Nature and to love her. And here I have not much companionship, and do not even desire it. We are too little acquainted with one another to do more than joke a bit and play poker or nap in the evenings.

Alongside our camp is the big Russian prison camp. It is separated from us by a wire fence, but in spite of this the prisoners come across to us. They seem nervous and fearful, though most of them are big fellows with beards—they look like meek, scolded St. Bernard dogs.

They slink about our camp and pick over the garbage tins. One can imagine what they find there. With us food is pretty scarce and none too good at that—turnips cut into six pieces and boiled in water, and unwashed carrot tops; moldy potatoes are tidbits, and the chief luxury is a thin rice soup in which float little bits of beef sinew, but these are cut up so small that they take a lot of finding.

Everything gets eaten, notwithstanding, and if ever anyone is so well off as not to want all his share, there are a dozen others standing by ready to relieve him of it. Only the dregs that the ladle cannot reach are tipped out and thrown into the garbage tins. Along with that sometimes go a few turnip peelings, moldy bread crusts and all kinds of muck.

This thin, miserable, dirty garbage is the objective of the prisoners. They pick it out of the stinking tins greedily and go off with it under their blouses.

It is strange to see these enemies of ours so close up. They have faces that make one think—honest peasant faces, broad foreheads, broad noses, broad mouths, broad hands, and thick hair.

They ought to be put to threshing, reaping, and apple picking. They look just as kindly as our own peasants in Friesland.

It is distressing to watch their movements, to see them begging for something to eat. They are all rather feeble, for they only get enough nourishment to keep them from starving. Ourselves we have not had sufficient to eat for long enough. They have dysentery; furtively many of them display the blood-stained tails of their shirts. Their backs, their necks are bent, their knees sag, their heads droop as they stretch out their hands and beg in the few words of German that they know—beg with those soft, deep, musical voices that are like warm stoves and cozy rooms at home.

Some men there are who give them a kick, so that they fall over—but those are not many. The majority do nothing to them, just ignore them. Occasionally, when they are too groveling, it makes a man mad and then he kicks them. If only they would not look at one so—— What great misery can be in two such small spots, no bigger than a man's thumb—in their eyes!

They come over to the camp in the evenings and trade. They exchange whatever they possess for bread. Often they have fair success, because they have very good boots and ours are bad. The leather of their knee boots is wonderfully soft, like suede. The peasants among us who get tidbits sent from home can afford to trade. The price of a pair of boots is about two or three loaves of army bread, or a loaf of bread and a small, tough ham sausage.

But most of the Russians have long since parted with whatever things they had. Now they wear only the most pitiful clothing, and try to exchange little carvings and objects that they have made out of shell fragments and copper driving bands. Of course, they don't get much for such things, though they may have taken immense pains with them—they go for a slice or two of bread. Our peasants are hard and cunning when they bargain. They hold the piece of bread or sausage right under the nose of the Russian till he grows pale with greed and his eyes bulge and then he will give anything for it. The peasants wrap up their booty with the utmost solemnity, and then get out their big pocket knives, and slowly and deliberately cut off a slice of bread for themselves from their supply and with every mouthful take a piece of the good, tough sausage and so reward themselves with a good feed. It is distressing to watch them take their afternoon meal thus; one would like to crack them over their thick pates. They rarely give anything away. How little we understand one another!

I am often on guard over the Russians. In the darkness one sees their forms move like sick storks, like great birds. They come close up to the wire fence and lean their faces against it; their fingers hook round the mesh. Often many stand side by side and breathe the wind that comes down from the moors and the forest.

They rarely speak and then only a few words. They are more human and more brotherly toward one another, it seems to me, than we are. But perhaps that is merely because they feel themselves to be more unfortunate than us. Anyway, the war is over so far as they are concerned. But to wait for dysentery is not much of a life either.

The Territorials who are in charge of them say that they were much more lively at first. They used to have intrigues among themselves, as always happens, and it would often come to blows and knives. But now they are quite apathetic, and listless.

They stand at the wire fence; sometimes one goes away and then another at once takes his place in the line. Most of them are silent; occasionally one begs a cigarette butt.

I see their dark forms, their beards move in the wind. I know nothing of them except that they are prisoners, and that is exactly what troubles me. Their life is obscure and guiltless—if I could know more of them, what their names are, how they live, what they are waiting for, what are their burdens, then my emotion would have an object and might become sympathy. But as it is I perceive behind them only the suffering of the creature, the awful melancholy of life and the pitilessness of men.

A word of command has made these silent figures our enemies; a word of command might transform them into our friends. At some table a document is signed by some persons whom none of us knows, and then for years together that very crime on which formerly the world's condemnation and severest penalty fell, becomes our highest aim. But who can draw such a distinction when he looks at these quiet men with their childlike faces and apostles' beards. Any noncommissioned officer is more of an enemy to a recruit, any schoolmaster to a pupil than they are to us. And yet we would shoot at them again and they at us if they were free.

I am frightened: I dare think this way no more. This way lies the abyss. It is not now the time; but I will not lose these thoughts, I will keep them, shut them away until the war is ended. My heart beats fast: this is the aim, the great, the sole aim, that I have thought of in the trenches; that I have looked for as the only possibility of existence after this annihilation of all human feeling; this is a task that will make life afterward worthy of these hideous years.

I take out my cigarettes, break each one in half, and give them to the Russians. They bow to me and then they light the cigarettes. Now red points glow in every face. They comfort me; it looks as though there were little windows in dark village cottages saying that behind them are rooms full of peace.

The days go by. On a foggy morning another of the Russians is buried;

almost every day one of them dies. I am on guard during the burial. The prisoners sing a chorale, they sing in parts, and it sounds almost as if there were no voices, but an organ far away on the moor.

The burial is quickly over.

In the evening they stand again at the wire fence and the wind comes down to them from the beech woods. The stars are cold.

I now know a few of those who speak a little German. There is a musician among them, he says he used to be a violinist in Berlin. When he hears that I can play the piano he fetches his violin and plays. The others sit down and lean their backs against the fence. He stands up and plays, sometimes he has that absent expression which violinists get when they close their eyes; or again he sways the instrument to the rhythm and smiles across to me.

He plays mostly folk songs and the others hum with him. They are like a country of dark hills that sing far down under the ground. The sound of the violin stands like a slender girl above it and is clear and alone. The voices cease and the violin continues alone. In the night it is so thin it sounds frozen; one must stand close up; it would be much better in a room —out here it makes a man grow sad.

Because I have already had a long leave I get none on Sundays. So the last Sunday before I go back to the front my father and eldest sister come over to see me. All day we sit in the Soldiers' Home. Where else could we go, we don't want to stay in the camp. About midday we go for a walk on the moors.

The hours are a torture; we do not know what to talk about, so we speak of my mother's illness. It is now definitely cancer, she is already in the hospital and will be operated on shortly. The doctors hope she will recover, but we have never heard of cancer being cured.

"Where is she then?" I ask.

"In the Luisa Hospital," says my father.

"In which class?"

"Third. We must wait till we know what the operation costs. She wanted to be in the third herself. She said that then she would have some company. And besides it is cheaper."

"So she is lying there with all those people. If only she could sleep properly."

My father nods. His face is broken and full of furrows. My mother has always been sickly; and though she has only gone to the hospital when she has been compelled to, it has cost a great deal of money, and my father's life has been practically given up to it.

"If only I knew how much the operation costs," says he.

"Have you not asked?"

"Not directly, I cannot do that—the surgeon might take it amiss and that would not do, he must operate on Mother."

Yes, I think bitterly, that's how it is with us, and with all poor people. They don't dare to ask the price, but worry themselves dreadfully beforehand about it; but the others, for whom it is not important, they settle the price first as a matter of course. And the doctor does not take it amiss from them.

"And the dressings afterwards are so expensive," says my father.

"Doesn't the Invalids' Fund pay anything toward it, then?" I ask.

"Mother has been ill too long."

"Have you any money at all?"

He shakes his head: "No, but I can do some overtime."

I know. He will stand at his desk folding and pasting and cutting until twelve o'clock at night. At eight o'clock in the evening he will eat some of the miserable rubbish they get in exchange for their food tickets, then he will take a powder for his headache and work on.

In order to cheer him up a bit I tell him a few stories, soldiers' jokes, and the like, about generals and sergeant majors.

Afterwards I accompany them both to the railway station. They give me a pot of jam and a bag of potato cakes that my mother has made for me.

Then they go off and I return to the camp.

In the evening I spread the jam on the cakes and eat some. But I have no taste for them. So I go out to give them to the Russians. Then it occurs to me that my mother cooked them herself and that she was probably in pain as she stood before the hot stove. I put the bag back in my pack and take only two cakes to the Russians.

Chapter IX

WE travel for several days. The first airplanes appear in the sky. We roll on past transport lines. Guns, guns. The light railway picks us up. I search for my regiment. No one knows exactly where it lies. Somewhere or other I put up for the night, somewhere or other I receive provisions and a few vague instructions. And so with my pack and my rifle I set out again on the way.

By the time I come up they are no longer in that devastated place. I hear we have become one of the flying divisions that are pushed in wherever it is hottest. That does not sound cheerful to me. They tell me of heavy losses that we have been having. I inquire after Kat and Albert. No one knows anything of them.

I search farther and wander about here and there; it is a wonderful feeling. One night and then another I camp out like a Red Indian. Then at last I get some definite information, and by the afternoon I am able to report to the Orderly Room.

The sergeant major detains me there. The company comes back in two days' time. There is no object in sending me up now.

"What was it like on leave?" he asks, "pretty good, eh?"

"In parts," I say.

"Yes," he sighs, "yes, if a man didn't have to come away again. The second half is always rather messed up by that."

I loaf around until the company comes back in the early morning, gray, dirty, soured, and gloomy. Then I jump up, push in among them, my eyes searching. There is Tjaden, there is Müller blowing his nose, and there are Kat and Kropp. We arrange our sacks of straw side by side. I have an uneasy conscience when I look at them, and yet without any good reason. Before we turn in I bring out the rest of the potato cakes and jam so that they can have some too.

The two outer cakes are moldy, still it is possible to eat them. I keep those for myself and give the fresh ones to Kat and Kropp.

Kat chews and says: "These are from your mother?"

I nod.

"Good," says he, "I can tell by the taste."

I could almost weep. I can hardly control myself any longer. But it will soon be all right again back here with Kat and Albert. This is where I belong.

"You've been lucky," whispers Kropp to me before we drop off to sleep, "they say we are going to Russia."

To Russia. It's not much of a war over there.

In the distance the front thunders. The walls of the hut rattle.

There's a great deal of polishing being done. We are inspected at every turn. Everything that is torn is exchanged for new. I score a spotless new tunic out of it and Kat, of course, an entire outfit. A rumor is going round that there may be peace, but the other story is more likely—that we are bound for Russia. Still, what do we need new things for in Russia? At last it leaks out—the Kaiser is coming to review us. Hence all the inspections.

For eight whole days one would suppose we were in a base camp, there is so much drill and fuss. Everyone is peevish and touchy, we do not take kindly to all this polishing, much less to parades. Such things exasperate a soldier more than the front line.

At last the moment arrives. We stand up stiff and the Kaiser appears. We are curious to see what he looks like. He stalks along the line, and I am really rather disappointed; judging from his pictures I imagined him to be bigger and more powerfully built, and above all to have a thundering voice.

He distributes Iron Crosses and speaks to this man and to that. Then we march off.

Afterwards we discuss it. Tjaden says with astonishment:

"So that is the All-Highest! And everyone, bar nobody, has to stand up stiff in front of him!" He meditates: "Hindenburg too, he has to stand up stiff to him, eh?"

"Sure," says Kat.

Tjaden hasn't finished yet. He thinks for a while and then asks: "And would a king have to stand up stiff to an emperor?"

None of us is quite sure about it, but we don't suppose so. They are both so exalted that standing strictly to attention is probably not insisted on.

"What rot you do hatch out," says Kat. "The main point is that you have to stand stiff yourself."

But Tjaden is quite fascinated. His otherwise prosy fancy is blowing bubbles. "But look," he announces, "I simply can't believe that an emperor has to go to the latrine the same as I have."

"You can bet your boots on it."

"Four and a half-wit make seven," says Kat. "You've got a maggot in your brain, Tjaden, just you run along to the latrine quick, and get your head clear, so that you don't talk like a two-year-old."

Tjaden disappears.

"But what I would like to know," says Albert, "is whether there would not have been a war if the Kaiser had said No."

"I'm sure of this much," I interject, "he was against it from the first."

"Well, if not him alone, then perhaps if twenty or thirty people in the world had said No."

"That's probable," I agree, "but they damned well said Yes."

"It's queer, when one thinks about it," goes on Kropp, "we are here to protect our fatherland. And the French are over there to protect their fatherland. Now, who's in the right?"

"Perhaps both," say I, without believing it.

"Yes, well now," pursues Albert, and I see that he means to drive me into a corner, "but our professors and parsons and newspapers say that we are the only ones that are right, and let's hope so—but the French professors and parsons and newspapers say that the right is on their side, what about that?"

"That I don't know," I say, "but whichever way it is there's war all the same and every month more countries coming in."

Tjaden reappears. He is still quite excited and again joins the conversation, wondering just how a war gets started.

"Mostly by one country badly offending another," answers Albert with a slight air of superiority.

Then Tjaden pretends to be obtuse. "A country? I don't follow. A mountain in Germany cannot offend a mountain in France. Or a river, or a wood, or a field of wheat."

"Are you really as stupid as that, or are you just pulling my leg?" growls Kropp. "I don't mean that at all. One people offends the other——"

"Then I haven't any business here at all," replies Tjaden; "I don't feel myself offended."

"Well, let me tell you," says Albert sourly, "it doesn't apply to tramps like you."

"Then I can be going home right away," retorts Tjaden, and we all laugh.

"Ach, man! he means the people as a whole, the State——" exclaims Müller.

"State, State"—Tjaden snaps his fingers contemptuously—"gendarmes, police, taxes, that's your State!—if that's what you are talking about, no thank you."

"That's right," says Kat, "you've said something for once, Tjaden. State and home country, there's a big difference."

"But they go together," insists Kropp, "without the State there wouldn't be any home country."

"True, but just you consider, almost all of us are simple folk. And in France, too, the majority of men are laborers, workmen, or poor clerks. Now just why would a French blacksmith or a French shoemaker want to attack us? No, it is merely the rulers. I had never seen a Frenchman before I came here, and it will be just the same with the majority of Frenchmen as regards us. They weren't asked about it any more than we were."

"Then what exactly is the war for?" asks Tjaden.

Kat shrugs his shoulders. "There must be some people to whom the war is useful."

"Well, I'm not one of them," grins Tjaden.

"Not you, nor anybody else here."

"Who are they, then?" persists Tjaden. "It isn't any use to the Kaiser either. He has everything he can want already."

"I'm not so sure about that," contradicts Kat; "he has not had a war up till now. And every full-grown emperor requires at least one war, otherwise he wouldn't become famous. You look in your schoolbooks."

"And generals too," adds Detering, "they become famous through war."

"Even more famous than emperors," adds Kat.

"There are other people back behind there who profit by the war, that's certain," growls Detering.

"I think it is more a kind of fever," says Albert. "No one in particular wants it, and then all at once there it is. We didn't want the war, the others say the same thing—and yet half the world is in it all the same."

"But there are more lies told by the other side than by us," say I; "just think of those pamphlets the prisoners have on them, where it says that we eat Belgian children. The fellows who write that ought to go and hang themselves. They are the real culprits."

Müller gets up. "Anyway, it is better that the war is here instead of in Germany. Just you take a look at the shell holes."

"True," assents Tjaden, "but no war at all would be better still."

He is quite proud of himself because he has for once scored over us volunteers. And his opinion is quite typical here, one meets it time and again, and there is nothing with which one can properly counter it, because that is the limit of their comprehension of the factors involved. The national feeling of the soldier resolves itself into this—here he is. But that is the end of it; everything else from joining up onwards he criticizes from a practical point of view.

Albert lies down on the grass and growls angrily: "The best thing is not to talk about the rotten business."

"It won't make any difference, that's sure," agrees Kat.

As for the windfall, we have to return almost all the new things and take back our old rags again. The good ones were merely for the inspection.

Instead of going to Russia, we go up the line again. On the way we pass through a devastated wood with the tree trunks shattered and the ground plowed up.

At several places there are tremendous craters. "Great guns, something's hit that," I say to Kat.

"Trench mortars," he replies, and then points up at one of the trees.

In the branches dead men are hanging. A naked soldier is squatting in the fork of a tree, he still has his helmet on, otherwise he is entirely unclad. There is only half of him sitting up there, the top half, the legs are missing.

"What can that mean?" I ask.

"He's been blown out of his clothes," mutters Tjaden.

"It's funny," says Kat, "we have seen that a couple of times now. If a mortar gets you it blows you almost clean out of your clothes. It's the concussion that does it."

I search around. And so it is. Here hang bits of uniform, and somewhere else is plastered a bloody mess that was once a human limb. Over there lies a body with nothing but a piece of the underpants on one leg and the collar of the tunic around its neck. Otherwise it is naked and the clothes are hanging up in the tree. Both arms are missing as though they had been pulled out. I discover one of them twenty yards off in a shrub.

The dead man lies on his face. There, where the arm wounds are, the earth is black with blood. Underfoot the leaves are scratched up as though the man had been kicking.

"That's no joke, Kat," say I.

"No more is a shell splinter in the belly," he replies, shrugging his shoulders.

"But don't get tenderhearted," says Tjaden.

All this can only have happened a little while ago, the blood is still fresh. As everybody we see there is dead we do not waste any more time, but report the affair at the next stretcher bearers' post. After all, it is not our business to take these stretcher bearers' jobs away from them.

A patrol has to be sent out to discover just how far the enemy position is advanced. Since my leave I feel a certain strange attachment to the other fellows, and so I volunteer to go with them. We agree on a plan, slip out through the wire, and then divide and creep forward separately. After a while I find a shallow shell hole and crawl into it. From here I peer forward.

There is moderate machine-gun fire. It sweeps across from all directions, not very heavy, but always sufficient to make one keep down.

A parachute star shell opens out. The ground lies stark in the pale light, and then the darkness shuts down again blacker than ever. In the trenches we were told there were black troops in front of us. That is nasty, it is hard to see them; they are very good at patrolling, too. And oddly enough they are often quite stupid; for instance, both Kat and Kropp were once able to shoot down a black enemy patrol because the fellows in their enthusiasm for cigarettes smoked while they were creeping about. Kat and Albert had simply to aim at the glowing ends of the cigarettes.

A bomb or something lands close beside me. I have not heard it coming and am terrified. At the same moment a senseless fear takes hold on me. Here I am alone and almost helpless in the dark—perhaps two other eyes have been watching me for a long while from another shell hole in front of me, and a bomb lies ready to blow me to pieces. I try to pull myself together. It is not my first patrol and not a particularly risky one. But it is the first since my leave, and besides, the lie of the land is still rather strange to me.

I tell myself that my alarm is absurd, that there is probably nothing at all there in the darkness watching me, because otherwise the missile would not have landed so flat.

It is in vain. In whirling confusion my thoughts hum in my brain—I hear the warning voice of my mother, I see the Russians with the flowing beards leaning against the wire fence, I have a bright picture of a canteen with stools, of a cinema in Valenciennes; tormented, terrified, in my imagination I see the gray, impalpable muzzle of a rifle which moves noiselessly before me whichever way I try to turn my head. The sweat breaks out from every pore.

I still continue to lie in my shallow bowl. I look at the time; only a few minutes have passed. My forehead is wet, the sockets of my eyes are damp, my hands tremble, and I am panting softly. It is nothing but an awful spasm of fear, a simple animal fear of poking out my head and crawling on farther.

All my efforts subside like froth into the one desire to be able just to stay lying there. My limbs are glued to the earth. I make a vain attempt—they refuse to come away. I press myself down on the earth, I cannot go forward, I make up my mind to stay lying there.

But immediately the wave floods over me anew, a mingled sense of shame, of remorse, and yet at the same time of security. I raise myself up a little to take a look around.

My eyes burn with staring into the dark. A star shell goes up; I duck down again.

I wage a wild and senseless fight, I want to get out of the hollow and yet slide back into it again; I say: "You must, it is your comrades, it is not any idiotic command," and again: "What does it matter to me, I have only one life to lose——"

That is the result of all this leave, I reproach myself bitterly. But I cannot convince myself, I become terribly faint. I raise myself slowly and reach forward with my arms, dragging my body after me and then lie on the edge of the shell hole, half in and half out.

There I hear sounds and drop back. Suspicious sounds can be detected clearly despite the noise of the artillery fire. I listen; the sound is behind me. They are our people moving along the trench. Now I hear muffled voices. To judge by the tone that might be Kat talking.

At once a new warmth flows through me. These voices, these few quiet words, these footsteps in the trench behind me recall me at a bound from the terrible loneliness and fear of death by which I had been almost destroyed. They are more to me than life, these voices, they are more than motherliness and more than fear; they are the strongest, most comforting thing there is anywhere: they are the voices of my comrades.

I am no longer a shuddering speck of existence, alone in the darkness— I belong to them and they to me, we all share the same fear and the same life, we are nearer than lovers, in a simpler, a harder way; I could bury my face in them, in these voices, these words that have saved me and will stand by me.

Cautiously I glide out over the edge and snake my way forward. I shuffle along on all fours a bit farther, I keep track of my bearings, look around me, and observe the distribution of the gunfire so as to be able to find my way back. Then I try to get in touch with the others.

I am still afraid, but it is an intelligent fear, an extraordinarily heightened caution. The night is windy and shadows flit hither and thither in the flicker of the gunfire. It reveals too little and too much. Often I peer ahead, but always for nothing. Thus I advance a long way and then turn back in a wide curve. I have not established touch with the others. Every yard nearer our trench fills me with confidence—and with haste, too. It would be bad to get lost now.

Then a new fear lays hold of me. I can no longer remember the direction. Quiet, I squat in a shell hole and try to locate myself. More than once it has happened that some fellow has jumped joyfully into a trench only then to discover that it was the wrong one.

After a little time I listen again, but still I am not sure. The confusion of shell holes now seems so bewildering that I can no longer tell in my agitation which way I should go. Perhaps I am crawling parallel to the lines, and that might go on forever. So I crawl round once again in a wide curve.

These damned rockets! They seem to burn for an hour, and a man cannot make the least movement without bringing the bullets whistling round.

But there is nothing for it, I must get out. Falteringly, I work my way farther, I move off over the ground like a crab and rip my hands sorely on the jagged splinters, as sharp as razor blades. Often I think that the sky is becoming lighter on the horizon, but it may be merely my imagination. Then gradually I realize that to crawl in the right direction is a matter of life or death.

A shell crashes. Almost immediately two others. And then it begins in earnest. A bombardment. Machine guns rattle. Now there is nothing for it but to stay lying low. Apparently an attack is coming. Everywhere the rockets shoot up. Unceasing.

I lie huddled in a large shell hole, my legs in the water up to the belly. When the attack starts I will let myself fall into the water, with my face as deep in the mud as I can keep it without suffocating. I must pretend to be dead.

Suddenly I hear the barrage lift. At once I slip down into the water, my helmet on the nape of my neck and my mouth just clear so that I can get a breath of air.

I lie motionless; somewhere something clanks, it stamps and stumbles nearer—all my nerves become taut and icy. It clatters over me and away, the first wave has passed. I have but this one shattering thought: What will you do if someone jumps into your shell hole?—Swiftly I pull out my little dagger, grasp it fast, and bury it in my hand once again under the mud. If anyone jumps in here I will go for him—it hammers in my forehead—at once, stab him clean through the throat, so that he cannot call out; that's the only way; he will be just as frightened as I am, when in terror we fall upon one another—then I must be first.

Now our batteries are firing. A shell lands near me. That makes me savage with fury, all it needs now is to be killed by our own shells; I curse and grind my teeth in the mud; it is a raving frenzy; in the end all I can do is groan and pray.

The crash of the shells bursts in my ears. If our fellows make a counter-raid I will be saved. I press my head against the earth and listen to the muffled thunder, like the explosions of quarrying—and raise it again to listen for the sounds on top.

The machine guns rattle. I know our barbed-wire entanglements are strong and almost undamaged—parts of them are charged with a powerful electric current. The riflefire increases. They have not broken through; they have to retreat.

I sink down again, huddled, strained to the uttermost. The banging, the creeping, the clanging becomes audible. One single cry yelling among it all. They are raked with fire, the attack is repulsed.

Already it has become somewhat lighter. Steps hasten over me. The first. Gone. Again, another. The rattle of machine guns becomes an unbroken chain. Just as I am about to turn around a little, something heavy stumbles, and with a crash a body falls over me into the shell hole, slips down, and lies across me——

I do not think at all, I make no decision—I strike madly home, and feel only how the body suddenly convulses, then becomes limp, and collapses. When I recover myself, my hand is sticky and wet.

The man gurgles. It sounds to me as though he bellows, every gasping breath is like a cry, a thunder—but it is only my heart pounding. I want to stop his mouth, stuff it with earth, stab him again, he must be quiet, he is betraying me; now at last I regain control of myself, but have suddenly become so feeble that I cannot anymore lift my hand against him.

So I crawl away to the farthest corner and stay there, my eyes glued on him, my hand grasping the knife—ready, if he stirs, to spring at him again. But he won't do so anymore, I can hear that already in his gurgling.

I can see him indistinctly. I have but one desire, to get away. If it is not soon it will be too light; it will be difficult enough now. Then as I try to raise up my head I see it is impossible already. The machine-gun fire so sweeps the ground that I would be shot through and through before I could make one jump.

I test it once with my helmet, which I take off and hold up to find out the level of the shots. The next moment it is knocked out of my hand by a bullet. The fire is sweeping very low over the ground. I am not far enough from the enemy line to escape being picked off by one of the snipers if I attempt to get away.

The light increases. Burning I wait for our attack. My hands are white at the knuckles, I clench them so tightly in my longing for the fire to cease so that my comrades may come.

Minute after minute trickles away. I dare not look again at the dark figure in the shell hole. With an effort I look past it and wait, wait. The bullets hiss, they make a steel net, never ceasing, never ceasing.

Then I notice my bloody hand and suddenly feel nauseated. I take some earth and rub the skin with it, now my hand is muddy and the blood cannot be seen anymore.

The fire does not diminish. It is equally heavy from both sides. Our fellows have probably given me up for lost long ago.

It is early morning, clear and gray. The gurgling continues; I stop my ears, but soon take my fingers away again, because then I cannot hear the other sound.

The figure opposite me moves. I shrink together and involuntarily look at it. Then my eyes remain glued to it. A man with a small pointed beard lies there, his head is fallen to one side, one arm is half bent, his head rests helplessly upon it. The other hand lies on his chest, it is bloody.

He is dead, I say to myself, he must be dead, he doesn't feel anything anymore; it is only the body that is gurgling there. Then the head tries to raise itself, for a moment the groaning becomes louder, his forehead sinks back upon his arm. The man is not dead, he is dying, but he is not dead. I drag myself toward him, hesitate, support myself on my hands, creep a bit farther, wait, again a terrible journey of three yards, a long, a terrible journey. At last I am beside him.

Then he opens his eyes. He must have heard me and gazes at me with a look of utter terror. The body lies still, but in the eyes there is such an extraordinary expression of flight that for a moment I think they have power enough to carry the body off with them. Hundreds of miles away with one bound. The body is still, perfectly still, without sound, the gurgle has ceased, but the eyes cry out, yell, all the life is gathered together in them for one tremendous effort to flee, gathered together there in a dreadful terror of death, of me.

My legs give way and I drop on my elbows. "No, no," I whisper.

The eyes follow me. I am powerless to move so long as they are there.

Then his hand slips slowly from his breast, only a little bit, it sinks just a few inches, but this movement breaks the power of the eyes. I bend forward, shake my head, and whisper: "No, no, no." I raise one hand, I must show him that I want to help him, I stroke his forehead.

The eyes shrink back as the hand comes, then they lose their stare, the eyelids droop lower, the tension is past. I open his collar and place his head more comfortably upright.

His mouth stands half open, it tries to form words. The lips are dry. My water bottle is not there. I have not brought it with me. But there is water in the mud, down at the bottom of the crater. I climb down, take out my handkerchief, spread it out, push it under, and scoop up the yellow water that strains through into the hollow of my hand.

He gulps it down. I fetch some more. Then I unbutton his tunic in order to bandage him if it is possible. In any case I must do it, so that if the fellows over there capture me they will see that I wanted to help him, and so will not shoot me. He tries to resist, but his hand is too feeble. The shirt is stuck and will not come away, it is buttoned at the back. So there is nothing for it but to cut it off.

I look for the knife and find it again. But when I begin to cut the shirt the eyes open once more and the cry is in them again and the demented expression, so that I must close them, press them shut and whisper: "I want to help you, Comrade, *camerade, camerade, camerade*——" eagerly repeating the word, to make him understand.

There are three stabs. My field dressing covers them, the blood runs out under it, I press it tighter; he groans.

That is all I can do. Now we must wait, wait.

These hours. . . . The gurgling starts again—but how slowly a man dies! For this I know—he cannot be saved. Indeed, I have tried to tell myself that he will be, but at noon this pretense breaks down and melts before his groans. If only I had not lost my revolver crawling about, I would shoot him. Stab him I cannot.

By noon I am groping on the outer limits of reason. Hunger devours me, I could almost weep for something to eat, I cannot struggle against it. Again and again I fetch water for the dying man and drink some myself.

This is the first man I have killed with my hands, whom I can see close at hand, whose death is my doing. Kat and Kropp and Müller have experienced it already, when they have hit someone; it happens to many, in hand-to-hand fighting especially——

But every gasp lays my heart bare. This dying man has time with him, he has an invisible dagger with which he stabs me: Time and my thoughts.

I would give much if he would but stay alive. It is hard to lie here and to have to see and hear him.

In the afternoon, about three, he is dead.

I breathe freely again. But only for a short time. Soon the silence is more unbearable than the groans. I wish the gurgling were there again, gasping, hoarse, now whistling softly and again hoarse and loud.

It is mad, what I do. But I must do something. I prop the dead man up again so that he lies comfortably, although he feels nothing anymore. I close his eyes. They are brown, his hair is black and a bit curly at the sides.

The mouth is full and soft beneath his moustache; the nose is slightly arched, the skin brownish—it is now not so pale as it was before, when he was still alive. For a moment the face seems almost healthy—then it collapses suddenly into the strange face of the dead that I have so often seen, strange faces, all alike.

No doubt his wife still thinks of him; she does not know what has happened. He looks as if he would often have written to her; she will still be getting mail from him—tomorrow, in a week's time—perhaps even a stray letter a month hence. She will read it, and in it he will be speaking to her.

My state is getting worse, I can no longer control my thoughts. What would his wife look like? Like the little brunette on the other side of the canal? Does she belong to me now? Perhaps by this act she becomes mine. I wish Kantorek were sitting here beside me. If my mother could see me —— The dead man might have had thirty more years of life if only I had impressed the way back to our trench more sharply on my memory. If only he had run two yards farther to the left, he might now be sitting in the trench over there and writing a fresh letter to his wife.

But I will get no further that way; for that is the fate of all of us: if Kemmerich's leg had been six inches to the right; if Haie Westhus had bent his back three inches farther forward——

The silence spreads. I talk and must talk. So I speak to him and say to him: "Comrade, I did not want to kill you. If you jumped in here again, I would not do it, if you would be sensible too. But you were only an idea to me before, an abstraction that lived in my mind and called forth its appropriate response. It was that abstraction I stabbed. But now, for the first time, I see you are a man like me. I thought of your hand grenades, of your bayonet, of your rifle; now I see your wife and your face and our fellowship. Forgive me, comrade. We always see it too late. Why do they never tell us that you are just poor devils like us, that your mothers are just as anxious as ours, and that we have the same fear of death, and the same dying and the same agony—— Forgive me, comrade; how could you be my enemy? If we threw away these rifles and this uniform you could be my brother just like Kat and Albert. Take twenty years of my life, comrade, and stand up—take more, for I do not know what I can even attempt to do with it now.

It is quiet, the front is still except for the crackle of riflefire. The bullets rain over, they are not fired haphazard, but shrewdly aimed from all sides. I cannot get out.

"I will write to your wife," I say hastily to the dead man, "I will write to her, she must hear it from me, I will tell her everything I have told you, she shall not suffer, I will help her, and your parents too, and your child——"

His tunic is half open. The pocketbook is easy to find. But I hesitate to open it. In it is the book with his name. So long as I do not know his name perhaps I may still forget him, time will obliterate it, this picture. But his name, it is a nail that will be hammered into me and never come out again. It has the power to recall this forever, it will always come back and stand before me.

Irresolutely I take the wallet in my hand. It slips out of my hand and falls open. Some pictures and letters drop out. I gather them up and want to put them back again, but the strain I am under, the uncertainty, the hunger, the danger, these hours with the dead man have confused me; I want to hasten the relief, to intensify and to end the torture, as one strikes an unendurably painful hand against the trunk of a tree, regardless of everything.

There are portraits of a woman and a little girl, small amateur photographs taken against an ivy-clad wall. Along with them are letters. I take them out and try to read them. Most of it I do not understand, it is so hard to decipher and I know scarcely any French. But each word I translate pierces me like a shot in the chest—like a stab in the chest.

My brain is taxed beyond endurance. But I realize this much, that I will never dare to write to these people as I intended. Impossible. I look at the portraits once more; they are clearly not rich people. I might send them money anonymously if I earn anything later on. I seize upon that, it is at least something to hold on to. This dead man is bound up with my life, therefore I must do everything, promise everything, in order to save myself; I swear blindly that I mean to live only for his sake and his family, with wet lips I try to placate him—and deep down in me lies the hope that I may buy myself off in this way and perhaps even yet get out of this; it is a little strategem: if only I am allowed to escape, then I will see to it. So I open the book and read slowly: Gérard Duval, compositor.

With the dead man's pencil I write the address on an envelope, then swiftly thrust everything back into his tunic.

I have killed the printer, Gérard Duval. I must be a printer, I think confusedly, be a printer, printer——

By afternoon I am calmer. My fear was groundless. The name troubles me no more. The madness passes. "Comrade," I say to the dead man, but I say it calmly, "today you, tomorrow me. But if I come out of it, comrade, I will fight against this, that has struck us both down; from you, taken life —and from me——? Life also. I promise you, comrade. It shall never happen again."

The sun strikes low. I am stupefied with exhaustion and hunger. Yesterday is like a fog to me, there is no hope of getting out of this yet. I fall into a doze and do not at first realize that evening is approaching. The twilight comes. It seems to me to come quickly now. One hour more. If it were summer, it would be three hours more. One hour more.

Now suddenly I begin to tremble; something might happen in the interval. I think no more of the dead man, he is of no consequence to me now. With one bound the lust to live flares up again and everything that has filled my thoughts goes down before it. Now, merely to avert any ill luck, I babble mechanically: "I will fulfill everything, fulfill everything I have promised you——" But already I know that I shall not do so.

Suddenly it occurs to me that my own comrades may fire on me as I creep up; they do not know I am coming. I will call out as soon as I can so that they will recognize me. I will stay lying in front of the trench until they answer me.

The first star. The front remains quiet. I breathe deeply and talk to myself in my excitement: "No foolishness now, Paul—quiet, Paul, quiet— then you will be saved, Paul." When I use my Christian name, it works as though someone else spoke to me, it has more power.

The darkness grows. My excitement subsides, I wait cautiously until the first rocket goes up. Then I crawl out of the shell hole. I have forgotten the dead man. Before me lies the oncoming night and the pale gleaming field. I fix my eye on a shell hole; the moment the light dies I scurry over into it, grope farther, spring into the next, duck down, scramble onward.

I come nearer. There, by the light of a rocket, I see something move in the wire, then it stiffens and lies still. Next time I see it again, yes, they are men from our trench. But I am suspicious until I recognize our helmets. Then I call. And immediately an answer rings out, my name: "Paul— Paul———"

I call again in answer. It is Kat and Albert who have come out with a stretcher to look for me.

"Are you wounded?"

"No, no———"

We drop into the trench. I ask for something to eat and wolf it down. Müller gives me a cigarette. In a few words I tell what happened. There is nothing new about it; it happens quite often. The night attack is the only unusual feature of the business. In Russia Kat once lay for two days behind the enemy lines before he could make his way back.

I do not mention the dead printer.

But by next morning I can keep it to myself no longer. I must tell Kat and Albert. They both try to calm me. "You can't do anything about it. What else could you have done? That is what you are here for."

I listen to them and feel comforted, reassured by their presence. It was mere driveling nonsense that I talked out there in the shell hole.

"Look there for instance," points Kat.

On the fire step stand some snipers. They rest their rifles with telescopic sights on the parapet and watch the enemy front. Once and again a shot cracks out.

Then we hear the cry: "That's found a billet!" "Did you see how he leaped in the air?" Sergeant Oellrich turns round proudly and scores his points. He heads the shooting list for today with three unquestionable hits.

"What do you say to that?" asks Kat.

I nod.

"If he keeps that up he will get a little colored bird for his buttonhole by this evening," says Albert.

"Or rather he will soon be made acting sergeant major," says Kat.

We look at one another. "I would not do it," I say.

"All the same," says Kat, "it's very good for you to see it just now."

Sergeant Oellrich returns to the fire step. The muzzle of his rifle searches to and fro.

"You don't need to lose any more sleep over your affair," nods Albert.

And now I hardly understand it myself anymore.

"It was only because I had to lie there with him so long," I say. "After all, war is war."

Oellrich's rifle cracks out sharp and dry.

Chapter X

WE have dropped in for a good job. Eight of us have to guard a village that has been abandoned because it is being shelled too heavily.

In particular we have to watch the supply dump as that is not yet empty. We are supposed to provision ourselves from the same store. We are just the right people for that—Kat, Albert, Müller, Tjaden, Detering, our whole gang is there. Haie is dead, though. But we are mighty lucky all the same, all the other squads have had more casualties than we have.

We select, as a dugout, a reinforced concrete cellar into which steps lead down from above. The entrance is protected by a separate concrete wall.

Now we develop an immense industry. This is an opportunity not only to stretch one's legs, but to stretch one's soul also. We make the best use of such opportunities. The war is too desperate to allow us to be sentimental for long. That is only possible so long as things are not going too badly. After all, we cannot afford to be anything but matter-of-fact. So matter-of-fact, indeed, that I often shudder when a thought from the days before the war comes momentarily into my head. But it does not stay long.

We have to take things as lightly as we can, so we make the most of every opportunity, and nonsense stands stark and immediate beside horror. It cannot be otherwise, that is how we hearten ourselves. So we zealously set to work to create an idyll—an idyll of eating and sleeping, of course.

The floor is first covered with mattresses which we haul in from the houses. Even a soldier's behind likes to sit soft. Only in the middle of the floor is there any clear space. Then we furnish ourselves with blankets and eiderdowns, luxurious soft affairs. There is plenty of everything to be had in the town. Albert and I find a mahogany bed which can be taken to pieces, with a sky of blue silk and a lace coverlet. We sweat like monkeys moving it in, but a man cannot let a thing like that slip, and it would certainly be shot to pieces in a day or two.

Kat and I do a little patrolling through the houses. In a very short time we have collected a dozen eggs and two pounds of fairly fresh butter. Suddenly there is a crash in the drawing room, and an iron stove hurtles through the wall past us and on, a yard from us out through the wall behind. Two holes. It comes from the house opposite where a shell has just landed. "The swine," grimaces Kat, and we continue our search. All at once we prick up our ears, hurry across, and suddenly stand petrified—there running up and down in a little sty are two live suckling pigs. We rub our eyes and look once again to make certain. Yes, they are still there. We seize hold of them—no doubt about it, two real young pigs.

This will make a grand feed. About twenty yards from our dugout there is a small house that was used as an officers' billet. In the kitchen is an immense fireplace with two ranges, pots, pans, and kettles—everything, even to a stack of small chopped wood in an outhouse—a regular cook's paradise.

Two of our fellows have been out in the fields all the morning hunting for potatoes, carrots, and green peas. We are quite uppish and sniff at the tinned stuff in the supply dump, we want fresh vegetables. In the dining room there are already two heads of cauliflower.

The suckling pigs are slaughtered. Kat sees to them. We want to make potato cakes to go with the roast. But we cannot find a grater for the potatoes. However, that difficulty is soon got over. With a nail we punch a lot of holes in a potlid and there we have a grater. Three fellows put on thick gloves to protect their fingers against the grater, two others peel the potatoes, and the business gets going.

Kat samples the suckling pigs, the carrots, the peas, and the cauliflower. He even mixes a white sauce for the cauliflower. I fry the pancakes, four at a time. After ten minutes I get the knack of tossing the pan so that the pancakes which are done on the one side sail up, turn in the air and are caught again as they come down. The suckling pigs are baked whole. We all stand round them as before an altar.

In the meantime we receive visitors, a couple of radiomen, who are generously invited to the feed. They sit in the living room where there is a piano. One of them plays, the other sings "An der Weser." He sings feelingly, but with a rather Saxon accent. All the same it moves us as we stand at the fireplace preparing the good things.

Then we begin to realize that we are in for trouble. The observation balloons have spotted the smoke from our chimney, and the shells start to drop on us. They are those damned spraying little daisy cutters that make only a small hole and scatter widely close to the ground. They keep dropping closer and closer all round us; still we cannot leave the grub in the lurch. A couple of splinters whizz through the top of the kitchen window. The roast is already cooked. But frying the pancakes is getting difficult. The explosions come so fast that the splinters strike oftener and oftener against the wall of the house and sweep in through the window. Whenever I hear a shell coming I drop down on one knee with the pan and the pancakes, and duck behind the wall of the window. Immediately afterwards I am up again and going on with the frying.

The Saxons stop singing—a fragment has smashed into the piano. At last everything is ready and we organize the transport of it back to the dugout. After the next explosion two men dash across the fifty yards to the dugout with the pots of vegetables. We see them disappear.

The next shot. Everyone ducks and then two more trot off, each with a big can of finest grade coffee, and reach the dugout before the next explosion.

Then Kat and Kropp seize the masterpiece—the big dish with the brown, roasted suckling pigs. A screech, a knee bend, and away they race over the fifty yards of open country.

I stay to finish frying my last four pancakes; twice I have to drop on the floor—after all, it means four pancakes more, and they are my favorite dish.

Then I grab the plate with the great pile of cakes and squeeze myself behind the housedoor. A hiss, a crash, and I gallop off with the plate clamped against my chest with both hands. I am almost in, I run like a deer, sweep round the wall, fragments clatter against the concrete, I tumble down the cellar steps, my elbows are skinned, but I have not lost a single pancake, nor even broken the plate.

About two o'clock we start the meal. It lasts till six. We drink coffee until half-past seven—officers' coffee from the supply dump—and smoke officers' cigars and cigarettes—also from the supply dump. Punctually at half-past seven we begin the evening meal. About ten o'clock we throw the bones of the suckling pigs outside the door. Then there is cognac and rum— also from the blessed supply dump—and once again long, fat cigars with bellybands. Tjaden suggests that it lacks only one thing: girls from an officers' brothel.

Late in the evening we hear mewing. A little gray cat sits in the entrance. We entice it in and give it something to eat. And that wakes up our own appetites once more. Still chewing, we lie down to sleep. But the night is bad. We have eaten too much fat. Fresh baby pig is very griping to the bowels. There is an everlasting coming and going in the dugout.

Burning houses stand out like torches against the night. Shells lumber across and crash down. Munition columns tear along the street. On one side the supply dump has been ripped open. In spite of all the flying fragments the drivers of the munition columns pour in like a swarm of bees and pounce on the bread. We let them have their own way. If we said anything it would only mean a good hiding for us. So we go differently about it. We explain that we are the guard and so know our way about, we get hold of the tinned stuff and exchange it for things we are short of. What does it matter anyhow—in a while it will all be blown to pieces. For ourselves we take some chocolate from the depot and eat it in slabs. Kat says it is good for loose bowels.

Almost a fortnight passes thus in eating, drinking, and roaming about.

No one disturbs us. The town gradually vanishes under the shells and we lead a charmed life. So long as any part of the supply dump still stands we don't worry, we desire nothing better than to stay here till the end of the war.

Tjaden has become so fastidious that he only half smokes his cigars. With his nose in the air he explains to us that he was brought up that way. And Kat is most cheerful. In the morning his first call is: "Emil, bring in the caviar and coffee." We put on extraordinary airs, every man treats the other as his valet, bounces him and gives him orders. "There is something itching under my foot; Kropp, my man, catch that louse at once," says Leer, poking out his leg at him like a ballet girl, and Albert drags him up the stairs by the foot. "Tjaden!"—"What?"—"Stand at ease, Tjaden; and what's more, don't say 'What,' say 'Yes, Sir'—now: Tjaden!" Tjaden retorts in the well-known phrase from Goethe's "Götz von Berlichingen," with which he is always very free.

After eight more days we receive orders to go back. The palmy days are over. Two big motor trucks take us away. They are stacked high with planks. Nevertheless, Albert and I erect on top our four-poster bed complete with blue silk canopy, mattress, and two lace coverlets. And behind it at the head is stowed a bagful of choice edibles. We often dip into it, and the tough ham sausages, the tins of liver sausages, the conserves, the boxes of cigarettes rejoice our hearts. Each man has a bag to himself.

Kropp and I have rescued two big red armchairs as well. They stand inside the bed, and we sprawl back in them as in a theater box. Above us swells the silken cover like a baldachin. Each man has a long cigar in his mouth. And thus from aloft we survey the scene.

Between us stands a parrot cage that we found for the cat. She is coming with us, and lies in the cage before her saucer of meat, and purrs.

Slowly the trucks roll down the road. We sing. Behind us the shells are sending up fountains from the now utterly abandoned town.

A few days later we are sent out to evacuate a village. On the way we meet the fleeing inhabitants trundling their goods and chattels along with them in wheelbarrows, perambulators, and on their backs. Their figures are bent, their faces full of grief, despair, haste, and resignation. The children hold on to their mothers' hands, and often an older girl leads the little ones, who stumble onward and are forever looking back. A few carry miserable-looking dolls. All are silent as they pass us by.

We are marching in column; the French do not fire on a town in which there are still inhabitants. But a few minutes later the air screams, the earth heaves, cries ring out; a shell has landed among the rear squad. We scatter and fling ourselves down on the ground, but at that moment I feel the instinctive alertness leave me which hitherto has always made me do unconsciously the right thing under fire; the thought leaps up with a terrible, throttling fear: "You are lost"—and the next moment a blow sweeps like a whip over my left leg. I hear Albert cry out; he is beside me.

"Quick, up, Albert!" I yell, for we are lying unsheltered in the open field.

He staggers up and runs. I keep beside him. We have to get over a hedge; it is higher than we are. Kropp seizes a branch, I heave him up by the leg, he cries out, I give him a swing and he flies over. With one leap I follow him and fall into a ditch that lies behind the hedge.

Our faces are smothered with duckweed and mud, but the cover is good. So we wade in up to our necks. Whenever a shell whistles we duck our heads under the water. After we have done this a dozen times, I am exhausted.

"Let's get away, or I'll fall in and drown," groans Albert.

"Where has it got you?" I ask him.

"In the knee, I think."

"Can you run?"

"I think——"

"Then out!"

We make for the ditch beside the road, and stooping, run along it. The shelling follows us. The road leads toward the munition dump. If that goes up there won't be a man of us with his head left on his shoulders. So we change our plan and run diagonally across country.

Albert begins to drag. "You go, I'll come on after," he says, and throws himself down.

I seize him by the arm and shake him. "Up, Albert, if once you lie down you'll never get any farther. Quick, I'll hold you up."

At last we reach a small dugout. Kropp pitches in and I bandage him up. The shot is just a little above his knee. Then I take a look at myself. My trousers are bloody and my arm, too. Albert binds up my wounds with his field dressing. Already he is no longer able to move his leg, and we both wonder how we managed to get this far. Fear alone made it possible; we would have run even if our feet had been shot off—we would have run on the stumps.

I can still crawl a little. I call out to a passing ambulance wagon, which picks us up. It is full of wounded. There is an army medical lance corporal with it who sticks an antitetanus needle into our chests.

At the dressing station we arrange matters so that we lie side by side. They give us a thin soup which we spoon down greedily and scornfully, because we are accustomed to better times but are hungry all the same.

"Now for home, Albert," I say.

"Let's hope so," he replies; "I only wish I knew what I've got."

The pain increases. The bandages burn like fire. We drink and drink, one glass of water after another.

"How far above the knee am I hit?" asks Kropp.

"At least four inches, Albert," I answer. Actually it is perhaps one.

"I've made up my mind," he says after a while, "if they take off my leg, I'll put an end to it. I won't go through life as a cripple."

So we lie there with our thoughts and wait.

In the evening we are hauled onto the chopping block. I am frightened and think quickly what I ought to do; for everyone knows that the surgeons in the dressing stations amputate on the slightest provocation. Under the great pressure of business that is much simpler than complicated patching. I think of Kemmerich. Whatever happens I will not let them chloroform me, even if I have to crack a couple of their skulls.

It is all right. The surgeon pokes around in the wound and a blackness comes before my eyes. "Don't carry on so," he says gruffly, and hacks away. The instruments gleam in the bright light like malevolent animals. The pain is insufferable. Two orderlies hold my arms fast, but I break loose with one of them and try to crash into the surgeon's spectacles just as he notices and springs back. "Chloroform the scoundrel," he roars madly.

Then I become quiet. "Pardon me, Herr Doctor, I will keep still, but do not chloroform me."

"Well now," he cackles, and takes up his instrument again. He is a fair fellow, not more than thirty years old, with scars and disgusting gold spectacles. Now I see that he is tormenting me, he is merely raking about in the wound and looking up surreptitiously at me over his glasses. My hands squeeze around the grips—I'll kick the bucket before he will get a squeak out of me.

He has fished out a piece of shell and tosses it to me. Apparently he is pleased at my self-control, for he seems to be more considerate of me now and says: "Tomorrow you'll be off home." Then I am put in plaster. When I am back again with Kropp I tell him that apparently a hospital train comes in tomorrow morning.

"We must work the army medical sergeant major so that we can keep together, Albert."

I manage to slip the sergeant major two of my cigars with bellybands, and then tip the word to him. He smells the cigars and says: "Have you got any more of them?"

"Another good handful," I say, "and my comrade," I point to Kropp, "he has some as well. We might possibly be glad to hand them to you out of the window of the hospital train in the morning."

He understands, of course, smells them once again and says: "Done."

We cannot get a minute's sleep all night. Seven fellows die in our ward. One of them sings hymns in a high cracked tenor before he begins to gurgle. Another has crept out of his bed to the window. He lies in front of it as though he wants to look out for the last time.

Our stretchers stand on the platform. We wait for the train. It rains and the station has no roof. Our covers are thin. We have waited already two hours.

The sergeant major looks after us like a mother. Although I feel pretty bad I do not let our scheme out of my mind. Occasionally I let him see the packet and give him one cigar in advance. In exchange the sergeant major covers us over with a waterproof sheet.

"Albert, old man, I suddenly bethink myself, our four-poster and the cat——"

"And the club chairs," he adds.

Yes, the club chairs with red plush. In the evening we used to sit in them like lords, and intended later on to let them out by the hour. One cigarette per hour. It might have turned into a regular business, a real good living.

"And our bags of grub, too, Albert."

We grow melancholy. We might have made some use of the things. If only the train left one day later Kat would be sure to find us and bring us the stuff.

What damned hard luck! In our bellies there is gruel, mean hospital stuff, and in our bags roast pork. But we are so weak that we cannot work up any more excitement about it.

The stretchers are sopping wet by the time the train arrives in the morning. The sergeant major sees to it that we are put in the same car. There is a crowd of Red Cross nurses. Kropp is stowed in below. I am lifted up and put into the bed above him.

"Good God!" I exclaim suddenly.

"What is it?" asks the sister.

I cast a glance at the bed. It is covered with clean snow-white linen, that even has the marks of the iron still on it. And my shirt has gone six weeks without being washed and is terribly muddy.

"Can't you get in by yourself?" asks the sister gently.

"Why yes," I say in a sweat, "but take off the bed cover first."

"What for?"

I feel like a pig. Must I get in there?—"It will get——" I hesitate.

"A little bit dirty?" she suggests helpfully. "That doesn't matter, we will wash it again afterwards."

"No, no, not that——" I say excitedly. I am not equal to such overwhelming refinement.

"When you have been lying out there in the trenches, surely we can wash a sheet," she goes on.

I look at her, she is young and crisp, spotless and neat, like everything here; a man cannot realize that it isn't for officers only, and feels himself strange and in some way even alarmed.

All the same, the woman is a tormentor, she is going to force me to say it. "It is only——" I try again—surely she must know what I mean.

"What is it, then?"

"Because of the lice," I bawl out at last.

She laughs. "Well, they must have a good day for once, too."

Now I don't care anymore. I scramble into bed and pull up the covers.

A hand gropes over the bedcover. The sergeant major. He goes off with the cigars.

An hour later we notice that we are moving.

At night I cannot sleep. Kropp is restless too. The train rides easily over the rails. I cannot realize it all yet; a bed, a train, home. "Albert!" I whisper.

"Yes——"

"Do you know where the latrine is?"

"Over to the right of the door, I think."

"I'm going to have a look." It is dark, I grope for the edge of the bed and cautiously try to slide down. But my foot finds no support, I begin to slip, the plaster leg is no help, and with a crash I lie on the floor.

"Damn!" I say.

"Have you bumped yourself?" asks Kropp.

"You could hear that well enough for yourself," I growl, "my head——"

A door opens in the rear of the car. The sister comes with a light and looks at me.

"He has fallen out of bed——"

She feels my pulse and smoothes my forehead. "You haven't any fever, though."

"No," I agree.

"Have you been dreaming then?" she asks.

"Perhaps——" I evade. The interrogation starts again. She looks at me with her clear eyes, and the more wonderful and sweet she is the less am I able to tell her what I want.

I am lifted up into bed again. That will be all right. As soon as she goes I must try to climb down again. If she were an old woman, it might be easier to say what a man wants, but she is so very young, at the most twenty-five—it can't be done, I cannot possibly tell her.

Then Albert comes to my rescue, he is not bashful, it makes no difference to him who is upset. He calls to the sister. She turns around. "Sister, he wants——" but no more does Albert know how to express it modestly and decently. Out there we say it in a single word, but here, to such a lady —— All at once he remembers his school days and finishes hastily: "He wants to leave the room, sister."

"Ah!" says the sister, "but he shouldn't climb out of his bed with his plaster bandage. What do you want then?" she says, turning to me.

I am in mortal terror at this new turn, for I haven't any idea what the things are called professionally. She comes to my help.

"Little or big?"

This shocking business! I sweat like a pig and say shyly: "Well, only quite a little one——"

At any rate, it produces the effect.

I get a bottle. After a few hours I am no longer the only one, and by morning we are quite accustomed to it and ask for what we want without any false modesty.

The train travels slowly. Sometimes it halts and the dead are unloaded. It halts often.

Albert is feverish. I feel miserable and have a good deal of pain, but the worst of it is that apparently there are still lice under the plaster bandage. They itch terribly, and I cannot scratch myself.

We sleep through the days. The country glides quietly past the window. The third night we reach Herstal. I hear from the sister that Albert is to be put off at the next station because of his fever. "How far does the train go?" I ask.

"To Cologne."

"Albert," I say, "we stick together; you see."

On the sister's next round I hold my breath and press it up into my head. My face swells and turns red. She stops. "Are you in pain?" "Yes," I groan, "all of a sudden."

She gives me a thermometer and goes on. I would not have been under Kat's tuition if I did not know what to do now. These army thermometers are not made for old soldiers. All one has to do is to drive the quicksilver up and then it stays there without falling again.

I stick the thermometer under my arm at a slant, and flip it steadily with my forefinger. Then I give it a shake. I send it up to 100.2°. But that is not enough. A match held cautiously near to it brings it up to 101.6°.

As the sister comes back, I blow myself out, breathe in short gasps, goggle at her with vacant eyes, toss about restlessly, and mutter in a whisper: "I can't bear it any longer——"

She notes me down on a slip of paper. I know perfectly well my plaster bandage will not be reopened if it can be avoided.

Albert and I are put off together.

We are in the same room in a Catholic hospital. That is a piece of luck, the Catholic infirmaries are noted for their good treatment and good food. The hospital has been filled up from our train, there are a great many bad cases among them. We do not get examined today because there are too few surgeons. The flat trolleys with the rubber wheels pass continually along the corridor, and always with someone stretched at full length upon them. A damnable position, stretched out at full length like that—the only time it is good is when one is asleep.

The night is very disturbed. No one can sleep. Toward morning we doze a little. I wake up just as it grows light. The door stands open and I hear voices from the corridor. The others wake up too. One fellow, who has been there a couple of days already, explains it to us: "Up here in the corridor every morning the sisters say prayers. They call it Morning Devotion. And so that you can get your share, they leave the door open."

No doubt it is well meant, but it gives us aches in our heads and bones.

"Such an absurdity!" I say. "Just when a man dropped off to sleep."

"All the light cases are up here, that's why they do it here," he replies.

Albert groans. I get furious and call out: "Be quiet out there!"

A minute later a sister appears. In her black and white dress she looks like a beautiful tea cozy. "Shut the door, will you, sister?" says someone.

"We are saying prayers, that is why the door is open," she responds.

"But we want to go on sleeping——"

"Prayer is better than sleep." She stands there and smiles innocently. "And it is seven o'clock already."

Albert groans again. "Shut the door," I snort.

She is quite disconcerted. Apparently she cannot understand. "But we are saying prayers for you too."

"Shut the door, anyway."

She disappears, leaving the door open. The intoning of the Litany proceeds.

I feel savage, and say: "I'm going to count up to three. If it doesn't stop before then I'll let something fly."

"Me, too," says another.

I count up to five. Then I take hold of a bottle, aim, and heave it through the door into the corridor. It smashes into a thousand pieces. The praying stops. A swarm of sisters appear and reproach us in concert.

"Shut the door!" we yell.

They withdraw. The little one who came first is the last to go. "Heathen," she chirps, but shuts the door all the same. We have won.

At noon the hospital inspector arrives and abuses us. He threatens us with clink and all the rest of it. But a hospital inspector is just the same as a commissariat inspector, or anyone else who wears a long dagger and shoulder straps, but is really a clerk, and is never considered even by a recruit as a real officer. So we let him talk. What can they do to us, anyway——

"Who threw the bottle?" he asks.

Before I can think whether I should report myself, someone says: "I did."

A man with a bristling beard sits up. Everyone is excited; why should he report himself?

"You?"

"Yes. I was annoyed because we were waked up unnecessarily and lost my senses so that I did not know what I was doing."

He talks like a book.

"What is your name?"

"Reinforcement-Reservist Josef Hamacher."

The inspector departs.

We are all curious. "But why did you say you did it? It wasn't you at all!"

He grins. "That doesn't matter. I have a shooting license."

Then, of course, we all understand. Whoever has a shooting license can do just whatever he pleases.

"Yes," he explains, "I got a crack in the head and they presented me with a certificate to say that I was periodically not responsible for my actions. Ever since then I've had a grand time. No one dares to annoy me. And nobody does anything to me.

"I reported myself because the shot amused me. If they open the door again tomorrow we will pitch another."

We are overjoyed. With Josef Hamacher in our midst we can now risk anything.

Then come the soundless, flat trollies to take us away.

The bandages are stuck fast. We bellow like steers.

There are eight men in our room. Peter, a curly black-haired fellow, has the worst injury—a severe lung wound. Franz Wächter, alongside him, has a shot in the arm which didn't look too bad at first. But the third night he calls out to us, telling us to ring, he thinks he has a hemorrhage.

I ring loudly. The night sister does not come. We have been making rather heavy demands on her during the night, because we have all been freshly bandaged, and so have a good deal of pain. One wants his leg placed so, another so, a third wants water, a fourth wants her to shake up his pillow—in the end the buxom old body grumbled bad-temperedly and slammed the doors. Now, no doubt, she thinks it is something of the same sort and so she is not coming.

We wait. Then Franz says: "Ring again."

I do so. Still she does not put in an appearance. In our wing there is only one night sister, perhaps she has something to do in one of the other rooms. "Franz, are you quite sure you are bleeding?" I ask. "Otherwise we shall be getting cursed again."

"The bandage is wet. Can't anybody make a light?"

That cannot be done either. The switch is by the door and none of us can stand up. I hold my thumb against the button of the bell till it becomes numb. Perhaps the sister has fallen asleep. They certainly have a great deal to do and are overworked day after day. And added to that is the everlasting praying.

"Should we smash a bottle?" asks Josef Hamacher of the shooting license.

"She wouldn't hear that any more than the bell."

At last the door opens. The old lady appears, mumbling. When she perceives Franz's trouble she begins to bustle, and says: "Why did not someone say I was wanted?"

"We did ring. And none of us here can walk."

He has been bleeding badly and she binds him up. In the morning we look at his face; it has become sharp and yellow, whereas the evening before he looked almost healthy. Now a sister comes oftener.

Sometimes there are Red Cross voluntary-aid sisters. They are pleasant, but often rather unskilled. They frequently give us pain when remaking our beds, and then are so frightened that they hurt us still more.

The nuns are more reliable. They know how they must take hold of us, but we would be more pleased if they were somewhat more cheerful. A few of them have real spirit, they are superb. There is no one who would not do anything for Sister Libertine, this marvelous sister, who spreads good cheer through the whole wing even when she can only be seen in the distance. And there are others like her. We would go through fire for her. A man cannot really complain, here he is treated by the nuns exactly like a civilian. On the other hand, just to think of a garrison hospital gives a man the creeps.

Franz Wächter does not regain his strength. One day he is taken away and does not come back. Josef Hamacher knows all about it: "We shan't see him again. They have put him in the Dead Room."

"What do you mean, Dead Room?" asks Kropp.

"Well, Dying Room——"

"What is that, then?"

"A little room at the corner of the building. Whoever is about to kick the bucket is put in there. There are two beds in it. It is generally called the Dying Room."

"But what do they do that for?"

"They don't have so much work to do afterwards. It is more convenient, too, because it lies right beside the lift to the mortuary. Perhaps also they do it for the sake of the others, so that no one in the ward dies in sympathy. And they can look after him better, too, if he is by himself."

"But what about him?"

Josef shrugs his shoulders. "Usually he doesn't take much notice anymore."

"Does everybody know about it, then?"

"Anyone who has been here long enough knows, of course."

In the afternoon Franz Wächter's bed has a fresh occupant. A couple of days later they take the new man away too. Josef makes a significant gesture. We see many come and go.

Often relatives sit by the beds and weep or talk softly and awkwardly. One old woman will not go away, but she cannot stay there the whole night through. Another morning she comes very early, but not early enough; for as she goes up to the bed, someone else is in it already. She has to go to the mortuary. The apples that she has brought with her she gives to us.

And then little Peter begins to get worse. His temperature chart looks bad, and one day the flat trolley stands beside his bed. "Where to?" he asks.

"To the bandaging ward."

He is lifted out. But the sister makes the mistake of removing his tunic from the hook and putting it on the trolley too, so that she should not have to make two journeys. Peter understands immediately and tries to roll off the trolley. "I'm stopping here!"

They push him back. He cries out feebly with his shattered lung. "I won't go to the Dying Room."

"But we are going to the bandaging ward."

"Then what do you want my tunic for?" He can speak no more. Hoarse, agitated, he whispers: "Stopping here!"

They do not answer but wheel him out. At the door he tries to raise himself up. His black curly head sways, his eyes are full of tears. "I will come back again! I will come back again!" he cries.

The door shuts. We are all excited; but we say nothing. At last Josef says: "Many a man has said that. Once a man is in there, he never comes through."

I am operated on and vomit for two days. My bones will not grow together, so the surgeon's secretary says. Another fellow's have grown crooked; his are broken again. It is disgusting.

Among our new arrivals there are two young soldiers with flat feet. The chief surgeon discovers them on his rounds and is overjoyed. "We'll soon put that right," he tells them, "we will just do a small operation, and then you will have perfectly sound feet. Enter them down, sister."

As soon as he is gone, Josef, who knows everything, warns them: "Don't you let him operate on you! That is a special scientific stunt of the old boy's. He goes absolutely crazy whenever he can get hold of anyone to do it on. He operates on you for flat feet, and there's no mistake, you don't have them anymore; you have club feet instead, and have to walk all the rest of your life on sticks."

"What should a man do, then?" asks one of them.

"Say No. You are here to be cured of your wound, not your flat feet. Did you have any trouble with them in the field? No, well, there you are! At present you can still walk, but if once the old boy gets you under the knife you'll be cripples. What he wants is little dogs to experiment with, so the war is a glorious time for him, as it is for all the surgeons. You take a look down below at the staff; there are a dozen fellows hobbling around that he has operated on. A lot of them have been here all the time since 'fourteen and 'fifteen. Not a single one of them can walk better than he could before, almost all of them worse, and most only with plaster legs. Every six months he catches them again and breaks their bones afresh, and every time is going to be the successful one. You take my word, he won't dare to do it if you say No."

"Ach, man," says one of the two unfortunates, "better your feet than your brain box. There's no telling what you'll get if you go back out there again. They can do with me just as they please, so long as I get back home. Better to have a club foot than be dead."

The other, a young fellow like ourselves, won't have it done. One morning the old man has the two hauled up and lectures and jaws at them so long that in the end they consent. What else could they do?—They are mere privates, and he is a big bug. They are brought back chloroformed and plastered.

It is going badly with Albert. They have taken him and amputated his leg. The whole leg has been taken off from the thigh. Now he hardly speaks anymore. Once he says he will shoot himself the first time he can get hold of his revolver again.

A new convoy arrives. Our room gets two blind men. One of them is a very youthful musician. The sisters never have a knife with them when they feed him; he has already snatched one from a sister. But in spite of this caution there is an incident. In the evening, while he is being fed, the sister is called away and leaves the plate with the fork on his table. He gropes for the fork, seizes it, and drives it with all his force against his heart, then he snatches up a shoe and strikes with it against the handle as hard as he can. We call for help and three men are necessary to take the fork away from him. The blunt prongs had already penetrated deep. He abuses us all night so that no one can go to sleep. In the morning he has lockjaw.

Again beds become empty. Day after day goes by with pain and fear, groans and death gurgles. Even the Death Room is no use anymore, it is too small; fellows die during the night in our room. They go even faster than the sisters can cope with them.

But one day the door flies open, the flat trolley rolls in, and there on the stretcher, pale, thin, upright and triumphant, with his shaggy head of curls, sits Peter. Sister Libertine with beaming looks pushes him over to his former bed. He is back from the Dying Room. We have long supposed him dead.

He looks round: "What do you say now?"

And even Josef has to admit that it is the first time he has ever known of such a thing.

Gradually a few of us venture to stand up. And I am given crutches to hobble around on. But I do not make much use of them; I cannot bear Albert's gaze as I move about the room. His eyes always follow me with such a strange look. So I sometimes escape to the corridor—there I can move about more freely.

On the next floor below are the abdominal and spine cases, head wounds, and double amputations. On the right side of the wing are the jaw wounds, gas cases, nose, ear, and neck wounds. On the left the blind and the lung wounds, pelvis wounds, wounds in the joints, wounds in the testicles, wounds in the intestines. Here a man realizes for the first time in how many places a man can get hit.

Two fellows die of tetanus. Their skin turns pale, their limbs stiffen, at last only their eyes live—stubbornly. Many of the wounded have their shattered limbs hanging free in the air from a gallows; underneath the wound a basin is placed into which the pus drips. Every two or three hours the vessel is emptied. Other men lie in stretching bandages with heavy weights hanging from the end of the bed. I see intestine wounds that are constantly full of excreta. The surgeon's clerk shows me X-ray photographs of completely smashed hipbones, knees, and shoulders.

A man cannot realize that above such shattered bodies there are still human faces in which life goes its daily round. And this is only one hospital, one single station; there are hundreds of thousands in Germany, hundreds of thousands in France, hundreds of thousands in Russia. How senseless is everything that can ever be written, done, or thought, when such things are possible. It must all be lies and of no account when the culture of a thousand years could not prevent this stream of blood being poured out, these torture chambers in their hundreds of thousands. A hospital alone shows what war is.

I am young, I am twenty years old; yet I know nothing of life but despair, death, fear, and fatuous superficiality cast over an abyss of sorrow. I see how peoples are set against one another, and in silence, unknowingly, foolishly, obediently, innocently slay one another. I see that the keenest brains of the world invent weapons and words to make it yet more refined and enduring. And all men of my age, here and over there, throughout the whole world, see these things; all my generation is experiencing these things with me. What would our fathers do if we suddenly stood up and came before them and proffered our account? What do they expect of us if a time ever comes when the war is over? Through the years our business has been killing—it was our first calling in life. Our knowledge of life is limited to death. What will happen afterwards? And what shall come out of us?

After a few weeks I have to go each morning to the massage department. There my leg is harnessed up and made to move. The arm has healed long since.

New convoys arrive from the line. The bandages are no longer made of cloth, but of white crêpe paper. Rag bandages have become scarce at the front.

Albert's stump heals well. The wound is almost closed. In a few weeks he should go off to an institute for artificial limbs. He continues not to talk much and is much more solemn than formerly. He often breaks off in his speech and stares in front of him. If he were not here with us he would have shot himself long ago. But now he is over the worst of it, and he often looks on while we play skat.

I get convalescent leave.

My mother does not want to let me go away. She is so feeble. It is all much worse than it was last time.

Then I am sent on from the base and return once more to the line.

Parting from my friend Albert Kropp was very hard. But a man gets used to that sort of thing in the army.

Chapter XI

WE count the weeks no more. It was winter when I came up, and when the shells exploded the frozen clods of earth were just as dangerous as the fragments. Now the trees are green again. Our life alternates between billets and the front. We have almost grown accustomed to it; war is a cause of death—like cancer and tuberculosis, like influenza and dysentery. The deaths are merely more frequent, more varied and terrible.

Our thoughts are clay, they are molded with the changes of the days—when we are resting they are good; under fire, they are dead. Fields of craters within and without.

Everyone is so, not only ourselves here—the things that existed before are no longer valid, and one practically knows them no more. Distinctions, breeding, education are changed, are almost blotted out and hardly recognizable any longer. Sometimes they give an advantage for profiting by a situation—but they also bring consequences along with them, in that they arouse prejudices which have to be overcome. It is as though formerly we were coins of different provinces; and now we are melted down, and all bear the same stamp. To rediscover the old distinctions, the metal itself must be tested. First we are soldiers and afterwards, in a strange and shamefaced fashion, individual men as well.

It is a great brotherhood, which to a condition of life arising out of the midst of danger, out of the tension and forlornness of death, adds something of the good-fellowship of the folk song, of the feeling of solidarity of convicts, and of the desperate loyalty to one another of men condemned to death—seeking in a wholly unpathetic way a fleeting enjoyment of the hours as they come. If one wants to appraise it, it is at once heroic and banal—but who wants to do that?

It is this, for example, that makes Tjaden spoon down his ham-and-pea soup in such tearing haste when an enemy attack is reported, simply because he cannot be sure that in an hour's time he will still be alive. We have discussed at length whether it is right or not to do so. Kat condemns it, because, he says, a man has to reckon with the possibility of an abdominal wound, and that is more dangerous on a full stomach than on an empty one.

Such things are real problems, they are serious matters to us, they cannot be otherwise. Here, on the borders of death, life follows an amazingly simple course, it is limited to what is most necessary, all else lies buried in gloomy sleep—in that lies our primitiveness and our survival. Were we more subtly differentiated we must long since have gone mad, have deserted, or have fallen. As in a polar expedition, every expression of life must serve only the preservation of existence and is absolutely focused on that. All else is banished because it would consume energies unnecessarily. That is the only way to save ourselves. In the quiet hours when the puzzling reflection of former days, like a blurred mirror, projects beyond me the figure of my present existence, I often sit over against myself, as before a stranger, and wonder how the unnameable active principle that calls itself Life has adapted itself even to this form. All other expressions lie in a winter sleep; life is simply one continual watch against the menace of death—it has transformed us into unthinking animals in order to give us the weapon of instinct—it has reinforced us with dullness so that we do not go to pieces before the horror, which would overwhelm us if we had clear, conscious thought—it has awakened in us the sense of comradeship, so that we escape the abyss of solitude—it has lent us the indifference of wild creatures so that in spite of all, we perceive the positive in every moment and store it up as a reserve against the onslaught of nothingness. Thus we live a closed, hard existence of the utmost superficiality, and rarely does an incident strike out a spark. But then unexpectedly a flame of grievous and terrible yearning flares up.

Those are the dangerous moments. They show us that the adjustment is only artificial, that it is not simple rest, but sharpest struggle for rest. In the outward form of our life we are hardly distinguishable from Bushmen; but whereas the latter can be so always, because they are so truly, and at best may develop further by exertion of their spiritual forces, with us it is the reverse—our inner forces are not exerted toward regeneration, but toward degeneration. The Bushmen are primitive and naturally so, but we are primitive in an artificial sense, and by virtue of the utmost effort.

And at night, waking out of a dream, overwhelmed and bewitched by the crowding faces, a man perceives with alarm how slight is the support, how thin the boundary that divides him from the darkness. We are little flames poorly sheltered by frail walls against the storm of dissolution and madness, in which we flicker and sometimes almost go out. Then the muffled roar of the battle becomes a ring that encircles us, we creep in upon ourselves, and with big eyes stare into the night. Our only comfort is the steady breathing of our comrades asleep, and thus we wait for the morning.

Every day and every hour, every shell and every death cuts into this thin support, and the years waste it rapidly. I see how it is already gradually breaking down around me.

There is the mad story of Detering.

He was one of those who kept himself to himself. His misfortune was that he saw a cherry tree in a garden. We were just coming back from the front line, and at a turning of the road near our new billets, marvelous in the morning twilight, stood this cherry tree before us. It had no leaves, but was one white mass of blossom.

In the evening Detering was not to be seen. Then at last he came back and had a couple of branches of cherry blossom in his hand. We made fun of him, and asked whether he was going to a wedding. He made no answer, but laid them on his bed. During the night I heard him making a noise, he seemed to be packing. I sensed something amiss and went over to him. He made out it was nothing, and I said to him: "Don't do anything silly, Detering."

"Ach, why—it's merely that I can't sleep——"

"What did you pick the cherry branches for?"

"I might have been going to get some more cherry branches," he replied, evasively—and after a while: "I have a big orchard with cherry trees at home. When they are in blossom, from the hay loft they look like one single sheet, so white. It is just the time."

"Perhaps you will get leave soon. You may even be sent back as a farmer."

He nodded, but he was far away. When these peasants are excited they have a curious expression, a mixture of cow and yearning god, half stupid and half rapt. In order to turn him away from his thoughts I asked him for a piece of bread. He gave it to me without a murmur. That was suspicious, for he is usually tightfisted. So I stayed awake. Nothing happened; in the morning he was as usual.

Apparently he had noticed that I had been watching him—but the second morning after, he was gone. I noticed it but said nothing, in order to give him time; he might perhaps get through. Various fellows have already got into Holland.

But at roll call he was missed. A week after, we heard that he had been caught by the field gendarmes, those despicable military police. He had headed toward Germany, that was hopeless, of course—and, of course, he did everything else just as idiotically. Anyone might have known that his flight was only homesickness and a momentary aberration. But what does a court-martial hundreds of miles behind the front line know about it? We have heard nothing more of Detering.

But sometimes it broke out in other ways, this danger, these pent-up things, as from an overheated boiler. It will be enough to tell how Berger met his end.

Our trenches have now for some time been shot to pieces, and we have an elastic line, so that there is practically no longer any proper trench warfare. When attack and counterattack have waged backwards and forwards there remains a broken line and a bitter struggle from crater to crater. The front line has been penetrated, and everywhere small groups have established themselves—the fight is carried on from clusters of shell holes.

We are in a crater, the English are coming down obliquely, they are turning our flank and working in behind us. We are surrounded. It is not easy to surrender, fog and smoke hang over us, no one would recognize that we wanted to give ourselves up, and perhaps we don't want to, a man doesn't even know himself at such moments. We hear the explosions of the hand grenades coming toward us. Our machine gun sweeps over the semi-circle in front of us. The cooling-water evaporates, we hastily pass round the case, every man urinates in it, and thus we again have water, and are able to continue firing. But behind us the attack crashes ever nearer.

A few minutes and we are lost.

Then, at closest range, a second machine gun bursts out. It is set up in a crater alongside us; Berger has fetched it, and now the counterattack comes over from behind; we are set free and make contact with the rear.

Afterwards, as we lie in comparatively good cover, one of the food carriers reports that a couple of hundred yards distant there lies a wounded messenger dog.

"Where?" asks Berger.

The other describes the place to him. Berger goes off either to fetch the beast in or to shoot it. Six months ago he would not have cared, he would have been reasonable. We try to prevent him. Then, as he goes off grimly, all we can say is: "You're mad," and let him go. For these cases of front-line madness become dangerous if one is not able to fling the man to the ground and hold him fast. And Berger is six feet and the most powerful man in the company.

He is absolutely mad, for he has to pass through the barrage; but this lightning that lowers somewhere above us all has struck him and made him demented. It affects others so that they begin to rave, to run away—there was one man who even tried to dig himself into the ground with hands, feet, and teeth.

It is true, such things are often simulated, but the pretense itself is a symptom. Berger, who means to finish off the dog, is carried off with a wound in the pelvis, and one of the fellows who carry him gets a bullet in the cheek while doing it.

Müller is dead. Someone shot him point blank with a Verey light[6] in the stomach. He lived for half an hour, quite conscious, and in terrible pain.

---

[6] *Verey light*: a flare.

Before he died he handed over his pocketbook to me, and bequeathed me his boots—the same that he once inherited from Kemmerich. I wear them, for they fit me quite well. After me Tjaden will get them, I have promised them to him.

We have been able to bury Müller, but he is not likely to remain long undisturbed. Our lines are falling back. There are too many fresh English and American regiments over there. There's too much corned beef and white wheaten bread. Too many new guns. Too many airplanes.

But we are emaciated and starved. Our food is so bad and mixed up with so much substitute stuff that it makes us ill. The factory owners in Germany have grown wealthy—dysentery dissolves our bowels. The latrine poles are always densely crowded; the people at home ought to be shown these gray, yellow, miserable, wasted faces here, these bent figures from whose bodies the colic wrings out the blood, and who with lips trembling and distorted with pain, grin at one another and say: "It is not much sense pulling up one's trousers again——"

Our artillery is fired out, it has too few shells and the barrels are so worn that they shoot uncertainly, and scatter so widely as even to fall on ourselves. We have too few horses. Our fresh troops are anemic boys in need of rest, who cannot carry a pack, but merely know how to die. By thousands. They understand nothing about warfare, they simply go on and let themselves be shot down. A single flyer routed two companies of them for a joke, just as they came fresh from the train—before they had ever heard of such a thing as cover.

"Germany ought to be empty soon," says Kat.

We have given up hope that someday an end may come. We never think so far. A man can stop a bullet and be killed; he can get wounded, and then the hospital is his next stop. There, if they do not amputate him, he sooner or later falls into the hands of one of those staff surgeons who, with the War Service Cross in his buttonhole, says to him: "What, one leg a bit short? If you have any pluck you don't need to run at the front. The man is A1. Dismiss!"

Kat tells a story that has traveled the whole length of the front from the Vosges to Flanders—of the staff surgeon who reads the names on the list, and when a man comes before him, without looking up says: "A1. We need soldiers up there." A fellow with a wooden leg comes up before him, the staff surgeon again says A1——"And then," Kat raises his voice, "the fellow says to him: 'I already have a wooden leg, but when I go back again and they shoot off my head, then I will get a wooden head made and become a staff surgeon.'" This answer tickles us all immensely.

There may be good doctors, and there are, lots of them; all the same, every soldier some time during his hundreds of inspections falls into the clutches of one of these countless hero-grabbers who pride themselves on changing as many C3's and B3's as possible into A1's.

There are many such stories, they are mostly far more bitter. All the same, they have nothing to do with mutiny or lead-swinging. They are merely honest and call a thing by its name; for there is a very great deal of fraud, injustice, and baseness in the army.——Is it nothing that regiment after regiment returns again and again to the ever more hopeless struggle, that attack follows attack along the weakening, retreating, crumbling line?

From a mockery the tanks have become a terrible weapon. Armored they come rolling on in long lines, and more than anything else embody for us the horror of war.

We do not see the guns that bombard us; the attacking lines of the enemy infantry are men like ourselves; but these tanks are machines, their caterpillars run on as endless as the war, they are annihilation, they roll without feeling into the craters, and climb up again without stopping, a fleet of roaring, smoke-belching armor-clads, invulnerable steel beasts squashing the dead and the wounded—we shrivel up in our thin skin before them, against their colossal weight our arms are sticks of straw, and our hand grenades matches.

Shells, gas clouds, and flotillas of tanks—shattering, starvation, death.

Dysentery, influenza, typhus—murder, burning, death.

Trenches, hospitals, the common grave—there are no other possibilities.

In one attack our company commander, Bertinck, falls. He was one of those superb front-line officers who are foremost in every hot place. He was with us for two years without being wounded, so that something had to happen in the end.

We occupy a crater and get surrounded. The stink of petroleum or oil blows across with the fumes of powder. Two fellows with a flamethrower are seen, one carries the tin on his back, the other has the hose in his hands from which the fire spouts. If they get so near that they can reach us we are done for, we cannot retreat yet.

We open fire on them. But they work nearer and things begin to look bad. Bertinck is lying in the hole with us. When he sees that we cannot escape because under the sharp fire we must make the most of this cover, he takes a rifle, crawls out of the hole, and lying down propped on his elbows, he takes aim. He fires—the same moment a bullet smacks into him, they have got him. Still he lies and aims again—once he shifts and again takes his aim; at last the rifle cracks. Bertinck lets the gun drop and says: "Good," and slips back into the hole. The hindmost of the two flame-throwers is hit, he falls, the hose slips away from the other fellow, the fire squirts about on all sides, and the man burns.

Bertinck has a chest wound. After a while a fragment smashes away his chin, and the same fragment has sufficient force to tear open Leer's hip. Leer groans as he supports himself on his arm, he bleeds quickly, no one can help him. Like an emptying tube, after a couple of minutes he collapses.

What use is it to him now that he was such a good mathematician at school?

The months pass by. The summer of 1918 is the most bloody and the most terrible. The days stand like angels in gold and blue, incomprehensible, above the ring of annihilation. Every man here knows that we are losing the war. Not much is said about it. We are falling back, we will not be able to attack again after this big offensive, we have no more men and no more ammunition.

Still the campaign goes on—the dying goes on——

Summer of 1918— Never has life in its niggardliness seemed to us so desirable as now—the red poppies in the meadows round our billets, the smooth beetles on the blades of grass, the warm evenings in the cool, dim rooms, the black, mysterious trees of the twilight, the stars and the flowing waters, dreams and long sleep—— O Life, life, life!

Summer of 1918—Never was so much silently suffered as in the moment when we depart once again for the front line. Wild, tormenting rumors of an armistice and peace are in the air, they lay hold on our hearts and make the return to the front harder than ever.

Summer of 1918—Never was life in the line more bitter and more full of horror than in the hours of the bombardment, when the blanched faces lie in the dirt, and the hands clutch at the one thought: No! No! Not now! Not now at the last moment!

Summer of 1918—Breath of hope that sweeps over the scorched fields, raging fever of impatience, of disappointment, of the most agonizing terror of death, insensate question: Why? Why do they not make an end? And why do these rumors of an end fly about?

There are so many airmen here, and they are so sure of themselves that they give chase to single individuals, just as though they were hares. For every one German plane there come at least five English and American. For one hungry, wretched German soldier come five of the enemy, fresh and fit. For one German army loaf there are fifty tins of canned beef over there. We are not beaten, for as soldiers we are better and more experienced; we are simply crushed and driven back by overwhelmingly superior forces.

Behind us lie rainy weeks—gray sky, gray fluid earth, gray dying. If we go out, the rain at once soaks through our overcoat and clothing—and we remain wet all the time we are in the line. We never get dry. Those who still wear high boots tie sandbags round the top so that the mud does not pour in so fast. The rifles are caked, the uniforms caked, everything is fluid and dissolved, the earth one dripping, soaked, oily mass in which lie the yellow pools with red spiral streams of blood and into which the dead, wounded, and survivors slowly sink down.

The storm lashes us, out of the confusion of gray and yellow the hail of splinters whips forth the childlike cries of the wounded, and in the night shattered life groans wearily to the silence.

Our hands are earth, our bodies clay, and our eyes pools of rain. We do not know whether we still live.

Then the heat sinks heavily into our shell holes like a jellyfish, moist and oppressive, and on one of these late summer days, while bringing food, Kat falls. We two are alone. I bind up his wound; his shin seems to be smashed. It has got the bone, and Kat groans desperately: "At last—just at the last——"

I comfort him. "Who knows how long the mess will go on yet! Now you are saved——"

The wound begins to bleed fast. Kat cannot be left by himself while I try to find a stretcher. Anyway, I don't know of a stretcher bearers' post in the neighborhood.

Kat is not very heavy; so I take him up on my back and start off to the dressing station with him.

Twice we rest. He suffers acutely on the way. We do not speak much. I have opened the collar of my tunic and breathe heavily, I sweat and my face is swollen with the strain of carrying. All the same I urge him to let us go on, for the place is dangerous.

"Shall we go on again, Kat?"

"Must, Paul."

"Then come."

I raise him up, he stands on the uninjured leg and supports himself against a tree. I take up the wounded leg carefully, then he gives a jump and I take the knee of the sound leg also under my arm.

The going is more difficult. Often a shell whistles across. I go as quickly as I can, for the blood from Kat's wound drips to the ground. We cannot shelter ourselves properly from the explosions; before we can take cover the danger is all over.

We lie down in a small shell hole to rest. I give Kat some tea from my water bottle. We smoke a cigarette. "Well, Kat," I say gloomily, "we are going to be separated at last."

He is silent and looks at me.

"Do you remember, Kat, how we commandeered the goose? And how you brought me out of the barrage when I was still a young recruit and was wounded for the first time? I cried then. Kat, that is almost three years ago."

He nods.

The anguish of solitude rises up in me. When Kat is taken away I will not have one friend left.

"Kat, in any case we must see one another again, if it is peacetime before you come back."

"Do you think that I will be marked A1 again with this leg?" he asks bitterly.

"With rest it will get better. The joint is all right. It may limp a bit."

"Give me another cigarette," he says.

"Perhaps we could do something together later on, Kat." I am very miserable, it is impossible that Kat—Kat my friend, Kat with the drooping shoulders and the poor, thin moustache, Kat, whom I know as I know no other man, Kat with whom I have shared these years—it is impossible that perhaps I shall not see Kat again.

"In any case give me your address at home, Kat. And here is mine, I will write it down for you."

I write his address in my pocketbook. How forlorn I am already, though he still sits here beside me. Couldn't I shoot myself quickly in the foot so as to be able to go with him?

Suddenly Kat gurgles and turns green and yellow. "Let us go on," he stammers.

I jump up, eager to help him. I take him up and start off at a run, a slow steady pace, so as not to jolt his leg too much.

My throat is parched; everything dances red and black before my eyes; I stagger on doggedly and pitilessly and at last reach the dressing station.

There I drop down on my knees, but have still enough strength to fall onto the side where Kat's sound leg is. After a few minutes I straighten myself up again. My legs and my hands tremble. I have trouble in finding my water bottle, to take a pull. My lips tremble as I try to drink. But I smile—Kat is saved.

After a while I begin to sort out the confusion of voices that falls on my ears.

"You might have spared yourself that," says an orderly.

I look at him without comprehending.

He points to Kat. "He is stone dead."

I do not understand him. "He has been hit in the shin," I say.

The orderly stands still. "That as well."

I turn around. My eyes are still dulled, the sweat breaks out on me again, it runs over my eyelids. I wipe it away and peer at Kat. He lies still. "Fainted," I say quickly.

The orderly whistles softly. "I know better than that. He is dead. I'll lay any money on that."

I shake my head: "Not possible. Only ten minutes ago I was talking to him. He has fainted."

Kat's hands are warm, I pass my arm under his shoulders in order to rub his temples with some tea. I feel my fingers become moist. As I draw them away from behind his head, they are bloody. "You see——" The orderly whistles once more through his teeth.

On the way without my having noticed it, Kat has caught a splinter in the head. There is just one little hole, it must have been a very tiny, stray splinter. But it has sufficed. Kat is dead.

Slowly I get up.

"Would you like to take his paybook and his things?" the lance corporal asks me.

I nod, and he gives them to me.

The orderly is mystified. "You are not related, are you?"

No, we are not related. No, we are not related.

Do I walk? Have I feet still? I raise my eyes, I let them move round and turn myself with them, one circle, one circle, and I stand in the midst. All is as usual. Only the Militiaman Stanislaus Katczinsky has died.

Then I know nothing more.

Chapter XII

IT is autumn. There are not many of the old hands left. I am the last of the seven fellows from our class.

Everyone talks of peace and armistice. All wait. If it again proves an illusion, then they will break up; hope is high, it cannot be taken away again without an upheaval. If there is not peace, then there will be revolution.

I have fourteen days' rest, because I have swallowed a bit of gas; in a little garden I sit the whole day long in the sun. The armistice is coming soon, I believe it now too. Then we will go home.

Here my thoughts stop and will not go any further. All that meets me, all that floods over me are but feelings—greed of life, love of home, yearning of the blood, intoxication of deliverance. But no aims.

Had we returned home in 1916, out of the suffering and the strength of our experiences we might have unleashed a storm. Now if we go back we will be weary, broken, burned out, rootless, and without hope. We will not be able to find our way anymore.

And men will not understand us—for the generation that grew up before us, though it has passed these years with us here, already had a home and a calling; now it will return to its old occupations, and the war will be forgotten—and the generation that has grown up after us will be strange to us and push us aside. We will be superfluous even to ourselves, we will grow older, a few will adapt themselves, some others will merely submit, and most will be bewildered—the years will pass by and in the end we shall fall into ruin.

But perhaps all this that I think is mere melancholy and dismay, which will fly away as the dust, when I stand once again beneath the poplars and listen to the rustling of their leaves. It cannot be that it has gone, the yearning that made our blood unquiet, the unknown, the perplexing, the oncoming things, the thousand faces of the future, the melodies from dreams and from books, the whispers and divinations of women—it cannot be that this has vanished in bombardment, in despair, in brothels.

Here the trees show gay and golden, the berries of the rowan stand red among the leaves, country roads run white out to the skyline, and the canteens hum like beehives with rumors of peace.

I stand up.

I am very quiet. Let the months and years come—they bring me nothing more, they can bring me nothing more. I am so alone, and so without hope that I can confront them without fear. The life that has borne me through these years is still in my hands and my eyes. Whether I have subdued it, I know not. But so long as it is there it will seek its own way out, heedless of the will that is within me.

He fell in October, 1918, on a day that was so quiet and still on the whole front, that the army report confined itself to the single sentence: All quiet on the Western Front.

He had fallen forward and lay on the earth as though sleeping. Turning him over one saw that he could not have suffered long; his face had an expression of calm, as though almost glad the end had come.

LOVE

Chienniang

LIN YUTANG

W ANG CHOU, a young boy of seventeen, had lost his father and was now alone. Steady and more mature than his age indicates, he was old enough to shift for himself. His father had told him on his deathbed that he should go to live with his aunt, who was living in the south at Hengchow, and had reminded him that he was betrothed to his cousin. This was a promise between his father and the father's sister when the babies were being expected; they had said that in case one was a boy and the other a girl, they would be betrothed to each other. Wang Chou disposed of the house and set out to the south accordingly. The young boy's mind was enlivened by the hope of seeing a girl cousin whom he had not seen since the age of six, when his father received an appointment in the north. He wondered how she had grown and whether she was still the fragile, affectionate child who used to cling to him as a play companion and wonder at all his doings. He had better hurry, Wang Chou thought, for a girl of seventeen might be betrothed to someone else if he did not show up. But the voyage was slow, and it took him a full month to come down the Hsiang River and then the Tungting Lake and finally reach the mountain city of Hengchow.

His uncle, Chang Yi, ran a shop dealing in herbs and medicinal products. He was a broad-jowled, heavy-voiced man. Every day for the past twenty-five years, he had gone to the shop as regularly as a clock, and he had never traveled or taken a holiday. Cautious, thrifty, and conservative, he had slowly built up his business until he was now quite well-to-do. He had expanded his shop to do wholesale business, added to his property, and built a new house. When Wang Chou saw him at the shop, the uncle growled, "What do you come here for?"

Wang Chou told him. He knew his uncle was a simple and timid man at heart, who wanted only to pay his taxes and have the good opinion of his neighbors. Sober and unimaginative, he had never relaxed from his stern appearance as an elder, having enough trouble keeping himself in the straight and narrow path.

He was taken to the uncle's new house, and announced himself as a relative from Taiyuan. The aunt was away at the moment.

Soon he saw a young girl in a blue dress come into the parlor. Chien-niang had grown up into a beautiful girl with a very slender figure; she wore a braid of black hair over her shoulder. Her silken smooth face flushed at the sight of her cousin. After a moment's hesitation, she let out a small scream and cried, "You are brother Chou!"

"You are sister Chien!"

The girl was so excited that her eyes filled with tears. "How you have grown!" cried the young girl, eyeing her handsome cousin.

"And so have you!" exclaimed Wang Chou.

Wang Chou looked at the girl with unconcealed admiration, especially with his father's dying words in mind. Soon they were lost in a busy exchange of news of the families and random recollections of their childhood. She had a younger brother, several years her junior, who was greatly surprised to see a total stranger who called himself his cousin. They had been separated so long that the family hardly ever spoke of him.

When the mother came back, she gave a hearty, warm welcome to this son of her deceased brother. She was a woman with clear-cut features, a very delicate complexion, and graying hair. A shy, sensitive woman, her lips constantly quivered when she smiled. He informed her that he had finished the district school and did not know what he was going to do next, and she informed him in turn that his uncle's business was doing well.

"I can see that. You are living in such a beautiful house," said the nephew.

"Your uncle is a very funny man. It took a long time of persuasion on my part and that of the children to get him to move into the new house after he had built it. He is even now regretting how many dollars he is losing by not renting it out. You stay with us. I will ask your uncle to give you a job at the shop. Do your part and don't be afraid of his big voice."

The uncle never came home until evening, and when he did, he was as gruff and as uncommunicative as he had been that morning. The death of his brother-in-law did not seem to concern him, and Wang Chou felt very much like a poor relative and an orphaned young man to be put to the test of apprenticeship. But the aunt was kind and a gentle creature. She was much better educated than her husband and seemed to look upon her husband's businesslike and authoritative attitude with light amusement, although she always obeyed his wishes. She had seen to it, too, that Chienniang received a perfect education through private tutoring. There was just nothing to talk about at dinner, because the mother and daughter did not understand business, and the father was not much interested in anything else. With his stern appearance and his naturally big voice, he had established himself as the head of the family.

In time, the nephew settled down as a permanent member of the family. Nothing was said about the promised betrothal, which was of course verbal between the aunt and her brother when they were both expecting babies. To Wang Chou, the girl in the blue dress would be his choice even if there had been no such promise. Chienniang found Wang Chou's quiet and reserved disposition very much to her liking, too, and as they were thrown into each other's company, before long she had given her heart completely to him.

The mother saw the new happiness on Chienniang's face. When Chienniang cooked something special for the family, she felt as if she were cooking for Wang Chou alone, and a new happiness and pride welled up in her heart. Step by step, she forgot her youthful bashfulness and took over the mending of his clothing and looking after his laundry; she assumed a sort of prior right to take care of him. There was no definite division of jobs, for the daughter was being trained to look after the general household, although they had several maids, but the business of cleaning his room and looking after his comforts fell naturally to her. Chienniang would not even permit her younger brother to upset things in his room.

The mother knew that she loved him. One day she said to her daughter dryly, "Chienniang, I see that our dishes are getting more and more salty these days."

Chienniang blushed, for Wang Chou had several times complained that the dishes were not salty enough.

Wang Chou had never dreamed that life could be so sweet and beautiful. He did not mind putting up with his gruff uncle at the shop; he would do anything for the sake of Chienniang and to be near her. Loving Chienniang, he loved all that was connected with her. He felt toward his aunt as if she were his own mother and played with the little boy as if he were his own brother. The father seldom talked at dinner or indulged in jokes with the family, but he was away all day, and was often invited out to business dinners in the evenings.

The Hengchow climate was changeful, varying to extremes between sudden storms coming over the mountains and a scorching heat when the sun was out. Once Wang Chou fell sick and found it so comfortable to lie in bed all day at home, served by his cousin, that he stayed in bed longer than was necessary.

"Now you must go to the shop, or my father will be angry," Chienniang said to him.

"Must I?" asked Wang Chou reluctantly.

One day Chienniang said to him, "You must put more clothing on. I think it is going to rain. If you get sick again, I will be angry with you."

"I would love to," replied Wang Chou impishly, and she understood what he meant.

"Don't be silly," said Chienniang, pouting her lips, and she made him put on extra clothing.

One day Chienniang's elder aunt, the wife of her father's brother, arrived from Changan for a visit. The brother was an extremely wealthy man. He had helped Chang Yi, the girl's father, found the shop with his money; their property was not yet divided and Chang Yi still retained that devotion to his brother which amounted to fear and servile respect for the head of the family. The aunt was royally treated. Family devotion, and Chang Yi's timid nature and natural respect for wealth, both could account for his attitude toward this elder aunt. The best dinners were served every day, and Chang Yi talked and joked at dinner and tried to make himself pleasant to the elder aunt in a way that he had not talked and joked with his wife.

The elder aunt found nothing more pleasant and agreeable than to arrange a match with a rich family for her niece. One day returning from a party with the wealthiest family of the town, the Tsiangs, she said to the girl's mother, in the girl's hearing, "Chienniang is a sweet girl and she is eighteen. I am arranging a match for her with the second son of the Tsiangs. You know of course who the Tsiangs are, and I mean *the* Tsiangs."

"My dear sister-in-law, I have betrothed Chienniang to my brother's son," replied the mother.

"You mean that nephew staying with you? But your brother is already dead."

"That does not make any difference. They seem wonderfully suited to each other." Chienniang, hearing her mother taking the nephew's side, blushed.

The elder aunt broke into loud laughter. "You are crazy! What has he got? I am talking about a respectable match with a decent family with some social standing like ourselves."

Chienniang rose from her seat, left the room, and slammed the door.

"What an ungrateful girl!" the elder aunt shouted after her. "She does not realize what I am doing for her. You have never seen their garden home. Don't be a weak mother. You will thank me when you see the inside of their house. Why, their mistress wears a diamond ring almost as big as mine."

The mother did not reply, and excused herself. But the elder aunt, having thought of this match as her best recreation during her stay, would not give up. An engagement would mean dinners and parties, her holiday would be filled with social activities, and she would be happy to have accomplished something memorable during her short stay. But if the mother resisted her suggestion, the elder aunt found in the father of the girl a ready, appreciative, and delighted listener. Chang Yi could not conceive of anything more gratifying to his social ambition and purpose in life. He had always envied one family in the city and that was the Tsiangs. They were an old family and old Mr. Tsiang had been an official in the capital. He had wanted to move in the circle of the Tsiangs and had not once been invited by them. The result was that Chienniang's betrothal to the second son of the Tsiang family was celebrated over the protest of the mother, while the girl lay in bed on a hunger strike.

"No good will come of this," said the mother to her husband. "It is against the girl's wish. You should have gone in and seen the girl crying her heart out in bed. It is her life we have to consider. You have fallen for the Tsiang money."

In time Chienniang was persuaded to eat and get up from bed. She went about the house like one condemned.

The young lover did not care what happened now. He took leave and disappeared for three weeks, trying to drown his sorrow in the Heng Mountains. After three weeks, he could not resist the idea of coming back to see his love. When he came back, he found Chienniang suffering from a curious, unknown disease. The day after his departure, the girl lost her memory and did not know who she was. She lay in bed and refused to get up. She did not recognize her own mother and father or her maid. She mumbled words which they did not understand. They feared she had gone out of her mind. But there was something worse. She had no fever, no pains, but she lay in bed all day without food, without drink. They tried to talk to her but her eyes were blank. It was as if her soul had departed from her body, and the body, without the master, stopped functioning altogether. A white pallor settled over her face and the doctors confessed that they had never seen a case like this, and did not know what it was.

With the mother's permission, Wang Chou rushed in to see her. "Chienniang, Chienniang!" he called. The mother watched anxiously. The girl's blank eyes seemed to focus again, her eyelashes moved, and a tinge of red returned to her cheeks.

"Chienniang, Chienniang!" he called again.

Her lips moved and parted in a glad, sure smile.

"It's you," she said quietly.

Tears filled the mother's eyes. "Chienniang, your spirit has returned. You know your mother, don't you?"

"Of course, Mother. What's the matter? What are you crying about? Why am I lying in bed?"

The girl apparently did not know all that had happened. When her mother told her that she had been lying in bed and had not recognized her own mother she could not believe it.

The girl became strong again in a few days. When she was sick, her father had been really frightened, but seeing that she had recovered, he settled back into his authoritative manner again. When the mother described how color returned to Chienniang's cheeks—which she had seen personally—when the nephew came to the girl's bedside, he said, "A fake! The doctors have never seen such a disease. Not knowing her own parents! I do not believe it."

"My dear husband, you have seen the girl lying in bed without food and drink for days. It is in her heart. You should reconsider the engagement——"

"The ceremony is over. Besides, you don't mean that I should break the engagement with the Tsiang family. They will not believe the story. I don't believe it myself."

The aunt, who was still staying with them, was heard to make sarcastic remarks, implying that the girl's sickness was feigned. "I have lived for fifty years and have never heard of a person not knowing her father and mother."

The father refused to reopen the question. The lovers were miserable and saw no way out. Wang Chou found the situation intolerable. There was nothing he could do. Chagrined and in despair, he informed his uncle that he was leaving for the capital, to be on his own.

"Maybe that is a good idea," replied the uncle curtly.

The night before his departure, the family gave him a farewell dinner. But Chienniang was heartbroken. She had been lying in bed for two days and refused to get up.

Wang Chou had the mother's permission to go into the girl's room and say good-bye. She had not eaten for two days and she was really ill with a high fever. Touching her gently, he said, "I am leaving and have come to say good-bye. There is nothing we can do."

"I will die, brother Chou. I have no desire to live when you are gone. But I only know this—living or dead, my spirit shall always be with you wherever you are."

Wang Chou could find no words to comfort her. They parted in tears, and the young man started on his way with an open wound in his heart, believing he should never come back to the house.

His boat had gone about a mile. It was about suppertime, and the boat was anchored for the night. Wang Chou lay in bed, sad and lonely, and shedding futile tears. Toward midnight, he heard footsteps drawing nearer and nearer on the bank.

"Brother Chou," he heard a girl whisper. He thought he was dreaming, for he knew she was ill in bed. He peeped out over the gunwale and saw Chienniang standing on the bank. In utter amazement, he jumped ashore.

"I have run away from home," said the girl weakly, and fell into his arms. He carried her into the boat quickly, unable to understand how she could cover that distance in her condition except by a superhuman willpower, and then he discovered she had come barefooted. How they cried together for joy!

Lying close to his body, caressed with kisses and restored by the warmth, she soon recovered. "Nothing can stop me from following you," she said to him when she opened her eyes again. It was as if she had completely recovered, and now that they were together and sure of each other, nothing mattered.

It was a long voyage, and during the whole trip, Chienniang expressed only one regret: she felt very sorry for her mother, who would be heartbroken when she found that her daughter had disappeared.

They finally arrived at a town in distant Szechuen, where Wang Chou found a small job with a salary barely large enough to support them. In order to make both ends meet, he rented a room in a farmhouse about a mile from the city, a distance which he had to cover on foot daily to and from his office. But he was unbelievably happy. Chienniang washed and cooked and she was contented and happy with him. He looked at his small room, furnished with rustic chairs, a table, and a simple bed, and said that he had all he wanted in life. The farmer who let him have a room upstairs was a simple man and his wife was kind to them. They offered them vegetables from their garden, which helped them to save money for food, and they in turn offered to help in the garden.

Then winter came and Chienniang gave birth to a baby boy, sweet and plump. When spring came, Wang Chou would return to find his wife holding the fat baby in her arms, breast-feeding him. His cup of happiness was full. He never apologized to his wife for making her live like a poor man's wife, for he knew he did not have to. Nevertheless, he knew that she was used to more comfortable living, and was surprised that she had adapted herself to the circumstances so well.

"I wish I could earn more money and hire a maid for you."

His wife stopped him with a soft pressure on his cheeks. It was a complete answer. "You didn't ask me to come. I ran away to follow you," she said simply.

Then they went through that delightful period when every week revealed something new and amazing in their child. The baby was adorable. Now he could grab what he wanted; now he could point to his nose and grab his ear and twitch it. Then the baby learned to crawl and smack his lips, and to say "mamma" and demonstrate those daily miracles of growing intelligence. He was an endless joy who filled their lives. The farmer couple, who were without children, loved the baby and helped Chienniang take care of him.

There was only one thing which marred their happiness. Chienniang kept thinking of her mother and little brother, though she cared not much for her father. Wang Chou was so much in love with her that he could sense her thoughts.

"You are thinking of your mother, I know. If you wish, I will take you home. We are married now and have a baby, and there's nothing they can do about it. At least, it will make your mother happy to see you again."

Chienniang wept with gratitude for his kindness and solicitude for her happiness.

"Let us do it. My mother must have gone crazy thinking that I am lost. And I have this beautiful grandchild to present to my parents."

They started out on the voyage again. After a month on the boat, they arrived at Hengchow.

"You go up first and prepare my parents to receive me," said Chienniang. Taking a gold hair brooch, she gave it to him and said, "Bring this as a token, in case they are still angry and deny your entrance or refuse to believe your story."

The boat anchored on the sandy bank. With Chienniang waiting in the boat, Wang Chou trudged the short distance to her home.

It was about suppertime and the father was at home. Wang Chou knelt on the ground and implored his forgiveness for running away with his daughter. The mother was there and seemed glad to see him, though she looked older, and her hair had turned completely white. He told them that they had now returned and their daughter was waiting in a boat.

"What are you talking about?" replied the father. "Forgive you for what? My daughter has been ill in bed for this entire year."

"Chienniang has never been able to leave her bed since you were gone," said the mother. "It has been sad this long year. She was so ill that at times she went without food for weeks. I could never forgive myself. I promised her that I would break off the engagement, but she was so weak she didn't seem to hear me, as if her spirit had already departed from her body. I was daily hoping for your return."

"I assure you that Chienniang is well and in the boat at this moment. Look, here is her token."

He presented the gold hair brooch. The mother examined it closely and recognized it. The family was greatly confused.

"I tell you she is in the boat. Send a servant to come along with me and see."

The parents were puzzled, but a servant was sent to go with Wang Chou and a sedan chair was ordered. The servant came to the boat and recognized the girl who looked exactly like Chienniang.

"Are my parents well?" the girl asked.

"They are well," replied the servant.

When the family was thus held in suspense and confusion, waiting for the return of the servant, a maid had taken the hair brooch and gone in to see the sick daughter. When the latter heard that Wang Chou had returned, her eyes opened and she smiled. She saw the hair brooch and said, "Indeed I have lost it," and put the brooch in her hair.

Without the maid's notice, the girl got up from her bed, walked out of the house silently, like a somnambulist, and went straight toward the bank, with a smiling face. Chienniang was leaving the boat already. Wang Chou was holding the baby, waiting for her to get into the sedan chair. He saw the girl on the bank come steadily nearer, and when the two girls met, they merged into one body and Chienniang's dresses became double.

The family was greatly excited when the maid reported that the sick daughter in bed had disappeared. When they saw Chienniang step out of the sedan chair, healthy and well and holding a plump baby in her arms, they were not more delighted than they were astonished and bewildered. They understood then that the girl's spirit, her real self, had gone to live with him. For love had wings which broke prison bars. What they had seen in the sick daughter lying in bed was no more than an empty shadow left behind, a body without a soul, from which the conscious spirit had wandered away.

The incident happened in the year A.D. 692. The family kept the story of this strange happening a secret from their neighbors. In time, Chienniang gave birth to several other children, and Wang Chou and Chienniang lived to a happy old age, loving each other more the older they grew.

Half a Sheet of Paper

AUGUST STRINDBERG

THE last moving van had gone. The tenant, a young man with a mourning band around his hat, wandered through the empty rooms to see if anything had been left behind. No, nothing had been forgotten, nothing. He went out into the corridor, determined never to think again of all he had passed through in this apartment. But there, on the wall, near the telephone, was a slip of paper covered with writing. The entries were in several handwritings: some quite legible, in black ink; some, pencil scrawls in black and red and blue. There stood recorded the whole beautiful romance that had been lived in the short space of two years. All that he had resolved to forget was written there—a bit of human history on half a sheet of paper.

He took the sheet down. It was a piece of sun-yellow scratch paper that casts a sheen. He laid it on the mantel of the fireplace in the living room, and, bending over, he began to read.

First stood her name: Alice—the most beautiful name he knew, because it was the name of his sweetheart. Beside it was a number, 15,111—it looked like a chant number on the hymnboard in church.

Underneath was scribbled: The Bank. It was there his work lay, the sacred work which for him had meant bread, home, family—the foundations of life. A heavy black line had been drawn across the number, for the bank had failed, and he had been taken on at another, after a short period of much anxiety.

Then followed the livery stable and the florist—that was when they were engaged, and he had a pocketful of money.

The furniture dealer—the decorator—— They furnish their apartment. Express Bureau—they move in. Opera House Box Office, 50,50—they are newly married and go to the opera on Sunday evenings. Their most delightful hours are those spent there, sitting quietly, while their hearts commune in the beauty and harmony of the fairyland on the other side of the footlights.

Here followed the name of a man (crossed out), a friend who had risen high, but who fell—dazzled by prosperity—fell irremediably, and had to flee the country. So ephemeral is that will-o'-the-wisp, Success!

Now something new came into the lives of the couple. Entered with a pencil in a woman's hand stands The Sister. What sister? Ah! the one with the long gray cloak and the sweet, sympathetic face, who comes so softly and never goes through the drawing room, but takes the corridor way to the bedroom. Below her name is written: Dr. L———

Here first appeared on the list a relative—Mother. That is his mother-in-law, who had discreetly kept away so as not to disturb the newly married. But now she has been called, and comes gladly, since she is needed.

Then came some entries in red and blue pencil. Employment Agency. The maid has left, and a new one must be engaged. The Apothecary—— Hm! It begins to look dark. The Dairy—milk is ordered, sterilized milk. The grocer, the butcher, and others. The household affairs are being conducted by telephone. Then the mistress of the house is not at her usual post? No. She is confined to her bed.

That which followed he could not read, for it grew dim before his eyes, as it must for the drowning man at sea who would look through salt water. But there it stood recorded, in plain black letters: The Undertaker.

That tells enough!——a larger and a smaller casket. And in parenthesis was written: "Of dust."

There is nothing more. It ended in dust, the way of all flesh.

He took up the sun-yellow paper, kissed it, folded it carefully, and put it in his breast pocket.

In two minutes he had relived two years of his life.

But he was not bowed down as he walked out. On the contrary, he carried his head high, like a proud and happy man, for he knew that for a little while he had held the best that life can bestow on man. How many there were, alas! who had not had this.

Love: Three Pages from a Sportsman's Book

GUY DE MAUPASSANT

I HAVE just read among the general news in one of the papers a drama of passion. He killed her and then he killed himself, so he must have loved her. What matters He or She? Their love alone matters to me, and it does not interest me because it moves me or astonishes me or because it softens me or makes me think, but because it recalls to my mind a remembrance of my youth, a strange recollection of a hunting adventure where Love appeared to me, as the Cross appeared to the early Christians, in the midst of the heavens.

I was born with all the instincts and the senses of primitive man, tempered by the arguments and the restraints of a civilized being. I am passionately fond of shooting, yet the sight of the wounded animal, of the blood on its feathers and on my hands, affects my heart so as almost to make it stop.

That year the cold weather set in suddenly toward the end of autumn, and I was invited by one of my cousins, Karl de Rauville, to go with him and shoot ducks on the marshes at daybreak.

My cousin was a jolly fellow of forty with red hair, very stout and bearded, a country gentleman, an amiable semi-brute of a happy disposition and endowed with that Gallic wit which makes even mediocrity agreeable. He lived in a house, half farmhouse, half chateau, situated in a broad valley through which a river ran. The hills right and left were covered with woods, old manorial woods where magnificent trees still remained and where the rarest feathered game in that part of France was to be found. Eagles were shot there occasionally, and birds of passage, such as rarely venture into our overpopulated part of the country, invariably lighted amid these giant oaks as if they knew or recognized some little corner of a primeval forest which had remained there to serve them as a shelter during their short nocturnal halts.

In the valley there were large meadows watered by trenches and separated by hedges; then, farther on, the river, which up to that point had been kept between banks, expanded into a vast marsh. That marsh was the best shooting ground I ever saw. It was my cousin's chief care, and he kept it as a preserve. Through the rushes that covered it, and made it rustling and rough, narrow passages had been cut, through which the flat-bottomed boats, impelled and steered by poles, passed along silently over dead water, brushing up against the reeds and making the swift fish take refuge in the weeds and the wild-fowl, with their pointed black heads, dive suddenly.

I am passionately fond of the water: of the sea, though it is too vast, too full of movement, impossible to hold; of the rivers which are so beautiful but which pass on and flee away; and above all of the marshes, where the whole unknown existence of aquatic animals palpitates. The marsh is an entire world in itself on the world of earth—a different world which has its own life, its settled inhabitants and its passing travelers, its voices, its noises, and above all its mystery. Nothing is more impressive, nothing more disquieting, more terrifying occasionally, than a fen. Why should a vague terror hang over these low plains covered with water? Is it the low rustling of the rushes, the strange will-o'-the-wisp lights, the silence which prevails on calm nights, the still mists which hang over the surface like a shroud; or is it the almost inaudible splashing, so slight and so gentle, yet sometimes more terrifying than the cannons of men or the thunders of the skies, which make these marshes resemble countries one has dreamed of, terrible countries holding an unknown and dangerous secret?

No, something else belongs to it—another mystery, profounder and graver, floats amid these thick mists, perhaps the mystery of the creation itself! For was it not in stagnant and muddy water, amid the heavy humidity of moist land under the heat of the sun, that the first germ of life pulsated and expanded to the day?

I arrived at my cousin's in the evening. It was freezing hard enough to split the stones.

During dinner, in the large room whose sideboards, walls, and ceiling were covered with stuffed birds with wings extended or perched on branches to which they were nailed—hawks, herons, owls, nightjars, buzzards, tiercels, vultures, falcons—my cousin, who, dressed in a sealskin jacket, himself resembled some strange animal from a cold country, told me what preparations he had made for that same night.

We were to start at half-past three in the morning so as to arrive at the place which he had chosen for our watching place at about half-past four. On that spot a hut had been built of lumps of ice so as to shelter us somewhat from the trying wind which precedes daybreak, a wind so cold as to tear the flesh like a saw, cut it like the blade of a knife, prick it like a poisoned sting, twist it like a pair of pincers, and burn it like fire.

My cousin rubbed his hands. "I have never known such a frost," he said; "it is already twelve degrees below zero at six o'clock in the evening."

I threw myself onto my bed immediately after we had finished our meal and went to sleep by the light of a bright fire burning in the grate.

At three o'clock he woke me. In my turn I put on a sheepskin and found my cousin Karl covered with a bearskin. After having each swallowed two cups of scalding coffee, followed by glasses of liqueur brandy, we started, accompanied by a gamekeeper and our dogs, Plongeon and Pierrot.

From the first moment that I got outside, I felt chilled to the very marrow. It was one of those nights on which the earth seems dead with cold. The frozen air becomes resisting and palpable, such pain does it cause; no breath of wind moves it, it is fixed and motionless; it bites you, pierces through you, dries you, kills the trees, the plants, the insects, the small birds, who fall from the branches onto the hard ground and become stiff under the grip of the cold.

The moon, which was in her last quarter and was inclining all to one side, seemed fainting in the midst of space, so weak that she was unable to wane, forced to stay up yonder, seized and paralyzed by the severity of the weather. She shed a cold, mournful light over the world, that dying and wan light which she gives us every month at the end of her period.

Karl and I walked side by side, our backs bent, our hands in our pockets and our guns under our arms. Our boots, which were wrapped in wool so that we might be able to walk without slipping on the frozen river, made no sound, and I looked at the white vapor which our dogs' breath made.

We were soon on the edge of the marsh and entered one of the lanes of dry rushes which ran through the low forest.

Our elbows, which touched the long, ribbonlike leaves, left a slight noise behind us, and I was seized, as I had never been before, by the powerful and singular emotion which marshes cause in me. This one was dead, dead from cold, since we were walking on it in the middle of its population of dried rushes.

Suddenly, at the turn of one of the lanes, I perceived the ice hut which had been constructed to shelter us. I went in, and as we had nearly an hour to wait before the wandering birds would awake, I rolled myself up in my rug in order to try and get warm. Then, lying on my back, I began to look at the misshapen moon, which had four horns through the vaguely transparent walls of this polar house. But the frost of the frozen marshes, the cold of these walls, the cold from the firmament, penetrated me so terribly that I began to cough. My cousin Karl became uneasy.

"No matter if we do not kill much today," he said. "I do not want you to catch cold; we will light a fire." And he told the gamekeeper to cut some rushes.

We made a pile in the middle of our hut, which had a hole in the middle of the roof to let out the smoke, and when the red flames rose up to the clear crystal blocks, they began to melt, gently, imperceptibly, as if they were sweating. Karl, who had remained outside, called out to me: "Come and look here!" I went out of the hut and remained struck with astonishment. Our hut, in the shape of a cone, looked like an enormous diamond with a heart of fire which had been suddenly planted there in the midst of the frozen water of the marsh. And inside we saw two fantastic forms, those of our dogs, who were warming themselves at the fire.

But a peculiar cry, a lost, a wandering cry, passed over our heads, and the light from our hearth showed us the wild birds. Nothing moves one so much as the first clamor of a life which one does not see, which passes through the somber air so quickly and so far off, just before the first streak of a winter's day appears on the horizon. It seems to me, at this glacial hour of dawn, as if that passing cry which is carried away by the wings of a bird is the sigh of a soul from the world!

"Put out the fire," said Karl; "it is getting daylight."

The sky was, in fact, beginning to grow pale, and the flights of ducks made long, rapid streaks which were soon obliterated on the sky.

A stream of light burst out into the night; Karl had fired, and the two dogs ran forward.

And then, nearly every minute, now he, now I, aimed rapidly as soon as the shadow of a flying flock appeared above the rushes. And Pierrot and Plongeon, out of breath but happy, retrieved the bleeding birds, whose eyes still, occasionally, looked at us.

The sun had risen, and it was a bright day with a blue sky, and we were thinking of taking our departure, when two birds with extended necks and outstretched wings glided rapidly over our heads. I fired, and one of them fell almost at my feet. It was a teal with a silver breast, and then, in the blue space above me, I heard a voice, the voice of a bird. It was a short, repeated, heart-rending lament; and the bird, the little animal that had been spared, began to turn round in the blue sky over our heads, looking at its dead companion which I was holding in my hand.

Karl was on his knees, his gun to his shoulder, watching it eagerly until it should be within shot. "You have killed the duck," he said, "and the drake will not fly away."

He certainly did not fly away; he circled over our heads continually and continued his cries. Never have any groans of suffering pained me so much as that desolate appeal, as that lamentable reproach of this poor bird which was lost in space.

Occasionally he took flight under the menace of the gun which followed his movements and seemed ready to continue his flight alone, but as he could not make up his mind to this he returned to find his mate.

"Leave her on the ground," Karl said to me; "he will come within shot by and by." And he did indeed come near us, careless of danger, infatuated by his animal love, by his affection for his mate, which I had just killed.

Karl fired, and it was as if somebody had cut the string which held the bird suspended. I saw something black descend, and I heard the noise of a fall among the rushes. And Pierrot brought it to me.

I put them—they were already cold—into the same game bag, and I returned to Paris the same evening.

Our Lady's Juggler

ANATOLE FRANCE

IN the days of King Louis there lived a poor juggler by the name of Barnabas, a native of Compiègne, who wandered from city to city performing tricks of skill and prowess.

On fair days he would lay down in the public square a worn and aged carpet, and after having attracted a group of children and idlers by certain amusing remarks which he had learned from an old juggler, and which he invariably repeated in the same fashion without altering a word, he would assume the strangest postures, and balance a pewter plate on the tip of his nose. At first the crowd regarded him with indifference, but when, with his hands and head on the ground, he threw into the air and caught with his feet six copper balls that glittered in the sunlight, or when, throwing himself back until his neck touched his heels, he assumed the form of a perfect wheel and in that position juggled with twelve knives, he elicited a murmur of admiration from his audience, and small coins rained on his carpet.

Still, Barnabas of Compiègne, like most of those who exist by their accomplishments, had a hard time making a living. Earning his bread by the sweat of his brow, he bore rather more than his share of those miseries we are all heir to through the fault of our Father Adam.

Besides, he was unable to work as much as he would have liked, for in order to exhibit his wonderful talents, he required—like the trees—the warmth of the sun and the heat of the day. In wintertime he was no more than a tree stripped of its leaves, in fact, half-dead. The frozen earth was too hard for the juggler. Like the cicada mentioned by Marie de France,

351

he suffered during the bad season from hunger and cold. But, since he
had a simple heart, he suffered in silence.

He had never thought much about the origin of wealth nor about the
inequality of human conditions. He firmly believed that if this world was
evil, the next could not but be good, and this faith upheld him. He was not
like the clever fellows who sell their souls to the devil; he never took the
name of God in vain; he lived the life of an honest man, and though he
had no wife of his own, he did not covet his neighbor's, for woman is the
enemy of strong men, as we learn by the story of Samson, which is written in the Scriptures.

Verily, his mind was not turned in the direction of carnal desire, and it
caused him far greater pain to renounce drinking than to forgo the
pleasure of women. For, though he was not a drunkard, he enjoyed drinking when the weather was warm. He was a good man, fearing God, and
devout in his adoration of the Holy Virgin. When he went into a church he
never failed to kneel before the image of the Mother of God and to address
her with this prayer:

"My Lady, watch over my life until it shall please God that I die, and
when I am dead, see that I have the joys of Paradise."

One evening, after a day of rain, as he walked sad and bent with his juggling balls under his arm and his knives wrapped up in his old carpet
seeking some barn where he might go supperless to bed, he saw a monk
going in his direction, and respectfully saluted him. As they were both walking at the same pace, they fell into conversation.

"Friend," said the monk, "how does it happen that you are dressed all in
green? Are you perchance going to play the part of the fool in some
mystery?"[1]

"No, indeed, Father," said Barnabas. "My name is Barnabas, and my
business is that of juggler. It would be the finest calling in the world if I
could eat every day."

"Friend Barnabas," answered the monk, "be careful what you say. There
is no finer calling than the monastic. The priest celebrates the praise of
God, the Virgin, and the saints; the life of a monk is a perpetual hymn to
the Lord."

And Barnabas replied: "Father, I confess I spoke like an ignorant man.
My estate cannot be compared to yours, and though there may be some
merit in dancing and balancing a stick with a denier[2] on top of it on the
end of your nose, it is in no wise comparable to your merit. Father, I wish

---

[1] *mystery*: a mystery play.
[2] *denier*: a small coin of France from the time of Pepin the Short to the French
Revolution.

I might, like you, sing the Office every day, especially the Office of the Very Holy Virgin, to whom I am specially and piously devoted. I would willingly give up the art by which I am known from Soissons to Beauvais, in more than six hundred cities and villages, in order to enter the monastic life."

The monk was touched by the simplicity of the juggler, and as he was not lacking in discernment, he recognized in Barnabas one of those well-disposed men of whom Our Lord has said, "Let peace be with them on earth." And he made answer therefore:

"Friend Barnabas, come with me and I will see that you enter the monastery of which I am the Prior. He who led Mary the Egyptian through the desert put me across your path in order that I might lead you to salvation."

Thus did Barnabas become a monk. In the monastery which he entered, the monks celebrated most magnificently the cult of the Holy Virgin, each of them bringing to her service all the knowledge and skill which God had given him.

The Prior, for his part, wrote books, setting forth, according to the rules of scholasticism, all the virtues of the Mother of God. Brother Maurice copied these treatises with a cunning hand on pages of parchment, while Brother Alexandre decorated them with delicate miniatures representing the Queen of Heaven seated on the throne of Solomon, with four lions on guard at the foot of it. Around Her head, which was encircled by a halo, flew seven doves, the seven gifts of the Holy Spirit: fear, piety, knowledge, power, judgment, intelligence, and wisdom. With Her were six golden-haired virgins: Humility, Prudence, Retirement, Respect, Virginity, and Obedience. At Her feet two little figures, shining white and quite naked, stood in suppliant attitudes. They were souls imploring, not in vain, Her all-powerful intercession for their salvation. On another page Brother Alexandre depicted Eve in the presence of Mary, that one might see at the same time sin and its redemption, woman humiliated, and the Virgin exalted. Among the other much-prized pictures in his book were the Well of Living Waters, the Fountain, the Lily, the Moon, the Sun, and the Closed Garden, of which much is said in the Canticle; the Gate of Heaven and the City of God. These were all images of the Virgin.

Brother Marbode, too, was one of the cherished children of Mary. He was ever busy cutting images of stone, so that his beard, his eyebrows, and his hair were white with the dust, and his eyes perpetually swollen and full of tears. But he was a hardy and a happy man in his old age, and there was no doubt that the Queen of Paradise watched over the declining days of Her child. Marbode represented Her seated in a pulpit, Her forehead encircled by a halo, with an orb of pearls. He was at great pains to make the folds of Her robe cover the feet of Her of whom the prophet has said, "My beloved is like a closed garden."

At times he represented Her as a graceful child, and Her image seemed to say, "Lord, Thou art My Lord!"

There were also in the monastery poets who composed prose writings in Latin and hymns in honor of the Most Gracious Virgin Mary; there was, indeed, one among them—a Picard—who translated the Miracles of Our Lady into rhymed verses in the vulgar tongue.

Perceiving so great a competition in praise and so fine a harvest of good works, Barnabas fell to lamenting his ignorance and simplicity.

"Alas!" he sighed as he walked by himself one day in the littie garden shaded by the monastery wall. "I am so unhappy because I cannot, like my brothers, give worthy praise to the Holy Mother of God to whom I have consecrated all the love in my heart. Alas, I am a stupid fellow, without art, and for Your service, Madame, I have no edifying sermons, no fine treatises nicely prepared according to the rules, no beautiful paintings, no cunningly carved statues, and no verses counted off by feet and marching in measure! Alas, I have nothing!"

Thus did he lament and abandon himself to his misery.

One evening when the monks were talking together by way of diversion, he heard one of them tell of a monk who could not recite anything but the *Ave Maria.* He was scorned for his ignorance, but after he died there sprang from his mouth five roses, in honor of the five letters in the name Maria. Thus was his holiness made manifest.

In listening to this story, Barnabas was conscious once more of the Virgin's beneficence, but he was not consoled by the example of the happy miracle, for his heart was full of zeal and he wanted to celebrate the glory of his Lady in Heaven.

He sought for a way in which to do this, but in vain, and each day brought him greater sorrow, until one morning he sprang joyously from his cot and ran to the chapel, where he remained alone for more than an hour. He returned thither again after dinner, and from that day onward he would go into the chapel every day the moment it was deserted, passing the greater part of the time which the other monks dedicated to the pursuit of the liberal arts and the sciences. He was no longer sad and he sighed no more. But such singular conduct aroused the curiosity of the other monks, and they asked themselves why Brother Barnabas retired alone so often, and the Prior, whose business it was to know everything that his monks were doing, determined to observe Barnabas. One day, therefore, when Barnabas was alone in the chapel, the Prior entered in company with two of the oldest brothers, in order to watch, through the bars of the door, what was going on within.

They saw Barnabas before the image of the Holy Virgin, his head on the floor and his feet in the air, juggling with six copper balls and twelve knives. In honor of the Holy Virgin he was performing the tricks which had in former days brought him the greatest fame. Not understanding that he was thus putting his best talents at the service of the Holy Virgin, the aged brothers cried out against such sacrilege. The Prior knew that Barnabas had a simple soul, but he believed that the man had lost his wits. All three set about to remove Barnabas from the chapel, when they saw the Virgin slowly descend from the altar and, with a fold of Her blue mantle, wipe the sweat that streamed over the juggler's forehead.

Then the Prior, bowing his head down to the marble floor, repeated these words:

"Blessed are the pure in heart, for they shall see God."

"Amen," echoed the brothers, bowing down to the floor.

The Book of Ruth

OLD TESTAMENT

CHAPTER 1

Now it came to pass in the days when the judges ruled, that there was a famine in the land. And a certain man of Bethlehem-judah went to sojourn in the country of Moab, he, and his wife, and his two sons.

And the name of the man was Elimelech, and the name of his wife Naomi, and the name of his two sons Mahlon and Chilion, Ephrathites of Bethlehem-judah. And they came into the country of Moab, and continued there.

And Elimelech Naomi's husband died; and she was left, and her two sons.

And they took them wives of the women of Moab; the name of the one was Orpah, and the name of the other Ruth: and they dwelled there about ten years.

And Mahlon and Chilion died also both of them; and the woman was left of her two sons and her husband.

Then she arose with her daughters in law, that she might return from the country of Moab: for she had heard in the country of Moab how that the Lord had visited his people in giving them bread.

Wherefore she went forth out of the place where she was, and her two daughters in law with her; and they went on the way to return unto the land of Judah.

And Naomi said unto her two daughters in law, Go, return each to her mother's house: the Lord deal kindly with you, as ye have dealt with the dead, and with me.

The Lord grant you that ye may find rest, each of you in the house of her husband. Then she kissed them; and they lifted up their voice, and wept.

And they said unto her, Surely we will return with thee unto thy people.

And Naomi said, Turn again, my daughters: why will ye go with me? are there yet any more sons in my womb, that they may be your husbands?

Turn again, my daughters, go your way; for I am too old to have an husband. If I should say, I have hope, if I should have an husband also to night, and should also bear sons;

Would ye tarry for them till they were grown? would ye stay for them from having husbands? nay, my daughters; for it grieveth me much for your sakes that the hand of the Lord is gone out against me.

And they lifted up their voice, and wept again: and Orpah kissed her mother in law; but Ruth clave unto her.

And she said, Behold, thy sister in law is gone back unto her people, and unto her gods: return thou after thy sister in law.

And Ruth said, Intreat me not to leave thee, or to return from following after thee: for whither thou goest, I will go; and where thou lodgest, I will lodge: thy people shall be my people, and thy God my God:

Where thou diest, will I die, and there will I be buried: the Lord do so to me, and more also, if ought but death part thee and me.

When she saw that she was stedfastly minded to go with her, then she left speaking unto her.

So they two went until they came to Bethlehem. And it came to pass, when they were come to Bethlehem, that all the city was moved about them, and they said, Is this Naomi?

And she said unto them, Call me not Naomi, call me Mara: for the Almighty hath dealt very bitterly with me.

I went out full, and the Lord hath brought me home again empty: why then call ye me Naomi, seeing the Lord hath testified against me, and the Almighty hath afflicted me?

So Naomi returned, and Ruth the Moabitess, her daughter in law, with her, which returned out of the country of Moab: and they came to Bethlehem in the beginning of barley harvest.

CHAPTER 2

And Naomi had a kinsman of her husband's, a mighty man of wealth, of the family of Elimelech; and his name was Boaz.

And Ruth the Moabitess said unto Naomi, Let me now go to the field, and glean ears of corn after him in whose sight I shall find grace. And she said unto her, Go, my daughter.

And she went, and came, and gleaned in the field after the reapers: and her hap was to light on a part of the field belonging unto Boaz, who was of the kindred of Elimelech.

And, behold, Boaz came from Bethlehem, and said unto the reapers, The Lord be with you. And they answered him, The Lord bless thee.

Then said Boaz unto his servant that was set over the reapers, Whose damsel is this?

And the servant that was set over the reapers answered and said, It is the Moabitish damsel that came back with Naomi out of the country of Moab:

And she said, I pray you, let me glean and gather after the reapers among the sheaves: so she came, and hath continued even from the morning until now, that she tarried a little in the house.

Then said Boaz unto Ruth, Hearest thou not, my daughter? Go not to glean in another field, neither go from hence, but abide here fast by my maidens:

Let thine eyes be on the field that they do reap, and go thou after them: have I not charged the young men that they shall not touch thee? and when thou art athirst, go unto the vessels, and drink of that which the young men have drawn.

Then she fell on her face, and bowed herself to the ground, and said unto him, Why have I found grace in thine eyes, that thou shouldest take knowledge of me, seeing I am a stranger?

And Boaz answered and said unto her, It hath fully been shewed me, all that thou hast done unto thy mother in law since the death of thine husband: and how thou hast left thy father and thy mother, and the land of thy nativity, and art come unto a people which thou knewest not heretofore.

The Lord recompense thy work, and a full reward be given thee of the Lord God of Israel, under whose wings thou art come to trust.

Then she said, Let me find favour in thy sight, my lord: for that thou hast comforted me, and for that thou hast spoken friendly unto thine handmaid, though I be not like unto one of thine handmaidens.

And Boaz said unto her, At mealtime come thou hither, and eat of the bread, and dip thy morsel in the vinegar. And she sat beside the reapers: and he reached her parched corn, and she did eat, and was sufficed, and left.

And when she was risen up to glean, Boaz commanded his young men, saying, Let her glean even among the sheaves, and reproach her not:

And let fall also some of the handfuls of purpose for her, and leave them, that she may glean them, and rebuke her not.

So she gleaned in the field until even, and beat out that she had gleaned: and it was about an ephah of barley.

And she took it up, and went into the city: and her mother in law saw what she had gleaned: and she brought forth, and gave to her that she had reserved after she was sufficed.

And her mother in law said unto her, Where hast thou gleaned to day? and where wroughtest thou? blessed be he that did take knowledge of thee. And she shewed her mother in law with whom she had wrought, and said, The man's name with whom I wrought to day is Boaz.

And Naomi said unto her daughter in law, Blessed be he of the Lord, who hath not left off his kindness to the living and to the dead. And Naomi said unto her, The man is near of kin unto us, one of our next kinsman.

And Ruth the Moabitess said, He said unto me also, Thou shalt keep fast by my young men, until they have ended all my harvest.

And Naomi said unto Ruth her daughter in law, It is good, my daughter, that thou go out with his maidens, that they meet thee not in any other field.

So she kept fast by the maidens of Boaz to glean unto the end of barley harvest and of wheat harvest; and dwelt with her mother in law.

CHAPTER 3

Then Naomi her mother in law said unto her, My daughter, shall I not seek rest for thee, that it may be well with thee?

And now is not Boaz of our kindred, with whose maidens thou wast? Behold, he winnoweth barley to night in the threshingfloor.

Wash thyself therefore, and anoint thee, and put thy raiment upon thee, and get thee down to the floor: but make not thyself known unto the man, until he shall have done eating and drinking.

And it shall be, when he lieth down, that thou shalt mark the place where he shall lie, and thou shalt go in, and uncover his feet, and lay thee down; and he will tell thee what thou shalt do.

And she said unto her, All that thou sayest unto me I will do.

And she went down unto the floor, and did according to all that her mother in law bade her.

And when Boaz had eaten and drunk, and his heart was merry, he went to lie down at the end of the heap of corn: and she came softly, and uncovered his feet, and laid her down.

And it came to pass at midnight, that the man was afraid, and turned himself: and, behold, a woman lay at his feet.

And he said, Who art thou? And she answered, I am Ruth thine handmaid: spread therefore thy skirt over thine handmaid; for thou art a near kinsman.

And he said, Blessed be thou of the Lord, my daughter: for thou hast shewed more kindness in the latter end than at the beginning, inasmuch as thou followedst not young men, whether poor or rich.

And now, my daughter, fear not; I will do to thee all that thou requirest: for all the city of my people doth know that thou art a virtuous woman.

And now it is true that I am thy near kinsman: howbeit there is a kinsman nearer than I.

Tarry this night, and it shall be in the morning, that if he will perform unto thee the part of a kinsman, well; let him do the kinsman's part: but if he will not do the part of a kinsman to thee, then will I do the part of a kinsman to thee, as the Lord liveth: lie down until the morning.

And she lay at his feet until the morning: and she rose up before one could know another. And he said, Let it not be known that a woman came into the floor.

Also he said, Bring the vail that thou hast upon thee, and hold it. And when she held it, he measured six measures of barley, and laid it on her: and she went into the city.

And when she came to her mother in law, she said, Who art thou, my daughter? And she told her all that the man had done to her.

And she said, These six measures of barley gave he me; for he said to me, Go not empty unto thy mother in law.

Then said she, Sit still, my daughter, until thou know how the matter will fall: for the man will not be in rest, until he have finished the thing this day.

CHAPTER 4

Then went Boaz up to the gate, and sat him down there: and, behold, the kinsman of whom Boaz spake came by; unto whom he said, Ho, such a one! turn aside, sit down here. And he turned aside, and sat down.

And he took ten men of the elders of the city, and said, Sit ye down here. And they sat down.

And he said unto the kinsman, Naomi, that is come again out of the country of Moab, selleth a parcel of land, which was our brother Elimelech's:

And I thought to advertise thee, saying, Buy it before the inhabitants, and before the elders of my people. If thou wilt redeem it, redeem it: but if thou wilt not redeem it, then tell me, that I may know: for there is none to redeem it beside thee; and I am after thee. And he said, I will redeem it.

Then said Boaz, What day thou buyest the field of the hand of Naomi, thou must buy it also of Ruth the Moabitess, the wife of the dead, to raise up the name of the dead upon his inheritance.

And the kinsman said, I cannot redeem it for myself, lest I mar mine own inheritance: redeem thou my right to thyself; for I cannot redeem it.

Now this was the manner in former time in Israel concerning redeeming and concerning changing, for to confirm all things; a man plucked off his shoe, and gave it to his neighbour: and this was a testimony in Israel.

Therefore the kinsman said unto Boaz, Buy it for thee. So he drew off his shoe.

And Boaz said unto the elders, and unto all the people, Ye are witnesses this day, that I have bought all that was Elimelech's, and all that was Chilion's and Mahlon's, of the hand of Naomi.

Moreover Ruth the Moabitess, the wife of Mahlon, have I purchased to be my wife, to raise up the name of the dead upon his inheritance, that the name of the dead be not cut off from among his brethren, and from the gate of his place: ye are witnesses this day.

And all the people that were in the gate, and the elders, said, We are witnesses. The Lord make the woman that is come into thine house like Rachel and like Leah, which two did build the house of Israel: and do thou worthily in Ephratah, and be famous in Bethlehem:

And let thy house be like the house of Pharez, whom Tamar bare unto Judah, of the seed which the Lord shall give thee of this young woman.

So Boaz took Ruth, and she was his wife: and when he went in unto her, the Lord gave her conception, and she bare a son.

And the women said unto Naomi, Blessed be the Lord, which hath not left thee this day without a kinsman, that his name may be famous in Israel.

And he shall be unto thee a restorer of thy life, and nourisher of thine old age: for thy daughter in law, which loveth thee, which is better to thee than seven sons, hath born him.

And Naomi took the child, and laid it in her bosom, and became nurse unto it.

And the women her neighbours gave it a name, saying, There is a son born to Naomi; and they called his name Obed: he is the father of Jesse, the father of David.

Now these are the generations of Pharez: Pharez begat Hezron,

And Hezron begat Ram, and Ram begat Amminadab,

And Amminadab begat Nahshon, and Nahshon begat Salmon,

And Salmon begat Boaz, and Boaz begat Obed,

And Obed begat Jesse, and Jesse begat David.

Selected Psalms

OLD TESTAMENT

Psalm 1

Blessed is the man that walketh not in the counsel of the ungodly, nor standeth in the way of sinners, nor sitteth in the seat of the scornful.

But his delight is in the law of the Lord; and in his law doth he meditate day and night.

And he shall be like a tree planted by the rivers of water, that bringeth forth his fruit in his season; his leaf also shall not wither; and whatsoever he doeth shall prosper.

The ungodly are not so: but are like the chaff which the wind driveth away.

Therefore the ungodly shall not stand in judgment, nor sinners in the congregation of the righteous.

For the Lord knoweth the way of the righteous: but the way of the ungodly shall perish.

Psalm 8

O Lord our Lord, how excellent is thy name in all the earth! who hast set thy glory above the heavens.

Out of the mouth of babes and sucklings hast thou ordained strength because of thine enemies, that thou mightest still the enemy and the avenger.

When I consider thy heavens, the work of thy fingers, the moon and the stars, which thou hast ordained;

What is man, that thou art mindful of him? and the son of man, that thou visitest him?

For thou hast made him a little lower than the angels, and hast crowned him with glory and honour.

Thou madest him to have dominion over the works of thy hands; thou hast put all things under his feet:

All sheep and oxen, yea, and the beasts of the field;

The fowl of the air, and the fish of the sea, and whatsoever passeth through the paths of the seas.

O Lord our Lord, how excellent is thy name in all the earth!

Psalm 15

Lord, who shall abide in thy tabernacle? who shall dwell in thy holy hill?

He that walketh uprightly, and worketh righteousness, and speaketh the truth in his heart.

He that backbiteth not with his tongue, nor doeth evil to his neighbour, nor taketh up a reproach against his neighbour.

In whose eyes a vile person is contemned; but he honoureth them that fear the Lord. He that sweareth to his own hurt, and changeth not.

He that putteth not out his money to usury, nor taketh reward against the innocent. He that doeth these things shall never be moved.

Psalm 19

The heavens declare the glory of God; and the firmament sheweth his handywork.

Day unto day uttereth speech, and night unto night sheweth knowledge.

There is no speech nor language, where their voice is not heard.

Their line is gone out through all the earth, and their words to the end of the world. In them hath he set a tabernacle for the sun,

Which is as a bridegroom coming out of his chamber, and rejoiceth as a strong man to run a race.

His going forth is from the end of the heaven, and his circuit unto the ends of it: and there is nothing hid from the heat thereof.

The law of the Lord is perfect, converting the soul: the testimony of the Lord is sure, making wise the simple.

The statutes of the Lord are right, rejoicing the heart: the commandment of the Lord is pure, enlightening the eyes.

The fear of the Lord is clean, enduring for ever: the judgments of the Lord are true and righteous altogether.

More to be desired are they than gold, yea, than much fine gold: sweeter also than honey and the honeycomb.

Moreover by them is thy servant warned: and in keeping of them there is great reward.

Who can understand his errors? cleanse thou me from secret faults.

Keep back thy servant also from presumptuous sins; let them not have dominion over me: then shall I be upright, and I shall be innocent from the great transgression.

Let the words of my mouth, and the meditation of my heart, be acceptable in thy sight, O Lord, my strength, and my redeemer.

Psalm 23

The Lord is my shepherd; I shall not want.

He maketh me to lie down in green pastures: he leadeth me beside the still waters.

He restoreth my soul: he leadeth me in the paths of righteousness for his name's sake.

Yea, though I walk through the valley of the shadow of death, I will fear no evil: for thou art with me; thy rod and thy staff they comfort me.

Thou preparest a table before me in the presence of mine enemies: thou anointest my head with oil; my cup runneth over.

Surely goodness and mercy shall follow me all the days of my life: and I will dwell in the house of the Lord for ever.

Psalm 24

The earth is the Lord's, and the fulness thereof; the world, and they that dwell therein.

For he hath founded it upon the seas, and established it upon the floods

Who shall ascend into the hill of the Lord? or who shall stand in his holy place?

He that hath clean hands, and a pure heart; who hath not lifted up his soul unto vanity, nor sworn deceitfully.

He shall receive the blessing from the Lord, and righteousness from the God of his salvation.

This is the generation of them that seek him, that seek thy face, O Jacob. Selah.

Lift up your heads, O ye gates; and be ye lift up, ye everlasting doors; and the King of glory shall come in.

Who is this King of glory? The Lord strong and mighty, the Lord mighty in battle.

Lift up your heads, O ye gates; even lift them up, ye everlasting doors; and the King of glory shall come in.

Who is this King of glory? The Lord of hosts, he is the King of glory. Selah.

Psalm 46

God is our refuge and strength, a very present help in trouble.

Therefore will not we fear, though the earth be removed, and though the mountains be carried into the midst of the sea;

Though the waters thereof roar and be troubled, though the mountains shake with the swelling thereof. Selah.

There is a river, the streams whereof shall make glad the city of God, the holy place of the tabernacles of the most High.

God is in the midst of her; she shall not be moved: God shall help her, and that right early.

The heathen raged, the kingdoms were moved: he uttered his voice, the earth melted.

The Lord of hosts is with us: the God of Jacob is our refuge. Selah.

Come, behold the works of the Lord, what desolations he hath made in the earth.

He maketh wars to cease unto the end of the earth; he breaketh the bow, and cutteth the spear in sunder; he burneth the chariot in the fire.

Be still, and know that I am God: I will be exalted among the heathen, I will be exalted in the earth.

The Lord of hosts is with us; the God of Jacob is our refuge. Selah.

Psalm 95

O come, let us sing unto the Lord: let us make a joyful noise to the rock of our salvation.

Let us come before his presence with thanksgiving, and make a joyful noise unto him with psalms.

For the Lord is a great God, and a great King above all gods.

In his hand are the deep places of the earth: the strength of the hills is his also.

The sea is his, and he made it: and his hands formed the dry land.

O come, let us worship and bow down: let us kneel before the Lord our maker.

For he is our God; and we are the people of his pasture, and the sheep of his hand. To day if ye will hear his voice,

Harden not your heart, as in the provocation, and as in the day of temptation in the wilderness:

When your fathers tempted me, proved me, and saw my work.

Forty years long was I grieved with this generation, and said, It is a people that do err in their heart, and they have not known my ways:

Unto whom I sware in my wrath that they should not enter into my rest.

Psalm 100

Make a joyful noise unto the Lord, all ye lands.

Serve the Lord with gladness: come before his presence with singing.

Know ye that the Lord he is God: it is he that hath made us, and not we ourselves; we are his people, and the sheep of his pasture.

Enter into his gates with thanksgiving, and into his courts with praise: be thankful unto him, and bless his name.

For the Lord is good; his mercy is everlasting; and his truth endureth to all generations.

Psalm 121

I will lift up mine eyes unto the hills, from whence cometh my help.

My help cometh from the Lord, which made heaven and earth.

He will not suffer thy foot to be moved: he that keepeth thee will not slumber.

Behold, he that keepeth Israel shall neither slumber nor sleep.

The Lord is thy keeper: the Lord is thy shade upon thy right hand.

The sun shall not smite thee by day, nor the moon by night.

The Lord shall preserve thee from all evil: he shall preserve thy soul.

The Lord shall preserve thy going out and thy coming in from this time forth, and even for evermore.

Hymn of Love to God

RABINDRANATH TAGORE

When you were alone, you did not know yourself;
There was then no waiting by the wayside,
And the winds charged with tears
Did not blow from this bank to the other.
I came and your sleep vanished,
And flowers of joy blossomed everywhere.
You made me bloom in countless flowers
And rocked me in a cradle of many forms.
Scattering me amidst the countless stars
You gathered me up again in your lap.
Hiding me behind the curtain of death
You find me ever anew.

I came,
And your heart trembled.
I came,
And with it came your sorrows
And your fiery joy
And ardent spring,
Raising storms of life and death.
I came,
And therefore you came too.
Seeing me,
And touching me,

You felt your own touch.
In my eyes is shame
And in my heart fear,
And a veil covers my face.
I tremble to look at you.
Yet I know, O lord,
You are longing to meet me;
Otherwise all suns and stars
Were created in vain.

Song of Praise to the Creator

FROM THE SOTHO

Invocation

Perfection ever rising to perfection,
The man who fashioned mountains and rocks!
Purity Immaculate,
Wood white and unblemished.

Guardian of nation upon nation,
Lone creator of firmament and horizon!
Origin of nation upon nation!
Even before birth the King!

The one of there! The one of here!
The one of here! The one of there!
The one of everywhere, above and below!
The knower of all!
The beautiful, knower of the innermost!
Lord of wisdom, above and below!
The depth too deep for the measure stick.

Lord of heaven's vault!
Lord of that which endeth not! Lord of the everlasting!
The rock which has withstood the fire!
Lord of that which endeth not, both the going out and the
    coming back.

That which endeth not is never understood.
King of kings, an unfathomable thought!
I, the mother, even though scandal is spoken,
Yet ever and again we clap hands,
And all slides off my shoulders.

The rock has been fashioned a shining beacon on the
   mountain top.
Thither we flee from raging storms.
Knife carving portions for others,
Yet, the while, carving for the master himself.
Where the front hoof has trod,
There also shall the back hoof tread.

The Praise

I, the revered of all nations,
I, for ever the same,
I, the leader to pastures and guide back to the kraal,
I am the origin of all sustenance,
I am the mother of all nurture,
'Tis I that reign, father of all bounty,
I, the bellow of the bull.
Ye are fed, ye are satisfied.
I, the great elephant, am your mother,
Your mother, see how great my breasts!

I embrace unlimited spaces,
I am not as small as you,
You little urchins dancing round the cooking pot,
Eyes fixed on the dishing up.
I am your foster-mother.
Ye and I are head and cheek,
Never can they be parted.
I am the royal bead on the brow of kings, the beautiful
   raiment.
Master-tutor above and below,
Rock that has withstood all tests.

I Corinthians

NEW TESTAMENT

CHAPTER 13

Though I speak with the tongues of men and of angels, and have not charity, I am become as sounding brass, or a tinkling cymbal.

And though I have the gift of prophecy, and understand all mysteries, and all knowledge; and though I have all faith, so that I could remove mountains, and have not charity, I am nothing.

And though I bestow all my goods to feed the poor, and though I give my body to be burned, and have not charity, it profiteth me nothing.

Charity suffereth long, and is kind; charity envieth not; charity vaunteth not itself, is not puffed up,

Doth not behave itself unseemly, seeketh not her own, is not easily provoked, thinketh no evil;

Rejoiceth not in iniquity, but rejoiceth in the truth;

Beareth all things, believeth all things, hopeth all things, endureth all things.

Charity never faileth: but whether there be prophecies, they shall fail; whether there be tongues, they shall cease; whether there be knowledge, it shall vanish away.

For we know in part, and we prophesy in part.

But when that which is perfect is come, then that which is in part shall be done away.

When I was a child, I spake as a child, I understood as a child, I thought as a child: but when I became a man, I put away childish things.

For now we see through a glass, darkly; but then face to face: now I know in part; but then shall I know even as also I am known.

And now abideth faith, hope, charity, these three; but the greatest of these is charity.

The Cadet Picture of My Father

RAINER MARIA RILKE

There's absence in the eyes. The brow's in touch
with something far. Now distant boyishness
and seduction shadow his enormous lips,
the slender aristocratic uniform
with its Franz Josef braid; both the hands bulge
like gloves upon the saber's basket hilt.
The hands are quiet, they reach out toward nothing—
I hardly see them now, as if they were
the first to grasp distance and disappear,
and all the rest lies curtained in itself,
and so withdrawn, I cannot understand
my father as he bleaches on this page——

Oh quickly disappearing photograph
in my more slowly disappearing hand!

Distant Footsteps

CESAR VALLEJO

My father sleeps. His august face
Expresses a peaceful heart.
He is so sweet now . . .
If there is anything bitter in him, it will be I.

There is solitude in the house; there is prayer;
There is no news of his sons today.
My father rouses, he listens
To the flight into Egypt, the stanching farewell.
He is so close now;
If there is anything distant in him, it will be I.

My mother walks in the orchard yonder,
Tasting a taste already tasteless.
She is so gentle now,
So much wing, so much departure, so much love.

There is solitude in the house, without a sound,
Without news, without greenness, without childhood,
And if there is anything broken this afternoon
And if it falls or creaks,
It is two old roadways, white and curving,
And my heart goes walking down them.

373

Sentimental Dialogue

PAUL VERLAINE

In the old park, frozen and deserted,
Two shapes have just slipped by.

Their eyes are dead and their lips are limp,
And their words can scarcely be heard.

In the old park, frozen and deserted,
Two wraiths have recalled the past.

"Do you remember our old delight?"
"Whyever should I remember it?"

"Does your heart still throb at my very name?
Do you still see my soul in your dreams?" "No."

"Ah, the fine days of unspeakable joy
When our lips met!" "Perhaps."

"How beautiful the sky was, how great our hope!"
"Hope has fled, defeated, to the dark sky."

They wandered on through the wild oats
And only the night listened to their words.

Tāj-Mahal

RABINDRANATH TAGORE

This you knew, O Emperor Shajahan,
That youth, glory and riches all pass away
In the stream of Time.
Might the sorrow of his heart
Be made deathless,
That was the desire of the Emperor.
Let the pomp of regal power
Vanish like the last glow of the sunset sky,
But may one deep sigh
Make tender the heavens,
This was your wish.
The lustre of all your diamonds and pearls
Is like the rainbow,
Spreading enchantment over the distant sky;
If that lustre dims, let it vanish,
But may this *Tāj-Mahal*[1] glisten bright
Like a tear drop on the cheek of Time.
Oh mind of Man,
You have no time to look backwards,
You hurry along the stream of life from port to port,
Taking up burdens at one
And laying them down at the other.
At the whisper of the south wind,
The spring flowers that fill the skirt of the forest,

[1] *Tāj-Mahal*: the mausoleum built by the Emperor Shajahan in memory of his dearly loved queen, Mumtāj, who died in childbirth.

375

Are scattered to dust
At the approach of twilight.
There is no time to linger.
Therefore in the wintry night the *Kunda*[2]
Blossoms anew to adorn tearful autumn's tray of delight.
O Heart, you must leave all your gatherings by the wayside,
At the end of the day,
At the end of the night.
There is no time to linger and to look backward.
And so, Emperor, your anxious heart
Had desired to steal the heart of Time
Through Beauty's enchantment.
Flinging what garland round her neck,
Have you given to death that is formless,
A form immortal.
There is no time to mourn in the busy flow of the years,
Therefore you have prisoned your restless cry
With the silent net of stern marble.
The love-names you used to call your beloved
On moon-light nights in the privacy of your chamber,
Those whispering love-calls you have here left behind
In the ear of the Infinite.
The tearful tenderness of love has blossomed
In these quiet stones as the flowers of Beauty.
O Poet-Emperor, this dream-picture of your heart,
This new 'Cloud-Messenger'[3]
In soaring songs and rhythms toward that Unseen,
Where your beloved has become one
With the glow of early dawn,
The tender sigh of the weary eventide,
The ethereal loveliness of the *Chameli*[4] in the moonlight,
And the shoreless region beyond all words
Whence the hungering eye returns baffled
From its quest.
Your messenger of Beauty,

---

[2] *Kunda*: a place where a holy fire is lit, or a place, like a dam, where a small stream breaks into a larger body of water.
[3] *Cloud-Messenger*: The name of a drama by Kalidasa in Sanskrit, immortalizing the longing of a banished prince for his beloved wife. It is one of the classics of Sanskrit literature.
[4] *Chameli*: a fragrant flower peculiar to northern India.

Eluding the watchman of Time,
Proclaims eternally: "I have not forgotten,
I have not forgotten, O beloved."

You have passed away, O Emperor.
Your empire has vanished like a dream
And your throne lies in the dust.
The memory of your warriors
Under whose tramp the earth once shuddered,
Is borne on the dust-laden winds of Delhi.
Your musicians sing no more,
The strains of the *nahabat*[5] mingle no more
With the ripples of the Jumna.[6]
The jingling music of the princesses' anklets
Which died down amidst the forsaken ruins,
Reappears in the cry of the crickets
And resounds in the darkness of the night.
Still your messenger, untired and unfailing,
Ignoring the rise and fall of empires,
The rhythm of life and death,
Proclaims through the ages
With the voice of the eternal-bereaved:
"I have not forgotten, I have not forgotten,
O beloved."

It is a lie!
Who says that you have not forgotten?
That you have not opened the doors of the cage of memory?
Does your mind still cleave
To the twilight gloom of the past?
Through the liberating path of forgetfulness
Has it not yet come out into the open?
The shrine stands firm in the dust of the earth
And gently covers death with the veil of memory.
Who can keep life still?
Every star of the sky beckons it on.
Its call vibrates from world to world
In the surging light of ever new dawns.

---

[5] *nahabat*: a small orchestra played at a rich man's house on festive occasions.
[6] *Jumna*: a river in northern India.

Breaking the bonds of remembrance,
It surges forth.
Free and unburdened,
Along the open road of the Universe.
Emperor,
No empire has ever been able to keep you in bondage;
This sea-girt earth cannot satisfy you,
O Mighty One!
Therefore at the end of life's feast
You leave this earth behind,
Pushing it aside with your feet
Like an outworn earthen vessel.
You are mightier than your deeds,
Therefore the chariot of your life again and again
Leaves those deeds behind.
Therefore only traces of you remain,
But you yourself are not here.
That love which cannot urge one forward,
That love which sets its throne in the common highway,
The allurements of its sensuous pleasure
Cling round your feet like the dust of the wayside.
All that you have given back again to dust.
Into that dust where your footprint fell,
Suddenly unawares, wafted on the wings of air,
A seed dropped from the garland of life.
You have travelled far away,
But that seed, taking immortal life, raises itself to the sky[7]
And chants in solemn melody:
"However far I look, he is not there, the traveller.
The beloved could not keep him back,
The empire made free the path for him to go,
The mountains and the oceans did not bar his way.
Today his chariot is moving at the call of the night
To the music of the stars,
Towards the open portal of the morn.
Heavy with the burden of memory, I remain behind,
But he, the free, the unburdened,
Is not here."

---

[7] *That love which cannot urge . . . raises itself to the sky*: See note at end
of poem.

Note: In a letter the poet admits that the above lines are rather ambiguous, and at one time he seriously thought of omitting them from the final text. But he goes on to say that a poem may not always be quite clear to the poet himself; the work of creation goes on unconsciously and at its end, the poet is as much an outsider toward his poem as the reader, and the judgment of the former has not more validity than that of the latter. With this reservation he offers the following explanation:

"The love of a Moghul Emperor, surrounded by his many wives, is of rather an earthly kind—its pleasure-house is built upon dust. Just because she died at the right time, Queen Mumtāj left behind a seed of sad parting which fell upon the dust of that pleasure garden; it did not turn to dust, but breaking through the evanescence of cloyed luxury, sprouted into blossom. Through its inherent quality, that supreme remembrance, embracing a mortal object, has become immortal. And with the sadness, this remembrance proclaims yet another message: Both Shajahan and Mumtāj have vanished, but on the dust of the path they travelled together stands Tāj-Mahal, echoing for ever the cry that lies at the heart of life."

Three Poems

HEINRICH HEINE

I

'Twas tea-time; the mildly aesthetic
    Ensemble took Love as their theme.
The mood of the guests was poetic;
    They gushed like a lyrical stream.

"True love must be always platonic,"
    A hardened old councilor cried.
With a laugh that was almost ironic,
    His wife looked upward and sighed.

A canon spoke, "We must resist 'em,
    These pleasures that rouse and harass,
Or else they will ruin the system."
    And a pretty young thing lisped, "Alas."

The countess, drooping and yearning,
    Said, "Love must sweep on like the sea!"
As, elegantly turning,
    She handed the baron his tea.

Still, it was not quite complete, dear;
    Your place stood empty above.
And, oh, it would have been sweet, dear,
    To hear *you* prattle of love.

II

My songs, you say, are poisoned.
    How else, love, could it be?
You have, with deadly magic,
    Poured poison into me.

My songs, you say, are poisoned.
    And well I know it, too.
I carry a thousand serpents
    And, love, among them—you.

III

Again the old dream came to me:
    'Twas May; the world was vernal;
We sat beneath the linden tree
    And pledged a faith eternal.

Great love and a deathless oath we swore.
    And that I might never forget it,
With a passionate kiss and a thousand more
    You took my hand, and bit it.

Oh, sweetheart with the lips that cling,
    With eyes so clear and merry,
The oath was quite the proper thing—
    The bite, unnecessary.

Carmen

PROSPER MÉRIMÉE

PART I

I HAVE always suspected the geographers of not knowing what they were talking about when they placed the battlefield of Munda within the country of the Bastuli-Poeni, near the modern Ronda, a few leagues north of Marbella. According to my own conjectures, based on the text of the anonymous author of *Bellum Hispaniense,* and some information gathered in the excellent library of the Duke of Ossuna, I decided that one must seek in the environs of Montilla the memorable spot where, for the last time, Caesar played double or quits against the champions of the Republic. Finding myself in Andalusia at the commencement of autumn in 1830, I made a rather long excursion to dispel a few lingering doubts. A pamphlet that I shall soon publish will dispel, I trust, any uncertainty in the minds of all honest archaeologists. While waiting for my dissertation to solve at last the geographical problem which holds all scientific Europe in suspense, I wish to tell you a short story. It will in no wise prejudice you on the interesting question of the site of Munda.

I had hired at Cordova a guide and two horses, and had taken the field—my sole baggage a few shirts and the Commentaries of Caesar. One day, while wandering in the higher parts of the plain of Cachena, weary with fatigue, parched with thirst, broiling under a noonday sun, I was heartily consigning Caesar and the sons of Pompey to the devil, when I saw at some distance from the path I was following a little green space dotted with reeds and rushes. This showed me that a spring was near. In fact, on drawing nearer I saw that the seeming greensward was a little bog, in which a rivulet

lost itself after issuing apparently from a narrow gorge between two high
buttresses of the Sierra de Cabra. I concluded that by following it up I
should find cooler water, fewer frogs and leeches, and perhaps a little shade
amid the rocks. At the entrance of the gorge my horse neighed and was
immediately answered by another horse that I could not see. I had scarcely
gone a hundred paces when the gorge suddenly widened and displayed a
sort of natural amphitheater wholly shaded by the height of the enclosing
cliffs. It would have been impossible to find a nook which promised to the
traveler a more agreeable halting place. At the foot of perpendicular cliffs
the spring gushed bubbling forth, and tumbled into a little basin lined with
sand as white as snow. Five or six beautiful green oaks, ever sheltered from
the wind and watered by the spring, rose from its banks and spread over
it the curtain of their deep shade; and finally, around the basin a fine lus-
trous grass offered a bed better than could be found in any inn ten leagues
round.

To me did not belong the honor of discovering so beautiful a spot. A
man was already resting there, no doubt asleep when I entered. Aroused by
the neighing of the horses, he had arisen and approached his steed, which
had profited by his master's slumber to make a good meal from the surrounding grass. He was a young gallant of medium height but robust make,
with a look haughty and sad. His complexion, which might have been
good, was from exposure to the sun become even darker than his hair. In
one hand he held the bridle of his horse, and in the other a brass blunderbuss. I admit that at first the blunderbuss and the fierce air of its owner
startled me a little; but I believed no more in brigands, from having heard
so much talk about them and yet having never seen a single one. Besides,
I had seen so many honest farmers arm themselves to the teeth when only
going to market that the sight of firearms did not warrant me in doubting
the honesty of the unknown. And then, thought I, what in the world could
he do with my shirts and my Elzevir Commentaries? So I saluted the man
with the blunderbuss with a familiar nod, and asked with a smile if I had
disturbed his siesta. Without answering he surveyed me searchingly from
head to foot, and then, seemingly satisfied by his examination, he considered with the same attention my advancing guide. I saw the latter turn
pale and pause in evident terror. An unlucky meeting! said I to myself.
But prudence counseled me at the same time to show no uneasiness. So I
dismounted, and telling my guide to unbridle, I knelt beside the spring and
plunged into it my head and hands; then I took a good long drink lying flat
on my belly like the bad soldiers of Gideon.

Meanwhile I kept an eye on my guide and the stranger. The former came
forward plainly against his will, and the latter seemed to intend us no evil,

for he had released his horse, and his blunderbuss, which he had before held ready, now pointed peacefully to the ground.

Not thinking it worthwhile to take offense at the slighting manner in which I was received, I stretched myself upon the grass, and nonchalantly asked the man with the blunderbuss if he had not a tinderbox about him. At the same time I took out my cigar case. Still silent, he fumbled about in his pocket, brought forth his tinderbox, and set eagerly at work to strike me a light. Evidently he was becoming more civilized, for he sat down opposite me, yet never laid down his weapon. My cigar lighted, I chose the best one remaining and asked him if he smoked.

"Yes, señor," he replied. They were his first words, and I noticed that he did not pronounce the *s*'s after the manner of the Andalusians.[1] From which I concluded that he was a traveler like myself, only less archaeologically inclined.

"You will find that pretty good," said I, giving him a real Havana regalia.

He made me a slight bow, lighted his cigar from mine, thanked me with another bow, and began to smoke with every sign of pleasure.

"Ah!" cried he, letting the smoke of his first puff stream forth from his lips and nostrils, "how long it is since I have smoked!"

In Spain, a cigar offered and accepted establishes hospitable relations, as in the East does the sharing of bread and salt. My man became more talkative than I had hoped. Although he claimed to be a native of the province of Montilla, he knew little about the neighborhood. He could not tell the name of the charming valley in which we were; he could not name any neighboring village; and finally, when I asked him if about there he had seen any old broken-down walls, large flanged tiles, or sculptured stones, he confessed that he had never noticed any such things. To make amends, however, he showed himself an expert in horseflesh. He criticized mine, which was not a difficult task, and then gave me the pedigree of his own, which came from the celebrated steed of Cordova, a noble animal—in fact, of such endurance, his master asserted, that he had once ridden him thirty leagues in a day at a gallop or fast trot. In the middle of his tirade, my unknown suddenly checked himself, as if surprised and vexed at having said too much. "You see, I was in great haste to get to Cordova," resumed he with some embarrassment. . . . "I had a lawsuit there. . . ." He looked searchingly at Antonio, who kept his eyes fixed on the ground.

The shade and the spring so charmed me that I remembered some slices

---

[1] *pronounce . . . Andalusians*: The Andalusians aspirate the *s*, and confound it with the soft *c* and *z* which the Spaniards pronounce like the English *th*. By the word *señor* alone one may distinguish an Andalusian. [Author's note]

of ham that some friends of mine at Montilla had put in my guide's wallet. I had them brought, and invited the stranger to share with us the impromptu collation. If he had not smoked for a long time, it seemed to me that he had not eaten for at least forty-eight hours. He fell to like a famished wolf, and I considered that our meeting must have been providential for the poor devil. My guide meanwhile ate little, drank less, and spoke not at all; though at the commencement of our journey he had shown himself a regular old gossip. The presence of our guest seemed to annoy him, and a certain mutual distrust kept them apart, without my being able to positively divine the cause.

When the last crumbs of bread and ham had disappeared, and we had each smoked another cigar, I ordered my guide to bridle our horses; and was just going to bid our new friend adieu, when he asked me where I expected to pass the night.

Before I could heed a sign that my guide made me, I had answered that I was going to the Venta del Cuervo.

"A poor shelter for a person like you, señor. I am going there, too, and if you will permit it we will go together."

"With pleasure," said I, mounting my horse. My guide, who held my stirrup, made me another sign with his eyes. I replied by shrugging my shoulders to assure him of my tranquillity, and we set out.

Antonio's mysterious signs, his uneasiness, the few words which had escaped the unknown—particularly his famous ride of thirty leagues, and the doubtful explanation he had given of it—had already formed my opinion of our new traveling companion. I had no doubt but that I had to do with a smuggler, perhaps a robber; but what did it matter? I knew the Spanish character well enough to fear no evil of a man with whom I had smoked and eaten. His company even was a sure protection against all evil comers. Besides, I was glad to know what a real brigand was like. One does not meet them every day, and there is a certain charm in being near a dangerous being, above all when one finds him good-natured and subdued.

I hoped that by degrees I might win the confidence of the unknown; so despite my guide's winks I turned the conversation to the subject of highwaymen. You may imagine with what respect I spoke of them. At that time there was in Andalusia a famous bandit named José-Maria, whose exploits were the talk of the country. Suppose I am really with José-Maria! thought I. Then I told all the stories I knew of that hero—but all to his credit, you may be sure; and I expressed my great admiration for his bravery and his generosity.

"José-Maria is only a rogue," the stranger replied coldly.

Does he do himself justice, or is it mock modesty? I asked myself; for from examining so closely my companion I had come to identify him with the description of José-Maria that I had seen posted on the gates of many towns of Andalusia. Yes, thought I, it is he indeed: blond hair, blue eyes, large mouth, beautiful teeth, small hands, fine linen, a velvet vest with silver buttons, gaiters of white skin, and a bay horse—there is no doubt of it; but let us respect his incognito.

We arrived at the venta. It was just what he had described to me, one of the worst I had yet seen. One large room served as kitchen, dining room, and chamber. On a stone flag in the middle of the room the fire was made, and the smoke passed out through a hole cut in the roof, or rather hung in clouds a few feet above the floor. Along the wall five or six old mule blankets were stretched out upon the floor. These were the beds for travelers. About twenty paces from the house, or rather from the single room I have just described, was built a kind of shed used for a stable. In this charming retreat there were no other persons just then except an old woman and a little girl, both as black as soot and horribly ragged. Behold! cried I to myself, all that remains of the population of the ancient Munda Baetica! O Caesar! O Sextus Pompey! amazed would you be, could you come back to this world!

When she saw my companion the old woman gave a cry of surprise, "Ah! Señor Don José."

Don José frowned, and raised his hand with a gesture of command which stopped the old woman at once. I turned to my guide, and by a covert sign I made him understand that he could tell me nothing about the man with whom I was going to pass the night. The supper was better than I had anticipated there. They served us, upon a little table about a foot high, an old cock fricasseed with rice and pimentos, then pimentos in oil, and finally *gazpacho*—a sort of salad of pimentos. Three courses thus seasoned forced us to have recourse very often to a skin of Montilla wine which seemed delicious. After supper, seeing a mandolin hanging from the wall—there are mandolins everywhere in Spain—I asked the little girl, who had waited upon us, if she could play.

"No," she answered, "but Don José can play—oh, so well!"

"Will you be so good as to sing me something?" said I to him. "I love passionately your national music."

"I can refuse nothing to so polite a man, who gives me such good cigars," cried Don José with an air of good humor; and being given the instrument, he sang and accompanied himself. His voice was harsh, but nevertheless agreeable; the air sad and weird; as for the words, I did not understand a single one.

"If I am not mistaken," I said, "that is not a Spanish song which you have just sung. It resembles the *zorzicos* which I have heard in the Provinces,[2] and the words seem to be Basque."

"Yes," answered Don José with a somber air. He laid the mandolin on the ground and, with folded arms, contemplated the embers of the dying fire with a singular expression of sadness. Illumined by a lamp on the little table, his face, at once noble and ferocious, reminded me of Milton's Satan. Like him, perhaps, my companion dreamed of the abode he had left, of the exile he now suffered for his sin. I tried to reanimate the conversation, but he did not reply, so absorbed was he in his sad thoughts. Already the old crone had retired to a corner of the room screened off by a tattered old blanket stretched across a rope; and the little girl had followed her to this retreat reserved for the fair sex. Then my guide, rising, asked me to accompany him to the stable; but at this Don José, as if suddenly awakened, asked in a brusque tone where he was going.

"To the stable," replied the guide.

"What for? The horses are fed. Sleep here. The gentleman will permit it."

"I am afraid that the gentleman's horse may be ailing. I want him to see it; perhaps he will know what to do."

Evidently Antonio wished to speak to me in private, but I cared not to arouse Don José's suspicions; in our position it seemed to me better to show the greatest confidence. I answered Antonio, then, that I had no fear for the horses and that I was sleepy. Don José followed him to the stable and soon came back alone. He told me that the horse was all right, but that the guide valued the beast so highly that he was rubbing it down with his vest to make it perspire, and that it was to be expected he would pass the night in this delightful occupation. I had stretched myself out upon the mule blankets, taking care to wrap myself carefully in my mantle, so that I should not touch them. After asking pardon for the liberty of lying near me, Don José lay down before the door, after he had placed a fresh cap on his blunderbuss, which he took care to place beneath the wallet which served him for a pillow. Five minutes after, having wished each other good night, we were both sound asleep.

I thought I was tired enough to sleep even in such a hovel, but in an hour's time I was awakened from my first nap by a disagreeable itching. As soon as I discovered the cause I got up, persuaded that it would be better to pass the night under the stars than under such an inhospitable roof. On tiptoe then I reached the door, stepping over Don José, who was

---

[2] *Provinces*: The provinces enjoying peculiar *fueros* (privileges or exemptions); that is to say, Alava, Biscay, Guipuzcoa, and a part of Navarre. Basque is the language of these countries. [Author's note]

sleeping the sleep of the just, and I managed so well that I left the house without disturbing him. Near the door was a large wooden bench. I stretched myself out upon it and arranged myself as comfortably as possible to pass the rest of the night. I was about to shut my eyes for the second time, when it seemed to me that there passed before me the shadow of a horse and the shadow of a man, both walking without the least noise. I sat up, and thought that I recognized Antonio. Surprised to find him outside the stable at that time, I jumped up and went to meet him. He had stopped, having seen me first.

"Where is he?" asked Antonio in a whisper.

"In the inn, sleeping; he doesn't mind the fleas. Why have you taken the horse out?"

I noticed then, that in order to make no noise in coming out of the shed, Antonio had carefully wrapped his horse's feet in the remnants of an old blanket.

"Speak lower, for God's sake," said Antonio. "You don't know who that man is. 'Tis José Navarro, the most notorious bandit in Andalusia. All day have I been making you signs which you would not understand."

"Bandit or not," I answered, "what does it matter to me? He hasn't robbed us, and I'll wager he does not intend to."

"So much the better, but there is a reward of two hundred ducats for his arrest. I know where there is a post of lancers, a league and a half from here, and before the break of day I'll bring back a squad of stout fellows. I would have taken his horse, too, but it is so vicious that no one but the Navarro can come near it."

"What the devil are you up to?" said I. "What wrong has this poor fellow done you that you should betray him? Besides, are you sure he is the brigand you pretend?"

"Perfectly sure. Just now he followed me to the stable and said, 'You seem to know me; tell this gentleman who I am, and I will blow your brains out.' Stay with him, señor; lie down beside him and fear nothing. So long as he knows you are there he will suspect nothing."

While we were thus talking we had gone so far from the inn that the horse's hooves would be out of hearing. In the twinkling of an eye, Antonio had torn the rags from his horse's feet and was preparing to mount. I tried both prayers and threats to detain him.

"I am a poor devil, señor," said he; "two hundred ducats are not to be thrown away, especially when it helps to rid the country of such vermin. But take care! If the Navarro awakes he will jump for his gun, so look out for yourself! As for me, I have gone too far to turn back; shift for yourself as best you can."

The rascal was in the saddle and, driving both spurs into his horse, was soon lost to my sight in the obscurity of night.

I was very angry with my guide and quite uneasy. After a moment of reflection I determined to return to the inn. Don José still slept, recuperating, no doubt, from the fatigues and vigils of many adventurous days. I was obliged to shake him roughly to awaken him. Never shall I forget the ferocious look and the movement he made to seize his gun, which I had taken the precaution to remove a short distance from his couch.

"Señor caballero," said I, "I have a silly question to ask: Would you care to see a half-dozen lancers ride up here?"

He sprang to his feet and in a terrible voice cried out, "Who told you that?"

"What matters it whence comes the advice, provided it is good?"

"Your guide has betrayed me, but he shall pay for this. Where is he?"

"I do not know. In the stable, I think—but someone told me——"

"Who, who?—not the old woman?"

"Someone whom I know not. But, without further words, have you, yes or no, reasons for not awaiting the soldiers? If you have, lose no time; and so good-bye, and I beg pardon for having disturbed you."

"Ah, your guide! your guide! I mistrusted him from the first. But I will pay him back! Adieu, señor; God requite you what I owe you. I am not so bad as you believe me; yes, there is yet something in me to merit the pity of a gallant man. Adieu, señor—I have only one regret: that I cannot repay you for this service."

"For payment, Don José, promise me to suspect no one, and dream not of vengeance. Wait a moment; take these cigars for your trip. A pleasant journey!" and I offered him my hand.

He shook it without speaking, grasped his weapon and his wallet, and after he had spoken a few words to the old hag in an argot which I did not understand, he ran to the stable, and in a few moments I heard him gallop off into the open country.

As for me, I lay down again on my bench, but I could not get to sleep. I asked myself if I had done right in saving a robber, perhaps a murderer, from the gallows, and solely because I had eaten with him a little ham and some rice *à la valencienne*. Had I not betrayed my guide who upheld the law? Had not I exposed him to the vengeance of a ruffian? But the laws of hospitality! Prejudice of a savage, said I to myself; I must now answer for all the future crimes of this bandit. And yet, is it a prejudice—this instinctive conscience which defies all reasoning? Perhaps, in such a delicate case, may I not be able to extricate myself without remorse? Thus I vacillated in the greatest uncertainty in regard to the morality of my action, when I saw approaching a half-dozen cavaliers, with Antonio prudently bringing up the rear. I went to meet them, and informed them that the bandit had taken flight more than two hours before.

The old crone, questioned by the corporal, answered that she knew the Navarro when he came to her house, but that, living alone, she had never dared to risk her life by denouncing him. She added that his habit was, when at her house, always to depart in the dead of night. As for me, I was obliged to go several leagues from there, show my passport, and sign a declaration before a magistrate; after which I was permitted to resume my archaeological researches. Antonio nursed a grudge against me, for he suspected me of having prevented his earning the two hundred ducats. However, we parted good friends at Cordova, and there I gave him as generous a tip as the state of my purse permitted.

PART II

I spent several days at Cordova. I had been told of a certain manuscript in the library of the Dominicans, in which I ought to find interesting information about the ancient Munda. Cordially received by the good priests, I spent several days in their monastery, and in the evenings I strolled about the city.

At sunset, in Cordova, there are many idlers on the quay which borders the left bank of the Guadalquivir. There one still breathes the odors from a tannery which preserves the ancient renown of the country for the manufacture of leather; but to compensate for this, one enjoys there a spectacle which has its merits. Some moments before the Angelus, a great number of women congregate on the bank of the stream, at the foot of the quay, which is quite high. Not a man dares to mingle with this troop. As soon as the Angelus rings it is supposed to be night. At the last stroke of the bell all the women undress and plunge into the water. Then such cries, such laughter, such an infernal uproar. From the top of the quay the men contemplate the bathers, straining their eyes, but seeing little. Nevertheless, these white and uncertain forms, traced on the somber azure of the flood, set working a poetic mind, and with a little imagination it is not difficult to imagine Diana and her nymphs at the bath, without fearing the fate of Actaeon.

I was told that several wretched scapegraces once made up a purse to bribe the bell ringer of the cathedral to ring the Angelus twenty minutes before the legal time. Though it was still broad daylight, the nymphs of the Guadalquivir did not hesitate, and trusting more to the Angelus than to the sun, in perfect innocence they made their toilette for the bath, and 'tis

always of the most simple description. I was not there. In my time the bell
ringer was incorruptible, the twilight dim, and only a cat could have told
the oldest orange peddler from the prettiest grisette of Cordova.

One evening, at the hour when one can see no more, I was leaning upon
the parapet of the quay, smoking, when a woman ascended the staircase
which leads to the river and came to sit near me. In her hair she wore a
large bunch of jasmine, the petals of which exhaled an intoxicating odor.
She was simply, perhaps poorly, clad, all in black, like most of the grisettes
in the evening. Women of fashion wear black only in the morning; in the
evening they dress *a la francesa*. When near me, my bather let slip to her
shoulders the mantilla which covered her head, and by the faint light of
the stars I saw that she was petite, well formed, and had very large eyes.
I threw my cigar away at once. She understood this attention, a politeness
wholly French, and hastened to tell me that she was very fond of the odor
of tobacco, and that she even smoked herself when she could find any very
mild *papelitos*. Luckily, I had some such mild cigarettes in my case, and
I eagerly offered her some. She deigned to accept one, and lighted it at the
end of a burning cord which an urchin brought us for a sou. Smoking together, we chatted so long, the beautiful bather and I, that we found ourselves almost alone on the quay. I did not think it indiscreet to ask her to
take an ice with me at the *neveria*.[3] After a moment's modest hesitation she
accepted; but, before accepting, she wished to know what time it was. I
made my repeater strike the hour, and this seemed to astonish her
greatly.

"What inventions you have in your countries, you foreigners! From what
country are you, señor? English, without doubt?"[4]

"French, and your humble servant. And you, mademoiselle, or madame,
you are probably of Cordova?"

"No."

"At least of Andalusia? I think I detect that from your soft accent."

"If you note everyone's accent so well, you should be able to divine what
I am."

"I think that you are from the country of Jesus, two steps from Paradise." I had learned this figure of speech, which designates Andalusia, from
my friend Francisco Sevilla, the well-known picador.

---

[3] *neveria*: a café provided with an icehouse, or, rather, with a supply of snow. There is
hardly a village which has not its *neveria*. [Author's note]
[4] *English, without doubt*: In Spain every traveler who does not lug around samples
of calico or silk passes for an Englishman, *Inglesito*. It is the same in the East.
At Chalcis I have had the honor of being introduced as a Μιλόοδος Φραυτξέσος
(French lord). [Author's note]

"Bah! Paradise—— People here say that it is not for such as we."

"Why, then you must be a Moor, or——" I hesitated, not daring to say a Jewess.

"Oh, come now! you know well enough that I am a Gypsy: shall I tell you *la baji?*[5] Have you never heard of La Carmencita? I am she."

I was at that time—it is fifteen years ago—such a miscreant that I did not draw back in horror at finding myself beside a sorceress. Good! thought I. Last week I supped with a highway robber; now I am going to take an ice with a servant of the devil. When traveling, one should see everything. I had still another motive for cultivating her acquaintance. When I left college, I confess to my shame that I had already lost some time in studying the occult sciences; several times, even, I had tried to conjure up the spirit of darkness. Cured long ago of the passion for such pursuits, I retained, nevertheless, a certain curiosity about all superstitions, and I congratulated myself on the chance of learning just how much the black art had flourished among the Gypsies.

While chatting we had entered the *neveria* and had seated ourselves at a little table which was lighted by a candle burning in a glass globe. I had time then to examine my gitana, while several respectable citizens, eating their ices, stared in amazement to see me in such company.

I doubt very much whether Mademoiselle Carmen was of pure blood; at least, she was infinitely prettier than any of her race that I have ever met. That a woman may be beautiful, say the Spaniards, she must unite thirty *si,* or, if you please, she must merit description by the use of ten adjectives, each of them applicable to three parts of her person. For example, she should have three things black: eyes, lashes, and eyebrows; three things elegant: hands, lips, and tresses—etc. For the rest, see Brantôme.[6] My Gypsy could not pretend to so many perfections. Her skin, though otherwise free from blemish, was nearly the color of copper; her eyes oblique, but large and full; her lips a little thick, but admirably formed, and disclosing teeth whiter than blanched almonds. Her hair, perhaps a little too coarse, was black, with blue reflections like a crow's wing, long and glossy. Not to tire you with a description too minute, I will say, briefly, that to each defect she joined an excellency enhanced by the contrast. It was a wild and savage beauty, a face which astonished you at first, and was never to be forgotten. Her eyes especially had an expression, at once voluptuous and fierce, that I have never met since in any other human glance. "Eye of a Gypsy, eye of a wolf," is a Spanish saying which shows careful

[5] *la baji:* fortune.
[6] *Brantôme*: French historian and biographer who traveled extensively in Spain and wrote about his travels.

observation. If you have not time to go to the zoological gardens and study a wolf's expression, look at your cat while she is watching a bird.

As everyone knows, it would have been ridiculous to have your fortune told in a café, so I asked the pretty witch to permit me to accompany her home; she consented without trouble, but she wished again to know how the time was passing and asked me to again make my repeater strike the hour.

"Is it really gold?" she asked, while she examined it with an excessive interest.

When we resumed our walk it was really night; most of the shops were closed, and the streets nearly deserted. We crossed the bridge over the Guadalquivir, and at the end of the suburb we stopped before a house which, to say the least, did not look like a palace. A child let us in. The Gypsy spoke to him a few words in a language I did not understand, but which I have since learned was the *rommani*, or *chipe calli*, the idiom of the Gypsies. The child immediately left us in a good-sized room furnished with a small table, two stools, and a chest. I should not forget, however, a jar of water, a pile of oranges, and a string of onions.

As soon as we were alone the Gypsy took from the chest a pack of cards which had evidently seen long service, a magnet, a dried chameleon, and several other objects necessary to her art. Then she told me to make a cross in my left hand with a piece of money, and the magic ceremonies commenced. It is useless to repeat to you her predictions, and as to her manner, it was evident that she was no prentice hand.

Unfortunately we were soon interrupted. Suddenly the door was opened violently, and a man, wrapped to his eyes in a brown mantle, strode into the room apostrophizing my Gypsy in no gentle terms. I did not understand what he said, but the tone of his voice indicated that he was in a very bad humor. At sight of him the fortune-teller showed neither anger nor surprise, but ran to meet him, and with an extraordinary volubility she addressed him in that tongue which she had already used before me. The word *payllo,* often repeated, was the sole word that I understood. I knew that the Gypsies thus designated men not of their own race. Supposing that it was all about me, I was expecting a rather delicate explanation; already I had grasped the leg of one of the stools and was communing with myself as to the exact moment when it would be expedient to hurl it at the intruder's head. The latter pushed the Gypsy rudely aside and strode toward me; then, recoiling a step, he exclaimed.

"Ah! señor, it is you, then!"

I looked in my turn and recognized my acquaintance, Don José, and at that moment I regretted a little that I had saved him from hanging.

"Eh? so it is you, my good fellow!" I cried, laughing with the best grace I could summon. "You have interrupted mademoiselle just as she was revealing to me the most interesting things."

"Always the same! This shall end," said he between his teeth, fixing upon her a ferocious look.

Nevertheless the Gypsy continued to talk to him in her own tongue. By degrees she became more and more excited. Her eyes became bloodshot and terrible; her features contracted; she stamped with her foot. It seemed to me that she was urging him to do something at which he hesitated. What this was I thought that I understood only too well from seeing her pass and repass her little hand under her chin. I was tempted to believe that there was a throat that needed cutting, and I had a strong suspicion that it was no other than mine own.

To all this torrent of eloquence Don José answered only by two or three words sharply spoken. The Gypsy flashed at him a look of profound contempt; then, sitting down *à la turque* in a corner of the room, she peeled an orange and commenced to eat it. Don José took me by the arm, opened the door, and led me into the street. We went about two hundred paces in deep silence. Then, extending his hand, "Keep straight on," he said, "and you will come to the bridge."

At the same time he turned his back and walked quickly away. I returned to my inn, a little abashed and in very bad humor. The worst of it was, that when I undressed I found that my watch was missing.

Several reasons prevented me from going to reclaim it the following day, or to put the police upon the lookout. I finished my work upon the Dominicans' manuscript, and departed for Seville. After several months' wandering in Andalusia, I wished to return to Madrid, and it was necessary to pass through Cordova. I had no intention to make a long wait there, for I had taken a strong dislike to that beautiful city and the nymphs of the Guadalquivir. Nevertheless, several friends to visit, some commissions to execute, would keep me at least three or four days in the ancient capital of the Mussulman princes.

As soon as I reappeared at the monastery of the Dominicans, one of the fathers, who had always shown a great interest in my researches concerning the site of Munda, welcomed me with open arms, crying:

"Blessed be the name of the Lord! Welcome, dear friend! We thought you dead; and I, who am now talking to you, I have recited many *Paters* and *Aves,* which I regret not, for the salvation of your soul. So! you have not been assassinated, but we know that you have been robbed."

"What do you mean?" I asked, a little surprised.

"Yes, you remember—the beautiful watch! the one you used to make strike in the library when we used to tell you it was time to go to the service. Ah, well! it has been recovered and will be given back to you."

"That is to say," I interrupted, "I had mislaid it———"

"The rascal is behind bars, and as everyone knew him to be a man who would shoot a Christian for a farthing, we were terribly afraid that he had killed you. I will go with you to the *corregidor* and we will get you back your watch. And then consider whether you should say that justice is not done in Spain!"

"I confess," I said, "that I would rather lose my watch than give evidence which might justly bring any poor wretch to the gallows; above all, because———"

"Oh, have no fear! he is well recommended, and they can't hang him more than once. When I say hang, I say wrongly, for he is an hidalgo, your robber; so he will be garroted[7] day after tomorrow without fail. You see that a robbery more or less would make little difference in his case. Would to God that he had only robbed! But he has committed several murders, each one more horrible than the last."

"What is his name?"

"He is known here as José Navarro; but he has a Basque name which neither you nor I could ever pronounce. I tell you, he is a man worth seeing, and you who like so much to see the curiosities of the country should not neglect this chance of learning how in Spain these rascals make their exit from this world. He is in the chapel,[8] and Padre Martinez will conduct you thither."

My Dominican insisted so strongly upon my seeing the apparatus for the *pepit pendement pien choli*[9] that I could not resist him. I went then to see the prisoner, taking with me a bunch of cigars, which I hoped might lead him to excuse my intrusion.

They admitted me to the presence of Don José, whom we found at a repast. He nodded coldly and thanked me politely for the gift I brought him. After counting the cigars in the package, he chose a certain number and gave me back the rest, observing that he had need of no more.

I asked him whether with a little money or the influence of my friends I might not in some way soften his lot. At first he shrugged his shoulders, smiling sadly; and then, thinking better of it, he begged me to have a Mass said for the salvation of his soul.

[7] *garroted*: In 1830 this was a privilege of the nobility. Today, under constitutional rule, the common people have acquired the right to the garrote. [Author's note]

[8] *chapel*: In the Spanish prisons there is usually a chapel in which the condemned prisoners are confined and prepared spiritually for death.

[9] *pepit . . . choli*: This is the Dominican's poor pronunciation of the French phrase *petit pendement bien joli* (very pretty little scaffold).

"Would you"—he added timidly—"would you have another said for a woman who has wronged you?"

"Surely," I replied; "but no one that I know of has wronged me in this country."

He took my hand and pressed it gravely. After a moment's silence he continued:

"Dare I also ask of you a favor? . . . When you return into your country you will perhaps pass through Navarre. At least you will pass through Vitoria, which is not far from it."

"Yes," I said, "I shall go certainly by Vitoria, and it is not unlikely that I may turn aside to visit Pamplona; and for your sake I will willingly make this detour."

"Well, if you go to Pamplona you will see more than one thing to interest you. . . . It is a beautiful city. . . . I will give you this medal." He showed me a silver medal suspended from his neck. "You will wrap it in paper"—he paused a moment to master his emotion—"and you will carry it or have it sent to a good woman whose address I will give you. Say that I am dead, but say not how I died."

I promised to carry out his wishes. I saw him again on the morrow and passed a part of the day in his company. It was from his lips that I learned the sad story you are going to read.

PART III

"I was born," he said, "at Elizondo, in the valley of Baztan. My name is Don José Lizarrabengoa, and you know Spain well enough, señor, to understand from my name that I am a Basque and of the old Christian faith. If I call myself Don it is because I have that right, and if I were at Elizondo I would show you my genealogy upon parchment. I was intended for the Church, and forced to study for it; but this profited me little. I was too fond of playing *paume*,[10] and that was my undoing. When we play at *paume,* we Navarros, we forget everything else. One day when I had won, a youth of Alava picked a quarrel with me. We resorted to our *maquilas,*[11] and at that I again beat him; but this obliged me to leave the country. I fell in with some dragoons and enlisted in the cavalry regiment of Almanza. The men from our mountains learn quickly a soldier's trade. I soon became a corporal, and they were promising to make me a quartermaster when, to my misfortune, I was put on guard at the tobacco factory at Seville.

[10] *paume*: tennis.
[11] *maquilas*: staffs shod with iron.

"If you have ever been at Seville you must have noticed the great building outside the ramparts near the Guadalquivir. It seems to me I can see still the door and the guardhouse beside it. When they are not on duty the Spaniards play cards or sleep; but I, a free Navarro, strove always to keep busy. One day I was making a chain, from brass wire, for my eping-lette.[12] All at once my comrades cried: 'There's the bell ringing: the girls are coming back to work!' You know, señor, that there are as many as four or five hundred women employed in the building. It is they who roll the cigars in a great room into which no man can enter without permission from a *vingt-quatre*,[13] because the women, especially the young ones, in warm weather work in a very free-and-easy costume. After the dinner hour, when they return to work, many young men go to watch them pass, and they are of all sorts. There are few of these ladies who would refuse a silk mantilla, and the amateur at that sort of game has only to stoop to win the prize. While the others looked on, I remained on my bench near the door. I was young then and always dreaming of home, and did not believe that there were any pretty girls without blue skirts and hair falling in braids on their shoulders.[14] Besides, the Andalusians frightened me. I was not then accustomed to their manners—always bantering and jesting, never a word of sense or reason. There I was, busy with my chain, when I heard some of the people say: 'There comes the *gitanella!*' I looked up and saw her. It was on a Friday, and I shall never forget it. I saw that Carmen whom you know, in whose house I found you some months ago.

"She wore a red skirt, very short, which displayed her white silk stockings, with more than one hole in them, and tiny shoes of red morocco, tied with flame-colored ribbon. She threw back her mantilla in order to show her shoulders and a great bunch of cassia flowers that she wore in her chemise. She had also a cassia flower in the corner of her mouth, and she came prancing along like a thoroughbred filly from the stud of Cordova. In my country, a woman in such a costume would have made everyone cross himself. At Seville, everyone paid her some gallant compliment on her figure. She answered them all with side glances, her hand on her hip, as bold as the true Gypsy that she was. At first she did not please me, and I resumed my work; but she, after the custom of women and cats, who come not when called but come unasked, stopped before me and accosted me.

" 'Friend,' she said, in the Andalusian manner, 'will you give me the chain to hang the keys of my strongbox on?'

---

[12] *epinglette*: priming needle for his firearm.
[13] *vingt-quatre*: a municipal and police magistrate.
[14] *blue skirts . . . shoulders*: the ordinary costume of the girls in the Basque provinces and in Navarre. [Author's note]

" 'It's to hang my epinglette on with,' I answered.

" 'Your epinglette!' she cried, laughing. 'Ah! the gentleman makes lace, since he has need of epingles.'[15] Everyone there burst out laughing, and I felt the blood rush to my cheeks, but could find nothing to reply.

" 'Well, my hearty,' she continued, 'make me seven yards of black lace for a mantilla, pinmaker of my soul.' And taking the cassia flower from her mouth, she threw it with a twist of her thumb and struck me right between the eyes.

"It seemed to me, señor, that a bullet had hit me. . . . I did not know what to do with myself, and stood as stiff as a post. When she had gone into the factory I saw the flower, which had fallen on the ground between my feet. I do not know what possessed me, but I picked it up, unseen by my comrades, and placed it carefully in my vest. That was my first act of folly.

"Two or three hours after, while I was still thinking it over, a porter rushed into the guardroom, all out of breath and greatly agitated. He told us that a woman had been assassinated in the great room where the cigars were made, and that we must send in the guard. The sergeant told me to take two men and look into the matter.

"I took my men and went up. Imagine, señor! On entering the room I found as many as two or three hundred women *en chemise,* or with only what was absolutely necessary on, all crying, screeching, gesticulating, and making such a tumult that you couldn't have heard God's thunder. At one side, one of them sprawled on the floor, covered with blood, and with a cross cut on her face that someone had just made with two cuts of a knife. Opposite the wounded one, who was being tended by the best of the band, I saw Carmen in the hands of five or six stout dames. The wounded woman kept bawling out, 'A priest! Confess me! I am dying!' Carmen said nothing: she clenched her teeth and rolled her eyes about like a chameleon.

" 'What is the matter here?' I asked. I was at great trouble to find out what had happened, for all the women talked at once. It seems that the wounded woman had boasted that she had enough money in her pocket to buy a donkey at the Triana market. 'O ho!' cried out Carmen, who had a tongue of her own, 'thou hast not then enough for a broom?'

"The other, stung by the reproach, perhaps because she felt that a reference to that article touched her in a weak spot, answered that she was not a judge of brooms, not having the honor to be either a Gypsy or a daughter of Satan; but that Señorita Carmen would soon make the donkey's acquaintance when the *corregidor* sent her out for an airing with two stout lackeys behind to beat off the flies.

" 'Well, for my part, then,' said Carmen, 'I will make drinking troughs

[15] *epingles*: pins

for the flies on your cheeks, for I feel like painting a checkerboard upon them.'[16] With that—criss, cross, she began, with the knife she used for trimming the ends of the cigars, to slash a St. Andrew's cross on the girl's face.

" 'Twas a clear case. I took Carmen by the arm. 'Sister,' said I politely, 'you must come with me.' She gave me a look as if she remembered me, but said resignedly, 'Let us go, then. Where is my mantilla?'

"She threw it over her head so as to show only one of her great eyes, and followed my two men as gently as a lamb. When we reached the guard-house the quartermaster said it was a grave affair, and that she must be taken to prison. 'Twas I, too, who must conduct her there. I placed her between two dragoons, and I marched behind, as a corporal should in such a case. Thus we started for the city. At first the Gypsy kept silence, but in the Street of the Serpent—you know the street, and how well it merits its name by all the windings it makes—in the Street of the Serpent she commenced by letting her mantilla drop upon her shoulders, so as to show me her pretty, wheedling face, and turning toward me as much as she could, she said:

" 'My officer, where are you taking me?'

" 'To prison, my poor child,' I replied, as gently as I could, as a true soldier should speak to a prisoner, above all to a woman.

" 'Alas! what will become of me? Noble officer, have pity upon me! You are so young, so gentle.' Then, in a lower tone, 'Let me escape,' she said; 'I will give you a piece of the bar-lachi,[17] which will make you beloved of all women.'

"The bar-lachi, señor, is the lodestone, with which the Gypsies pretend that one can work charms if one knows how to use it. Give a woman a pinch of it grated in a glass of white wine, and she cannot resist you.

"I replied as seriously as I could, 'We are not here to talk nonsense. You must go to prison; that's the order, and there is no help for it.'

"Now we Basque people have an accent by which the Spaniards can easily tell us; but in revenge there is scarcely one of them who can learn

[16] *painting . . . them*: "pintar un javeque"—to paint in checkers. The Spanish checkerboards are usually painted in red and white squares. [Author's note]

[17] *bar-lachi*: "If the Gitánas in general be addicted to any one superstition, it is certainly with respect to this stone, to which they attribute all kinds of miraculous powers. . . . They believe that he who is in possession of it has nothing to fear from steel or lead, from fire or water, and that death itself has no power over him. . . . Extraordinary things are related of its power in exciting the amorous passions, and on this account it is in great request amongst the gipsy hags; all these women are procuresses, and find persons of both sexes weak and wicked enough to make use of their pretended knowledge in the composition of love-draughts and decoctions. In the case of the loadstone, however, there is no pretence, the Gitánas believing all they say respecting it, and still more." (George Borrow, *The Zincali, an Account of the Gipsies of Spain*.) [Author's note]

to say even *Bài, jaona*.[18] 'Twas not hard then for Carmen to know that I came from the Provinces. You know, señor, that the Gypsies, having no country of their own, and always wandering from one place to another, speak all languages; and the most of them are equally at home in Portugal, in France, in the Provinces, in Catalonia—everywhere, in fact; even with the Moors and the English they can make themselves understood. Carmen knew the Basque dialect well enough.

" '*Laguna ene bihotsarena*, comrade of my heart,' said she, suddenly, 'are you from our country?'

"Our language, señor, is so beautiful that when we hear it in a strange country it thrills our hearts. . . . I wish I might have a confessor from the Provinces," the bandit added more softly. After a silence he continued:

" 'I am from Elizondo,' I answered her in Basque, very much moved to hear my native tongue.

" 'And I, I am from Etchalar,' said she. That is a place some four hours' journey from us. 'I was carried away to Seville by the Gypsies. I was working in the tobacco factory to gain enough to take me home to Navarre to my poor old mother, who has no one to support her but me and the little *barratcea*[19] with its twenty cider-apple trees. Ah! were I only at home before the white mountain! They insulted me because I am not one of this nation of swindlers, peddlers of rotten oranges; and these vile women are all against me because I told them that not all their *jacques*[20] at Seville with their knives could frighten one of our boys with his blue beret and his *maquila*. Comrade, friend, can you do nothing for a countrywoman?'

"She lied, señor, she lied always. I do not know whether in all her life that girl ever spoke one word of truth; but when she spoke I believed her: she was too much for me. She spoke the Basque brokenly, yet I believed she came from Navarre; her eyes alone, her mouth, and her complexion stamped her a Gypsy. I was bewitched and no longer paid attention to anything. I reflected that if the Spaniards had spoken aught against my country to me, I would have slashed them across the face as she had just treated her comrade. In brief, I was like a drunken man: I began to talk foolishly, and was ready to act likewise.

" 'If I were to push you, and you tumbled down, my countryman,' she said in Basque, 'it would not be these two Castilian conscripts who could hold me.'

"Faith! I forgot my orders, everything, and I replied:

[18] *Bài, jaona*: Yes, sir.
[19] *barratcea*: garden.
[20] *jacques*: bullies.

" 'Well, my friend, my countrywoman, try it, and may Our Lady of the Mountain aid you!' At that moment we were passing before one of those narrow alleys of which there are so many in Seville. Suddenly Carmen turned about and struck me with her clenched fist in the chest. I fell backwards on purpose. With one bound she jumped over me and fled, showing us a pair of legs. . . . Well, they talk of 'Basque legs,' but hers surpassed them all, as fleet as they were shapely. I picked myself up quickly, but I managed to get my lance[21] crosswise in the alley, and so well did it bar the passage that at the very start my comrades were hindered for the moment from the pursuit. Then I started off running myself, and they after me; but catch her!—there was no risk of it, with our spurs, our sabers, and our lances! In less time than I can tell you, the prisoner had disappeared. Besides, all the gossips of the neighborhood helped her flight, jeered at us, and put us on the wrong scent. After many marches and countermarches we were obliged to return to the guardhouse without a receipt from the governor of the prison.

"My men, to escape punishment, said that Carmen had spoken with me in Basque, and that it did not seem natural that a blow from so slight a girl would knock down so easily a man of my strength. All this looked suspicious, or rather, too clear. When the guard was relieved, I was reduced to the ranks and sent to prison for a month. That was my first punishment since I had enlisted. Farewell, then, to the quartermaster's stripes which I deemed already in my grasp!

"My first days of imprisonment passed very sadly. When I became a soldier I had pictured to myself that I should at least become an officer. Longa, Mina, my compatriots, have even become captains general; Chapalangarra, who is a Negro, and, like Mina, a refugee in your country— Chapalangarra was a colonel, and I have played *paume* a score of times with his brother, who was a poor devil like myself. 'Now,' said I to myself, 'all the time you have served without punishment is all time lost. Here you are with a bad reputation. To regain the good opinion of your officers, you must work ten times as hard as when you were a raw recruit. And for what have you brought this punishment upon yourself? For a jade of a Gypsy who mocked you, and who at this moment goes scot-free in some quarter of the city.' Nevertheless I could not help thinking about her. Will you believe it, señor, her silk stockings, so full of holes, and which she so freely showed in her flight, were always before my eyes. Between my prison bars I looked out upon the street, and among all the women who passed I saw not one the equal of that little she-devil. And then, in spite of

[21] *lance*: All the cavalry in Spain were then armed with lances. [Author's note]

myself, I would smell of the cassia flower she had thrown at me, and which,
though withered, still kept its sweet perfume. . . . If there are witches,
that girl was one.

"One day the jailer entered and gave me a loaf of Alcalá[22] bread.
'Look,' said he, 'see what your cousin has sent you.' I took the bread, very
much astonished, for I had no cousin at Seville. Perhaps it is a mistake,
I thought, regarding the bread; but it was so appetizing, and smelled so
good, that without bothering myself about where it came from or for
whom it was intended, I determined to eat it. In trying to cut it, my knife
struck against something hard. I examined it and found a small English
file which someone had slipped into the loaf before it was baked. There
was also in it a goldpiece of two piasters. No more doubt then; it was a
present from Carmen. To the people of her race, liberty is everything,
and they would burn a city to avoid a day's imprisonment. Besides, the girl
was cunning, and with bread like that one could laugh at jailers. In an hour
the thickest bar might be cut with the little file, and with the two piasters,
at the first slopshop I could exchange my uniform for plain clothes. You
can imagine that a man who had so many times stolen the young eagles
from their nests on our crags would make little of dropping to the street
from a window scarcely thirty feet from the ground. Yet I still kept my
honor as a soldier, and to desert seemed to me a great crime. Still, I was
touched by this token of remembrance. When one is in prison, one loves
to think that outside one has a friend who still thinks of you. The goldpiece
offended me a little. I would have liked well to send it back; but how
could I find my creditor? That did not seem so easy.

"After the ceremony of my degradation, I thought that there was nothing
further for me to suffer; but there remained yet another humiliation: that
was when, after my release, I was put on guard duty as a common soldier.
You cannot imagine what a man of spirit feels in such a situation. I believe I would rather have been shot. Then, at least, one marches at the
head of his squad; one feels like somebody; everyone looks at you.

"I was placed as sentry at the colonel's door. He was a young man—
rich, a good fellow, and fond of pleasures. All the young officers were at
his house, and many citizens; women also—actresses, so it was said. As
for me, it seemed that the whole city had made a rendezvous at his door to
stare at me. And then comes the colonel's carriage with his *valet de cham-
bre* on the box. Whom do I see alight? *La gitanella!* She was dressed to
kill this time, adorned like a Madonna, bedecked and bedizened—a span-

---

[22] *Alcalá*: Alcalá de los Panaderos, a town two leagues from Seville, where delicious
rolls of bread are made. It is claimed that their excellency is due to the water of
Alcalá, and great quantities of them are each day carried to Seville. [Author's note]

gled dress, blue shoes, also spangled, flowers and furbelows all over her. In her hand she held a Basque tambourine. With her were two other Gypsy women, one young, and one old. There is always an old woman to lead them about; then old man with a guitar, a Gypsy also, to play and make them dance. You know that people of quality often amuse themselves by bidding Gypsies to their parties that they may make them dance the *romalis,* their national dance—and sometimes for something quite different.

"Carmen remembered me, and we exchanged a look. I know not why, but at that moment I wished myself a hundred feet underground. '*Agur, laguna!*'[23] said she. 'My officer, you mount guard then, like a raw recruit!' and before I could find a word to reply she was within the house.

"All the guests were in the patio, and notwithstanding the crowd, I could see through the gate[24] nearly all that happened. I heard the sound of the castanets, the tambourine, the laughter, and the applause; and at times I could see her head when she leaped with her tambourine. Then I heard the officers saying gallant things to her that made the blood rush to my cheeks. What she replied I know not. 'Twas from that day I think that I commenced to love her in earnest; for three or four times the notion came to me to rush into the patio and cut down with my saber all those coxcombs who were flirting with her. My torment lasted a good hour; then the Gypsies came out, and the carriage carried them away.

"Carmen, in passing, gave me a look with those eyes of hers—you know them—and said to me in a low voice: 'Compatriot, when one likes a good *fritura,*[25] one goes to Lillas Pastia's at Triana.' As lightly as a kid she bounded into the carriage, the coachman whipped up his mules, and all the joyous band drove off, I know not where.

"You will guess that as soon as I was relieved I went to Triana,[26] but

[23] *Agur, laguna!*: Good-day, comrade!
[24] *gate*: Most of the houses in Seville have an interior open court surrounded by porticoes. The people live there in summer. Over the court is spread an awning which is sprinkled with water by day and removed at night. The street door is almost always open, and the passage to the court *zaguán* (entrance hall) is closed by an iron gate often very elegantly wrought.
[25] *fritura*: dish of small fried fish.
[26] *Triana*: "The faubourg of Triana, in Seville, has from time immemorial been noted as a favourite residence of the Gitanos; and here, at the present day, they are to be found in greater number than in any other town in Spain. This faubourg is indeed chiefly inhabited by desperate characters, as, besides the Gitanos, the principal part of the robber population of Seville is here congregated. Perhaps there is no part, even of Naples, where crime so much abounds, and the law is so little respected, as at Triana, the character of whose inmates was so graphically delineated two centuries and a half back by Cervantes, in one of the most amusing of his tales, *Rinconete and Cortadillo.*" (George Borrow, *Gipsies of Spain.*)

first I got shaved and brushed myself up as if for parade. She was at Lillas Pastia's, an old *fritura* seller, a Gypsy as black as a Moor, to whose house came many of the citizens to eat fried fish; especially, I think, since Carmen had taken up her quarters there.

" 'Lillas,' she said, as soon as she saw me, 'I shall do no more today. Tomorrow it will be day again. Come, my countryman, let us take a stroll.'

"She threw her mantilla over her face, and we were in the street before I knew where I was going.

" 'Señorita,' I said, 'I think I have you to thank for a present sent me while I was in prison. I have eaten the bread, the file will do to sharpen my lance—I will keep it in remembrance of you; but the money, here it is.'

" 'Goodness!' she cried, bursting with laughter, 'he has kept the money. Well, so much the better, for I am none too flush; but what's the odds? a wandering dog will not starve. Come along, let us eat it all. You shall treat me.'

"We had taken the road back to Seville. At the commencement of the Street of the Serpent she bought a dozen oranges, which she made me put in my handkerchief. A little farther on she bought, besides, a loaf of bread, a sausage, and a bottle of Manzanilla. Finally she entered a confectioner's shop. There she threw on the counter the goldpiece I had returned to her, with another which she had in her pocket, and some silver. Then she asked me for all I had, too. I had only a few small pieces, which I gave her, feeling much ashamed to have no more. I thought she wanted to buy out the shop. She took all there was of the finest and dearest *yemas*,[27] *turon*,[28] preserved fruits, as long as the money lasted. All this I had to carry off in paper bags. Perhaps you know the Street of the Candilejo, where is a bust of the King Don Pedro, the Guardian of Justice. That should have made me think what I was about. We stopped before an old house in this street. She entered the passage and rapped at the ground floor. A Gypsy, true servant of Satan, came to open it. Carmen spoke some words in Romany to her. The old hag grumbled at first. To appease her Carmen gave her two oranges, a fistful of bonbons, and also a sip of wine. Then she put her cloak on her back and led her to the door, which she secured with a bar of wood. As soon as we were alone she commenced to dance and laugh like one possessed, singing, 'Thou art my *rom,* and I thy *romi.*'[29]

[27] *yemas*: yolks of eggs prepared with a crust of sugar.
[28] *turon*: a kind of nougat.
[29] *rom, romi*: husband, wife.

"There I stood in the middle of the room, loaded with all our purchases, and not knowing where to put them. She dumped them all on the floor, and clasping me round the neck, cried out, 'I pay my debts, I pay my debts; 'tis the law of the Calés.'[30] Ah! senor, that day! that day! . . . When I think of it, I forget tomorrow!"

The bandit was silent a moment; then, after he had relighted his cigar, he continued:

"We remained together the whole day, eating, drinking—and the rest. When she had eaten bonbons like a six-year-old child, she stuffed handfuls into the old woman's water jar—'to make her a sorbet,' she said. She smashed the *yemas* by throwing them against the wall—'so that the flies may leave us in peace,' she said. There was no trick or folly that she did not commit. I said I would like to see her dance, but what would we do for castanets? At once she took the old woman's only plate, broke it in pieces, and behold! there she was dancing the *romalis,* clacking the pieces of the plate together as well as if she had castanets of ebony or ivory. One would never be bored in that girl's company, I warrant you. Evening came, and I heard drums beating the 'retreat.'

" 'I must return to my quarters for roll call,' I said.

" 'To your quarters!' she cried with an air of contempt. 'Are you then a Negro slave, to let yourself be driven about with a whip? You are a real canary, in character as well as clothes.[31] Get out! You are chickenhearted.'

"Well, I stayed, resigned beforehand to the guardroom. In the morning, she was the first to speak of our parting.

" 'Listen, Joselito,' she said; 'have I repaid you? According to our laws, I owed you nothing, for you are a *payllo*; but you are good-looking, you have pleased me. We are quits. Good-day.'

"I asked her when I might see her again.

" 'When you are less stupid,' she said, laughing.

"Then in a more serious tone she continued: 'Do you know, comrade, that I believe I love you a little bit? But that could not last. Dog and wolf can't keep house together long. Perhaps if you conformed to Gypsy law I should like to become your *romi*. But this is all nonsense. It cannot be. Bah! my lad, believe me, you are well out of it. You have met the devil— yes, the devil; he isn't always black, and he has not twisted your neck. I am dressed in wool, but I am not a lamb. Go, burn a candle before your *majari*;[32] she has earned it. Come, let us go. Good-bye once again. Think

[30] *Calés: calo,* feminine *calli,* plural *calés*; literally, "black." A name the Gypsies give themselves in their own tongue.
[31] *You . . . clothes*: The Spanish dragoons are uniformed in yellow. [Author's note]
[32] *majari*: the Virgin Mary.

no more of Carmencita, or she may make you wed a widow with wooden legs.'[33]

"Thus speaking, she unbarred the door, and once in the street, wrapped herself in her mantilla and showed me her heels.

"She spoke truly. I would have been wise had I thought no more about her; but after that day in the Street of the Candilejo I could think of nothing else. I wandered about all day long, hoping to meet her again. I inquired about her of the old woman and the *fritura* seller. They both said that she had gone to Laloro,[34] as they call Portugal. Probably they followed Carmen's instructions in replying thus; but I was not long finding out that they both lied. Several weeks after my day in the Street of the Candilejo, I was on guard at one of the city gates. A little distance from this gate a breach had been made in the enclosing wall; workmen were busy there during the day, and at night a sentry was placed there to guard against smuggling. During the day I saw Lillas Pastia loitering about the guardhouse, chatting with several of my comrades; they all knew him well, and his fish and his fritters still better. He approached me and asked me if I had yet heard from Carmen.

" 'No,' I answered.

" 'Well, you soon will, comrade.'

"He was not mistaken. That night I was placed on duty in the breach. As soon as the corporal had left, I saw a woman coming near. My heart told me that it was Carmen. Nevertheless, I cried out, 'Be off; there is no passing here.'

" 'Come, don't be cross,' said she, making herself known to me.

" 'What! is it you, Carmen?'

" 'Yes, my countryman. Let us talk a little, but to the point. Do you wish to earn a *duro*? Some people are coming with packs; let them pass.'

" 'No,' I replied; 'I must stop them—'tis my orders.'

" 'Your orders! Your orders! You did not think of orders in the Street of the Candilejo.'

" 'Ah!' I cried, quite upset by this sole reminder, 'for that it was worthwhile to forget my orders; but I want no smugglers' money.'

" 'Let us see, then. If you don't want the money, would you like to dine again at old Dorothea's house?'

" 'No,' I replied, half strangled by the effort I was making—'I cannot.'

" 'Very well! Since you are so obstinate, I know whom to ask. I will offer to go to Dorothea's with your officer. He seems to be a good fellow,

---

[33] *widow . . . legs*: the gallows.
[34] *Laloro*: the red land.

and he will put on duty here a lad who will see no more than he should. Adieu, Canary; I shall laugh well when the orders are to hang you.'

"I had the weakness to call her back; and I promised to let the whole race of Gypsies pass, if necessary, provided that I obtained the only reward I coveted. She immediately swore to meet me the next day and ran to apprise her friends who were close by. There were five of them, among them Pastia, all well loaded with English goods. Carmen kept watch. She was to give the alarm with her castanets as soon as she saw the guards; but of this she had no need. The smugglers accomplished their affair in an instant.

"On the morrow I went to the Street of the Candilejo. Carmen was awaiting me, and in a very bad humor.

" 'I do not like people of whom one must beg a favor,' she said. 'The first time, you rendered me a great service without the thought of gaining aught. Yesterday you bargained with me. I don't know why I have come, for I love you no more. Come, get out! There is a *duro* for your trouble!'

"A little more and I should have hurled the money at her head; and I was obliged to exercise great self-control to keep from beating her. After we had disputed together for an hour, I rushed out in a furious rage. I wandered awhile about the city, walking here and there like a madman; at last I entered a church, and seating myself in the darkest corner, I burst into tears. Suddenly I heard a voice, saying:

" 'A dragon's tears.[35] I should like to make a philter of them.'

"I looked up; Carmen was before me.

" 'Well, my countryman,' said she. 'Do you still want me? Surely I must love you, in spite of all; for since you have left me I know not what is the matter with me. Come, now! this time it is I who asks you if you wish to go to the Street of the Candilejo.

"So we made it up. But Carmen's temper was like the weather in our country: never is the storm so nigh as when the sun is shining brightest. She had promised to meet me again at Dorothea's, but she came not; and Dorothea asserted that she had gone to Laloro on business for Egypt.[36]

"Knowing by experience how much dependence to place on that, I searched everywhere for Carmen where she might be; twenty times a day I passed through the Street of the Candilejo. One evening I was at Dorothea's, whom I had almost tamed by treating her occasionally to a glass of anisette, when Carmen entered, followed by a young man, a lieutenant in our regiment.

---

[35] *A dragon's tears*: a play upon the French word *dragon*, which means both dragon and dragoon.
[36] *business for Egypt*: Gypsy business.

" 'Get out of this,' she said to me in Basque.

"I stood stupefied with rage in my heart.

" 'What are you doing here?' cried the lieutenant. 'Decamp; get out of this.'

"I could not budge. I was like one paralyzed. The officer, seeing that I did not move and had not even uncovered, seized me angrily by the collar and shook me roughly. I know not what I said to him. He drew his sword, and I drew mine. The old woman seized my arm and the lieutenant gave me a cut on my forehead, the scar of which I carry to this day. I stepped back, and with my elbow sent Dorothea sprawling on the floor; then, as the lieutenant followed me up, I gave him the point of my sword, and he sheathed it in his bosom. Then Carmen blew out the lamp and called out in her own tongue to Dorothea to fly. I myself escaped to the street and ran on I knew not whither. It seemed to me that someone was following me. When I recovered my wits, I found that Carmen had not left me.

" 'You great stupid canary,' she said; 'all you know is to commit follies. I told you that I should bring misfortune upon you. Yet there is a remedy for every ill if one has for a sweetheart a Fleming of Rome.[37] Begin by tying this handkerchief about your head, and give me your belt. Wait for me in this alley. I will be back in two minutes.'

"She disappeared, and soon brought me a striped cloak, which she had found I know not where. She made me doff my uniform and put the cloak over my shirt. Thus attired, I looked enough like the peasants of Valencia as they come to Seville to sell their chufas.[38] Then she brought me to a house somewhat like Dorothea's, at the foot of a narrow court. She and another Gypsy woman washed and dressed my wound better than could a surgeon major, and gave me something to drink, I know not what. At last they laid me upon a mattress, and I fell asleep.

"Probably these women had put in my drink one of those soporific drugs of which they know the secret, for I did not awake until very late the next day. I had a fearful headache and a slight fever. It was some time before I recalled the terrible drama in which I had been an actor the evening before. After they had dressed my wound, Carmen and her friend, both crouching by my mattress, exchanged a few words in *chipe calli* which seemed to be a medical consultation. Then they both assured me that I would soon be well, but that I had better quit Seville in the shortest time possible, for if I was taken I would certainly be shot.

---

[37] *Fleming of Rome*: "Flamenca de Roma," a slang term for Gypsies. Rome here does not refer to the Eternal City, but to the *romi*, or married folks, as the Gypsies call themselves. Those first seen in Spain came probably from the Netherlands: hence their name of Flemings. [Author's note]

[38] *chufa*: a bulbous root, of which an agreeable drink is made. [Author's note]

" 'My lad,' said Carmen, 'the king will no longer give you either rice or salt cod,[39] and you must do something; you must be thinking of earning your living. You are too stupid to steal a *pastesas*;[40] but you are active and strong; if you have the courage, make your way to the coast and become a smuggler. Have I not promised to get you hanged? That is better than being shot. Besides, if you know how to manage, you may live like a prince so long as the *miñones*[41] and the coast guard do not collar you.'

"It was in this engaging manner that that devil of a girl showed me the new career for which she destined me; to tell the truth, the only one left me, now that I had incurred the penalty of death. Need I tell you that she decided me without much trouble? It seemed to me that I should bind myself more closely to her by this life of risk and lawlessness. Henceforth I thought myself sure of her love. I had often heard of a band of smugglers who infested Andalusia—well mounted, blunderbuss in hand, and their mistresses seated on the croup behind them. Already I could see myself trotting over hill and dale with this pretty Gypsy behind me. When I spoke to her of this she must needs laugh till she held her sides, telling me that there was nothing so fine as a night passed in bivouac, when each *rom* retired with his *romi* beneath the little tent made of a blanket stretched over three hoops.

" 'If I keep always in the mountains,' said I to her, 'I shall be sure of you. No lieutenant will be there to share with me.'

" 'Ah! you are jealous,' she replied. 'So much the worse for you. How can you be so stupid! Can you not see that I love you, since I have never asked you for any money?'

"When she talked in that fashion I felt like strangling her.

"To make a short story, señor, Carmen procured for me a civilian's dress, in which I escaped from Seville unrecognized. I went to Jerez, with a letter from Pastia to an anisette seller at whose house the smugglers used to meet. I was presented to these gentry, whose chief, called Dancaïre, received me into his band. We departed for Gaucin, where I again saw Carmen, who had agreed to meet me there. In our expeditions she served as a spy for us men, and a better one there never was. She had just returned from Gibraltar, and had already arranged with a ship's captain for the landing of certain English goods which we were expected to receive on the coast. We waited for them near Estepona; then we hid a part of them in the mountains, and laden with the rest we proceeded to Ronda. Carmen was already there: it was she again who told us the moment when we might safely enter the town. This first expedition and some others were fortunate

---

[39] *rice . . . cod*: the ordinary rations of the Spanish soldiers.
[40] *a pastesas*: "Ustilar a pastesas," to rob skillfully, without violence.
[41] *miñones*: a kind of free corps.

—a smuggler's life pleased me better than a soldier's. I made Carmen presents—I had money and a sweetheart. I felt little remorse, for, as the Gypsies say, the itch of pleasure does not itch at all. Everywhere we were well received; my comrades treated me well, even showing me some respect. This was because I had 'killed my man,' and among them all there was not one with a similar exploit on his conscience. But what affected me the most in my new life was that I was often with Carmen. She showed me more friendship than ever; nevertheless, before our comrades she never admitted our intimacy, and had even made me swear with all sorts of oaths to say nothing to them on my own account. I was so feeble in the hands of this creature that I obeyed her every caprice. Besides, this was the first time she ever showed me any of the reserve of an honest woman, and I was simple enough to believe that she had really corrected her former ways.

"Our troop, which was composed of eight or ten men, seldom met together, and only at decisive moments; we were usually scattered about by twos and threes in the towns and villages. Each of us pretended to follow a trade: this one was a tinker, another a horse dealer; I was a peddler, but I seldom showed myself in the large towns because of my bad affair at Seville. One day, or rather one night, our rendezvous was at Vejer. Dancaïre and I found ourselves there before the others. He seemed very gay.

" 'We are going to have another comrade,' he told me. 'Carmen has just made one of her best strokes. She has just managed the escape of her *rom,* who was in the presidio at Tarifa.'

"I was beginning already to understand the Gypsy dialect which nearly all my comrades spoke, and this word *rom* gave me a chill.

" 'What—her husband! Is she then married?' I asked of the captain.

" 'Yes,' he replied; 'to Garcia, the One-eyed, a Gypsy as artful as she is herself. The poor fellow was in the galleys. Carmen so bewitched the surgeon of the presidio that she obtained the liberty of her *rom.* Ah! that girl is worth her weight in gold. For two years she has been contriving his escape. Nothing succeeded until they took the notion to change the commandant. With this one it seems that she has come quickly to an understanding.'

"You can imagine with what pleasure I heard this news. I soon met Garcia, the One-eyed; he was the ugliest monster that Bohemia ever reared, with a black skin and a soul still blacker; he was the most thoroughbred rascal that I have ever met. Carmen came with him, and when she called him her *rom* before me, you should have seen the eyes she made at me and her grimaces when Garcia's back was turned. I was indignant, and did not speak to her the whole night. In the morning, we made up our bales and were already on our way, when we discovered that a dozen horsemen were at our heels. These Andalusian braggarts, who were always talking murder, at once showed the white feather. 'Twas a regular stampede. Only Dancaïre, Garcia, a fine-looking fellow from Ecija named Remendado, and Carmen did not lose their heads. The others abandoned their mules and threw themselves into the ravines, where the horses could not pursue them. We could not save our beasts, and hastened to unstrap the most valuable of our booty and to load it on our shoulders; then we tried to escape over the rocks by the steepest and roughest slopes. We cast our bales before us and followed them as best we could, sliding along on our heels. During this time the enemy peppered us, and for the first time I heard the whistling of bullets; but I did not mind them. When one is under a woman's eyes there is no merit in defying death. We all escaped except poor Remendado, who received a bullet in his loins. I dropped my packet and tried to carry him.

" 'Fool!' cried Garcia, 'what have we to do with carrion? Drop him and save the cotton stockings.'

" 'Drop him!' cried Carmen.

"Fatigue obliged me to lay him for a moment in the shelter of a rock. The One-eyed advanced and discharged his blunderbuss at the poor fellow's head.

" 'He will be clever who will recognize him now,' said Garcia, regarding the face which a dozen balls had torn in fragments.

"Such, señor, was the delightful life I led. In the evening we found ourselves in a thicket, worn out with fatigue, with nothing to eat, and ruined by the loss of our mules. What did that infernal Garcia do?—he pulled a pack of cards from his pocket and began to play with Dancaïre by the light of a fire that they had kindled. Meanwhile I lay down, gazing at the stars, thinking of Remendado, and wishing myself in his place. Carmen crouched near me, and from time to time she rattled her castanets, humming a tune. Then, approaching me as if to whisper, she kissed me two or three times, almost against my will.

" 'You are the devil,' said I.

" 'Yes,' she answered.

"After a few hours' rest she left for Gaucin, and the following morning a little goatherd brought us some bread. We remained there all day, and in the night moved toward Gaucin. We waited for news from Carmen. None came. At daybreak we saw a muleteer guiding a well-dressed woman, with a parasol, and a little girl who seemed to be her domestic. Garcia said to us:

" 'There are two mules and two women that Saint Nicholas sends us. I should prefer four mules; but never mind, I will attend to this business.'

"He took his blunderbuss and went down toward the path, hiding in the bushes. We followed him at a little distance, Dancaïre and I. When we were within range we showed ourselves, crying to the muleteer to halt. The woman, instead of being frightened at our appearance—and our dress should have sufficed for that—burst into a peal of laughter.

" 'Ah! the *lillipendi;* they take me for an *erani!*'[42]

" 'Twas Carmen, but so well disguised that I should not have known her had she spoken in any other tongue. She sprang from her mule and in a low voice conversed for some time with Dancaïre and Garcia; then, turning to me: 'Canary, we will meet again before you are hanged. I am going to Gibraltar, on the "affairs of Egypt." You will soon have news of me.'

"We separated after she had shown us a place where we could find shelter for several days. That girl was the salvation of our troop. We soon received some money she sent us, and information which was of more value to us: this was that on such a day two English gentlemen would pass by such a road; a word to the wise is sufficient—they had money in plenty. Garcia wished to assassinate them, but Dancaïre and I opposed it. We took nothing from them but their money and watches, except their shirts, of which we had great need.

"Señor, one becomes a rascal without thinking much about it. You lose your head over a pretty girl, you fight for her, misfortune comes upon you, you must needs live in the mountains, and from a smuggler you become a robber without reflection. We judged it would not be well for us to remain in the neighborhood of Gibraltar, after the affair with the English gentlemen, and we hid ourselves in the Sierra de Ronda.

"You have spoken to me of José-Maria; well, it was there that I made his acquaintance. He took his mistress with him on his expeditions. She was a pretty girl, wise, modest, and good-mannered; never a vulgar word, and so devoted! . . . In return he made her miserable. He was always running after other girls, he bullied her, then sometimes he took the notion to be jealous of her. Once he struck her with his knife. Ah, well! she only loved him the more for that. Why, that girl was proud of the scar on her arm, and showed it as if it were the most beautiful thing on earth. And then, to crown all, José-Maria was the very worst of comrades. In an expedition that we made, he managed so well that all the profit of the affair fell to him, and to us the trouble and the blows. But I must go back to my story.

"We heard no more from Carmen. Dancaïre said: 'One of us must go to Gibraltar for news of her; she must have arranged some affair. I would go willingly, but I am too well known at Gibraltar.'

[42] *"Ah! . . . erani!"*: "Ah! the fools; they take me for a real lady!"

"The One-eyed said: 'Me, too; they know me there. I have played too many tricks on the lobsters[43] there! And as I have only one eye, it is hard for me to disguise myself.'

" 'Then I must go,' I said in my turn, delighted at the very idea of seeing Carmen again. 'Let us see! what must be done?'

"The others told me. 'You may go either by sea or by Saint Roque, as you prefer. And when you come to Gibraltar, ask at the port where a chocolate vendor named Rollona lives; when you have found her, she will tell you all that is happening there.'

"It was agreed that we should all depart for the Sierra of Gaucin; that I should leave my two comrades there and proceed to Gibraltar disguised as a fruit seller. At Ronda a man who was in our interest had procured me a passport. At Gaucin they gave me a donkey; I loaded him with melons and oranges, and then took the road. On my arrival at Gibraltar I found that Rollona was well known, but that she was dead or had gone to *finibus terrae*;[44] and her disappearance explained, to my notion, how we had lost our means of communication with Carmen. I put up my donkey in a stable, and taking my oranges, wandered about the city as if trying to sell them, but in reality to see if I could not encounter some familiar face. At Gibraltar there are many vagrants of all nations. 'Tis the Tower of Babel over again; for one cannot go ten paces in a street without hearing as many tongues spoken. I met plenty of Gypsies, but I did not dare to trust any of them. They sounded me and I them; we each divined that we were rogues—the important thing was to know if we were of the same band. After two days of fruitless wanderings I had learned nothing of either Rollona or Carmen, and I was thinking of returning to my comrades after making a few purchases, when, as I was walking down a street at sunset, I heard a woman's voice calling to me from a window.

" 'Orange seller!'

"I looked up and saw Carmen on a balcony, leaning over the rail, and beside her an officer in scarlet, with gold epaulettes, curled hair, and the bearing of a great milord. As for her, she was dressed superbly: a shawl over her shoulders, a gold comb in her hair, in silk attire, and—the darling! the same as ever—gay with laughter. The Englishman in barbarous Spanish ordered me to come up, for madame wished some oranges; and Carmen called to me in Basque:

" 'Come up, and do not be astonished at anything.'

"In fact, nothing could astonish me that she did. I cannot say whether

---

[43] *lobsters*: a name given by the Spaniards to the English because of their red uniforms.

[44] *to finibus terrae*: to the galleys or "to the devil."

I felt more joy than sorrow at finding her. At the door there stood a big powdered English servant, who led me into a magnificent room. Carmen immediately said in Basque:

" 'Remember! you do not understand a word of Spanish, nor know me.'

"Then turning to the Englishman: 'There! I told you so: I saw from the first that he was a Basque. You shall now hear a droll jargon. How stupid he looks!—ah! one would say a cat surprised in a cupboard.'

" 'And thou,' said I, in my own tongue, 'thou hast the air of a brazen-faced jade, and I have a good mind to slash thy face before thy gallant.'

" 'My gallant!' she cried. 'So you have found that out all by yourself. And you are jealous of that imbecile there! Well, you are more stupid than you were before our soirées at the Street of the Candilejo. Do you not see, fool that you are, that at this moment I am arranging an affair of Egypt, and in the most brilliant style, too? This house is mine; this lobster's guineas will be mine. I lead him about by the nose, and I will soon lead him whence he will never return.'

" 'And I,' I replied, 'if you arrange the affairs of Egypt after that fashion, I will arrange it so that you will never commence again.'

" 'Ah! so then! Are you my *rom* that you command me? The One-eyed is satisfied. What business have you here? Ought not you to be content to be the only one that can call himself my *minchorro?*'[45]

" 'What does he say?' asked the Englishman.

" 'He says that he is dry, and that he could down a good drink,' replied Carmen. And she threw herself back on a sofa, bursting with merriment over her translation.

"Señor, when that girl laughed there was no chance to talk sense. Everyone laughed with her. The great Englishman laughed with her, like the fool that he was, and ordered that some drink should be brought me.

"While I was drinking, 'Do you see that ring on his finger?' said Carmen. 'If you wish, I will give it to you.'

"I answered: 'I would give one of my fingers to have milord in the mountains, each of us with a *maquila* in his hand.'

" '*Maquila,* what does that mean?' asked the Englishman.

" '*Maquila,*' replied Carmen, laughing all the time, 'is an orange. Isn't it a droll word for an orange? He says that he would like to make you eat an orange.'

" 'Yes?' replied the Englishman. 'Very well! Bring some more *maquilas* tomorrow.'

"While we were talking, the domestic entered and announced that din-

---

[45] *minchorro*: slang term for a lover.

ner was ready. Then the Englishman arose, gave me a piaster, and offered
his arm to Carmen—as if she could not walk in alone! Carmen, always
laughing, said to me:

" 'My lad, I cannot invite you to dinner; but tomorrow, as soon as you
hear the drums beat for parade, come here with the oranges. You will find
a chamber better furnished than that of the Street of the Candilejo, and
you will see that I am as ever thine own Carmencita, and then we can
talk of the affairs of Egypt.'

"I did not reply, and was already in the street when the Englishman
called to me, 'Bring some *maquilas* tomorrow!' and I heard the peals of
Carmen's laughter.

"I went out, not knowing what I was doing, and slept scarcely any; and
in the morning I found myself so incensed against the traitress that I resolved to quit Gibraltar without seeing her again; but at the first roll of the
drums all my fortitude deserted me: I took my basket of oranges and ran to
Carmen's. Through the half-opened blind I saw her great black eyes
watching me. The powdered footman let me in at once. Carmen sent him
away on an errand, and as soon as we were alone she burst into one of
her peals of crocodile laughter, and threw herself in my arms. I had never
seen her so beautiful. Dressed like a Madonna, perfumed . . . silken furniture, embroidered curtains . . . ah! . . . and I, dressed like the robber that
I was.

" '*Minchorro!*' said Carmen, 'I would like to smash everything here, set
fire to the house, and fly to the sierra!'

"And then it was caresses! . . . then laughter! . . . then she danced, she
tore her furbelows; never did monkey perform more gambols, make
more grimaces, commit more deviltries. When she became serious again:

" 'Listen,' she said; 'about Egypt. I want him to take me to Ronda,
where I have a sister a nun' (here a fresh burst of laughter). 'We will pass
by a place I will tell you of; you fall on him and rob him of everything.
. . . The best way would be to wring his neck; but,' she added, with a
diabolical smile that she sometimes had—and that smile never a soul then
wished to imitate—'do you know what you must do? Let the One-eyed go
first; hold back a little yourself. The lobster is brave and skillful: he has
good pistols. . . . Do you understand?' . . . She interrupted herself with
another peal of laughter that made my flesh creep.

" 'No,' I said; 'I hate Garcia, but he is my comrade. Someday, perhaps,
I will rid you of him; but we will settle our accounts after the manner of
my own country. I am only an Egyptian by chance, and for certain things
I shall always be a true Navarro, as the proverb says.'

"She replied: 'You are a fool, an idiot, a true *payllo*. You are like the dwarf who thought himself tall because he could spit a long way. You do not love me. Get out!'

"When she told me to get out I could not go. I promised to return to my comrades and await the Englishman; for her part, she promised to be indisposed until the time of departure for Ronda. I remained two days longer at Gibraltar. She had the audacity to come in disguise to see me at my inn. I departed—I also had a project. I returned to our rendezvous, knowing the hour at which the Englishman and Carmen should pass. I found Dancaïre and Garcia awaiting me. We passed the night in a wood by a fire of pinecones which burned splendidly. I asked Garcia to play cards. He accepted. At the second game I told him he cheated; he laughed at me. I threw the cards in his face. He tried to seize his blunderbuss; I put my foot on it, and said:

" 'They say that you can handle a knife with the best knave in Málaga. Will you try it on with me?'

Dancaïre wished to separate us. I had given Garcia two or three blows with my fist. Rage gave him courage: he had drawn his knife and I mine. We both called out to Dancaïre to give us room and to see fair play. He saw that he could not stop us, and drew back. Garcia was already crouching like a cat ready to spring on a mouse. He held his hat in his left hand, as a guard, his knife in advance. That is the Andalusian guard. I stood on guard in the Navarro manner, right in front of him, the left arm raised, the left leg advanced, the knife along the right thigh. I felt stronger than a giant. He threw himself upon me like a flash. I turned on my left foot and he found nothing before him; but I struck him in the throat, and my knife went so deep that my hand came right up under his chin. I drew back the blade so forcibly that it broke. 'Twas all over. The blade was pushed from the wound by a jet of blood as large as your arm. He fell on his face as dead as a log.

" 'What hast thou done!' cried Dancaïre.

" 'Listen,' said I; 'we could not live together. I love Carmen, and I wish to be the only one. Besides, Garcia was a villain, and I have not forgotten how he served poor Remendado. There are now but two of us; but we are good fellows. Come, will you be my friend for life, for death?'

"Dancaïre held out his hand. He was a man fifty years old.

" 'To the devil with love affairs!' cried he. 'If you had asked him for Carmen, he would have sold her to you for a piaster. We are only two now; how shall we manage tomorrow?'

" 'Leave me to manage it by myself,' I answered; 'now I care not for the whole world.'

"We buried Garcia, and pitched our tent two hundred paces farther on.

The next day, Carmen and her Englishman came along with two mule-teers and a servant. I said to Dancaïre, 'I will take care of the Englishman. Frighten the others, they are unarmed.' The Englishman had a stout heart. If Carmen had not pushed his arm he would have killed me. In short, I reconquered Carmen that day, and my first words were to tell her that she was a widow. When she found out how it had happened:

" 'You will always be a *lillipendi!*' she said. 'Garcia should have killed you. Your Navarre guard is all nonsense, and he has sent to the other world cleverer men than thou. But his time had come. Yours will come, too.'

" 'And yours,' I said, 'if you are not a true wife to me.'

" 'So much the better,' she replied; 'I have often seen in the coffee grounds that we two must die together. Bah! he who sows, reaps!' and she rattled her castanets, which she always did when she wished to drive away unpleasant thoughts.

"One is apt to forget oneself when speaking of his own affairs. All these details must bore you; but I shall soon finish. The life we led lasted long enough. Dancaïre and I joined with us several comrades more trusty than our old ones, and we busied ourselves smuggling; sometimes, I must admit, we also stopped people on the highway, but only at the last extrem-ity, when we could not live otherwise. Besides, we did not maltreat travelers; we confined ourselves to taking their money. During several months I was content with Carmen: she continued to be useful in our oper-ations by advising us of good strokes that we might make. She stayed sometimes at Málaga, sometimes at Cordova, and sometimes at Granada; but at a word from me she left all, and came to meet me at some isolated inn, or even in camp. Once only—'twas at Málaga—she gave me some anxiety. I knew that she had cast her wiles about a very rich merchant, with whom she proposed, probably, to repeat the pleasantry of Gibraltar. In spite of all Dancaïre could say to dissuade me, I set out and entered Málaga in plain daylight. I looked Carmen up, and brought her away at once. We had a very warm explanation.

" 'Do you know,' she said, 'that since you are really my *rom*, I love you less than when you were my *minchorro?* I won't be tormented, much less commanded. What I wish is to be free, and do what I like. Take care not to push me too far. If you annoy me, I will find some good fellow who will serve you as you served the One-eyed.'

"Dancaïre reconciled us to one another. Shortly after, misfortune fell upon us. The soldiers surprised us. Dancaïre was killed, as were two others of my comrades; two more were captured. I myself was sorely wounded, and without my good horse I would have been taken by the soldiers. Worn out with fatigue, with a bullet in my body, I hid myself in a wood with the only comrade left me. I fainted when I dismounted, and I thought I was going to die like a wounded hare in the underbrush. My comrade carried me to a cave known to us, and then went to seek Carmen. She was at Granada, and came on the instant. She did not leave me a single moment for fifteen days—she did not close an eye; and nursed me with a skill and attention never shown by other woman for the man she loved best. As soon as I could use my legs, she fetched me to Granada in great secrecy. Gypsies can find safe retreats everywhere, and I passed more than six weeks in a house two doors removed from the judge who was seeking for me. More than once from behind the blinds I saw him pass. At length my strength came back; but I had reflected while on my bed of pain, and I intended to mend my ways. I spoke to Carmen of quitting Spain and trying to live honestly in the New World. She laughed at me.

" 'We were not made to grow cabbages,' she said; 'our destiny is to live at the expense of the *payllos*. Come, I have arranged an affair with Nathan-ben-Joseph, of Gibraltar. He has some cotton stuffs which only await you to smuggle them in. He knows that you are alive. He counts on you. What will our correspondents in Gibraltar say if you break your word?'

"I let myself be persuaded, and resumed my wicked career.

"While I was in hiding at Granada, there were some bullfights which Carmen attended. When she came back she talked a good deal about a very adroit picador named Lucas. She knew his horse's name, and how much his embroidered vest had cost him. I did not pay much attention to this. Juanito, my remaining comrade, told me several days afterwards that he had seen Carmen with Lucas at the house of a merchant of Zacatin. This began to alarm me. I demanded of Carmen how and why she had become acquainted with the picador.

" 'He is a fellow,' said she, 'with whom one may arrange an affair. The river that makes a noise has either water or pebbles. He has earned 1,200 reals in the bullring. One of two things must happen: we must have this money; or, as he is a fine rider and a brave fellow, we might enroll him in our band. So-and-so are dead; you must needs replace them. Take him with you.'

" 'I do not want his money or himself, and I forbid you to speak to him,' I cried.

" 'Take care!' she replied. 'When one forbids me to do a thing, it is soon done.'

"Happily, the picador left for Málaga, and I set to work to smuggle in the cotton for the Jew. I had a great deal to do on that expedition, and Carmen, too; and I forgot Lucas. Perhaps she also forgot him—for the moment, at least. It was about this time, señor, that I met you—first near Montilla, then afterwards at Cordova. I will not speak to you of our last interview. You perhaps know more about it than I. Carmen robbed you of your watch; she also wanted your money—above all, the ring that I see now upon your finger, and which she said was a magic ring and of great importance to possess. We had a violent dispute, and I struck her. She turned pale and wept. 'Twas the first time I ever saw her cry, and it gave me a terrible shock. I asked her to forgive me, but she sulked all one day; and when I left for Montilla she did not wish to kiss me.

"I had a heavy heart when, three days after, she came to see me, with a laughing air as gay as a lark. All was forgotten, and we were like a pair of lovers for two days. When we were parting she said to me:

" 'There is to be a fête at Cordova. I am going to see it; so I shall find out what men leave with money, and I will tell you.'

"I let her go. When alone I thought over this fête, and the great change in Carmen's humor. She must have already revenged herself, I thought, since she has given in first.

"A peasant told me that there was a bullfight at Cordova. My blood boiled, and like a madman I set out for the place. Someone pointed out Lucas, and on a bench near the barrier I saw Carmen. I had only to look at her a minute to confirm my suspicions. Lucas with the first bull acted the gallant, as I had expected. He tore the cockade[46] from the bull and carried it to Carmen, who pinned it in her hair immediately. The bull charged him, as if to avenge me. Lucas was overturned, with his horse on his breast and the bull on top of both. I looked for Carmen, but she was no longer in her place. As it was impossible for me to get out, I was forced to await the end of the fight. Then I went to the house which you know of, and remained there quietly all the evening and a part of the night. About two o'clock in the morning Carmen returned, and was a little surprised to see me.

" 'Come with me,' I said to her.

" 'Very well,' she said; 'let us go.'

"I went to fetch my horse and put her behind me, and we traveled all the night without exchanging a single word. At daybreak we halted at a solitary inn, near a little hermitage. There I said to Carmen:

" 'Listen. I forget all. Of the past I will not speak a word. But swear to

---

[46] *cockade*: "La divisa," a knot of ribbons indicating by its color from which pasture the bull comes. This knot is affixed to the skin of the bull by a steel hook. It is the height of gallantry to tear it from the living animal and offer it to a woman. [Author's note]

me one thing: that you will follow me to America, and that you will there lead a quiet life.'

" 'No,' she replied in a sulky voice; 'I do not wish to go to America. I am well satisfied here.'

" " 'Tis because you are close to Lucas,' I said. 'But reflect well; if he recovers, 'twill be only to make old bones. Yet, after all, why should I bother myself about him? I am tired of killing your lovers; it is you whom I will kill next.'

"She regarded me fixedly, with her wild air, and said:

" 'I have always thought that you would kill me. The first time I saw you I had just met a priest at the door of my dwelling, and tonight, while leaving Cordova, saw you nothing?—a hare crossed the road between your horse's feet. It is fate!'

" 'Carmencita,' I asked, 'is it true that you no longer love me?'

"She did not reply. She was seated cross-legged on a mat and tracing figures on the ground with her finger.

" 'Let us change our life,' I cried, in a supplicating voice. 'Come, let us live together somewhere where we will never be parted. You know that we have a hundred and twenty *onzas* buried under an oak nearby. . . . Besides, we still have money in the hands of Ben-Joseph the Jew.'

"She began to smile, and replied:

" 'Me first, then you; I knew well 'twould happen thus.'

" 'Reflect!' I continued. 'I am at the end of my patience and my courage; make up your mind, or I will make up mine.'

"I left her and walked toward the hermitage. I found the hermit at prayer. I waited until his prayer was done; I would have liked very much to pray, but I could not. When he arose I drew near him.

" 'Father,' said I, 'will you pray for one who is in great peril?'

" 'I pray for all the afflicted,' he replied.

" 'Could you say a Mass for a soul about to appear before its Creator?'

" 'Yes,' he answered, regarding me fixedly. And as there was something strange in my looks, he wished to make me talk.

" 'It seems to me that I have seen you before,' he said.

"I put a piaster on his bench.

" 'When will you say the Mass?' I asked.

" 'In half an hour. The innkeeper's son from over there comes to serve it. Tell me, young man, have you not something on your conscience which torments you? Won't you listen to the counsels of a Christian?'

"I felt ready to cry. I told him I would return, and fled. I laid me down upon the grass until I heard the bell. Then I drew near, but I remained outside the chapel. When Mass was said I went back to the inn. I hoped that Carmen had fled—she might have taken my horse and escaped; but I found her still there. She did not wish that anyone might say that I had frightened her. While I was away she had ripped the hem of her dress and taken out the lead. Now she was before a table, gazing into a bowlful of water at the lead, which she had melted and that moment cast in. So absorbed was she with her enchantment that she did not at first notice my return. Sometimes she took a piece of lead and turned it in every direction with a sad air; sometimes she sang one of her mystic songs, in which the Gypsies invoke Marie Padilla, the mistress of Don Pedro, who was, they say, the *Bari Crallisa,* or the queen of the Gypsies.[47]

" 'Carmen,' I said, 'will you come with me?'

"She arose, threw away her bowl, and drew her mantilla over her head as if ready to go. They brought me my horse. She sprang up behind me, and we departed.

" 'So, my Carmen,' I said, after we had gone a little way, 'you really wish to follow me, don't you?'

" 'I will follow you to death, yes; but I will never live with you again.'

"We were in a solitary gorge. I pulled up my horse.

" 'Is it here?' she cried, and with one bound she sprang to the ground. She threw off her mantilla, cast it at her feet, and stood motionless, with one hand on her hip, looking me steadily in the eyes.

" 'You wish to kill me, I can well see,' she said. 'It is decreed; but you shall never make me yield.'

" 'I beseech you,' I said to her, 'be reasonable. Listen to me. All the past is forgotten. Nevertheless, you know well that it is you who have ruined me. 'Tis for you I have become a robber and a murderer. Carmen! my own Carmen! let me save you, and with you save myself.'

" 'José,' she replied, 'you ask the impossible. I love you no more; you, you love me still, and for this you wish to kill me. I might yet tell you some lie, but I do not care to take the trouble. All is over between us. As my *rom,* you have the right to kill your *romi*; but Carmen will be always free. *Calli* she was born and *calli* she will die.'

" 'So, then, you love Lucas?' I demanded.

" 'Yes; I have loved him, like you, for a moment—less, perhaps, than you. Now I love nothing, and I hate myself for ever having loved you at all.'

"I threw myself at her feet. I took her hands in mine, I bedewed them

---

[47] *Marie Padilla . . . Gypsies*: They accuse Marie Padilla of having bewitched the King Don Pedro. A popular tradition asserts that she gave Queen Blanche of Bourbon a girdle of gold which seemed to the eyes of the bewitched king a living serpent. From that arose the repugnance that he always showed for the unhappy princess.

with tears. I reminded her of all the happy times we had spent together. I offered to remain always a brigand, to please her. Everything, señor, everything, if only she would love me again.

"She said, 'To love you, it is impossible. To live with you, I do not wish it.'

"Fury seized me. I drew my knife. I would have liked her to be afraid or to plead for mercy; but that woman was a demon.

" 'For the last time,' I cried—'will you stay with me?'

" 'No! no! no!' she cried, stamping her foot; and she drew from her finger a ring I had given her, and threw it among the bushes.

"I struck her twice. 'Twas Garcia's knife, which I had taken when I broke mine in his throat. She fell at the second thrust, without a cry. It seems to me that I can still see her great black eyes steadily fixed on me; then they became dimmed and closed. I remained completely prostrated for a good hour beside the body. Then I remembered that Carmen had often told me that she would like to be buried in a wood. I dug her a grave with my knife, and placed her in it. I searched a long time for her ring, and at last I found it. I placed it in the grave beside her, and also a small cross. Perhaps I did wrong. Then I mounted my horse, galloped straight to Cordova, and at the first guardhouse I made myself known. I told them that I had killed Carmen, but I did not wish to tell them where her body lay. The hermit was a holy man. He prayed for her. He said a Mass for her soul. . . . Poor girl! It is the Gypsies who are to blame, for having reared her as they did."

Cyrano de Bergerac

EDMOND ROSTAND

CHARACTERS

CYRANO DE BERGERAC
CHRISTIAN DE NEUVILLETTE
COMTE DE GUICHE
RAGUENEAU
LE BRET
CAPTAIN CARBON
   DE CASTEL-JALOUX
LIGNIÈRE
DE VALVERT
MONTFLEURY
BELLEROSE
JODELET
CUIGY
BRISSAILLE
A BORE
A MOUSQUETAIRE
OTHER MOUSQUETAIRES
A SPANISH OFFICER
A LIGHT-CAVALRY MAN
A DOORKEEPER
A BURGHER
HIS SON
A PICKPOCKET
A SPECTATOR
A WATCHMAN
BERTRANDOU THE FIFER
A CAPUCHIN

TWO MUSICIANS
SEVEN CADETS
THREE MARQUISES
POETS
PASTRYCOOKS

ROXANE
SISTER MARTHA
LISE
THE SWEETMEAT VENDOR
MOTHER MARGARET
THE DUENNA
SISTER CLAIRE
AN ACTRESS
A SOUBRETTE
A FLOWER GIRL
PAGES

The crowd, bourgeois, marquises, mousquetaires, pickpockets, pastrycooks, poets, Gascony Cadets, players, fiddlers, pages, children, Spanish soldiers, spectators, précieuses, actresses, bourgeoises, nuns, etc.

The first four acts take place in 1640; the fifth in 1655.

ACT ONE

The great hall of the Hôtel de Bourgogne, in 1640. A sort of tennis court arranged and decorated for theatrical performances.

The hall is a long rectangle, seen obliquely, so that one side of it consti-tutes the background, which runs from the position of the front wing at the right, to the line of the farthest wing at the left, and forms an angle with the stage, which is equally seen obliquely.

This stage is furnished, on both sides, along the wings, with benches. The drop curtain is composed of two tapestry hangings, which can be drawn apart. Above a Harlequin cloak, the royal escutcheon. Broad steps lead from the raised platform of the stage into the house. On either side of these steps, the musicians' seats. A row of candles fills the office of footlights.

Two galleries run along the side; the lower one is divided into boxes. No seats in the pit, which is the stage proper. At the back of the pit, that is to say, at the right, in the front, a few seats raised like steps, one above the other; and, under a stairway which leads to the upper seats, and of which the lower end only is visible, a stand decked with small candelabra, jars full of flowers, flagons and glasses, dishes heaped with sweetmeats, etc.

In the center of the background, under the box tier, the entrance to the theater, a large door which half opens to let in the spectators. On the panels of this door, and in several corners, and above the sweetmeat stand, red playbills announcing "LA CLORISE."

[At the rise of the curtain, the house is nearly dark, and still empty. The chandeliers are let down in the middle of the pit, until time to light them. The audience, arriving gradually. Cavaliers, burghers,

lackeys, pages, the fiddlers, etc. A tumult of voices is heard beyond the door; enter brusquely a CAVALIER.]

DOORKEEPER (*running in after him*): Not so fast! Your fifteen pence!

CAVALIER: I come in admission free!

DOORKEEPER: And why?

CAVALIER: I belong to the king's light cavalry!

DOORKEEPER (*to another* CAVALIER *who has entered*): You?

SECOND CAVALIER: I do not pay!

DOORKEEPER: But . . .

SECOND CAVALIER: I belong to the mousquetaires!

FIRST CAVALIER (*to the* SECOND): It does not begin before two. The floor is empty. Let us have a bout with foils.

> [*They fence with foils they have brought.*]

A LACKEY (*entering*): Pst! . . . Flanquin!

OTHER LACKEY (*arrived a moment before*): Champagne? . . .

FIRST LACKEY (*taking a pack of cards from his doublet and showing it to* SECOND LACKEY): Cards. Dice. (*Sits down on the floor.*) Let us have a game.

SECOND LACKEY (*sitting down likewise*): You rascal, willingly!

FIRST LACKEY (*taking from his pocket a bit of candle which he lights and sticks on the floor*): I filched an eyeful of my master's light!

ONE OF THE WATCH (*to a* FLOWER GIRL, *who comes forward*): It is pleasant getting here before the lights.

> [*Puts his arm around her waist.*]

ONE OF THE FENCERS (*taking a thrust*): Hit!

ONE OF THE GAMBLERS: Clubs!

THE WATCHMAN (*pursuing the girl*): A kiss!

THE FLOWER GIRL (*repulsing him*): We shall be seen!

THE WATCHMAN (*drawing her into dark corner*): No, we shall not!

A MAN (*sitting down on the floor with others who have brought provisions*): By coming early, you get a comfortable chance to eat.

A BURGHER (*leading his son*): This should be a good place, my boy. Let us stay here.

ONE OF THE GAMBLERS: Ace wins!

A MAN (*taking a bottle from under his cloak and sitting down*): A proper toper, toping Burgundy (*drinks*), I say, should tope it in Burgundy House!

THE BURGHER (*to his son*): Might one not suppose we had stumbled into some house of evil fame? (*Points with his cane at the drunkard.*) Guzzlers! . . . (*In breaking guard one of the fencers jostles him.*) Brawlers! . . . (*He falls between the gamblers.*) Gamesters! . . .

THE WATCHMAN (*behind him, still teasing the* FLOWER GIRL): A kiss!

THE BURGHER (*dragging his son precipitately away*): Bless my soul! . . . And to reflect that in this very house, my son, were given the plays of the great Rotrou!

THE YOUTH: And those of the great Corneille!

[*A band of* PAGES *holding hands rush in performing a farandole and singing.*]

PAGES: Tra la la la la la la la! . . .

DOORKEEPER (*severely to the* PAGES): Look, now! . . . you pages, you! none of your tricks!

FIRST PAGE (*with wounded dignity*): Sir! . . . this want of confidence . . . (*As soon as the* DOORKEEPER *has turned away, briskly to the* SECOND PAGE) Have you a string about you?

SECOND PAGE: With a fishhook at the end!

FIRST PAGE: We will sit up there and angle for wigs!

A PICKPOCKET (*surrounded by a number of individuals of dubious appearance*): Come now, my little hopefuls, and learn your ABC's of trade. Being as you're not used to hooking . . .

SECOND PAGE (*shouting to other* PAGES *who have already taken seats in the upper gallery*): Ho! . . . Did you bring any peashooters?

THIRD PAGE (*from above*): Yes! . . . And peas!

[*Shoots down a volley of peas.*]

THE YOUTH (*to his father*): What are we going to see?

THE BURGHER: *Clorise.*

THE YOUTH: By whom?

THE BURGHER: By Balthazar Baro. Ah, what a play it is! . . .

[*Goes toward the back on his son's arm.*]

PICKPOCKET (*to his disciples*): Particularly the lace ruffles at the knees . . . You're to snip off carefully!

A SPECTATOR (*to another, pointing toward an upper seat*): Look! On the first night of *The Cid*, I was perched up there!

PICKPOCKET (*with pantomimic suggestion of spiriting away*): Watches . . .

THE BURGHER (*coming forward again with his son*): The actors you are about to see, my son, are among the most illustrious . . .

PICKPOCKET (*with show of abstracting with furtive little tugs*): Pocket handkerchiefs . . .

THE BURGHER: Montfleury . . .

SOMEBODY (*shouting from the upper gallery*): Make haste, and light the chandeliers!

THE BURGHER: Bellerose, l'Epy, the Beaupré, Jodelet . . .

A PAGE (*in the pit*): Ah! . . . Here comes the goody seller!

THE SWEETMEAT VENDOR (*appearing behind the stand*): Oranges . . .
Milk . . . Raspberry cordial . . . citron wine . . .

[*Hubbub at the door.*]

FALSETTO VOICE (*outside*): Make room, ruffians!

ONE OF THE LACKEYS (*astonished*): The marquises . . . in the pit!

OTHER LACKEY: Oh, for an instant only!

[*Enter a band of foppish* YOUNG MARQUISES.]

ONE OF THE MARQUISES (*looking around the half-empty house*): What?
. . . We happen in like so many linen drapers? Without disturbing anybody? Treading on any feet? . . . Too bad! too bad! too bad! (*He finds
himself near several other gentlemen, come in a moment before.*) Cuigy,
Brissaille!

[*Effusive embraces.*]

CUIGY: We are of the faithful indeed. We are here before the lights.

THE MARQUIS: Ah, do not speak of it! . . . It has put me in such a humor!

OTHER MARQUIS: Be comforted, Marquis . . . here comes the candlelighter!

THE AUDIENCE (*greeting the arrival of the candlelighter*): Ah . . .

[*Many gather around the chandeliers while they are being lighted. A
few have taken seats in the galleries.* LIGNIÈRE *enters, arm in arm with*
CHRISTIAN DE NEUVILLETTE. LIGNIÈRE, *in somewhat disordered ap-
parel; appearance of gentlemanly drunkard.* CHRISTIAN, *becomingly
dressed, but in clothes of a slightly obsolete elegance.*]

CUIGY: Lignière!

BRISSAILLE (*laughing*): Not tipsy yet?

LIGNIÈRE (*low to* CHRISTIAN): Shall I present you? (CHRISTIAN *nods as-
sent.*) Baron de Neuvillette . . .

[*Exchange of bows.*]

THE AUDIENCE (*cheering the ascent of the first lighted chandelier*): Ah! . .

CUIGY (*to* BRISSAILLE, *looking at* CHRISTIAN): A charming head . . .
charming!

FIRST MARQUIS (*who has overheard*): Pooh! . . .

LIGNIÈRE (*presenting* CHRISTIAN): Messieurs de Cuigy . . . de Brissaille . . .

CHRISTIAN (*bowing*): Delighted! . . .

FIRST MARQUIS (*to* SECOND): He is a pretty fellow enough, but is dressed
in the fashion of some other year!

LIGNIÈRE (*to* CUIGY): Monsieur is lately arrived from Touraine.

CHRISTIAN: Yes, I have been in Paris not over twenty days. I enter the
Guards tomorrow, the Cadets.

FIRST MARQUIS (*looking at those who appear in the boxes*): There comes
the Présidente Aubry!

SWEETMEAT VENDOR: Oranges! Milk!

THE FIDDLERS (*tuning*): La . . . la . . .

CUIGY (*to* CHRISTIAN, *indicating the house, which is filling*): A good house! . . .

CHRISTIAN: Yes, crowded.

FIRST MARQUIS: The whole of fashion!

> [*They give the names of the women, as, very brilliantly attired, these enter the boxes. Exchange of bows and smiles.*]

SECOND MARQUIS: Mesdames de Guéménée . . .

CUIGY: De Bois-Dauphin . . .

FIRST MARQUIS: Whom . . . time was . . . we loved! . . .

BRISSAILLE: . . . de Chavigny . . .

SECOND MARQUIS: Who still plays havoc with our hearts!

LIGNIÈRE: *Tiens!* Monsieur de Corneille has come back from Rouen!

THE YOUTH (*to his father*): The Academy is present?

THE BURGHER: Yes . . . I perceive more than one member of it. Yonder are Boudu, Boissat, and Cureau . . . Porchères, Colomby, Bourzeys, Bourdon, Arbaut . . . All names of which not one will be forgotten. What a beautiful thought it is!

FIRST MARQUIS: Attention! Our *précieuses* are coming into their seats . . . Barthénoide, Urimédonte, Cassandace, Félixérie . . .

SECOND MARQUIS: Ah, how exquisite are their surnames! . . . Marquis, can you tell them off, all of them?

FIRST MARQUIS: I can tell them off, all of them, Marquis!

LIGNIÈRE (*drawing* CHRISTIAN *aside*): Dear fellow, I came in here to be of use to you. The lady does not come. I revert to my vice!

CHRISTIAN (*imploring*): No! No! . . . You who turn into ditties Town and Court, stay by me: you will be able to tell me for whom it is I am dying of love!

THE LEADER OF THE VIOLINS (*rapping on his desk with his bow*): Gentlemen! . . .

> [*He raises his bow.*]

SWEETMEAT VENDOR: Macaroons . . . Citronade . . .

> [*The fiddles begin playing.*]

CHRISTIAN: I fear . . . oh, I fear to find that she is fanciful and subtle! I dare not speak to her, for I am of a simple wit. The language written and spoken in these days bewilders and baffles me. I am a plain soldier . . . shy, to boot. . . . She is always at the right, there, the end: the empty box.

LIGNIÈRE (*with show of leaving*): I am going.

CHRISTIAN (*still attempting to detain him*): Oh, no! . . . Stay, I beseech you!

LIGNIÈRE: I cannot. D'Assoucy is expecting me at the pothouse. Here is a mortal drought!

SWEETMEAT VENDOR (*passing before him with a tray*): Orangeade? . . .

LIGNIÈRE: Ugh!

SWEETMEAT VENDOR: Milk? . . .

LIGNIÈRE: Pah! . . .

SWEETMEAT VENDOR: Lacrima? . . .

LIGNIÈRE: Stop! (*To* CHRISTIAN) I will tarry a bit. . . . Let us see this
lacrima?

> [*Sits down at the sweetmeat stand. The* VENDOR *pours him a glass of
> lacrima. Shouts among the audience at the entrance of a little, merry-
> faced, roly-poly man.*]

AUDIENCE: Ah, Ragueneau! . . .

LIGNIÈRE (*to* CHRISTIAN): Ragueneau, who keeps the great cookshop.

RAGUENEAU (*attired like a pastrycook in his Sunday best, coming quickly
toward* LIGNIÈRE): Monsieur, have you seen Monsieur de Cyrano?

LIGNIÈRE (*presenting* RAGUENEAU *to* CHRISTIAN): The pastrycook of poets
and of players!

RAGUENEAU (*abashed*): Too much honor.

LIGNIÈRE: No modesty! . . . Mecaenas! . . .

RAGUENEAU: It is true, those gentlemen are among my customers. . . .

LIGNIÈRE: Debtors! . . . A considerable poet himself. . . .

RAGUENEAU: It has been said! . . .

LIGNIÈRE: Daft on poetry! . . .

RAGUENEAU: It is true that for an ode. . . .

LIGNIÈRE: You are willing to give at any time a tart!

RAGUENEAU: . . . let. A tart-let.

LIGNIÈRE: Kind soul, he tries to cheapen his charitable acts! And for a
triolet were you not known to give . . . ?

RAGUENEAU: Rolls. Just rolls.

LIGNIÈRE (*severely*): Buttered! . . . And the play, you are fond of the
play?

RAGUENEAU: It is with me a passion!

LIGNIÈRE: And you settle for your entrance fee with a pastry currency.
Come now, among ourselves, what did you have to give today for admit-
tance here?

RAGUENEAU: Four custards . . . eighteen ladyfingers. (*He looks all around.*)
Monsieur de Cyrano is not here. I wonder at it.

LIGNIÈRE: And why?

RAGUENEAU: Montfleury is billed to play.

LIGNIÈRE: So he is, indeed. That ton of man will today entrance us in the
part of Phoedo . . . Phoedo! . . . But what is that to Cyrano?

RAGUENEAU: Have you not heard? He forbade Montfleury, whom he has
taken in aversion, to appear for one month upon the stage.

LIGNIÈRE (*who is at his fourth glass*): Well?

RAGUENEAU: Montfleury is billed to play.

CUIGY (*who has drawn near with his companions*): He cannot be prevented.

RAGUENEAU: He cannot? . . . Well, I am here to see!

FIRST MARQUIS: What is this Cyrano?

CUIGY: A crackbrain!

SECOND MARQUIS: Of quality?

CUIGY: Enough for daily uses. He is a cadet in the Guards. (*Pointing out a gentleman who is coming and going about the pit, as if in search of somebody*) But his friend Le Bret can tell you. (*Calling*) Le Bret! . . . (LE BRET *comes toward them.*) You are looking for Bergerac?

LE BRET: Yes. I am uneasy.

CUIGY: Is it not a fact that he is a most uncommon fellow?

LE BRET (*affectionately*): The most exquisite being he is that walks beneath the moon!

RAGUENEAU: Poet!

CUIGY: Swordsman!

BRISSAILLE: Physicist!

LE BRET: Musician!

LIGNIÈRE: And what an extraordinary aspect he presents!

RAGUENEAU: I will not go so far as to say that I believe our grave Philippe de Champaigne will leave us a portrait of him; but, the bizarre, excessive, whimsical fellow that he is would certainly have furnished the late Jacques Callot with a type of madcap fighter for one of his masques. Hat with triple feather, doublet with twice-triple skirt, cloak which his interminable rapier lifts up behind, with pomp, like the insolent tail of a cock; prouder than all the Artabans that Gascony ever bred, he goes about in his stiff Punchinello ruff, airing a nose. . . . Ah, gentlemen, what a nose is that! One cannot look upon such a specimen of the nasigera without exclaiming, "No! truly, the man exaggerates" . . . After that, one smiles, one says: "He will take it off." . . . But Monsieur de Bergerac never takes it off at all.

LE BRET (*shaking his head*): He wears it always . . . and cuts down whoever breathes a syllable in comment.

RAGUENEAU (*proudly*): His blade is half the shears of Fate!

FIRST MARQUIS (*shrugging his shoulders*): He will not come!

RAGUENEAU: He will. I wager you a chicken à la Ragueneau.

FIRST MARQUIS (*laughing*): Very well!

> [*Murmur of admiration in the house.* ROXANE *has appeared in her box. She takes a seat in the front, her* DUENNA *at the back.* CHRISTIAN, *engaged in paying the* SWEETMEAT VENDOR, *does not look.*]

SECOND MARQUIS (*uttering a series of small squeals*): Ah, gentlemen, she is horrifically enticing!

FIRST MARQUIS: A strawberry set in a peach, and smiling!

SECOND MARQUIS: So fresh that, being near her, one might catch cold in his heart!

CHRISTIAN (*looks up, sees* ROXANE, *and, agitated, seizes* LIGNIÈRE *by the arm*): That is she!

LIGNIÈRE (*looking*): Ah, that is she! . . .

CHRISTIAN: Yes. Tell me at once. . . . Oh, I am afraid! . . .

LIGNIÈRE (*sipping his wine slowly*): Magdeleine Robin, surnamed Roxane. Subtle. Euphuistic.

CHRISTIAN: Alack-a-day!

LIGNIÈRE: Unmarried. An orphan. A cousin of Cyrano's . . . the one of whom they were talking.
> [*While he is speaking, a richly dressed nobleman, wearing the order of the Holy Ghost on a blue ribbon across his breast, enters* ROXANE'S *box, and, without taking a seat, talks with her a moment.*]

CHRISTIAN (*starting*): That man? . . .

LIGNIÈRE (*who is beginning to be tipsy, winking*): Hé! Hé! Comte de Guiche. Enamored of her. But married to the niece of Armand de Richelieu. Wishes to manage a match between Roxane and a certain sorry lord, one Monsieur de Valvert, vicomte and . . . easy. She does not subscribe to his views, but De Guiche is powerful: he can persecute to some purpose a simple commoner. But I have duly set forth his shady machinations in a song which . . . Ho! he must bear me a grudge! The end was wicked . . . Listen! . . .
> [*He rises, staggering, and lifting his glass, is about to sing.*]

CHRISTIAN: No. Good evening.

LIGNIÈRE: You are going? . . .

CHRISTIAN: To find Monsieur de Valvert.

LIGNIÈRE: Have a care. You are the one who will get killed. (*Indicating* ROXANE *by a glance*) Stay. Someone is looking . . .

CHRISTIAN: It is true . . .
> [*He remains absorbed in the contemplation of* ROXANE. *The* PICK-POCKETS, *seeing his abstracted air, draw nearer to him.*]

LIGNIÈRE: Ah, you are going to stay. Well, I am going. I am thirsty! And I am looked for . . . at all the public houses!
> [*Exit unsteadily.*]

LE BRET (*who has made the circuit of the house, returning toward* RAGUENEAU, *in a tone of relief*): Cyrano is not here.

RAGUENEAU: And yet . . .

LE BRET: I will trust to Fortune he has not seen the announcement.

THE AUDIENCE: Begin! Begin!

ONE OF THE MARQUISES (*watching* DE GUICHE, *who comes from* ROXANE'S *box, and crosses the pit, surrounded by obsequious satellites, among them the* VICOMTE DE VALVERT): Always a court about him, De Guiche!

OTHER MARQUIS: Pf! . . . Another Gascon!

FIRST MARQUIS: A Gascon of the cold and supple sort. That sort succeeds. Believe me, it will be best to offer him our duty.

[*They approach* DE GUICHE.]

SECOND MARQUIS: These admirable ribbons! What color, Comte de Guiche? Should you call it Kiss-me-Sweet or . . . Expiring Fawn?

DE GUICHE: This shade is called Sick Spaniard.

FIRST MARQUIS: Appropriately called, for shortly, thanks to your valor, the Spaniard will be sick indeed, in Flanders!

DE GUICHE: I am going upon the stage. Are you coming? (*He walks toward the stage, followed by all the* MARQUISES *and men of quality. He turns and calls.*) Valvert, come!

CHRISTIAN (*who has been listening and watching them, starts on hearing that name*): The Vicomte! . . . Ah, in his face . . . in his face I will fling my . . . (*He puts his hand to his pocket and finds the* PICKPOCKET'S *hand. He turns.*) Hein?

PICKPOCKET: Aï!

CHRISTIAN (*without letting him go*): I was looking for a glove.

PICKPOCKET (*with an abject smile*): And you found a hand. (*In a different tone, low and rapid*) Let me go . . . I will tell you a secret.

CHRISTIAN (*without releasing him*): Well?

PICKPOCKET: Lignière, who has just left you . . .

CHRISTIAN (*as above*): Yes? . . .

PICKPOCKET: . . . has not an hour to live. A song he made annoyed one of the great, and a hundred men—I am one of them—will be posted to-night . . .

CHRISTIAN: A hundred? . . . By whom?

PICKPOCKET: Honor . . .

CHRISTIAN (*shrugging his shoulders*): Oh! . . .

PICKPOCKET (*with great dignity*): Among rogues!

CHRISTIAN: Where will they be posted?

PICKPOCKET: At the Porte de Nesle, on his way home. Inform him.

CHRISTIAN (*letting him go*): But where can I find him?

PICKPOCKET: Go to all the taverns—the Golden Vat, the Pine-Apple, the Belt and Bosom, the Twin Torches, the Three Funnels—and in each one leave a scrap of writing warning him.

CHRISTIAN: Yes. I will run! . . . Ah, the blackguards! A hundred against

one! . . . (*Looks lovingly toward* ROXANE) Leave her! . . . (*Furiously, looking toward* VALVERT) And him! . . . But Lignière must be prevented.
[*Exit running.*]

[DE GUICHE, *the* MARQUISES, *all the gentry have disappeared behind the curtain, to place themselves on the stage seats. The pit is crowded. There is not an empty seat in the boxes or the gallery.*]

THE AUDIENCE: Begin!

A BURGHER (*whose wig goes sailing off at the end of a string held by one of the pages in the upper gallery*): My wig!

SCREAMS OF DELIGHT: *He is bald! . . . The pages! . . . Well done! . . . Ha, ha, ha! . . .*

THE BURGHER (*furious, shaking his fist*): Imp of Satan. . . .
[*Laughter and screams, beginning very loud and decreasing suddenly. Dead silence.*]

LE BRET (*astonished*): This sudden hush? . . . (*One of the spectators whispers in his ear*) Ah? . . .

THE SPECTATOR: I have it from a reliable quarter.

RUNNING MURMURS: Hush! . . . Has he come? No! . . . Yes, he has! . . . In the box with the grating . . . The Cardinal! . . . the Cardinal! . . . the Cardinal! . .

ONE OF THE PAGES: What a shame! . . . Now we shall have to behave!
[*Knocking on the stage. Complete stillness. Pause.*]

VOICE OF ONE OF THE MARQUISES (*breaking the deep silence, behind the curtain*): Snuff that candle!

OTHER MARQUIS (*thrusting his head out between the curtains*): A chair!
[*A chair is passed from hand to hand, above the heads. The* MARQUIS *takes it and disappears, after kissing his hand repeatedly toward the boxes.*]

A SPECTATOR: Silence!
[*Once more, the three knocks. The curtain opens. Tableau. The* MARQUISES *seated at the sides, in attitudes of languid haughtiness. The stage setting is the faint-colored bluish sort usual in a pastoral. Four small crystal candelabra light the stage. The violins play softly.*]

LE BRET (*to* RAGUENEAU, *under breath*): Is Montfleury the first to appear?

RAGUENEAU (*likewise under breath*): Yes. The opening lines are his.

LE BRET: Cyrano is not here.

RAGUENEAU: I have lost my wager.

LE BRET: Let us be thankful. Let us be thankful.
[*A bagpipe is heard.* MONTFLEURY *appears upon the stage, enormous, in a conventional shepherd's costume, with a rose-wreathed hat set jauntily on the side of his head, breathing into a beribboned bagpipe.*]

THE PIT (*applauding*): Bravo, Montfleury! Montfleury!
MONTFLEURY (*after bowing, proceeds to play the part of* PHOEDO):

> Happy the man who, freed from Fashion's fickle sway,
> In exile self-prescribed whiles peaceful hours away;
> Who when Zephyrus sighs amid the answering trees. . . .

A VOICE (*from the middle of the pit*): Rogue! Did I not forbid you for one month?

> [*Consternation. Everyone looks around. Murmurs.*]

VARIOUS VOICES: *Hein?* What? What is the matter?

> [*Many in the boxes rise to see.*]

CUIGY: It is he!
LE BRET (*alarmed*): Cyrano!
THE VOICE: King of the Obese! Incontinently vanish! . . .
THE WHOLE AUDIENCE (*indignant*): Oh!
MONTFLEURY: But . . .
THE VOICE: You stop to muse upon the matter?
SEVERAL VOICES (*from the pit and the boxes*): Hush! . . . Enough! . . . Proceed, Montfleury. . . . Fear nothing!
MONTFLEURY (*in an unsteady voice*):

> Happy the man who freed from Fashion's f——— . . .

THE VOICE (*more threatening than before*): How is this? Shall I be constrained, Man of the Monster Belly, to enforce my regulation . . . regularly?

> [*An arm holding a cane leaps above the level of the heads.*]

MONTFLEURY (*in a voice growing fainter and fainter*):

> Happy the man . . .

> [*The cane is wildly flourished.*]

THE VOICE: Leave the stage!
THE PIT: Oh! . . .
MONTFLEURY (*choking*):

> Happy the man who freed . . .

CYRANO (*appearing above the audience, standing upon a chair, his arms folded on his chest, his hat at a combative angle, his moustache on end, his nose terrifying*): Ah! I shall lose my temper!

> [*Sensation at sight of him.*]

MONTFLEURY (*to the* MARQUISES): Messieurs, I appeal to you!
ONE OF THE MARQUISES (*languidly*): But go ahead! . . . Play!

CYRANO: Fat man, if you attempt it, I will dust the paint off you with this!

THE MARQUIS: Enough!

CYRANO: Let every little lordling keep silence in his seat, or I will ruffle his ribbons with my cane!

ALL THE MARQUISES (*rising*): This is too much! . . . Montfleury. . .

CYRANO: Let Montfleury go home; or stay, and, having cut his ears off, I will disembowel him!

A VOICE: But . . .

CYRANO: Let him go home, I said!

OTHER VOICE: But after all . . .

CYRANO: It is not yet done? (*With show of turning up his sleeves*) Very well, upon that stage, as on a platter trimmed with green, you shall see me carve that mount of brawn. . . .

MONTFLEURY (*calling up his whole dignity*): Monsieur, you cast indignity, in my person, upon the Muse!

CYRANO (*very civilly*): Monsieur, if that lady, with whom you have naught to do, had the pleasure of beholding you . . . just as you stand there like a decorated pot! . . . she could not live, I do protest, but she hurled her buskin at you!

THE PIT: Montfleury! . . . Montfleury! . . . Give us Baro's piece!

CYRANO (*to those shouting around him*): I beg you will show some regard for my scabbard: it is ready to give up the sword!

[*The space round him widens.*]

THE CROWD (*backing away*): Hey . . . softly, there!

CYRANO (*to* MONTFLEURY): Go off!

THE CROWD (*closing again, and grumbling*): Oh! . . . Oh!

CYRANO (*turning suddenly*): Has somebody objections?

[*The crowd again pushes away from him.*]

A VOICE (*at the back, singing*):

> Monsieur de Cyrano, one sees,
> Inclines to be tyrannical;
> In spite of that Cyrannical
> We shall see *La Clorise*!

THE WHOLE AUDIENCE (*catching up the tune*): *La Clorise! La Clorise!*

CYRANO: Let me hear that song again, and I will do you all to death with my stick!

A BURGHER: Samson come back! . . .

CYRANO: Lend me your jaw, good man!

A LADY (*in one of the boxes*): This is unheard of!

A MAN: It is scandalous!

A BURGHER: It is irritating, to say no more.

A PAGE: What fun it is!

THE PIT: Ksss! . . . Montfleury! . . . Cyrano! . . .

CYRANO: Be still! . . .

THE PIT (*in uproar*): Hee-haw. . . . Baaaaah! . . . Bow-wow! . . . Cocka-doodledoooooo!

CYRANO: I will . . .

A PAGE: Meeeow!

CYRANO: I order you to hold your tongues! . . . I dare the floor collectively to utter another sound! . . . I challenge you, one and all! . . . I will take down your names . . . Step forward, budding heroes! Each in his turn. You shall be given numbers. Come, which one of you will open the joust with me? You, Monsieur? No! You? No! The first that offers is promised all the mortuary honors due the brave. Let all who wish to die hold up their hands! (*Silence.*) It is modesty that makes you shrink from the sight of my naked sword? Not a name? Not a hand?—Very good. Then I proceed. (*Turning toward the stage where* MONTFLEURY *is waiting in terror*) As I was saying, it is my wish to see the stage cured of this tumor. Otherwise . . . (*clapping hand to his sword*) . . . the lancet!

MONTFLEURY: I . . .

CYRANO (*getting down from his chair and sitting in the space that has become vacant around him, with the ease of one at home*): Thrice will I clap my hands, O plenilune! At the third clap . . . eclipse!

THE PIT (*diverted*): Ah! . . .

CYRANO (*clapping his hands*): One! . . .

MONTFLEURY: I . . .

A VOICE (*from one of the boxes*): Do not go! . . .

THE PIT: He will stay! . . . He will go! . . .

MONTFLEURY: Messieurs, I feel . . .

CYRANO: Two! . . .

MONTFLEURY: I feel it will perhaps be wiser . . .

CYRANO: Three! . . .

    [MONTFLEURY *disappears, as if through a trapdoor. Storm of laughter, hissing, catcalls.*]

THE HOUSE: Hoo! . . . Hoo! . . . Milksop! . . . Come back! . . .

CYRANO (*beaming, leans back in his chair and crosses his legs*): Let him come back, if he dare!

A BURGHER: The spokesman of the company!

    [BELLEROSE *comes forward on the stage and bows.*]

THE BOXES: Ah, here comes Bellerose!

BELLEROSE (*with elegant bearing and diction*): Noble ladies and gentlemen . . .

THE PIT: No! No! Jodelet! . . . We want Jodelet! . . .

JODELET (*comes forward, speaks through his nose*): Pack of swine!

THE PIT: That is right! . . Well said! . . . Bravo!

JODELET: Don't bravo me! . . . The portly tragedian, whose paunch is your delight, felt sick! . . .

THE PIT: He is a poltroon! . . .

JODELET: He was obliged to leave . . .

THE PIT: Let him come back!

SOME: No!

OTHERS: Yes! . . .

A YOUTH (*to* CYRANO): But, when all is said, Monsieur, what good grounds have you for hating Montfleury?

CYRANO (*amiably, sitting as before*): Young gosling, I have two, whereof each, singly, would be ample. Primo: He is an execrable actor, who bellows, and with grunts that would disgrace a water carrier launches the verse that should go forth as if on pinions! . . . Secundo: is my secret.

THE OLD BURGHER (*behind* CYRANO): But without compunction you deprive us of hearing *La Clorise*. I am determined . . .

CYRANO (*turning his chair around so as to face the old gentleman; respectfully*): Venerable mule, old Baro's verses being what they are, I do it without compunction, as you say.

THE PRÉCIEUSES (*in the boxes*): Ha! . . . Ho! . . . Our own Baro! . . . My dear, did you hear that? How can such a thing be said? . . . Ha! . . . Ho! . . .

CYRANO (*turning his chair so as to face the boxes; gallantly*): Beautiful creatures, do you bloom and shine, be ministers of dreams, your smiles our anodyne. Inspire poets, but poems . . . spare to judge!

BELLEROSE: But the money which must be given back at the door!

CYRANO (*turning his chair to face the stage*): Bellerose, you have said the only intelligent thing that has, as yet, been said! Far from me to wrong by so much as a fringe the worshipful mantle of Thespis. . . . (*He rises and flings a bag upon the stage.*) Catch! . . . and keep quiet!

THE HOUSE (*dazzled*): Ah! . . . Oh! . . .

JODELET (*nimbly picking up the bag, weighing it with his hand*): For such a price, you are authorized, Monsieur, to come and stop the performance every day!

THE HOUSE: Hoo! . . . Hoo! . . .

JODELET: Should we be hooted in a body! . . .

BELLEROSE: The house must be evacuated!

JODELET: Evacuate it!

[*The audience begins to leave,* CYRANO *looking on with a satisfied air. The crowd, however, becoming interested in the following scene, the exodus is suspended. The women in the boxes who were already standing, and had put on their wraps, stop to listen and end by resuming their seats.*]

LE BRET (*to* CYRANO): What you have done . . . is mad!

A BORE: Montfleury! . . . the eminent actor! . . . What a scandal! . . . But the Duc de Candale is his patron! . . . Have you a patron, you?

CYRANO: No!

THE BORE: You have not?

CYRANO: No!

THE BORE: What? You are not protected by some great nobleman under the cover of whose name. . . .

CYRANO (*exasperated*): No, I have told you twice. Must I say the same thing thrice? No, I have no protector . . . (*hand on sword*) . . . but this will do.

THE BORE: Then, of course, you will leave town.

CYRANO: That will depend.

THE BORE: But the Duc de Candale has a long arm . . .

CYRANO: Not so long as mine . . . (*pointing to his sword*) . . . pieced out with this!

THE BORE: But you cannot have the presumption . . .

CYRANO: I can, yes.

THE BORE: But . . .

CYRANO: And now . . . face about!

THE BORE: But . . .

CYRANO: Face about, I say . . . or else, tell me why you are looking at my nose.

THE BORE (*bewildered*): I . . .

CYRANO (*advancing upon him*): In what is it unusual?

THE BORE (*backing*): Your worship is mistaken.

CYRANO (*same business as above*): Is it flabby and pendulous, like a proboscis?

THE BORE: I never said . . .

CYRANO: Or hooked like a hawk's beak?

THE BORE: I . . .

CYRANO: Do you discern a mole upon the tip?

THE BORE: But . . .

CYRANO: Or is a fly disporting himself thereon? What is there wonderful about it?

THE BORE: Oh . . .

CYRANO: Is it a freak of nature?

THE BORE: But I had refrained from casting so much as a glance at it!

CYRANO: And why, I pray, should you not look at it?

THE BORE: I had . . .

CYRANO: So it disgusts you?

THE BORE: Sir . . .

CYRANO: Its color strikes you as unwholesome?

THE BORE: Sir . . .

CYRANO: Its shape, unfortunate?

THE BORE: But far from it!

CYRANO: Then wherefore that depreciating air? . . . Perhaps monsieur thinks it a shade too large?

THE BORE: Indeed not. No, indeed. I think it small . . . small—I should have said, minute!

CYRANO: What? How? Charge me with such a ridiculous defect? Small, my nose? Ho! . . .

THE BORE: Heavens!

CYRANO: Enormous, my nose! . . . Contemptible stutterer, snub-nosed and flat-headed, be it known to you that I am proud, proud of such an appendage! inasmuch as a great nose is properly the index of an affable, kindly, courteous man, witty, liberal, brave, such as I am! and such as you are for evermore precluded from supposing yourself, deplorable rogue! For the inglorious surface my hand encounters above your ruff is no less devoid . . .

[Strikes him.]

THE BORE: Aï! aï! . . .

CYRANO: . . . of pride, alacrity, and sweep, of perception and of gift, of heavenly spark, of sumptuousness, to sum up all, of *NOSE,* than that (*turns him around by the shoulders and suits the action to the word*) which stops my boot below your spine!

THE BORE (*running off*): Help! The watch! . . .

CYRANO: Warning to the idle who might find entertainment in my organ of smell. . . . And if the facetious fellow be of birth, my custom is, before I let him go, to chasten him, in front, and higher up, with steel, and not with hide!

DE GUICHE (*who has stepped down from the stage with the* MARQUISES): He is becoming tiresome!

VALVERT (*shrugging his shoulders*): It is empty bluster!

DE GUICHE: Will no one take him up?

VALVERT: No one? . . . Wait! I will have one of those shots at him! (*He approaches* CYRANO, *who is watching him, and stops in front of him, in an attitude of silly swagger.*) Your . . . nose is . . . er . . . Your nose . . . is very large!

CYRANO (*gravely*): Very.

VALVERT (*laughs*): Ha! . . .

CYRANO (*imperturbable*): Is that all?

VALVERT: But . . .

CYRANO: Ah, no, young man, that is not enough! You might have said, dear me, there are a thousand things . . . varying the tone . . . For instance . . . here you are—Aggressive: "I, Monsieur, if I had such a nose, nothing would serve but I must cut it off!" Amicable: "It must be in your way while drinking; you ought to have a special beaker made!" Descriptive: "It is a crag! . . . a peak! . . . a promontory! . . . A promontory, did I say? . . . It is a peninsula!" Inquisitive: "What may the office be of that oblong receptacle? Is it an inkhorn or a scissor case?" Mincing: "Do you so dote on birds, you have, fond as a father, been at pains to fit the little darlings with a roost?" Blunt: "Tell me, Monsieur, you, when you smoke, is it possible you blow the vapor through your nose without a neighbor crying, 'The chimney is afire'?" Anxious: "Go with caution, I beseech, lest your head, dragged over by that weight, should drag you over!" Tender: "Have a little sunshade made for it! It might get freckled!" Learned: "None but the beast, Monsieur, mentioned by Aristophanes, the hippocampelephantocamelos, can have borne beneath his forehead so much cartilage and bone!" Offhand: "What, comrade, is that sort of peg in style? Capital to hang one's hat upon!" Emphatic: "No wind can hope, O lordly nose, to give the whole of you a cold, but the Nor'-Wester!" Dramatic: "It is the Red Sea when it bleeds!" Admiring: "What a sign for a perfumer's shop!" Lyrical: "Art thou a Triton, and is that thy conch?" Simple: "A monument! When is admission free?" Deferent: "Suffer, Monsieur, that I should pay you my respects: that is what I call possessing a house of your own!" Rustic: "Hi, boys! Call that a nose? Ye don't gull me! It's either a prize carrot or else a stunted gourd!" Military: "Level against the cavalry!" Practical: "Will you put it up for raffle? Indubitably, sir, it will be the feature of the game!" And finally in parody of weeping Pyramus: "Behold, behold the nose that traitorously destroyed the beauty of its master! and is blushing for the same!"—That, my dear sir, or something not unlike, is what you would have said to me, had you the smallest leaven of letters or of wit; but of wit, O most pitiable of objects made by God, you never had a rudiment, and of letters, you have just those that are needed to spell "fool"! . . . But, had it been otherwise, and had you been possessed of the fertile fancy requisite to shower upon me, here, in this noble company, that volley of sprightly pleasantries, still should you not have delivered yourself of so much as a quarter of the tenth part of the begin-

ning of the first. . . . For I let off these good things at myself, and with
sufficient zest, but do not suffer another to let them off at me!

DE GUICHE (*attempting to lead away the amazed* VICOMTE): Let be,
Vicomte!

VALVERT: That insufferable haughty bearing! . . . A clodhopper without . . .
without so much as gloves . . . who goes abroad without points . . . or
bowknots! . . .

CYRANO: My foppery is of the inner man. I do not trick myself out like a
popinjay, but I am more fastidious, if I am not so showy. I would not
sally forth, by any chance, not washed quite clean of an affront; my conscience foggy about the eye, my honor crumpled, my nicety black-
rimmed. I walk with all upon me furbished bright. I plume myself with
independence and straightforwardness. It is not a handsome figure, it is
my soul that I hold erect as in a brace. I go decked with exploits in place
of ribbon bows. I taper to a point my wit like a moustache. And at my
passage through the crowd true sayings ring like spurs!

VALVERT: But, sir . . .

CYRANO: I am without gloves? . . . a mighty matter! I only had one left, of
a very ancient pair, and even that became a burden to me . . . I left it in
somebody's face.

VALVERT: Villain, clodpoll, flatfoot, refuse of the earth!

CYRANO (*taking off his hat and bowing as if the* VICOMTE *had been intro-
ducing himself*): Ah! . . . And mine, Cyrano-Savinien-Hercule de Bergerac!

VALVERT (*exasperated*): Buffoon!

CYRANO (*giving a sudden cry, as if seized with a cramp*): Aï! . . .

VALVERT (*who has started toward the back, turning*): What is he saying
now?

CYRANO (*screwing his face as if in pain*): It must have leave to stir . . . it
has a cramp! It is bad for it to be kept still so long!

VALVERT: What is the matter?

CYRANO: My rapier prickles like a foot asleep!

VALVERT (*drawing*): So be it!

CYRANO: I shall give you a charming little hurt!

VALVERT (*contemptuous*): A poet!

CYRANO: Yes, a poet . . . and to such an extent, that while we fence, I will,
hop! extempore, compose you a ballade!

VALVERT: A ballade?

CYRANO: I fear you do not know what that is.

VALVERT: But . . .

CYRANO (*as if saying a lesson*): The ballade is composed of three stanzas of eight lines each. . . .

VALVERT (*stamps with his feet*): Oh! . . .

CYRANO (*continuing*): And an envoi of four.

VALVERT: You . . .

CYRANO: I will with the same breath fight you and compose one. And at the last line, I will hit.

VALVERT: Indeed you will not!

CYRANO: No? . . . (*declaiming*) "Ballade of the Duel Which in Burgundy House Monsieur de Bergerac Fought with a Jackanapes."

VALVERT: And what is that, if you please?

CYRANO: That is the title.

THE AUDIENCE (*at the highest pitch of excitement*): Make room! . . . Good sport! . . . Stand aside! . . . Keep still! . . .

[*Tableau. A ring, in the pit, of the interested; the* MARQUISES *and* OFFICERS *scattered among the* BURGHERS *and* COMMON PEOPLE. *The* PAGES *have climbed on the shoulders of various ones, the better to see. All the women are standing in the boxes. At the right,* DE GUICHE *and his attendant gentlemen. At the left,* LE BRET, RAGUENEAU, CUIGY, *etc.*]

CYRANO (*closing his eyes a second*): Wait. I am settling upon the rhymes. There. I have them.

[*In declaiming, he suits the action to the word.*]

> Of my broad belt made lighter,
> I cast my mantle broad,
> And stand, poet and fighter,
> To do and to record.
> I bow, I draw my sword,
> En garde! with steel and wit
> I play you at first abord . . .
> At the last line, I hit!
> > [*They begin fencing.*]
>
> You should have been politer;
> Where had you best be gored?
> The left side or the right—ah?
> Or next your azure cord?
> Or where the spleen is stored?
> Or in the stomach pit?
> Come we to quick accord . . .
> At the last line, I hit!

You falter, you turn whiter?
You do so to afford
Your foe a rhyme in "iter"? . . .
You thrust at me—I ward—
And balance is restored.
Laridon! Look to your spit! . . .
No, you shall not be floored
Before my cue to hit!
[*He announces solemnly.*]

ENVOI

Prince, call upon the Lord! . . .
I skirmish . . . feint a bit . . .
I lunge! . . . I keep my word!
[*The* VICOMTE *staggers;* CYRANO *bows.*]
At the last line, I hit!

[*Acclamations. Applause from the boxes. Flowers and handkerchiefs are thrown. The* OFFICERS *surround and congratulate* CYRANO. *RAGUE-NEAU dances with delight.* LE BRET *is tearfully joyous and at the same time highly troubled. The friends of the* VICOMTE *support him off the stage.*]

THE CROWD (*in a long shout*): Ah! . . .

A LIGHT-CAVALRY MAN: Superb!

A WOMAN: Sweet!

RAGUENEAU: Astounding!

A MARQUIS: Novel!

LE BRET: Insensate!

THE CROWD (*pressing around* CYRANO): Congratulations! . . . Well done! . . . Bravo! . . .

A WOMAN'S VOICE: He is a hero!

A MOUSQUETAIRE (*striding swiftly toward* CYRANO, *with outstretched hand*): Monsieur, will you allow me? It was quite, quite excellently done, and I think I know whereof I speak. But, as a fact, I expressed my mind before, by making a huge noise. . . .
[*He retires.*]

CYRANO (*to* CUIGY): Who may the gentleman be?

CUIGY: D'Artagnan.

LE BRET (*to* CYRANO, *taking his arm*): Come, I wish to talk with you.

CYRANO: Wait till the crowd has thinned. (*To* BELLEROSE) I may remain?

BELLEROSE (*deferentially*): Why, certainly! . . .

                    [*Shouts are heard outside.*]

JODELET (*after looking*): They are hooting Montfleury.

BELLEROSE (*solemnly*): *Sic transit!* . . . (*In a different tone, to the* DOOR-
KEEPER *and the* CANDLESNUFFER) Sweep and close. Leave the lights.
We shall come back, after eating, to rehearse a new farce for tomorrow.

    [*Exeunt* JODELET *and* BELLEROSE, *after bowing very low to* CYRANO.]

THE DOORKEEPER (*to* CYRANO): Monsieur will not be going to dinner?

CYRANO: I? . . . No.

                [*The* DOORKEEPER *withdraws.*]

LE BRET (*to* CYRANO): And this, because? . . .

CYRANO (*proudly*): Because . . . (*in a different tone, having seen that the*
DOORKEEPER *is too far to overhear*) I have not a penny!

LE BRET (*making the motion of flinging a bag*): How is this? The bag of
crowns. . . .

CYRANO: Monthly remittance, you lasted but a day!

LE BRET: And to keep you the remainder of the month? . . .

CYRANO: Nothing is left!

LE BRET: But then, flinging that bag, what a child's prank!

CYRANO: But what a gesture! . . .

THE SWEETMEAT VENDOR (*coughing behind her little counter*): Mm! . . .
(CYRANO *and* LE BRET *turn toward her. She comes timidly forward.*)
Monsieur, to know you have not eaten . . . makes my heart ache. (*Pointing to the sweetmeat stand*) I have there all that is needed. . . . (*Impul-
sively*) Help yourself!

CYRANO (*taking off his hat*): Dear child, despite my Gascon pride, which
forbids that I should profit at your hand by the most inconsiderable of
dainties, I would not offend you by declining: I will accept therefore . . .
(*He goes to the stand and selects.*) Oh, a trifle! . . . A grape off this . . .
(*She proffers the bunch, he takes a single grape.*) No . . . one! This glass
of water . . . (*She starts to pour wine into it, he stops her.*) No . . . clear!
And half a macaroon.

      [*He breaks in two the macaroon and returns half.*]

LE BRET: This comes near being silly!

SWEETMEAT VENDOR: Oh, you will take something more! . . .

CYRANO: Yes. Your hand to kiss.

    [*He kisses the hand she holds out to him, as if it were that of a princess.*]

SWEETMEAT VENDOR: Monsieur, I thank you. (*Curtseys.*) Good evening!

                  [*Exit.*]

CYRANO (*to* LE BRET): I am listening. (*He establishes himself before the
stand, sets the macaroon before him.*) Dinner! (*Does the same with the*

glass of water.) Drink! (*And with the grape.*) Dessert! (*He sits down.*) La! let me begin! I was as hungry as a wolf! (*Eating*) You were saying?

LE BRET: That if you listen to none but those great boobies and swash-bucklers your judgment will become wholly perverted. Inquire, will you, of the sensible, concerning the effect produced today by your bravado.

CYRANO (*finishing his macaroon*): Enormous!

LE BRET: The Cardinal . . .

CYRANO (*beaming*): He was there, the Cardinal?

LE BRET: Must have found what you did . . .

CYRANO: To a degree, original.

LE BRET: Still . . .

CYRANO: He is a poet. It cannot be distasteful to him wholly that one should deal confusion to a fellow poet's play.

LE BRET: But, seriously, you make too many enemies!

CYRANO (*biting into the grape*): How many, thereabouts, should you think I made tonight?

LE BRET: Eight and forty. Not mentioning the women.

CYRANO: Come, tell them over!

LE BRET: Montfleury, the old merchant, De Guiche, the Vicomte, Baro, the whole Academy . . .

CYRANO: Enough! You steep me in bliss!

LE BRET: But whither will the road you follow lead you? What can your object be?

CYRANO: I was wandering aimlessly; too many roads were open . . . too many resolves, too complex, offered a choice. I took . . .

LE BRET: Which?

CYRANO: By far the simplest of them all. I decided to be, in every matter, always admirable!

LE BRET (*shrugging his shoulders*): Very well. . . . But tell me, will you not, the motive—look, the true one!—of your dislike to Montfleury.

CYRANO (*rising*): That old Silenus, who has not seen his knees this many a year, still believes himself a danger to the fair. And as he struts and burrs upon the stage, he makes sheep's eyes at them with his moist frog's eyes. And I have hated him . . . oh, properly! . . . since the night he was so daring as to cast his glance on her. . . . her, who—Oh, I thought I saw a slug crawl over a flower!

LE BRET (*amazed*): Hey? What? Is it possible? . . .

CYRANO (*with a bitter laugh*): That I should love? (*In a different tone, seriously*) I love.

LE BRET: And may one know? . . . You never told me. . . .

CYRANO: Whom I love? . . . Come, think a little. The dream of being beloved, even by the beautiless, is made to me an empty dream indeed by this good nose, my forerunner ever by a quarter of an hour. Hence, whom should I love? . . . It seems superfluous to tell you! . . . I love . . . it was inevitable! . . . the most beautiful that breathes!

LE BRET: The most beautiful? . . .

CYRANO: No less, in the whole world! And the most resplendent, and the most delicate of wit, and among the golden-haired . . . (*with overwhelming despair*) . . . still the superlative!

LE BRET: Dear me, what is this fair one?

CYRANO: All unawares, a deadly snare, exquisite without concern to be so. A snare of nature's own, a musk rose, in which ambush Love lies low. Who has seen her smile remembers the ineffable! There is not a thing so common but she turns it into prettiness; and in the merest nod or beck she can make manifest all the attributes of a goddess. No, Venus! you cannot step into your iridescent shell, nor, Dian, you, walk through the blossoming groves, as she steps into her chair and walks in Paris!

LE BRET: *Sapristi!* I understand! It is clear!

CYRANO: It is pellucid.

LE BRET: Magdeleine Robin, your cousin?

CYRANO: Yes, Roxane.

LE BRET: But, what could be better? You love her? Tell her so! You covered yourself with glory in her sight a moment since.

CYRANO: Look well at me, dear friend, and tell me how much hope you think can be justly entertained with this protuberance. Oh, I foster no illusions! . . . Sometimes, indeed, yes, in the violet dusk, I yield, even I! to a dreamy mood. I penetrate some garden that lies sweetening the hour. With my poor great devil of a nose I sniff the April . . . and as I follow with my eyes some woman passing with some cavalier, I think how dear to have such a one walk beside me, linked like that, slowly, in the soft moonlight! I kindle—I forget—and then . . . then suddenly I see the shadow of my profile upon the garden wall!

LE BRET (*touched*): My friend . . .

CYRANO: Friend, I experience a bad half hour sometimes, in being so unsightly . . . and alone.

LE BRET (*in quick sympathy, taking his hand*): You weep?

CYRANO: Ah, God forbid! That? Never! No, that would be unsightly to excess! That a tear should course the whole length of this nose! Never, so long as I am accountable, shall the divine loveliness of tears be implicated with so much gross ugliness! Mark me well, nothing is so holy as are tears, nothing! and never shall it be that, rousing mirth through me, a single one of them shall seem ridiculous!

LE BRET: Come, do not despond! Love is a lottery.

CYRANO (*shaking his head*): No! I love Cleopatra: do I resemble Caesar? I worship Berenice: do I put you in mind of Titus?

LE BRET: But your courage . . . and your wit! . . . The little girl who but a moment ago bestowed on you that very modest meal, her eyes—you must have seen as much—did not exactly hate you!

CYRANO (*impressed*): That is true!

LE BRET: You see? So, then!—But Roxane herself, in following your duel, went lily-pale.

CYRANO: Lily-pale? . . .

LE BRET: Her mind, her heart as well, are struck with wonder! Be bold, speak to her, in order that she may . . .

CYRANO: Laugh in my face! . . . No, there is but one thing upon earth I fear. . . . It is that.

THE DOORKEEPER (*admitting the* DUENNA *to* CYRANO): Monsieur, you are inquired for.

CYRANO (*seeing the* DUENNA): Ah, my God! . . . her duenna!

THE DUENNA (*with a great curtsey*): Somebody wishes to know of her valorous cousin where one may see him in private.

CYRANO (*upset*): See me?

THE DUENNA (*with curtsey*): See you. There are things for your ear.

CYRANO: There are . . . ?

THE DUENNA (*another curtsey*): Things.

CYRANO (*staggering*): Ah, my God! . . .

THE DUENNA: Somebody intends, tomorrow, at the earliest roses of the dawn, to hear Mass at Saint Roch.

CYRANO (*upholds himself by leaning on* LE BRET): Ah, my God!

THE DUENNA: That over, where might one step for a moment . . . have a little talk?

CYRANO (*losing his senses*): Where? . . . I . . . But . . . Ah, by God!

THE DUENNA: Expedition, if you please.

CYRANO: I am casting about . . .

THE DUENNA: Where?

CYRANO: At . . . at . . . at Ragueneau's . . . the pastrycook's.

THE DUENNA: He lodges?

CYRANO: In . . . in Rue . . . Ah, my God! my God! . . . St. Honoré.

THE DUENNA (*retiring*): We will be there. Do not fail. At seven.

CYRANO: I will not fail.

[*Exit* DUENNA.]

CYRANO (*falling on* LE BRET'S *neck*): To me . . . from her . . . a meeting!

LE BRET: Well, your gloom is dispelled?

CYRANO: Oh, to whatever end it may be, she is aware of my existence!

LE BRET: And now you will be calm?

CYRANO (*beside himself*): Now, I shall be fulminating and frenetical! I want an army all complete to put to rout! I have ten hearts and twenty arms. . . . I cannot now be suited with felling dwarfs to earth . . . (*at the top of his lungs*) . . . giants are what I want!

    [*During the last lines, on the stage at the back, shadowy shapes of players have been moving about. The rehearsal has begun; the* FIDDLERS *have resumed their places.*]

A VOICE (*from the stage*): Hey! Psst! Over there! A little lower. We are trying to rehearse!

CYRANO (*laughing*): We are going.

    [*He goes toward the back. Through the street door enter* CUIGY, BRISSAILLE, *several* OFFICERS *supporting* LIGNIÈRE *in a state of complete intoxication.*]

CUIGY: Cyrano!

CYRANO: What is this?

CUIGY: A drunken sot we are bringing you.

CYRANO (*recognizing him*): Lignière! Hey, what has happened to you?

CUIGY: He is looking for you.

BRISSAILLE: He cannot go home.

CYRANO: Why?

LIGNIÈRE (*in a thick voice, showing him a bit of crumpled paper*): This note bids me beware. . . . A hundred men against me . . . on account of lampoon. . . . Grave danger threatening me . . . Porte de Nesle . . . must pass it to get home. Let me come and sleep under your roof.

CYRANO: A hundred, did you say? . . . You shall sleep at home!

LIGNIÈRE (*frightened*): But . . .

CYRANO (*in a terrible voice, pointing to the lighted lantern which the* DOORKEEPER *stands swinging as he listens to this scene*): Take that lantern (LIGNIÈRE *hurriedly takes it.*) and walk! . . . I swear to tuck you in your bed tonight myself. (*To the* OFFICERS) You, follow at a distance. You may look on!

CUIGY: But a hundred men . . .

CYRANO: Are not one man too many for my mood tonight!

    [*The players, in their several costumes, have stepped down from the stage and come nearer.*]

LE BRET: But why take under your especial care . . .

CYRANO: Still Le Bret is not satisfied!

LE BRET: . . . that most commonplace of sots?

CYRANO (*slapping* LIGNIÈRE *on the shoulder*): Because this sot, this cask of muscatel, this hogshead of rosolio, once upon a time did a wholly pretty thing. On leaving Mass, having seen her whom he loved take holy water, as the rite prescribes, he, whom the sight of water puts to flight, ran to the holy-water bowl, and stooping over, drank it dry. . . .

AN ACTRESS (*in the costume of soubrette*): *Tiens,* that was nice!

CYRANO: Was it not, soubrette?

THE SOUBRETTE (*to the others*): But why are they, a hundred, all against one poor poet?

CYRANO: Let us start! (*To the* OFFICERS) And you, gentlemen, when you see me attack, whatever you may suppose to be my danger, do not stir to second me!

ANOTHER OF THE ACTRESSES (*jumping from the stage*): Oh, I will not miss seeing this!

CYRANO: Come!

ANOTHER ACTRESS (*likewise jumping from the stage, to an elderly actor*): Cassandre, will you not come?

CYRANO: Come, all of you! the Doctor, Isabel, Leander, all! and you shall lend, charming fantastic swarm, an air of Italian farce to the Spanish drama in view. Yes, you shall be a tinkling heard above a roar, like bells about a tambourine!

ALL THE WOMEN (*in great glee*): Bravo! . . . Hurry! . . . A mantle! . . . A hood!

JODELET: Let us go!

CYRANO (*to the* FIDDLERS): You will favor us with a tune, messieurs the violinists!

[*The* FIDDLERS *fall into the train. The lighted candles which furnished the footlights are seized and distributed. The procession becomes a torchlight procession.*]

CYRANO: Bravo! Officers, beauty in fancy dress, and, twenty steps ahead . . . (*he takes the position he describes*) . . . I, by myself, under the feather stuck, with her own hand, by Glory, in my hat! Proud as a Scipio trebly Nasica![1]—It is understood? Formal interdiction to interfere with me!—We are ready? One! Two! Three! Doorkeeper, open the door!

[*The* DOORKEEPER *opens wide the folding door. A picturesque corner of Old Paris appears, bathed in moonlight.*]

CYRANO: Ah! . . . Paris floats in dim nocturnal mist. . . . The sloping bluish roofs are washed with moonlight. . . . A setting, exquisite indeed, offers itself for the scene about to be enacted. . . . Yonder, under silvery vapor

---

[1] *Scipio . . . Nasica*: Scipio Nasica (the "large-nosed") was the leader of a successful revolt in Rome against the supporters of Tiberius Gracchus, 133 B.C.

wreaths, like a mysterious magic mirror, glimmers the Seine. . . . And you shall see what you shall see!

ALL: To the Porte de Nesle!

CYRANO (*standing on the threshold*): To the Porte de Nesle! (*Before crossing it, he turns to the* SOUBRETTE) Were you not asking, mademoiselle, why upon that solitary rhymester a hundred men were set? (*He draws his sword, and tranquilly*) Because it was well known he is a friend of mine!

[*Exit* CYRANO. *To the sound of the violins, by the flickering light of the candles, the procession*—LIGNIÈRE *staggering at the head, the* ACTRESSES *arm in arm with the* OFFICERS, *the players capering behind—follows out into the night.*]

CURTAIN

ACT TWO

THE COOKSHOP OF POETS

RAGUENEAU'S *shop, vast kitchen at the corner of Rue St. Honoré and Rue de l'Arbre-Sec, which can be seen at the back, through the glass door, gray in the early dawn.*

At the left, in front, a counter overhung by a wrought-iron canopy from which geese, ducks, and white peacocks are hanging. In large china jars, tall nosegays composed of the simpler flowers, mainly sunflowers. On the same side, in the middle distance, an enormous fireplace, in front of which, between huge andirons, each of which supports a small iron pot, roasting meats drip into appropriate pans.

At the right, door in the front wing. In the middle distance, a staircase leading to a loft, the interior of which is seen through open shutters; a spread table, lighted by a small Flemish candelabrum, shows it to be an

*eating room. A wooden gallery continuing the stairway suggests other sim-
ilar rooms to which it may lead.*

*In the center of the shop, an iron hoop—which can be lowered by means
of a rope—to which large roasts are hooked.*

*In the shadow, under the stairway, ovens are glowing. Copper molds and
saucepans are shining; spits turning, hams swinging, pastry pyramids showing fair. It is the early beginning of the workday. Bustling of hurried scul-
lions, portly cooks, and young cooks' assistants; swarming of caps decorated with hen feathers and guinea-fowl wings. Wicker crates and broad
sheets of tin are brought in loaded with brioches and tarts.*

*There are tables covered with meats and cakes; others, surrounded by
chairs, await customers. In a corner, a smaller table, littered with papers.*

> [*At the rise of the curtain,* RAGUENEAU *is discovered seated at this
> table, writing with an inspired air, and counting upon his fingers.*]

FIRST PASTRYCOOK (*bringing in a tall molded pudding*): Nougat of fruit!

SECOND PASTRYCOOK (*bringing in the dish he names*): Custard!

THIRD PASTRYCOOK (*bringing in a fowl roasted in its feathers*): Peacock!

FOURTH PASTRYCOOK (*bringing in a tray of cakes*): Mince pies!

FIFTH PASTRYCOOK (*bringing in a deep earthen dish*): Beef stew!

RAGUENEAU (*laying down his pen and looking up*): Daybreak already
    plates with silver the copper pans! Time, Ragueneau, to smother within
    thee the singing divinity! The hour of the lute will come anon—now is
    that of the ladle! (*He rises, speaking to one of the cooks*) You, sir, be so
    good as to lengthen this gravy—it is too thick!

THE COOK: How much?

RAGUENEAU: Three feet.

> [*Goes farther.*]

THE COOK: What does he mean?

FIRST PASTRYCOOK: Let me have the tart!

SECOND PASTRYCOOK: The dumpling!

RAGUENEAU (*standing before the fireplace*): Spread thy wings, Muse, and
    fly farther, that thy lovely eyes may not be reddened at the sordid
    kitchen fire! (*To one of the* COOKS, *pointing at some small loaves of
    bread*) You have improperly placed the cleft in those loaves; the caesura
    belongs in the middle—between the hemistichs! (*To another of the* COOKS,
    pointing at an unfinished pastry) This pastry palace requires a roof! (*To
    a young* COOK'S APPRENTICE, *who, seated upon the floor, is putting fowls
    on a spit*) And you, on that long spit, arrange, my son, in pleasing alter-
    nation, the modest pullet and the splendid turkey cock—even as our wise
    Malherbe alternated of old the greater with the lesser lines, and so with
    roasted fowls compose a poem!

ANOTHER APPRENTICE (*coming forward with a platter covered by a napkin*): Master, in your honor, see what I have baked. . . . I hope you are pleased with it!

RAGUENEAU (*ecstatic*): A lyre!

THE APPRENTICE: Of pie crust!

RAGUENEAU (*touched*): With candied fruits!

THE APPRENTICE: And the strings, see—of spun sugar!

RAGUENEAU (*giving him money*): Go, drink my health! (*Catching sight of* LISE, *who is entering*) Hush! My wife! . . . Move on, and hide that money. (*To* LISE, *showing her the lyre, with a constrained air*) Fine, is it not?

LISE: Ridiculous!

[*She sets a pile of wrapping paper on the counter.*]

RAGUENEAU: Paper bags? Good. Thanks. (*He examines them.*) Heavens! My beloved books! The masterpieces of my friends—dismembered—torn! —to fashion paper bags for penny pies! . . . Ah, the abominable case is reenacted of Orpheus and the Maenads! [2]

LISE (*drily*): And have I not an unquestionable right to make what use I can of the sole payment ever got from your paltry scribblers of uneven lines?

RAGUENEAU: Pismire! Forbear to insult those divine, melodious crickets!

LISE: Before frequenting that low crew, my friend, you did not use to call me a Maenad—no, nor yet a pismire!

RAGUENEAU: Put poems to such a use!

LISE: To that use and no other!

RAGUENEAU: If with poems you do this, I should like to know, Madame, what you do with prose!

[*Two* CHILDREN *have come into the shop.*]

RAGUENEAU: What can I do for you, little ones?

FIRST CHILD: Three patties.

RAGUENEAU (*waiting on them*): There you are! Beautifully browned and piping hot.

SECOND CHILD: Please, will you wrap them for us?

RAGUENEAU (*starting, aside*): There goes one of my bags! (*To the* CHILDREN) You want them wrapped, do you? (*He takes one of the paper bags, and as he is about to put in the patties, reads*) "*No otherwise, Ulysses from Penelope departing. . . .*" Not this one! (*He lays it aside*

---

[2] *Orpheus . . . Maenads*: Orpheus was torn to pieces by Maenads, female attendants upon Dionysus, for neglect of women.

and takes another. At the moment of putting in the patties, he reads)
"Phoebus of the aureate locks. . . ." Not that one!

[*Same business.*]

LISE (*out of patience*): Well, what are you waiting for?

RAGUENEAU: Here we are. Here we are. Here we are. (*He takes a third bag and resigns himself.*) The sonnet to Phyllis! . . . It is hard, all the same.

LISE: It is lucky you made up your mind. (*Shrugging her shoulders*) Nicodemus!

[*She climbs on a chair and arranges dishes on the sideboard.*]

RAGUENEAU (*taking advantage of her back being turned, calls back the* CHILDREN, *who have already reached the door*): Psst! . . . Children! Give me back the sonnet to Phyllis, and you shall have six patties instead of three! (*The* CHILDREN *give back the paper bag, joyfully take the patties, and exeunt.* RAGUENEAU *smoothes out the crumpled paper and reads declaiming*) *"Phyllis!"* . . . Upon that charming name, a grease spot! . . . *"Phyllis!"* . . .

[*Enter brusquely* CYRANO.]

CYRANO: What time is it?

RAGUENEAU (*bowing with eager deference*): Six o'clock.

CYRANO (*with emotion*): In an hour!

[*He comes and goes in the shop.*]

RAGUENEAU (*following him*): Bravo! I too was witness. . . .

CYRANO: Of what?

RAGUENEAU: Your fight.

CYRANO: Which?

RAGUENEAU: At the Hôtel de Bourgogne.

CYRANO (*with disdain*): Ah, the duel!

RAGUENEAU (*admiringly*): Yes—the duel in rhyme.

LISE: He can talk of nothing else.

CYRANO: Let him! . . . It does no harm.

RAGUENEAU (*thrusting with a spit he has seized*): *"At the last line, I hit!"* *"At the last line, I hit!"*—How fine that is! (*With growing enthusiasm*) *"At the last line, I. . . ."*

CYRANO: What time, Ragueneau?

RAGUENEAU (*remaining fixed in the attitude of thrusting, while he looks at the clock*): Five minutes past six. . . .*"I hit!"* (*He recovers from his dueling posture.*) Oh, to be able to make a ballade!

LISE (*to* CYRANO, *who in passing her counter has absentmindedly shaken hands with her*): What ails your hand?

CYRANO: Nothing. A scratch.

RAGUENEAU: You have been exposed to some danger?

CYRANO: None whatever.

LISE (*shaking her finger at him*): I fear that is a fib!

CYRANO: From the swelling of my nose? The fib in that case must have been good-sized. . . . (*In a different tone*) I am expecting someone. You will leave us alone in here.

RAGUENEAU: But how can I contrive it? My poets shortly will be coming . . .

LISE (*ironically*): For breakfast!

CYRANO: When I sign to you, you will clear the place of them. . . . What time is it?

RAGUENEAU: It is ten minutes past six.

CYRANO (*seating himself nervously at* RAGUENEAU'S *table and helping himself to paper*): A pen?

RAGUENEAU (*taking one from behind his ear and offering it*): A swan's quill.

A MOUSQUETAIRE (*with enormous moustachios, enters; in a stentorian voice*): Good morning!

        [LISE *goes hurriedly to him, toward the back.*]

CYRANO (*turning*): What is it?

RAGUENEAU: A friend of my wife's—a warrior—terrible, from his own report.

CYRANO (*taking up the pen again and waving* RAGUENEAU *away*): Hush! . . . (*To himself*) Write to her . . . fold the letter . . . hand it to her . . . and make my escape. . . . (*Throwing down the pen*) Coward! . . . But may I perish if I have the courage to speak to her . . . to say a single word. . . . (*To* RAGUENEAU) What time is it?

RAGUENEAU: A quarter past six.

CYRANO (*beating his breast*): A single word of all I carry here! . . . Whereas in writing. . . . (*He takes up the pen again.*) Come, let us write it then, in very deed, the love letter I have written in thought so many times. I have but to lay my soul beside my paper, and copy!

        [*He writes.*]

[*Beyond the glass door, shadowy, lank, hesitating shabby forms are seen moving. Enter the* POETS, *clad in black, with hanging hose, sadly mud-splashed.*]

LISE (*coming forward, to* RAGUENEAU): Here they come, your scarecrows!

FIRST POET (*entering, to* RAGUENEAU): Brother in art! . . .

SECOND POET (*shaking both of* RAGUENEAU'S *hands*): Dear fellow bard. . . .

THIRD POET: Eagle of pastrycooks (*sniffs the air*), your eyrie smells divine!

FOURTH POET: Phoebus turned baker!

FIFTH POET: Apollo, master cook!

RAGUENEAU (*surrounded, embraced, shaken by the hand*): How at his ease a man feels at once with them!

FIRST POET: The reason we are late is the crowd at the Porte de Nesle!

SECOND POET: Eight ugly ruffians, ripped open with the sword, lie weltering on the pavement.

CYRANO (*raising his head a second*): Eight? I thought there were only seven.

[*Goes on with his letter.*]

RAGUENEAU (*to* CYRANO): Do you happen to know who is the hero of this event?

CYRANO (*negligently*): I? . . . No.

LISE (*to the* MOUSQUETAIRE): Do you?

THE MOUSQUETAIRE (*turning up the ends of his moustache*): Possibly!

CYRANO (*writing, from time to time he is heard murmuring a word or two*): . . . "I love you . . ."

FIRST POET: A single man, we were told, put a whole gang to flight!

SECOND POET: Oh, it was a rare sight! The ground was littered with pikes, and cudgels. . . .

CYRANO (*writing*): . . . "Your eyes . . ."

THIRD POET: Hats were strewn as far as the Goldsmiths' Square!

FIRST POET: *Sapristi!* He must have been a madman of mettle. . . .

CYRANO (*as above*): ". . . your lips . . ."

FIRST POET: An infuriate giant, the doer of that deed!

CYRANO (*same business*): ". . . but when I see you, I come near to swooning with a tender dread . . ."

SECOND POET (*snapping up a tart*): What have you lately written, Ragueneau?

CYRANO (*same business*): ". . . who loves you devotedly . . ." (*In the act of signing the letter, he stops, rises, and tucks it inside his doublet.*) No need to sign it. I deliver it myself.

RAGUENEAU (*to* SECOND POET): I have rhymed a recipe.

THIRD POET (*establishing himself beside a tray of cream puffs*): Let us hear this recipe!

FOURTH POET (*examining a brioche of which he has possessed himself*): It should not wear its cap so saucily on one side . . . it scarcely looks well! . . .

[*Bites off the top.*]

FIRST POET: See, the spice cake there, ogling a susceptible poet with eyes of almond under citron brows! . . .

[*He takes the spice cake.*]

SECOND POET: We are listening!

THIRD POET (*slightly squeezing a cream puff betwen his fingers*): This puff creams at the mouth. . . . I water!

SECOND POET (*taking a bite out of the large pastry lyre*): For once the Lyre will have filled my stomach!

RAGUENEAU (*who has made ready to recite, has coughed, adjusted his cap, struck an attitude*): A recipe in rhyme!

SECOND POET (*to* FIRST POET, *nudging him*): Is it breakfast, with you?

FIRST POET (*to* SECOND POET): And with you, is it dinner?

RAGUENEAU: *"How Almond Cheesecakes Should Be Made."*

> Briskly beat to lightness due,
>   Eggs, a few;
> With the eggs so beaten, beat—
> Nicely strained for this same use—
>   Lemon juice,
> Adding milk of almonds, sweet.
>
> With fine pastry dough, rolled flat,
>   After that,
> Line each little scalloped mold;
> Round the sides, light-fingered, spread
>   Marmalade;
> Pour the liquid eggy gold,
>
> Into each delicious pit;
>   Prison it
> In the oven—and, by-and-by,
> Almond cheesecakes will in gay
>   Blond array
> Bless your nostril and your eye!

THE POETS (*their mouths full*): Exquisite! . . . Delicious!

ONE OF THE POETS (*choking*): Humph!

[*They go toward the back, eating.* CYRANO, *who has been watching them, approaches* RAGUENEAU.]

CYRANO: While you recite your works to them, have you a notion how they stuff?

RAGUENEAU (*low, with a smile*): Yes, I see them . . . without looking, lest they should be abashed. I get a double pleasure thus from saying my verses over: I satisfy a harmless weakness of which I stand convicted, at the same time giving those who have not fed a needed chance to feed!

CYRANO (*slapping him on the shoulder*): You . . . I like you! (RAGUENEAU *joins his friends.* CYRANO *looks after him; then, somewhat sharply*) Hey, Lise! (LISE, *absorbed in tender conversation with the* MOUSQUETAIRE, *starts and comes forward toward* CYRANO.) Is that Captain . . . laying siege to you?

LISE (*offended*): My eyes, sir, have ever with a glance been able to frown down those who meant hurt to my character. . . .

CYRANO: For eyes so resolute . . . I thought yours looked a little languishing!

LISE (*choking with anger*): But . . .

CYRANO (*bluntly*): I like your husband. Wherefore, Madame Lise, I say he shall not be sc . . . horned!

LISE: But . . .

CYRANO (*raising his voice so as to be heard by the* MOUSQUETAIRE): A word to the wise!

[*He bows to the* MOUSQUETAIRE, *and after looking at the clock, goes to the door at the back and stands on watch.*]

LISE (*to the* MOUSQUETAIRE, *who has simply returned* CYRANO'S *bow*): Really . . . I am astonished at you. . . . Defy him . . . to his face!

THE MOUSQUETAIRE: To his face, indeed! . . . to his face! . . .

[*He quickly moves off.* LISE *follows him.*]

CYRANO (*from the door at the back, signaling to* RAGUENEAU *that he should clear the room*): Pst! . . .

RAGUENEAU (*urging the* POETS *toward the door at the right*): We shall be much more comfortable in there. . . .

CYRANO (*impatiently*): Pst! . . . Pst! . . .

RAGUENEAU (*driving along the* POETS): I want to read you a little thing of mine. . . .

FIRST POET (*despairingly, his mouth full*): But the provisions. . . .

SECOND POET: . . . shall not be parted from us!

[*They follow* RAGUENEAU *in procession, after making a raid on the eatables.*]

CYRANO: If I feel that there is so much as a glimmer of hope—I will out with my letter! . . .

[ROXANE, *masked, appears behind the glass door followed by the* DUENNA.]

CYRANO (*instantly opening the door*): Welcome! (*Approaching the* DUENNA) Madame, a word with you!

THE DUENNA: A dozen.

CYRANO: Are you fond of sweets?

THE DUENNA: To the point of indigestion!

CYRANO (*snatching some paper bags off the counter*): Good. Here are two sonnets of Benserade's. . . .

THE DUENNA: Pooh!

CYRANO: . . . which I fill for you with grated almond drops.

THE DUENNA (*with a different expression*): Ha!

CYRANO: Do you look with favor upon the cake they call a trifle?

THE DUENNA: I affect it out of measure, when it has whipped cream inside.

CYRANO: Six shall be yours, thrown in with a poem by Saint-Amant. And in these verses of Chapelain I place this wedge of fruit cake, light by the side of them. . . . Oh! And do you like tarts . . . little jam ones . . . fresh?

THE DUENNA: I dream of them at night!

CYRANO (*loading her arms with crammed paper bags*): Do me the favor to go and eat these in the street.

THE DUENNA: But . . .

CYRANO (*pushing her out*): And do not come back till you have finished! (*He closes the door upon her, comes forward toward* ROXANE, *and stands, bareheaded, at a respectful distance.*) Blessed for evermore among all hours the hour in which, remembering that so lowly a being still draws breath, you were so gracious as to come to tell me . . . to tell me? . . .

ROXANE (*who has removed her mask*): First of all, that I thank you. For that churl, that coxcomb yesterday, whom you taught manners with your sword, is the one whom a great nobleman, who fancies himself in love with me. . .

CYRANO: De Guiche?

ROXANE (*dropping her eyes*): . . . has tried to force upon me as a husband.

CYRANO: Honorary? (*Bowing*) It appears, then, that I fought—and I am glad of it—not for my graceless nose, but your thrice-beautiful eyes.

ROXANE: Further than that . . . I wished . . . But, before I can make the confession I have in mind to make, I must find in you once more the . . . almost brother, with whom as a child I used to play, in the park—do you remember?—by the lake!

CYRANO: I have not forgotten. Yes . . . you came every summer to Bergerac.

ROXANE: You used to fashion lances out of reeds. . . .

CYRANO: The silk of the tasseled corn furnished hair for your doll. . . .

ROXANE: It was the time of long delightful games. . . .

CYRANO: And somewhat sour berries. . . .

ROXANE: The time when you did everything I bade you!

CYRANO: Roxane, wearing short frocks, was known as Magdeleine.

ROXANE: Was I pretty in those days?

CYRANO: You were not ill-looking.

ROXANE: Sometimes, in your venturesome climbings you used to hurt yourself. You would come running to me, your hand bleeding. And, playing at being your mamma, I would harden my voice and say (*taking his hand*) "Will you never keep out of mischief?" (*She stops short, amazed.*) Oh, it is too much! Here you have done it again! (CYRANO *tries to draw back his hand.*) No! Let me look at it! . . . Aren't you ashamed! A great boy like you! . . . How did this happen, and where?

CYRANO: Oh, fun . . . near the Porte de Nesle.

ROXANE (*sitting down at a table and dipping her handkerchief into a glass of water*): Let me have it.

CYRANO (*sitting down too*): So prettily, so cheerfully maternal!

ROXANE: And tell me, while I wash this naughty blood away . . . with how many were you fighting?

CYRANO: Oh, not quite a hundred.

ROXANE: Tell me about it.

CYRANO: No. What does it matter? You tell me, you . . . what you were going to tell me before, and did not dare. . . .

ROXANE (*without releasing his hand*): I do dare, now. I have breathed in courage with the perfume of the past. Oh, yes, now I dare. Here it is. There is someone whom I love.

CYRANO: Ah! . . .

ROXANE: Oh, he does not know it.

CYRANO: Ah! . . .

ROXANE: As yet. . . .

CYRANO: Ah! . . .

ROXANE: But if he does not know it, he soon will.

CYRANO: Ah! . . .

ROXANE: A poor boy who until now has loved me timidly, from a distance, without daring to speak. . . .

CYRANO: Ah! . . .

ROXANE: No, leave me your hand. It is hot, this will cool it. . . . But I have read his heart in his face.

CYRANO: Ah! . . .

ROXANE (*completing the bandaging of his hand with her small pocket handkerchief*): And, cousin, is it not a strange coincidence—that he should serve exactly in your regiment!

CYRANO: Ah! . . .

ROXANE (*laughing*): Yes. He is a Cadet, in the same company!

CYRANO: Ah! . . .

ROXANE: He bears plain on his forehead the stamp of wit, of genius! He is proud, noble, young, brave, handsome . . .

CYRANO (*rising, pale*): Handsome! . . .

ROXANE: What . . . what is the matter?

CYRANO: With me? . . . Nothing! . . . It is . . . it is . . . (*showing his hand, smiling*) . . . you know! . . . It smarts a little. . . .

ROXANE: In short, I love him. I must tell you, however, that I have never seen him save at the play.

CYRANO: Then you have never spoken to each other?

ROXANE: Only with our eyes.

CYRANO: But, then . . . how can you know? . . .

ROXANE: Oh, under the lindens of the Place Royale, people will talk. A trustworthy gossip told me many things!

CYRANO: A Cadet, did you say?

ROXANE: A Cadet, in your company.

CYRANO: His name?

ROXANE: Baron Christian de Neuvillette.

CYRANO: What? He is not in the Cadets.

ROXANE: He is! He certainly is, since morning. Captain Carbon de Castel-Jaloux . . .

CYRANO: And quickly, quickly, she throws away her heart! . . . But my poor little girl . . .

THE DUENNA (*opening the door at the back*): Monsieur de Bergerac, I have eaten them, every one!

CYRANO: Now read the poetry printed upon the bags! (*The* DUENNA *disappears.*) My poor child, you who can endure none but the choicest language, who savor eloquence and wit . . . if he should be a barbarian!

ROXANE: No! No! . . . He has hair like one of D'Urfé's heroes!

CYRANO: If he had, on proof, as homely a wit as he has pretty hair!

ROXANE: No! No! . . . I can see at a single glance, his utterances are fine, pointed . . .

CYRANO: Ah, yes! A man's utterances are invariably like his moustache! . . . Still, if he *were* a ninny? . . .

ROXANE (*stamping with her foot*): I should die, there!

CYRANO (*after a time*): You bade me come here that you might tell me this? I scarcely see the appropriateness, Madame.

ROXANE: Ah, it was because someone yesterday let death into my soul by telling me that in your company you are all Gascons . . . all!

CYRANO: And that we pick a quarrel with every impudent fledgling, not Gascon, admitted by favor to our thoroughbred Gascon ranks? That is what you heard?

ROXANE: Yes, and you can imagine how distracted I am for him!

CYRANO (*through his teeth*): You well may be!

ROXANE: But I thought, yesterday, when you towered up, great and invincible, giving his due to that miscreant, standing your ground against those caitiffs, I thought, "Were he but willing, he of whom all are in awe . . ."

CYRANO: Very well, I will protect your little baron.

ROXANE: Ah, you will . . . you will protect him for me? . . . I have always felt for you the tenderest regard!

CYRANO: Yes, yes.

ROXANE: You will be his friend?

CYRANO: I will!

ROXANE: And never shall he have to fight a duel?

CYRANO: I swear it.

ROXANE: Oh, I quite love you! . . . Now I must go. (*She hurriedly resumes her mask, throws a veil over her head; says absentmindedly*) But you have not yet told me about last night's encounter. It must have been amazing! . . . Tell him to write to me. (*She kisses her hand to him.*) I love you dearly!

CYRANO: Yes, yes.

ROXANE: A hundred men against you? . . . Well, adieu. We are fast friends.

CYRANO: Yes, yes.

ROXANE: Tell him to write me! . . . A hundred men! . . . You shall tell me another time. I must not linger now. . . . A hundred men! What a heroic thing to do!

CYRANO (*bowing*): Oh, I have done better since!

[*Exit* ROXANE. CYRANO *stands motionless, staring at the ground. Silence. The door at the right opens.* RAGUENEAU *thrusts in his head.*]

RAGUENEAU: May we come back?

CYRANO (*without moving*): Yes. . . .

[RAGUENEAU *beckons, his friends come in again. At the same time, in the doorway at the back, appears* CARBON DE CASTEL-JALOUX, *in the costume of a Captain of the Guards. On seeing* CYRANO, *he gesticulates exaggeratedly by way of signal to someone out of sight.*]

CARBON DE CASTEL-JALOUX: He is here!

CYRANO (*looking up*): Captain!

CARBON DE CASTEL-JALOUX (*exultant*): Hero! We know all! . . . About thirty of my Cadets are out there! . . .

CYRANO (*drawing back*): But . . .

CARBON DE CASTEL-JALOUX (*trying to lead him off*): Come! . . . You are in request!

CYRANO: No!

CARBON DE CASTEL-JALOUX: They are drinking across the way, at the Cross of the Hilt.

CYRANO: I . . .

CARBON DE CASTEL-JALOUX (*going to the door and shouting toward the street corner, in a voice of thunder*): The hero refuses. He is not in the humor!

A VOICE (*outside*): Ah, sandious! [3]

[*Tumult outside, noise of clanking swords and of boots drawing nearer.*]

CARBON DE CASTEL-JALOUX (*rubbing his hands*): Here they come, across the street.

THE CADETS (*entering the cookshop*): *Mille dious! . . . Capdedious! . . . Mordious! . . . Pocapdedious!* [3]

RAGUENEAU (*backing in alarm*): Messieurs, are you all natives of Gascony?

THE CADETS: All!

ONE OF THE CADETS (*to* CYRANO): Bravo!

CYRANO: Baron.

OTHER CADET (*shaking both* CYRANO'S *hands*): Vivat!

CYRANO: Baron!

THIRD CADET: Let me hug you to my heart!

CYRANO: Baron!

SEVERAL GASCONS: Let us hug him!

CYRANO (*not knowing which one to answer*): Baron! . . . Baron! . . . your pardon!

RAGUENEAU: Messieurs, are you all barons?

THE CADETS: All!

RAGUENEAU: Are they truly?

FIRST CADET: Our coats of arms piled up would dwindle in the clouds!

LE BRET (*entering, running to* CYRANO): They are looking for you! A crowd, gone mad as March, led by those who were with you last night.

CYRANO (*alarmed*): You never told them where to find me? . . .

LE BRET (*rubbing his hands*): I did.

A BURGHER (*entering, followed by a number of others*): Monsieur, the Marais is coming in a body!

[*The street outside has filled with people. Sedan chairs, coaches, stop before the door.*]

[3] *sandious, etc.*: oaths in the Gascon dialect.

LE BRET (*smiling, low to* CYRANO): And Roxane?

CYRANO (*quickly*): Be quiet!

THE CROWD (*outside*): Cyrano!

[*A rabble bursts into the cookshop. Confusion. Shouting.*]

RAGUENEAU (*standing upon a table*): My shop is invaded! They are breaking everything! It is glorious!

PEOPLE (*pressing round* CYRANO): My friend . . . my friend. . . .

CYRANO: I had not so many friends . . . yesterday!

LE BRET: This is success!

A YOUNG MARQUIS (*running toward* CYRANO, *with outstretched hands*): If you knew, my dear fellow . . .

CYRANO: Dear? . . . Fellow? . . . Where was it we stood sentinel together?

OTHER MARQUIS: I wish to present you, sir, to several ladies, who are outside in my coach. . . .

CYRANO (*coldly*): But you, to me—by whom will you first be presented?

LE BRET (*astonished*): But what is the matter with you?

CYRANO: Be still!

A MAN OF LETTERS (*with an inkhorn*): Will you kindly favor me with the details of . . .

CYRANO: No.

LE BRET (*nudging him*): That is Theophrastus Renaudot, the inventor of the gazette.

CYRANO: Enough!

LE BRET: A sheet close-packed with various information! It is an idea, they say, likely to take firm root and flourish!

A POET (*coming forward*): Monsieur . . .

CYRANO: Another!

THE POET: I am anxious to make a pentacrostic on your name.

SOMEBODY ELSE (*likewise approaching* CYRANO): Monsieur . . .

CYRANO: Enough, I say!

[*At the gesture of impatience which* CYRANO *cannot repress, the crowd draws away.* DE GUICHE *appears, escorted by officers; among them* CUIGY, BRISSAILLE, *those who followed* CYRANO *at the end of the first act.* CUIGY *hurries toward* CYRANO.]

CUIGY (*to* CYRANO): Monsieur de Guiche! (*Murmurs. Everyone draws back.*) He comes at the request of the Marshal de Gaussion . . .

DE GUICHE (*bowing to* CYRANO): . . . who wishes to express his admiration for your latest exploit, the fame of which has reached him.

THE CROWD: Bravo!

CYRANO (*bowing*): The Marshal is qualified to judge of courage.

DE GUICHE: He would scarcely have believed the report, had these gentlemen not been able to swear they had seen the deed performed.

CUIGY: With our own eyes!

LE BRET (*low to* CYRANO, *who wears an abstracted air*): But . . .

CYRANO: Be silent!

LE BRET: You appear to be suffering . . .

CYRANO (*starting, and straightening himself*): Before these people? . . . (*His moustache bristles; he expands his chest.*) I . . . suffering? . . . You shall see!

DE GUICHE (*in whose ear* CUIGY *has been whispering*): But this is by no means the first gallant achievement marking your career. You serve in the madcap Gascon company, do you not?

CYRANO: In the Cadets, yes.

ONE OF THE CADETS (*in a great voice*): Among his countrymen!

DE GUICHE (*considering the* GASCONS, *in line behind* CYRANO): Ah, ha!— all these gentlemen, then, of the formidable aspect, are the famous . . .

CARBON DE CASTEL-JALOUX: Cyrano!

CYRANO: Captain? . . .

CARBON DE CASTEL-JALOUX: My company, I believe, is here in total. Be so obliging as to present it to the Count.

CYRANO (*taking a step toward* DE GUICHE *and pointing at the* CADETS):

> They are the Gascony Cadets
> Of Carbon de Castel-Jaloux;
> Famed fighters, liars, desperates,
> They are the Gascony Cadets!
> All, better-born than pickpockets,
> Talk couchant, rampant . . . pendent, too!
> They are the Gascony Cadets
> Of Carbon de Castel-Jaloux!
>
> Cat-whiskered, eyed like falconets,
> Wolf-toothed and heron-legged, they hew
> The rabble down that snarls and threats . . .
> Cat-whiskered, eyed like falconets!
> Great pomp of plume hides and offsets
> Holes in those hats they wear askew . . .
> Cat-whiskered, eyed like falconets,
> They drive the snarling mob, and hew!
>
> The mildest of their sobriquets
> Are Crack-my-crown and Run-me-through;
> Mad drunk on glory Gascon gets!

These boasters of soft sobriquets
Wherever rapier rapier whets
Are met in punctual rendezvous. . . .
The mildest of their sobriquets
Are Crack-my-crown and Run-me-through!

They are the Gascony Cadets
That give the jealous spouse his due!
Lean forth, adorable coquettes,
They are the Gascony Cadets,
With plumes and scarfs and aigulettes!
The husband gray may well look blue. . . .
They are the Gascony Cadets
That give the jealous spouse his due!

DE GUICHE (*nonchalantly seated in an armchair which* RAGUENEAU *has hurriedly brought for him*): A gentleman provides himself today, by way of luxury, with a poet. May I look upon you as mine?

CYRANO: No, your lordship, as nobody's.

DE GUICHE: My uncle Richelieu yesterday found your spontaneity diverting. I shall be pleased to be of use to you with him.

LE BRET (*dazzled*): Great God!

DE GUICHE: I cannot think I am wrong in supposing that you have rhymed a tragedy?

LE BRET (*whispering to* CYRANO): My boy, your *Agrippina* will be played!

DE GUICHE: Take it to him. . . .

CYRANO (*tempted and pleased*): Really.

DE GUICHE: He has taste in such matters. He will no more than, here and there, alter a word, recast a passage. . . .

CYRANO (*whose face has instantly darkened*): Not to be considered, Monsieur! My blood runs cold at the thought of a single comma added or suppressed.

DE GUICHE: On the other hand, my dear sir, when a verse finds favor with him, he pays for it handsomely.

CYRANO: He scarcely can pay me as I pay myself, when I have achieved a verse to my liking, by singing it over to myself!

DE GUICHE: You are proud.

CYRANO: You have observed it?

ONE OF THE CADETS (*coming in with a number of disreputable, draggled tattered hats threaded on his sword*): Look, Cyrano, at the remarkable feathered game we secured this morning near the Porte de Nesle! The hats of the fugitives!

CARBON DE CASTEL-JALOUX: *Spolia opima!*

ALL (*laughing*): Ha! Ha! Ha! . . .

CUIGY: The one who planned that military action, my word! must be proud of it today!

BRISSAILLE: Is it known who did it?

DE GUICHE: I! . . . (*The laughter stops short.*) They had instructions to chastise—a matter one does not attend to in person—a drunken scribbler.

[*Constrained silence.*]

THE CADET (*under breath, to* CYRANO, *indicating the hats*): What can we do with them? They are oily. . . . Make them into a hotchpot?

CYRANO (*taking the sword with the hats, and bowing, as he shakes them off at* DE GUICHE'S *feet*): Monsieur, if you should care to return them to your friends? . . .

DE GUICHE (*rises, and in a curt tone*): My chair and bearers, at once. (*To* CYRANO, *violently*) As for you, sir . . .

A VOICE (*in the street, shouting*): The chairmen of Monseigneur the Comte de Guiche!

DE GUICHE (*who has recovered control over himself, with a smile*): Have you read *Don Quixote?*

CYRANO: I have. And at the name of that divine madman I uncover . . .

DE GUICHE: My advice to you is to ponder . . .

A CHAIRMAN (*appearing at the back*): The chair is at the door!

DE GUICHE: . . . the chapter of the windmills.

CYRANO (*bowing*): Chapter thirteen.

DE GUICHE: For when a man attacks them, it often happens . . .

CYRANO: I have attacked, am I to infer, a thing that veers with every wind?

DE GUICHE: . . . that one of their far-reaching canvas arms pitches him down into the mud!

CYRANO: Or up among the stars!

[*Exit* DE GUICHE. *He is seen getting into his chair. The gentlemen withdraw, whispering.* LE BRET *goes to the door with them. The crowd leaves. The* CADETS *remain seated at the right and left at tables where food and drink is brought to them.*]

CYRANO (*bowing with a derisive air to those who depart without daring to take leave of him*): Gentlemen . . . gentlemen . . . gentlemen. . . .

LE BRET (*coming forward, greatly distressed, lifting his hands to Heaven*): Oh, in what a pretty pair of shoes . . .

CYRANO: Oh, you! . . . I expect you to grumble!

LE BRET: But yourself, you will agree with me that invariably to cut the throat of opportunity becomes excessive! . . .

CYRANO: Yes. I agree. I am excessive.

LE BRET (*triumphant*): You see, you admit it! . . .

CYRANO: But for the sake of principle, and of example, as well, I think it a good thing to exceed as I do!

LE BRET: Could you but leave apart, once in a while, your mousquetaire of a soul, fortune, undoubtedly, fame . . .

CYRANO: And what should a man do? Seek some grandee, take him for patron, and like the obscure creeper clasping a tree trunk, and licking the bark of that which props it up, attain to height by craft instead of strength? No, I thank you. Dedicate, as they all do, poems to financiers? Wear motley in the humble hope of seeing the lips of a minister distend for once in a smile not ominous of ill? No, I thank you. Eat every day a toad? Be threadbare at the belly with groveling? Have his skin dirty soonest at the knees? Practice feats of dorsal elasticity? No, I thank you. With one hand stroke the goat while with the other he waters the cabbage? Make gifts of senna that countergifts of rhubarb may accrue, and indefatigably swing his censer in some beard? No, I thank you. Push himself from lap to lap, become a little great man in a great little circle, propel his ship with madrigals for oars and in his sails the sighs of the elderly ladies? No, I thank you. Get the good editor Sercy to print his verses at his own expense? No, I thank you. Contrive to be nominated Pope in conclaves held by imbeciles in wineshops? No, I thank you. Work to construct a name upon the basis of a sonnet, instead of constructing other sonnets? No, I thank you. Discover talent in tyros, and in them alone? Stand in terror of what gazettes may please to say, and say to himself, "At whatever cost, may I figure in the *Paris Mercury!*" No, I thank you. Calculate, cringe, peak, prefer making a call to a poem—petition, solicit, apply? No, I thank you! No, I thank you! No, I thank you! But . . . sing, dream, laugh, loaf, be single, be free, have eyes that look squarely, a voice with a ring; wear, if he chooses, his hat hindside afore; for a yes, for a no, fight a duel or turn a ditty! . . . Work, without concern of fortune or of glory, to accomplish the heart's-desired journey to the moon! Put forth nothing that has not its spring in the very heart, yet, modest, say to himself, "Old man, be satisfied with blossoms, fruits, yea, leaves alone, so they be gathered in your garden and not another man's!" Then, if it happen that to some small extent he triumph, be obliged to render of the glory, to Caesar not one jot, but honestly appropriate it all. In short, scorning to be the parasite, the creeper, if even failing to be the oak, rise, not perchance to a great height . . . but rise alone!

LE BRET: Alone? Good! but not one against all! How the devil did you contract the mania that possesses you for making enemies, always, everywhere?

CYRANO: By seeing you make friends, and smile to those same flocks of friends with a mouth that takes for model an old purse! I wish not to be troubled to return bows in the street, and I exclaim with glee, "An enemy the more!"

LE BRET: This is mental aberration!

CYRANO: I do not dispute it. I am so framed. To displease is my pleasure. I love that one should hate me. Dear friend, if you but knew how much better a man walks under the exciting fire of hostile eyes, and how amused he may become over the spots on his doublet, spattered by Envy and Cowardice! . . . The facile friendship wherewith you surround yourself, resembles those wide Italian collars, loose and easy, with a perforated pattern, in which the neck looks like a woman's. They are more comfortable, but of less high effect; for the brow not held in proud position by any constraint from them, falls to nodding this way and that. . . . But for me every day Hatred starches and flutes the ruff whose stiffness holds the head well in place. Every new enemy is another plait in it, adding compulsion, but adding, as well, a ray: for, similar in every point to the Spanish ruff, Hatred is a bondage . . . but is a halo, too!

LE BRET (*after a pause, slipping his arm through* CYRANO'S): To the hearing of all be proud and bitter . . . but to me, below breath, say simply that she does not love you!

CYRANO (*sharply*): Not a word!

> [CHRISTIAN *has come in and mingled with the* CADETS; *they ignore him; he has finally gone to a little table by himself, where* LISE *waits on him.*]

ONE OF THE CADETS (*seated at a table at the back, glass in hand*): Hey, Cyrano! (CYRANO *turns toward him.*) Your story!

CYRANO: Presently!

> [*He goes toward the back on* LE BRET'S *arm. They talk low.*]

THE CADET (*rising and coming toward the front*): The account of your fight! It will be the best lesson (*stopping in front of the table at which* CHRISTIAN *is sitting*) for this timorous novice!

CHRISTIAN (*looking up*): . . . Novice?

OTHER CADET: Yes, sickly product of the North!

CHRISTIAN: Sickly?

FIRST CADET (*impressively*): Monsieur de Neuvillette, it is a good deed to warn you that there is a thing no more to be mentioned in our company than rope in the hangman's house!

CHRISTIAN: And what is it?

OTHER CADET (*in a terrifying voice*): Look at me! (*Three times, darkly, he places his finger upon his nose.*) You have understood?

CHRISTIAN: Ah, it is the . . .

OTHER CADET: Silence! . . . Never must you so much as breathe that word, or . . . (*He points toward* CYRANO *at the back talking with* LE BRET.) . . . you will have him, over there, to deal with!

OTHER CADET (*who, while* CHRISTIAN *was turned toward the first, has noiselessly seated himself on the table behind him*): Two persons were lately cut off in their pride by him for talking through their noses. He thought it personal.

OTHER CADET (*in a cavernous voice, as he rises from under the table where he had slipped on all fours*): Not the remotest allusion, ever, to the fatal cartilage . . . unless you fancy an early grave!

OTHER CADET: A word will do the business! What did I say? . . . A word? . . . A simple *gesture!* Make use of your pocket handkerchief, you will shortly have use for your shroud!

[*Silence. All around* CHRISTIAN *watch him, with folded arms. He rises and goes to* CARBON DE CASTEL-JALOUX, *who, in conversation with an* OFFICER, *affects to notice nothing.*]

CHRISTIAN: Captain!

CARBON (*turning and looking him rather contemptuously up and down*): Monsieur?

CHRISTIAN: What is the proper course for a man when he finds gentlemen of the South too boastful?

CARBON: He must prove to them that one can be of the North, yet brave.

[*He turns his back upon him.*]

CHRISTIAN: I am much obliged.

FIRST CADET (*to* CYRANO): And now, the tale of your adventure!

ALL: Yes, yes, now let us hear!

CYRANO (*coming forward among them*): My adventure? (*All draw their stools nearer, and sit around him, with craned necks.* CHRISTIAN *sits astride a chair.*) Well, then, I was marching to meet them. The moon up in the skies was shining like a silver watch, when suddenly I know not what careful watchmaker having wrapped it in a cottony cloud, there occurred the blackest imaginable night; and, the streets being nowise lighted—*mordious!*—you could see no farther than . . .

CHRISTIAN: Your nose.

[*Silence. Everyone slowly gets up; all look with terror at* CYRANO. *He has stopped short, amazed. Pause.*]

CYRANO: Who is that man?

ONE OF THE CADETS (*low*): He joined this morning.

CYRANO (*taking a step toward* CHRISTIAN): This morning?

CARBON (*low*): His name is Baron de Neuvill . . .

CYRANO (*stopping short*): Ah, very well. . . . (*He turns pale, then red, gives evidence of another impulse to throw himself upon* CHRISTIAN.) . . . I . . . (*He conquers it, and says in a stifled voice*) Very well. (*He takes up his tale.*) As I was saying . . . (*with a burst of rage*) Mordious! . . . (*He continues in a natural tone*) One could not see at all. (*Consternation. All resume their seats, staring at one another.*) And I was walking along, reflecting that for a very insignificant rogue I was probably about to offend some great prince who would bear me a lasting grudge, that, in brief, I was about to thrust my . . .

CHRISTIAN: nose. . . .

> [*All get up.* CHRISTIAN *has tilted his chair and is rocking on the hind legs.*]

CYRANO (*choking*): . . . finger . . . between the tree and the bark;[4] for the aforesaid prince might be of sufficient power to trip me and throw me . . .

CHRISTIAN: on my nose. . . .

CYRANO (*wipes the sweat from his brow*): But, said I, "Gascony forward! Never falter when duty prompts! Forward, Cyrano!" and, saying this, I advance—when suddenly, in the darkness, I barely avoid a blow . . .

CHRISTIAN: upon the nose. . . .

CYRANO: I ward it. . . . and thereupon find myself . . .

CHRISTIAN: nose to nose. . . .

CYRANO (*springing toward him*): *Ventre-Saint-Gris!* . . . (*All the* GASCONS *rush forward to see;* CYRANO, *on reaching* CHRISTIAN, *controls himself and proceeds*) . . . with a hundred drunken brawlers, smelling . . .

CHRISTIAN: to the nose's limit. . . .

CYRANO (*deathly pale, and smiling*): . . . of garlic and of grease. I leap forward, head lowered . . .

CHRISTIAN: nose to the wind! . . .

CYRANO: And I charge them. I knock two breathless and run a third through the body. One lets off at me: Paf! and I retort . . .

CHRISTIAN: Pif!

CYRANO (*exploding*): Death and damnation! Go—all of you!

> [*All the* CADETS *make for the door.*]

FIRST CADET: The tiger is roused at last!

CYRANO: All! and leave me with this man.

SECOND CADET: *Bigre!* When we see him again, it will be in the shape of mincemeat!

---

[4] *finger . . . bark*: *Entre l'arbre et l'écorce il ne faut pas mettre le doigt* is the French proverb ("It is impossible to put your finger between the tree and the bark").

RAGUENEAU: Mincemeat? . . .

OTHER CADET: In one of your pies.

RAGUENEAU: I feel myself grow white and flabby as a table napkin!

CARBON: Let us go!

OTHER CADET: Not a smudge of him will be left!

OTHER CADET: What these walls are about to behold gives me gooseflesh to think upon!

OTHER CADET (*closing the door at the right*): Ghastly! . . . Ghastly!

[*All have left, by the back or the sides, a few up the stairway.* CYRANO *and* CHRISTIAN *remain face to face, and look at each other a moment.*]

CYRANO: Embrace me!

CHRISTIAN: Monsieur . . .

CYRANO: Brave fellow.

CHRISTIAN: But what does this . . .

CYRANO: Very brave fellow. I wish you to.

CHRISTIAN: Will you tell me? . . .

CYRANO: Embrace me, I am her brother.

CHRISTIAN: Whose?

CYRANO: Hers!

CHRISTIAN: What do you mean?

CYRANO: Roxane's!

CHRISTIAN (*running to him*): Heavens! You, her brother?

CYRANO: Or the same thing: her first cousin.

CHRISTIAN: And she has . . .

CYRANO: Told me everything!

CHRISTIAN: Does she love me?

CYRANO: Perhaps!

CHRISTIAN (*seizing his hands*): How happy I am, Monsieur, to make your acquaintance! . . .

CYRANO: That is what I call a sudden sentiment!

CHRISTIAN: Forgive me! . . .

CYRANO (*looking at him, laying his hand upon his shoulder*): It is true that he is handsome, the rascal!

CHRISTIAN: If you but knew, Monsieur, how greatly I admire you! . . .

CYRANO: But all those noses which you . . .

CHRISTIAN: I take them back!

CYRANO: Roxane expects a letter tonight. . . .

CHRISTIAN: Alas!

CYRANO: What is the matter?

CHRISTIAN: I am lost if I cease to be dumb!

CYRANO: How is that?

CHRISTIAN: Alas! I am such a dunce that I could kill myself for shame!

CYRANO: But, no . . . no. . . . You are surely not a dunce, if you believe you are! Besides, you scarcely attacked me like a dunce.

CHRISTIAN: Oh, it is easy to find words in mounting to the assault! Indeed, I own to a certain cheap military readiness, but when I am before women, I have not a word to say. . . . Yet their eyes, when I pass by, express a kindness toward me. . . .

CYRANO: And do their hearts not express the same when you stop beside them?

CHRISTIAN: No! . . . for I am of those—I recognize it, and am dismayed!— who do not know how to talk of love.

CYRANO: *Tiens!* . . . It seems to me that if Nature had taken more pains with my shape, I should have been of those who do know how to talk of it.

CHRISTIAN: Oh, to be able to express things gracefully!

CYRANO: Oh, to be a graceful little figure of a mousquetaire!

CHRISTIAN: Roxane is a *précieuse* . . . there is no chance but that I shall disillusion Roxane!

CYRANO (*looking at* CHRISTIAN): If I had to express my soul, such an interpreter! . . .

CHRISTIAN (*desperately*): I ought to have eloquence! . . .

CYRANO (*abruptly*): Eloquence I will lend you! . . . And you, to me, shall lend all-conquering physical charm . . . and between us we will compose a hero of romance!

CHRISTIAN: What?

CYRANO: Should you be able to say as your own things which I day by day would teach you?

CHRISTIAN: You are suggesting? . . .

CYRANO: Roxane shall not be disillusioned! Tell me, shall we win her heart, we two as one? Will you submit to feel, transmitted from my leather doublet into your doublet stitched with silk, the soul I wish to share?

CHRISTIAN: But Cyrano! . . .

CYRANO: Christian, will you?

CHRISTIAN: You frighten me!

CYRANO: Since you fear, left to yourself, to chill her heart, will you consent —and soon it will take fire, I vouch for it!—to contribute your lips to my phrases? . . .

CHRISTIAN: Your eyes shine! . . .

CYRANO: Will you?

CHRISTIAN: What, would it please you so much?

CYRANO (*with rapture*): It would . . . (*remembering, and confining himself to expressing an artistic pleasure*) . . . amuse me! It is an experiment fit surely to tempt a poet. Will you complete me, and let me in exchange complete you? We will walk side by side: you in full light, I in your shadow. . . . I will be wit to you . . . you, to me, shall be good looks!

CHRISTIAN: But the letter, which should be sent to her without delay? . . . Never shall I be able . . .

CYRANO (*taking from his doublet the letter written in the first part of the act*): The letter? Here it is!

CHRISTIAN: How? . . .

CYRANO: It only wants the address.

CHRISTIAN: I . . .

CYRANO: You can send it without uneasiness. It is a good letter.

CHRISTIAN: You had? . . .

CYRANO: You shall never find us—poets!—without epistles in our pockets to the Chlorises . . . of our imagining! For we are those same that have for mistress a dream blown into the bubble of a name! Take it—you shall convert this feigning into earnest; I was sending forth at random these confessions and laments: you shall make the wandering birds to settle . . . Take it! You shall see . . . I was as eloquent as if I had been sincere! Take, and have done!

CHRISTIAN: But will it not need to be altered in any part? . . . Written without object, will it fit Roxane?

CYRANO: Like a glove!

CHRISTIAN: But . . .

CYRANO: Trust to the blindness of love . . . and vanity! Roxane will never question that it was written for her.

CHRISTIAN: Ah, my friend!

[*He throws himself into* CYRANO'S *arms. They stand embraced.*]

ONE OF THE CADETS (*opening the door a very little*): Nothing more. . . . The stillness of death. . . . I dare not look. . . . (*He thrusts in his head.*) What is this?

ALL OF THE CADETS (*entering and seeing* CYRANO *and* CHRISTIAN *locked in each other's arms*): Ah! . . . Oh! . . .

ONE OF THE CADETS: This passes bounds!

[*Consternation.*]

THE MOUSQUETAIRE (*impudent*): Ouais?

CARBON: Our demon is waxen mild as an apostle; smitten upon one nostril, he turns the other also!

THE MOUSQUETAIRE: It is in order now to speak of his nose, is it? (*Calling* LISE, *with a swaggering air*) Hey, Lise! now listen and look. (*Pointedly*

sniffing the air) Oh . . . oh . . . it is surprising! . . . what an odor! (*Going to* CYRANO) But monsieur must have smelled it, too? Can you tell me what it is, so plain in the air?
CYRANO (*beating him*) : Why, sundry blows!
   [*Joyful antics of the* CADETS *in beholding* CYRANO *himself again.*]

CURTAIN

ACT THREE

ROXANE'S KISS

A small square in the old Marais. Old-fashioned houses. Narrow streets seen in perspective. At the right, ROXANE'S *house and the wall of her garden, above which spreading treetops. Over the housedoor, a balcony and window. A bench beside the doorstep.*
   The wall is overclambered by ivy, the balcony wreathed with jasmine.
   By means of the bench and projecting stones in the wall, the balcony can easily be scaled.
   On the opposite side, an old house in the same style of architecture, brick and stone, with an entrance door. The doorknocker is swaddled in linen.
      [*At the rise of the curtain, the* DUENNA *is seated on the bench. The window on* ROXANE'S *balcony is wide open.* RAGUENEAU, *in a sort of livery, stands near the* DUENNA; *he is finishing the tale of his misfortunes, drying his eyes.*]

RAGUENEAU: And then she eloped with a mousquetaire! Ruined, forsaken, I was hanging myself. I had already taken leave of earth, when Monsieur de Bergerac happening along, unhanged me, and proposed me to his cousin as her steward. . . .

THE DUENNA: But how did you fall into such disaster?

RAGUENEAU: Lise was fond of soldiers; I, of poets! Mars ate up all left over by Apollo. Under those circumstances, you conceive, the pantry soon was bare.

THE DUENNA (*rising and calling toward the open window*): Roxane, are you ready? . . . They are waiting for us! . . .

ROXANE'S VOICE (*through the window*): I am putting on my mantle!

THE DUENNA (*to* RAGUENEAU, *pointing at the door opposite*): It is over there, opposite, we are expected. At Clomire's. She holds a meeting in her little place. A disquisition upon the Softer Sentiments is to be read.

RAGUENEAU: Upon the Softer Sentiments?

THE DUENNA (*coyly*): Yes! . . . (*Calling toward the window*) Roxane, you must make haste, or we shall miss the disquisition upon the Softer Sentiments!

ROXANE'S VOICE: I am coming!

    [*A sound of string instruments is heard, drawing nearer.*]

CYRANO'S VOICE (*singing in the wings*): La! la! la! la! la! . . .

THE DUENNA (*surprised*): We are to have music?

CYRANO (*enters followed by two* PAGES *with theorbos*[5]): I tell you it is a demi-semi-quaver! . . . you demi-semi-noddle!

FIRST PAGE (*ironically*): Monsieur knows then about quavers, semi and demi?

CYRANO: I know music, as do all Gassendi's disciples!

THE PAGE (*playing and singing*): La! la!

CYRANO (*snatching the theorbo from him and continuing the musical phrase*): I can carry on the melody. . . . La, la, la, la . . .

ROXANE (*appearing on the balcony*): It is you?

CYRANO (*singing upon the tune he is continuing*): I, indeed, who salute your lilies and present my respects to your ro-o-oses! . . .

ROXANE: I am coming down!

    [*She leaves the balcony.*]

THE DUENNA (*pointing at the* PAGES): What is the meaning of these two virtuosi?

CYRANO: A wager I won, from D'Assoucy. We were disputing upon a question of grammar. Yes! No! Yes! No! Suddenly pointing at these two tall knaves, expert at clawing strings, by whom he constantly goes attended, he said, "I wager a day long of music!" He lost. Until, therefore, the next rise of the sun, I shall have dangling after me these arch-lute players, harmonious witnesses of all I do! . . . At first I liked it very well, but

---

[5] *theorbos*: bass lutes.

now it palls a little. (*To the* MUSICIANS) Hey! . . . Go, from me, to Montfleury, and play him a pavane![6] . . . (*The* PAGES *go toward the back. To the* DUENNA) I have come to inquire of Roxane, as I do every evening. . . . (*To the* PAGES, *who are leaving*) Play a long time . . . and out of tune! (*to the* DUENNA) . . . whether in the friend of her soul she can still detect no fault?

ROXANE (*coming out of the house*): Ah, how beautiful he is, what wit he has, how deeply I love him!

CYRANO (*smiling*): Christian has so much wit? . . .

ROXANE: Cousin, more than yourself!

CYRANO: I grant you.

ROXANE: There is not one alive, I truly believe, more apt at turning those pretty nothings which yet are everything. . . . Sometimes he is of an absent mood, his muse is woolgathering; then, suddenly, he will say the most enchanting things!

CYRANO (*incredulous*): Come! . . .

ROXANE: Oh, it is too bad! Men are all alike, narrow, narrow: because he is handsome, he cannot possibly be witty!

CYRANO: So he talks of the heart in acceptable fashion?

ROXANE: "Talks," cousin, is feeble. . . . He dissertates!

CYRANO: And writes? . . .

ROXANE: Still better! Listen now to this. . . . (*Declaiming*) "*The more of my heart you steal from me, the more heart I have!*" (*Triumphantly to* CYRANO) Well? . . .

CYRANO: Pooh!

ROXANE: And to this: "*Since you have stolen my heart, and since I must suffer, to suffer with, send me your own!*"

CYRANO: Now he has too much heart, now he has not enough . . . just what does he want, in the matter of quantity?

ROXANE: You vex me! You are eaten up with jealousy. . . .

CYRANO (*starting*): *Hein?*

ROXANE: Author's jealousy! And this, could anything be more exquisitely tender? "*Believe it, my heart cries out to you, and if kisses could be sent in writing, Love, you should read my letter with your lips. . . .*"

CYRANO (*in spite of himself smiling with satisfaction*): Ha! Ha! Those particular lines seem to me . . . ho! . . . ho! . . . (*remembering himself, disdainfully*) . . . puny, pretty . . .

ROXANE: This, then . . .

CYRANO (*delighted*): You know his letters by heart?

ROXANE: All!

[6] *pavane*: a dance with a slow, stately measure.

CYRANO: It is flattering, one cannot deny.

ROXANE: In this art of expressing love he is a master!

CYRANO (*modest*): Oh . . . a master!

ROXANE (*peremptorily*): A master!

CYRANO: As you please, then . . . a master!

THE DUENNA (*who had gone toward the back, coming quickly forward*): Monsieur de Guiche! (*To* CYRANO, *pushing him toward the house*) Go in! It is perhaps better that he should not see you here! it might put him on the scent. . . .

ROXANE (*to* CYRANO): Yes, of my dear secret! He loves me, he is powerful . . . he must not find out! He might cut in sunder our loves . . . with an ax!

CYRANO (*going into the house*): Very well, very well.

[DE GUICHE *appears.*]

ROXANE (*to* DE GUICHE, *with a curtsey*): I was leaving the house.

DE GUICHE: I have come to bid you farewell.

ROXANE: You are going away?

DE GUICHE: To war.

ROXANE: Ah!

DE GUICHE: I have my orders. Arras is besieged.

ROXANE: Ah! . . . it is besieged?

DE GUICHE: Yes. . . . I see that my departure does not greatly affect you.

ROXANE: Oh! . . .

DE GUICHE: As for me, I own it wrings my heart. Shall I see you again? . . . When? . . . You know that I am made Commander-in-General?

ROXANE (*uninterested*): I congratulate you.

DE GUICHE: Of the Guards.

ROXANE (*starting*): Ah! . . . of the Guards?

DE GUICHE: Among whom your cousin serves—the man of the boasts and tirades. I shall have opportunity in plenty to retaliate upon him down there.

ROXANE (*suffocating*): What? The Guards are going down there?

DE GUICHE: Surely. It is my regiment.

ROXANE (*falls sitting upon the bench; aside*): Christian!

DE GUICHE: What is it troubles you?

ROXANE (*greatly moved*): This departure . . . grieves me mortally. When one cares for a person . . . to know him away at the war!

DE GUICHE (*surprised and charmed*): For the first time you utter a kind and feeling word, when I am leaving!

ROXANE (*in a different tone, fanning herself*): So . . . you are thinking of revenge upon my cousin?

DE GUICHE (*smiling*): You side with him?

ROXANE: No . . . against him.

DE GUICHE: Do you see much of him?

ROXANE: Very little.

DE GUICHE: He is everywhere to be met, with one of the Cadets . . . (*trying to remember*) . . . that Neu . . . villen . . . viller . . .

ROXANE: A tall man?

DE GUICHE: Light-haired.

ROXANE: Red-haired.

DE GUICHE: Good-looking.

ROXANE: Pooh!

DE GUICHE: But a fool!

ROXANE: He looks like one. (*In a different tone*) Your vengeance upon Cyrano is then to place him within reach of shot, which is the thing of all he loves! . . . A miserable vengeance! . . . I know, I do, what would more seriously concern him!

DE GUICHE: And that is?

ROXANE: Why . . . that the regiment should march, and leave him behind with his beloved Cadets, arms folded, the whole war through, in Paris! That is the only way to cast down a man like him. You wish to punish him? Deprive him of danger.

DE GUICHE: A woman! A woman! None but a woman could devise a vengeance of that sort!

ROXANE: His friends will gnaw their fists, and he his very soul, with chagrin at not being under fire; and you will be abundantly avenged!

DE GUICHE (*coming nearer*): Then you do love me a little? (ROXANE *smiles.*) I think I see in your espousing my grudge a proof of affection, Roxane. . . .

ROXANE: You may!

DE GUICHE (*showing several folded papers*): I have here upon me the orders to be transmitted at once to each of the companies . . . except . . . (*taking one from among the others*) . . . this one! . . . the company of the Cadets . . . (*He puts it in his pocket.*) This, I will keep. (*Laughing*) Ah, ah, ah! Cyrano! his belligerent humor! . . . So you sometimes play tricks upon people, you? . . .

ROXANE: Sometimes.

DE GUICHE (*very near her*): I love you to distraction! This evening . . . listen . . . it is true that I must be gone. But to go when I feel it is evident you care! Listen! . . . There is, not far from here, in Rue Orléans, a convent founded by the Capuchins. Father Athanasius. A layman may not enter. But the good fathers—I fear no difficulty with them! They will hide me up their sleeve—their sleeve is wide. They are the Capuchins that serve Richelieu at home. Fearing the uncle, they proportionately fear the nephew. I shall be thought to have left. I will come to you masked. Let me delay by a single day, wayward enchantress!

ROXANE: But if it should transpire . . . your fame . . .

DE GUICHE: Bah!

ROXANE: But . . . the siege . . . Arras! . . .

DE GUICHE: Must wait! Allow me, I beg . . .

ROXANE: No!

DE GUICHE: I beseech!

ROXANE (*tenderly*): No! Love itself bids me forbid you!

DE GUICHE: Ah!

ROXANE: You must go! (*Aside*) Christian will stay! (*Aloud*) For my sake, be heroic . . . Antony!

DE GUICHE: Ah, heavenly word upon your lips! . . . Then you love the one who . . .

ROXANE: Who shall have made me tremble for his sake . . .

DE GUICHE (*in a transport of joy*): Ah, I will go! (*He kisses her hand.*) Are you satisfied with me?

ROXANE: My friend, I am.

[*Exit* DE GUICHE.]

THE DUENNA (*dropping a mocking curtsey toward his back*): My friend, we are!

ROXANE (*to the* DUENNA): Not a word of what I have done: Cyrano would never forgive me for defrauding him of his war! (*She calls toward the house.*) Cousin! (CYRANO *comes out.*) We are going to Clomire's. (*She indicates the house opposite.*) Alcandre has engaged to speak, and so has Lysimon.

THE DUENNA (*putting her little finger to her ear*): Yes, but my little finger tells me that we shall be too late to hear them!

CYRANO (*to* ROXANE): Of all things do not miss the trained monkeys.

[*They have reached* CLOMIRE'S *door.*]

THE DUENNA: See! . . . See! they have muffled the doorknocker! (*To the doorknocker*) You have been gagged, that your voice should not disturb the beautiful lecture . . . little brutal disturber!

[*She lifts it with infinite care and knocks softly.*]

ROXANE (*seeing the door open*): Come! (*From the threshold to* CYRANO) If Christian should come, as probably he will, say he must wait!

CYRANO (*hurriedly, as she is about to disappear*): Ah! (*She turns.*) Upon what shall you, according to your custom, question him today?

ROXANE: Upon . . .

CYRANO (*eagerly*): Upon? . . .

ROXANE: But you will be silent . . .

CYRANO: As that wall!

ROXANE: Upon nothing! I will say: Forward! Free rein! No curb! Improvise! Talk of love! Be magnificent!

CYRANO (*smiling*): Good.

ROXANE: Hush!

CYRANO: Hush!

ROXANE: Not a word!

[*She goes in and closes the door.*]

CYRANO (*bowing, when the door is closed*): A thousand thanks!

[*The door opens again and* ROXANE *looks out.*]

ROXANE: He might prepare his speeches . . .

CYRANO: Ah, no! . . . the devil, no!

BOTH (*together*): Hush! . . .

[*The door closes.*]

CYRANO (*calling*): Christian! (*Enter* CHRISTIAN.) I know all that we need to. Now make ready your memory. This is your chance to cover yourself with glory. Let us lose no time. Do not look sullen, like that. Quick! Let us go to your lodging and I will rehearse you . . .

CHRISTIAN: No!

CYRANO: What?

CHRISTIAN: No, I will await Roxane here.

CYRANO: What insanity possesses you? Come quickly and learn . . .

CHRISTIAN: No, I tell you! I am weary of borrowing my letters, my words . . . of playing a part, and living in constant fear. . . . It was very well at first, but now I feel that she loves me. I thank you heartily. I am no longer afraid. I will speak for myself. . . .

CYRANO: *Ouais?* . . .

CHRISTIAN: And what tells you that I shall not know how? I am not such an utter blockhead, after all! You shall see! Your lessons have not been altogether wasted. I can shift to speak without your aid! And, that failing, by Heaven! I shall still know enough to take her in my arms! (*Catching sight of* ROXANE, *who is coming out from* CLOMIRE'S) She is coming! Cyrano, no, do not leave me! . . .

CYRANO (*bowing to him*): I will not meddle, Monsieur.

[*He disappears behind the garden wall.*]

ROXANE (*coming from* CLOMIRE'S *house with a number of people from whom she is taking leave; curtseys and farewells*): Barthénoide! . . . Alcandre! . . . Grémione! . . .

THE DUENNA (*comically desperate*): We missed the disquisition upon the Softer Sentiments!

[*She goes into* ROXANE'S *house.*]

ROXANE (*still taking leave of this one and that*): Urimédonte! . . .
  Good-bye!
  [*All bow to* ROXANE, *to one another, separate, and go off by the
  various streets.* ROXANE *sees* CHRISTIAN.]
ROXANE: You are here! (*She goes to him.*) Evening is closing round. . . .
  Wait! . . . They have all gone. . . . The air is so mild. . . . Not a passer in
  sight. . . . Let us sit here. . . . Talk! . . . I will listen.
CHRISTIAN (*sits beside her, on the bench; silence*): I love you.
ROXANE (*closing her eyes*): Yes. Talk to me of love.
CHRISTIAN: I love you.
ROXANE: Yes. That is the theme. Play variations upon it.
CHRISTIAN: I love . . .
ROXANE: Variations!
CHRISTIAN: I love you so much . . .
ROXANE: I do not doubt it. What further? . . .
CHRISTIAN: And further . . . I should be so happy if you loved me! Tell me,
  Roxane, that you love me . . .
ROXANE (*pouting*): You proffer cider to me when I was hoping for
  champagne! . . . Now tell me a little *how* you love me?
CHRISTIAN: Why . . . very, very much.
ROXANE: Oh! . . . unravel, disentangle your sentiments!
CHRISTIAN: Your throat! . . . I want to kiss it! . . .
ROXANE: Christian!
CHRISTIAN: I love you! . . .
ROXANE (*attempting to rise*): Again! . . .
CHRISTIAN (*hastily, holding her back*): No, I do not love you! . . .
ROXANE (*sitting down again*): That is fortunate!
CHRISTIAN: I adore you!
ROXANE (*rising and moving away*): Oh!
CHRISTIAN: Yes . . . love makes me into a fool!
ROXANE (*drily*): And I am displeased at it! as I should be displeased at
  your no longer being handsome.
CHRISTIAN: But . . .
ROXANE: Go, and rally your routed eloquence!
CHRISTIAN: I . . .
ROXANE: You love me. I have heard it. Good evening.
  [*She goes toward the house.*]
CHRISTIAN: No, no, not yet! . . . I wish to tell you . . .
ROXANE (*pushing open the door to go in*): That you adore me. Yes, I
  know. No! No! Go away! . . . Go! . . . Go! . . .
CHRISTIAN: But I . . .
  [*She closes the door in his face.*]

CYRANO (*who has been on the scene a moment, unnoticed*): Unmistakably a success.

CHRISTIAN: Help me!

CYRANO: No, sir, no.

CHRISTIAN: I will go kill myself if I am not taken back into favor at once— at once!

CYRANO: And how can I—how, the devil?—make you learn on the spot. . . .

CHRISTIAN (*seizing him by the arm*): Oh, there! . . . Look! . . . See!

[*Light has appeared in the balcony window.*]

CYRANO (*with emotion*): Her window!

CHRISTIAN: Oh, I shall die!

CYRANO: Not so loud!

CHRISTIAN (*in a whisper*): I shall die!

CYRANO: It is a dark night. . . .

CHRISTIAN: Well?

CYRANO: All may be mended. But you do not deserve. . . There! stand there, miserable boy! . . . in front of the balcony! I will stand under it and prompt you.

CHRISTIAN: But . . .

CYRANO: Do as I bid you!

THE PAGES (*reappearing at the back, to* CYRANO): Hey!

CYRANO: Hush!

[*He signs to them to lower their voices.*]

FIRST PAGE (*in a lower voice*): We have finished serenading Montfleury!

CYRANO (*low, quickly*): Go and stand out of sight. One at this street corner, the other at that; and if anyone comes near, play! . . .

SECOND PAGE: What sort of tune, Monsieur the Gassendist?

CYRANO: Merry if it be a woman, mournful if it be a man. (*The* PAGES *disappear, one at each street corner; to* CHRISTIAN) Call her!

CHRISTIAN: Roxane!

CYRANO (*picking up pebbles and throwing them at the windowpane*): Wait! A few pebbles . . .

ROXANE (*opening the window*): Who is calling me?

CHRISTIAN: It is I . . .

ROXANE: Who is . . . I?

CHRISTIAN: Christian!

ROXANE (*disdainfully*): Oh, you!

CHRISTIAN: I wish to speak with you.

CYRANO (*under the balcony, to* CHRISTIAN): Speak low! . . .

ROXANE: No, your conversation is too common. You may go home!

CHRISTIAN: In mercy! . . .

ROXANE: No . . . you do not love me anymore!

CHRISTIAN (*whom* CYRANO *is prompting*): You accuse me . . . just Heaven!
of loving you no more . . . when I can love you no more!

ROXANE (*who was about to close her window, stopping*): Ah, that is a
little better!

CHRISTIAN (*same business*): To what a . . . size has Love grown in my . . .
sigh-rocked soul which the . . . cruel cherub has chosen for his cradle!

ROXANE (*stepping nearer to the edge of the balcony*): That is distinctly
better! . . . But, since he is so cruel, this Cupid, you were unwise not to
smother him in his cradle!

CHRISTIAN (*same business*): I tried to, but, Madame, the . . . attempt was
futile. This . . . new-born Love is . . . a little Hercules . . .

ROXANE: Much, much better!

CHRISTIAN (*same business*): . . . who found it merest baby play to . . .
strangle the serpents . . . twain, Pride and . . . Mistrust.

ROXANE (*leaning her elbows on the balcony rail*): Ah, that is very good
indeed! . . . But why do you speak so slowly and stintedly? Has your
imagination gout in its wings?

CYRANO (*drawing* CHRISTIAN *under the balcony and taking his place*):
Hush! It is becoming too difficult!

ROXANE: Tonight your words come falteringly. . . . Why is it?

CYRANO (*talking low like* CHRISTIAN): Because of the dark. They have to
grope to find your ear.

ROXANE: My words do not find the same difficulty.

CYRANO: They reach their point at once? Of course they do! That is because I catch them with my heart. My heart, you see, is very large, your
ear particularly small. . . . Besides, your words drop . . . they fall quickly;
mine have to climb . . . and that takes longer!

ROXANE: They have been climbing more nimbly, however, in the last few
minutes.

CYRANO: They are becoming used to this gymnastic feat!

ROXANE: It is true that I am talking with you from a very mountaintop!

CYRANO: It is sure that a hard word dropped from such a height upon my
heart would shatter it!

ROXANE (*with the motion of leaving*): I will come down.

CYRANO (*quickly*): Do not!

ROXANE (*pointing at the bench at the foot of the balcony*): Then do you
get up on the seat! . . .

CYRANO (*drawing away in terror*): No!

ROXANE: How do you mean . . . no?

CYRANO (*with ever-increasing emotion*): Let us profit a little by this chance of talking softly together without seeing each other. . . .

ROXANE: Without seeing each other? . . .

CYRANO: Yes, to my mind, delectable! Each guesses at the other, and no more. You discern but the trailing blackness of a mantle, and I a dawn-gray glimmer which is a summer gown. I am a shadow merely, a pearly phantom are you! You can never know what these moments are to me! If ever I was eloquent . . .

ROXANE: You were!

CYRANO: My words never till now surged from my very heart. . . .

ROXANE: And why?

CYRANO: Because, till now, they must strain to reach you through . . .

ROXANE: What?

CYRANO: Why, the bewildering emotion a man feels who sees you, and whom you look upon! . . . But this evening, it seems to me that I am speaking to you for the first time!

ROXANE: It is true that your voice is altogether different.

CYRANO (*coming nearer, feverishly*): Yes, altogether different, because, protected by the dark, I dare at last to be myself. I dare . . . (*he stops, and distractedly*) . . . What was I saying? . . . I do not know. . . . All this . . . forgive my incoherence! . . . is so delicious . . . is so new to me!

ROXANE: So new? . . .

CYRANO (*in extreme confusion, still trying to mend his expressions*): So new . . . yes, new, to be sincere; the fear of being mocked always constrains my heart. . . .

ROXANE: Mocked. . . . for what?

CYRANO: Why . . . for its impulses, its flights! . . . Yes, my heart always cowers behind the defense of my wit. I set forth to capture a star . . . and then, for dread of laughter, I stop and pick a flower . . . of rhetoric!

ROXANE: That sort of flower has its pleasing points. . . .

CYRANO: But yet, tonight, let us scorn it!

ROXANE: Never before had you spoken as you are speaking! . . .

CYRANO: Ah, if far from Cupid darts and quivers, we might seek a place of somewhat fresher things! If instead of drinking, flat sip by sip, from a chiseled golden thimble, drops distilled and dulcified, we might try the sensation of quenching the thirst of our souls by stooping to the level of the great river, and setting our lips to the stream!

ROXANE: But yet, wit . . . fancy . . . delicate conceits. . . .

CYRANO: I gave my fancy leave to frame conceits, before, to make you linger . . . but now it would be an affront to this balm-breathing night, to Nature and the hour, to talk like characters in a pastoral performed at

Court! . . . Let us give Heaven leave, looking at us with all its earnest stars, to strip us of disguise and artifice: I fear . . . oh, fear! . . . lest in our mistaken alchemy sentiment should be subtilized to evaporation; lest the life of the heart should waste in these empty pastimes, and the final refinement of the fine be the undoing of the refined!

ROXANE: But yet, wit . . . aptness . . . ingenuity. . . .

CYRANO: I hate them in love! Criminal, when one loves, to prolong overmuch that paltry thrust and parry! The moment, however, comes inevitably—and I pity those for whom it never comes!—in which, we apprehending the noble depth of the love we harbor, a shallow word hurts us to utter!

ROXANE: If . . . if, then, that moment has come for us two, what words will you say to me?

CYRANO: All those, all those, all those that come to me! Not in formal nosegay order . . . I will throw them to you in a wild sheaf! I love you, choke with love, I love you, dear . . . My brain reels, I can bear no more, it is too much. . . . Your name is in my heart the golden clapper in a bell; and as I know no rest, Roxane, always the heart is shaken, and ever rings your name! . . . Of you, I remember all, all have I loved! Last year, one day, the twelfth of May, in going out at morning you changed the fashion of your hair. . . . I have taken the light of your hair for my light, and as having stared too long at the sun, on everything one sees a scarlet wheel, on everything when I come from my chosen light, my dazzled eye sets swimming golden blots! . . .

ROXANE (*in a voice unsteady with emotion*): Yes . . . this is love. . . .

CYRANO: Ah, verily! The feeling which invades me, terrible and jealous, is love . . . with all its mournful frenzy! It is love, yet self-forgetting more than the wont of love! Ah, for your happiness how readily would I give mine, though you should never know it, might I but, from a distance, sometimes, hear the happy laughter bought by my sacrifice! Every glance of yours breeds in me new strength, new valor! Are you beginning to understand? Tell me, do you grasp my love's measure? Does some little part of my soul make itself felt of you there in the darkness? . . . Oh, what is happening to me this evening is too sweet, too deeply dear! I tell you all these things, and you listen to me, you! Not in my least modest hoping did I ever hope so much! I have now only to die! It is because of words of mine that she is trembling among the dusky branches. For you are trembling, like a flower among leaves! Yes, you tremble . . . for whether you will or no, I have felt the worshiped trembling of your hand all along this thrilled and blissful jasmine bough!

[*He madly kisses the end of a pendent bough.*]

ROXANE: Yes, I tremble . . . and weep . . . and love you . . . and am yours!
. . . For you have carried me away . . . away! . . .

CYRANO: Then, let death come! I have moved you, I! . . . There is but one
thing more I ask. . . .

CHRISTIAN (*under the balcony*): A kiss!

ROXANE (*drawing hastily back*): What?

CYRANO: Oh!

ROXANE: You ask? . . .

CYRANO: Yes . . . I . . . (*To* CHRISTIAN) You are in too great haste!

CHRISTIAN: Since she is so moved, I must take advantage of it!

CYRANO (*to* ROXANE): I . . . Yes, it is true I asked . . . but, merciful
heavens! . . . I knew at once that I had been too bold.

ROXANE (*a shade disappointed*): You insist no more than so?

CYRANO: Indeed, I insist . . . without insisting! Yes! yes! but your modesty
shrinks! . . . I insist, but yet . . . the kiss I begged . . . refuse it me!

CHRISTIAN (*to* CYRANO, *pulling at his mantle*): Why?

CYRANO: Hush, Christian!

ROXANE (*bending over the balcony rail*): What are you whispering?

CYRANO: Reproaches to myself for having gone too far; I was saying
"Hush, Christian!" (*The theorbos are heard playing.*) Your pardon! . . .
a second! . . . Someone is coming!

[ROXANE *closes the window.* CYRANO *listens to the theorbos, one of
which plays a lively, and the other a lugubrious tune.*]

CYRANO: A dance? . . . A dirge? . . . What do they mean? Is it a man or a
woman? . . . Ah, it is a monk!

[*Enter a* CAPUCHIN MONK, *who goes from house to house, with a lantern, examining the doors.*]

CYRANO (*to the* CAPUCHIN): What are you looking for, Diogenes?

THE CAPUCHIN: I am looking for the house of Madame . . .

CHRISTIAN: He is in the way!

THE CAPUCHIN: Magdeleine Robin. . . .

CYRANO (*pointing up one of the streets*): This way! . . . Straight ahead . . .
go straight ahead. . . .

THE CAPUCHIN: I thank you. I will say ten Aves for your peace.

[*Exit.*]

CYRANO: My good wishes speed your cowl!

[*He comes forward toward* CHRISTIAN.]

CHRISTIAN: Insist upon the kiss! . . .

CYRANO: No, I will not!

CHRISTIAN: Sooner or later . . .

CYRANO: It is true! It must come, the moment of inebriation when your lips
shall imperiously be impelled toward each other, because the one is

fledged with youthful gold and the other is so soft a pink! . . . (*To himself*) I had rather it should be because . . .

[*Sound of the window reopening*; CHRISTIAN *hides under the balcony.*]

ROXANE (*stepping forward on the balcony*): Are you there? We were speaking of . . . of . . . of a . . .

CYRANO: Kiss. The word is sweet. Why does your fair lip stop at it? If the mere word burns it, what will be of the thing itself? Do not make it into a fearful matter, and then fear! Did you not a moment ago insensibly leave playfulness behind and slip without trepidation from a smile to a sigh, from a sigh to a tear? Slip but a little further in the same blessed direction: from a tear to a kiss there is scarcely a dividing shiver!

ROXANE: Say no more!

CYRANO: A kiss! When all is said, what is a kiss? An oath of allegiance taken in closer proximity, a promise more precise, a seal on a confession, a rose-red dot upon the letter *i* in loving; a secret which elects the mouth for ear; an instant of eternity murmuring like a bee; balmy communion with a flavor of flowers; a fashion of inhaling each other's heart, and of tasting, on the brink of the lips, each other's soul!

ROXANE: Say no more . . . no more!

CYRANO: A kiss, Madame, is a thing so noble that the Queen of France, on the most fortunate of lords, bestowed one—the queen herself!

ROXANE: If that be so . . .

CYRANO (*with increasing fervor*): Like Buckingham I have suffered in long silence, like him I worship a queen, like him I am sorrowful and unchanging. . . .

ROXANE: Like him you enthrall through the eyes of the heart that follows you!

CYRANO (*to himself, sobered*): True, I am handsome . . . I had forgotten!

ROXANE: Come then and gather it, the supreme flower . . .

CYRANO (*pushing* CHRISTIAN *toward the balcony*): Go!

ROXANE: . . . tasting of the heart . . .

CYRANO: Go! . . .

ROXANE: . . . murmuring like a bee . . .

CYRANO: Go!

CHRISTIAN (*hesitating*): But now I feel as if I ought not!

ROXANE: . . . making eternity an instant . . .

CYRANO (*pushing* CHRISTIAN): Scale the balcony, you donkey!

[CHRISTIAN *springs toward the balcony, and climbs by means of the bench, the vine, the posts, and balusters.*]

CHRISTIAN: Ah, Roxane!

[*He clasps her to him and bends over her lips.*]

CYRANO: Ha! . . . What a turn of the screw to my heart! . . . A kiss!—a banquet of Love at which I am Lazarus, a crumb drops from your table even to me, here in the shade. . . . Yes, in my outstretched heart a little falls, as I feel that upon the lip pressing her lip Roxane kisses the words spoken by me! . . . (*The theorbos are heard.*) A merry tune . . . a mournful one. . . . The monk! (*He goes through the pretense of arriving on the spot at a run, as if from a distance; calling*) Ho, there!

ROXANE: What is it?

CYRANO: It is I. I was passing this way. Is Christian there?

CHRISTIAN (*astonished*): Cyrano!

ROXANE: Good evening, cousin!

CYRANO: Cousin, good evening!

ROXANE: I will come down.

> [ROXANE *disappears in the house. The* CAPUCHIN *reenters at the back.*]

CHRISTIAN (*seeing him*): Oh, again!

> [*He follows* ROXANE.]

THE CAPUCHIN: It is here she lives, I am certain . . . Magdeleine Robin.

CYRANO: You said Rolin.

THE CAPUCHIN: No, bin . . . *b, i, n,* bin!

ROXANE (*appearing upon the threshold, followed by* RAGUENEAU, *carrying a lantern, and* CHRISTIAN): What is it?

THE CAPUCHIN: A letter.

CHRISTIAN: What?

THE CAPUCHIN (*to* ROXANE): Oh, the contents can be only of a sacred character! It is from a worthy nobleman who . . .

ROXANE (*to* CHRISTIAN): It is from De Guiche!

CHRISTIAN: He dares to . . .?

ROXANE: Oh, he will not trouble me much longer! (*Opening the letter*) I love you, and if . . . (*by the light of* RAGUENEAU'S *lantern she reads, aside, low*) "*Mademoiselle: The drums are beating. My regiment is buckling on its corselet. It is about to leave. I am thought to have left already, but lag behind. I am disobeying you. I am in the convent here. I am coming to you, and send you word by a friar, silly as a sheep, who has no suspicion of the import of this letter. You smiled too sweetly upon me an hour ago: I must see you smile again. Arrange to be alone, and deign graciously to receive the audacious worshiper, forgiven already, I can but hope, who signs himself your*—etc. . . . (*To the* CAPUCHIN) Father, this is what the letter tells me . . . Listen: (*All draw nearer; she reads aloud*) "*Mademoiselle: The wishes of the Cardinal may not be disregarded, however hard compliance with them prove. I have therefore chosen as bearer of this letter a most reverend, holy, and sagacious*

Capuchin; it is our wish that he should at once, in your own dwelling, pronounce the nuptial blessing over you. Christian must secretly become your husband. I send him to you. You dislike him. Bow to Heaven's will in resignation, and be sure that it will bless your zeal, and sure, likewise, Mademoiselle, of the respect of him who is and will be ever your most humble and . . ." etc.

THE CAPUCHIN (*beaming*): The worthy gentleman! . . . I knew it! You remember that I said so: the contents of that letter can be only of a sacred character!

ROXANE (*low, to* CHRISTIAN): I am a fluent reader, am I not?

CHRISTIAN: Hm!

ROXANE (*with feigned despair*): Ah . . . it is horrible!

THE CAPUCHIN (*who has turned the light of his lantern upon* CYRANO): You are the one?

CHRISTIAN: No, I am.

THE CAPUCHIN (*turning the light upon him, and as if his good looks aroused suspicion*): But . . .

ROXANE (*quickly*): "*Postscript: You will bestow upon the convent two hundred and fifty crowns.*"

THE CAPUCHIN: The worthy, worthy gentleman! (*To* ROXANE) Be reconciled!

ROXANE (*with the expression of a martyr*): I will endeavor! (*While* RAGUENEAU *opens the door for the* CAPUCHIN, *whom* CHRISTIAN *is showing into the house,* ROXANE *says low to* CYRANO) De Guiche is coming! . . . Keep him here! Do not let him enter until . . .

CYRANO: I understand! (*To the* CAPUCHIN) How long will it take to marry them?

THE CAPUCHIN: A quarter of an hour.

CYRANO (*pushing all toward the house*): Go in! I shall be here!

ROXANE (*to* CHRISTIAN): Come!

[*They go in.*]

CYRANO: How can I detain De Guiche for a quarter of an hour? (*He jumps upon the bench, climbs the wall toward the balcony rail.*) So! . . . I climb up here! . . . I know what I will do! . . . (*The theorbos play a melancholy tune.*) Ho, it is a man! (*The tune quavers lugubriously.*) Ho, ho, this time there is no mistake! (*He is on the balcony; he pulls the brim of his hat over his eyes, takes off his sword, wraps his cloak about him, and bends over the balcony rail.*) No, it is not too far! (*He climbs over the balcony rail, and reaching for a long bough that projects beyond the garden wall, holds on to it with both hands, ready to let himself drop.*) I shall make a slight commotion in the atmosphere!

DE GUICHE (*enters masked, groping in the dark*): What can that thrice-damned Capuchin be about?

CYRANO: The devil! if he should recognize my voice? (*Letting go with one hand, he makes show of turning a key.*) Cric! crac! (*Solemnly*) Cyrano resume the accent of Bergerac!

DE GUICHE (*looking at* ROXANE'S *house*): Yes, that is it. I can scarcely see. This mask bothers my eyes!

[*He is about to enter* ROXANE'S *house;* CYRANO *swings from the balcony, holding on to the bough, which bends and lets him down between the door and* DE GUICHE. *He intentionally drops very heavily, to give the effect of dropping from a great height, and lies flattened upon the ground, motionless, as if stunned.*]

DE GUICHE: What is it? (*When he looks up, the bough has swung into place; he sees nothing but the sky.*) Where did this man drop from?

CYRANO (*rising to a sitting posture*): From the moon!

DE GUICHE: From the . . . ?

CYRANO (*in a dreamy voice*): What time is it?

DE GUICHE: Is he mad?

CYRANO: What time? What country? What day? What season?

DE GUICHE: But . . .

CYRANO: I am dazed!

DE GUICHE: Monsieur . . .

CYRANO: I have dropped from the moon like a bomb!

DE GUICHE (*impatiently*): What are you babbling about?

CYRANO (*rising, in a terrible voice*): I tell you I have dropped from the moon!

DE GUICHE (*backing a step*): Very well. You have dropped from the moon! . . . He is perhaps a lunatic!

CYRANO (*walking up close to him*): Not metaphorically, mind that!

DE GUICHE: But . . .

CYRANO: A hundred years ago, or else a minute—for I have no conception how long I have been falling—I was up there, in that saffron-colored ball!

DE GUICHE (*shrugging his shoulders*): You were. Now, let me pass!

CYRANO (*standing in his way*): Where am I? Be frank with me! Keep nothing from me! In what region, among what people, have I been shot like an aerolite?

DE GUICHE: I wish to pass!

CYRANO: While falling I could not choose my way and have no notion where I have fallen! Is it upon a moon, or is it upon an earth, I have been dragged by my posterior weight?

DE GUICHE: I tell you, sir . . .

CYRANO (*with a scream of terror at which* DE GUICHE *starts backward a step*): Great God! . . . In this country men's faces are soot-black!

DE GUICHE (*lifting his hand to his face*): What does he mean?

CYRANO (*still terrified*): Am I in Algeria? Are you a native? . . .

DE GUICHE (*who has felt his mask*): Ah, my mask!

CYRANO (*pretending to be easier*): So I am in Venice! . . . Or am I in Genoa?

DE GUICHE (*attempting to pass*): A lady is expecting me!

CYRANO (*completely reassured*): Ah, then I am in Paris.

DE GUICHE (*smiling in spite of himself*): The rogue is not far from amusing!

CYRANO: Ah, you are laughing!

DE GUICHE: I laugh . . . but intend to pass!

CYRANO (*beaming*): To think I should strike Paris! (*Quite at his ease, laughing, brushing himself, bowing*) I arrived—pray, pardon my appearance!—by the last whirlwind. I am rather unpresentable—travel, you know! My eyes are still full of stardust. My spurs are clogged with bristles off a planet. (*Appearing to pick something off his sleeve*) See, on my sleeve, a comet's hair!

[*He makes a feint of blowing it away.*]

DE GUICHE (*beside himself*): Sir . . .

CYRANO (*as* DE GUICHE *is about to pass, stretching out his leg as if to show something on it, thereby stopping him*): Embedded in my calf, I have brought back one of the Great Bear's teeth . . . and as, falling too near the Trident, I strained aside to clear one of its prongs, I landed sitting in Libra . . . yes, one of the scales! . . . and now my weight is registered up there! (*Quickly preventing* DE GUICHE *from passing, and taking hold of a button on his doublet*) And if, Monsieur, you should take my nose between your fingers and compress it . . . milk would result!

DE GUICHE: What are you saying? Milk? . . .

CYRANO: of the Milky Way.

DE GUICHE: Go to the devil!

CYRANO: No! I am sent from Heaven, literally. (*Folding his arms*) Will you believe—I discovered it in passing—that Sirius at night puts on a nightcap? (*Confidentially*) The lesser Bear is too little yet to bite. . . . (*Laughing*) I tumbled plump through Lyra, and snapped a string! . . . (*Magnificently*) But I intend setting all this down in a book, and the golden stars I have brought back caught in my shaggy mantle, when the book is printed, will be seen serving as asterisks!

DE GUICHE: I have stood this long enough! I want . . .

CYRANO: I know perfectly what you want!

DE GUICHE: Man . . .

CYRANO: You want to know, from me, at first hand, what the moon is made of, and whether that monumental pumpkin is inhabited?

DE GUICHE (*shouting*): Not in the very least! I want . . .

CYRANO: to know how I got there? I got there by a method of my own invention.

DE GUICHE (*discouraged*): He is mad! . . . stark!

CYRANO (*disdainfully*): Do not imagine that I resorted to anything so absurd as Regiomontanus's eagle, or anything so lacking in enterprise as Archytas's pigeon![7] . . .

DE GUICHE: The madman is erudite. . . .

CYRANO: I drew up nothing that had ever been thought of before! (DE GUICHE *has succeeded in getting past* CYRANO *and is nearing* ROXANE'S *door*; CYRANO *follows him, ready to buttonhole him.*) I invented no less than six ways of storming the blue fort of Heaven!

DE GUICHE (*turning around*): Six, did you say?

CYRANO (*volubly*): One way was to stand naked in the sunshine, in a harness thickly studded with glass phials, each filled with morning dew. The sun in drawing up the dew, you see, could not have helped drawing me up, too!

DE GUICHE (*surprised, taking a step toward* CYRANO): True. That is one!

CYRANO (*taking a step backward, with a view of drawing* DE GUICHE *away from the door*): Or else, I could have let the wind into a cedar coffer, then rarefied the imprisoned element by means of cunningly adjusted burning glasses, and soared up with it!

DE GUICHE (*taking another step toward* CYRANO): Two!

CYRANO (*backing*): Or else, mechanic as well as artificer, I could have fashioned a giant grasshopper, with steel joints, which, impelled by successive explosions of saltpeter, would have hopped with me to the azure meadows where graze the starry flocks!

DE GUICHE (*unconsciously following* CYRANO *and counting on his fingers*): That makes three!

CYRANO: Since smoke by its nature ascends, I could have blown into an appropriate globe a sufficient quantity to ascend with me!

DE GUICHE (*as above, more and more astonished*): Four!

CYRANO: Since Phoebe, the moon goddess, when she is at wane, is greedy,

---

[7] *Archytas's pigeon*: Regiomontanus, a German astronomer of the fifteenth century, A.D., and Archytas, a Greek philosopher of the fifth century, B.C., constructed flying machines of the shapes here mentioned.

O beeves! of your marrow . . . with that marrow I could have besmeared myself!

DE GUICHE (*amazed*): Five!

CYRANO (*who while talking has backed, followed by* DE GUICHE, *to the farther side of the square, near a bench*): Or else, I could have placed myself upon an iron plate, have taken a magnet of suitable size, and thrown it in the air! That way is a very good one! The magnet flies upward, the iron instantly after; the magnet no sooner overtaken than you fling it up again. . . . The rest is clear! You can go upward indefinitely.

DE GUICHE: Six! . . . But here are six excellent methods! Which of the six, my dear sir, did you select?

CYRANO: A seventh!

DE GUICHE: Did you, indeed? And what was that?

CYRANO: I give you a hundred guesses!

DE GUICHE: I must confess that I should like to know!

CYRANO (*imitating the noise of the surf, and making great mysterious gestures*): Hoo-ish! hoo-ish!

DE GUICHE: Well! What is that?

CYRANO: Cannot you guess?

DE GUICHE: No!

CYRANO: The tide! . . . At the hour in which the moon attracts the deep, I lay down upon the sands, after a sea bath . . . and, my head being drawn up first—the reason of this, you see, that the hair will hold a quantity of water in its mop!—I rose in the air, straight, beautifully straight, like an angel. I rose . . . I rose softly . . . without an effort . . . when, suddenly, I felt a shock. Then . . .

DE GUICHE (*lured on by curiosity, taking a seat on the bench*): Well . . . then?

CYRANO: Then . . . (*resuming his natural voice*) . . . the time is up, Monsieur, and I release you. They are married.

DE GUICHE (*getting to his feet with a leap*): I am dreaming or drunk! That voice? (*The door of* ROXANE'S *house opens;* LACKEYS *appear carrying lighted candelabra.* CYRANO *removes his hat.*) And that nose! . . . Cyrano!

CYRANO (*bowing*): Cyrano. They have exchanged rings within the quarter of the hour.

DE GUICHE: Who have? (*He turns round. Tableau. Behind the* LACKEYS *stand* ROXANE *and* CHRISTIAN *holding hands. The* CAPUCHIN *follows them, smiling.* RAGUENEAU *holds high a flambeau. The* DUENNA *closes the procession, bewildered, in her bedgown.*) Heavens! (*To* ROXANE) You! (*Recognizing* CHRISTIAN *with amazement*) He? (*Bowing to* ROX-

ANE) Your astuteness compels my admiration! (*To* CYRANO) My compliments to you, ingenious inventor of flying machines. Your experiences would have beguiled a saint on the threshold of Paradise! Make a note of them. . . . They can be used again, with profit, in a book!

CYRANO (*bowing*): I will confidently follow your advice.

THE CAPUCHIN (*to* DE GUICHE, *pointing at the lovers, and wagging his great white beard with satisfaction*): A beautiful couple, my son, brought together by you!

DE GUICHE (*eyeing him frigidly*): As you say! (*To* ROXANE) And now proceed, Madame, to take leave of your husband.

ROXANE: What?

DE GUICHE (*to* CHRISTIAN): The regiment is on the point of starting. You are to join it!

ROXANE: To go to war?

DE GUICHE: Of course!

ROXANE: But the Cadets are not going!

DE GUICHE: They are! (*Taking out the paper which he had put in his pocket*) Here is the order. (*To* CHRISTIAN) I beg you will take it to the Captain, Baron, yourself.

ROXANE (*throwing herself in* CHRISTIAN's *arms*): Christian!

DE GUICHE (*to* CYRANO, *with a malignant laugh*): The wedding night is somewhat far as yet!

CYRANO (*aside*): He thinks that he is giving me great pain!

CHRISTIAN (*to* ROXANE): Oh, once more, dear! . . . Once more!

CYRANO: Be reasonable . . . Come! . . . Enough!

CHRISTIAN (*still clasping* ROXANE): Oh, it is hard to leave her. . . . You cannot know. . . .

CYRANO (*trying to draw him away*): I know.

[*Drums are heard in the distance sounding a march.*]

DE GUICHE (*at the back*): The regiment is on its way!

ROXANE (*to* CYRANO, *while she clings to* CHRISTIAN, *whom he is trying to draw away*): Oh! . . . I entrust him to your care! Promise that under no circumstance shall his life be placed in danger!

CYRANO: I will endeavor . . . but obviously cannot promise . . .

ROXANE (*same business*): Promise that he will be careful of himself!

CYRANO: I will do my best, but . . .

ROXANE (*as above*): . . . that during this terrible siege he shall not take harm from the cold!

CYRANO: I will try, but . . .

ROXANE (*as above*): . . . that he will be true to me!

CYRANO: Of course, but yet, you see . . .

ROXANE (*as above*): . . . that he will write to me often!
CYRANO (*stopping*): Ah, that . . . I promise freely!

CURTAIN

ACT FOUR

THE GASCONY CADETS

The post occupied at the siege of Arras by the company of CARBON DE CASTEL-JALOUX. *At the back, across the whole stage, sloping earthwork. Beyond this is seen a plain stretching to the horizon; the country is covered with constructions relating to the siege. In the distance, against the sky, the outlines of the walls and roofs of Arras. Tents; scattered arms; drums, etc. It is shortly before sunrise. The East is yellow.*

Sentinels at even intervals. Campfires. The GASCONY CADETS *lie asleep, rolled in their cloaks.* CARBON DE CASTEL-JALOUX *and* LE BRET *are watching. All are very pale and gaunt.* CHRISTIAN *lies sleeping among the others, in his military cape, in the foreground, his face lighted by one of the campfires. Silence.*

LE BRET: It is dreadful!
CARBON: Yes. Nothing left.
LE BRET: *Mordious!*
CARBON (*warning him by a gesture to speak lower*): Curse in a whisper! You will wake them! . . . (*To the* CADETS) Hush! Go to sleep! (*To* LE BRET) Who sleeps dines.
LE BRET: Who lies awake misses two good things. . . . What a situation!
[*A few shots are heard in the distance.*]
CARBON: The devil take their popping! They will wake my young ones! . . . (*To the* CADETS *who lift their heads*) Go to sleep!
[*The* CADETS *lie down again. Other shots are heard, nearer.*]

ONE OF THE CADETS (*stirring*): The devil! Again?

CARBON: It is nothing. It is Cyrano getting home.

[*The heads which had started up go down again.*]

A SENTINEL (*outside*): *Ventrebieu!* Who goes there?

CYRANO'S VOICE: Bergerac!

THE SENTINEL (*upon the embankment*): *Ventrebieu!* Who goes there?

CYRANO (*appearing at the top of the embankment*): Bergerac, blockhead!

[*He comes down.* LE BRET *goes to him, uneasy.*]

LE BRET: Ah, thank God!

CYRANO (*warning him by a sign to wake no one*): Hush!

LE BRET: Wounded?

CYRANO: Do you not know that it has become a habit with them to miss me?

LE BRET: To me, it seems a little excessive that you should, every morning, for the sake of taking a letter, risk . . .

CYRANO (*stopping in front of* CHRISTIAN): I promised that he would write often. (*He looks at* CHRISTIAN.) He sleeps. He has grown pale. If the poor little girl could know that he is starving. . . . But handsome as ever!

LE BRET: Go at once and sleep.

CYRANO: Le Bret, do not grumble! Learn this: I nightly cross the Spanish lines at a point where I know beforehand everyone will be drunk.

LE BRET: You ought sometime to bring us back some victuals!

CYRANO: I must be lightly burdened to flit through! . . . But I know that there will be events before the evening. The French, unless I am much mistaken, will eat or die.

LE BRET: Oh, tell us!

CYRANO: No, I am not certain. . . . You will see!

CARBON: What a shameful reversal of the order of things, that the besieger should be starved!

LE BRET: Alas! never was more complicated siege than this of Arras: We besiege Arras, and, caught in a trap, are ourselves besieged by the Cardinal-Prince of Spain. . . .

CYRANO: Someone now ought to come and besiege him.

LE BRET: I am not joking!

CYRANO: Oh, oh!

LE BRET: To think, ungrateful boy, that every day you risk a life precious as yours, solely to carry . . . (CYRANO *goes toward one of the tents.*) Where are you going?

CYRANO: I am going to write another.

[*He lifts the canvas flap, and disappears in the tent. Daybreak has brightened. Rosy flush. The city of Arras at the horizon catches a golden light. The report of a cannon is heard, followed at once by a drum call, very far away, at the left. Other drums beat, nearer. The drum calls answer one another, come nearer, come very near, and go off, decreasing, dying in the distance, toward the right, having made the circuit of the camp. Noise of general awakening. Voices of* OFFI-CERS *in the distance.*]

CARBON (*with a sigh*): The reveille. . . . Ah, me! . . . (*The* CADETS *stir in their cloaks, stretch.*) An end to the succulent slumbers! I know but too well what their first word will be!

ONE OF THE CADETS (*sitting up*): I am famished!

OTHER CADET: I believe I am dying!

ALL: Oh! . . .

CARBON: Get up!

THIRD CADET: I cannot go a step!

FOURTH CADET: I have not strength to stir!

FIRST CADET (*looking at himself in a bit of armor*): My tongue is coated: it must be the weather that is indigestible!

OTHER CADET: Anyone who wants them can have all my titles of nobility for a Chester cheese . . . or part of one!

OTHER CADET: If my stomach does not have something put into it to take up the attention of my gastric juice, I shall retire into my tent before long . . . like Achilles!

OTHER CADET: Yes, they ought to provide us with bread!

CARBON (*going to the tent into which* CYRANO *has retired; low*): Cyrano!

OTHER CADETS: We cannot stand this much longer!

CARBON (*as above, at the door of the tent*): To the rescue, Cyrano! You who succeed so well always in cheering them, come and make them pluck up spirits!

SECOND CADET (*falling upon* FIRST CADET *who is chewing something*): What are you chewing, man?

FIRST CADET: A bit of gun tow fried in axle grease . . . using a burganet[8] as frying pan. The suburbs of Arras are not precisely rich in game. . . .

OTHER CADET (*entering*): I have been hunting!

OTHER CADET (*entering*): I have been fishing!

ALL (*rising and falling upon the newcomers*): What?—what did you catch?—A pheasant?—A carp? . . . Quick! quick!—Let us see!

THE HUNTSMAN: A sparrow!

THE ANGLER: A gudgeon!

ALL (*exasperated*): Enough of this! Let us revolt!

---

[8] *burganet*: light helmet.

CARBON: To the rescue, Cyrano!

[*It is now broad daylight.*]

CYRANO (*coming out of the tent, tranquil, a pen behind his ear, a book in his hand*): What is the matter? (*Silence; to* FIRST CADET) Why do you go off like that, with that slouching gait?

THE CADET: I have something away down in my heels which inconveniences me.

CYRANO: And what is that?

THE CADET: My stomach.

CYRANO: That is where mine is, too.

THE CADET: Then you, too, must be inconvenienced.

CYRANO: No. The size of the hollow within me merely increases my sense of my size.

SECOND CADET: I happen to have teeth, long ones!

CYRANO: The better will you bite . . . in good time!

THIRD CADET: I reverberate like a drum!

CYRANO: You will be of use . . . to sound the charge!

OTHER CADET: I have a buzzing in my ears!

CYRANO: A mistake. Empty belly, no ears. You hear no buzzing.

OTHER CADET: Ah, a trifling article to eat . . . and a little oil upon it!

CYRANO (*taking off the* CADET'S *morion and placing it in his hand*): That is seasoned.

OTHER CADET: What is there we could devour?

CYRANO (*tossing him the book he has been holding*): Try *The Iliad!*

OTHER CADET: The minister, in Paris, makes his four meals a day!

CYRANO: You feel it remiss in him not to send you a bit of partridge?

THE SAME: Why should he not? And some wine!

CYRANO: Richelieu, some Burgundy, if you please?

THE SAME: He might, by one of his Capuchins!

CYRANO: By His Eminence, perhaps, in sober gray?

OTHER CADET: No ogre was ever so hungry!

CYRANO: You may have your fill yet of humble pie!

FIRST CADET (*shrugging his shoulders*): Forever jests! . . . puns! . . . *mots!*

CYRANO: *Le mot* forever, indeed! And I would wish to die, on a fine evening, under a rose-flushed sky, delivering myself of a good *mot* in a good cause! . . . Ah, yes, the best were indeed, far from feverbed and potion, pierced with the only noble weapon, by an adversary worthy of oneself, to fall upon a glorious field, the point of a sword through his heart, the point of a jest on his lips! . . .

ALL (*in a wail*): I am hungry!

CYRANO (*folding his arms*): God have mercy! can you think of nothing but eating? . . . Come here, Bertrandou the fifer, once the shepherd! Take from the double case one of your fifes: Breathe into it, play to this pack of guzzlers and of gluttons our homely melodies, of haunting rhythm, every note of which appeals like a little sister, through whose every strain are heard strains of beloved voices . . . mild melodies whose slowness brings to mind the slowness of the smoke upcurling from our native hamlet hearths . . . melodies that seem to speak to a man in his native dialect! . . . (*The old* FIFER *sits down and makes ready his fife.*) Today let the fife, martial unwillingly, be reminded, while your fingers upon its slender stem flutter like birds in a delicate minuet, that before being ebony it was reed; surprise itself by what you make it sing . . . let it feel restored to it the soul of its youth, rustic and peaceable! (*The old man begins playing Languedoc tunes.*) Listen, Gascons! It is no more, beneath his fingers, the shrill fife of the camp, but the soft flute of the woodland! It is no more, between his lips, the whistling note of battle, but the lowly lay of goatherds leading their flocks to feed! . . . Hark! . . . It sings of the valley, the heath, the forest! . . . of the little shepherd, sunburned under his crimson cap! . . . the green delight of evening on the river! . . . Hark, Gascons all! It sings of Gascony!

[*Every head has drooped; all eyes have grown dreamy; tears are furtively brushed away with a sleeve, the hem of a cloak.*]

CARBON (*to* CYRANO, *low*): You are making them weep!

CYRANO: With homesickness! . . . a nobler pain than hunger—not physical: mental! I am glad the seat of their suffering should have removed—that the gripe should now afflict their hearts!

CARBON: But you weaken them, making them weep!

CYRANO (*beckoning to a* DRUMMER): Never fear! The hero in their veins is quickly roused. It is enough to . . .

[*He signs to the* DRUMMER *who begins drumming.*]

ALL (*starting to their feet and snatching up their arms*): Hein? . . . What? . . . What is it?

CYRANO (*smiling*): You see? . . . The sound of the drum was enough! Farewell dreams, regrets, old homestead, love. . . . What comes with the fife with the drum may go. . . .

ONE OF THE CADETS (*looking off at the back*): Ah! ah! . . . Here comes Monsieur de Guiche!

ALL THE CADETS (*grumbling*): Hoo . . .

CYRANO (*smiling*): Flattering murmur . . .

ONE OF THE CADETS: He bores us! . . .

OTHER CADET: Showing himself off, with his broad point collar on top of his armor! . . .

OTHER CADET: As if lace were worn with steel!

FIRST CADET: Convenient, if you have a boil on your neck to cover. . . .

SECOND CADET: There is another courtier for you!

OTHER CADET: His uncle's own nephew!

CARBON: He is a Gascon, nevertheless!

FIRST CADET: Not genuine! . . . Never trust him. For a Gascon, look you, must be something of a madman—nothing is so deadly to deal with as a Gascon who is completely rational!

LE BRET: He is pale!

OTHER CADET: He is hungry, as hungry as any poor devil of us! But his corselet being freely embellished with gilt studs, his stomach ache is radiant in the sun!

CYRANO (*eagerly*): Let us not appear to suffer, either! You, your cards, your pipes, your dice . . . (*All briskly set themselves to playing with cards and dice, on the heads of drums, on stools, on cloaks spread over the ground. They light long tobacco pipes.*) . . . and I will be reading Descartes. . . .

> [*He walks to and fro, forward and backward, reading a small book which he has taken from his pocket. Tableau. Enter* DE GUICHE. *Everyone appears absorbed and satisfied.* DE GUICHE *is very pale. He goes toward* CARBON DE CASTEL-JALOUX.]

DE GUICHE (*to* CARBON): Ah, good morning. (*They look at each other attentively. Aside, with satisfaction*) He is pale as plaster.

CARBON (*same business*): His eyes are all that is left of him.

DE GUICHE (*looking at the* CADETS): So here are the wrongheaded rascals? . . . Yes, gentlemen, it is reported to me on every side that I am your scoff and derision; that the Cadets, highland nobility, Béarn clodhoppers, Périgord baronets, cannot express sufficient contempt for their colonel; call me intriguer, courtier, find it irksome to their taste that I should wear, with my cuirass, a collar of Genoese point, and never cease to air their wondering indignation that a man should be a Gascon without being a vagabond. (*Silence. The* CADETS *continue smoking and playing.*) Shall I have you punished by your Captain? . . . I do not like to.

CARBON: Did you otherwise, however . . . I am free, and punish only . . .

DE GUICHE: Ah? . . .

CARBON: My company is paid by myself, belongs to me. I obey no orders but such as relate to war.

DE GUICHE: Ah, is it so? Enough, then. I will treat your taunts with simple scorn. My fashion of deporting myself under fire is well known. You are not unaware of the manner in which yesterday, at Bapaume, I forced

back the columns of the Comte de Bucquoi; gathering my men together
to plunge forward like an avalanche, three times I charged him. . . .

CYRANO (*without lifting his nose from his book*): And your white scarf?

DE GUICHE (*surprised and self-satisfied*): You heard of that circumstance?
. . . In fact, it happened that as I was wheeling about to collect my men
for the third charge, I was caught in a stream of fugitives which bore me
onward to the edge of the enemy. I was in danger of being captured and
cut off with an arquebus, when I had the presence of mind to untie and
let slip to the ground the white scarf which proclaimed my military
grade. Thus was I enabled, undistinguished, to withdraw from among
the Spaniards, and thereupon returning with my reinspirited men, to
defeat them. Well? . . . What do you say to the incident?

> [*The* CADETS *have appeared not to be listening; at this point, however
> hands with cards and dice boxes remain suspended in the air; no pipe
> smoke is ejected; all expresses expectation.*]

CYRANO: That never would Henry the Fourth, however great the number
of his opponents, have consented to diminish his presence by the size of
his white plume.

> [*Silent joy. Cards fall, dice rattle, smoke upwreathes.*]

DE GUICHE: The trick was successful, however!

> [*As before, expectation suspends gambling and smoking.*]

CYRANO: Very likely. But one should not resign the honor of being a target.
(*Cards, dice, smoke, fall, rattle, and upwreathe, as before, in expression
of increasing glee.*) Had I been at hand when you allowed your scarf to
drop—the quality of our courage, Monsieur, shows different in this—I
would have picked it up and worn it. . . .

DE GUICHE: Ah, yes—more of your Gascon bragging! . . .

CYRANO: Bragging? . . . Lend me the scarf. I engage to mount, ahead of all,
to the assault, wearing it crosswise upon my breast!

DE GUICHE: A Gascon's offer, that too! You know that the scarf was left
in the enemy's camp, by the banks of the Scarpe, where bullets since then
have hailed . . . whence no one can bring it back!

CYRANO (*taking a white scarf from his pocket and handing it to* DE
GUICHE): Here it is.

> [*Silence. The* CADETS *smother their laughter behind cards and in dice
> boxes.* DE GUICHE *turns around, looks at them; instantly they become
> grave; one of them, with an air of unconcern, whistles the tune played
> earlier by the* FIFER.]

DE GUICHE (*taking the scarf*): I thank you. I shall be able with this shred
of white to make a signal . . . which I was hesitating to make. . . .

> [*He goes to the top of the bank and waves the scarf.*]

ALL: What now? . . . What is this?

THE SENTINEL (*at the top of the bank*): A man . . . over there . . . running off. . . .

DE GUICHE (*coming forward again*): It is a supposed Spanish spy. He is very useful to us. The information he carries to the enemy is that which I give him—so that their decisions are influenced by us.

CYRANO: He is a scoundrel!

DE GUICHE (*coolly tying on his scarf*): He is a convenience. We were saying? . . . Ah, I was about to tell you. Last night, having resolved upon a desperate stroke to obtain supplies, the Marshal secretly set out for Dourlens. The royal sutlers are encamped there. He expects to join them by way of the tilled fields; but, to provide against interference, he took with him troops in such number that, certainly, if we were now attacked, the enemy would find easy work. Half of the army is absent from the camp.

CARBON: If the Spaniards knew that, it might be serious. But they do not know.

DE GUICHE: They do. And are going to attack us.

CARBON: Ah!

DE GUICHE: My pretended spy came to warn me of their intention. He said, moreover: "I can direct the attack. At what point shall it be? I will lead them to suppose it the least strong, and they will center their efforts against it." I answered: "Very well. Go from the camp. Look down the line. Let them attack at the point I signal from."

CARBON (*to the* CADETS): Gentlemen, get ready!

[*All get up. Noise of swords and belts being buckled on.*]

DE GUICHE: They will be here in an hour.

FIRST CADET: Oh! . . . if there is a whole hour! . . .

[*All sit down again, and go on with their games.*]

DE GUICHE (*to* CARBON): The main object is to gain time. The Marshal is on his way back.

CARBON: And to gain time?

DE GUICHE: You will be so obliging as to keep them busy killing you.

CYRANO: Ah, this is your revenge!

DE GUICHE: I will not pretend that if I had been fond of you, I would have thus singled out you and yours; but, as your bravery is unquestionably beyond that of others, I am serving my King at the same time as my inclination.

CYRANO: Suffer me, Monsieur, to express my gratitude.

DE GUICHE: I know that you affect fighting one against a hundred. You will not complain of lacking opportunity.

[*He goes toward the back with* CARBON.]

CYRANO (*to the* CADETS): We shall now be able, gentlemen, to add to the Gascon escutcheon, which bears, as it is, six chevrons, or and azure, the chevron that was wanting to complete it—blood-red!

[DE GUICHE *at the back speaks low with* CARBON. *Orders are given. All is made ready to repel an attack.* CYRANO *goes toward* CHRISTIAN, *who stands motionless, with folded arms.*]

CYRANO (*laying his hand on* CHRISTIAN'S *shoulder*): Christian?

CHRISTIAN (*shaking his head*): Roxane!

CYRANO: Ah me!

CHRISTIAN: I wish I might at least put my whole heart's last blessing in a beautiful letter!

CYRANO: I mistrusted that it would come today . . . (*he takes a letter from his doublet*) . . . and I have written your farewells.

CHRISTIAN: Let me see!

CYRANO: You wish to see it? . . .

CHRISTIAN (*taking the letter*): Yes! (*He opens the letter, begins to read, stops short.*) Ah? . . .

CYRANO: What?

CHRISTIAN: That little round blister?

CYRANO (*hurriedly taking back the letter and looking at it with an artless air*): A blister?

CHRISTIAN: It is a tear!

CYRANO: It looks like one, does it not? . . . A poet, you see, is sometimes caught in his own snare—that is what constitutes the interest, the charm! . . . This letter, you must know, is very touching. In writing it I apparently made myself shed tears.

CHRISTIAN: Shed tears? . . .

CYRANO: Yes, because . . . well, to die is not terrible at all . . . but never to see her again . . . never! . . . that, you know, is horrible beyond all thinking. . . . And, things having taken the turn they have, I shall not see her. . . . (CHRISTIAN *looks at him.*) We shall not see her. . . . (*Hastily*) You will not see her. . . .

CHRISTIAN (*snatching the letter from him*): Give me the letter!

[*Noise in the distance.*]

VOICE OF A SENTINEL: *Ventrebleu*, who goes there?

[*Shots. Noise of voices, tinkling of bells.*]

CARBON: What is it?

THE SENTINEL (*on the top of the bank*): A coach!

[*All run to see.*]

THE CADETS (*noisy exclamations*): What?—In the camp?—It is driving into the camp!—It comes from the direction of the enemy! The devil!

Fire upon it!—No! the coachman is shouting something!—What does he say?—He shouts: "Service of the King!"

DE GUICHE: What? Service of the King?

[*All come down from the bank and fall into order.*]

CARBON: Hats off, all!

DE GUICHE (*at the corner*): Service of the King! Stand back, low rabble, and give it room to turn around with a handsome sweep!

[*The coach comes in at a trot. It is covered with mud and dust. The curtains are drawn. Two* LACKEYS *behind. It comes to a standstill.*]

CARBON (*shouting*): Salute!

[*Drums roll. All the* CADETS *uncover.*]

DE GUICHE: Let down the steps!

[*Two men hurry forward. The coach door opens.*]

ROXANE (*stepping from the carriage*): Good morning!

[*At the sound of a feminine voice, all the men, in the act of bowing low, straighten themselves. Consternation.*]

DE GUICHE: Service of the King! You?

ROXANE: Of the only King! . . . of Love!

CYRANO: Ah, great God!

CHRISTIAN (*rushing to her*): You? Why are you here?

ROXANE: The siege lasted too long!

CHRISTIAN: Why have you come?

ROXANE: I will tell you!

CYRANO (*who at the sound of her voice has started, then stood motionless without venturing to look her way*): God! . . . can I trust myself to look at her?

DE GUICHE: You cannot remain here.

ROXANE: But I can—I can, indeed! Will you favor me with a drum? (*She seats herself upon a drum brought forward for her.*) There! I thank you! (*She laughs.*) They fired upon my carriage. (*Proudly*) A patrol!—It does look rather as if it were made out of a pumpkin, does it not? like Cinderella's coach! and the footmen made out of rats! (*Blowing a kiss to* CHRISTIAN) How do you do? (*Looking at them all*) You do not look overjoyed! . . . Arras is a long way from Paris, do you know it? (*Catching sight of* CYRANO) Cousin, delighted!

CYRANO (*coming toward her*): But how did you . . . ?

ROXANE: How did I find the army? Dear me, cousin, that was simple: I followed straight along the line of devastation. . . . Ah, I should never have believed in such horrors had I not seen them! Gentlemen, if that is the service of your King, I like mine better!

CYRANO: But this is mad! . . . By what way did you come?

ROXANE: Way? . . . I drove through the Spaniards' camp.

FIRST CADET: Ah, what will keep a lovely woman from her way!

DE GUICHE: But how did you contrive to get through their lines?

LE BRET: That must have been difficult . . .

ROXANE: No, not very. I simply drove through them, in my coach, at a trot. If an hidalgo, with arrogant front, showed likely to stop us, I put my face at the window, wearing my sweetest smile, and, those gentlemen being—let the French not grudge my saying so—the most gallant in the world . . . I passed!

CARBON: Such a smile is a passport, certainly! . . . But you must have been not unfrequently bidden to stand and deliver where you were going?

ROXANE: Not unfrequently, you are right. Whereupon I would say, "I am going to see my lover!" At once, the fiercest-looking Spaniard of them all would gravely close my carriage door; and, with a gesture the King might emulate, motion aside the musket barrels leveled at me; and, superb at once for grace and haughtiness, bringing his spurs together, and lifting his plumed hat, bow low and say, "Pass, Señorita, pass!"

CHRISTIAN: But, Roxane . . .

ROXANE: I said, "My lover!" yes, forgive me! . . . You see, if I had said, "My husband!" they would never have let me by!

CHRISTIAN: But . . .

ROXANE: What troubles you?

DE GUICHE: You must leave at once.

ROXANE: I?

CYRANO: At once!

LE BRET: As fast as you can.

CHRISTIAN: Yes, you must.

ROXANE: But why?

CHRISTIAN (*embarrassed*): Because . . .

CYRANO (*embarrassed too*): In three-quarters of an hour . . .

DE GUICHE (*the same*): Or an hour . . .

CARBON (*the same*): You had much better . . .

LE BRET (*the same*): You might . . .

ROXANE: I shall remain. You are going to fight.

ALL: Oh, no! . . . No!

ROXANE: He is my husband! (*She throws herself in* CHRISTIAN'S *arms.*) Let me be killed with you!

CHRISTIAN: How your eyes shine!

ROXANE: I will tell you why they shine!

DE GUICHE (*desperately*): It is a post of horrible probabilities!

ROXANE (*turning toward him*): What—of horrible . . . ?

CYRANO: In proof of which he appointed us to it! . . .

ROXANE: Ah, you wish me made a widow?

DE GUICHE: I swear to you . . .

ROXANE: No! Now I have lost all regard. . . . Now I will surely not go. . . . Besides, I think it fun!

CYRANO: What? The *précieuse* contained a heroine?

ROXANE: Monsieur de Bergerac, I am a cousin of yours!

ONE OF THE CADETS: Never think but that we will take good care of you!

ROXANE (*more and more excited*): I am sure you will, my friends!

OTHER CADET: The whole camp smells of iris!

ROXANE: By good fortune I put on a hat that will look well in battle! (*Glancing toward* DE GUICHE) But perhaps it is time the Count should go—the battle might begin.

DE GUICHE: Ah, it is intolerable! . . . I am going to inspect my guns, and coming back. . . . You still have time: think better of it!

ROXANE: Never!

[*Exit* DE GUICHE.]

CHRISTIAN (*imploring*): Roxane!

ROXANE: No!

FIRST CADET: She is going to stay!

ALL (*hurrying about, pushing one another, snatching things from one another*): A comb!—Soap!—My jacket is torn, a needle!—A ribbon!— Lend me your pocket mirror!—My cuffs!—Curling irons!—A razor!

ROXANE (*to* CYRANO, *who is still pleading with her*): No! Nothing shall prevail upon me to stir from this spot!

CARBON (*after having, like the others, tightened his belt, dusted himself, brushed his hat, straightened his feather, pulled down his cuffs, approaches* ROXANE, *and ceremoniously*): It is, perhaps, proper, since you are going to stay, that I should present to you a few of the gentlemen about to have the honor of dying in your presence. . . . (ROXANE *bows, and stands waiting, with her arm through* CHRISTIAN'S.) Baron Peyrescous de Colignac!

THE CADET (*bowing*): Madame!

CARBON (*continuing to present the* CADETS): Baron de Casterac de Cahuzac—Vidame de Malgouyre Estressac Lesbas d'Escarabiot—Chevalier d'Antignac-Juzet—Baron Hillot de Blagnac-Saléchan de Castel Crabioules . . .

ROXANE: But how many names have you apiece?

BARON HILLOT: Innumerable!

CARBON (*to* ROXANE): Open your hand with the handkerchief!

ROXANE (*opens her hand; the handkerchief drops*): Why?

[*The whole company starts forward to pick it up.*]

CARBON (*instantly catching it*): My company had no flag! Now, my word, it will have the prettiest one in the army!

ROXANE (*smiling*): It is rather small!

CARBON (*fastening the handkerchief on the staff of his captain's spear*): But it is lace!

ONE OF THE CADETS (*to the others*): I could die without a murmur, having looked upon that beautiful face, if I had so much as a walnut inside me! . . .

CARBON (*who has overheard, indignant*): Shame! . . . to talk of food when an exquisite woman . . .

ROXANE: But the air of the camp is searching, and I myself am hungry: Patties, jellied meat, light wine . . . are what I should like best! Will you kindly bring me some?

[*Consternation.*]

ONE OF THE CADETS: Bring you some?

OTHER CADET: And where, great God, shall we get them?

ROXANE (*quietly*): In my coach.

ALL: What?

ROXANE: But there is much to be done, carving and boning and serving. Look more closely at my coachman, gentlemen, and you will recognize a precious individual: the sauces, if we wish, can be warmed over. . . .

THE CADETS (*springing toward the coach*): It is Ragueneau! (*Cheers.*) Oh! Oh!

ROXANE (*watching them*): Poor fellows!

CYRANO (*kissing her hand*): Kind fairy!

RAGUENEAU (*standing upon the box seat like a vendor at a public fair*): Gentlemen!

[*Enthusiasm.*]

THE CADETS: Bravo! Bravo!

RAGUENEAU: How should the Spaniards, when so much beauty passed, suspect the repast?

[*Applause.*]

CYRANO (*low to* CHRISTIAN): Hm! Hm! Christian!

RAGUENEAU: Absorbed in gallantry, no heed took they . . . (*he takes a dish from the box seat*) . . . of galantine!

[*Applause. The galantine is passed from hand to hand.*]

CYRANO (*low to* CHRISTIAN): A word with you . . .

RAGUENEAU: Venus kept their eyes fixed upon herself, while Diana slipped past with the . . . (*he brandishes a joint*) . . . game!

[*Enthusiasm. The joint is seized by twenty hands at once.*]

CYRANO (*low to* CHRISTIAN): I must speak with you.

ROXANE (*to the* CADETS *who come forward, their arms full of provisions*): Spread it all upon the ground!

[*Assisted by the two imperturbable footmen who were on the back of the coach, she arranges everything on the grass.*]

ROXANE (*to* CHRISTIAN, *whom* CYRANO *is trying to draw aside*): Make yourself useful, sir!

[CHRISTIAN *comes and helps her.* CYRANO *gives evidence of uneasiness.*]

RAGUENEAU: A truffled peacock!

FIRST CADET (*radiant, comes forward cutting off a large slice of ham*): Praise the pigs, we shall not go to our last fight with nothing in our b . . . (*correcting himself at sight of* ROXANE) . . . hm . . . stomachs!

RAGUENEAU (*flinging the carriage cushions*): The cushions are stuffed with snipe!

[*Tumult. The cushions are ripped open. Laughter. Joy.*]

RAGUENEAU (*flinging bottles of red wine*): Molten ruby! (*Bottles of white wine.*) Fluid topaz!

ROXANE (*throwing a folded tablecloth to* CYRANO): Unfold the cloth: Hey! . . . be nimble!

RAGUENEAU (*waving one of the coach lanterns*): Each lantern is a little larder!

CYRANO (*low to* CHRISTIAN, *while together they spread the cloth*): I must speak with you before you speak with her. . . .

RAGUENEAU: The handle of my whip, behold, is a sausage!

ROXANE (*pouring wine, dispensing it*): Since we are the ones to be killed, *morbleu,* we will not fret ourselves about the rest of the army! Everything for the Gascons! . . . And if De Guiche comes, nobody must invite him! (*Going from one to the other*) Gently! You have time. . . . You must not eat so fast! There, drink. What are you crying about?

FIRST CADET: It is too good!

ROXANE: Hush! White wine or red?—Bread for Monsieur de Carbon!— A knife!—Pass your plate!—You prefer crust?—A little more?—Let me help you.—Champagne?—A wing? . . .

CYRANO (*following* ROXANE, *his hands full of dishes, helping her*): I adore her!

ROXANE (*going to* CHRISTIAN): What will you take?

CHRISTIAN: Nothing!

ROXANE: Oh, but you must take something! This biscuit—in a little Muscatel—just a little?

CHRISTIAN (*trying to keep her from going*): Tell me what made you come?

ROXANE: I owe myself to those poor fellows. . . . Be patient. . . . By and by . . .

LE BRET (*who had gone toward the back to pass a loaf of bread on the end of a pike to the* SENTINEL *upon the earthwork*): De Guiche!

CYRANO: Presto! Vanish basket, flagon, platter, and pan! Hurry! Let us look as if nothing were! (*To* RAGUENEAU) Take a flying leap onto your box! . . . Is everything hidden?

[*In a wink, all the eatables have been pushed into the tents, or hidden under clothes, cloaks, hats. Enter* DE GUICHE, *hurriedly; he stops short, sniffing the air. Silence.*]

DE GUICHE: What a good smell!

ONE OF THE CADETS (*singing, with effect of mental abstraction*): To lo lo lo. . . .

DE GUICHE (*stopping and looking at him closely*): What is the matter with you—you, there? You are red as a crab.

THE CADET: I? Nothing. . . . It is just my blood. . . . We are going to fight: it tells . . .

OTHER CADET: Poom . . . poom . . . poom. . . .

DE GUICHE (*turning*): What is this?

THE CADET (*slightly intoxicated*): Nothing. . . . A song . . . just a little song.

DE GUICHE: You look in good spirits, my boy!

THE CADET: Danger affects me that way!

DE GUICHE (*calling* CARBON DE CASTEL-JALOUX *to give an order*): Captain, I . . . (*He stops at sight of his face.*) Peste! You look in good spirits, too.

CARBON (*flushed, holding a bottle behind him; with an evasive gesture*): Oh! . . .

DE GUICHE: I had a cannon left over, which I have ordered them to place (*he points in the wing*) there, in that corner, and which your men can use, if necessary. . . .

ONE OF THE CADETS (*swaying from one foot to the other*): Charming attention!

OTHER CADET (*smiling sugarily*): Our thanks for your gracious thoughtfulness!

DE GUICHE: Have they gone mad? (*Drily*) As you are not accustomed to handling a cannon, look out for its kicking. . . .

FIRST CADET: Ah, pfft! . . .

DE GUICHE (*going toward him, furious*): But . . .

THE CADET: A cannon knows better than to kick a Gascon!

DE GUICHE (*seizing him by the arm and shaking him*): You are all tipsy . . . on what?

THE CADET (*magnificently*): The smell of powder!

DE GUICHE (*shrugs his shoulders, pushes aside the* CADET, *and goes rapidly toward* ROXANE): Quick, Madame! what have you condescended to decide?

ROXANE: I remain.

DE GUICHE: Retire, I beseech you!

ROXANE: No.

DE GUICHE: If you are determined, then. . . . Let me have a musket!

CARBON: What do you mean?

DE GUICHE: I, too, will remain.

CYRANO: At last, Monsieur, an instance of pure and simple bravery!

FIRST CADET: Might you be a Gascon, lace collar notwithstanding?

DE GUICHE: I do not leave a woman in danger.

SECOND CADET (*to* FIRST CADET): Look here! I think he might be given something to eat!

[*All the food reappears, as if by magic.*]

DE GUICHE (*his eyes brightening*): Provisions?

THIRD CADET: Under every waistcoat!

DE GUICHE (*mastering himself haughtily*): Do you imagine that I will eat your leavings?

CYRANO (*bowing*): You are improving!

DE GUICHE (*proudly, falling at the last of the sentence into a slightly Gascon accent*): I will fight before I eat!

FIRST CADET (*exultant*): Fight! Eat! . . . He spoke with an accent!

DE GUICHE (*laughing*): I did?

THE CADET: He is one of us!

[*All fall to dancing.*]

CARBON (*who a moment before disappeared behind the earthworks, reappearing at the top*): I have placed my pikemen. They are a determined troop. . . .

[*He points at a line of pikes projecting above the bank.*]

DE GUICHE (*to* ROXANE, *bowing*): Will you accept my hand and pass them in review?

[*She takes his hand; they go toward the bank. Everyone uncovers and follows.*]

CHRISTIAN (*going to* CYRANO, *quickly*): Speak! Be quick!

[*As* ROXANE *appears at the top of the bank, the pikes disappear, lowered in a salute, and a cheer goes up;* ROXANE *bows.*]

PIKEMEN (*outside*): Vivat!

CHRISTIAN: What did you want to tell me?

CYRANO: In case Roxane . . .

CHRISTIAN: Well?

CYRANO: Should speak to you of the letters . . .

CHRISTIAN: Yes, the letters. I know!

CYRANO: Do not commit the blunder of appearing surprised . . .

CHRISTIAN: At what?

CYRANO: I must tell you! . . . It is quite simple, and merely comes into my mind today because I see her. You have . . .

CHRISTIAN: Hurry!

CYRANO: You . . . you have written to her oftener than you suppose. . . .

CHRISTIAN: Oh, have I?

CYRANO: Yes. It was my business, you see. I had undertaken to interpret your passion, and sometimes I wrote without having told you I should write.

CHRISTIAN: Ah?

CYRANO: It is very simple.

CHRISTIAN: But how did you succeed, since we have been so closely surrounded, in . . . ?

CYRANO: Oh, before daybreak I could cross the lines. . . .

CHRISTIAN (*folding his arms*): Ah, that is very simple, too? . . . And how many times a week have I been writing? Twice ? Three times? Four? . . .

CYRANO: More.

CHRISTIAN: Every day?

CYRANO: Yes, every day . . . twice.

CHRISTIAN (*violently*): And you cared so much about it that you were willing to brave death. . . .

CYRANO (*seeing* ROXANE *who returns*): Be still. . . . Not before her!

[*He goes quickly into his tent.* CADETS *come and go at the back.* CARBON *and* DE GUICHE *give orders.*]

ROXANE (*running to* CHRISTIAN): And now, Christian . . .

CHRISTIAN (*taking her hands*): And now, you shall tell me why, over these fearful roads, through these ranks of rough soldiery, you risked your dear self to join me?

ROXANE: Because of the letters!

CHRISTIAN: The . . . ? What did you say?

ROXANE: It is through your fault that I have been exposed to such and so many dangers. It is your letters that have gone to my head! Ah, think how many you have written me in a month, each one more beautiful . . .

CHRISTIAN: What? . . . Because of a few little love letters . . .

ROXANE: Say nothing! You cannot understand! Listen: The truth is that I took to idolizing you one evening, when, below my window, in a voice I did not know before, your soul began to reveal itself. . . . Think then what the effect should be of your letters, which have been like your voice heard constantly for one month, your voice of that evening, so ten-

der, caressing. . . . You must bear it as you can, I have come to you!
Prudent Penelope would not have stayed at home with her eternal tapes-
try, if Ulysses, her lord, had written as you write . . . but, impulsive as
Helen, would have tossed aside her yarns and flown to join him!

CHRISTIAN: But . . .

ROXANE: I read them, I reread them, in reading I grew faint . . . I became
your own indeed! Each fluttering leaf was like a petal of your soul wafted
to me. . . . In every word of those letters, love is felt as a flame would be
felt—love, compelling, sincere, profound. . . .

CHRISTIAN: Ah, sincere, profound? . . . You say that it can be felt, Roxane?

ROXANE: He asks me!

CHRISTIAN: And so you came?

ROXANE: I came—oh Christian, my own, my master! If I were to kneel at
your feet you would lift me, I know. It is my soul, therefore, which
kneels, and never can you lift it from that posture! . . . I came to implore
your pardon—as it is fitting, for we are both perhaps about to die!—your
pardon for having done you the wrong, at first, in my shallowness, of
loving you . . . for mere looking!

CHRISTIAN (*in alarm*): Ah, Roxane! . . .

ROXANE: Later, dear one, grown less shallow—similar to a bird which
flutters before it can fly—your gallant exterior appealing to me still, but
your soul appealing equally, I loved you for both! . . .

CHRISTIAN: And now?

ROXANE: Now at last yourself are vanquished by yourself: I love you for
your soul alone. . . .

CHRISTIAN (*drawing away*): Ah, Roxane!

ROXANE: Rejoice! For to be loved for that wherewith we are clothed so
fleetingly must put a noble heart to torture. . . . Your dear thought at
last casts your dear face in shadow: the harmonious lineaments whereby
at first you pleased me, I do not see them, now my eyes are open!

CHRISTIAN: Oh!

ROXANE: You question your own triumph?

CHRISTIAN (*sorrowfully*): Roxane!

ROXANE: I understand, you cannot conceive of such a love in me?

CHRISTIAN: I do not wish to be loved like that! I wish to be loved quite
simply . . .

ROXANE: . . . for that which other women till now have loved in you? Ah,
let yourself be loved in a better way.

CHRISTIAN: No . . . I was happier before! . . .

ROXANE: Ah, you do not understand! It is now that I love you most, that
I truly love you. It is that which makes you, you—can you not grasp

it?—that I worship. . . . And did you no longer walk our earth like a young martial Apollo . . .

CHRISTIAN: Say no more!

ROXANE: Still would I love you! . . . Yes, though a blight should have fallen upon your face and form . . .

CHRISTIAN: Do not say it!

ROXANE: But I do say it—I do!

CHRISTIAN: What? If I were ugly, distinctly, offensively?

ROXANE: If you were ugly, dear, I swear it!

CHRISTIAN: God!

ROXANE: And you are glad, profoundly glad?

CHRISTIAN (*in a smothered voice*): Yes . . .

ROXANE: What is it?

CHRISTIAN (*pushing her gently away*): Nothing. I have a word or two to say to someone . . . your leave, for a second . . .

ROXANE: But . . .

CHRISTIAN (*pointing at a group of* CADETS *at the back*): In my selfish love, I have kept you from those poor brothers. . . . Go, smile on them a little, before they die, dear . . . go!

ROXANE (*moved*): Dear Christian!

[*She goes toward the* GASCONS *at the back; they respectfully gather around her.*]

CHRISTIAN (*calling toward* CYRANO's *tent*): Cyrano!

CYRANO (*appears, armed for battle*): What is it? . . . How pale you are!

CHRISTIAN: She does not love me anymore!

CYRANO: What do you mean?

CHRISTIAN: She loves you.

CYRANO: No!

CHRISTIAN: She only loves my soul!

CYRANO: No!

CHRISTIAN: Yes! Therefore it is you she loves . . . and you love her. . . .

CYRANO: I . . .

CHRISTIAN: I know it!

CYRANO: It is true.

CHRISTIAN: To madness!

CYRANO: More.

CHRISTIAN: Tell her then.

CYRANO: No!

CHRISTIAN: Why not?

CYRANO: Look at me!

CHRISTIAN: She would love me grown ugly.

CYRANO: She told you so?

CHRISTIAN: With the utmost frankness!

CYRANO: Ah! I am glad she should have told you that! But, believe me, believe me, place no faith in such a mad avowal! Dear God, I am glad such a thought should have come to her, and that she should have spoken it—but believe me, do not take her at her word. Never cease to be the handsome fellow you are. . . . She would not forgive me!

CHRISTIAN: That is what I wish to discover.

CYRANO: No! no!

CHRISTIAN: Let her choose between us! You shall tell her everything.

CYRANO: No . . . No . . . I refuse the ordeal!

CHRISTIAN: Shall I stand in the way of your happiness because my outside is not so much amiss?

CYRANO: And I? Shall I destroy yours, because thanks to the hazard that sets us upon earth, I have the gift of expressing . . . what you perhaps feel?

CHRISTIAN: You shall tell her everything!

CYRANO: He persists in tempting me. . . . It is a mistake . . . and cruel!

CHRISTIAN: I am weary of carrying about, in my own self, a rival!

CYRANO: Christian!

CHRISTIAN: Our marriage . . . contracted without witnesses . . . can be annulled . . . if we survive!

CYRANO: He persists! . . .

CHRISTIAN: Yes. I will be loved for my sole self, or not at all! . . . I am going to see what they are about. Look! I will walk to the end of the line and back. . . . Tell her, and let her pronounce between us.

CYRANO: She will pronounce for you.

CHRISTIAN: I can but hope she will! (*Calling*) Roxane!

CYRANO: No! No!

ROXANE (*coming forward*): What is it?

CHRISTIAN: Cyrano has something to tell you . . . something important!

      [ROXANE *goes hurriedly to* CYRANO. *Exit* CHRISTIAN.]

ROXANE: Something important?

CYRANO (*distracted*): He is gone! . . . (*To* ROXANE) Nothing whatever! He attaches—but you must know him of old!—he attaches importance to trifles. . . .

ROXANE (*quickly*): He did not believe what I told him a moment ago? . . . I saw that he did not believe . . .

CYRANO (*taking her hand*): But did you tell him all the truth?

ROXANE: Yes. Yes. I should love him even . . .

      [*She hesitates a second.*]

CYRANO (*smiling sadly*): You do not like to say it before me?

ROXANE: But . . .

CYRANO: I shall not mind! . . . Even if he were ugly?

ROXANE: Yes . . . ugly. (*Musket shots outside.*) They are firing!

CYRANO (*ardently*): Dreadfully ugly?

ROXANE: Dreadfully.

CYRANO: Disfigured?

ROXANE: Disfigured!

CYRANO: Grotesque?

ROXANE: Nothing could make him grotesque . . . to me.

CYRANO: You would love him still?

ROXANE: I believe that I should love him more . . . if that were possible!

CYRANO (*losing his head, aside*): My God, perhaps she means it . . . perhaps it is true . . . and that way is happiness! (*To* ROXANE) I . . . Roxane . . . listen!

LE BRET (*comes in hurriedly; calls softly*): Cyrano!

CYRANO (*turning*): *Hein?*

LE BRET: Hush!

[*He whispers a few words to* CYRANO.]

CYRANO (*letting* ROXANE'S *hand drop, with a cry*): Ah! . . .

ROXANE: What ails you?

CYRANO (*to himself, in consternation*): It is finished!

[*Musket reports.*]

ROXANE: What is it? What is happening? Who is firing?

[*She goes to the back to look off.*]

CYRANO: It is finished. . . . My lips are sealed for evermore!

[CADETS *come in, attempting to conceal something they carry among them; they surround it, preventing* ROXANE'S *seeing it.*]

ROXANE: What has happened?

CYRANO (*quickly stopping her as she starts toward them*): Nothing!

ROXANE: These men? . . .

CYRANO (*drawing her away*): Pay no attention to them!

ROXANE: But what were you about to say to me before?

CYRANO: What was I about to say? . . . Oh, nothing! . . . Nothing whatever, I assure you. (*Solemnly*) I swear that Christian's spirit, that his soul, were . . . (*in terror, correcting himself*) . . . are the greatest that . . .

ROXANE: Were? . . . (*With a great cry*) Ah! . . .

[*Runs to the group of* CADETS *and thrusts them aside.*]

CYRANO: It is finished!

ROXANE (*seeing* CHRISTIAN *stretched out in his cloak*): Christian!

LE BRET (*to* CYRANO): At the enemy's first shot!

[ROXANE *throws herself on* CHRISTIAN'S *body. Musket reports. Clashing of swords. Tramping. Drums.*]

CARBON (*sword in hand*): The attack! To your muskets!

[*Followed by the* CADETS *he goes to the farther side of the earthworks.*]

ROXANE: Christian!

CARBON'S VOICE (*beyond the earthworks*): Make haste!

ROXANE: Christian!

CARBON: Fall into line!

ROXANE: Christian!

CARBON: Measure . . . match!

[RAGUENEAU *has come running in with water in a steel cap.*]

CHRISTIAN (*in a dying voice*): Roxane!

CYRANO (*quick, low in* CHRISTIAN'S *ear, while* ROXANE, *distracted, dips into the water a fragment of linen torn from her breast to bind his wound*): I have told her everything! . . . You are still the one she loves!

[CHRISTIAN *closes his eyes.*]

ROXANE: What, dear love?

CARBON: Muzzle . . . high!

ROXANE (*to* CYRANO): He is not dead? . . .

CARBON: Open charge . . . with teeth!

ROXANE: I feel his cheek grow cold against my own!

CARBON: Take aim!

ROXANE: A letter on his breast. . . . (*She opens it.*) To me!

CYRANO (*aside*): My letter!

CARBON: Fire!

[*Musket shots. Cries. Roar of battle.*]

CYRANO (*trying to free his hand which* ROXANE *clasps, kneeling*): But, Roxane, they are fighting.

ROXANE (*clinging*): No! . . . Stay with me a little! . . . He is dead. You are the only one that truly knew him. . . . (*She cries subduedly.*) Was he not an exquisite being . . . an exceptional, marvelous being? . . .

CYRANO (*standing bareheaded*): Yes, Roxane.

ROXANE: A poet without his peer . . . one verily to reverence?

CYRANO: Yes, Roxane.

ROXANE: A sublime spirit?

CYRANO: Yes, Roxane.

ROXANE: A profound heart, such as the profane could never have understood . . . a soul as noble as it was charming? . . .

CYRANO (*firmly*): Yes, Roxane.

ROXANE (*throwing herself on* CHRISTIAN'S *body*): And he is dead!

CYRANO (*aside, drawing his sword*): And I have now only to die, since, without knowing it, she mourns my death in his!

[*Trumpets in the distance.*]

DE GUICHE (*reappears on the top of the bank, bareheaded, his forehead bloody; in a thundering voice*): The signal they promised! The flourish of trumpets! . . . The French are entering the camp with supplies! . . . Stand fast a little longer!

ROXANE: Upon his letter . . . blood . . . tears!

A VOICE (*outside, shouting*): Surrender!

VOICES OF THE CADETS: No!

RAGUENEAU (*who from the top of the coach is watching the battle beyond the bank*): The conflict rages hotter! . . .

CYRANO (*to* DE GUICHE *pointing at* ROXANE): Take her away! . . . I am going to charge.

ROXANE (*kissing the letter, in a dying voice*): His blood! . . . his tears!

RAGUENEAU (*leaping from the coach and running to* ROXANE): She is fainting!

DE GUICHE (*at the top of the bank, to the* CADETS, *madly*): Stand fast!

VOICE (*outside*): Surrender!

VOICES OF THE CADETS: No!

CYRANO (*to* DE GUICHE): Your courage none will question. . . . (*Pointing to* ROXANE) Fly for the sake of saving her!

DE GUICHE (*runs to* ROXANE *and lifts her in his arms*): So be it! But we shall win the day if you can hold out a little longer. . . .

CYRANO: We can. (*To* ROXANE, *whom* DE GUICHE, *helped by* RAGUENEAU, *is carrying off insensible.*) Good-bye, Roxane!

[*Tumult. Cries.* CADETS *reappear wounded and fall upon the stage.* CYRANO *dashing forward to join the combatants is stopped on the crest of the bank by* CARBON, *covered with blood.*]

CARBON: We are losing ground . . . have got two halberd wounds. . . .

CYRANO (*yelling to the* GASCONS): Steadfast! . . . Never give them an inch! . . . Brave boys! (*To* CARBON) Fear nothing! I have various deaths to avenge: Christian's and all my hopes'! (*They come down.* CYRANO *brandishes the spear at the head of which* ROXANE'S *handkerchief is fastened.*) Float free, little cobweb flag, embroidered with her initials! (*He drives the spear staff into the earth; shouts to the* CADETS) Fall on them, boys! . . . Crush them! (*To the* FIFER) Fifer, play!

[*The* FIFER *plays. Some of the wounded get to their feet again. Some of the* CADETS, *coming down the bank, group themselves around* CYRANO *and the little flag. The coach, filled and covered with men, bristles with muskets and becomes a redoubt.*]

ONE OF THE CADETS (*appears upon the top of the bank, backing while he fights; he cries*): They are coming up the slope!

[*Falls dead.*]

CYRANO: We will welcome them!

[*Above the bank suddenly rises a formidable array of enemies. The great banners of the Imperial Army appear.*]

CYRANO: Fire!

[*General discharge.*]

CRY (*among the hostile ranks*): Fire!

[*Shots returned.* CADETS *drop on every side.*]

A SPANISH OFFICER (*taking off his hat*): What are these men, so determined all to be killed?

CYRANO (*declaiming, as he stands in the midst of flying bullets*):

> They are the Gascony Cadets
> Of Carbon de Castel-Jaloux;
> Famed fighters, liars, desperates . . .
> [*He leaps forward, followed by a handful of survivors.*]
> They are the Gascony Cadets! . . .
> [*The rest is lost in the confusion of battle.*]

CURTAIN

ACT FIVE

CYRANO'S GAZETTE

Fifteen years later, 1655. The park belonging to the convent of the Sisters of the Cross, in Paris.

Superb shade trees. At the left, the house; several doors opening onto a broad terrace with steps. In the center of the stage, huge trees standing alone in a clear oval space. At the right, first wing, a semicircular stone seat, surrounded by large box trees.

All along the back of the stage, an avenue of chestnut trees, which leads, at the right, fourth wing, to the door of a chapel seen through trees. Through the double row of trees overarching the avenue are seen lawns, other avenues, clumps of trees, the farther recesses of the park, the sky.

The chapel opens by a small side door into a colonnade, overrun by a scarlet creeper; the colonnade comes forward and is lost to sight behind the box trees at the right.

It is autumn. The leaves are turning, above the still-fresh grass. Dark patches of evergreens, box and yew. Under each tree a mat of yellow leaves. Fallen leaves litter the whole stage, crackle underfoot, lie thick on the terrace and the seats.

Between the seat at the right and the tree in the center, a large embroidery frame, in front of which a small chair. Baskets full of wools, in skeins and balls. On the frame, a piece of tapestry, partly done.

[*At the rise of the curtain, nuns come and go in the park; a few are seated on the stone seat around an older nun; leaves are falling.*]

SISTER MARTHA (*to* MOTHER MARGARET): Sister Claire, after putting on her cap, went back to the mirror, to see herself again.

MOTHER MARGARET (*to* SISTER CLAIRE): It was unbecoming, my child.

SISTER CLAIRE: But Sister Martha, today, after finishing her portion, went back to the tart for a plum. I saw her!

MOTHER MARGARET (*to* SISTER MARTHA): My child, it was ill done.

SISTER CLAIRE: I merely glanced! . . .

SISTER MARTHA: The plum was about so big! . . .

MOTHER MARGARET: This evening, when Monsieur Cyrano comes, I will tell him.

SISTER CLAIRE (*alarmed*): No! He will laugh at us!

SISTER MARTHA: He will say that nuns are very vain!

SISTER CLAIRE: And very greedy!

MOTHER MARGARET: And really very good.

SISTER CLAIRE: Mother Margaret, is it not true that he has come here every Saturday in the last ten years?

MOTHER MARGARET: Longer! Ever since his cousin brought among our linen coifs her coif of crape, the worldly symbol of her mourning, which settled like a sable bird amidst our flock of white some fourteen years ago.

SISTER MARTHA: He alone, since she took her abode in our cloister, has art to dispel her never-lessening sorrow.

ALL THE NUNS: He is so droll!—It is merry when he comes!—He teases us! —He is delightful!—We are greatly attached to him!—We are making Angelica paste to offer him!

SISTER MARTHA: He is not, however, a very good Catholic!

SISTER CLAIRE: We will convert him.

THE NUNS: We will! We will!

MOTHER MARGARET: I forbid your renewing that attempt, my children. Do not trouble him: he might not come so often!

SISTER MARTHA: But . . . God!

MOTHER MARGARET: Set your hearts at rest: God must know him of old!

SISTER MARTHA: But every Saturday, when he comes, he says to me as soon as he sees me, "Sister, I ate meat, yesterday!"

MOTHER MARGARET: Ah, that is what he says? . . . Well, when he last said it, he had eaten nothing for two days.

SISTER MARTHA: Mother!

MOTHER MARGARET: He is poor.

SISTER MARTHA: Who told you?

MOTHER MARGARET: Monsieur Le Bret.

SISTER MARTHA: Does no one offer him assistance?

MOTHER MARGARET: No, he would take offense.

[*In one of the avenues at the back appears* ROXANE, *in black, wearing a widow's coif and long mourning veil;* DE GUICHE *markedly older, magnificently dressed, walks beside her. They go very slowly.* MOTHER MARGARET *gets up.*]

MOTHER MARGARET: Come, we must go within. Madame Magdeleine is walking in the park with a visitor.

SISTER MARTHA (*low to* SISTER CLAIRE): Is not that the Marshal-Duke de Grammont?

SISTER CLAIRE (*looking*): I think it is!

SISTER MARTHA: He has not been to see her in many months!

THE NUNS: He is much engaged! . . . The Court!—The camp! . . .

SISTER CLAIRE: Cares of this world!

[*Exeunt.* DE GUICHE *and* ROXANE *come forward silently, and stop near the embroidery frame. A pause.*]

DE GUICHE: And so you live here, uselessly fair, always in mourning?

ROXANE: Always.

DE GUICHE: As faithful as of old?

ROXANE: As faithful.

DE GUICHE (*after a time*): Have you forgiven me?

ROXANE: Since I am here.

[*Another silence.*]

DE GUICHE: And he was really such a rare being?

ROXANE: To understand, one must have known him!

DE GUICHE: Ah, one must have known him! . . . Perhaps I did not know him well enough. And his last letter, still and always, against your heart?

ROXANE: I wear it on this velvet, as a more holy scapular.

DE GUICHE: Even dead, you love him?

ROXANE: It seems to me sometimes he is but half dead, that our hearts have not been severed, that his love still wraps me round, no less than ever living!

DE GUICHE (*after another silence*): Does Cyrano come here to see you?

ROXANE: Yes, often. That faithful friend fulfills for me the office of gazette. His visits are regular. He comes: when the weather is fine, his armchair is brought out under the trees. I wait for him here with my work; the hour strikes; on the last stroke, I hear—I do not even turn to see who comes!—his cane upon the steps; he takes his seat; he rallies me upon my never-ending tapestry; he tells of the events of the week, and . . . (LE BRET *appears on the steps.*) Ah, Le Bret! (LE BRET *comes down the steps.*) How does your friend?

LE BRET: Ill.

DE GUICHE: Oh!

ROXANE: He exaggerates! . . .

LE BRET: All is come to pass as I foretold: neglect! poverty! his writings ever breeding him new enemies! Fraud he attacks in every embodiment: usurpers, pious pretenders, plagiarists, asses in lions' skins . . . all! He attacks all!

ROXANE: No one, however, but stands in profound respect of his sword. They will never succeed in silencing him.

DE GUICHE (*shaking his head*): Who knows?

LE BRET: What I fear is not the aggression of man; what I fear is loneliness and want and winter creeping upon him like stealthy wolves in his miserable attic; they are the insidious foes that will have him by the throat at last! . . . Every day he tightens his belt by an eyelet; his poor great nose is pinched, and turned the sallow of old ivory; the worn black serge you see him in is the only coat he has!

DE GUICHE: Ah, there is one who did not succeed! . . . Nevertheless, do not pity him too much.

LE BRET (*with a bitter smile*): Marshal! . . .

DE GUICHE: Do not pity him too much: he signed no bonds with the world; he has lived free in his thoughts as in his actions.

LE BRET (*as above*): Duke . . .

DE GUICHE (*haughtily*): I know, yes: I have everything, he has nothing. . . . But I should like to shake hands with him. (*Bowing to* ROXANE) Good-bye.

ROXANE: I will go with you to the door.

    [DE GUICHE *bows to* LE BRET *and goes with* ROXANE *toward the ter-race steps.*]

DE GUICHE (*stopping, while she goes up the steps*): Yes, sometimes I envy him. You see, when a man has succeeded too well in life, he is not un-likely to feel—dear me! without having committed any very serious wrong!—a multitudinous disgust at himself, the sum of which does not constitute a real remorse, but an obscure uneasiness; and a ducal mantle, while it sweeps up the stairs of greatness, may trail in its furry lining a rustling of sere illusions and regrets, as, when you slowly climb toward those doors, your black gown trails the withered leaves.

ROXANE (*ironically*): Are you not unusually pensive? . . .

DE GUICHE: Ah, yes! (*As he is about to leave, abruptly*) Monsieur Le Bret! (*To* ROXANE) Will you allow me? A word. (*He goes to* LE BRET, *and lowering his voice*) It is true that no one will dare overtly to attack your friend, but many have him in particular disrelish; and someone was saying to me yesterday, at the Queen's, "It seems not unlikely that this Cyrano will meet with an accident."

LE BRET: Ah? . . .

DE GUICHE: Yes. Let him keep indoors. Let him be cautious.

LE BRET (*lifting his arms toward Heaven*): Cautious! . . . He is coming here. I will warn him. Warn him! . . . Yes, but . . .

ROXANE (*who has been standing at the head of the steps, to a* NUN *who comes toward her*): What is it?

THE NUN: Ragueneau begs to see you, Madame.

ROXANE: Let him come in. (*To* DE GUICHE *and* LE BRET) He comes to plead distress. Having determined one day to be an author, he became in turn precentor . . .

LE BRET: Bathhouse keeper . . .

ROXANE: Actor . . .

LE BRET: Beadle . . .

ROXANE: Barber . . .

LE BRET: Arch-lute teacher . . .

ROXANE: I wonder what he is now!

RAGUENEAU (*entering precipitately*): Ah, Madame! (*He sees* LE BRET.) Monsieur!

ROXANE (*smiling*): Begin telling your misfortunes to Le Bret. I am com-ing back.

RAGUENEAU: But, Madame . . .

    [ROXANE *leaves without listening, with the* DUKE. RAGUENEAU *goes to* LE BRET.]

RAGUENEAU: It is better so. Since you are here, I had rather not tell her! Less than half an hour ago, I was going to see your friend. I was not thirty feet from his door, when I saw him come out. I hurried to catch up with him. He was about to turn the corner. I started to run, when from a window below which he was passing—was it pure mischance? It may have been!—a lackey drops a block of wood . . .

LE BRET: Ah, the cowards! . . . Cyrano!

RAGUENEAU: I reach the spot and find him . . .

LE BRET: Horrible!

RAGUENEAU: Our friend, Monsieur, our poet, stretched upon the ground, with a great hole in his head!

LE BRET: He is dead?

RAGUENEAU: No, but . . . God have mercy! I carried him to his lodging. . . . Ah, his lodging! You should see that lodging of his!

LE BRET: Is he in pain?

RAGUENEAU: No, Monsieur, he is unconscious.

LE BRET: Has a doctor seen him?

RAGUENEAU: One came . . . out of good nature.

LE BRET: My poor, poor Cyrano! . . . We must not tell Roxane outright. And the doctor? . . .

RAGUENEAU: He talked . . . I hardly grasped . . . of fever . . . cerebral inflammation! Ah, if you should see him, with his head done up in cloths! . . . Let us hurry . . . No one is there to tend him . . . And he might die if he attempted to get up!

LE BRET (*dragging* RAGUENEAU *off at the right*): This way. Come, it is shorter through the chapel.

ROXANE (*appearing at the head of the steps, catching sight of* LE BRET *hurrying off through the colonnade which leads to the chapel side door*): Monsieur Le Bret! (LE BRET *and* RAGUENEAU *make their escape without answering.*) Le Bret not turning back when he is called? . . . Poor Ragueneau must be in some new trouble! (*She comes down the steps.*) How beautiful . . . how beautiful, this golden-hazy waning day of September at its wane! My sorrowful mood, which the exuberant gladness of April offends, autumn, the dreamy and subdued, lures on to smile. . . . (*She sits down at her embroidery frame. Two* NUNS *come from the house bringing a large armchair which they place under the tree.*) Ah, here comes the classic armchair in which my old friend always sits!

SISTER MARTHA: The best in the convent parlor!

ROXANE: I thank you, Sister. (*The* NUNS *withdraw.*) He will be here in a moment. (*She adjusts the embroidery frame before her.*) There! The clock is striking . . . My wools! . . . The clock has struck? . . . I wonder at this! . . . Is it possible that for the first time he is late? . . . It must be that the Sister who keeps the door—my thimble, ah, here it is!—is detaining him to exhort him to repentance. . . . (*A pause.*) She exhorts him at some length! . . . He cannot be much longer. . . . A withered leaf! (*She brushes away the dead leaf which has dropped on the embroidery.*) Surely nothing could keep—my scissors? . . . in my workbag!—could keep him from coming!

A NUN (*appearing at the head of the steps*): Monsieur de Bergerac!

ROXANE (*without turning round*): What was I saying? . . . (*She begins to embroider. CYRANO appears, exceedingly pale, his hat drawn down over his eyes. The NUN who has shown him into the garden withdraws. He comes down the steps very slowly, with evident difficulty to keep on his feet, leaning heavily on his cane. ROXANE proceeds with her sewing.*) Ah, these dull soft shades! . . . How shall I match them? (*To CYRANO, in a tone of friendly chiding*) After fourteen years, for the first time you are late!

CYRANO (*who has reached the armchair and seated himself, in a jolly voice which contrasts with his face*): Yes, it seems incredible! I am savage at it. I was detained, spite of all I could do! . . .

ROXANE: By . . . ?

CYRANO: A somewhat inopportune call.

ROXANE (*absentmindedly sewing*): Ah, yes . . . some troublesome fellow!

CYRANO: Cousin, it was a troublesome Madame.

ROXANE: You excused yourself?

CYRANO: Yes. I said, "Your pardon, but this is Saturday, on which day I am due in a certain dwelling. On no account do I ever fail. Come back in an hour!"

ROXANE (*lightly*): Well, she will have to wait some time to see you. I shall not let you go before evening.

CYRANO: Perhaps . . . I shall have to go a little earlier.

[*He closes his eyes and is silent a moment. SISTER MARTHA is seen crossing the park from the chapel to the terrace. ROXANE sees her and beckons to her by a slight motion of her head.*]

ROXANE (*to CYRANO*): Are you not going to tease Sister Martha today?

CYRANO (*quickly, opening his eyes*): I am indeed! (*In a comically gruff voice*) Sister Martha, come nearer! (*The NUN demurely comes toward him.*) Ha! ha! ha! Beautiful eyes, ever studying the ground!

SISTER MARTHA (*lifting her eyes and smiling*): But . . . (*She sees his face and makes a gesture of surprise.*) Oh!

CYRANO (*low, pointing at ROXANE*): Hush! . . . It is nothing! (*In a swaggering voice, aloud*) Yesterday, I ate meat!

SISTER MARTHA: I am sure you did! (*Aside*) That is why he is so pale!
   (*Quickly, low*) Come to the refectory presently. I shall have ready for
   you there a good bowl of broth. . . . You will come!

CYRANO: Yes, yes, yes.

SISTER MARTHA: Ah, you are more reasonable today!

ROXANE (*hearing them whisper*): She is trying to convert you?

SISTER MARTHA: Indeed I am not!

CYRANO: It is true, you, usually almost discursive in the holy cause, are
   reading me no sermon! You amaze me! (*With comical fury*) I will
   amaze you, too! Listen, you are authorized . . . (*with the air of casting
   about in his mind, and finding the jest he wants*) . . . Ah, now I shall
   amaze you! to . . . pray for me, this evening . . . in the chapel.

ROXANE: Oh! oh!

CYRANO (*laughing*): Sister Martha . . . lost in amazement!

SISTER MARTHA (*gentle*): I did not wait for your authorization.

                    [*She goes in.*]

CYRANO (*turning to* ROXANE, *who is bending over her embroidery*): The
   devil, tapestry . . . the devil, if I hope to live to see the end of you!

ROXANE: I was waiting for that jest.

            [*A slight gust of wind makes the leaves fall.*]

CYRANO: The leaves!

ROXANE (*looking up from her work and gazing off toward the avenues*):
   They are the russet gold of a Venetian beauty's hair. . . . Watch them
   fall!

CYRANO: How consummately they do it! In that brief fluttering from bough
   to ground, how they contrive still to put on beauty! And though fore-
   doomed to molder upon the earth that draws them, they wish their fall
   invested with the grace of a free bird's flight!

ROXANE: Serious, you?

CYRANO (*remembering himself*): Not at all, Roxane!

ROXANE: Come, never mind the falling leaves! Tell me the news, instead.
   . . . Where is my budget?[9]

CYRANO: Here it is!

ROXANE: Ah!

CYRANO (*growing paler and paler, and struggling with pain*): Saturday, the
   nineteenth: The King having filled his dish eight times with Cette preserves, and emptied it, was taken with a fever; his distemper, for high
   treason, was condemned to be let blood, and now the royal pulse is rid
   of febriculosity! On Sunday: at the Queen's great ball were burned

---

[9] *budget*: here, a small leather bag, which Roxane has about her neck.

seven hundred and sixty-three wax candles; our troops, it is said, defeated Austrian John; four sorcerers were hanged; Madame Athis's little dog had a distressing turn, the case called for a . . .

ROXANE: Monsieur de Bergerac, leave out the little dog!

CYRANO: Monday . . . nothing, or next to it: Lygdamire took a fresh lover.

ROXANE: Oh!

CYRANO (*over whose face is coming a change more and more marked*): Tuesday: the whole Court assembled at Fontainebleau. Wednesday: the fair Monglat said to Count Fiesco "No!" Thursday: Mancini, Queen of France . . . or little less. Twenty-fifth: the fair Monglat said to Count Fiesco "Yes!" And Saturday, the twenty-sixth . . .

  [*He closes his eyes. His head drops on his breast. Silence.*]

ROXANE (*surprised at hearing nothing further, turns, looks at him and starts to her feet in alarm*): Has he fainted? (*She runs to him, calling*) Cyrano!

CYRANO (*opening his eyes, in a faint voice*): What is it? . . . What is the matter? (*He sees* ROXANE *bending over him, hurriedly readjusts his hat, pulling it more closely over his head, and shrinks back in his armchair in terror.*) No! no! I assure you, it is nothing! . . . Do not mind me!

ROXANE: But surely . . .

CYRANO: It is merely the wound I received at Arras. . . . Sometimes . . . you know . . . even now . . .

ROXANE: Poor friend!

CYRANO: But it is nothing . . . it will pass. . . . (*He smiles with effort.*) It has passed.

ROXANE: Each one of us has his wound. I too have mine. It is here, never to heal, that ancient wound . . . (*placing her hand on her breast*) . . . it is here beneath the yellowing letter on which are still faintly visible teardrops and drops of blood!

  [*The light is beginning to grow less.*]

CYRANO: His letter? . . . Did you not once say that someday . . . you might show it to me?

ROXANE: Ah! . . . Do you wish? . . . His letter?

CYRANO: Yes . . . today . . . I wish to . . .

ROXANE (*handing him the little bag from her neck*): Here!

CYRANO: I may open it?

ROXANE: Open it . . . read!

  [*She goes back to her embroidery frame, folds it up, orders her wools.*]

CYRANO: "Good-bye, Roxane! I am going to die!"

ROXANE (*stopping in astonishment*): You are reading it aloud?

CYRANO (*reading*): "It is fated to come this evening, beloved, I believe!

My soul is heavy, oppressed with love it had not time to utter . . . and now Time is at end! Never again, never again shall my worshiping eyes . . ."

ROXANE: How strangely you read his letter!

CYRANO (*continuing*): " . . . whose passionate revel it was, kiss in its fleeting grace your every gesture. One, usual to you, of tucking back a little curl, comes to my mind . . . and I cannot refrain from crying out . . ."

ROXANE: How strangely you read his letter! . . .

[*The darkness gradually increases.*]

CYRANO: ". . . and I cry out: Good-bye!"

ROXANE: You read it . . .

CYRANO: ". . . my dearest, my darling . . . my treasure . . ."

ROXANE: . . . in a voice . . .

CYRANO: ". . . my love! . . ."

ROXANE: . . . in a voice . . . a voice which I am not hearing for the first time!

[ROXANE *comes quietly nearer to him, without his seeing it; she steps behind his armchair, bends noiselessly over his shoulder, looks at the letter. The darkness deepens.*]

CYRANO: ". . . My heart never desisted for a second from your side . . . and I am and shall be, in the world that has no end, the one who loved you without measure, the one . . ."

ROXANE (*laying her hand on his shoulder*): How can you go on reading? It is dark. (CYRANO *starts, and turns around; sees her close to him, makes a gesture of dismay and hangs his head. Then, in the darkness which has completely closed round them, she says slowly, clasping her hands*) And he, for fourteen years, has played the part of the comical old friend who came to cheer me!

CYRANO: Roxane!

ROXANE: So it was you.

CYRANO: No, no, Roxane!

ROXANE: I ought to have divined it, if only by the way in which he speaks my name!

CYRANO: No, it was not I!

ROXANE: So it was you!

CYRANO: I swear to you . . .

ROXANE: Ah, I detect at last the whole generous imposture. The letters . . . were yours!

CYRANO: No!

ROXANE: The tender fancy, the dear folly . . . yours!

CYRANO: No!

ROXANE: The voice in the night, was yours!

CYRANO: I swear to you that it was not!

ROXANE: The soul . . . was yours!

CYRANO: I did not love you, no!

ROXANE: And you loved me!

CYRANO: Not I . . . it was the other!

ROXANE: You loved me!

CYRANO: No!

ROXANE: Already your denial comes more faintly!

CYRANO: No, no, my darling love, I did not love you!

ROXANE: Ah, how many things within the hour have died . . . how many have been born! Why, why have you been silent these long years, when on this letter, in which he had no part, the tears were yours?

CYRANO (*handing her the letter*): Because . . . the blood was his.

ROXANE: Then why let the sublime bond of this silence be loosed today?

CYRANO: Why?

[LE BRET *and* RAGUENEAU *enter running.*]

LE BRET: Madness! Monstrous madness! . . . Ah, I was sure of it! There he is!

CYRANO (*smiling and straightening himself*): Tiens! Where else?

LE BRET: Madame, he is likely to have got his death by getting out of bed!

ROXANE: Merciful God! A moment ago, then . . . that faintness . . . that . . . ?

CYRANO: It is true. I had not finished telling you the news. And on Saturday, the twenty-sixth, an hour after sundown, Monsieur de Bergerac died of murder done upon him.

[*He takes off his hat; his head is seen wrapped in bandages.*]

ROXANE: What is he saying? . . . Cyrano? . . . Those bandages about his head? . . . Ah, what have they done to you? . . . Why? . . .

CYRANO: "Happy who falls, cut off by a hero, with an honest sword through his heart!" I am quoting from myself! . . . Fate will have his laugh at us! . . . Here am I killed, in a trap, from behind, by a lackey, with a log! Nothing could be completer! In my whole life I shall have not had anything I wanted . . . not even a decent death!

RAGUENEAU: Ah, Monsieur! . . .

CYRANO: Ragueneau, do not sob like that! (*Holding out his hand to him*) And what is the news with you, these latter days, fellow poet?

RAGUENEAU (*through his tears*): I am candlesnuffer at Molière's theater.

CYRANO: Molière!

RAGUENEAU: But I intend to leave no later than tomorrow. Yes, I am indignant! Yesterday, they were giving *Scapin,* and I saw that he has appropriated a scene of yours.

LE BRET: A whole scene?

RAGUENEAU: Yes, Monsieur. The one in which occurs the famous "What the devil was he doing in . . ."

LE BRET: Molière has taken that from you!

CYRANO: Hush! hush! He did well to take it! (*To* RAGUENEAU) The scene was very effective, was it not?

RAGUENEAU: Ah, Monsieur, the public laughed . . . laughed!

CYRANO: Yes, to the end, I shall have been the one who prompted . . . and was forgotten! (*To* ROXANE) Do you remember that evening on which Christian spoke to you from below the balcony? There was the epitome of my life: while I have stood below in darkness, others have climbed to gather the kiss and glory! It is well done, and on the brink of my grave I approve it: Molière has genius . . . Christian was a fine fellow! (*At this moment, the chapel bell having rung, the* NUNS *are seen passing at the back, along the avenue, on their way to service.*) Let them hasten to their prayers . . . the bell is summoning them. . . .

ROXANE (*rising and calling*): Sister! Sister!

CYRANO (*holding her back*): No! No! do not leave me to fetch anybody! When you came back I might not be here to rejoice. . . . (*The* NUNS *have gone into the chapel; the organ is heard.*) I longed for a little music . . . it comes in time!

ROXANE: I love you . . . you shall live!

CYRANO: No! for it is only in the fairy tale that the shy and awkward prince when he hears the beloved say "I love you!" feels his ungainliness melt and drop from him in the sunshine of those words! . . . But you would always know full well, dear Heart, that there had taken place in your poor slave no beautifying change!

ROXANE: I have hurt you . . . I have wrecked your life, I! . . . I!

CYRANO: You? . . . The reverse! Woman's sweetness I had never known. My mother . . . thought me unflattering. I had no sister. Later, I shunned Love's crossroad in fear of mocking eyes. To you I owe having had, at least, among the gentle and fair, a friend. Thanks to you there has passed across my life the rustle of a woman's gown.

LE BRET (*calling his attention to the moonlight peering through the branches*): Your other friend, among the gentle and fair, is there . . . she comes to see you!

CYRANO (*smiling to the moon*): I see her!

ROXANE: I never loved but one . . . and twice I lose him!

CYRANO: Le Bret, I shall ascend into the opalescent moon, without need this time of a flying machine!

ROXANE: What are you saying?

CYRANO: Yes, it is there, you may be sure, I shall be sent for my Paradise.

More than one soul of those I have loved must be apportioned there. . . .
There I shall find Socrates and Galileo!

LE BRET (*in revolt*): No! No! It is too senseless, too cruel, too unfair! So
true a poet! So great a heart! To die . . . like this! To die! . . .

CYRANO: As ever . . . Le Bret is grumbling!

LE BRET (*bursting into tears*): My friend! My friend!

CYRANO (*lifting himself, his eyes wild*): They are the Gascony Cadets! . . .
Man in the gross . . . Eh, yes! . . . the weakness of the weakest point . . .

LE BRET: Learned . . . even in his delirium! . . .

CYRANO: Copernicus said . . .

ROXANE: Oh!

CYRANO: But what the devil was he doing . . . and what the devil was he
doing in that galley?

> Philosopher and physicist,
> Musician, rhymester, duelist,
> Explorer of the upper blue,
> Retorter apt with point and point,
> Lover as well—not for his peace!
> Here lies Hercule-Savinien
> De Cyrano de Bergerac,
> Who was everything . . . but of account!

But, your pardons, I must go . . . I wish to keep no one waiting. . . . See,
a moonbeam, come to take me home! (*He has dropped in his chair;*
ROXANE's *weeping calls him back to reality; he looks at her and gently
strokes her mourning veil.*) I do not wish . . . indeed, I do not wish . . .
that you should sorrow less for Christian, the comely and the kind! Only
I wish that when the everlasting cold shall have seized upon my fibers,
this funereal veil should have a twofold meaning, and the mourning you
wear for him be worn for me too . . . a little!

ROXANE: I promise. . . .

CYRANO (*seized with a great shivering, starts to his feet*): Not there! No!
Not in an elbow chair! (*All draw nearer to help him.*) Let no one stay
me! No one. (*He goes and stands against the tree.*) Nothing but this
tree! (*Silence.*) She comes. Mors, the indiscriminate Madame! . . . Already I am booted with marble . . . gauntleted with lead! (*He stiffens
himself.*) Ah, since she is on her way, I will await her standing . . .
(*drawing his sword*) . . . sword in hand!

LE BRET: Cyrano!

ROXANE (*swooning*): Cyrano!

> [*All start back, terrified.*]

CYRANO: I believe she is looking at me . . . that she dares to look at my nose, the bony baggage who has none! (*He raises his sword.*) What are you saying? That it is no use? . . . I know it! But one does not fight because there is hope of winning! No! . . . no! . . . it is much finer to fight when it is no use! . . . What are all those? You are a thousand strong? . . . Ah, I know you now . . . all my ancient enemies! . . . Hypocrisy? . . . (*He beats with his sword, in the vacancy.*) Take this! and this! Ha! Ha! Compromises? . . . and Prejudices? and dastardly Expedients? (*He strikes.*) That I should come to terms, I? . . . Never! Never! . . . Ah, you are there, too, you bloated and pompous Silliness! I know full well that you will lay me low at last. . . . No matter: whilst I have breath, I will fight you, I will fight you, I will fight you! (*He waves his sword in great sweeping circles, and stops, panting.*) Yes, you have wrested from me everything, laurel as well as rose. . . . Work your wills! . . . Spite of your worst, something will still be left me to take whither I go . . . and to-night when I enter God's house, in saluting, broadly will I sweep the azure threshold with what despite of all I carry forth unblemished and unbent . . . (*starting forward, with lifted sword*) . . . and that is . . .

[*The sword falls from his hands, he staggers, drops in the arms of* LE BRET *and* RAGUENEAU.]

ROXANE (*bending over him and kissing his forehead*): That is? . . .

CYRANO (*opens his eyes again, recognizes her and says with a smile*): . . . my white plume!

CURTAIN

HEROISM

The Iliad

HOMER

GODS, GODDESSES, GREEKS, AND TROJANS

Gods and Goddesses:

JOVE (ZEUS), *son of Saturn, king of the gods, ruler of the sky*

NEPTUNE (POSEIDON), *son of Saturn, king of the sea; on the side of the Greeks*

PLUTO (HADES), *son of Saturn, ruler of the underworld of the dead*

JUNO (HERA), *daughter of Saturn, wife of Jove; on the side of the Greeks*

MINERVA (ATHENA), *daughter of Jove; on the side of the Greeks*

APOLLO (PHŒBUS APOLLO), *son of Jove; on the side of the Trojans*

VENUS (APHRODITE), *daughter of Jove; on the side of the Trojans*

MARS (ARES), *son of Jove; on the side of the Trojans*

VULCAN (HEPHÆSTUS), *son of Jove and Juno; on the side of the Greeks*

MERCURY (HERMES), *son of Jove; on the side of the Trojans*

IRIS, *messenger of the gods*

THETIS, *a sea-goddess, wife of Peleus and mother of Achilles*

Greeks (also called Achæans, Danaans, Argives):

AGAMEMNON, *son of Atreus; King of Argos and Mycenæ*

MENELAUS, *son of Atreus; King of Sparta and Lacedæmon; husband of Helen*

ACHILLES, *son of Peleus and Thetis*

NESTOR, *son of Neleus*

ULYSSES, *son of Laertes*

AJAX, *son of Telamon;* AJAX THE LESSER, *son of Oileus*

535

DIOMED, *son of Tydeus*
PATROCLUS, *son of Menœtius*
PHŒNIX, *teacher of Achilles*
CALCHAS, *a seer*
MACHAON, *a surgeon*
TALTHYBIUS *and* EURYBATES, *heralds*

Trojans (*also called Dardanians*):

PRIAM, *son of Laomedon, King of Troy*
HECTOR, *son of Priam*
PARIS, *son of Priam* (*also called* ALEXANDRUS)
HELENUS, *son of Priam; a seer*
DEIPHOBUS, LYCAON, *and* POLYDORUS, *sons of Priam*
SARPEDON, *son of Jove; chief of the Lycians*
GLAUCUS, *a Lycian*
ÆNEAS, *son of Anchises and Venus; chief of the Dardanians*
PANDARUS, *a bowman*
POLYDAMAS, *adviser to Hector*
HECUBA, *wife of Priam; Queen of Troy*
HELEN, *wife of Menelaus; brought by Paris to Troy*
ANDROMACHE, *daughter of Eëtion; wife of Hector*

BOOK I

SING, O goddess, the anger of Achilles son of Peleus, that brought countless ills upon the Achæans. Many a brave soul did it send hurrying down to Hades, and many a hero did it yield a prey to dogs and vultures, for so were the counsels of Jove fulfilled from the day on which the son of Atreus,[1] king of men, and great Achilles, first fell out with one another.

And which of the gods was it that set them on to quarrel? It was the son of Jove and Leto;[2] for he was angry with the king and sent a pestilence upon the host to plague the people, because the son of Atreus had dishonored Chryses his priest. Now Chryses had come to the ships of the Achæans to free his daughter, and had brought with him a great ransom: moreover he bore in his hand the scepter of Apollo wreathed with a suppliant's wreath, and he besought the Achæans, but most of all the two sons of Atreus, who were their chiefs.

"Sons of Atreus," he cried, "and all other Achæans, may the gods who dwell in Olympus grant you to sack the city of Priam, and to reach your homes in safety; but free my daughter, and accept a ransom for her, in reverence to Apollo, son of Jove."

On this the rest of the Achæans with one voice were for respecting the priest and taking the ransom that he offered; but not so Agamemnon, who spoke fiercely to him and sent him roughly away. "Old man," said he, "let me not find you tarrying about our ships, nor yet coming hereafter. Your

[1] *son of Atreus*: Agamemnon, commander-in-chief of the Greek forces.
[2] *son . . . Leto*: Apollo.

scepter of the god and your wreath shall profit you nothing. I will not free her. She shall grow old in my house at Argos far from her own home, busying herself with her loom and visiting my couch; so go, and do not provoke me or it shall be the worse for you."

The old man feared him and obeyed. Not a word he spoke, but went by the shore of the sounding sea and prayed apart to King Apollo whom lovely Leto had borne. "Hear me," he cried, "O god of the silver bow, that protectest Chryses and holy Cilla and rulest Tenedos with thy might, hear me oh thou of Sminthe. If I have ever decked your temple with garlands, or burned your thighbones in fat of bulls or goats, grant my prayer, and let your arrows avenge these my tears upon the Danaans."

Thus did he pray, and Apollo heard his prayer. He came down furious from the summits of Olympus, with his bow and his quiver upon his shoulder, and the arrows rattled on his back with the rage that trembled within him. He sat himself down away from the ships with a face as dark as night, and his silver bow rang death as he shot his arrow in the midst of them. First he smote their mules and their hounds, but presently he aimed his shafts at the people themselves, and all day long the pyres of the dead were burning.

For nine whole days he shot his arrows among the people, but upon the tenth day Achilles called them in assembly—moved thereto by Juno, who saw the Achæans in their death throes and had compassion upon them. Then, when they were got together, he rose and spoke among them.

"Son of Atreus," said he, "I deem that we should now turn roving home if we would escape destruction, for we are being cut down by war and pestilence at once. Let us ask some priest or prophet, or some reader of dreams (for dreams, too, are of Jove) who can tell us why Phœbus Apollo is so angry, and say whether it is for some vow that we have broken, or hecatomb[3] that we have not offered, and whether he will accept the savor of lambs and goats without blemish, so as to take away the plague from us."

With these words he sat down, and Calchas son of Thestor, wisest of augurs, who knew things past present and to come, rose to speak. He it was who had guided the Achæans with their fleet to Ilius,[4] through the prophesyings with which Phœbus Apollo had inspired him. With all sincerity and goodwill he addressed them thus:—

"Achilles, loved of heaven, you bid me tell you about the anger of King Apollo, I will therefore do so; but consider first and swear that you will stand by me heartily in word and deed, for I know that I shall offend one

[3] *hecatomb*: animal sacrifice, typically of 100 oxen or cattle.
[4] *Ilius*: Troy.

who rules the Argives with might, and to whom all the Achæans are in subjection. A plain man cannot stand against the anger of a king, who if he swallow his displeasure now, will yet nurse revenge till he has wreaked it. Consider, therefore, whether or no you will protect me."

And Achilles answered, "Fear not, but speak as it is borne in upon you from heaven, for by Apollo, Calchas, to whom you pray, and whose oracles you reveal to us, not a Danaan at our ships shall lay his hand upon you, while I yet live to look upon the face of the earth—no, not though you name Agamemnon himself, who is by far the foremost of the Achæans."

Thereon the seer spoke boldly. "The god," he said, "is angry neither about vow nor hecatomb, but for his priest's sake, whom Agamemnon has dishonored, in that he would not free his daughter nor take a ransom for her; therefore has he sent these evils upon us, and will yet send others. He will not deliver the Danaans from this pestilence till Agamemnon has restored the girl without fee or ransom to her father, and has sent a holy hecatomb to Chryses. Thus we may perhaps appease him."

With these words he sat down, and Agamemnon rose in anger. His heart was black with rage, and his eyes flashed fire as he scowled on Calchas and said, "Seer of evil, you never yet prophesied smooth things concerning me, but have ever loved to foretell that which was evil. You have brought me neither comfort nor performance; and now you come seeing among the Danaans, and saying that Apollo has plagued us because I would not take a ransom for this girl, the daughter of Chryses. I have set my heart on keeping her in my own house, for I love her better even than my own wife Clytemnestra, whose peer she is alike in form and feature, in understanding and accomplishments. Still I will give her up if I must, for I would have the people live, not die; but you must find me a prize instead, or I alone among the Argives shall be without one. This is not well; for you behold, all of you, that my prize is to go elsewhither."

And Achilles answered, "Most noble son of Atreus, covetous beyond all mankind, how shall the Achæans find you another prize? We have no common store from which to take one. Those we took from the cities have been awarded; we cannot disallow the awards that have been made already. Give this girl, therefore, to the god, and if ever Jove grants us to sack the city of Troy we will requite you three and fourfold."

Then Agamemnon said, "Achilles, valiant though you be, you shall not thus outwit me. You shall not overreach and you shall not persuade me. Are you to keep your own prize, while I sit tamely under my loss and give up the girl at your bidding? Let the Achæans find me a prize in fair exchange to my liking, or I will come and take your own, or that of Ajax or of Ulysses; and he to whomsoever I may come shall rue my coming. But of this we will take thought hereafter; for the present, let us draw a ship into the sea, and find a crew for her expressly; let us put a hecatomb on board, and let us send Chryseis also; further, let some chief man among us be in command, either Ajax, or Idomeneus, or yourself, son of Peleus, mighty warrior that you are, that we may offer sacrifice and appease the anger of the god."

Achilles scowled at him and answered, "You are steeped in insolence and lust of gain. With what heart can any of the Achæans do your bidding, either on foray or in open fighting? I came not warring here for any ill the Trojans had done me. I have no quarrel with them. They have not raided my cattle nor my horses, nor cut down my harvests on the rich plains of Phthia; for between me and them there is a great space, both mountain and sounding sea. We have followed you, Sir Insolence! for your pleasure, not ours—to gain satisfaction from the Trojans for your shameless self and for Menelaus. You forget this, and threaten to rob me of the prize for which I have toiled, and which the sons of the Achæans have given me. Never when the Achæans sack any rich city of the Trojans do I receive so good a prize as you do, though it is my hands that do the better part of the fighting. When the sharing comes, your share is far the largest, and I, forsooth, must go back to my ships, take what I can get and be thankful, when my labor of fighting is done. Now, therefore, I shall go back to Phthia; it will be much better for me to return home with my ships, for I will not stay here dishonored to gather gold and substance for you."

And Agamemnon answered, "Fly if you will, I shall make you no prayers to stay you. I have others here who will do me honor, and above all Jove, the lord of counsel. There is no king here so hateful to me as you are, for you are ever quarrelsome and ill affected. What though you be brave? Was it not heaven that made you so? Go home, then, with your ships and comrades to lord it over the Myrmidons.[5] I care neither for you nor for your anger; and thus will I do: since Phœbus Apollo is taking Chryseis from me, I shall send her with my ship and my followers, but I shall come to your tent and take your own prize Briseis, that you may learn how much stronger I am than you are, and that another may fear to set himself up as equal or comparable with me."

The son of Peleus was furious, and his heart within his shaggy breast was divided whether to draw his sword, push the others aside, and kill the son of Atreus, or to restrain himself and check his anger. While he was thus in two minds, and was drawing his mighty sword from its scabbard, Minerva came down from heaven (for Juno had sent her in the love she bore to

[5] *Myrmidons*: a people of Thessaly, Achilles' followers.

them both), and seized the son of Peleus by his yellow hair, visible to him alone, for of the others no man could see her. Achilles turned in amaze, and by the fire that flashed from her eyes at once knew that she was Minerva. "Why are you here," said he, "daughter of ægis-bearing Jove? To see the pride of Agamemnon, son of Atreus? Let me tell you—and it shall surely be—he shall pay for this insolence with his life."

And Minerva said, "I come from heaven, if you will hear me, to bid you stay your anger. Juno has sent me, who cares for both of you alike. Cease, then, this brawling, and do not draw your sword; rail at him if you will, and your railing will not be vain, for I tell you—and it shall surely be—that you shall hereafter receive gifts three times as splendid by reason of this present insult. Hold, therefore, and obey."

"Goddess," answered Achilles, "however angry a man may be, he must do as you two command him. This will be best, for the gods ever hear the prayers of him who has obeyed them."

He stayed his hand on the silver hilt of his sword, and thrust it back into the scabbard as Minerva bade him. Then she went back to Olympus among the other gods, and to the house of ægis-bearing Jove.

But the son of Peleus again began railing at the son of Atreus, for he was still in a rage. "Wine bibber," he cried, "with the face of a dog and the heart of a hind, you never dare to go out with the host in fight, nor yet with our chosen men in ambuscade. You shun this as you do death itself. You had rather go round and rob his prizes from any man who contradicts you. You devour your people, for you are king over a feeble folk; otherwise, son of Atreus, henceforward you would insult no man. Therefore I say, and swear it with a great oath—nay, by this my scepter which shall sprout neither leaf nor shoot, nor bud anew from the day on which it left its parent stem upon the mountains—for the ax stripped it of leaf and bark, and now the sons of the Achæans bear it as judges and guardians of the decrees of heaven—so surely and solemnly do I swear that hereafter they shall look fondly for Achilles and shall not find him. In the day of your distress, when your men fall dying by the murderous hand of Hector, you shall not know how to help them, and shall rend your heart with rage for the hour when you offered insult to the bravest of the Achæans."

With this the son of Peleus dashed his gold-bestudded scepter on the ground and took his seat, while the son of Atreus was beginning fiercely from his place upon the other side. Then uprose smooth-tongued Nestor, the facile speaker of the Pylians, and the words fell from his lips sweeter than honey. Two generations of men born and bred in Pylos had passed away under his rule, and he was now reigning over the third. With all sincerity and goodwill, therefore, he addressed them thus:—

"Of a truth," he said, "a great sorrow has befallen the Achæan land. Surely Priam with his sons would rejoice, and the Trojans be glad at heart if they could hear this quarrel between you two, who are so excellent in fight and counsel. I am older than either of you; therefore be guided by me. Moreover I have been the familiar friend of men even greater than you are, and they did not disregard my counsels. Never again can I behold such men as Pirithoüs and Dryas shepherd of his people, or as Cæneus, Exadius, godlike Polyphemus, and Theseus son of Ægeus, peer of the immortals. These were the mightiest men ever born upon this earth: mightiest were they, and when they fought the fiercest tribes of mountain savages they utterly overthrew them. I came from distant Pylos, and went about among them, for they would have me come, and I fought as it was in me to do. Not a man now living could withstand them, but they heard my words, and were persuaded by them. So be it also with yourselves, for this is the more excellent way. Therefore, Agamemnon, though you be strong, take not this girl away, for the sons of the Achæans have already given her to Achilles; and you, Achilles, strive not further with the king, for no man who by the grace of Jove wields a scepter has like honor with Agamemnon. You are strong, and have a goddess for your mother; but Agamemnon is stronger than you, for he has more people under him. Son of Atreus, check your anger, I implore you; end this quarrel with Achilles, who in the day of battle is a tower of strength to the Achæans."

And Agamemnon answered, "Sir, all that you have said is true, but this fellow must needs become our lord and master: he must be lord of all, king of all, and captain of all, and this shall hardly be. Granted that the gods have made him a great warrior, have they also given him the right to speak with railing?"

Achilles interrupted him. "I should be a mean coward," he cried, "were I to give in to you in all things. Order other people about, not me, for I shall obey no longer. Furthermore I say—and lay my saying to your heart —I shall fight neither you nor any man about this girl, for those that take were those also that gave. But of all else that is at my ship you shall carry away nothing by force. Try, that others may see; if you do, my spear shall be reddened with your blood."

When they had quarreled thus angrily, they rose, and broke up the assembly at the ships of the Achæans. The son of Peleus went back to his tents and ships with the son of Menœtius and his company, while Agamemnon drew a vessel into the water and chose a crew of twenty oarsmen. He escorted Chryseis on board and sent moreover a hecatomb for the god. And Ulysses went as captain.

These, then, went on board and sailed their ways over the sea. But the son of Atreus bade the people purify themselves; so they purified themselves and cast their filth into the sea. Then they offered hecatombs of bulls and goats without blemish on the seashore, and the smoke with the savor of their sacrifice rose curling up toward heaven.

Thus did they busy themselves throughout the host. But Agamemnon did not forget the threat that he had made Achilles, and called his trusty messengers and squires Talthybius and Eurybates. "Go," said he, "to the tent of Achilles, son of Peleus; take Briseis by the hand and bring her hither; if he will not give her I shall come with others and take her—which will press him harder."

He charged them straightly further and dismissed them, whereon they went their way sorrowfully by the seaside, till they came to the tents and ships of the Myrmidons. They found Achilles sitting by his tent and his ships, and ill-pleased he was when he beheld them. They stood fearfully and reverently before him, and never a word did they speak, but he knew them and said, "Welcome, heralds, messengers of gods and men; draw near; my quarrel is not with you but with Agamemnon who has sent you for the girl Briseis. Therefore, Patroclus, bring her and give her to them, but let them be witnesses by the blessed gods, by mortal men, and by the fierceness of Agamemnon's anger, that if ever again there be need of me to save the people from ruin, they shall seek and they shall not find. Agamemnon is mad with rage and knows not how to look before and after that the Achæans may fight by their ships in safety."

Patroclus did as his dear comrade had bidden him. He brought Briseis from the tent and gave her over to the heralds, who took her with them to the ships of the Achæans—and the woman was loth to go. Then Achilles went all alone by the side of the hoar sea, weeping and looking out upon the boundless waste of waters. He raised his hands in prayer to his immortal mother. "Mother," he cried, "you bore me doomed to live but for a little season; surely Jove, who thunders from Olympus, might have made that little glorious. It is not so. Agamemnon, son of Atreus, has done me dishonor, and has robbed me of my prize by force."

As he spoke he wept aloud, and his mother heard him where she was sitting in the depths of the sea hard by the old man her father. Forthwith she rose as it were a gray mist out of the waves, sat down before him as he stood weeping, caressed him with her hand, and said, "My son, why are you weeping? What is it that grieves you? Keep it not from me, but tell me, that we may know it together."

Achilles drew a deep sigh and said, "You know it; why tell you what you know well already? We went to Thebes the strong city of Eëtion, sacked it, and brought hither the spoil. The sons of the Achæans shared it duly among themselves, and chose lovely Chryseis as the meed of Agamemnon; but Chryses, priest of Apollo, came to the ships of the Achæans to free his daughter, and brought with him a great ransom: moreover he bore in his hand the scepter of Apollo, wreathed with a suppliant's wreath, and he besought the Achæans, but most of all the two sons of Atreus who were their chiefs.

"On this the rest of the Achæans with one voice were for respecting the priest and taking the ransom that he offered; but not so Agamemnon, who spoke fiercely to him and sent him roughly away. So he went back in anger, and Apollo, who loved him dearly, heard his prayer. Then the god sent a deadly dart upon the Argives, and the people died thick on one another, for the arrow went everywhither among the wide host of the Achæans. At last a seer in the fullness of his knowledge declared to us the oracles of Apollo, and I was myself first to say that we should appease him. Whereon the son of Atreus rose in anger, and threatened that which he has since done. The Achæans are now taking the girl in a ship to Chryses and sending gifts of sacrifice to the god; but the heralds have just taken from my tent the daughter of Briseus, whom the Achæans had awarded to myself.

"Help your brave son, therefore, if you are able. Go to Olympus, and if you have ever done him service in word or deed, implore the aid of Jove. Ofttimes in my father's house have I heard you glory in that you alone of the immortals saved the son of Saturn from ruin, when the others, with Juno, Neptune, and Pallas Minerva, would have put him in bonds. It was you, goddess, who delivered him by calling to Olympus the hundred-handed monster whom gods call Briareus, but men Ægæon, for he is stronger even than his father; when therefore he took his seat all-glorious beside the son of Saturn, the other gods were afraid, and did not bind him. Go, then, to him, remind him of all this, clasp his knees, and bid him give succor to the Trojans. Let the Achæans be hemmed in at the sterns of their ships, and perish on the seashore, that they may reap what joy they may of their king, and that Agamemnon may rue his blindness in offering insult to the foremost of the Achæans."

Thetis wept and answered, "My son, woe is me that I should have borne or suckled you. Would indeed that you had lived your span free from all sorrow at your ships, for it is all too brief; alas, that you should be at once short of life and long of sorrow above your peers: woe, therefore, was the hour in which I bore you; nevertheless I will go to the snowy heights of Olympus, and tell this tale to Jove, if he will hear our prayer: meanwhile stay where you are with your ships, nurse your anger against the Achæans, and hold aloof from fight. For Jove went yesterday to Oceanus, to a feast among the Ethiopians, and the other gods went with him. He will return to

Olympus twelve days hence; I will then go to his mansion paved with bronze and will beseech him; nor do I doubt that I shall be able to persuade him."

On this she left him, still furious at the loss of her that had been taken from him. Meanwhile Ulysses reached Chryses with the hecatomb. When they had come inside the harbor they furled the sails and laid them in the ship's hold; they slackened the forestays, lowered the mast into its place, and rowed the ship to the place where they would have her lie; there they cast out their mooring stones and made fast the hawsers. They then got out upon the seashore and landed the hecatomb for Apollo; Chryseis also left the ship, and Ulysses led her to the altar to deliver her into the hands of her father. "Chryses," said he, "King Agamemnon has sent me to bring you back your child, and to offer sacrifice to Apollo on behalf of the Danaans, that we may propitiate the god, who has now brought much sorrow upon the Argives."

So saying he gave the girl over to her father, who received her gladly, and they ranged the holy hecatomb all orderly round the altar of the god. They washed their hands and took up the barley meal to sprinkle over the victims, while Chryses lifted up his hands and prayed aloud on their behalf. "Hear me," he cried, "O god of the silver bow, that protectest Chryses and holy Cilla, and rulest Tenedos with thy might. Even as thou didst hear me aforetime when I prayed, and didst press hardly upon the Achæans, so hear me yet again, and stay this fearful pestilence from the Danaans."

Thus did he pray, and Apollo heard his prayer. When they had done praying and sprinkling the barley meal, they drew back the heads of the victims and killed and flayed them. They cut out the thighbones, wrapped them round in two layers of fat, set some pieces of raw meat on the top of them, and then Chryses laid them on the wood fire and poured wine over them, while the young men stood near him with five-pronged spits in their hands. When the thighbones were burned and they had tasted the inward meats, they cut the rest up small, put the pieces upon the spits, roasted them till they were done, and drew them off: then, when they had finished their work and the feast was ready, they ate it, and every man had his full share, so that all were satisfied. As soon as they had had enough to eat and drink, pages filled the mixing bowl with wine and water and handed it round, after giving every man his drink-offering.

Thus all day long the young men worshiped the god with song, hymning him and chanting the joyous pæan, and the god took pleasure in their voices; but when the sun went down, and it came on dark, they laid themselves down to sleep by the stern cables of the ship, and when the child of morning, rosy-fingered Dawn, appeared they again set sail for the host of the Achæans. Apollo sent them a fair wind, so they raised their mast and hoisted their white sails aloft. As the sail bellied with the wind the ship flew through the deep blue water, and the foam hissed against her bows as she sped onward. When they reached the wide-stretching host of the Achæans, they drew the vessel ashore, high and dry upon the sands, set her strong props beneath her, and went their ways to their own tents and ships.

But Achilles abode at his ships and nursed his anger. He went not to the honorable assembly, and sallied not forth to fight, but gnawed at his own heart, pining for battle and the war cry.

Now after twelve days the immortal gods came back in a body to Olympus, and Jove led the way. Thetis was not unmindful of the charge her son had laid upon her, so she rose from under the sea and went through great heaven with early morning to Olympus, where she found the mighty son of Saturn sitting all alone upon its topmost ridges. She sat herself down before him, and with her left hand seized his knees, while with her right she caught him under the chin, and besought him, saying—

"Father Jove, if I ever did you service in word or deed among the immortals, hear my prayer, and do honor to my son, whose life is to be cut short so early. King Agamemnon has dishonored him by taking his prize and keeping her. Honor him then yourself, Olympian lord of counsel, and grant victory to the Trojans, till the Achæans give my son his due and load him with riches in requital."

Jove sat for a while silent, and without a word, but Thetis still kept firm hold of his knees, and besought him a second time. "Incline your head," said she, "and promise me surely, or else deny me—for you have nothing to fear—that I may learn how greatly you disdain me."

At this Jove was much troubled and answered, "I shall have trouble if you set me quarreling with Juno, for she will provoke me with her taunting speeches; even now she is always railing at me before the other gods and accusing me of giving aid to the Trojans. Go back now, lest she should find out. I will consider the matter, and will bring it about as you wish. See, I incline my head that you may believe me. This is the most solemn token that I can give to any god. I never recall my word, or deceive, or fail to do what I say, when I have nodded my head."

As he spoke the son of Saturn bowed his dark brows, and the ambrosial locks swayed on his immortal head, till vast Olympus reeled.

When the pair had thus laid their plans, they parted—Jove to his own house, while the goddess quitted the splendor of Olympus, and plunged into the depths of the sea. The gods rose from their seats, before the coming of their sire. Not one of them dared to remain sitting, but all stood up as he came among them. There, then, he took his seat. But Juno, when she saw him, knew that he and the old merman's daughter, silver-footed Thetis, had been hatching mischief, so she at once began to upbraid him. "Trickster," she cried, "which of the gods have you been taking into your counsels now? You are always settling matters in secret behind my back, and have never yet told me, if you could help it, one word of your intentions."

"Juno," replied the sire of gods and men, "you must not expect to be informed of all my counsels. You are my wife, but you would find it hard to understand them. When it is proper for you to hear, there is no one, god or man, who will be told sooner, but when I mean to keep a matter to myself, you must not pry nor ask questions."

"Dread son of Saturn," answered Juno, "what are you talking about? I? Pry and ask questions? Never. I let you have your own way in everything. Still, I have a strong misgiving that the old merman's daughter Thetis has been talking you over, for she was with you and had hold of your knees this selfsame morning. I believe, therefore, that you have been promising her to give glory to Achilles, and to kill much people at the ships of the Achæans."

"Wife," said Jove, "I can do nothing but you suspect me and find it out. You will take nothing by it, for I shall only dislike you the more, and it will go harder with you. Granted that it is as you say; I mean to have it so; sit down and hold your tongue as I bid you, for if I once begin to lay my hands about you, though all heaven were on your side it would profit you nothing."

On this Juno was frightened, so she curbed her stubborn will and sat down in silence. But the heavenly beings were disquieted throughout the house of Jove, till the cunning workman Vulcan began to try and pacify his mother Juno. "It will be intolerable," said he, "if you two fall to wrangling and setting heaven in an uproar about a pack of mortals. If such ill counsels are to prevail, we shall have no pleasure at our banquet. Let me then advise my mother—and she must herself know that it will be better—to make friends with my dear father Jove, lest he again scold her and disturb our feast. If the Olympian Thunderer wants to hurl us all from our seats, he can do so, for he is far the strongest, so give him fair words, and he will then soon be in a good humor with us."

As he spoke, he took a double cup of nectar, and placed it in his mother's hand. "Cheer up, my dear mother," said he, "and make the best of it. I love you dearly, and should be very sorry to see you get a thrashing; however grieved I might be, I could not help you, for there is no standing against Jove. Once before when I was trying to help you, he caught me by the foot and flung me from the heavenly threshold. All day long from morn till eve was I falling, till at sunset I came to ground in the island of Lemnos, and there I lay, with very little life left in me, till the Sintians came and tended me."

Juno smiled at this, and as she smiled she took the cup from her son's hands. Then Vulcan drew sweet nectar from the mixing bowl, and served it round among the gods, going from left to right; and the blessed gods laughed out a loud applause as they saw him bustling about the heavenly mansion.

Thus through the livelong day to the going down of the sun they feasted, and everyone had his full share, so that all were satisfied. Apollo struck his lyre, and the Muses lifted up their sweet voices, calling and answering one another. But when the sun's glorious light had faded, they went home to bed, each in his own abode, which lame Vulcan with his consummate skill had fashioned for them. So Jove, the Olympian Lord of Thunder, hied him to the bed in which he always slept; and when he had got onto it he went to sleep, with Juno of the golden throne by his side.

BOOK VI

THE fight between Trojans and Achæans was now left to rage as it would, and the tide of war surged hither and thither over the plain as they aimed their bronze-shod spears at one another between the streams of Simois and Xanthus.

First, Ajax son of Telamon, tower of strength to the Achæans, broke a phalanx of the Trojans, and came to the assistance of his comrades by killing Acamas son of Eussorus, the best man among the Thracians, being both brave and of great stature. The spear struck the projecting peak of his helmet: its bronze point then went through his forehead into the brain, and darkness veiled his eyes.

Then Diomed killed Axylus son of Teuthranus, a rich man who lived in the strong city of Arisbe, and was beloved by all men; for he had a house by the roadside, and entertained everyone who passed; howbeit not one of his guests stood before him to save his life, and Diomed killed both him and his squire Calesius, who was then his charioteer—so the pair passed beneath the earth.

Euryalus killed Dresus and Opheltius, and then went in pursuit of Æsepus and Pedasus, whom the naiad nymph Abarbarea had borne to noble Bucolion. Bucolion was eldest son to Laomedon, but he was a bastard. While tending his sheep he had converse with the nymph, and she conceived twin sons; these the son of Mecisteus now slew, and he stripped the armor from their shoulders. Polypœtes then killed Astyalus, Ulysses Pidytes of Percote, and Teucer Aretaon. Ablerus fell by the spear of Nestor's son Antilochus, and Agamemnon, king of men, killed Elatus who dwelt in Pedasus by the banks of the river Satnioeis. Leïtus killed Phylacus as he was flying, and Eurypylus slew Melanthus.

Then Menelaus of the loud war cry took Adrestus alive, for his horses ran into a tamarisk bush, as they were flying wildly over the plain, and broke the pole from the car; they went on toward the city along with the others in full flight, but Adrestus rolled out, and fell in the dust flat on his face by the wheel of his chariot. Menelaus came up to him spear in hand, but Adrestus caught him by the knees begging for his life. "Take me alive," he cried, "son of Atreus, and you shall have a full ransom for me: my father is rich and has much treasure of gold, bronze, and wrought iron laid by in his house. From this store he will give you a large ransom should he hear of my being alive and at the ships of the Achæans."

Thus did he plead, and Menelaus was for yielding and giving him to a squire to take to the ships of the Achæans, but Agamemnon came running up to him and rebuked him. "My good Menelaus," said he, "this is no time for giving quarter. Has, then, your house fared so well at the hands of the Trojans? Let us not spare a single one of them—not even the child unborn and in its mother's womb; let not a man of them be left alive, but let all in Ilius perish, unheeded and forgotten."

Thus did he speak, and his brother was persuaded by him, for his words were just. Menelaus, therefore, thrust Adrestus from him, whereon King Agamemnon struck him in the flank, and he fell: then the son of Atreus planted his foot upon his breast to draw his spear from the body.

Meanwhile Nestor shouted to the Argives, saying, "My friends, Danaan warriors, servants of Mars, let no man lag that he may spoil the dead, and bring back much booty to the ships. Let us kill as many as we can; the bodies will lie upon the plain, and you can despoil them later at your leisure."

With these words he put heart and soul into them all. And now the Trojans would have been routed and driven back into Ilius, had not Priam's son Helenus, wisest of augurs, said to Hector and Æneas, "Hector and Æneas, you two are the mainstays of the Trojans and Lycians, for you are foremost at all times, alike in fight and counsel; hold your ground here, and go about among the host to rally them in front of the gates, or they will fling themselves into the arms of their wives, to the great joy of our foes. Then, when you have put heart into all our companies, we will stand firm here and fight the Danaans however hard they press us, for there is nothing else to be done. Meanwhile do you, Hector, go to the city and tell our mother what is happening. Tell her to bid the matrons gather at the temple of Minerva in the acropolis; let her then take her key and open the doors of the sacred building; there, upon the knees of Minerva, let her lay the largest, fairest robe she has in her house—the one she sets most store by; let her, moreover, promise to sacrifice twelve yearling heifers that have never yet felt the goad, in the temple of the goddess, if she will take pity on the town, with the wives and little ones of the Trojans, and keep the son of Tydeus from falling on the goodly city of Ilius; for he fights with fury and fills men's souls with panic. I hold him mightiest of them all; we did not fear even their great champion Achilles, son of a goddess though he be, as we do this man: his rage is beyond all bounds, and there is none can vie with him in prowess."

Hector did as his brother bade him. He sprang from his chariot, and went about everywhere among the host, brandishing his spears, urging the men on to fight, and raising the dread cry of battle. Thereon they rallied and again faced the Achæans, who gave ground and ceased their murderous onset, for they deemed that some one of the immortals had come down from starry heaven to help the Trojans, so strangely had they rallied. And Hector shouted to the Trojans, "Trojans and allies, be men, my friends, and fight with might and main, while I go to Ilius and tell the old men of our council and our wives to pray to the gods and vow hecatombs in their honor."

With this he went his way, and the black rim of hide that went round his shield beat against his neck and his ankles.

Then Glaucus, son of Hippolochus, and the son of Tydeus went into the open space between the hosts to fight in single combat. When they were close up to one another Diomed of the loud war cry was the first to speak. "Who, my good sir," said he, "who are you among men? I have never seen you in battle until now, but you are daring beyond all others if you abide my onset. Woe to those fathers whose sons face my might. If, however, you are one of the immortals and have come down from heaven, I will not fight you; for even valiant Lycurgus, son of Dryas, did not live long when he took to fighting with the gods. He it was that drove the nursing women who were in charge of frenzied Bacchus through the land of Nysa, and they flung their thyrsi on the ground as murderous Lycurgus beat them with his oxgoad. Bacchus himself plunged terror-stricken into the sea, and Thetis took him to her bosom to comfort him, for he was scared by the fury with which the man reviled him. Thereon the gods who live at ease were angry with Lycurgus and the son of Saturn struck him blind, nor did he live much longer after he had become hateful to the immortals. Therefore I will not fight with the blessed gods; but if you are of them that eat the fruit of the ground, draw near and meet your doom."

And the son of Hippolochus answered, "Mighty son of Tydeus, why ask me of my lineage? Men come and go as leaves year by year upon the trees. Those of autumn the wind sheds upon the ground, but when spring returns the forest buds forth with fresh ones. Even so is it with the generations of mankind, the new spring up as the old are passing away. If, then, you would learn my descent, it is one that is well known to many. There is a city in the heart of Argos, pastureland of horses, called Ephyra, where Sisyphus lived, who was the crafticst of all mankind. He was the son of Æolus, and had a son named Glaucus, who was father to Bellerophon, whom heaven endowed with the most surpassing comeliness and beauty. But Prœtus devised his ruin, and being stronger than he, drove him from the land of the Argives, over which Jove had made him ruler. For Antea, wife of Prœtus, lusted after him, and would have had him lie with her in secret; but Bellerophon was an honorable man and would not, so she told lies about him to Prœtus. 'Prœtus,' said she, 'kill Bellerophon or die, for he would have had converse with me against my will.' The king was angered, but shrank from killing Bellerophon, so he sent him to Lycia with lying letters of introduction, written on a folded tablet, and containing much ill against the bearer. He bade Bellerophon show these letters to his father-in-law, to the end that he might thus perish; Bellerophon therefore went to Lycia, and the gods convoyed him safely.

"When he reached the river Xanthus, which is in Lycia, the king received him with all goodwill, feasted him nine days, and killed nine heifers in his honor, but when rosy-fingered morning appeared upon the tenth day, he questioned him and desired to see the letter from his son-in-law Prœtus. When he had received the wicked letter he first commanded Bellerophon to kill that savage monster, the Chimæra, who was not a human being, but a goddess, for she had the head of a lion and the tail of a serpent, while her body was that of a goat, and she breathed forth flames of fire; but Bellerophon slew her, for he was guided by signs from heaven. He next fought the far-famed Solymi, and this, he said, was the hardest of all his battles. Thirdly, he killed the Amazons, women who were the peers of men, and as he was returning thence the king devised yet another plan for his destruction; he picked the bravest warriors in all Lycia, and placed them in ambuscade, but not a man ever came back, for Bellerophon killed every one of them. Then the king knew that he must be the valiant offspring of a god, so he kept him in Lycia, gave him his daughter in marriage, and made him of equal honor in the kingdom with himself; and the Lycians gave him a piece of land, the best in all the country, fair with vineyards and tilled fields, to have and to hold.

"The king's daughter bore Bellerophon three children, Isander, Hippolochus, and Laodameia. Jove, the lord of counsel, lay with Laodameia, and she bore him noble Sarpedon; but when Bellerophon came to be hated by all the gods, he wandered all desolate and dismayed upon the Alean plain, gnawing at his own heart, and shunning the path of man. Mars, insatiate of battle, killed his son Isander while he was fighting the Solymi; his daughter was killed by Diana of the golden reins, for she was angered with her; but Hippolochus was father to myself, and when he sent me to Troy he urged me again and again to fight ever among the foremost and outvie my peers, so as not to shame the blood of my fathers who were the noblest in Ephyra and in all Lycia. This, then, is the descent I claim."

Thus did he speak, and the heart of Diomed was glad. He planted his spear in the ground, and spoke to him with friendly words. "Then," he said, "you are an old friend of my father's house. Great Œneus once entertained Bellerophon for twenty days, and the two exchanged presents. Œneus gave a belt rich with purple, and Bellerophon a double cup, which I left at home when I set out for Troy. I do not remember Tydeus, for he was taken from us while I was yet a child, when the army of the Achæans was cut to pieces before Thebes. Henceforth, however, I must be your host in middle Argos, and you mine in Lycia, if I should ever go there; let us avoid one another's spears even during a general engagement; there are many noble Trojans and allies whom I can kill, if I overtake them and heaven delivers them into my hand; so again with yourself, there are many Achæans whose lives you may take if you can; we two, then, will exchange armor, that all present may know of the old ties that subsist between us."

With these words they sprang from their chariots, grasped one another's hands, and plighted friendship. But the son of Saturn made Glaucus take leave of his wits, for he exchanged golden armor for bronze, the worth of a hundred head of cattle for the worth of nine.

Now when Hector reached the Scæan gates and the oak tree, the wives and daughters of the Trojans came running toward him to ask after their sons, brothers, kinsmen, and husbands: he told them to set about praying to the gods, and many were made sorrowful as they heard him.

Presently he reached the splendid palace of King Priam, adorned with colonnades of hewn stone. In it there were fifty bedchambers—all of hewn stone—built near one another, where the sons of Priam slept, each with his wedded wife. Opposite these, on the other side the courtyard, there were twelve upper rooms also of hewn stone for Priam's daughters, built near one another, where his sons-in-law slept with their wives. When Hector got there, his fond mother came up to him with Laodice, the fairest of her daughters. She took his hand within her own and said, "My son, why have you left the battle to come hither? Are the Achæans, woe betide them, pressing you hard about the city that you have thought fit to come and uplift your hands to Jove from the citadel? Wait till I can bring you wine that you may make offering to Jove and to the other immortals, and may then drink and be refreshed. Wine gives a man fresh strength when he is wearied, as you now are with fighting on behalf of your kinsmen."

And Hector answered, "Honored mother, bring no wine, lest you unman me and I forget my strength. I dare not make a drink-offering to Jove with unwashed hands; one who is bespattercd with blood and filth may not pray to the son of Saturn. Get the matrons together, and go with offerings to the temple of Minerva, driver of the spoil; there, upon the knees of Minerva, lay the largest and fairest robe you have in your house—the one you set most store by; promise, moreover, to sacrifice twelve yearling heifers that have never yet felt the goad, in the temple of the goddess, if she will take pity on the town, with the wives and little ones of the Trojans, and keep the son of Tydeus from off the goodly city of Ilius, for he fights with fury, and fills men's souls with panic. Go, then, to the temple of Minerva, while I seek Paris and exhort him, if he will hear my words. Would that the earth might open her jaws and swallow him, for Jove bred him to be the bane of the Trojans, and of Priam and Priam's sons. Could I but see him go down into the house of Hades, my heart would forget its heaviness."

His mother went into the house and called her waiting women who gathered the matrons throughout the city. She then went down into her fragrant storeroom, where her embroidered robes were kept, the work of Sidonian women, whom Alexandrus had brought over from Sidon when he sailed the seas upon that voyage during which he carried off noble Helen. Hecuba took out the largest robe, and the one that was most beautifully enriched with embroidery, as an offering to Minerva: it glittered like a star, and lay at the very bottom of the chest. With this she went on her way and many matrons with her.

When they reached the temple of Minerva, lovely Theano, daughter of Cisseus and wife of Antenor, opened the doors, for the Trojans had made her priestess of Minerva. The women lifted up their hands to the goddess with a loud cry, and Theano took the robe to lay it upon the knees of

Minerva, praying the while to the daughter of great Jove. "Holy Minerva," she cried, "protectress of our city, mighty goddess, break the spear of Diomed and lay him low before the Scæan gates. Do this, and we will sacrifice twelve heifers that have never yet known the goad, in your temple, if you will have pity upon the town, with the wives and little ones of the Trojans." Thus she prayed, but Pallas Minerva granted not her prayer.

While they were thus praying to the daughter of great Jove, Hector went to the fair house of Alexandrus, which he had built for him by the foremost builders in the land. They had built him his house, storehouse, and court-yard near those of Priam and Hector on the acropolis. Here Hector entered, with a spear eleven cubits long in his hand; the bronze point gleamed in front of him, and was fastened to the shaft of the spear by a ring of gold. He found Alexandrus within the house, busied about his armor, his shield, and cuirass, and handling his curved bow; there, too, sat Argive Helen with her women, setting them their several tasks; and as Hector saw him he rebuked him with words of scorn. "Sir," said he, "you do ill to nurse this rancor; the people perish fighting round this our town; you would yourself chide one whom you saw shirking his part in the combat. Up then, or ere long the city will be in a blaze."

And Alexandrus answered, "Hector, your rebuke is just; listen therefore, and believe me when I tell you that I am not here so much through rancor or ill-will toward the Trojans, as from a desire to indulge my grief. My wife was even now gently urging me to battle, and I hold it better that I should go, for victory is ever fickle. Wait, then, while I put on my armor, or go first and I will follow. I shall be sure to overtake you."

Hector made no answer, but Helen tried to soothe him. "Brother," said she, "to my abhorred and sinful self, would that a whirlwind had caught me up on the day my mother brought me forth, and had borne me to some mountain or to the waves of the roaring sea that should have swept me away ere this mischief had come about. But, since the gods have devised these evils, would, at any rate, that I had been wife to a better man—to one who could smart under dishonor and men's evil speeches. This fellow was never yet to be depended upon, nor never will be, and he will surely reap what he has sown. Still, brother, come in and rest upon this seat, for it is you who bear the brunt of that toil that has been caused by my hateful self and by the sin of Alexandrus—both of whom Jove has doomed to be a theme of song among those that shall be born hereafter."

And Hector answered, "Bid me not be seated, Helen, for all the goodwill you bear me. I cannot stay. I am in haste to help the Trojans, who miss me greatly when I am not among them; but urge your husband, and of his own self also let him make haste to overtake me before I am out of the city. I must go home to see my household, my wife, and my little son, for I know not whether I shall ever again return to them, or whether the gods will cause me to fall by the hands of the Achæans."

Then Hector left her, and forthwith was at his own house. He did not find Andromache, for she was on the wall with her child and one of her maids, weeping bitterly. Seeing, then, that she was not within, he stood on the threshold of the women's rooms and said, "Women, tell me, and tell me true, where did Andromache go when she left the house? Was it to my sisters, or to my brothers' wives? or is she at the temple of Minerva where the other women are propitiating the awful goddess?"

His good housekeeper answered, "Hector, since you bid me tell you truly, she did not go to your sisters nor to your brothers' wives, nor yet to the temple of Minerva, where the other women are propitiating the awful goddess, but she is on the high wall of Ilius, for she had heard the Trojans were being hard pressed, and that the Achæans were in great force: therefore she went to the wall in frenzied haste, and the nurse went with her carrying the child."

Hector hurried from the house when she had done speaking, and went down the streets by the same way that he had come. When he had gone through the city and had reached the Scæan gates through which he would go out onto the plain, his wife came running toward him, Andromache, daughter of great Eëtion who ruled in Thebes under the wooded slopes of Mount Placus, and was king of the Cilicians. His daughter had married Hector, and now came to meet him with a nurse who carried his little child in her bosom—a mere babe, Hector's darling son, and lovely as a star. Hector had named him Scamandrius, but the people called him Astyanax,[1] for his father stood alone as chief guardian of Ilius. Hector smiled as he looked upon the boy, but he did not speak, and Andromache stood by him weeping and taking his hand in her own. "Dear husband," said she, "your valor will bring you to destruction; think on your infant son, and on my hapless self who ere long shall be your widow—for the Achæans will set upon you in a body and kill you. It would be better for me, should I lose you, to lie dead and buried, for I shall have nothing left to comfort me when you are gone, save only sorrow. I have neither father nor mother now. Achilles slew my father when he sacked Thebes, the goodly city of the Cilicians. He slew him, but did not for very shame despoil him; when he had burned him in his wondrous armor, he raised a barrow over his

---

[1] *Astyanax*: meaning "king of the city."

ashes and the mountain nymphs, daughters of ægis-bearing Jove, planted a grove of elms about his tomb. I had seven brothers in my father's house, but on the same day they all went within the house of Hades. Achilles killed them as they were with their sheep and cattle. My mother—her who had been queen of all the land under Mount Placus—he brought hither with the spoil, and freed her for a great sum, but the archer-queen Diana took her in the house of your father. Nay—Hector—you who to me are father, mother, brother, and dear husband—have mercy upon me; stay here upon this wall; make not your child fatherless, and your wife a widow; as for the host, place them near the fig tree, where the city can be best scaled, and the wall is weakest. Thrice have the bravest of them come thither and assailed it, under the two Ajaxes, Idomeneus, the sons of Atreus, and the brave son of Tydeus, either of their own bidding, or because some sooth-sayer had told them."

And Hector answered, "Wife, I too have thought upon all this, but with what face should I look upon the Trojans, men or women, if I shirked battle like a coward? I cannot do so: I know nothing save to fight bravely in the forefront of the Trojan host and win renown alike for my father and myself. Well do I know that the day will surely come when mighty Ilius shall be destroyed with Priam and Priam's people, but I grieve for none of these—not even for Hecuba, nor King Priam, nor for my brothers many and brave who may fall in the dust before their foes—for none of these do I grieve as for yourself when the day shall come on which some one of the Achæans shall rob you forever of your freedom, and bear you weeping away. It may be that you will have to ply the loom in Argos at the bidding of a mistress, or to fetch water from the springs Messeïs or Hypereia, treated brutally by some cruel taskmaster; then will one say who sees you weeping, 'She was wife to Hector, the bravest warrior among the Trojans during the war before Ilius.' On this your tears will break forth anew for him who would have put away the day of captivity from you. May I lie dead under the barrow that is heaped over my body ere I hear your cry as they carry you into bondage."

He stretched his arms toward his child, but the boy cried and nestled in his nurse's bosom, scared at the sight of his father's armor, and at the horse-hair plume that nodded fiercely from his helmet. His father and mother laughed to see him, but Hector took the helmet from his head and laid it all gleaming upon the ground. Then he took his darling child, kissed him, and dandled him in his arms, praying over him the while to Jove and to all the gods. "Jove," he cried, "grant that this my child may be even as myself, chief among the Trojans; let him be not less excellent in strength, and let him rule Ilius with his might. Then may one say of him as he comes from battle, 'The son is far better than the father.' May he bring back the blood-stained spoils of him whom he has laid low, and let his mother's heart be glad."

With this he laid the child again in the arms of his wife, who took him to her own soft bosom, smiling through her tears. As her husband watched her his heart yearned toward her and he caressed her fondly, saying, "My own wife, do not take these things too bitterly to heart. No one can hurry me down to Hades before my time, but if a man's hour is come, be he brave or be he coward, there is no escape for him when he has once been born. Go, then, within the house, and busy yourself with your daily duties, your loom, your distaff, and the ordering of your servants; for war is man's matter, and mine above all others of them that have been born in Ilius."

He took his plumed helmet from the ground, and his wife went back again to her house, weeping bitterly and often looking back toward him. When she reached her home she found her maidens within, and bade them all join in her lament; so they mourned Hector in his own house though he was yet alive, for they deemed that they should never see him return safe from battle, and from the furious hands of the Achæans.

Paris did not remain long in his house. He donned his goodly armor overlaid with bronze, and hasted through the city as fast as his feet could take him. As a horse, stabled and full fed, breaks loose and gallops glo-riously over the plain to the place where he is wont to bathe in the fair-flowing river—he holds his head high, and his mane streams upon his shoulders as he exults in his strength and flies like the wind to the haunts and feeding ground of the mares—even so went forth Paris from high Pergamus, gleaming like sunlight in his armor, and he laughed aloud as he sped swiftly on his way. Forthwith he came upon his brother Hector, who was then turning away from the place where he had held converse with his wife, and he was himself the first to speak. "Sir," said he, "I fear that I have kept you waiting when you are in haste, and have not come as quickly as you bade me."

"My good brother," answered Hector, "you fight bravely, and no man with any justice can make light of your doings in battle. But you are care-less and willfully remiss. It grieves me to the heart to hear the ill that the Trojans speak about you, for they have suffered much on your account. Let us be going, and we will make things right hereafter, should Jove vouchsafe us to set the cup of our deliverance before the ever-living gods of heaven in our own homes, when we have chased the Achæans from Troy."

Note: Jove, with the gods in council, forbids help to either Trojans or Greeks. He then goes to Mount Ida to watch the two camps. Thundering, Jove seems to favor the Trojans, and Juno, enraged, consults with Neptune about help for the Greeks. So the battle continues as the gods alternately put heart and strength into both armies. At length Juno and Minerva arm themselves to help the Greeks, who are hard pressed. Jove forbids and they are angry. Night falls and the battle ends, but the two goddesses now determine to "make serviceable suggestions" to the Greeks. The Trojans rejoice, sure of victory on the morrow.

BOOK IX

THUS did the Trojans watch. But Panic, comrade of bloodstained Rout, had taken fast hold of the Achæans, and their princes were all of them in despair. As when the two winds that blow from Thrace—the north and the northwest—spring up of a sudden and rouse the fury of the main—in a moment the dark waves uprear their heads and scatter their sea wrack in all directions—even thus troubled were the hearts of the Achæans.

The son of Atreus in dismay bade the heralds call the people to a council man by man, but not to cry the matter aloud; he made haste also himself to call them, and they sat sorry at heart in their assembly. Agamemnon shed tears as it were a running stream or cataract on the side of some sheer cliff; and thus, with many a heavy sigh he spoke to the Achæans. "My friends," said he, "princes and councillors of the Argives, the hand of heaven has been laid heavily upon me. Cruel Jove gave me his solemn promise that I should sack the city of Troy before returning, but he has played me false, and is now bidding me go ingloriously back to Argos with the loss of much people. Such is the will of Jove, who has laid many a proud city in the dust as he will yet lay others, for his power is above all. Now, therefore, let us all do as I say and sail back to our own country, for we shall not take Troy."

Thus he spoke, and the sons of the Achæans for a long while sat sorrowful there, but they all held their peace, till at last Diomed of the loud battle cry made answer saying, "Son of Atreus, I will chide your folly, as is my right in council. Be not then aggrieved that I should do so. In the first place you attacked me before all the Danaans and said that I was a coward and no soldier. The Argives young and old know that you did so. But the son of scheming Saturn endowed you by halves only. He gave you honor as the chief ruler over us, but valor, which is the highest both right and might, he did not give you. Sir, think you that the sons of the Achæans are indeed as unwarlike and cowardly as you say they are? If your own mind is set upon going home—go—the way is open to you; the many ships that followed you from Mycenae stand ranged upon the seashore; but the rest of us will stay here till we have sacked Troy. Nay though these too should turn homeward with their ships, Sthenelus and myself will still fight on till we reach the goal of Ilius, for heaven was with us when we came."

The sons of the Achæans shouted applause at the words of Diomed, and presently Nestor rose to speak. "Son of Tydeus," said he, "in war your prowess is beyond question, and in council you excel all who are of your own years; no one of the Achæans can make light of what you say nor gainsay it, but you have not yet come to the end of the whole matter. You are still young—you might be the youngest of my own children—still you have spoken wisely and have counseled the chief of the Achæans not without discretion; nevertheless I am older than you and I will tell you everything; therefore let no man, not even King Agamemnon, disregard my saying, for he that foments civil discord is a clanless, heartless outlaw.

"Now, however, let us obey the behests of night and get our suppers, but let the sentinels every man of them camp by the trench that is without the wall. I am giving these instructions to the young men; when they have been attended to, do you, son of Atreus, give your orders, for you are the most royal among us all. Prepare a feast for your councillors; it is right and reasonable that you should do so; there is abundance of wine in your tents, which the ships of the Achæans bring from Thrace daily. You have everything at your disposal wherewith to entertain guests, and you have many subjects. When many are got together, you can be guided by him whose counsel is wisest—and sorely do we need shrewd and prudent counsel, for the foe has lit his watchfires hard by our ships. Who can be other than dismayed? This night will either be the ruin of our host, or save it."

Thus did he speak, and they did even as he had said. The sentinels went out in their armor under command of Nestor's son Thrasymedes, a captain of the host, and of the bold warriors Ascalaphus and Ialmenus: there were also Meriones, Aphareus, and Deïpyrus, and the son of Creion, noble Lycomedes. There were seven captains of the sentinels, and with each there went a hundred youths armed with long spears: they took their places midway between the trench and the wall, and when they had done so they lit their fires and got every man his supper.

The son of Atreus then bade many councillors of the Achæans to his quarters and prepared a great feast in their honor. They laid their hands on the good things that were before them, and as soon as they had had enough to eat and drink, old Nestor, whose counsel was ever truest, was the first to lay his mind before them. He, therefore, with all sincerity and goodwill addressed them thus:

"With yourself, most noble son of Atreus, king of men, Agamemnon, will I both begin my speech and end it, for you are king over much people. Jove, moreover, has vouchsafed you to wield the scepter and to uphold righteousness, that you may take thought for your people under you; therefore it behooves you above all others both to speak and to give ear, and to carry out the counsel of another who shall have been minded to speak wisely. All turns on you and on your commands, therefore I will say what I think will be best. No man will be of a truer mind than that which has been mine from the hour when you, sir, angered Achilles by taking the girl Briseis from his tent against my judgment. I urged you not to do so, but you yielded to your own pride, and dishonored a hero whom heaven itself had honored—for you still hold the prize that had been awarded to him. Now, however, let us think how we may appease him, both with presents and fair speeches that may conciliate him."

And King Agamemnon answered, "Sir, you have reproved my folly justly. I was wrong. I own it. One whom heaven befriends is in himself a host, and Jove has shown that he befriends this man by destroying much people of the Achæans. I was blinded with passion and yielded to my worser mind; therefore I will make amends, and will give him great gifts by way of atonement. I will tell them in the presence of you all. I will give him seven tripods that have never yet been on the fire, and ten talents of gold. I will give him twenty iron caldrons and twelve strong horses that have won races and carried off prizes. Rich, indeed, both in land and gold is he that has as many prizes as my horses have won me. I will give him seven excellent workwomen, Lesbians, whom I chose for myself when he took Lesbos— all of surpassing beauty. I will give him these, and with them her whom I erewhile took from him, the daughter of Briseus; and I swear a great oath that I never went up into her couch, nor have been with her after the manner of men and women.

"All these things will I give him now down, and if hereafter the gods vouchsafe me to sack the city of Priam, let him come when we Achæans are dividing the spoil, and load his ship with gold and bronze to his liking; furthermore let him take twenty Trojan women, the loveliest after Helen herself. Then, when we reach Achæan Argos, wealthiest of all lands, he shall be my son-in-law and I will show him like honor with my own dear son Orestes, who is being nurtured in all abundance. I have three daughters, Chrysothemis, Laodice, and Iphianassa, let him take the one of his choice, freely and without gifts of wooing, to the house of Peleus; I will add such dower to boot as no man ever yet gave his daughter, and will give him seven well-established cities, Cardamyle, Enope, and Hire, where there is grass; holy Pheræ and the rich meadows of Anthea; Æpea also, and the vine-clad slopes of Pedasus, all near the sea, and on the borders of sandy Pylos. The men that dwell there are rich in cattle and sheep; they will honor him with gifts as though he were a god, and be obedient to his comfortable ordinances. All this will I do if he will now forgo his anger. Let him then yield—it is only Hades who is utterly ruthless and unyielding —and hence he is of all gods the one most hateful to mankind. Moreover I am older and more royal than himself. Therefore, let him now obey me."

Then Nestor answered, "Most noble son of Atreus, king of men, Agamemnon. The gifts you offer are no small ones, let us then send chosen messengers, who may go to the tent of Achilles son of Peleus without delay. Let those go whom I shall name. Let Phœnix, dear to Jove, lead the way; let Ajax and Ulysses follow, and let the heralds Odius and Eurybates go with them. Now bring water for our hands, and bid all keep silence while we pray to Jove the son of Saturn, if so be that he may have mercy upon us."

Thus did he speak, and his saying pleased them well. Menservants poured water over the hands of the guests, while pages filled the mixing bowls with wine and water, and handed it round after giving every man his drink-offering; then, when they had made their offerings, and had drunk each as much as he was minded, the envoys set out from the tent of Agamemnon son of Atreus; and Nestor, looking first to one and then to another, but most especially at Ulysses, was instant with them that they should prevail with the noble son of Peleus.

They went their way by the shore of the sounding sea, and prayed earnestly to earth-encircling Neptune that the high spirit of the son of Æacus might incline favorably toward them. When they reached the ships and tents of the Myrmidons, they found Achilles playing on a lyre, fair, of cunning workmanship, and its crossbar was of silver. It was part of the spoils which he had taken when he sacked the city of Eëtion, and he was now diverting himself with it and singing the feats of heroes. He was alone with Patroclus, who sat opposite to him and said nothing, waiting till he should cease singing. Ulysses and Ajax now came in—Ulysses leading the way—and stood before him. Achilles sprang from his seat with the lyre still in his hand, and Patroclus, when he saw the strangers, rose also. Achilles then greeted them saying, "All hail and welcome—you must come upon some great matter, you, who for all my anger are still dearest to me of the Achæans."

With this he led them forward, and bade them sit on seats covered with purple rugs; then he said to Patroclus who was close by him, "Son of Menœtius, set a larger bowl upon the table, mix less water with the wine, and give every man his cup, for these are very dear friends, who are now under my roof."

Patroclus did as his comrade bade him; he set the chopping block in front of the fire, and on it he laid the loin of a sheep, the loin also of a goat, and the chine of a fat hog. Automedon held the meat while Achilles chopped it; he then sliced the pieces and put them on spits while the son of Menœtius made the fire burn high. When the flame had died down, he spread the embers, laid the spits on top of them, lifting them up and setting them upon the spit racks; and he sprinkled them with salt. When the meat was roasted, he set it on platters, and handed bread round the table in fair baskets, while Achilles dealt them their portions. Then Achilles took his seat facing Ulysses against the opposite wall, and bade his comrade Patroclus offer sacrifice to the gods; so he cast the offerings into the fire, and they laid their hands upon the good things that were before them. As soon as they had had enough to eat and drink, Ajax made a sign to Phœnix, and when he saw this, Ulysses filled his cup with wine and pledged Achilles.

"Hail," said he, "Achilles, we have had no scant of good cheer, neither in the tent of Agamemnon, nor yet here; there has been plenty to eat and drink, but our thought turns upon no such matter. Sir, we are in the face of great disaster, and without your help know not whether we shall save our fleet or lose it. The Trojans and their allies have camped hard by our ships and by the wall; they have lit watchfires throughout their host and deem that nothing can now prevent them from falling on our fleet. Jove, moreover, has sent his lightnings on their right; Hector, in all his glory, rages like a maniac; confident that Jove is with him he fears neither god nor man, but is gone raving mad, and prays for the approach of day. He vows that he will hew the high sterns of our ships in pieces, set fire to their hulls, and make havoc of the Achæans while they are dazed and smothered in smoke; I much fear that heaven will make good his boasting, and it will prove our lot to perish at Troy far from our home in Argos. Up, then, and late though it be, save the sons of the Achæans who faint before the fury of the Trojans. You will repent bitterly hereafter if you do not, for when the harm is done there will be no curing it; consider ere it be too late, and save the Danaans from destruction.

"My good friend, when your father Peleus sent you from Phthia to

Agamemnon, did he not charge you saying, 'Son, Minerva and Juno will make you strong if they choose, but check your high temper, for the better part is in goodwill. Eschew vain quarreling, and the Achæans old and young will respect you more for doing so.' These were his words, but you have forgotten them. Even now, however, be appeased, and put away your anger from you. Agamemnon will make you great amends if you will forgive him; listen, and I will tell you what he has said in his tent that he will give you. He will give you seven tripods that have never yet been on the fire, and ten talents of gold; twenty iron caldrons, and twelve strong horses that have won races and carried off prizes. Rich indeed both in land and gold is he who has as many prizes as these horses have won for Agamemnon. Moreover he will give you seven excellent workwomen, Lesbians, whom he chose for himself, when you took Lesbos—all of surpassing beauty. He will give you these, and with them her whom he erewhile took from you, the daughter of Briseus, and he will swear a great oath, he has never gone up into her couch nor been with her after the manner of men and women. All these things will he give you now down, and if hereafter the gods vouchsafe him to sack the city of Priam, you can come when we Achæans are dividing the spoil, and load your ship with gold and bronze to your liking. You can take twenty Trojan women, the loveliest after Helen herself. Then, when we reach Achæan Argos, wealthiest of all lands, you shall be his son-in-law, and he will show you like honor with his own dear son Orestes, who is being nurtured in all abundance. Agamemnon has three daughters, Chrysothemis, Laodice, and Iphianassa; you may take the one of your choice, freely and without gifts of wooing, to the house of Peleus; he will add such dower to boot as no man ever yet gave his daughter, and will give you seven well-established cities, Cardamyle, Enope, and Hire, where there is grass; holy Pheræ and the rich meadows of Anthea; Æpea also, and the vine-clad slopes of Pedasus, all near the sea, and on the borders of sandy Pylos. The men that dwell there are rich in cattle and sheep; they will honor you with gifts as though you were a god, and be obedient to your comfortable ordinances. All this will he do if you will now forgo your anger. Moreover, though you hate both him and his gifts with all your heart, yet pity the rest of the Achæans who are being harassed in all their host; they will honor you as a god, and you will earn great glory at their hands. You might even kill Hector; he will come within your reach, for he is infatuated, and declares that not a Danaan whom the ships have brought can hold his own against him."

Achilles answered, "Ulysses, noble son of Laertes, I should give you formal notice plainly and in all fixity of purpose that there be no more of this cajoling, from whatsoever quarter it may come. Him do I hate even as the gates of hell who says one thing while he hides another in his heart; therefore I will say what I mean. I will be appeased neither by Agamemnon son of Atreus nor by any other of the Danaans, for I see that I have no thanks for all my fighting. He that fights fares no better than he that does not; coward and hero are held in equal honor, and death deals like measure to him who works and him who is idle. I have taken nothing by all my hardships—with my life ever in my hand; as a bird when she has found a morsel takes it to her nestlings, and herself fares hardly, even so many a long night have I been wakeful, and many a bloody battle have I waged by day against those who were fighting for their women. With my ships I have taken twelve cities, and eleven round about Troy have I stormed with my men by land; I took great store of wealth from every one of them, but I gave all up to Agamemnon son of Atreus. He stayed where he was by his ships, yet of what came to him he gave little, and kept much himself.

"Nevertheless he did distribute some meeds¹ of honor among the chieftains and kings, and these have them still; from me alone of the Achæans did he take the woman in whom I delighted—let him keep her and sleep with her. Why, pray, must the Argives needs fight the Trojans? What made the son of Atreus gather the host and bring them? Was it not for the sake of Helen? Are the sons of Atreus the only men in the world who love their wives? Any man of common right feeling will love and cherish her who is his own, as I this woman, with my whole heart, though she was but a fruitling of my spear. Agamemnon has taken her from me; he has played me false; I know him; let him tempt me no further, for he shall not move me. Let him look to you, Ulysses, and to the other princes to save his ships from burning. He has done much without me already. He has built a wall; he has dug a trench deep and wide all round it, and he has planted it within the stakes; but even so he stays not the murderous might of Hector. So long as I fought among the Achæans Hector suffered not the battle to range far from the city walls; he would come to the Scæan gates and to the oak tree, but no further. Once he stayed to meet me—and hardly did he escape my onset: now, however, since I am in no mood to fight him, I will tomorrow offer sacrifice to Jove and to all the gods; I will draw my ships into the water and then victual them duly; tomorrow morning, if you care to look, you will see my ships on the Hellespont, and my men rowing out to sea with might and main. If great Neptune vouchsafes me a fair passage, in three days I shall be in Phthia. I have much there that I left behind me when I came here to my sorrow, and I shall bring back still further store

¹ *meeds*: rewards.

of gold, of red copper, of fair women, and of iron, my share of the spoils
that we have taken; but one prize, he who gave has insolently taken away.
Tell him all as I now bid you, and tell him in public that the Achæans may
hate him and beware of him should he think that he can yet dupe others—
for his effrontery never fails him.

"As for me, hound that he is, he dares not look me in the face. I will
take no counsel with him, and will undertake nothing in common with him.
He has wronged me and deceived me enough, he shall not cozen me further; let him go his own way, for Jove has robbed him of his reason. I
loathe his presents, and for himself care not one straw. He may offer me
ten or even twenty times what he has now done, nay—not though it be all
that he has in the world, both now or ever shall have; he may promise me
the wealth of Orchomenus or of Egyptian Thebes, which is the richest city
in the whole world, for it has a hundred gates through each of which two
hundred men may drive at once with their chariots and horses; he may
offer me gifts as the sands of the sea or the dust of the plain in multitude,
but even so he shall not move me till I have been revenged in full for the
bitter wrong he has done me. I will not marry his daughter; she may be
fair as Venus, and skillful as Minerva, but I will have none of her: let
another take her, who may be a good match for her and who rules a larger
kingdom. If the gods spare me to return home, Peleus will find me a wife;
there are Achæan women in Hellas and Phthia, daughters of kings that
have cities under them; of these I can take whom I will and marry her.
Many a time was I minded when at home in Phthia to woo and wed a
woman who would make me a suitable wife, and to enjoy the riches of my
old father Peleus. My life is more to me than all the wealth of Ilius while
it was yet at peace before the Achæans went there, or than all the treasure
that lies on the stone floor of Apollo's temple beneath the cliffs of Pytho.
Cattle and sheep are to be had for harrying, and a man may buy both
tripods and horses if he wants them, but when his life has once left him it
can neither be bought nor harried back again.

"My mother Thetis tells me that there are two ways in which I may meet
my end. If I stay here and fight, I shall not return alive but my name will
live forever: whereas if I go home my name will die, but it will be long ere
death shall take me. To the rest of you, then, I say, 'Go home, for you will
not take Ilius.' Jove has held his hand over her to protect her, and her
people have taken heart. Go, therefore, as in duty bound, and tell the
princes of the Achæans the message that I have sent them; tell them to find
some other plan for the saving of their ships and people, for so long as my
displeasure lasts the one that they have now hit upon may not be. As for

Phœnix, let him sleep here that he may sail with me in the morning if he so will. But I will not take him by force."

They all held their peace, dismayed at the sternness with which he had denied them, till presently the old knight Phœnix in his great fear for the ships of the Achæans, burst into tears and said, "Noble Achilles, if you are now minded to return, and in the fierceness of your anger will do nothing to save the ships from burning, how, my son, can I remain here without you? Your father Peleus bade me go with you when he sent you as a mere lad from Phthia to Agamemnon. You knew nothing neither of war nor of the arts whereby men make their mark in council, and he sent me with you to train you in all excellence of speech and action. Therefore, my son, I will not stay here without you—no, not though heaven itself vouchsafe to strip my years from off me, and make me young as I was when I first left Hellas the land of fair women. I was then flying the anger of my father Amyntor, son of Ormenus, who was furious with me in the matter of his concubine, of whom he was enamored to the wronging of his wife my mother. My mother, therefore, prayed me without ceasing to lie with the woman myself, that so she might hate my father, and in the course of time I yielded. But my father soon came to know, and cursed me bitterly, calling the dread Erinyes[2] to witness. He prayed that no son of mine might ever sit upon my knees—and the gods, Jove of the world below and awful Proserpine, fulfilled his curse. I took counsel to kill him, but some god stayed my rashness and bade me think on men's evil tongues and how I should be branded as the murderer of my father: nevertheless I could not bear to stay in my father's house with him so bitter against me. My cousins and clansmen came about me, and pressed me sorely to remain; many a sheep and many an ox did they slaughter, and many a fat hog did they set down to roast before the fire; many a jar, too, did they broach of my father's wine. Nine whole nights did they set a guard over me taking it in turns to watch, and they kept a fire always burning, both in the cloister of the outer court and in the inner court at the doors of the room wherein I lay; but when the darkness of the tenth night came, I broke through the closed doors of my room, and climbed the wall of the outer court after passing quickly and unperceived through the men on guard and the women-servants. I then fled through Hellas till I came to fertile Phthia, mother of sheep, and to King Peleus, who made me welcome and treated me as a father treats an only son who will be heir to all his wealth. He made me rich and set me over much people, establishing me on the borders of Phthia where I was chief ruler over the Dolopians.

---

[2] *Erinyes*: the Furies.

"It was I, Achilles, who had the making of you; I loved you with all my heart: for you would eat neither at home nor when you had gone out elsewhere, till I had first set you upon my knees, cut up the dainty morsel that you were to eat, and held the wine cup to your lips. Many a time have you slobbered your wine in baby helplessness over my shirt; I had infinite trouble with you, but I knew that heaven had vouchsafed me no offspring of my own, and I made a son of you, Achilles, that in my hour of need you might protect me. Now, therefore, I say battle with your pride and beat it; cherish not your anger forever; the might and majesty of heaven are more than ours, but even heaven may be appeased; and if a man has sinned he prays the gods, and reconciles them to himself by his piteous cries and by frankincense, with drink-offerings and the savor of burnt sacrifice. For prayers are as daughters to great Jove; halt, wrinkled, with eyes askance, they follow in the footsteps of sin, who, being fierce and fleet of foot, leaves them far behind him, and ever baneful to mankind outstrips them even to the ends of the world; but nevertheless the prayers come hobbling and healing after. If a man has pity upon these daughters of Jove when they draw near him, they will bless him and hear him too when he is praying; but if he deny them and will not listen to them, they go to Jove the son of Saturn and pray that he may presently fall into sin—to his ruing bitterly hereafter. Therefore, Achilles, give these daughters of Jove due reverence, and bow before them as all good men will bow. Were not the son of Atreus offering you gifts and promising others later—if he were still furious and implacable—I am not he that would bid you throw off your anger and help the Achæans, no matter how great their need; but he is giving much now, and more hereafter; he has sent his captains to urge his suit, and has chosen those who of all the Argives are most acceptable to you; make not then their words and their coming to be of none effect. Your anger has been righteous so far. We have heard in song how heroes of old time quarreled when they were roused to fury, but still they could be won by gifts, and fair words could soothe them.

"I have an old story in my mind—a very old one—but you are all friends and I will tell it. The Curetes and the Ætolians were fighting and killing one another round Calydon—the Ætolians defending the city and the Curetes trying to destroy it. For Diana of the golden throne was angry and did them hurt because Œneus had not offered her his harvest first-fruits. The other gods had all been feasted with hecatombs, but to the daughter of great Jove alone he had made no sacrifice. He had forgotten her, or somehow or other it had escaped him, and this was a grievous sin. Thereon the archer-goddess in her displeasure sent a prodigious creature against him—a savage wild boar with great white tusks that did much harm to his orchard lands, uprooting apple trees in full bloom and throwing them to the ground. But Meleager son of Œneus got huntsmen and hounds from many cities and killed it—for it was so monstrous that not a few were needed, and many a man did it stretch upon his funeral pyre. On this the goddess set the Curetes and the Ætolians fighting furiously about the head and skin of the boar.

"So long as Meleager was in the field things went badly with the Curetes, and for all their numbers they could not hold their ground under the city walls; but in the course of time Meleager was angered as even a wise man will sometimes be. He was incensed with his mother Althæa, and therefore stayed at home with his wedded wife fair Cleopatra, who was daughter of Marpessa daughter of Euenus, and of Ides the strongest man then living. He it was who took his bow and faced King Apollo himself for fair Marpessa's sake; her father and mother then named her Alcyone, because her mother had mourned with the plaintive strains of the halcyon bird when Phœbus Apollo had carried her off. Meleager, then, stayed at home with Cleopatra, nursing the anger which he felt by reason of his mother's curses. His mother, grieving for the death of her brother, prayed the gods, and beat the earth with her hands, calling upon Hades and on awful Proserpine; she went down upon her knees and her bosom was wet with tears as she prayed that they would kill her son—and Erinys that walks in darkness and knows no ruth heard her from Erebus.

"Then was heard the din of battle about the gates of Calydon, and the dull thump of the battering against their walls. Thereon the elders of the Ætolians besought Meleager; they sent the chiefest of their priests, and begged him to come out and help them, promising him a great reward. They bade him choose fifty ploughgates, the most fertile in the plain of Calydon, the one-half vineyard and the other open ploughland. The old warrior Œneus implored him, standing at the threshold of his room and beating the doors in supplication. His sisters and his mother herself besought him sore, but he the more refused them; those of his comrades who were nearest and dearest to him also prayed him, but they could not move him till the foe was battering at the very doors of his chamber, and the Curetes had scaled the walls and were setting fire to the city. Then at last his sorrowing wife detailed the horrors that befall those whose city is taken; she reminded him how the men are slain, and the city is given over to the flames, while the women and children are carried into captivity; when he heard all this, his heart was touched, and he donned his armor to go forth. Thus of his own inward motion he saved the city of the Ætolians; but they now gave him nothing of those rich rewards that they had offered earlier, and though he saved the city he took nothing by it. Be not then, my son, thus minded; let not heaven lure you into any such course. When the ships are burning it will be a harder matter to save them. Take the gifts, and go, for the Achæans will then honor you as a god; whereas if you fight without taking them, you may beat the battle back, but you will not be held in like honor."

And Achilles answered, "Phœnix, old friend and father, I have no need of such honor. I have honor from Jove himself, which will abide with me at my ships while I have breath in my body, and my limbs are strong. I say further—and lay my saying to your heart—vex me no more with this weeping and lamentation, all in the cause of the son of Atreus. Love him so well, and you may lose the love I bear you. You ought to help me rather in troubling those that trouble me; be king as much as I am, and share like honor with myself; the others shall take my answer; stay here yourself and sleep comfortably in your bed; at daybreak we will consider whether to remain or go."

On this he nodded quietly to Patroclus as a sign that he was to prepare a bed for Phœnix, and that the others should take their leave. Ajax son of Telamon then said, "Ulysses, noble son of Laertes, let us be gone, for I see that our journey is vain. We must now take our answer, unwelcome though it be, to the Danaans who are waiting to receive it. Achilles is savage and remorseless; he is cruel, and cares nothing for the love his comrades lavished upon him more than on all the others. He is implacable—and yet if a man's brother or son has been slain he will accept a fine by way of amends from him that killed him, and the wrongdoer having paid in full remains in peace among his own people; but as for you, Achilles, the gods have put a wicked unforgiving spirit in your heart, and this, all about one single girl, whereas we now offer you the seven best we have, and much else into the bargain. Be then of a more gracious mind, respect the hospitality of your own roof. We are with you as messengers from the host of the Danaans, and would fain be held nearest and dearest to yourself of all the Achæans."

"Ajax," replied Achilles, "noble son of Telamon, you have spoken much to my liking, but my blood boils when I think it all over, and remember how the son of Atreus treated me with contumely as though I were some vile tramp, and that too in the presence of the Argives. Go, then, and deliver your message; say that I will have no concern with fighting till Hector, son of noble Priam, reaches the tents of the Myrmidons in his murderous course, and flings fire upon their ships. For all his lust of battle, I take it he will be held in check when he is at my own tent and ship."

On this they took every man his double cup, made their drink-offerings, and went back to the ships, Ulysses leading the way. But Patroclus told his men and the maidservants to make ready a comfortable bed for Phœnix; they therefore did so with sheepskins, a rug, and a sheet of fine linen. The old man then laid himself down and waited till morning came. But Achilles slept in an inner room, and beside him the daughter of Phorbas, lovely Diomedè, whom he had carried off from Lesbos. Patroclus lay on the other side of the room, and with him fair Iphis whom Achilles had given him when he took Scyros the city of Enyeüs.

When the envoys reached the tents of the son of Atreus, the Achæans rose, pledged them in cups of gold, and began to question them. King Agamemnon was the first to do so. "Tell me, Ulysses," said he, "will he save the ships from burning, or did he refuse, and is he still furious?"

Ulysses answered, "Most noble son of Atreus, king of men, Agamemnon, Achilles will not be calmed, but is more fiercely angry than ever, and spurns both you and your gifts. He bids you take counsel with the Achæans to save the ships and host as you best may; as for himself, he said that at daybreak he should draw his ships into the water. He said further that he should advise everyone to sail home likewise, for that you will not reach the goal of Ilius. 'Jove,' he said, 'has laid his hand over the city to protect it, and the people have taken heart.' This is what he said, and the others who were with me can tell you the same story—Ajax and the two heralds, men, both of them, who may be trusted. The old man Phœnix stayed where he was to sleep, for so Achilles would have it, that he might go home with him in the morning if he so would; but he will not take him by force."

They all held their peace, sitting for a long time silent and dejected, by reason of the sternness with which Achilles had refused them, till presently Diomed said, "Most noble son of Atreus, king of men, Agamemnon, you ought not to have sued the son of Peleus nor offered him gifts. He is proud enough as it is, and you have encouraged him in his pride still further. Let him stay or go as he will. He will fight later when he is in the humor, and heaven puts it in his mind to do so. Now, therefore, let us all do as I say; we have eaten and drunk our fill, let us then take our rest, for in rest there is both strength and stay. But when fair rosy-fingered morn appears, forthwith bring out your host and your horsemen in front of the ships, urging them on, and yourself fighting among the foremost."

Thus he spoke, and the other chieftains approved his words. They then made their drink-offerings and went every man to his own tent, where they lay down to rest and enjoyed the boon of sleep.

BOOK XVI

THUS did they fight about the ship of Protesilaus. Then Patroclus drew near to Achilles with tears welling from his eyes, as from some spring whose crystal stream falls over the ledges of a high precipice. When Achilles saw him thus weeping he was sorry for him and said, "Why, Patroclus, do you stand there weeping like some silly child that comes running to her mother, and begs to be taken up and carried—she catches hold of her mother's dress to stay her though she is in a hurry, and looks tearfully up until her mother carries her—even such tears, Patroclus, are you now shedding. Have you anything to say to the Myrmidons or to myself? or have you had news from Phthia which you alone know? They tell me Menœtius son of Actor is still alive, as also Peleus son of Æacus, among the Myrmidons—men whose loss we two should bitterly deplore; or are you grieving about the Argives and the way in which they are being killed at the ships, through their own high-handed doings? Do not hide anything from me but tell me that both of us may know about it."

Then, O knight Patroclus, with a deep sigh you answered, "Achilles, son of Peleus, foremost champion of the Achæans, do not be angry, but I weep for the disaster that has now befallen the Argives. All those who have been their champions so far are lying at the ships, wounded by sword or spear. Brave Diomed son of Tydeus has been hit with a spear, while famed Ulysses and Agamemnon have received sword wounds; Eurypylus again has been struck with an arrow in the thigh; skilled apothecaries are attending to these heroes, and healing them of their wounds; are you still, O Achilles, so inexorable? May it never be my lot to nurse such a passion as you have done, to the baning of your own good name. Who in future story will speak well of you unless you now save the Argives from ruin? You know no pity; knight Peleus was not your father nor Thetis your mother, but the gray sea bore you and the sheer cliffs begot you, so cruel and remorseless are you. If however you are kept back through knowledge of some oracle, or if your mother Thetis has told you something from the mouth of Jove, at least send me and the Myrmidons with me, if I may bring deliverance to the Danaans. Let me moreover wear your armor; the Trojans may thus mistake me for you and quit the field, so that the hard-pressed sons of the Achæans may have breathing time—which while they are fighting may hardly be. We who are fresh might soon drive tired men back from our ships and tents to their own city."

He knew not what he was asking, nor that he was suing for his own destruction. Achilles was deeply moved and answered, "What, noble Patroclus, are you saying? I know no prophesyings which I am heeding, nor has my mother told me anything from the mouth of Jove, but I am cut to the very heart that one of my own rank should dare to rob me because he is more powerful than I am. This, after all that I have gone through, is more than I can endure. The girl whom the sons of the Achæans chose for me, whom I won as the fruit of my spear on having sacked a city—her has King Agamemnon taken from me as though I were some common vagrant. Still, let bygones be bygones: no man may keep his anger forever; I said I would not relent till battle and the cry of war had reached my own ships; nevertheless, now gird my armor about your shoulders, and lead the Myrmidons to battle, for the dark cloud of Trojans has burst furiously over our fleet; the Argives are driven back onto the beach, cooped within a narrow space, and the whole people of Troy has taken heart to sally out against them, because they see not the visor of my helmet gleaming near them. Had they seen this, there would not have been a creek nor grip[1] that had not been filled with their dead as they fled back again. And so it would have been, if only King Agamemnon had dealt fairly by me. As it is the Trojans have beset our host. Diomed son of Tydeus no longer wields his spear to defend the Danaans, neither have I heard the voice of the son of Atreus coming from his hated head, whereas that of murderous Hector rings in my ears as he gives orders to the Trojans, who triumph over the Achæans and fill the whole plain with their cry of battle. But even so, Patroclus, fall upon them and save the fleet, lest the Trojans fire it and prevent us from being able to return. Do, however, as I now bid you, that you may win me great honor from all the Danaans, and that they may restore the girl to me again and give me rich gifts into the bargain. When you have driven the Trojans from the ships, come back again. Though Juno's thundering husband should put triumph within your reach, do not fight the Trojans further in my absence, or you will rob me of glory that should be mine. And do not for lust of battle go on killing the Trojans nor lead the Achæans on to Ilius, lest one of the ever-living gods from Olympus attack you—for Phœbus Apollo loves them well: return when you have freed the ships from peril, and let others wage war upon the plain. Would by father Jove, Minerva, and Apollo, that not a single man of all the Trojans might be left alive, nor yet of the Argives, but that we two might be alone left to tear aside the mantle that veils the brow of Troy."

Thus did they converse. But Ajax could no longer hold his ground for

---

[1] *grip*: ditch.

the shower of darts that rained upon him; the will of Jove and the javelins of the Trojans were too much for him; the helmet that gleamed about his temples rang with the continuous clatter of the missiles that kept pouring onto it and onto the cheekpieces that protected his face. Moreover his left shoulder was tired with having held his shield so long, yet for all this, let fly at him as they would, they could not make him give ground. He could hardly draw his breath, the sweat rained from every pore of his body, he had not a moment's respite, and on all sides he was beset by danger upon danger.

And now, tell me, O Muses that hold your mansions on Olympus, how fire was thrown upon the ships of the Achæans. Hector came close up and let drive with his great sword at the ashen spear of Ajax. He cut it clean in two just behind where the point was fastened onto the shaft of the spear. Ajax, therefore, had now nothing but a headless spear, while the bronze point flew some way off and came ringing down onto the ground. Ajax knew the hand of heaven in this, and was dismayed at seeing that Jove had now left him utterly defenseless and was willing victory for the Trojans. Therefore he drew back, and the Trojans flung fire upon the ship which was at once wrapped in flame.

The fire was now flaring about the ship's stern, whereon Achilles smote his two thighs and said to Patroclus, "Up, noble knight, for I see the glare of hostile fire at our fleet; up, lest they destroy our ships, and there be no way by which we may retreat. Gird on your armor at once while I call our people together."

As he spoke Patroclus put on his armor. First he greaved his legs with greaves of good make, and fitted with ankle clasps of silver; after this he donned the cuirass of the son of Æacus, richly inlaid and studded. He hung his silver-studded sword of bronze about his shoulders, and then his mighty shield. On his comely head he set his helmet, well wrought, with a crest of horsehair that nodded menacingly above it. He grasped two redoubtable spears that suited his hands, but he did not take the spear of noble Achilles, so stout and strong, for none other of the Achæans could wield it, though Achilles could do so easily. This was the ashen spear from Mount Pelion, which Chiron had cut upon a mountaintop and had given to Peleus, wherewith to deal out death among heroes. He bade Automedon yoke his horses with all speed, for he was the man whom he held in honor next after Achilles, and on whose support in battle he could rely most firmly. Automedon therefore yoked the fleet horses Xanthus and Balius, steeds that could fly like the wind: these were they whom the harpy Podarge bore to the west wind, as she was grazing in a meadow by the waters of the river Oceanus. In the side traces he set the noble horse Pedasus, whom Achilles had brought away with him when he sacked the city of Eëtion, and who, mortal steed though he was, could take his place along with those that were immortal.

Meanwhile Achilles went about everywhere among the tents, and bade his Myrmidons put on their armor. Even as fierce ravening wolves that are feasting upon a horned stag which they have killed upon the mountains, and their jaws are red with blood—they go in a pack to lap water from the clear spring with their long thin tongues; and they reek of blood and slaughter; they know not what fear is, for it is hunger drives them—even so did the leaders and councillors of the Myrmidons gather round the good squire of the fleet descendant of Æacus, and among them stood Achilles himself cheering on both men and horses.

Fifty ships had noble Achilles brought to Troy, and in each there was a crew of fifty oarsmen. Over these he set five captains whom he could trust, while he was himself commander over them all. Menesthius of the gleaming corselet, son to the river Spercheius that streams from heaven, was captain of the first company. Fair Polydora daughter of Peleus bore him to ever-flowing Spercheius—a woman mated with a god—but he was called son of Borus son of Perieres, with whom his mother was living as his wedded wife, and who gave great wealth to gain her. The second company was led by noble Eudorus, son to an unwedded woman. Polymele, daughter of Phylas the graceful dancer, bore him; the mighty slayer of Argos was enamored of her as he saw her among the singing women at a dance held in honor of Diana the rushing huntress of the golden arrows; he therefore— Mercury, giver of all good—went with her into an upper chamber, and lay with her in secret, whereon she bore him a noble son Eudorus, singularly fleet of foot and in fight valiant. When Ilithuia goddess of the pains of childbirth brought him to the light of day, and he saw the face of the sun, mighty Echecles son of Actor took the mother to wife, and gave great wealth to gain her, but her father Phylas brought the child up, and took care of him, doting as fondly upon him as though he were his own son. The third company was led by Pisander son of Mæmalus, the finest spearman among all the Myrmidons next to Achilles' own comrade Patroclus. The old knight Phœnix was captain of the fourth company, and Alcimedon, noble son of Laërceus, of the fifth.

When Achilles had chosen his men and had stationed them all with their captains, he charged them straitly saying, "Myrmidons, remember your threats against the Trojans while you were at the ships in the time of my anger, and you were all complaining of me. 'Cruel son of Peleus,' you would say, 'your mother must have suckled you on gall, so ruthless are you. You keep us here at the ships against our will; if you are so relentless it were better we went home over the sea.' Often have you gathered and thus chided with me. The hour is now come for those high feats of arms that you have so long been pining for, therefore keep high hearts each one of you to do battle with the Trojans."

With these words he put heart and soul into them all, and they serried their companies yet more closely when they heard the words of their king. As the stones which a builder sets in the wall of some high house which is to give shelter from the winds—even so closely were the helmets and bossed shields set against one another. Shield pressed on shield, helm on helm, and man on man; so close were they that the horsehair plumes on the gleaming ridges of their helmets touched each other as they bent their heads.

In front of them all two men put on their armor—Patroclus and Automedon—two men, with but one mind to lead the Myrmidons. Then Achilles went inside his tent and opened the lid of the strong chest which silver-footed Thetis had given him to take on board ship, and which she had filled with shirts, cloaks to keep out the cold, and good thick rugs. In this chest he had a cup of rare workmanship, from which no man but himself might drink, nor would he make offering from it to any other god save only to father Jove. He took the cup from the chest and cleansed it with sulfur; this done he rinsed it in clean water, and after he had washed his hands he drew wine. Then he stood in the middle of the court and prayed, looking toward heaven, and making his drink-offering of wine; nor was he unseen of Jove whose joy is in thunder. "King Jove," he cried, "lord of Dodona, god of the Pelasgi, who dwellest afar, you who hold wintry Dodona in your sway, where your prophets the Selli dwell around you with their feet unwashed and their couches made upon the ground—if you heard me when I prayed to you aforetime, and did me honor while you sent disaster on the Achæans, vouchsafe me now the fulfillment of yet this further prayer. I shall stay here where my ships are lying, but I shall send my comrade into battle at the head of many Myrmidons. Grant, O all-seeing Jove, that victory may go with him; put your courage into his heart that Hector may learn whether my squire is man enough to fight alone, or whether his might is only then so indomitable when I myself enter the turmoil of war. Afterwards when he has chased the fight and the cry of battle from the ships, grant that he may return unharmed, with his armor and his comrades, fighters in close combat."

Thus did he pray, and all-counseling Jove heard his prayer. Part of it he did indeed vouchsafe him—but not the whole. He granted that Patroclus should thrust back war and battle from the ships, but refused to let him come safely out of the fight.

When he had made his drink-offering and had thus prayed, Achilles went inside his tent and put back the cup into his chest.

Then he again came out, for he still loved to look upon the fierce fight that raged between the Trojans and Achæans.

Meanwhile the armed band that was about Patroclus marched on till they sprang high in hope upon the Trojans. They came swarming out like wasps whose nests are by the roadside, and whom silly children love to tease, whereon anyone who happens to be passing may get stung—or again, if a wayfarer going along the road vexes them by accident, every wasp will come flying out in a fury to defend his little ones—even with such rage and courage did the Myrmidons swarm from their ships, and their cry of battle rose heavenwards. Patroclus called out to his men at the top of his voice, "Myrmidons, followers of Achilles son of Peleus, be men my friends, fight with might and with main, that we may win glory for the son of Peleus, who is far the foremost man at the ships of the Argives—he, and his close-fighting followers. The son of Atreus King Agamemnon will thus learn his folly in showing no respect to the bravest of the Achæans."

With these words he put heart and soul into them all, and they fell in a body upon the Trojans. The ships rang again with the cry which the Achæans raised, and when the Trojans saw the brave son of Menœtius and his squire all gleaming in their armor, they were daunted and their battalions were thrown into confusion, for they thought the fleet son of Peleus must now have put aside his anger, and have been reconciled to Agamemnon; everyone, therefore, looked round about to see whither he might fly for safety.

Patroclus first aimed a spear into the middle of the press where men were packed most closely, by the stern of the ship of Protesilaus. He hit Pyræchmes who had led his Pæonian horsemen from the Amydon and the broad waters of the river Axius; the spear struck him on the right shoulder, and with a groan he fell backwards in the dust; on this his men were thrown into confusion, for by killing their leader, who was the finest soldier among them. Patroclus struck panic into them all. He thus drove them from the ship and quenched the fire that was then blazing—leaving the half-burnt ship to lie where it was. The Trojans were now driven back with a shout that rent the skies, while the Danaans poured after them from their ships, shouting also without ceasing. As when Jove, gatherer of the thundercloud, spreads a dense canopy on the top of some lofty mountain, and all the peaks, the jutting headlands, and forest glades show out in the great light that flashes from the bursting heavens, even so when the Danaans had now driven back the fire from their ships, they took breath for a little while; but the fury of the fight was not yet over, for the Trojans were not driven back in utter rout, but still gave battle, and were ousted from their ground only by sheer fighting.

The fight then became more scattered, and the chieftains killed one another when and how they could. The valiant son of Menœtius first drove his spear into the thigh of Areïlycus just as he was turning round; the point went clean through, and broke the bone so that he fell forward. Meanwhile Menelaus struck Thoas in the chest, where it was exposed near the rim of his shield, and he fell dead. The son of Phyleus saw Amphiclus about to attack him, and ere he could do so took aim at the upper part of his thigh, where the muscles are thicker than in any other part; the spear tore through all the sinews of the leg, and his eyes were closed in darkness. Of the sons of Nestor one, Antilochus, speared Atymnius, driving the point of the spear through his throat, and down he fell. Maris then sprang on Antilochus in hand-to-hand fight to avenge his brother, and bestrode the body spear in hand; but valiant Thrasymedes was too quick for him, and in a moment had struck him in the shoulder ere he could deal his blow; his aim was true, and the spear severed all the muscles at the root of his arm, and tore them right down to the bone, so he fell heavily to the ground and his eyes were closed in darkness. Thus did these two noble comrades of Sarpedon go down to Erebus slain by the two sons of Nestor; they were the warrior sons of Amisodorus, who had reared the invincible Chimæra, to the bane of many. Ajax son of Oïleus sprang on Cleobulus and took him alive as he was entangled in the crush; but he killed him then and there by a sword blow on the neck. The sword reeked with his blood, while dark death and the strong hand of fate gripped him and closed his eyes.

Peneleos and Lycon now met in close fight, for they had missed each other with their spears. They had both thrown without effect, so now they drew their swords. Lycon struck the plumed crest of Peneleos' helmet but his sword broke at the hilt, while Peneleos smote Lycon on the neck under the ear. The blade sank so deep that the head was held on by nothing but the skin, and there was no more life left in him. Meriones gave chase to Acamas on foot and caught him up just as he was about to mount his chariot; he drove a spear through his right shoulder so that he fell headlong from the car, and his eyes were closed in darkness. Idomeneus speared Erymas in the mouth; the bronze point of the spear went clean through it beneath the brain, crashing in among the white bones and smashing them up. His teeth were all of them knocked out and the blood came gushing in a stream from both his eyes; it also came gurgling up from his mouth and nostrils, and the darkness of death enfolded him round about.

Thus did these chieftains of the Danaans each of them kill his man. As ravening wolves seize on kids or lambs, fastening on them when they are alone on the hillsides and have strayed from the main flock through the carelessness of the shepherd—and when the wolves see this they pounce upon them at once because they cannot defend themselves—even so did the Danaans now fall on the Trojans, who fled with ill-omened cries in their panic and had no more fight left in them.

Meanwhile great Ajax kept on trying to drive a spear into Hector, but Hector was so skillful that he held his broad shoulders well under cover of his oxhide shield, ever on the lookout for the whizzing of the arrows and the heavy thud of the spears. He well knew that the fortunes of the day had changed, but still stood his ground and tried to protect his comrades.

As when a cloud goes up into heaven from Olympus, rising out of a clear sky when Jove is brewing a gale—even with such panic-stricken rout did the Trojans now fly, and there was no order in their going. Hector's fleet horses bore him and his armor out of the fight, and he left the Trojan host penned in by the deep trench against their will. Many a yoke of horses snapped the pole of their chariots in the trench and left their master's car behind them. Patroclus gave chase, calling impetuously on the Danaans and full of fury against the Trojans, who, being now no longer in a body, filled all the ways with their cries of panic and rout; the air was darkened with the clouds of dust they raised, and the horses strained every nerve in their flight from the tents and ships toward the city.

Patroclus kept on heading his horses wherever he saw most men flying in confusion, cheering on his men the while. Chariots were being smashed in all directions, and many a man came tumbling down from his own car to fall beneath the wheels of that of Patroclus, whose immortal steeds, given by the gods to Peleus, sprang over the trench at a bound as they sped onward. He was intent on trying to get near Hector, for he had set his heart on spearing him, but Hector's horses were now hurrying him away. As the whole dark earth bows before some tempest on an autumn day when Jove rains his hardest to punish men for giving crooked judgment in their courts, and driving justice therefrom without heed to the decrees of heaven—all the rivers run full and the torrents tear many a new channel as they roar headlong from the mountains to the dark sea, and it fares ill with the works of men—even such was the stress and strain of the Trojan horses in their flight.

Patroclus now cut off the battalions that were nearest to him and drove them back to the ships. They were doing their best to reach the city, but he would not let them, and bore down on them between the river and the ships and wall. Many a fallen comrade did he then avenge. First he hit Pronoüs with a spear on the chest where it was exposed near the rim of his shield, and he fell heavily to the ground. Next he sprang on Thestor son of Enops, who was sitting all huddled up in his chariot, for he had lost his head and the reins had been torn out of his hands. Patroclus went up to him and drove a spear into his right jaw; he thus hooked him by the teeth and the spear pulled him over the rim of his car, as one who sits at the end of some jutting rock and draws a strong fish out of the sea with a hook and a line—even so with his spear did he pull Thestor all gaping from his chariot; he then threw him down on his face and he died while falling. On this, as Erylaus was coming on to attack him, he struck him full on the head with a stone, and his brains were all battered inside his helmet, whereon he fell headlong to the ground and the pangs of death took hold upon him. Then he laid low, one after the other, Erymas, Amphoterus, Epaltes, Tlepolemus, Echius son of Damastor, Pyris, Ipheus, Euippus, and Polymelus son of Argeas.

Now when Sarpedon saw his comrades, men who wore ungirdled tunics, being overcome by Patroclus son of Menœtius, he rebuked the Lycians saying, "Shame on you, where are you flying to? Show your mettle; I will myself meet this man in fight and learn who it is that is so masterful; he has done us much hurt, and has stretched many a brave man upon the ground."

He sprang from his chariot as he spoke, and Patroclus, when he saw this, leaped onto the ground also. The two then rushed at one another with loud cries like eagle-beaked crook-taloned vultures that scream and tear at one another in some high mountain fastness.

The son of scheming Saturn looked down upon them in pity and said to Juno who was his wife and sister, "Alas, that it should be the lot of Sarpedon whom I love so dearly to perish by the hand of Patroclus. I am in two minds whether to catch him up out of the fight and set him down safe and sound in the fertile land of Lycia, or to let him now fall by the hand of the son of Menœtius."

And Juno answered, "Most dread son of Saturn, what is this that you are saying? Would you snatch a mortal man whose doom has long been fated, out of the jaws of death? Do as you will, but we shall not all of us be of your mind. I say further, and lay my saying to your heart, that if you send Sarpedon safely to his own home, some other of the gods will be also wanting to escort his son out of battle, for there are many sons of gods fighting round the city of Troy, and you will make every one jealous. If, however, you are fond of him and pity him, let him indeed fall by the hand of Patroclus, but as soon as the life is gone out of him, send Death and sweet Sleep to bear him off the field and take him to the broad lands of Lycia, where his brothers and his kinsmen will bury him with mound and pillar, in due honor to the dead."

The sire of gods and men assented, but he shed a rain of blood upon the earth in honor of his son whom Patroclus was about to kill on the rich plain of Troy far from his home.

When they were now come close to one another Patroclus struck Thrasydemus, the brave squire of Sarpedon, in the lower part of the belly, and killed him. Sarpedon then aimed a spear at Patroclus and missed him, but he struck the horse Pedasus in the right shoulder, and it screamed aloud as it lay, groaning in the dust until the life went out of it. The other two horses began to plunge; the pole of the chariot cracked, and they got entangled in the reins through the fall of the horse that was yoked along with them; but Automedon knew what to do; without the loss of a moment he drew the keen blade that hung by his sturdy thigh and cut the third horse adrift; whereon the other two righted themselves, and pulling hard at the reins again went together into battle.

Sarpedon now took a second aim at Patroclus, and again missed him, the point of the spear passed over his left shoulder without hitting him. Patroclus then aimed in his turn, and the spear sped not from his hand in vain, for he hit Sarpedon just where the midriff surrounds the ever-beating heart. He fell like some oak or silver poplar or tall pine to which woodsmen have laid their axes upon the mountains to make timber for shipbuilding—even so did he lie stretched at full length in front of his chariot and horses, moaning and clutching at the bloodstained dust. As when a lion springs with a bound upon a herd of cattle and fastens on a great black bull which dies bellowing in its clutches—even so did the leader of the Lycian warriors struggle in death as he fell by the hand of Patroclus. He called on his trusty comrade and said, "Glaucus, my brother, hero among heroes, put forth all your strength, fight with might and main, now if ever quit² yourself like a valiant soldier. First go about among the Lycian captains and bid them fight for Sarpedon; then yourself also do battle to save my armor from being taken. My name will haunt you henceforth and forever if the Achæans rob me of my armor now that I have fallen at their ships. Do your very utmost and call all my people together."

Death closed his eyes as he spoke. Patroclus planted his heel on his breast and drew the spear from his body, whereon his senses came out along with it, and he drew out both spearpoint and Sarpedon's soul at the same time. Hard by the Myrmidons held his snorting steeds, who were wild with panic at finding themselves deserted by their lords.

---

² *quit*: acquit.

Glaucus was overcome with grief when he heard what Sarpedon said, for he could not help him. He had to support his arm with his other hand, being in great pain through the wound which Teucer's arrow had given him when Teucer was defending the wall as he, Glaucus, was assailing it. Therefore he prayed to far-darting Apollo saying, "Hear me O king from your seat, maybe in the rich land of Lycia, or maybe in Troy, for in all places you can hear the prayer of one who is in distress, as I now am. I have a grievous wound; my hand is aching with pain, there is no stanching the blood, and my whole arm drags by reason of my hurt, so that I cannot grasp my sword nor go among my foes and fight them, though our prince, Jove's son Sarpedon, is slain. Jove defended not his son, do you, there-fore, O king, heal me of my wound, ease my pain and grant me strength both to cheer on the Lycians and to fight along with them round the body of him who has fallen."

Thus did he pray, and Apollo heard his prayer. He eased his pain, stanched the black blood from the wound, and gave him new strength. Glaucus perceived this, and was thankful that the mighty god had answered his prayer; forthwith, therefore, he went among the Lycian captains, and bade them come to fight about the body of Sarpedon. From these he strode on among the Trojans to Polydamas son of Panthoüs and Agenor; he then went in search of Æneas and Hector, and when he had found them he said, "Hector, you have utterly forgotten your allies, who languish here for your sake far from friends and home while you do nothing to support them. Sarpedon leader of the Lycian warriors has fallen—he who was at once the right and might of Lycia; Mars has laid him low by the spear of Patroclus. Stand by him, my friends, and suffer not the Myrmidons to strip him of his armor, nor to treat his body with contumely in revenge for all the Danaans whom we have speared at the ships."

As he spoke the Trojans were plunged in extreme and ungovernable grief; for Sarpedon, alien though he was, had been one of the mainstays of their city, both as having much people with him, and as himself the fore-most among them all. Led by Hector, who was infuriated by the fall of Sarpedon, they made instantly for the Danaans with all their might, while the undaunted spirit of Patroclus son of Menœtius cheered on the Achæans. First he spoke to the two Ajaxes, men who needed no bidding. "Ajaxes," said he, "may it now please you to show yourselves the men you always have been, or even better—Sarpedon is fallen—he who was first to over-leap the wall of the Achæans; let us take the body and outrage it; let us strip the armor from his shoulders, and kill his comrades if they try to rescue his body."

He spoke to men who of themselves were full eager; both sides, therefore, the Trojans and Lycians on the one hand, and the Myrmidons and Achæans on the other, strengthened their battalions, and fought desperately about the body of Sarpedon, shouting fiercely the while. Mighty was the din of their armor as they came together, and Jove shed a thick darkness over the fight, to increase the fury of the battle over the body of his son.

At first the Trojans made some headway against the Achæans, for one of the best men among the Myrmidons was killed, Epeigeus son of noble Agacles who had erewhile been king in the good city of Budeum; but presently, having killed a valiant kinsman of his own, he took refuge with Peleus and Thetis, who sent him to Ilius the land of noble steeds to fight the Trojans under Achilles. Hector now struck him on the head with a stone just as he had caught hold of the body, and his brains inside his helmet were all battered in, so that he fell face foremost upon the body of Sarpedon, and there died. Patroclus was enraged by the death of his comrade, and sped through the front ranks as swiftly as a hawk that swoops down on a flock of daws or starlings. Even so swiftly, O noble knight Patroclus, did you make straight for the Lycians and Trojans to avenge your comrade. Forthwith he struck Sthenelaus the son of Ithæmenes on the neck with a stone, and broke the tendons that join it to the head and spine. On this Hector and the front rank of his men gave ground. As far as a man can throw a javelin when competing for some prize, or even in battle—so far did the Trojans now retreat before the Achæans. Glaucus, captain of the Lycians, was the first to rally them, by killing Bathycles son of Chalcon who lived in Hellas and was the richest man among the Myrmidons. Glaucus turned round suddenly, just as Bathycles who was pursuing him was about to lay hold of him, and drove his spear right into the middle of his chest, whereon he fell heavily to the ground, and the fall of so good a man filled the Achæans with dismay, while the Trojans were exultant, and came up in a body round the corpse. Nevertheless the Achæans, mindful of their prowess, bore straight down upon them.

Meriones then killed a helmed warrior of the Trojans, Laogonus son of Onetor, who was priest of Jove of Mount Ida, and was honored by the people as though he were a god. Meriones struck him under the jaw and ear, so that life went out of him and the darkness of death laid hold upon him. Æneas then aimed a spear at Meriones, hoping to hit him under the shield as he was advancing, but Meriones saw it coming and stooped forward to avoid it, whereon the spear flew past him and the point stuck in the ground, while the butt end went on quivering till Mars robbed it of its force. The spear, therefore, sped from Æneas's hand in vain and fell quivering to the ground. Æneas was angry and said, "Meriones, you are a good dancer, but if I had hit you my spear would soon have made an end of you."

And Meriones answered, "Æneas, for all your bravery, you will not be able to make an end of everyone who comes against you. You are only a mortal like myself, and if I were to hit you in the middle of your shield with my spear, however strong and self-confident you may be, I should soon vanquish you, and you would yield your life to Hades of the noble steeds."

On this the son of Menœtius rebuked him and said, "Meriones, hero though you be, you should not speak thus; taunting speeches, my good friend, will not make the Trojans draw away from the dead body; some of them must go underground first; blows for battle, and words for council; fight, therefore, and say nothing."

He led the way as he spoke and the hero went forward with him. As the sound of woodcutters in some forest glade upon the mountains—and the thud of their axes is heard afar—even such a din now rose from earth—clash of bronze armor and of good oxhide shields, as men smote each other with their swords and spears pointed at both ends. A man had need of good eyesight now to know Sarpedon, so covered was he from head to foot with spears and blood and dust. Men swarmed about the body, as flies that buzz round the full milk-pails in spring when they are brimming with milk—even so did they gather round Sarpedon; nor did Jove turn his keen eyes away for one moment from the fight, but kept looking at it all the time, for he was settling how best to kill Patroclus, and considering whether Hector should be allowed to end him now in the fight round the body of Sarpedon, and strip him of his armor, or whether he should let him give yet further trouble to the Trojans. In the end, he deemed it best that the brave squire of Achilles son of Peleus should drive Hector and the Trojans back toward the city and take the lives of many. First, therefore, he made Hector turn fainthearted, whereon he mounted his chariot and fled, bidding the other Trojans fly also, for he saw that the scales of Jove had turned against him. Neither would the brave Lycians stand firm; they were dismayed when they saw their king lying struck to the heart amid a heap of corpses—for when the son of Saturn made the fight wax hot many had fallen above him. The Achæans, therefore, stripped the gleaming armor from his shoulders and the brave son of Menœtius gave it to his men to take to the ships. Then Jove lord of the storm cloud said to Apollo, "Dear Phœbus, go, I pray you, and take Sarpedon out of range of the weapons; cleanse the black blood from off him, and then bear him a long way off where you may wash him in the river, anoint him with ambrosia, and clothe him in immortal raiment; this done, commit him to the arms of

the two fleet messengers, Death and Sleep, who will carry him straightway
to the rich land of Lycia, where his brothers and kinsmen will inter him,
and will raise both mound and pillar to his memory, in due honor to the
dead."

Thus he spoke. Apollo obeyed his father's saying, and came down from
the heights of Ida into the thick of the fight; forthwith he took Sarpedon
out of range of the weapons, and then bore him a long way off, where he
washed him in the river, anointed him with ambrosia and clothed him in
immortal raiment; this done, he committed him to the arms of the two
fleet messengers, Death and Sleep, who presently set him down in the rich
land of Lycia.

Meanwhile Patroclus, with many a shout to his horses and to Automedon, pursued the Trojans and Lycians in the pride and foolishness of his
heart. Had he but obeyed the bidding of the son of Peleus, he would have
escaped death and have been scatheless; but the counsels of Jove pass
man's understanding; he will put even a brave man to flight and snatch
victory from his grasp, or again he will set him on to fight, as he now did
when he put a high spirit into the heart of Patroclus.

Who then first, and who last, was slain by you, O Patroclus, when the
gods had now called you to meet your doom? First Adrestus, Autonoüs,
Echeclus, Perimus the son of Megas, Epistor, and Melanippus; after these
he killed Elasus, Mulius, and Pylartes. These he slew, but the rest saved
themselves by flight.

The sons of the Achæans would now have taken Troy by the hands of
Patroclus, for his spear flew in all directions, had not Phœbus Apollo taken
his stand upon the wall to defeat his purpose and to aid the Trojans. Thrice
did Patroclus charge at an angle of the high wall, and thrice did Apollo
beat him back, striking his shield with his own immortal hands. When
Patroclus was coming on like a god for yet a fourth time, Apollo shouted
to him with an awful voice and said, "Draw back, noble Patroclus, it is
not your lot to sack the city of the Trojan chieftains, nor yet will it be that
of Achilles who is a far better man than you are." On hearing this, Patroclus withdrew to some distance and avoided the anger of Apollo.

Meanwhile Hector was waiting with his horses inside the Scæan gates,
in doubt whether to drive out again and go on fighting, or to call the army
inside the gates. As he was thus doubting Phœbus Apollo drew near him
in the likeness of a young and lusty warrior Asius, who was Hector's uncle,
being own brother to Hecuba, and son of Dymas who lived in Phrygia by
the waters of the river Sangarius; in his likeness Jove's son Apollo now
spoke to Hector saying, "Hector, why have you left off fighting? It is ill

done of you. If I were as much better a man than you, as I am worse, you should soon rue your slackness. Drive straight toward Patroclus, if so be that Apollo may grant you a triumph over him, and you may kill him."

With this the god went back into the hurly-burly, and Hector bade Cebriones drive again into the fight. Apollo passed in among them, and struck panic into the Argives, while he gave triumph to Hector and the Trojans. Hector let the other Danaans alone and killed no man, but drove straight at Patroclus. Patroclus then sprang from his chariot to the ground, with a spear in his left hand, and in his right a jagged stone as large as his hand could hold. He stood still and threw it, nor did it go far without hitting someone; the cast was not in vain, for the stone struck Cebriones, Hector's charioteer, a bastard son of Priam, as he held the reins in his hands. The stone hit him on the forehead and drove his brows into his head, for the bone was smashed, and his eyes fell to the ground at his feet. He dropped dead from his chariot as though he were diving, and there was no more life left in him. Over him did you then vaunt, O knight Patroclus, saying, "Bless my heart, how active he is, and how well he dives. If we had been at sea this fellow would have dived from the ship's side and brought up as many oysters as the whole crew could stomach, even in rough water, for he has dived beautifully off his chariot onto the ground. It seems, then, that there are divers also among the Trojans."

As he spoke he flung himself on Cebriones with the spring, as it were, of a lion that while attacking a stockyard is himself struck in the chest, and his courage is his own bane—even so furiously, O Patroclus, did you then spring upon Cebriones. Hector sprang also from his chariot to the ground. The pair then fought over the body of Cebriones. As two famished lions fight fiercely on some high mountain over the body of a stag that they have killed, even so did these two mighty warriors, Patroclus son of Menœtius and brave Hector, hack and hew at one another over the corpse of Cebriones. Hector would not let him go when he had once got him by the head, while Patroclus kept fast hold of his feet, and a fierce fight raged between the other Danaans and Trojans. As the east and south wind buffet one another when they beat upon some dense forest on the mountains— there is beech and ash and spreading cornel; the tops of the trees roar as they beat on one another, and one can hear the boughs cracking and breaking—even so did the Trojans and Achæans spring upon one another and lay about each other, and neither side would give way. Many a pointed spear fell to ground and many a winged arrow sped from its bowstring about the body of Cebriones; many a great stone, moreover, beat on many a shield as they fought around his body, but there he lay in the whirling clouds of dust, all huge and hugely, heedless of his driving now.

So long as the sun was still high in mid-heaven the weapons of either side were alike deadly, and the people fell; but when he went down toward the time when men loose their oxen, the Achæans proved to be beyond all forecast stronger, so that they drew Cebriones out of range of the darts and tumult of the Trojans, and stripped the armor from his shoulders. Then Patroclus sprang like Mars with fierce intent and a terrific shout upon the Trojans, and thrice did he kill nine men; but as he was coming on like a god for a fourth time, then, O Patroclus, was the hour of your end approaching, for Phœbus fought you in fell earnest. Patroclus did not see him as he moved about in the crush, for he was enshrouded in thick darkness, and the god struck him from behind on his back and his broad shoulders with the flat of his hand, so that his eyes turned dizzy. Phœbus Apollo beat the helmet from off his head, and it rolled rattling off under the horses' feet, where its horsehair plumes were all begrimed with dust and blood. Never indeed had that helmet fared so before, for it had served to protect the head and comely forehead of the godlike hero Achilles. Now, however, Zeus delivered it over to be worn by Hector. Nevertheless the end of Hector also was near. The bronze-shod spear, so great and so strong, was broken in the hand of Patroclus, while his shield that covered him from head to foot fell to the ground as did also the band that held it, and Apollo undid the fastenings of his corselet.

On this his mind became clouded; his limbs failed him, and he stood as one dazed; whereon Euphorbus son of Panthoüs a Dardanian, the best spearman of his time, as also the finest horseman and fleetest runner, came behind him and struck him in the back with a spear, midway between the shoulders. This man as soon as ever he had come up with his chariot had dismounted twenty men, so proficient was he in all the arts of war—he it was, O knight Patroclus, that first drove a weapon into you, but he did not quite overpower you. Euphorbus then ran back into the crowd, after drawing his ashen spear out of the wound; he would not stand firm and wait for Patroclus, unarmed though he now was, to attack him; but Patroclus unnerved, alike by the blow the god had given him and by the spear wound, drew back under cover of his men in fear for his life. Hector on this, seeing him to be wounded and giving ground, forced his way through the ranks, and when close up with him struck him in the lower part of the belly with a spear, driving the bronze point right through it, so that he fell heavily to the ground to the great grief of the Achæans. As when a lion has fought some fierce wild boar and worsted him—the two fight furiously upon the mountains over some little fountain at which they would both drink, and the lion has beaten the boar till he can hardly breathe—even so did Hector son of Priam take the life of the brave son of Menœtius who had killed so many, striking him from close at hand, and vaunting over him the while. "Patroclus," said he, "you deemed that you should sack our city, rob our Trojan women of their freedom, and carry them off in your ships to your own country. Fool; Hector and his fleet horses were ever straining their utmost to defend them. I am foremost of all the Trojan warriors to stave the day of bondage from off them; as for you, vultures shall devour you here. Poor wretch, Achilles with all his bravery availed you nothing; and yet I ween when you left him he charged you straitly saying, 'Come not back to the ships, knight Patroclus, till you have rent the bloodstained shirt of murderous Hector about his body.' Thus I ween did he charge you, and your fool's heart answered him 'yea' within you."

Then, as the life ebbed out of you, you answered, O knight Patroclus: "Hector, vaunt as you will, for Jove the son of Saturn and Apollo have vouchsafed you victory; it is they who have vanquished me so easily, and they who have stripped the armor from my shoulders; had twenty such men as you attacked me, all of them would have fallen before my spear. Fate and the son of Leto have overpowered me, and among mortal men Euphorbus; you are yourself third only in the killing of me. I say further, and lay my saying to your heart, you too shall live but for a little season; death and the day of your doom are close upon you, and they will lay you low by the hand of Achilles son of Æacus."

When he had thus spoken his eyes were closed in death, his soul left his body and flitted down to the house of Hades, mourning its sad fate and bidding farewell to the youth and vigor of its manhood. Dead though he was, Hector still spoke to him saying, "Patroclus, why should you thus foretell my doom? Who knows but Achilles, son of lovely Thetis, may be smitten by my spear and die before me?"

As he spoke he drew the bronze spear from the wound, planting his foot upon the body, which he thrust off and let lie on its back. He then went spear in hand after Automedon, squire of the fleet descendant of Æacus, for he longed to lay him low, but the immortal steeds which the gods had given as a rich gift to Peleus bore him swiftly from the field.

Note: Antilochus, the son of Nestor, has been sent to inform Achilles of Patroclus' death.

BOOK XVIII

THUS then did they fight as it were a flaming fire. Meanwhile the fleet runner Antilochus, who had been sent as messenger, reached Achilles, and found him sitting by his tall ships and boding that which was indeed too surely true. "Alas," said he to himself in the heaviness of his heart, "why are the Achæans again scouring the plain and flocking toward the ships? Heaven grant the gods be not now bringing that sorrow upon me of which my mother Thetis spoke, saying that while I was yet alive the bravest of the Myrmidons should fall before the Trojans, and see the light of the sun no longer. I fear the brave son of Menœtius has fallen through his own daring—and yet I bade him return to the ships as soon as he had driven back those that were bringing fire against them, and not join battle with Hector."

As he was thus pondering, the son of Nestor came up to him and told his sad tale, weeping bitterly the while. "Alas," he cried, "son of noble Peleus, I bring you bad tidings, would indeed that they were untrue. Patroclus has fallen, and a fight is raging about his naked body—for Hector holds his armor."

A dark cloud of grief fell upon Achilles as he listened. He filled both hands with dust from off the ground, and poured it over his head, disfiguring his comely face, and letting the refuse settle over his shirt so fair and new. He flung himself down all huge and hugely at full length, and tore his hair with his hands. The bondswomen whom Achilles and Patroclus had taken captive screamed aloud for grief, beating their breasts, and with their limbs failing them for sorrow. Antilochus bent over him the while, weeping and holding both his hands as he lay groaning for he feared that he might plunge a knife into his own throat. Then Achilles gave a loud cry and his mother heard him as she was sitting in the depths of the sea by the old man her father, whereon she screamed, and all the goddesses-daughters of Nereus that dwelt at the bottom of the sea came gathering round her. There were Glauce, Thalia and Cymodoce, Nesaia, Speo, Thoë and dark-eyed Halië, Cymothoë, Actæa and Limnorea, Melite, Iæra, Amphithoë and Agave, Doto and Proto, Pherusa and Dynamene, Dexamene, Amphinome and Callianeira, Doris, Panope and the famous sea-nymph Galatea, Nemertes, Apseudes and Callianassa. There were also Clymene, Ianeira and Ianassa, Mæra, Oreithuia and Amatheia of the lovely locks, with other Nereids who dwell in the depths of the sea. The crystal cave was filled with their multitude and they all beat their breasts while Thetis led them in their lament.

"Listen," she cried, "sisters, daughters of Nereus, that you may hear the burden of my sorrows. Alas, woe is me, woe in that I have borne the most glorious of offspring. I bore him fair and strong, hero among heroes, and he shot up as a sapling; I tended him as a plant in a goodly garden, and sent him with his ships to Ilius to fight the Trojans, but never shall I welcome him back to the house of Peleus. So long as he lives to look upon the light of the sun he is in heaviness, and though I go to him I cannot help him. Nevertheless I will go, that I may see my dear son and learn what sorrow has befallen him though he is still holding aloof from battle."

She left the cave as she spoke, while the others followed weeping after, and the waves opened a path before them. When they reached the rich plain of Troy, they came up out of the sea in a long line onto the sands, at the place where the ships of the Myrmidons were drawn up in close order round the tents of Achilles. His mother went up to him as he lay groaning; she laid her hand upon his head and spoke piteously, saying, "My son, why are you thus weeping? What sorrow has now befallen you? Tell me; hide it not from me. Surely Jove has granted you the prayer you made him, when you lifted up your hands and besought him that the Achæans might all of them be pent up at their ships, and rue it bitterly in that you were no longer with them."

Achilles groaned and answered, "Mother, Olympian Jove has indeed vouchsafed me the fulfillment of my prayer, but what boots it to me, seeing that my dear comrade Patroclus has fallen—he whom I valued more than all others, and loved as dearly as my own life? I have lost him; aye, and Hector when he had killed him stripped him of the wondrous armor, so glorious to behold, which the gods gave to Peleus when they laid you in the couch of a mortal man. Would that you were still dwelling among the immortal sea nymphs, and that Peleus had taken to himself some mortal bride. For now you shall have grief infinite by reason of the death of that son whom you can never welcome home—nay, I will not live nor go about among mankind unless Hector fall by my spear, and thus pay me for having slain Patroclus son of Menœtius."

Thetis wept and answered, "Then, my son, is your end near at hand—for your own death awaits you full soon after that of Hector."

Then said Achilles in his great grief, "I would die here and now, in that I could not save my comrade. He has fallen far from home, and in his hour of need my hand was not there to help him. What is there for me? Return to my own land I shall not, and I have brought no saving neither to Patroclus nor to my other comrades of whom so many have been slain by mighty Hector; I stay here by my ships a bootless burden upon the earth, I, who in fight have no peer among the Achæans, though in council there are better than I. Therefore, perish strife both from among gods and men, and anger, wherein even a righteous man will harden his heart—which rises up in the soul of a man like smoke, and the taste thereof is sweeter than drops of honey. Even so has Agamemnon angered me. And yet—so be it, for it is over; I will force my soul into subjection as I needs must; I will go; I will pursue Hector who has slain him whom I loved so dearly, and will then abide my doom when it may please Jove and the other gods to send it. Even Hercules, the best beloved of Jove—even he could not escape the hand of death, but fate and Juno's fierce anger laid him low, as I too shall lie when I am dead if a like doom awaits me. Till then I will win fame, and will bid Trojan and Dardanian women wring tears from their tender cheeks with both their hands in the grievousness of their great sorrow; thus shall they know that he who has held aloof so long will hold aloof no longer. Hold me not back, therefore, in the love you bear me, for you shall not move me."

Then silver-footed Thetis answered, "My son, what you have said is true. It is well to save your comrades from destruction, but your armor is in the hands of the Trojans; Hector bears it in triumph upon his own shoulders. Full well I know that his vaunt shall not be lasting, for his end is close at hand; go not, however, into the press of battle till you see me return hither; tomorrow at break of day I shall be here, and will bring you goodly armor from King Vulcan."

On this she left her brave son, and as she turned away she said to the sea-nymphs her sisters, "Dive into the bosom of the sea and go to the house of the old sea-god my father. Tell him everything; as for me, I will go to the cunning workman Vulcan on high Olympus, and ask him to provide my son with a suit of splendid armor."

When she had so said, they dived forthwith beneath the waves, while silver-footed Thetis went her way that she might bring the armor for her son.

Thus, then, did her feet bear the goddess to Olympus, and meanwhile the Achæans were flying with loud cries before murderous Hector till they reached the ships and the Hellespont, and they could not draw the body of Mars' servant Patroclus out of reach of the weapons that were showered upon him, for Hector son of Priam with his host and horsemen had again caught up to him like the flame of a fiery furnace; thrice did brave Hector seize him by the feet, striving with might and main to draw him away and calling loudly on the Trojans, and thrice did the two Ajaxes, clothed in valor as with a garment, beat him from off the body; but all undaunted he would now charge into the thick of the fight, and now again he would stand still and cry aloud, but he would give no ground. As upland shepherds that cannot chase some famished lion from a carcass, even so could not the two Ajaxes scare Hector son of Priam from the body of Patroclus.

And now he would even have dragged it off and have won imperishable glory, had not Iris fleet as the wind, winged her way as messenger from Olympus to the son of Peleus and bidden him arm. She came secretly without the knowledge of Jove and of the other gods, for Juno sent her, and when she had got close to him she said, "Up, son of Peleus, mightiest of all mankind; rescue Patroclus about whom this fearful fight is now raging by the ships. Men are killing one another, the Danaans in defense of the dead body, while the Trojans are trying to hale it away, and take it to windy Ilius: Hector is the most furious of them all; he is for cutting the head from the body and fixing it on the stakes of the wall. Up, then, and bide here no longer; shrink from the thought that Patroclus may become meat for the dogs of Troy. Shame on you, should his body suffer any kind of outrage."

And Achilles said, "Iris, which of the gods was it that sent you to me?"

Iris answered, "It was Juno the royal spouse of Jove, but the son of Saturn does not know of my coming, nor yet does any other of the immortals who dwell on the snowy summits of Olympus."

Then fleet Achilles answered her saying, "How can I go up into the battle? They have my armor. My mother forbade me to arm till I should see her come, for she promised to bring me goodly armor from Vulcan; I know no man whose arms I can put on, save only the shield of Ajax son of Telamon, and he surely must be fighting in the front rank and wielding his spear about the body of dead Patroclus."

Iris said, "We know that your armor has been taken, but go as you are; go to the deep trench and show yourself before the Trojans, that they may fear you and cease fighting. Thus will the fainting sons of the Achæans gain some brief breathing time, which in battle may hardly be."

Iris left him when she had so spoken. But Achilles dear to Jove arose, and Minerva flung her tasseled ægis round his strong shoulders; she crowned his head with a halo of golden cloud from which she kindled a glow of gleaming fire. As the smoke that goes up into heaven from some city that is being beleaguered on an island far out at sea—all day long do men sally from the city and fight their hardest, and at the going down of the sun the line of beacon fires blazes forth, flaring high for those that dwell near them to behold, if so be that they may come with their ships and succor them—even so did the light flare from the head of Achilles, as he stood by the trench, going beyond the wall—but he did not join the Achæans for he heeded the charge which his mother laid upon him.

There did he stand and shout aloud. Minerva also raised her voice from afar, and spread terror unspeakable among the Trojans. Ringing as the note of a trumpet that sounds alarm when the foe is at the gates of a city, even so brazen was the voice of the son of Æacus, and when the Trojans heard its clarion tones they were dismayed; the horses turned back with their chariots for they boded mischief, and their drivers were awestruck by the steady flame which the gray-eyed goddess had kindled above the head of the great son of Peleus.

Thrice did Achilles raise his loud cry as he stood by the trench, and thrice were the Trojans and their brave allies thrown into confusion; whereon twelve of their noblest champions fell beneath the wheels of their chariots and perished by their own spears. The Achæans to their great joy then drew Patroclus out of reach of the weapons, and laid him on a litter: his comrades stood mourning round him, and among them fleet Achilles who wept bitterly as he saw his true comrade lying dead upon his bier. He had sent him out with horses and chariots into battle, but his return he was not to welcome.

Then Juno sent the busy sun, loath though he was, into the waters of Oceanus; so he set, and the Achæans had rest from the tug and turmoil of war.

Now the Trojans when they had come out of the fight, unyoked their horses and gathered in assembly before preparing their supper. They kept their feet, nor would any dare to sit down, for fear had fallen upon them all because Achilles had shown himself after having held aloof so long from battle. Polydamas son of Panthoüs was first to speak, a man of judgment, who alone among them could look both before and after. He was comrade to Hector, and they had been born upon the same night; with all sincerity and goodwill, therefore, he addressed them thus:—

"Look to it well, my friends; I would urge you to go back now to your city and not wait here by the ships till morning, for we are far from our walls. So long as this man was at enmity with Agamemnon the Achæans were easier to deal with, and I would have gladly camped by the ships in the hope of taking them; but now I go in great fear of the fleet son of Peleus; he is so daring that he will never bide here on the plain whereon the Trojans and Achæans fight with equal valor, but he will try to storm our city and carry off our women. Do then as I say, and let us retreat. For this is what will happen. The darkness of night will for a time stay the son of Peleus, but if he find us here in the morning when he sallies forth in full armor, we shall have knowledge of him in good earnest. Glad indeed will he be who can escape and get back to Ilius, and many a Trojan will become meat for dogs and vultures—may I never live to hear it. If we do as I say, little though we may like it, we shall have strength in counsel during the night, and the great gates with the doors that close them will protect the city. At dawn we can arm and take our stand on the walls; he will then rue it if he sallies from the ships to fight us. He will go back when he has given his horses their fill of being driven all whithers under our walls, and will be in no mind to try and force his way into the city. Neither will he ever sack it, dogs shall devour him ere he do so."

Hector looked fiercely at him and answered, "Polydamas, your words are not to my liking in that you bid us go back and be pent within the city. Have you not had enough of being cooped up behind walls? In the old days the city of Priam was famous the whole world over for its wealth of gold and bronze, but our treasures are wasted out of our houses, and much goods have been sold away to Phrygia and fair Meonia, for the hand of Jove has been laid heavily upon us. Now, therefore, that the son of scheming Saturn has vouchsafed me to win glory here and to hem the Achæans in at their ships, prate no more in this fool's wise among the people. You will have no man with you; it shall not be; do all of you as I now say;— take your suppers in your companies throughout the host, and keep your watches and be wakeful every man of you. If any Trojan is uneasy about his possessions, let him gather them and give them out among the people. Better let these, rather than the Achæans, have them. At daybreak we will arm and fight about the ships; granted that Achilles has again come forward to defend them, let it be as he will, but it shall go hard with him. I shall not shun him, but will fight him, to fall or conquer. The god of war deals out like measure to all, and the slayer may yet be slain."

Thus spoke Hector; and the Trojans, fools that they were, shouted in applause, for Pallas Minerva had robbed them of their understanding. They gave ear to Hector with his evil counsel, but the wise words of Polydamas no man would heed. They took their supper throughout the host, and meanwhile through the whole night the Achæans mourned Patroclus, and the son of Peleus led them in their lament. He laid his murderous hands upon the breast of his comrade, groaning again and again as a bearded lion when a man who was chasing deer has robbed him of his young in some dense forest; when the lion comes back he is furious, and searches dingle and dell to track the hunter if he can find him, for he is mad with rage— even so with many a sigh did Achilles speak among the Myrmidons saying, "Alas! vain were the words with which I cheered the hero Menœtius in his own house; I said that I would bring his brave son back again to Opöeis after he had sacked Ilius and taken his share of the spoils—but Jove does not give all men their heart's desire. The same soil shall be reddened here at Troy by the blood of us both, for I too shall never be welcomed home by the old knight Peleus, nor by my mother Thetis, but even in this place shall the earth cover me. Nevertheless, O Patroclus, now that I am left behind you, I will not bury you, till I have brought hither the head and armor of mighty Hector who has slain you. Twelve noble sons of Trojans will I behead before your bier to avenge you; till I have done so you shall lie as you are by the ships, and fair women of Troy and Dardanus, whom we have taken with spear and strength of arm when we sacked men's goodly cities, shall weep over you both night and day."

Then Achilles told his men to set a large tripod upon the fire that they might wash the clotted gore from off Patroclus. Thereon they set a tripod full of bathwater on to a clear fire: they threw sticks onto it to make it blaze, and the water became hot as the flame played about the belly of the tripod. When the water in the caldron was boiling they washed the body, anointed it with oil, and closed its wounds with ointment that had been kept nine years. Then they laid it on a bier and covered it with a linen cloth from head to foot, and over this they laid a fair white robe. Thus all night long did the Myrmidons gather round Achilles to mourn Patroclus.

Then Jove said to Juno his sister-wife, "So, Queen Juno, you have gained your end, and have roused fleet Achilles. One would think that the Achæans were of your own flesh and blood."

And Juno answered, "Dread son of Saturn, why should you say this thing? May not a man though he be only mortal and knows less than we do, do what he can for another person? And shall not I—foremost of all goddesses both by descent and as wife to you who reign in heaven—devise evil for the Trojans if I am angry with them?"

Thus did they converse. Meanwhile Thetis came to the house of Vulcan, imperishable, star-bespangled, fairest of the abodes in heaven, a house of bronze wrought by the lame god's own hands. She found him busy with his bellows, sweating and hard at work, for he was making twenty tripods that were to stand by the wall of his house, and he set wheels of gold under them all that they might go of their own selves to the assemblies of the gods, and come back again—marvels indeed to see. They were finished all but the ears of cunning workmanship which yet remained to be fixed to them: these he was now fixing, and he was hammering at the rivets. While he was thus at work silver-footed Thetis came to the house. Charis, of graceful headdress, wife to the far-famed lame god, came toward her as soon as she saw her, and took her hand in her own, saying, "Why have you come to our house, Thetis, honored and ever welcome—for you do not visit us often? Come inside and let me set refreshment before you."

The goddess led the way as she spoke, and bade Thetis sit on a richly decorated seat inlaid with silver; there was a footstool also under her feet. Then she called Vulcan and said, "Vulcan, come here, Thetis wants you"; and the far-famed lame god answered, "Then it is indeed an august and honored goddess who has come here; she it was that took care of me when I was suffering from the heavy fall which I had through my cruel mother's anger—for she would have got rid of me because I was lame. It would have gone hardly with me had not Eurynome, daughter of the ever-encircling waters of Oceanus, and Thetis, taken me to their bosom. Nine years did I stay with them, and many beautiful works in bronze, brooches, spiral armlets, cups, and chains did I make for them in their cave, with the roaring waters of Oceanus foaming as they rushed ever past it; and no one knew, neither of gods nor men, save only Thetis and Eurynome who took care of me. If, then, Thetis has come to my house I must make her due requital for having saved me; entertain her, therefore, with all hospitality, while I put by my bellows and all my tools."

On this the mighty monster hobbled off from his anvil, his thin legs plying lustily under him. He set the bellows away from the fire, and gathered his tools into a silver chest. Then he took a sponge and washed his face and hands, his shaggy chest and brawny neck; he donned his shirt, grasped his strong staff, and limped toward the door. There were golden handmaids also who worked for him, and were like real young women, with sense and reason, voice also and strength, and all the learning of the immortals; these busied themselves as the king bade them, while he drew near to Thetis, seated her upon a goodly seat, and took her hand in his own, saying, "Why have you come to our house, Thetis honored and ever welcome—for you do not visit us often? Say what you want, and I will do it for you at once if I can, and if it can be done at all."

Thetis wept and answered, "Vulcan, is there another goddess in Olympus whom the son of Saturn has been pleased to try with so much affliction as he has me? Me alone of the marine goddesses did he make subject to a mortal husband, Peleus son of Æacus, and sorely against my will did I submit to the embraces of one who was but mortal, and who now stays at home worn out with age. Neither is this all. Heaven vouchsafed me a son, hero among heroes, and he shot up as a sapling. I tended him as a plant in a goodly garden and sent him with his ships to Ilius to fight the Trojans, but never shall I welcome him back to the house of Peleus. So long as he lives to look upon the light of the sun, he is in heaviness, and though I go to him I cannot help him; King Agamemnon has made him give up the maiden whom the sons of the Achæans had awarded him, and he wastes with sorrow for her sake. Then the Trojans hemmed the Achæans in at their ships' sterns and would not let them come forth; the elders, therefore, of the Argives besought Achilles and offered him great treasure, whereon he refused to bring deliverance to them himself, but put his own armor on Patroclus and sent him into the fight with much people after him. All day long they fought by the Scæan gates and would have taken the city there and then, had not Apollo vouchsafed glory to Hector and slain the valiant son of Menœtius after he had done the Trojans much evil. Therefore I am suppliant at your knees if haply you may be pleased to provide my son, whose end is near at hand, with helmet and shield, with goodly greaves fitted with ankle clasps, and with a breastplate, for he lost his own when his true comrade fell at the hands of the Trojans, and he now lies stretched on earth in the bitterness of his soul."

And Vulcan answered, "Take heart, and be no more disquieted about this matter; would that I could hide him from death's sight when his hour is come, so surely as I can find him armor that shall amaze the eyes of all who behold it."

When he had so said he left her and went to his bellows, turning them toward the fire and bidding them do their office. Twenty bellows blew upon the melting pots, and they blew blasts of every kind, some fierce to help him when he had need of them, and others less strong as Vulcan willed it in the course of his work. He threw tough copper into the fire, and tin, with silver and gold; he set his great anvil on its block, and with one hand grasped his mighty hammer while he took the tongs in the other.

First he shaped the shield so great and strong, adorning it all over and binding it round with a gleaming circuit in three layers; and the baldric was made of silver. He made the shield in five thicknesses, and with many a wonder did his cunning hand enrich it.

He wrought the earth, the heavens, and the sea; the moon also at her full and the untiring sun, with all the signs that glorify the face of heaven—the Pleiads, the Hyads, huge Orion, and the Bear, which men also call the Wain and which turns round ever in one place, facing Orion, and alone never dips into the stream of Oceanus.

He wrought also two cities, fair to see and busy with the hum of men. In the one were weddings and wedding feasts, and they were going about the city with brides whom they were escorting by torchlight from their chambers. Loud rose the cry of Hymen, and the youths danced to the music of flute and lyre, while the women stood each at her house door to see them.

Meanwhile the people were gathered in assembly, for there was a quarrel, and two men were wrangling about the blood money for a man who had been killed, the one saying before the people that he had paid damages in full, and the other that he had not been paid. Each was trying to make his own case good, and the people took sides, each man backing the side that he had taken; but the heralds kept them back, and the elders sat on their seats of stone in a solemn circle, holding the staves which the heralds had put into their hands. Then they rose and each in his turn gave judgment, and there were two talents laid down, to be given to him whose judgment should be deemed the fairest.

About the other city there lay encamped two hosts in gleaming armor, and they were divided whether to sack it, or to spare it and accept the half of what it contained. But the men of the city would not yet consent, and armed themselves for a surprise; their wives and little children kept guard upon the walls, and with them were the men who were past fighting through age; but the others sallied forth with Mars and Pallas Minerva at their head—both of them wrought in gold and clad in golden raiment, great and fair with their armor as befitting gods, while they that followed were smaller. When they reached the place where they would lay their ambush, it was on a riverbed to which livestock of all kinds would come from far and near to water; here, then, they lay concealed, clad in full armor. Some way off them there were two scouts who were on the lookout for the coming of sheep or cattle, which presently came, followed by two shepherds who were playing on their pipes, and had not so much as a thought of danger. When those who were in ambush saw this, they cut off the flocks and herds and killed the shepherds. Meanwhile the besiegers, when they heard much noise among the cattle as they sat in council, sprang to their horses, and made with all speed toward them; when they reached them they set battle in array by the banks of the river, and the hosts aimed their bronze-shod spears at one another. With them were Strife and Riot, and fell Fate who was dragging three men after her, one with a fresh wound, and the other unwounded, while the third was dead, and she was dragging him along by his heel: and her robe was bedrabbled in men's blood. They went in and out with one another and fought as though they were living people hauling away one another's dead.

He wrought also a fair fallow field, large and thrice ploughed already. Many men were working at the plough within it, turning their oxen to and fro, furrow after furrow. Each time that they turned on reaching the headland a man would come up to them and give them a cup of wine, and they would go back to their furrows looking forward to the time when they should again reach the headland. The part that they had ploughed was dark behind them, so that the field, though it was of gold, still looked as if it were being ploughed—very curious to behold.

He wrought also a field of harvest corn, and the reapers were reaping with sharp sickles in their hands. Swath after swath fell to the ground in a straight line behind them, and the binders bound them in bands of twisted straw. There were three binders, and behind them there were boys who gathered the cut corn in armfuls and kept on bringing them to be bound: among them all the owner of the land stood by in silence and was glad. The servants were getting a meal ready under an oak, for they had sacrificed a great ox, and were busy cutting him up, while the women were making a porridge of much white barley for the laborers' dinner.

He wrought also a vineyard, golden and fair to see, and the vines were loaded with grapes. The bunches overhead were black, but the vines were trained on poles of silver. He ran a ditch of dark metal all round it, and fenced it with a fence of tin; there was only one path to it, and by this the vintagers went when they would gather the vintage. Youths and maidens all blithe and full of glee, carried the luscious fruit in plaited baskets; and with them there went a boy who made sweet music with his lyre, and sang the Linus-song[1] with his clear boyish voice.

He wrought also a herd of horned cattle. He made the cows of gold and tin, and they lowed as they came full speed out of the yards to go and feed among the waving reeds that grow by the banks of the river. Along with the cattle there went four shepherds, all of them in gold, and their nine fleet dogs went with them. Two terrible lions had fastened on a bellowing bull that was with the foremost cows, and bellow as he might they haled him, while the dogs and men gave chase: the lions tore through the bull's thick hide and were gorging on his blood and bowels, but the herdsmen were afraid to do anything, and only hounded on their dogs; the dogs dared not fasten on the lions but stood by barking and keeping out of harm's way.

The god wrought also a pasture in a fair mountain dell, and a large flock of sheep, with a homestead and huts, and sheltered sheepfolds.

Furthermore he wrought a green, like that which Dædalus once made in Cnossus for lovely Ariadne. Hereon there danced youths and maidens whom all would woo, with their hands on one another's wrists. The maidens wore robes of light linen, and the youths well-woven shirts that were slightly oiled. The girls were crowned with garlands, while the young men had daggers of gold that hung by silver baldrics; sometimes they would dance deftly in a ring with merry twinkling feet, as it were a potter sitting at his work and making trial of his wheel to see whether it will run, and sometimes they would go all in line with one another, and much people was gathered joyously about the green. There was a bard also to sing to them and play his lyre, while two tumblers went about performing in the midst of them when the man struck up with his tune.

All round the outermost rim of the shield he set the mighty stream of the river Oceanus.

Then when he had fashioned the shield so great and strong, he made a breastplate also that shone brighter than fire. He made a helmet, close fitting to the brow, and richly worked, with a golden plume overhanging it; and he made greaves also of beaten tin.

Lastly, when the famed lame god had made all the armor, he took it

---

[1] *Linus-song*: an ancient dirge named after Linus, a legendary musician who was the son of Apollo.

and set it before the mother of Achilles; whereon she darted like a falcon from the snowy summits of Olympus and bore away the gleaming armor from the house of Vulcan.

Note: Achilles has driven his battle chariot to the front.

BOOK XX

THUS, then, did the Achæans arm by their ships round you, O son of Peleus, who were hungering for battle; while the Trojans over against them armed upon the rise of the plain.

Meanwhile Jove from the top of many-delled Olympus bade Themis gather the gods in council, whereon she went about and called them to the house of Jove. There was not a river absent except Oceanus, nor a single one of the nymphs that haunt fair groves, or springs of rivers and meadows of green grass. When they reached the house of cloud-compelling Jove, they took their seats in the arcades of polished marble which Vulcan with his consummate skill had made for father Jove.

In such wise, therefore, did they gather in the house of Jove. Neptune also, lord of the earthquake, obeyed the call of the goddess, and came up out of the sea to join them. There, sitting in the midst of them, he asked what Jove's purpose might be. "Why," said he, "wielder of the lightning, have you called the gods in council? Are you considering some matter that concerns the Trojans and Achæans—for the blaze of battle is on the point of being kindled between them?"

And Jove answered, "You know my purpose, shaker of earth, and wherefore I have called you hither. I take thought for them even in their destruction. For my own part I shall stay here seated on Mount Olympus and look on in peace, but do you others go about among Trojans and Achæans, and help either side as you may be severally disposed. If Achilles fights the Trojans without hindrance they will make no stand against him; they have ever trembled at the sight of him, and now that he is roused to such fury about his comrade, he will override fate itself and storm their city."

Thus spoke Jove and gave the word for war, whereon the gods took their several sides and went into battle. Juno, Pallas Minerva, earth-encircling Neptune, Mercury bringer of good luck and excellent in all cunning—all these joined the host that came from the ships; with them also came Vulcan in all his glory, limping, but yet with his thin legs plying lustily under him. Mars of gleaming helmet joined the Trojans, and with him Apollo of locks unshorn, and the archer-goddess Diana, Leto, Xanthus, and laughter-loving Venus.

So long as the gods held themselves aloof from mortal warriors the Achæans were triumphant, for Achilles who had long refused to fight was now with them. There was not a Trojan but his limbs failed him for fear as he beheld the fleet son of Peleus all glorious in his armor, and looking like Mars himself. When, however, the Olympians came to take their part among men, forthwith uprose strong Strife, rouser of hosts, and Minerva raised her loud voice, now standing by the deep trench that ran outside the wall, and now shouting with all her might upon the shore of the sounding sea. Mars also bellowed out upon the other side, dark as some black thundercloud, and called on the Trojans at the top of his voice, now from the acropolis, and now speeding up the side of the river Simois till he came to the hill Callicolone.

Thus did the gods spur on both hosts to fight, and rouse fierce contention also among themselves. The sire of gods and men thundered from heaven above, while from beneath Neptune shook the vast earth, and bade the high hills tremble. The spurs and crests of many-fountained Ida quaked, as also the city of the Trojans and the ships of the Achæans. Hades, king of the realms below, was struck with fear; he sprang panic-stricken from his throne and cried aloud in terror lest Neptune, lord of the earthquake, should crack the ground over his head, and lay bare his moldy mansions to the sight of mortals and immortals—mansions so ghastly grim that even the gods shudder to think of them. Such was the uproar as the gods came together in battle. Apollo with his arrows took his stand to face King Neptune, while Minerva took hers against the god of war; the archer-goddess Diana with her golden arrows, sister of far-darting Apollo, stood to face Juno; Mercury the lusty bringer of good luck faced Leto, while the mighty eddying river whom men call Scamander, but gods Xanthus, matched himself against Vulcan.

The gods, then, were thus ranged against one another. But the heart of Achilles was set on meeting Hector son of Priam, for it was with his blood that he longed above all things else to glut the stubborn lord of battle. Meanwhile Apollo set Æneas on to attack the son of Peleus, and put courage into his heart, speaking with the voice of Lycaon son of Priam. In his likeness, therefore, he said to Æneas, "Æneas, counselor of the Trojans, where are now the brave words with which you vaunted over your wine before the Trojan princes, saying that you would fight Achilles son of Peleus in single combat?"

And Æneas answered, "Why do you thus bid me fight the proud son of Peleus, when I am in no mind to do so? Were I to face him now, it would not be for the first time. His spear has already put me to flight from Ida, when he attacked our cattle and sacked Lyrnessus and Pedasus; Jove indeed saved me in that he vouchsafed me strength to fly, else had I fallen by the hands of Achilles and Minerva, who went before him to protect him and urged him to fall upon the Lelegæ and Trojans. No man may fight Achilles, for one of the gods is always with him as his guardian angel, and even were it not so, his weapon flies ever straight, and fails not to pierce the flesh of him who is against him; if heaven would let me fight him on even terms he should not soon overcome me, though he boasts that he is made of bronze."

Then said King Apollo, son to Jove, "Nay, hero, pray to the ever-living gods, for men say that you were born of Jove's daughter Venus, whereas Achilles is son to a goddess of inferior rank. Venus is child to Jove, while Thetis is but daughter to the old man of the sea. Bring, therefore, your spear to bear upon him, and let him not scare you with his taunts and menaces."

As he spoke he put courage into the heart of the shepherd of his people, and he strode in full armor among the ranks of the foremost fighters. Nor did the son of Anchises escape the notice of white-armed Juno, as he went forth into the throng to meet Achilles. She called the gods about her, and said, "Look to it, you two, Neptune and Minerva, and consider how this shall be; Phœbus Apollo has been sending Æneas clad in full armor to fight Achilles. Shall we turn him back at once, or shall one of us stand by Achilles and endow him with strength so that his heart fail not, and he may learn that the chiefs of the immortals are on his side, while the others who have all along been defending the Trojans are but vain helpers? Let us all come down from Olympus and join in the fight, that this day he may take no hurt at the hands of the Trojans. Hereafter let him suffer whatever Fate may have spun out for him when he was begotten and his mother bore him. If Achilles be not thus assured by the voice of a god, he may come to fear presently when one of us meets him in battle, for the gods are terrible if they are seen face to face."

Neptune lord of the earthquake answered her saying, "Juno, restrain your fury; it is not well; I am not in favor of forcing the other gods to fight us, for the advantage is too greatly on our own side; let us take our places on some hill out of the beaten track, and let mortals fight it out among themselves. If Mars or Phœbus Apollo begin fighting, or keep Achilles in check so that he cannot fight, we, too, will at once raise the cry of battle, and in that case they will soon leave the field and go back vanquished to Olympus among the other gods."

With these words the dark-haired god led the way to the high earth barrow of Hercules, built round solid masonry, and made by the Trojans and Pallas Minerva for him to fly to when the sea monster was chasing him from the shore onto the plain. Here Neptune and those that were with him took their seats, wrapped in a thick cloud of darkness; but the other gods seated themselves on the brow of Callicolone round you, O Phœbus, and Mars the waster of cities.

Thus did the gods sit apart and form their plans, but neither side was willing to begin battle with the other, and Jove from his seat on high was in command over them all. Meanwhile the whole plain was alive with men and horses, and blazing with the gleam of armor. The earth rang again under the tramp of their feet as they rushed toward each other, and two champions, by far the foremost of them all, met between the hosts to fight —to wit, Æneas son of Anchises, and noble Achilles.

Æneas was first to stride forward in attack, his doughty helmet tossing defiance as he came on. He held his strong shield before his breast, and brandished his bronze spear. The son of Peleus from the other side sprang forth to meet him, like some fierce lion that the whole countryside has met to hunt and kill—at first he bodes no ill, but when some daring youth has struck him with a spear, he crouches open-mouthed, his jaws foam, he roars with fury, he lashes his tail from side to side about his ribs and loins, and glares as he springs straight before him, to find out whether he is to slay, or be slain among the foremost of his foes—even with such fury did Achilles burn to spring upon Æneas.

When they were now close up with one another Achilles was first to speak. "Æneas," said he, "why do you stand thus out before the host to fight me? Is it that you hope to reign over the Trojans in the seat of Priam? Nay, though you kill me Priam will not hand his kingdom over to you. He is a man of sound judgment, and he has sons of his own. Or have the Trojans been allotting you a demesne of passing richness, fair with orchard lawns and corn lands, if you should slay me? This you shall hardly do. I have discomfited you once already. Have you forgotten how when you were alone I chased you from your herds helter-skelter down the slopes of Ida? You did not turn round to look behind you; you took refuge in Lyrnessus, but I attacked the city, and with the help of Minerva and father Jove I sacked it and carried its women into captivity, though Jove and the other gods rescued you. You think they will protect you now, but they will not do so; therefore I say go back into the host, and do not face me, or you will rue it. Even a fool may be wise after the event."

Then Æneas answered, "Son of Peleus, think not that your words can scare me as though I were a child. I too, if I will, can brag and talk unseemly. We know one another's race and parentage as matters of common fame, though neither have you ever seen my parents nor I yours. Men say that you are son to noble Peleus, and that your mother is Thetis, fair-haired daughter of the sea. I have noble Anchises for my father, and Venus for my mother; the parents of one or other of us shall this day mourn a son, for it will be more than silly talk that shall part us when the fight is over. Learn, then, my lineage if you will—and it is known to many.

"In the beginning Dardanus was the son of Jove, and founded Dardania, for Ilius was not yet established on the plain for men to dwell in, and her people still abode on the spurs of many-fountained Ida. Dardanus had a son, king Erichthonius, who was wealthiest of all men living; he had three thousand mares that fed by the water meadows, they and their foals with them. Boreas was enamored of them as they were feeding, and covered them in the semblance of a dark-maned stallion. Twelve filly foals did they conceive and bear him, and these, as they sped over the rich plain, would go bounding on over the ripe ears of corn and not break them; or again when they would disport themselves on the broad back of Oceanus they could gallop on the crest of a breaker. Erichthonius begat Tros, king of the Trojans, and Tros had three noble sons, Ilus, Assaracus, and Ganymede who was comeliest of mortal men; wherefore the gods carried him off to be Jove's cupbearer, for his beauty's sake, that he might dwell among the immortals. Ilus begat Laomedon, and Laomedon begat Tithonus, Priam, Lampus, Clytius, and Hiketaon of the stock of Mars. But Assaracus was father to Capys, and Capys to Anchises, who was my father, while Hector is son to Priam.

"Such do I declare my blood and lineage, but as for valor, Jove gives it or takes it as he will, for he is lord of all. And now let there be no more of this prating in mid-battle as though we were children. We could fling taunts without end at one another; a hundred-oared galley would not hold them. The tongue can run all whithers and talk all wise; it can go here and there, and as a man says, so shall he be gainsaid. What is the use of our bandying hard words, like women who when they fall foul of one another go out and wrangle in the streets, one half true and the other lies, as rage inspires them? No words of yours shall turn me now that I am fain to fight—therefore let us make trial of one another with our spears."

As he spoke he drove his spear at the great and terrible shield of Achilles, which rang out as the point struck it. The son of Peleus held the shield before him with his strong hand, and he was afraid, for he deemed that Æneas' spear would go through it quite easily, not reflecting that the god's glorious gifts were little likely to yield before the blows of mortal men; and indeed Æneas' spear did not pierce the shield, for the layer of gold, gift of the god, stayed the point. It went through two layers, but the god had made the shield in five, two of bronze, the two innermost ones of tin, and one of gold; it was in this that the spear was stayed.

Achilles in his turn threw, and struck the round shield of Æneas at the very edge, where the bronze was thinnest; the spear of Pelian ash went clean through, and the shield rang under the blow; Æneas was afraid, and crouched backwards, holding the shield away from him; the spear, however, flew over his back, and stuck quivering in the ground, after having gone through both circles of the sheltering shield. Æneas though he had avoided the spear, stood still, blinded with fear and grief because the weapon had gone so near him; then Achilles sprang furiously upon him, with a cry as of death and with his keen blade drawn, and Æneas seized a great stone, so huge that two men, as men now are, would be unable to lift it, but Æneas wielded it quite easily.

Æneas would then have struck Achilles as he was springing toward him, either on the helmet, or on the shield that covered him, and Achilles would have closed with him and dispatched him with his sword, had not Neptune lord of the earthquake been quick to mark, and said forthwith to the immortals, "Alas, I am sorry for great Æneas, who will now go down to the house of Hades, vanquished by the son of Peleus. Fool that he was to give ear to the counsel of Apollo. Apollo will never save him from destruction. Why should this man suffer when he is guiltless, to no purpose, and in another's quarrel? Has he not at all times offered acceptable sacrifice to the gods that dwell in heaven? Let us then snatch him from death's jaws, lest the son of Saturn be angry should Achilles slay him. It is fated, moreover, that he should escape, and that the race of Dardanus, whom Jove loved above all the sons born to him of mortal women, shall not perish utterly without seed or sign. For now indeed has Jove hated the blood of Priam, while Æneas shall reign over the Trojans, he and his children's children that shall be born hereafter."

Then answered Juno, "Earthshaker, look to this matter yourself, and consider concerning Æneas, whether you will save him, or suffer him, brave though he be, to fall by the hand of Achilles son of Peleus. For of a truth we two, I and Pallas Minerva, have sworn full many a time before all the immortals, that never would we shield Trojans from destruction, not even when all Troy is burning in the flames that the Achæans shall kindle."

When earth-encircling Neptune heard this he went into the battle amid the clash of spears, and came to the place where Achilles and Æneas were. Forthwith he shed a darkness before the eyes of the son of Peleus, drew the bronze-headed ashen spear from the shield of Æneas, and laid it at the feet of Achilles. Then he lifted Æneas on high from off the earth and hurried him away. Over the heads of many a band of warriors both horse and foot did he soar as the god's hand sped him, till he came to the very fringe of the battle where the Cauconians were arming themselves for fight. Neptune, shaker of the earth, then came near to him and said, "Æneas, what god has egged you on to this folly in fighting the son of Peleus, who is both a mightier man of valor and more beloved of heaven than you are? Give way before him whensoever you meet him, lest you go down to the house of Hades even though Fate would have it otherwise. When Achilles is dead you may then fight among the foremost undaunted, for none other of the Achæans shall slay you."

The god left him when he had given him these instructions, and at once removed the darkness from before the eyes of Achilles, who opened them wide indeed and said in great anger, "Alas! what marvel am I now beholding? Here is my spear upon the ground, but I see not him whom I meant to kill when I hurled it. Of a truth Æneas also must be under heaven's protection, although I had thought his boasting was idle. Let him go hang; he will be in no mood to fight me further, seeing how narrowly he has missed being killed. I will now give my orders to the Danaans and attack some other of the Trojans."

He sprang forward along the line and cheered his men on as he did so. "Let not the Trojans," he cried, "keep you at arm's length, Achæans, but go for them and fight them man for man. However valiant I may be, I cannot give chase to so many and fight all of them. Even Mars, who is an immortal, or Minerva, would shrink from flinging himself into the jaws of such a fight and laying about him; nevertheless, so far as in me lies I will show no slackness of hand or foot nor want of endurance, not even for a moment; I will utterly break their ranks, and woe to the Trojan who shall venture within reach of my spear."

Thus did he exhort them. Meanwhile Hector called upon the Trojans and declared that he would fight Achilles. "Be not afraid, proud Trojans," said he, "to face the son of Peleus; I could fight gods myself if the battle were one of words only, but they would be more than a match for me, if we had to use our spears. Even so the deed of Achilles will fall somewhat short of his word; he will do in part, and the other part he will clip short. I will go up against him though his hands be as fire—though his hands be fire and his strength iron."

Thus urged the Trojans lifted up their spears against the Achæans, and raised the cry of battle as they flung themselves into the midst of their ranks. But Phœbus Apollo came up to Hector and said, "Hector, on no account must you challenge Achilles to single combat; keep a lookout for him while you are under cover of the others and away from the thick of the fight, otherwise he will either hit you with a spear or cut you down at close quarters."

Thus he spoke, and Hector drew back within the crowd, for he was afraid when he heard what the god had said to him. Achilles then sprang upon the Trojans with a terrible cry, clothed in valor as with a garment. First he killed Iphition son of Otrynteus, a leader of much people whom a naiad nymph had borne to Otrynteus waster of cities, in the land of Hydè under the snowy heights of Mount Tmolus. Achilles struck him full on the head as he was coming on toward him, and split it clean in two; whereon he fell heavily to the ground and Achilles vaunted over him saying, "You lie low, son of Otrynteus, mighty hero; your death is here, but your lineage is on the Gygæan lake where your father's estate lies, by Hyllus, rich in fish, and the eddying waters of Hermus."

Thus did he vaunt, but darkness closed the eyes of the other. The chariots of the Achæans cut him up as their wheels passed over him in the front of the battle, and after him Achilles killed Demoleon, a valiant man of war and son to Antenor. He struck him on the temple through his bronze-cheeked helmet. The helmet did not stay the spear, but it went right on, crushing the bone so that the brain inside was shed in all directions, and his lust of fighting was ended. Then he struck Hippodamas in the midriff as he was springing down from his chariot in front of him, and trying to escape. He breathed his last, bellowing like a bull bellows when young men are dragging him to offer him in sacrifice to the King of Helice, and the heart of the earthshaker is glad: even so did he bellow as he lay dying. Achilles then went in pursuit of Polydorus son of Priam, whom his father had always forbidden to fight because he was the youngest of his sons, the one he loved best, and the fastest runner. He, in his folly and showing off the fleetness of his feet, was rushing about among the front ranks until he lost his life, for Achilles struck him in the middle of the back as he was darting past him: he struck him just at the golden fastenings of his belt and where the two pieces of the double breastplate overlapped. The point of the spear pierced him through and came out by the navel, whereon he fell groaning onto his knees and a cloud of darkness overshadowed him as he sank holding his entrails in his hands.

When Hector saw his brother Polydorus with his entrails in his hands and sinking down upon the ground, a mist came over his eyes, and he could not bear to keep longer at a distance; he therefore poised his spear and darted toward Achilles like a flame of fire. When Achilles saw him he bounded forward and vaunted saying, "This is he that has wounded my heart most deeply and has slain my beloved comrade. Not for long shall we two quail before one another on the highways of war."

He looked fiercely on Hector and said, "Draw near, that you may meet your doom the sooner." Hector feared him not and answered, "Son of Peleus, think not that your words can scare me as though I were a child; I too if I will can brag and talk unseemly; I know that you are a mighty warrior, mightier by far than I, nevertheless the issue lies in the lap of heaven whether I, worse man though I be, may not slay you with my spear, for this too has been found keen ere now."

He hurled his spear as he spoke, but Minerva breathed upon it, and though she breathed but very lightly she turned it back from going toward Achilles, so that it returned to Hector and lay at his feet in front of him. Achilles then sprang furiously on him with a loud cry, bent on killing him, but Apollo caught him up easily as a god can, and hid him in a thick darkness. Thrice did Achilles spring toward him spear in hand, and thrice did he waste his blow upon the air. When he rushed forward for the fourth time as though he were a god, he shouted aloud saying, "Hound, this time too you have escaped death—but of a truth it came exceedingly near you. Phœbus Apollo, to whom it seems you pray before you go into battle, has again saved you; but if I too have any friend among the gods I will surely make an end of you when I come across you at some other time. Now, however, I will pursue and overtake other Trojans."

On this he struck Dryops with his spear, about the middle of his neck, and he fell headlong at his feet. There he let him lie and stayed Demouchus son of Philetor, a man both brave and of great stature, by hitting him on the knee with a spear; then he smote him with his sword and killed him. After this he sprang on Laogonus and Dardanus, sons of Bias, and threw them from their chariot, the one with a blow from a thrown spear, while the other he cut down in hand-to-hand fight. There was also Tros the son of Alastor—he came up to Achilles and clasped his knees in the hope that he would spare him and not kill him but let him go, because they were both of the same age. Fool, he might have known that he should not prevail with him, for the man was in no mood for pity or forbearance but was in grim earnest. Therefore when Tros laid hold of his knees and sought a hearing for his prayers, Achilles drove his sword into his liver, and the liver came rolling out, while his bosom was all covered with the black blood that welled from the wound. Thus did death close his eyes as he lay lifeless.

Achilles then went up to Mulius and struck him on the ear with a spear, and the bronze spearhead came right out at the other ear. He also struck Echeclus son of Agenor on the head with his sword, which became warm with the blood, while death and stern fate closed the eyes of Echeclus. Next in order the bronze point of his spear wounded Deucalion in the forearm where the sinews of the elbow are united, whereon he waited Achilles' onset with his arm hanging down and death staring him in the face. Achilles cut his head off with a blow from his sword and flung it helmet and all away from him, and the marrow came oozing out of his back-bone as he lay. He then went in pursuit of Rhigmus, noble son of Peires, who had come from fertile Thrace, and struck him through the middle with a spear which fixed itself in his belly, so that he fell headlong from his chariot. He also speared Areïthous squire to Rhigmus in the back as he was turning his horses in flight, and thrust him from his chariot, while the horses were struck with panic.

As a fire raging in some mountain glen after long drought—and the dense forest is in a blaze, while the wind carries great tongues of fire in every direction—even so furiously did Achilles rage, wielding his spear as though he were a god, and giving chase to those whom he would slay, till the dark earth ran with blood. Or as one who yokes broad-browed oxen that they may tread barley in a threshing floor—and it is soon bruised small under the feet of the lowing cattle—even so did the horses of Achilles trample on the shields and bodies of the slain. The axle underneath and the railing that ran round the car were bespattered with clots of blood thrown up by the horses' hooves, and from the tires of the wheels; but the son of Peleus pressed on to win still further glory, and his hands were bedrabbled with gore.

> *Note*: Achilles, maddened and set for revenge because of Patroclus' death, meets Lycaon, a son of Priam, in battle and, despite the youth's pleas for mercy, kills him. The same happens with Asteropaeus, son of the river Axius. In revenge, the Scamander River rises and menaces the life of Achilles, but Achilles is fated to die under the walls of Troy, not to drown. Neptune and Minerva, disguised, urge Achilles on to further battle. Vulcan heats the Scamander to boiling in punishment for its threat to Achilles. Jove laughs as the gods fall to fighting among themselves over the mortal combat going on below. Meanwhile, King Priam watches sadly from the walls of Troy as Achilles drives the Trojans in a rout toward their waiting open gates.

BOOK XXII

THUS the Trojans in the city, scared like fawns, wiped the sweat from off them and drank to quench their thirst, leaning against the goodly battlements, while the Achæans with their shields laid upon their shoulders drew close up to the walls. But stern Fate bade Hector stay where he was before Ilius and the Scæan gates. Then Phœbus Apollo spoke to the son of Peleus saying, "Why, son of Peleus, do you, who are but man give chase to me who am immortal? Have you not yet found out that it is a god whom you pursue so furiously? You did not harass the Trojans whom you had routed, and now they are within their walls, while you have been decoyed hither away from them. Me you cannot kill, for death can take no hold upon me."

Achilles was greatly angered and said, "You have balked me, Far-Darter, most malicious of all gods, and have drawn me away from the wall, where many another man would have bitten the dust ere he got within Ilius; you have robbed me of great glory and have saved the Trojans at no risk to yourself, for you have nothing to fear, but I would indeed have my revenge if it were in my power to do so."

On this, with fell intent he made toward the city, and as the winning horse in a chariot race strains every nerve when he is flying over the plain, even so fast and furiously did the limbs of Achilles bear him onward. King Priam was first to note him as he scoured the plain, all radiant as the star which men call Orion's Hound, and whose beams blaze forth in time of harvest more brilliantly than those of any other that shines by night; brightest of them all though he be, he yet bodes ill for mortals, for he brings fire and fever in his train—even so did Achilles' armor gleam on his breast as he sped onward. Priam raised a cry and beat his head with his hands as he lifted them up and shouted out to his dear son, imploring him to return; but Hector still stayed before the gates, for his heart was set upon doing battle with Achilles. The old man reached out his arms toward him and bade him for pity's sake come within the walls. "Hector," he cried, "my son, stay not to face this man alone and unsupported, or you will meet death at the hands of the son of Peleus, for he is mightier than you. Monster that he is; would indeed that the gods loved him no better than I do, for so, dogs and vultures would soon devour him as he lay stretched on earth, and a load of grief would be lifted from my heart, for many a brave son has he reft from me, either by killing them or selling them away in the islands that are beyond the sea: even now I miss two sons from among the Trojans who have thronged within the city, Lycaon and Polydorus, whom Laothoë peeress among women bore me. Should they be still alive and in the hands of the Achæans, we will ransom them with gold and bronze, of which we have store, for the old man Altes endowed his daughter richly; but if they are already dead and in the house of Hades, sorrow will it be to us two who were their parents; albeit the grief of others will be more short-lived unless you too perish at the hands of Achilles. Come, then, my son, within the city, to be the guardian of Trojan men and Trojan women, or you will both lose your own life and afford a mighty triumph to the son of Peleus. Have pity also on your unhappy father while life yet remains to him—on me, whom the son of Saturn will destroy by a terrible doom on the threshold of old age, after I have seen my sons slain and my daughters haled away as captives, my bridal chambers pillaged, little children dashed to earth amid the rage of battle, and my sons' wives dragged away by the cruel hands of the Achæans; in the end fierce hounds will tear me in pieces at my own gates after someone has beaten the life out of my body with sword or spear—hounds that I myself reared and fed at my own table to guard my gates, but who will yet lap my blood and then lie all distraught at my doors. When a young man falls by the sword in battle, he may lie where he is and there is nothing unseemly; let what will be seen, all is honorable in death, but when an old man is slain there is nothing in this world more pitiable than that dogs should defile his gray hair and beard and all that men hide for shame."

The old man tore his gray hair as he spoke, but he moved not the heart of Hector. His mother hard by wept and moaned aloud as she bared her bosom and pointed to the breast which had suckled him. "Hector," she cried, weeping bitterly the while, "Hector, my son, spurn not this breast, but have pity upon me too: if I have ever given you comfort from my own bosom, think on it now, dear son, and come within the wall to protect us from this man; stand not without to meet him. Should the wretch kill you, neither I nor your richly dowered wife shall ever weep, dear offshoot of myself, over the bed on which you lie, for dogs will devour you at the ships of the Achæans."

Thus did the two with many tears implore their son, but they moved not the heart of Hector, and he stood his ground awaiting huge Achilles as he drew nearer toward him. As a serpent in its den upon the mountains, full fed with deadly poisons, waits for the approach of man—he is filled with fury and his eyes glare terribly as he goes writhing round his den—even so Hector leaned his shield against a tower that jutted out from the wall and stood where he was, undaunted.

"Alas," said he to himself in the heaviness of his heart, "if I go within the gates, Polydamas will be the first to heap reproach upon me, for it was he that urged me to lead the Trojans back to the city on that awful night when Achilles again came forth against us. I would not listen, but it would have been indeed better if I had done so. Now that my folly has destroyed the host, I dare not look Trojan men and Trojan women in the face, lest a worse man should say, 'Hector has ruined us by his self-confidence.' Surely it would be better for me to return after having fought Achilles and slain him, or to die gloriously here before the city. What, again, if I were to lay down my shield and helmet, lean my spear against the wall and go straight up to noble Achilles? What if I were to promise to give up Helen, who was the fountainhead of all this war, and all the treasure that Alexandrus brought with him in his ships to Troy, aye, and to let the Achæans divide the half of everything that the city contains among themselves? I might make the Trojans, by the mouths of their princes, take a solemn oath that they would hide nothing, but would divide into two shares all that is within the city—but why argue with myself in this way? Were I to go up to him he would show me no kind of mercy; he would kill me then and there as easily as though I were a woman, when I had put off my armor. There is no parleying with him from some rock or oak tree as young men and maidens prattle with one another. Better fight him at once, and learn to which of us Jove will vouchsafe victory."

Thus did he stand and ponder, but Achilles came up to him as it were Mars himself, plumed lord of battle. From his right shoulder he brandished his terrible spear of Pelian ash, and the bronze gleamed around him like flashing fire or the rays of the rising sun. Fear fell upon Hector as he beheld him, and he dared not stay longer where he was, but fled in dismay from before the gates, while Achilles darted after him at his utmost speed. As a mountain falcon, swiftest of all birds, swoops down upon some cowering dove—the dove flies before him but the falcon with a shrill scream follows close after, resolved to have her—even so did Achilles make straight for Hector with all his might, while Hector fled under the Trojan wall as fast as his limbs could take him.

On they flew along the wagon road that ran hard by under the wall, past the lookout station, and past the weather-beaten wild fig tree, till they came to two fair springs which feed the river Scamander. One of these two springs is warm, and steam rises from it as smoke from a burning fire, but the other even in summer is as cold as hail or snow, or the ice that forms on water. Here, hard by the springs, are the goodly washing troughs of stone, where in the time of peace before the coming of the Achæans the wives and fair daughters of the Trojans used to wash their clothes. Past these did they fly, the one in front and the other giving chase behind him: good was the man that fled, but better far was he that followed after, and swiftly indeed did they run, for the prize was no mere beast for sacrifice or bullock's hide, as it might be for a common footrace, but they ran for the life of Hector. As horses in a chariot race speed round the turning posts when they are running for some great prize—a tripod or woman—at the games in honor of some dead hero, so did these two run full speed three times round the city of Priam. All the gods watched them, and the sire of gods and men was the first to speak.

"Alas," said he, "my eyes behold a man who is dear to me being pursued round the walls of Troy; my heart is full of pity for Hector, who has burned the thighbones of many a heifer in my honor, at one while on the crests of many-valleyed Ida, and again on the citadel of Troy; and now I see noble Achilles in full pursuit of him round the city of Priam. What say you? Consider among yourselves and decide whether we shall now save him or let him fall, valiant though he be, before Achilles son of Peleus."

Then Minerva said, "Father, wielder of the lightning, lord of cloud and storm, what mean you? Would you pluck this mortal whose doom has long been decreed out of the jaws of death? Do as you will, but we others shall not be of a mind with you."

And Jove answered, "My child, Trito-born,[1] take heart. I did not speak in full earnest, and I will let you have your way. Do without let or hindrance as you are minded."

Thus did he urge Minerva who was already eager, and down she darted from the topmost summits of Olympus.

Achilles was still in full pursuit of Hector, as a hound chasing a fawn which he has started from its covert on the mountains, and hunts through glade and thicket. The fawn may try to elude him by crouching under cover of a bush, but he will scent her out and follow her up until he gets her—even so there was no escape for Hector from the fleet son of Peleus. Whenever he made a set to get near the Dardanian gates and under the walls, that his people might help him by showering down weapons from above, Achilles would gain on him and head him back toward the plain, keeping himself always on the city side. As a man in a dream who fails to lay hands upon another whom he is pursuing—the one cannot escape nor the other overtake—even so neither could Achilles come up with Hector, nor Hector break away from Achilles; nevertheless he might even yet have escaped death had not the time come when Apollo, who thus far had sustained his strength and nerved his running, was now no longer to stay by him. Achilles made signs to the Achæan host, and shook his head to show that no man was to aim a dart at Hector, lest another might win the glory of having hit him and he might himself come in second. Then, at last, as they were nearing the fountains for the fourth time, the father of all balanced his golden scales and placed a doom in each of them, one for Achilles and the other for Hector. As he held the scales by the middle, the doom of Hector fell down deep into the house of Hades—and then Phœbus Apollo left him. Thereon Minerva went close up to the son of Peleus and said, "Noble Achilles, favored of heaven, we two shall surely take back to the ships a triumph for the Achæans by slaying Hector, for all his lust of battle. Do what Apollo may as he lies groveling before his

[1] *Trito-born*: referring to Minerva (Athena) who, according to one legend, was born on the shores of Lake Tritonis in Libya.

father, ægis-bearing Jove, Hector cannot escape us longer. Stay here and take breath, while I go up to him and persuade him to make a stand and fight you."

Thus spoke Minerva. Achilles obeyed her gladly, and stood still, leaning on his bronze-pointed ashen spear, while Minerva left him and went after Hector in the form and with the voice of Deïphobus. She came close up to him and said, "Dear brother, I see you are hard pressed by Achilles who is chasing you at full speed round the city of Priam, let us await his onset and stand on our defense."

And Hector answered, "Deïphobus, you have always been dearest to me of all my brothers, children of Hecuba and Priam, but henceforth I shall rate you yet more highly, inasmuch as you have ventured outside the wall for my sake when all the others remain inside."

Then Minerva said, "Dear brother, my father and mother went down on their knees and implored me, as did all my comrades, to remain inside, so great a fear has fallen upon them all; but I was in an agony of grief when I beheld you; now, therefore, let us two make a stand and fight, and let there be no keeping our spears in reserve, that we may learn whether Achilles shall kill us and bear off our spoils to the ships, or whether he shall fall before you."

Thus did Minerva inveigle him by her cunning, and when the two were now close to one another great Hector was first to speak. "I will no longer flee you son of Peleus," said he, "as I have been doing hitherto. Three times have I fled round the mighty city of Priam, without daring to withstand you, but now, let me either slay or be slain, for I am in the mind to face you. Let us, then, give pledges to one another by our gods, who are the fittest witnesses and guardians of all covenants; let it be agreed between us that if Jove vouchsafes me the longer stay and I take your life, I am not to treat your dead body in any unseemly fashion, but when I have stripped you of your armor, I am to give up your body to the Achæans. And do you likewise."

Achilles glared at him and answered, "Fool, prate not to me about covenants. There can be no covenants between men and lions, wolves and lambs can never be of one mind, but hate each other out and out all through. Therefore there can be no understanding between you and me, nor may there be any covenants between us, till one or other shall fall and glut grim Mars with his life's blood. Put forth all your strength; you have need now to prove yourself indeed a bold soldier and man of war. You have no more chance, and Pallas Minerva will forthwith vanquish you by my spear: you shall now pay me in full for the grief you have caused me on account of my comrades whom you have killed in battle."

He poised his spear as he spoke and hurled it. Hector saw it coming and avoided it; he watched it and crouched down so that it flew over his head and stuck in the ground beyond; Minerva then snatched it up and gave it back to Achilles without Hector's seeing her; Hector thereon said to the son of Peleus, "You have missed your aim, Achilles, peer of the gods, and Jove has not yet revealed to you the hour of my doom, though you made sure that he had done so. You were a false-tongued liar when you deemed that I should forget my valor and quail before you. You shall not drive your spear into the back of a runaway—drive it, should heaven so grant you power, drive it into me as I make straight toward you; and now for your own part avoid my spear if you can—would that you might receive the whole of it into your body; if you were once dead the Trojans would find the war an easier matter, for it is you who have harmed them most."

He poised his spear as he spoke and hurled it. His aim was true for he hit the middle of Achilles' shield, but the spear rebounded from it, and did not pierce it. Hector was angry when he saw that the weapon had sped from his hand in vain, and stood there in dismay for he had no second spear. With a loud cry he called Deïphobus and asked him for one, but there was no man; then he saw the truth and said to himself, "Alas! the gods have lured me on to my destruction. I deemed that the hero Deïphobus was by my side, but he is within the wall, and Minerva has inveigled me; death is now indeed exceedingly near at hand and there is no way out of it—for so Jove and his son Apollo the far-darter have willed it, though heretofore they have been ever ready to protect me. My doom has come upon me; let me not then die ingloriously and without a struggle, but let me first do some great thing that shall be told among men hereafter."

As he spoke he drew the keen blade that hung so great and strong by his side, and gathering himself together he sprang on Achilles like a soaring eagle which swoops down from the clouds onto some lamb or timid hare— even so did Hector brandish his sword and spring upon Achilles. Achilles mad with rage darted toward him, with his wondrous shield before his breast, and his gleaming helmet, made with four layers of metal, nodding fiercely forward. The thick tresses of gold with which Vulcan had crested the helmet floated round it, and as the evening star that shines brighter than all others through the stillness of night, even such was the gleam of the spear which Achilles poised in his right hand, fraught with the death of noble Hector. He eyed his fair flesh over and over to see where he could best wound it, but all was protected by the goodly armor of which Hector had spoiled Patroclus after he had slain him, save only the throat where the collarbones divide the neck from the shoulders, and this is a most deadly place: here then did Achilles strike him as he was coming on toward him, and the point of his spear went right through the fleshy part of the neck, but it did not sever his windpipe so that he could still speak. Hector fell headlong, and Achilles vaunted over him saying, "Hector, you deemed that you should come off scatheless when you were spoiling Patroclus, and recked not of myself who was not with him. Fool that you were: for I, his comrade, mightier far than he, was still left behind him at the ships, and now I have laid you low. The Achæans shall give him all due funeral rites, while dogs and vultures shall work their will upon yourself."

Then Hector said, as the life ebbed out of him, "I pray you by your life and knees, and by your parents, let not dogs devour me at the ships of the Achæans, but accept the rich treasure of gold and bronze which my father and mother will offer you, and send my body home, that the Trojans and their wives may give me my dues of fire when I am dead."

Achilles glared at him and answered, "Dog, talk not to me neither of knees nor parents; would that I could be as sure of being able to cut your flesh into pieces and eat it raw, for the ill you have done me, as I am that nothing shall save you from the dogs—it shall not be, though they bring ten or twenty-fold ransom and weigh it out for me on the spot, with promise of yet more hereafter. Though Priam son of Dardanus should bid them offer me your weight in gold, even so your mother shall never lay you out and make lament over the son she bore, but dogs and vultures shall eat you utterly up."

Hector with his dying breath then said, "I know you what you are, and was sure that I should not move you, for your heart is hard as iron; look to it that I bring not heaven's anger upon you on the day when Paris and Phœbus Apollo, valiant though you be, shall slay you at the Scæan gates."

When he had thus said the shrouds of death enfolded him, whereon his soul went out of him and flew down to the house of Hades, lamenting its sad fate that it should enjoy youth and strength no longer. But Achilles said, speaking to the dead body, "Die; for my part I will accept my fate whensoever Jove and the other gods see fit to send it."

As he spoke he drew his spear from the body and set it on one side; then he stripped the bloodstained armor from Hector's shoulders while the other Achæans came running up to view his wondrous strength and beauty; and no one came near him without giving him a fresh wound. Then would one turn to his neighbor and say, "It is easier to handle Hector now than when he was flinging fire onto our ships"—and as he spoke he would thrust his spear into him anew.

When Achilles had done spoiling Hector of his armor, he stood among the Argives and said, "My friends, princes and counselors of the Argives, now that heaven has vouchsafed us to overcome this man, who has done us more hurt than all the others together, consider whether we should not attack the city in force, and discover in what mind the Trojans may be.

We should thus learn whether they will desert their city now that Hector has fallen, or will still hold out even though he is no longer living. But why argue with myself in this way, while Patroclus is still lying at the ships unburied, and unmourned—he whom I can never forget so long as I am alive and my strength fails not? Though men forget their dead when once they are within the house of Hades, yet not even there will I forget the comrade whom I have lost. Now, therefore, Achæan youths, let us raise the song of victory and go back to the ships taking this man along with us; for we have achieved a mighty triumph and have slain noble Hector to whom the Trojans prayed throughout their city as though he were a god."

On this he treated the body of Hector with contumely: he pierced the sinews at the back of both his feet from heel to ankle and passed thongs of oxhide through the slits he had made: thus he made the body fast to his chariot, letting the head trail upon the ground. Then when he had put the goodly armor on the chariot and had himself mounted, he lashed his horses on and they flew forward nothing loath. The dust rose from Hector as he was being dragged along, his dark hair flew all abroad, and his head once so comely was laid low on earth, for Jove had now delivered him into the hands of his foes to do him outrage in his own land.

Thus was the head of Hector being dishonored in the dust. His mother tore her hair, and flung her veil from her with a loud cry as she looked upon her son. His father made piteous moan, and throughout the city the people fell to weeping and wailing. It was as though the whole of frowning Ilius was being smirched with fire. Hardly could the people hold Priam back in his hot haste to rush without the gates of the city. He groveled in the mire and besought them, calling each one of them by his name. "Let be, my friends," he cried, "and for all your sorrow, suffer me to go single-handed to the ships of the Achæans. Let me beseech this cruel and terrible man, if maybe he will respect the feeling of his fellow men, and have compassion on my old age. His own father is even such another as myself—Peleus, who bred him and reared him to be the bane of us Trojans, and of myself more than of all others. Many a son of mine has he slain in the flower of his youth, and yet, grieve for these as I may, I do so for one—Hector—more than for them all, and the bitterness of my sorrow will bring me down to the house of Hades. Would that he had died in my arms, for so both his ill-starred mother who bore him, and myself, should have had the comfort of weeping and mourning over him."

Thus did he speak with many tears, and all the people of the city joined in his lament. Hecuba then raised the cry of wailing among the Trojans. "Alas, my son," she cried, "what have I left to live for now that you are no more? Night and day did I glory in you throughout the city, for you were a tower of strength to all in Troy, and both men and women alike hailed you as a god. So long as you lived you were their pride, but now death and destruction have fallen upon you."

Hector's wife had as yet heard nothing, for no one had come to tell her that her husband had remained without the gates. She was at her loom in an inner part of the house, weaving a double purple web, and embroidering it with many flowers. She told her maids to set a large tripod on the fire, so as to have a warm bath ready for Hector when he came out of battle; poor woman, she knew not that he was now beyond the reach of baths, and that Minerva had laid him low by the hands of Achilles. She heard the cry coming as from the wall, and trembled in every limb; the shuttle fell from her hands, and again she spoke to her waiting women. "Two of you," she said, "come with me that I may learn what it is that has befallen; I heard the voice of my husband's honored mother; my own heart beats as though it would come into my mouth and my limbs refuse to carry me; some great misfortune for Priam's children must be at hand. May I never live to hear it, but I greatly fear that Achilles has cut off the retreat of brave Hector and has chased him onto the plain where he was single-handed; I fear he may have put an end to the reckless daring which possessed my husband, who would never remain with the body of his men, but would dash on far in front, foremost of them all in valor."

Her heart beat fast, and as she spoke she flew from the house like a maniac, with her waiting women following after. When she reached the battlements and the crowd of people, she stood looking out upon the wall, and saw Hector being borne away in front of the city—the horses dragging him without heed or care over the ground toward the ships of the Achæans. Her eyes were then shrouded as with the darkness of night and she fell fainting backwards. She tore the tiring[2] from her head and flung it from her, the frontlet and net with its plaited band, and the veil which golden Venus had given her on the day when Hector took her with him from the house of Eëtion, after having given countless gifts of wooing for her sake. Her husband's sisters and the wives of his brothers crowded round her and supported her, for she was fain to die in her distraction; when she again presently breathed and came to herself, she sobbed and made lament among the Trojans saying, "Woe is me, O Hector; woe, indeed, that to share a common lot we were born, you at Troy in the house of Priam, and I at Thebes under the wooded mountain of Placus in the house of Eëtion who brought me up when I was a child—ill-starred sire of an ill-starred daughter—would that he had never begotten me. You are now going into the house of Hades under the secret places of the earth, and you leave me a sorrowing widow in your house. The child, of whom you and I are the

[2] *tiring*: headband.

unhappy parents, is as yet a mere infant. Now that you are gone, O Hector, you can do nothing for him nor he for you. Even though he escape the horrors of this woeful war with the Achæans, yet shall his life henceforth be one of labor and sorrow, for others will seize his lands. The day that robs a child of his parents severs him from his own kind; his head is bowed, his cheeks are wet with tears, and he will go about destitute among the friends of his father, plucking one by the cloak and another by the shirt. Some one or other of these may so far pity him as to hold the cup for a moment toward him and let him moisten his lips, but he must not drink enough to wet the roof of his mouth; then one whose parents are alive will drive him from the table with blows and angry words. 'Out with you,' he will say, 'you have no father here,' and the child will go crying back to his widowed mother—he, Astyanax, who erewhile would sit upon his father's knees, and have none but the daintiest and choicest morsels set before him. When he had played till he was tired and went to sleep, he would lie in a bed, in the arms of his nurse, on a soft couch, knowing neither want nor care, whereas now that he has lost his father his lot will be full of hardship—he, whom the Trojans name Astyanax, because you, O Hector, were the only defense of their gates and battlements. The wriggling writhing worms will now eat you at the ships, far from your parents, when the dogs have glutted themselves upon you. You will lie naked, although in your house you have fine and goodly raiment made by the hands of women. This will I now burn; it is of no use to you, for you can never again wear it, and thus you will have respect shown you by the Trojans both men and women."

In such wise did she cry aloud amid her tears, and the women joined in her lament.

Note: The Greeks have held funeral games for Patroclus.

BOOK XXIV

THE assembly now broke up and the people went their ways each to his own ship. There they made ready their supper, and then bethought them of the blessed boon of sleep; but Achilles still wept for thinking of his dear comrade, and sleep, before whom all things bow, could take no hold upon him. This way and that did he turn as he yearned after the might and manfulness of Patroclus; he thought of all they had done together, and all they had gone through both on the field of battle and on the waves of the weary sea. As he dwelt on these things he wept bitterly and lay now on his side, now on his back, and now face downwards, till at last he rose and went out as one distraught to wander upon the seashore. Then, when he saw dawn breaking over beach and sea, he yoked his horses to his chariot, and bound the body of Hector behind it that he might drag it about. Thrice did he drag it round the tomb of the son of Menœtius, and then went back into his tent, leaving the body on the ground full length and with its face downwards. But Apollo would not suffer it to be disfigured, for he pitied the man, dead though he now was; therefore he shielded him with his golden ægis continually, that he might take no hurt while Achilles was dragging him.

Thus shamefully did Achilles in his fury dishonor Hector; but the blessed gods looked down in pity from heaven, and urged Mercury, slayer of Argus, to steal the body. All were of this mind save only Juno, Neptune, and Jove's gray-eyed daughter, who persisted in the hate which they had ever borne toward Ilius with Priam and his people; for they forgave not the wrong done them by Alexandrus in disdaining the goddesses who came to him when he was in his sheepyards, and preferring her who had offered him a wanton to his ruin.

When, therefore, the morning of the twelfth day had now come, Phœbus Apollo spoke among the immortals saying, "You gods ought to be ashamed of yourselves; you are cruel and hardhearted. Did not Hector burn you thighbones of heifers and of unblemished goats? And now dare you not rescue even his dead body, for his wife to look upon, with his mother and child, his father Priam, and his people, who would forthwith commit him to the flames, and give him his due funeral rites? So, then, you would all be on the side of mad Achilles, who knows neither right nor ruth? He is like some savage lion that in the pride of his great strength and daring springs upon men's flocks and gorges on them. Even so has Achilles flung aside all pity, and all that conscience which at once so greatly banes yet greatly boons him that will heed it. A man may lose one far dearer than Achilles has lost—a son, it may be, or a brother born from his own mother's womb; yet when he has mourned him and wept over him he will let him bide, for it takes much sorrow to kill a man; whereas Achilles, now that he has slain noble Hector, drags him behind his chariot round the tomb of his comrade. It were better of him, and for him, that he should not do so, for brave though he be we gods may take it ill that he should vent his fury upon dead clay."

Juno spoke up in a rage. "This were well," she cried, "O lord of the silver bow, if you would give like honor to Hector and to Achilles; but Hector was mortal and suckled at a woman's breast, whereas Achilles is the offspring of a goddess whom I myself reared and brought up. I married her to Peleus, who is above measure dear to the immortals; you gods came all of you to her wedding; you feasted along with them yourself and brought your lyre—false, and fond of low company, that you have ever been."

Then said Jove, "Juno, be not so bitter. Their honor shall not be equal, but of all that dwell in Ilius, Hector was dearest to the gods, as also to myself, for his offerings never failed me. Never was my altar stinted of its dues, nor of the drink-offerings and savor of sacrifice which we claim of right. I shall therefore permit the body of mighty Hector to be stolen; and yet this may hardly be without Achilles coming to know it, for his mother keeps night and day beside him. Let some one of you, therefore, send Thetis to me, and I will impart my counsel to her, namely that Achilles is to accept a ransom from Priam, and give up the body."

On this Iris fleet as the wind went forth to carry his message. Down she plunged into the dark sea midway between Samos and rocky Imbrus; the waters hissed as they closed over her, and she sank into the bottom as the lead at the end of an oxhorn, that is sped to carry death to fishes. She found Thetis sitting in a great cave with the other sea-goddesses gathered around her; there she sat in the midst of them weeping for her noble son who was to fall far from his own land, on the rich plains of Troy. Iris went up to her and said, "Rise, Thetis; Jove, whose counsels fail not, bids you come to him." And Thetis answered, "Why does the mighty god so bid me? I am in great grief, and shrink from going in and out among the immortals. Still, I will go, and the word that he may speak shall not be spoken in vain."

The goddess took her dark veil, than which there can be no robe more somber, and went forth with fleet Iris leading the way before her. The waves of the sea opened them a path, and when they reached the shore they flew up into the heavens, where they found the all-seeing son of Saturn with the blessed gods that live forever assembled near him. Minerva gave up her seat to her, and she sat down by the side of father Jove. Juno then placed a fair golden cup in her hand, and spoke to her in words of comfort, whereon Thetis drank and gave her back the cup; and the sire of gods and men was the first to speak.

"So, goddess," said he, "for all your sorrow, and the grief that I well know reigns ever in your heart, you have come hither to Olympus, and I will tell you why I have sent for you. This nine days past the immortals have been quarreling about Achilles waster of cities and the body of Hector. The gods would have Mercury slayer of Argus steal the body, but in furtherance of our peace and amity henceforward, I will concede such honor to your son as I will now tell you. Go, then, to the host and lay these commands upon him; say that the gods are angry with him, and that I am myself more angry than them all, in that he keeps Hector at the ships and will not give him up. He may thus fear me and let the body go. At the same time I will send Iris to great Priam to bid him go to the ships of the Achæans, and ransom his son, taking with him such gifts for Achilles as may give him satisfaction."

Silver-footed Thetis did as the god had told her, and forthwith down she darted from the topmost summits of Olympus. She went to her son's tents where she found him grieving bitterly, while his trusty comrades round him were busy preparing their morning meal, for which they had killed a great woolly sheep. His mother sat down beside him and caressed him with her hand saying, "My son, how long will you keep on thus grieving and making moan? You are gnawing at your own heart, and think neither of food nor of woman's embraces; and yet these too were well, for you have no long time to live, and death with the strong hand of fate are already close beside you. Now, therefore, heed what I say, for I come as a messenger from Jove; he says that the gods are angry with you, and himself more angry than them all, in that you keep Hector at the ships and will not give him up. Therefore let him go, and accept a ransom for his body."

And Achilles answered, "So be it. If Olympian Jove of his own motion thus commands me, let him that brings the ransom bear the body away."

Thus did mother and son talk together at the ships in long discourse with one another. Meanwhile the son of Saturn sent Iris to the strong city of Ilius. "Go," said he, "fleet Iris, from the mansions of Olympus, and tell King Priam in Ilius, that he is to go to the ships of the Achæans and free the body of his dear son. He is to take such gifts with him as shall give satisfaction to Achilles, and he is to go alone, with no other Trojan, save only some honored servant who may drive his mules and wagon, and bring back the body of him whom noble Achilles has slain. Let him have no thought nor fear of death in his heart, for we will send the slayer of Argus to escort him, and bring him within the tent of Achilles. Achilles will not kill him nor let another do so, for he will take heed to his ways and sin not, and he will entreat a suppliant with all honorable courtesy."

On this Iris, fleet as the wind, sped forth to deliver her message. She went to Priam's house, and found weeping and lamentation therein. His sons were seated round their father in the outer courtyard, and their raiment was wet with tears: the old man sat in the midst of them with his mantle wrapped close about his body, and his head and neck all covered with the filth which he had clutched as he lay groveling in the mire. His daughters and his sons' wives went wailing about the house, as they thought of the many and brave men who lay dead, slain by the Argives. The messenger of Jove stood by Priam and spoke softly to him, but fear fell upon him as she did so. "Take heart," she said, "Priam offspring of Dardanus, take heart and fear not. I bring no evil tidings, but am minded well toward you. I come as a messenger from Jove, who though he be not near, takes thought for you and pities you. The lord of Olympus bids you go and ransom noble Hector, and take with you such gifts as shall give satisfaction to Achilles. You are to go alone, with no other Trojan, save only some honored servant who may drive your mules and wagon, and bring back to the city the body of him whom noble Achilles has slain. You are to have no thought, nor fear of death, for Jove will send the slayer of Argus to escort you. When he has brought you within Achilles' tent, Achilles will not kill you nor let another do so, for he will take heed to his ways and sin not, and he will entreat a suppliant with all honorable courtesy."

Iris went her way when she had thus spoken, and Priam told his sons to get a mule wagon ready, and to make the body of the wagon fast upon the top of its bed. Then he went down into his fragrant storeroom, high-vaulted, and made of cedarwood, where his many treasures were kept, and he called Hecuba his wife. "Wife," said he, "a messenger has come to me from Olympus, and has told me to go to the ships of the Achæans to ransom my dear son, taking with me such gifts as shall give satisfaction to Achilles. What think you of this matter? for my own part I am greatly moved to pass through the host of the Achæans and go to their ships."

His wife cried aloud as she heard him, and said, "Alas, what has become of that judgment for which you have been ever famous both among strangers and your own people? How can you venture alone to the ships of the Achæans, and look into the face of him who has slain so many of your brave sons? You must have iron courage, for if the cruel savage sees you and lays hold on you, he will know neither respect nor pity. Let us then weep Hector from afar here in our own house, for when I gave him birth the threads of overruling fate were spun for him that dogs should eat his flesh far from his parents, in the house of that terrible man on whose liver I would fain fasten and devour it. Thus would I avenge my son, who showed no cowardice when Achilles slew him, and thought neither of flight nor of avoiding battle as he stood in defense of Trojan men and Trojan women."

Then Priam said, "I would go, do not therefore stay me nor be as a bird of ill omen in my house, for you will not move me. Had it been some mortal man who had sent me—some prophet or priest who divines from sacrifice—I should have deemed him false and have given him no heed;

but now I have heard the goddess and seen her face to face, therefore I will go and her saying shall not be in vain. If it be my fate to die at the ships of the Achæans even so would I have it; let Achilles slay me, if I may but first have taken my son in my arms and mourned him to my heart's comforting."

So saying he lifted the lids of his chests, and took out twelve goodly vestments. He took also twelve cloaks of single fold, twelve rugs, twelve fair mantles, and an equal number of shirts. He weighed out ten talents of gold, and brought moreover two burnished tripods, four caldrons, and a very beautiful cup which the Thracians had given him when he had gone to them on an embassy; it was very precious, but he grudged not even this, so eager was he to ransom the body of his son. Then he chased all the Trojans from the court and rebuked them with words of anger. "Out," he cried, "shame and disgrace to me that you are. Have you no grief in your own homes that you are come to plague me here? Is it a small thing, think you, that the son of Saturn has sent this sorrow upon me, to lose the bravest of my sons? Nay, you shall prove it in person, for now he is gone the Achæans will have easier work in killing you. As for me, let me go down within the house of Hades, ere mine eyes behold the sacking and wasting of the city."

He drove the men away with his staff, and they went forth as the old man sped them. Then he called to his sons, upbraiding Helenus, Paris, noble Agathon, Pammon, Antiphonus, Polites of the loud battle cry, Deïphobus, Hippothoüs, and Dius. These nine did the old man call near him. "Come to me at once," he cried, "worthless sons who do me shame; would that you had all been killed at the ships rather than Hector. Miserable man that I am, I have had the bravest sons in all Troy—noble Nestor, Troïlus the dauntless charioteer, and Hector who was a god among men, so that one would have thought he was son to an immortal—yet there is not one of them left. Mars has slain them and those of whom I am ashamed are alone left me. Liars, and light of foot, heroes of the dance, robbers of lambs and kids from your own people, why do you not get a wagon ready for me at once, and put all these things upon it that I may set out on my way?"

Thus did he speak, and they feared the rebuke of their father. They brought out a strong mule wagon, newly made, and set the body of the wagon fast on its bed. They took the mule yoke from the peg on which it hung, a yoke of boxwood with a knob on the top of it and rings for the reins to go through. Then they brought a yokeband eleven cubits long, to bind the yoke to the pole; they bound it on at the far end of the pole, and put the ring over the upright pin making it fast with three turns of the band on either side the knob, and bending the thong of the yoke beneath it. This done, they brought from the storechamber the rich ransom that was to purchase the body of Hector, and they set it all orderly on the wagon; then they yoked the strong harness mules which the Mysians had on a time given as a goodly present to Priam; but for Priam himself they yoked horses which the old king had bred, and kept for his own use.

Thus heedfully did Priam and his servant see to the yoking of their cars at the palace. Then Hecuba came to them all sorrowful, with a golden goblet of wine in her right hand, that they might make a drink-offering before they set out. She stood in front of the horses and said, "Take this, make a drink-offering to father Jove, and since you are minded to go to the ships in spite of me, pray that you may come safely back from the hands of your enemies. Pray to the son of Saturn lord of the whirlwind, who sits on Ida and looks down over all Troy, pray him to send his swift messenger on your right hand, the bird of omen which is strongest and most dear to him of all birds, that you may see it with your own eyes and trust it as you go forth to the ships of the Danaans. If all-seeing Jove will not send you this messenger, however set upon it you may be, I would not have you go to the ships of the Argives."

And Priam answered, "Wife, I will do as you desire me; it is well to lift hands in prayer to Jove, if so be he may have mercy upon me."

With this the old man bade the servingwoman pour pure water over his hands, and the woman came, bearing the water in a bowl. He washed his hands and took the cup from his wife; then he made the drink-offering and prayed, standing in the middle of the courtyard and turning his eyes to heaven. "Father Jove," he said, "that rulest from Ida, most glorious and most great, grant that I may be received kindly and compassionately in the tents of Achilles; and send your swift messenger upon my right hand, the bird of omen which is strongest and most dear to you of all birds, that I may see it with my own eyes and trust it as I go forth to the ships of the Danaans."

So did he pray, and Jove the lord of counsel heard his prayer. Forthwith he sent an eagle, the most unerring portent of all birds that fly, the dusky hunter that men also call the Black Eagle. His wings were spread abroad on either side as wide as the well-made and well-bolted door of a rich man's chamber. He came to them flying over the city upon their right hands, and when they saw him they were glad and their hearts took comfort within them. The old man made haste to mount his chariot, and drove out through the inner gateway and under the echoing gatehouse of the outer court. Before him went the mules drawing the four-wheeled wagon, and driven by wise Idæus; behind these were the horses, which the old man lashed with his whip and drove swiftly through the city, while his friends followed after, wailing and lamenting for him as though he were on his road to death. As soon as they had come down from the city and had reached the plain, his sons and sons-in-law who had followed him went back to Ilius.

But Priam and Idæus as they showed out upon the plain did not escape the ken of all-seeing Jove, who looked down upon the old man and pitied him; then he spoke to his son Mercury and said, "Mercury, for it is you who are the most disposed to escort men on their way, and to hear those whom you will hear, go, and so conduct Priam to the ships of the Achæans that no other of the Danaans shall see him nor take note of him until he reach the son of Peleus."

Thus he spoke and Mercury, guide and guardian, slayer of Argus,[1] did as he was told. Forthwith he bound on his glittering golden sandals with which he could fly like the wind over land and sea; he took the wand with which he seals men's eyes in sleep, or wakes them just as he pleases, and flew holding it in his hand till he came to Troy and to the Hellespont. To look at, he was like a young man of noble birth in the heyday of his youth and beauty with the down just coming upon his face.

Now when Priam and Idæus had driven past the great tomb of Ilius, they stayed their mules and horses that they might drink in the river, for the shades of night were falling, when, therefore, Idæus saw Mercury standing near them he said to Priam, "Take heed, descendant of Dardanus; here is matter which demands consideration. I see a man who I think will presently fall upon us; let us fly with our horses, or at least embrace his knees and implore him to take compassion upon us?"

When he heard this the old man's heart failed him, and he was in great fear; he stayed where he was as one dazed, and the hair stood on end over his whole body; but the bringer of good luck came up to him and took him by the hand, saying, "Whither, father, are you thus driving your mules and horses in the dead of night when other men are asleep? Are you not afraid of the fierce Achæans who are hard by you, so cruel and relentless? Should some one of them see you bearing so much treasure through the darkness of the flying night, what would not your state then be? You are no longer young, and he who is with you is too old to protect you from those who would attack you. For myself, I will do you no harm, and I will defend you from anyone else, for you remind me of my own father."

And Priam answered, "It is indeed as you say, my dear son; nevertheless some god has held his hand over me, in that he has sent such a wayfarer as yourself to meet me so opportunely; you are so comely in mien and figure, and your judgment is so excellent that you must come of blessed parents."

[1] *Argus*: a giant, said to have one hundred eyes; killed by Mercury at Juno's request.

Then said the slayer of Argus, guide and guardian, "Sir, all that you have said is right; but tell me and tell me true, are you taking this rich treasure to send it to a foreign people where it may be safe, or are you all leaving strong Ilius in dismay now that your son has fallen who was the bravest man among you and was never lacking in battle with the Achæans?"

And Priam said, "Who are you, my friend, and who are your parents, that you speak so truly about the fate of my unhappy son?"

The slayer of Argus, guide and guardian, answered him, "Sir, you would prove me, that you question me about noble Hector. Many a time have I set eyes upon him in battle when he was driving the Argives to their ships and putting them to the sword. We stood still and marveled, for Achilles in his anger with the son of Atreus suffered us not to fight. I am his squire, and came with him in the same ship. I am a Myrmidon, and my father's name is Polyctor: he is a rich man and about as old as you are; he has six sons besides myself, and I am the seventh. We cast lots, and it fell upon me to sail hither with Achilles. I am now come from the ships onto the plain, for with daybreak the Achæans will set battle in array about the city. They chafe at doing nothing, and are so eager that their princes cannot hold them back."

Then answered Priam, "If you are indeed the squire of Achilles son of Peleus, tell me now the whole truth. Is my son still at the ships, or has Achilles hewn him limb from limb, and given him to his hounds?"

"Sir," replied the slayer of Argus, guide and guardian, "neither hounds nor vultures have yet devoured him; he is still just lying at the tents by the ship of Achilles, and though it is now twelve days that he has lain there, his flesh is not wasted nor have the worms eaten him although they feed on warriors. At daybreak Achilles drags him cruelly round the sepulcher of his dear comrade, but it does him no hurt. You should come yourself and see how he lies fresh as dew, with the blood all washed away, and his wounds every one of them closed though many pierced him with their spears. Such care have the blessed gods taken of your brave son, for he was dear to them beyond all measure."

The old man was comforted as he heard him and said, "My son, see what a good thing it is to have made due offerings to the immortals; for as sure as that he was born my son never forgot the gods that hold Olympus, and now they requite it to him even in death. Accept therefore at my hands this goodly chalice; guard me and with heaven's help guide me till I come to the tent of the son of Peleus."

Then answered the slayer of Argus, guide and guardian, "Sir, you are tempting me and playing upon my youth, but you shall not move me, for you are offering me presents without the knowledge of Achilles whom I fear and hold it great guiltiness to defraud, lest some evil presently befall me; but as your guide I would go with you even to Argos itself, and would guard you so carefully whether by sea or land, that no one should attack you through making light of him who was with you."

The bringer of good luck then sprang onto the chariot, and seizing the whip and reins he breathed fresh spirit into the mules and horses. When they reached the trench and the wall that was before the ships, those who were on guard had just been getting their suppers, and the slayer of Argus threw them all into a deep sleep. Then he drew back the bolts to open the gates, and took Priam inside with the treasure he had upon his wagon. Ere long they came to the lofty dwelling of the son of Peleus for which the Myrmidons had cut pine and which they had built for their king; when they had built it they thatched it with coarse tussock grass which they had mown out on the plain, and all round it they made a large courtyard, which was fenced with stakes set close together. The gate was barred with a single bolt of pine which it took three men to force into its place, and three to draw back so as to open the gate, but Achilles could draw it by himself. Mercury opened the gate for the old man, and brought in the treasure that he was taking with him for the son of Peleus. Then he sprang from the chariot onto the ground and said, "Sir, it is I, immortal Mercury, that am come with you, for my father sent me to escort you. I will now leave you, and will not enter into the presence of Achilles, for it might anger him that a god should befriend mortal men thus openly. Go you within, and embrace the knees of the son of Peleus: beseech him by his father, his lovely mother, and his son; thus you may move him."

With these words Mercury went back to high Olympus. Priam sprang from his chariot to the ground, leaving Idæus where he was, in charge of the mules and horses. The old man went straight into the house where Achilles, loved of the gods, was sitting. There he found him with his men seated at a distance from him: only two, the hero Automedon, and Alcimus of the race of Mars, were busy in attendance about his person, for he had but just done eating and drinking, and the table was still there. King Priam entered without their seeing him, and going right up to Achilles he clasped his knees and kissed the dread murderous hands that had slain so many of his sons.

As when some cruel spite has befallen a man that he should have killed someone in his own country, and must fly to a great man's protection in a land of strangers, and all marvel who see him, even so did Achilles marvel as he beheld Priam. The others looked one to another and marveled also, but Priam besought Achilles saying, "Think of your father, O Achilles like unto the gods, who is such even as I am, on the sad threshold of old age. It may be that those who dwell near him harass him, and there is none to keep war and ruin from him. Yet when he hears of you as being still alive, he is glad, and his days are full of hope that he shall see his dear son come home to him from Troy; but I, wretched man that I am, had the bravest in all Troy for my sons, and there is not one of them left. I had fifty sons when the Achæans came here; nineteen of them were from a single womb, and the others were borne to me by the women of my household. The greater part of them has fierce Mars laid low, and Hector, him who was alone left, him who was the guardian of our city and ourselves, him have you lately slain; therefore I am now come to the ships of the Achæans to ransom his body from you with a great ransom. Fear, O Achilles, the wrath of heaven; think on your own father and have compassion upon me, who am the more pitiable, for I have steeled myself as no man has ever yet steeled himself before me, and have raised to my lips the hand of him who slew my son."

Thus spoke Priam, and the heart of Achilles yearned as he bethought him of his father. He took the old man's hand and moved him gently away. The two wept bitterly—Priam, as he lay at Achilles' feet, weeping for Hector, and Achilles now for his father and now for Patroclus, till the house was filled with their lamentation. But when Achilles was now sated with grief and had unburdened the bitterness of his sorrow, he left his seat and raised the old man by the hand, in pity for his white hair and beard; then he said, "Unhappy man, you have indeed been greatly daring; how could you venture to come alone to the ships of the Achæans, and enter the presence of him who has slain so many of your brave sons? You must have iron courage; sit now upon this seat, and for all our grief we will hide our sorrows in our hearts, for weeping will not avail us. The immortals know no care, yet the lot they spin for man is full of sorrow; on the floor of Jove's palace there stand two urns, the one filled with evil gifts, and the other with good ones. He for whom Jove the lord of thunder mixes the gifts he sends, will meet now with good and now with evil fortune; but he to whom Jove sends none but evil gifts will be pointed at by the finger of scorn, the hand of famine will pursue him to the ends of the world, and he will go up and down the face of the earth, respected neither by gods nor men. Even so did it befall Peleus; the gods endowed him with all good things from his birth upwards, for he reigned over the Myrmidons excelling all men in prosperity and wealth, and mortal though he was they gave him a goddess for his bride. But even on him too did heaven send misfortune, for there is no race of royal children born to him in his house, save one son who is doomed to die all untimely; nor may I take care of him now that he is growing old, for I must stay here at Troy to be the bane of you and of your children. And you too, O Priam, I have heard that you were aforetime happy. They say that in wealth and plenitude of offspring you surpassed all that is in Lesbos, the realm of Makar to the northward,

Phrygia that is more inland, and those that dwell upon the great Hellespont; but from the day when the dwellers in heaven sent this evil upon
you, war and slaughter have been about your city continually. Bear up
against it, and let there be some intervals in your sorrow. Mourn as you
may for your brave son, you will take nothing by it. You cannot raise him
from the dead, ere you do so yet another sorrow shall befall you."

And Priam answered, "O king, bid me not be seated, while Hector is
still lying uncared for in your tents, but accept the great ransom which I
have brought you, and give him to me at once that I may look upon him.
May you prosper with the ransom and reach your own land in safety, seeing that you have suffered me to live and to look upon the light of the sun."

Achilles looked at him sternly and said, "Vex me, sir, no longer; I am of
myself minded to give up the body of Hector. My mother, daughter of the
old man of the sea, came to me from Jove to bid me deliver it to you.
Moreover I know well, O Priam, and you cannot hide it, that some god has
brought you to the ships of the Achæans, for else, no man however strong
and in his prime would dare to come to our host; he could neither pass our
guard unseen, nor draw the bolt of my gates thus easily; therefore, provoke
me no further, lest I sin against the word of Jove, and suffer you not, suppliant though you are, within my tents."

The old man feared him and obeyed. Then the son of Peleus sprang like
a lion through the door of his house, not alone, but with him went his two
squires Automedon and Alcimus who were closer to him than any others
of his comrades now that Patroclus was no more. These unyoked the
horses and mules, and bade Priam's herald and attendant be seated within
the house. They lifted the ransom for Hector's body from the wagon, but
they left two mantles and a goodly shirt, that Achilles might wrap the
body in them when he gave it to be taken home. Then he called to his
servants and ordered them to wash the body and anoint it, but he first took
it to a place where Priam should not see it, lest if he did so, he should
break out in the bitterness of his grief, and enrage Achilles, who might
then kill him and sin against the word of Jove. When the servants had
washed the body and anointed it, and had wrapped it in a fair shirt and
mantle, Achilles himself lifted it onto a bier, and he and his men then laid
it on the wagon. He cried aloud as he did so and called on the name of his
dear comrade. "Be not angry with me, Patroclus," he said, "if you hear
even in the house of Hades that I have given Hector to his father for a
ransom. It has been no unworthy one, and I will share it equitably with
you."

Achilles then went back into the tent and took his place on the richly
inlaid seat from which he had risen, by the wall that was at right angles to
the one against which Priam was sitting. "Sir," he said, "your son is now

laid upon his bier and is ransomed according to your desire; you shall look upon him when you take him away at daybreak; for the present let us prepare our supper. Even lovely Niobe had to think about eating, though her twelve children—six daughters and six lusty sons—had been all slain in her house. Apollo killed the sons with arrows from his silver bow, to punish Niobe, and Diana slew the daughters, because Niobe had vaunted herself against Leto; she said Leto had borne two children only, whereas she had herself borne many—whereon the two killed the many. Nine days did they lie weltering, and there was none to bury them, for the son of Saturn turned the people into stone; but on the tenth day the gods in heaven themselves buried them, and Niobe then took food, being worn out with weeping. They say that somewhere among the rocks on the mountain pastures of Sipylus, where the nymphs live that haunt the river Acheloüs, there, they say, she lives in stone and still nurses the sorrows sent upon her by the hand of heaven. Therefore, noble sir, let us two now take food; you can weep for your dear son hereafter as you are bearing him back to Ilius—and many a tear will he cost you."

With this Achilles sprang from his seat and killed a sheep of silvery whiteness, which his followers skinned and made ready all in due order. They cut the meat carefully up into smaller pieces, spitted them, and drew them off again when they were well roasted. Automedon brought bread in fair baskets and served it round the table, while Achilles dealt out the meat, and they laid their hands on the good things that were before them. As soon as they had had enough to eat and drink, Priam, descendant of Dardanus, marveled at the strength and beauty of Achilles for he was as a god to see, and Achilles marveled at Priam as he listened to him and looked upon his noble presence. When they had gazed their fill Priam spoke first. "And now, O king," he said, "take me to my couch that we may lie down and enjoy the blessed boon of sleep. Never once have my eyes been closed from the day your hands took the life of my son; I have groveled without ceasing in the mire of my stableyard, making moan and brooding over my countless sorrows. Now, moreover, I have eaten bread and drunk wine; hitherto I have tasted nothing."

As he spoke Achilles told his men and the womenservants to set beds in the room that was in the gatehouse, and make them with good red rugs, and spread coverlets on the top of them with woolen cloaks for Priam and Idæus to wear. So the maids went out carrying a torch and got the two beds ready in all haste. Then Achilles said laughingly to Priam, "Dear sir, you shall lie outside, lest some counselor of those who in due course keep coming to advise with me should see you here in the darkness of the flying night, and tell it to Agamemnon. This might cause delay in the delivery of the body. And now tell me and tell me true, for how many days would you celebrate the funeral rites of noble Hector? Tell me, that I may hold aloof from war and restrain the host."

And Priam answered, "Since, then, you suffer me to bury my noble son with all due rites, do thus, Achilles, and I shall be grateful. You know how we are pent up within our city; it is far for us to fetch wood from the mountain, and the people live in fear. Nine days, therefore, will we mourn Hector in my house; on the tenth day we will bury him and there shall be a public feast in his honor; on the eleventh we will build a mound over his ashes, and on the twelfth, if there be need, we will fight."

And Achilles answered, "All, King Priam, shall be as you have said. I will stay our fighting for as long a time as you have named."

As he spoke he laid his hand on the old man's right wrist, in token that he should have no fear; thus then did Priam and his attendant sleep there in the forecourt, full of thought, while Achilles lay in an inner room of the house, with fair Briseis by his side.

And now both gods and mortals were fast asleep through the livelong night, but upon Mercury alone, the bringer of good luck, sleep could take no hold for he was thinking all the time how to get King Priam away from the ships without his being seen by the strong force of sentinels. He hovered therefore over Priam's head and said, "Sir, now that Achilles has spared your life, you seem to have no fear about sleeping in the thick of your foes. You have paid a great ransom, and have received the body of your son; were you still alive and a prisoner the sons whom you have left at home would have to give three times as much to free you; and so it would be if Agamemnon and the other Achæans were to know of your being here."

When he heard this the old man was afraid and roused his servant. Mercury then yoked their horses and mules, and drove them quickly through the host so that no man perceived them. When they came to the ford of eddying Xanthus, begotten of immortal Jove, Mercury went back to high Olympus, and dawn in robe of saffron began to break over all the land. Priam and Idæus then drove on toward the city lamenting and making moan, and the mules drew the body of Hector. No one neither man nor woman saw them, till Cassandra, fair as golden Venus standing on Pergamus, caught sight of her dear father in his chariot, and his servant that was the city's herald with him. Then she saw him that was lying upon the bier, drawn by the mules, and with a loud cry she went about the city saying, "Come hither Trojans, men and women, and look on Hector; if ever you rejoiced to see him coming from battle when he was alive, look now on him that was the glory of our city and all our people."

At this there was not man nor woman left in the city, so great a sorrow had possessed them. Hard by the gates they met Priam as he was bringing in the body. Hector's wife and his mother were the first to mourn him: they flew toward the wagon and laid their hands upon his head, while the crowd stood weeping round them. They would have stayed before the gates, weeping and lamenting the livelong day to the going down of the sun, had not Priam spoken to them from the chariot and said, "Make way for the mules to pass you. Afterwards when I have taken the body home you shall have your fill of weeping."

On this the people stood asunder, and made a way for the wagon. When they had borne the body within the house they laid it upon a bed and seated minstrels round it to lead the dirge, whereon the women joined in the sad music of their lament. Foremost among them all Andromache led their wailing as she clasped the head of mighty Hector in her embrace. "Husband," she cried, "you have died young, and leave me in your house a widow; he of whom we are the ill-starred parents is still a mere child, and I fear he may not reach manhood. Ere he can do so our city will be razed and overthrown, for you who watched over it are no more—you who were its savior, the guardian of our wives and children. Our women will be carried away captives to the ships, and I among them; while you, my child, who will be with me will be put to some unseemly tasks, working for a cruel master. Or, maybe, some Achæan will hurl you (O miserable death) from our walls, to avenge some brother, son, or father whom Hector slew; many of them have indeed bitten the dust at his hands, for your father's hand in battle was no light one. Therefore do the people mourn him. You have left, O Hector, sorrow unutterable to your parents, and my own grief is greatest of all, for you did not stretch forth your arms and embrace me as you lay dying, nor say to me any words that might have lived with me in my tears night and day for evermore."

Bitterly did she weep the while, and the women joined in her lament. Hecuba in her turn took up the strains of woe. "Hector," she cried, "dearest to me of all my children. So long as you were alive the gods loved you well, and even in death they have not been utterly unmindful of you; for when Achilles took any other of my sons, he would sell him beyond the seas, to Samos Imbrus or rugged Lemnos; and when he had slain you too with his sword, many a time did he drag you round the sepulcher of his comrade—though this could not give him life—yet here you lie all fresh as dew, and comely as one whom Apollo has slain with his painless shafts."

Thus did she too speak through her tears with bitter moan, and then Helen for a third time took up the strain of lamentation. "Hector," said she, "dearest of all my brothers-in-law—for I am wife to Alexandrus who brought me hither to Troy—would that I had died ere he did so—twenty years are come and gone since I left my home and came from over the sea, but I have never heard one word of insult or unkindness from you. When another would chide with me, as it might be one of your brothers or sisters or of your brothers' wives, or my mother-in-law—for Priam was as kind to me as though he were my own father—you would rebuke and check them with words of gentleness and goodwill. Therefore my tears flow both for you and for my unhappy self, for there is no one else in Troy who is kind to me but all shrink and shudder as they go by me."

She wept as she spoke and the vast crowd that was gathered round her joined in her lament. Then King Priam spoke to them saying, "Bring wood, O Trojans, to the city, and fear no cunning ambush of the Argives, for Achilles when he dismissed me from the ships gave me his word that they should not attack us until the morning of the twelfth day."

Forthwith they yoked their oxen and mules and gathered together before the city. Nine days long did they bring in great heaps of wood, and on the morning of the tenth day with many tears they took brave Hector forth, laid his dead body upon the summit of the pile, and set the fire thereto. Then when the child of morning rosy-fingered dawn appeared on the eleventh day, the people again assembled, round the pyre of mighty Hector. When they were got together, they first quenched the fire with wine wherever it was burning, and then his brothers and comrades with many a bitter tear gathered his white bones, wrapped them in soft robes of purple, and laid them in a golden urn, which they placed in a grave and covered over with large stones set close together. Then they built a barrow hurriedly over it keeping guard on every side lest the Achæans should attack them before they had finished. When they had heaped up the barrow they went back again into the city, and being well assembled they held high feast in the house of Priam their king.

Thus, then, did they celebrate the funeral of Hector tamer of horses.

The Story of Moses

OLD TESTAMENT

EXODUS

CHAPTER 1

Now there arose up a new king over Egypt, which knew not Joseph.

And he said unto his people, Behold, the people of the children of Israel are more and mightier than we:

Come on, let us deal wisely with them; lest they multiply, and it come to pass, that, when there falleth out any war, they join also unto our enemies, and fight against us, and so get them up out of the land.

Therefore they did set over them taskmasters to afflict them with their burdens. . . .

And Pharaoh charged all his people, saying, Every son that is born ye shall cast into the river, and every daughter ye shall save alive.

CHAPTER 2

And there went a man of the house of Levi, and took to wife a daughter of Levi.

And the woman conceived, and bare a son: and when she saw him that he was a goodly child, she hid him three months.

And when she could not longer hide him, she took for him an ark of bulrushes, and daubed it with slime and with pitch, and put the child therein; and she laid it in the flags by the river's brink.

And his sister stood afar off, to wit what would be done to him.

And the daughter of Pharaoh came down to wash herself at the river; and her maidens walked along by the river's side; and when she saw the ark among the flags, she sent her maid to fetch it.

And when she had opened it, she saw the child: and, behold, the babe wept. And she had compassion on him, and said, This is one of the Hebrews' children.

Then said his sister to Pharaoh's daughter, Shall I go and call to thee a nurse of the Hebrew women, that she may nurse the child for thee?

And Pharaoh's daughter said to her, Go. And the maid went and called the child's mother.

And Pharaoh's daughter said unto her, Take this child away, and nurse it for me, and I will give thee thy wages. And the woman took the child, and nursed it.

And the child grew, and she brought him unto Pharaoh's daughter, and he became her son. And she called his name Moses: and she said, Because I drew him out of the water.

And it came to pass in those days, when Moses was grown, that he went out unto his brethren, and looked on their burdens: and he spied an Egyptian smiting an Hebrew, one of his brethren.

And he looked this way and that way, and when he saw that there was no man, he slew the Egyptian, and hid him in the sand.

And when he went out the second day, behold, two men of the Hebrews strove together: and he said to him that did the wrong, Wherefore smitest thou thy fellow?

And he said, Who made thee a prince and a judge over us? intendest thou to kill me, as thou killedst the Egyptian? And Moses feared, and said, Surely this thing is known.

Now when Pharaoh heard this thing, he sought to slay Moses. But Moses fled from the face of Pharaoh, and dwelt in the land of Midian: and he sat down by a well.

Now the priest of Midian had seven daughters: and they came and drew water, and filled the troughs to water their father's flock.

And the shepherds came and drove them away: but Moses stood up and helped them, and watered their flock.

And when they came to Reuel their father, he said, How is it that ye are come so soon to day?

And they said, An Egyptian delivered us out of the hand of the shepherds, and also drew water enough for us, and watered the flock.

And he said unto his daughters, And where is he? why is it that ye have left the man? call him, that he may eat bread.

And Moses was content to dwell with the man: and he gave Moses Zipporah his daughter.

And she bare him a son, and he called his name Gershom: for he said, I have been a stranger in a strange land.

And it came to pass in process of time, that the king of Egypt died: and the children of Israel sighed by reason of the bondage, and they cried, and their cry came up unto God by reason of the bondage.

And God heard their groaning, and God remembered his covenant with Abraham, with Isaac, and with Jacob.

And God looked upon the children of Israel, and God had respect unto them.

CHAPTER 3

Now Moses kept the flock of Jethro his father in law, the priest of Midian: and he led the flock to the backside of the desert, and came to the mountain of God, even to Horeb.

And the angel of the Lord appeared unto him in a flame of fire out of the midst of a bush: and he looked, and, behold, the bush burned with fire, and the bush was not consumed.

And Moses said, I will now turn aside, and see this great sight, why the bush is not burnt.

And when the Lord saw that he turned aside to see, God called unto him out of the midst of the bush, and said, Moses, Moses. And he said, Here am I.

And he said, Draw not nigh hither: put off thy shoes from off thy feet, for the place whereon thou standest is holy ground.

Moreover he said, I am the God of thy father, the God of Abraham, the God of Isaac, and the God of Jacob. And Moses hid his face; for he was afraid to look upon God.

And the Lord said, I have surely seen the affliction of my people which are in Egypt, and have heard their cry by reason of their taskmasters; for I know their sorrows . . .

Come now therefore, and I will send thee unto Pharaoh, that thou mayest bring forth my people the children of Israel out of Egypt.

And Moses said unto God, Who am I, that I should go unto Pharaoh, and that I should bring forth the children of Israel out of Egypt?

And he said, Certainly I will be with thee; and this shall be a token unto thee, that I have sent thee: When thou hast brought forth the people out of Egypt, ye shall serve God upon this mountain.

CHAPTER 4

And Moses answered and said, But, behold, they will not believe me, nor hearken unto my voice: for they will say, The Lord hath not appeared unto thee.

And the Lord said unto him, What is that in thine hand? And he said, A rod.

And he said, Cast it on the ground. And he cast it on the ground, and it became a serpent; and Moses fled from before it.

And the Lord said unto Moses, Put forth thine hand, and take it by the tail. And he put forth his hand, and caught it, and it became a rod in his hand . . .

And the Lord said furthermore unto him, Put now thine hand into thy bosom. And he put his hand into his bosom: and when he took it out, behold, his hand was leprous as snow.

And he said, Put thine hand into thy bosom again. And he put his hand into his bosom again; and plucked it out of his bosom, and, behold, it was turned again as his other flesh.

And it shall come to pass, if they will not believe thee, neither hearken to the voice of the first sign, that they will believe the voice of the latter sign.

And it shall come to pass, if they will not believe also these two signs, neither hearken unto thy voice, that thou shalt take of the water of the river, and pour it upon the dry land: and the water which thou takest out of the river shall become blood upon the dry land.

And Moses said unto the Lord, O my Lord, I am not eloquent, neither heretofore, nor since thou hast spoken unto thy servant: but I am slow of speech, and of a slow tongue.

And the Lord said unto him, Who hath made man's mouth? or who maketh the dumb, or deaf, or the seeing, or the blind? have not I the Lord?

Now therefore go, and I will be with thy mouth, and teach thee what thou shalt say.

And he said, O my Lord, send, I pray thee, by the hand of him whom thou wilt send.

And the anger of the Lord was kindled against Moses, and he said, Is not Aaron the Levite thy brother? I know that he can speak well. And also, behold, he cometh forth to meet thee: and when he seeth thee, he will be glad in his heart.

And thou shalt speak unto him, and put words in his mouth: and I will be with thy mouth, and with his mouth, and will teach you what ye shall do.

And he shall be thy spokesman unto the people: and he shall be, even he shall be to thee instead of a mouth, and thou shalt be to him instead of God.

And thou shalt take this rod in thine hand, wherewith thou shalt do signs.

CHAPTER 5

And afterward Moses and Aaron went in, and told Pharaoh, Thus saith the Lord God of Israel, Let my people go, that they may hold a feast unto me in the wilderness.

And Pharaoh said, Who is the Lord, that I should obey his voice to let Israel go? I know not the Lord, neither will I let Israel go.

And they said, the God of the Hebrews hath met with us: let us go, we pray thee, three days' journey into the desert, and sacrifice unto the Lord our God; lest he fall upon us with pestilence, or with the sword.

And the king of Egypt said unto them, Wherefore do ye, Moses and Aaron, let the people from their works? get you unto your burdens. . . .

And Pharaoh commanded the same day the taskmasters of the people, and their officers, saying,

Ye shall no more give the people straw to make brick, as heretofore: let them go and gather straw for themselves.

And the tale of the bricks, which they did make heretofore, ye shall lay upon them; ye shall not diminish ought thereof: for they be idle; therefore they cry, saying, Let us go and sacrifice to our God.

Let there more work be laid upon the men, that they may labour therein; and let them not regard vain words.

CHAPTER 7

And the Lord said unto Moses, See, I have made thee a god to Pharaoh: and Aaron thy brother shall by thy prophet.

Thou shalt speak all that I command thee: and Aaron thy brother shall speak unto Pharaoh, that he send the children of Israel out of his land.

And I will harden Pharaoh's heart, and multiply my signs and my wonders in the land of Egypt.

But Pharaoh shall not hearken unto you, that I may lay my hand upon Egypt, and bring forth mine armies, and my people the children of Israel, out of the land of Egypt by great judgments.

And the Egyptians shall know that I am the Lord, when I stretch forth mine hand upon Egypt, and bring out the children of Israel from among them. . . .

And the Lord spake unto Moses and unto Aaron, saying,

When Pharaoh shall speak unto you, saying, Shew a miracle for you: then thou shalt say unto Aaron, Take thy rod, and cast it before Pharaoh, and it shall become a serpent.

And Moses and Aaron went in unto Pharaoh, and they did so as the Lord had commanded: and Aaron cast down his rod before Pharaoh, before his servants, and it became a serpent.

Then Pharaoh also called the wise men and the sorcerers: now the magicians of Egypt, they also did in like manner with their enchantments.

For they cast down every man his rod, and they became serpents: but Aaron's rod swallowed up their rods.

And he hardened Pharaoh's heart, that he hearkened not unto them; as the Lord had said. . . .

And the Lord spake unto Moses, Say unto Aaron, Take thy rod, and stretch out thine hand upon the waters of Egypt, upon their streams, upon their rivers, and upon their ponds, and upon all their pools of water, that they may become blood; and that there may be blood throughout all the land of Egypt, both in vessels of wood, and in vessels of stone.

And Moses and Aaron did so, as the Lord commanded; and he lifted up the rod, and smote the waters that were in the river, in the sight of Pharaoh, and in the sight of his servants; and all the waters that were in the river were turned to blood.

And the fish that was in the river died; and the river stank, and the Egyptians could not drink of the water of the river; and there was blood throughout all the land of Egypt.

And the magicians of Egypt did so with their enchantments: and Pharaoh's heart was hardened, neither did he hearken unto them; as the Lord had said.

And Pharaoh turned and went into his house, neither did he set his heart to this also.

And all the Egyptians digged round about the river for water to drink; for they could not drink of the water of the river.

And seven days were fulfilled, after that the Lord had smitten the river.

CHAPTER 8

And the Lord spake unto Moses, Say unto Aaron, Stretch forth thine hand with thy rod over the streams, over the rivers, and over the ponds, and cause frogs to come up upon the land of Egypt.

And Aaron stretched out his hand over the waters of Egypt; and the frogs came up, and covered the land of Egypt.

And the magicians did so with their enchantments, and brought up frogs upon the land of Egypt.

Then Pharaoh called for Moses and Aaron, and said, Intreat the Lord, that he may take away the frogs from me, and from my people; and I will let the people go, that they may do sacrifice unto the Lord.

And Moses said unto Pharaoh, Glory over me: when shall I intreat for thee, and for thy servants, and for thy people, to destroy the frogs from thee and thy houses, that they may remain in the river only?

And he said, To morrow. And he said, Be it according to thy word: that thou mayest know that there is none like unto the Lord our God.

And the frogs shall depart from thee, and from thy houses, and from thy servants, and from thy people; they shall remain in the river only.

And Moses and Aaron went out from Pharaoh: and Moses cried unto the Lord because of the frogs which he had brought against Pharaoh.

And the Lord did according to the word of Moses; and the frogs died out of the houses, out of the villages, and out of the fields.

And they gathered them together upon heaps: and the land stank.

But when Pharaoh saw that there was respite, he hardened his heart, and hearkened not unto them; as the Lord had said.

CHAPTER 11

. . . And the Lord said unto Moses, Pharaoh shall not hearken unto you; that my wonders may be multiplied in the land of Egypt.

And Moses and Aaron did all these wonders before Pharaoh: and the Lord hardened Pharaoh's heart, so that he would not let the children of Israel go out of his land.

CHAPTER 12

. . . Then Moses called for all the elders of Israel, and said unto them, Draw out and take you a lamb according to your families, and kill the passover.

And ye shall take a bunch of hyssop, and dip it in the blood that is in the bason, and strike the lintel and the two side posts with the blood that is in the bason; and none of you shall go out at the door of his house until the morning.

For the Lord will pass through to smite the Egyptians; and when he seeth the blood upon the lintel, and on the two side posts, the Lord will pass over the door, and will not suffer the destroyer to come in unto your houses to smite you.

And ye shall observe this thing for an ordinance to thee and to thy sons for ever.

And it shall come to pass, when ye be come to the land which the Lord will give you, according as he hath promised, that ye shall keep this service.

And it shall come to pass, when your children shall say unto you, What mean ye by this service?

That ye shall say, It is the sacrifice of the Lord's passover, who passed over the houses of the children of Israel in Egypt, when he smote the Egyptians, and delivered our houses. And the people bowed the head and worshipped.

And the children of Israel went away, and did as the Lord had commanded Moses and Aaron, so did they.

And it came to pass, that at midnight the Lord smote all the firstborn in the land of Egypt, from the firstborn of Pharaoh that sat on his throne unto the firstborn of the captive that was in the dungeon; and all the firstborn of cattle.

And Pharaoh rose up in the night, he, and all his servants, and all the Egyptians; and there was a great cry in Egypt; for there was not a house where there was not one dead.

And he called for Moses and Aaron by night, and said, Rise up, and get you forth from among my people, both ye and the children of Israel; and go, serve the Lord, as ye have said.

Also take your flocks and your herds, as ye have said, and be gone; and bless me also.

And the Egyptians were urgent upon the people, that they might send them out of the land in haste; for they said, We be all dead men. . . .

And the children of Israel journeyed from Rameses to Succoth, about six hundred thousand on foot that were men, beside children.

And a mixed multitude went up also with them; and flocks, and herds, even very much cattle.

And they baked unleavened cakes of the dough which they brought forth out of Egypt, for it was not leavened; because they were thrust out of Egypt, and could not tarry, neither had they prepared for themselves any victual.

CHAPTER 13

. . . And the Lord went before them by day in a pillar of a cloud, to lead them the way; and by night in a pillar of fire, to give them light; to go by day and night:

He took not away the pillar of the cloud by day, nor the pillar of fire by night, from before the people.

CHAPTER 14

. . . And it was told the king of Egypt that the people fled: and the heart of Pharaoh and of his servants was turned against the people, and they said, Why have we done this, that we have let Israel go from serving us?

And he made ready his chariot, and took his people with him:

And he took six hundred chosen chariots, and all the chariots of Egypt, and captains over every one of them.

And the Lord hardened the heart of Pharaoh king of Egypt, and he pursued after the children of Israel: and the children of Israel went out with an high hand.

But the Egyptians pursued after them, all the horses and chariots of Pharaoh, and his horsemen, and his army, and overtook them encamping by the sea, beside Pi-hahiroth, before Baal-zephon.

And when Pharaoh drew nigh, the children of Israel lifted up their eyes, and, behold, the Egyptians marched after them; and they were sore afraid: and the children of Israel cried out unto the Lord.

And they said unto Moses, Because there were no graves in Egypt, hast thou taken us away to die in the wilderness? wherefore hast thou dealt thus with us, to carry us forth out of Egypt?

Is not this the word that we did tell thee in Egypt, saying, Let us alone, that we may serve the Egyptians? For it had been better for us to serve the Egyptians, than that we should die in the wilderness.

And Moses said unto the people, Fear ye not, stand still, and see the salvation of the Lord, which he will shew to you to day: for the Egyptians whom ye have seen to day, ye shall see them again no more for ever.

The Lord shall fight for you, and ye shall hold your peace. . . .

And the angel of God, which went before the camp of Israel, removed and went behind them; and the pillar of the cloud went from before their face, and stood behind them:

And it came between the camp of the Egyptians and the camp of Israel; and it was a cloud and darkness to them, but it gave light by night to these: so that the one came not near the other all the night.

And Moses stretched out his hand over the sea; and the Lord caused the sea to go back by a strong east wind all that night, and made the sea dry land, and the waters were divided.

And the children of Israel went into the midst of the sea upon the dry ground: and the waters were a wall unto them on their right hand, and on their left.

And the Egyptians pursued, and went in after them to the midst of the sea, even all Pharaoh's horses, his chariots, and his horsemen.

And it came to pass, that in the morning watch the Lord looked unto the host of the Egyptians through the pillar of fire and of the cloud, and troubled the host of the Egyptians,

And took off their chariot wheels, that they drave them heavily: so that the Egyptians said, Let us flee from the face of Israel; for the Lord fighteth for them against the Egyptians.

And the Lord said unto Moses, Stretch out thine hand over the sea, that the waters may come again upon the Egyptians, upon their chariots, and upon their horsemen.

And Moses stretched forth his hand over the sea, and the sea returned to his strength when the morning appeared; and the Egyptians fled against it; and the Lord overthrew the Egyptians in the midst of the sea.

And the waters returned, and covered the chariots, and the horsemen, and all the host of Pharaoh that came into the sea after them; there remained not so much as one of them.

But the children of Israel walked upon dry land in the midst of the sea; and the waters were a wall unto them on their right hand, and on their left.

CHAPTER 15

Then sang Moses and the children of Israel this song unto the Lord, and spake, saying, I will sing unto the Lord, for he hath triumphed gloriously: the horse and his rider hath he thrown into the sea.

The Lord is my strength and song, and he is become my salvation: he is my God, and I will prepare him an habitation; my father's God, and I will exalt him.

The Lord is a man of war: the Lord is his name.

Pharaoh's chariots and his host hath he cast into the sea: his chosen captains also are drowned in the Red sea.

The depths have covered them: they sank into the bottom as a stone.

Thy right hand, O Lord, is become glorious in power: thy right hand, O Lord, hath dashed in pieces the enemy.

And in the greatness of thine excellency thou hast overthrown them that rose up against thee: thou sentest forth thy wrath, which consumed them as stubble.

And with the blast of thy nostrils the waters were gathered together, the floods stood upright as an heap, and the depths were congealed in the heart of the sea.

The enemy said, I will pursue, I will overtake, I will divide the spoil; my lust shall be satisfied upon them; I will draw my sword, my hand shall destroy them.

Thou didst blow with thy wind, the sea covered them: they sank as lead in the mighty waters.

CHAPTER 19

. . . And the Lord said unto Moses, Go unto the people, and sanctify them to day and to morrow, and let them wash their clothes,

And be ready against the third day: for the third day the Lord will come down in the sight of all the people upon mount Sinai.

And thou shalt set bounds unto the people round about, saying, Take heed to yourselves, that ye go not up into the mount, or touch the border of it: whosoever toucheth the mount shall be surely put to death:

There shall not an hand touch it, but he shall surely be stoned, or shot through; whether it be beast or man, it shall not live: when the trumpet soundeth long, they shall come up to the mount.

And Moses went down from the mount unto the people, and sanctified the people; and they washed their clothes.

And he said unto the people, Be ready against the third day: come not at your wives.

And it came to pass on the third day in the morning, that there were thunders and lightnings, and a thick cloud upon the mount, and the voice of the trumpet exceeding loud; so that all the people that was in the camp trembled.

And Moses brought forth the people out of the camp to meet with God; and they stood at the nether part of the mount.

And mount Sinai was altogether on a smoke, because the Lord descended upon it in fire: and the smoke thereof ascended as the smoke of a furnace, and the whole mount quaked greatly.

And when the voice of the trumpet sounded long, and waxed louder and louder, Moses spake, and God answered him by a voice.

And the Lord came down upon mount Sinai, on the top of the mount: and the Lord called Moses up to the top of the mount; and Moses went up.

CHAPTER 20

And God spake all these words, saying,

I am the Lord thy God, which have brought thee out of the land of Egypt, out of the house of bondage.

Thou shalt have no other gods before me.

Thou shalt not make unto thee any graven image, or any likeness of anything that is in heaven above, or that is in the earth beneath, or that is in the water under the earth:

Thou shalt not bow down thyself to them, nor serve them: for I the Lord thy God am a jealous God, visiting the iniquity of the fathers upon the children unto the third and fourth generation of them that hate me;

And shewing mercy unto thousands of them that love me, and keep my commandments.

Thou shalt not take the name of the Lord thy God in vain; for the Lord will not hold him guiltless that taketh his name in vain.

Remember the sabbath day, to keep it holy.

Six days shalt thou labour, and do all thy work:

But the seventh day is the sabbath of the Lord thy God: in it thou shalt not do any work, thou, nor thy son, nor thy daughter, thy manservant, nor thy maidservant, nor thy cattle, nor thy stranger that is within thy gates:

For in six days the Lord made heaven and earth, the sea, and all that in them is, and rested the seventh day: wherefore the Lord blessed the sabbath day, and hallowed it.

Honour thy father and thy mother: that thy days may be long upon the land which the Lord thy God giveth thee.

Thou shalt not kill.

Thou shalt not commit adultery.

Thou shalt not steal.

Thou shalt not bear false witness against thy neighbour.

Thou shalt not covet thy neighbour's house, thou shalt not covet thy neighbour's wife, nor his manservant, nor his maidservant, nor his ox, nor his ass, nor any thing that is thy neighbour's.

CHAPTER 31

. . . And he gave unto Moses, when he had made an end of communing with him upon mount Sinai, two tables of testimony, tables of stone, written with the finger of God.

CHAPTER 32

And when the people saw that Moses delayed to come down out of the mount, the people gathered themselves together unto Aaron, and said unto him, Up, make us gods, which shall go before us; for as for this Moses, the man that brought us up out of the land of Egypt, we wot not what is become of him.

And Aaron said unto them, Break off the golden earrings, which are in the ears of your wives, of your sons, and of your daughters, and bring them unto me.

And all the people brake off the golden earrings which were in their ears, and brought them unto Aaron.

And he received them at their hand, and fashioned it with a graving tool, after he had made it a molten calf: and they said, These be thy gods, O Israel, which brought thee up out of the land of Egypt.

And when Aaron saw it, he built an altar before it; and Aaron made proclamation, and said, To morrow is a feast to the Lord.

And they rose up early on the morrow, and offered burnt offerings, and brought peace offerings; and the people sat down to eat and to drink, and rose up to play. . . .

And the Lord said unto Moses, I have seen this people, and, behold, it is a stiffnecked people:

Now therefore let me alone, that my wrath may wax hot against them, and that I may consume them: and I will make of thee a great nation. . . .

And the Lord repented of the evil which he thought to do unto his people.

And Moses turned, and went down from the mount, and the two tables of the testimony were in his hand: the tables were written on both their sides; on the one side and on the other were they written.

And the tables were the work of God, and the writing was the writing of God, graven upon the tables.

And when Joshua heard the noise of the people as they shouted, he said unto Moses, There is a noise of war in the camp.

And he said, It is not the voice of them that shout for mastery, neither is it the voice of them that cry for being overcome: but the noise of them that sing do I hear.

And it came to pass, as soon as he came nigh unto the camp, that he saw the calf, and the dancing: and Moses' anger waxed hot, and he cast the tables out of his hands, and brake them beneath the mount.

And he took the calf which they had made, and burnt it in the fire, and ground it to powder, and strawed it upon the water, and made the children of Israel drink of it. . . .

And it came to pass on the morrow, that Moses said unto the people, Ye have sinned a great sin: and now I will go up unto the Lord; peradventure I shall make an atonement for your sin. . . .

And the Lord plagued the people, because they made the calf, which Aaron made.

CHAPTER 33

And the Lord said unto Moses, Depart, and go up hence, thou and the people which thou hast brought up out of the land of Egypt, unto the land which I sware unto Abraham, to Isaac, and to Jacob, saying, Unto thy seed will I give it . . .

Unto a land flowing with milk and honey: for I will not go up in the midst of thee; for thou art a stiffnecked people: lest I consume thee in the way.

And when the people heard these evil tidings, they mourned: and no man did put on him his ornaments. . . .

And the children of Israel stripped themselves of their ornaments by the mount Horeb.

And Moses took the tabernacle, and pitched it without the camp, afar off from the camp, and called it the Tabernacle of the congregation. And it came to pass, that every one which sought the Lord went out unto the tabernacle of the congregation, which was without the camp.

And it came to pass, when Moses went out unto the tabernacle, that all the people rose up, and stood every man at his tent door, and looked after Moses, until he was gone into the tabernacle.

And it came to pass, as Moses entered into the tabernacle, the cloudy pillar descended, and stood at the door of the tabernacle, and the Lord talked with Moses.

And all the people saw the cloudy pillar stand at the tabernacle door: and all the people rose up and worshipped, every man in his tent door.

And the Lord spake unto Moses face to face, as a man speaketh unto his friend. . . .

And Moses said unto the Lord, See, thou sayest unto me, Bring up this people: and thou hast not let me know whom thou wilt send with me. Yet thou hast said, I know thee by name, and thou hast also found grace in my sight.

Now therefore, I pray thee, if I have found grace in thy sight, shew me now thy way, that I may know thee, that I may find grace in thy sight: and consider that this nation is thy people.

And he said, My presence shall go with thee, and I will give thee rest.

And he said unto him, If thy presence go not with me, carry us not up hence.

For wherein shall it be known here that I and thy people have found grace in thy sight? is it not in that thou goest with us? so shall we be separated, I and thy people, from all the people that are upon the face of the earth.

And the Lord said unto Moses, I will do this thing also that thou hast spoken: for thou hast found grace in my sight, and I know thee by name.

And he said, I beseech thee, shew me thy glory.

And he said, I will make all my goodness pass before thee, and I will proclaim the name of the Lord before thee; and will be gracious to whom I will be gracious, and will shew mercy on whom I will shew mercy.

And he said, Thou canst not see my face: for there shall no man see me, and live.

And the Lord said, Behold, there is a place by me, and thou shalt stand upon a rock:

And it shall come to pass, while my glory passeth by, that I will put thee in a clift of the rock, and will cover thee with my hand while I pass by:

And I will take away mine hand, and thou shalt see my back parts: but my face shall not be seen.

CHAPTER 34

And the Lord said unto Moses, Hew thee two tables of stone like unto the first: and I will write upon these tables the words that were in the first tables, which thou brakest.

And be ready in the morning, and come up in the morning unto mount Sinai, and present thyself there to me in the top of the mount.

And no man shall come up with thee, neither let any man be seen throughout all the mount; neither let the flocks nor herds feed before that mount.

And he hewed two tables of stone like unto the first; and Moses rose up early in the morning, and went up unto mount Sinai, as the Lord had commanded him, and took in his hand the two tables of stone. . . .

And it came to pass, when Moses came down from mount Sinai with the two tables of testimony in Moses' hand, when he came down from the mount, that Moses wist not that the skin of his face shone while he talked with him. . . .

And afterward all the children of Israel came nigh: and he gave them in commandment all that the Lord had spoken with him in mount Sinai.

NUMBERS

CHAPTER 12

And Miriam and Aaron spake against Moses because of the Ethiopian woman whom he had married: for he had married an Ethiopian woman.

And they said, Hath the Lord indeed spoken only by Moses? hath he not spoken also by us? And the Lord heard it.

(Now the man Moses was very meek, above all the men which were upon the face of the earth.)

And the Lord spake suddenly unto Moses, and unto Aaron, and unto Miriam, Come out ye three unto the tabernacle of the congregation. And they three came out.

And the Lord came down in the pillar of the cloud, and stood in the door of the tabernacle, and called Aaron and Miriam: and they both came forth.

And he said, Hear now my words: If there be a prophet among you, I the Lord will make myself known unto him in a vision, and will speak unto him in a dream.

My servant Moses is not so, who is faithful in all mine house.

With him will I speak mouth to mouth, even apparently, and not in dark speeches; and the similitude of the Lord shall he behold: wherefore then were ye not afraid to speak against my servant Moses?

And the anger of the Lord was kindled against them; and he departed.

And the cloud departed from off the tabernacle; and, behold, Miriam became leprous, white as snow: and Aaron looked upon Miriam, and, behold, she was leprous.

And Aaron said unto Moses, Alas, my lord, I beseech thee, lay not the sin upon us, wherein we have done foolishly, and wherein we have sinned.

Let her not be as one dead, of whom the flesh is half consumed when he cometh out of his mother's womb.

And Moses cried unto the Lord, saying, Heal her now, O God, I beseech thee.

And the Lord said unto Moses, If her father had but spit in her face, should she not be ashamed seven days? let her be shut out from the camp seven days, and after that let her be received in again.

And Miriam was shut out from the camp seven days: and the people journeyed not till Miriam was brought in again.

CHAPTER 20

Then came the children of Israel, even the whole congregation, into the desert of Zin in the first month: and the people abode in Kadesh; and Miriam died there, and was buried there.

And there was no water for the congregation: and they gathered themselves together against Moses and against Aaron.

And the people chode with Moses, and spake, saying, Would God that we had died when our brethren died before the Lord!

And why have ye brought up the congregation of the Lord into this wilderness, that we and our cattle should die there?

And wherefore have ye made us to come up out of Egypt, to bring us in unto this evil place? it is no place of seed, or of figs, or of vines, or of pomegranates; neither is there any water to drink.

And Moses and Aaron went from the presence of the assembly unto the door of the tabernacle of the congregation, and they fell upon their faces: and the glory of the Lord appeared unto them.

And the Lord spake unto Moses, saying,

Take the rod, and gather thou the assembly together, thou, and Aaron, thy brother, and speak ye unto the rock before their eyes; and it shall give forth his water, and thou shalt bring forth to them water out of the rock: so thou shalt give the congregation and their beasts drink.

And Moses took the rod from before the Lord, as he commanded him.

And Moses and Aaron gathered the congregation together before the rock, and he said unto them, Hear now, ye rebels; must we fetch you water out of this rock?

And Moses lifted up his hand, and with his rod he smote the rock twice: and the water came out abundantly, and the congregation drank, and their beasts also.

And the Lord spake unto Moses and Aaron, Because ye believed me not, to sanctify me in the eyes of the children of Israel, therefore ye shall not bring this congregation into the land which I have given them.

CHAPTER 21

. . . And they journeyed from mount Hor by the way of the Red sea, to compass the land of Edom: and the soul of the people was much discouraged because of the way.

And the people spake against God, and against Moses, Wherefore have ye brought us up out of Egypt to die in the wilderness? for there is no bread, neither is there any water; and our soul loatheth this light bread.

And the Lord sent fiery serpents among the people, and they bit the people; and much people of Israel died.

Therefore the people came to Moses, and said, We have sinned, for we have spoken against the Lord, and against thee; pray unto the Lord, that he take away the serpents from us. And Moses prayed for the people.

And the Lord said unto Moses, Make thee a fiery serpent, and set it upon a pole: and it shall come to pass, that every one that is bitten, when he looketh upon it, shall live.

And Moses made a serpent of brass, and put it upon a pole, and it came to pass, that if a serpent had bitten any man, when he beheld the serpent of brass, he lived.

DEUTERONOMY

CHAPTER 31

. . . And the Lord said unto Moses, Behold, thy days approach that thou must die: call Joshua, and present yourselves in the tabernacle of the congregation, that I may give him a charge. . . .

Moses therefore wrote this song the same day, and taught it the children of Israel.

CHAPTER 32

Give ear, O ye heavens, and I will speak; and hear, O earth, the words of my mouth.

My doctrine shall drop as the rain, my speech shall distil as the dew, as the small rain upon the tender herb, and as the showers upon the grass:

Because I will publish the name of the Lord: ascribe ye greatness unto our God.

He is the Rock, his work is perfect: for all his ways are judgment: a God of truth and without iniquity, just and right is he.

They have corrupted themselves, their spot is not the spot of his children: they are a perverse and crooked generation.

Do ye thus requite the Lord, O foolish people and unwise? is not he thy father that hath bought thee? hath he not made thee, and established thee?

Remember the days of old, consider the years of many generations: ask thy father, and he will shew thee; thy elders, and they will tell thee.

When the Most High divided to the nations their inheritance, when he separated the sons of Adam, he set the bounds of the people according to the number of the children of Israel.

For the Lord's portion is his people; Jacob is the lot of his inheritance.

He found him in a desert land, and in the waste howling wilderness; he led him about, he instructed him, he kept him as the apple of his eye.

As an eagle stirreth up her nest, fluttereth over her young, spreadeth abroad her wings, taketh them, beareth them on her wings:

So the Lord alone did lead him, and there was no strange god with him.

He made him ride on the high places of the earth, that he might eat the increase of the fields; and he made him to suck honey out of the rock, and oil out of the flinty rock;

Butter of kine, and milk of sheep, with fat of lambs, and rams of the breed of Bashan, and goats, with the fat of kidneys of wheat; and thou didst drink the pure blood of the grape.

But Jeshurun waxed fat, and kicked: thou art waxen fat, thou art grown thick, thou art covered with fatness; then he forsook God which made him, and lightly esteemed the Rock of his salvation.

They provoked him to jealousy with strange gods, with abominations provoked they him to anger.

They sacrificed unto devils, not to God; to gods whom they knew not, to new gods that came newly up, whom your fathers feared not.

Of the Rock that begat thee thou art unmindful, and hast forgotten God that formed thee.

And when the Lord saw it, he abhorred them, because of the provoking of his sons, and of his daughters.

And he said, I will hide my face from them, I will see what their end shall be: for they are a very froward generation, children in whom is no faith.

They have moved me to jealousy with that which is not God; they have provoked me to anger with their vanities: and I will move them to jealousy with those which are not a people; I will provoke them to anger with a foolish nation.

For a fire is kindled in mine anger, and shall burn unto the lowest hell, and shall consume the earth with her increase, and set on fire the foundations of the mountains.

I will heap mischiefs upon them; I will spend mine arrows upon them.

They shall be burnt with hunger, and devoured with burning heat, and with bitter destruction: I will also send the teeth of beasts upon them, with the poison of serpents of the dust.

The sword without, and terror within, shall destroy both the young man and the virgin, the suckling also with the man of gray hairs.

I said, I would scatter them into the corners, I would make the remembrance of them to cease from among men:

Were it not that I feared the wrath of the enemy, lest their adversaries should behave themselves strangely, and lest they should say, Our hand is high, and the Lord hath not done all this.

For they are a nation void of counsel, neither is there any understanding in them.

O that they were wise, that they understood this, that they would consider their latter end!

How should one chase a thousand, and two put ten thousand to flight, except their Rock had sold them, and the Lord had shut them up?

For their rock is not as our Rock, even our enemies themselves being judges.

For their vine is of the vine of Sodom, and of the fields of Gomorrah: their grapes are grapes of gall, their clusters are bitter:

Their wine is the poison of dragons, and the cruel venom of asps.

Is not this laid up in store with me, and sealed up among my treasures?

To me belongeth vengeance, and recompence; their foot shall slide in due time: for the day of their calamity is at hand, and the things that shall come upon them make haste.

For the Lord shall judge his people, and repent himself for his servants, when he seeth that their power is gone, and there is none shut up, or left.

And he shall say, Where are their gods, their rock in whom they trusted,

Which did eat the fat of their sacrifices, and drank the wine of their drink offerings? let them rise up and help you, and be your protection.

See now that I, even I, am he, and there is no god with me: I kill, and I make alive; I wound, and I heal: neither is there any that can deliver out of my hand.

For I lift up my hand to heaven, and say, I live for ever.

If I whet my glittering sword, and mine hand take hold on judgment; I will render vengeance to mine enemies, and will reward them that hate me.

I will make mine arrows drunk with blood, and my sword shall devour flesh; and that with the blood of the slain and of the captives, from the beginning of revenges upon the enemy.

Rejoice, O ye nations, with his people: for he will avenge the blood of his servants, and will render vengeance to his adversaries, and will be merciful unto his land, and to his people.

And Moses came and spake all the words of this song in the ears of the people, he, and Hoshea the son of Nun. . . .

And the Lord spake unto Moses that selfsame day, saying,

Get thee up into this mountain Abarim, unto mount Nebo, which is in the land of Moab, that is over against Jericho; and behold the land of Canaan, which I give unto the children of Israel for a possession:

And die in the mount whither thou goest up, and be gathered unto thy people; as Aaron thy brother died in mount Hor, and was gathered unto his people:

Because ye trespassed against me among the children of Israel at the waters of Meribah-Kadesh, in the wilderness of Zin; because ye sanctified me not in the midst of the children of Israel.

Yet thou shalt see the land before thee; but thou shalt not go thither unto the land which I give the children of Israel.

CHAPTER 33

And this is the blessing, wherewith Moses the man of God blessed the children of Israel before his death.

And he said, The Lord came from Sinai, and rose up from Seir unto them; he shined forth from mount Paran, and he came with ten thousands of saints: from his right hand went a fiery law for them.

Yea, he loved the people; all his saints are in thy hand: and they sat down at thy feet; every one shall receive of thy words. . . .

Let Reuben live, and not die; and let not his men be few.

And this is the blessing of Judah: and he said, Hear, Lord, the voice of Judah, and bring him unto his people: let his hands be sufficient for him; and be thou an help to him from his enemies.

And of Levi he said, Let thy Thummim and thy Urim be with thy holy one, whom thou didst prove at Massah, and with whom thou didst strive at the waters of Meribah;

Who said unto his father and to his mother, I have not seen him; neither did he acknowledge his brethren, nor knew his own children: for they have observed thy word, and kept thy covenant.

They shall teach Jacob thy judgments, and Israel thy law: they shall put incense before thee, and whole burnt sacrifice upon thine altar.

Bless, Lord, his substance, and accept the work of his hands: smite through the loins of them that rise against him, and of them that hate him, that they rise not again.

And of Benjamin he said, The beloved of the Lord shall dwell in safety by him; and the Lord shall cover him all the day long, and he shall dwell between his shoulders.

And of Joseph he said, Blessed of the Lord be his land, for the precious things of heaven, for the dew, and for the deep that coucheth beneath,

And for the precious fruits brought forth by the sun, and for the precious things put forth by the moon,

And for the chief things of the ancient mountains, and for the precious things of the lasting hills,

And for the precious things of the earth and fulness thereof, and for the good will of him that dwelt in the bush: let the blessing come upon the head of Joseph, and upon the top of the head of him that was separated from his brethren.

His glory is like the firstling of his bullock, and his horns are like the horns of unicorns: with them he shall push the people together to the ends of the earth: and they are the ten thousands of Ephraim, and they are the thousands of Manasseh.

And of Zebulun he said, Rejoice, Zebulun, in thy going out; and, Issachar, in thy tents.

They shall call the people unto the mountain; there they shall offer sacrifices of righteousness: for they shall suck of the abundance of the seas, and of treasures hid in the sand.

And of Gad he said, Blessed be he that enlargeth Gad: he dwelleth as a lion, and teareth the arm with the crown of the head.

And he provided the first part for himself, because there, in a portion of the lawgiver, was he seated; and he came with the heads of the people, he executed the justice of the Lord, and his judgments with Israel.

And of Dan he said, Dan is a lion's whelp: he shall leap from Bashan.

And of Naphtali he said, O Naphtali, satisfied with favour, and full with the blessing of the Lord: possess thou the west and the south.

And of Asher he said, Let Asher be blessed with children; let him be acceptable to his brethren, and let him dip his foot in oil.

Thy shoes shall be iron and brass; and as thy days, so shall thy strength be.

There is none like unto the God of Jeshurun, who rideth upon the heaven in thy help, and in his excellency on the sky.

The eternal God is thy refuge, and underneath are the everlasting arms: and he shall thrust out the enemy from before thee; and shall say, Destroy them.

Israel then shall dwell in safety alone: the fountain of Jacob shall be upon a land of corn and wine; also his heavens shall drop down dew.

Happy art thou, O Israel: who is like unto thee, O people saved by the Lord, the shield of thy help, and who is the sword of thy excellency! and thine enemies shall be found liars unto thee; and thou shalt tread upon their high places.

CHAPTER 34

And Moses went up from the plains of Moab unto the mountain of Nebo, to the top of Pisgah, that is over against Jericho. And the Lord shewed him all the land of Gilead, unto Dan.

And all Naphtali, and the land of Ephraim, and Manasseh, and all the land of Judah, unto the utmost sea,

And the south, and the plain of the valley of Jericho, the city of palm trees, unto Zoar.

And the Lord said unto him, This is the land which I sware unto Abraham, unto Isaac, and unto Jacob, saying, I will give it unto thy seed: I have caused thee to see it with thine eyes, but thou shalt not go over thither.

So Moses the servant of the Lord died there in the land of Moab, according to the word of the Lord.

And he buried him in a valley in the land of Moab, over against Bethpeor: but no man knoweth of his sepulchre unto this day.

The Song of Roland

EDITED BY NORMA L. GOODRICH

ROLLANZ

Carles li reis, nostre emperere magnes,
Set anz tuz pleins ad estet en Espaigne:
Tresqu'en la mer cunquist la tere altaigne.
N'i ad castel ki devant lui remaigne;
Mur ne citet n'i est remes a fraindre,
Fors Sarraguce, ki est en une muntaigne.
Li reis Marsilie la tient, ki Deu nen aimet.
Mahumet sert e Apollin recleimet:
Nes poet guarder que mals ne l'i ateignet.

[Verses 1–9]

Carles the King, our great Charlemagne,
Seven full years has campaigned in Spain,
Up to the sea has conquered proud domains.
There is not a castle that before him remains,
Not a rampart nor city has he to gain
Save Saragossa, which is on a mountain.
King Marsilie holds it whom God disdains;
He serves Mohammed and Apollo acclaims
Marsilie found *they* were not sovereign!

[V. 815] High are the peaks and the valleys dark! The Pyrenees tower into the clouds above their dizzy passes. All day long Carlemagne[1] and the

---

[1] *Carlemagne*: Proper names have often been left in Old French because of their musical effect: Rollanz, Carles, Carlemagne, etc.

Franks ride northward through the mountains in such great numbers that the very earth shakes. Straining their eyes, the knights gaze across the foot-hills, hoping to catch their first sight of France. Thoughts of their home and families whom they left seven years before bring tears to their eyes. More than his knights is King Carles full of grief, for behind him, at the gates of Spain, he has stationed his nephew Rollanz. The twelve peers of France and twenty thousand knights are still back in Spain to assure the rear guard!

Now Carlemagne weeps; he cannot hide his tears. "I feel danger behind me!" says the king. "I fear Rollanz is in danger, for Guenes named him to command the rear guard. . . . If I lose Rollanz, I shall never have exchange!"

[V. 999] Clear is the day in Spain, and radiant the sun! Four hundred thousand Sarrazins, under King Marsilie of Saragossa, spur their horses northward! Crimson, blue, and white flash their banners in the sun. A thousand trumpets shrill as they ride in serried ranks. Their clarions call through the thin mountain air, and alert the rear guard of the Franks, who are almost at the pass.

"Sir Companion," asked Oliviers of his friend Rollanz, "can it be that the Sarrazins have followed?"

"If they have," Rollanz answered Oliviers, "then it is the will of God. We shall make our stand here. Every vassal knows what he must suffer for his king—distress, and heat and cold. Let every baron strike great blows for Carlemagne!"

Oliviers climbed a hill to look toward the south. There he saw such a host of Sarrazins coming that he could not even count them. Their helmets glittered in the sun and their shields; their satin banners floated over a sea of rhythmic, mounted knights. "Rollanz, sound the horn!" cried Oliviers. "Carlemagne will hear it and come back!"

"I shall not call for aid! I shall not sound the horn!" Rollanz answered his friend. "In doing so I would lose my good name in my beloved France. Durendal will run in blood today up to its golden hilt! Let the pagans spur northward to the portals! I swear to you here; they are bent unto death. May neither God nor the angels suffer shame because of us! Halt! Let us wheel about and fight them!"

Among the twelve peers was the Archbishop Turpins. Standing on a hillock, he called the Franks to him. "Dismount and pray, for the battle draws near." Then he blessed the valiant knights and gave them absolution. "As penance I command you to strike a blow for God!"

The sunny-faced, the smiling Rollanz reviewed the peers. He rode his swift war charger and brandished high his lance. Its pennants were pure white with long, streaming tassels. "Sir Barons, before evening we shall have won a wealthy prize. These pagans that spur after us are seeking martyrdom." As Rollanz, sheathed in armor, cantered Veillantif down the line of the Franks, their battle cry "Mountjoy" rose from twenty thousand throats. They knew Guenes had sold them to King Marsilie of Saragossa. Then Guenes had appointed Rollanz to the rear guard. They knew they were betrayed.

Opposite the Franks lined up the hosts from Spain, vassals and allies of Marsilie of Saragossa. "Cowardly French, ride forth and tilt with us! Today your Carlemagne will lose his *right hand*. Foolish was your king to leave his nephew Rollanz at the pass! Do you know you were sold and betrayed into our ambush by your own Baron Guenes?"

Rollanz struck the first blow that day at Roncevals. With his sword Durendal he split the taunter's body. "No, son of a slave, our King Carles knew whom to trust! No shame shall fall on him, on us, or on our gentle France!" Second to Rollanz, Oliviers marked out his man, dug his golden spurs into his horse's flanks and charged the pagan foe. Third into their ranks lumbered the Archbishop Turpins, marked out a prince of Barbary, and slew him with his boar spear. Then the good Sir Gerin sent a heathen's soul to Satan. Gerin's friend, the Knight Gerier, next pierced a pagan peer. Duke Sansun attacked next, and after him Anseïs. "That was a worthy arm," cheered Rollanz. Then Engelers of Gascony, Oton, and Berengier accounted for three more. Of the twelve Spanish peers, only Margariz and Chernubles still lived a few minutes more.

The twelve peers of France fought like lions on that field. With each blow Rollanz split a Sarrazin's skull, sectioned his body, and severed the horse's spine. He swung about him in scythe strokes. At one moment he passed Oliviers, who was braining enemies with his shivered lance. "Where's Halteclere, your sword?" Oliviers had been too busy to unsheathe it! . . . By hundreds, then by thousands, they strewed the field with pagan dead. Many a gallant French knight also gave up his young life at Roncevals.

Across the Pyrenees all France waited. All France knew that it was a tragic day. From the Mont-Saint-Michel to Saints, and from Besançon to Ouessant, walls crumbled in every house! At noon there grew a darkness in the sky and a great hush broken only by streaks of chainfire and thunder. A hollow wind swept from mountain to seacoast. Huge chunks of hail rattled on the thatch. People crowded together for comfort. They spoke only in whispers. "Here has come the day of judgment and the end of the world!" They did not know and therefore could not say the truth: it was grief sweeping across fair France for the coming death of Rollanz!

Even as the Frankish peers stood masters of the field, they heard a distant rumbling like the waves of the seacoast. Then hove into sight the main body of the Spanish army, twenty battalions on the double, and seven thousand trumpets sounding the charge. At their head galloped, his dragon pennant streaming in the hot summer sun, Abisme, the daring leader of the infidels. The Archbishop Turpins marked him well. "That Sarrazin is a heretic. Much better I should kill him, for I have always hated cowards!" Turpins spurred his yellow-maned Danish charger and smashed his lance into the amethysts and topazes that gleamed on Abisme's shield. Turpins ran him through. Then he wheeled back and encouraged the Franks, "Sir Barons, go not with somber thoughts! Beyond this last day we shall live no more on earth. Therefore strike your blows today for God and for France! I am here to guarantee you all a seat in Paradise."

Then a count of Saragossa, Climborins by name—he who had kissed Guenes on the mouth for his treason—unhorsed and killed Engelers of Gascony. What a loss was that for the Franks! Oliviers saw it and took revenge. Then the heathen Valdabrun—he who had taken Jerusalem by treachery, violated the temple of Solomon, and killed the Patriarch before his fonts—slaughtered the distinguished Duke Sansun. "God! What a baron was he!" moaned the Franks. Rollanz struck down Baldabrun, split his skull, his byrnie, his jeweled saddle, and his horse's spine. Then charged from the Spanish ranks an African son of a king, who cut the vermilion-and-azure shield of Anseïs, killed that noble baron. "Baron Anseïs, what a pity is your death!" moaned the Franks. Then from the middle rode out the Archbishop Turpins. Never tonsured priest ever did such deeds of prowess. "You have just killed a baron whom my heart regrets," said Turpins as he struck the African dead.

Grandonie, the heathen son of Cappadocia's king, crushed the crimson shield of Gerin, then killed Gerier his companion, and after them Berengier. "See how our numbers dwindle!" moaned the Franks. Rollanz saw those heathen blows. Grandonie had never seen Rollanz in his life, and yet he recognized him. Despite the noise and confusion of battle, Grandonie knew Rollanz at once. Rollanz was the open-faced, proud-eyed, the graceful, handsome knight. All at once Grandonie was afraid. Rollanz did not let him escape. With one stroke of Durendal he slit the helmet of Toledo steel as far as the nose, then cut through the teeth and lips, unthreaded the chain mail, ripped through the silver pommel, and crushed the horse's spine. Then cried the Franks, "Carles's *right hand* guarantees us!" Drops of bright blood trickled through the green field of Roncevals.

In the Book of Deeds it is well written that the Franks had killed up to this moment four thousand of their foes. They stemmed the first four attacks, but the fifth one cost them dear. All the Franks were dead, except for sixty knights whom God had thus far spared. They saw what there was to do: they must fetch a high price!

"Sir Knight and dear companions," shouted Rollanz to Oliviers, "with all these knights dead, France will remain a desert! I shall now wind the horn!"

"To sound it now would be unworthy of us all! . . . How bloody are your arms, dear Rollanz!"

"I have been dealing bloody blows. . . . Why are you angry with me now?"

"All this carnage is your fault! You outstretched yourself today. If you had listened when I spoke, King Carles would be here now. You have lost us by your pride, Rollanz. Before evening you and I will say farewell."

As Rollanz and Oliviers stood quarreling, the Archbishop Turpins came between them. "Sir Rollanz! Sir Oliviers! By God, I beg you to stop! The horn can no longer save us. Yet, on the other hand, it would still be better for Rollanz to sound it. Why? Because the Franks will return with our army. They will gather up our bodies and carry them over the mountains. They will not leave us as carrion for wild dogs and wolves. They will inter us in the crypts of our cathedrals."

"Sir, well spoken," answered Rollanz. He lifted the horn to his lips and blew with all his might, until his temples burst and the salt blood burst through his throat.

High are the peaks and loud the voice of the horn! For thirty leagues around its shrill tongue blared. Far up on the passes of the Pyrenees, Carlemagne heard it and halted. "Our men do battle!" cried King Carles.

"No," answered the traitor Guenes. "You know how playful Rollanz is. He'd blow his horn all day on the track of a hare. Who'd dare to attack our rear guard? Let's ride forward into France."

"Listen," commanded Carles. "That horn was winded long!"

Duke Naimes agreed with Carles. "Rollanz does battle. I am sure of it. And that man, Guenes, beside you, Sir King, has betrayed him! God, Sire, do you hear that desperate horn?"

"Answer Rollanz," cried Carles. "Sound the horns and arm yourselves all!" In haste the Franks dismounted, slipped on their mail shirts, grasped their spears, and mounted their war horses. Under their breaths they prayed Rollanz would live to see their avenging arms. What is the use of words? They were too late.

Already the vesper shadows crept down the mountain slopes. At the head of his army Carlemagne galloped hard, his face intent and angry as he leaned forward on his horse's neck. Before turning southward, Carles had ordered Guenes seized and put in the guard of the cooks and kitchen knaves. "Watch him closely," commanded the king, "for he is a base felon!

He has handed one of mine over to the enemy today!" The kitchen boys pulled out Guenes's hair and his whiskers. They fastened a peg and chain about his neck, the sort a bear wears. Then they hoisted him on a pack animal and beat him with switches and sticks.

[V. 1830] High are the hills and shadowy and dark, the valleys deep and the torrents swift! Rollanz looked over his shoulder toward the mountain peaks and then at the dead lords of France who lay at his feet. "I saw you lay your sweet lives down for me, and yet I could not save you. May God bear you all to Paradise. May he rest your gallant souls in sainted flowers! Greater barons than you have I never seen." Then Rollanz returned to battle, so terrible and swift that the archbishop gasped to see him drive the heathen like packs of yelping dogs before him.

"That's what a true knight should be," thought Turpins, "either strong and proud like Rollanz, or else I wouldn't give four cents for him. Either let him be like Rollanz, or let him go to a monastery and pray for our sins." Rollanz gave no quarter that day and took no prisoners. Through the thick of battle he spied the King of Saragossa. "May God damn you!" cried Rollanz as he struck off King Marsilie's right hand. Then he cut off his prince's head. At that one hundred thousand pagans, screaming to Mohammed for aid, fled from the field of battle. . . . Call them, as you will! They will not return!

Then Marsilie's uncle, a king who held lands all the way from Carthage to Ethiopia, led his troops against the Franks. His warriors were black and fierce; only their teeth showed white under their helms. When Rollanz saw them coming, he knew that he was lost. They were gallant, those men! Rallying the few remaining Franks, however, Rollanz plunged dauntlessly into their midst. As the African king rode past on his sorrel, he struck Oliviers a deathblow in the back. Before he fell, however, Oliviers turned and killed that king. "You shall never go brag to some lady how you killed Oliviers," he cried. Then he summoned Rollanz, for he knew he soon would die.

Hurrying to Oliviers' side, Rollanz scanned his friend's face sadly. Oliviers' cheeks were already pale and bloodless. Great clots of blood dripped from his body to the ground. Rollanz' eyes blurred, and his head swam at the sight. Oliviers did not even recognize Rollanz. Thinking he was an enemy knight, Oliviers swung his sword at him and dented his helmet. When Rollanz spoke, then Oliviers came to his senses, knew the voice, and asked forgiveness. "I have no injury, Oliviers," said Rollanz gently. "I pardon you here and before God." Then each knight bowed to the other. So did Rollanz and Oliviers part in their lifetimes.

"Sir Companion," murmured Rollanz in farewell, "what a pity for one so brave! Together have we two been both in years and in days. When you are dead, it is pain for me to live!" In his grief Rollanz would have fallen from the saddle if his golden spurs had not held him upright.

There were only three French barons left alive. One was Gualter of Hum, who had fought all day on the mountains. Now, a sole survivor, he rode down to the plain toward Rollanz. "Where are you, gentle Count? Where are you, Rollanz? I was never afraid when I could fight beside you!" Side by side, Rollanz, Gualter, and the Archbishop Turpins of Rheims faced the Sarrazin host. None of them would abandon the others. Forty thousand mounted Sarrazins face them, and one thousand on foot. No pagan stirs a foot to meet them. Instead, they shower volleys of spears, lances, arrows, and darts; Gualter falls. The archbishop's horse falls. The archbishop's body is pierced through with four spears!

Yet the gallant archbishop still struggled to his feet. His eyes sought Rollanz. He gasped, "I am not defeated! I do not surrender!" Then the huge Turpins advanced boldly toward the enemy, swinging his sword about his head in a frenzy of anger and will to defy them. The Book says he injured four hundred more, and so says the eyewitness, the Baron Gilie who built the monastery at Laon. Anyone who doesn't know this, understands nothing about History!

Count Rollanz stood alone. He trembled from fatigue, from the heat of battle, and from his bursting temples. He still did not know whether or not Carlemagne had heard his call. He tried once more to sound the horn, but his strength was almost gone. Even so, the emperor heard the feeble notes. "Sirs!" called King Carles. "That was my nephew's last breath! I can tell by the sound that he is near death! Ride on, whoever wishes to see him yet alive! Sound all our horns at once!" Then sixty thousand trumpets blared full-tongued through the hills and echoing vales.

On the plain of Roncevals the pagans stopped to hear that blast. "Carles will soon be upon us! Then there will be havoc. If Rollanz lives one hour more, we are lost and so is Spain." Then four hundred banded together and advanced toward Turpins and Rollanz.

Count Rollanz of France, nephew of the king, drew himself up cold and haughty. He clenched his teeth and waited. He would never retreat an inch while breath stayed in his lungs. "I am on horseback while you have lost your mount," said Rollanz to the archbishop. "Therefore let Durendal bear the brunt. Know only that I am beside you, whatever happens."

Turpins laughed and answered stanchly, "He is a felon who will still not strike them hard! Carles is coming. He will avenge us."

The four hundred Sarrazins stood face to face with Rollanz. Not a man of them dared attack, and yet there was not a moment to lose. Even then they could hear the advance body of the Franks thundering down the mountain. The blaring war cry "Mountjoy" floated to their ears. Instead of rushing the two French barons, the Sarrazins let fly another volley of spears, arrows, lances, and beribboned darts. Then they turned tail and fled for their lives across the field.

Rollanz stood alone on the field of battle. His armor, his helmet, his mail were pierced and shattered. His valiant war horse Veillantif was dead of thirty wounds. Rollanz turned to the archbishop. As gently as he could, he lifted off his armor and stanched his wounds. Then raising the prelate in his arms, Rollanz laid him on thick grass. "Take leave of me, gentle sir," pleaded Rollanz. "All our friends and companions, all are dead. I shall go and carry their bodies here before you. I shall lay them in a row here on the sod."

Still the archbishop lived and so did his great heart. "Go and return, Rollanz. This field is ours, thank God—yours and mine!"

Rollanz walked across the battlefield. He searched through the vales and he searched through the hills. First he found Sir Gerin and Sir Gerier, then Sir Berengier, Sir Anseïs, and Sir Sansun. Then he found the body of that great hero Sir Gerard of Rusillun. These he laid at the archbishop's feet so that they could be blessed. Then Rollanz sought and found his dear friend, Sir Oliviers the Wise. As he carried Oliviers in his arms, Rollanz spoke soft words to his friend, and wept. After he had laid Oliviers on the earth, Rollanz could endure no more. His face became drained and white. He sank to the ground.

"How I pity you, Baron," said the Archbishop Turpins. The compassion he felt for Rollanz was the sharpest pain he had felt all that day. Unsteadily the worthy prelate rose to his feet. He wanted to bring water for Rollanz from the little stream that flows at Roncevals, but he had lost too much blood. Before he had traversed the length of an acre, his heart faltered and stopped beating. The throes of death gripped him. He fell forward on the grass.

As Rollanz struggled to regain consciousness, he saw the archbishop join his hands and raise them to the heavens imploring God to give him Paradise. Then his head fell, and he died. Through many great battles, and many fine sermons, he had campaigned all his life against the pagans. May God grant him his sainted benediction! AOI[2]

Rollanz was alone. Sensing that his own death was near, he prayed for the archbishop. He saw how he lay, his beautiful white hands crossed on his breast. "Ah, gentle man, knight of illustrious ancestry, I recommend thee today to the celestial Glory. Never will any man do more willingly your service. Nor has any prophet equaled thee since the Apostles in

---

[2] *AOI*: Scholars do not know what these letters mean, probably "Alleluia."

keeping the faith and attracting men to it. May your soul suffer no hardship. May the gate of Paradise be open when you come."

Rollanz feels death very close. His brains bubble out through his ears. His every thought is a prayer to God to summon to Him the dead peers of France. He prays to the Angel Gabriel, who is near. Then taking his ivory war horn in one hand, and his sword Durendal in the other, Rollanz walks in the direction of Spain toward a hill where there are four marble steps. There he falls over backward on the green turf.

High are the peaks and very tall the trees. Four marble steps there were shimmering and white. On the bright green grass the Count Rollanz falls fainting. Now a Sarrazin, who had smeared his face and body with blood, pretending to be dead among the dead, had all this time been watching Rollanz. As soon as he sees the count lying alone, the heathen in his pride and folly rushes over to him. He tugs at Durendal. Rollanz feels his hands and recovers his strength long enough to strike one last blow with his war horn, so true that the pagan's brains come oozing out his eye sockets.

Rollanz' one thought is for his sword. He cannot risk its falling into enemy hands. Ten times he brings the steel blade down upon a rock, but in vain. It neither blunts nor breaks. "Holy Mother, help me! Ah, Durendal! How sad I am for you. With you in my hand how many lands, how many kingdoms have I subdued that Carles of the curly white beard now holds in sway! You must never fall into the grasp of a man who would flee before the foe!" Even though he strikes the blade full against brown chalcedony, it neither shivers nor cracks!

Rollanz gazes at the twinkling sword, murmuring to himself, "Ah, Durendal, how beautiful you are, how you shine, how white you shine! How against the sun you gleam and return fire for fire! How well I remember that day God commanded Carlemagne to bestow you upon a count and captain. Then gave he you to me, King Carles the Great. Together we have conquered Anjou and Brittany. Together we have won Poitou and Maine, and fair Normandie, Provence and Aquitaine, Lombardy and Romagna,[3] Bavaria and Flanders, and even Burgundy! Together we have won Constantinople and Poland. Saxony. Scotland. England. All these lands does Carles hold, who has the whitest beard. For you, Durendal, I feel such heavy grief. May France never have to say that you are in pagan hands!"

Desperately Rollanz strikes the brown rock with all his power and might. The sword neither splinters nor breaks, only bounces away from the rock. Rollanz speaks to it again, "Ah! Durendal, how lovely and how holy art thou! Thy hilt holds the most holy relics: Saint Peter's tooth, Saint

---

[3] *Romagna*: Rumania.

Basil's blood, Saint Denis's[4] hair, and a precious remnant from Saint Mary's own robe. No pagan must ever lord it with you! I pray that a coward's hand may never defile you! By your aid I have conquered so many fair lands!"

Now Rollanz feels that death, stealing its way from head to heart, creeps over his whole body. He runs toward a tall pine tree, where he falls face downward on the ground, his sword and horn safely under his body, his face pointing toward the enemy. He confesses his sins. In atonement he holds out his gauntlet toward God. *"Mea culpa. Mea culpa.* Forgive me my sins, the great and the small, throughout my life from birth to death." Again he offers his right gauntlet to God. . . . The angels from heaven hover softly over him. AOI

Count Rollanz of France lies under a pine tree. Toward Spain he has turned his sweet face. All his memories surge through his mind—how many lands he has won, his beloved France, the strong men of his lineage, his liege lord, and King Carles who raised him and fed him from childhood at his own table. "True Father, Thou who never lied, Thou who called back Lazarun from the dead, Thou who saved Daniel from the lions, guard my soul from perdition despite the sins of my life." Rollanz holds forth his right glove to God. . . . It is Saint Gabriel himself who stoops and takes the glove from the hand of Rollanz. Then, and only then, Rollanz drops his weary head to his arm. Hands joined, he goes to his end. God sends his angel cherubim. He also sends Saint Michael-of-the-Peril. With them comes Saint Gabriel. Together they bear the soul of Rollanz to Paradise.

[V. 2397] Rollanz is dead. God has his soul in Heaven. . . . Now the emperor reaches Roncevals. There is not a road or a path, not an ell or an inch of ground where does not lie a Frenchman or a pagan. Carles cried aloud, "Where are you, my fine nephew? Where is the Archbishop? Where is the Count Oliviers? Where is Gerin, and Gerier, and Berengier, the Gascon Engelers, Duke Sansun, the worthy Anseïs, and that great hero, Gerard de Rusillun the Old? Where are my Twelve Peers of France whom I left at the pass? No matter how I call, will no voice answer mine? Answer me! . . . How greatly am I dismayed that I was not here when this battle commenced!" King Carles tears at his beard, so appalled is he. His twenty thousand Franks kneel upon the sod and weep.

Upon the field of Roncevals the Frankish army weeps. They mourn aloud their sons, their brothers, and their nephews. They weep for dear friends and honored liege lords. Then Duke Naimes first of all speaks to

---

[4] *St. Denis*: patron saint of France.

Carlemagne. "Sire, lift your head. Do you see that cloud of dust not two leagues away? That's the pagan host retreating! Let us first avenge our grief."

"That far away already?" mused King Carles of France. "Grant us this grace, O God. These men have stripped from me the gentlest flowers of France." Then Carles summons four knights, "Guard this field of combat, with its hills and its vales. Let these dead be, exactly as they lie. Let neither beast nor lion come near them. Let neither squire nor servant lay a finger on these dead! Let no man touch a one of them until God lets me return." A thousand knights patrolled and mounted guard.

Bugles sounded. Ranks formed. Carles rode to the head of the columns and signaled them to ride. He set a hard pace against the Sarrazins' backs. Not until vespers did the army slacken speed. Then the king dismounted in a meadow to pray. He knelt and touched his forehead to the earth. There he asked *his* Sovereign Lord to hold back the night, to stretch out the day. Then came to Carles that angel who communed with him and directed his prayers. The angel's words were rapid and clear: "Carles, mount. The daylight shall not lack. God knows you have just lost the finest flower of France. Vengeance is yours today upon these criminals." The emperor set out at once. AOI

For Carles the king, God made a mighty show. He held back the sun, as it was. Less than two leagues ahead the pagan host rode hard. Carlemagne followed harder. Mile after mile the Franks closed the gap. In the Valley of the Shadow the Franks caught up with the Sarrazins. With bursting hearts they wielded swords and axes upon their backs. Detachments forged a circular path ahead on either side and barred the main road and the paths to the south. The pagans were trapped with the dark waters of the Ebro River behind them. The stream was deep and marvelously swift; there was neither barge nor ferry nor warship standing by with ready oar. The pagans called upon their god Tervagant to help them. Then they plunged into the Ebro.

No god helped them. Those who wore rich armor and mail sank first, swifter than rocks, to the bottom. Others floated downstream, gulping great draughts of river water before they drowned in agony. The Franks lined the river-bank and cried aloud, "Ah, Rollanz, what grief we feel for you!"

As soon as Carles was certain that not a pagan lived, that all had perished either by sword or by water, he dismounted and like a noble king lay on the ground to thank God. His men looked about them. They were astonished at the amount of riches that strewed the field. By the time Carles had finished his devotions, the sun had set! He spoke then to his knights, "Let us find shelter here for the night. It is too late to return today to Roncevals. Our horses are weary and worn. Unloose their girths, lift off the saddles, and unfasten their golden bridles. Let them graze in these fields."

"Sire, you speak well," answered the Knights.

The emperor took lodging there by the Ebro waters. His Franks dismounted in that wasteland, lifted off the ornate saddles, and slipped the bridles from their horses' heads. Then they turned the animals loose to pasture. They could give them no more attention than that. The knights were so tired that they slept there on the ground. Not even a guard was set on their camp.

The emperor also slept in that meadow, his boar spear close to his head. He would not even disarm. He slept in his white hauberk, his jeweled helmet still tightly laced and his massive sword Joyous cinched to his belt. The great sword of Carlemagne lay in beauty, it that changed colors thirty times a day. In its pommel lay encased the point of the lance which had pierced Our Lord on the Cross. Because of the treasure it enclosed, the sword of Carles was called Joyous. It was this joy that the Franks were remembering when they called their battle cry, "Mountjoy!" This is the reason that no people can stand against them.

Clear is the night and the moon glimmering. Carles lies on the ground grieving for his nephew Rollanz. His heart is heavy too for Oliviers, for the Twelve Peers of France, and for the French knights whom he has left dead and blood-smeared on the field of Roncevals. He cannot change his nature; therefore he weeps for them and laments. He begs God to guarantee their salvation. The weight of his affliction wears him so sorely that he finally falls asleep. Even the horses have lain down. Those that have the strength to eat, champ the grass where they lie. *Mult ad apris ki bien conuist ahan*—that man has learned much who has known agony deeply.

Carles sleeps like a man in travail. Then God sends Saint Gabriel to watch over the emperor. All night long the angel stands close by his head. He sends Carles a dream of a great battle he will fight, and of the deaths he will still see. Then in his dream Carlemagne sees mighty cold winds and frosts, storms and marvelous huge tempests, and a monstrous wall of fire and flame that engulfs his whole army. As the ash and apple-wood spears catch fire in the hands of the men, Carles groans. Then the bucklers catch fire up to their golden hasps. The boar-spear shafts explode! The steel and mail and helmets curl and buckle in the flames. Carles sees his knights in torment.

Then the scene changes. Bears and ravenous leopards leap out of the woods and devour the Franks. Serpents and fabled vipers, dragons and demons come to feed on the bodies! More than thirty thousand winged griffins swoop down upon the host! Carles's Franks cry out to him frantically, "Carlemagne! Help us! Help!" The king, though wracked with grief and anxious to go to their aid, is hindered. Finally from a wood lumbers a huge lion, enraged, lordly, treacherous, dauntless. It leaps upon the emperor himself! They fall to the ground, struggle, tumble, fight. Carles cannot tell which one is uppermost. . . . Even through this dream Carles does not awaken.

Then the scene changes. In his next dream Carles is in his castle at Aix. There he sees before him a bear held by two chains. All of a sudden, from the forest of Ardennes he sees thirty bears burst! They seem to speak in the language of men, for Carles hears them say to him, "Sire! Give him back to us! It is not just to keep him any longer! He is our relative. He deserves our succor!" Even as the bears grow angry and threaten, a greyhound runs down the palace steps toward them, darts between the chained bear and his relatives. It leaps for the chained bear's throat. The two fight furiously, but Carles cannot tell which one is vanquished. . . . All these presages the angel of God shows the noble king. Then Carles sleeps dreamlessly until the broad daylight.

[V. 2845] The next morning at the very break of day Carlemagne awakens. Saint Gabriel, who has watched him all the night, makes his sign over the king's head. Carles stands up. His first act is to lay down his weapons and to divest himself of his armor. All the Franks watch him and do likewise. Then they mount their horses and return by high road and byroad to Roncevals. They are going to see by morning light the terrible damage there where the battle was. AOI

When Carles finally comes to Roncevals itself, he can no longer refrain from tears. Holding up his gauntlet, he stops the troops behind him. Then he turns in the saddle and tells them, "Sirs, advance at a walk, for I myself must go ahead of you, especially now. I should like to find my nephew's body first. I remember one day at Aix there was a splendid feast day. My knights were boasting of their chivalry, of their great battles, and of the escarpments they had stormed. Then I overheard my young nephew Rollanz talking. Rollanz said, 'If ever I trespass, if ever I die in a strange land you will know where to find me. You will find me lying farther into enemy territory than any other man in our ranks. You will find me lying in death with my face turned not away, but full toward our foes. Thus in the very act of conquering, I swear I shall die like a baron.' "

The emperor of the Franks walked his horse forward, not much farther than one could throw a stick. He climbed a mound. The flowers of the field, between his horse's feet, were every one stained with scarlet blood. Tears ran down the old king's cheeks. He rode slowly along until he came to two trees. There he saw on the brown stone the cuts from Rollanz' sword. There he saw stretched in death upon the greensward his nephew Rollanz.

A shudder ran over the king. He dismounted and ran toward his nephew. In his two hands he held the knight's body and rocked back and forth in bitter convulsions of grief. When his sobs had begun to subside, Duke Naimes, Count Acelin, Geoffrey of Anjou, and his brother Tierri lifted the king from the body and bore him under a pine tree. From there Carles looked down upon his boy and said to him softly, "My friend, my Rollanz, God have mercy on thee! For no man ever saw a knight like thee joust and tilt so nobly in such awful wars. *La meie honor est turnet en declin*—my honor is turned to its decline."

The four knights clasped the old king's hands. Again he spoke to Rollanz, "My friend, my Rollanz, may God put thy soul in flowers, in Paradise, among the glorious! Not a day shall henceforth dawn but I shall suffer because of thee. No one now will uphold my honor. I have not a friend left on this earth. Relatives perhaps, but none noble like thee.

"My friend, my Rollanz, I shall go from here to France. When I am in my own estates at Laon, foreign vassals will inquire, 'Where is your count, the Captain?' I shall have to answer that he died in Spain.

"My friend, my Rollanz, valorous and beautiful knight, when I am at Aix in my Chapel, men will come to me asking for news of thee. Then I shall have to say to them, 'Dead is that youth who conquered so many domains for me.' Then will rise up the Saxons, the Hungarians, the Rumanians, the Bulgars, the Poles, the Italians, the Africans, and those of Califerne. . . . I wish that I were dead."

Geoffrey of Anjou said to the king, "Do you not, Sire, abandon yourself entirely to your grief. Let us seek our knights, our priests, our abbots, and our bishops, and let us inter them honorably according to our rites."

Carles stood by as the bodies of Rollanz, Oliviers, and the Archbishop Turpins were opened, their hearts wrapped in silk, and their bodies enfolded in deerhides. He ordered them placed on three carts and draped in silk gauze.

He had hardly taken these dispositions when messengers from Saragossa announced the approach of the Sarrazin reinforcements from Arabia. Carles turned toward them and pursued the war.

[V. 2980]

THE VENGEANCE OF CARLEMAGNE

[V. 3633] White is the heat and high the clouds of dust. The pagans are in flight, and the Franks press them hard. The chase lasts right to the gates of Saragossa.

To the highest tower of the palace Brandimonie, wife of King Marsilie of Saragossa, has climbed. With her are her scholars[5] and her canons of the false faith, those who are neither tonsured nor ordained. When Brandimonie sees the Arabian forces so confounded, she screams aloud, "Mohammed, help us! Ah, gentle Marsilie, they are vanquished, our men! Our emir has been killed, to our great sorrow. And you have been wounded by Rollanz, to our great shame!" Upon hearing her wild words Marsilie turned his face to the wall. He shed tears, his face clouded over, and he died of sorrow. Loaded as he was with sin, he gave up his soul to living devils.

The pagans are finally dead, and King Carles has won the war. First he orders the portals of Saragossa to be burst wide open. He knows perfectly well that it will not be defended. He takes possession of the city. His troops file through its streets and find lodging for the night. Proud is King Carles of the flowerlike white beard. From Queen Brandimonie herself Carlemagne receives the towers and the dungeons, the ten large and fifty small ones. He whom God aids can carry out his plans.

That day passes, and the night is full of stars. The emperor of the Franks has captured Saragossa! By orders of the king, the pagan idols are destroyed so that neither evil nor sorcery can work any more harm. The bishops bless the waters and convert the heathen. If any man protests, he is burned or put to the sword. More than one hundred thousand listen to exhortations and accept the faith. Carles makes exception for the Queen Brandimonie. She will be carried captive back to France. Carles wishes her to be converted also, but through love. Swiftly sped the night, and dawned a cloudless day. Carles left one thousand trusty, proven knights to rule the city in his name. He garrisoned its towers. Then mounting at the head of his troops, taking beside him Brandimonie—to whom he only wished well—Carles set out happy and joyous. On the way home he seized Narbonne and passed by. Then he came to Bordeaux where he left in the Church of Saint Seurin the ivory war horn which pilgrims go to see even today. He crossed the Gironde on great ships. He bore his nephew's body, that of his highborn friend and companion Sir Oliviers, and that of the Archbishop Turpins to the Church of Saint Romain at Blaye. In white sarcophagi he laid them to rest, the valorous barons. Then over mountain and down dale he journeyed, without stopping, to his own city of Aix.

As soon as Carles arrives in his capital, he orders the presence of ponderous and learned judges from all parts of his empire. He requests the instant attendance of ambassadors, both authoritative and wise, from Bavaria, from Saxony, from Lorraine, from Friesland, from Germany, from

---

[5] *scholars*: *Clerc* is "scholar" or "intellectual" in Old French; *clergie* is "learning" or "scholars."

Burgundy, from Poitou, from Normandy, from Brittany, and from France
(they are the wisest). Then he declares in session (October 16) the court
that will sit in judgment upon Guenes.

[V. 3705] The Emperor Carles has returned home from Spain; he has
made his way to Aix, the chief seat of his empire. He climbs the degrees to
his throne, where he sits in regal state. Then hastens to his presence the
lovely damsel Alde. "Where," Alde asks the king, "where is Rollanz, our
noble captain? Where is he who swore to take me as his wife?"

Tears come to Carles's eyes. Averting his eyes, he pulls at his long, white
beard. "Sister, dear young friend, after whom do you inquire?"

"Rollanz."

"Do you seek from me a dead man? My nephew Rollanz died in Spain.
I will grant your suit, however, in the person of my son Louis. I can do no
more than that for you, dear lady. Accept my son and heir Louis, a count
of the marches."[6]

Alde replied to Carles in swift, breathless words, "Your answer rings
strangely in my ears, O King. May it please God. May it please the Saints.
May it please the angels in heaven that after Rollanz, I do not remain in
this world at all. . . ." Color drained from Alde's cheeks, and she slipped to
the marble floor at the king's feet. She was already dead, this promised
wife of Rollanz. God have mercy on her soul.

Carles the king did not know that the damsel had died. He thinks she
only swooned. He is so sorry for the pretty maiden that he weeps. He rises
from the throne and chafes her hands. Then he lifts her in his arms. Only
when her head droops on his shoulder does he realize that she is dead.
Carles summons four countesses. He orders the maiden's slender body
borne to a minister, laid in state by an altar, and waked by nuns. He has
Alde buried there. He can do no more to honor this maiden.

The emperor Carles has returned to Aix from his seven-year campaign
in Spain. The felon Guenes, attached to a stake, has been brought before
the palace. Serfs have tied his hands with deerhide thongs; they beat him
with sticks and switches. Guenes has not merited better treatment. There
the traitor awaits the commencement of his trial. As the Book of Deeds
records, Carles has summoned his leading vassals, who have convened in
the Chapel at Aix. It is the high feast day of that great baron of France,
Saint Silvestre. On that day begins the judgment to which the traitor
Guenes has been carted.

"Sir Barons," says Carlemagne the king, "judge me the case of Guenes.
He was in my host all the way to Spain. He stripped from me twenty

---

[6] *marches*: marquis.

thousand of my Frankish warriors, and my own nephew whom your eyes shall never more behold. He caused the death of Sir Oliviers, the chivalrous, the courageous. He betrayed my Twelve Peers for goods and for gold."

"Felon indeed," shouted Guenes defiantly, "if I hide that fact! Rollanz did me wrong both in goods and in gold. It was for that I sought his death and his distress. But treason, no! That did I never do!"

Answer the Franks, "We will take it under advisement."

Before Carles the king stands Guenes on his feet. He is a strapping fellow with a high-colored face. If he were only loyal, you would call him a noble man. He holds the gaze of all Franks and of his judges. Thirty of his family have come to be with him. Then Guenes shouts loudly, in a very deep voice, "Sirs, I was in the host when the emperor whom I serve still with fidelity and love received hostages from Marsilie of Saragossa. We all suspected the Sarrazin was lying. Carles asked for a messenger from among us to send into Spain, into almost certain death, since our previous heralds had been slain. His nephew Rollanz proposed me for the post. I went, since I was so named and commanded; and I managed to survive. Before all the host, I openly swore vengeance upon Rollanz. I got my revenge, but there was no treason in that!"

Answer the Franks, "We shall see."

Guenes understands that upon their decision hangs his life. Thirty of his relatives are there, but one among them is most reliable and influential. This is the knight Pinabel, who knows not only how to plead well, but also how to compose an excellent brief. Pinabel, in addition, is courageous. He handles weapons extremely well. Guenes tells him, "Friend, get me off. Get me out of here, out of death and calumny!"

Pinabel reassures Guenes, "You will certainly be saved. If any French baron here present casts his vote for your death, rather than see you hanged, I shall meet him sword to sword, my body for yours. In such a trial I shall demonstrate your innocence. Never fear." Guenes bows low to Pinabel.

Judges from all the territories of the Carolingian Empire debate what they are to do, and lower their voices when Pinabel is present. They are finally unanimous in their verdict, all except the young Count Tierri. This count and his brother Geoffrey of Anjou had lifted the body of Rollanz on the field of Roncevals. Tierri voted for the death of Guenes.

The judges advance to Carles, saying, "Sire, we beg you to call it quits with Count Guenes, who will henceforward serve you in all good faith and honor. Leave him his life, for he is a very gentle man. You cannot have back Rollanz, not for lands or for gold."

The king replies, "You are felons!" When Carles sees that they have all failed him, his heart and brow grow sad.

Then steps before the king the younger brother of Geoffrey of Anjou, the youngster Tierri. He is a slender youth and not very tall. His skin is dark, and his hair very black. He says courteously to Carlemagne, "Sire, great King, do not lose your spirits so. You know how long and how willingly I have served you. According to the tradition of my ancestors, I am bound personally to uphold your accusation before this court. No matter what the forfeits of Rollanz to Guenes may have been, the Count Rollanz acted in your service, which should therefore have guaranteed his safety. Guenes, in so betraying Rollanz to his death, broke both his feudal oath and our laws. Let him therefore be viewed and treated as a perjurer. If he has a champion from among his family, let that man advance with his sword against mine, let us put the innocence of Guenes here to trial again before this court and our king. Accordingly, I also claim my right. I ask to challenge Guenes."

Answer the Franks, "You have spoken well."

Then strides before the king the tall, strong Pinabel. He is a valorous baron. He says, "Sir King, this court has convened at your instance to judge your accusation. Let this affair make less stir. I see before me Tierri, and I hear his request. I cancel his vote, and herewith ask to fight him." Pinabel strips off his right gauntlet of deerhide and hands it to the king.

Carles says, "I require now a guarantee. Who will give his word and bond for this man!" The thirty relatives of Guenes step forward.

"I shall set you at liberty on your oaths," announces Carles. Then he assigns guards to watch them. When Tierri sees that there will be a trial by conflict, he also presents his right gauntlet to Carles and gives bondsmen who are placed under like surveillance.

The king orders four benches to be set up before the palace, and there the challengers and their bondsmen to sit. In due procedure and plain sight of all, the quarrel is provoked. The great hero, Ogier of Denmark, bears the challenges from each to the other. The knights ask for horses and arms. When they are dressed, they each confess and are absolved. Each one makes generous bequests to the ministers of his preference. Both bow before the king. They wear spurs, white hauberks, gleaming helmets, and shields with coat of arms. Their swords are sheathed. Their boar spears are ready. Then each is raised to the saddle of his war horse. One hundred thousand knights weep for love of Rollanz and pity for the young Tierri. What the outcome will be, only God knows.

Before the palace at Aix, the meadow is very wide. There the two knights meet to render justice. They are both great vassals and both of them valorous. Each one mounts a horse that is savage and aggressive. Both knights spur forward, slackening the reins. Each one strikes the other with all his strength and might. At the first well-aimed blow the shields are shivered, the hauberks split open, the girths broken, the cantles turned, and the saddles thrown to the ground. The spectators weep to behold this awful sight.

Both knights fall heavily to the ground. Quickly both rise to their feet, however. Pinabel is much swifter, lighter-footed, and more agile. Each one looks about for the other. Their horses are gone. They unsheathe their swords with golden hilts and strike great, ringing blows at each other's heads. Both helmets are crushed and pierced. The Franks who watch moan aloud. "Oh, God," says Carlemagne, "may the right triumph!"

Pinabel speaks first. "Tierri, call off the fight. I will be your vassal in all love and faith. At your pleasure I will give you my wealth. Only let Guenes be reconciled with the king."

Tierri answers, "I take no thought of what you propose. May I be dishonored if I consent to such a thing! Between us two today must God *show* who is right. You, Pinabel, are chivalrous, strong, and brave. This I know. Your body is well molded. The peers hold you as a peer among them. Therefore do you break off this combat. Such Justice will be done to Guenes as men will remember every day of their lives from now forward."

"May God not so please," replies Pinabel. "It is my duty to uphold my family. I will never unsay myself for any man alive. I prefer death to dishonor."

Then they renew their struggle so violently that sparks fly from their swords. No man can come between them. They are fighting to the death. Pinabel of Sorence is of very great valor. On his helmet from Provence he strikes Tierri so hard that sparks land in the grass and set fire to it. He thrusts the point of his sword in Tierri's face so fiercely that he cuts a gash the length of the young knight's cheek. He slits open Tierri's hauberk down to the belly.

Tierri feels the hot blood running down his face. He sees it dripping into the grass. Then he strikes Pinabel a blow that severs the nosepiece from his helmet and lets the sword pierce his skull. Tierri stirs the blade about in the brain and so kills the valiant Pinabel. The Franks cry loudly, "It is a sign from God! Let Guenes be hanged and also his relatives, who answered for his good faith!"

Carles, accompanied by four of his greatest knights—Duke Naimes, Ogier of Denmark, Geoffrey of Anjou, and Guillaume of Blaye—strides to Tierri and enfolds him in his arms. With his own sable tippet Carles wipes the blood from Tierri's face. Squires hasten to disarm Tierri gently.

Then they place him upon an Arabian mule and lead him among great shouting to the palace.

Again Carles sits in session with his judges, of whom he enquires, "What is your will for those I hold in bond? They came to swear for Guenes."

Answer the Franks, "Not one of them has the right to live."

Carles orders all of Guenes's relatives strung up on the hangman's tree. One hundred sergeants carry out this sentence promptly. The man who betrays, kills others along with himself.

The court then turns its attention to Guenes. Their verdict is that he should die in the most excruciating agony. Four horses are brought. Guenes is tied to each one by his hands and feet. Then four sergeants whip up the horses, driving them toward a stream. Guenes dies, indeed, in great pain. When a man betrays another, it is not right that he live to brag of it.

Then Carles asks the court its pleasure concerning the captive Queen Brandimonie. "I have in my palace a noble lady prisoner. She has heard so many sermons that she desires to be baptized."

Answer the Franks, "Let godmothers be found. Receive her into the church." They rechristened her Juliane. Then the judges were dismissed.

Carlemagne retires to sleep in his high-vaulted chamber. As he rests, Saint Gabriel descends to him, saying, "Carles, arise! Call up your army! Christianity needs you and cries aloud for you!"

Carles did not want to rise. "O God," prayed the king, "you see how painful is my life!" Then he pulled at his long, white beard and wept.

CI FALT LA GESTE QUE TURDOLDUS DECLINET.[7] [V. 4002]

---

[7] *CI . . . DECLINET*: This is the last line of the Oxford manuscript. It is highly controversial. It seems to say, "Here ends the Deeds [poem] that Turold recites [or composes, or writes]."

The Cid

EDITED BY NORMA L. GOODRICH

Note: Rodrigo Diaz de Bivar, known as the Cid, was the foremost Spanish soldier of the eleventh century. Serving King Sancho of Castile, he sided with Sancho in the struggle against the king's brother, Alfonso. In 1072, Sancho was killed in battle and Alfonso ascended to the throne. Several years later, while Don Rodrigo was away on a mission to collect tribute for the king, a nobleman, Garcia Ordoñez, accused the Cid of keeping part of the tribute for himself. King Alfonso supported the charge and banished the Cid from Castile.

THEN weeping and distressed Mio Cid[1] said, "Father in heaven, you see what my wicked enemies have done to me!"

Mio Cid and his dear friend Alvar Fañez rode forth from Vivar. There was a black crow on their right; as they entered Burgos, there was a black crow on their left. Even so, Mio Cid shrugged his shoulders and held his head high. "Alvar Fañez," he sighed, *"we have been exiled from Castile!"*

Sixty of his knights, all bearing pennants, fell quietly in behind Mio Cid as he rode through the streets of Burgos, up to his own palace. The city dwellers watched them from their balconies; no one dared greet Mio Cid on pain of the king's displeasure. Mio Cid dismounted before his own door. He knocked loudly on its panels. He knocked loudly and again. There was no answer from his people within the walls. Mio Cid turned away from his own door. Even that was barred against him.

[1] *Mio Cid*: my hero or lord.

That night Mio Cid camped outside the city, on the banks of the Arlan-
zon, just as if he were campaigning in the mountains. There Martin Antolinez of Burgos joined him, and supplied food for the company, in defiance
of the king's injunction. Mio Cid was able to borrow six hundred marks
from Señors Rachel and Vidas. At cockcrow he and his companions, those
who had freely chosen an exile's wandering life with him, rode to the
monastery of San Pero de Cardeña, where their ladies had taken refuge.

"From this moment," said Mio Cid to those who still followed him,
"since the king of Castile has seen fit to banish me, I am about to depart
from this kingdom. I do not know whether I shall ever in my life enter my
home again. Queen of glory, sustain me!"

He and his loyal knights arrived in the courtyard of the monastery just
before daybreak. Doña Ximena, the wife of Mio Cid, and her two daughters, Doña Elvira and Doña Sol, were kneeling at matins when the word
came of the knights' arrival. Joyously they ran into the dark courtyard,
where by the flare of candles and torches they recognized Mio Cid. Doña
Ximena fell on her knees before her husband. She kissed his hands.

"I see that you are leaving us," she wept, "and that you and I must part,
even in our lifetimes."

Weeping also, Mio Cid put his arms about his two young daughters. He
pressed them close to him. "Yes, most accomplished Lady, whom I love
as I love my soul, I see that we must, indeed, part in our lifetimes. I must
leave you here, Lady. May God grant me a few more days of life and
happiness in this world. May He grant me to earn dowries for our young
daughters. May He grant me life so that I may do you service and homage,
most honored Lady, my wife."

During that day heralds rode about the countryside announcing the
present departure of Mio Cid from the lands of King Alfonso of Castile,
and inviting all men who so desired to rally to his banner. Within six days,
115 men-at-arms had joined Mio Cid. They knew he had no money, for he
had left his cash at the monastery for the care of his wife and daughters.
Whatever he still possessed, they knew he would share gladly, down to the
last coin. Since only three days remained before Mio Cid would be arrested
by the king, his whole party prepared to ride at daybreak toward the
frontiers of Castile.

Doña Ximena prayed, "Glorious Father, who art in heaven. Thou who
appeared in Bethlehem, Thou whom Melchior, Gaspar and Balthazar
came to adore, Thou who spent thirty-two years upon this earth, Thou who
upon the cross did a wonderful deed! Longinos, who had been blind from
birth, pricked Thee with the point of his lance so that Thy blood streamed
down the lance's point and dripped on his hands. When Longinos lifted

his hands to his eyes, they were *healed* and he saw! I adore Thee and believe in Thee with all my heart. I pray Saint Peter to keep Mio Cid from harm and to make us united again in this lifetime."

After Doña Ximena and her husband had heard mass together, they rose and left the chapel. Mio Cid kissed his wife tenderly, for she was weeping so hard she did not know what to do. He entrusted her and his daughters to the abbot, promising to reward the monastery for their trouble and expense. Then he tore himself from his family painfully, like a fingernail from the finger, and rode away over the eastern mountains at the head of his knights.

One night as Mio Cid lay sleeping alone and exiled, near the Duero River, the Angel Gabriel appeared to him in a dream. "Ride forward, Cid, good Campeador![2] Never did baron ride into the eastern lands with such a promise as I now make you: as long as you live, Cid, your life will turn out well for you!"

By the time that Mio Cid had reached the Sierras, he could count three hundred lances behind him. How could he feed such a host? . . . He took the town of Casteion, captured its fortress, and received three thousand marks as a tribute. All this money, herds also, fell to Mio Cid who cared nothing for wealth. To each of his knights he gave one hundred silver marks and to each footsoldier fifty marks. Then he restored their freedom to the Moors he had vanquished, and to their women also, so that people would never speak badly of Mio Cid. He then set out again, for King Alfonso of Castile was still close behind him. Mio Cid would never have raised his lance against his liege lord.

Before the walls of Alcocer, Mio Cid camped for fifteen weeks. He finally took that city also, by artifice. He left one tent pitched before the town, folded his other baggage, and set off down the riverbanks. The people of Alcocer, thinking that he had run out of bread for his men and barley for his animals, spurred after him. When he had drawn them far enough away from the gates, Mio Cid wheeled about, cut a path through his pursuers, and entered the city ahead of them. The banner of Mio Cid was raised over the citadel. He allowed the Moors to re-enter as his subjects.

When the neighboring cities of Teca, Teruel, and Calatayud heard of this victory, they sent a messenger to King Tanin at Valencia, asking for aid before they too were seized. Two Moorish kings set out with three thousand well-armed Moors. They recruited supporters and came to besiege Mio Cid in Alcocer. They cut off the water supply to the city and waited. After three weeks Mio Cid and Alvar Fañez put all the Moors out of the city one night. Then they armed themselves for battle. They were six

---

[2] *Campeador*: champion in battle.

hundred. The honor of carrying their banner was accorded to Pero Bermuez. At daybreak they threw open their gate and plunged without warning into the Moors' encampment. . . . You should have seen the Moors scurry about to arm themselves! At the roll of their drums you would have thought the earth wanted to split!

The men of Mio Cid clutched their shields against their chests. They lowered their lances, from which bright pennants streamed. They did this as one man. They bent their faces over their horses' necks. In stirring tones Mio Cid called to them, "Strike them, Knights, for the love of charity! I am Ruy Díaz, the Cid Campeador of Vivar!"

> *Trescientas lanzas son, todas tienen pendones.*
> *Sennos Moros mataron, todos de sennos colpes.*
> *A la tornada que facen otros tantos son.*
> *Veriedes tantas lanzas premer è alzar,*
> *Tanta adarga aforadar é pasar,*
> *Tanta loriga falsa desmanchar,*
> *Tantos pendones blancos salir bermeios en sangre,*
> *Tantos buenos cavallos sin sos dueños andar.*
> *Los Moros laman Mafomat: los Christianos Sanctiague.*

> They are three hundred lances, all bearing pennants.
> Each man killed a Moor, each one at one carom.
> At the turning, as they wheel, they are still as many.
> You should have seen those lances, lowered and raised,
> So many bucklers pierced, so many perforated,
> So many coats of mail broken and unlaced,
> So many white pennants with red blood defaced,
> So many fine horses without their riders stray.
> The Moors call on Mohammed: the Christians on
>   Saint James.

That day there were the following brave men with Mio Cid: Alvar Fañez, Martin Antolinez, Muño Gustioz, Martin Muñoz, Alvar Salvadores, Galin Garcia, and Felez Muñoz, who was the Cid's nephew. They fought so valiantly that the Moorish kings fled the field of battle and rode for dear life into Teruel and Calatayud to nurse their wounds. Mio Cid pursued them right to the gates of Calatayud. Then he returned to the battlefield, where the Moors lay dead and dying. Sword in hand, he waited for his Castilians to rally around him. "Grace be to God that we have won this pitched battle," said Mio Cid. So much wealth lay in the Moorish camp that it seemed one could not count it.

Mio Cid allowed the Moorish people to return to their city. He also ordered that they should each be given something. Mio Cid's part of the spoils was one-fifth. In his share were one hundred war horses. He said to

Alvar Fañez, "Ride back to Castile. Announce to my lord and king the news of this battle. Take him thirty caparisoned horses, each with a fine sword hanging from the pommel. Ask him to receive this gift from me. Take also this purse of gold and pay for the thousand masses I promised at Saint Mary of Burgos. Give what is left to my lady wife and to my daughters. Say to them that if I live, they shall all three become wealthy ladies."

In all Mio Cid's party now there was not a needy man. However, the Campeador could not stay in Alcocer, for the country was too bare and the land too poor to sustain him and his growing forces. When he prepared to ride forth, the Moors and their women sent their prayers along with him. They wept to see Mio Cid go. The Castilians camped on the high hill of Mont Real and sent requests for tribute to Teruel.

Meanwhile Alvar Fañez had arrived in Castile. Kneeling before the king, he begged him to accept Mio Cid's gift. "It is too early," said the king, "to pardon a vassal who has incurred my displeasure. However, I accept his offering, and I am happy for his success. I reinstate you, Alvar Fañez, in your fiefs. As for the Campeador, I have nothing to say except that I hereby declare that any knight who wishes to join him is free to do so. I also ordain that the hill of Mont Real where Mio Cid is encamped be duly and legally called from this day forth the Hill of Mio Cid." Alvar Fañez took two hundred more knights to his lord, who had moved north to Saragossa and put it to ransom. Saragossa paid willingly; it congratulated itself to be acquitted so easily.

The news of Mio Cid's incursions in the north reached the Count of Barcelona, Raymond Bérenger. This Frankish nobleman was highly insulted and deeply offended. "Mio Cid de Vivar," said Count Raymond, who was a rash sort of fellow, "is dashing through lands which are under my protection. I never sent him a challenge. I never acted as the aggressor. Since he has dared to provoke me, I think I shall have to go ask him why."

Large forces of Christians and Moors flocked to the banner of this Frankish count. They caught up with Mio Cid as he was winding his way, heavily loaded with spoils, down a sierra into a valley. To the count's angry message Mio Cid sent this answer: "Tell the Count not to take it so badly. I am carrying away nothing that belongs to him. Tell him to let me go in peace."

Count Raymond replied haughtily. "He shall have to pay me now. This exile must learn that he has dishonored a count!"

Then Mio Cid ordered that the baggage be unloaded. He saw that Count Raymond would not let him escape without a battle. When Mio Cid observed the silken hose and cushioned saddles of the Franks, and compared them to his sturdy wooden saddles and coats of armor, he did not doubt but that three Franks would fall before each Castilian lance. In the ensuing short encounter Mio Cid easily won 1,000 silver marks, and took Count Raymond prisoner. The Frank was escorted to his captor's tent and served a delicious dinner.

As each dish was presented to him, Count Raymond turned up his nose in disdain. "I would not touch a mouthful of your food for all there is in Spain," he said scornfully. "I prefer to leave here both body and soul rather than to confess I was defeated by such a motley band of . . . leggings!"

Then Mio Cid told him, "Eat some of this bread, Count, and drink some wine. If you do what I advise, you will escape from your captivity. If not, then you will never see your Christian land again."

Count Raymond answered, "You eat, Don Rodrigo, and enjoy yourself. I prefer to die, for I refuse your food and your drink." For three days, while the Castilians were apportioning the booty, the Frankish count sulked and fasted.

Mio Cid watched him all this time. Again he said, "Eat something, Count, for if you do not eat you will never see Christians again. If you do eat enough to satisfy my honor, I will liberate you and two of your gentlemen as well. You shall be freed."

When he heard that, Count Raymond exulted. "If you really do it, Cid, I shall be marvelously pleased with you as long as I live."

"Then eat, Count, for when you have done so, I shall set you free with two others. However, know that of all the spoils I have taken from you, I shall not return a red cent. The men who follow me would be poverty-stricken if I did not provide. Therefore I need this plunder for myself and for them. We have to live by taking what we can find. Not only that! We have to lead this kind of life as long as it shall please our Holy Father, since I am a man who has incurred his sovereign's displeasure, for which I was banished."

Mio Cid was seated in his tent, higher than the count. "If you do not eat enough of my food to satisfy my honor, Sir, you and I shall never be free, the one of the other."

"I accept with all my heart," said Count Raymond, "your gracious hospitality." Mio Cid was pleased when he saw the Frank call for water, wash his hands, and then plunge his flashing white fingers into the meats that were set before him. When both had dined, Count Raymond courteously thanked Mio Cid. "Since the day I was dubbed, I don't recall such a delicious meal," he said. "The pleasure it has afforded me will not soon be forgotten."

Three palfreys with beautiful saddles were brought, and heavy cloaks and furs. His Castilian host escorted the three Franks to the edge of the camp. "Are you leaving me so soon?" inquired Mio Cid. "And in such a Frankish manner? Let me thank you again for all the rich gifts you have left behind you. If it ever occurs to you to wish for revenge, and if you come looking for me, I am sure that you will find me. If you do not, on the other hand, send after me, but leave me alone, I shall see that you receive something from my wealth or from that of yours which I have."

"Give not a thought to it, Mio Cid," laughed Count Raymond. "You have nothing to fear from me. I have paid you enough tribute for one year. And as for seeking you out, I doubt if it will ever cross my mind."

Then the Frankish count dug both spurs into his palfrey's sides and looked over his shoulder, expecting that Mio Cid would repent and chase after him. His Highness (*el Caboso*) would never have committed such a disloyalty for anything in the world! Mio Cid returned to his camp where he spent many more days distributing the plunder from this battle. He and his men were so rich now that they couldn't tell how much they had.

> *Aquí s conpieza la gesta de Mio Cid el de Bibar.*
> Here begins the story of Mio Cid of Vivar.

THE SIEGE OF VALENCIA

Mio Cid, leaving Saragossa and its lands far behind him, turned toward the sea, toward the east from which rises the sun. The more towns he seized on his passage, the more he came to understand that God was with him. His triumphs weighed heavily upon those in the princely city of Valencia; you may as well know it. Those of Valencia therefore took the initiative. They left their rich city and advanced to besiege the Castilians in Murviedro. Mio Cid was delighted. "Here we are," he said, "in their land, drinking their wine and eating their bread. They have every right to question our presence. If we wish to remain here, we must chastise them thoroughly. Let this night pass. On the morrow we shall advance and then see who among my followers is worth his pay."

Now listen to what Alvar Fañez replied. "Campeador, let us do what pleases you. Give me a hundred knights—I ask for no more. Attack them full in the face, and I know you will not flinch. I will circle round and strike them from the rear." His spirit always pleased Mio Cid.

At the very break of dawn Mio Cid aroused his men. Each one knew where to go and what to do. "Hit them hard," cried Mio Cid. "In the name of our Maker and the Apostle James, strike them, knights, with all your will and heart. For I am Ruy Díaz, Mio Cid of Vivar!"

There you would have seen the Castilians spur between the Moors' tents, slash the ropes, and topple the pegs! As the Moors tried to search for their leaders through the confusion of falling pavilions, Alvar Fañez struck them from behind. They had a choice then—to surrender or to run! Two

Moorish kings were killed. Mio Cid pursued those who escaped all the way to Valencia; those who made it to that haven had only the fleetness of their horses to thank. Great was the joy of the Castilians, for they were rich beyond all their hopes. Nor did they stop there. Sleeping during the day and marching at night, Mio Cid spent three years taking one Moorish city after another. He gave them a good lesson in Valencia.

The news of his victories traveled across the sea to Morocco. The people of Valencia complained bitterly as they saw Mio Cid tightening the circle he had drawn around them. They no longer knew what to do, for all the roads were cut. No bread came into the city anymore. Father no longer fed son, nor son father. Friend no longer helped friend. They found no crumb of consolation. It is a disastrous state of affairs, sirs, not to have bread and to watch your women and children starve before your eyes. The king of Morocco knew this, and yet he sent them no aid.

When Mio Cid saw no reinforcements disembark, his heart was gladdened. He dispatched heralds throughout Aragon, Navarre, and Castile to proclaim far and wide: "He who wishes to lose all care and arrive at great riches, let him rally to Mio Cid, who desires to take a daring ride! Mio Cid intends to besiege lordly Valencia itself! He wants it to be in Christian hands. He will wait three days by the Canal of Celfa. Let each man who joins him do it of his own free will, and not under duress!"

After knights and footsoldiers had swollen his ranks, Mio Cid led his army to the very ramparts of Valencia. He besieged that great city honorably, without trickery, simply allowing no one to leave and no one to enter. He established and announced the delay he would grant the city: nine months and no more. He thought that their reinforcements, if any, would have ample time to succor the besieged if that was their intent. At the beginning of the tenth month the lordly Valencia fell to Mio Cid. As he rode through its streets, those of his followers who had joined his ranks as simple footsoldiers were mounted and equipped as gallantly as knights. Who could begin to tell you the quantities of gold and silver each had earned? How happy was he as he watched his banner being raised to the top of the Alcazar!

Within a short time thereafter the king of Seville rode forth to challenge Mio Cid's possession of Valencia. Although this king had thirty thousand warriors under his banner, Mio Cid vanquished him. His share from Valencia, which was thirty thousand minted marks, plus this second landfall, surpassed his dreams. Each Castilian took from this battle one hundred silver marks, so you can imagine what Mio Cid's fifth was!

Then Mio Cid vowed that he would never pull a hair from his ample beard or cut it in any way. This would show his long trials, his great love for his lord Alfonso of Castile, and would be a subject of marvel for Moors and Christians alike. Next he decreed that any man who deserted Valencia without permission, and without having first kissed his hand, should be hanged and his wealth donated to the public coffers. He also appointed Alvar Fañez to have a census made of his followers, their lands and estates, and the amount of wealth they had earned. He found that his forces totaled 3,600. Smiling and satisfied at how his position had improved, he then asked Alvar Fañez to take one hundred horses as a gift to King Alfonso of Castile.

"Beg my king to spare me my lady and my daughters, so that I may now enjoy their gracious presence here in Valencia. Now that I am lord of this proud city, I can begin to do them honor. Therefore urge my suit before the king. . . . I can entrust my family's safety to you, dear Alvar Fañez, during the journey where they must be honorably escorted. Let no indignity fall upon them." Mio Cid dispatched one hundred men with Alvar Fañez and a gift of one thousand marks to the monastery which had provided shelter and care to his family.

While these deliberations were being taken, there arrived in Valencia from the Holy Land a distinguished priest and scholar named Don Jerome. Mio Cid was struck by this priest's learning and prudence; he observed also how Jerome[3] sat a horse as skillfully as a knight, and how he bore himself in all situations requiring learning and diplomacy. This erudite Jerome explained to Mio Cid that he was a militant priest, who wished to share their fortunes and their rude trials. He said he expressly forbade any Christian to weep for him if ever he fell under a Moorish sword. Mio Cid studied this Frankish priest, his speech and his actions, and judged him to be honorable and holy. He therefore decided to elevate Jerome to the rank of bishop and to create a diocese for him in the city of Valencia. This decision was also to be announced to King Alfonso of Castile. There was great happiness in the city when the people learned that they now had within their walls their own Lord Bishop.

Alvar Fañez found the king of Castile in the estates of Carrion. He fell on his knees and presented Mio Cid's gift in full view of the populace one day as the king came out from mass. King Alfonso smiled as he heard from Alvar Fañez' lips the list of Mio Cid's conquests—Xerica, Onda, Almenar, Murviedro, Cebola, Casteion, Peña Cadiella, *and* Valencia—when he learned of the five pitched battles he had won, and of the wealth he had acquired for himself and his men. With his right hand King Alfonso made the sign of the cross at such good news. "My heart is glad," said the king.

---

[3] *Jerome*: This priest, so similar to the Archbishop Turpins in the *Roland*, probably came from France instead of from the Orient, or Holy Land. He died around 1126.

"I am pleased at the prowess of the Campeador. He brings me glory. I accept his gift."

Then Garcia Ordoñez, long a bitter enemy of Mio Cid, added his acid comment, "It seems to me, Sire, that the Cid Campeador has not left us a single man alive in the land of the Moors."

"Stop such talk," commanded the king. "He serves me better than you do."

"Mio Cid craves your mercy," continued Alvar Fañez, "if such a request does not displease you. He asks that you permit his lady and daughters to leave their monastery and to journey to Valencia."

"I accede to his request," answered King Alfonso. "I wish also to provide for these noble ladies while they remain within my lands. See that neither insult, nor evil, nor dishonor fall upon them. Let your Mio Cid look to their safety at the frontier of Castile. Think of it, and make your plans accordingly.

"Now hear you all," continued the king, "I wish Mio Cid to be deprived of nothing. I hereby reinstate his vassals in all their lands and privileges and exempt them from my jurisdiction in cases of capital punishment. I do this so that they may be free to serve their feudal lord."

The two young princes, or Infantes, of Carrion were present at this interview. They spoke to each other secretly. "The fortunes of the Cid Campeador are increasing steadily. Perhaps we should marry his daughters. . . . However, how should we, Infantes of Carrion, propose such a thing to this adventurer, this Mio Cid, who is only from Vivar?"

"Tell your lord," said the crafty Infantes to Alvar Fañez, "that we greet him, that we are at his service as much as princes are able, and that he should think kindly of us. He could not lose thereby."

"I shall transmit your words," replied Alvar Fañez. "There is no trouble in that."

After he had humbled himself before Doña Ximena, and told her of her coming travels, Alvar Fañez sent three knights toward Valencia to tell Mio Cid that his family would be leaving Castile and that within five days he should have an escort waiting for them at the frontier. Then he spent five hundred marks in Burgos on palfreys for the ladies and their attendants, upon the saddles and accouterments so that they would suffer no indignity from their appearance.

Mio Cid, you may be sure, sent his most courageous and most trusted vassals to escort his precious ladies. He dispatched Muño Gustioz, Pero Bermuez, and Martin Antolinez with one hundred knights armed to the teeth, and he also asked Bishop Jerome to join their party. He instructed them to pass through Molina, which was ruled by the Moor Abengalvon, long a personal friend of Mio Cid. The Moor would surely add another hundred knights to the escort. "Tell my old companion Abengalvon that I count on him to do full honors to my family. I shall remain in Valencia because it is now my hereditary fief," declared Mio Cid. "I spent years to win this realm and will not lose it now."

The Moor Abengalvon, understanding the weight of his responsibility, set out to meet the ladies himself. Not satisfied with one hundred knights, he took two hundred with him. Nor would he accept any money for their maintenance. He ordered stores, lodgings, horses, servants for the entire company plus that of Alvar Fañez, all at his own expense. In this way were the ladies of Mio Cid honored. Their attendants rode the finest horses. Their palfreys were draped with satins and damasks. Silver bells hung from their saddles. Every knight's equipment was elaborate. Each lance bore a silken pannet. Every knight wore his shield hung about his neck. Their polish reflected the sunlight proudly. Alvar Fañez rode up and down the columns. He left nothing to chance. Abengalvon was equally vigilant, and openhanded. He would not let Mio Cid's party pay for even a horseshoe!

When Mio Cid heard that the party was approaching the gates of Valencia, that his family were all well and not too tired from their travels over the Sierras, that they had been greeted everywhere with the greatest ceremony and show of respect, it was the happiest moment in his life! Immediately he dispatched two hundred knights to ride forth from the gates. Mio Cid still remained in the Citadel, watching and standing guard. Then when he was notified that the party was almost at the gate, he chose men to stand guard in his stead. He deputed armed sentinels for every tower of the Alcazar, for every entrance and every exit, where they could within instants spread the alarm.

Then Mio Cid called for his horse, a new one named Babieca,[4] which he had acquired recently. He did not know whether or not the horse was swift, whether or not it would stand for him. Mio Cid wanted to remain at attention just outside the city's main gate, where with his back to the wall he would be safe enough. Don Jerome arrived first and hastened to the chapel to put on his vestments and take the silver cross so that he could welcome the ladies.

Mio Cid put Babieca through his paces, guided him through intricate figures, and stopped him short at the gate. The new horse performed beautifully before all eyes. Then Mio Cid dismounted and advanced on foot toward the party. Babieca stood as still as stone. From that day forth the honor and reputation of this war horse traveled throughout Spain. What man did not dream of seeing the bearded Mio Cid astride Babieca!

[4] *Babieca*: a masculine noun meaning "idiot, fool."

Doña Ximena and her daughters wept so hard they could hardly see Mio Cid. "Thank you, Campeador," cried Doña Ximena, kneeling at her husband's feet. "You were, indeed, born at a marvelous hour! You have rescued me and my daughters from ugly humiliations! Here are your daughters. With God's aid and yours, they are well trained and good."

"Dear and esteemed Lady," said Mio Cid, "and daughters who are my heart and soul, I salute you. Do me the honor of allowing me to escort you into your new heritage, which I won only for you."

The lady and her daughters kissed Mio Cid's hand. They rode into the city, receiving the respect and honors due them. Mio Cid conducted them first to the highest tower of the Alcazar, from which they could look down on Valencia's white streets spread out below them, and also eastward toward the blue Mediterranean. When they saw the beauty of their new home, how surrounded they were with thick groves of perfumed lemon and orange trees, the ladies lifted their hands to God in prayer. Mio Cid and his knights felt their hearts swell with pride. The winter sped by happily, and we come to the month of March.

Now I want to tell you about Morocco across the sea, and about its King Yucef, who lost his royal temper because of Mio Cid, Don Rodrigo. "He has entered my domains by violence," cried King Yucef. "And he only honors Jesus Christ!" The king of Morocco embarked with fifty thousand warriors to seek Valencia. He pitched his tents on the beach beside the city. Mio Cid saw him and was not afraid.

"All I have in this world is right before my eyes," mused Mio Cid. "I conquered Valencia fairly. I shall not abandon it except when I die. This city is my inheritance. I shall fight these Moors with my wife and daughters watching me. They will then see how an outcast gets a home in a strange land, and with their own eyes learn how an exile earns his bread."

He sent for Doña Ximena and her daughters to come to the tower of the Alcazar. Then he pointed downward where the Moorish tents blanketed the earth as far as one could see. "God save you!" they cried. "What is it, Mio Cid?"

"Why, that, honored wife, is no cause for alarm. That is more wealth about to drop into our coffers. Since you are newly arrived, the Moors are bringing you a gift. Since you have daughters to marry, they are bringing them African dowries. Watch the battle, if you like, here from the Alcazar. Have no fear on my account, Lady. I shall win it."

By the end of the second day the Moors were defeated and their treasure carted within the walls of Valencia. Mio Cid rode back from the battle, sword in hand. His face was dark and tired. He reined in Babieca before the ladies and dismounted. They knelt before him. "While you ladies kept Valencia for me," smiled Mio Cid, "I fought out in the orchards. Look at this bloody sword and sweating horse! With such a steed as Babieca, the Moors defeat themselves! Pray to God that Babieca lives for several more years. You may then be sure that many will humbly kneel to kiss your fingers!"

After they had entered their palace, Mio Cid, seated on his expensive bench, which had a backrest to it, announced welcome news. "I should like all in Castile to know that those ladies who escorted my señora and her daughters in days of misfortune have been amply rewarded. I hereby bestow a dowry of one hundred marks on each one of them. As for your daughters, Lady, that will come later."

Mio Cid was so enriched by this victory that no proper count of his wealth could be taken. The Moors who dwelled near Valencia were also bettered, particularly as Mio Cid let them keep the stray horses. Mio Cid decided to send King Yucef's pavilion—so large it was upheld by two posts inlaid in gold—to King Alfonso of Castile. From his fifth part Mio Cid granted one-tenth to the church. Don Jerome was delighted, he who had fought side by side with the Campeador, he who had killed uncounted enemies. The next morning Alvar Fañez set out for Castile, taking the tent and this time two hundred horses as a gift. He found the king in Valladolid.

Don Alfonso was overjoyed at the presents and wondered how he could reward the Mio Cid. Don Garcia, who hated the Campeador, regretted his successes. The young princes of Carrion again took counsel with each other. "The fortune of this Cid is still better," said they. "Sire, consent to ask for the hands of the Cid's daughters. We consent to marry them. It will be an honor for them and an advantage for us."

After an hour's reflection King Alfonso replied, "I exiled this good Campeador. I have done him only harm; he has returned only good for evil. I do not know whether he desires these marriages. Let us broach the subject." Then to Alvar Fañez and Pero Bermuez he said, "I pardon Mio Cid. Let him come to see me. Diego and Ferrando Gonzalez, the Infantes of Carrion, desire to wed his daughters. Tell your lord this union would do him great honor. Tell your lord to meet me at the frontier."

When Mio Cid heard the king's proposal, he thought for an hour. "These princes are haughty and have wide influence at court. I should not have desired these marriages. However, since he who is above us all has counseled it, we will with God's inspiration discuss the matter with him." Then Mio Cid sent a letter saying that he would meet the king at the Tagus River.

In three weeks' time both parties, magnificently attired, met at the river. The Infantes of Carrion rode beside the king in high spirits. They paid for this and that, right and left, on credit, knowing that they would soon have gold enough to last them all their lives. What sturdy mules there were in the two retinues! What prancing palfreys! What handsome coats of mail! What galloping horses! What gorgeous cloaks and satin cloaks and fur cloaks! Young and old, tall and short, wore robes of dazzling colors! Mio Cid rode gaily too, for he had left Valencia well defended, with strict orders that not a person was to enter or leave the city until his return.

When he had come before the king, Mio Cid dismounted with fifteen of his chosen knights. He advanced on foot. He threw himself face down before his lord. He fastened his teeth on a clump of grass and wept bitterly, so happy was he! In this way, thudding his knees and his hands flat on the earth, he made his gesture of submission to Don Alfonso.

The king was pained. "Stand on your feet, Cid Campeador. Kiss my hands. As for my feet, no! Obey me, or you shall not receive my love."

Mio Cid did not rise. "I crave your mercy, my lawful lord. With me prostrate before you, give me back once more your love, so all present may hear you."

"Gladly," said the king, raising his voice. "I hereby pardon you, Mio Cid, and accord you my love. From this day forth receive access to all my domains."

"Thanks, great lord," cried Mio Cid, "I accept. Now surely God will protect me day and night." Rising, he kissed the king's hand. "Be my guest, Don Alfonso, my liege lord."

"That would not be fitting," replied the king. "We have been here since yesterday while you arrived only now. Tomorrow we shall do as you please. Today you are my guest."

Then the Infantes of Carrion humbled themselves before Mio Cid. "You were born in a good hour, Cid. As far as we are able, we shall walk toward your welfare."

"God willing," replied Mio Cid.

After two days of entertaining, during which the king feasted his eyes admiringly on the magnificent beard of Mio Cid and could not praise it enough, they heard mass celebrated by Don Jerome and then settled down to the weighty business at hand.

"Give us your daughters in marriage," said the king. "These princes ask it and I order it."

"I have no daughters to wed," replied Mio Cid. "I engendered them, but they are not mine. They are also of a tender age. These Infantes of Carrion could look for a much more honorable match, owing to their high birth. We are all of us at your mercy, Sire, Doña Elvira and Doña Sol as much as I am. Therefore here are the hands of your daughters, Don Alfonso. Bestow them as *you* please, and I shall be content."

"With these words then," ordained the king, "I bestow Doña Elvira and

Doña Sol upon the Infantes of Carrion. Their troths are plighted. Take these sons-in-law to Valencia with you."

"I thank you, Sire," replied Mio Cid. "It is you who give my daughters in marriage, and not I." There was a celebration then for all present. Mio Cid bestowed gifts on every man who asked. Then leaping on Babieca, Mio Cid cried, "Let all who desire rich presents attend these weddings in Valencia!" It had been decided that Alvar Fañez would act in proxy for Don Alfonso, since Mio Cid repeated that he would not give away his daughters at the altar. As he rode back to Valencia, his party greatly increased and the king's diminished by those who accepted the cordial wedding invitation. Mio Cid asked Pero Bermuez and Muño Gustioz to watch the Infantes carefully, to report their personal habits to him, even after they were lodged in the palace he assigned to them in Valencia.

The wedding celebration was lavish and festive. Mio Cid outdid himself in generosity. For fifteen days he entertained his guests at tournaments and feasts. Everyone was pleased with the Infantes of Carrion. They remained in Valencia for two years.

> *Las coplas deste cantar aqui s van acabando.*
> The couplets of this song are just ending now.

May the Creator and all his Saints save you and keep you.

DISHONOR AND REVENGE

Mio Cid was in Valencia with his vassals, and also with his sons-in-law, the two princes of Carrion.

One afternoon as Mio Cid lay sleeping on his high-backed bench, a frightful event occurred. A lion burst from its cage, broke its chain, and started roaming through the palace. Those brave men of the Campeador threw their capes over their right arms and retreated cautiously until they had formed a barrier between the huge cat and their master. The Infante Ferrando saw no place to hide, no tower stairway unbolted, no chamber door open. In terror he crawled under the settee where the Campeador lay resting. The second Infante, Diego, darted out a door and squeezed himself between a beam and the wall, moaning, "Now I shall never see Carrion again!"

At this moment he-who-was-born-in-that-good-hour awoke. He saw his barons encircling his couch. "What is it, friends?" asked Mio Cid. "What do you want?"

"It is only, honored Sir, that a lion has escaped."

Mio Cid had his wide cloak about his shoulders. Rising to his feet, he walked deliberately toward the lion. The beast, seeing that man approach so confidently, was cowed. It drooped its head and looked toward the floor. Then Mio Cid grasped it by the mane and succeeded in turning it and forcing it back into the cage. All present were amazed. When they had recovered from their excitement, Mio Cid asked where his sons were. No one knew. Up and down the palace people called them. Neither one nor the other answered. Finally they were discovered hiding. Don Diego had soiled his shirt and his cloak. Both Infantes were as pale as sheets. You never saw such amusement as the looks of them caused at the court. Mio Cid had to forbid conversation on that subject! He saw that the Infantes were sensitive.

Before these jokes had ceased being remembered, a new force of fifty thousand Moors under King Bucar of Morocco—I suppose you have heard of him—came to besiege Valencia. From the Alcazar, Mio Cid saw their tents spread through his orchards, and their sight delighted him. He thanked his Maker that more booty was about to fall into his hands. The Infantes, on the contrary, were panic-stricken! "We'll be expected to leave our palace and advance to battle! What will happen to us then? These Moors could not have come at a better time! Now we shall certainly never see Carrion again!"

Muño Gustioz reported their conversation to his lord. "Your sons-in-law are so brave that they are frightened," he told Mio Cid. "They are so homesick that they can't go to battle! You should go and console them now, and may the Creator help you! Let them sit home and receive no share of the spoils. We will win this engagement also, if our Maker wishes!"

With a pleasant face Mio Cid strode to the Infantes. "Good day, my sons-in-law, Princes of Carrion. Why do you not today hold my daughters, they who are as bright as sunlight, in your arms while I go out to meet the Moors. You know I am for the war, and you are for Carrion. Amuse yourselves today here in Valencia. Do whatever you like for your pleasure. Leave the Moors to me. I am an old hand at this sort of nastiness. I assure you, the Moors shall be vanquished."

[Here the manuscript is torn; at least one page is missing, but the story of this day is told later by Pero Bermuez.]

The Infantes armed themselves for battle. Mio Cid asked his nephew Pero Bermuez to watch over the princes. Alvar Fañez stood ready to ride when Bishop Jerome rode through the press to Mio Cid.

"Today I said mass for you at Holy Trinity. Now you understand that I left France to fight the Moors. I came here to Valencia for that express purpose because here I could best serve my order. I demand the right to strike the first blow on this field. You see that I have raised my own pennant. You see that my arms are of the finest. If you refuse me this right to try my worth against our foes, I shall never serve you again!"

"I am pleased with your words," replied Mio Cid. "There the Moors are, right in front of you, Lord Bishop. By all means, go and test them. We shall watch from here how an abbot wages war."

Then all alone Bishop Jerome spurred into the enemy. He killed two at the first lance thrust and five more with his sword. Blows fell upon him from all sides; his armor was proof against them. He struck about him with heavy, ringing swings of his sword arm. Mio Cid waited until he saw that the bishop was heavily surrounded. Then, followed by his knights, Mio Cid spurred Babieca into the foe. What a battle was that! Heads and helmets fell to the ground and rolled in the grass! Riderless horses, maddened with wounds, plunged through the falling tents.

Mio Cid marked the African King Bucar. He gave chase, calling, "Wait for me, Bucar! You have traveled so far to meet me! Come greet the Cid of the long beard! We should salute each other like true knights! Who knows? We might strike up a friendship!"

"God damn such a friendship!" cried Bucar. "I know what you want to strike! If my mount neither falters nor stumbles, you will find me in the sea!"

"That's a lie, Bucar. I'll overtake you first!" cried Mio Cid. He spurred Babieca to great, thundering strides. Little by little he overtook the Moorish king, caught up with him about three lengths from the water. With one stroke of his sword Mio Cid dashed the jewels in the golden helm of Bucar over the sand, split the helm and all that was under it down to the waist. That blow ended the battle quickly, for the Moors hastened to lay down their arms. Mio Cid rode back through the tents. His forehead was wrinkled. Then he met the two Infantes, in full armor, there on the field. The sight of them delighted his heart.

"Come," smiled Mio Cid. "You are both of you now my real sons. Good news and high praise shall travel to Castile. All men shall know that you conquered Bucar, the king of Morocco. We shall all come out of this victory with pleasure and honor." Every good word Mio Cid said the two princes twisted into evil. When they had received their share of the booty, however, they saw that they would never need any more wealth as long as they lived.

"I thank God humbly," said Mio Cid. "I see laid out before me everything I have wished for all my life. My sons fought beside me on the field of honor. Once I was poor, and now I am a rich man. My dear daughters are wedded to princes. I win battles, one after another, thanks to my

Creator. Over there in Morocco, where the mosques are, men fear that some dark night I may take it into my head to cross the sea and besiege their cities. They have no basis for their suspicions. I never think of it. I shall never go to seek them. I shall live in Valencia, and allow them to send me tribute instead."

Then the two princes—truly they were brothers—withdrew and whispered to each other. "Let us return to Carrion. We have stayed here long enough. We could never spend all this gold our whole lives long. Let us ask the Cid for our wives. We could tell him that we want to take them to Carrion. We have stayed here long enough. We could tell him we wish to show his daughters our lands and castles. Yes, say we want them to see their inheritance. Only let us escape his vigilance! Once on the road we'll go where we like and do as we please. Let us go before someone mentions that incident of the lion again. We were born princes of Carrion.

"We will transport out of Valencia all the wealth that we now have. Then let us humiliate these daughters of the Campeador. Let us revile them! We are rich enough at present. Let us think of marrying only the heiresses of kings and emperors. We are princely by birth and by taste. Let us abuse his daughters before anyone mentions the incident of the lion again!"

At once they put their request, very courteously framed and delivered, to Mio Cid and to his favorites. The Campeador made no difficulty at all about granting their suit. He had no suspicions about their real intentions. "Yes, I shall give you my daughters, and something of mine also," he said proudly. "Let people up and down Castile see how richly my sons are wed. I am pleased that you have settled estates and revenues upon Doña Elvira and Doña Sol, who are the very coverings of my heart. I grant you 3,000 silver marks as an additional dowry. I present you with two fabled swords, which I wrested hardly from my foes. Here they are, Colada and Tizon. Serve my daughters well, for they are yours in holy wedlock. Honor them, and I shall reward you for it."

When Doña Elvira and Doña Sol were ready to take their leave, they knelt before their parents and said, "We beg your favor, father who engendered us, and mother who bore us. Señor and Señora, you are sending us now to the lands of Carrion. We are honored to do your bidding."

"Go, daughters," replied Doña Ximena, "and may the Lord preserve you. You have our favor, mine and your father's. Go now to Carrion where lie your inheritances. I think we have married you nobly."

Mio Cid and his knights escorted the girls out of the sunny city and through its surrounding orange groves with all the panoply of chivalry. Although their father rode joyfully before his knights, his mind was not entirely at ease because he had seen from omens that these marriages would not be without sorrow. However, he could not retract the contracts;

both girls had been duly wedded. Because of his deep concern, however, he asked Felez Muñoz to accompany the girls to Carrion and then to bring him back word how they were received and how honored.

It was hard for Mio Cid to break away from his daughters, very painful for him to be obliged to turn his back on them, and return to Valencia. He wept, and so did his two girls. "We commit you to God's care, Doña Elvira and Doña Sol," he said. "Bear yourselves in such a way that we here in Valencia shall be happy."

The princes replied, "God willing."

Still Mio Cid could not depart. The separation was as painful to him as if a nail were being torn from his finger. "Listen, my nephew," he instructed Felez Muñoz, "pass through Molina. Tell my friend, the Moor Abengalvon, that my daughters are entering their estates at Carrion. Ask him to receive them, and to furnish them with anything whatsoever that they may require or desire. Tell him I wish his Moors to escort my children to the frontier. He will do this for love of me. He knows that I repay my debts. He knows what my word is worth."

The Infantes of Carrion, once Mio Cid had turned his back, thought only of covering ground as fast as possible. They soon arrived at Molina, where Abengalvon met them with every sign of joy. God! How he served this company! Early next morning he awaited their departure, and accompanied them with two hundred knights, for they had to cross high and lonely mountains in order to reach Castile. Abengalvon spared no expense. Every rich sword and jeweled helm in his kingdom was paraded in order to honor Doña Elvira and Doña Sol. He escorted them as if they had been born of princely rank, like their husbands.

"Look," whispered the brothers to each other, "since we have decided to leave the Campeador's daughters, we could kill this Moor Abengalvon; all his wealth would then accrue to us. As sure as we stand here, if the sum were added to what we now have, not even the Cid could bring us to a reckoning."

While they were plotting, a certain Moor who was a good Latinist overheard their conversation. Instead of keeping this secret to himself, he naturally hastened to Abengalvon. "Master," he warned, "be on your guard, as you are my liege. I heard the Infantes conspiring your death."

Abengalvon was a man of no uncertain courage. He did not stand on ceremony, even with princes. With his knights in close ranks behind him, and with his own sword drawn, he rode up to the princes, face to face. "Now tell me, Infantes of Carrion, what I have done to incur your wrath. I have gone to some inconvenience to do you service, without guile or malice. And you are planning to murder me! If I were not bound to refrain because of Mio Cid of Vivar, I would whip you now so soundly that the reports would re-echo about the world! I would then escort his daughters back to Mio Cid. And as for you, you wouldn't get to Carrion at all!

"I take leave of you here and now, for I see your rascality and your treachery! By your leave, Doña Elvira and Doña Sol, I shall retire from your company. I care little for the reports that may come from Carrion. May God ordain that Mio Cid have joy from these alliances." Leaving the Infantes highly outraged, Abengalvon like a sensible man returned home to Molina.

After the Moor had disappeared down the road, the Infantes ordered their party forward on the double. Not content with their previous rate of speed, they pushed on day and night until they were high in the Sierras de Miedes. Through these high, white peaks they hastened, forcing their horses and setting a hard pace. They passed gigantic caverns and precipices that dropped off into the dark forests below them until they came one evening to the deep woods where the trees were of a tremendous height. Their branches seemed to reach to the clouds. In a clearing they came upon a grove and a spring of clear water. Wild animals hunted for food even up to the edge of this encampment.

The Infantes selected a spot for their tent and allowed their weary wives to dismount. The whole company settled down for the night. The brothers from Carrion caressed their wives in their arms that night and gave them evidences of their love. . . . They will prove it to the poor Doña Elvira and to the poor Doña Sol when day breaks!

Early in the morning the horses and pack animals were saddled, the baggage was reloaded, the tents were folded and packed, and the party set off through the woods. The princes ordered everyone to leave. They said that not a man or a woman should remain at the campsite except themselves and their wives. They wanted to be quite alone with their ladies. According to their wishes, everyone rode ahead down the forest trail, leaving the four under the trees. . . . What do you think the Infantes of Carrion had been hatching?

"You may believe us when we tell you, Doña Sol and Doña Elvira, that you are now going to be disgraced," said the princes. "Here in these forbidding mountains you are both about to be debased. We shall continue on our journey; first of all, we have an account to settle before we abandon you here. This is as much portion of the princely domains of Carrion as you shall ever inherit. We want the news of your fate to reach the Cid Campeador. We intend to take our revenge here for that adventure of the lion."

Then before the horrified eyes of the two young ladies, the Infantes of Carrion took off their fur cloaks, and then their jackets. That was not all! They next proceeded to strip the ladies of their rich mantles. They ripped off their cloaks, their dresses, and left them naked in their thin shirts and tunics. They buckled on their spurs and unhooked the leather girths from their horses!

When Doña Sol saw them approaching herself and her sister with these straps in their hands, she spoke. Doña Sol said, "In the name of Heaven, Don Diego and Don Ferrando, do not use straps on us! Hear my plea! You both have swords that are strong and trenchant. I should know because I have often seen these blades in my father's hands. They are called Colada and Tizon. . . . Then use them on us! Cut off our heads, and give us martyr-dom! Moors and Christians alike will declare that we have earned it. Even though we do not deserve to die, even though you will not treat us accord-ing to our actions, do not, I pray you, make upon our persons such a bad example. If you beat us here in the forest, you will only abase yourselves, not us! . . . You will be called to account for it too, either man to man or at the court of Castile!"

Doña Sol's prayer did not help either herself or her sister. Suddenly the Infantes raised the leather straps and began to rain stinging blows upon their naked shoulders. Leaving the girths unknotted and at their full length, they whipped the girls so unmercifully that both fainted. After both had fallen to the ground, the princes tore their shirts from their backs with their spurs and bruised the girls' hips and thighs. The bright, red blood flowed over their rags of tunics. The weeping girls felt each blow all the way to their hearts. What a blessing it would have been, had the Creator so willed, if the Cid Campeador had suddenly appeared riding through the trees!

The princes beat those ladies until they lay totally unconscious on the ground, their shirts and their tunics drenched with blood. They struck them until their arms were tired, for each one tried to get in the hardest strokes. For a long time neither Doña Sol nor Doña Elvira had made a sound. Then the Infantes picked up the girls' robes and cloaks, picked up their ermine shawls, mounted the palfreys, and rode away, leaving their wives for dead where they lay. They abandoned their bloody remains to the birds of the mountain peaks and to the beasts of prey. They left them for dead, hear, and not for alive! What a blessing it would have been if the Cid Campeador had suddenly appeared before them, riding through the trees! Oh!

The Infantes of Carrion left the poor girls under the trees. Neither girl could even crawl to help her sister anymore. Down the trails and out into patches of sunlight the brothers rode laughing and congratulating each other. "Now we have exacted our revenge for such marriages! We shouldn't have even welcomed such girls as these for concubines, unless, of course, their father begged us to do so on bended knee! They were not our equals. And to think we actually had to hold them in our arms! Another score too! We have also avenged ourselves for the lion." So they rode down the mountainside, joking and thumping each other on the back.

Now I am going to tell you about Felez Muñoz, who was the nephew of Mio Cid the Campeador. He had been ordered that morning to ride ahead with the others, and he did so, but not of his own accord. As he followed the path, his heart ached and pained him so that he gradually slipped away from the others, down side paths. Then he stole backward along the trail, keeping to the thick underbrush, and making no noise. After a while he not only saw the Infantes riding down the trail; he also was able to overhear snatches of their banter. They neither saw Felez Muñoz nor suspected his presence. You may be sure that if they had, he would not have escaped with his life!

Felez Muñoz waited just long enough to let them get a good distance away. Then he dug his spurs into his horse's flanks and galloped frantically back up the trail. There he saw the pitifully wounded girls lying on the earth.

"Cousins! Cousins!" he cried, leaping from his horse and tying its bridle to a tree. "Cousins! My dear Cousins! Doña Elvira! Doña Sol! Oh, what evil have these princes done! I pray to God and to the holy Saint Mary that they receive as bad a punishment!" As gently as he could, Felez Muñoz turned each girl over on her back. Their eyes were closed. They did not breathe. Not a sound, not even a whimper came from either one. It would have broken your heart. "Cousins, live! Wake up! Awaken while it is daylight, while the forest creatures are in their lairs asleep. Wake up before the wild beasts eat us all!"

Then Felez Muñoz saw that the girls were coming to consciousness. Little by little their eyelids began to quiver. Then they opened their eyes and recognized their cousin leaning over them. "Take courage, Cousins, in the name of the Creator!" he urged them. "As soon as the Infantes of Carrion notice that I am no longer with them, they will send after me. If God does not provide for us, we shall all die here."

Then painfully Doña Sol said, "If our father the Campeador has ever merited your love, Cousin, bring us a little water . . . and may God bless you."

With his sombrero, which was a new and clean one he had recently bought in Valencia, Felez Muñoz fetched water and poured it over the deep cuts on the two girls' bodies. He then helped them to sit up. He kept talking to them and encouraging them. He comforted them as best he could, for their bodies were bruised and torn. He pleaded and exhorted them to be brave. The girls with his help finally managed to limp to his horse, where he gently lifted each one to the saddle. Then wrapping them in his wide cloak, telling them all the time how proud he was of their courage, he left the campsite. Leading his horse by the bridle, he plunged under the trees and away from that bloody soil as fast as he could walk. At the hour between daylight and dusk they came down out of the mountain, up to the banks of the Duero River. He found shelter for the girls, for everyone knew their father, at the first castle on the river. Then he spurred hotly down the dusty road and into the nearest town to seek strong friends.

While Doña Elvira and Doña Sol were recovering from their wounds, surrounded by sympathetic and distressed friends, the news of their humiliation traveled westward to the king and eastward to Mio Cid the Campeador. When their father heard all the details of this premeditated outrage, he raised his hand, enjoining silence upon his court. For an hour he sat, stern and alone, digesting the awful news. Then, gripping his beard, he spoke. "Thanks be to Christ, Lord of the world, that the Infantes of Carrion have done me this signal honor. I shall see that their joy is short-lived. As for my daughters, I vow that they shall never again wed counts, only kings!" Then he dispatched two hundred knights under Alvar Fañez' command to bring home his beloved children.

Tears came to Alvar Fañez' eyes when he next looked upon the ladies Doña Sol and Doña Elvira. They said to him, "We are as happy to see you as if we were looking on the face of our Creator! Give thanks to Him that we are even alive! Please take us home. We will tell you all that happened when we are safely home again."

"Dry your tears, dear Ladies. It is enough for all of us that you are alive and well. Your father and mother send you their love. The day shall come very soon when we in Valencia shall have our revenge!"

There was a holiday in Valencia the day the daughters of Mio Cid rode into their home city again. Mio Cid smiled contentedly to see his dear girls safe in his palace again. Then he drew up a message to King Alfonso of Castile. "Tell the king that I sympathize with his affliction," dictated Mio Cid. "Say that I lament his dishonor, for it was he who gave my daughters in marriage. Ask Don Alfonso to summon these Infantes of Carrion to a tournament or to a plenary session of his court, for I am about to seek retribution for their insults, to say nothing of the wealth they took from me under false pretenses. Rancor lodges deep in the heart of a man like me."

When Don Alfonso heard Mio Cid's messengers, he deliberated and then announced that he would convene his court at Toledo. The king acted promptly. He sent his cards into all of his vast realms—throughout Castile, León, Saint-James, Portugal, and Galicia—summoning his vassals to Toledo in seven weeks' time. He who failed to appear would lose at least his titles and lands.

The Infantes of Carrion, having taken counsel with their family, asked to be excused from attending. They feared having to face Mio Cid. However, King Alfonso replied, "Absolutely not! You will attend my court or else leave my kingdom. You must give satisfaction to Mio Cid, who has complained to me about you." Don Garcia collected his friends, summoned all the great nobles who made up his faction to support the Infantes. Don Garcia, who had always hated Mio Cid, saw in this assembly an opportunity to insult Mio Cid himself.

The assembled court had to wait for five days until Alvar Fañez came to announce Mio Cid's arrival. Don Alfonso rode out of Toledo to meet him. Mio Cid came, escorted by all his chosen companions, all fully dressed in armor, all ready to defend their Campeador with every ounce of the strength and skill they possessed. As soon as he had come in plain sight of the king, Mio Cid dismounted and fell to his knees.

"By Saint Isidore," cried the king, "I will not allow you to humble yourself to me today. Mount up, or you will incur my displeasure. Let us greet each other in all sincerity of heart and soul. Know that my own heart is heavy with the weight that hangs upon you. May God grant that your presence may grace my court, Mio Cid."

"Amen," replied Mio Cid the Campeador. "I prostrate myself before you, Sire, and before these great nobles who accompany you. My wife, Doña Ximena, who is a lady of property, kisses your hand. My two daughters greet you humbly. May what has happened to us weigh heavily upon you."

"I shall attend to your plea," answered Don Alfonso, "and may God oversee us all."

King Alfonso of Castile returned to the city of Toledo, but Mio Cid remained that night by the banks of the Tagus River. He explained that he needed to await his men before crossing the river and entering the city. He also desired to spend the night in vigil in a holy place. "I shall present myself at court before dinner at noon," he promised.

"I consent willingly," answered the king.

All that night Mio Cid remained kneeling and praying in a holy place. He lighted taper after taper, taking counsel with his Lord as to how he should proceed on the following day. He knew that he had the faction of Don Garcia to outwit and intimidate. He realized what powerful friends and allies the Infantes of Carrion claimed among the great nobles. At daybreak Alvar Fañez found Mio Cid still at his devotions. He and his men then worshipped together. The mass was ended at sunrise. Mio Cid then made a handsome donation to the chapel and addressed his followers. He named his dearest, oldest companions as his escort and asked them to bring their number up to one hundred by designating others.

"Wear undergarments that will keep your full armor from chafing," said Mio Cid. "Dress yourselves as for battle in complete suits of armor and coats of mail underneath. Let your breastplates be as radiant as the sun. Then put over all this your ermine and your fur cloaks. Fasten them carefully at throat and waist so that the armor does not show. Under your cloaks be sure that your swords are sharp and ready. Wear them loose to-day. Thus garbed shall we fare to the court where I may say my say and demand justice; in the case that our princes of Carrion seek a quarrel, I shall have no fear with one hundred warriors like you. We know each other's worth, I think."

They answered to a man, "We shall do it, Señor."

While his knights were dressing, Mio Cid attired himself to go before the court. He drew on tights of fine wool, and a shirt of white linen as dazzling as sunlight. Its tucks were edged with gold and silver. Over his armor he wore a gold-brocaded tunic, bordered with so much gold that you would have said he gleamed like the sun itself. Then over his shoulders he draped a red fur scalloped with gold. On his head he fitted a cap of scarlet linen worked with gold and so cut that it covered all his hair that had not been trimmed. To protect his beard in like fashion he tied it with a scarlet rib-bon and tucked it inside his tunic. Over this he fastened a sweeping cloak that fell from his shoulders to the ground in such ample folds that it hid his sword perfectly. He leaped to Babieca's back and rode into the city of Toledo at a sharp clip.

Mio Cid dismounted at the palace door. Surrounded on all sides by his hundred magnificently attired knights, he entered the audience hall. Cour-teously the king arose, and so did most of his nobles. Not so Don Garcia and the Infantes of Carrion.

"Come sit beside me," invited the King Don Alfonso. "You shall take this seat of honor, here upon this bench which has a backrest. It is the one you so thoughtfully presented me. Certain people here may be afflicted because of the honor I do you, but sit down. You will be more comfortable than all of us."

"Pray keep your seat," answered Mio Cid humbly. "Sit on your high-backed bench as a king and great liege lord should do. I shall sit here with my men around me." When Mio Cid had taken his place, all eyes in the room were free to inspect his splendid attire. Such elegance had never be-fore been paraded, except by the king. They noticed how full his beard was and how he had tied it with a satin cord. They were impressed by his manner, that of a great baron accustomed to rule. The Infantes alone could not meet his gaze. When they felt Mio Cid direct his glance in their direc-tion, they bowed their heads. They were ashamed to meet his eyes.

"Hear ye, gentlemen of my house, if you wish the Creator to hear you," began King Alfonso of Castile. "Since my coronation I have held only two plenary sessions of all my vassals, one at Burgos and one at Carrion. I have seen fit to convoke this third at Toledo out of love for Mio Cid, who was born in a good hour, in order that he may receive his right from the Infantes of Carrion. They did him a great wrong; we know this. Let the Count Don Anrrich and the Count Don Remond be our judges; they are unaffiliated with either faction. You will all hear this case, inasmuch as you are thoughtful and experienced, so that justice may be done; I shall sanction no injustice. Let the one side be for this day at peace with the other. I swear by Saint Isidore that whoever causes commotion in my court today shall be exiled from my realm. I shall side with the right. Let us hear the demands of Mio Cid first and then the replies of the Infantes of Carrion."

Mio Cid rose and kissed the king's hand. "I give you thanks for having convened this assembly out of love for me. Here is what I demand: in the case of my daughters that these princes have left me, I feel no dishonor; for you married them, Sire, and you will know what to do about them today. However, when these princes led my daughters out of lordly Valencia, because I loved them in my heart and in my soul, I gave them two swords, Colada and Tizon. I had won these blades like a baron with the intention of using them for your glory and vassalage, Sire. Now since these princes have abandoned my daughters in the woods, it is clear that they no longer care about me. In consequence they have lost my love. I ask that they return the swords to me since they are no longer my sons-in-law."

The judges decreed, "All is reasonable."

Then the Count Don Garcia spoke for his faction. "We must deliberate this point." After he, the Infantes, and their friends had spoken together, and had decreed, Don Garcia counseled them secretly, "This Cid Campeador still shows us his love, since he does not call for a reckoning today concerning his daughters. We shall give Don Alfonso satisfaction on that score. Let us give up the swords since this Cid limits himself to that penalty. After he receives them, the court will be adjourned. The Cid Campeador will have lost his opportunity; he will never extort satisfaction from us then!"

The party of Don Garcia and the Infantes replied in open court, "Thanks, King Don Alfonso. We do not deny that he gave us the swords. Since he calls for them and desires them, we wish to deliver them to him in your presence." They unsheathed the swords and laid them on the king's hands. A murmur of admiration moved the courtiers. The pommels of these blades were so bright that they lighted up the room. When Mio Cid took them, he smiled at their beauty, perhaps at the pleasant memories of his victories.

The swords sparkled in the hands of Mio Cid, who smiled broadly and thought to himself, "By this beard which no man has ever dared pluck, we shall see how Doña Elvira and Doña Sol shall be avenged!" Mio Cid called his nephew by name. Holding out Tizon to him, he said, "Felez Muñoz, take this beauty. You are worthier of her." He then stretched out Colada. "Martin Antolinez, vassal of renown, Colada is for you. I earned her from a gentleman, Count Raymond the Frank of Barcelona. I entrust her to you. Care for her well. If you have occasion to wield her, she will earn you fame and high esteem." Martin Antolinez took Colada reverently, bent low, and kissed Mio Cid's hand.

Mio Cid then rose to his feet again. "Thanks be to God, and to you also, King, that I have been put at rest concerning Colada and Tizon! When they led my daughters out of Valencia, I gave them 3,000 silver marks. While I was thinking of gifts for them, they were planning to execute another project. Let them return my money since they are no longer my sons-in-law." You should have heard the complaints of the Infantes then!

Count Don Remond instructed them, "Answer yes or no."

Then the Infantes replied, "We returned his swords to the Cid Campeador so that he would not ask for anything else. That was all he demanded. May it please the King; that is our answer."

The king intervened, "To this demand of the Cid, you must also give satisfaction. I decree it."

Alvar Fañez then said hotly, "Insist, oh Mio Cid, Campeador. Part of that money was mine. I also demand restitution."

The Infantes took counsel together. It was a staggering sum of silver, which they had already spent. They pleaded with the court, "He is pressing us sorely, this Cid who conquered Valencia. Now he covets our wealth! We shall have to pay him later, out of our lands at Carrion."

"You must pay him here and now, before this court," advised the judges.

"Mio Cid is right," said the king, "and he must be paid. The Infantes of Carrion gave me two hundred marks, which I now return. Since they are to transmit this money, I don't want it."

The Infantes' faction complained, "We don't have the money."

The judges answered, "You mean you have spent it. Then pay its equivalent in kind." When the Infantes understood that there was no other alternative, they began to round up whatever they could. You should have seen their finest charges, mules, palfreys, swords, equipment, furs! Mio Cid accepted it all at the court's evaluation, except for the two hundred marks of King Alfonso. The Infantes paid him the whole sum finally, even though they were obliged to strip themselves and borrow right and left in order to adjust the amount. You may as well know; they came off badly jolted.

"Ah, thanks, Sire, for your love and kindness to me!" said Mio Cid, again rising to his feet. "However, I still cannot forget my wrongs. Let me speak to you now about my greatest source of grievance. Hear me, nobles, and then assess my injury. . . . Without a challenge I cannot dismiss these Infantes of Carrion who have so basely dishonored me. Infantes, tell me how I offended you! Did I do it in banter? Did I do it maliciously? In what way did I do you wrong? Where was my crime? I want to hear it *now*!

"When you led my daughters out of Valencia, why did you tear in such a way the very coverings of my heart? I gave you my daughters. I gave you my wealth without stinting; openhanded I poured my riches and my love upon you! If you no longer wanted my daughters, treacherous dogs, why did you take them out of their fief at Valencia? Why did you strike my daughters with leather straps and with your spurs? Why did you abandon them in the deep woods where they were to fall prey to ravening beasts and flesh-eating birds? All this you did to my daughters, which has by so much diminished your manhoods! Let this court now sentence you for this crime, and give me satisfaction."

Don Garcia replied to Mio Cid's demands. "Greatest King of Spain, here is before you this Cid, who has had his entrance proclaimed by heralds, who has let his beard grow so long that it frightens some and amazes others! Our Infantes of Carrion are such that they could not accept his daughters even as concubines! Who would have given them such women as their wives? In deserting them, these princes were within their rights. We take no account whatsoever of the Cid's accusations."

Mio Cid leaped to his feet and stood stroking his beard. "What insolence is this for you of all people to criticize my beard? My beard has never been plucked by any man of woman born, by neither Moor nor Christian! Can you say as much? Is it not the plain truth that I once pulled your beard, Don Garcia, the day I stormed your castle?"

Ferrando Gonzalez of Carrion rose to his feet. In a loud voice he interrupted, "Enough talk, Cid. You have been paid. There is no more quarrel between us. We were born Infantes; that is our princely nature. We should rather have been married to the daughters of kings and emperors. Daughters from your station were not highly born enough for us. In so deserting them we were within our rights. We have grown in self-esteem because of this action, not sunk!"

"Very well," replied Mio Cid. "We have been polite long enough. Pero Bermuez the Mute, you may now speak, if you wish."

"You are a liar, Ferrando of Carrion," cried Pero Bermuez, "a liar in every word you utter! Had you remained with the Campeador, and only then, your true natures would have been concealed! Now let me remind you what sort of man you are! Think back to the battle we fought at Valencia. You asked the Campeador to let you fight, and he instructed me to watch over you. Suddenly, brave Infante, you spied a Moor. You started toward him! Then what? Then you wheeled about and ran! That's what! I took your place. I slew the Moor. I gave you his horse, which you promptly showed Mio Cid, saying that you had done this brave deed. I kept your secret. Right until this day I never broke faith, never spread abroad the tale of your cowardice. I let you brag how brave you were! People believed you out of love for Mio Cid. You may be handsome, but you are surely not manly! You are all tongue, with no hands to act! Say, Ferrando, do I speak the truth about you?

"Let's also gossip about the lion, Ferrando. Where were you hiding when the lion threatened Mio Cid? Ferrando, I challenge you to a single combat because you are a liar and a traitor. I shall fight you here before Don Alfonso of Castile to test my statements. As for the daughters of Mio Cid, you lie! The both of you have sunk, not risen, because of that action. They are only women, and you are supposed to be men! Whichever way you look at it, they are worth more than you! The day we meet in combat, I shall force you to admit all this publicly."

Diego of Carrion then addressed the court. "We are by birth the purest of counts. If only it had not pleased God to saddle us with such alliances! Imagine, having this Cid, Don Rodrigo, for a father-in-law! That we deserted his daughters, we have today no compunction. As long as they live, let them sigh after us! They should be reproached to have thought of touching us! I am ready to fight the most valiant man there is to prove that we were right!"

Martin Antolinez jumped up and cried, "Shut your mouth, you liar, you mouth-without-truth! Don't forget the incident of the lion, Diego Gonzalez! You squeezed yourself in between the pillar and the wall! You never again could wear the clothes you had on that day! I shall fight you for it! I want to know from you why you deserted the daughters of Mio Cid. Know in any case, they are worth more than you are! When you leave the field of combat, I shall hear you admit it too, plus the fact that you are a traitor, and that you have lied today in every word that you have uttered!"

At that moment appeared in the courtroom Asur Gonzalez. He strolled into the room, dragging his cloak on the floor behind him. His face was scarlet, for he had just finished eating. In any event, he had no reputation for intelligence. "Well! Well! Barons!" scoffed Asur Gonzalez. "Did you ever see such a fuss about nobody? Somebody tell me about this Cid of Vivar. Where is he, out filling up feedbags with grain? Out at his mill? That's the way he lives, you know. Whoever put it into his head to aspire to alliances with Carrion?"

"Shut up, you traitor! Liar! Scoundrel!" shouted Muño Gustioz. "You've been out stuffing yourself instead of praying, as you should have been doing. Every time you get close enough to a man to open your mouth, you disgust him! You speak the truth neither to friend nor to lord. You are false to all, even to your Creator. I wish to have no share of your friendship. I propose to make you own up to what you are."

"Let all talk stop here," decreed King Alfonso. "Those who have challenged will fight. Otherwise, may God help them!"

He had hardly uttered these words when two handsome young knights entered the courtroom. All eyes turned in their direction, watched them approach the king. It was the two royal Infantes, one named Oiarra and the other Yenego Simenez. One was the heir apparent to the kingdom of Navarre and the other the heir of the kingdom of Aragon. Bending low to kiss the hand of Don Alfonso, the two crown princes asked that he bestow upon them the hands of Doña Elvira and Doña Sol in marriage. The king so ordained. Mio Cid, you may be sure, submitted joyously to the king's will.

Then Alvar Fañez asked permission to say what was on his mind. "My resentment against the Infantes of Carrion," began Alvar Fañez, "is great. It was I who at the request of King Alfonso gave these ladies at the altar. I am glad that they shall now become queens of Spain. Now you Infantes of Carrion will have to kiss their hands and call them Señora. No matter what spite you feel, you will now have to attend upon them. So have we seen, from day to day, the honor of Mio Cid increase. As for you, Infantes, you are none the less liars and traitors! Will no one stand up and fight me for my words?"

"Enough," said the king. "Not another word. Let the three challengers appear at dawn tomorrow. The issue will be settled on the field of combat."

"Please, Sire," then pleaded the Infantes, "give us a delay. Those of the Cid are armed and ready, but we must return to Carrion first!"

"Will you name the place and the time?" King Alfonso asked Mio Cid.

He replied with a smile, "Why, yes. Let them come to Valencia."

"Be reassured," answered the king. "Entrust your knights to me. I will guarantee their safety. I hereby decree that the combats will take place in my presence three weeks from today at Carrion. He who does not present himself accordingly shall forfeit the privilege and be branded a traitor."

Mio Cid then thanked the judges, gave rich gifts to those who loved him, and prepared to take his leave. The king told Mio Cid that he was the finest baron in all his realm. As Mio Cid bade farewell, he made one last gesture to show his love for Don Alfonso. "You ordered me, Sire, to ride Babieca into your enemies, Moors and Christians alike. This horse has not his like in all the world. I give him to you now, Sire. Have him led away to your stables."

"I have no such desire," replied the king. "Such a splendid horse and such a splendid rider belong together. I am not the man to mount your Babieca! If any person else were to ride him, God would surely not come to his aid! It is because of you, Mio Cid, and because of your horse that our realm has been so favored."

Mio Cid then took leave of his vassals, the three challengers. "Stand firm on that field," he told them. "Fight like barons. Let the news that reaches me in Valencia be good."

"Why do you say that, Señor?" asked Martin Antolinez. "We made this contract ourselves, and we shall fulfill it. You may learn that we were killed, but you will never learn that we were defeated!" Mio Cid was pleased at those words. Light at heart, he set out for his fief at Valencia.

In three weeks' time the king and his challengers waited at the field of combat. The Infantes were two days late. Finally they came, escorted by their relatives and friends. If they could have murdered Mio Cid's men, they would have done so. Fortunately, they did not attempt it, so great was their fear of King Alfonso of León. That night was spent in vigil.

By morning a large crowd of knights thronged the field to see these trials and to hear Don Alfonso's verdict as to which party could claim the right on its side. On one end of the field Mio Cid's men were armed. The Infantes prepared themselves on the opposite side. As they were being dressed, Count Garcia Ordoñez briefed them. Then the Infantes sent word to Don Alfonso entreating him to debar Colada and Tizon, the two trenchant swords, from the combat. They regretted having returned these wonderfully cutting blades to Mio Cid.

"I did not see you draw these swords when you wore them to my court," the king replied shortly. "If you possess other good swords, they will give you their aid. The same will be true for the Campeador's men. Therefore stand up, Infantes of Carrion, and enter the lists. You are now obliged to combat. Therefore acquit yourselves like noblemen. If you ride victorious from this field, great honor will accrue to you. Be sure that your opponents have overlooked nothing, and that they intend to win. If you are vanquished, don't complain to me about it; for everyone here knows that you brought it all upon yourselves."

When the Infantes heard the reply of King Alfonso, they sorely repented their past deeds. They would not have committed them again, had they to relive that past year, for all their estates at Carrion.

Meanwhile the king in like measure had instructed Mio Cid's knights. They replied, "We kiss your hand, since you are our king and lord. Be our judge today. Protect us with your might and justice against any unfair play. The Infantes are on their home ground, surrounded by their vassals. We don't know whether or not they are plotting against us. Mio Cid entrusted us to you, Señor. Uphold the right in the name of the Creator."

"With heart and soul," pledged the king.

The three knights mounted. They adjusted their shields and checked their stirrups. They raised their lances so that the pennants blew in the breeze. Then, making the sign of the cross over their saddles, they rode, all three side by side, up to the barrier. There they waited silently until the Gonzalez brothers rode to the barrier opposite, and halted while the king appointed judges so that there could be no recourse. The king then harangued the combatants carefully and clearly.

"Listen to what I say, Infantes of Carrion," began Don Alfonso. "You were to have competed this trial at Toledo, but you would hear of no such thing. Remember that I am the sponsor of these three vassals of Mio Cid, and that I conducted them to your estates. Seek only your due. If you overstep the bounds of justice, I shall mishandle you badly from one end of my realm to another."

Then the judges measured off the lists as the crowd stepped back away from the barriers. They called out the rules, saying that any knight who left the lists was adjudged to have forfeited the contest. They ascertained that the spectators were maintaining a safe distance of six lance lengths on all sides. Lots were drawn for positions so that those who were lucky had the sun at their backs instead of in their faces. Then the judges retired from the center of the arena.

The three of Mio Cid faced the three from Carrion. Each man glared fixedly at his adversary. Each man clutched his shield against his chest, lowered his lance until the pennants hung straight down, bent forward with his body over the pommel of his saddle, dug his spurs into his horse's sides, and shot forward. . . . The spurt was so great that the ground thundered underfoot. Each man aimed at his foe. They joined in a shock of metal. . . . The watchers were sure that all six were dead.

Pero Bermuez, who first had challenged his man, met Ferrando Gonzalez face to face. Each one struck the other's shield, with no decisive result. On the second exchange Ferrando Gonzalez pierced the shield of Pero Bermuez, but his lance came out into air instead of into flesh. In two places he broke the wood of his lance. Pero Bermuez sat firm in the saddle. He was not even jolted. Since he had taken a blow, he gave one in return. His stroke broke the shield strap from Ferrando Gonzalez' neck. The shield fell to one side. Then Pero Bermuez pierced him, for his cover was gone. Then he pierced his chest, for the cover was gone. Ferrando wore three thicknesses of mail, which stood him in good stead. Two were shattered, but the third held well. The lance, however, had driven his shirt and the padded doublet he wore under his armor into his chest, to about the depth of a man's hand. Blood spurted from Ferrando Gonzalez' mouth. His stirrup straps broke; neither one held firm. Pero Bermuez threw him to earth over his horse's haunches. The spectators thought he was wounded to death. Pero Bermuez dropped his lance and grasped his sword. Then Ferrando Gonzalez, looking up at him, recognized Tizon! Instead of awaiting its blow, he cried, "I am vanquished." The judges acknowledged his submission and called Pero Bermuez from the lists.

Meanwhile Martin Antolinez and Diego Gonzalez were dealing each other heavy blows—so hard, in fact, that both their lances were shivered. When Martin Antolinez then unsheathed Colada, the light from this blade, flashing in the sunlight, flooded the field of combat, so clear and white was it! At the first swift stroke he severed the straps of Diego Gonzalez' helmet. Then he knocked it from his head. Next he lifted off his mail hood. He then snipped off the top of his cloth hat. With a swishing sound that was almost a whistle, he lopped off his hair and cut to the scalp. Pieces of flesh fell to the ground. When Diego Gonzalez saw with what precision Colada could be wielded, he realized that he would not escape her alive. He yanked the reins of his horse away from the blows. Then Martin Antolinez whacked him with the flat of the blade, not with the point! Although Diego Gonzalez had his own sword in hand, he made no effort to use it. "Help me, glorious God! . . . Señor, save me from that blade!" Turning his horse's head about in a desperate effort, he bounded out of the lists!

"Come, Pero Bermuez, beside me," called the king. "You have won decisively." The judges concurred. Two knights from Valencia had triumphed, and I shall now tell you of the third.

Muño Gustioz was matched against Asur Gonzalez, who was agile, strong, and courageous. Both knights dealt telling blows upon each other's shields. Asur Gonzalez broke the shield of Muño Gustioz, and also broke his armor. When the lance pierced the broken shield, however, it passed into empty air on the other side. Then Muño Gustioz at the next exchange cracked Asur Gonzalez' shield in the middle. Aiming carefully, he drove his lance as he rushed forward right through the shield with such a momentum that it passed through his opponent's body and came out, pennants and all, on the other side. It came out about two arms' length on the back of Asur Gonzalez' body. Then Muño Gustioz toppled him from the saddle and let him slip the length of the lance to the ground. The lance came out red with blood, tip, wood, pennants! Muño Gustioz sat over his opponent, his lance pointed downward until the judges shouted, "In the name of God, do not strike him! You have won the trial." Everyone thought Asur Gonzalez was dead.

The good King Alfonso ordered the field to be cleared and the weapons lost there to be confiscated for himself. The champions of Mio Cid left the lists amid warm congratulations. The sorrow in Carrion was great.

That very night the king dispatched Mio Cid's three knights to Valencia so that they might risk no reprisal nor any fear of such. Like devoted vassals they rode day and night to make their report. They had proven the Infantes of Carrion to be evil men, and they had accomplished the duty required of them by their lord.

Mio Cid the Campeador was satisfied. Then was he satisfied. Great, indeed, was the shame that had fallen publicly upon the Infantes of Carrion. May a similar punishment, or a worse one, fall upon any man who so jeers at a fine lady, and then deserts her!

Now let us leave to themselves the Infantes of Carrion and concern ourselves rather with him who was born in such a favorable hour. . . . The beautiful city of Valencia laughed and rejoiced because of the honor their champions had brought upon every one. Mio Cid stroked his beard contentedly and said, "Thanks to the King of Heaven, my daughters have been avenged. I shall be able without shame to marry them to men of great rank or not, as I wish."

Meanwhile the Princes of Navarre and Aragon pursued their courtships of Doña Elvira and Doña Sol. They had a new interview with King Don Alfonso. They made before him new marriage vows, more solemn than the first. You see how the reputation and honor of Mio Cid had increased!

Now, the daughters of Mio Cid became the queens of Navarre and Aragon! The king of Spain today is one of their descendants. Everything he touched turned to glory for Mio Cid, who was born at such a good hour.

Mio Cid departed from this world at a Pentecost. May Christ have mercy on his soul. May He have mercy on us all, the righteous as well as the sinners.

This is the story of Mio Cid, the Campeador. Here ends the tale.

May God be pleased to grant Paradise also to him who wrote this book. Amen.

The Abbot Per wrote it in the month of May in the year of our Lord MCCXLV.

Julius Caesar

WILLIAM SHAKESPEARE

* *triumvirs:* members of a three-man government, the triumvirate.

710

VARRO
CLITUS
CLAUDIUS
STRATO
LUCIUS   } *servants to Brutus*
DARDANIUS
LABEO
FLAVIUS

PINDARUS, *servant to Cassius*
SERVANT *to Octavius*

CALPHURNIA, *wife of Caesar*
PORTIA, *wife of Brutus*

SENATORS, CITIZENS, GUARDS, ATTENDANTS, SOLDIERS, *&c.*

SCENE: *Rome; near Sardis; near Philippi.*

ACT I

[*Rome. A public place. Enter* FLAVIUS, MARULLUS, *and* CITIZENS.]

FLAVIUS: Hence! Home you idle creatures, get you home.
    Is this a holiday? What, know you not,
    Being mechanical,* you ought not walk
    Upon a labouring day without the sign
    Of your profession?* Speak, what trade art thou?
FIRST CITIZEN: Why sir, a carpenter.
MARULLUS: Where is thy leather apron, and thy rule?
    What dost thou with thy best apparel on?
    You sir, what trade are you?
SECOND CITIZEN: Truly sir, in respect of a fine workman, I am but as you   10
    would say, a cobbler.*
MARULLUS: But what trade art thou? Answer me directly.
SECOND CITIZEN: A trade sir, that I hope I may use with a safe conscience;
    which is indeed sir, a mender of bad soles.
FLAVIUS: What trade thou knave? Thou naughty* knave, what trade?
SECOND CITIZEN: Nay I beseech you sir, be not out with me; yet if you be
    out* sir, I can mend you.
MARULLUS: What mean'st thou by that? Mend me, thou saucy fellow?
SECOND CITIZEN: Why sir, cobble you.
FLAVIUS: Thou art a cobbler, art thou?   20
SECOND CITIZEN: Truly sir, all that I live by is with the awl. I meddle with
    no tradesman's matters, nor women's matters, but withal, I am indeed
    sir, a surgeon to old shoes; when they are in great danger, I recover
    them. As proper men as ever trod upon neat's leather have gone upon
    my handiwork.
FLAVIUS: But wherefore art not in thy shop to-day?
    Why dost thou lead these men about the streets?

---

3. *mechanical:* of the artisan class.   5. *profession:* In Elizabethan times, an artisan was required to wear or carry some distinctive sign of his trade.   11. *cobbler:* In Shakespeare's time, "cobbler" meant not only "shoemaker" but "clumsy workman."   15. *naughty:* worthless.   17. *out:* In Shakespeare's time, "out" meant not only "out-at-the-heels" but "angry."

SECOND CITIZEN: Truly sir, to wear out their shoes, to get myself into more
    work. But indeed sir, we make holiday to see Caesar, and to rejoice in
    his triumph.   30
MARULLUS: Wherefore rejoice? What conquest brings he home?
    What tributaries* follow him to Rome,
    To grace in captive bonds his chariot wheels?
    You blocks, you stones, you worse than senseless things!
    O you hard hearts, you cruel men of Rome,
    Knew you not Pompey? Many a time and oft
    Have you climbed up to walls and battlements,
    To towers and windows, yea, to chimney tops,
    Your infants in your arms, and there have sat
    The livelong day, with patient expectation,   40
    To see great Pompey pass the streets of Rome.
    And when you saw his chariot but appear,
    Have you not made an universal shout,
    That Tiber trembled underneath her banks,
    To hear the replication of your sounds
    Made in her concave shores?
    And do you now put on your best attire?
    And do you now cull out a holiday?
    And do you now strew flowers in his way,
    That comes in triumph over Pompey's blood?   50
    Be gone!
    Run to your houses, fall upon your knees,
    Pray to the gods to intermit* the plague
    That needs must light on this ingratitude.
FLAVIUS: Go, go, good countrymen, and for this fault,
    Assemble all the poor men of your sort;
    Draw them to Tiber banks, and weep your tears
    Into the channel, till the lowest stream
    Do kiss the most exalted shores of all.
                       [*Exeunt* CITIZENS.]
    See whe'r their basest metal be not moved;   60
    They vanish tongue-tied in their guiltiness.
    Go you down that way towards the Capitol;
    This way will I. Disrobe the images,
    If you do find them decked with ceremonies.*

32. *tributaries:* captives.   53. *intermit:* turn aside.   64. *ceremonies:* wreaths
placed on statues of Caesar to honor him.

MARULLUS: May we do so?
   You know it is the feast of Lupercal.*
FLAVIUS: It is no matter; let no images
   Be hung with Caesar's trophies. I'll about,
   And drive away the vulgar* from the streets.
   So do you too, where you perceive them thick.   70
   These growing feathers plucked from Caesar's wing
   Will make him fly an ordinary pitch,
   Who else would soar above the view of men,
   And keep us all in servile fearfulness.
                              [*Exeunt.*]

                         SCENE TWO

   [*The same. Music. Enter* CAESAR, ANTONY *girt for the course,** CAL-
   PHURNIA, PORTIA, DECIUS, CICERO, BRUTUS, CASSIUS, and CASCA; SOOTH-
   SAYER and CITIZENS, FLAVIUS and MARULLUS following.*]

CAESAR: Calphurnia.
CASCA: Peace ho! Caesar speaks.
                         [*Music ceases.*]
CAESAR: Calphurnia.
CALPHURNIA: Here my lord.
CAESAR: Stand you directly in Antonius' way,
   When he doth run his course. Antonius.
ANTONY: Caesar, my lord.
CAESAR: Forget not, in your speed, Antonius,
   To touch Calphurnia;* for our elders say,
   The barren, touched in this holy chase,
   Shake off their sterile curse.
ANTONY: I shall remember.
   When Caesar says, do this, it is performed.
CAESAR: Set on, and leave no ceremony out.   10
                         [*Music.*]
SOOTHSAYER: Caesar!
CAESAR: Ha! Who calls?

66. *feast of Lupercal:* a feast held in February in honor of the god Lupercus.
69. *vulgar:* common people.

Stage direction. *girt for the course:* dressed for a race. On the feast of the Lupercal, a
race was held in which young men of noble birth competed.   8. *To touch Calphurnia:* She is childless and Caesar wants a son to succeed him.

CASCA: Bid every noise be still. Peace yet again!
> *[Music ceases.]*
CAESAR: Who is it in the press that calls on me?
  I hear a tongue shriller than all the music
  Cry Caesar. Speak; Caesar is turned to hear.
SOOTHSAYER: Beware the ides of March.*
CAESAR: What man is that?
BRUTUS: A soothsayer bids you beware the ides of March.   20
CAESAR: Set him before me, let me see his face.
CASSIUS: Fellow, come from the throng, look upon Caesar.
CAESAR: What sayst thou to me now? Speak once again.
SOOTHSAYER: Beware the ides of March.
CAESAR: He is a dreamer, let us leave him. Pass.
> *[Sennet.* Exeunt all but BRUTUS and CASSIUS.]*
CASSIUS: Will you go see the order of the course?*
BRUTUS: Not I.
CASSIUS: I pray you do.
BRUTUS: I am not gamesome. I do lack some part
  Of that quick spirit that is in Antony.   30
  Let me not hinder, Cassius, your desires;
  I'll leave you.
CASSIUS: Brutus, I do observe you now of late;
  I have not from your eyes that gentleness
  And show of love as I was wont to have.
  You bear too stubborn and too strange a hand
  Over your friend, that loves you.
BRUTUS: Cassius,
  Be not deceived. If I have veiled my look,*
  I turn the trouble of my countenance
  Merely upon myself. Vexed I am   40
  Of late, with passions of some difference,*
  Conceptions only proper to myself,
  Which give some soil,* perhaps, to my behaviors.
  But let not therefore my good friends be grieved,
  Among which number, Cassius, be you one,
  Nor construe any further my neglect,
  Than that poor Brutus with himself at war,
  Forgets the shows of love to other men.

---

19. *ides of March:* March 15.   Stage direction. *Sennet:* trumpet call.   26. *order of the course:* outcome of the race.   38. *veiled my look:* grown secretive.
41. *passions of some difference:* conflicting emotions.   43. *soil:* blemish.

CASSIUS: Then Brutus, I have much mistook your passion;*
By means whereof this breast of mine hath buried   50
Thoughts of great value, worthy cogitations.
Tell me good Brutus, can you see your face?
BRUTUS: No Cassius; for the eye sees not itself
But by reflection, by some other things.
CASSIUS: 'Tis just,
And it is very much lamented Brutus,
That you have no such mirrors as will turn
Your hidden worthiness into your eye,
That you might see your shadow. I have heard,
Where many of the best respect* in Rome—   60
Except immortal Caesar—speaking of Brutus,
And groaning underneath this age's yoke,
Have wished that noble Brutus had his eyes.
BRUTUS: Into what dangers would you lead me Cassius,
That you would have me seek into myself
For that which is not in me?
CASSIUS: Therefore, good Brutus, be prepared to hear.
And since you know you cannot see yourself
So well as by reflection, I your glass,
Will modestly discover* to yourself   70
That of yourself which you yet know not of.
And be not jealous* on me, gentle Brutus.
Were I a common laughter,* or did use
To stale with ordinary oaths my love
To every new protester;* if you know,
That I do fawn on men, and hug them hard,
And after scandal* them; or if you know,
That I profess myself in banqueting
To all the rout,* then hold me dangerous.
                    [Flourish* and shout.]
BRUTUS: What means this shouting? I do fear, the people   80
Choose Caesar for their king.
CASSIUS: Ay, do you fear it?
Then I must think you would not have it so.

---

49. *passion:* emotions.   60. *respect:* reputation.   70. *discover:* reveal.
72. *jealous:* suspicious.   73. *common laughter:* person lacking seriousness.
73–75. *did use . . . protester:* were in the habit of swearing oaths of friendship with
every new acquaintance.   77. *scandal:* slander.   78–79. *profess . . . rout:* profess
friendship to all those I meet at banquets (or dinner parties). Stage direction. *Flourish:* trumpet call.

BRUTUS: I would not Cassius, yet I love him well.
But wherefore do you hold me here so long?
What is it that you would impart to me?
If it be aught toward the general good,
Set honour in one eye, and death i' th' other,
And I will look on both indifferently;
For let the gods so speed me, as I love
The name of honour more than I fear death. 90
CASSIUS: I know that virtue to be in you Brutus,
As well as I do know your outward favour.*
Well, honour is the subject of my story.
I cannot tell what you and other men
Think of this life; but for my single self,
I had as lief* not be, as live to be
In awe of such a thing as I myself.
I was born free as Caesar, so were you;
We both have fed as well, and we can both
Endure the winter's cold as well as he. 100
For once, upon a raw and gusty day,
The troubled Tiber chafing with her shores,
Caesar said to me, dar'st thou Cassius now
Leap in with me into this angry flood,
And swim to yonder point? Upon the word,
Accoutred* as I was, I plunged in,
And bade him follow; so indeed he did.
The torrent roared, and we did buffet it
With lusty sinews, throwing it aside,
And stemming it with hearts of controversy:* 110
But ere we could arrive the point proposed,
Caesar cried, help me Cassius, or I sink.
I, as Æneas, our great ancestor,
Did from the flames of Troy upon his shoulder
The old Anchises bear,* so from the waves of Tiber
Did I the tired Caesar. And this man
Is now become a god, and Cassius is
A wretched creature, and must bend his body,
If Caesar carelessly but nod on him.
He had a fever when he was in Spain, 120

92. *favour:* good looks.   96. *as lief:* as soon.   106. *Accoutred:* dressed as a
soldier.   110. *hearts of controversy:* in competition with each other.
113–15. *as Æneas . . . Anchises:* In Virgil's *Æneid*, the hero Æneas tells how he
carried his father out of the burning city.

And when the fit was on him, I did mark
How he did shake. 'Tis true, this god did shake;
His coward lips did from their colour fly,
And that same eye, whose bend doth awe the world,
Did lose his* lustre; I did hear him groan.
Ay, and that tongue of his, that bade the Romans
Mark him, and write his speeches in their books,
Alas, it cried, give me some drink Titinius,*
As a sick girl. Ye gods, it doth amaze me,
A man of such a feeble temper* should   130
So get the start* of the majestic world,
And bear the palm* alone.
                    [*Shout and flourish.*]
BRUTUS: Another general shout?
   I do believe that these applauses are
   For some new honours that are heaped on Caesar.
CASSIUS: Why man, he doth bestride the narrow world
   Like a Colossus,* and we petty men
   Walk under his huge legs, and peep about
   To find ourselves dishonourable graves.
   Men at some time are masters of their fates.   140
   The fault, dear Brutus, is not in our stars,*
   But in ourselves, that we are underlings.
   Brutus and Caesar. What should be in that Caesar?
   Why should that name be sounded more than yours?
   Write them together, yours is as fair a name.
   Sound them, it doth become the mouth as well.
   Weigh them, it is as heavy. Conjure* with 'em,
   Brutus will start a spirit as soon as Caesar.
   Now in the names of all the gods at once,
   Upon what meat doth this our Caesar feed,   150
   That he is grown so great? Age, thou art shamed.
   Rome, thou hast lost the breed of noble bloods.
   When went there by an age, since the great flood,
   But it was famed with more than with one man?
   When could they say, till now, that talked of Rome,
   That her wide walls encompassed but one man?

125. *his:* its.   128. *Titinius:* a friend of Cassius who appears later in the play.
130. *temper:* constitution.   131. *get the start:* be the leader.   132. *palm:* honors.
137. *Colossus:* a huge statue in the harbor of Rhodes.   141. *stars:* the influence
of the stars over men's lives.   147. *Conjure:* referring to a superstition that by
chanting a name, one would be able to call a spirit from the grave.

Now is it Rome indeed, and room enough,
When there is in it but one only man.
O you and I have heard our fathers say,
There was a Brutus once,* that would have brooked*   160
Th' eternal devil to keep his state in Rome,
As easily as a king.
BRUTUS: That you do love me, I am nothing jealous;
What you would work me to, I have some aim;*
How I have thought of this, and of these times,
I shall recount hereafter. For this present,
I would not, so with love I might entreat you,
Be any further moved.* What you have said,
I will consider; what you have to say,
I will with patience hear, and find a time   170
Both meet to hear and answer such high things.
Till then, my noble friend, chew upon this;
Brutus had rather be a villager,
Than to repute himself a son of Rome
Under these hard conditions as this time
Is like to lay upon us.
CASSIUS: I am glad
That my weak words have struck but this much show
Of fire from Brutus.

[*Enter* CAESAR *and his train.*]

BRUTUS: The games are done, and Caesar is returning.
CASSIUS: As they pass by, pluck Casca by the sleeve,   180
And he will, after his sour fashion, tell you
What hath proceeded worthy note to-day.
BRUTUS: I will do so. But look you Cassius,
The angry spot doth glow on Caesar's brow,
And all the rest look like a chidden train.*
Calphurnia's cheek is pale, and Cicero
Looks with such ferret* and such fiery eyes
As we have seen him in the Capitol,
Being crossed in conference* by some senators.
CASSIUS: Casca will tell us what the matter is.   190
CAESAR: Antonius.
ANTONY: Caesar.

160. *There . . . once:* Brutus' ancestor, Junius Brutus, who led a revolt against a tyrant.   160. *brooked:* tolerated.   164. *What . . . aim:* I have some idea of what you are persuading me to do.   168. *moved:* persuaded.   185. *train:* of followers.   187. *ferret:* The ferret has small red eyes.   189. *conference:* debate.

CAESAR: Let me have men about me that are fat,
Sleek-headed men, and such as sleep a nights.
Yond Cassius has a lean and hungry look;
He thinks too much. Such men are dangerous.
ANTONY: Fear him not Caesar, he's not dangerous.
He is a noble Roman, and well given.*
CAESAR: Would he were fatter. But I fear him not.
Yet if my name were liable to fear,   200
I do not know the man I should avoid
So soon as that spare Cassius. He reads much,
He is a great observer, and he looks
Quite through the deeds of men. He loves no plays,
As thou dost Antony; he hears no music;
Seldom he smiles, and smiles in such a sort*
As if he mocked himself, and scorned his spirit
That could be moved to smile at any thing.
Such men as he be never at heart's ease,
Whiles they behold a greater than themselves,   210
And therefore are they very dangerous.
I rather tell thee what is to be feared,
Than what I fear; for always I am Caesar.
Come on my right hand, for this ear is deaf,
And tell me truly what thou think'st of him.
          [*Sennet. Exeunt* CAESAR *and all his train but* CASCA.]
CASCA: You pulled me by the cloak; would you speak with me?
BRUTUS: Ay Casca, tell us what hath chanced* to-day
That Caesar looks so sad.
CASCA: Why you were with him, were you not?
BRUTUS: I should not then ask Casca what had chanced.   220
CASCA: Why there was a crown offered him; and being offered him, he put
it by with the back of his hand thus, and then the people fell
a-shouting.
BRUTUS: What was the second noise for?
CASCA: Why for that too.
CASSIUS: They shouted thrice. What was the last cry for?
CASCA: Why for that too.
BRUTUS: Was the crown offered him thrice?
CASCA: Ay marry* was't, and he put it by thrice, every time gentler than
other; and at every putting by mine honest neighbours shouted.   230

198. *well given:* reliable.   206. *sort:* manner.   217. *chanced:* happened.
229. *marry:* indeed.

CASSIUS: Who offered him the crown?

CASCA: Why Antony.

BRUTUS: Tell us the manner of it, gentle Casca.

CASCA: I can as well be hanged as tell the manner of it. It was mere foolery; I did not mark it. I saw Mark Antony offer him a crown, yet 'twas not a crown neither, 'twas one of these coronets;* and as I told you, he put it by once; but for all that, to my thinking, he would fain* have had it. Then he offered it to him again; then he put it by again: but to my thinking, he was very loth to lay his fingers off it. And then he offered it the third time; he put it the third time by, and still as he refused it, the 240 rabblement hooted, and clapped their chopped* hands, and threw up their sweaty nightcaps, and uttered such a deal of stinking breath because Caesar refused the crown, that it had almost choked Caesar; for he swounded,* and fell down at it. And for my own part, I durst not laugh, for fear of opening my lips, and receiving the bad air.

CASSIUS: But soft I pray you; what, did Caesar swound?

CASCA: He fell down in the market place, and foamed at mouth, and was speechless.

BRUTUS: 'Tis very like* he hath the falling sickness.*

CASSIUS: No, Caesar hath it not; but you, and I, 250
And honest Casca, we have the falling sickness.

CASCA: I know not what you mean by that, but I am sure Caesar fell down. If the tag-rag people did not clap him, and hiss him, according as he pleased, and displeased them, as they use to do the players in the theatre, I am no true man.

BRUTUS: What said he, when he came unto himself?

CASCA: Marry, before he fell down, when he perceived the common herd was glad he refused the crown, he plucked me ope his doublet, and offered them his throat to cut. An* I had been a man of any occupation,* if I would not have taken him at a word* I would I might go to hell 260 among the rogues. And so he fell. When he came to himself again, he said, if he had done or said any thing amiss, he desired their worships to think it was his infirmity. Three or four wenches where I stood cried, alas good soul, and forgave him with all their hearts. But there's no heed to be taken of them; if Caesar had stabbed their mothers, they would have done no less.

BRUTUS: And after that, he came thus sad away?

CASCA: Ay.

236. *coronets:* small crowns.   237. *fain:* gladly.   241. *chopped:* rough.
244. *swounded:* fainted.   249. *like:* likely.   249. *falling sickness:* epilepsy.
259. *An:* if.   259. *occupation:* enterprise.   260. *at a word:* at his word.

CASSIUS: Did Cicero say any thing?

CASCA: Ay, he spoke Greek.   270

CASSIUS: To what effect?

CASCA: Nay, an I tell you that, I'll ne'er look you i' th' face again. But those that understood him smiled at one another, and shook their heads; but for mine own part, it was Greek to me. I could tell you more news too: Marullus and Flavius, for pulling scarfs* off Caesar's images, are put to silence.* Fare you well. There was more foolery yet, if I could remember it.

CASSIUS: Will you sup with me to-night, Casca?

CASCA: No, I am promised forth.*

CASSIUS: Will you dine with me to-morrow?   280

CASCA: Ay, if I be alive, and your mind hold,* and your dinner worth the eating.

CASSIUS: Good; I will expect you.

CASCA: Do so. Farewell both.

[Exit.]

BRUTUS: What a blunt fellow is this grown to be!
    He was quick mettle,* when he went to school.

CASSIUS: So is he now, in execution
    Of any bold or noble enterprise,
    However he puts on this tardy form.*
    This rudeness is a sauce to his good wit,   290
    Which gives men stomach to digest his words
    With better appetite.

BRUTUS: And so it is. For this time I will leave you.
    To-morrow, if you please to speak with me,
    I will come home to you; or if you will,
    Come home to me, and I will wait for you.

CASSIUS: I will do so. Till then, think of the world.

[Exit BRUTUS.]

    Well Brutus, thou art noble; yet I see
    Thy honourable mettle may be wrought
    From that it is disposed.* Therefore it is meet   300
    That noble minds keep ever with their likes;
    For who so firm that cannot be seduced?

---

275. *scarfs:* wreaths.   276. *put to silence:* commanded not to speak on political matters.   279. *am promised forth:* have a prior invitation.   281. *your mind hold:* you don't change your mind.   286. *quick mettle:* quick-spirited. 289. *tardy form:* slow-witted manner.   299–300. *Thy . . . disposed:* Your mind may be bent to a course of action to which it would otherwise not be inclined. There is a pun here on mettle (metal).

Caesar doth bear me hard, but he loves Brutus.
If I were Brutus now, and he were Cassius,
He should not humour* me. I will this night,
In several hands,* in at his windows throw,
As if they came from several citizens,
Writings, all tending* to the great opinion
That Rome holds of his name; wherein obscurely
Caesar's ambition shall be glanced* at. 310
And after this, let Caesar seat him sure,
For we will shake him, or worse days endure.

[*Exit.*]

SCENE THREE

[*The same. Thunder and lightning. Enter* CASCA *and* CICERO *at several doors.*]

CICERO: Good even, Casca. Brought you Caesar home?
Why are you breathless, and why stare you so?
CASCA: Are you not moved, when all the sway of earth
Shakes, like a thing unfirm? O Cicero,
I have seen tempests, when the scolding winds
Have rived the knotty oaks, and I have seen
Th' ambitious ocean swell, and rage, and foam,
To be exalted* with the threat'ning clouds;
But never till to-night, never till now,
Did I go through a tempest dropping fire.*
Either there is a civil strife in heaven, 10
Or else the world, too saucy* with the gods,
Incenses them to send destruction.
CICERO: Why, saw you any thing more wonderful?
CASCA: A common slave—you know him well by sight—
Held up his left hand, which did flame and burn
Like twenty torches joined; and yet his hand,
Not sensible of fire, remained unscorched.
Besides—I ha' not since put up my sword—
Against the Capitol I met a lion,
Who glazed upon me, and went surly by, 20

305. *humour:* be persuaded by.   306. *hands:* handwritings.   308. *tending:*
referring.   310. *glanced:* hinted.
8. *exalted:* lifted up.   10. *tempest dropping fire:* perhaps a shower of meteors.
12. *saucy:* rebellious.

Without annoying me. And there were drawn
Upon a heap, a hundred ghastly women,
Transformed with their fear, who swore they saw
Men, all in fire, walk up and down the streets.
And yesterday the bird of night did sit,
Even at noonday, upon the market place,
Hooting, and shrieking. When these prodigies*
Do so conjointly meet, let not men say,
These are their reasons—they are natural.   30
For I believe, they are portentous things
Unto the climate that they point upon.
CICERO: Indeed, it is a strange-disposed time.
  But men may construe things after their fashion,
  Clean* from the purpose of the things themselves.
  Comes Caesar to the Capitol to-morrow?
CASCA: He doth; for he did bid Antonius
  Send word to you he would be there to-morrow.
CICERO: Good night then, Casca; this disturbed sky
  Is not to walk in.
CASCA: Farewell Cicero.   40
                    [*Exit* CICERO. *Enter* CASSIUS.]
CASSIUS: Who's there?
CASCA: A Roman.
CASSIUS: Casca, by your voice.
CASCA: Your ear is good. Cassius, what night is this!
CASSIUS: A very pleasing night to honest men.
CASCA: Who ever knew the heavens menace so?
CASSIUS: Those that have known the earth so full of faults.
  For my part, I have walked about the streets,
  Submitting me unto the perilous night;
  And thus unbraced,* Casca, as you see,
  Have bared my bosom to the thunder-stone;*
  And when the cross blue lightning seemed to open   50
  The breast of heaven, I did present myself
  Even in the aim and very flash of it.
CASCA: But wherefore did you so much tempt the heavens?
  It is the part of men to fear and tremble,
  When the most mighty gods by tokens send
  Such dreadful heralds to astonish us.

28. *prodigies:* remarkable events.   35. *Clean:* here, far.   48. *unbraced:* uncovered.   49. *thunder-stone:* thunderbolt.

CASSIUS: You are dull, Casca; and those sparks of life
   That should be in a Roman you do want,*
   Or else you use not. You look pale, and gaze,
   And put on fear, and cast yourself in wonder,*   60
   To see the strange impatience of the heavens.
   But if you would consider the true cause,
   Why all these fires, why all these gliding ghosts,
   Why birds and beasts from quality and kind,
   Why old men, fools, and children calculate;*
   Why all these things change from their ordinance,
   Their natures, and pre-formed faculties,
   To monstrous quality; why you shall find
   That heaven hath infused them with these spirits,
   To make them instruments of fear and warning   70
   Unto some monstrous state.
   Now could I, Casca, name to thee a man,
   Most like this dreadful night,
   That thunders, lightens, opens graves, and roars
   As doth the lion in the Capitol;
   A man no mightier than thyself, or me,
   In personal action; yet prodigious grown,
   And fearful, as these strange eruptions are.
CASCA: 'Tis Caesar that you mean. Is it not, Cassius?
CASSIUS: Let it be who it is; for Romans now   80
   Have thews and limbs, like to their ancestors;
   But, woe the while, our fathers' minds are dead,
   And we are governed with our mothers' spirits;
   Our yoke and sufferance* show us womanish.
CASCA: Indeed, they say, the senators to-morrow
   Mean to establish Caesar as a king;
   And he shall wear his crown by sea and land,
   In every place, save here in Italy.
CASSIUS: I know where I will wear this dagger then;
   Cassius from bondage will deliver Cassius.   90
   Therein, ye gods, you make the weak most strong;
   Therein, ye gods, you tyrants do defeat.
   Nor stony tower, nor walls of beaten brass,
   Nor airless dungeon, nor strong links of iron,
   Can be retentive to the strength of spirit;

58. *want:* lack.   60. *cast . . . wonder:* look amazed.   65. *calculate:* speculate
about causes.   84. *sufferance:* tolerance.

But life, being weary of these worldly bars,
Never lacks power to dismiss itself.
If I know this, know all the world besides,
That part of tyranny that I do bear
I can shake off at pleasure.

         [Thunder still.]

CASCA: So can I.   100
So every bondman in his own hand bears
The power to cancel his captivity.

CASSIUS: And why should Caesar be a tyrant then?
Poor man, I know he would not be a wolf,
But that he sees the Romans are but sheep;
He were no lion, were not Romans hinds.*
Those that with haste will make a mighty fire
Begin it with weak straws. What trash is Rome,
What rubbish, and what offal, when it serves
For the base matter to illuminate
So vile a thing as Caesar! But O grief,   110
Where hast thou led me? I perhaps speak this
Before a willing bondman; then I know
My answer must be made. But I am armed,
And dangers are to me indifferent.

CASCA: You speak to Casca, and to such a man
That is no fleering tell-tale. Hold, my hand.
Be factious* for redress of all these griefs,
And I will set this foot of mine as far,
As who* goes farthest.

CASSIUS: There's a bargain made.   120
Now know you, Casca, I have moved already
Some certain of the noblest minded Romans
To undergo with me an enterprise
Of honourable-dangerous consequence;
And I do know, by this they stay for me
In Pompey's Porch;* for now, this fearful night,
There is no stir or walking in the streets;
And the complexion of the element*
Is favoured like the work we have in hand,
Most bloody, fiery and most terrible.   130

---

106. *hinds:* does. 118. *Be factious:* form a faction. 120. *who:* whoever.
126. *Pompey's Porch:* the entrance to a theater that was built by Pompey.
128. *element:* weather.

[Enter CINNA.]

CASCA: Stand close* awhile, for here comes one in haste.

CASSIUS: 'Tis Cinna, I do know him by his gait;
  He is a friend. Cinna, where haste you so?

CINNA: To find out you. Who's that? Metellus Cimber?

CASSIUS: No, it is Casca, one incorporate
  To our attempts. Am I not stayed for,* Cinna?

CINNA: I am glad on't. What a fearful night is this!
  There's two or three of us have seen strange sights.

CASSIUS: Am I not stayed for? Tell me.

CINNA: Yes, you are.
  O Cassius, if you could   140
  But win the noble Brutus to our party—

CASSIUS: Be you content. Good Cinna, take this paper,
  And look you lay it in the praetor's chair,*
  Where Brutus may but find it. And throw this
  In at his window. Set this up with wax
  Upon old Brutus' statue. All this done,
  Repair to Pompey's Porch, where you shall find us.
  Is Decius Brutus and Trebonius there?

CINNA: All but Metellus Cimber, and he's gone
  To seek you at your house. Well, I will hie,   150
  And so bestow these papers as you bade me.

CASSIUS: That done, repair to Pompey's Theatre.
                              [Exit CINNA.]
  Come Casca, you and I will yet, ere day,
  See Brutus at his house. Three parts of him
  Is ours already; and the man entire,
  Upon the next encounter, yields him ours.

CASCA: O he sits high in all the people's hearts;
  And that which would appear offence in us,
  His countenance, like richest alchemy,*
  Will change to virtue, and to worthiness.   160

CASSIUS: Him, and his worth, and our great need of him,
  You have right well conceited.* Let us go,
  For it is after midnight, and ere day,
  We will awake him, and be sure of him.
                              [Exeunt.]

---

131. *close:* hidden.   136. *stayed for:* worth waiting for.   143. *praetor's chair:*
The praetor was a high government position that Brutus held.   159. *alchemy:* a
medieval attempt to transmute base metals into gold.   162. *conceited:* expressed.

ACT II

[*Rome.* BRUTUS' *house.* BRUTUS *is discovered in his orchard.*]

BRUTUS: What Lucius, ho!
  I cannot, by the progress of the stars,
  Give guess how near to day. Lucius I say!
  I would it were my fault to sleep so soundly.
  When Lucius, when? Awake, I say; what Lucius!
                     [*Enter* LUCIUS.]
LUCIUS: Called you my lord?
BRUTUS: Get me a taper in my study, Lucius.
  When it is lighted, come and call me here.
LUCIUS: I will my lord.
                         [*Exit.*]
BRUTUS: It must be by his death;* and for my part,   10
  I know no personal cause to spurn* at him,
  But for the general.* He would be crowned.
  How that might change his nature, there's the question.
  It is the bright day that brings forth the adder,
  And that craves* wary walking. Crown him that,*
  And then I grant we put a sting in him,
  That at his will he may do danger with.
  Th' abuse of greatness is, when it disjoins
  Remorse from power. And to speak truth of Caesar,
  I have not known when his affections swayed*   20
  More than his reason. But 'tis a common proof,*
  That lowliness is young ambition's ladder,
  Whereto the climber-upward turns his face;
  But when he once attains the upmost round,*
  He then unto the ladder turns his back,
  Looks in the clouds, scorning the base degrees
  By which he did ascend: so Caesar may;
  Then lest he may, prevent. And since the quarrel

---

10. *It . . . death:* Caesar's death is the only solution.   11. *spurn:* strike.
12. *general:* public.   15. *craves:* requires.   15. *that:* king.   20. *swayed:* held
sway.   21. *proof:* truth.   24. *round:* rung.

Will bear no colour* for the thing he is,
Fashion it thus; that what he is, augmented,   30
Would run to these and these extremities.
And therefore think him as a serpent's egg,
Which hatched, would as his kind grow mischievous;
And kill him in the shell.
                    [*Enter* LUCIUS.]
LUCIUS: The taper burneth in your closet* sir.
   Searching the window for a flint, I found
   This paper, thus sealed up; and I am sure
   It did not lie there when I went to bed.
                    [*Gives him the letter.*]
BRUTUS: Get you to bed again, it is not day.
   Is not to-morrow, boy, the ides of March?   40
LUCIUS: I know not sir.
BRUTUS: Look in the calendar, and bring me word.
LUCIUS: I will sir.
                    [*Exit.*]
BRUTUS: The exhalations,* whizzing in the air,
   Give so much light, that I may read by them.
   Brutus, thou sleep'st; awake, and see thyself:
   Shall Rome, &c. Speak, strike, redress.
   Brutus, thou sleep'st: awake.
   Such instigations* have been often dropped,
   Where I have took them up.   50
   Shall Rome, &c. Thus must I piece it out:
   Shall Rome stand under one man's awe? What, Rome?
   My ancestors did from the streets of Rome
   The Tarquin* drive, when he was called a king.
   Speak, strike, redress. Am I entreated
   To speak, and strike? O Rome, I make thee promise,
   If the redress will follow, thou receivest
   Thy full petition at the hand of Brutus.
                    [*Enter* LUCIUS.]
LUCIUS: Sir, March is wasted fifteen days.
                    [*Knock within.*]
BRUTUS: 'Tis good. Go to the gate; somebody knocks.   60
                    [*Exit* LUCIUS.]

29. *bear no colour:* cannot be justified.   35. *closet:* small room.   44. *exhala-*
tions: meteors.   49. *instigations:* urgings.   54. *Tarquin:* the tyrant whom Brutus' ancestor overthrew. (See page 719.)

Since Cassius first did whet me against Caesar,
I have not slept.
Between the acting of a dreadful thing,
And the first motion,* all the interim is
Like a phantasma, or a hideous dream.
The Genius, and the mortal instruments,*
And then in council; and the state of man,
Like to a little kingdom, suffers then
The nature of an insurrection.

[Enter LUCIUS.]

LUCIUS: Sir, 'tis your brother* Cassius at the door,   70
  Who doth desire to see you.
BRUTUS: Is he alone?
LUCIUS: No sir, there are moe* with him.
BRUTUS: Do you know them?
LUCIUS: No sir, their hats are plucked about their ears,
  And half their faces buried in their cloaks,
  That by no means I may discover them
  By any mark of favour.*
BRUTUS: Let 'em enter.

[Exit LUCIUS.]

They are the faction. O conspiracy,
Sham'st thou to show thy dangerous brow by night,
When evils are most free? O then, by day
Where wilt thou find a cavern dark enough
To mask thy monstrous visage? Seek none, conspiracy;
Hide it in smiles and affability.
For if thou put thy native semblance* on,
Not Erebus* itself were dim enough,   80
To hide thee from prevention.*

[Enter CASSIUS, CASCA, DECIUS, CINNA, METELLUS CIMBER, and TRE-
BONIUS.]

CASSIUS: I think we are too bold upon your rest.
  Good morrow Brutus, do we trouble you?
BRUTUS: I have been up this hour, awake all night.
  Know I these men that come along with you?
CASSIUS: Yes, every man of them; and no man here   90
  But honours you; and every one doth wish

---

64. *motion:* intention to act.   66. *Genius . . . instruments:* mind and body.
70. *brother:* Cassius is Brutus' brother-in-law.   72. *moe:* more.   76. *favour:*
appearance.   83. *native semblance:* natural appearance.   84. *Erebus:* according
to Greek myth, the darkest part of Hell.   85. *prevention:* exposure.

You had but that opinion of yourself
Which every noble Roman bears of you.
This is Trebonius.
BRUTUS: He is welcome hither.
CASSIUS: This, Decius Brutus.
BRUTUS: He is welcome too.
CASSIUS: This, Casca; this, Cinna; and this, Metellus Cimber.
BRUTUS: They are all welcome.
    What watchful cares do interpose themselves
    Betwixt your eyes and night?
CASSIUS: Shall I entreat a word?   100
             [CASSIUS *and* BRUTUS *whisper aside.*]
DECIUS: Here lies the east. Doth not the day break here?
CASCA: No.
CINNA: O pardon sir, it doth; and yon gray lines
    That fret* the clouds are messengers of day.
CASCA: You shall confess that you are both deceived.
    Here, as I point my sword, the sun arises,
    Which is a great way growing on* the south,
    Weighing* the youthful season of the year.
    Some two months hence, up higher toward the north
    He first presents his fire, and the high* east   110
    Stands as the Capitol, directly here.
BRUTUS: Give me your hands all over, one by one.
CASSIUS: And let us swear our resolution.
BRUTUS: No, not an oath. If not the face of men,
    The sufferance of our souls, the time's abuse—
    If these be motives weak, break off betimes,*
    And every man hence to his idle bed.
    So let high-sighted* tyranny range on,
    Till each man drop by lottery. But if these,
    As I am sure they do, bear fire* enough   120
    To kindle cowards, and to steel with valour
    The melting spirits of women; then countrymen,
    What need we any spur, but our own cause,
    To prick us to redress? What other bond
    Than secret Romans, that have spoke the word,
    And will not palter?* And what other oath
    Than honesty to honesty engaged,

104. *fret:* break up.   107. *growing on:* moving toward.   108. *Weighing:* considering.   110. *high:* true.   116. *betimes:* this moment.   118. *high-sighted:* arrogant.   120. *bear fire:* arouse.   126. *palter:* equivocate.

That this shall be,* or we will fall for it?
Swear priests and cowards and men cautelous,*
Old feeble carrions, and such suffering souls   130
That welcome wrongs; unto bad causes swear
Such creatures as men doubt; but do not stain
The even virtue of our enterprise,
Nor th' insuppressive* mettle of our spirits,
To think that or our cause or* our performance
Did need an oath; when every drop of blood
That every Roman bears, and nobly bears,
Is guilty of a several bastardy,
If he do break the smallest particle
Of any promise that hath passed from him.   140
CASSIUS: But what of Cicero? Shall we sound him?
    I think he will stand very strong with us.
CASCA: Let us not leave him out.
CINNA: No, by no means.
METELLUS: O let us have him, for his silver hairs
    Will purchase us a good opinion,
    And buy men's voices to commend our deeds.
    It shall be said, his judgement ruled our hands;
    Our youths and wildness shall no whit appear,
    But all be buried in his gravity.
BRUTUS: O name him not; let us not break with* him,   150
    For he will never follow anything
    That other men begin.
CASSIUS: Then leave him out.
CASCA: Indeed he is not fit.
DECIUS: Shall no man else be touched, but only Caesar?
CASSIUS: Decius, well urged. I think it is not meet,*
    Mark Antony, so well beloved of Caesar,
    Should outlive Caesar. We shall find of him
    A shrewd contriver; and you know, his means,
    If he improve them, may well stretch so far
    As to annoy us all; which to prevent,   160
    Let Antony and Caesar fall together.
BRUTUS: Our course will seem too bloody, Caius Cassius,
    To cut the head off, and then hack the limbs,

---

128. *this shall be:* we shall succeed.   129. *cautelous:* cunning.   134. *insuppressive:* unsuppressable.   135. *or . . . or:* either . . . or.   150. *break with:* suggest the idea to.   155. *meet:* right.

Like wrath in death, and envy afterwards;
For Antony is but a limb of Caesar.
Let's be sacrificers, but not butchers, Caius.
We all stand up against the spirit of Caesar,
And in the spirit of men there is no blood.
O that we then could come by Caesar's spirit,
And not dismember Caesar! But alas,   170
Caesar must bleed for it. And gentle friends,
Let's kill him boldly, but not wrathfully;
Let's carve him as a dish fit for the gods,
Not hew him as a carcass fit for hounds.
And let our hearts, as subtle masters do,
Stir up their servants to an act of rage,
And after seem to chide 'em. This shall make
Our purpose necessary, and not envious;
Which so appearing to the common eyes,
We shall be called purgers, not murderers.   180
And for Mark Antony, think not of him;
For he can do no more than Cacsar's arm
When Caesar's head is off.
CASSIUS: Yet I fear him,
For in the ingrafted* love he bears to Caesar—
BRUTUS: Alas good Cassius, do not think of him.
If he love Caesar, all that he can do
Is to himself, take thought, and die for Caesar;
And that were much he should,* for he is given
To sports, to wildness, and much company.
TREBONIUS: There is no fear in him; let him not die,   190
For he will live, and laugh at this hereafter.
                     [*Clock strikes.*]
BRUTUS: Peace, count the clock.
CASSIUS: The clock hath stricken three.
TREBONIUS: 'Tis time to part.
CASSIUS: But it is doubtful yet,
Whether Caesar will come forth to-day or no;
For he is superstitious grown of late,
Quite from the main opinion he held once
Of fantasy, of dreams, and ceremonies.*

---

184. *ingrafted:* deep-rooted.   188. *much he should:* much to expect of him.
197. *ceremonies:* rites where animals were sacrificed and their entrails examined for omens.

It may be, these apparent prodigies,*
The unaccustomed terror of this night,
And the persuasion of his augurers,*   200
May hold him from the Capitol to-day.
DECIUS: Never fear that. If he be so resolved,
I can o'ersway him;* for he loves to hear
That unicorns may be betrayed with trees,*
And bears with glasses,* elephants with holes,
Lions with toils,* and men with flatterers;
But when I tell him he hates flatterers,
He says he does, being then most flattered.
Let me work;
For I can give his humour the true bent,*   210
And I will bring him to the Capitol.
CASSIUS: Nay, we will all of us be there to fetch him.
BRUTUS: By the eighth hour; is that the uttermost?
CINNA: Be that the uttermost, and fail not then.
METELLUS: Caius Ligarius doth bear Caesar hard,
Who rated* him for speaking well of Pompey;
I wonder none of you have thought of him.
BRUTUS: Now good Metellus go along by* him.
He loves me well, and I have given him reasons.
Send him but hither, and I'll fashion* him.   220
CASSIUS: The morning comes upon's. We'll leave you, Brutus;
And friends disperse yourselves; but all remember
What you have said, and show yourselves true Romans.
BRUTUS: Good gentlemen, look fresh and merrily.
Let not our looks put on* our purposes,
But bear it as our Roman actors do,
With untired spirits and formal constancy;*
And so, good morrow to you every one.
                [*Exeunt all but* BRUTUS.]
Boy! Lucius! Fast asleep? It is no matter;

198. *prodigies:* strange occurrences.   200. *augurers:* priests who examined the sacrificed animals for omens.   203. *o'ersway him:* change his mind.   204. *unicorns . . . trees:* It was believed that this mythical animal could be tricked into impaling himself on a tree, if the hunter were nimble enough to dodge his attack.   205. *bears . . . glasses:* It was believed that bears could be confused to the point of submission by showing them their reflections in a mirror.   206. *toils:* nets.   210. *give . . . bent:* bend him in the right direction.   216. *rated:* scolded.   218. *by:* to.   220. *fashion:* persuade.   224. *put on:* reveal.   227. *formal constancy:* steadfast appearance.

Enjoy the honey-heavy dew of slumber.   230
Thou hast no figures* nor no fantasies,
Which busy care draws in the brains of men;
Therefore thou sleep'st so sound.

[*Enter* PORTIA.]

PORTIA: Brutus my lord.
BRUTUS: Portia! What mean you? Wherefore rise you now?
It is not for your health, thus to commit
Your weak condition to the raw cold morning.
PORTIA: Nor for yours neither. Y'have ungently,* Brutus,
Stole from my bed; and yesternight at supper
You suddenly arose, and walked about,
Musing and sighing, with your arms across;   240
And when I asked you what the matter was,
You stared upon me, with ungentle looks.
I urged you further, then you scratched your head,
And too impatiently stamped with your foot.
Yet I insisted, yet you answered not,
But, with an angry wafture of your hand
Gave sign for me to leave you. So I did,
Fearing to strengthen that impatience
Which seemed too much enkindled; and withal*
Hoping it was but an effect of humour,*   250
Which sometime hath his hour with every man.
It will not let you eat, nor talk, nor sleep;
And could it work so much upon your shape,*
As it hath much prevailed on your condition,*
I should not know you Brutus. Dear my lord,
Make me acquainted with your cause of grief.
BRUTUS: I am not well in health, and that is all.
PORTIA: Brutus is wise, and were he not in health,
He would embrace the means to come by it.
BRUTUS: Why so I do. Good Portia go to bed.   260
PORTIA: Is Brutus sick, and is it physical*
To walk unbraced, and suck up the humours*
Of the dank morning? What, is Brutus sick,
And will he steal out of his wholesome bed
To dare the vile contagion of the night,

231. *figures:* visions.   237. *ungently:* rudely.   249. *withal:* yet.   250. *humour:*
mood.   253. *shape:* appearance.   254. *condition:* mood.   261. *physical:* healthy.   262. *humours:* vapors.

And tempt the rheumy and unpurged* air,
To add unto his sickness? No, my Brutus,
You have some sick offence within your mind,
Which by the right and virtue of my place
I ought to know of; and upon my knees,   270
I charm you, by my once commended beauty,
By all your vows of love, and that great vow
Which did incorporate and make us one,
That you unfold to me, your self, your half,
Why you are heavy; and what men to-night
Have had resort to you; for here have been
Some six or seven, who did hide their faces
Even from darkness.
BRUTUS: Kneel not, gentle Portia.
PORTIA: I should not need, if you were gentle Brutus.
  Within the bond of marriage, tell me, Brutus,   280
  Is it excepted I should know no secrets
  That appertain to you? Am I your self,
  But as it were in sort or limitation?*
  To keep with you at meals, comfort your bed,
  And talk to you sometimes? Dwell I but in the suburbs
  Of your good pleasure? If it be no more,
  Portia is Brutus' harlot, not his wife.
BRUTUS: You are my true and honourable wife,
  As dear to me as are the ruddy drops
  That visit my sad heart.   290
PORTIA: If this were true, then should I know this secret.
  I grant I am a woman; but withal,
  A woman that Lord Brutus took to wife.
  I grant I am a woman; but withal,
  A woman well reputed—Cato's* daughter.
  Think you I am no stronger than my sex,
  Being so fathered, and so husbanded?
  Tell me your counsels, I will not disclose 'em.
  I have made strong proof of my constancy,
  Giving myself a voluntary wound   300
  Here, in the thigh. Can I bear that with patience,
  And not my husband's secrets?
BRUTUS: O ye gods,

266. *unpurged:* unhealthful.   283 *in sort . . . limitation:* only in some limited
way.   295. *Cato:* a distinguished Roman patriot.

Render me worthy of this noble wife.
          [*Knock.*]
Hark, hark, one knocks. Portia go in awhile,
And by and by thy bosom shall partake
The secrets of my heart.
All my engagements I will construe* to thee,
All the charactery of* my sad brows.
Leave me with haste.
          [*Exit* PORTIA. *Enter* LUCIUS *and* LIGARIUS.]
          Lucius, who's that knocks?
LUCIUS: Here is a sick man that would speak with you.   310
BRUTUS: Caius Ligarius, that Metellus spake of.
     Boy, stand aside. Caius Ligarius, how?
LIGARIUS: Vouchsafe good morrow from a feeble tongue.
BRUTUS: O what a time have you chose out brave Caius,
     To wear a kerchief!* Would you were not sick.
LIGARIUS: I am not sick, if Brutus have in hand
     Any exploit worthy the name of honour.
BRUTUS: Such an exploit have I in hand Ligarius,
     Had you a healthful ear to hear of it.
LIGARIUS: By all the gods that Romans bow before,   320
     I here discard my sickness. Soul of Rome,
     Brave son, derived from honourable loins,
     Thou like an exorcist* hast conjured up
     My mortified spirit. Now bid me run,
     And I will strive with things impossible,
     Yea get the better of them. What's to do?
BRUTUS: A piece of work that will make sick men whole.
LIGARIUS: But are not some whole that we must make sick?
BRUTUS: That must we also. What it is, my Caius,
     I shall unfold to thee, as we are going   330
     To whom it must be done.
LIGARIUS: Set on your foot,
     And with a heart new-fired I follow you,
     To do I know not what; but it sufficeth
     That Brutus leads me on.
BRUTUS: Follow me then.
          [*Exeunt.*]

307. *construe:* explain.   308. *charactery of:* what is written on.   315. *ker-chief:* worn as a remedy for sickness, as was the custom in Shakespeare's time.
323. *exorcist:* one who calls up and drives away spirits.

SCENE TWO

[*Rome.* CAESAR's *house. Thunder and lightning. Enter* CAESAR *in his nightgown.*]

CAESAR: Nor heaven nor earth have been at peace to-night.
  Thrice hath Calphurnia in her sleep cried out,
  Help ho, they murder Caesar! Who's within?
                    [*Enter* SERVANT.]
SERVANT: My lord.
CAESAR: Go bid the priests do present sacrifice,*
  And bring me their opinions of success.
SERVANT: I will my lord.
                  [*Exit. Enter* CALPHURNIA.]
CALPHURNIA: What mean you, Caesar? Think you to walk forth?
  You shall not stir out of your house to-day.
CAESAR: Caesar shall forth; the things that threatened me   10
  Ne'er looked but on my back. When they shall see
  The face of Caesar, they are vanished.
CALPHURNIA: Caesar, I never stood on ceremonies,
  Yet now they fright me. There is one within,
  Besides the things that we have heard and seen,
  Recounts most horrid sights seen by the watch.
  A lioness hath whelped* in the streets;
  And graves have yawned, and yielded up their dead;
  Fierce fiery warriors fought upon the clouds,
  In ranks and squadrons and right form of war,   20
  Which drizzled blood upon the Capitol.
  The noise of battle hurtled in the air;
  Horses did neigh, and dying men did groan,
  And ghosts did shriek and squeal about the streets.
  O Caesar, these things are beyond all use,*
  And I do fear them.
CAESAR: What can be avoided
  Whose end is purposed by the mighty gods?*
  Yet Caesar shall go forth; for these predictions
  Are to* the world in general, as to Caesar.

---

5. *priests . . . sacrifice:* to discover omens. (See page 733.)   17. *whelped:* given birth.   25. *use:* experience.   26–27. *What . . . gods:* Who can avoid what is destined?   29. *to:* about.

CALPHURNIA: When beggars die, there are no comets* seen;   30
   The heavens themselves blaze forth the death of princes.
CAESAR: Cowards die many times before their deaths,
   The valiant never taste of death but once.
   Of all the wonders that I yet have heard,
   It seems to me most strange that men should fear,
   Seeing that death, a necessary end,
   Will come when it will come.
                [*Enter* SERVANT.]
                What say the augurers?
SERVANT: They would not have you to stir forth to-day.
   Plucking the entrails of an offering forth,
   They could not find a heart within the beast.   40
CAESAR: The gods do this in shame of* cowardice.
   Caesar should be a beast without a heart
   If he should stay at home to-day for fear.
   No, Caesar shall not. Danger knows full well
   That Caesar is more dangerous than he.
   We were two lions littered in one day,
   And I the elder and more terrible.
   And Caesar shall go forth.
CALPHURNIA: Alas my lord,
   Your wisdom is consumed in confidence.
   Do not go forth to-day. Call it my fear   50
   That keeps you in the house, and not your own.
   We'll send Mark Antony to the Senate House,
   And he shall say you are not well to-day.
   Let me upon my knee prevail in this.
CAESAR: Mark Antony shall say I am not well,
   And for thy humour I will stay at home.
                [*Enter* DECIUS.]
   Here's Decius Brutus, he shall tell them so.
DECIUS: Caesar, all hail. Good morrow, worthy Caesar,
   I come to fetch you to the Senate House.
CAESAR: And you are come in very happy time,   60
   To bear my greeting to the senators,
   And tell them that I will not come to-day.
   Cannot, is false; and that I dare not, falser.
   I will not come to-day, tell them so Decius.

---

30. *comets:* It was believed that comets foretold great events.   41. *in shame of:*
to shame.

CALPHURNIA: Say he is sick.
CAESAR: Shall Caesar send a lie?
   Have I in conquest stretched mine arm so far
   To be afeard to tell greybeards the truth?
   Decius, go tell them, Caesar will not come.
DECIUS: Most mighty Caesar, let me know some cause,
   Lest I be laughed at when I tell them so.   70
CAESAR: The cause is in my will; I will not come,
   That is enough to satisfy the senate.
   But for your private satisfaction,
   Because I love you, I will let you know.
   Calphurnia here, my wife, stays me at home.
   She dreamt to-night, she saw my statue,
   Which like a fountain with an hundred spouts
   Did run pure blood; and many lusty Romans
   Came smiling, and did bathe their hands in it.
   And these does she apply for warnings and portents,   80
   And evils imminent; and on her knee
   Hath begged that I will stay at home to-day.
DECIUS: This dream is all amiss interpreted;
   It was a vision fair and fortunate.
   Your statue spouting blood in many pipes,
   In which so many smiling Romans bathed,
   Signifies that from you great Rome shall suck
   Reviving blood, and that great men shall press
   For tinctures, stains, relics, and cognizance.*
   This by Calphurnia's dream is signified.   90
CAESAR: And this way have you well expounded it.
DECIUS: I have, when you have heard what I can say;
   And know it now—the senate have concluded
   To give this day a crown to mighty Caesar.
   If you shall send them word you will not come,
   Their minds may change. Besides, it were a mock*
   Apt to be rendered,* for some one to say,
   Break up the senate till another time,
   When Caesar's wife shall meet with better dreams.
   If Caesar hide himself, shall they not whisper,   100

89. *tinctures . . . cognizance:* relics of Caesar.   96. *mock:* joke.   97. *rendered:*
made.

Lo Caesar is afraid?
Pardon me, Caesar, for my dear dear love
To your proceeding bids me tell you this;
And reason to my love is liable.*
CAESAR: How foolish do your fears seem now, Calphurnia!
I am ashamed I did yield to them.
Give me my robe, for I will go.
  [*Enter* BRUTUS, LIGARIUS, METELLUS, CASCA, TREBONIUS, CINNA, *and*
  PUBLIUS.]
And look where Publius is come to fetch me.
PUBLIUS: Good morrow, Caesar.   110
CAESAR: Welcome, Publius.
What, Brutus, are you stirred so early too?
Good morrow, Casca. Caius Ligarius,
Caesar was ne'er so much your enemy
As that same ague which hath made you lean.
What is't a clock?
BRUTUS: Caesar, 'tis strucken eight.
CAESAR: I thank you for your pains and courtesy.
                    [*Enter* ANTONY.]
See, Antony, that revels long a nights,
Is notwithstanding up. Good morrow, Antony.
ANTONY: So to most noble Caesar.
CAESAR: Bid them prepare within;   120
I am to blame to be thus waited for.
Now Cinna, now Metellus. What, Trebonius,
I have an hour's talk in store for you;
Remember that you call on* me to-day.
Be near me, that I may remember you.
TREBONIUS: Caesar I will. (*Aside*) And so near will I be,
That your best friends shall wish I had been further.
CAESAR: Good friends, go in, and taste some wine with me,
And we, like friends, will straightway go together.
BRUTUS (*aside*): That every like is not the same,* O Caesar,
The heart of Brutus earns* to think upon.
                    [*Exeunt.*]

104. *reason . . . liable:* love overrules my caution.   122. *call on:* have an appointment with.   128. *every . . . same:* everyone who seems to be a friend is not (a
reference to Caesar's phrase "like friends").   129. *earns:* grieves.

SCENE THREE

[*Rome. Before* CAESAR'S *house. Enter* ARTEMIDORUS *with a paper.*]

ARTEMIDORUS (*reads*):

> *Caesar, beware of Brutus, take heed of Cassius; come not near Casca,*
> *have an eye to Cinna, trust not Trebonius, mark well Metellus Cimber,*
> *Decius Brutus loves thee not: thou hast wronged Caius Ligarius. There is*
> *but one mind in all these men, and it is bent against Caesar. If thou beest*
> *not immortal, look about you. Security gives way to conspiracy.* The*
> *mighty gods defend thee.   Thy lover, Artemidorus.*

Here will I stand, till Caesar pass along,
And as a suitor* will I give him this.
My heart laments, that virtue cannot live
Out of the teeth of emulation.*   10
If thou read this, o Caesar, thou mayst live;
If not, the Fates with traitors do contrive.
                              [*Exit.*]

SCENE FOUR

[*Rome. Before* BRUTUS' *house. Enter* PORTIA *and* LUCIUS.]

PORTIA: I prithee, boy, run to the Senate House;
    Stay not to answer me, but get thee gone.
    Why dost thou stay?
LUCIUS: To know my errand, madam.
PORTIA: I would have had thee there and here again,
    Ere I can tell thee what thou shouldst do there.
    (*Aside*) O constancy, be strong upon my side,
    Set a huge mountain 'tween my heart and tongue.
    I have a man's mind, but a woman's might.
    How hard it is for women to keep counsel!*
    Art thou here yet?
LUCIUS: Madam, what should I do?
    Run to the Capitol, and nothing else?
    And so return to you, and nothing else?   10

---

5. *Security . . . conspiracy:* Overconfidence makes you vulnerable.   8. *suitor:* a
pleader for a favor.   10. *emulation:* jealousy.
9. *counsel:* a secret.

PORTIA: Yes, bring me word, boy, if thy lord look well,
   For he went sickly forth; and take good note
   What Caesar doth, what suitors press to him.
   Hark, boy, what noise is that?
LUCIUS: I hear none, madam.
PORTIA: Prithee, listen well.
   I heard a bustling rumour like a fray,
   And the wind brings it from the Capitol.
LUCIUS: Sooth, madam, I hear nothing.   20

                 [*Enter* SOOTHSAYER.]

PORTIA: Come hither, fellow, which way hast thou been?
SOOTHSAYER: At mine own house, good lady.
PORTIA: What is't a clock?
SOOTHSAYER: About the ninth hour, lady.
PORTIA: Is Caesar yet gone to the Capitol?
SOOTHSAYER: Madam, not yet, I go to take my stand,
   To see him pass on to the Capitol.
PORTIA: Thou hast some suit to* Caesar, hast thou not?
SOOTHSAYER: That I have, lady, if it will please Caesar
   To be so good to Caesar as to hear me,
   I shall beseech him to befriend himself.   30
PORTIA: Why, know'st thou any harm's intended towards him?
SOOTHSAYER: None that I know will be, much that I fear may chance.
   Good morrow to you. Here the street is narrow.
   The throng that follows Caesar at the heels,
   Of senators, of praetors, common suitors,
   Will crowd a feeble man almost to death.
   I'll get me to a place more void, and there
   Speak to great Caesar as he comes along.
                     [*Exit.*]
PORTIA: I must go in. Ay me! How weak a thing
   The heart of woman is! O Brutus,   40
   The heavens speed thee in thine enterprise—
   Sure the boy heard me—Brutus hath a suit
   That Caesar will not grant. O, I grow faint.
   Run, Lucius, and commend me to my lord;
   Say I am merry.* Come to me again,
   And bring me word what he doth say to thee.
                [*Exeunt severally.**]

27. *suit to:* petition for.   45. *merry:* cheerful.   Stage direction. *severally:* in different directions.

ACT III

SCENE ONE

[*Rome. Before the Capitol.* SENATORS *discovered sitting. Enter* CITIZENS, ARTEMIDORUS, *and* SOOTHSAYER. *Flourish. Enter* CAESAR, BRUTUS, CASSIUS, CASCA, DECIUS, METELLUS, TREBONIUS, CINNA, ANTONY, LEPIDUS, POPILIUS, *and* PUBLIUS.]

CAESAR: The ides of March are come.

SOOTHSAYER: Ay Caesar, but not gone.

ARTEMIDORUS: Hail, Caesar. Read this schedule.*

DECIUS: Trebonius doth desire you to o'er-read
At your best leisure this his humble suit.

ARTEMIDORUS: O Caesar, read mine first; for mine's a suit
That touches Caesar nearer. Read it, great Caesar.

CAESAR: What touches us ourself shall be last served.

ARTEMIDORUS: Delay not, Caesar, read it instantly.

CAESAR: What, is the fellow mad?

PUBLIUS: Sirrah, give place.   10

CASSIUS: What, urge you your petitions in the street?
Come to the Capitol.

POPILIUS: I wish your enterprise to-day may thrive.

CASSIUS: What enterprise, Popilius?

POPILIUS: Fare you well.

BRUTUS: What said Popilius Lena?

CASSIUS: He wished to-day our enterprise might thrive.
I fear our purpose is discovered.

BRUTUS: Look how he makes to Caesar. Mark him.

CASSIUS: Casca
Be sudden, for we fear prevention.
Brutus, what shall be done? If this be known,   20
Cassius or Caesar never shall turn back,
For I will slay myself.

BRUTUS: Cassius, be constant.
Popilius Lena speaks not of our purposes,
For look, he smiles, and Caesar doth not change.

CASSIUS: Trebonius knows his time; for look you, Brutus,

3. *schedule:* paper.

He draws Mark Antony out of the way.

[*Exeunt* ANTONY *and* TREBONIUS. CAESAR *enters the Capitol and takes
the chair of state*.]

DECIUS: Where is Metellus Cimber? Let him go,
And presently prefer his suit to Caesar.

BRUTUS: He is addressed; press near and second* him.

CINNA: Casca, you are the first that rears your hand.*   30

CAESAR: Are we all ready? What is now amiss,
That Caesar and his senate must redress?

METELLUS: Most high, most mighty, and most puissant* Caesar,
Metellus Cimber throws before thy seat
An humble heart.

CAESAR: I must prevent thee Cimber.
These couchings,* and these lowly courtesies,
Might fire the blood of ordinary men,
And turn pre-ordinance and first decree*
Into the law of children.* Be not fond,*
To think that Caesar bears such rebel blood   40
That will be thawed from the true quality
With that which melteth fools; I meant sweet words,
Low-crooked curtsies, and base spaniel fawning.
Thy brother by decree is banished.
If thou dost bend, and pray, and fawn for him,
I spurn thee like a cur out of my way.
Know, Caesar doth not wrong, nor without cause
Will he be satisfied.

METELLUS: Is there no voice more worthy than my own,
To sound more sweetly in great Caesar's ear,   50
For the repealing of my banished brother?

BRUTUS: I kiss thy hand, but not in flattery, Caesar;
Desiring thee that Publius Cimber* may
Have an immediate freedom of repeal.

CAESAR: What, Brutus?

CASSIUS: Pardon, Caesar; Caesar, pardon.
As low as to thy foot doth Cassius fall,
To beg enfranchisement* for Publius Cimber.

CAESAR: I could be well moved, if I were as you;

29. *second:* support.   30. *rears . . . hand:* strike.   33. *puissant:* powerful.
36. *couchings:* kneelings.   38. *pre-ordinance . . . decree:* law and custom.
39. *law of children:* childish or silly laws.   39. *fond:* foolish.   53. *Publius Cimber:*
Metellus Cimber's brother, who has been exiled from Rome.   57. *enfranchisement:* restoration of rights.

If I could pray to move, prayers would move me.
But I am constant as the northern star,   60
Of whose true-fixed and resting quality
There is no fellow in the firmament.*
The skies are painted with unnumbered sparks,
They are all fire, and every one doth shine;
But there's but one in all doth hold his place.
So in the world; 'tis furnished well with men,
And men are flesh and blood, and apprehensive;*
Yet in the number I do know but one
That unassailable holds on his rank,
Unshaked of motion: and that I am he,   70
Let me a little show it, even in this—
That I was constant Cimber should be banished,
And constant do remain to keep him so.
CINNA: O Caesar—
CAESAR: Hence! Wilt thou lift up Olympus?
DECIUS: Great Caesar—
CAESAR: Doth not Brutus bootless* kneel?
CASCA: Speak hands for me.
                    [*They stab* CAESAR, BRUTUS *last.*]
CAESAR: Et tu, Brute?* Then fall Caesar.
                    [*Dies.*]
CINNA: Liberty! Freedom! Tyranny is dead.
    Run hence, proclaim, cry it about the streets.
CASSIUS: Some to the common pulpits,* and cry out,   80
    Liberty, freedom, and enfranchisement!
BRUTUS: People and senators, be not affrighted.
    Fly not, stand still. Ambition's debt is paid.
CASCA: Go to the pulpit, Brutus.
DECIUS: And Cassius too.
BRUTUS: Where's Publius?
CINNA: Here, quite confounded* with this mutiny.
METELLUS: Stand fast together, lest some friend of Caesar's
    Should chance—
BRUTUS: Talk not of standing. Publius, good cheer,   90
    There is no harm intended to your person,
    Nor to no Roman else: so tell them, Publius.

62. *firmament:* heavens.   67. *apprehensive:* rational.   75. *bootless:* to no avail.
77. *Et tu, Brute:* And you, Brutus?   80. *common pulpits:* public platforms.
86. *confounded:* confused, frightened.

CASSIUS: And leave us, Publius, lest that the people
  Rushing on us should do your age some mischief.
BRUTUS: Do so; and let no man abide* this deed,
  But we the doers.

                   [Enter TREBONIUS.]
CASSIUS: Where is Antony?
TREBONIUS: Fled to his house amazed.
  Men, wives, and children stare, cry out, and run,
  As it were doomsday.
BRUTUS: Fates, we will know your pleasures.
  That we shall die we know, 'tis but the time,
  And drawing days out, that men stand upon.*   100
CASCA: Why he that cuts off twenty years of life
  Cuts off so many years of fearing death.
BRUTUS: Grant that, and then is death a benefit;
  So are we Caesar's friends, that have abridged
  His time of fearing death. Stoop, Romans, stoop,
  And let us bathe our hands in Caesar's blood
  Up to the elbows, and besmear our swords;
  Then walk we forth, even to the market place,
  And waving our red weapons o'er our heads,
  Let's all cry, peace, freedom, and liberty!   110
CASSIUS: Stoop then, and wash. How many ages hence
  Shall this our lofty scene be acted over,
  In states unborn and accents yet unknown.
BRUTUS: How many times shall Caesar bleed in sport,*
  That now on Pompey's basis* lies along,
  No worthier than the dust.
CASSIUS: So oft as that shall be,
  So often shall the knot of us be called,
  The men that gave their country liberty.
DECIUS: What, shall we forth?
CASSIUS: Ay, every man away.
  Brutus shall lead, and we will grace his heels   120
  With the most boldest and best hearts of Rome.

                   [Enter SERVANT.]
BRUTUS: Soft, who comes here? A friend of Antony's.
SERVANT: Thus, Brutus, did my master bid me kneel;

---

94. *abide:* be held responsible for.   100. *stand upon:* worry over.   114. *in sport:*
performed by actors.   115. *Pompey's basis:* the base of Pompey's statue.

Thus did Mark Antony bid me fall down,
And being prostrate, thus he bade me say:
Brutus is noble, wise, valiant, and honest;
Caesar was mighty, bold, royal, and loving.
Say, I love Brutus, and I honour him;
Say, I feared Caesar, honoured him, and loved him.
If Brutus will vouchsafe* that Antony　　　　　130
May safely come to him, and be resolved*
How Caesar hath deserved to lie in death,
Mark Antony shall not love Caesar dead
So well as Brutus living; but will follow
The fortunes and affairs of noble Brutus
Thorough the hazards of this untrod state*
With all true faith. So says my master Antony.
BRUTUS: Thy master is a wise and valiant Roman;
　　I never thought him worse.
　　Tell him, so please him come unto this place,　　　　　140
　　He shall be satisfied; and by my honour
　　Depart untouched.
SERVANT:　　　　　I'll fetch him presently.
　　　　　　　　　[Exit.]
BRUTUS: I know that we shall have him well to friend.
CASSIUS: I wish we may. But yet have I a mind
　　That fears him much; and my misgiving still
　　Falls shrewdly to the purpose.*
　　　　　　　　[Enter ANTONY.]
BRUTUS: But here comes Antony. Welcome, Mark Antony.
ANTONY: O mighty Caesar! Dost thou lie so low?
　　Are all thy conquests, glories, triumphs, spoils,
　　Shrunk to this little measure? Fare thee well.　　　　　150
　　I know not, gentlemen, what you intend,
　　Who else must be let blood, who else is rank:
　　If I myself, there is no hour so fit
　　As Caesar's death's hour; nor no instrument
　　Of half that worth as those your swords, made rich
　　With the most noble blood of all this world.
　　I do beseech ye, if you bear me hard,
　　Now, whilst your purpled hands do reek and smoke,

130. *vouchsafe:* guarantee.　　131. *resolved:* satisfied.　　136. *untrod state:* new government (which Brutus and Cassius are trying to establish).　　145–146. *my misgiving . . . purpose:* My suspicions are still justified.

Fulfil your pleasure. Live a thousand years,
I shall not find myself so apt* to die.   160
No place will please me so, no mean* of death,
As here by Caesar, and by you cut off,
The choice and master spirits of this age.
BRUTUS: O Antony, beg not your death of us.
Though now we must appear bloody and cruel,
As by our hands, and this our present act,
You see we do; yet see you but our hands,
And this the bleeding business they have done.
Our hearts you see not, they are pitiful;*
And pity to the general wrong of Rome—   170
As fire drives out fire, so pity pity—
Hath done this deed on Caesar. For your part,
To you, our swords have leaden* points, Mark Antony;
Our arms in strength of malice,* and our hearts,
Of brothers' temper, do receive you in
With all kind love, good thoughts, and reverence.
CASSIUS: Your voice shall be as strong as any man's,
In the disposing of new dignities.*
BRUTUS: Only be patient, till we have appeased
The multitude, beside themselves with fear,   180
And then we will deliver you* the cause,
Why I, that did love Caesar when I struck him,
Have thus proceeded.
ANTONY: I doubt not of your wisdom.
Let each man render me his bloody hand.
First Marcus Brutus, will I shake with you;
Next Caius Cassius do I take your hand;
Now Decius Brutus yours; now yours Metellus;
Yours Cinna; and my valiant Casca, yours;
Though last, not least in love, yours good Trebonius.
Gentlemen all—alas, what shall I say?   190
My credit now stands on such slippery ground,
That one of two bad ways you must conceit* me,
Either a coward, or a flatterer.
That I did love thee, Caesar, O 'tis true.
If then thy spirit look upon us now,

160. *apt:* ready.   161. *mean:* means.   169. *pitiful:* full of pity.   173. *leaden:* blunted.   174. *in strength of malice:* with power to harm.   178. *In . . . dignities:* in appointing officials of the new government.   181. *deliver you:* explain to you.   192. *conceit:* imagine.

Shall it not grieve thee dearer than thy death,
To see thy Antony making his peace,
Shaking the bloody fingers of thy foes,
Most noble, in the presence of thy corse?*
Had I as many eyes as thou hast wounds,   200
Weeping as fast as they stream forth thy blood,
It would become me better than to close
In terms of friendship with thine enemies.
Pardon me, Julius! Here wast thou bayed, brave hart;*
Here didst thou fall; and here thy hunters stand,
Signed in thy spoil, and crimsoned in thy lethe.*
O world, thou wast the forest to this hart,
And this indeed, O world, the heart of thee.
How like a deer, strucken by many princes,
Dost thou here lie.   210

CASSIUS: Mark Antony—
ANTONY: Pardon me, Caius Cassius.
The enemies of Caesar shall say this;
Then, in a friend, it is cold modesty.

CASSIUS: I blame you not for praising Caesar so,
But what compact mean you to have with us?
Will you be pricked* in number of our friends,
Or shall we on, and not depend on you?

ANTONY: Therefore I took your hands, but was indeed
Swayed from the point, by looking down on Caesar.
Friends am I with you all, and love you all,   220
Upon this hope, that you shall give me reasons
Why, and wherein, Caesar was dangerous.

BRUTUS: Or else* were this a savage spectacle.
Our reasons are so full of good regard,
That were you, Antony, the son of Caesar,
You should be satisfied.

ANTONY: That's all I seek;
And am moreover suitor, that I may
Produce his body to the market place,
And in the pulpit, as becomes a friend,
Speak in the order* of his funeral.   230

---

199. *corse:* corpse.   204. *bayed . . . hart:* brought to bay, as a stag is trapped by hounds.   206. *lethe:* blood (literally, the river of forgetfulness in the Underworld of Greek mythology).   216. *pricked:* marked.   223. *Or else:* otherwise.
230. *order:* ceremony.

BRUTUS: You shall, Mark Antony.

CASSIUS: Brutus, a word with you.
  (*aside to* BRUTUS) You know not what you do. Do not consent
  That Antony speak in his funeral.
  Know you how much the people may be moved
  By that which he will utter?

BRUTUS (*aside to* CASSIUS): By your pardon.
  I will myself into the pulpit first,
  And show the reason of our Caesar's death.
  What Antony shall speak, I will protest*
  He speaks by leave, and by permission;
  And that we are contented Caesar shall   240
  Have all true rites, and lawful ceremonies.
  It shall advantage more than do us wrong.

CASSIUS (*aside to* BRUTUS): I know not what may fall,* I like it not.

BRUTUS: Mark Antony, here take you Caesar's body.
  You shall not in your funeral speech blame us,
  But speak all good you can devise of Caesar,
  And say you do't by our permission;
  Else shall you not have any hand at all
  About his funeral. And you shall speak
  In the same pulpit whereto I am going,   250
  After my speech is ended.

ANTONY: Be it so.
  I do desire no more.

BRUTUS: Prepare the body, then, and follow us.

               [*Exeunt all but* ANTONY.]

ANTONY: O pardon me, thou bleeding piece of earth,
  That I am meek and gentle with these butchers.
  Thou art the ruins of the noblest man
  That ever lived in the tide of times.
  Woe to the hand that shed this costly blood!
  Over thy wounds now do I prophesy,
  Which like dumb mouths do ope* their ruby lips,   260
  To beg the voice and utterance of my tongue,
  A curse shall light upon the limbs of men;
  Domestic fury, and fierce civil strife,
  Shall cumber* all the parts of Italy.
  Blood and destruction shall be so in use,*

238. *protest:* explain.   243. *fall:* happen.   260. *ope:* open.   264. *cumber:* burden.   265. *in use:* habitual.

And dreadful objects so familiar,
That mothers shall but smile when they behold
Their infants quartered with the hands of war;
All pity choked with custom of fell* deeds;
And Caesar's spirit ranging for revenge,   270
With Ate* by his side, come hot from hell,
Shall in these confines, with a monarch's voice,
Cry havoc,* and let slip the dogs of war,
That this foul deed shall smell above the earth
With carrion men, groaning for burial.
                    [*Enter* OCTAVIUS' SERVANT.]
You serve Octavius Caesar, do you not?
SERVANT: I do, Mark Antony.
ANTONY: Caesar did write for him to come to Rome.
SERVANT: He did receive his letters, and is coming,
    And bid me say to you by word of mouth—   280
    O Caesar!*
ANTONY: Thy heart is big. Get thee apart and weep.
    Passion I see is catching, for mine eyes,
    Seeing those beads of sorrow stand in thine,
    Began to water. Is thy master coming?
SERVANT: He lies to-night within seven leagues of Rome.
ANTONY: Post back with speed, and tell him what hath chanced.
    Here is a mourning Rome, a dangerous Rome,
    No Rome of safety for Octavius yet;
    Hie hence, and tell him so. Yet stay awhile,   290
    Thou shalt not back, till I have borne this corse
    Into the market place. There shall I try*
    In my oration, how the people take
    The cruel issue of these bloody men;
    According to the which, thou shalt discourse
    To young Octavius of the state of things.
    Lend me your hand.
                    [*Exeunt with* CAESAR'S *body.*]

269. *fell:* foul.   271. *Ate:* Greek goddess of strife.   273. *Cry havoc:* a battle
cry signifying that no prisoners were to be taken and that all the enemy would be
killed.   281. *O Caesar:* at seeing the body.   292. *try:* test.

SCENE TWO

[*Rome. The Forum. Enter* BRUTUS *and* CASSIUS, *and* CITIZENS.]

CITIZENS: We will be satisfied. Let us be satisfied.
BRUTUS: Then follow me, and give me audience, friends.
   Cassius, go you into the other street,
   And part the numbers.
   Those that will hear me speak, let 'em stay here;
   Those that will follow Cassius, go with him;
   And public reasons shall be rendered
   Of Caesar's death.
FIRST CITIZEN: I will hear Brutus speak.
SECOND CITIZEN: I will hear Cassius, and compare their reasons,
   When severally we hear them rendered.   10
     [*Exit* CASSIUS, *with some* CITIZENS. BRUTUS *goes into the pulpit.*]
THIRD CITIZEN: The noble Brutus is ascended. Silence!
BRUTUS: Be patient till the last.
   Romans, countrymen, and lovers, hear me for my cause, and be silent,
that you may hear. Believe me for mine honour, and have respect to
mine honour, that you may believe. Censure* me in your wisdom, and
awake your senses, that you may the better judge. If there be any in this
assembly, any dear friend of Caesar's, to him I say, that Brutus' love to
Caesar was no less than his. If then, that friend demand, why Brutus
rose against Caesar, this is my answer—not that I loved Caesar less; but
that I loved Rome more. Had you rather Caesar were living, and die all 20
slaves, than that Caesar were dead, to live all free men? As Caesar
loved me, I weep for him; as he was fortunate, I rejoice at it; as he was
valiant, I honour him: but as he was ambitious, I slew him. There is
tears, for his love; joy, for his fortune; honour, for his valour; and death,
for his ambition. Who is here so base, that would be a bondman? If any,
speak, for him have I offended. Who is here so rude,* that would not be
a Roman? If any, speak, for him have I offended. Who is here so vile,
that will not love his country? If any, speak, for him have I offended. I
pause for a reply.
CITIZENS: None, Brutus, none.   30
BRUTUS: Then none have I offended. I have done no more to Caesar than
   you shall do to Brutus. The question of his death is enrolled* in the
   Capitol; his glory not extenuated,* wherein he was worthy; nor his

15. *Censure:* judge.   26. *rude:* primitive.   32. *enrolled:* on record.   33. *extenuated:* lessened.

offences enforced,* for which he suffered death. (*Enter* ANTONY *with* CAESAR'S *body.*) Here comes his body, mourned by Mark Antony, who though he had no hand in his death, shall receive the benefit of his dying, a place in the commonwealth, as which of you shall not? With this I depart, that as I slew my best lover for the good of Rome, I have the same dagger for myself, when it shall please my country to need my death.   40

CITIZENS: Live, Brutus, live, live!

FIRST CITIZEN: Bring him with triumph home unto his house.

SECOND CITIZEN: Give him a statue with his ancestors.

THIRD CITIZEN: Let him be Caesar.

FOURTH CITIZEN: Caesar's better parts*
    Shall be crowned in Brutus.

FIRST CITIZEN: We'll bring him to his house, with shouts and clamours.

BRUTUS: My countrymen—

SECOND CITIZEN: Peace, silence, Brutus speaks.

FIRST CITIZEN: Peace ho!

BRUTUS: Good countrymen, let me depart alone,   50
    And for my sake, stay here with Antony:
    Do grace to Caesar's corpse, and grace his speech
    Tending to Caesar's glories, which Mark Antony
    By our permission is allowed to make.
    I do entreat you, not a man depart,
    Save I alone, till Antony have spoke.
                            [*Exit.*]

FIRST CITIZEN: Stay ho, and let us hear Mark Antony.

THIRD CITIZEN: Let him go up into the public chair,
    We'll hear him. Noble Antony, go up.

ANTONY: For Brutus' sake, I am beholding to you.   60
                    [*Goes up.*]

FOURTH CITIZEN: What does he say of Brutus?

THIRD CITIZEN: He says, for Brutus' sake
    He finds himself beholding to us all.

FOURTH CITIZEN: 'Twere best he speak no harm of Brutus here.

FIRST CITIZEN: This Caesar was a tyrant.

THIRD CITIZEN: Nay, that's certain.
    We are blest that Rome is rid of him.

SECOND CITIZEN: Peace, let us hear what Antony can say.

ANTONY: You gentle Romans—

---

34. *enforced:* exaggerated.   45. *parts:* qualities.

CITIZENS: Peace ho, let us hear him.
ANTONY: Friends, Romans, countrymen, lend me your ears.
  I come to bury Caesar, not to praise him.
  The evil that men do, lives after them,   70
  The good is oft interred with their bones;
  So let it be with Caesar. The noble Brutus
  Hath told you Caesar was ambitious;
  If it were so, it was a grievous fault,
  And grievously hath Caesar answered it.
  Here, under leave of Brutus, and the rest—
  For Brutus is an honourable man,
  So are they all, all honourable men—
  Come I to speak in Caesar's funeral.
  He was my friend, faithful, and just to me;   80
  But Brutus says, he was ambitious,
  And Brutus is an honourable man.
  He hath brought many captives home to Rome,
  Whose ransoms did the general coffers* fill.
  Did this in Caesar seem ambitious?
  When that the poor have cried, Caesar hath wept.
  Ambition should be made of sterner stuff,
  Yet Brutus says, he was ambitious;
  And Brutus is an honourable man.
  You all did see, that on the Lupercal   90
  I thrice presented him a kingly crown,
  Which he did thrice refuse. Was this ambition?
  Yet Brutus says, he was ambitious;
  And sure he is an honourable man.
  I speak not to disprove what Brutus spoke,
  But here I am, to speak what I do know;
  You all did love him once, not without cause,
  What cause withholds you then to mourn for him?
  O judgement, thou art fled to brutish beasts,
  And men have lost their reason. Bear with me;   100
  My heart is in the coffin there with Caesar,
  And I must pause, till it come back to me.
FIRST CITIZEN: Methinks there is much reason in his sayings.
SECOND CITIZEN: If thou consider rightly of the matter,
  Caesar has had great wrong.

84. *general coffers:* public treasury.

THIRD CITIZEN: Has he masters?
    I fear there will a worse come in his place.
FOURTH CITIZEN: Marked ye his words? He would not take the crown,
    Therefore 'tis certain, he was not ambitious.
FIRST CITIZEN: If it be found so, some will dear abide it.*
SECOND CITIZEN: Poor soul, his eyes are red as fire with weeping.   110
THIRD CITIZEN: There's not a nobler man in Rome than Antony.
FOURTH CITIZEN: Now mark him, he begins again to speak.
ANTONY: But yesterday, the word of Caesar might
    Have stood against the world. Now lies he there,
    And none so poor to do him reverence.
    O masters, if I were disposed to stir
    Your hearts and minds to mutiny and rage,
    I should do Brutus wrong, and Cassius wrong,
    Who you all know are honourable men.
    I will not do them wrong. I rather choose   120
    To wrong the dead, to wrong myself and you,
    Than I will wrong such honourable men.
    But here's a parchment, with the seal of Caesar,
    I found it in his closet, 'tis his will.
    Let but the commons* hear this testament—
    Which, pardon me, I do not mean to read—
    And they would go and kiss dead Caesar's wounds,
    And dip their napkins* in his sacred blood;
    Yea, beg a hair of him for memory,
    And dying, mention it within their wills,   130
    Bequeathing it as a rich legacy
    Unto their issue.*
FOURTH CITIZEN: We'll hear the will, read it, Mark Antony.
CITIZENS: The will, the will! We will hear Caesar's will.
ANTONY: Have patience gentle friends, I must not read it.
    It is not meet you know how Caesar loved you.
    You are not wood, you are not stones, but men;
    And being men, hearing the will of Caesar,
    It will inflame you, it will make you mad.
    'Tis good you know not that you are his heirs,   140
    For if you should, O what would come of it?
FOURTH CITIZEN: Read the will, we'll hear it, Antony.
    You shall read us the will, Caesar's will.

109. *abide it:* pay for it.   125. *commons:* common people.   128. *napkins:*
handkerchiefs.   132. *issue:* heirs.

ANTONY: Will you be patient? Will you stay awhile?
I have o'ershot myself to tell you of it.
I fear I wrong the honourable men,
Whose daggers have stabbed Caesar; I do fear it.
FOURTH CITIZEN: They were traitors. Honourable men?
CITIZENS: The will! The testament!
SECOND CITIZEN: They were villains, murderers. The will, read the will.   150
ANTONY: You will compel me then to read the will?
Then make a ring about the corpse of Caesar,
And let me show you him that made the will.
Shall I descend? And will you give me leave?
CITIZENS: Come down.
SECOND CITIZEN: Descend.
THIRD CITIZEN: You shall have leave.
                    [ANTONY *comes down.*]
FOURTH CITIZEN: A ring, stand round.
FIRST CITIZEN: Stand from the hearse, stand from the body.
SECOND CITIZEN: Room for Antony, most noble Antony.   160
ANTONY: Nay, press not so upon me; stand far off.
CITIZENS: Stand back; room; bear back.
ANTONY: If you have tears, prepare to shed them now.
You all do know this mantle, I remember
The first time ever Caesar put it on;
'Twas on a summer's evening in his tent,
That day he overcame the Nervii.*
Look, in this place ran Cassius' dagger through.
See what a rent the envious Casca made.
Through this, the well-beloved Brutus stabbed.   170
And as he plucked his cursed steel away,
Mark how the blood of Caesar followed it,
As rushing out of doors, to be resolved
If Brutus so unkindly knocked, or no;
For Brutus, as you know, was Caesar's angel.
Judge, O you gods, how dearly Caesar loved him.
This was the most unkindest cut of all;
For when the noble Caesar saw him stab,
Ingratitude, more strong than traitors' arms,
Quite vanquished him. Then burst his mighty heart,   180
And in his mantle muffling up his face,
Even at the base of Pompey's statue,

167. *the Nervii:* a Belgian tribe that Caesar conquered.

Which all the while ran blood, great Caesar fell.
O what a fall was there, my countrymen!
Then I, and you, and all of us fell down,
Whilst bloody treason flourished over us.
O now you weep, and I perceive you feel
The dint of pity. These are gracious drops.
Kind souls, what weep you, when you but behold
Our Caesar's vesture wounded*? Look you here.   190
Here is himself, marred as you see with traitors.

FIRST CITIZEN: O piteous spectacle!

SECOND CITIZEN: O noble Caesar!

THIRD CITIZEN: O woeful day!

FOURTH CITIZEN: O traitors, villains!

FIRST CITIZEN: O most bloody sight!

SECOND CITIZEN: We will be revenged.

CITIZENS: Revenge! About! Seek! Burn! Fire! Kill! Slay! Let not a traitor
live.

ANTONY: Stay, countrymen.   200

FIRST CITIZEN: Peace there, hear the noble Antony.

SECOND CITIZEN: We'll hear him, we'll follow him, we'll die with him.

ANTONY: Good friends, sweet friends, let me not stir you up
To such a sudden flood of mutiny.
They that have done this deed are honourable.
What private griefs they have, alas I know not,
That made them do it. They are wise, and honourable,
And will no doubt with reasons answer you.
I come not friends, to steal away your hearts,
I am no orator as Brutus is;   210
But as you know me all, a plain blunt man,
That love my friend, and that they know full well,
That gave me public leave to speak of him.
For I have neither wit, nor words, nor worth,
Action, nor utterance, nor the power of speech,
To stir men's blood. I only speak right on.
I tell you that which you yourselves do know,
Show you sweet Caesar's wounds, poor poor dumb mouths,
And bid them speak for me. But were I Brutus,
And Brutus Antony, there were an Antony   220
Would ruffle up your spirits, and put a tongue
In every wound of Caesar, that should move

190. *vesture wounded:* torn clothing.

The stones of Rome, to rise and mutiny.

CITIZENS: We'll mutiny.

FIRST CITIZEN: We'll burn the house of Brutus.

THIRD CITIZEN: Away then, come, seek the conspirators.

ANTONY: Yet hear me, countrymen, yet hear me speak.

CITIZENS: Peace ho, hear Antony, most noble Antony.

ANTONY: Why friends, you go to do you know not what.
  Wherein hath Caesar thus deserved your loves?   230
  Alas you know not, I must tell you then.
  You have forgot the will I told you of.

CITIZENS: Most true, the will, let's stay and hear the will.

ANTONY: Here is the will, and under Caesar's seal.
  To every Roman citizen he gives,
  To every several* man, seventy-five drachmas.

SECOND CITIZEN: Most noble Caesar, we'll revenge his death.

THIRD CITIZEN: O royal Caesar!

ANTONY: Hear me with patience.

CITIZENS: Peace ho!   240

ANTONY: Moreover, he hath left you all his walks,
  His private arbours, and new-planted orchards,
  On this side Tiber; he hath left them you,
  And to your heirs for ever—common pleasures,
  To walk abroad, and recreate yourselves.
  Here was a Caesar! When comes such another?

FIRST CITIZEN: Never, never. Come, away, away!
  We'll burn his body in the holy place,
  And with the brands fire the traitors' houses.
  Take up the body.   250

SECOND CITIZEN: Go fetch fire.

THIRD CITIZEN: Pluck down benches.

FOURTH CITIZEN: Pluck down forms,* windows, any thing.

                    [*Exeunt* CITIZENS *with the body.*]

ANTONY: Now let it work. Mischief thou art afoot,
  Take thou what course thou wilt.

                    [*Enter* SERVANT.]

  How now, fellow?

SERVANT: Sir, Octavius is already come to Rome.

ANTONY: Where is he?

SERVANT: He and Lepidus* are at Caesar's house.

236. *every several:* each.   253. *forms:* benches.   259. *Lepidus:* a Roman of high
family who, with Antony and Octavius, was to form a new government in Rome.

ANTONY: And thither will I straight to visit him.   260
　　He comes upon a wish. Fortune is merry,
　　And in this mood will give us anything.
SERVANT: I heard him say, Brutus and Cassius
　　Are rid* like madmen through the gates of Rome.
ANTONY: Belike* they had some notice of the people
　　How I had moved them. Bring me to Octavius.
　　　　　　　　　　[*Exeunt.*]

SCENE THREE

[*The same. Enter* CINNA *the poet, and after him* CITIZENS.]

CINNA: I dreamt to-night that I did feast with Caesar,
　　And things unluckily charge my fantasy.
　　I have no will to wander forth of doors,
　　Yet something leads me forth.
FIRST CITIZEN: What is your name?
SECOND CITIZEN: Whither are you going?
THIRD CITIZEN: Where do you dwell?
FOURTH CITIZEN: Are you a married man, or a bachelor?
SECOND CITIZEN: Answer every man directly.
FIRST CITIZEN: Ay, and briefly.   10
FOURTH CITIZEN: Ay, and wisely.
THIRD CITIZEN: Ay, and truly, you were best.*
CINNA: What is my name? Whither am I going? Where do I dwell? Am I
　　a married man, or a bachelor? Then to answer every man, directly and
　　briefly, wisely and truly—wisely I say, I am a bachelor.
SECOND CITIZEN: That's as much as to say, they are fools that marry.
　　You'll bear me a bang* for that I fear. Proceed directly.
CINNA: Directly I am going to Caesar's funeral.
FIRST CITIZEN: As a friend, or an enemy?
CINNA: As a friend.   20
SECOND CITIZEN: That matter is answered directly.
FOURTH CITIZEN: For your dwelling—briefly.
CINNA: Briefly, I dwell by the Capitol.
THIRD CITIZEN: Your name sir, truly.
CINNA: Truly, my name is Cinna.
FIRST CITIZEN: Tear him to pieces, he's a conspirator.

264. *Are rid:* have ridden.　　265. *Belike:* probably.
12. *you were best:* you'd better.　　17. *bear . . . bang:* be hit by me.

CINNA: I am Cinna the poet, I am Cinna the poet.

FOURTH CITIZEN: Tear him for his bad verses, tear him for his bad verses.

CINNA: I am not Cinna the conspirator.

FOURTH CITIZEN: It is no matter, his name's Cinna, pluck but his name out 30 of his heart, and turn him going.

THIRD CITIZEN: Tear him, tear him! Come, brands, ho! Firebrands! To Brutus', to Cassius', burn all. Some to Decius' house, and some to Casca's; some to Ligarius'. Away, go!

[*Exeunt.*]

ACT IV

SCENE ONE

[*Rome.* ANTONY'S *house.* ANTONY, OCTAVIUS, *and* LEPIDUS.]

ANTONY: These many then shall die; their names are pricked.*

OCTAVIUS: Your brother too must die; consent you Lepidus?

LEPIDUS: I do consent.

OCTAVIUS: Prick him down Antony.

LEPIDUS: Upon condition Publius shall not live,
    Who is your sister's son, Mark Antony.

ANTONY: He shall not live; look, with a spot I damn him.
    But Lepidus, go you to Caesar's house.
    Fetch the will hither, and we shall determine
    How to cut off some charge in legacies.*

LEPIDUS: What, shall I find you here?   10

OCTAVIUS: Or here, or at the Capitol.

[*Exit* LEPIDUS.]

ANTONY: This is a slight unmeritable man,
    Meet to be sent on errands. Is it fit,
    The threefold world divided, he should stand
    One of the three to share it?

OCTAVIUS: So you thought him,
    And took his voice who should be pricked to die,

---

1. *pricked:* Marks have been made after these names. The new rulers of Rome are drawing up a list of enemies to be executed.   9. *How . . . legacies:* how to reduce Caesar's bequests to the citizens of Rome.

In our black sentence and proscription.*
ANTONY: Octavius, I have seen more days than you;
    And though we lay these honours on this man,
    To ease ourselves of divers* sland'rous loads,   20
    He shall but bear them as the ass bears gold,
    To groan and sweat under the business,
    Either led or driven, as we point the way;
    And having brought our treasure where we will,
    Then take we down his load, and turn him off,
    Like to the empty ass, to shake his ears,
    And graze in commons.*
OCTAVIUS: You may do your will.
    But he's a tried and valiant soldier.
ANTONY: So is my horse, Octavius, and for that
    I do appoint him store of provender.   30
    It is a creature that I teach to fight,
    To wind,* to stop, to run directly on,
    His corporal* motion governed by my spirit,
    And in some taste, is Lepidus but so;
    He must be taught, and trained, and bid go forth.
    A barren-spirited fellow; one that feeds
    On objects, arts, and imitations,
    Which, out of use and staled by other men,
    Begin his fashion.* Do not talk of him
    But as a property. And now Octavius,   40
    Listen great things. Brutus and Cassius
    Are levying powers; we must straight make head.*
    Therefore let our alliance be combined,
    Our best friends made, our means stretched,
    And let us presently go sit in council,
    How covert matters may be best disclosed,
    And open perils surest answered.
OCTAVIUS: Let us do so; for we are at the stake,
    And bayed about* with many enemies,
    And some that smile have in their hearts, I fear,   50
    Millions of mischiefs.

[Exeunt.]

17. *proscription:* the execution list.   20. *divers:* various.   27. *commons:* the common pastures (owned by the community as a whole).   32. *wind:* turn.
33. *corporal:* bodily.   39. *Begin his fashion:* that is, Lepidus takes up these fashions after other men have grown tired of them.   42. *head:* headway.
48–49. *we . . . bayed about:* a reference to bear-baiting, a popular Elizabethan amusement. The bear was tied to a stake and attacked by (baying) dogs.

SCENE TWO

[*Before* BRUTUS' *tent, in the camp near Sardis.* Drum. Enter* BRUTUS
and LUCIUS *from the tent. Enter* LUCILIUS *and* SOLDIERS *at one door,
and* TITINIUS *and* PINDARUS *at the other.*]

BRUTUS: Stand ho!
LUCILIUS: Give the word ho, and stand.
BRUTUS: What now, Lucilius, is Cassius near?
LUCILIUS: He is at hand, and Pindarus is come
    To do you salutation from his master.
BRUTUS: He greets me well. Your master, Pindarus,
    In his own change, or by ill officers,
    Hath given me some worthy cause to wish
    Things done, undone. But if he be at hand
    I shall be satisfied.*
PINDARUS: I do not doubt   10
    But that my noble master will appear
    Such as he is, full of regard and honour.
BRUTUS: He is not doubted. A word Lucilius,
    How he received you; let me be resolved.
LUCILIUS: With courtesy, and with respect enough,
    But not with such familiar instances,*
    Nor with such free and friendly conference
    As he hath used of old.
BRUTUS: Thou hast described
    A hot friend cooling. Ever note Lucilius,
    When love begins to sicken and decay   20
    It useth an enforced* ceremony.
    There are no tricks in plain and simple faith;
    But hollow men, like horses hot at hand,*
    Make gallant show, and promise of their mettle;
    But when they should endure the bloody spur,
    They fall their crests, and like deceitful jades*
    Sink in the trial. Comes his army on?
LUCILIUS: They mean this night in Sardis to be quartered.
    The greater part, the horse in general,*
    Are come with Cassius.
                    [*Low march within.*]

Setting. *Sardis:* an ancient Greek city in Asia Minor, part of Roman territory.
10. *be satisfied:* be given reasons.   16. *familiar instances:* familiarity.   21. *enforced:* artificial.   23. *hot at hand:* high-spirited at first.   26. *jades:* nags.
29. *the horse in general:* the cavalry.

BRUTUS: Hark, he is arrived.   30
    March gently on to meet him.
                        [*Enter* CASSIUS *and* SOLDIERS.]
CASSIUS: Stand ho!
BRUTUS: Stand ho, speak the word along.
FIRST SOLDIER: Stand.
SECOND SOLDIER: Stand.
THIRD SOLDIER: Stand.
CASSIUS: Most noble brother, you have done me wrong.
BRUTUS: Judge me, you gods; wrong I mine enemies?
    And if not so, how should I wrong a brother?
CASSIUS: Brutus, this sober form of yours hides wrongs,   40
    And when you do them—
BRUTUS: Cassius, be content,
    Speak your griefs softly, I do know you well.
    Before the eyes of both our armies here,
    Which should perceive nothing but love from us,
    Let us not wrangle. Bid them move away.
    Then in my tent, Cassius, enlarge your griefs,
    And I will give you audience.
CASSIUS: Pindarus,
    Bid our commanders lead their charges* off
    A little from this ground.
BRUTUS: Lucius, do you the like, and let no man   50
    Come to our tent, till we have done our conference.
    Lucilius and Titinius guard our door.
        [*Exeunt* LUCIUS *and* PINDARUS *with* SOLDIERS. BRUTUS *and* CASSIUS
        enter the tent.]

SCENE THREE

[*Within the tent.*]

CASSIUS: That you have wronged me doth appear in this:
    You have condemned and noted Lucius Pella
    For taking bribes here of the Sardians;
    Wherein my letters, praying on his side,
    Because I knew the man, was slighted off.*
BRUTUS: You wronged yourself to write in such a case.

48. *charges:* soldiers.
5. *slighted off:* disregarded.

CASSIUS: In such a time as this it is not meet
   That every nice* offence should bear his comment.*
BRUTUS: Let me tell you, Cassius, you yourself
   Are much condemned to have an itching palm,   10
   To sell and mart your offices* for gold
   To undeservers.
CASSIUS: I, an itching palm?
   You know that you are Brutus that speaks this,
   Or by the gods, this speech were else your last.
BRUTUS: The name of Cassius honours this corruption,
   And chastisement* doth therefore hide his head.
CASSIUS: Chastisement?
BRUTUS: Remember March, the ides of March remember.
   Did not great Julius bleed for justice' sake?
   What villain touched his body, that did stab,   20
   And not for justice? What, shall one of us,
   That struck the foremost man of all this world
   But for supporting robbers,* shall we now
   Contaminate our fingers with base bribes,
   And sell the mighty space of our large honours
   For so much trash as may be grasped thus?
   I had rather be a dog, and bay the moon,
   Than such a Roman.
CASSIUS: Brutus, bait not me,
   I'll not endure it. You forget yourself,
   To hedge me in. I am a soldier, I,   30
   Older in practice,* abler than yourself
   To make conditions.*
BRUTUS: Go to! You are not, Cassius.
CASSIUS: I am.
BRUTUS: I say, you are not.
CASSIUS: Urge me no more, I shall forget myself.
   Have mind upon your health. Tempt me no farther.
BRUTUS: Away slight man.
CASSIUS: Is't possible?
BRUTUS: Hear me, for I will speak.
   Must I give way and room to your rash choler?*

---

8. *nice:* small.   8. *bear . . . comment:* be noticed.   11. *offices:* appointments.
16. *chastisement:* punishment.   23. *for supporting robbers:* for allowing corrupt
officials.   31. *practice:* experience.   32. *make conditions:* manage matters.
39. *choler:* anger.

Shall I be frighted, when a madman stares?   40

CASSIUS: O ye gods, ye gods! Must I endure all this?

BRUTUS: All this? Ay more. Fret till your proud heart break.
Go show your slaves how choleric you are,
And make your bondmen tremble. Must I budge?
Must I observe you? Must I stand and crouch
Under your testy humour*? By the gods,
You shall digest the venom of your spleen,*
Though it do split you. For from this day forth,
I'll use you for my mirth, yea for my laughter,
When you are waspish.

CASSIUS: Is it come to this?   50

BRUTUS: You say you are a better soldier.
Let it appear so; make your vaunting* true,
And it shall please me well. For mine own part,
I shall be glad to learn of* noble men.

CASSIUS: You wrong me every way; you wrong me, Brutus.
I said, an elder soldier, not a better.
Did I say, better?

BRUTUS: If you did, I care not.

CASSIUS: When Caesar lived, he durst not thus have moved me.

BRUTUS: Peace, peace, you durst not so have tempted him.

CASSIUS: I durst not?   60

BRUTUS: No.

CASSIUS: What, durst not tempt him?

BRUTUS: For your life you durst not.

CASSIUS: Do not presume too much upon my love;
I may do that I shall be sorry for.

BRUTUS: You have done that you should be sorry for.
There is no terror, Cassius, in your threats;
For I am armed so strong in honesty,
That they pass by me, as the idle wind,
Which I respect not. I did send to you
For certain sums of gold, which you denied me;   70
For I can raise no money by vile means.
By heaven, I had rather coin my heart,
And drop my blood for drachmas, than to wring
From the hard hands of peasants their vile trash
By any indirection.* I did send

46. *testy humour:* bad temper.   47. *spleen:* evil mood.   52. *vaunting:* boasting.
54. *of:* from.   75. *indirection:* corrupt means.

To you for gold to pay my legions,
Which you denied me. Was that done like Cassius?
Should I have answered Caius Cassius so?
When Marcus Brutus grows so covetous,
To lock such rascal counters* from his friends, 80
Be ready, gods, with all your thunder-bolts;
Dash him to pieces.
CASSIUS: I denied you not.
BRUTUS: You did.
CASSIUS: I did not. He was but a fool that brought
My answer back. Brutus hath rived* my heart.
A friend should bear his friend's infirmities;
But Brutus makes mine greater than they are.
BRUTUS: I do not, till you practise them on me.
CASSIUS: You love me not.
BRUTUS: I do not like your faults. 90
CASSIUS: A friendly eye could never see such faults.
BRUTUS: A flatterer's would not, though they do appear
As huge as high Olympus.
CASSIUS: Come, Antony, and young Octavius, come,
Revenge yourselves alone on Cassius,
For Cassius is aweary of the world:
Hated by one he loves, braved* by his brother,
Checked like a bondman, all his faults observed,
Set in a note-book, learned, and conned by rote,*
To cast into my teeth. Oh I could weep
My spirit from mine eyes. There is my dagger, 100
And here my naked breast; within, a heart
Dearer than Pluto's* mine, richer than gold.
If that thou beest a Roman, take it forth.
I that denied thee gold, will give my heart.
Strike as thou didst at Caesar. For I know,
When thou didst hate him worst, thou lovedst him better
Than ever thou lovedst Cassius.
BRUTUS: Sheathe your dagger.
Be angry when you will, it shall have scope.*
Do what you will, dishonour shall be humour.*
O Cassius, you are yoked with a lamb 110

---

80. *counters:* coins.   85. *rived:* split.   96. *braved:* defied.   98. *conned by rote:* memorized.   102. *Pluto:* god of the underworld.   108. *have scope:* be tolerated.   109. *shall be humour:* shall be tolerated as a quirk of temperament.

That carries anger as the flint bears* fire,
Who much enforced* shows a hasty spark,
And straight is cold again.

CASSIUS: Hath Cassius lived
To be but mirth and laughter to his Brutus,
When grief and blood ill-tempered vexeth him?

BRUTUS: When I spoke that, I was ill-tempered too.

CASSIUS: Do you confess so much? Give me your hand.

BRUTUS: And my heart too.

CASSIUS: O Brutus!

BRUTUS: What's the matter?

CASSIUS: Have you not love enough to bear with me,
When that rash humour* which my mother gave me   120
Makes me forgetful?

BRUTUS: Yes Cassius, and from henceforth,
When you are over-earnest with your Brutus,
He'll think your mother chides, and leave you so.
                    [*Enter* POET, *and* LUCIUS *following.*]

POET: Let me go in to see the generals.
There is some grudge between 'em, 'tis not meet
They be alone.

LUCIUS: You shall not come to them.

POET: Nothing but death shall stay* me.

CASSIUS: How now? What's the matter?

POET: For shame, you generals, what do you mean?
Love, and be friends, as two such men should be,   130
For I have seen more years I'm sure than ye.

CASSIUS: Ha, ha, how vilely doth this cynic* rhyme!

BRUTUS: Get you hence, sirrah. Saucy* fellow, hence!

CASSIUS: Bear with him, Brutus, 'tis his fashion.

BRUTUS: I'll know his humour, when he knows his time.*
What should the wars do with these jigging fools?
Companion, hence!

CASSIUS: Away, away, be gone.
                    [*Exit* POET.]

BRUTUS: Lucilius and Titinius, bid the commanders
Prepare to lodge their companies to-night.

CASSIUS: And come yourselves, and bring Messala with you   140
Immediately to us.

111. *bears:* strikes.   112. *much enforced:* struck hard.   120. *humour:* temper.
127. *stay:* stop.   132. *cynic:* rude fellow.   133. *Saucy:* insolent.   135. *time:*
here, meter. (The poet's lines reveal him to be a clumsy versifier.)

[*Exeunt* LUCILIUS *and* TITINIUS.]

BRUTUS: Lucius, a bowl of wine.

[*Exit* LUCIUS.]

CASSIUS: I did not think you could have been so angry.

BRUTUS: O Cassius, I am sick of many griefs.

CASSIUS: Of your philosophy* you make no use,
If you give place to accidental evils.

BRUTUS: No man bears sorrow better. Portia is dead.

CASSIUS: Ha! Portia?

BRUTUS: She is dead.

CASSIUS: How 'scaped I killing when I crossed you so?
O insupportable and touching loss!   150
Upon what sickness?

BRUTUS: Impatient of my absence,
And grief that young Octavius with Mark Antony
Have made themselves so strong. For with her death
That tidings came. With this she fell distract,
And, her attendants absent, swallowed fire.

CASSIUS: And died so?

BRUTUS: Even so.

CASSIUS: O ye immortal gods!

[*Enter* LUCIUS, *with wine and tapers.*]

BRUTUS: Speak no more of her. Give me a bowl of wine.
In this I bury all unkindness Cassius.

CASSIUS: My heart is thirsty for that noble pledge.
Fill Lucius, till the wine o'erswell the cup.   160
I cannot drink too much of Brutus' love.

[*Exit* LUCIUS. *Enter* TITINIUS *and* MESSALA.]

BRUTUS: Come in Titinius. Welcome good Messala.
Now sit we close about this taper here,
And call in question our necessities.*

CASSIUS: Portia, art thou gone?

BRUTUS: No more I pray you.
Messala, I have here received letters,
That young Octavius and Mark Antony
Come down upon us with a mighty power,*
Bending their expedition toward Philippi.*

MESSALA: Myself have letters of the selfsame tenour.*   170

144. *philosophy:* Brutus, a stoic, believed that a man should train himself to remain
unmoved by misfortune.   164. *call . . . necessities:* discuss what must be done.
168. *power:* force of men.   169. *Philippi:* a city in Macedonia.   170. *tenour:*
drift.

BRUTUS: With what addition?

MESSALA: That by proscription and bills of outlawry,
　Octavius, Antony, and Lepidus
　Have put to death an hundred senators.

BRUTUS: Therein our letters do not well agree.
　Mine speak of seventy senators that died
　By their proscriptions, Cicero being one.

CASSIUS: Cicero one?

MESSALA:　　　　　　　　Cicero is dead,
　And by that order of proscription.

BRUTUS: Well, to our work alive. What do you think　　　　180
　Of marching to Philippi presently?

CASSIUS: I do not think it good.

BRUTUS:　　　　　　　　　　Your reason?

CASSIUS:　　　　　　　　　　　　　This it is:
　'Tis better that the enemy seek us;
　So shall he waste his means, weary his soldiers,
　Doing himself offence,* whilst we lying still,
　Are full of rest, defence, and nimbleness.*

BRUTUS: Good reasons must of force give place to better.
　The people 'twixt Philippi and this ground
　Do stand but in a forced affection;*
　For they have grudged us contribution,*　　　　190
　The enemy, marching along by them,
　By them shall make a fuller number up,
　Come on refreshed, new-added, and encouraged;
　From which advantage shall we cut him off,
　If at Philippi we do face him there,
　These people* at our back.

CASSIUS:　　　　　　　　Hear me, good brother.

BRUTUS: Under your pardon. You must note beside,
　That we have tried the utmost of our friends;
　Our legions are brim-full, our cause is ripe.
　The enemy increaseth every day;　　　　200
　We, at the height, are ready to decline.
　There is a tide in the affairs of men,
　Which taken at the flood* leads on to fortune;
　Omitted, all the voyage of their life
　Is bound in shallows and in miseries.
　On such a full sea are we now afloat,

185. *offence:* harm.　　186. *nimbleness:* energy.　　189. *affection:* loyalty.
190. *contribution:* that is, supplies.　　196. *These people:* the natives.　　203. *flood:*
high tide.

And we must take the current when it serves,
Or lose our ventures.

CASSIUS: Then with your will* go on.
We'll along ourselves, and meet them at Philippi.

BRUTUS: The deep of night is crept upon our talk, 210
And nature must obey necessity,
Which we will niggard with a little rest.
There is no more to say.

CASSIUS: No more. Good night:
Early to-morrow will we rise, and hence.

BRUTUS: Lucius! (*Enter* LUCIUS.) My gown.* (*Exit* LUCIUS.)
Farewell good Messala.
Good night, Titinius. Noble, noble Cassius,
Good night, and good repose.

CASSIUS: O my dear brother!
This was an ill beginning of the night.
Never come such division 'tween our souls;
Let it not, Brutus.

[*Enter* LUCIUS, *with the gown.*]

BRUTUS: Every thing is well. 220

CASSIUS: Good night, my lord.

BRUTUS: Good night, good brother.

TITINIUS *and* MESSALA: Good night, Lord Brutus.

BRUTUS: Farewell, every one.

[*Exeunt* CASSIUS, TITINIUS, *and* MESSALA.]

Give me the gown. Where is thy instrument*?

LUCIUS: Here in the tent.

BRUTUS: What, thou speak'st drowsily?
Poor knave, I blame thee not; thou art o'erwatched.*
Call Claudius and some other of my men;
I'll have them sleep on cushions in my tent.

LUCIUS: Varro and Claudius!

[*Enter* VARRO *and* CLAUDIUS.]

VARRO: Calls my lord?

BRUTUS: I pray you, sirs, lie in my tent and sleep; 230
It may be I shall raise you by and by
On business to my brother Cassius.

VARRO: So please you, we will stand and watch your pleasure.

BRUTUS: I will not have it so. Lie down, good sirs;
It may be I shall otherwise bethink me.*

---

208. *with your will:* as you wish.   215. *gown:* robe.   223. *instrument:* lute.
225. *o'erwatched:* kept watch too long.   235. *otherwise bethink me:* change my
mind.

Look, Lucius, here's the book I sought for so;
I put it in the pocket of my gown.
LUCIUS: I was sure your lordship did not give it me.
BRUTUS: Bear with me, good boy, I am much forgetful.
Canst thou hold up thy heavy eyes a while,   240
And touch thy instrument a strain* or two?
LUCIUS: Ay, my lord, an't* please you.
BRUTUS: It does, my boy.
I trouble thee too much, but thou art willing.
LUCIUS: It is my duty, sir.
BRUTUS: I should not urge thy duty past thy might,
I know young bloods look for a time of rest.
LUCIUS: I have slept, my lord, already.
BRUTUS: It was well done, and thou shalt sleep again;
I will not hold thee long. If I do live,
I will be good to thee. (*Music, and a song.*)   250
This is a sleepy tune. O murd'rous slumber,
Layest thou thy leaden mace upon my boy,
That plays thee music? Gentle knave, good night:
I will not do thee so much wrong to wake thee.
If thou dost nod, thou break'st thy instrument;
I'll take it from thee, and, good boy, good night.
Let me see, let me see; is not the leaf turned down
Where I left reading? Here it is, I think.
                        [*Enter* GHOST OF CAESAR.]
How ill this taper burns! Ha! Who comes here?
I think it is the weakness of mine eyes   260
That shapes this monstrous apparition.
It comes upon me. Art thou anything?
Art thou some god, some angel, or some devil,
That mak'st my blood cold, and my hair to stare*?
Speak to me what thou art.
GHOST OF CAESAR: Thy evil spirit, Brutus.
BRUTUS: Why com'st thou?
GHOST OF CAESAR: To tell thee thou shalt see me at Philippi.
BRUTUS: Well; then I shall see thee again?
GHOST OF CAESAR: Ay, at Philippi.
BRUTUS: Why I will see thee at Philippi then.   270
                        [*Exit* GHOST.]
Now I have taken heart thou vanishest.
Ill spirit, I would hold more talk with thee.

241. *strain:* melody.   242. *an't:* if it.   264. *stare:* stand.

Boy, Lucius! Varro! Claudius! Sirs, awake.
  Claudius!
LUCIUS: The strings, my lord, are false.*
BRUTUS: He thinks he still is at his instrument.
  Lucius, awake.
LUCIUS: My lord.
BRUTUS: Didst thou dream, Lucius, that thou so criedst out?
LUCIUS: My lord, I do not know that I did cry.   280
BRUTUS: Yes, that thou didst. Didst thou see anything?
LUCIUS: Nothing, my lord.
BRUTUS: Sleep again, Lucius. Sirrah Claudius! (*To* VARRO)
  Fellow thou, awake.
VARRO: My lord.
CLAUDIUS: My lord.
BRUTUS: Why did you so cry out, sirs, in your sleep?
VARRO *and* CLAUDIUS: Did we, my lord?
BRUTUS: Ay. Saw you any thing?
VARRO: No, my lord, I saw nothing.
CLAUDIUS: Nor I, my lord.
BRUTUS: Go and commend me to my brother Cassius.   290
  Bid him set on his powers betimes before,*
  And we will follow.
VARRO *and* CLAUDIUS: It shall be done my lord.
              [*Exeunt.*]

ACT V

SCENE ONE

[*A plain near Philippi. Enter* OCTAVIUS, ANTONY, *and* SOLDIERS.]

OCTAVIUS: Now Antony, our hopes are answered.
  You said the enemy would not come down,
  But keep the hills and upper regions.

275. *false:* badly tuned.   291. *Bid . . . before:* Ask him to get his army moving
well ahead of mine.

It proves not so; their battles* are at hand;
They mean to warn* us at Philippi here,
Answering before we do demand of them.
ANTONY: Tut, I am in their bosoms, and I know
Wherefore they do it. They could be content
To visit other places, and come down
With fearful bravery, thinking by this face*   10
To fasten in our thoughts that they have courage;
But 'tis not so.

[Enter MESSENGER.]

MESSENGER: Prepare you, generals;
The enemy comes on in gallant show.
Their bloody sign of battle is hung out,
And something to be done immediately.
ANTONY: Octavius, lead your battle softly on,
Upon the left hand of the even field.*
OCTAVIUS: Upon the right hand I, keep thou the left.
ANTONY: Why do you cross me in this exigent*?   20
OCTAVIUS: I do not cross you; but I will do so.

[*March. Drum. Enter* BRUTUS, CASSIUS, *and* SOLDIERS; LUCILIUS, TI-
TINIUS, MESSALA, *and others.*]

BRUTUS: They stand, and would have parley.
CASSIUS: Stand fast, Titinius, we must out and talk.
OCTAVIUS: Mark Antony, shall we give sign of battle?
ANTONY: No, Caesar, we will answer on their charge.
Make forth; the generals would have some words.
OCTAVIUS: Stir not until the signal.
BRUTUS: Words before blows: is it so, countrymen?
OCTAVIUS: Not that we love words better, as you do.
BRUTUS: Good words are better than bad strokes, Octavius.   30
ANTONY: In your bad strokes, Brutus, you give good words;
Witness the hole you made in Caesar's heart,
Crying, long live, hail Caesar!
CASSIUS: Antony,
The posture of your blows are yet unknown;
But for your words, they rob the Hybla* bees,
And leave them honeyless.
ANTONY: Not stingless too.
BRUTUS: O yes, and soundless too.
For you have stolen their buzzing, Antony,

4. *battles:* forces.   5. *warn:* challenge.   10. *face:* show.   18. *even field:* level
plain.   20. *exigent:* crisis.   35. *Hybla:* a Sicilian city famous for its honey.

And very wisely threat before you sting.

ANTONY: Villains, you did not so, when your vile daggers 40
Hacked one another in the sides of Caesar.
You showed your teeth like apes, and fawned like hounds,
And bowed like bondmen, kissing Caesar's feet;
Whilst damned Casca, like a cur, behind
Struck Caesar on the neck. O you flatterers!

CASSIUS: Flatterers? Now, Brutus, thank yourself;
This tongue had not offended so to-day,
If Cassius might have ruled.*

OCTAVIUS: Come, come, the cause.* If arguing make us sweat,
The proof of it will turn to redder drops. 50
Look,
I draw a sword against conspirators:
When think you that the sword goes up again?
Never, till Caesar's three and thirty wounds
Be well avenged; or till another Caesar
Have added slaughter to the sword of traitors.*

BRUTUS: Caesar, thou canst not die by traitors' hands,
Unless thou bring'st them with thee.

OCTAVIUS: So I hope.
I was not born to die on Brutus' sword.

BRUTUS: O if thou wert the noblest of thy strain, 60
Young man, thou couldst not die more honourable.

CASSIUS: A peevish schoolboy, worthless of such honour,
Joined with a masquer and a reveller.

ANTONY: Old Cassius still.

OCTAVIUS: Come, Antony; away!
Defiance, traitors, hurl we in your teeth.
If you dare fight to-day, come to the field;
If not, when you have stomachs.*
                    [*Exeunt* OCTAVIUS, ANTONY, *and* SOLDIERS.]

CASSIUS: Why now blow wind, swell billow, and swim bark.*
The storm is up, and all is on the hazard.*

BRUTUS: Ho Lucilius, hark, a word with you.

LUCILIUS: My lord. (*They speak apart.*) 70

CASSIUS: Messala.

MESSALA: What says my general?

---

48. *If . . . ruled:* about whether or not to permit Antony to speak at Caesar's funeral.
49. *the cause:* to the point.   55–56. *or till . . . traitors:* or until you have killed
me.   67. *stomachs:* appetite for battle.   68. *bark:* boat.   69. *all . . . hazard:*
all is being risked.

CASSIUS: Messala,
   This is my birth-day; as this very day
   Was Cassius born. Give me thy hand, Messala.
   Be thou my witness, that against my will,
   As Pompey was,* am I compelled to set
   Upon one battle all our liberties.
   You know that I held Epicurus strong,
   And his opinion.* Now I change my mind,
   And partly credit things that do presage.*
   Coming from Sardis, on our former ensign*   80
   Two mighty eagles fell, and there they perched,
   Gorging and feeding from our soldiers' hands,
   Who to Philippi here consorted* us.
   This morning are they fled away and gone,
   And in their steads do ravens, crows, and kites,*
   Fly o'er our heads, and downward look on us
   As we were sickly prey; their shadows seem
   A canopy most fatal, under which
   Our army lies, ready to give up the ghost.
MESSALA: Believe not so.
CASSIUS: I but believe it partly,   90
   For I am fresh of spirit, and resolved
   To meet all perils very constantly.
BRUTUS: Even so Lucilius.*
CASSIUS: Now most noble Brutus,
   The gods to-day stand friendly, that we may,
   Lovers in peace, lead on our days to age.
   But since the affairs of men rest still incertain,
   Let's reason with* the worst that may befall.
   If we do lose this battle, then is this
   The very last time we shall speak together.
   What are you then determined to do?   100
BRUTUS: Even by the rule of that philosophy*
   By which I did blame Cato* for the death

---

75. *As Pompey was:* Pompey was forced to fight Caesar at the battle of Pharsalia and was defeated.   77–78. *Epicurus . . . opinion:* The philosopher Epicurus scoffed at the practice of foretelling the future by omens.   79. *presage:* foretell. 80. *former ensign:* leading flag.   83. *consorted:* accompanied.   85. *kites:* birds believed to be bad omens.   93. *Even . . . Lucilius:* Brutus has finished talking to Lucilius and rejoins Cassius.   97. *reason with:* discuss.   101. *that philosophy:* Brutus as a Stoic disapproved of the Roman practice of commiting suicide as a means of ending one's misery.   102. *Cato:* Brutus' father-in-law was an ally of Pompey and committed suicide rather than fall into Caesar's hands.

Which he did give himself. I know not how,
But I do find it cowardly and vile,
For fear of what might fall, so to prevent
The time of life—arming myself with patience
To stay the providence of some high powers
That govern us below.
CASSIUS: Then, if we lose this battle,
  You are contented to be led in triumph
  Thorough the streets of Rome?   110
BRUTUS: No, Cassius, no. Think not, thou noble Roman,
  That ever Brutus will go bound to Rome;
  He bears too great a mind. But this same day
  Must end that work the ides of March begun,
  And whether we shall meet again I know not.
  Therefore our everlasting farewell take.
  For ever, and for ever, farewell Cassius.
  If we do meet again, why we shall smile;
  If not, why then this parting was well made.
CASSIUS: For ever, and for ever, farewell Brutus.   120
  If we do meet again, we'll smile indeed;
  If not, 'tis true this parting was well made.
BRUTUS: Why then lead on. O that a man might know
  The end of this day's business ere it come.
  But it sufficeth that the day will end,
  And then the end is known. Come ho, away!
                       [*Exeunt.*]

SCENE TWO

[*The same. Alarums.* * *Enter* BRUTUS *and* MESSALA.]

BRUTUS: Ride, ride Messala, ride and give these bills*
  Unto the legions on the other side. (*Alarum.*)
  Let them set on at once; for I perceive
  But cold demeanour* in Octavius' wing,
  And sudden push gives them the overthrow.
  Ride, ride Messala, let them all come down.
                      [*Exeunt.*]

Stage direction. *Alarums:* bugle calls.   1. *bills:* messages.   4. *cold demeanour:*
low spirits.

SCENE THREE

[The same. Alarums. Enter CASSIUS *and* TITINIUS.]

CASSIUS: O look, Titinius, look, the villains fly.*
  Myself have to mine own turned enemy:
  This ensign* here of mine was turning back;
  I slew the coward, and did take it from him.
TITINIUS: O Cassius, Brutus gave the word too early,
  Who having some advantage on Octavius,
  Took it too eagerly: his soldiers fell to spoil,*
  Whilst we by Antony are all enclosed.
                      [Enter PINDARUS.]
PINDARUS: Fly further off, my lord, fly further off;
  Mark Antony is in your tents, my lord.   10
  Fly therefore, noble Cassius, fly far off.
CASSIUS: This hill is far enough. Look, look, Titinius;
  Are those my tents where I perceive the fire?
TITINIUS: They are, my lord.
CASSIUS: Titinius, if thou lovest me,
  Mount thou my horse, and hide thy spurs in him,
  Till he have brought thee up to yonder troops
  And here again, that I may rest assured
  Whether yond troops are friend or enemy.
TITINIUS: I will be here again, even with* a thought.
                        [Exit.]
CASSIUS: Go, Pindarus, get higher on that hill.   20
  My sight was ever thick. Regard, Titinius,
  And tell me what thou not'st* about the field.
                  *[*PINDARUS *goes up.]*
  This day I breathed first: time is come round,
  And where I did begin, there shall I end;
  My life is run his compass. Sirrah, what news?
PINDARUS (*above*): O my lord!
CASSIUS: What news?
PINDARUS (*above*): Titinius is enclosed round about
  With horsemen, that make to him on the spur,
  Yet he spurs on. Now they are almost on him.   30
  Now Titinius! Now some light.* O he lights too.
  He's ta'en. (*Shout.*) And hark, they shout for joy.*

---

1. *villains fly:* Cassius' own men are fleeing.   3. *ensign:* standard-bearer.
7. *spoil:* looting.   19. *even with:* as quickly as.   22. *not'st:* observe.
31. *light:* dismount.   32. *they . . . joy:* Pindarus is mistaken. Titinius has not been
taken prisoner, but has encountered allies.

CASSIUS: Come down, behold no more.
    O coward that I am, to live so long,
    To see my best friend ta'en before my face.
                [PINDARUS *descends.*]
    Come hither, sirrah.
    In Parthia* did I take thee prisoner,
    And then I swore thee, saving of thy life,
    That whatsoever I did bid thee do,
    Thou shouldst attempt it. Come now, keep thine oath.   40
    Now be a freeman, and with this good sword
    That ran through Caesar's bowels, search this bosom.
    Stand* not to answer. Here, take thou the hilts,
    And when my face is covered, as 'tis now,
    Guide thou the sword.—Caesar, thou art revenged,
    Even with the sword that killed thee.
                [*Dies.*]
PINDARUS: So, I am free; yet would not so have been,
    Durst I have done my will. O Cassius!
    Far from this country Pindarus shall run,
    Where never Roman shall take note of him.   50
          [*Exit. Enter* TITINIUS *and* MESSALA.]
MESSALA: It is but change,* Titinius; for Octavius
    Is overthrown by noble Brutus' power,
    As Cassius' legions are by Antony.
TITINIUS: These tidings will well comfort Cassius.
MESSALA: Where did you leave him?
TITINIUS: All disconsolate,
    With Pindarus his bondman, on this hill.
MESSALA: Is not that he that lies upon the ground?
TITINIUS: He lies not like the living. O my heart!
MESSALA: Is not that he?
TITINIUS: No, this was he, Messala,
    But Cassius is no more. O setting sun,   60
    As in thy red rays thou dost sink to night,
    So in his red blood Cassius' day is set.
    The sun of Rome is set. Our day is gone;
    Clouds, dews and dangers come;* our deeds are done.
    Mistrust of my success hath done this deed.
MESSALA: Mistrust of good success hath done this deed.
    O hateful Error, Melancholy's child,

---

37. *Parthia:* an ancient country in Asia.   43. *Stand:* wait.   51. *change:* fair exchange.   64. *Clouds . . . come:* Let come what may.

Why dost thou show to the apt thoughts of men
The things that are not? O Error soon conceived,
Thou never com'st unto a happy birth,   70
But kill'st the mother that engendered* thee.
TITINIUS: What, Pindarus! Where art thou, Pindarus?
MESSALA: Seek him, Titinius, whilst I go to meet
    The noble Brutus, thrusting this report
    Into his ears: I may say, thrusting it;
    For piercing steel, and darts envenomed,
    Shall be as welcome to the ears of Brutus
    As tidings of this sight.
TITINIUS: Hie you, Messala,
    And I will seek for Pindarus the while.
                    [*Exit* MESSALA.]
    Why didst thou send me forth, grave Cassius?   80
    Did I not meet thy friends, and did not they
    Put on my brows this wreath of victory,
    And bid me give it thee? Didst thou not hear their shouts?
    Alas, thou hast misconstrued every thing.
    But hold thee, take this garland on thy brow;
    Thy Brutus bid me give it thee, and I
    Will do his bidding. Brutus, come apace,
    And see how I regarded Caius Cassius.
    By your leave, gods—this is a Roman's part.
    Come Cassius' sword, and find Titinius' heart.   90
        [*Dies. Alarum. Enter* MESSALA, *with* BRUTUS, YOUNG CATO, LUCILIUS,
        LABEO, FLAVIUS, *and others.*]
BRUTUS: Where, where Messala, doth his body lie?
MESSALA: Lo yonder, and Titinius mourning it.
BRUTUS: Titinius' face is upward.
CATO: He is slain.
BRUTUS: O Julius Caesar, thou art mighty yet;
    Thy spirit walks abroad, and turns our swords
    In our own proper entrails.
                    [*Low alarums.*]
CATO: Brave Titinius!
    Look whe'r* he have not crowned dead Cassius.
BRUTUS: Are yet two Romans living such as these?
    The last of all the Romans, fare thee well.

71. *engendered:* gave birth.   97. *wh'r:* whether.

It is impossible that ever Rome   100
Should breed thy fellow. Friends, I owe moe tears
To this dead man than you shall see me pay.
I shall find time, Cassius; I shall find time.
Come therefore, and to Thasos send his body.
His funerals shall not be in our camp,
Lest it discomfort us. Lucilius, come,
And come, young Cato, let us to the field.
Labeo and Flavius, set our battles on.
'Tis three a clock; and Romans, yet ere night
We shall try fortune in a second fight.   110

                             [*Exeunt.*]

SCENE FOUR

[*The same. Alarum. Enter* BRUTUS, MESSALA, YOUNG CATO, LUCILIUS,
FLAVIUS, *and* SOLDIERS, *fighting.*]
BRUTUS: Yet countrymen, O yet hold up your heads.
            [*Exit, fighting, followed by* MESSALA.]
CATO: What bastard doth not? Who will go with me?
  I will proclaim my name about the field—
  I am the son of Marcus Cato, ho!
  A foe to tyrants, and my country's friend.
  I am the son of Marcus Cato, ho!
           [*Enter more* SOLDIERS *fighting.*]
LUCILIUS: And I am Brutus, Marcus Brutus, I;
  Brutus my country's friend. Know me for Brutus!
            [CATO *is slain.*]
  O young and noble Cato, art thou down?
  Why now thou diest as bravely as Titinius,   10
  And mayst be honoured, being Cato's son.
FIRST SOLDIER: Yield, or thou diest.
LUCILIUS: Only I yield to die.*
  There is so much, that thou wilt kill me straight;
            [*Offers money.*]
  Kill Brutus, and be honoured in his death.
FIRST SOLDIER: We must not. A noble prisoner.
SECOND SOLDIER: Room ho! Tell Antony, Brutus is ta'en.

12. *Only . . . die:* I yield only that I may die.

[*Enter* ANTONY.]

FIRST SOLDIER: I'll tell the news. Here comes the general.
    Brutus is ta'en, Brutus is ta'en, my lord.
ANTONY: Where is he?
LUCILIUS: Safe, Antony, Brutus is safe enough.   20
    I dare assure thee that no enemy
    Shall ever take alive the noble Brutus.
    The gods defend him from so great a shame.
    When you do find him, or alive, or dead,
    He will be found like Brutus, like himself.
ANTONY: This is not Brutus, friend, but I assure you,
    A prize no less in worth; keep this man safe,
    Give him all kindness. I had rather have
    Such men my friends than enemies. Go on,
    And see whe'r Brutus be alive or dead,   30
    And bring us word unto Octavius' tent
    How every thing is chanced.
                   [*Exeunt.*]

SCENE FIVE

[*The same. Enter* BRUTUS, DARDANIUS, CLITUS, STRATO, *and* VOLUM-
    NIUS.]

BRUTUS: Come, poor remains of friends, rest on this rock.
CLITUS: Statilius showed the torch-light,* but my lord,
    He came not back: he is or ta'en, or slain.
BRUTUS: Sit thee down, Clitus. Slaying is the word,
    It is a deed in fashion. Hark thee, Clitus.
                   [*Whispers.*]
CLITUS: What I, my lord? No, not for all the world.
BRUTUS: Peace then, no words.
CLITUS: I'll rather kill myself.
BRUTUS: Hark thee, Dardanius.
                   [*Whispers.*]
DARDANIUS: Shall I do such a deed?
CLITUS: O Dardanius!
DARDANIUS: O Clitus!   10
CLITUS: What ill request did Brutus make to thee?
DARDANIUS: To kill him, Clitus. Look, he meditates.

---

2. *showed the torch-light:* gave the signal.

CLITUS: Now is that noble vessel full of grief,
   That it runs over even at his eyes.
BRUTUS: Come hither, good Volumnius, list a word.
VOLUMNIUS: What says my lord?
BRUTUS: Why this, Volumnius.
   The ghost of Caesar hath appeared to me
   Two several times by night—at Sardis once,
   And this last night, here in Philippi fields.
   I know my hour is come.
VOLUMNIUS: Not so, my lord.   20
BRUTUS: Nay I am sure it is, Volumnius.
   Thou seest the world, Volumnius, how it goes,
   Our enemies have beat* us to the pit.
                [*Low alarums.*]
   It is more worthy to leap in ourselves,
   Than tarry till they push us. Good Volumnius,
   Thou know'st that we two went to school together;
   Even for that our love of old, I prithee
   Hold thou my sword-hilts, whilst I run on it.
VOLUMNIUS: That's not an office for a friend, my lord.
               [*Alarm still.*]
CLITUS: Fly, fly my lord, there is no tarrying here.   30
BRUTUS: Farewell to you; and you; and you Volumnius.
   Strato, thou hast been all this while asleep;
   Farewell to thee too, Strato. Countrymen,
   My heart doth joy, that yet in all my life
   I found no man but he was true to me.
   I shall have glory by this losing day,
   More than Octavius and Mark Antony
   By this vile conquest shall attain unto.
   So fare you well at once, for Brutus' tongue
   Hath almost ended his life's history.   40
   Night hangs upon mine eyes, my bones would rest,
   That have but laboured to attain this hour.
         [*Alarums. Cry within,* Fly, fly, fly!]
CLITUS: Fly, my lord, fly.
BRUTUS: Hence! I will follow.
      [*Exeunt* CLITUS, DARDANIUS, *and* VOLUMNIUS.]
   I prithee, Strato, stay thou by thy lord.
   Thou art a fellow of a good respect;

23. *beat:* driven.

Thy life hath had some smatch* of honour in it.
Hold then my sword, and turn away thy face,
While I do run upon it. Wilt thou, Strato?

STRATO: Give me your hand first. Fare you well, my lord.

BRUTUS: Farewell, good Strato. (*Runs on his sword.*) Caesar now be still; 50
I killed not thee with half so good a will.

    [*Dies. Alarum. Retreat. Enter* OCTAVIUS, ANTONY, MESSALA, LUCI-
    LIUS, *and* SOLDIERS.]

OCTAVIUS: What man is that?

MESSALA: My master's man. Strato, where is thy master?

STRATO: Free from the bondage you are in, Messala;
The conquerors can but make a fire of him.
For Brutus only* overcame himself,
And no man else hath honour by his death.

LUCILIUS: So Brutus should be found. I thank thee, Brutus,
That thou has proved Lucilius' saying* true.

OCTAVIUS: All that served Brutus, I will entertain* them. 60
Fellow, wilt thou bestow thy time with me?

STRATO: Ay, if Messala will prefer* me to you.

OCTAVIUS: Do so, good Messala.

MESSALA: How died my master, Strato?

STRATO: I held the sword, and he did run on it.

MESSALA: Octavius, then take him to follow thee,
That did the latest* service to my master.

ANTONY: This was the noblest Roman of them all.
All the conspirators save only he
Did that they did, in envy of great Caesar; 70
He only, in a general* honest thought,
And common good to all, made one of them.
His life was gentle,* and the elements
So mixed in him, that Nature might stand up,
And say to all the world, this was a man.

OCTAVIUS: According to his virtue let us use him,
With all respect, and rites of burial.
Within my tent his bones to-night shall lie,
Most like a soldier, ordered honourably.
So call the field to rest, and let's away, 80
To part* the glories of this happy day.

             [*Exeunt.*]

---

46. *smatch:* trace.   56. *only:* alone.   59. *saying:* See Act V, Scene IV, lines
21–22.   60. *entertain:* enlist.   62. *prefer:* recommend.   67. *latest:* last.
71. *general:* unselfish.   73. *gentle:* noble.   81. *part:* share.

Mateo Falcone

PROSPER MÉRIMÉE

O N leaving Portovecchio from the northwest and directing his steps toward the interior of the island, the traveler will notice that the land rises rapidly, and after three hours' walking over tortuous paths obstructed by great masses of rock and sometimes cut by ravines, he will find himself on the border of a great maquis. The maquis is the domain of the Corsican shepherds and of those who are at variance with justice. It must be known that, in order to save himself the trouble of manuring his field, the Corsican husbandman sets fire to a piece of woodland.

If the flame spread farther than is necessary, so much the worse! In any case he is certain of a good crop from the land fertilized by the ashes of the trees which grow upon it. He gathers only the heads of his grain, leaving the straw, which it would be unnecessary labor to cut. In the following spring the roots that have remained in the earth without being destroyed send up their tufts of sprouts, which in a few years reach a height of seven or eight feet. It is this kind of tangled thicket that is called a maquis. They are made up of different kinds of trees and shrubs, so crowded and mingled together at the caprice of nature that only with an ax in hand can a man open a passage through them, and maquis are frequently seen so thick and bushy that the wild sheep themselves cannot penetrate them.

If you have killed a man, go into the maquis of Portovecchio. With a good gun and plenty of powder and balls, you can live there in safety. Do not forget a brown cloak furnished with a hood, which will serve you for both cover and mattress. The shepherds will give you chestnuts, milk, and cheese, and you will have nothing to fear from justice nor the relatives of the dead except when it is necessary for you to descend to the city to replenish your ammunition.

When I was in Corsica in 18——, Mateo Falcone had his house half a league from this maquis. He was rich enough for that country, living in noble style—that is to say, doing nothing—on the income from his flocks, which the shepherds, who are a kind of nomads, lead to pasture here and there on the mountains. When I saw this, two years after the event that I am about to relate, he appeared to me to be about fifty years old or more. Picture to yourself a man, small but robust, with curly hair, black as jet, an aquiline nose, thin lips, large, restless eyes, and a complexion the color of tanned leather. His skill as a marksman was considered extraordinary even in his country, where good shots are so common. For example, Mateo would never fire at a sheep with buckshot; but at a hundred and twenty paces, he would drop it with a ball in the head or shoulder, as he chose. He used his arms as easily at night as during the day. I was told this feat of his skill, which will, perhaps, seem impossible to those who have not traveled in Corsica. A lighted candle was placed at eighty paces, behind a paper transparency about the size of a plate. He would take aim, then the candle would be extinguished, and, at the end of a moment, in the most complete darkness, he would fire and hit the paper three times out of four.

With such a transcendent accomplishment, Mateo Falcone had acquired a great reputation. He was said to be as good a friend as he was a dangerous enemy; accommodating and charitable, he lived at peace with all the world in the district of Portovecchio. But it is said of him that in Corte, where he had married his wife, he had disembarrassed himself very vigorously of a rival who was considered as redoubtable in war as in love; at least, a certain gunshot which surprised this rival as he was shaving before a little mirror hung in his window was attributed to Mateo. The affair was smoothed over and Mateo was married. His wife, Giuseppa, had given him at first three daughters (which infuriated him), and finally a son, whom he named Fortunato, and who became the hope of his family, the inheritor of the name. The daughters were well married: their father could count at need on the poniards and carbines of his sons-in-law. The son was only ten years old, but he already gave promise of fine attributes.

On a certain day in autumn, Mateo set out at an early hour with his wife to visit one of his flocks in a clearing of the maquis. The little Fortunato wanted to go with them, but the clearing was too far away; moreover, it was necessary someone should stay to watch the house; therefore the father refused: it will be seen whether or not he had reason to repent.

He had been gone some hours, and the little Fortunato was tranquilly stretched out in the sun, looking at the blue mountains, and thinking that the next Sunday he was going to dine in the city with his uncle, the Caporal,[1] when he was suddenly interrupted in his meditations by the firing of a musket. He got up and turned to that side of the plain whence the noise came. Other shots followed, fired at irregular intervals, and each time nearer; at last, in the path which led from the plain to Mateo's house, appeared a man wearing the pointed hat of the mountaineers, bearded, covered with rags, and dragging himself along with difficulty by the support of his gun. He had just received a wound in his thigh.

This man was an outlaw, who, having gone to the town by night to buy powder, had fallen on the way into an ambuscade of Corsican light infantry. After a vigorous defense he was fortunate in making his retreat, closely followed and firing from rock to rock. But he was only a little in advance of the soldiers, and his wound prevented him from gaining the maquis before being overtaken.

He approached Fortunato and said: "You are the son of Mateo Falcone?"—"Yes."

"I am Gianetto Saupiero. I am followed by the yellow-collars.[2] Hide me, for I can go no farther."

"And what will my father say if I hide you without his permission?"

"He will say that you have done well."

"How do you know?"

"Hide me quickly; they are coming."

"Wait till my father gets back."

"How can I wait? *Maledizione!* They will be here in five minutes. Come, hide me, or I will kill you."

Fortunato answered him with the utmost coolness:

"Your gun is empty, and there are no more cartridges in your belt."

"I have my stiletto."

"But can you run as fast as I can?"

He gave a leap and put himself out of reach.

"You are not the son of Mateo Falcone! Will you then let me be captured before your house?"

The child appeared moved.

"What will you give me if I hide you?" said he, coming nearer.

The outlaw felt in a leather pocket that hung from his belt, and took out a five-franc piece, which he had doubtless saved to buy ammunition with. Fortunato smiled at the sight of the silver piece; he snatched it, and said to Gianetto:

"Fear nothing."

Immediately he made a great hole in a pile of hay that was near the

---

[1] *Caporal*: civic official.
[2] *yellow-collars:* slang for policemen.

house. Gianetto crouched down in it and the child covered him in such a way that he could breathe without it being possible to suspect that the hay concealed a man. He bethought himself further, and, with the subtlety of a tolerably ingenious savage, placed a cat and her kittens on the pile, that it might not appear to have been recently disturbed. Then, noticing the traces of blood on the path near the house, he covered them carefully with dust, and, that done, he again stretched himself out in the sun with the greatest tranquillity.

A few moments afterwards, six men in brown uniforms with yellow collars, and commanded by an Adjutant, were before Mateo's door. This Adjutant was a distant relative of Falcone's. (In Corsica the degrees of relationship are followed much further than elsewhere.) His name was Tiodoro Gamba; he was an active man, much dreaded by the outlaws, several of whom he had already entrapped.

"Good day, little cousin," said he, approaching Fortunato; "how tall you have grown. Have you seen a man go past here just now?"

"Oh! I am not yet so tall as you, my cousin," replied the child with a simple air.

"You soon will be. But haven't you seen a man go by here, tell me?"

"If I have seen a man go by?"

"Yes, a man with a pointed hat of black velvet, and a vest embroidered with red and yellow."

"A man with a pointed hat, and a vest embroidered with red and yellow?"

"Yes, answer quickly, and don't repeat my questions!"

"This morning the curé passed before our door on his horse Piero. He asked me how papa was, and I answered him——"

"Ah, you little scoundrel, you are playing sly! Tell me quickly which way Gianetto went? We are looking for him, and I am sure he took this path."

"Who knows?"

"Who knows? It is I know that you have seen him."

"Can anyone see who passes when they are asleep?"

"You were not asleep, rascal; the shooting woke you up."

"Then you believe, cousin, that your guns make so much noise? My father's carbine has the advantage of them."

"The devil take you, you cursed little scapegrace! I am certain that you have seen Gianetto. Perhaps, even, you have hidden him. Come, comrades, go into the house and see if our man is there. He could only go on one foot, and the knave has too much good sense to try to reach the maquis limping like that. Moreover, the bloody tracks stop here."

"And what will papa say?" asked Fortunato with a sneer. "What will he say if he knows that his house has been entered while he was away?"

"You rascal," said the Adjutant, taking him by the ear, "do you know

that I can easily make you change your tone? Perhaps you will speak differently after I have given you twenty blows with the flat of my sword."

Fortunato continued to sneer.

"My father is Mateo Falcone," said he with emphasis.

"You little scamp, you know very well that I can carry you off to Corte
or to Bastia. I will make you lie in a dungeon, on straw, with your feet
in shackles, and I will have you guillotined if you don't tell me where
Gianetto is."

The child burst out laughing at this ridiculous menace. He repeated:

"My father is Mateo Falcone."

"Adjutant," said one of the soldiers in a low voice, "let us have no quarrels with Mateo."

Gamba appeared evidently embarrassed. He spoke in an undertone with
the soldiers who had already visited the house. This was not a very long
operation, for the cabin of a Corsican consists only of a single square
room, furnished with a table, some benches, chests, housekeeping utensils
and those of the chase. In the meantime, little Fortunato petted his cat
and seemed to take a wicked enjoyment in the confusion of the soldiers and
of his cousin.

One of the men approached the pile of hay. He saw the cat, and gave the
pile a careless thrust with his bayonet, shrugging his shoulders as if he felt
that his precaution was ridiculous. Nothing moved; the boy's face betrayed
not the slightest emotion.

The Adjutant and his troop were cursing their luck. Already they were
looking in the direction of the plain, as if disposed to return by the way
they had come, when their chief, convinced that menaces would produce no
impression on Falcone's son, determined to make a last effort, and try the
effect of caresses and presents.

"My little cousin," said he, "you are a very wide-awake little fellow. You
will get along. But you are playing a naughty game with me; and if I wasn't
afraid of making trouble for my cousin Mateo, the devil take me, but I
would carry you off with me."

"Bah!"

"But when my cousin comes back I shall tell him about this, and he will
whip you till the blood comes for having told such lies."

"You don't say so!"

"You will see. But hold on!—be a good boy and I will give you something."

"Cousin, let me give you some advice: if you wait much longer Gianetto
will be in the maquis and it will take a smarter man than you to follow
him."

The Adjutant took from his pocket a silver watch worth about ten crowns, and noticing that Fortunato's eyes sparkled at the sight of it, said, holding the watch by the end of its steel chain:

"Rascal! you would like to have such a watch as that hung round your neck, wouldn't you, and to walk in the streets of Portovecchio proud as a peacock? People would ask you what time it was, and you would say: 'Look at my watch.' "

"When I am grown up, my uncle, the Caporal, will give me a watch."

"Yes; but your uncle's little boy has one already; not so fine as this, either. But then, he is younger than you."

The child sighed.

"Well! Would you like this watch, little cousin?"

Fortunato, casting sidelong glances at the watch, resembled a cat that has been given a whole chicken. It feels that it is being made sport of, and does not dare to use its claws; from time to time it turns its eyes away so as not to be tempted, licking its jaws all the while, and has the appearance of saying to its master, "How cruel your joke is!"

However, the Adjutant seemed in earnest in offering his watch. Fortunato did not reach out his hand for it, but said with a bitter smile:

"Why do you make fun of me?"

"Good God! I am not making fun of you. Only tell me where Gianetto is and the watch is yours."

Fortunato smiled incredulously, and fixing his black eyes on those of the Adjutant tried to read there the faith he ought to have had in his words.

"May I lose my epaulettes," cried the Adjutant, "if I do not give you the watch on this condition. These comrades are witnesses; I cannot deny it."

While speaking he gradually held the watch nearer till it almost touched the child's pale face, which plainly showed the struggle that was going on in his soul between covetousness and respect for hospitality. His breast swelled with emotion; he seemed about to suffocate. Meanwhile the watch was slowly swaying and turning, sometimes brushing against his cheek. Finally, his right hand was gradually stretched toward it; the ends of his fingers touched it; then its whole weight was in his hand, the Adjutant still keeping hold of the chain. The face was light blue; the cases newly burnished. In the sunlight it seemed to be all on fire. The temptation was too great. Fortunato raised his left hand and pointed over his shoulder with his thumb at the hay against which he was reclining. The Adjutant understood him at once. He dropped the end of the chain and Fortunato felt himself the sole possessor of the watch. He sprang up with the agility of a deer and stood ten feet from the pile, which the soldiers began at once to overturn.

There was a movement in the hay, and a bloody man with a sword in his hand appeared. He tried to rise to his feet, but his stiffened leg would not permit it and he fell. The Adjutant at once grappled with him and took away his stiletto. He was immediately secured, notwithstanding his resistance.

Gianetto, lying on the earth and bound like a fagot, turned his head toward Fortunato, who had approached.

"Son of ——!" said he, with more contempt than anger.

The child threw him the silver piece which he had received, feeling that he no longer deserved it; but the outlaw paid no attention to the movement, and with great coolness said to the Adjutant:

"My dear Gamba, I cannot walk; you will be obliged to carry me to the city."

"Just now you could run faster than a buck," answered the cruel captor; "but be at rest. I am so pleased to have you that I would carry you a league on my back without fatigue. Besides, comrade, we are going to make a litter for you with your cloak and some branches, and at the Crespoli farm we shall find horses."

"Good," said the prisoner. "You will also put a little straw on your litter that I may be more comfortable."

While some of the soldiers were occupied in making a kind of stretcher out of some chestnut boughs and the rest were dressing Gianetto's wound, Mateo Falcone and his wife suddenly appeared at a turn in the path that led to the maquis. The woman was staggering under the weight of an enormous sack of chestnuts, while her husband was sauntering along, carrying one gun in his hands, while another was slung across his shoulders, for it is unworthy of a man to carry other burdens than his arms.

At the sight of the soldiers Mateo's first thought was that they had come to arrest him. But why this thought? Had he then some quarrels with justice? No. He enjoyed a good reputation. He was said to have a particularly good name, but he was a Corsican and a highlander, and there are few Corsican highlanders who, in scrutinizing their memory, cannot find some peccadillo, such as a gunshot, dagger thrust, or similar trifles. Mateo more than others had a clear conscience; for more than ten years he had not pointed his carbine at a man, but he was always prudent, and put himself into a position to make a good defense if necessary. "Wife," said he to Giuseppa, "put down the sack and hold yourself ready."

She obeyed at once. He gave her the gun that was slung across his shoulders, which would have bothered him, and, cocking the one he held in his hands, advanced slowly toward the house, walking among the trees that bordered the road, ready at the least hostile demonstration, to hide behind the largest, whence he could fire from under cover. His wife followed closely behind, holding his reserve weapon and his cartridge box. The duty of a good housekeeper, in case of a fight, is to load her husband's carbines.

On the other side the Adjutant was greatly troubled to see Mateo advance in this manner, with cautious steps, his carbine raised, and his finger on the trigger.

"If by chance," thought he, "Mateo should be related to Gianetto, or if he should be his friend and wish to defend him, the contents of his two guns would arrive among us as certainly as a letter in the post; and if he should see me, notwithstanding the relationship!"

In this perplexity he took a bold step. It was to advance alone toward Mateo and tell him of the affair while accosting him as an old acquaintance, but the short space that separated him from Mateo seemed terribly long.

"Hello! old comrade," cried he. "How do you do, my good fellow? It is I, Gamba, your cousin."

Without answering a word, Mateo stopped, and in proportion as the other spoke, slowly raised the muzzle of his gun so that it was pointing upward when the Adjutant joined him.

"Good-day, brother," said the Adjutant, holding out his hand. "It is a long time since I have seen you."

"Good-day, brother."

"I stopped while passing, to say good-day to you and to cousin Pepa here. We have had a long journey today, but have no reason to complain, for we have captured a famous prize. We have just seized Gianetto Saupiero."

"God be praised!" cried Giuseppa. "He stole a milch goat from us last week."

These words reassured Gamba.

"Poor devil!" said Mateo. "He was hungry."

"The villain fought like a lion," continued the Adjutant, a little mortified. "He killed one of my soldiers, and not content with that, broke Caporal Chardon's arm; but that matters little, he is only a Frenchman. Then, too, he was so well hidden that the devil couldn't have found him. Without my little cousin Fortunato, I should never have discovered him."

"Fortunato!" cried Mateo.

"Fortunato!" repeated Giuseppa.

"Yes, Gianetto was hidden under the haypile yonder, but my little cousin showed me the trick. I shall tell his uncle, the Caporal, that he may send him a fine present for his trouble. Both his name and yours will be in the report that I shall send to the Attorney-General."

"*Maledizione!*" said Mateo in a low voice.

They had rejoined the detachment. Gianetto was already lying on the litter ready to set out. When he saw Mateo and Gamba in company he smiled a strange smile; then, turning his head toward the door of the house, he spat on the sill, saying:

"House of a traitor."

Only a man determined to die would dare pronounce the word "traitor" to Falcone. A good blow with the stiletto, which there would be no need of repeating, would have immediately paid the insult. However, Mateo made no other movement than to place his hand on his forehead like a man who is dazed.

Fortunato had gone into the house when his father arrived, but now he reappeared with a bowl of milk which he handed with downcast eyes to Gianetto.

"Get away from me!" cried the outlaw, in a loud voice. Then, turning to one of the soldiers, he said:

"Comrade, give me a drink."

The soldier placed his gourd in his hands, and the prisoner drank the water handed to him by a man with whom he had just exchanged bullets. He then asked them to tie his hands across his breast instead of behind his back.

"I like," said he, "to lie at my ease."

They hastened to satisfy him; then the Adjutant gave the signal to start, said adieu to Mateo, who did not respond, and descended with rapid steps toward the plain.

Nearly ten minutes elapsed before Mateo spoke. The child looked with restless eyes, now at his mother, now at his father, who was leaning on his gun and gazing at him with an expression of concentrated rage.

"You begin well," said Mateo at last with a calm voice, but frightful to one who knew the man.

"Oh, father!" cried the boy, bursting into tears, and making a forward movement as if to throw himself on his knees. But Mateo cried, "Away from me!"

The little fellow stopped and sobbed, immovable, a few feet from his father.

Giuseppa drew near. She had just discovered the watch chain, the end of which was hanging out of Fortunato's jacket.

"Who gave you that watch?" demanded she in a severe tone.

"My cousin, the Adjutant."

Falcone seized the watch and smashed it in a thousand pieces against a rock.

"Wife," said he, "is this my child?"

Giuseppa's cheeks turned a brick red.

"What are you saying, Mateo? Do you know to whom you speak?"

"Very well, this child is the first of his race to commit treason."

Fortunato's sobs and gasps redoubled as Falcone kept his lynx-eyes upon him. Then he struck the earth with his gunstock, shouldered the weapon, and turned in the direction of the maquis, calling to Fortunato to follow. The boy obeyed. Giuseppa hastened after Mateo and seized his arm.

"He is your son," said she with a trembling voice, fastening her black eyes on those of her husband to read what was going on in his heart.

"Leave me alone," said Mateo. "I am his father."

Giuseppa embraced her son, and bursting into tears entered the house. She threw herself on her knees before an image of the Virgin and prayed ardently. In the meanwhile Falcone walked some two hundred paces along the path and only stopped when he reached a little ravine which he descended. He tried the earth with the butt end of his carbine, and found it soft and easy to dig. The place seemed to be convenient for his design.

"Fortunato, go close to that big rock there."

The child did as he was commanded, then he kneeled.

"Say your prayers."

"Oh, father, father, do not kill me!"

"Say your prayers!" repeated Mateo in a terrible voice.

The boy, stammering and sobbing, recited the Pater and the Credo. At the end of each prayer the father loudly answered, "Amen!"

"Are those all the prayers you know?"

"Oh! father, I know the Ave Maria and the litany that my aunt taught me."

"It is very long, but no matter."

The child finished the litany in a scarcely audible tone.

"Are you finished?"

"Oh! my father, have mercy! Pardon me! I will never do so again. I will beg my cousin the Caporal to pardon Gianetto."

He was still speaking. Mateo raised his gun, and, taking aim, said:

"May God pardon you!"

The boy made a desperate effort to rise and grasp his father's knees, but there was not time. Mateo fired and Fortunato fell dead.

Without casting a glance on the body, Mateo returned to the house for a spade with which to bury his son. He had gone but a few steps when he met Giuseppa, who, alarmed by the shot, was hastening hither.

"What have you done?" cried she.

"Justice."

"Where is he?"

"In the ravine. I am going to bury him. He died a Christian. I shall have a mass said for him. Have my son-in-law, Tiodoro Bianchi, sent for to come and live with us."

Two Poems

TYRTAEUS OF SPARTA

Courage: heros mortuus: heros vivus

I would not say anything for a man nor take account of him
    for any speed of his feet or wrestling skill he might have,
not if he had the size of a Cyclops and strength to go with it,
    not if he could outrun Boreas, the North Wind of Thrace,
not if he were more handsome and gracefully formed than Tithonos,
    or had more riches than Midas had, or Kinyras too,
not if he were more of a king than Tantalid Pelops,
    or had the power of speech and persuasion Adrastos had,
not if he had all splendors except for a fighting spirit.
    For no man ever proves himself a good man in war
unless he can endure to face the blood and the slaughter,
    go close against the enemy and fight with his hands.
Here is courage, mankind's finest possession, here is
    the noblest prize that a young man can endeavor to win,
and it is a good thing his city and all the people share with him
    when a man plants his feet and stands in the foremost spears
relentlessly, all thought of foul flight completely forgotten,
    and has well trained his heart to be steadfast and to endure,
and with words encourages the man who is stationed beside him.
    Here is a man who proves himself to be valiant in war.
With a sudden rush he turns to flight the rugged battalions
    of the enemy, and sustains the beating waves of assault.

And he who so falls among the champions and loses his sweet life,
    so blessing with honor his city, his father, and all his people,
with wounds in his chest, where the spear that he was facing has transfixed
    that massive guard of his shield, and gone through his breastplate as well,
why, such a man is lamented alike by the young and the elders,
    and all his city goes into mourning and grieves for his loss.
His tomb is pointed to with pride, and so are his children,
    and his children's children, and afterward all the race that is his.
His shining glory is never forgotten, his name is remembered,
    and he becomes an immortal, though he lies under the ground,
when one who was a brave man has been killed by the furious War God
    standing his ground and fighting hard for his children and land.
But if he escapes the doom of death, the destroyer of bodies,
    and wins his battle, and bright renown for the work of his spear,
all men give place to him alike, the youth and the elders,
    and much joy comes his way before he goes down to the dead.
Aging, he has reputation among his citizens. No one
    tries to interfere with his honors or all he deserves;
all men withdraw before his presence, and yield their seats to him,
    the youth, and the men his age, and even those older than he.
Thus a man should endeavor to reach this high place of courage
    with all his heart, and, so trying, never be backward in war.

To the Soldiers, After a Defeat

Now, since you are the seed of Herakles the invincible,
    courage! Zeus has not yet turned away from us. Do not
fear the multitude of their men, nor run away from them.
    Each man should bear his shield straight at the foremost ranks
and make his heart a thing full of hate, and hold the black flying
    spirits of death as dear as he holds the flash of the sun.
You know what havoc is the work of the painful War God,
    you have learned well how things go in exhausting war,
for you have been with those who ran and with the pursuers,
    O young men, you have had as much of both as you want.
Those who, standing their ground and closing their ranks together,
    endure the onset at close quarters and fight in the front,
they lose fewer men. They also protect the army behind them.

Once they flinch, the spirit of the whole army falls apart.
And no man could count over and tell all the number of evils,
  all that can come to a man, once he gives way to disgrace.
For once a man reverses and runs in the terror of battle,
  he offers his back, a tempting mark to spear from behind,
and it is a shameful sight when a dead man lies in the dust there,
  driven through from behind by the stroke of an enemy spear.
No, no, let him take a wide stance and stand up strongly against them,
  digging both heels in the ground, biting his lip with his teeth,
covering thighs and legs beneath, his chest and his shoulders
  under the hollowed-out protection of his broad shield,
while in his right hand he brandishes the powerful war-spear,
  and shakes terribly the crest high above his helm.
Our man should be disciplined in the work of the heavy fighter,
  and not stand out from the missiles when he carries a shield,
but go right up and fight at close quarters and, with his long spear
  or short sword, thrust home and strike his enemy down.
Let him fight toe to toe and shield against shield hard driven,
  crest against crest and helmet on helmet, chest against chest;
let him close hard and fight it out with his opposite foeman,
  holding tight to the hilt of his sword, or to his long spear.
And you, O light-armed fighters, from shield to shield of your fellows
  dodge for protection and keep steadily throwing great stones,
and keep on pelting the enemy with your javelins, only
  remember always to stand near your own heavy-armed men.

Courage and *To the Soldiers, After a Defeat* by Tyrtaeus of Sparta: Reprinted from *Greek Lyrics* by Richmond Lattimore, by permission of The University of Chicago Press. Copyright 1940, 1955 and 1960 by Richmond Lattimore.

Russia 1812

VICTOR HUGO

The snow fell, and its power was multiplied.
For the first time the Eagle bowed its head—
dark days! Slowly the Emperor returned—
behind him Moscow! Its onion domes still burned.
The snow rained down in blizzards—rained and froze.
Past each white waste a further white waste rose.
None recognized the captains or the flags.
Yesterday the Grand Army, today its dregs!
No one could tell the vanguard from the flanks.
The snow! The hurt men struggled from the ranks,
hid in the bellies of dead horse, in stacks
of shattered caissons. By the bivouacs,
one saw the picket dying at his post,
still standing in his saddle, white with frost,
the stone lips frozen to the bugle's mouth!
Bullets and grapeshot mingled with the snow,
that hailed . . . The Guard, surprised at shivering, march
in a dream now; ice rimes the gray mustache.
The snow falls, always snow! The driving mire
submerges; men, trapped in that white empire,
have no more bread and march on barefoot—gaps!
They were no longer living men and troops,
but a dream drifting in a fog, a mystery,
mourners parading under the black sky.
The solitude, vast, terrible to the eye,
was like a mute avenger everywhere,
as snowfall, floating through the quiet air,
buried the huge army in a huge shroud.
Could anyone leave this kingdom? A crowd—
each man, obsessed with dying, was alone.
Men slept—and died! The beaten mob sludged on,

ditching the guns to burn their carriages.
Two foes. The North, the Czar. The North was worse.
In hollows where the snow was piling up,
one saw whole regiments fallen asleep.
Attila's dawn, Cannaes of Hannibal![1]
The army marching to its funeral!
Litters, wounded, the dead, deserters—swarm,
crushing the bridges down to cross a stream.
They went to sleep ten thousand, woke up four.
Ney,[2] bringing up the former army's rear,
hacked his horse loose from three disputing Cossacks . . .
All night, the *qui vive?* The alert! Attacks;
retreats! White ghosts would wrench away our guns,
or we would see dim, terrible squadrons,
circles of steel, whirlpools of savages,
rush sabering through the camp like dervishes.
And in this way, whole armies died at night.

The Emperor was there, standing—he saw.
This oak already trembling from the axe,
watched his glories drop from him branch by branch:
chiefs, soldiers. Each one had his turn and chance—
they died! Some lived. These still believed his star,
and kept their watch. They loved the man of war,
this small man with his hands behind his back,
whose shadow, moving to and fro, was black
behind the lighted tent. Still believing, they
accused their destiny of *lèse-majesté.*
His misfortune had mounted on their back.
The man of glory shook. Cold stupefied
him, then suddenly he felt terrified.
Being without belief, he turned to God:
"God of armies, is this the end?" he cried.
And then at last the expiation came,
as he heard some one call him by his name,
some one half-lost in shadow, who said, "No,
Napoleon." Napoleon understood,
restless, bareheaded, leaden, as he stood
before his butchered legions in the snow.

---

[1] *Cannaes of Hannibal*: In 216 B.C., the Roman army was badly defeated by Hannibal at the village of Cannae.
[2] *Ney*: one of Napoleon's chief generals.

Master and Man

LEO TOLSTOY

Chapter I

IT happened in the seventies, in winter, on the day after St. Nicholas'
Day.[1] There was a holiday in the parish, and the village landowner and
second-guild merchant, Vasili Andreyitch Brekhunof, could not be absent,
as he had to attend church—he was a churchwarden—and receive and entertain friends and acquaintances at home.

But at last all the guests were gone, and Vasili Andreyitch began preparations for a drive over to see a neighboring landed proprietor about
buying from him the forest for which they had been bargaining this long
while. He was in great haste to go, so as to forestall the town merchants,
who might snatch away this profitable purchase.

The youthful landowner asked ten thousand rubles for the forest, simply
because Vasili Andreyitch offered seven thousand. In reality, seven thousand
was but a third of the real worth of the forest. Vasili Andreyitch might,
perhaps, even now make the bargain, because the forest stood in his district, and by an old standing agreement between him and the other village
merchants, no one of them competed in another's territory. But Vasili Andreyitch had learned that the timber-merchants from the capital town of the
province intended to bid for the Goryatchkin forest, and he decided to go
at once and conclude the bargain. Accordingly, as soon as the feast was
over, he took seven hundred rubles of his own from the strong box, added to
them twenty-three hundred belonging to the church, so as to make three

[1] *St. Nicholas' Day*: St. Nicholas' Day is December 6 (Old Style).

thousand, and, after carefully counting the whole, he put the money into his pocket-book and made haste to be gone.

Nikita, the laborer, the only one of Vasili Andreyitch's men who was not drunk that day, ran to harness the horse. He was not drunk on this occasion, because he had been a drunkard, and now since the last day before the fast, when he spent his coat and leather boots in drink, he had sworn off and for two months had not tasted liquor. He was not drinking even now, in spite of the temptation arising from the universal consumption of alcohol during the first two days of the holiday.

Nikita was a fifty-year-old peasant from a neighboring village; no manager, as folk said of him, but one who lived most of his life with other people, and not at his own home. He was esteemed everywhere for his industry, dexterity, and strength, and still more for his kindliness and pleasantness. But he never lived long in one place, because twice a year, or even oftener, he took to drinking; and at such times, besides spending all he had, he became turbulent and quarrelsome. Vasili Andreyitch had dismissed him several times, and afterward engaged him again, valuing his honesty and kindness to animals, but chiefly his cheapness. The merchant did not pay Nikita eighty rubles, the worth of such a man, but forty; and even that he paid without regular account, in small installments, and mostly not in cash, but in high-priced goods from his own shop.

Nikita's wife, Marfa, a vigorous and once beautiful woman, carried on the home, with a boy almost fully grown and two girls. She never urged Nikita to live at home: first, because she had lived for about twenty years with a cooper, a peasant from another village, who lodged with them; and secondly, because, although she treated her husband as she pleased when he was sober, she feared him like fire when he was drinking.

Once, when drunk at home, Nikita, apparently to revenge himself for all the submissiveness he had shown his wife when sober, broke open her box, took her best clothes, and, seizing an ax, cut to shreds all her dresses and garments. All the wages Nikita earned went to his wife, and he made no objection to this arrangement. Thus it was that Marfa, two days before the holiday, came to Vasili Andreyitch, and got from him wheat flour, tea, sugar, and a pint of vodka—about three rubles' worth in all—and five rubles in cash; and she thanked him as for a special favor, although, at the lowest figure, Vasili Andreyitch owed twenty rubles.

"What agreement did I make with you?" said Vasili Andreyitch to Nikita. "If you want anything, take it; you will work it out. I am not like other folks, with their delays, and accounts, and fines. We are dealing straightforwardly. You work for me, and I'll stand by you."

Talking in this way, Vasili Andreyitch was honestly convinced of his beneficence to Nikita; and he was so plausible that all those who depended on him for their money, beginning with Nikita, confirmed him in this conviction that he was not only not cheating them, but was doing them a service.

"I understand, Vasili Andreyitch; I do my best, I try to do as I would for my own father. I understand all right," answered Nikita, though he understood very well that Vasili Andreyitch was cheating him; at the same time he felt that it was useless to try to get the accounts cleared up. While there was nowhere else to go, he must stay where he was, and take what he could get.

Now, on receiving his master's orders to put the horse in, Nikita, willingly and cheerfully as always, and with a firm and easy stride, stepped to the cart-shed, took down from the nail the heavy, tasseled leather bridle, and, jingling the rings of the bit, went to the closed stable where by himself stood the horse which Vasili Andreyitch had ordered harnessed.

"Well, silly, were you lonely?" said Nikita, in answer to the soft, welcoming whinny which greeted him from the stallion, a fairly good dark bay of medium height, with sloping quarters, who stood solitary in his stall. "No, no! Quiet, quiet, there's plenty of time! Let me give you a drink first," he went on, addressing the horse as if he were speaking to a creature which could understand human speech. With the skirt of his coat he swept down the horse's broad, double-ridged back, rough and dusty as it was; then he put the bridle on the handsome young head, arranged his ears and mane, and throwing off the rope, led him away to drink.

Picking his way out of the dung-cumbered stall, Mukhortui began to plunge, making play with his hind foot, pretending that he wanted to kick Nikita, who was hurrying him to the well.

"Now, then, behave yourself, you rogue," said Nikita, knowing how careful Mukhortui was that the hind foot should only just touch his greasy sheepskin coat, but do no hurt; and Nikita himself especially enjoyed this sport.

After drinking the cold water, the horse drew a deep sigh, and moved his wet, strong lips from which transparent drops fell into the trough; then, after standing a moment as if in thought, he suddenly gave a loud neigh.

"If you want no more, you needn't take it. Well, let it be at that; but don't ask again for more," said Nikita, with perfect seriousness, emphasizing to Mukhortui the consequences of his behavior. Then he briskly ran back to the shed, pulling the rein on the gay young horse, who lashed out all the way along the yard.

No other men were about, except a stranger to the place, the husband of the cook, who had come for the holiday.

"Go and ask, there's a good fellow, which sledge is wanted, the wide one or the little one," said Nikita to him.

The cook's husband went into the high-perched, iron-roofed house, and soon returned with the answer that the small one was ordered. By this time Nikita had put on the brass-studded saddle, and carrying in one hand the light, painted yoke, with the other hand he led the horse toward the two sledges which stood under the shed.

"All right, the small one it is," said he, backing into the shafts the intelligent horse, which all the time pretended to bite at him; and, with the help of the cook's husband, he began to harness.

When all was nearly ready, and only the reins needed attention, Nikita sent the cook's husband to the shed for straw and to the storehouse for some sacking.

"That's great! There, there; don't bristle up so!" said Nikita, squeezing into the sledge the freshly thrashed oat straw which the cook's husband had brought. "Now give me the sacking, while we spread it out, and put the cloth over it. That's all right, just the thing, comfortable to sit on," said he, doing that which he was talking about, and making the cloth tight over the straw all round.

"Thanks, my dear fellow," said Nikita to the cook's husband. "When two work, it's done quicker."

Then, disentangling the leather reins, the ends of which were brought together and tied on a ring, he took the driver's seat on the sledge, and shook up the good horse, who stirred himself, eager to make across the frozen refuse that littered the yard, toward the gate.

"Uncle Mikit, uncle!" came a shout behind him, from a seven-year-old boy in a black fur cloak, new white, felt boots, and warm cap, who came hurrying out from the entrance-hall toward the yard. "Put me in?" he asked in a shrill voice, buttoning his little coat as he ran.

"All right, come, my dove," said Nikita; and, stopping the sledge, he put in the master's son, whose face grew radiant with joy, and drove out into the road.

It was three o'clock, and cold—about ten degrees of frost—gloomy and windy. Half the sky was shrouded by a low-hanging dark cloud. In the yard it seemed quiet, but in the street the wind was more noticeable. The snow blew down from the roof of the barn close by, and at the corner by the baths flew whirling round. Nikita had scarcely driven out and turned round by the front door, when Vasili Andreyitch, too, with a cigarette in his mouth, wearing a sheepskin overcoat tightly fastened by a girdle placed low, came out from the entrance-hall. He strode down the trampled snow of the high steps, which creaked under his leather-trimmed felt boots,

and stopped. Drawing in one final puff of smoke, he flung down his cigarette and trampled it underfoot; then, breathing out the smoke through his
mustaches and critically surveying the horse, he began to turn in the corners of his overcoat collar on both sides of his ruddy face, clean-shaven,
except for a mustache, so as to keep the fur clear from the moisture of his
breath.

"See there! What a funny little rascal! He's all ready!" said he, as he
caught sight of his little pale, thin son in the sledge. Vasili Andreyitch
was excited by the wine he had taken with his guests, and was therefore
more than usually satisfied with everything which belonged to him, and with
everything he did. The sight of his son, whom he always in his own mind
thought of as his heir, now caused him great satisfaction. He looked at
him, and as he did so he smirked and showed his long teeth.

His wife, a pale and meager woman, about to become a mother, stood
behind him in the entrance-hall with a woolen shawl so wrapped about her
head and shoulders that only her eyes could be seen.

"Would it not be better to take Nikita with you?" she asked, timidly
stepping out from the door.

Vasili Andreyitch made no reply, but merely spat, scowling angrily at
her words, which evidently were disagreeable to him.

"You have money with you," the wife continued, in the same plaintive
voice. "What if the weather should get worse! Be careful, for God's sake."

"Do you think I don't know the road, that I need a guide?" retorted
Vasili Andreyitch, with that affected compression of the lips with which he
ordinarily addressed dealers in the market, and bringing out every syllable
with extraordinary precision, as if he valued his own speech.

"Really, I would take him. I beg of you, for God's sake!" repeated his
wife, folding her shawl closer.

"Just listen! She sticks to it like a leaf in the bath! . . . Why, where
must I take him to?"

"Well, Vasili Andreyitch, I'm ready," said Nikita, cheerfully. "If I'm
away, there are only the horses to be fed," he added, turning to his
mistress.

"I'll look after that, Nikitushka; I'll tell Semyon," answered the mistress.

"Well, then, shall I come, Vasili Andreyitch?" asked Nikita, waiting.

"It seems we must have some regard for the old woman. But if you
come, go and put on something warmer," said Vasili Andreyitch, smiling
once more, and winking at Nikita's sheepskin coat, which was torn under
the arms and down the back, and soiled and patched and frayed into
fringes round the skirts.

"Hey, dear soul, come and hold the horse awhile!" shouted Nikita to
the cook's husband, in the yard.

"I'll hold him myself," said the little boy, taking his half-frozen red hands out of his pockets, and seizing the cold leather reins.

"Only don't be too long putting your best coat on! Be quick!" shouted Vasili Andreyitch, grinning at Nikita.

"In a moment, Father, Vasili Andreyitch!" said Nikita, and, with his trousers stuffed into his old patched felt boots, he swiftly ran down the yard to the laborers' quarters.

"Here, Arinushka, give me my coat off the oven. I have to go with the master!" said Nikita, hastening into the room, and taking his girdle down from the nail.

The cook, who had just finished her after-dinner nap, and was about to get ready the samovar for her husband, turned cheerily to Nikita, and, catching his haste, moved about quickly, just as he was doing, took the well-worn woolen khalat off the oven, where it was drying, and shook and rubbed it.

"There now, you'll have a chance to spread and have a good time with your husband here," said Nikita to the cook; always, as part of his good-natured politeness, ready to say something to anyone whom he came across.

Then, putting round himself the narrow shrunken girdle, he drew in his breath and tightened it about his spare body as much as he could.

"There," he said afterward, addressing himself, not to the cook, but to the girdle, while tucking the ends under his belt, "this way, you won't jump out." Then, working his shoulders up and down to get his arms loose, he put on the coat, again stretching his back to free his arms, and poked up under his sleeves and took his mittens from the shelf.

"Now, we're all right."

"You ought to change your boots," said the cook; "those boots are very bad."

Nikita stopped, as if remembering something.

"Yes, I ought. . . . But it will go as it is; it's not far."

And he ran out into the yard.

"Won't you be cold, Nikitushka?" said the mistress, as he came up to the sledge.

"Why should I be cold? It is quite warm," answered Nikita, arranging the straw in the fore part of the sledge, so as to bring it over his legs, and stowing under it the whip which the good horse would not need.

Vasili Andreyitch had already taken his place in the sledge, almost filling up the whole of the curved back with the bulk of his body wrapped in two shubas; and, taking up the reins, he started at once. Nikita jumped in, seating himself in front, to the left, and hanging one leg over the side.

Chapter II

THE good stallion took the sledge along at a brisk pace over the smooth frozen road through the village, the runners creaking faintly as they went.

"Look at him there, hanging on! Give me the whip, Nikita," shouted Vasili Andreyitch, evidently enjoying the sight of his boy holding to the sledge-runners, behind. "I'll give it to you! Run to your mamma, you young dog!"

The boy jumped off. Mukhortui began to pace and then, getting his breath, broke into a trot.

Krestui, the village where Vasili Andreyitch lived, consisted of six houses. Scarcely had they passed the blacksmith's hut, the last in the village, when they suddenly remarked that the wind was much stronger than they had thought. The road was by this time scarcely visible. The tracks of the sledge were instantly covered with snow, and the road was to be distinguished only by the fact that it was higher than anything else. There was a whirl of snow over the fields, and the line where the earth and sky join could not be distinguished. The Telyatin forest, always plainly in sight, loomed dimly through the driving snow-dust. The wind came from the left hand, persistently blowing to one side the mane on Mukhortui's powerful neck, turning away even his knotted tail, and pressing Nikita's high collar—he sat on the windward side—against his face and nose.

"There is no chance of showing his speed, with this snow," said Vasili Andreyitch, proud of his good horse. "I once went to Pashutino with him, and we got there in half an hour."

"What?" said Nikita, who could not hear on account of his collar.

"Pashutino, I said; and he did it in half an hour," shouted Vasili Andreyitch.

"A good horse that, no question," said Nikita.

They became silent. But Vasili Andreyitch wanted to talk.

"Say, I suppose you told your wife not to give any drink to the cooper?" said Vasili Andreyitch in the same loud voice, being perfectly convinced that Nikita must feel flattered, talking with such an important and sensible man as himself, and he was so pleased with his jest that it never entered his head that the subject might be unpleasant to Nikita.

Again the man failed to catch his master's words, the voice being carried away by the wind.

Vasili Andreyitch, in his loud clear voice, repeated the jest about the cooper.

"God help them, Vasili Andreyitch, I don't meddle in these matters. I only hope that she does no harm to the lad; if she does—then God help her!"

"That is right," said Vasili Andreyitch. "Well, are you going to buy a horse in the spring?" Thus he began a new topic of conversation.

"Yes, I must buy one," answered Nikita, turning down his collar, and leaning toward his master. Now the conversation became interesting to him, and he did not wish to lose a word.

"My lad is grown up; he must plow for himself, but now he is hired out all the time," said he.

"Well, then, take the horse with the thin loins; the price will not be high," shouted Vasili Andreyitch, feeling himself excited and consequently eagerly entering into his favorite business of horse-dealing, to which he gave all his intellectual powers.

"You give me fifteen rubles, and I'll buy in the market," said Nikita, who knew that at the highest price the horse which Vasili Andreyitch called "Bezkostretchnui" and wanted to sell him, was not worth more than seven rubles, but would cost him at his master's hands twenty-five; and that meant half a year's wages gone.

"The horse is a good one. I treat you as I would myself. Conscientiously. Brekhunof injures no man. Let me stand the loss, and me only. Honestly," he shouted in the voice which he used in cheating his customers, "a genuine horse."

"As you think," said Nikita, sighing, and convinced that it was useless to listen further, he again drew the collar over his ear and face.

They drove in silence for about half an hour. The wind cut sharply into Nikita's side and arm, where his shuba was torn. He huddled himself up and breathed into his coat-collar, which covered his mouth, and was not wholly cold!

"What do you think; shall we go through Karamuishevo, or keep the straight road?" said Vasili Andreyitch.

The road through Karamuishevo was more frequented and staked on both sides; but it was longer. The straight road was nearer, but it was little used, and either there were no stakes, or they were poor ones left standing covered with snow.

Nikita thought awhile.

"Through Karamuishevo is farther, but it is better going," he said.

"But straight on we have only to be careful not to lose the road in passing the little valley, and then the way is fairly good, sheltered by the forest," said Vasili Andreyitch, who favored the direct road.

"As you wish," replied Nikita, and again he rolled up his collar.

So Vasili Andreyitch took this way, and after driving about half a verst, he came to a place where there was a long oak stake which shook in the wind, and to which a few dry leaves were clinging, and there he turned to the left.

On turning, the wind blew almost directly against them, and the snow showered from on high. Vasili Andreyitch stirred up his horse, and inflated his cheeks, blowing his breath upon his mustaches. Nikita dozed.

They drove thus silently for about ten minutes. Suddenly Vasili Andreyitch began to say something.

"What?" asked Nikita, opening his eyes.

Vasili Andreyitch did not answer, but bent himself about, looking behind them, and then ahead of the horse. The sweat had curled the animal's coat on the groin and neck, and he was going at a walk.

"I say, what's the matter?" repeated Nikita.

"What is the matter?" mocked Vasili Andreyitch, irritated. "I see no stakes. We must be off the road."

"Well, pull up then, and I will find the road," said Nikita and lightly jumping down, he drew out the whip from the straw and started off to the left, from his own side of the sledge.

The snow was not deep that season, so that one could travel anywhere, but in places it was up to one's knee, and got into Nikita's boots. He walked about, feeling with his feet and the whip, but no road was to be found.

"Well?" said Vasili Andreyitch, when Nikita returned to the sledge.

"There is no road on this side. I must try the other."

"There's something dark there in front. Go and see what it is," said Vasili Andreyitch.

Nikita walked ahead; got near the dark patch; and found it was black earth which the wind had strewn over the snow, from some fields of winter wheat. After searching to the right also, he returned to the sledge, shook the snow off himself, cleared his boots, and took his seat.

"We must go to the right," he said decidedly. "The wind was on our left before, now it is straight in my face. To the right," he repeated, with the same decision.

Vasili Andreyitch heeded him and turned to the right. But yet no road was found. He drove on in this direction for some time. The wind did not diminish, and the snow still fell.

"We seem to be astray altogether, Vasili Andreyitch," suddenly exclaimed Nikita, as if he were announcing some pleasant news. "What is that?" he said, pointing to some black potato-leaves, which thrust themselves through the snow.

Vasili Andreyitch stopped the horse, which by this time was in a heavy perspiration and stood with its deep sides heaving.

"What can it mean?" asked he.

"It means that we are on the Zakharovsky lands. Why, we are ever so far astray!"

"You lie!" remarked Vasili Andreyitch.

"I am not lying, Vasili Andreyitch; it is the truth," said Nikita. "You can feel that the sledge is moving over a potato-field, and there are the heaps of old leaves. It is the Zakharovsky factory-land."

"What a long way we are out!" said Vasili Andreyitch. "What are we to do?"

"Go straight ahead, that's all. We shall reach some place," said Nikita. "If we do not get to Zakharovka, we shall come out at the owner's farm."

Vasili Andreyitch assented, and let the horse go as Nikita had said. They drove in this way for a long while. At times they passed over winter wheat fields all bare, and the sledge creaked over the humps of frozen soil. Sometimes they passed a stubble-field, sometimes a corn-field, where they could see the upstanding wormwood and straw beaten by the wind; sometimes they drove into deep and even white snow on all sides, with nothing visible above it.

The snow whirled down from on high, and sometimes seemed to rise up from below. The horse was evidently tiring; his coat grew crisp and white with frozen sweat, and he walked. Suddenly he stumbled in some ditch or water-course, and went down. Vasili Andreyitch wanted to halt, but Nikita cried to him:—

"Why should we stop? We have gone astray, and we must find our road. Hey, old fellow, hey," he shouted in an encouraging voice to the horse; and he jumped from the sledge, sinking into the ditch.

The horse dashed forward, and quickly landed upon a frozen heap. Obviously it was a man-made ditch.

"Where are we, then?" said Vasili Andreyitch.

"We shall see," answered Nikita. "Go ahead, we shall get to somewhere."

"Is not that the Goryatchkin forest?" asked Vasili Andreyitch, pointing out a dark mass which showed across the snow in front of them.

"When we get nearer, we shall see what forest it is," said Nikita.

He noticed that from the side of the dark mass, long, dry willow leaves were fluttering toward them; and so he knew that it was no forest, but a settlement; yet he chose not to say so. And, in fact, they had scarcely gone twenty-five yards beyond the ditch, when they distinctly made out the trees, and heard a new and melancholy sound. Nikita was right; it was not a forest but a row of tall willow trees, whereon a few scattered leaves still shivered. The willows were evidently ranged along the ditch of a threshing-floor. Coming up to the trees, through which the wind moaned and sighed, the horse suddenly planted his forefeet above the height of the sledge, then drew up his hind legs after him, turned to the left and leaped, sinking up to his knees in the snow. It was a road.

"Here we are," said Nikita, "but I don't know where."

The horse without erring ran along the snow-covered road, and they had not gone eighty yards when they saw the straight strip of a wattled fence, from which the snow was flying in the wind. Passing under a deeply drifted roof of a granary, the road turned in the direction of the wind, and brought them upon a snowdrift. But ahead of them was a passage between two houses; the drift was merely blown across the road, and had to be crossed. Indeed, after passing the drift, they came into a village street. In front of the end house of the village, the wind was shaking desperately the frozen linen which hung there: shirts, one red, one white, some leg-cloths, and a skirt. The white shirt especially shook frantically, tugging at the sleeves.

"Look there, either a lazy woman or a dead one left her linen out over the holiday," said Nikita, seeing the fluttering shirts.

Chapter III

A T the beginning of the street, the wind was still fierce, and the road was snow-covered; but well within the village, it was calm, warm, and cheerful. At one house a dog was barking; at another, a woman, with a sleeveless coat over her head, came running out from somewhere, and stopped at the door of an izba[2] to see who was driving past. In the middle of the village could be heard the sound of girls singing.

Here, in the village, the wind and the snow and the frost seemed subdued.

"Why, this is Grishkino," said Vasili Andreyitch.

"It is," said Nikita.

Grishkino it was. So they had strayed eight versts too far to the left, and traveled out of their proper direction; still, they had got somewhat nearer to their destination. From Grishkino to Goryatchkino was about five versts more.

In the middle of the village they almost ran into a tall man, walking in the center of the road.

"Who is driving?" said this man, and he held the horse. Then, recognizing

---

[2] *izba*: a log hut.

Vasili Andreyitch, he took hold of the shaft, and reached the sledge, where he sat himself on the driver's seat.

It was the peasant Isaï, well known to Vasili Andreyitch, and known throughout the district as the most notorious horse-thief.

"Ah, Vasili Andreyitch, where is God sending you?" said Isaï, from whom Nikita caught the smell of vodka.

"We are going to Goryatchkino."

"You've come a long way round! You should have gone through Malakhovo."

" 'Should have' is right, but we got astray," said Vasili Andreyitch, pulling up.

"A good horse," said Isaï, examining him, and dexterously tightening the loosened knot in his thick tail. "Are you going to stay the night here?"

"No, friend, we must go on."

"Your business must be pressing. And who is that? Ah, Nikita Stepanuich!"

"Who else?" answered Nikita. "Look here, good friend, can you tell us how not to miss the road again?"

"How can you possibly miss it? Just turn back straight along the street, and then outside the houses; keep straight ahead. Don't go to the left. When you reach the highroad, then turn to the right."

"And which turning do we take out of the highroad—the summer or the winter road?" asked Nikita.

"The winter road. As soon as you get clear of the village there are some bushes, and opposite them is a way-mark, an oaken one, all branches. There is the road."

Vasili Andreyitch turned the horse back, and drove through the village.

"You had better stay the night," Isaï shouted after them. But Vasili Andreyitch did not answer, and started up the horse; five versts of smooth road, two versts of it through the forest, was easy enough to drive over, especially as the wind seemed quieter and the snow had apparently ceased falling.

After once more passing along the street, darkened and trodden with fresh horse-tracks, and after passing the house where the linen was hung out—the white shirt was by this time torn, and hung by one frozen sleeve —they came to the weirdly moaning and sighing willows, and then were again in the open country.

Not only had the snow-storm not ceased, but it seemed to have gained strength. The whole road was under snow, and only the stakes proved that they were keeping right. But even these signs of the road were difficult to make out, for the wind blew straight into their faces.

Vasili Andreyitch screwed up his eyes, and bent his head, examining the way-marks; but for the most part, he left the horse alone, trusting to his sagacity. And, in fact, the creature went truly, turning now to the left, now to the right, along the windings of the road which he sensed under his feet. So that in spite of the thickening snow and strengthening wind, the way-marks were still to be seen, now on the left, now on the right.

They had driven thus for ten minutes, when suddenly, straight in front of their horse, appeared a black object moving through the obliquely flying whirlwind of snow. It was a party of travelers. Mukhortui had overtaken them, and he struck his forefeet against the cross-bar of their sledge.

"Drive round! . . . a-a-r! . . . Go ahead!" cried voices from the sledge.

Vasili Andreyitch started to go round them. In the sledge were four peasants, three men and a woman, evidently returning from a festival visit. One of the men was whipping the snow-plastered rump of their little horse with a switch, while two of them, waving their arms from the fore part of the sledge, shouted out something. The woman, muffled up and covered with snow, sat quiet and rigid at the back.

"Where are you from?" asked Vasili Andreyitch.

"A-a-a-skiye!" was all that could be heard.

"I say, where are you from?"

"A-a-a-skiye!" shouted one of the peasants, with all his strength; but nevertheless it was impossible to make out the name.

"Go on! don't give up!" cried another, the one who kept beating his poor little horse.

"So you have come from the festival, have you?"

"Get on! get on! Up, Semka! drive round! Up, up!"

The sledges struck together, almost locked their sides, then fell apart, and the peasants' sledge began to drop behind.

The shaggy, snow-covered, big-bellied pony, laboriously breathing under the duga-bow, and evidently at the end of his strength in his vain efforts to escape from the switch belaboring him, staggered along on his short legs through the deep snow, which he trod down with difficulty. With distended nostrils, and ears set back in distress, and with his lower lip stuck out like a fish's, he kept his muzzle near Nikita's shoulder for a moment; then he began to fall behind.

"See what drink does," said Nikita. "They have tired that horse to death. What heathens!"

For a few minutes, the pantings of the tired-out horse could be heard, with the drunken shouts of the peasants. Then the pantings became inaudible, and the shouts, also. Again nothing could be heard round about except the wind whistling in their ears, and the occasional scrape of the sledge-runners on a bare spot of road.

This encounter enlivened and encouraged Vasili Andreyitch, and he drove more boldly, not examining the way-marks, and again trusting to his horse.

Nikita had nothing to occupy him, and dozed just as he always did in such circumstances, thus wasting much good daylight. Suddenly the horse stopped, and Nikita was jerked forward, knocking his nose against the front.

"It seems we are going wrong again," said Vasili Andreyitch.

"What is the matter?"

"The way-marks are not to be seen. We must be out of the road."

"Well, if we've lost the road, we must look for it," said Nikita, laconically; and again stepping easily in his great bark overshoes, he started out to explore the snow.

He walked for a long time, now out of sight, now reappearing, then disappearing; at last, he returned.

"There is no road here; it may be farther on," said he, sitting down in the sledge.

It was already beginning to grow dark. The storm was neither increasing, nor did it diminish.

"I should like to hear those peasants again," said Vasili Andreyitch.

"Yes, but they won't pass near us; we must be a good distance off the road. Maybe they are astray, too," said Nikita.

"Where shall we make for, then?"

"Leave the horse to himself. He will find his way. Give me the reins."

Vasili Andreyitch handed over the reins; the more willingly because his hands, in spite of his warm gloves, were beginning to freeze.

Nikita took the reins, and held them lightly, trying to give no pressure; he was glad to prove the good sense of his favorite. And in fact, the intelligent horse, turning one ear and then the other, first in this and then in that direction, presently began to wheel round.

"He just doesn't speak," said Nikita. "Look how he manages it! Go on, go on, that's good."

The wind was now at their backs; they felt warmer.

"Is he not wise?" continued Nikita, delighted with his horse. "A Kirghiz beast is strong, but stupid. But this one—see what he does with his ears. There is no need of a telegraph-wire; he can feel through a mile."

Hardly half an hour had gone, when a forest, or a village, or something, loomed up in front; and, to their right, the way-marks again showed. Evidently they were on the road again.

"We are back at Grishkino, are we not?" exclaimed Nikita, suddenly.

Indeed, on the left hand rose the same granary, with the snow flying from it; and farther on was the same line with the frozen washing—the shirts and drawers, so fiercely shaken by the wind.

Again they drove through the street, again felt the quiet, warmth, and cheerfulness, again saw the road with the horse-tracks; heard voices, songs, the barking of a dog. It was now so dark that a few windows were lighted.

Halfway down the street, Vasili Andreyitch turned the horse toward a large two-storied brick house, and drew up at the steps.

Nikita went to the snow-dimmed window, in the light from which glittered the flitting flakes, and knocked with the handle of the whip.

"Who is there?" a voice answered to his knock.

"The Brekhunofs, from Krestui, my good man," answered Nikita. "Come out for a minute."

Some one moved from the window, and in about two minutes the door in the entrance-hall was heard to open, the latch of the front door clicked, and holding the door against the wind, there peeped out a tall, old, white-bearded muzhik, who had thrown a sheepskin coat over his white holiday shirt. Behind him was a young fellow in a red shirt and leather boots.

"What, is it you, Andreyitch?" said the old man.

"We have lost our road, friend," said Vasili Andreyitch. "We set out for Goryatchkino, and found ourselves here. Then we went on, but lost the road again."

"Why, how you've wandered!" answered the old man. "Petrukha, go, open the gates," he said to the young man in the red shirt.

"Of course I will," said the young fellow, cheerfully, as he ran off through the entrance-hall.

"We are not stopping for the night, friend," said Vasili Andreyitch.

"Where can you go in the night-time? You had better stop."

"Should be very glad to spend the night, but I must go on business, friend; it's impossible!"

"Well, then, at least warm yourself a little; the samovar is just ready," said the old man.

"Warm ourselves? We can do that," said Vasili Andreyitch. "It cannot get darker, and when the moon is up, it will be still lighter. Come, Mikit, let us go in and warm up a bit."

"Why, yes, let us warm ourselves," said Nikita, who was very cold, and whose great desire was to thaw out his benumbed limbs in a well-heated room.

Vasili Andreyitch went with the old man into the house. Nikita drove through the gates opened by Petrukha, by whose advice he stood the horse under the pent-roof of the shed, the floor of which was strewn with stable-litter. The high bow over the head of the horse caught the roof-beam, and the hens and a cock, already gone to roost up there, began to cackle angrily and scratch on the wood. Some startled sheep, pattering their feet on the frozen dung-heap, huddled themselves out of the way. A dog yelped desperately in fright, after the manner of young hounds, and barked fiercely at the stranger.

Nikita held conversation with them all. He begged pardon of the fowls, and calmed them with assurances that he would give them no more trouble; he reproved the sheep for being needlessly frightened; and while fastening up the horse, he kept on exhorting the little dog.

"That will do," said he, shaking the snow from himself. "Hear, how he is barking!" added he, for the dog's benefit. "That's quite enough for you, quite enough, stupid! That will do! Why do you bother yourself? There are no thieves or strangers about."

"It is like the tale of the Three Domestic Counselors," said the young man, thrusting the sledge under the shed with his strong arms.

"What about the counselors?"

"The tale is in Paulson. A thief sneaks up to a house; the dog barks—that means 'Be on your guard'; the cock crows—that means 'Get up'; the cat washes itself—that means 'A welcome guest is coming, be ready for him,' " said the young man, with a smile.

Petrukha could read and write, and knew, almost by heart, the only book he possessed, which was Paulson's primer; and he liked, especially when, as now, he had been drinking a little too much, to quote from the book some saying which seemed appropriate to the occasion.

"Quite true," said Nikita.

"I suppose you are cold, uncle," said Petrukha.

"Yes, something that way," said Nikita. They both crossed the yard and entered the house.

Chapter IV

THE house at which Vasili Andreyitch had drawn up was one of the richest in the village. The family had five allotments of land, and hired still more outside. Their establishment owned six horses, three cows, two yearling heifers, and twenty head of sheep. In the house lived twenty-two souls; four married sons, six grandchildren (of whom one, Petrukha, was married), two great-grandchildren, three orphans, and four daughters-in-law with their children. It was one of the few families living together in one household; yet even here was that indefinable interior work of disintegration—beginning, as usual, among the women—infallibly bound to bring about speedy separation. Two sons were water-carriers in Moscow; one was in the army. At present, those at home were the old man, his wife, the second son who managed the household, the oldest son who had come from Moscow on a holiday, and all the women and children. Besides the family there was a guest, a neighbor, who was an intimate friend.

Over the table in the living-room hung a shaded lamp, which threw a bright light down on the tea-service, a bottle of vodka, and some eatables, and on the brick walls, where, in the "red corner," hung the ikons with pictures on each side of them.

At the head of the table sat Vasili Andreyitch, in his black fur coat, sucking his frozen mustaches, and scrutinizing the people and the room with his bulging, hawk-like eyes. Beside him at the table sat the white-bearded, bald, old father of the house, in a white homespun shirt; next him sat the son from Moscow, with his sturdy back and shoulders, clad in a thin cotton shirt; then the other son, the broad-shouldered eldest brother, who acted as head of the house; then a lean and red-haired muzhik—the visiting neighbor.

The peasants, having drunk and eaten, prepared to take tea, and the samovar was already boiling as it stood on the floor near the oven. The children were to be seen on the oven and on the bunks. On the wall bench sat a woman with a cradle beside her. The aged mother of the house, whose face was covered with a network of fine wrinkles even to the lips, waited on Vasili Andreyitch.

As Nikita entered the room, she was just filling a coarse glass with vodka, and handing it to Vasili Andreyitch.

"No harm done, Vasili Andreyitch, but you must wish our good health," said she. "Have a drink, dear!"

The sight and smell of vodka, especially in his cold and tired condition, greatly disturbed Nikita's mind. He frowned, and after shaking the snow from his coat and hat, stood before the holy images; without apparently seeing any one, he made the sign of the cross thrice, and bowed to the images; then, turning to the old man, he bowed to him first, afterward to all who sat at table, and again to the women beside the oven; and saying, "Good fortune to your feast," he began to take off his overcoat without looking at the table.

"Why, you are all over frost, uncle," said the eldest brother, looking at the snow which crowned Nikita's face, eyes, and beard.

Nikita took off his coat, shook it again, hung it near the oven, and came to the table. They offered him vodka also. There was a moment's bitter struggle; he came very near taking the glass and pouring the fragrant, transparent liquid into his mouth, but he looked at Vasili Andreyitch, remembered his vow, remembered the lost boots, the cooper, his son for whom he had promised to buy a horse when the spring came; he sighed, and refused.

"I don't drink, thank you humbly," he said gloomily, and sat down on the bench, near the second window.

"Why not?" asked the eldest brother.

"I don't drink, that's all," said Nikita, not daring to raise his eyes, and looking at his thin beard and mustache, and at the thawing icicles clinging to them.

"It is not good for him," said Vasili Andreyitch, munching a biscuit after emptying his glass.

"Then have some tea," said the kindly old woman. "I dare say you are quite benumbed, good soul. How lazy you women are with the samovar!"

"It is ready," answered the youngest, and wiping round the samovar with an apron, she bore it heavily to the table, and set it down with a thud.

Meanwhile, Vasili Andreyitch told how they had gone astray and worked back twice to the same village; what mistakes they had made, and how they had met the drunken peasants. Their hosts expressed surprise, showed why and where they had missed the road, told them the names of the revelers they had met, and made plain how they ought to go.

"From here to Molchanovka, a child might go; the only thing is to make sure to turn out of the highroad; you'll see a bush there. But yet you did not get there," said the neighbor.

"You ought to stop here. The women will make a bed," said the old woman, persuasively.

"You would make a better start in the morning; much pleasanter, that," said the old man, affirming what his wife had said.

"Impossible, friend! Business!" said Vasili Andreyitch. "If you let an hour go, you may not be able to make it up in a year," added he, remembering the forest and the dealers who might do him out of his purchase. "We shall get there, shan't we?" he said, turning to Nikita.

"We may lose ourselves again," said Nikita, gloomily. He was gloomy, because of the intense longing he felt for the vodka; and the tea, the only thing which could quench that longing, had not yet been offered to him.

"We have only to reach the turning, and there is no more danger of losing the road, as it goes straight through the forest," said Vasili Andreyitch.

"Just as you say, Vasili Andreyitch; if you want to go, let us go," said Nikita, taking the glass of tea offered to him.

"Well, let us drink up our tea, and then forward march!"

Nikita said nothing, but shook his head; and carefully pouring the tea into the saucer, began to warm his hands and his swollen fingers over the steam. Then, taking a small bite of sugar in his mouth, he turned to their hosts, said, "Your health," and drank down the warming liquid.

"Couldn't some one come with us to the turning?" asked Vasili Andreyitch.

"Why not? Certainly," said the eldest son. "Petrukha will put in the horse, and go with you as far as the turning."

"Then put in your horse, and I shall be in your debt."

"My dear man," said the kindly old woman, "we are right glad to do it."

"Petrukha, go and put in the mare," said the eldest son.

"All right," said Petrukha, smiling; and, without delay, taking his cap from the nail, he hurried away to harness up.

While the harnessing was in progress, the talk turned back to the point where it stood when Vasili Andreyitch arrived. The old man had complained to his neighbor, the village-elder, about the conduct of his third son, who had sent him no present this holiday-time, though he had sent a French shawl to his wife.

"These young folk are getting worse and worse," said the old man.

"Very much worse!" said the neighbor. "They are unmanageable. They know too much. There's Demotchkin, now, who broke his father's arm. It all comes from too much learning."

Nikita listened, watched the faces, and it was evident that he, too, would like to have a share in the conversation, had he not been so busy with his tea; as it was, he only nodded his head approvingly. He emptied glass after glass, growing warmer and warmer, and more and more comfortable. The talk continued in one strain, all about the harm that comes from family division; and it was clearly no theoretical discussion, but concerned with a rupture in this very house, arising through the second son, who sat there in his place, morosely silent. The question was a painful one, and absorbed the whole family; but out of politeness they refrained from discussing their private affairs before strangers.

At last, however, the old man could endure it no longer. In a tearful voice, he began to say that there should be no break-up of the family while he lived; that the house had much to thank God for, but if they fell apart—they must become beggars.

"Just like the Matveyefs," said the neighbor. "There was plenty among them all, but when they broke up the family, there was nothing for any of them."

"That's just what you want to do," said the old man to his son.

The son answered nothing, and there was a painful pause. The silence was broken by Petrukha, who had by this time harnessed the horse and returned to the room, where he had been standing for a few minutes, smiling all the time.

"There is a tale in Paulson, just like this," said he. "A father gave his sons a broom to break. They could not break it while it was bound together, but they broke it easily by taking every switch by itself. That's the way here," he said, with his broad smile. "All's ready!" he added.

"Well, if we're ready, let us start," said Vasili Andreyitch. "As to this quarrel, don't you give in, grandfather. You got everything together, and you are the master. Apply to the magistrate; he will show you how to keep your authority."

"And he gives himself such airs, such airs," continued the old man, in his complaining voice. "There is no ordering him! It is as if Satan lived in him."

Meanwhile, Nikita, having drunk his fifth glass of tea, did not stand it upside down, in sign that he had finished, but laid it on its side, hoping they might fill it a sixth time. But there was no longer any water in the samovar, and the hostess did not fill up for him again, and then Vasili Andreyitch began to put on his things. There was no help; Nikita also rose, put back into the sugar-basin the little lump of sugar, which he had nibbled on all sides, wiped the moisture from his face with the skirt of his coat, and went to put on his overcoat.

After getting into the garment, he sighed heavily: then, having thanked their hosts and said good-bye, he went out from the warm, bright room, and through the dark, cold entrance-hall, where the wind creaked the doors and drove the snow in at the chinks, into the dark yard.

Petrukha, in his sheepskin, stood in the center of the yard with the horse, and smiling, recited verses from Paulson:

> *Storm-clouds veil the sky with darkness,*
> *Swiftly whirl the snowblasts wild,*
> *Now the storm roars like a wild beast,*
> *Now it waileth like a child.*

Nikita nodded appreciatively and arranged the reins.

The old man, coming out with Vasili Andreyitch, brought a lantern into the entry to show the way, but the wind put it out at once. Even in the enclosed yard, one could see that the storm had become much more violent.

"What weather!" thought Vasili Andreyitch. "I'm afraid we shall not get there. But it must be! Business! And then, I have put our friend to the trouble of harnessing his horse. God helping, we shall get there."

Their aged host also thought it better not to go; but he had offered his arguments already, and they had not listened to him. It was useless to ask them again.

"Maybe it is old age makes me overcautious; they will get there all right," thought he. "And we can all go to bed at proper time. It will be less bother."

As for Petrukha, he had no thought of danger: he knew the way so well and the whole region, and then besides, the lines about "the snowblasts wild" encouraged him, because they were a true description of what was going on out-of-doors. Nikita had no wish to go at all; but he was long used to follow other people's wishes, and to give up his own. Therefore no one withheld the travelers.

Chapter V

VASILI Andreyitch went over to his sledge, found it with some difficulty in the darkness, got in, and took the reins.

"Go ahead!" he shouted.

Petrukha, kneeling in his sledge, started the horse. Mukhortui, who had before been whinnying, aware of the mare's nearness, now dashed after her, and they drove out into the street. They rode once more through the village, down the same road, past the space where the frozen linen had hung, but was no longer to be seen; past the same barn, now snowed-up almost as high as the roof, from which the snow flew incessantly; past the moaning, whistling, and bending willows; and again they came to where the sea of snow raged from above and below. The wind was so violent that, taking the travelers sidewise when they were crossing its direction, it heeled the sledge over and pushed the horse aside. Petrukha drove his good mare in front, at an easy trot, giving her an occasional lively shout of encouragement. Mukhortui pressed after her.

After driving thus for about ten minutes, Petrukha turned around and called out something. But neither Vasili Andreyitch nor Nikita could hear for the wind, but they guessed that they had reached the turning. In fact, Petrukha had turned to the right; the wind which had been at their side again blew in their faces, and to the right, through the snow, loomed something black. It was the bush beside the turning.

"Well, good-bye to you!"

"Thanks, Petrukha!"

" 'The storm-clouds veil the sky with darkness!' " shouted Petrukha, and disappeared.

"Quite a poet," said Vasili Andreyitch, and shook the reins.

"Yes, a fine young man, a genuine peasant," said Nikita.

They drove on.

Nikita, protecting his head by crouching it down between his shoulders, so that his short beard covered up his throat, sat silent, trying not to lose the warmth which the tea had given him. Before him, he saw the straight lines of the shafts, which to his eyes looked like the ruts of the road; he saw the shifting quarters of the horse, with the knotted tail blown off in one direction by the wind; beyond, he saw the high duga-bow between the shafts, and the horse's rocking head and neck, with the floating mane. From time to time he noticed the stakes, and knew that, thus far, they had kept to the road, and he need not concern himself.

Vasili Andreyitch drove on, trusting to the horse to keep to the road. But Mukhortui, although he had rested a little in the village, went unwillingly, and seemed to shirk from the road, so that Vasili Andreyitch had to press him at times.

"Here is a stake on the right, here's another, and there's a third," reckoned Vasili Andreyitch, "and here, in front, is the forest," he thought, examining a dark patch ahead. But that which he took for a forest was only a bush. They passed the bush, drove about fifty yards farther, and there was neither the fourth stake nor the forest.

"We must reach the forest soon," thought Vasili Andreyitch; and buoyed up by the vodka and the tea, he shook the reins. The good, obedient animal responded, and now at an amble, now at an easy trot, made in the direction he was sent, although he knew it was not the way in which he should have been going. Ten minutes went by, still no forest.

"I'm afraid we are astray again!" said Vasili Andreyitch, pulling up.

Nikita silently got out from the sledge, and holding with his hand the flaps of his khalat, which now pressed against him and then flew from him as he stood and turned in the wind, began to tread the snow; first he went to one side, then to the other. Three times he went out of sight altogether. At last he returned, and took the reins from Vasili Andreyitch's hands.

"We must go to the right," he said sternly and peremptorily; and he turned the horse.

"Well, if it must be to the right, let us go to the right," said Vasili Andreyitch, passing over the reins and thrusting his frozen hands into his sleeves.

Nikita did not answer.

"Now then, old fellow, stir yourself," he called to the horse; but Mukhortui, in spite of the shake of the reins, went on only slowly. In places the snow was knee-deep, and the sledge jerked at every movement of the horse.

Nikita took the whip, which hung in front of the sledge, and struck once. The good creature, unused to the knout, sprang forward at a trot, but soon fell again to a slow amble, and then began to walk. Thus they went for five minutes. All was so dark, and so blurred with snow from above and below, that sometimes they could not make out the duga-bow. At times it seemed as if the sledge was standing, and the ground running back. Suddenly the horse stopped short, evidently perceiving something a little distance in front of him. Nikita once more lightly jumped out, throwing down the reins, and went in front to find out what was the matter. But hardly had he taken a pace clear ahead, when his feet slipped, and he went rolling down some steep place.

"Whoa, whoa, whoa!" he said to himself, falling and trying to stop his fall. There was nothing to seize hold of, and he brought up only when his feet plunged into a deep bed of snow which lay in the ravine.

The fringe of drifted snow which hung on the edge of the ravine, disturbed by Nikita's fall, showered down on him, and got into his neck.

"What a way of doing!" cried Nikita, reproachfully addressing the snow and the ravine, as he cleared out his coat-collar.

"Mikit, hey, Mikit," shouted Vasili Andreyitch, from above.

But Nikita did not answer.

He was too much occupied in shaking away the snow, than in looking for the whip, which he had lost in rolling down the bank. Having found the whip, he started to climb up the bank where he had rolled down, but it was a perfect impossibility; he slipped back every time; so that he was compelled to go along the foot of the bank to find a way up. About ten yards from the place where he fell, he managed to struggle up again on all fours, and then he turned back along the bank toward the place where the horse should have been. He could not see horse or sledge; but by going with the wind, he heard Vasili Andreyitch's voice and Mukhortui's whinny calling him, before he saw them.

"I'm coming; I'm coming. What are you cackling for!" he said.

Only when he had approached quite near the sledge could he make out the horse and Vasili Andreyitch, who stood close by, and looked gigantic.

"Where the devil have you been hiding? We've got to drive back. We must get back to Grishkino anyway," the master began to rebuke him angrily.

"I should be glad to get there, Vasili Andreyitch, but how are we to do it? Here is a ravine where if we once get in, we shall never come out. I pitched in there in such a way that I could hardly get out."

"Well, assuredly we can't stay here; somewhere we must go," said Vasili Andreyitch.

Nikita made no answer. He sat down on the sledge with his back to the wind, took off his boots and emptied them of snow; then, with a little straw which he took from the sledge, he stopped from the inside a gap in the left boot.

Vasili Andreyitch was silent, as if leaving everything to Nikita alone. Having got his boots on, Nikita drew his feet into the sledge, put on his mittens again, took the reins, and turned the horse along the ravine. But they had not driven a hundred paces when the horse stopped again. Another ravine confronted him.

Nikita got out again and began to explore the snow. He was gone a long while. At last he reappeared on the side opposite to that on which he started.

"Andreyitch, are you alive?" he called.

"Here!" shouted Vasili Andreyitch. "What is the matter?"

"I can't make anything out, it is too dark; except some ravines. We must drive to windward again."

They set off once more; Nikita explored again, stumbling through the snow. Again he sat down, again he crept forward, and at last, out of breath, he stopped beside the sledge.

"How now?" asked Vasili Andreyitch.

"Well, I'm quite tired out. And the horse is done up."

"What are we to do?"

"Wait a minute."

Nikita moved off again, and soon returned.

"Follow me," he said, going in front of the horse.

Vasili Andreyitch no longer gave orders, but implicitly did what Nikita told him.

"Here, this way!" shouted Nikita, stepping quickly to the right. Seizing Mukhortui by the bridle, he turned him toward a snowdrift.

At first the horse resisted, then dashed forward, hoping to leap the drift, but failed, and sank in snow up to the hams.

"Get out!" called Nikita to Vasili Andreyitch, who still sat in the sledge; and taking hold of one shaft, he tried to push the sledge after the horse.

"It's a pretty hard job, brother," he said to Mukhortui, "but it can't be helped. Na! na! Stir yourself! Just a little!" he called out.

The horse leaped forward, once, twice, but failed to clear himself, and sat back again as if thinking out something.

"Well, friend, this is no good," urged Nikita to Mukhortui. "Now, once more!"

Nikita pulled on the shaft again; Vasili Andreyitch did the same on the opposite side. The horse lifted his head, and made a sudden dash.

"Nu! na! You won't sink; don't be afraid," shouted Nikita.

One plunge, a second, a third, and at last the horse was out from the snowdrift, and stood still, breathing heavily and shaking himself clear. Nikita wanted to lead him on farther, but Vasili Andreyitch, in his two shubas, had so lost his breath that he could walk no more, and dropped into the sledge.

"Let me get my breath a little," he said, unbinding the handkerchief with which, at the village, he had tied the collar of his coat.

"We are all right here; you might as well lie down," said Nikita. "I'll lead him along"; and with Vasili Andreyitch in the sledge, he led the horse by the head about ten paces farther, then up a slight rise, and stopped.

The place where Nikita drew up was not in a hollow, where the snow, swept from the drifts and piled up, might perfectly shelter them; but nevertheless it was partly protected from the wind by the edge of the ravine.

There were moments when the wind seemed to become quieter; but these intervals did not last long, and after them the storm, as if to make up for such a rest, rushed on with tenfold vigor, and tore and whirled the more angrily.

Such a gust of wind swept past as Vasili Andreyitch, with recovered breath, got out of the sledge, and went up to Nikita to talk over the situation. They both instinctively bowed themselves, and waited until the stress should be over. Mukhortui laid back his ears and shook his head. When the blast had abated a little, Nikita took off his mittens, stuck them in his girdle, and having breathed a little on his hands, began to undo the strap from the shaft bow.

"Why are you doing that?" asked Vasili Andreyitch.

"I'm taking out the horse. What else can we do? I'm done up," said Nikita, as if apologizing.

"But couldn't we drive somewhere?"

"No, we could not. We should only do harm to the horse. The poor beast is worn out," said Nikita, pointing to the creature, who stood there, with heavily heaving sides, submissively waiting for whatever should come. "We must put up for the night here," he repeated, as if they were at their inn. He began to undo the collar-straps.

The buckles fell apart.

"But we shall be frozen, shan't we?" queried Vasili Andreyitch.

"Well, if we are, we cannot help it," said Nikita.

Chapter VI

IN his two fur coats, Vasili Andreyitch was quite warm; especially after his exertion in the snowdrift. But a cold shiver ran down his back when he learned that they really had to spend the night where they were. To calm himself, he sat down in the sledge, and got out his cigarettes and matches.

Meanwhile Nikita went on taking out the horse. He undid the belly-band, took away the reins and collar-strap, and removed the shaft-bow, continuing to encourage the horse by speaking to him.

"Now, come out, come out," he said, leading him clear of the shafts. "We must tie you here. I'll put a bit of straw for you, and take off your bridle," he went on, doing as he said. "After a bite, you'll feel ever so much better."

But Mukhortui was not calmed by Nikita's words; uneasily, he shifted his feet, pressed against the sledge, turned his back to the wind, and rubbed his head on Nikita's sleeve.

As if not wholly to reject the treat of straw which Nikita put under his nose, Mukhortui just once seized a wisp out of the sledge, but quickly deciding that there was more important business than to eat straw, he threw it down again, and the wind instantly tore it away and hid it in the snow.

"Now we must make a signal," said Nikita, turning the front of the sledge against the wind; and having tied the shafts together with a strap, he set them on end in front of the sledge. "If the snow covers us, the good folk will see the shafts, and dig us out," said Nikita, slapping his mittens together and pulling them on. "That's what old hands advise."

Vasili Andreyitch had meanwhile opened his coat, and making a shelter with its folds, he rubbed match after match on the steel box. But his hands trembled, and the kindled matches were blown out by the wind, one after another, some when just struck, others when he thrust them to the cigarette. At last one match burned fully, and lighted up for a moment the fur of his coat, his hand with the gold ring on the bent forefinger, and the snow-sprinkled straw which stuck out from under the sacking. The cigarette lighted. Twice he eagerly whiffed the smoke, swallowed it, blew it through his mustaches, and would have gone on, but the wind tore away the burning tobacco and sent it whirling after the straw. Even these few whiffs of tobacco-smoke cheered up Vasili Andreyitch.

"Well, we will stop here," he said authoritatively.

"Wait a minute, and I'll make a flag," he said, picking up the handkerchief which he had taken from round his collar and put down in the sledge. Drawing off his gloves, and reaching up, he tied the handkerchief tightly to the strap that held the shafts together.

The handkerchief at once began to beat about wildly; now clinging round a shaft, now streaming out, and cracking like a whip.

"That's a clever piece of work," said Vasili Andreyitch, pleased with what he had done, and getting into the sledge. "We should be warmer together, but there's not room for two," he said.

"I can find a place," said Nikita, "but the horse must be covered; he's sweating, the good fellow. Excuse me," he added, going to the sledge, and drawing the sacking from under Vasili Andreyitch. This he folded, and after taking off the saddle and breeching, covered Mukhortui with it.

"Anyway, it will be a bit warmer, silly," he said, putting the saddle and heavy breeching over the sacking.

"You won't need the cloth, will you? and give me a little straw," said Nikita, coming back to the sledge after he had finished his work.

Taking these from beneath Vasili Andreyitch, Nikita went behind the sledge, dug there a hole in the snow, stuffed in the straw, and pulling down his hat, wrapping his kaftan well around him, and covering himself with the coarse matting, sat down on the straw, leaning against the bark back of the sledge, which kept off the wind and snow.

Vasili Andreyitch shook his head disapprovingly at what Nikita was doing, as he usually found fault with the peasants' ignorance and stupidity; and he began to make his own arrangements for the night.

He smoothed the remaining straw and heaped it thicker under his side; then he thrust his hands into his sleeves, and settled his head in the corner of the sledge sheltered from the wind in front.

He did not feel sleepy. He lay and thought; thought about one thing only, which was the aim, reason, pleasure, and pride of his life: about how much money he had made and might make, and how much other men whom he knew had made and possessed, and the means whereby they gained it and were gaining it; and how he, in like manner, might gain a good deal more. The purchase of the Goryatchkin forest was for him an affair of the utmost importance. He counted on making from this transaction as much as ten thousand! And he began mentally to estimate the value of the forest, which he had inspected in the autumn so carefully as to count all the trees on five acres.

"The oak will make sledge-runners. The small stuff will take care of itself. And there'll be thirty cords of wood to the acre," said he to himself. "At the very worst there'll be a little less than eighty rubles an acre. There are one hundred and fifty acres."

He reckoned it up mentally and saw that it amounted to about twelve thousand rubles; but without his abacus he could not calculate it exactly.

"But for all that, I won't pay ten thousand; say eight thousand; besides, one must allow for the bare spaces. I'll oil the surveyor—a hundred rubles will do—a hundred and fifty, if necessary; he'll deduct about thirteen acres out of the forest. He is sure to sell for eight; three thousand down. Never fear; he will weaken at that," he thought, pressing his forearm on the pocket-book beneath.

"And how we lost our way after we left the turning, God only knows! The forest and the woodman's hut should be near by. I should like to hear the dogs, but they never bark when they're wanted, the cursed brutes."

He opened his collar a little from his ear and tried to listen; all he could hear was the same whistle of the wind, the flapping and cracking of the handkerchief on the shafts, and the pelting of the falling snow on the bark matting of the sledge.

He covered himself again.

"If one had only known this beforehand, we had better have stayed where we were. But no matter, we shall get there tomorrow. It is only a day lost. In this weather, the others won't get there either."

Then he remembered that on the twenty-first he had to receive the price for some gelded rams, from the butcher.

"I wanted to be there myself, for if he doesn't find me, my wife won't know how to receive the money. She's very inexperienced, she doesn't know about the right way of doing things," he continued to reflect, remembering how she had failed in her behavior toward a commissary of police, who had come to pay them a visit the day before, at the feast. "Just a woman, of course. What has she ever seen anywhere? In my father's time, what a house we had! Nothing out of the way, a well-to-do countryman's: a barn and an inn, and that was the whole property. And now in these fifteen years what have I done? A general store, two taverns, a flour-mill, a granary, two farms rented, a house and warehouse all iron-roofed," he remembered proudly. "Not as it was in father's time! Who is known over the whole place? Brekhunof.

"And why is this? Because I know my business, I look after things; not like others, who idle or waste their time in foolishness. I don't sleep at night. Storm or no storm, I start out. And of course, the thing is done. People think it's fun making money. Not at all; you work and rack your brains. You spend your night this way outdoors, and go without sleep! The thoughts whirling in your head are as good as a cushion!" he exclaimed with pride. "They think men get on through luck. Look at the Mironofs, who have their millions, now. Why? They worked. Then God gives. If God only grants me health!"

And the idea that he, also, might become a millionaire like Mironof, who began with nothing, so excited Vasili Andreyitch that he suddenly felt a need to talk to some one. But there was no one. . . . If he could only have reached Goryatchkino, he might have talked with the landowner, and "put spectacles on him."

"Whew! how it blows! It will snow us up so that we can't get out in the morning," he thought, as he listened to the rush of the wind, which blew against the front of the sledge, bending it back, and lashed the snow against the bark matting. He lifted himself and looked out: in the white whirling darkness all he could see was Mukhortui's black head, and his back covered with the fluttering matting, and his thick twisted tail; all around, on every side, in front and behind, was the same monotonous white waving mist, occasionally appearing to grow a little lighter, then again growing thicker and denser.

"I was foolish enough yielding to Nikita," he thought. "We ought to have driven on, we should have come out somewhere. We might have gone back to Grishkino, and stayed at Taras's. Now we must sit here all night. Well, what was I thinking about? Yes, that God gives to the industrious, and not to the lazy, not to loafers and fools. It's time for a smoke, too."

He sat up, got his cigarette-case, and stretched himself flat on his stomach, to protect the light from the wind with the flaps of his coat; but the wind got in and put out one match after another. At last he managed to get a cigarette lit, and he began to smoke. The fact that he succeeded greatly delighted him. Though the wind smoked more of his cigarette than he did, nevertheless he got about three puffs, and felt better.

He again threw himself back in the sledge, wrapped himself up, and returned to his recollections and dreams; very unexpectedly he lost himself and fell asleep.

But suddenly something touched him and woke him up. Whether it was Mukhortui pulling the straw from under him, or something within him that startled him, at all events he awoke, and his heart began to beat so quickly and violently that the sledge seemed to be shaking under him.

He opened his eyes. Everything around was the same as before; only it seemed a little lighter.

"The dawn," he said to himself; "it must be nearly morning."

But he instantly remembered that the light was only due to the rising of the moon.

He lifted himself, and looked first at the horse. Mukhortui was standing with his back to the wind, and shivering all over. The snow-covered sacking had fallen off on one side; the breeching had slipped down; the snowy head and the fluttering crest and mane, all were now clearly visible.

Vasili Andreyitch bent over the back of the sledge and looked behind. Nikita was still sitting in the old position which he had first taken. The sacking with which he had protected himself and his feet were covered with snow.

"I'm afraid the muzhik will be frozen; his clothes are so wretched. I might be held responsible. I declare they're such senseless people! They truly haven't the slightest forethought!" reflected Vasili Andreyitch; and he was tempted to take the sacking from the horse, to put over Nikita; but it was cold to get out and stir around, and besides, the horse might freeze to death.

"What made me bring him? It is all her stupidity!" thought Vasili Andreyitch, remembering his unattractive wife; and he turned again to his former place in the front of the sledge.

"My uncle once sat in snow all night, like this," he reflected, "and no harm came of it. And Sevastian also was dug out," he went on, remembering another case, "but he was dead, stiff like a frozen carcass. If we had only stopped at Grishkino, nothing would have happened."

Carefully covering himself, so that the warmth of the fur might not be wasted, but might protect his neck, knees, and the soles of his feet, he shut his eyes, trying to sleep again. But however much he tried, this time he could not lose himself; on the contrary, he felt alert and excited. Again he began to count his gains and the debts due to him; again he began to boast of his success, and to feel proud of himself and his position; but he was all the while disturbed by a lurking fear, and by the unpleasant regret that he had not stopped for the night at Grishkino.

"It would have been good to lie on the bench in a warm room!" He turned from side to side several times; he curled himself up trying to find a better position, more sheltered from the wind and snow, but all the time he felt uncomfortable; he rose again and changed his position, crossed his feet, shut his eyes, and lay silent; but either his crossed feet, in their high felt boots, began to ache, or the wind blew in somewhere; and thus lying for a short time, he again began the disagreeable reflection, how comfortably he would have rested in the warm house at Grishkino. Again he rose, changed his position, wrapped himself up, and again tucked himself in.

Once Vasili Andreyitch fancied he heard a distant cockcrow. He felt glad, and threw back his coat, and strained his ear to listen; but in spite of all his efforts he could hear nothing but the sound of the wind whistling against the shafts, and flapping the handkerchief, and the snow lashing the bark matting of the sledge.

Nikita had been motionless all the time, just as he had sat from the first, not stirring or even answering Vasili Andreyitch, though he spoke to him twice.

"He doesn't care in the least; he must be asleep," Vasili Andreyitch thought angrily, looking behind the sledge at Nikita, deeply covered with snow.

Twenty times Vasili Andreyitch thus rose and lay down. It seemed to him this night would never end.

"It must be near morning now," he thought once as he rose and glanced round him. "Let me look at my watch. I shall freeze if I unbutton my coat; but if I only know it is near morning, I shall feel better. We could begin to harness the horse."

At the bottom of his mind, Vasili Andreyitch knew that it could not be anywhere near morning; but he began to feel more and more afraid, and he chose both to assure himself and to deceive himself. He cautiously undid the hooks of his short coat, then putting his hand in at the bosom, he felt about until he got at the waistcoat. With great trouble, he drew out his silver watch enameled with flowers, and tried to examine it. Without a light, he could make out nothing.

Again he lay down flat on his elbows and his knees, as when he lighted the cigarette; got the matches, and proceeded to strike. This time he was more careful, and feeling for a match with the largest head, ignited it at the first stroke. When he brought the face of the watch into the light he could not believe his eyes. . . . It was not later than ten minutes past twelve. The whole night was still before him.

"Oh, what a long night!" thought Vasili Andreyitch, feeling the cold run down his back; and buttoning up again and wrapping his fur coat round him, he snuggled into the corner of the sledge with the intention of waiting patiently.

Suddenly, above the monotonous roar of the wind, he distinctly heard a new and a living sound. It grew gradually louder, and became quite clear; then began to die away with equal regularity. There could be no doubt it was a wolf. And this wolf was so near, that down the wind one could hear how he changed his cry by the movement of his jaws. Vasili Andreyitch turned back his collar and listened attentively. Mukhortui listened likewise, pricking up his ears, and when the wolf had ceased his chant he shifted his feet, and neighed warningly.

After this Vasili Andreyitch not only was unable to sleep, but even to keep calm. The more he tried to think of his accounts, of his business, reputation, importance, and property, more and more fear grew upon him; and above all his thoughts, one thought stood out predominantly and penetratingly: the thought of his rashness in not stopping at Grishkino.

"The forest—what do I care about the forest? There is plenty of business without that, thank God! Ah, if we had only stayed for the night!" said he to himself. "They say drunken men soon freeze to death," he thought, "and I have had some drink."

Then testing his own sensations, he felt that he began to shiver, either from cold or fear. He tried to wrap himself up and to lie down, as before; but he could not any longer do that. He could not stay in one position, wanted to rise, to do something so as to suppress his gathering fears, against which he felt helpless. Again he got his cigarettes and matches; but only three of the latter remained, and these were bad ones. All three rubbed away without lighting.

"The devil take you, curse you!" he objurgated, himself not knowing whom or what, and he threw away the cigarette. He was about to throw away the matchbox also, but stayed his hand, and thrust it into his pocket instead. He was so agitated that he could no longer remain in his place. He got out of the sledge, and standing with his back to the wind, set his girdle again, tightly, and low down.

"What is the use of lying down? It is only waiting for death; much better mount the horse and get away!" the thought suddenly flashed into his mind. "The horse will not stand still with some one on his back. It's all the same to *him*"—thinking of Nikita—"if he does die. What sort of a life has he! He does not care much even about his life, but as for me—thank God, I have something to live for!" . . .

Untying the horse from the sledge, he threw the reins over his neck, and tried to mount, but his coats and his boots were so heavy that he failed. Then he clambered on the sledge, and tried to mount from that; but the sledge tilted under his weight, and he failed again. At last, on a third attempt, he backed the horse to the sledge, and, cautiously balancing on the edge, got his body across the horse's back. Lying thus for a moment, he pushed himself once, twice, and finally threw one leg over and seated himself, supporting his feet on the loose breeching straps in place of stirrups. The shaking of the sledge roused Nikita, and he got up; Vasili Andreyitch thought he was speaking.

"Listen to you, fool? What, must I die in this way, for nothing?" exclaimed Vasili Andreyitch. Tucking under his knees the loose skirts of his coat, he turned the horse round, and rode away from the sledge in the direction where he expected to find the forest and the keeper's hut.

Chapter VII

NIKITA had not stirred since he had covered himself with the matting and taken his seat behind the sledge. Like all men who live with nature, and are acquainted with poverty, he was patient, and could wait for hours, even days, without growing restless or irritated. When his master called him, he heard, but made no answer, because he did not want to stir. Although he still felt the warmth from the tea he had taken, and from the exercise of struggling through the snowdrifts, he knew the warmth would not last long, and that he could not warm himself again by moving about, for he was exhausted, and felt as a horse does when, in spite of the whip, it stops, and its master perceives that it must have food before it can work again. His foot, the one in the torn boot, was numb, and he could no longer feel his great toe. And, moreover, his whole body kept growing colder and colder.

The thought that he might and in all probability would die that night came upon him, but this thought did not seem especially unpleasant or especially awful. It did not seem to him especially unpleasant, because his life had not been a perpetual festival, but rather an incessant round of toil of which he was beginning to weary. And this thought did not seem to him especially awful, because, beyond the masters whom he served here, like Vasili Andreyitch, he felt himself dependent upon the Great Master; upon Him who had sent him into this life, and he knew that even after death he must remain in the power of that Master, and that that Master would not treat him badly.

"Is it a pity to leave what you are practiced in, and used to? Well, what's to be done about it? You must get used to new things as well."

"Sins?" he thought, and recollected his drunkenness, the money wasted in drink, his ill-treatment of his wife, his profanity, neglect of church and of the fasts, and all things for which the priest reprimanded him at the confessional. "Of course, these are sins. But then, did I bring them on myself? Whatever I am, I suppose God made me so. Well, and about these sins? How can one help it?"

Thus ran his reflections, and after he had considered what might happen to him that night, he let it have the go-by, and gave himself up to whatever notions and memories came of their own accord into his mind. He remembered Marfa's visit, and the drunkenness among the peasants, and his own abstinence from drink; then he recalled how they had started on their present journey; Taras's house, and the talk about the break-up of the family; that reminded him of his own lad; then he thought of Mukhortui, with the sacking over him for warmth; and his master, rolling round in the sledge, and making it creak.

"I suppose he is vexed and angry because he started out," said Nikita to himself. "A man who lives such a life as his does not want to die; not like people of my kind."

And all these recollections and thoughts interwove and jumbled themselves in his brain, until he fell asleep.

When Vasili Andreyitch mounted the horse, he twisted aside the sledge, and the back of it, against which Nikita was leaning, slid away, and one of the runner-ends struck him in the side. Nikita awoke, and was compelled to change his position. Straightening his legs with difficulty, and throwing off the snow which covered them, he got up. Instantly an agonizing cold penetrated his whole frame. On making out what was happening, he wanted Vasili Andreyitch to leave him the sacking, which was no longer needed for the horse, so that he might put it round himself.

But Vasili Andreyitch did not wait, and disappeared in the mist of snow.

Thus left alone, Nikita considered what he should do. He felt that he had not strength enough to start off in search of some house; and it was no longer possible for him to sit down in his former place, for it was already covered with snow; and he knew he could not get warm in the sledge, having nothing to cover him. There seemed no warmth at all from his coat and sheepskin. It was a bitter moment. He felt as cold as if he had only his shirt on. "Our Father, who art in Heaven," he repeated; and the consciousness that he was not alone but that Some One heard him and would not desert him comforted him. He drew a deep sigh, and keeping the matting over his head, he crept into the sledge and lay down in the place where his master had lain.

But he could not possibly keep warm in the sledge. At first he shivered all over, then the shivering ceased, and little by little, he began to lose consciousness. Whether he was dying, or falling asleep, he knew not; but he was as ready for the one as for the other.

Chapter VIII

MEANWHILE Vasili Andreyitch, using his feet and the straps of the harness, urged the horse in the direction where he, for some cause, expected to find the forest and the forester's hut. The snow blinded his eyes, and the wind, it seemed, was bent on staying him, but with head bent forward, and all the time pulling up his shuba between him and the cold pad, on which he could not settle himself, he kept urging on the horse. The dark bay, though with difficulty, obediently ambled on in the direction to which he was turned.

For five minutes he rode on; as it seemed to him, in a straight line; seeing nothing but the horse's head and the white waste, and hearing only the whistling of the wind about the horse's ears and collar of his own coat.

Suddenly a dark patch showed in front of him. His heart began to beat with joy, and he rode on toward the object, already seeing in it the walls of village houses. But the dark patch was not stationary, it kept moving, and it was not a village but a patch of tall wormwood, growing on a strip of land and protruding through the snow, and shaking desperately under the blast of the wind which bent their heads all in one direction and whistled through them.

The sight of this wormwood tormented by the pitiless wind somehow made Vasili Andreyitch tremble, and he started to ride away hastily; not perceiving that in approaching the patch of wormwood, he had quite turned out of his first direction, and that now he was heading the opposite way, though he still supposed that he was riding toward where the forester's hut should be. But the horse seemed always to make toward the right, and so Vasili Andreyitch had to guide it toward the left.

Again a dark patch appeared before him; again he rejoiced, believing that now surely this was a village. But once more it was a patch of tall wormwood, once more the dry grass was shaking desperately, and, as before, frightening Vasili Andreyitch. But it could not be the same patch of grass, for near it was a horse-track, now disappearing in the snow. Vasili Andreyitch stopped, bent down, and looked carefully; a horse-track, not yet snow-covered; it could only be the hoof-prints of his own horse. He had evidently gone round in a small circle.

"And I shall perish in this way," he thought.

To overcome his terror, he urged on the horse with still greater energy, peering into the white mist of snow, wherein he saw nothing but flitting and fitful points of light which vanished the instant he looked at them. Once he thought he heard either the barking of dogs or the howling of wolves, but the sounds were so faint and indistinct, that he could not be sure whether he had heard them or imagined them; and he stopped and began to strain his ears and listen.

Suddenly a terrible, deafening cry beat upon his ears, and everything began to tremble and quake about him. Vasili Andreyitch seized the horse's neck, but that also shook, and the terrible cry grew still more frightful. For some seconds, Vasili Andreyitch could not collect himself, or understand what had happened. It was only this: Mukhortui, whether to encourage himself or to call for help, had neighed, loudly and resonantly.

"Ugh! Plague take you! You cursed brute, how you frightened me!" said Vasili Andreyitch to himself. But even when he understood the cause of his terror, he could not shake it off.

"I must consider and steady my nerves," he said to himself again, and saw at the same time he could not regain his self-control, but kept urging forward the horse without noting that he was now going with the wind, instead of against it. Especially when the horse walked slowly, his body, where it was exposed and where it touched the pad, was freezing and ached. His hands and legs shook and he was short of breath. He could see that he was likely to perish in the midst of this horrible snowy waste, and he could see no way of rescue. He forgot all about the forester's hut, and desired one thing only—to get back to the sledge, that he might not perish alone, like that wormwood in the midst of the terrible waste of snow.

Suddenly the horse stumbled under him, caught in a snowdrift, and began to plunge, and fell on his side. Vasili Andreyitch jumped off as he did so, dragging with him the breeching on which his foot was supported, and turned the pad round by holding to it as he jumped.

As soon as Vasili Andreyitch was off his back, the horse struggled to his feet, plunged forward one leap and then another, and neighing again, with the sacking and breeching trailing after him, disappeared, leaving Vasili Andreyitch alone in the snowdrift.

He pressed on in pursuit of the horse, but the snow was so deep, and his coats were so heavy, that after he had gone not more than twenty paces, sinking over the knee at each step, he was out of breath, and stopped.

"The forest, the sheep, the farms, the shop, the taverns, the iron-roofed house and granary, my son!" thought he, "how can I leave them all? What does this really mean! It cannot be!"

These words flashed through his mind. Then somehow or other he recalled the wind-shaken wormwood which he had ridden past twice, and such a panic seized him that he lost all sense of the reality of what was happening. He asked himself, "Is not this all a dream?"—and tried to wake up. But there was nothing to wake up from! It was actual snow lashing his face and covering him and benumbing his right hand, from which he had dropped the glove; and it was a real desert in which he was now alone, like that wormwood, waiting for inevitable, speedy, and incomprehensible death.

"Queen in heaven, St. Nicholas, teacher of temperance!"

He recalled the Te Deums of the day; the shrine with the black image in a golden chasuble; the tapers which he sold for the shrine, and which, when they were at once returned to him hardly touched by the flame, he used to put back into the store-chest.[3] And he began to implore that same Nicholas —the miracle-worker—to save him, vowing to the saint a Te Deum and tapers.

---

[3] *the store-chest*: As churchwarden, he would put away the tapers to resell for church revenue.

But in some way, here, he clearly and without a doubt realized that the image, chasuble, tapers, priests, masses, though they were all very important and necessary in their place, in the church, were of no service to him now; and that between those tapers and Te Deums, and his present disastrous plight, there could be no possible connection.

"I must not give up," he said to himself, "I must follow the horse's tracks, or they, too, will be snowed over." This idea struck him, and he made on. "He'll get away if I don't overtake him. But I mustn't hurry or else I shall be worse off and perish still more miserably."

But notwithstanding his resolution to walk quietly, he kept hurrying on, running, falling down every minute, rising and falling again. The hoofprints were already almost indistinguishable where the snow was not deep. "I am lost!" thought Vasili Andreyitch, "if I lose this track and don't overtake the horse."

But at that instant, casting a glance in front, he saw something dark. It was Mukhortui, and not merely Mukhortui, but the sledge, and the shafts with the handkerchief.

Mukhortui, with the pad twisted round to one side, and the trailed breeching and sacking, was standing, not in his former place, but nearer to the shafts; and was shaking his head, which was drawn down by the bridle beneath his feet.

It turned out that Vasili Andreyitch had stuck in the same ravine into which he and Nikita had previously plunged, that the horse had led him back to the sledge, and that he had dismounted at not more than fifty paces from the place where the sledge lay.

Chapter IX

VASILI Andreyitch struggled back to the sledge, clutched hold of it, and stood so, motionless for a long time, trying to calm himself and to get back his breath. There was no sign of Nikita in his former place, but something covered with snow was lying in the sledge, and Vasili Andreyitch conjectured that it was Nikita. Vasili Andreyitch's terror had now altogether disappeared; if he felt any fear, it was of that state of terror which he had experienced when on the horse, and especially when he was alone in the snowdrift. By any and every means, he must keep away that terror; and in order to keep it away it was necessary for him to do something, to occupy himself with something.

Accordingly, the first thing he did was to turn his back to the wind and throw open his coat. As soon as he felt a little rested, he shook out the snow from his boots and from his left-hand glove—the right-hand glove was lost beyond recovery and was undoubtedly already buried somewhere deep in the snow—then he bound up his girdle again, tight and low-down, as he always did when he was going out of his shop to buy grain from the peasants' carts. He tightened his belt and prepared for action. The first thing which appeared to him necessary to do was to free the horse's leg. So Vasili Andreyitch did this; then, clearing the bridle, he tied Mukhortui to the iron cramp in front of the sledge, as before, and walking round the horse's quarters, he adjusted the pad, the breeching, and the sacking.

But as he did this, he perceived a movement in the sledge, and Nikita's head rose out of the snow that covered it. Obviously with great difficulty, the half-frozen peasant rose and sat up; and in a strange fashion, as if he were driving away flies, waved his hand before his face. He waved his hand and said something which Vasili Andreyitch interpreted as a call to himself.

Vasili Andreyitch left the sack unadjusted, and went to the sledge.

"What is the matter with you?" he asked. "What are you saying?"

"I am dy-y-ing, that's what's the matter," said Nikita, brokenly, struggling for speech. "Give what I have earned to the lad. Or to the wife; it's all the same."

"What, are you really frozen?" asked Vasili Andreyitch.

"I can feel I've got my death. Forgive . . . for Christ's sake . . ." said Nikita, in a sobbing voice, continuing to wave his hand before his face, as if driving away flies.

Vasili Andreyitch stood for half a minute silent and motionless; then suddenly, with the same resolution with which he used to strike hands over a good bargain, he took a step back, turned up the sleeves of his coat, and using both hands, began to rake the snow from off Nikita and the sledge. When he had brushed out, Vasili Andreyitch quickly took off his girdle, opened out his coat, and moving Nikita with a push, he lay down on him, covering him not only with the fur coat, but with the full length of his own body, which glowed with warmth.

Adjusting with his hands the skirts of his coat, so as to come between Nikita and the bark matting of the sledge, and tucking the tail of the coat between his knees, Vasili Andreyitch lay flat, with his head against the bark matting in the sledge-front; and now he no longer could hear either the stirring of the horse or the whistling of the wind; all he could hear was Nikita's breathing. At first, and for a long time, Nikita lay without a sign; then he gave a loud sigh, and moved.

"Ah, there you are! And yet you say 'die.' Lie still, get warm, and somehow we shall . . ." began Vasili Andreyitch.

But, to his own surprise, he could not speak: because his eyes were filled with tears, and his lower jaw began to quiver violently. He said no more— only gulped down something which rose in his throat.

"I was well scared, that is clear, and how weak I feel!" he thought of himself. But this weakness not only was not unpleasant to him, but rather gave him a peculiar and hitherto unknown delight.

"That's what we are!" he said to himself, experiencing a strange triumph and emotion. He lay quiet for some time, wiping his eyes with the fur of his coat and tucking under his knees the right skirt, which the wind kept turning up.

He felt a passionate desire to let some one else know of his happy condition.

"Nikita!" he said.

"It's comfortable, it's warm," came an answer from below.

"So it is, friend! I was nearly lost. And you would have been frozen, and I should have. . . ."

But here again his face began to quiver, and his eyes once more filled with tears, and he could say no more.

"Well, never mind," he thought, "I know well enough about myself, what I know."

And he kept quiet. Thus he lay for a long time.

Nikita warmed him from below, and the fur coat warmed him from above; but his hands, with which he held the coatskirts down on both sides of Nikita, and his feet, from which the wind kept lifting the coat, began to freeze. Especially cold was his right hand, unprotected by a glove. But he did not think either of his legs or of his hands. He thought only of how to warm the peasant who lay beneath him.

Several times he looked at the horse, and saw that his back was uncovered, and the sacking and breeching were hanging down nearly to the snow. He ought to get up and cover the horse; but he could not bring himself to leave Nikita for even a moment, and so disturb that happy situation in which he felt himself; he now no longer had any sense of terror.

"Never fear, we shan't lose him this time," he said to himself, about his way of warming Nikita, and with the same boastfulness as he used to speak of buying and selling.

Thus Vasili Andreyitch continued lying an hour and then another and then a third, but he was unconscious of the passage of time.

At first his thoughts were filled with impressions of the snow-storm, the shafts of the sledge, the horse under the shaft-bow, all in confusion before his eyes; he remembered Nikita, lying under him; then mingling with these recollections rose others, of the festival, his wife, the commissary of police, the taper-box; then again of Nikita, this time lying under the taper-box. Then came apparitions of peasants selling and buying, and white walls, the iron-roofed houses, with Nikita lying underneath; then all was confused, one thing blending with another; and, like the colors in the rainbow, uniting in one white light, all the different impressions fused into one nothing; and he fell asleep.

For a long time he slept dreamlessly; but before daybreak visions visited him again. It seemed to him that he was once more standing beside the taper-box, and Tikhon's wife was asking him for a five-kopek candle for the festival-day; he wanted to take the taper and give it to her, but he could not move his hands, which hung down, thrust tightly into his pockets. He wanted to walk round the box, but his feet would not move; his galoshes, new and shiny, had grown to the stone floor, and he could neither move them, nor take out his feet.

All at once the box ceased to be a taper-box, and turned into a bed; and Vasili Andreyitch sees himself lying, face downward, on the taper-box, and yet it is his own bed in his own house. And thus he lies and is unable to get up; and yet he must get up, because Ivan Matveyitch, the commissary of police, will soon come for him, and he must go with Ivan Matveyitch either to bargain for the forest, or to set the breeching right on Mukhortui.

He asks his wife:

"Well, Mikolavna, has he not come yet?"

"No," she says, "he has not."

He hears some one drive up to the front steps. It must be he. No, he has gone past.

"Mikolavna, Mikolavna! what, has he not come yet?"

"No."

And he lies on the bed and is still unable to rise, and is still waiting. And this waiting is painful, and yet pleasant.

All at once, his joy is fulfilled: the expected one has come; not Ivan Matveyitch, the police officer, but some one else, and yet the one for whom he has been waiting. He has come, and he calls to him; and he that called is he who had bidden him lie down on Nikita.

And Vasili Andreyitch is glad because that one has visited him.

"I am coming," he cries joyfully. And the cry awakens him!

He wakes; but wakes an entirely different person from what he had been when he fell asleep. He wants to rise, and cannot; to move his arm, and cannot—his leg, and he cannot do that. He wants to turn his head, and cannot do even so much. He is surprised but not at all disturbed by this. He divines that this is death, and is not at all disturbed even by that. And he remembers that Nikita is lying under him, and that he has got warm, and is alive; and it seems to him that he is Nikita, and Nikita is he; that his life is not in himself, but in Nikita. He makes an effort to listen, and hears Nikita's breathing, even his slight snoring.

"Nikita is alive, and therefore I also am alive!" he says to himself, triumphantly.

He remembers his money, his shop, his house, his purchases and sales, the Mironofs' millions; and it is hard for him to understand why that man called Vasili Brekhunof had troubled himself with all those things with which he had troubled himself.

"Well, he did not know what it was all about," he thinks, concerning this Vasili Brekhunof. "I did not know; but now I do know. No mistake this time; *now I know.*"

And again he hears the summons of that one who had before called him. "I am coming, I am coming," he says with his whole joy-thrilled being. And he feels himself free, with nothing to encumber him more.

And nothing more, in this world, was seen, or heard, or felt by Vasili Andreyitch.

Round about the storm still eddied. The same whirlwinds of snow covered the dead Vasili Andreyitch's coat, and Mukhortui, all of a tremble, and the sledge, now hardly to be seen, with Nikita lying in the bottom of it, kept warm beneath his dead master.

Chapter X

JUST before morning Nikita awoke. He was aroused by the cold again creeping along his back. He had dreamt that he was driving from the mill with a cartload of his master's flour, and that in crossing the brook, as he went past the bridge, the cart got stuck. And he sees himself go beneath the cart, and lift it, straightening up his back. But, wonderful!—the cart does not stir, it sticks to his back, so that he can neither lift it nor get out from under it. It was crushing his loins. And how cold it was! He must get away somehow.

"There! Stop!" he cries to whoever it is that presses his back with the load. "Take the sacks out!"

But the cart still presses him, always colder and colder; and suddenly a peculiar knocking awakes him completely, and he remembers everything. The cold cart—that was his dead and frozen master, lying upon him. The knocking was from Mukhortui, who had struck twice on the sledge with his hoofs.

"Andreyitch, eh, Andreyitch!" calls Nikita, softly, straightening his back, and already having a suspicion of the truth.

But Andreyitch does not answer, and his body and legs are hard, and cold, and heavy, like iron weights.

"He must be dead. May his be the Kingdom of Heaven!" thinks Nikita.

He turns his head, digs with his hand through the snow about him, and opens his eyes. It is daylight. The wind still whistles through the shafts, and the snow is still falling; but with a difference, not lashing upon the bark matting, as before, but silently covering the sledge and horse, ever deeper and deeper; and the horse's breathing and stirring are no more to be heard.

"He must be frozen, too," thinks Nikita.

And, in fact, those hoof-strokes on the sledge were the last struggles of Mukhortui, by that time quite benumbed, to keep on his legs.

"God, Father, it seems Thou callest me as well," says Nikita, to himself. "Let Thy holy will be done. But it is hard. . . . Still you can't die twice, and you must die once. If it would only come quicker!" . . .

And he draws in his arm again, shutting his eyes; and he loses consciousness, with the conviction that this time he is really going to die altogether.

At dinner-time on the next day, the peasants with their shovels dug out Vasili Andreyitch and Nikita, only seventy yards from the road, and half a verst from the village. The snow had hidden the sledge, but the shafts and the handkerchief were still visible. Mukhortui, up to his belly in snow, with the breeching and sacking trailing from his back, stood all whitened, his dead head pressed in on the apple of his throat; his nostrils were fringed with icicles, his eyes filled with frost and frozen round as with tears. In that one night he had become so thin, that he was nothing but skin and bones.

Vasili Andreyitch was stiffened like a frozen carcass, and he lay with his legs spread apart, just as he was when they rolled him off Nikita. His prominent hawk-eyes were frozen, and his open mouth under his clipped mustache was filled with snow.

But Nikita, though chilled through, was alive. When he was roused, he imagined he was already dead, and that what they were doing with him was happening, not in this world, but in another. When he heard the shouts of the peasants who were digging him out and pulling the frozen Vasili An-dreyitch from him he was surprised, at first, to think that in the other world, also, peasants should be shouting so, and that they had the same kind of a body. But when he understood that he was still here, in this world, he was sorry rather than glad; especially when he realized that the toes of both his feet were frozen.

Nikita lay in the hospital for two months. They cut off three toes from him, and the others recovered, so that he was able to work. For twenty years more he went on living, first as a farm-laborer, then as a watchman. He died at home, just as he wished, only this year—laid under the holy images, with a lighted wax taper in his hands.

Before his death, he asked forgiveness from his old wife, and forgave her for the cooper; he took leave of his son and the grandchildren; and went away truly pleased that, in dying, he released his son and daughter-in-law from the added burden of his keep, and that he himself was, this time, really going out of a life grown wearisome to him, into that other one which with every passing year had grown clearer and more desirable to him.

Whether he is better off, or worse off, there, in the place where he awoke after that real death, whether he was disappointed or found things there just as he expected, is what we shall all of us soon learn.

Biographical Notes

ABRAHAMS, PETER (1919–   )   Although he was born in South Africa, the son of an Abyssinian father and a half-European mother, Peter Abrahams escaped from the squalor of native life in South Africa to live and write in London. His books have been influential in helping the world to understand the native life of South Africa. They include *A Black Man Speaks for Freedom* (1939), *Mine Boy* (1946), *The Path of Thunder* (1948), and *Tell Freedom: Memories of Africa* (1954).

CAVAFY, C. P. (1863–1933)   Cavafy was a poet of honesty and sensitivity. He published only two volumes of verse in his lifetime, and these have been available in English only since 1961. Born of Greek parents residing in Alexandria, Egypt, he lived most of his life there, where his principal job was as provisional clerk in the Ministry of Irrigation. Since his death he has come to be regarded as one of the significant European poets of the early 20th century.

CHEKHOV, ANTON (1860–1904)   Chekhov was one of the most important writers to emerge in prerevolutionary Russia. He worked best in the shorter forms of literature—the drama and the short story. *Uncle Vanya, The Cherry Orchard,* and *The Seagull* are among his best-known plays. The last named had a triumphant production under the guidance of the famous director Stanislavsky. Chekhov's subtlety and low-keyed drama have influenced such other dramatists as Eugene O'Neill and Tennessee Williams. As a fiction writer, he is regarded as a pioneer of the modern short story; and his stories, which emphasize characterization and insight into human situations rather than intricate plots, have been models for later writers.

FRANCE, ANATOLE (1844–1924) The most piercing satirist of his generation, France was also a religious skeptic and a social reformer. Taking as subject matter for his biting satire early Christianity and modern society, France wrote stories such as the famous "Procurator of Judea" and the well-known allegory *Penguin Island*. But mixed with his ironic wit and social criticism was a romantic fervor, a love of the beauty in the world, and a tenderness for humanity.

HEINE, HEINRICH (1797–1856) Heine was the son of an intelligent, middle-class German-Jewish family. He studied at the universities of Bonn, Göttingen, and Berlin. Most famous as a lyric poet (*Book of Songs, Romancero*, and *Last Poems*), he also wrote in other forms—travel sketches, satires, and narrative poems. He ended his life in illness and squalor in Paris, but he had done much to help in the mutual understanding between France and Germany in his time. Schubert, Schumann, and Brahms set many of his poems to music. "Die Lorelei," one of his most famous song-poems, combines the romantic and the folk traditions. It defied even Hitler's attempts to suppress this most German of songs written by a Jew.

HESSE, HERMANN (1877–1962) Of German-Swiss origins, Hesse was novelist, poet, essayist, and literary critic. He spent most of his life in Switzerland and became a citizen there in 1923. Hesse began his long writing career conventionally, but from *Demian* on he wrote a series of intense, psychological, and spiritual novels and stories, all centered on the quest for knowledge of the self. *Siddhartha, Steppenwolf*, and *Magister Ludi* are now widely read and studied. In 1946 Hesse was awarded both the Goethe Prize and the Nobel Prize for literature.

HOMER (c. 850 B.C.) *The Iliad* and *The Odyssey*, the two oldest works of literature extant in European literature, are traditionally attributed to the Greek poet Homer. But whether there was such a poet, or whether the two works are the product of refined legends and several authors, is not known for certain. As did earlier traditions, the Middle Ages continued to picture Homer as a blind poet; but recent scholarship has cast serious doubt upon this picture. Whatever we say of their author or authors, however, the two poems remain giants among works of Western literature.

HUGO, VICTOR (1802–1885) Hugo became the father of the Romantic movement in France. He believed that truth lay in the juxtaposition of the beautiful and the ugly, and he admired Shakespeare greatly for his mixture of the comic and tragic. Hugo produced some 50 volumes of plays, novels, poems, and essays. *Notre-Dame de Paris* and *Les Misé-rables,* two of his major novels, are still widely read, but his lasting fame in France seems to rest with the volumes of lyric poetry.

HUSSEIN, TĀHĀ (1889–   ) Tāhā Hussein became blind in childhood, but went to al-Azhar University at the age of 13, and later studied in Cairo and Paris. He is now the foremost Egyptian-Arabic writer of our time. In 1925 he became Professor of Arabic Literature at Cairo University and in 1950, Minister of Education. He is a humanist and a force for modernism in contemporary Egypt. His work includes symbolic, romantic novels about the early history of Islam, essays, and works of literary criticism.

IBSEN, HENRIK (1828–1906) Without doubt the greatest playwright of Norway, and many would say one of the greatest since Shakespeare, Ibsen wrote more than twenty plays, of which some of the most famous are *Peer Gynt, A Doll's House, Ghosts,* and *Hedda Gabler.* His plays opened up what might be called the Modern Theater, and almost all playwrights since his time have been influenced by his realism and his use of symbols in drama.

LEOPARDI, GIACOMO (1798–1837) Leopardi, a classicist writing in an essentially romantic era, was the son of a noble family. He weakened his already frail health by excessive study, and perhaps as a consequence, his essentially pessimistic view of life was strengthened. He believed that love, knowledge, and all that man seeks is essentially illusion, but that we must cultivate these illusions if we are to survive. His poems, collected as *Canti (Songs),* and his moral essays reflect these thoughts.

LIN YUTANG (1895–   ) Lin Yutang, a third-generation Christian, was born in Amoy, Fukien Province, China. After marriage he and his wife went abroad to learn together. He holds an M.A. from Harvard and a Ph.D. from the University of Leipzig. He returned to China in 1923 and became a revolutionary, but he tired of the intrigue, turned to literature, and returned to Europe and the United States. His works of fiction and philosophy have been very popular and influential in helping the West understand China. They include *My Country and My People, The Importance of Living, The Wisdom of Confucius,* and the novel *Moment in Peking.*

MAUPASSANT, GUY DE (1850–1893) Maupassant is often called the master short-story writer of all time; he wrote three hundred stories, six novels, and several dramatic works. His stories concern French life in all of its aspects, from the incidents of high society to the tragedies of the Franco-Prussian War. Like the later American short-story writer O. Henry, he often contrived a surprise ending which was both ironical and effective.

MÉRIMÉE, PROSPER (1803–1870) One of France's masters of imaginative prose in the 19th century, Mérimée trained in the law but became a civil servant instead of practicing law. In 1831 he was appointed Inspector of Ancient Monuments for France. He was fascinated by Spain and its folklore from the beginning of his writing career. A melancholy, skeptical, and sensitive man with a powerful intellect, he wrote many volumes of personal reminiscence, as well as *Colomba,* a novel about Corsica. His most famous book in France is called *Letters to an Unknown Woman.*

MOTOKIYO, SEAMI (1363–1444) Seami and his father, Kanami Kiyotsugu (1333–1384) were largely responsible for transforming the Japanese *Nō* plays from mere entertainment to a sophisticated art form combining dance, music, poetry, and spectacle. Seami was both an active playwright and a performer. He received careful training from his father, and grew up in the cultivated aristocracy of his time. Ideas from Buddhism, Japanese and Chinese literature, Japanese history, and a familiarity with nature mingle in his plays to form masterpieces in one of the most subtle and complex art forms of the Far East.

NICOL, ABIOSEH Born in Sierra Leone of African parents, and educated in Africa and abroad, Mr. Nicol, an educator, has traveled and lectured widely. Much of what he writes about Africa is based on his own experiences.

PO CHÜ-I (772–846) Po lived during the T'ang dynasty of ancient China and is now ranked among the very greatest of her lyric poets. Born the son of a minor government official in Honan Province of east central China, he received a traditional education, passed the government examinations, and served in various administrative posts during his lifetime. His poetry is simple, direct, and unusual in that it conforms to the Confucian ideal that one of the principal concerns of poetry should be social criticism.

REMARQUE, ERICH MARIA (1897–   ) Though German-born, Remarque is of French extraction and is now an American citizen. He was wounded several times during World War I, while fighting in the German army. An outspoken critic of Hitler, he was deprived of German citizenship and has divided his time between Switzerland and the United States since then. In addition to *All Quiet on the Western Front*, he has had great popular success with several other realistic novels—*The Road Back, Arch of Triumph*, and *Spark of Life*.

RILKE, RAINER MARIA (1875–1926) Rilke ranks as one of the finest of 20th-century European lyric poets. He was a wanderer and spent much of his life in travel and residence abroad—Paris, Italy, Russia. He broke with many of the conventions of traditional poetry, and his aim was to render as freshly as possible the facts and activities of daily life. Among his most famous works are *Sonnets to Orpheus* and *The Duino Elegies*, both published in 1923, and *The Tale of the Love and Death of Cornet Christopher Rilke*, an impressionistic account of a military ancestor.

ROSTAND, EDMOND (1868–1918) Without doubt Rostand was one of the most popular writers of his time in France, and in the English-speaking world as well. He had little success as a poet, but his early verse plays were popular. *Cyrano* (1898) played a record 500 consecutive performances in Paris, with the famous actor Coquelin in the title role. He later wrote *L'Aiglon*, as a vehicle for Sarah Bernhardt, who toured the United States in the lead role. Rostand was the youngest person ever admitted to the French Academy. He contributed largely to the renaissance of verse drama in the 20th century, not only in France but in England and the United States as well.

SHAKESPEARE, WILLIAM (1564–1616) Shakespeare is without question the greatest writer in English, and some would say the greatest writer who ever lived. His plays, ranging from light comedies to tragedies, from historical plays to allegories, reveal human life at its most intense. The characters spring to life and their conflicts become of immediate concern to readers and audiences alike. *Macbeth, King Lear, Hamlet, A Midsummer Night's Dream, Richard II*, and *The Tempest* are only a few of Shakespeare's plays which have been popular with readers and audiences ever since their original productions.

STRINDBERG, AUGUST (1849–1912)   Sweden's foremost writer, and one of the outstanding dramatists of modern times, Strindberg lived a personal life of great conflict and suffering. His continual struggle was for self-realization in a chaotic world, and his plays reflect this struggle. *Miss Julie, The Father, The Dance of Death,* and *The Dream Play* continue to fascinate theater audiences all over the world. Strindberg's own tortured life is revealed in the eight volumes of his autobiography.

TAGORE, RABINDRANATH (1861–1941)   Tagore was the youngest son of a prominent and artistic Bengal family and received most of his education from private tutors. He was equally fluent in Bengali, Sanskrit, and English. Trained as a poet, he became a philosopher and a leader for nationalism in India. His writings and his life were admired the world over, and his accomplishments have often been compared to those of Goethe and Tolstoy.

TOLSTOY, LEO (1828–1910)   Count Leo Tolstoy was one of the most celebrated Russian writers of his time, and his novel *War and Peace* is often called the greatest novel ever written. Author of *Anna Karenina*, other novels, and a group of very fine short stories, Tolstoy was also interested in the condition of the serfs in Russia, in land reform, and in the ethical power of Christianity. He became the beloved leader of the Russian youth of his day. Tolstoy's death was a tragedy for the entire world.

TURGENEV, IVAN (1818–1883)   Son of a wealthy Russian landowning family, Turgenev led a sophisticated life which included many years of travel and residence in western Europe, notably France. He attended the universities of St. Petersburg and Moscow, and was known for his attempts to "westernize" Russia. He is the author of a number of sensitive, realistic stories and novels, the most famous of which is *Fathers and Sons*. In it he reflects the revolutionary ideas of the younger generation and the onset of the radical changes which were to sweep over his country in the early 20th century.

TYRTAEUS OF SPARTA (c. 650 B.C.)   According to legend, Tyrtaeus was a lame schoolteacher from Athens. Actually, he was a native of the island of Lesbos. He inspired Spartans with his patriotic elegies and war songs. His poems constituted a kind of sacred book from which young Spartans were admonished to learn courage.

VALLEJO, CESAR (1892–1938)   A journalist, novelist, playwright, and poet, Vallejo was born in Peru, but spent the later part of his life in France, where he died. He began his career as a poet with traditional romantic works, but with his collection of poems called *Trilce* (1922) he broke with conventions and tried many experimental techniques. He visited Russia in the 1920's and afterward wrote a proletarian novel, *Tungsten*, which attempts to dignify the Peruvian Indians and give political power to workers and peasants. A posthumous book called *Human Poems* deals with the Spanish Civil War. All of his poems mix the realistic, romantic, and symbolist elements in an individual and often very successful way.

VERLAINE, PAUL (1844–1896)   Verlaine's poetry is delicate, sensitive, and highly colored—the strange product of a life of vagabondage and decadence. With Rimbaud and Baudelaire, Verlaine remains as one of the best of the French Symbolist poets. Books of poetry like *Fêtes Galantes, The Good Song,* and *Romances without Words* express Verlaine's mood of gentle, vague melancholy which eventually attracted a large public to his work.

XENOPHANES OF COLOPHON (c. 538–500 B.C.)   Xenophanes was both philosopher and poet. He was founder of the Eleatic School of philosophy, which held that there is only one controlling Godhead, the Absolute (the Pure Being), and that knowledge of the world through the senses is illusion and error. He defended idealism in his poetry, and protested against the anthropomorphic representations of God in the works of Homer and Hesiod.

ACKNOWLEDGMENTS

We offer grateful acknowledgment to publishers and authors for their permission to use the following works:

THE STRANGER'S NOTE and CHIENNIANG by Lin Yutang: Copyright © 1948, 1951, 1952 by Lin Yutang. Reprinted from *Famous Chinese Stories* by Lin Yutang by permission of The John Day Company, Inc. and Curtis Brown Ltd., London.

THE STREAM OF DAYS by Tāhā Hussein: Reprinted by permission of the author.

THE BET by Anton Chekhov: Reprinted from *Short Fiction of the Masters* edited by Leo Hamalian and Frederick R. Karl. Copyright © 1963 by G. P. Putnam's Sons and used by permission of the publishers.

YOUTH, BEAUTIFUL YOUTH by Hermann Hesse: Reprinted by permission of the publishers. Copyright 1954 by Suhrkamp Verlag, Berlin and Frankfurt. Reprinted by permission of Robert Pick and Richard and Clara Winston.

AN ENEMY OF THE PEOPLE by Henrik Ibsen: Reprinted from *Plays* of Henrik Ibsen. Translated by R. Farquharson Sharp. Everyman's Library Edition. Reprinted by permission of E. P. Dutton & Co., Inc. and J. M. Dent & Sons Ltd.

BIRYUK by Ivan Turgenev: Reprinted from *A Sportsman's Sketches* by Ivan Turgenev, translated by Constance Garnett, by permission of William Heinemann Ltd.

GOLDEN BELLS, REMEMBERING GOLDEN BELLS and THE PRISONER by Po Chü-i: From *Translations from the Chinese* translated by Arthur Waley. Copyright 1919 by Alfred A. Knopf, Inc. and renewed 1947 by Arthur Waley. Reprinted by permission of Alfred A. Knopf, Inc. and George Allen & Unwin Ltd.

MY LORD THE BABY by Rabindranath Tagore: Reprinted with permission of The Macmillan Company from *The Hungry Stones and Other Stories* by Rabindranath Tagore. Copyright 1916 by The Macmillan Company, renewed 1944 by Rathindranath Tagore. Reprinted by permission of Macmillan & Co. Ltd., London, and the Trustees of the Tagore Estate.

RETURN: TWO POEMS by Abioseh Nicol: Reprinted by permission of the author and David Higham Associates from *An African Treasury*.

850

TELL FREEDOM by Peter Abrahams: From *Tell Freedom* by Peter Abrahams. Copyright 1954 by Peter Abrahams. Reprinted by permission of Alfred A. Knopf, Inc. and John Farquharson Ltd.

THE DWARF TREES by Seami Motokiyo: Reprinted from *The Nō Plays of Japan* by Arthur Waley by permission of George Allen & Unwin Ltd.

ALL QUIET ON THE WESTERN FRONT by Erich Maria Remarque: Grateful acknowledgment is made to Mr. Remarque for granting permission to reprint his work. *Im Westen Nichts Neues* copyright 1928 by Ullstein A. G.; copyright renewed 1956 by Erich Maria Remarque. *All Quiet on the Western Front* copyright 1929, 1930 by Little Brown and Company; copyright renewed 1957, 1958 by Erich Maria Remarque.

WAITING FOR THE BARBARIANS by C. P. Cavafy: From *Six Poets of Modern* GREECE translated by Edmund Keeley and Philip Sherrard. Copyright © 1960 by Edmund Keeley and Philip Sherrard. Reprinted by permission of Alfred A. Knopf, Inc. and Thames and Hudson Ltd.

THE ATHLETE AND THE PHILOSOPHER by Xenophanes of Colophon: Reprinted from *Greek Lyrics* by Richmond Lattimore by permission of The University of Chicago Press. Copyright 1940, 1955, and 1960 by Richmond Lattimore.

SATURDAY NIGHT IN THE VILLAGE by Giacomo Leopardi, RUSSIA 1812 by Victor Hugo and THE CADET PICTURE OF MY FATHER by Rainer Maria Rilke: Reprinted with permission of Farrar, Straus & Giroux, Inc. from *Imitations* by Robert Lowell. Copyright © 1958, 1959, 1960, 1961 by Robert Lowell. Reprinted by permission of Faber & Faber, Ltd.

HALF A SHEET OF PAPER by August Strindberg: Reprinted by permission of the American-Scandinavian Foundation.

OUR LADY'S JUGGLER by Anatole France: From *Great Short Stories of the World*, edited by Barrett H. Clark and Maxim Lieber. Copyright © 1925 by Robert M. McBride & Company. Published by arrangement with The World Publishing Company, Cleveland and New York.

HYMN OF LOVE TO GOD and TĀJ MAHAL by Rabindranath Tagore: Reprinted from *A Flight of Swans* translated by Aurobindo Bose, edited by J. L. Cranmer-Byng by permission of John Murray Ltd.

SONG OF PRAISE TO THE CREATOR by G. H. Franz: Reprinted by permission of Afrika Publishers, Cape Town, South Africa.

SENTIMENTAL DIALOGUE by Paul Verlaine: Reprinted by permission of Angel Flores from *An Anthology of French Poetry from Nerval to Valery*, translated by Muriel Kittel. Anchor Books.

CARMEN by Prosper Mérimée: Reprinted from *Three Famous French Romances* by permission of Random House, Inc.

SIE SASSEN UND TRANKEN AM TEETISCH, VERGIFTET SIND MEINE LIEDER and MIR TRÄUMTE WIEDER DER ALTE TRAUM by Heinrich Heine: From *Heinrich Heine: Paradox and Poet, The Poems,* translated by Louis Untermeyer, copyright 1937 by Harcourt, Brace & World, Inc.; renewed, 1965, by Louis Untermeyer. Reprinted by permission of the publishers.

DISTANT FOOTSTEPS by Cesar Vallejo: Translated by H. R. Hays. Reprinted from *12 Spanish American Poets*, Yale University Press, by permission of the translator.

THE SONG OF ROLAND and THE CID: Used by permission of The Orion Press, Inc.

JULIUS CAESAR by William Shakespeare: From *William Shakespeare The Complete Works* edited by Charles Jasper Sisson. Reprinted by permission of Harper & Row, Publishers and Odhams Books Ltd.

MASTER AND MAN by Leo Tolstoy: Published in *The Complete Works of Leo Tolstoy* by Thomas Y. Crowell Company, and used by courtesy of the publisher.

COURAGE and TO THE SOLDIERS AFTER A DEFEAT by Tyrtaeus of Sparta: Reprinted from *Greek Lyrics* by Richmond Lattimore by permission of The University of Chicago Press. Copyright 1940, 1955 and 1960 by Richmond Lattimore.